# THE
# BOOK COLLECTOR'S
# HANDBOOK
# OF VALUES

# THE
# BOOK COLLECTOR'S
# HANDBOOK
# OF VALUES

## THIRD EDITION
## 1978–1979

By VAN ALLEN BRADLEY
*Revised and Enlarged*

*G.P.Putnam's Sons*
*New York*

*This is for Sharon and
Gremlyn Angelica*

**Library of Congress Catalog Card Number:**      75-13906
Bradley, Van Allen
    The Book Collector's Handbook of Values 1976–1977
New York
June 1975

G.P. Putnam
5-16-75

SBN: 399-12110-2

# PREFACE
## TO THE THIRD EDITION

FRIDAY, April 7, 1978, was a landmark day in the history of rare book sales. In just twenty-seven seconds the General Theological Seminary's Gutenberg Bible, one of a small number of copies of the first book printed from movable type, was sold at auction to the highest bidder for a world-record price for a printed book—$2,200,000, including a $200,000 surcharge (10 percent) to the buyer by the auction house.

The scene was the New York gallery of Christie, Manson & Woods. The buyer was Martin Breslauer, a bookseller acting as agent for the Stuttgart Museum. The bidding opened at $500,000. From the time John H. Jenkins, a Texas dealer bidding for a New York investment house, stood up and shouted a bid of $1,000,000 until the auctioneer's final hammer, only seven seconds elapsed. Warren R. Howell, a San Francisco bookseller, was the recorded underbidder at $1,900,000, although Jenkins also was signaling the same final bid for his client. (Jenkins told a group of us at poker that evening that he acted without authority to go beyond $1,700,000 and with a willingness to sacrifice his own commission.)

At the same auction house in 1977, elephant folio copies of John J. Audubon's *The Birds of America* came up at two separate sales. The first copy was sold for $352,000 and the second for $396,000, including in each instance the 10 percent surcharge. Each sale set a world record for a book by an American.

These sensational events were fitting high points of the feverish excitement that has dominated the world of rare books throughout the 1970's and that seems certain to make this one of the great decades of book collecting. When the first edition of *The Book Collector's Handbook of Values* appeared in 1972, we had just come through the stimulating period of the late 1960's and the early 1970's in which the interest in scarce and rare Americana surged to previously undreamed-of heights with the dispersal at auction of the library of the late Thomas W. Streeter. A continuing rise in values throughout the early 1970's made it imperative for me to revise and update this *Handbook* for a second edition in 1975. Book prices as well as an interest in book collecting, both as a hobby and, quite likely, as an investment in this period of general inflation, have continued to advance to an astonishing degree over the four years since the work on the 1975 revision was done. Modern first editions soared to new all-time records in the fall of 1977 and the spring of 1978 with the sale at the New

York galleries of Sotheby Parke Bernet of the library of Jonathan Goodwin. The advances of the last four years have been most sharp in the
areas of fine Americana, literary first editions, and color plate books. For
these reasons I have again gone through this book, entry by entry and line
by line, with a threefold purpose: to bring the price ranges in line with the
current market as of 1978; to make needed corrections and revisions; and
to expand the scope of the book while at the same time eliminating some
of the less useful items.

As I noted in the Introduction to the First Edition (which I am letting
stand), it is inevitable that in a compilation of this kind, gathered from
various sources, there will be errors, bibliographical and otherwise. It has
been my goal to eliminate them wherever possible, and I herewith thank
all the collectors, librarians and booksellers who have generously aided
my efforts. I welcome further corrections and comments.

This does not pretend to be a bibliography but is only a guidebook. The
large number of entries and their range over innumerable specialties make
it obviously impossible for me to have personally examined each book
listed. I have examined many thousands of these books personally, but in
other cases I have relied upon dealer and auction catalogues and an as-
sortment of bibliographical references, my own and others I was able to
consult. Even the best bibliographies have their errors and omissions, as
was made evident recently when a dealer in modern first editions issued a
list of almost 100 errors he had detected in a major bibliographical work in
the field.

Booksellers are notoriously inconsistent in their methods of catalogu-
ing, and the catalogues from which many of these entries are drawn have
in some cases presented problems for this compiler. A lack of complete-
ness in catalogue entries is a principal problem, while outright errors
(which possibly have been repeated or compounded here) are another. As
an example of incompleteness, many booksellers list books with no description of the binding (boards, cloth, leather, wrappers, etc.), while others say simply "hardcover," which could mean anything. Other booksellers pay no attention to the general bibliographical custom which holds
that a title-page date is listed without brackets or parentheses, while a
copyright date or a known date of publication is placed in parentheses if it
does not appear on the title page.

Another inconsistency among booksellers concerns limitation notices.
Example: If a book is issued in an edition of 185 copies, twenty-five of
them in a special binding and signed, and fifteen of them in a super-deluxe
edition signed and with a page of manuscript, some dealers simply say,
"One of 185 copies." Others who may have the twenty-five-copy or
fifteen-copy issues may say, "One of twenty-five copies." or, "One of
fifteen copies." In each case the three dealers may feel that no other information is necessary, yet each of the entries may present a confusing
picture to the reader. In the first instance, why not subtract the forty

signed copies from 185 and simply say, "One of 140 ordinary copies (of an edition of 185)"? Or, "One of 140 unsigned copies (from an edition of 185)"? Certainly the reader of the catalogue is entitled to know that there are extant more desirable copies (i.e., signed ones), if he wishes to go after one. The reverse situation arises with the cataloguer of signed editions. He certainly should let the reader know that there are unsigned copies of the book in the marketplace. Finally, anyone unfamiliar with the book in question should be able to discover from the entry the total number of copies of the edition published.

A word about dust jackets: Wherever possible I have sought to include dust-jacketed copies of modern books in the entries, although in a great many cases no entries for dust-jacketed books could be found. It must be assumed that in these listings if no jacket is mentioned, the cost of a jacketed copy would be higher than the price I have listed. Additionally, one should make an allowance for the *condition* of the dust jacket, as well as for the condition of the book it protects. A frayed, chipped, torn, or soiled jacket would add considerably less value to a bare book than a mint dust jacket, of course. In general, most modern books since about 1920 ideally should have jackets. In the period before that the surviving dust jackets are relatively scarce. When one does show up it may create an astonishing situation. Example: In October, 1977, Maurice F. Neville, a Santa Barbara (Calif.) bookseller, paid a world-record price of $2,500 at auction for a dust-jacketed first edition of Edgar Rice Burroughs' *Tarzan of the Apes.* He tells me he sold it early this year to a collector for $3,350.

How much difference does the condition of the jacket make? One answer is supplied by the entries for two different copies of J.D. Salinger's *Nine Stories* in a recent catalogue issued by Peter B. Howard (Serendipity Books). His first entry: "A copy of surpassing beauty, flawless in perfect dust jacket. $325." A second entry: "Another copy. Fine in dust jacket. $145."

It is most important when consulting this handbook as a guide to values of your own books that you take into consideration the fact that the price ranges given herein are for *fine or relatively fine* copies only and that copies less than fine must be evaluated at lower prices. More than ever in today's market, it is the superior copy of a book that brings a premium price. For a further understanding of the principles used in this handbook, please give careful attention to the Introduction to the First Edition, which follows the section of "Acknowledgments."

In general, throughout this book I have tried to supply when possible bibliographical help in the identification of first editions. For this edition I have added in the Acknowledgments the titles of a number of reference books which will be of aid in identifying books.

What I said in a Preface to the Second Edition applies even more strongly today: "Book collecting is advancing steadily in general interest and importance, and 'the quest for the perfect book' is more difficult than ever because of the dwindling supply of good books and the growing so-phistication of the collector. Now, perhaps more than ever, the collector should strive to obtain the finest possible copy of a wanted book.''

Rarity and condition remain the two prime influences in the determina-tion of values in the world of books.

VAN ALLEN BRADLEY
Barrington, Illinois
April 19, 1978

# ACKNOWLEDGMENTS

WORK on the first (1972) edition of this book began in 1964, and in its first eight years before publication the manuscript went through three complete drafts, including an updating of prices. Revisions of the published book have been a continuing process, and the work on this new edition has occupied most of my available free time for more than a year. The list of those colleagues and friends, including booksellers, librarians, and collectors, who have generously contributed to those efforts, has lengthened steadily. To all these I wish again to acknowledge an indebtedness and to express my thanks.

The list begins with my best and severest critic, my wife Sharon; my editor William Targ; and my publisher Walter J. Minton. It includes, for special help on this edition, my bookseller friends Andreas Brown, Michael Ginsberg, John H. Jenkins, and Ray S. Walton. It also includes the following: the late Ben Abramson; the late Ramon F. Adams; Milton Altman; the late John E. Baker, Jr.; the late Jacob S. Blanck; Nelson Bond; William Boozer; the late Frances Brewer; Matthew J. Bruccoli; Joseph Camardo; the late John Carter; Leland Case; George Charney; Jacob L. Chernofsky; C.E. Frazer Clark, Jr.; Mrs. Louis H. Cohn; Lloyd W. Currey; Jeff Dykes; J.M. Edelstein; Jane Faul; Charles Feinberg; the late Lew D. Feldman; Ralph D. Gardner; the late Adrian H. Goldstone; the late Everett D. Graff; Lawrence Gutter; the late Joseph Haas; William Hanzel; Peggy Halda; Nancy Harris; Richard Harwell; W.R. Hasbrouck; Irwin T. Holtzman; Peter B. Howard; Warren R. Howell; the late Wright Howes; Mary Johnsen; Thomas Joyce; John S. Van E. Kohn; Dean Krakel; Adolph Kroch and his son, Carl; Lawrence Kunetka; Donald LaChance; the late Richard Leekley; Jennifer Licht; Robert Liska; Mary Ann and Sol M. Malkin; Lawrence McGilvery; Richard Mohr; Harry T. Moore; Lawrence Moskowitz; Howard S. Mott; Kenneth Nebenzahl; Ralph G. Newman; Thomas Orlando; Carl Petersen; the late David A. Randall; Mrs. George A. Ratz; William S. Reese; Fred Rosenstock; Justin G. Schiller, Ralph B. Sipper; Harold Byron Smith, Sr.; the late Vincent Starrett; the late Arthur Swann; Terence Tanner; Lawrence W. Towner; the late Ernest J. Wessen; James M. Wells; Fred White, Jr.; Robert A. Wilson; and Jake Zeitlin.

From all the others to whom I am indebted but have not mentioned here, I beg indulgence while at the same time expressing gratitude.

Catalogues from booksellers throughout the world have been freely consulted and drawn upon for much of the information contained here.

Among those whose catalogues have proved most helpful are the following: American: Alta California Bookstore, Argosy Book Store, Bennett & Marshall, Black Sun Books, L.W. Currey Rare Books, Dawson's Book Shop, Philip C. Duschnes, Inc., Peter Decker, Jeff Dykes, Doris Frohnsdorf, Frontier America Corporation, Michael Ginsberg Rare Books, Goodspeed's Book Shop, Gotham Book Mart and Gallery, Guidon Books, Lathrop C. Harper, Inc., Robert G. Hayman, Heritage Book Shop, Holmes Book Company, House of Books, Ltd., House of El Dieff, John Howell—Books, International Bookfinders, J.&S. Graphics (now J. Stephan Lawrence), the Jenkins Company, Literary Heritage, T.N. Luther, M.&.S. Rare Books, George S. Macmanus Company, Midland Rare Book Company, Edward Morrill & Son, Howard S. Mott, Inc., Kenneth Nebenzahl, Inc., Phoenix Book Shop, William Pieper, Justin G. Schiller, Ltd., Barry Scott, Serendipity Books, Seven Gables Bookshop, C.A. Stonehill, Inc., W. Thomas Taylor, Van Norman Book Company, Western Hemisphere, J. Howard Woolmer, William P. Wreden, and Zeitlin & Ver Brugge. English: Beeleigh Abbey Books, Deighton Bell & Company, Bow Windows Book Shop, Francis Edwards, Ltd., W.&G. Foyle, Ltd., Frank Hammond, Kew Books, Maggs Brothers, Ltd., Stanley Noble, Bernard Quaritch, Ltd., Bertram Rota, Ltd., Chas. J. Sawyer, Henry Sotheran, Ltd., Henry Stevens, Son & Stiles, and Charles W. Traylen.

The catalogues of several auction houses have also been most useful, especially those of Christie, Manson & Woods, Sotheby Parke Bernet, and Swann Galleries, all of New York City, as well as the London catalogues of Christie's and Sotheby's. For quick reference, of course, the indispensable guides to the auction market remain the annual and cumulative index volumes of *American Book-Prices Current,* now back on schedule under the able editorship of Katharine Kyes Leab and Daniel J. Leab, and its equivalent English series *Book Auction Records,* published by Dawson's of Pall Mall.

Basic bibliographical works I have consulted range upwards into the thousands of books, but perhaps the two most valuable series have been the first six volumes of Jacob Blanck's *Bibliography of American Literature* (Yale University Press) and the eight-volume catalogue of *The Celebrated Collection of Americana Formed by the Late Thomas Winthrop Streeter* (Parke-Bernet). A few of the individual works that have served me well include Whitman Bennett's *A Practical Guide to American Book Collecting* (Bennett Book Studios); William Targ's books *Modern English First Editions and Their Prices, 10,000 Rare Books and Their Prices,* and *American First Editions and Their Prices* (all published by the Black Archer Press); Percy H. Muir's *Points, 1874–1930* (Constable); Robert W. Henderson's *Early American Sport* (Barnes); John C. Eckel's *The First Editions of the Writings of Charles Dickens* (Inman); T.W. Field's *An Essay Towards an Indian Bibliography* (Scribner, Armstrong); Ramon F. Adams' two fine compilations, *The Rampaging Herd* and *Six-Guns and*

*Saddle Leather* (Oklahoma); Ralph D. Gardner's *Road to Success: The Bibliography of the Works of Horatio Alger* (Wayside); Percy Muir's *English Children's Books, 1600–1900* (Praeger); Jacob S. Blanck's *Peter Parley to Penrod* (Bowker); Henry S. Boutell's *First Editions of Today and How to Tell Them* (Peacock Press); Merle Johnson's *American First Editions* (Mark Press); Wright Howes' *U.S.-iana* (Bowker); Henry R. Wagner's *The Plains and the Rockies*, revised by Charles L. Camp (Grabhorn Press); Lyle H. Wright's three volumes, *American Fiction, 1774–1850*, *American Fiction, 1851–1875*, and *American Fiction, 1876–1900* (Huntington Library); the Lilly Library exhibition catalogue *Three Centuries of American Poetry* (Indiana); Solon J. Buck's *Travel and Description, 1765–1865* (Illinois State Historical Society); Cecil J. Byrd's *A Bibliography of Illinois Imprints, 1814–58* (Chicago); Colton J. Storm's *A Catalogue of the Everett D. Graff Collection of Western Americana* (Chicago); Peter Decker's catalogue of the library of George W. Soliday (Antiquarian Press); the fourth edition of *The Oxford Companion to English Literature*, edited by Sir Paul Harvey, and its counterpart, *The Oxford Companion to American Literature*, edited by James D. Hart (both published by Oxford); Gary M. Lepper's *A Bibliographical Introduction to 75 Modern American Authors* (Serendipty); Gale Research's two helpful series, the annual *Bookman's Price Index* and the first two volumes of *First Printings of American Authors;* William S. Reese's *Six-Score: The 120 Best Books on the Range Cattle Industry* (Jenkins); Donald Gallup's *A Bibliography of Ezra Pound* (Hart-Davis) and *T.S. Eliot: A Bibliography* (Faber & Faber); Allan Wade's *A Bibliography of the Writings of W.B. Yeats* (Hart-Davis); Warren Roberts' *A Bibliography of D.H. Lawrence* (Hart-Davis); Matthew J. Bruccoli's *F. Scott Fitzgerald: A Bibliography* (Pittsburgh); Adrian H. Goldstone's and John R. Payne's *John Steinbeck: A Bibliographical Catalogue of the Adrian H. Goldstone Collection* (Texas); Audre Hanneman's *Ernest Hemingway: A Comprehensive Bibilography* (Princeton); B.D. Cutler's and Villa Stiles' *Modern British Authors: Their First Editions* (Greenberg); I.R. Brussel's *Anglo-American First Editions, 1826-1900, East to West* (Constable); G.F. Wilson's *A Bibliography of the Writings of W.H. Hudson* (Bookman's Journal); Jay Monaghan's *Lincoln Biography*, 2 volumes (Illinois State Historical Society); Jacob Schwartz's *1100 Obscure Points* (Ulysses Bookshop); Robert A. Wilson's *Gertrude Stein: A Bibliography* (Phoenix Bookshop); Flora V. Livingston's *Bibliography of the Works of Rudyard Kipling* (Wells); B.D. Cutler's *Sir James M. Barrie: A Bibliography* (Greenberg); Michael Sadleir's *Trollope: A Bibliography* (Dawson's of Pall Mall); Howard Haycraft's *Murder for Pleasure* (Appleton-Century-Crofts); Jack D. Rittenhouse's *The Santa Fe Trail: A Historical Bibliography* (New Mexico); the catalogue of the Thomas Wayne Norris collection of books on California and the Far West (Holmes); Chris Steinbrunner's and Otto Penzler's *Encyclopedia of Mystery and Detection* (McGraw-Hill); Everett F. Bleiler's

*Checklist of Fantastic Literature* (Shasta); Carl Petersen's *Each in Its Ordered Place: A Faulkner Collector's Notebook* (Ardis); Linton D. Massey's *"Man Working," 1919–1962: William Faulkner* (Virginia); Sidney Kramer's *A History of Stone & Kimball and Herbert S. Stone & Company* (Forgue); Jack Laurence Chalker's "Howard Phllips Lovecraft: A Bibliography," as published in Arkham House's *The Dark Brotherhood and Other Pieces* (by Lovecraft and others); the Lilly Library exhibition catalogue *The First Hundred Years of Detective Fiction, 1841–1941* (Indiana); Dwight Lowell Dumond's *A Bibliography of Anti-Slavery in America* (Michigan); David Kherdian's *Six Poets of the San Francisco Renaissance* (Giligia); B.J. Kirkpatrick's *A Bibliography of E.M. Forster* (Hart-Davis); Ernst L. Flintje's *Government Publications on Western Explorations* (Howes); Robert Ernest Cowan's *A Bibliography of the History of California and the Far West* (Long's); J. Leonard Jenewein's *Black Hills Booktrails* (Dakota Wesleyan); Tal Luther's *High Spots of Custer and Battle of the Little Big Horn Literature* (Kansas City Westerners); E.I. Edwards' *Desert Voices: A Descriptive Bibliography* (Westernlore); Eric Quayle's *The Collector's Book of Books* (Potter) and *The Collector's Book of Detective Fiction* (Studio Vista); Thomas J. Wise's *A Bibliography of the Writings of Joseph Conrad* (Dawson's of Pall Mall); George Robert Minkoff's *A Bibliography of the Black Sun Press* (Minkoff); George Dowden's *A Bibliography of Works by Allen Ginsberg* (City Lights); Robert Greenwood's *California Imprints, 1833–1862*, as compiled by Seiko June Suzuki and Marjorie B.C. Bloomfield's and Edward Mendelson's *W.H. Auden:* Pulham (Talisman); *A Bibliography* (Virginia); and Lawrence Lande's *A Bibliography of Canadiana* (McGill).

This random listing could go on indefinitely. Many other references in my own library and from other sources were consulted in the effort to make this compilation as broadly useful as possible. It is not, however, intended to be a bibliographical substitute for the more detailed original sources. New and more definitive bibliographical works are appearing year after year, and the serious dealer, librarian, and collector should be on the alert for them. The best single guide to such literature is the book-review section of the journal of the antiquarian book trade, *AB Bookman's Weekly*, Box AB, Clifton, New Jersey 07015.

A final title which I would like to add to this list will serve to ilustrate the importance of keeping up with the new offerings in the bibliographical field. It is a little book published in 1977 by the compilers, Edward N. Zempel and Linda A. Virkler, *A First Edition?* (Spoon River Press, Box 3635, Peoria, Illinois 61614), a most useful adjunct to Boutell's *First Editions* (mentioned in this section and in the "Introduction" to the *First Edition,* which follows). It updates the information in Boutell and is most useful in identifying first editions of both American and English publishers not included in the Boutell volume.

# INTRODUCTION

WHAT THIS BOOK IS ALL ABOUT: From December, 1957, until mid-May, 1971, I wrote for the Chicago *Daily News* and other newspapers in the United States and Canada a weekly syndicated column about rare books and their prices under the title "Gold in Your Attic" (in some newspapers "Rare Book Hunter"). So far as I know, it was the longest sustained series of its kind ever published anywhere, and the response from readers eager for information on the little-known rare book trade was enormous—a warning of which was given to me in advance by the distinguished English bookman John Carter and others with whom I had discussed the project. The mail was far greater than it was physically possible for me to respond to with personal answers, although I did try to reply to as many readers as possible, by personal letter, by notes in the column, or by means of various kinds of form letters which I designed to cover information of a generalized nature. The inadequacy of these means of communication prompted me to publish in 1958 my first book on the subject, *Gold in Your Attic* (Fleet), which reappeared ten years later in a revised edition as *The New Gold in Your Attic*. One story on that first book, by Hal Boyle of the Associated Press, brought countless letters to add to my communications problem. A sequel, *More Gold in Your Attic*, appeared in 1961. Each of these books, much smaller than the present volume, was designed primarily for the general public and bore alphabetical indexes to roughly 2,500 American books and pamphlets (with minimal detail and with no mention of English books). Despite their limited scope, they continue to have wide general use.

It was on the basis of my experiences with the column and these books that I began to prepare some six or seven years ago a much larger index, with the intention of including not only a great deal of additional information about individual books (binding data, bibliographical points, etc.), but a cross section not only of American books and pamphlets but also English books, for which my mail had indicated a heavy reader demand. I have also included a few books published elsewhere in Europe by English and American authors. So far as I know, the only comparable books of the kind I contemplated have been Seymour de Ricci's 1921 *The Book Collector's Guide* (Rosenbach) and *10,000 Rare Books and Their Prices*, by William Targ, published in 1936.

My aim was to prepare a comprehensive work that would be of use not only to the general reader, but also to the serious and sophisticated collector and to libraries, scholars, and booksellers as well. It was obvious almost from the start that in order to keep the project from becoming too formidable, I must establish a set of ground rules, which I have more or less followed.

THE SCOPE AND METHOD OF THE BOOK: My first decision was to limit the entries primarily to nineteenth- and twentieth-century books—*i.e.*, to use the year 1800 as a starting point. Since a compilation of this kind is not a bibliography in the true sense, I decided, as with the *Attic* series, to discard orthodox bibliographical form and list books simply in an author-title alphabetical form as an expedient method of making the book useful to the largest number of readers. In other words, if a book has an author named on the title page, it will be found, if included here, under the author's name as published, even though that may be a pseudonym. Thus, while most bibliographical works list Mark Twain's books under his real name, Samuel Langhorne Clemens, you will find him here under Twain. Another example: Mary Baker Eddy is widely known, but *Science and Health* is listed here under the name she used on the title page of that famous book, Mary Baker Glover. If an author's book is anonymous, it will be found listed here under its title, even though its authorship may be generally well known. An example is T.S. Eliot's anonymous *Ezra Pound His Metric and Poetry*, which is listed here under the title rather than under Eliot's name. In most cases in which this unorthodox method has been used, I have provided cross-references for the quick use of anyone who may be trying to locate a book.

A third ground rule I established was to exclude, with some exceptions, books with a retail value in the current market of less than $25, because to have included lower-priced books would have made necessary an index running into the hundreds of thousands of entries—an obviously impossible work without the cooperation of a large research staff and one that no commercial publishing house could possibly price within the means of the readers I wanted to reach.

A fourth ground rule was to limit the inclusions wherever possible to books *in fine condition and in their original binding* and to describe both the bindings and the editions (including bibliographical points of identification). Thus, with the exception of limited or signed editions issued as a regular part of publishing procedure, I have eliminated in most cases signed copies, unique or presentation copies, books annotated in the author's hand, etc. The reasons for these decisions are, first, that *in most cases rebound copies are worth less* than copies in original binding and, second, that an author's signature or other writing by the author may greatly enhance the value of the book. In other words, my chief aim was to include only books in their original condition—*i.e.*, as issued by the publisher and unaffected by anything that may have been done with or to them after publication.

The final ground rule was to provide as accurately as possible through examining the catalogues (and often the stocks) of leading booksellers in both England and America, as well as the book auction records of the major galleries, an up-to-date range of prices within which a scarce or rare book might be expected to be available at retail. (The auction prices are indicated with a capital A, followed by the auction season concerned; example: "$150 (A, 1971).") The decision to include some auction records was intended as both a support and a background for the use of experienced collectors, librarians, and booksellers, as well as an aid to the general reader in understanding and interpreting the book market. In many cases—especially with rare and very expensive books—the only price information available to layman or professional is in the auction records. Parenthetically, I should add that in general, as I have pointed out in my column and my other books, auction prices in the case of the majority of books that appear on the market in America and England are in most cases at what should be considered the "wholesale" level—prices paid by dealers—since it is the dealers who make up most of the audience at rare book auctions. Thus, a book that brings $25 at auction will generally wind up in some dealer's catalogue at half again or twice that price, and often more. An example I have witnessed within the month was the purchase by a dealer at auction for $50 of a copy of an art book containing two original lithographs; it was later priced by the purchaser at $225. I should add, however, that auction prices in the case of books in the higher brackets— in the retail range of roughly $500 and upward—quite frequently are fairly close to retail values. The reason for this is that collectors, libraries, and institutions commonly authorize major booksellers to bid for them at auctions on a 10 percent fee arrangement. In other words, a library may authorize a dealer to pay $1,000 for a book for which, if obtained, it will pay the dealer $1,100 (plus travel or other allowances), the extra $100 representing the dealer's 10 percent commission for acting as representative. One other point to be made about the auction records is that they often present problems confusing even to the most experienced bookman, such as wide variations in the prices on the same book in the same year—for example, $15 to $85. In general there are reasons for these variations (usually a matter of condition), which one can solve only by consulting the auction catalogue (or through the happenstance of having attended the sale). From these comments then, it should be obvious that the book auction records, as accurate as their compilers try to make them, are not an absolute guide to values and must be used with caution and interpreted with a fairly sophisticated knowledge of the book trade in general.

CONDITION IS THE KEY: Let me underscore the fact that the price ranges indicated herein are for books *in original binding and in fine condition.* The price spreads are included because the book market is a free market in which each dealer is at liberty to price a book as he personally values it in relation to his own knowledge of scarcity and demand and basic value. Thus a New York dealer may have a book priced at $75, a London dealer at $110, and a San Francisco dealer at $65. From this, it should be obvious that shopping around may sometimes be advisable. In general, however, the international rare book trade is a vast, loose network of independent dealers in which there is, with certain limits, a general unanimity of opinion concerning the values of books.

By and large it is *condition* that determines the price asked for a scarce or rare book. In recent years I have noted a very strong trend among collectors (and sometimes libraries) to accept only the finest copies available—regardless of price. Thus I observed in one shop a customer who was offered a fine first-edition copy of John Steinbeck's *The Grapes of Wrath* without dust jacket for $10 and turned it down for an absolutely mint copy in dust jacket at $75.

In considering the prices included in this compilation, it should always be kept in mind that inferior copies—poor, average, or even good to very good copies—may be worth less than the prices I have noted, as will be rebound copies. Obviously, books with defects—lacking dust jackets (if originally included, as with most books published since 1900) or having torn pages, soiled covers, or pages written on or underlined—are going to be worth less than the prices I have shown. Additionally, it should be kept in mind that the book market is steadily changing and that quite often the value of a book will rise sharply within a short space of time, so that even before this book is in your hands, the prices on some items listed herein may be considered low. This will be true despite the fact that every effort has been made to include catalogue prices and, where useful, auction records into the 1972 season.

POINTS: Bibliography is not an exact science, and no library, least of all my own, could possibly contain a complete bibliographical guide to the 15,000 to 18,000 separate items I have listed herein. Wherever possible, I have included the most reliable data I could find in order to assist the reader in identifying the first editions, as well as first issues, first states, etc. More detailed information on many of the major works listed may be consulted in bibliographies.

HOW DOES ONE TELL A FIRST EDITION? This is the question asked most frequently, and it is one of the more difficult questions to answer. There is, in fact, no single statement that will serve as an adequate answer. In general, it can be said that if the date on the title page of a book agrees with the date on the verso, or back, of the title page, the book may be assumed to be a first edition, provided there are no indications to the contrary. The question is, however, much more complicated than that; this is one of the reasons why it is necessary to include in many of the entries herein the bibliographical points of identification.

There is unfortunately no unanimity of method among either English or American publishers of identifying their first editions. Henry S. Boutell's *First Editions of Today and How to Tell Them* (Peacock Press), in its 1965 fourth edition, revised, contains a relatively up-to-date list of American and English publisher statements concerning their various methods of identifying their books. For example, Atheneum, Bobbs-Merrill, Doubleday, Dutton, Farrar, Straus & Giroux, Harcourt Brace Jovanovich, Harper & Row, Holt, Rinehart & Winston, Houghton Mifflin, Alfred A. Knopf, Lippincott, Little, Brown, Macmillan, W.W. Norton, Prentice-Hall, Random House, and the University of Oklahoma Press are among the larger American publishers who in general currently indicate on the copyright page (or elsewhere) the first appearances of their books with the words "First edition," "First printing," or other equivalent terminology. (In the case of some of these publishers these conditions have not always applied.) Other publishers use different methods, such as, for example, Putnam's, which reports that it does not indicate on its first editions that they are such (meaning they are) and adds, "When a book is reprinted, we as a rule print under the copyright notice the words 'Second Impression,' or whatever number the printing may be." Many publishers frankly state that they have no means of identifying their first editions. Indeed, New Directions, the publishers of some of the more collectible of modern authors, including Dylan Thomas, have been the despair of collectors who have been unable to untangle their various printings. (I have seen one New Directions book exactly identical with another copy except that the binding was of an entirely different color and style. The company itself told the Boutell editors in 1964 that "we are trying to remember to mark First Edition on copyright pages," but I have seen few so marked.) The situation with English publishers is just as chaotic, with practices varying from publisher to publisher. Most of the English trade houses, such as Faber & Faber and André Deutsch, seem to favor a simple line "First Published 1972" (or some similar equivalent) on the copyright page, with notations of later printings or "impressions" being made on subsequent issues.

In the case of nineteenth-century books, the practices of publishers were equally various, so that, in summary, I must say that aside from the rule of thumb about title page and copyright page agreement, every book must be considered as an individual problem. Unless the book itself is somehow identifiable as a first edition, if may be necessary to consult author bibliographies (and other library or bookseller resources, including catalogues) for exact information unless I have included it herein.

ABOUT SELLING YOUR BOOKS: The rare book trade, like most antiquarian businesses, is a relatively small market operated by dealers of varying degrees of competence, style, and temperament. The prices given in this handbook are prices at the retail level and are *not* prices that a dealer can be expected to pay for them. Whether you sell at retail to collectors or at wholesale to dealers is your own choice. In my experience, most dealers are willing to pay about 50 percent of retail value (and sometimes more) for books for which they have immediate customers or a relatively steady demand. In general, they incline to pay less—20 percent to, say, 35 percent—for books for stock. This, I think, is what one must expect when it is considered that they often must sit with books for years before finding a customer for them. Meanwhile, rent and salaries and all the other items of overhead, including the frightfully high present cost of printing catalogues, goes on and on. The net profit in the rare book trade is not noticeably large.

One final word: *Never be guilty of asking a dealer to price your books for you* (asking for a free appraisal). Most dealers will make appraisals—but probably they will expect to be paid a fee. One dealer I know charges $500 a day for appraising large collections. Another has a flat fee of $25 for appraising a single book. The best thing to do is to prepare your own list of books, identifying them as best you can, and decide what you want for them. Do not take a large lot of books to a dealer and ask him to look at them. He simply doesn't have the time. It is far better to list them first and show him the list, asking if he has a possible interest in them. Your list should include the following information: author's name; title of book (from the title page); place and date of publication (from the title page); copyright date (from the back of the title page); a statement of the edition (if shown or known); a description of the binding (leather, cloth, paper, etc.); a description of the condition, noting all defects such as binding wear, torn pages, writing in the book, etc. If your books are right for the dealer, he will be glad to examine and buy them. In the event, finally, that you cannot price your own books, you may wish to ask him to make an offer, but do this only if you have confidence in the dealer and are willing to accept his judgment. Do not put him in a competitive position by taking a list around to his competitors to angle for the best price you can find.

BOOKS AS TREASURES: I have prepared this book, I hope, for readers who are interested in scarce and rare books as items to buy and treasure rather than to sell, although selling for profit is certainly an honorable practice! Whatever emphasis I have placed on price in all my writing about books has been with the hope of helping readers to identify scarce and rare items and of encouraging the collector to use caution in his buying and to obtain the finest possible copy within his means. I think it is wholly right for the book lover to cherish his prizes while at the same time conducting his search for fine books in such manner that they will always be worth at least as much as he pays for them. In fact, the whole history of book collecting shows that the really good books always increase in value as the years pass. There is a certain comfort, I think, in knowing that one has bought wisely and well.

# A

A. *Empedocles on Etna and Other Poems*. By A. Green cloth. London, 1852. (By Matthew Arnold.) First edition. $250-$350. London, 1896. Ballantyne Press. Boards. One of 210. $100-$150.

A. *Strayed Reveller (The), and Other Poems*. By A. Dark green cloth. London, 1849. (By Matthew Arnold.) First edition. $250-$350.

A., T.B. *The Bells: A Collection of Chimes*. By T.B.A. Brown cloth. New York, 1855. (By Thomas Bailey Aldrich.) First edition. $35-$50. (Note: Also supposed to exist with "Boston & New York & Cincinnati" imprint.)

ABBEY, James. *California. A Trip Across the Plains in the Spring of 1850*. 64 pp., printed wrappers. New Albany, Ind., 1850. First edition. $3,000-$4,000.

ABBEY, John Roland. *Scenery of Great Britain and Ireland in Aquatint and Lithography, 1770-1860*. Frontispiece in color, numerous other illustrations. Buckram. London, 1952. First edition. One of 500. In dust jacket. $500-$750.

ABBOT *(The)*. 3 vols., boards. Edinburgh, 1820. (By Sir Walter Scott.) First edition. $500-$750. Also, worn and stained, $325 (A, 1974).

ABBOTSFORD, *and Newstead Abbey*. By the Author of "The Sketch-Book." Boards. London, 1835. (By Washington Irving.) First edition. $200-$300. Philadelphia, 1835. Blue or green cloth, paper labels. First edition, first printing, with copyright notices on both pages 2 and 4. $400-$500.

ABBOTT, Jacob. See *Rollo Learning to Talk*.

A'BECKETT, Gilbert Abbott. *The Comic History of England*. Illustrated in color by John Leech. 20 parts in 19, blue wrappers. London, 1846-48. First edition. $400-$500. London, 1847-48. 2 vols., cloth. First edition in book form. $200-$250.

AB-SA-RA-KA, *Home of the Crows*. Folding map. Cloth. Philadelphia, 1868. (By Mrs. Henry B. Carrington.) First edition. $125-$200. Philadelphia, 1869. Cloth. Second edition. $40-$60. Philadelphia, 1878. Cloth. Third edition. $40-$80. Philadelphia, 1879. Fifth edition. $40-$60. Philadelphia, 1890. $75-$100.

ACELDAMA, *a Place to Bury Strangers In*. By a Gentleman of the University of Cambridge. Wrappers. London, 1898. (By Aleister Crowley.) First edition. $300-$400. Author's first book.

ACKERMANN, Rudolph. *A History of the University of Cambridge* [and] *A History of the University of Oxford*. Illustrated with color plates. 4 vols., red morocco. London, 1815-14. First editions. Together, $6,000-$8,000. Separately: *Cambridge*, $4,000-$4,500. *Oxford*, $2,000-$3,000.

ACKERMANN, Rudolph. *The Microcosm of London*. 104 colored aquatint plates by Pugin and Rowlandson. 3 vols., half morocco. London, (1808-10). First edition. $2,000-$6,000. Also, $4,160 (A, 1973). London, 1904. 3 vols., parchment and boards. $200-$300.

ACKLEY, Mary E. *Crossing the Plains and Early Days in California*. Illustrated. Boards, printed label on spine. San Francisco, 1928. First edition. $100-$125.

ACTIVE Anthology *(The)*. See Pound, Ezra.

ACTON, Harold. *The Last of the Medici.* Introduction by Norman Douglas. Portrait. Boards. Florence, Italy, 1930. First edition. One of 365 signed. In dust jacket. $60-$80.

*ACTS, Resolutions and Memorials, Adopted by the Second Legislative Assembly of the Territory of Arizona.* Boards. Prescott, Ariz., 1866. $400-$600. Prescott, 1867. *Acts*, etc., for 3d Assembly. Boards. $125-$200.

ADAMS, Andy. *The Log of a Cowboy.* Map, 6 plates. Brown pictorial cloth. Boston, 1903. First edition, first issue, with map and dated title page. In dust jacket. $150-$250. Lacking jacket, $85-$125.

ADAMS, Ansel. Portfolio Two: *The National Parks and Monuments.* San Francisco, 1950. Grabhorn printing. One of 100. $3,000-$5,000. Also, $2,600 (A, 1975).

ADAMS, Charles F., Jr., and Adams, Henry. *Chapters of Erie, and Other Essays.* Terracotta or green cloth. Boston, 1871. First edition. $50-$60.

ADAMS, Henry. See Adams, Charles F., Jr. Also see *Democracy; Mont Saint Michel and Chartres.*

ADAMS, Henry. *The Education of Henry Adams.* Blue cloth, leather spine label. Washington, 1907. First edition. One of 100. $2,000-$2,500. Boston, 1918. Revised and edited by Henry Cabot Lodge. Blue cloth. First trade edition. In dust jacket. $85-$100. New York, 1942. Limited Editions Club. Etchings by Samuel Chamberlain. Cloth. Boxed. $60-$75.

ADAMS, Henry. *A Letter to American Teachers of History.* Green or blue cloth. Washington, 1910. First edition. Signed by the author. (Blanck suggests that most copies were signed). $150-$200.

ADAMS, J.C. *Life of J.C. Adams.* (Cover title.) 29 pp., printed wrappers. (New York, 1860.) First edition. $1,500-$2,000. Lacking covers, and with caption title only: *The Hair-Breadth Escapes and Adventures of "Grizzly Adams."* $1,000-$1,500.

ADAMS, John Quincy. *Oration on the Life and Character of Gilbert Motier de Lafayette.* Wrappers. Washington, 1835. First edition. $75-$100. Another issue: One of a few on thick paper, specially bound in morocco. $200-$250. (Note: Inscribed copies bring more, of course, as with all Presidential items.)

ADAMS, Léonie. *High Falcon and Other Poems.* Cloth. New York, (1929). First edition. In dust jacket. $35-$40.

ADAMS, Léonie. *Those Not Elect.* Boards. New York, 1925. First edition. In dust jacket. $50-$75.

ADAMS, Will. *Errata: or, The Works of Will. Adams.* 2 vols., boards. New York, 1823. (By John Neal.) First edition. $100-$150.

ADAMS, William Taylor. See Ashton, Warren T.

ADE, George. *Artie.* Cloth. Chicago, 1896. First edition. $35-$50. Author's first book.

ADE, George. *Fables in Slang.* Tan decorated cloth. Chicago, 1900. First edition. $30-$50.

ADE, George. *One Afternoon with Mark Twain.* Stiff wrappers. Chicago, 1939. First edition. One of 350. $75-$100.

ADE, George. *Revived Remarks on Mark Twain.* 36 pp., wrappers. Chicago, 1936. First edition. One of 500 signed. $50-$75.

ADE, George. *Stories of the Streets and of the Town.* Edited by Franklin J. Meine. Cloth. Chicago, 1941. Caxton Club. One of 500. $40-$60.

ADE, George. *The Sultan of Sulu.* Illustrated. Pictorial cream wrappers. New York, 1903. First edition, with "Published May, 1903," on copyright page. $50-$75.

ADELER, Max. *Out of the Hurly-Burly.* Illustrated by A.B. Frost and others. Decorated cloth. Philadelphia, 1874. (By Charles Heber Clark.) First edition. $50-$75. Author's first book and first book illustrated by Frost.

ADMIRARI, Nil. *The Trollopiad; or, Travelling Gentlemen in America.* Half leather. New York, 1837. (By Frederick William Shelton.) First edition. $50-$75.

*ADVENTURES of a Brownie (The), as Told to My Child.* By the Author of "John Halifax, Gentleman." Cloth. London, 1872. (By Dinah Maria Mulock.) First edition. $75-$150.

*ADVENTURES of a Post Captain (The).* By a Naval Officer. 25 colored plates. Boards. London, (1817). (By Alfred Thornton.) First edition. $150-$250.

*ADVENTURES of Robin Day (The).* 2 vols., purple cloth, paper label on spine. Philadelphia, 1839. (By Robert Montgomery Bird.) First edition. $100-$150.

*ADVENTURES of Timothy Peacock, Esquire (The).* By a Member of the Vermont Bar. Cloth. Middlebury, Vt., 1835. (By Daniel Pierce Thompson.) First edition. $600. Author's first novel.

*ADVENTURES of Ulysses (The).* Frontispiece, engraved title page. Boards, paper label. London, 1808. (By Charles Lamb.) First edition. $200-$300.

*ADVENTURES of a Yankee (The), or The Singular Life of John Ledyard.* By a Yankee. Woodcuts. Boards and morocco. Boston, 1831. (By John Ledyard.) First edition. $150-$200.

*ADVENTURES of a Younger Son (The).* 3 vols. boards. London, 1831. (By Edward John Trelawny.) First edition. $300-$350. Author's first book.

AESCHYLUS. *Agamemnon: A Tragedy.* Translated by Edward FitzGerald. Wrappers. (London, 1865). First edition. $50-$75. London, 1876. Half leather. One of 250. $35-$50.

AESOP. *Fables.* Sir Roger L'Estrange translation. Illustrated by Stephen Gooden. Vellum. London, 1936. One of 500 signed by Gooden. Boxed. $600-$1,000. New York, 1933. Limited Editions Club. Samuel Croxall translation. Illustrated by Bruce Rogers. Boards and vellum. Boxed. $125-$150.

AGAPIDA, Fray Antonio. *A Chronicle of the Conquest of Granada.* 2 vols., boards and cloth, paper labels. Philadelphia, 1829. (By Washington Irving.) First edition. $150-$250. Large paper issue: $300-$400. London, 1829. 2 vols., boards. First English edition. $75-$100. New York, 1893. 2 vols., half morocco. Agapida Edition. One of 150. $50-$75.

AGASSIZ, Louis. *Lake Superior.* 16 plates. Cloth. Boston, 1850. First edition. $200-$250.

AGATE, James. *Ego: The Autobiography of James Agate.* Illustrated. Cloth. London, (1935). First edition. In dust jacket. $40-$60.

AGATE, James. *A Shorter Ego: The Autobiography of James Agate.* 2 vols., half morocco. London, (1945). One of 100 signed. $75-$100.

*AGE of Bronze (The).* Plain drab wrappers. London, 1823. (By George Gordon Noel, Lord Byron.) First edition. $400-$600.

AGEE, G.W. *Rube Burrows, King of Outlaws.* 194 pp., wrappers. (Cincinnati, 1890.) First edition. $50-$75. Chicago, (1890). $35-$45.

AGEE, James. See *Brooks-Bryce Anglo American Prize Essays—1927.*

AGEE, James. *A Death in the Family.* Blue cloth. New York, (1957). First edition, first issue, with title page printed in blue, "walking" for "waking" on page 80. In dust jacket. $30-$50. Advance issue: Blue wrappers. $150-$200.

AGEE, James. *Four Early Stories.* Boards and buckram. Iowa City, 1963. One of 285. In tissue dust jacket. $75-$125. West Branch, Iowa, 1964. Second issue. $50-$60.

4                                                                JAMES AGEE

AGEE, James. *Let Us Now Praise Famous Men*. Walker Evans photographs. Black cloth.
Boston, 1941. First edition. In dust jacket. $100-$125. Boston, 1960. Black cloth. In dust
jacket. $25-$35.

AGEE, James. *The Letters of James Agee to Father Flye*. Black cloth. New York, 1962.
First edition. In dust jacket. $25-$35.

AGEE, James. *The Morning Watch*. Boards. Boston, 1951. First edition. In dust jacket.
$75-$85.

AGEE, James. *Permit Me Voyage*. Cloth. New Haven, 1934. First edition. In dust jacket.
$250-$300. Author's first book.

AGRICOLA, Georgius. See Hoover, Herbert C. and Lou Henry.

AIKEN, Conrad. *Blue Voyage*. Boards. New York, 1927. First edition. One of 125 signed.
Boxed. $75. Trade edition: In dust jacket. $25.

AIKEN, Conrad. *The Coming Forth by Day of Osiris Jones*. Green cloth. New York, 1931.
First edition, first issue, with Scribner "A" on copyright page and "The Music" incorrectly printed as section title on page 37. In dust jacket. $45-$65.

AIKEN, Conrad. *Earth Triumphant and Other Tales in Verse*. Cloth. New York, 1914. First
edition. $75-$85. Author's first book.

AIKEN, Conrad. *The Jig of Forslin: A Symphony*. Cloth. Boston, 1916. First edition. In
dust jacket. $50-$100.

AIKEN, Conrad. *Preludes for Memnon*. Cloth. New York, 1931. First edition. In dust jacket. $30-$50.

AIKEN, Conrad. *Priapus and the Pool*. Boards. Cambridge, Mass., 1922. First edition.
Printed by Bruce Rogers. One of 425. $75. One of 50 (of the same edition) on handmade
paper and signed. $100-$150. New York, 1925. New edition, with added poems. $25.

AIKEN, Conrad. *Punch: The Immortal Liar*. Cloth. New York, 1921. First edition. In dust
jacket. $35-$50.

AIKEN, Conrad. *Scepticisms*. Green cloth, lettered in red. New York, 1919. First edition,
first binding. In dust jacket. $35-$40.

AIKEN, Conrad. *Selected Poems*. Cloth. New York, 1929. First edition. One of 210 on large
paper, signed. $150-$200. Trade edition: In dust jacket. $15-$25.

AIKEN, Conrad. *Thee*. Illustrated by Leonard Baskin. Boards. New York, (1967). First edition. One of 100 signed by author and artist. Boxed. $75-$150.

AIKEN, Conrad. *Turns and Movies and Other Tales in Verse*. Printed wrappers over
boards. Boston, 1916. First edition. $50-$75.

AINSWORTH, Ed. *The Cowboy in Art*. Illustrated, including color. Cloth. New York,
(1968). First trade edition. In dust jacket. $25-$35.

AINSWORTH, W. Harrison. *Cardinal Pole*. 3 vols., cloth. London, 1863. First edition.
$120.

AINSWORTH, W. Harrison. *Jack Sheppard*. Portrait and illustrations by George Cruikshank. 3 vols., green cloth. London, 1838-39. First edition. $250-$350. London, 1839-40.
Illustrated. 15 parts, wrappers. $300-$450.

AINSWORTH, W. Harrison. *Merry England: or, Nobles and Serfs*. 3 vols., green cloth.
London, 1874. First edition. $200-$225.

AINSWORTH, W. Harrison. *The Miser's Daughter*. Illustrated by George Cruikshank. 3
vols., black cloth. London, 1842. First edition. $150-$250.

AINSWORTH, W. Harrison. *Old Saint Paul's*. Illustrated by John Franklin and Phiz. 3

vols., cloth. London, 1841. First edition. $200-$250. (Also issued in 12 paperbound parts.) London, 1847. Red cloth. First octavo edition. $50-$60.

AINSWORTH, W. Harrison. *The Tower of London*. Illustrated by George Cruikshank. 13 parts in 12, wrappers. London, 1840. First edition. `$300-$400. London, 1840. Purple cloth. First book edition. $150-$200.

AKEN, David. *Pioneers of the Black Hills*. Pictorial wrappers. (Milwaukee, 1920?) First edition. $75-$125.

*ALARIC at Rome: A Prize Poem. Recited in Rugby School. June XII, MDCCCXL*. 12 pp., pink pictorial and printed wrappers. Rugby, England, 1840. (By Matthew Arnold.) First edition. $400-$500 and up. Author's first book of verse.

ALBEE, Edward. *The American Dream*. Cloth. New York, (1961). First edition. In dust jacket. $50-$65.

ALBEE, Edward. *Tiny Alice*. Cloth. New York, 1965. First edition. In dust jacket. $45-$60.

ALBEE, Edward. *Who's Afraid of Virginia Woolf?* Cloth. New York, 1962. First edition. In dust jacket. $45-$50.

ALBEE, Edward. *The Zoo Story. The Death of Bessie Smith. The Sandbox: Three Plays*. Blue cloth. New York, (1960). First edition. In dust jacket. $75-$100. Author's first book.

ALCOTT, A. Bronson. *Sonnets and Canzonets*. Illustrated with photographs. Cloth. Boston, 1882. First edition. One of 50 signed. $150-$200. (Note: The trade edition, lacking photographs, not especially valuable—about $35 in fine condition.)

ALCOTT, Louisa May. *Flower Fables*. Frontispiece and 5 plates. Cloth. Boston, 1855. First edition. $75-$100.

ALCOTT, Louisa May. *Hospital Sketches*. Printed green boards or cloth. Boston, 1863. First edition, first printing, in boards, with ad on back announcing Wendell Phillips' *Speeches* at $2.50 (not $2.25). $75-$150.

ALCOTT, Louisa May. *Kitty's Class Day*. 12 pp., printed buff wrappers. Boston, (1868). First edition. $200-$300. (Note: Issue points on this pamphlet are debatable; see Blanck's *Bibliography of American Literature*.)

ALCOTT, Louisa May. *Little Men*. Frontispiece. Blue cloth. London, 1871. First edition. $125-$150. Boston, 1871. Green cloth. First American edition, first issue, with ads at front listing *Pink and White Tyranny* as nearly ready. $200-$250.

ALCOTT, Louisa May. *Little Women*. Frontispiece and 3 plates, 2 vols., cloth. Boston, 1868-69. First edition, without "Part One" on spine of Vol. 1 and with Vol. 2 having no notice of *Little Women, Part First*, on page iv. $1,500-$2,000. Vol. 1 alone: $650 (A, 1974). New York, 1967. Limited Editions Club. Illustrated. Brocade cloth. Boxed. $40-$50.

ALCOTT, Louisa May. *Morning-Glories, and Other Stories*. Frontispiece and 3 plates. Cloth. Boston, 1868. First edition. $75.

ALCOTT, Louisa May. *An Old-Fashioned Girl*. Double frontispiece and 2 plates. Cloth. Boston, 1870. First edition, first issue, no ads on copyright page. $50-$75. Second issue, with ads on copyright page, $20.

ALCOTT, Louisa May. *The Rose Family*. 47 pp., printed wrappers, or cloth. Boston, 1864. First edition. Wrappers: $150-$200. Cloth: $100-$150.

ALDINGTON, Richard. *A.E. Housman and W.B. Yeats, Two Lectures*. Boards. (Hurst, England), 1955. Peacocks Press. One of 350. $40-$50.

ALDINGTON, Richard. *All Men Are Enemies*. Boards and buckram. London, 1933. One of 110 signed. $50-$75.

ALDINGTON, Richard. *At All Costs*. Boards and buckram. London, 1930. First edition. One of 275 signed. $35-$50.

ALDINGTON, Richard. *Balls and Another Book for Suppression*. Wrappers. London, 1930. Blue Moon Booklets No. 7. First edition. $40-$50. Also privately issued: (Westport), 1932. (Title: *Balls.)* Sewed, self-wrappers. One of "99 & a few others." $50-$85.

ALDINGTON, Richard. *The Colonel's Daughter: A Novel*. Green cloth. London, 1931. First edition. One of 210 signed. $50-$60.

ALDINGTON, Richard. *D.H. Lawrence*. Boards and buckram. London, 1930. First edition. One of 260 signed. In tissue dust jacket. $45-$50. Another issue: Orange wrappers. $20.

ALDINGTON, Richard. *Death of a Hero*. Cloth. London, 1929. First edition. In dust jacket. $35. Paris, 1930. 2 vols., printed wrappers. Unexpurgated text. One of 300. $200-$225.

ALDINGTON, Richard. *Ezra Pound and T.S. Eliot: A Lecture*. Boards. London, 1954. Peacocks Press. First edition. One of 350. $50-$75. Another issue: Full morocco. One of 10 trial copies on Azure paper, signed. $200-$300. Also, $175 (A, 1977).

ALDINGTON, Richard. *Fifty Romance Lyric Poems*. Black cloth. New York, 1928. First edition. One of 9 on green paper, signed. $100-$150. Another issue: One of 900. $25-$35.

ALDINGTON, Richard. *A Fool i' the Forest*. Cloth. London, 1925. First edition, limited, signed. In dust jacket. $60-$75.

ALDINGTON, Richard. *Images (1910-1915)*. Hand-colored wrappers. (London, 1915). First edition, $150-$175. Author's first book.

ALDINGTON, Richard. *Images of War*. Illustrated. Boards and cloth. London, 1919. First edition. One of 200. $100-$150.

ALDINGTON, Richard. *Images—Old and New*. Stiff boards. Boston, 1916. First edition. In dust jacket. $35-$50.

ALDINGTON, Richard. *Last Straws*. Green suede. Paris, 1930. Hours Press. First edition. One of 200 signed. $100-$150.

ALDINGTON, Richard. *Love and the Luxembourg*. Red buckram. New York, 1930. First edition. One of 475 signed. Boxed. $50-$60.

ALDINGTON, Richard. *The Love of Myrrhine and Konallis*. Cloth. Chicago, 1926. First edition. One of 150 signed. $50-$60.

ALDINGTON, Richard. *Stepping Heavenward*. Boards and cloth. Florence, Italy, 1931. One of 808 signed. In dust jacket. Boxed. $100-$150. London, 1931. Boards. $20-$25.

ALDRICH, Thomas Bailey. See A., T.B.

ALDRICH, Thomas Bailey. *The Ballad of Babie Bell and Other Poems*. Brown cloth. New York, 1859. First edition, first issue, with Broadway address for publisher. $50-$75.

ALDRICH, Thomas Bailey. *Friar Jerome's Beautiful Book*. Red vellum, linen ties. (Boston, 1836.) One of 250 on large paper. $50-$100.

ALDRICH, Thomas Bailey. *Judith and Holofernes*. Cloth. Boston, 1896. First edition. One of 50 with paper labels. $100-$150. Trade edition: $25.

ALDRICH, Thomas Bailey. *Prudence Palfrey*. Cloth. Boston, 1874. First edition. $35.

ALDRICH, Thomas Bailey. *The Story of a Bad Boy*. Cloth. Boston, 1870. First edition, first issue, with line 20 on page 14 reading "scattered" and line 10 on page 197 reading "abroad." $250-$500. Boston, 1895. Illustrated by A.B. Frost. Decorated cloth. $35-$50.

ALDRIDGE, Reginald. *Life on a Ranch.* Frontispiece and 3 plates. Stiff wrappers. New York, 1884. First edition. $225-$500.

ALDRIDGE, Reginald. *Ranch Notes in Kansas.* 4 plates. Pictorial cloth. London, 1884. First English edition (of *Life on a Ranch*; see above). $150-$200.

ALEXANDER, E.P. *Military Memoirs of a Confederate.* Maps, 3 plates. Cloth. New York, 1907. First edition. $50-$75.

ALEXANDER, Hartley B. (editor). *Sioux Indian Painting.* 50 color plates. 2 vols., large folio, loose in pictorial cloth portfolios, with ties. Nice, France, (1938). First edition. One of 400. $500-$800. Also, $425 (A, 1974).

ALEXANDER, John H. *Mosby's Men.* Illustrated. Cloth. New York, 1907. First edition. In dust jacket. $100-$125.

ALEXANDER, William. *Picturesque Representations of the Dress and Manners of the Austrians.* 50 color plates. Full contemporary morocco. London, (about 1813). $400-$500. Also, similar volumes, about 1814, covering the Chinese (50 color plates), Russians (64 plates), Turks (61), English (50), similar values.

ALEXANDRE, Arsène. *The Decorative Art of Leon Bakst.* Notes on the Ballets by Jean Cocteau. Translated by Harry Melvill. Portrait. 77 plates, 50 in color. Folio, half vellum. London, 1913. First edition. $750-$1,000. Another issue: One of 80 with an original watercolor. $676 (A, 1973).

ALGER, Horatio, Jr. See Putnam, Arthur Lee; Starr, Julian. Also see *Nothing to Do; Timothy Crump's Ward.*

ALGER, Horatio, Jr. *Abraham Lincoln, The Backwoods Boy.* Illustrated. Pictorial cloth. New York, 1883. First edition, first issue, with ads listing this book as No. 2 in "Boyhood and Manhood" series. $75-$100.

ALGER, Horatio, Jr. *Adrift in the City.* Illustrated. Tan cloth, stamped in blue and black. Philadelphia, (1865). First edition with Porter & Coates imprint. $50. Later issues, published by Henry T. Coates, $30.

ALGER, Horatio, Jr. *Bertha's Christmas Vision: An Autumn Sheaf.* Blind-stamped cloth. Boston, 1856. First edition. $300-$350. Also, $175 (A, 1973). Author's first book.

ALGER, Horatio, Jr. *Dan, the Detective.* Illustrated. Cloth. New York, 1884. First edition. $200-$250.

ALGER, Horatio, Jr. *Dean Dunham.* Stiff tan pictorial wrappers. New York, 1890. First edition. (No. 32 in weekly series of "Leather-Clad Tales of Adventure and Romance.") $75-$100.

ALGER, Horatio, Jr. *Digging for Gold.* Illustrated. Pictorial tan cloth. Philadelphia, (1892). First edition. $40-$50.

ALGER, Horatio, Jr. *The Errand Boy.* Red and black wrappers. New York, 1888. First edition. (Vol. 1, No. 14, of Boys' Home Library.) $50-$75.

ALGER, Horatio, Jr. *Falling in with Fortune.* Illustrated. Pictorial green cloth. New York, (1900). (By Edward Stratemeyer.) First edition, with no Alger titles in ads at back. $40-$50.

ALGER, Horatio, Jr. *Fame and Fortune.* Illustrated. Cloth. Boston, (1868). First edition, first state, with no frontispiece and with damaged type in "By" on title page. $50-$60.

ALGER, Horatio, Jr. *Finding a Fortune.* Illustrated. Pictorial tan cloth. Philadelphia, 1904. First edition, with interlocking script monogram on spine. $50-$60.

ALGER, Horatio, Jr. *The Five Hundred Dollar Check.* Pictorial tan cloth. New York, (1891). First book edition, first issue, with United States Book Co. imprint on title page and "Porter & Coates" on spine. $250-$300. Later issue, with "Lovell" on spine,

$100-$150. (Note: This book had appeared earlier as a paperback Leather-Clad Tale under the title *$500; or Jacob Marlowe's Secret*, 1890. Value: $50-$75.)

ALGER, Horatio, Jr. *Forging Ahead*. Illustrated. Tan cloth. Philadelphia, 1903. First edition, with date in Roman numerals at foot of title page. $50-$60.

ALGER, Horatio, Jr. *Frank and Fearless*. Illustrated. Tan cloth. Philadelphia, 1897. First edition, with dated title page. $50-$60. Later, title undated, $30-$35.

ALGER, Horatio, Jr. *Frank Fowler, the Cash Boy*. Wrappers. New York, (1887). First edition, A.L. Burt imprint, Boys' Home Library. $50-$60. Another issue, same year: Cloth. $30.

ALGER, Horatio, Jr. *Frank's Campaign*. Illustrated. Cloth. Boston, 1864. First edition, first state, with vertical lines on covers. $50. Second state, pebbled cloth. $35. (The second edition is so indicated on title page.)

ALGER, Horatio, Jr. *From Canal Boy to President*. Illustrated. Green cloth. New York, 1881. First edition, first issue, with pages 266 and 268 transposed and with erratum slip tipped to page 267. $40-$60. Later printings, about $20.

ALGER, Horatio, Jr. *Grand'ther Baldwin's Thanksgiving*. Purple cloth. Boston, (1875). First edition, published by Loring. $75-$100.

ALGER, Horatio, Jr. *In a New World*. Cloth. Philadelphia, (1893). First edition, with *Digging for Gold* as Alger title listed in ads at back. $30. (See *The Nugget Finders* for British reissue.)

ALGER, Horatio, Jr. *Joe's Luck*. Wrappers. New York, 1887. Boys' Home Library. $50-$75.

ALGER, Horatio, Jr. *Julius; or The Street Boy Out West*. Illustrated. Pictorial cloth. Boston, (1874). First edition, with no listing in ads of any volumes of the Brave and Bold series. $40.

ALGER, Horatio, Jr. *Luke Walton, or The Chicago Newsboy*. Cloth. Philadelphia, (1889). First edition. $35-$50.

ALGER, Horatio, Jr. *Making His Mark*. Illustrated. Dark blue cloth. Philadelphia, 1901. First edition, with only two Alger titles listed on last page of ads. $40-$45.

ALGER, Horatio, Jr. *Mark Stanton*. Wrappers. New York, 1890. (Leather-Clad paperback.) First edition $60-$75.

ALGER, Horatio, Jr. *The Nugget Finders*. Colored frontispiece. Green cloth. London, 1894. First English edition of *In a New World*, first state, with publisher's address as 48 Paternoster Row. $60. Later, with address as 3 Pilgrim Street. $40.

ALGER, Horatio, Jr. *Paul the Peddler*. Illustrated. Cloth. Boston, (1871). First edition with book ads at front listing *Phil, the Fiddler* for April, 1872, *Slow and Sure* for November, and *Strive and Succeed* for October. $40-$50.

ALGER, Horatio, Jr. *Phil, the Fiddler*. Illustrated. Cloth. Boston, (1872). First edition, with ads at front listing *Slow and Sure* for November, 1872, and *Strive and Succeed* for October. $50-$60.

ALGER, Horatio, Jr. *Ragged Dick; or Street Life in New York with the Boot-Blacks*. Pictorial title page, 3 illustrations. Cloth. Boston, (1868). First edition, first issue, with *Fame and Fortune* listed in ads for publication "In December." $450-$600.

ALGER, Horatio, Jr. *Ralph Raymond's Heir*. Printed brown wrappers. New York, (1892). (Idle Hour Series paperback.) First edition. $50-$60.

ALGER, Horatio, Jr. *Robert Coverdale's Struggle*. Pictorial colored cover. New York, (1910). New Medal Library No. 555. First edition. $500 and up. (One copy known.)

ALGER, Horatio, Jr. *Tom Thatcher's Fortune*. Wrappers. New York, 1888. Boys' Home Library. First edition. $50-$60.

ALGER, Horatio, Jr. *Tony, the Hero*. Cloth. New York, (1880). First edition, with J.S. Ogilvie imprint. $75.

ALGER, Horatio, Jr. *The Train Boy*. 36 pp., wrappers. New York, (1882). First edition. $35. New York, 1883. Cloth. First complete edition. $40-$45.

ALGER, Horatio, Jr. *The Western Boy*. Pictorial title. Cloth. (New York, 1878). First edition, with G.W. Carleton ad at front of book. $200-$300.

ALGER, Horatio, Jr. *The Young Acrobat*. Orange wrappers. New York, 1888. First edition. No. 8 in Munsey's Popular Series for Boys and Girls. $75.

ALGER, Horatio, Jr. *The Young Miner; or Tom Nelson in California*. Boards and cloth. San Francisco, 1965. Book Club of California. One of 450. $75-$85.

ALGER, Horatio, Jr. *The Young Musician*. Illustrated. Cloth. Philadelphia, 1906. First edition, with no book ads, $60-$70.

ALGER, Horatio, Jr., and Cheney, O. Augusta. *Seeking His Fortune and Other Dialogues*. Pictorial cloth. Boston, (1875). First edition. $500. New York, 1882. Boards. Reprint by Ward & Drummond. $50-$60.

ALGREN, Nelson. *The Man with the Golden Arm*. Cloth. Garden City, 1949. First edition. In dust jacket. $35-$50.

ALGREN, Nelson. *The Neon Wilderness*. Green cloth. New York, 1947. First edition. In dust jacket. $40-$60.

ALGREN, Nelson. *Never Come Morning*. Introduction by Richard Wright. Blue cloth. New York, (1942). First edition. In dust jacket. $75-$85.

ALGREN, Nelson. *Somebody in Boots*. Brown cloth. New York, (1935). First edition. In dust jacket. $300-$350. Author's first book.

ALGREN, Nelson. *A Walk on the Wild Side*. Boards. New York, (1956). First edition. In dust jacket. $35-$50.

*ALHAMBRA (The)*. See Crayon, Geoffrey.

ALKEN, Henry. *The National Sports of Great Britain*. 50 colored plates. Folio, boards (?) or morocco. London, 1820 (-21). First edition, first issue, with engraved 1820 title page and with watermarks dated 1816 and 1818. $6,000-$12,000. London, 1821. Second issue, without 1820 title page. $5,000-$10,000. London, 1823. Second edition. $4,000-$5,000. Also, $4,000 (A, 1975). London, 1824. Morocco. $750-$1,000. London, 1825. Boards. First octavo edition. $600-$750. Large paper issue: $800-$1,000. London, 1903. Boards and cloth. $150-$250. Another edition: (New York), 1904. Half morocco. $400-$600.

ALKEN, Henry. *Scraps from the Sketch-Books of Henry Alken*. 42 colored plates. Boards. London, 1821. First edition. $800-$1,500. London, 1822. Contemporary half morocco. $400-$500. London, 1825. Morocco. $350-$500.

ALKEN, Henry. *Shooting, or One Day's Sport of Three Real Good Ones, However Ignorant of Sporting Rules*. 6 color plates. Buff printed wrappers (dated 1824). London, 1823. First edition. $400-$600.

*ALLAHAKBARRIE Book of Broadway Cricket for 1899*. Illustrated. Parchment wrappers. (London, 1899). (By Sir James M. Barrie.) In cloth folder and slipcase. $300-$350.

ALLAN, J.T. (compiler). *Central and Western Nebraska, and the Experiences of Its Stock Growers*. (Cover title.) 16 pp., pictorial wrappers. Omaha, 1883. $100-$125. (Note: A Union Pacific land department pamphlet.)

ALLAN, J.T. (compiler). *Western Nebraska and the Experiences of Its Actual Settlers*. 16 pp., wrappers. Omaha, 1882. $100-$125.

ALLEN, Miss A.J. (compiler). *Ten Years in Oregon*. Portrait. Calf. Ithaca, N.Y., 1848. First edition. $150-$250. Second issue, same date, portrait omitted, pages added. Sheep, $150-$250. Ithaca, 1850. Pictorial cloth. $40-$50.

ALLEN, Hervey. See Allen, William Hervey.

ALLEN, Hervey, and Mabbott, Thomas O. (editors). *Poe's Brother*. Boards. New York, printing, with publisher's monogram on copyright page and with numerous typographical errors, among them "Xaxier" for "Xavier" in line 6 of page 352, "ship" for "shop" in line 18 of page 1086, and the word "found" repeated in line 22 of page 397. In dust jacket. $50-$60. De luxe issue: 3 vols., suede boards. One of 105 signed. $200-$300. New York, 1937. Limited Editions Club. 3 vols., orange cloth. One of 1,500. Boxed. $30-$50.

ALLEN, Hervey. *The Bride of Huitzil*. Boards and cloth. New York, 1922. First edition. One of 350 signed. $50-$60.

ALLEN, Hervey. *Israfel: The Life and Times of Edgar Allan Poe*. 2 vols., cloth. New York, 1926. First edition, first state, with wineglass on table in Longfellow portrait facing page 529. In dust jackets. $50-$75. De luxe issue: Three-quarters leather. One of 250. $75-$100.

ALLEN, Hervey. *Wampum and Old Gold*. Boards. New Haven, 1921. First edition. One of 500. $40-$50.

ALLEN, Hervey, and Mabbott, Thomas O. (editors). *Poe's Brother*. Boards. New York, (1926.) First edition. One of 1,000. Boxed. $35-$50.

ALLEN, Ira. *A Concise Summary of the Second Volume of the Olive Branch*. 24 pp., wrappers. Philadelphia, 1807. $100-$125.

ALLEN, J.A. *Notes on the Natural History of Portions of Montana and Dakota*. 61 pp., wrappers. Boston, 1874. $100-$125.

ALLEN, W.A. *The Sheep Eaters*. 6 plates. Cloth. New York, 1913. First edition. $25-$35.

ALLEN, William A. *Adventures with Indians and Game*. 25 plates. Cloth, or half leather. Chicago, 1903. First edition. $100-$125.

ALLEN, William Hervey. *Ballads of the Border*. Printed wrappers. (El Paso), 1916. (By Hervey Allen.) First edition, probable first state, with author's name misspelled "Hervy" on copyright page. $400-$600. There were many later printings. Author's first book.

*ALLIES' Fairy Book (The)*. 12 colored plates, other illustrations by Arthur Rackham. Buckram. London, (1916). One of 525 signed by the artist. $450-$600. Trade edition: Cloth. First issue, with pictorial end papers. In dust jacket. $100-$150.

ALLINGHAM, William. *Sixteen Poems*. Selected by William Butler Yeats. Boards and linen. Dundrum, Ireland, 1905. Dun Emer Press. One of 200. $100-$150.

ALLISON, William. *The British Thoroughbred Horse*. Cloth. London, 1901. First edition. $50-$85. London, 1907. Second edition. $40-$60.

ALMONTE, Juan Nepomuceno. *Noticia Estadistica sobre Tejas*. 3 folding tables. Boards or wrappers. Mexico, 1835. First edition. $1,250-$2,000.

*ALNWICK Castle, with Other Poems*. Printed tan wrappers. New York, 1827. (By Fitz-Greene Halleck.) First edition. $150-$200.

*ALONZO and Melissa*. Contemporary leather and boards. Brattleboro, Vt., 1824. (By Isaac Mitchell.) $25-$35. (Note: See author entry for first edition.)

*ALTA California*. By a Captain of Volunteers. 64 pp., cloth. Philadelphia, 1847. First edition. $450-$600.

ALTER, J. Cecil. *James Bridger: Trapper, Frontiersman, Scout, and Guide*. 18 plates.

Cloth. Salt Lake City, (1925). First edition. One of 1,000 signed. $60-$100. Columbus, Ohio, 1951. Cloth. In dust jacket. $25-$35.

ALTISONANT, Lorenzo. *Letters to Esq. Pedant, in the East*. Boards, Cambridge City, Ind., 1844. (By Samuel Klinefelter Hoshour.) First edition. $75-$150. Cincinnati, 1850. Boards. $50.

*ALTOWAN; Or Incidents of Life and Adventure in the Rocky Mountains*. By an Amateur Traveller. Edited by J. Watson Webb. 2 vols., cloth. New York, 1846. (By Sir William Drummond Stewart.) First edition. $350-$500. (Note: Howes says this was "probably actually written by Webb.")

ALVAREZ, A. *Lost*. Cloth. (London), 1968. First edition. One of 250 signed. $40-$60.

*AMERICAN Arguments for British Rights*. Wrappers. London, 1806. (By William Loughton Smith.) $75-$100.

*AMERICAN Caravan IV: A Yearbook of American Literature*. Cloth. New York, 1931. First edition. In dust jacket. $50-$60.

*AMERICAN Church Silver of the 17th and 18th Centuries*. Boards. Boston, 1911. Boston Museum of Fine Arts. $50-$75.

*AMERICAN Cruiser (The)*. Cloth. Boston, 1846. (By Capt. George Little.) First edition. $65.

*AMERICAN Shooter's Manual (The)*. By a Gentleman of Philadelphia County. Frontispiece, 2 plates, errata. Contemporary calf. Philadelphia, 1827. (By Dr. Jesse Y. Kester?) First edition. $600-$800. Also, repaired copy, $300 (A, 1975).

*AMERICANA—Beginnings: A Selection from the Library of Thomas W. Streeter*. 97 pp., wrappers. Morristown, N.J., 1952. One of 325. $125-$150.

AMES, John Henry. *Lincoln, the Capital of Nebraska*. Wrappers. Lincoln, 1870. First edition. $150.

AMMONS, A.R. *Ommateum: With Doxology*. Cloth. Philadelphia, (1955—actually 1954). First edition. $400-$500. The poet's first book.

AMSDEN, Charles A. *Navaho Weaving*. 122 plates, many in color. Cloth. Santa Ana, 1934. First edition. $75-$100. Albuquerque, 1948 (actually 1949). Cloth. $45. Chicago, (1964). Cloth. $20.

*ANALYSIS of the Hunting Field (The)*. 7 colored plates by Henry Alken, 43 woodcuts. Green or red cloth. London, 1846. (By Robert Smith Surtees.) First edition, first issue, green cloth (some copies with preface dated 1846, some dated 1847). $400-$600. Second

*ANCIENT and Modern Michilimackinac*. (Cover title.) 48 pp., wrappers. (St. James, Mich.), MDCCCLIV (1854). (By James Jesse Strang.) First edition, first issue. $1,000 and up. Another, dated 1854, but "obviously" (according to Howes) on later paper, $50 and up.

ANDERSEN, Hans Christian. *The Complete Andersen*. Translated by Jean Hersholt. Hand-colored illustrations by Fritz Kredel. 6 vols., buckram and boards. New York, 1949. Limited Editions Club. Boxed. $125-$150.

ANDERSEN, Hans Christian. *Fairy Tales*. 12 colored plates and numerous black-and-white illustrations by Arthur Rackham. Vellum. London, (1932). De luxe edition. One of 525 signed by the artist. $500-$600. Another edition: London, (about 1920). Illustrated by Kay Nielsen. Full vellum. One of 500 signed by Nielsen. $500-$600.

ANDERSEN, Hans Christian. *Stories from Hans Andersen*. 28 color plates by Edmund Dulac. Vellum, silk ties. London, (1911). One of 750 signed by Dulac. $300-$375. Another issue: Pigskin. One of 100 on Japan paper. $400-$500.

ANDERSON, David. *The Enchanted Galleon*. Signed frontispiece photo by Ansel Adams. (San Francisco, 1930.) First edition. One of 60. Boxed. $200-$225.

ANDERSON, Maxwell. *You Who Have Dreams*. Boards, paper labels. New York, 1925. First edition. One of 1,000. In dust jacket. $35-$50. Signed issue (25): $75-$100. Author's first book.

ANDERSON, Poul. *The Broken Sword*. Cloth. New York, (1954). First edition. In dust jacket. $40-$50.

ANDERSON, Sherwood, *Alice and the Lost Novel*. Boards. London, 1929. First edition. One of 530 signed. In dust jacket. $50-$75.

ANDERSON, Sherwood. *Beyond Desire*. Tan cloth. New York, (1932). First edition. One of 165 signed. $75-$85. Trade edition: Cloth. In dust jacket. $30-$40.

ANDERSON, Sherwood. *Dark Laughter*. Half vellum and boards. New York, 1925. First edition. One of 350 signed. Boxed. $100-$150. (There were also 20 copies lettered and signed by the author.) Trade edition: Black cloth. In dust jacket. $35.

ANDERSON, Sherwood. *Death in the Woods and Other Stories*. Boards. New York, (1933). First edition. In dust jacket. $60-$80.

ANDERSON, Sherwood. *Horses and Men*. Orange cloth. New York, 1923. First edition, first issue, with top edges stained orange. In dust jacket. $50-$75.

ANDERSON, Sherwood. *Many Marriages*. Black cloth. New York, 1923. First edition, first issue, with top edges stained orange. In dust jacket. $40-$60.

ANDERSON, Sherwood. *Marching Men*. Crimson cloth. New York, 1917. First edition. In dust jacket. $150-$200.

ANDERSON, Sherwood. *Mid-American Chants*. Yellow cloth. New York, 1918. First edition. In dust jacket. $75-$100.

ANDERSON, Sherwood. *The Modern Writer*. Boards. San Francisco, (1925). First edition. One of 950. Boxed. $50-$75. Another issue: One of 50 on vellum, signed. $200-$250.

ANDERSON, Sherwood. *Nearer the Grass Roots*. Half cloth. San Francisco, 1929. Grabhorn printing. First edition. One of 500 signed. $75-$85.

ANDERSON, Sherwood. *A New Testament*. Half vellum and boards. New York, 1927. First edition. One of 265 large paper copies, signed. In slipcase. $75-$125. Trade edition: Cloth. In dust jacket. $20-$25.

ANDERSON, Sherwood. *No Swank*. Cream-colored cloth. Philadelphia, 1934. First edition. One of 50 signed. $125-$200. Also, 950 unsigned. $40-$75.

ANDERSON, Sherwood. *Poor White*. Blue cloth. New York, 1920. First edition, first issue, with top edges stained blue. In dust jacket. $40-$60.

ANDERSON, Sherwood. *Sherwood Anderson's Notebook*. Boards and cloth. New York, 1936. One of 225 signed. In slipcase. $75.

ANDERSON, Sherwood. *Tar: A Midwest Childhood*. Boards and vellum. New York, 1926. First edition. One of 350 large paper copies, signed. Boxed. $50-$75. Trade edition: Cloth. In dust jacket. $15-$20.

ANDERSON, Sherwood. *The Triumph of the Egg*. Plates. Green cloth. New York, 1921. First edition, first issue, with top edges stained yellow. In dust jacket. $50-$65.

ANDERSON, Sherwood. *Windy McPherson's Son*. Decorated brown cloth. New York, 1916. First edition. In dust jacket. $500-$750. Also, $600 (A, 1977). Author's first book.

ANDERSON, Sherwood. *Winesburg, Ohio*. Yellow cloth, paper label on spine. New York, 1919. First edition, first issue, with top stained yellow, end paper map at front, line 5 of page 86 reading "lay," and with broken type in the word "the" in line 3 of page 251. In dust jacket. $400-$500. Lacking jacket. $200-$250. Second issue, top unstained. In dust jacket. $100-$150.

ANDRÉ, John. *Major André's Journal.* Edited by Henry Cabot Lodge. Facsimile maps, plans, and other illustrations. 2 vols. full vellum. Boston, 1903. First edition. One of 467. $485. Another issue: One of 10 on Japan vellum. $600-$750.

ANDREAS, A.T. *History of Chicago.* Illustrated. 3 vols., morocco and cloth. Chicago, 1884-86. First edition. $200-$300. Another issue: Full morocco. $300-$400.

ANDREAS, A.T. *History of the State of Kansas.* Morocco. Folding map. Chicago, 1883. First edition. $100-$150.

ANDREAS, A.T. *Illustrated Historical Atlas of the State of Iowa.* Colored maps and views. Three-quarters morocco. Chicago. 1875. $400-$600.

ANDREWS, Alfred. *Genealogical History of Deacon Stephen Hart and His Descendants, 1632-1875.* Portraits. Cloth. New Britain, Conn., 1875. $50.

ANDREWS, Eliza Frances. *The War-Time Journal of a Georgia Girl, 1864-65.* 16 plates. Cloth. New York, 1908. First edition. $50-$75.

ANDREWS, Jane. *Ten Boys Who Lived on the Road from Long Ago to Now.* Illustrated by Charles Copeland. Pictorial cloth. Boston, 1886. First edition. $75-$100.

ANDREWS, William Loring. *A Choice Collection of Books from the Aldine Presses.* Wrappers. New York, 1885. First edition. One of 50. $150-$200. Author's first book.

ANDREWS, William Loring. *An Essay on the Portraiture of the American Revolutionary War.* Green morocco. New York, 1896. First edition. One of 185. $40-$65. Another issue: One of 15 on Japan paper. $80-$100.

*ANGEL in the House (The).* Cloth, paper label. London, 1854. (By Coventry Patmore.) First edition. $75-$100. London, 1863. 2 vols., cloth. $50-$60.

*ANNE of Geierstein; or, The Maiden of the Mist.* 3 vols., boards, paper labels. Edinburgh, 1829. (By Sir Walter Scott.) First edition. $150-$250. Also, $100 (A, 1973).

*ANNUAL Anthology (The).* 2 vols., old mottled calf. Bristol, England, 1799 and 1800. First editions. With leaf C3 (page 37) of Vol. 2 uncanceled, printing the uncorrected version of line 3, stanza X, of Robert Southey's "Battle of Blenheim." $150-$200.

*ANNUAL Review: History of St. Louis, etc.* Folding map. 47 pp., wrappers. St. Louis, 1854. $100-$200.

ANSTEY, F. *Vice Versa: or a Lesson to Fathers.* Cloth. London, 1882. (By Thomas Anstey Guthrie.) First edition. $75.

*ANTHOLOGY of Younger Poets (An).* Boards and linen. Philadelphia, 1932. First edition. One of 500. $50-$75. Trade edition: Boards. $25-$30. (Note: Contains five poems by William Faulkner.)

*ANTIDOTE (An) to the Miseries of Human Life, in the History of the Widow Placid and Her Daughter Rachel.* Marbled boards, leather spine. New Haven, 1809. (By Harriet Corp.) Third (first American) edition. $65.

*ANTIQUARY (The).* 3 vols., boards. Edinburgh, 1816. (By Sir Walter Scott.) First edition, with pages 27-30 of Vol. 1 uncanceled. $250-$350.

*ANTI-TEXASS Legion (The): Protest of Some Free Men, States, and Presses Against the Texass Rebellion.* 72 pp., wrappers. New York, 1844. $200-$350.

ANTONINUS, Brother. *A Canticle to the Waterbirds.* Illustrated. Cloth. Berkeley, 1968. (By William Everson.) First edition. One of 200 signed. (Issued without dust jacket.) $50-$75. Trade issue: Wrappers (2,000 copies). $15-$20.

ANTONINUS, Brother. *The Last Crusade.* Half vellum and cloth. No place, 1969. (By William Everson.) One of 165 signed. $75-$125.

ANTONINUS, Brother. *Novum Psalterium PII XII*. Folio, blue morocco. Los Angeles, 1955. (By William Everson.) One of 48. $250-$350.

ANTONINUS, Brother. *The Poet Is Dead: A Memorial for Robinson Jeffers*. Boards and leather. San Francisco, 1964. Auerhahn Press. By William Everson.) First edition. One of 205 signed. In dust jacket. $75-$125. (Five copies were issued in a slipcase. Value: about $150.)

*APOCRYPHA (The)*. Authorized version. Full-page woodcuts by Stephen Gooden, Eric Jones, etc. Folio, black vellum. London, 1929. Cresset Press. One of 30 on handmade paper with an extra set of illustrations signed by the artists. Boxed. $400-$750. Another issue: Boards. One of 450. Boxed. $150-$225.

*APPEAL by the Convention of Michigan . . . in Relation to the Boundary Question Between Michigan and Ohio*. 176 pp., stitched. Detroit, 1835. $375. (A, 1967).

*APPEAL to the American People (An): Being an Account of the Persecutions of the Church of Latter Day Saints*. 60 pp., wrappers. Cincinnati, 1840. Second edition. $500-$600.

*APPEAL (An) to the Clergy of the Church of Scotland*. 12 pp., stitched, without wrappers. Edinburgh, 1875. (By Robert Louis Stevenson.) First edition. $5,000 and up. Also, $3,200 (A, 1925). (About 3 copies known.)

APPERLEY, C.J. See Nimrod. Also see *Memoirs of the Life of the Late John Mytton, Esq.*

APPLEGATE, Jesse. *A Day with the Cow Column in 1843*. Pictorial cloth. Chicago, 1934. Caxton Club. One of 300. $40-$60. Another edition: (Portland), 1952. One of 225. $45-$60.

APPLEGATE, Jesse. *Recollections of My Boyhood*. 99 pp., pictorial wrappers. Roseburg, Ore., 1914. First edition. $100-$200.

APULEIUS, Lucius. *The XI Bookes of the Golden Asse*. Translated by William Adlington. Printed on handmade paper in an Italian semi-gothic type, initial letters in red and blue. Folio, decorated green boards, linen spine. Chelsea (London), 1924. Ashendene Press. One of 165. Boxed. $500-$750. Also, spine label chipped, $250 (A, 1977). Another issue: One of 16 on vellum. Full morocco. $2,000-$2,500. Also, $1,500 (A, 1971).

ARISTOPHANES. *Lysistrata*. 8 plates by Aubrey Beardsley. Boards. London, 1896. One of 100. $400-$500. London, (1926). Translated by Jack Lindsay. Illustrated by Norman Lindsay. Half morocco. One of 725 signed by the artist. $75-$100. New York, 1934. Limited Editions Club. Translated by Gilbert Seldes. Illustrated by Pablo Picasso. Boards. Boxed. $850-$1,250. (Note: There is sometimes offered with this book a set of 6 proofs of the original Picasso etchings for the edition, each signed by Picasso. There were 150 issued in cloth portfolios. $2,000-$2,500, possibly more.)

ARISTOTLE. *Politics and Poetics*. Illustrated by Leonard Baskin. Buckram. (New York), 1964. Limited Editions Club. Boxed. $125-$150.

ARKWRIGHT, William. *The Pointer & His Predecessors*. Illustrated. Half or full morocco. London, 1906. First edition, deluxe issue. One of 750. $350-$400. Trade issue: cloth. $200-$250.

ARLEN, Michael. *The Green Hat*. Cloth. London, (1924). First edition. In dust jacket. $75-$100. New York, 1925. (Acting version.) Boards. One of 175 signed. $75-$100. (Note: The typography is by Bruce Rogers.)

ARLEN, Michael. *The London Venture*. Illustrated. Pictorial cloth. London, 1919. First edition. In dust jacket. $75-$100. Author's first book. London, 1920. Second edition. In dust jacket. $20.

ARLEN, Michael. *May Fair*. Cloth. London, (1925). First edition. In dust jacket. $35.

*ARMAGEDDON: A Fragment: Avalon*. Wrappers. Charleston, S.C., 1923. First edition. Contains poems by John Crowe Ransom and others. $200 and up.

ARMES, George A. *Ups and Downs of an Army Officer*. Illustrated. Pictorial cloth. Washington, 1900. First edition. $100-$150.

ARMITAGE, John. *The History of Brazil.* 2 portraits. 2 vols., boards. London, 1836. First edition. $400-$475.

ARMOUR, John P. *Edenindia; A Tale of Adventure.* Pictorial cloth. New York, 1907. First edition. $40-$50.

ARMOUR, Samuel. *History of Orange County, California.* Illustrated. Cloth. Los Angeles, 1921. $75-$85.

*ARMSMEAR: The Home, the Arm and the Armory of Col. Samuel Colt: A Memorial.* Plates, map. Cloth. New York, 1866. First edition. Inscribed by Mrs. Colt. $250-$350.

ARMSTRONG, A. N. *Oregon: A Brief History and Description of Oregon and Washington.* Cloth. Chicago, 1857. First edition. $225-$275.

ARMSTRONG, Moses K. *History and Resources of Dakota, Montana and Idaho.* Map. Printed wrappers. Yanktown, Dakota Territory, 1866. First edition. $3,500-$4,000.

ARNO, Peter. *Oops, Dearie!* Red cloth. New York, 1927. First edition. In dust jacket. $40. Author's first book.

ARNOLD, Henry V. *The Early History of the Devil's Lake Country,* 105 pp., printed wrappers. Larimore, N. D., 1920. First edition. $75-$100.

ARNOLD, Henry V. *The History of Old Pembina, 1780-1872.* Wrappers. Larimore, N. D., 1917. First edition. $85-$100.

ARNOLD, Matthew. See: A. (pseudonym—first entry in list). Also see *Alaric at Rome.*

ARNOLD, Matthew. *Cromwell: A Prize Poem.* Wrappers. Oxford, 1843. First edition. $300-$400.

ARNOLD, Matthew. *Culture and Anarchy.* Cloth. London, 1869. First edition. $75-$150.

ARNOLD, Matthew. *Discourses in America.* Cloth. London, 1885. First edition. $35-$40.

ARNOLD, Matthew. *Essays in Criticism.* Cloth. London, 1865. First edition, with one ad leaf. $100-$125. Second series: Cloth. London, 1888. First edition. $100-$125.

ARNOLD, Matthew. *God and the Bible.* Cloth. London, 1875. First edition. $50-$60.

ARNOLD, Matthew. *Last Essays on Church and Religion.* Cloth. London, 1877. First edition. $40-$50.

ARNOLD, Matthew. *Merope: A Tragedy.* Cloth. London, 1858. First edition. $50-$60.

ARNOLD, Matthew. *Mixed Essays.* Cloth. London, 1879. First edition. $40-$50.

ARNOLD, Matthew. *New Poems.* Green cloth. London, 1867. First edition. $100-$150.

ARNOLD, Matthew. *Poems.* Cloth. London, 1853. First edition. $50-$75. London, 1855. (Second Series.) Cloth. First edition. $50-$75. Boston, 1856. Cloth. $35.

*AROUND the Horn in '49.* See *Journal of the Hartford Union Mining and Trading Company.*

*ARRANGEMENT of Places. Will Each Gentleman Kindly Take in to Dinner the Lady Seated on His Right.* 12 pp., wrappers. (Program of 70th birthday dinner for Mark Twain at Delmonico's.) (New York), 1905. $75-$125.

ARRIGHI, Ludovico. *The Calligraphic Models of Ludovico degli Arrighi.* 64 pp., facsimile. Marbled boards and vellum. Paris, 1926. One of 300. $300-$400.

ARRINGTON, Alfred W. See Summerfield, Charles.

*ART of Domestick Happiness and Other Poems (The).* By the Recluse. Mottled calf. Pittsburgh, 1817. (By Aquilla M. Bolton.) First edition, with errata leaf. $25.

*ARTHUR Mervyn; or Memoirs of the Year 1793.* By the Author of Wieland. 2 vols., calf. Philadelphia, 1799-1800. (By Charles Brockden Brown.) First edition. $300-$400. (Note: The 1799 volume and the Second Part are usually listed separately in catalogues and bibliographies; relative values: $150 and up for the first, $100 and up for second. For first English edition, see author entry.)

ARTHUR, T. S. *Ten Nights in a Bar-Room, and What I Saw There.* Cloth. Philadelphia, 1854. First edition, first issue, with both Lippincott and Bradley named in imprint and woodcut frontispiece by Van Ingen. $50-$75.

ARTHUR, T.S. *True Riches.* Cloth. Boston, 1852. First edition. $35.

ARTHUR, T. S, *Words for the Wise.* Cloth. Philadelphia, 1851. First edition. $30.

*ARTICLES of Religion, as Established by the Bishops, the Clergy, and Laity of the Protestant Episcopal Church in the United States of America, etc.* 22 pp., half morocco. New York, 1802. $60.

ASHBEE, Henry Spencer. *An Iconography of Don Quixote, 1605–1895.* Half cloth. London, 1895. First edition. $75-$100.

ASHBERY, John. *The New Spirit.* Pictorial wrappers. New York, (1970). First edition. One of 65 signed. $60.

ASHBERY, John. *Some Trees.* Foreword by W. H. Auden. Cloth. New Haven, 1956. First edition. In dust jacket. $50-$65.

ASHBERY, John. *Turandot and Other Poems.* Illustrated. Wrappers. New York, 1953. First edition. One of 300. $100-$150. Author's first book.

ASHE, Thomas. *Travels in America.* 3 vols., boards. London, 1808. First edition. $700-$800.

ASHENDENE Press. See *Descriptive Bibliography, etc.*

ASHLEY, Clifford W. *The Yankee Whaler.* Plates, some in color. Half cloth and boards. Boston, 1926. First edition. One of 156 signed, with original drawing. Boxed. $500-$600. Also, $425 and $375 (A, 1977). Ordinary issue: $125-$150.

ASHLEY, William H. *The West of William H. Ashley.* Edited by Dale L. Morgan. Illustrated. Pictorial buckram. Denver, 1964. One of 750. $75-$100. De luxe issue: Half calf. One of 250 signed. $125-$150.

ASHTON, John. *Real Sailor-Songs.* Boards, vellum spine. London, 1891. First edition. $100-$150.

ASHTON, Warren T. *Hatchie, the Guardian Slave.* Illustrated. Black cloth. Boston, 1853. (By William Taylor Adams.) First edition. $75-$100.

*"ASK Mamma"; or, The Richest Commoner in England.* 13 full-page color plates and 69 woodcuts by John Leech. 13 parts, red wrappers. London, (1857) and 1858. (By Robert Smith Surtees.) First edition. $150-$250. London, 1858. Pictorial cloth. First book edition. $75-$100.

ASTON, James. *First Lesson.* Yellow cloth. London, (1932). (By T. H. White.) First edition. In dust jacket. $75-$100.

ASTON, James. *They Winter Abroad.* Yellow cloth. London, (1932). (By T. H. White.) First edition. In dust jacket. $75-$100. New York, 1932. First American edition. In dust jacket. $50-$75.

*ATALANTIS.* Wrappers. New York, 1832. (By William Gilmore Simms.) First edition. $150-$250. Philadelphia, 1848. Cloth. New edition. $100.

ATHERTON, Gertrude. See Lin, Frank.

ATHERTON, Gertrude. *Black Oxen.* Cloth. New York, (1923). First edition. One of 250 signed. In dust jacket. $40-$50.

ATHERTON, Gertrude. *The Conqueror.* Dark red cloth, gilt top. New York, 1902. First edition, first state, with page numerals on page 546 in upper left corner. $35-$50.

ATHERTON, Gertrude. *What Dreams May Come.* Cloth. London, 1889. First English edition (of author's first book, which was issued in America under the pseudonym Frank Lin, which see). $40-$60.

ATHERTON, William. *Narrative of the Suffering & Defeat of the North-Western Army, Under General Winchester.* Leather-backed boards, printed paper label. Frankfort, Ky., 1842. First edition. $100-$175.

ATHEY, Henry, and Bowers, Herbert. *With Gyves of Gold: A Novel.* Pictorial cloth. New York, 1898. First edition. $50-$75.

*ATHLETIC Sports for Boys.* Printed boards. New York, (1865). First edition. $50.

*ATTACHE (The); or, Sam Slick in England,* (Second Series.) 2 vols., ribbed plum-colored cloth. London, 1844. (By Thomas Chandler Haliburton.) First edition, with 48 pages of ads at end of Vol. 2. $100-$150.

ATTAWAY, William. *Blood on the Forge.* Cloth. New York, 1941. First edition. In dust jacket. $125.

ATTERLEY, Joseph. *A Voyage to the Moon.* Boards. New York, 1827. (By George Tucker.) First edition. $400-$500.

ATWATER, Caleb. *A History of the State of Ohio.* Calf. Cincinnati, (1838). First edition. $125-$150.

ATWATER, Caleb. *Mysteries of Washington City.* Boards and leather. Washington, 1844. First edition. $85-$125.

ATWATER, Caleb. *Remarks Made on a Tour to Prairie du Chien; Thence to Washington City.* Boards. Columbus, Ohio, 1831. First edition. $100-$125.

AUBREY, Frank. *King of the Dead; A Weird Adventure.* Cloth. London, 1903. First edition. $300-$350.

AUCHINCLOSS, Louis. See Lee, Andrew.

AUDEN, W. H. See Baudelaire, Charles; Rich, Adrienne Cecile.

AUDEN, W. H. *The Age of Anxiety.* Cloth. New York, (1947). First edition. In dust jacket. $40-$60. London, (1948). First English edition. In dust jacket. $25-$35.

AUDEN, W. H. *Another Time.* Cloth. New York, (1940). First edition. In dust jacket. $100-$125. London, (1940). First English edition. (Issued as *Poems by W. H. Auden: Another Time.)* In dust jacket. $75-$100.

AUDEN, W. H. *The Collected Poetry.* Cloth. New York, (1945). First edition, first printing, with title page in green and black. In dust jacket. $50-$75. Also, $45 (A, 1975).

AUDEN, W. H. *Collected Shorter Poems, 1930–1944.* Blue cloth. London, (1950). First edition. In dust jacket. $40-$65.

AUDEN, W.H. *Collected Shorter Poems, 1927–1957.* Cloth. London, (1966). First edition. In dust jacket. $35.

AUDEN, W.H. *The Dance of Death.* Boards. London, (1933). First edition. In dust jacket. $60-$75.

AUDEN, W. H. *Delia, or a Masque of Night.* Wrappers. Rome, 1953. First edition. $75-$100.

AUDEN, W.H. *Epithalamion.* Unbound sheet, printed both sides, folded. Princeton, 1939. First edition. $150-$200. (About 100 printed.)

AUDEN, W.H. *For the Time Being.* Boards and cloth. New York, (1944). First edition. In dust jacket. $25-$35. London, (1945). Cloth. First English edition. In dust jacket. $25.

AUDEN, W. H. *Good-Bye to the Mezzogiorno.* Text in English and Italian. Wrappers and printed band. Milan, Italy, 1958. First edition. One of 1,000. $35.

AUDEN, W. H. *Homage to Clio.* Printed wrappers. London, 1960. Advance uncorrected proof copy. $40. London, 1960. Plum-colored cloth. First published English edition. In dust jacket. $15-$20.

AUDEN, W. H. *Look, Stranger!* Cloth. London, (1936). First edition. $65-$80. (For first American edition, see Auden, *On This Island.*)

AUDEN, W. H. *Louis MacNeice: A Memorial Address.* Printed wrappers. London, 1963. First edition. $75-$100.

AUDEN, W. H. *Marginalia.* Engravings by Laurence Scott. Oblong, printed wrappers. (Cambridge, Mass., 1966). Ibex Press. First edition. One of 150 signed by author and artist. $125-$150. Another issue: One of 26 signed. $200-$250.

AUDEN, W. H. *On This Island.* Brown cloth. New York, (1937). First American edition. In dust jacket. $50. (Note: The first edition of this was published in London, 1936, as *Look, Stranger!,* which see.)

AUDEN, W. H. *The Orators: An English Study.* Cloth. London, (1932). First edition. In dust jacket. $125-$150.

AUDEN, W. H. *Our Hunting Fathers.* Wrappers. (Cambridge), 1935. First edition. One of 22. $300-$500.

AUDEN, W. H. *Poem.* Wrappers. (Bryn Mawr), 1933. First edition. One of 5 on Fabriano paper (from an edition of 22). (Note: I can find no sales record for this except for the copy inscribed to T. S. Eliot and with a presentation autograph letter, signed, sold at Sotheby's in 1966 to a New York dealer for $624.) Another issue: One of 5 on Kelmscott paper. $315 (catalogue price).

AUDEN, W. H. *Poems.* Printed blue-green wrappers. London, (1930). First edition. $300-$400. Also, $160 (A, 1976). Author's first published book. New York, (1934). Orange cloth. First American edition. In dust jacket. $50-$80. (Note: In 1928 Stephen Spender, the poet's friend, hand-printed "about 45" copies of a paperbound *Poems,* dated 1928 and printed at Frognal, Hampstead, England. A copy inscribed by Spender and later by Auden brought $8,500 at auction in 1973.)

AUDEN, W. H. *Selected Poems.* Cloth. London, (1938). First edition. In dust jacket. $50-$75. London, (1968). Boards. $15.

AUDEN, W. H. *Some Poems.* Board. London, (1940). First edition. In dust jacket. $35-$40.

AUDEN, W. H. *Sonnet.* Wrappers. (Cambridge), 1935. First edition. One of 5 on Normandie paper (from an edition of 22). $400-$600. Another issue: One of 5 on vellum. $312 (catalogue price).

AUDEN, W. H. *Spain.* Stiff covered wrappers. (London, 1937). First edition. $35-$50.

AUDEN, W. H. *Three Songs for St. Cecelia's Day.* Wrappers. (New York), 1941. First edition. $50-$75.

AUDEN, W. H., and Isherwood, Christopher. *The Ascent of F6.* Cloth. London, (1936). First edition. In dust jacket. $50-$75.

AUDEN, W. H., and Isherwood, Christopher. *The Dog Beneath the Skin, or, Where Is Francis?* Cloth. London, (1935). First edition. In dust jacket. $50-$75. New York, 1935. Cloth. First American edition. In dust jacket. $25.

AUDEN, W. H., and Isherwood, Christopher. *On the Frontier.* Cloth. London, (1938). First edition. In dust jacket. $60-$80.

AUDEN, W. H., and MacNeice, Louis. *Letters from Iceland.* Plates, folding map. Green cloth. London, (1927). First edition. In dust jacket. $75-$85.

AUDSLEY, George Ashdown. *The Art of Organ-Building*. Illustrated. 2 vols., cloth. New York, 1905. $200-$250.

AUDSLEY, George Ashdown. *The Ornamental Arts of Japan*. 70 plates in gold and colors, 31 in monochrome, loose in 5 cloth portfolios. 2 vols., folio. New York, 1882–84. Artist's proofs edition. One of 50 signed. $400-$500. Another issue: 2 vols., morocco. (Not signed.) $200-$250. New York, 1883–84. Plates loose in 4 folders. One of 500 signed. $200. New York, 1883–85. 2 vols. in 4 folders. One of 60. $150.

AUDSLEY, George Ashdown, and Bowes, J.L. *The Keramic Art of Japan*. 63 plates, 42 in gold and colors; 4 plates of potters' marks, other illustrations. Morocco and cloth. Liverpool, 1875. First edition. $200-$250. London, 1881. Cloth. $50-$75.

AUDUBON, John James. *The Birds of America from Original Drawings*. 435 double elephant folio hand-colored plates without text. 87 parts in wrappers, or 4 leatherbound double elephant folio volumes. London, 1827–38. First edition. Excessively rare in the original parts. The last known sale (1974) was at world record price of $246,500. Two sets of the four leatherbound volumes were sold at auction in New York City in 1977—one at $352,000 and another at $396,000 ($360,000 plus a 10 percent surcharge by Christie's auction gallery). These sales successively set a world record price for a printed book at auction. New York, 1840–44. 500 colored plates. 100 parts in wrappers (very rare); or 7 vols., octavo, full or half morocco; also half calf. First American and first octavo edition; also, first edition with all 500 plates and first edition with plates and text together (under the title *The Birds of America from Drawings Made in the United States and Their Territories)*; a reissue in smaller size of the plates from the original edition, with text, including changes, from the Edinburgh first edition of Audubon's *Ornithological Biography*, which see $8,500 (A, 1977); $6,500 (A, 1976); $6,000 (A, 1975). For various other 19th Century editions, many of which are imperfect when offered, consult the detailed records in the annual volumes of *American Book Prices Current*. New York, 1937. Edited by William Vogt. 500 plates in color. One-volume edition. Buckram. Limited issue on all-rag paper. Boxed. $100-$150. Trade edition: Buckram. $75-$100.

AUDUBON, John James. *Delineations of American Scenery and Character*. Cloth. New York, 1926. First edition. One of 42 large paper copies. $100-$150. Trade edition, same date. In dust jacket. $35-$50. (500 copies with London imprint.)

AUDUBON, John James. *Journal of John James Audubon, Made During His Trip to New Orleans in 1820–21*. Edited by Howard Corning. 2 plates. Boards and cloth. Boston, 1929. One of 250. $100-$125. (Note: This and the volume following, issued as a set by the Club of Odd Volumes, are most often offered together in the $200-$250 range.)

AUDUBON, John James. *Journal of John James Audubon, Made While Obtaining Subscriptions to His "Birds of America," 1840–1843*. Edited by Howard Corning. Plate. Boston, 1929. One of 250. $100-$125. (See note in preceding entry.)

AUDUBON, John James. *Ornithological Biography; or, An Account of the Habits of the Birds of the United States of America*. 5 vols., cloth. Edinburgh, 1831-49 (actually 1839). First edition of the text volume to accompany the double elephant folios of *The Birds of America*. $750-$1,000. Also, in half leather, $350 (A, 1977).

AUDUBON, John James. *The Quadrupeds of North America*. See Audubon and Bachman, *The Viviparous Quadrupeds, etc.*

AUDUBON, John James. *A Synopsis of the Birds of America*. Cloth, paper label. Edinburgh, 1839. First edition. $400-$500.

AUDUBON, John James, and Bachman, John. *The Viviparous Quadrupeds of North America*. 150 colored plates without text. 30 parts in wrappers, or 3 vols. (Vol. 1, 1845; Vol. 2, 1846; Vol. 3, 1848), folio, half morocco. New York, 1845–48. (Text issued, New York, 1846-53. 31 parts in wrappers or 3 vols., cloth, dated 1846, 1851, and 1853, the 3 vols. sometimes bound in 2. A 93-page supplement, with 6 colored plates was issued in 1854). First edition complete (consisting of the 3 plate volumes, the 3 text volumes, and the supplement). Rarely offered. The last complete set in the auction records brought $5,500 in 1970, but the recent sharp increases in color plate values make that price useless as a guide. More realistic: 6 vols., some broken, $19,000 (A,1975); imperfect 3 vol. sets, lacking text volumes, $25,000 and $18,500 in 1975. New York, 1849–54. Reissue under the title *The Quadrupeds of North America*. 155 colored plates (including all except one from the supplement to the original edition). 31 parts in wrappers, or 3 vols., morocco or half morocco, dated 1849, 1851, and 1854. First octavo edition. Wrappers: $5,000-$7,500. Also, with defects, $2,752 (A,1976). In book form: $4,000-$5,000. Also, $1,900 (A, 1977); $3,000 (A,1975). New York, 1854. 3 vols., contemporary bindings (morocco, half morocco, etc.). $3,000-$4,000. Also, with defects, $2,200 and $1,300 (A, 1975).

AUDUBON, John Woodhouse. *Audubon's Western Journal, 1849–50*. Edited by Maria R. Audubon. Folding map, 6 plates. Cloth. Cleveland, 1906. Reprint of Audubon's extremely rare and virtually unobtainable *Illustrated Notes of an Expedition Through Mexico and California*. $175-$200.

AUDUBON, John Woodhouse. *The Drawings of John Woodhouse Audubon, Illustrating His Adventures Through Mexico and California*. 34 full-page illustrations, including 2 in color. Folio, boards and cloth. San Francisco, 1957. Book Club of California. Grabhorn printing. One of 400. $200-$250.

AUDUBON, Maria R. *Audubon and His Journals*. Edited by Elliot Coues. Plates. 2 vols. cloth. New York, 1897. First edition. $100-$150.

AUSCHER, Ernest Simon. *A History and Description of French Porcelain*. 24 plates in color. Morocco. London, 1905. First edition, limited. $40-$50.

AUSTEN, Jane. See *Elizabeth Bennet; Emma; Mansfield Park; Northanger Abbey; Pride and Prejudice; Sense and Sensibility*.

AUSTIN, Edward S. *The Housekeepers' Manual*. Wrappers. Chicago, 1869. First edition. $75-$125.

AUSTIN, Jane G. *Standish of Standish*. Tan cloth. Boston, 1889. First edition. $35. (Note: Copies of the same date in gray-green cloth are of a later issue.)

AUSTIN, Mary. *The Flock*. Cloth. Boston, 1906. First edition. In dust jacket. $50-$60.

AUSTIN, Mary. *The Land of Little Rain*. Illustrated. Pictorial cloth. Boston, 1903. First edition. $75-$100. Author's first book.

AUSTIN, Mary. *What the Mexican Conference Really Means*. 14 pp., wrappers. New York, (1915). First edition. $50-$60.

AUSTIN, Mary, and Adams, Ansel. *Taos Pueblo*. Photographs by Adams and text by Mrs. Austin. Folio, cloth, pigskin spine. San Francisco, 1930. Grabhorn printing. First edition. One of 107 (Johnson says 108) signed by author and illustrator. $2,500-$4,500.

AUSTIN, Mary, and Martin, Ann. *Suffrage and Government*. 14 pp., printed wrappers. New York, 1914. $50.

AUSTIN, Stephen F. *Esposicion al Publico sobre los Asuntos de Tejas*. 32 pp., stitched. Mexico, 1835. First edition, with page 29 misnumbered 31. $7,500-$12,000. (A Texas dealer sold a copy to another dealer in 1977 for $8,000.) Presentation copy, $12,000 (sold by another Texas dealer in 1977).

*AUTHENTIC Narrative of the Seminole War (An), and of the Miraculous Escape of Mrs. Mary Godfrey, and Her Four Female Children*. Folding frontispiece in color, 24 pp., plain wrappers. Providence, R. I., 1836. $1,000. New York, 1836. $1,000.

*AUTHORS Take Sides on the Spanish War*. Wrappers. London, (1937). Left Review. $150-$200.

*AUTHORSHIP: A Tale*. Boards and cloth. Boston, 1930. (By John Neal.) First edition. $75-$100.

*AUTOCRAT of the Breakfast Table (The)*. Illustrated. Cloth. Boston, 1858. (By Oliver Wendell Holmes.) First edition, first issue, with engraved half title, with period after word "Company" in imprint, and with left end paper at back headed "Poetry and the Drama" and right "School Books." $250-$500. (An unsolved controversy still exists over whether the first binding bore a five-ring or four-ring decoration on the spine.) In presumed second binding (Blanck is not certain) with five rings on spine, $175 (A, 1971),

$270 (A, 1962). $250 (1974 dealer catalogue). Boston, 1859. Illustrated. Cloth. Large paper edition. $150-$200. New York, 1955. Limited Editions Club. Cloth. Boxed. $50-$65.

AVIRETT, James B. *The Memoirs of Gen. Turner Ashby and His Compeers.* Portrait. Cloth. Baltimore, 1867. First edition. $125-$150.

*AYESHA, The Maid of Kars.* By the Author of "Zohrab," etc. 3 vols., boards. London, 1834. (By James Morier.) First edition. $100-$150.

# B

B., A. *The Six Letters of A. B. on the Differences Between Great Britain and the United States of America.* Wrappers. London, 1807. First edition. $75-$100.

B., E. B. *Sonnets.* By E.B.B. 47 pp., without wrappers. Reading, England, 1847 (actually printed about 1883-90). (By Elizabeth Barrett Browning.) Thomas J. Wise's forgery—the fake first edition of "Sonnets from the Portuguese," which actually appeared first in the second edition of *Poems*, 1850, which see under author entry (Barrett and Browning); for later editions, see entry for *Sonnets from the Portuguese* under "Elizabeth Browning." The Wise forgery, bound in morocco, sold for a record (at the time) $1,250 at auction in 1930. Following its exposure as a fake in 1934, the value declined, but in 1967 at a sale in London featuring Wise forgeries a New York City dealer paid $1,680 at auction for a copy in morocco. This remarkable record continued in the 1976 auction season when a copy that had belonged to the late John Carter, who was chiefly instrumental in exposing Wise (see the entry under his name elsewhere in this book), came to auction in London and was sold to a book dealer for $3,096.

B., F. *The Kasidah of Haji Abdu El-Yezdi.* Translated and annotated by his friend and pupil, F. B. (Sir Richard Burton is translator). Yellow wrappers. London, (1880). First edition, first issue, without Quaritch imprint. $400-$800.

B., H. *The Bad Child's Book of Beasts.* Pictorial boards. Oxford, (1896). (By Hilaire Belloc.) First edition. $50.

B., J. K. *The Lorgnette.* By J. K. B. Illustrated. Oblong, cloth. New York, (1886). (By John Kendrick Bangs.) First edition. $100-$150. Author's first book.

BABB, James T. *A Bibliography of the Writings of William McFee.* Cloth. Garden City, 1931. First edition. One of 360 signed by McFee. Boxed. $100-$135.

BABBITT, E.D. *The Principles of Light and Color.* Illustrated. Cloth. New York, 1878. Second edition. $100. East Orange, N.J., (1896). Cloth. $50-$75.

BABBITT, E.L. *The Allegheny Pilot.* 16 maps. 64 pp., wrappers. Freeport, Pa., 1855. First edition. $150-$250.

BACA, Manuel Cabeza de. *Vincente Silva and His 40 Bandits.* Translated by Lane Kauffmann. Illustrated. Boards and cloth. Washington, 1947. First edition in English. One of 300 signed. $75-$100. Another issue: One of 25 bound in full goatskin, signed. $300-$400. Another issue: One of 175 in blue wrappers. $100-$150.

BACHELLER, Irving. *Eben Holden.* Cloth. Boston, (1900). First edition, first state, with line 13 on page 400 reading "go to fur," and with pine cones on spine with rounded top. $60-$80. (Later issue reads "go tew fur" and has flat-topped cones.)

BACHELLER, Irving. *The Story of a Passion.* Cloth. (East Aurora, 1899). One of 50. $50-$60.

BACON, Sir Francis. *Bacon's Essays.* Edited by Sydney Humphries. Portrait and woodcut initial letters. Vellum. London, 1912. One of 30. $75-$100.

BACON, Sir Francis. *The Essayes or Counsels Civill and Morall.* Folio, vellum. London, 1928. Cresset Press. Vellum. One of 250. $200-$400. Another issue: One of 8 on vellum. $1,650-$2,000.

BACON, Sir Francis. *Essays Moral, Economical and Political.* Boards, paper label. Boston, 1807. First American edition. $50-$75.

BAHR, Jerome. *All Good Americans*. Preface by Ernest Hemingway. Blue cloth. New York, 1937. First edition. In dust jacket. $40-$50. Reissued in yellow cloth, 1939 (with "A" on copyright page—an exception to the Scribner method of marking first editions with an "A"). $20.

BAILEY, Washington. *A Trip to California in 1853*. Portrait. Printed wrappers. (LeRoy, Ill.), 1915. First edition, with errata slip. $300-$350.

BAILY, Francis. *Journal of a Tour in Unsettled Parts of North America in 1796 & 1797*. Decorated cloth. London, 1856. First edition. $550-$750.

BAINBRIDGE, George C. *The Fly-Fisher's Guide*. Colored frontispiece and 7 colored plates. Half leather. Liverpool, 1816. First edition. $150-$200. Another issue: Morocco. One of 12. $400-$500.

BAIRD, Joseph A. *California's Pictorial Letter Sheets, 1849-1869*. San Francisco, 1967. Grabhorn printing. One of 475 signed. $200-$300.

BAIRD, Spencer F.; Brewer, T.M.; and Ridgway, R. *The Water Birds of North America*. Hand-colored illustrations. 2 vols., cloth. Boston, 1884. First edition. $300-$350.

BAKER, B. *The Torn Book*. 24 color plates. Pictorial boards. New York, 1913. First edition. $37.50.

BAKER, Charles H. Collins. *Lely and the Stuart Portrait Painters*. 240 reproductions, some in color. 2 vols., buckram. London, 1912. One of 375. $300-$325. Another issue: Vellum. One of 30, with an extra set of plates. $500-$600.

BAKER, Charles H. Collins, and Constable, W.G. *English Painting of the Sixteenth and Seventeenth Centuries*. 82 collotype plates. Half leather. London, 1930. $75-$100.

BAKER, D.W.C. (compiler). *A Texas Scrap-Book*. Cloth. New York, (1875). First edition. $100-$150.

BAKER, George P. *The Pilgrim Spirit: A Pageant . . . Landing of the Pilgrims*. Cloth. Boston, 1921. First edition, first issue, with the name "Brewster" on page 74. (Some with errata slip.) $50-$75. (Note: Contains contributions by Robert Frost and Edwin Arlington Robinson.)

BAKER, Hozial H. *Overland Journey to Carson Valley, Utah*. Woodcut frontispiece and other illustrations. 38 pp., yellow printed wrappers. Seneca Falls, N.Y., 1861. First edition. $3,500-$5,000.

BALDWIN, James. *Giovanni's Room*. Boards and cloth. New York, 1956. First edition. In dust jacket. $50-$60.

BALDWIN, James. *Go Tell It on the Mountain*. Cloth. New York, 1953. First edition. In dust jacket. $100-$175. Advance copy in jacket wrappers. $250-$350. Author's first book.

BALDWIN, James. *A Story of the Golden Age*. Illustrated by Howard Pyle. Decorated brown cloth. New York, 1887. First edition. $100-$150.

BALDWIN, James. *The Story of Siegfried*. Illustrated by Howard Pyle. Pictorial cloth. New York, 1882. First edition. $100-$150.

BALDWIN, Joseph G. *The Flush Times of Alabama and Mississippi*. Blue cloth. New York, 1853. First edition. $150-$200. Author's first book.

BALLOU, Hosea. *A Candid Review of a Pamphlet Entitled "A Candid Reply."* Calf. Portsmouth, N.H., (1809). First edition. $50-$60.

BALLOU, Hosea. *Treatise on Atonement*. Calf. Randolph, Vt., 1805. First edition. $40-$50.

BALME, J.R. *American States, Churches and Slavery*. Cloth. London, 1863. First edition. $40-$50.

BALWHIDDER, The Rev. Micah. *Annals of the Parish; or The Chronicle of Dalmailing.* Boards, printed label. Edinburgh, 1821. (By John Galt.) First edition. $150-$200.

BALZAC, Honoré de. *The Hidden Treasure.* Illustrated. Boards. Kentfield, Calif., 1953. Allen Press. One of 160. $200-$250.

BANCROFT, George. *Poems.* Tan boards. Cambridge, Mass., 1823. First edition. $35-$50.

BANDELIER, Adolph F. A. *The Gilded Man.* Cloth. New York, 1893. First edition. $85-$125.

BANDINI, Joseph. *A Description of California in 1828.* Illustrated. Boards and cloth. Berkeley, Calif., 1951. One of 400. $40-$60.

BANGS, John Kendrick. See B., J.K.

BANGS, John Kendrick. *Bikey the Skicycle and Other Tales of Jimmie Boy.* Illustrated by Peter Newell. Decorated cloth. New York, 1902. First edition. $65.

BANGS, John Kendrick. *A House-Boat on the Styx.* Illustrated. Cloth. New York, 1896. First edition. $35-$50.

BANGS, John Kendrick. *Mephistopheles: A Profanation.* Red wrappers. New York, 1889. First edition. $40-$50.

BANGS, John Kendrick. *Mr. Munchausen.* Cloth. Boston, 1901. First edition, first state, with Small, Maynard copyright. $35-$50.

BANGS, John Kendrick. *Mollie and the Unwisemen Abroad.* Illustrated. Cloth. Philadelphia, 1910. First edition. $55.

BANGS, John Kendrick. *Toppleton's Client.* Boards. London, 1893. First edition. $150. New York, 1893. Cloth. First American edition. $75-$100.

BANNERMAN, Helen. *The Story of Little Black Sambo.* Colored plates. Cloth. London, 1899. First edition. $800-$1,000. Also, stained and mended, $600 (A, 1977).

BARBE-MARBOIS, François. *The History of Louisiana, Particularly the Cession of That Colony to the U.S.A.* Cloth. Philadelphia, 1830. First American edition and first in English. $350-$450.

BARHAM, Richard Harris. See Ingoldsby, Thomas.

BARING, Alexander. *An Inquiry into the Causes and Consequences of the Orders in Council; and An Examination of the Conduct of Great Britain Towards the Neutral Commerce of America.* Wrappers. London, 1808. First edition. $75-$125.

BARING, Maurice. *Algae: An Anthology of Phrases.* Wrappers, paper label. London, 1928. First edition. One of 100 signed. In dust jacket. Boxed. $100-$125.

BARKER, Eugene, C. *The Life of Stephen F. Austin.* 2 maps, plan, 6 portraits. Boards and vellum. Nashville, 1925. First edition. One of 250 signed. $175-$300. Trade edition: $50-$85.

BARKER, George. *Poems.* Cloth. London, (1935). First edition. In dust jacket. $35-$50.

BARKER, Matthew Henry. *The Old Sailor's Jolly Boat.* 24 full-page engravings by George and Robert Cruikshank. London, 1844. $200-$300.

BARLOW, Joel. *The Columbiad: A Poem.* Portrait and 11 plates. Contemporary or later morocco. Philadelphia, 1807. (New edition of *The Vision of Columbus,* which see in entry below.) $100-$150.

BARLOW, Joel. *Joel Barlow to His Fellow Citizens of the United States.* (Caption title.) Wrappers. (Philadelphia, 1801.) First American edition. $75-$100.

BARLOW, Joel. *The Vision of Columbus: A Poem in Nine Books.* Sheep. Hartford, 1787. First edition. $200-$250. (Reprinted as *The Columbiad,* which see in entry above.)

BARNARD, George N. *Photographic View of Sherman's Campaign*. 61 gold-toned albumen prints, mounted, with lithographic captions. Oblong folio, morocco. New York, (1866). First edition. $10,000 and up. Also, $5,400 (A, 1970).

BARNES, Charles Merritt. *Combats and Conquest of Immortal Heroes*. Full morocco. San Antonio, 1910. First edition. $75-$125.

BARNES, David M. *The Draft Riots in New York, July, 1863*. 117 pp., wrappers, or cloth. New York, 1863. First edition. Wrappers: $100-$125. Cloth: $75-$100.

BARNES, Djuna. See *Ladies Almanack*.

BARNES, Djuna. *A Book*. 6 portraits, Black boards, paper label. New York, (1923). First edition. In dust jacket. $250-$300. Also, $130 (A, 1975).

BARNES, Djuna. *The Book of Repulsive Women*. Illustrated. Wrappers. (New York, 1915.) First edition. $250-$300. Also, $225 (A, 1977). Author's first book. New York, 1948. Stiff wrappers. One of 1,000. $75-$100.

BARNES, Djuna. *A Night Among the Horses*. Boards, cloth spine. New York, 1929. First edition. In dust jacket. $50-$75.

BARNES, Djuna. *Nightwood*. Cloth. London, (1936). First edition. In dust jacket. $40-$50. New York, (1937). First American edition. In dust jacket. $50-$65. Contains an introduction by T.S. Eliot.

BARNES, Djuna. *Ryder*. New York, 1928. Cloth. First edition. In dust jacket. $80-$125.

BARNES, Will C. *Apaches and Longhorns*. Edited by Frank C. Lockwood. Illustrated. Cloth. Los Angeles, 1941. First edition. In dust jacket. $50-$75.

BARNEY, James M. *Tales of Apache Warfare*. 45 pp., wrappers. (Phoenix), 1933. $75-$85.

BARNEY, Natalie C. *Actes et Entr'actes*. Wrappers. Paris, 1910. First edition. $135-$150.

BARNEY, Natalie C. *The One Who Is Legion*. Cloth. London, 1930. First edition. In dust jacket. $100-$125.

BARNEY, Natalie C. *Poems & Poemes*. Wrappers. Paris & New York, (1920). First edition. Limited edition. Copies on blue paper, $100-$125; white paper, $50-$75.

BARNFIELD, Richard. *Complete Poems*. Edited by Alexander B. Grosart, Frontispiece, 7 facsimiles of title pages. Half morocco. London, 1876. Roxburghe Club. $200.

BARNUM, H.L. *The Spy Unmasked; or, Memoirs of Enoch Crosby*. Map, 5 plates. Boards. New York, 1828. First edition. $50-$60.

BARREIRO, Antonio. *Ojeada sobre Nuevo-Mexico*. Illustrated, 3 tables. Marbled wrappers. Puebla, Mexico, 1832. First edition. $750-$1,000.

BARRETT, Elizabeth Barrett. *Poems*. 2 vols., dark green cloth, uncut. London, 1844. (By Elizabeth Barrett Browning.) First edition, with ads in Vol. 1 dated June 1. $500-$750. Later, 1844, no ads, $300-$400. Also, with ads dated January, 1845, $225 (A, 1974). London, 1850. 2 vols. brown cloth. Second edition, second issue, with single address in imprint. "New Edition." $500-$750. (First appearance of "Sonnets from the Portuguese" in a book.) London, 1856. 3 vols., cloth. $300-$400. London, 1873. 5 vols., cloth. $150-$250. (See entry under Browning, Elizabeth Barrett.)

BARRETT, Elizabeth B. *The Seraphim and Other Poems*. Purple cloth. London, 1838. (By Elizabeth Barrett Browning.) First edition. $150-$300.

BARRETT, Elizabeth, and Browning, Robert. *Two Poems*. Printed wrappers. London, 1854. (By Elizabeth Barrett Browning, etc.) First edition. $200-$300.

BARRETT, Ellen C. *Baja California, 1535-1956: A Bibliography*. Blue cloth. Los Angeles, 1957. First edition. One of 500. $60-$85.

BARRETT, Francis. *The Magus, or Celestial Intelligencer*. Illustrated. Boards and leathers. London, 1801. First edition. $250-$300.

BARRIE, Sir James M. See *The Allahakbarrie Book of Broadway Cricket for 1899.*

BARRIE, Sir James M. *The Admirable Crichton.* Illustrated by Hugh Thomson. Boards and cloth. London, (1914). $50-$75. Another issue: Vellum with ties. One of 500 signed by Thomson. $200-$250.

BARRIE, Sir James M. *Auld Licht Idylls.* Blue buckram. London, 1888. First edition, first issue, with black end papers. $80-$100. London, 1895. Illustrated by William Hole. Cloth. One of 550. $125-$150.

BARRIE, Sir James M. *Better Dead.* Pictorial glazed yellow (or buff) wrappers. London, 1888 (actually 1887). First edition. $200-$250. Author's first book.

BARRIE, Sir James M. *Courage: The Rectorial Address Delivered at St. Andrews University, May 3rd, 1922.* Cream cloth, gilt top. London, (1922). First edition. Limited issue on large paper. $50-$75. Also, with ALS about the speech, $90 (A, 1962).

BARRIE, Sir James M. *An Edinburgh Eleven.* Wrappers. London, 1889. First edition, first issue, with "Galvin Ogilvy" on front cover and "J.M. Barrie" on title page.$100. Later issue same date: Gray cloth. $25-$35.

BARRIE, Sir James M. *The Greenwood Hat: Being a Memoir of James Anon, 1885-1887.* 10 plates. Green leather, gilt top. London, 1930. First edition. One of 550. Boxed. $60-$80. (A number of inscribed copies have been noted.)

BARRIE, Sir James M. *"The Ladies' Shakespeare."* 7 pp., dark-red printed wrappers. London, 1925. First edition. One of 25. $60-$80.

BARRIE, Sir James M. *The Little Minister.* 3 vols., brown cloth. London, 1891. First edition, first issue, with 16 pages of ads in Vol. 1 dated "5G.9.91." $500-$750. Another set, unopened, with Barrie's autograph on front flyleaf of Vol. 1. $1,250. Also, "as new," $725 (A, 1957); "unopened," outer hinges rubbed, $300 (A, 1962); rebound, $130 (A, 1967). New York, (1891). Lovell, Coryell & Co. Wrappers. First American edition. $35-$50.

BARRIE, Sir James M. *The Little White Bird.* Cloth. London, 1902. First edition. In dust jacket. $35-$50.

BARRIE, Sir James M. *My Lady Nicotine.* Blue buckram. London, 1890. First edition, first issue, with 6 pages of ads at back. $35-$50. Inscribed by the author, $90.

BARRIE, Sir James M. *Peter and Wendy.* Illustrated. Green cloth. London, 1911. First edition, $100-$125. New York, (1911). Cloth. First American edition, first issue, from English sheets. $50. Later, printed in U.S. $25.

BARRIE, Sir James M. *Peter Pan in Kensington Gardens.* Illustrated in color and black and white by Arthur Rackham. Vellum. London, 1906. First edition. One of 500 signed by Rackham. $600-$750. Trade edition: Cloth. $250-$350. New York, 1906. First American trade edition. $150-250. New York, 1907. Green cloth. $150-$200. London, 1907. Cloth, $150-$200. Note: There were several other clothbound editions (1909, 1910, 1912, 1920, etc.) issued in New York and London, and these usually retail in the $100 and up range if in fine condition. Copies with original Rackham drawings occasionally reach the market. One such brought $1,100 at auction in 1974. There were also Paris editions in 1907 and 1911, and these bring very high prices. Example: $309 and $464 at auction in 1974 for two copies of the 1911 Paris edition (limited to 100).

BARRIE, Sir James M. *Quality Street.* Illustrated by Hugh Thomson. Vellum with silk ties. (London, 1913.) One of 1,000. $200-$300. Trade issue: Cloth. $100-$125.

BARRIE, Sir James M. *A Tillyloss Scandal.* Wrappers. New York, (1893). First edition, first issue, with publisher's address as "43, 45, 47 East 10th Street." $60-$100.

BARRIE, Sir James M. *Walker London.* Frontispiece. Green printed wrappers. New York, 1907. First edition. $75-$100.

BARRIE, Sir James M. *When a Man's Single: A Tale of Literary Life.* Blue buckram, gilt top. London, 1888. First edition, with ads at back. $75.

BARRIE, Sir James M. *A Window in Thrums*. Cloth. London, 1889. First edition. With 6 pages of ads at back. $50-$60. London, 1892. Illustrated by William Hole. Blue cloth. One of 50. $100-$150. Another issue: One of 500. $50.

BARROW, John. *A Chronological History of Voyages into the Arctic Regions*. Illustrated, folding map. Boards and cloth. London, 1818. First edition. $300-$350.

BARROW, John. *A Voyage to Cochinchina, 1792-1793*. Folding map, 20 colored aquatint plates. Contemporary calf. London, 1806. First edition. $400-$500. Also, $361 (A, 1976).

BARROWS, R.M. (compiler). *The Kitbook for Soldiers, Sailors, and Marines*. Pictorial boards. Chicago, (1943). First edition. In pictorial mailing box. $100-$150. (Contains J.D. Salinger's story "The Hang of It," his first book appearance.)

BARROWS, Willard. *Notes on Iowa Territory*. Folding map. 46 pp., cloth, printed front cover label. Cincinnati, 1845. First edition. $1,500. Map in facsimile, $1,250.

BARRY, T.A., and Patten, B.A. *Men and Memories of San Francisco, in the "Spring of '50."* 2 plates. Flexible cloth. San Francisco, 1873. First edition. $50.

BARTH, John. *Chimera*. New York, (1972). First edition. One of 300 signed. Boxed. $40.

BARTH, John. *The End of the Road*. Cloth. New York, 1958. First edition. In dust jacket. $50-$60.

BARTH, John. *The Floating Opera*. Cloth. New York, (1956). First edition, first issue, with "(1)" at foot of last page. In dust jacket. $150-$185. Author's first book.

BARTH, John. *Giles Goat-Boy*. Cloth. Garden City, 1966. First edition. One of 250 signed. Boxed. $75-$100.

BARTH, John. *Lost in the Fun House*. Cloth. Garden City, 1968. First edition. One of 250 signed. Boxed. $60-$75.

BARTH, John. *The Sot-Weed Factor*. Cloth. Garden City, 1960. First edition. In dust jacket. $150-$200.

BARTHELME, Donald. *Come Back, Dr. Caligari*. Cloth. Boston, (1964). First edition. In dust jacket. $50-$60. Author's first book.

BARTLETT, J.S., M.D. *The Physician's Pocket Synopsis*. Leather. Boston, 1822. First edition. $50-$75.

BARTLETT, John. See *A Collection of Familiar Quotations*.

BARTLETT, John Russell. *Personal Narrative of Explorations and Incidents in Texas, New Mexico, California, etc.*. Folding map. 44 plates, 2 vols., pictorial cloth. New York, 1854. First edition. $350-$600. Another issue (?): 2 vols. in one, cloth. $175-$250. London, 1854. 2 vols., cloth. $250-$300.

BARTON, James L. *Commerce of the Lakes*. Folding table. 80 pp., wrappers. Buffalo, 1847. First edition. $80-$100.

BARTON, James L. *Lake Commerce*. 34 pp., wrappers. Buffalo, 1846. First edition. $75.

BASKIN, Leonard. *Figures of Dead Men*. Preface by Archibald MacLeish. Illustrated. Boards and cloth. (Boston), 1968. One of 100 signed by Baskin, with an original signed woodcut. $150-$200.

BASKIN, Leonard. *LB—Some Engravings*. 17 woodcuts. Stiff boards. Gehenna Press, 1952. First edition, with each engraving signed and titled by Baskin. One of 10. In dust jacket. $1,500-$2,000.

BASS, W.W. (editor). *Adventures in the Canyons of the Colorado by Two of Its Earliest Explorers, James White and H.W. Hawkins*. Frontispiece, plate, facsimiles. 38 pp., wrappers. Grand Canyon, 1920. First edition. $80-$100.

BATES, Ed. F. *History . . . of Denton County, Texas.* plates. Denton, Tex., (1918). First edition. $100-$150.

BATES, H.E. *The Beauty of the Dead, and One Other Story.* Boards and cloth. London, 1941. Corvinus Press. One of 25. $75-$100.

BATES, H.E. *Flowers and Faces.* Engravings by John Nash. Boards. London, 1935. Golden Cockerel Press. One of 325. $150. Another issue: Full morocco. One of 60 with an extra set of plates. $300-$400.

BATES, H.E. *A German Idyll.* Engravings. Morocco and cloth. Waltham Saint Lawrence, 1932, Golden Cockerel Press. One of 307. $75-$100.

BATES, H.E. *The Last Bread: A Play in One Act.* Wrappers. London, (1926). First edition. $40-$50. Author's first book.

BATES, H.E. *Sally Go Round the Moon.* Vellum. London, 1932. White Owl Press. One of 21 signed. Boxed. $150-$200.

BATES, H.E. *The Story Without an End.* Parchment. (London), 1932. White Owl Press. One of 25 signed, with a leaf of manuscript. $150-$200.

BATES, H.W. *The Naturalist on the River Amazons.* Illustrated, including folding map. 2 vols., cloth. London, 1863. First edition. $160-$185.

BATES, J.H. *Notes of a Tour in Mexico and California.* Cloth. New York, 1887. First edition. $50-$65.

BAUDELAIRE, Charles. *Les Fleurs du Mal.* Illustrated by Auguste Rodin. Wrappers. New York, 1940. Limited Editions Club. Boxed $100-$125. Same: Illustrated by Matisse. Stiff illustrated wrappers. (Paris, 1947.) In slipcase. One of 320 copies, signed by Matisse. $1,000-$1,250.

BAUDELAIRE, Charles. *Flowers of Evil.* Edited by James Laver. Lithographs by Jacob Epstein. Buckram. New York, 1940. Limited Editions Club. Boxed. $100-$135.

BAUDELAIRE, Charles. *Intimate Journals.* Translated by Christopher Isherwood. Introduction by T.S. Eliot. Blue cloth, gilt top. London, 1930. First edition. One of 700. Boxed. $100-$150. Hollywood, 1947. Cloth. Revised edition (with W.H. Auden introduction). Signed by Isherwood. In dust jacket. $75-$100.

BAUER, Max. *Precious Stones.* Translated from the German by L.J. Spencer. Plates. Half morocco. London, 1903. First edition. $250-$350. London, 1904. $150-$250.

BAUM, L. Frank. See Stanton, Schuyler.

BAUM, L. Frank. *American Fairy Tales.* Illustrated. Pictorial cloth. Chicago, 1901. First edition. $100-$150.

BAUM, L. Frank. *The Army Alphabet.* Illustrated by Harry Kennedy. Pictorial boards. Chicago, 1900. First edition. $150-$200.

BAUM, L. Frank. *The Cowardly Lion and the Hungry Tiger.* Color plates. Boards. Chicago, (1913). First edition. $35-$50.

BAUM, L. Frank. *Dorothy and the Wizard of Oz.* Illustrated by John R. Neill. Cloth. Chicago, (1908). First edition, first issue, with "Reilly & Britton Co." at bottom of spine. $100-$150.

BAUM, L. Frank. *The Enchanted Island of Yew.* Illustrated by Fanny Y. Cory. Pictorial cloth. Indianapolis, (1903). First edition. $50-$75.

BAUM, L. Frank. *The Life and Adventures of Santa Claus.* Illustrated in color. Cloth. Indianapolis, 1902. First edition. $100-$135.

BAUM, L. Frank. *The Marvelous Land of Oz.* Illustrated by John R. Neill. Cloth. Chicago,

1904. First edition, first issue, without "Published July, 1904" on copyright page. In dust jacket. $200-$250.

BAUM, L. Frank. *The Master Key*. Illustrated in color by Fanny Cory. Olive-green cloth. Indianapolis, (1901). First edition, first issue, with signatures of 8 pp. and with copyright line 1 21/32 inches wide. $100-$125. Second issue, signatures of 16 pp. $75-$100. Third issue, copyright line 1 25/32 inches wide. $50-$75.

BAUM, L. Frank. *Mother Goose in Prose*. Illustrated by Maxfield Parrish. Pictorial cloth. Chicago, (1897). First edition. $400-$600. Chicago, (1901). 12 plates. Pictorial cloth. $75-$100.

BAUM, L. Frank. *A New Wonderland*. Illustrated by Frank Verbeck. Green cloth. New York, 1900. First edition. $150-$200.

BAUM, L. Frank. *Ozma of Oz*. Tan pictorial cloth. Chicago, (1907). First edition, first issue, with illustrations in color on p. 221. In dust jacket. $150-$200.

BAUM, L. Frank. *The Patchwork Girl of Oz*. Illustrated. Light green pictorial cloth. Chicago, (1913). First edition, first issue. $50-$75. Later issue, tan cloth. $40-$50.

BAUM, L. Frank. *Queen Zixi of Ix*. Illustrated in color. Pictorial cloth. New York, 1905. First edition. $35-$50.

BAUM, L. Frank. *The Road to Oz*. Illustrated by John R. Neill. Pictorial green cloth. Chicago, (1909). Reilly & Britton. First edition. $35.

BAUM, L. Frank. *Sea Fairies*. Illustrated. Light-green cloth. Chicago, (1911). First edition, first issue, with three heads on cover label. $50. Second issue, cover label showing girl on a sea horse. $25.

BAUM, L. Frank. *The Songs of Father Goose*. Illustrated by W. W. Denslow. Colored pictorial boards. Chicago, 1900. First edition. $50-$75.

BAUM, L. Frank. *The Songs of Father Goose for the Kindergarten*. 88 pp., pictorial boards and cloth. Indianapolis, (1909). $50-$60.

BAUM, L. Frank. *The Wonderful Wizard of Oz*. Illustrated by W.W. Denslow. Green cloth. Chicago and New York, 1900. First edition, first issue, with 11-line colophon (not 13) on back end paper. $1,000-$1,500. Also, $800 (A, 1972). (Note: Several binding states make this a difficult book to evaluate properly. If you find a copy with title page date of 1900, seek a specialist dealer's help.)

BAUM, L. Frank. *The Yellow Hen*. Illustrated. Pictorial boards. Chicago, (1916). First edition. $150.

BAX, Clifford (editor). *Florence Farr, Barnard Shaw and W.B. Yeats*. Boards, linen spine, paper label. Dublin, 1941. Cuala Press. First edition. One of 500. In tissue dust jacket. $75-$100.

BAXTER, William. *Pea Ridge and Prairie Grove*. Cloth. Cincinnati, 1864. First edition. $50-$65.

BAY, J. Christian. *The Fortune of Books*. Illustrated. Blue cloth. Chicago, (1941). In dust jacket. $50-$75.

BAY, J. Christian. *A Handful of Western Books *A Second Handful of Western Books* A Third Handful of Western Books*. Illustrated. 3 vols., boards and cloth. Cedar Rapids, Iowa, 1935-36-37. First editions. Limited to 350, 400, and 400 copies, respectively. (Note: Most of these bear the Torch Press imprint. An unknown number bear the imprint of the Chicago bookseller Walter M. Hill. Matched sets are to be preferred.) Together, the three volumes, in tissue dust jackets, $125-$175 at retail. Odd volumes, in jackets, $40-$50, or more at retail. (See following item.)

BAY, J. Christian. *Three Handfuls of Western Books*. (Combined one-volume edition of preceding items.) Boards. (Cedar Rapids), 1941. One of 35. $100-$125.

*BAYEUX Tapestry (The).* Facsimile in color, by James Basire after C.A. Stothard. 17 double page plates in color. Folio, half calf. (London, 1823). $200-$300.

BEAGLE, Peter S. *A Fine and Private Place.* Cloth. New York, 1960. First edition. In dust jacket. $50-$60. Author's first book.

BEALE, Charles Willing. *The Secret of the Earth.* Yellow cloth. New York, (1899). First edition. $75.

BEAN, Edwin F. (compiler). *Bean's History and Directory of Nevada County, California.* Half leather and boards. Nevada, Calif., 1867. First edition. $400-$750.

BEARD, Charles A. *An Economic Interpretation of the Constitution of the United States.* Cloth. New York, 1913. First edition. $200-$250.

BEARD, Charles R. *A Catalogue of the Collection of Martinware Formed by Frederick John Nettlefold.* 31 color plates, 46 in black and white. Half brown morocco. (London?), 1936. Privately printed. $150-$200.

BEARD, Daniel C. *American Boy's Handy Book: What to Do and How to Do It.* Illustrated. Pictorial cloth. New York, 1882. First edition. $50-$75.

BEARDSLEY, Aubrey. *A Book of Fifty Drawings.* Scarlet cloth. London, 1897. First edition. $150-$250. Another issue: One of 50 on vellum. $400-$600.

BEARDSLEY, Aubrey. *Fifty Drawings.* Pictorial cloth. New York, 1920. First edition. One of 500. $50-$75. (Beardsley experts doubt that these are Beardsley's drawings.)

BEARDSLEY, Aubrey. *Last Letters.* Cloth. London, 1904. First edition. $50-$60.

BEARDSLEY, Aubrey. *A Second Book of Fifty Drawings.* Cloth. London, 1899. First edition. One of 1,000. $150-$250. Another issue: One of 50 on vellum. $400-$500.

BEARDSLEY, Aubrey. *Six Drawings Illustrating Théophile Gautier's Romance, "Mademoiselle de Maupin."* 6 plates, loose in half cloth portfolio, silk ties. London, 1898. One of 50. $200-$300.

BEARDSLEY, Aubrey. *Some Unknown Drawings of Aubrey Beardsley.* Edited by R.A. Walker. 32 plates and facsimiles. Buckram. London, 1923. First edition. One of 500 signed. In dust jacket. $75-$100.

BEARDSLEY, Aubrey. *The Story of Venus and Tannhäuser.* Green cloth, label on front cover. London, 1907. One of 50 on vellum. (First complete edition.) $250-$300. Another issue: Gray boards, label. One of 300. $100-$150. (Note: On most copies seen the spine is defective.) New York, 1927. Boards and cloth. One of 750. $100-$125.

BEARDSLEY, Aubrey. *Under the Hill and Other Essays in Prose and Verse.* 16 illustrations by the author. Pictorial cloth. London, 1904. First edition. One of 50 on Japan paper. $250-$300. Trade edition: $100-$150.

BEATON, Cecil. *The Book of Beauty.* 27 photographic plates, 90 text drawings. Buckram. London, 1930. One of 110 signed. $150-$200.

BEATTIE, George W. and Helen P. *Heritage of the Valley.* Cloth. Pasadena, 1939. First edition. In dust jacket. $40-$50.

BEATTIE, William. *Switzerland Illustrated.* 107 plates by W.H. Bartlett, map. 2 vols., half calf. London, 1836. $500-$650.

*BEAUCHAMPE; or, the Kentucky Tragedy.* 2 vols., cloth. Philadelphia, 1842. (By William Gilmore Simms.) First edition. $150-$175.

BEAUMONT, Cyril W. *The History of Harlequin.* With a preface by Sacheverell Sitwell. 44 plates (5 colored), text decorations by Claudia Guercio. Decorated parchment boards, vellum spine. London, 1926. One of 325. In dust jacket. $150-$250.

BEAUMONT, Cyril W. *Puppets and the Puppet Stage.* 110 pp. of illustrations. Cloth. London, 1938. In dust jacket. $50-$60.

BEAUMONT, William. *Experiments and Observations on the Gastric Juice, and the Physiology of Digestion.* 3 engravings. Boards and cloth, paper spine label. Plattsburgh, N.Y., 1833. First edition. $1,750-$2,250. Also, presentation copy inscribed by the author, worn, $1,700 (A, 1969). Boston, 1834. Boards and cloth, paper label. Second issue (first edition copy with Boston title page). $750-$1,000. Edinburgh, 1838. Boards and calf. First English edition. $500-$750.

BEAUMONT, William. *The Physiology of Digestion.* Edited by Samuel Beaumont. Cloth. Burlington, Vt., 1847. Second edition of *Experiments and Observations on the Gastric Juice.* $400-$500.

*BEAUTY and the Beast.* Boards, in printed paper case. London, (about 1811 or 1813?). (By Charles Lamb?) First edition. $500 and up.

BECK, Lewis C. *A Gazetteer of the States of Illinois and Missouri.* Folding map, 5 plates. Boards, paper label. Albany, 1823. First edition. $600-$1,000.

BECKER, Robert H. *Diseños of California Ranchos.* San Francisco, 1964, Grabhorn printing. One of 400. $300-$400.

BECKETT, Samuel. See Crowder, Henry.

BECKETT, Samuel. *All Strange Away.* Illustrated by Edward Gorey. New York, 1976. One of 120 numbered and signed. $125-$150. One of 26 lettered and signed. $150-$200.

BECKETT, Samuel. *All That Fall: A Play.* 59 pp., stiff wrappers. New York, (1957). Special holiday greeting from Grove Press. First American edition. $100-$125. Another issue: Cloth. $25. London, 1957. Wrappers. First English edition. $25-$30.

BECKETT, Samuel. *Come and Go: Dramaticule.* Illustrated. Cloth. London, (1967). First edition. One of 100 signed. Boxed. $100-$125.

BECKETT, Samuel. *Comment C'est.* 177 pp., printed wrappers. Paris, (1961). Editions de Minuit. First edition. One of 100 for the Club de l'Edition Originale, signed. $125-$150. Trade edition, unsigned. In glassine dust jacket. $35.

BECKETT, Samuel. *Echo's Bones and Other Precipitates.* 30 pp., printed wrappers. Paris, 1935. Europa Press. First edition. One of 25 on Normandy vellum, signed. $500-$750. Also, $600 (A, 1977). Another issue: One of 250 on Alfa paper, unsigned. $200-$250.

BECKETT, Samuel. *En Attendant Godot.* Wrappers. Paris, 1952. Editions de Minuit. First edition (of *Waiting for Godot*). One of 35 numbered copies. $3,500-$4,000. (Inscribed copy, $12,500.) First trade edition: Wrappers. Paris, 1952. $150-$200.

BECKETT, Samuel. *Endgame.* Translated by the author. Dark red cloth. London, (1958). First English edition. In dust jacket. $35-$50. New York, (1958). Grove Press. First American edition. In dust jacket. $10-$15. Limited issue: One of 100. $60.

BECKETT, Samuel. *From an Abandoned Work.* Printed wrappers. London, (1958). First English edition. $20-$25.

BECKETT, Samuel. *How It Is.* (Series A and Series B.) Translated from the French by the author. 2 vols., vellum and morocco. London, (1964). First editions. Each, 100 signed. In tissue dust jackets. Boxed. $300-$450.

BECKETT, Samuel. *Imagination Dead Imagine.* Brown buckram. London, (1965). First English edition. One of 100 signed. Boxed. $100-$125.

BECKETT, Samuel. *Imagination Morte Imaginez.* Wrappers. Paris, (1965). First edition. One of 450 numbered copies. $45-$60. One of 112 for the publisher's friends, signed. $125-$150.

BECKETT, Samuel. *Krapp's Last Tape, and Embers.* Wrappers. London, 1959. First edition. $25-$35.

BECKETT, Samuel. *Malone Dies.* Translated by the author. 120 pp., cream-colored canvas. New York, (1956). First American edition. One of 500. In transparent dust jacket. $35-$50. London, 1958. Black cloth. First English edition. In dust jacket. $35.

BECKETT, Samuel. *Malone Meurt*. Wrappers. (Paris, 1951.) First edition (of *Malone Dies*). $200-$300.

BECKETT, Samuel. *Mercier Et Camier*. Wrappers. Paris, 1970. First edition. One of 92. $100-$125.

BECKETT, Samuel. *Molloy*. Printed wrappers. Paris, (1951). First edition. One of 500 on Alfa paper. $40-$60. Paris, (1955). Olympia Press. Wrappers. First edition in English. $50-$75.

BECKETT, Samuel. *Molloy. Malone Dies. The Unnamable: A Trilogy*. Wrappers. Paris, (1959). Olympia Press. First collected edition. $40-$60.

BECKETT, Samuel. *More Pricks Than Kicks*. Tan cloth. London, 1934. First edition. In dust jacket. $400-$500.

BECKETT, Samuel. *Murphy*. Cloth. London, (1938). First edition. In dust jacket. $50-$75. Paris, 1947. Wrappers. First edition in French. $100-$125. New York, (1957). Boards and cloth. First American edition. One of 100 signed. $100-$185.

BECKETT, Samuel. *No's Knife: Collected Shorter Prose, 1945-1966*. Full white calf, gilt. London, (1967). First edition. One of 100 signed. (Series A.) Boxed. $100-$110. Another issue: White calf and buckram. One of 100 signed. (Series B.) Boxed. $100-$125.

BECKETT, Samuel. *Nouvelles et Textes pour Rien*. Illustrated. Wrappers. Paris, (1958). Numbered edition. $35. (Note: The first edition appeared in Paris in 1955.)

BECKETT, Samuel. *Play and Two Short Pieces for Radio*. Red cloth. London, 1964. First English edition. In dust jacket. $20-$25. Advance proof copy in printed wrapper, $75-$100.

BECKETT, Samuel. *Poems in English*. Mottled tan leather-like cloth boards. London, (1961). One of 100 signed, "printed in advance of the first edition." $250-$350. Also, $225 (A, 1977). Also, a copy listed as "cloth, one of 100," inscribed to Nancy Cunard, $576 (A, 1969). Another issue: Cloth. One of 175 signed. In tissue dust jacket. $75-$125. First trade edition: Cloth. In dust jacket. $20-$25. New York, (1963). Green cloth. First American edition. In dust jacket. $20-$25.

BECKETT, Samuel. *Proust*. 72 pp., decorated boards. London, 1931. First edition. In dust jacket. $150-$200. Also, $150 (A, 1977).

BECKETT, Samuel. *The Unnamable*. Translated by the author. 179 pp., boards and cloth. New York, (1958). Grove Press. First American edition. One of 26 lettered copies, signed. $100-$150. One of 100 numbered copies. $75. Another issue: Printed wrappers. Review copy. $50.

BECKETT, Samuel. *Waiting for Godot*. Translated by the author. New York, 1954. In dust jacket. $125-$175. London, (1956). Yellow cloth. First English edition. In dust jacket. $125-$175. London, 1957. Printed wrappers. Acting edition, first printing. $35-$50.

BECKETT, Samuel. *Watt*. Printed wrappers. Paris, (1953). Collection Merlin: Olympia Press. First edition. One of 25, lettered A to Y, on fine paper and signed by Beckett. $350-$400. First trade edition: wrappers. Paris, (1953). $50-$75. New York, (1959). First American edition. $25-$35.

BECKETT, Samuel. *Whoroscope*. 6 pp., printed wrappers, with white (separate) band around the book. Paris, 1930. Hours Press. First edition. One of 100 signed and numbered (of a total edition of 300). $1,000-$1,500. Another issue: One of 200, unsigned. $300-$500; inscribed to Nancy Cunard, publisher of the book, with an autograph letter, signed, $2,280 (A, 1969). Author's first separately published work.

BECKETT, Samuel, and others. *Our Exagmination Round His Factification for Incamination of Work in Progress*. Printed wrappers. Paris, 1929. Shakespeare and Company. First edition. One of 96 (large paper) on verge d'Arches paper. $800-$1,000. Also, $600 (A, 1977). Ordinary issue: $150-$200.

BEDFORD, Hilory G. *Texas Indian Troubles*. Decorated cloth. Dallas, 1905. First edition. $300-$400.

BEEBE, Henry. *The History of Peru*. Leather. Peru, Ill., 1858. First edition. $100-$150.

BEEBE, Lucius. *Aspects of the Poetry of Edwin Arlington Robinson*. Cloth. Cambridge, Mass., 1928. First edition. One of 200. $25-$35.

BEEBE, Lucius, and Clegg, Charles M. *Mixed Train Daily*. Illustrated. Cloth. New York, 1947. First edition. In dust jacket. $35-$50.

BEEBE, William. *The Arcturus Adventure*. Boards and vellum. New York, 1926. Autograph (first) edition. One of 50 signed. $100-$150. First trade edition: Cloth. In dust jacket. $15-$20.

BEEBE, William. *Galapagos: World's End*. 9 color plates, 84 other illustrations. Buckram. New York, 1924. Autograph (first) edition. One of 100 signed. In dust jacket. $200-$300. First trade edition: Cloth. In dust jacket. $25.

BEEBE, William. *A Monograph of the Pheasants*. 90 color plates, 20 maps, other illustrations. 4 vols., folio, cloth. London, 1918-22. First edition. One of 600. $2,000-$2,500, possibly more. Also, $1,400, $1,200, $1,100, $1,118, $997, and $850 (A, 1975).

BEEBE, William. *Pheasants: Their Lives and Homes*. 64 plates (some in color). 2 vols., vellum. Garden City, 1926. First edition. One of 201 on large paper, signed. $250-$350. Trade edition: 2 vols., cloth. $125-$150. Garden City, 1931. 2 vols. $75-$100. Garden City, 1936. 2 vols. in one. $100-$125.

BEECHER, John. *And I Will Be Heard*. Wrappers. New York, (1940). First edition. $50-$60. Author's first book.

BEECHER, John. *Here I Stand*. Wrappers. (New York, 1941). First edition. One of 100 signed. $60.

BEECHER, Harriet Elizabeth. *Prize-Tale: A New England Sketch*. Plain wrappers, cloth spine. Lowell, Mass., 1834. First edition. $750. First book by Harriet Beecher Stowe.

BEECHEY, F.W. *An Account of a Visit to California*. Map, color plates. Half vellum. (San Francisco, 1941). Grabhorn printing. One of 350. $125-$175.

BEECHEY, F.W. *Narrative of a Voyage to the Pacific and Beering's Strait*. 23 plates, 3 maps. 2 vols., brown cloth, or boards and cloth. London, 1831. First edition. $1,000 and up. London, 1831. 2 vols. Second edition. $350-$500. Philadelphia, 1832. Boards and cloth. First American edition. $200.

BEECHEY, F.W. *A Voyage of Discovery Towards the North Pole*. Folding map, 6 plates. Half leather. London, 1843. First edition. $600-$800.

BEE-HUNTER (The); or, The Oak Openings. By the author of "The Pioneers," 3 vols., drab boards. London, 1848. (By James Fenimore Cooper.) First edition (of the novel published in America as *The Oak Openings*, which see as title entry). $100-$150.

BEER, Thomas. *The Mauve Decade*. Boards and cloth. New York, 1926. First edition. One of 165 signed. Boxed. $50-$60. Another issue: One of 15 signed. Boxed. $110.

BEERBOHM, Max. *A Book of Caricatures*. Frontispiece in color, 48 drawings. Folio, boards and cloth, paper label, gilt top. London, (1907). First edition. In dust jacket. $150-$200.

BEERBOHM, Max. *Caricatures of Twenty-Five Gentlemen*. 25 plates. Cloth. London, (1896). First edition. $75-$100.

BEERBOHM, Max. *Cartoons: "The Second Childhood of John Bull."* 15 full-page tinted plates. Cloth. London, (1901). First edition. $150-$200. Another issue: Second issue. Plates in cloth folder. $75-$100. London, (1911). Folio, boards and linen. $75-$100.

BEERBOHM, Max. *A Christmas Garland*. Violet cloth, with gilt lettering and decorations. London, 1912. First edition. $25-$35.

BEERBOHM, Max. *Collected Works*. 10 vols., cloth. London, 1922-28. One of 780, first volume signed by the author. In dust jackets, $300-$400. (See *The Works of Max Beerbohm*.)

BEERBOHM, Max. *Fifty Caricatures*. 50 plates. Pictorial green cloth. London, 1913. First edition. $100-$125.

BEERBOHM, Max. *The Happy Hypocrite: A Fairy Tale for Tired Men*. Printed green wrappers. New York, 1897. First edition. No. 1 of the Bodley Booklets. $150-$250. London, 1915. Illustrated by George Sheringham. Pictorial cloth. $25-$35. Another issue: Boards. One of 50 on Japan paper. $75-$100. London, (1918). 24 colored illustrations. Cloth. $100-$125.

BEERBOHM, Max. *More*. Green cloth, paper label (with extra label tipped in). London, 1899. First edition. $50-$75.

BEERBOHM, Max. *Observations*. Color frontispiece, 51 other illustrations. Cloth. London, 1925. First edition. In dust jacket. $50-$75. London, 1926. Buckram. One of 280 signed, and with an additional colored plate, signed. $100-$150.

BEERBOHM, Max. *The Poet's Corner*. Colored caricatures. Folio, pictorial boards. London, (1904). First edition, first issue. $75-$100. Second issue: Pictorial wrappers. $50-$75.

BEERBOHM, Max. *Rossetti and His Circle*. 23 colored caricatures. Blue cloth. London, (1922). First edition. One of 380 signed. In dust jacket. $100-$150. Trade edition: $50-$60.

BEERBOHM, Max. *Seven Men*. Blue cloth. London, 1919. First edition, first issue, in bright-blue cloth. In dust jacket. $35-$50. Second issue: Dark-blue cloth. In dust jacket. $20-$25.

BEERBOHM, Max. *A Survey*. 52 plates, including colored frontispiece. Purple cloth. London, 1921. First edition. One of 275 signed. In dust jacket. $100-$150. Trade edition: Cloth. In dust jacket. $50-$75. New York, 1921. Boards and cloth. First American edition. $25-$35.

BEERBOHM, Max. *Things New and Old*. Colored frontispiece, 49 other plates. White buckram. London, 1923. One of 380 signed and with extra signed plate. In dust jacket. $250-$300. Trade edition: Cloth. In dust jacket. $75-$100.

BEERBOHM, Max. *The Works of Max Beerbohm*. Cloth. London, 1896. First edition. $125-$200. (Also see Beerbohm, *Collected Works*.)

BEERBOHM, Max. *Zuleika Dobson*. Smooth brown cloth, or rough cloth. London, 1911. First edition. In dust jacket. $300-$400. Lacking jacket, $75-$150. (Note: Percy H. Muir says there is no priority of issue for smooth brown cloth over rough cloth; they were issued simultaneously, but rough cloth is scarcer.) New York, 1960. Limited Editions Club. Cloth. Boxed. $50-$60.

BEERS, F.W., and Co. *Atlas of the Counties of Lamoille and Orleans, Vermont*. Maps in color. Half leather. New York, 1878. First edition. $100.

BEETON, Mrs. Isabella. *The Book of Household Management*. Frontispiece and pictorial title in color, numerous other illustrations. 2 vols., cloth. London, 1861. First edition, first issue, with "18 Bouverie St." on title page. $500-$600.

*BEETON'S Christmas Annual. 28th Season*. Illustrated. Wrappers. London, 1887. (Contains first appearance of A. Conan Doyle's *A Study in Scarlet*.) $4,000-$6,000. Also, $1,872 and $1,740 (A, 1971).

BEHAN, Brendan. *The Hostage*. Boards and cloth. New York, (1958). First American edition. One of 26 signed. (Issued without dust jacket.) $50-$85.

BEHAN, Brendan. *The Quare Fellow*. Black cloth. London, (1956). First edition. In dust jacket. $35.

BEHN, Mrs. Aphra. *The Works of Mrs. Aphra Behn*. Edited by Montague Summers. Portrait. 6 vols., cloth-backed boards. London, 1915. One of 50 sets on handmade paper. $250-$300. Another issue: One of 760. $75-$100.

BELCHER, Sir Edward. *Narrative of a Voyage Round the World . . . 1836-1842.* 19 plates, 3 maps in pocket. 2 vols., cloth. London, 1843. First edition. $400-$500.

BELL, Acton. *Agnes Grey.* See Bell, Ellis and Acton, *Wuthering Heights.*

BELL, Acton. *The Tenant of Wildfell Hall.* 3 vols., dark claret-colored cloth. London, 1848. (By Anne Brontë.) First edition. $750-$1,000. Also, rebound in calf, $650 (A, 1974).

BELL, Currer (editor). *Jane Eyre: An Autobiography.* 3 vols., red, or claret, cloth. London, 1847. (By Charlotte Brontë.) First edition, first issue, with 36-page catalogue at back of first volume, dated June and October, with half titles, and with a leaf advertising the *Calcutta Review.* $2,000 and up. Also, $1,400 (A, 1974). London, 1847. Second edition. (Currer Bell as author instead of editor on title page.) $400-$600. London, 1848. Third edition. $200-$350. Paris, 1923. Illustrated by Ethel Gabain. Folio, wrappers. One of 460. $100-$150.

BELL, Currer. *The Professor.* 2 vols., plum-colored cloth. London, 1857. (By Charlotte Brontë.) First edition, with 2 pages of ads at end of Vol. 1 and 16 pages of ads at end of Vol. 2 dated June, 1857. $500-$750. Also, rubbed, $258 (A, 1974).

BELL, Currer. *Shirley: A Tale.* 3 vols., deep claret-colored cloth. London, 1849. (By Charlotte Brontë.) First edition, with 16 pages of ads dated October, 1849, at end of Vol. 1. $1,000 and up.

BELL, Currer. *Villette.* 3 vols., olive-brown cloth. London, 1853. (By Charlotte Brontë.) First edition, with 12 pages of ads dated January, 1853, in Vol. 1. $850-$1,200. Also, $600 (A, 1974).

BELL, Currer, Ellis, and Acton. *Poems.* Dark-green cloth. London, 1846. (By Charlotte, Emily and Anne Brontë.) First edition, first issue, published by Aylott and Jones. $2,000 and up. London, 1846 (actually 1848). Green cloth. Published by Smith, Elder & Co. Second issue, with 4-line errata slip. $500-$750. Philadelphia, 1848. Boards. First American edition. $400-$600.

BELL, Ellis (and Acton). *Wuthering Heights.* 3 vols., claret-colored cloth (third vol. titled *Agnes Grey,* by Acton Bell). London, 1847. (First two vols. by Emily Brontë, third by Anne Brontë.) First edition. (1,000 copies printed.) $15,000 and up. (A badly worn and defective set, with corrections in Charlotte Brontë's hand, was sold for $3,784 at a London auction house in June, 1975.)

BELL, Gertrude. *The Arab War.* Half linen. London, 1924. Golden Cockerel Press. One of 500. $250.

BELL, Horace. *On the Old West Coast.* Edited by Lanier Bartlett. Plates and facsimiles. Half buckram and boards. New York, 1930. First edition. One of 20 signed by the editor. Boxed. $75-$100. Trade edition: Cloth. In dust jacket. $25-$30.

BELL, Horace. *Reminiscences of a Ranger.* Pictorial cloth. Los Angeles, 1881. First edition. $100-$150. Santa Barbara, 1927. Green cloth. $25.

BELL, John. *Discourses on the Nature and Cure of Wounds.* 2 plates. 2 vols. in one, leather. Walpole, N.H., 1807. First American edition. $150-$200.

BELL, Solomon. *Tales of Travel West of the Mississippi.* Map, plates. Boards and cloth, leather label. Boston, 1830. (By William J. Snelling.) First edition. $300-$400.

BELL, William A. *New Tracks in North America.* Plates and maps, some in color. 2 vols., cloth. London, 1869. First English edition. $200-$225.

BELLAMY, Edward. *Equality.* Salmon-colored or blue cloth. New York, 1897. First edition. In dust jacket. $100-$125.

BELLAMY, Edward. *Looking Backward, 2000-1887.* Pea-green, orange-brown, or gray cloth. Boston, 1888. First edition, first state, with printer's imprint of "J.J. Arakelyan" on copyright page. $250-$300. Another (second) issue: Gray wrappers. $100-$150. New York, 1941. Limited Editions Club. Cloth. Boxed. $25-$35.

BELLAMY, Edward. *Miss Ludington's Sister*. Cloth. Boston, 1884. First edition. $50.

BELLAMY, Edward. *Six to One: A Nantucket Idyl*. Frontispiece. Printed wrappers or cloth. New York, 1878. First edition. Cloth. $85-$125. Author's first book.

BELLOC, Hilaire. See B., H.

BELLOC, Hilaire. *The Book of the Bayeux Tapestry*. 76 colored facsimiles. Cloth. New York, 1914. $50-$75.

BELLOC, Hilaire. *Cautionary Tales for Children*. Pictorial boards. London, (1908). First edition. $75-$100. Presentation copy, inscribed, $125.

BELLOC, Hilaire. *The Highway and Its Vehicles*. Illustrated. Buckram. London, 1926. One of 1,250. $100-$125.

BELLOC, Hilaire. *New Cautionary Tales*. Illustrated. Half cloth. London, 1930. First edition. One of 110 signed. In dust jacket. $80-$125.

BELLOC, Hilaire. *The Praise of Wine*. Loose sheets in printed wrappers. (London, 1931). First edition. $75-$100.

BELLOC, Hilaire. *Verse*. Edited by W.H. Roughead. Buckram. London, 1954. Nonesuch Press. $50-$75.

BELLOC, Hilaire. *Verses and Sonnets*. Green cloth. London, 1896. First edition. $75-$100. Author's first book.

BELLOW, Saul. *The Adventures of Augie March*. Cloth. New York, 1953. First edition. In dust jacket. $75-$100. Author's first book.

BELLOW, Saul. *Dangling Man*. Cloth. New York, (1944). First edition. In dust jacket. $250-$350. London, 1946. First English edition. In dust jacket. $75-$85.

BELLOW, Saul. *Henderson the Rain King*. Cloth. New York, 1959. First edition. In dust jacket. $50-$60.

BELLOW, Saul. *Seize the Day*. Cloth. New York, 1956. First edition. In dust jacket. $25-$35.

BELLOW, Saul. *The Victim*. Cloth. New York, (1947). First edition. In dust jacket. $100-$150.

BELTRAMI, J.C. *A Pilgrimage in Europe and America*. Portrait, folding map, other engravings. 2 vols., boards and linen. London, 1828. First English edition. $200-$250.

BEMELMANS, Ludwig. *Madeline*. Cloth. New York, 1930. First edition. In dust jacket. $50-$60.

BEMELMANS, Ludwig. *Now I Lay Me Down to Sleep*. Cloth, pictorial cloth label, leather spine label. New York, 1943. First edition. One of 500 signed. Boxed. $50-$60.

BEMELMANS, Ludwig. *Small Beer*. Cloth. New York, 1939. First edition. One of 75 with original colored illustrations. Boxed. $75.

BENAVIDES, Alonso de. *The Memorial of Fray Alonso de Benavides, 1630*. Facsimiles of Madrid edition of 1630. Boards. Chicago, 1916. One of 300. $225-$250.

BENDIRE, Charles. *Life Histories of North American Birds*. 19 color plates. 2 vols., folio, cloth. Washington, 1892-95. First edition. $75-$150.

BENEDICT, Almon H. *"Wide Awake" Poem*. 16 pp., wrappers. Cortland Village, N.Y., 1860. First edition. $60.

BENÉT, Rosemary, and Benét, Stephen Vincent. *A Book of Americans*. Illustrated. Cloth. New York, 1933. First edition. One of 125 signed. Boxed. $50-$75. Trade edition: Cloth.

First issue, with publisher's monogram on copyright page. In dust jacket. $15-$20. Second issue, in dust jacket, $7.50.

BENÉT, Stephen Vincent. See Rinehart, Mary Roberts, and Hopwood, Avery; Benét, Rosemary. Also see *The Yale Book of Student Verse, 1910-1919.*

BENÉT, Stephen Vincent. *The Ballad of the Duke's Mercy.* Cloth. New York, 1939. One of 250 signed. $40-$50. Trade edition: Cloth. In dust jacket. $20.

BENÉT, Stephen Vincent. *The Ballad of William Sycamore, 1790-1880.* Boards, paper label. New York-New Haven-Princeton, (1923). First edition. One of 500 signed. $40-$50.

BENÉT, Stephen Vincent. *Ballads and Poems: 1915-1930.* Pictorial boards. Garden City, 1931. First edition. One of 201 signed. Boxed. $100-$125. Trade edition: Cloth. In dust jacket. $15-$20.

BENÉT, Stephen Vincent. *The Barefoot Saint.* Decorations by Valenti Angelo. Cloth. Garden City, 1929. First edition. One of 367. Boxed. $50-$75.

BENÉT, Stephen Vincent. *Burning City.* Red fabrikoid. New York, (1936). First edition. One of 275 signed. In glassine dust jacket. Boxed. $75-$100. Trade edition: Cloth. In dust jacket. $25-$35.

BENÉT, Stephen Vincent. *The Devil and Daniel Webster.* Illustrated by Harold Denison. Buckram. Weston, Vt., (1937). First edition. One of 700 signed. In glassine dust jacket. Boxed. $100-$150. New York, (1937). Cloth. First trade edition. In dust jacket. $25.

BENÉT, Stephen Vincent. *The Drug Shop; or Endymion in Edmonstoun.* 24 pp., printed wrappers. (New Haven), 1917. First edition. 100 copies only. $100-$125.

BENÉT, Stephen Vincent. *Five Men and Pompey.* Wrappers over boards. Boston, 1915. First edition. First state, purple wrappers. $150-$200. Second state, brown wrappers. $50-$60. (Note: Johnson says there were "a few copies" on handmade paper.) Author's first book.

BENÉT, Stephen Vincent. *James Shore's Daughter.* Parchment boards. Garden City, 1934. First edition. One of 307 signed. Boxed. $50-$75. Trade edition: Cloth. In dust jacket. $15-$20.

BENÉT, Stephen Vincent. *John Brown's Body.* Vellum boards. (Garden City, 1928). First edition. One of 201 signed. Boxed. $275-$375. Trade edition: Cloth. In dust jacket. Boxed. $25-$35. New York, 1948. Limited Editions Club. John Steuart Curry illustrations. Cloth. One of 1,500. Boxed. $35-$40.

BENÉT, Stephen Vincent. *Johnny Pye and the Fool Killer.* Illustrated. Blue cloth, tan wrap-around band. Weston, Vt., (1938). First edition. One of 750 signed. In glassine box. $75-$100. New York, (1938). Green cloth. First trade edition. In dust jacket. $15-$25.

BENÉT, Stephen Vincent. *King David.* Printed boards, paper label. New York, 1923. First edition. One of 350 signed. $50-$75.

BENÉT, Stephen Vincent. *Nightmare at Noon.* Printed wrappers. New York, (1940). First edition, first printing, with publisher's monogram on coypright page. $100.

BENÉT, Stephen Vincent. *A Portrait and a Poem.* Half morocco. Paris, 1934. First edition. One of 50. $150-$200.

BENÉT, Stephen Vincent. *Tuesday, Nov. 5th, 1940.* 8 pp., wrappers. New York, 1941. First edition. One of 50. $100-$150.

BENÉT, William Rose. *Merchants from Cathay and Other Poems.* Green cloth. New York, 1913. First edition. $40-$50. Author's first book.

BENEZET, Anthony A. *The Family Physician.* Calf. Cincinnati, 1826. First edition. $275.

BENJAMIN, Asher. *The Architect, or Practical House Carpenter.* 64 plates. Sheep. Boston, 1845. $200-$300. Boston, 1848. $100-$150. Boston, 1850. $100-$150.

BENJAMIN, Asher. *The Builder's Guide*. Plates. Boards and calf. Boston, 1839. $200-$300. Boston, 1850. $150-$200.

BENJAMIN, Asher. *The Practical House Carpenter*. Illustrated. Contemporary calf. Boston, 1832. $200-$300.

BENJAMIN, Asher. *The Practice of Architecture*. 60 full-page plates. Sheep. Boston, 1833. First edition. $150-$250. Philadelphia, 1835. Sheep. Second edition. $85. Boston, 1835. Contemporary leather. $75.

BENJAMIN, Asher. *The Rudiments of Architecture*. 36 plates, one folding. Calf. Boston, 1814. First edition. $400-$500. Boston, 1820. Second edition. $300-$400.

BENJAMIN, Asher, and Reynard, Daniel. *The American Builder's Companion*. 44 plates. Calf, or boards. Boston, (1806). First edition. $400-$500. Also, $200 (A, 1974). Boston, 1826. 63 plates. Contemporary calf. Fifth edition, enlarged. $75-$150. Boston, 1827. Leather. Sixth edition. $75-$100.

BENNETT, Arnold. See Wadsworth, Edward.

BENNETT, Arnold. *Anna of the Five Towns*. Cloth. London, 1902. First edition. $35.

BENNETT, Arnold. *The Bright Island*. London, 1924. Golden Cockerel Press. One of 200 signed. $125-$150.

BENNETT, Arnold. *Clayhanger*. Cloth. London, (1910). First edition. In dust jacket. $75-$100.

BENNETT, Arnold. *The Clayhanger Family*. Cloth. London, 1925. One of 200 signed. In dust jacket. $100-$125.

BENNETT, Arnold. *Don Juan de Marana*. Frontispiece. Vellum and boards. London, 1923. One of 100 signed. In dust jacket. $100-$150.

BENNETT, Arnold. *Elsie and the Child*. Color illustrations. Cloth. London, 1929. One of 100 signed. $50-$60.

BENNETT, Arnold. *From the Log of the Velsa*. Illustrated. White cloth. London, 1920. One of 110 signed. $35-$50.

BENNETT, Arnold. *Hilda Lessways*. Cloth. London, (1911). First edition. In dust jacket. $25-$35.

BENNETT, Arnold. *Imperial Palace*. 2 vols., vellum. London, (1930). First edition. One of 100 signed. $100.

BENNETT, Arnold. *The Loot of Cities*. Wrappers. London, (1904). First edition. $200-$300.

BENNETT, Arnold. *A Man from the North*. Red cloth, stamped in white. London, (1898). First edition. $100-$125. Author's first book.

BENNETT, Arnold. *The Old Wives' Tale*. Lavender, or pink, cloth, white lettering. London 1908. First edition. $250-$300. London, 1927. 2 vols., parchment and cloth. Facsimile of the manuscript. One of 500. $150-$200. New York, 1941. Limited Editions Club. Illustrated by John Austen. 2 vols., cloth. Boxed. $40-$60.

BENNETT, Arnold. *Things That Interested Me, Being Leaves from a Journal*. Cloth. Burslem, England, 1906. One of 100. $50-$60. London, 1921. Second Series. Cloth. In dust jacket. $35-$50. London, 1926. Third Series. Cloth. In dust jacket. $35-$50.

BENNETT, Arnold. *Things Which Have Interested Me*. Second Series. Parchment and boards. Burslem, 1907. One of 100 signed. $50-$60.

BENNETT, Emerson. *The Bandits of the Osage*. Printed wrappers (?). Cincinnati, 1847. Published by Edwards & Goshorn. $150 and up. (Note: Blanck lists the first edition, same date, as published by Robinson & Jones. Estimated value at retail: $200-$300.)

BENNETT, Emerson. *Clara Moreland; or, Adventures in the Far South-West.* Printed wrappers or cloth. Philadelphia, (1863). First edition. $150-$200.

BENNETT, Emerson. *Leni-Leoti; or, Adventures in the Far West.* Printed orange wrappers. Cincinnati, 1849. First edition. $400-$500.

BENNETT, Emerson. *Mike Fink: A Legend of the Ohio.* Printed wrappers (?). Cincinnati, 1848. First edition. $500-$600. Cincinnati, (1852). Printed wrappers. Revised edition. $150-$200.

BENNETT, Emerson. *The Mysterious Marksman; or, The Outlaws of New York.* Wrappers. Cincinnati, (about 1855). First edition (?). $300 and up. (Note: This title not in Blanck.)

BENNETT, Emerson. *The Prairie Flower; or, Adventures in the Far West.* 128 pp., printed wrappers. Cincinnati, 1849. First edition. $400-$500. Later issue: Cloth. $250-$300. Cincinnati, 1850. Boards and cloth. New edition, revised. $200-$300.

BENNETT, George. *Gatherings of a Naturalist in Australasia.* 7 colored plates, one in sepia, numerous woodcuts. Cloth. London, 1860. $200-$250. Also, $94.60 (A, 1975).

BENNETT, John. *Barnaby Lee.* Illustrated by Clyde O. De Land. Decorated cloth. New York, 1902. First edition. $75.

BENNETT, John. *Master Skylark: A Story of Shakespeare's Time.* Illustrated by Reginald Birch. Pictorial cloth. New York, 1897. First edition. $50-$75.

BENNETT, Melba Berry. *Robinson Jeffers and the Sea.* Decorated boards, morocco spine. San Francisco, 1936. Grabhorn printing. First edition. One of 300. In mustard-colored dust jacket. $80-$125.

BENSON, A.C. *Le Cahier Jaune.* Yellow wrappers. Eton, 1892. Limited edition. $45-$50. Author's first book.

BENSON, Frank W. (illustrator). *Etchings and Drypoints.* 285 reproductions. Text by Adam E.M. Paff. 4 vols., boards. Boston, 1917-29. One of 275, with frontispiece signed by Benson. In dust jackets. $300-$350.

BENSON, Henry C. *Life Among the Choctaw Indians.* Cloth. Cincinnati, 1860. First edition. $100-$200.

BENTLEY, E.C. *Trent's Last Case.* Blue cloth. London, no date. First edition. $50-$60.

BENTON, Frank. *Cowboy Life on the Sidetrack.* Illustrated. Pictorial cloth. Denver, (1903). First edition. $75-$125.

BENTON, J.A. *California As She Was, As She Is, As She is to Be.* 16 pp., pictorial wrappers. Sacramento, 1850. First edition. $2,250.

*BEPPO, A Venetian Story.* Drab wrappers. London, 1818. (By George Gordon Noel, Lord Byron.) First edition. $750-$1,000. Also, torn, stained, and soiled, $310 (A, 1976); $375 (A, 1971).

BERENSON, Bernard. *The Drawings of the Florentine Painters.* 180 full-page tinted plates. 2 vols., folio, half morocco. London, 1903. One of 355. $200-$300. New York, 1903. 2 vols. folio, boards and morocco. $150. Chicago, 1938. 3 vols., small folio, boards, vellum spine. Amplified edition. $300-$350. Milan, Italy, 1961. Italian text. 3 vols., half morocco. $75-$100.

BERENSON, Bernard. *The Italian Painters of the Renaissance.* Illustrated. Cloth. London, (1952). Phaidon Press. $40-$60.

BERENSON, Bernard. *A Sienese Painter of the Franciscan Legend.* 26 color illustrations. Boards and cloth. London, 1909. First edition. $35-$40.

BERENSON, Bernard. *Studies in Medieval Painting.* Illustrated. Cloth. New Haven, 1930. First edition. $50-$75.

BERENSON, Bernard. *Three Essays in Method*. Illustrated. Cloth. Oxford, 1927. First edition. $50-$60.

BERNARD, Auguste. *Geofroy Tory, Painter and Engraver*. Translated by George B. Ives. Boards. (Cambridge, Mass.), 1909. One of 370 designed by Bruce Rogers. $250-$350. Also, $180 (A, 1976).

BERNARD, Auguste. *Geofroy Tory: Peintre et Graveur*. Morocco, gilt. Paris, 1865. One of a few printed on vellum. $300-$400.

BERNERS, Dame Juliana. *The Treatyse of Fysshynge with an Angle*. Woodcuts. Full green morocco. London (Chelsea), 1903. Ashendene Press. One of 25 on vellum. $3,000-$3,500. Another issue: Vellum. One of 150. Boxed. $400-$600.

BERNSTEIN, Aline. *Three Blue Suits*. Frontispiece. Tan-blue cloth, paper labels. New York, 1933. First edition. One of 600 signed. Boxed. $75-$100. Author's first book.

BERQUIN-DUVALLON. See *Travels in Louisiana and the Floridas*.

BERRIGAN, Daniel. *Time Without Number*. Boards and cloth. New York, 1957. First edition. In dust jacket with wraparound band. $25. Author's first book.

BERRY, Wendell. *November Twenty Six Nineteen Hundred Sixty Three*. Illustrated by Ben Shahn. Cloth. New York, (1964). First edition. Limited issue signed by Shahn and Berry. Boxed. $75-$100. Trade edition, not signed: $15-$20.

BERRYMAN, John. *The Dispossessed*. Cloth. New York, 1948. First edition. In dust jacket. $75-$100.

BERRYMAN, John. *His Thoughts Made Pockets & the Plane Buckt*. Boards, leather spine. Pawlet, Vt., 1958. First edition. One of 26 lettered copies signed by the author. $150-$200. Another issue: Wrappers. One of 500. In printed envelope. $50-$60.

BERRYMAN, John. *Homage to Mistress Bradstreet*. Cloth. New York, 1956. First edition. In dust jacket. $65-$75.

BERRYMAN, John. *Poems*. Printed blue wrappers. Norfolk, Conn., (1942). New Directions. First edition. Poet of the Month series. $50-$75. Another issue: Boards. In dust jacket. $40-$50. Author's first book.

BERT, Edmund. *Treatise of Hawks and Hawking*. Illustrated. Boards, leather spine. London, 1891. One of 100. $75-$100.

BESANT, Walter. *The Art of Fiction*. Yellow cloth. Boston, 1885. First edition. $40-$50. (Note: Contains an essay on fiction by Henry James.)

BESSIE, Alvah C. *Dwell in the Wilderness*. Cloth. New York, (1935). First edition. In dust jacket. $60. Author's first book.

BESTERMAN, Theodore. *A World Bibliography of Bibliographies*. 3 vols., buckram. London, 1947-49. Second edition. $100-$150.

BETJEMAN, John. See O'Betjeman, Deirdre.

BETJEMAN, John. *Antiquarian Prejudice*. Wrappers. London, 1939. Hogarth Press. First edition. In slipcase. $35-$60.

BETJEMAN, John. *John Betjeman's Collected Poems*. Compiled by the Earl of Birkenhead. Scarlet leather. London, 1958. First edition. One of 100 signed. In slipcase. $75-$100. Trade edition: Cream-colored cloth. In dust jacket. $30.

BETJEMAN, John. *Continual Dew*. Black cloth. London, (1937). First edition. In dust jacket. $100-$150.

BETJEMAN, John. *English Cities and Small Towns*. 8 color plates, 31 black and white illustrations. Brown boards. London, 1943. First edition. In dust jacket. $25.

BETJEMAN, John. *A Few Late Chrysanthemums.* White buckram. London, 1954. First edition. One of 50 signed. $100-$125. Trade edition: Purple cloth. In dust jacket. $25.

BETJEMAN, John. *First and Last Loves.* Illustrated. Cream-colored cloth. London, (1952). First edition. In dust jacket. $40-$50.

BETJEMAN, John. *Ghastly Good Taste.* Folding plate. Printed pink boards and cloth. London, 1933. First edition, first issue, with pages 119-120 not canceled. $80-$100. London, 1970. One of 200 signed, $100-$125.

BETJEMAN, John. *High and Low.* Buckram. London, (1966). First edition. One of 100 signed. $100-$125. Second printing: Yellow cloth. In dust jacket. $20.

BETJEMAN, John. *Mount Zion, or In Touch with the Infinite.* Illustrated. Red, white and blue striped boards, pictorial label on front cover. London, (1931). James Press. First edition. $300-$400. Author's first book.

BETJEMAN, John. *New Bats in Old Belfries.* Red cloth, paper label. London, 1945. One of a few signed copies on special paper with colored title page. In dust jacket. $75-$100. Unsigned, in dust jacket. $25-$35.

BETJEMAN, John. *Old Lights for New Chancels.* Portrait frontispiece. Wrappers. London, (1940). First edition. In dust jacket. $35-$50.

BETJEMAN, John. *An Oxford University Chest.* Photographs by Moholy-Nagy. Illustrations by Osbert Lancaster, etc. Marbled boards, cloth spine, gilt top. London, (1938). First edition. $85-$125.

BETJEMAN, John. *Poems in the Porch.* Illustrated. Pictorial wrappers. London, 1954. Talbot Press. First edition. $35-$50.

BETJEMAN, John. *Selected Poems.* Buckram. London, 1948. First edition. One of 18 signed. $250-$300. Trade edition: Red cloth. In dust jacket. $50-$60.

BETJEMAN, John. *Summoned by Bells.* Illustrated, Full green leather, gilt top. London, 1960. First edition. One of 125 signed. $100-$125. Proof copy: Decorated wrappers. $27.50. Trade edition: Green cloth. In dust jacket. $25.

BEVIER, Robert S. *History of the First and Second Missouri Confederate Brigades, 1861-1865.* 2 portraits. Cloth. St. Louis, 1879. First edition. $150-$200.

BEWICK, Thomas. (Note: The various works of this famous engraver exist in innumerable editions and issues. I have chosen only a few representative items here, omitting Bewick's *General History of Quadrupeds,* first published in 1790 and therefore not within the scope of this compilation.)

*BEWICK Gleanings.* Edited by Julia Boyd. 53 plates. Green morocco. Newcastle-on-Tyne, England, 1886. Large paper edition, signed, $150-$200.

BEWICK, Thomas. *A History of British Land and Water Birds.* Woodcuts. 2 vols., contemporary leather. Newcastle, 1797-1804. First edition. $350-$450. Newcastle, 1821. 2 vols., green morocco. Each volume signed by Bewick. $400-$450.

BEWICK, Thomas. *Select Fables.* Portraits and woodcuts. Boards. Newcastle, 1820. First edition. $200 and up. Edinburgh, 1879. Vellum and white boards. Edition De Luxe on Whatman paper. One of 100. $100. London, (1878). Brown cloth and leather. $35.

BEWICK, Thomas. *The Water Colour Drawings of Thomas Bewick.* 40 illustrations in color. Half pigskin. London, 1930. Alcuin Press. $75-$100.

BEY, Pilaff. *Venus in the Kitchen.* Edited by Norman Douglas, with foreword by Graham Greene. Illustrated. Wrappers. London, (1952). "Proof Copy for Your Personal Reading" (so imprinted on front cover). $50.

BEYER, Edward. *Album of Virginia.* 40 tinted lithograph views, plus decorated text. 2 vols., cloth, or half cloth (oblong folio plate volume and octavo text volume). Richmond,

1856. First edition. $6,000-$10,000, possibly more. (No copy of the first edition has appeared for public sale in modern times.) Richmond, 1857. $2,000 or more. Richmond, 1858. $1,820 (in a dealer's catalogue).

BIANCO, Margery Williams. *Poor Cecco*. 7 color plates by Arthur Rackham. Cloth. London, 1925. $400-$600. New York, (1925). Half vellum. One of 105 signed by Rackham. $1,000-$1,250.

*BIBLE*. Illustrated by Marc Chagall. 2 vols., paper folder within gray board folder and in slipcase. Teriade, 1956. One of 275 on Montval wove paper, signed by Chagall. $6,000.

BICKERSTAFF, Isaac. *The Rhode-Island Almanac for 1842*. Stitched. Providence, (1841). $75-$100. (Note: Contains "Indian Barbarity," about Miss Fleming's captivity.)

BIDDLE, Owen. *The Young Carpenter's Assistant*. 44 (of 46) plates. Morocco. Philadelphia, 1805. First edition. Worn, foxed, etc. $300 (A, 1969).

BIDWELL, John. *Echoes of the Past About California*. 3 photographic views. Wrappers. Chico, Calif., (1914). First edition. $35-$100. (A curious book: catalogued at as low as $25 and as high as $150!)

BIDWELL, John. *A Journey to California*. 48 pp., boards and cloth. San Francisco, 1937. $75-$100. (Note: One copy is known of the 1842 original of this narrative.)

BIERCE, Ambrose. See Grile, Dod; Herman, William; and Bowers, Mrs. Dr. J. Milton.

BIERCE, Ambrose. *Battle Sketches*. 8 wood engravings. Vellum. London, 1930. Shakespeare Head Press. One of 350. Boxed. $75-$100.

BIERCE, Ambrose. *Black Beetles in Amber*. Frontispiece. Light-gray or red cloth. San Francisco, 1892. First edition, first issue, with imprint of Western Authors Publishing Company. $100-$150. Second issue: Printed gray wrappers. Published by Johnson & Emigh. $150-$200.

BIERCE, Ambrose. *Can Such Things Be?* Golden brown cloth, or printed yellow wrappers. New York, (1893). First edition. Cloth: $35-$50. Wrappers: $75-$100. Washington, 1903. Maroon cloth. $10-$15.

BIERCE, Ambrose. *The Cynic's Word Book*. Olive-green cloth. New York, 1906. First edition, presumed first issue, without frontispiece. $75-$100. Another (later?) issue: Frontispiece inserted. $50-$100. (Note: Blanck had seen no such copy, although Vincent Starrett had reported the existence of a frontispiece in some copies. Priority unknown.)

BIERCE, Ambrose. *Fantastic Fables*. Pictorial brownish yellow cloth. New York, 1899. First edition, first printing, with ads at back headed by "By Anna Fuller." $50-$75. Later, blue cloth, with ads headed "New Fiction." $10-$15.

BIERCE, Ambrose. *A Horseman in the Sky*. Boards and cloth. San Francisco, 1920. John Henry Nash printing. One of 400. $50-$60.

BIERCE, Ambrose. *In the Midst of Life*. Blue cloth. London, 1892. First English edition (of *Tales of Soldiers and Civilians*). $25-$35. (Second issue appeared in colored boards.) New York, 1898. Cloth. (Reprint of the *Tales* with three added stories.) $25-$35.

BIERCE, Ambrose. *The Letters of Ambrose Bierce*. Edited by Bertha C. Pope. Frontispiece portrait. Boards and cloth. San Francisco, 1922. Book Club of California. Printed by John Henry Nash. One of 415. $75-$100.

BIERCE, Ambrose. *The Shadow on the Dial and Other Essays*. Edited by S.O. Howes. Green buckram. San Fancisco, 1909. First edition. In dust jacket. $50-$60.

BIERCE, Ambrose. *Shapes of Clay*. Portrait frontispiece. Blue or red cloth. San Francisco, 1903. First edition, first issue, with transposed lines on page 71. $150-$200.

BIERCE, Ambrose. *A Son of the Gods and a Horseman in the Sky*. Frontispiece. Vellum and boards. San Francisco, (1907). First separate edition. One of 1,000. $50-$60.

BIERCE, Ambrose. *Tales of Soldiers and Civilians*. Brown, green, or gray cloth. San Francisco, 1891. First edition. $200-$300. Some copies imprinted "Compliments of" on preliminary leaf and signed by Bierce—the so-called "limited" edition. $300-$400. New York, 1943. Limited Editions Club. Boards and leather. Boxed. $50-$60. (For first English edition see Bierce, *In the Midst of Life*.)

BIERCE, Ambrose. *Ten Tales*. Preface by A.J.A. Symons. Red cloth. London, 1925. First edition. In dust jacket. $25-$35.

BIERCE, Ambrose. *Write It Right: A Little Blacklist of Literary Faults*. Tan cloth. New York, 1909. First edition, first issue, 5¾ by 3 inches in size. In dust jacket. $75-$100. San Francisco, 1971. Grabhorn printing. One of 400. $50-$75.

BIERCE, Ambrose, and Danziger, Gustav Adolph. *The Monk and the Hangman's Daughter*. Illustrated by Theodore Hampe. Printed yellow wrappers, or gray cloth. Chicago, 1892. First edition. Wrappers: $100-$150. Cloth: $75-$100. (Note: Danziger was a pseudonym for Adolphe De Castro.) New York, 1907. Green cloth. $10. New York, 1926. $5. New York, 1967. Illustrated. Limited Editions Club. Boxed. $50-$60.

BIGELOW, Jacob. *American Medical Botany*. 60 color plates. Vols. 1-3 in 6 vols., cloth, paper labels, or 6 parts, printed boards. Boston, 1817-18-20. First edition. Cloth (6 vols.): $800-$1,000. Boards (6 parts): $1,000 and up.

BIGELOW, Jacob. *A Discourse of Self-Limited Diseases*. Wrappers. Boston, 1835. First edition. $400-$500.

BIGGERS, Don H. *From Cattle Range to Cotton Patch*. Illustrated. Stiff wrappers. Abilene, Tex., (about 1908). First edition. $400-$500. Bandera, Tex., 1944. Second edition. $65-$100.

BIGGS, William. *Narrative of William Biggs, While He Was a Prisoner with the Kickepoo Indians*. 22pp., wrappers. (Edwardsville, Ill.?), June, 1826. First edition. $2,500-$3,000. (Howes, who located two copies, gives the date as 1825. Byrd located a privately held copy in Vermont and fixed the date at 1826. In March, 1978, a fourth copy, with back wrapper only, was located in California. Careful examination of the blurred printing date of this copy and of the copy held by the Newberry Library leads me to believe 1826 is the correct date. The place of publication is an educated guess by both Byrd and Howes; it is not definitely known.)

BIGHAM, Clive. *The Roxburghe Club: Its History and Its Members, 1812-1927*. Half morocco. Oxford, 1928. First edition. $100-$150.

BIGMORE, E.C., and Wyman, C.W.H. *A Bibliography of Printing*. 3 vols., cloth, leather spine, London, 1880-86. First edition. One of 250 large paper copies. $300-$350. New York, 1945. 3 vols. in 2, buckram. Facsimile reprint, with type page enlarged. $200-$225.

BINGHAM, Caleb. *An Astronomical and Geographical Catechism for the Use of Children*. Wallpaper wrappers. Boston, 1802. Sixth edition. $75.

BINGHAM, Helen M. *History of Green County, Wisconsin*. Frontispiece. Cloth. Milwaukee, 1877. First edition. $65-$75.

BINYON, Laurence. *The Art of Botticelli*. Muirhead Bone etching, 23 color plates. Folio, cloth, vellum spine, London, 1913. One of 275. $150-$200.

BINYON, Laurence. *A Catalogue of Japanese and Chinese Woodcuts*. 39 illustrations. Cloth. London, 1916. $80-$100.

BINYON, Laurence. *The Court Painters of the Grand Moguls*. 39 full-page plates, 9 colored. Cloth. Oxford, 1921. First edition. $150-$175.

BINYON, Laurence. *The Drawings and Engravings of William Blake*. Plates, some in color. Folio, vellum portfolio with ties. London, 1922. One of 200. $200-$300. Another issue: Vellum and boards. $80-$100.

BINYON, Laurence. *Dream-Come-True*. Woodcut frontispiece. Boards. London, 1905. One of 175. In dust jacket. $275 and $460.

BINYON, Laurence. *The Engraved Designs of William Blake*. Plates. Half cloth and boards. London, 1926. One of 100 with an extra set of plates. $500-$600. Without the extra plates, $150-$200.

BINYON, Laurence. *The Followers of William Blake*. 79 plates, 7 colored. Cloth. London, 1925. First edition. $100-$150. Another issue: One of 100. $150-$175.

BINYON, Laurence. *The George Eumorfopolous Collection*. (Catalogue of the Chinese Frescoes.) 50 full-page color plates. Folio, gold and black cloth. London, 1927. One of 560. $250-$350.

BINYON, Laurence. *Little Poems from the Japanese Rendered into English Verse*. Wrappers. Leeds, England, 1925. Swan Press. First edition. One of 200. $75-$100.

BINYON, Laurence. *Painting in the Far East*. 30 plates. Cloth. London, 1908. First edition. $50-$75.

BINYON, Laurence. *Poems*. Wrappers. Oxford, 1895. Daniel Press. First edition. One of 200. $85-$125.

BINYON, Laurence, and Sexton, J.J. O'Brien. *Japanese Colour Prints*. 46 plates, some in color. Buckram. London, 1923. $100-$125. Another issue: Pigskin. One of 100 signed, with an extra set of plates. $400-$450.

BINYON, Laurence; Wilkinson, J.V.S.; and Gray, Basil. *Persian Miniature Painting*. Illustrated, including color plates. Folio, cloth. London, 1923. $200-$300.

*BIOGRAPHICAL Dictionary (A) of the Living Authors of Great Britain and Ireland*. Contemporary calf. London, 1816. (By John Watkins and Frederick Shoberl.) First edition. $125-$150.

*BIOGRAPHICAL Note of Commodore Jesse D. Elliott (A)*. By a Citizen of New York. Printed boards. Philadelphia, 1835. (By Russell Jarvis.) First edition. $50-$60.

*BIOGRAPHICAL Sketch, Words of the Songs, Ballads, etc., of the Composer and Vocalist, Stephen Massett, "Jeems Pipes, of Pipesville."* Portrait. 52 pp., wrappers. New York, 1858. First edition. $40.

*BIOGRAPHY of James Lawrence, Esq.* Portrait. Printed paper boards. New-Brunswick, N.J., 1813. (By Washington Irving?) First edition. $150-$250.

*BIOGRAPHY of Joseph Lane. By Western.* Three-quarters morocco. Washington, 1852. $350.

BIRD, Robert Montgomery. See *The Adventures of Robin Day; Calavar; The Infidel; Nick-of-the-Woods; Peter Pilgrim; Sheppard Lee.*

BIRKBECK, Morris. See *An Impartial Appeal; Remarks Addressed to the Citizens of Illinois.*

BIRKBECK, Morris. *An Appeal to the People of Illinois, on the Question of a Convention.* 25 pp., wrappers. Shawneetown, Ill., 1823. First edition. $500-$800. Also, $425 (A, 1967).

BIRKBECK, Morris. *Extracts from a Supplementary Letter from the Illinois.* 29 pp., half leather. New York, 1819. First edition. $600-$800. Also, disbound and foxed, $400 (A, 1967).

BIRKBECK, Morris. *Letters from Illinois.* 2 folding maps. Boards and calf. Philadelphia, 1818. First edition. $100-$200.

BIRKBECK, Morris. *Notes on a Journey in America from the Coast of Virginia to the Territory of Illinois.* Boards. Philadelphia, 1817. First edition. $300-$400. Also, $140 (A, 1973). London, 1818. Map. Boards and calf. First English edition. $100-$200. Issued also without map, same date: $35-$50. (There were three other English editions in 1818; all are valued in the $50-$75 range.) Philadelphia, 1819. $35.

BISHOP, Elizabeth. *North & South*. Cloth. Boston, 1946. First edition. In dust jacket. $50-$75. Author's first book.

BISHOP, Elizabeth. *Questions of Travel*. Cloth. New York, (1965). First edition. In dust jacket. $25-$30.

BISHOP, John Peale. *Act of Darkness*. Cloth. New York, 1935. First edition. In dust jacket. $35-$50. Author's first and only novel.

BISHOP, John Peale. *Green Fruit*. Boards and cloth. Boston, 1917. First edition. In dust jacket. $40-$50. Author's first book.

BISHOP, John Peale. *Minute Particulars*. Wrappers. New York, 1935. First edition. One of 165 signed. In glassine dust jacket. $50-$75.

BISHOP, Richard E. *Bishop's Birds: Etchings of Waterfowl and Upland Game Birds*. 73 reproductions. Pictorial cloth. Philadelphia, 1936. Limited edition. $100. Also, $55 (A, 1967). Another issue: Parchment. One of 125 signed, with signed Bishop etching tipped in. Boxed. $200-$250.

BISHOP, Richard E. *Bishop's Wildfowl . . . Etchings and Oil Painting Reproductions*. Text by E. Prestrud and R. Williams. Color plates. Full calf. (St. Paul) 1948. First edition. $150-$200.

BISHOP, Zealia. *The Curse of Yig*. Black cloth. Sauk City, Wis., 1953. Arkham House. First edition. In dust jacket. $50-$60.

BISLAND, Elizabeth (editor). *The Life and Letters of Lafcadio Hearn*. Illustrated. 2 vols., cloth, Boston, 1906. First edition. One of 200, with a page of an original manuscript by Hearn. $400-$500.

BLACKBIRD, Andrew J. *History of the Ottawa and Chippewa Indians of Michigan*. Cloth. Ypsilanti, Mich., 1887. First edition. $125-$150.

BLACKMORE, Richard D. *Lorna Doone: A Romance of Exmoor*. 3 vols., blue watered cloth. London, 1869. First edition. $750-$1,000.

BLACKMUR, R.P. *The Expense of Greatness*. Cloth. New York, 1940. First edition. In dust jacket. $30-$40.

BLACKMUR, R.P. *From Jordan's Delight*. New York, 1937. First edition. In dust jacket. $30-$40.

BLACKMUR, R.P. *The Good European & Other Poems*. Cloth, paper label. Cummington, Mass., 1947. First edition. One of 40 signed. $75-$100.

BLACKMUR, R.P. *The Second World*. Cloth. (Cummington), 1942. Cummington Press. First edition. One of 300. In dust jacket. $60-$80.

BLACKMUR, R.P. *T.S. Eliot*. Wrappers. (Cambridge, Mass.), 1928. First edition. $150. Author's first book.

BLACKWOOD, Algernon. *The Empty House and Other Ghost Stories*. Cloth. London, 1906. First edition. $100-$125. Author's first book.

*BLACKWATER Chronicle (The)*. By "The Clerke of Oxenforde." Illustrated. Cloth. New York, 1853. (By Pendleton Kennedy, or, as some suppose, by his brother John Pendleton Kennedy.) First edition. $200 and up.

BLAIR, Robert. *The Grave: A Poem*. Portrait and 12 etchings by Schiavonetti after designs by Blake. Boards. London, 1808. $400-$600. (There was a large paper issue as well as an ordinary issue. Either is rare and valuable.)

BLAKE, W.O. *The History of Slavery and the Slave Trade*. Illustrated. Roan. Columbus, Ohio, 1858. First edition. $50-$60.

BLAKE, William. See Binyon, Laurence. (Note: There have been innumerable facsimile reproductions of the illuminated books of William Blake, poet, mystic, artist, and engraver [1757-1827], the originals of which are of the greatest rarity. A few of the more popular editions are listed here. For more complete listings, see *American Book-Prices Current* and the British publication *Book Auction Records).*

BLAKE, William. *America, a Prophecy.* Facsimile by William Muir of the rare 1793 first edition. Wrappers. Edmonton, Alberta, Canada, 1887. One of 50. $150-$250. (New York), 1947. Cloth. $25. London (Paris), 1963. Facsimile, with 18 plates. Boards and leather. One of 480. Boxed. $300-$375.

BLAKE, William. *The Book of Thel.* Facsimile, with hand-colored pages by William Muir. Folio, wrappers. London, 1920. One of 50. $400-$500. (Paris, 1956). Trianon Press. 8 plates in color with additional material showing progressive stages in the platework. Full morocco. One of 20 sets. $500-$600. Another issue: Half morocco. One of 380. Boxed. $150-$200.

BLAKE, William. *The Book of Urizen.* Facsimile of the 1794 first edition, with 27 plates reproduced by color-collotype and stencil. Half morocco. London (Paris), 1958. One of 480. In slipcase. $500-$550. Another issue: Full morocco. One of 20, with 27 plates and a set of progressive stages, guide sheet stencil proofs, and other material used in making one of the plates. In handmade case. $800-$1,000.

BLAKE, William. *Genesis.* Cummington, Mass., 1952. One of 170. $75-$150.

BLAKE, William. *Illustrations of the Book of Job.* Title page and 21 other plates engraved by Blake. Folio. London, 1825. First edition, with plate No. 1 misdated 1828. (In various bindings—cloth folders, wrappers, morocco, etc.) $5,000-$7,500. London, 1902. Facsimile. Wrappers. $200-$250. New York, 1935. 6 parts, folio, wrappers. One of 200. Boxed. $1,500-$1,800.

BLAKE, William. *Jerusalem.* Facsimile of the original illuminated book of 1804. 10 full-page and 45 half-page watercolors, 45 pp. with colored designs. 5 parts, folio, wrappers. London (Paris), (1951). Trianon Press. One of 516. Boxed. $2,000-$2,500. In book form: Buckram. $1,000-$1,250.

BLAKE, William. *The Marriage of Heaven and Hell.* J.C. Hotten's facsimile of the 1790 original. 27 leaves hand-colored. Boards. (London, 1868). $75-$100. Other editions: (Edmonton, 1885). William Muir's facsimile. Wrappers. One of 50. $100-$150. London, 1960. Trianon Press facsimile. Folio, boards and morocco. One of 526. $350-$450. Another issue: One of 20 of the edition of 526 with a set of hand-colored plates (proofs, etc.). $1,000-$1,500.

BLAKE, William. *The Note-Book of William Blake Called the Rossetti Manuscript.* Edited by Geoffrey Keynes. 120 pp. in facsimile. Buckram. London, 1935. Nonesuch Press. One of 650. In dust jacket. $150-$200.

BLAKE, William. *Pencil Drawings.* Edited by Geoffrey Keynes. 82 facsimile plates. Half buckram. London, 1927. Nonesuch Press. Limited edition. In dust jacket. $200-$250. Second Series: London, 1956. Cloth. Limited. In dust jacket. $100-$135.

BLAKE, William. *Songs of Innocence.* Frontispiece. Half cloth. San Francisco, 1924. Grabhorn printing. One of 100. $100-$135.

BLAKE, William. *Songs of Innocence and of Experience.* Facsimile reproduction in collotype of the 54 plates from the 1794 original. Full morocco. London, 1955. Trianon Press. One of 526. In slipcase. $750-$1,000.

BLAKE, William. *The Writings of William Blake.* Edited by Geoffrey Keynes. 3 vols., half vellum and marbled boards. London, 1925. Nonesuch Press. One of 1,500. Boxed. $250-$300. Thin paper issue: 3 vols. in one, morocco or limp vellum. One of 75. $400-$500.

BLANCHARD, Rufus. *Discovery and Conquests of the North West.* 7 maps and plates. 6 parts, wrappers, or bound together in morocco or cloth. Wheaton, Ill., 1879. First edition. In parts: $250. Morocco or cloth: $50-$60. Wheaton (some copies say "Chicago"), 1880. (One 1880 copy noted with 1881 copyright.) Reprint edition. $40-$50. Chicago (some copies say "Wheaton"), 1881. Enlarged edition, with 11 maps and plates. $35-$50. Wheaton, 1898-1900 (actually 1903). 2 vols. $35-$50.

BLANCK, Jacob. *Peter Parley to Penrod*. Cloth. New York, 1938. One of 500. $50-$75. New York, 1956. Second edition. $50-$60. Cambridge, Mass., 1961. $25.

BLAND, David. *History of Book Illustration*. Illustrated. Cloth. Cleveland, (1958). First edition. In dust jacket. $100-$125.

BLAND, Jane Cooper. *Currier & Ives: A Manual for Collectors*. 24 pages of color plates, other illustrations. Cloth. New York, (1931). $75-$100.

BLANDEN, Charles G., and Mathison, Minna (editors). *The Chicago Anthology*. Cloth. Chicago, 1916. First edition. $40-$50.

BLAVATSKY, H.P. *Isis Unveiled: A Master Key to the Mysteries of Ancient and Modern Theology*. 2 vols., cloth. New York, 1877. First edition. With inserted autograph slip of certification. $200-$250. New York, 1923. 2 vols., cloth. $50. New York, (1950). 2 vols., cloth. $50.

BLAVATSKY, H.P. *Nightmare Tales*. Black cloth. London, 1892. First edition. $125-$175.

BLAVATSKY, H.P. *The Secret Doctrine*. 2 vols., cloth. London, 1888. First edition. $100-$150. London, 1893-98. 4 vols. (3 vols. with index), cloth. $100. London, (1928). 3 vols., cloth. $50-$60.

BLEDSOE, A.J. *History of Del Norte County, California*. Printed wrappers. Eureka, Calif., 1881. First edition. $2,000 and up.

BLEDSOE, A.J. *Indian Wars of the Northwest*. Cloth. San Francisco, 1885. First edition, $150-$200.

BLEW, William C.A. *A History of Steeple-Chasing*. 28 illustrations, 12 hand-colored plates. Cloth. London, 1901. $150-$200.

BLEW, William C.A. *The Quorn Hunt and Its Masters*. Map, 12 hand-colored plates. Cloth. London, 1899. First edition. $125-$150.

BLIGH, William *The Log of the Bounty*. Illustrated. 2 vols., buckram. London, (1937). Golden Cockerel Press. One of 300. $350-$500.

BLISS, Edward. *A Brief History of the New Gold Regions of Colorado Territory*. Map. 30 pp., wrappers. New York, 1864. First edition. $1,250-$1,500.

BLOCH, Robert. *The Opener of the Way*. Cloth. Sauk City, Wis., 1945. Arkham House. First edition. In dust jacket. $75-$100. Author's first book.

BLODGETT, Henry W. *Autobiography*. Cloth. Waukegan, Ill., 1906. First edition. $100-$125.

BLOME, Richard. *Hawking or Faulconry*. London, 1929. Cresset Press. One of 650. $100-$125.

*BLOSSOMS of Morality (The)*. 51 wood engravings. Half calf and boards. Philadelphia, 1810. (By Richard Johnson.) $45-$50.

BLOWE, Daniel. *A Geographical, Commercial, and Agricultural View of the United States of America*. Portrait, 2 maps, 4 plans. Calf. Liverpool, (1820). $200-$300.

*BLUE Grotto (The) and Its Literature*. 18 pp., printed red wrappers. London, 1904. (By Norman Douglas.) First edition. $50. Signed on title page by Douglas, $125.

BLUNDEN, Edmund. See Lloyd, Robert.

BLUNDEN, Edmund. *Dead Letters*. Decorated wrappers, paper label. London, 1923. Pelican Press. One of 50. $100-$150.

BLUNDEN, Edmund. *Japanese Garland*. 6 color plates. Boards and vellum. London, 1928. Beaumont Press. One of 80 signed. $50-$75.

BLUNDEN, Edmund. *Masks of Time*. Boards and vellum. London, 1925. Beaumont Press. One of 80 on vellum, signed. $60-$75. Another issue: One of 310 on paper. In plain dust jacket. $35.

BLUNDEN, Edmund. *Near and Far*. Cloth. London, 1929. One of 160 signed. In dust jacket. $50-$60. Trade edition: In dust jacket. $15-$20.

BLUNDEN, Edmund. *Pastorals: A Book of Verses*. Wrappers. London, (1916). First edition. $125-$175.

BLUNDEN, Edmund. *Poems, 1914-1930*. Buckram. London, 1930. First edition. One of 200 signed. In dust jacket. $50-$60.

BLUNDEN, Edmund. *Retreat: New Sonnets and Poems*. Cloth. (London, 1928). One of 112 signed. In dust jacket. $50-$100.

BLUNDEN, Edmund. *A Summer's Fancy*. Illustrated. Cloth, vellum spine. London, 1930. Beaumont Press. First edition. One of 80 signed. $60-$75.

BLUNDEN, Edmund. *To Nature*. Illustrated by Randolph Schwabe. Patterned boards, vellum spine. (London, 1923). Beaumont Press. One of 80 on vellum, signed. $48 and $45.

BLUNDEN, Edmund. *Undertones of War*. Cloth. London, 1928. First edition. In dust jacket. $100-$125.

BLUNDEN, Edmund. *Winter Nights*. Illustrated. Boards. London, 1928. First edition. One of 500 signed. $30-$40.

BLUNT, Edmund M. *Traveller's Guide to and Through the State of Ohio, with Sailing Directions for Lake Erie*. 16 pp., leather. New York, 1832. First edition. $500-$600. New York, 1833. Folding map in color. 28 pp., leather. $500-$600.

BLUNT, Wilfrid Scawen. See Proteus.

BLUNT, Wilfrid Scawen. *The Celebrated Romance of the Stealing of the Mare*. Translated from the Arabic by Lady Anne Blunt and done into verse by W.S.B. Boards and leather. Newtown, Wales, 1930. Gregynog Press. One of 275. $200-$300. One of 25 (of this edition) especially bound in morocco. $1,250-$1,500.

BLUNT, Wilfrid Scawen. *The Love-Lyrics and Songs of Proteus and the Love-Sonnets*. Woodcut borders and initals. Limp vellum with ties. London, 1892. Kelmscott Press. One of 300. $400-$500.

BLY, Robert. *The Light Around the Body*. Cloth. New York, 1967. First edition. In dust jacket. $25-$35.

BOCCACCIO, Giovanni. *The Decameron*. 1620 translation. Woodcuts by Fritz Kredel. 2 vols., boards and calf. New York, 1940. Limited Editions Club. One of 530. Boxed. $100-$125. Another Limited Editions Club edition: New York, 1930. Translated by Frances Winwar. 2 vols., cloth. Boxed. $50-$60. London, 1920. Ashendene Press. Folio, boards and linen. One of 105. $1,250-$1,500.

BOCCACCIO, Giovanni. *Life of Dante*. Translated by Philip Henry Wicksteed. Woodcut title portrait. Boards and vellum. (Boston, 1904). One of 325 designed by Bruce Rogers. $75-$100.

BODE, Winston. *A Portrait of Pancho*. Illustrated. Full leather. Austin, Tex., 1965. First edition. One of 150 signed. Boxed. $150-$200. Trade edition: Cloth. $25.

BODENHEIM, Maxwell. See Hecht, Ben, and Bodenheim, Maxwell.

BODENHEIM, Maxwell. *Minna and Myself*. Red cloth. New York, 1918. First edition, first issue, with "Master-Posner" for "Master-Poisoner" on page 67. In dust jacket. $100-$150. Author's first book.

BODENHEIM, Maxwell. *The Sardonic Arm*. Illustrated. Black cloth. Chicago, 1923. First edition. One of 575. $35-$50.

BOEHME, Jacob. *Christosophia*. Leather. Ephrata, Pa., 1811-12. $100-$150.

BOERSCHMANN, Ernst. *Chinesische Architektur*. 340 plates. 2 vols., cloth. New York, (1925). First American edition. $75-$100.

BOGAN, Louise. *Body of This Death: Poems*. Blue boards, linen spine, paper label. New York, 1923. First edition. In dust jacket. $75-$100. Author's first book.

BOGAN, Louise. *Dark Summer*. Cloth. New York, 1929. First edition. In dust jacket. $50-$75.

BOGAN, Louise. *Poems and New Poems*. Cloth. New York, 1941. First edition. In dust jacket. $40-$60.

BOGGS, Mae Helene Bacon (compiler). *My Playhouse Was a Concord Coach*. Maps, illustrations. Cloth. (Oakland, 1942.) First edition. $200-$300. (Most copies inscribed.)

*BOKE of Noblesse (The)*. *Addressed to King Edward IV on his Invasion of France in 1475*. Half morocco. London, 1860, Roxburghe Club. $150-$200.

*BOKE (The) Off the Revelacion Off Sanct Jhon the Devine done into Englysshe by William Tyndale*. Printed in black and red. Green vellum. London, 1900. Ashendene Press. One of 54. $500-$600.

BOKER, George Henry. *The Podesta's Daughter*. Purplish brown cloth. Philadelphia, 1852. First edition. $25-$30.

BOLDREWOOD [sic], Rolf (Bolderwood). *Robbery Under Arms: A Story of Life and Adventure in the Bush and in the Goldfields of Australia*. Decorated green cloth. London, 1888. (By Thomas A. Browne.) First edition. $400-$500.

BOLLER, Henry A. *Among the Indians*. Folding map, cloth, paper label. Philadelphia, 1868. First edition. $400-$500.

BOLTON, Herbert Eugene. *Anza's California Expeditions*. Folding map, illustrations. 5 vols., cloth. Berkeley, 1930. First edition. In dust jackets. $200-$250.

BOLTON, Herbert Eugene. *Athanase de Mezieres and the Louisiana-Texas Frontier*. Map, 2 facsimiles. 2 vols., cloth. Cleveland, 1914. First edition. $250-$350.

BOLTON, Herbert Eugene. *Coronado on the Turquoise Trail*. Illustrated. Cloth. Albuquerque, 1949. $45-$50.

BOLTON, Herbert Eugene. *Guide to Materials for the History of the United States in the Principal Archives of Mexico*. Printed wrappers. Washington, 1913. First edition. $150-$200.

BOLTON, Herbert Eugene. *The Rim of Christendom*. 12 plates, 3 facsimiles. Cloth. New York, 1936. First edition. $35-$50.

BOLTON, Herbert Eugene (translator). *Font's Complete Diary of the Second Anza Expedition*. Maps, plates, facsimiles. Cloth. Berkeley, 1931. First edition. $50-$75. Berkeley, 1933. Cloth. Second edition. $35-$50.

BOLTWOOD, Lucius M. *History and Genealogy of the Family of Thomas Noble*. Illustrated. Cloth. Hartford, 1878. First edition. $25-$30.

BOND, Henry. *Family Memorials*. Vol. 1. Buckram. Boston, 1855. (Watertown, Mass., genealogies, including Waltham and Weston.) $35-$50.

BOND, J. Wesley. *Minnesota and Its Resources*. Folding map, 6 plates. Cloth. Chicago, 1856. First edition. $50-$150.

BOND, Nelson. *Exiles of Time.* Cloth. Philadelphia, 1949. In dust jacket. $25-$35. Another issue: One of 112 signed. Boxed. $75-$100.

BOND, Nelson. *Mr. Mergenthwirker's Lobblies and Other Fantastic Tales.* Cloth. New York, (1946). In dust jacket. $35-$50.

BOND, Nelson. *The Thirty-first of February.* Cloth. New York, (1949). In dust jacket. $25-$30. Another issue: One of 112 signed. Boxed. $75-$100.

BONFILS, Winifred B. *The Life and Personality of Phoebe Apperson Hearst.* Vellum. San Francisco. 1928. John Henry Nash printing. One of 1,000. In original tan flannel bag. $25-$35.

BONNELL, George W. *Topographical Description of Texas.* Boards. Austin, 1840. First edition. $2,000-$3,000.

BONNER, T.D. *The Life and Adventures of James P. Beckwourth, Mountaineer, Scout and Pioneer, etc.* Frontispiece and plates. Cloth. New York, 1856. First edition. $200-$250.

BONNEY, Edward. *Banditti of the Prairies; or, The Murderer's Doom!* Plates. Pictorial wrappers. Chicago, 1850. First edition, with imprint "Chicago, W.W. Dannenhauer, 1850" on front cover. $2,500 and up. Also, $1,350 (A, 1963). Philadelphia, (1855). $100-$150. Philadelphia, 1856. Third edition. $150-$200. Chicago, 1856. $200-$250. Chicago, 1858. 13 plates. Wrappers. $300-$400.

*BOOK of Commandments (A), for the Government of the Church of Christ.* Boards. Zion (Independence, Mo.), 1833. (By Joseph Smith, Jr.) First edition. $7,500.

*BOOK of Job (The).* Illustrated in color by Arthur Szyk. Boards. New York, 1946. Limited Editions Club. Boxed. $85-$125.

*BOOK OF Jonah (The).* Illustrated by David Jones. Buckram. Waltham Saint Lawrence, 1926. Golden Cockerel Press. One of 175. In dust jacket. $400-$600.

*BOOK of Kells (The).* 48 color plates, 625 in black and white, 2 vols. facsimile, plus text volume, 3 vols. in all, vellum. Olten and Berne, Switzerland, 1950-51. One of 500. $5,000 and up. Also, $3,750 (A, 1974).

*BOOK of the Law of the Lord (The).* Saint James. A.R.I. (Beaver Island, Lake Michigan), (1851). (By James Jesse Strang.) First edition. $5,000 and up (3 copies known). (Beaver Island, 1856). Second edition, lacking title page (some supplied, and with preface, in modern type, circa 1920). $1,000. For a later edition, see James J. Strang entry.

*BOOK of the Poets' Club (The).* Orange wrappers. London, 1909. First edition. (Includes first printings of four Ezra Pound poems.) $475 (A, 1977).

*BOOK of Princeton Verse 1916 (A).* Edited by Alfred Noyes. Cloth. Princeton, 1916. First edition. In dust jacket. $100. (Includes poems by Edmund Wilson, John Peale Bishop, and others.)

*BOOK of Princeton Verse II (A).* Cloth. Princeton, (1919). First edition. (First book appearance of three poems by F. Scott Fitzgerald.) In dust jacket. $150-$200. Also, $150 (A, 1977).

*BOOK of Psalms (The).* Illustrated by Valenti Angelo. Morocco. New York, 1961. Limited Editions Club. Boxed. $50-$60.

*BOOK of Ruth (The).* Boards. London, 1923. Nonesuch Press. One of 250. $100-$125. New York, 1947. Limited Editions Club. Introduction by Mary Ellen Chase. Illustrated by Arthur Szyk. Boards. Boxed. $100-$110.

*BOOK of Tobit (The) and the History of Susanna.* Color plates by W. Russell Flint. Vellum, silk ties. London, 1929. One of 100 copies. With an extra set of plates. Boxed. $150-$200. One of 13 on vellum, signed by the artist. With duplicate plates in folder. $450-$500.

*BOOK-LOVER'S Almanac (The) for 1895.* Wrappers. New York, 1894. First edition. One of 100 on Japan paper. $100-$150.

BOOTH, Stephen. *The Book Called Holinshed's Chronicles*. Woodcut reproductions and original leaf from the 1587 edition. Decorated boards and cloth. San Francisco, 1968. One of 500. $100-$125.

BORDEN, Gail, Jr. *Letters of . . . to Dr. Ashbel Smith*. 9 pp., wrappers. Galveston, 1850. First edition. $750-$1,250.

BORDEN, Spencer. *The Arab Horse*. Cloth. New York, 1906. $75-$85.

*BORDER Beagles: A Tale of Mississippi*. 2 vols., boards and cloth, paper labels. Philadelphia, 1840. (By William Gilmore Simms.) First edition. $250-$350.

*BORDERERS (The): A Tale*. By the Author of "The Spy." 3 vols., drab tan boards, paper labels. London, 1829. (By James Fenimore Cooper.) First edition (of the novel published in America as *The Wept of Wish-Ton-Wish*.) $200-$250.

BORGES, Jorge Luis. *Deathwatch on the Southside*. Wrappers. Cambridge, (1968). One of 150 signed. $50.

BORNEMAN, Henry S. *Pennsylvania German Illuminated Manuscripts*. 38 colored reproductions. Oblong, cloth. Norristown, Pa., 1937. $200-$250.

BORROW, George. See Ewald, Johannes.

BORROW, George. *The Bible in Spain*. 3 vols., red cloth, paper labels. London, 1843. First edition. $300-$350.

BORROW, George. *Lavengro; the Scholar—the Gypsy—the Priest*. 3 vols., blue cloth, paper labels. London, 1851. First edition. $200-$225. New York, 1936. Limited Editions Club. 2 vols., cloth. Boxed. $70-$80.

BORROW, George. *Proud Signild and Other Ballads*. Wrappers. London, 1913. First edition. One of 30. $75-$100.

BORROW, George. *The Romany Rye*. 2 vols., blue cloth. London, 1875. First edition. $150.

BORROW, George. *Wild Wales: Its People, Language, and Scenery*. 3 vols., cloth, paper labels. London, 1862. First edition, with 32 pages of ads and without half titles in Vols. 2 and 3. $150-$200.

*BORZOI 1920 (The)*. Half cloth. New York, 1920. (By Alfred A. Knopf.) First edition. One of 100 on San Marco paper. $35-$50. New York, 1925. Half cloth. One of 500 large paper copies. $35-$50.

BOSCANA, Father Geronimo. *Chinigchinich*. Translated by Alfred Robinson. Color plates, maps. Folio, boards and cloth. Santa Ana, 1933. $200-$250.

BOSQUI, Edward. *Memoirs*. Half cloth. (Oakland), 1952. Grabhorn Press. One of 350. $75.

BOSSCHERE, Jean de. *12 Occupations*. Illustrated. Decorated wrappers. London, 1916. First edition. $200-$300. Also, $250 (A, 1977). (Translated anonymously by Ezra Pound.)

BOSSERT, Helmuth T. *Peasant Art in Europe*. 130 full-color plates and 32 plates in black and white. Folio, cloth. London, 1927. First English edition. $75-$100. New York, 1927. First American edition. $85-$100.

*BOSTON Prize Poems, and Other Specimens of Dramatic Poetry*. Printed boards. Boston, 1824. First edition. $150-$200. Also, $100 (A, 1974). Longfellow's first appearance in a book.

BOSWELL, James. *Boswell for the Defence*. Edited by W.K. Wimsatt and Frederick A. Pottle. Illustrated, folding maps. Blue buckram, gilt, calf spine, leather label. London, 1960. Yale de luxe edition. One of 350. Boxed. $35-$50.

BOSWELL, James. *Boswell in Holland, 1763-1764*. Edited by Frederick A. Pottle. Illustrated, folding map. Blue buckram and calf. London, 1952. Yale de luxe edition. One of 1,050. Boxed. $25-$35.

BOSWELL, James. *Boswell in Search of a Wife*. Edited by F. Brady and Frederick A. Pottle. Blue buckram and calf. London, 1957. Yale de luxe edition. One of 400. Boxed. $50-$75.

BOSWELL, James. *Boswell on the Grand Tour: Germany and Switzerland*. Edited by Frederick A. Pottle. Illustrated, folding map. Blue buckram and calf. London, 1953. Yale de luxe edition. One of 1,000. Boxed. $35-$50.

BOSWELL, James. *Boswell on the Grand Tour: Italy, Corsica, and France*. Edited by F. Brady and Frederick A. Pottle. Illustrated, folding maps. Blue buckram and calf. London, 1955. Yale de luxe edition. One of 400. Boxed. $35-$50.

BOSWELL, James. *Boswell's Journal of a Tour to the Hebrides with Samuel Johnson, LL.D.* Boards, cloth spine, paper label. New York, 1936. First complete edition. One of 816. Boxed. $35-$50.

BOSWELL, James. *The Life of Samuel Johnson*. Portrait, 2 folding plates. Contemporary sheep. Boston, 1807. First American edition. $100-$150. New York, 1938. Limited Editions Club. 3 vols., cloth. Boxed. $50. New York, 1945. Illustrated by Gordon Ross. Cloth. One of 1,000 signed by Ross. $70-$80.

BOSWORTH, Newton. *Hochelaga Depicta: The Early History and Present State of the City and Island of Montreal*. Illustrated, including 2 folding maps. Cloth. Montreal, 1839. $200-$250.

BOUCHETTE, Joseph. *A Topographical Description of the Province of Lower Canada, with Remarks Upon Upper Canada*. Maps and illustrations. Boards and calf. London, 1815. First English edition. $300-$350. London, 1832. Boards. $100-$150.

BOUGARD, R. *The Little Sea Torch*. Colored plates and charts. Half leather and boards. London, 1801. First English edition. $1,500-$2,000.

BOURDILLON, Francis W. *Among the Flowers, and Other Poems*. Decorated white cloth. London, 1878. First edition. $50-$75. Author's first book.

BOURKE, John G. *An Apache Campaign in the Sierra Madre*. Illustrated. Printed wrappers, or pictorial cloth. New York, 1886. First edition. Wrappers: $225-$400. Cloth: $150-$225.

BOURKE, John G. *Mackenzie's Last Fight with the Cheyennes*. Portrait. 44 pp., printed wrappers. Governor's Island, N.Y., 1890. First edition. $600-$1,000.

BOURKE, John G. *On the Border with Crook*. Frontispiece portrait, other plates. Cloth. New York, 1891. First edition. $100-$150.

BOURKE, John G. *Scatologic Rites of All Nations*. Cloth. Washington, 1891. First edition. $200-$300.

BOURKE, John G. *The Snake-Dance of the Moquis of Arizona*. Plates, some in color. Pictorial cloth. New York, 1884. First edition. $125-$150. New York, 1891. Cloth. $100-$125.

BOWDITCH, Nathaniel. *The New American Practical Navigator*. Folding frontispiece map, 6 plates. Boards or full leather. Newburyport, Mass., 1802. First edition. $1,500-$2,000. Also, $1,450 (A, 1972).

BOWEN, Abel. *The Naval Monument*. 25 woodcuts. Calf. Boston, 1816. First edition. With errata slip. $150-$200.

BOWEN, Elizabeth. *Ann Lee's and Other Stories*. Cloth. London, 1926. First edition. $100-$125. New York, 1927. First American edition. In dust jacket. $75.

BOWEN, Elizabeth. *Seven Winters*. Boards and linen. Dublin, 1942. Cuala Press. One of 450. In tissue dust jacket. $60-$85.

BOWERS, Mrs. Dr. J. Milton. *The Dance of Life: An Answer to the "Dance of Death."* Red or green cloth. San Francisco, 1877. (By Ambrose Bierce?) First edition. $50.

BOWLES, Jane. *Two Serious Ladies*. Cloth. New York, 1943. First edition. In dust jacket. $100-$150. Author's first book.

BOWLES, Paul. *The Sheltering Sky*. Cloth. London, 1949. First edition. In dust jacket. $50-$60. New York, (1949). Cloth. First American edition. In dust jacket. $40-$50.

BOWLES, Paul. *Two Poems*. Wrappers. New York, (about 1932). First edition. $100-$150. Author's first book.

BOWLES, Paul. *Yallah*. Illustrated with photos. Cloth. Zurich, 1956. First edition. $75-$100. New York, 1957. First American edition. $75-$125.

BOX, Capt. Michael James. *Capt. James Box's Adventures and Explorations in New and Old Mexico*. Cloth. New York, 1861. First edition. $800-$1,500, possibly more. New York, 1869. Cloth. Second edition. $350-$600, possibly more. (Both editions have become extremely difficult to find.)

BOYD, Belle. *Belle Boyd in Camp and Prison, Written by Herself*. Cloth. New York, 1865. (By Belle B. Hardinge.) First American edition. $50. (There was a two-volume London first edition in 1865. No recent price data seen.) New York, 1866. Cloth. $35.

BOYD, James. *Drums*. Green cloth. New York-London, 1925. First edition. In dust jacket. $35. Author's first book. New York, (1928). Illustrated by N.C. Wyeth. Cloth. One of 525 signed by author and artist. Boxed. $35-$50.

BOYD, Nancy. *Distressing Dialogues*. Cloth. New York, (1924). (By Edna St. Vincent Millay.) First edition (so stated). In dust jacket. $25-$35.

BOYLE, Kay. *The Crazy Hunter*. Cloth. New York, (1940). First edition. In dust jacket. $40-$50.

BOYLE, Kay. *Short Stories*. Printed wrappers in gold or silver protective boards. Paris, 1929. Black Sun Press. First edition. One of 15 on Japan paper, signed. $600-$750. Also, $600 (A, 1977). Another issue: One of 150 on Van Gelder paper. Boxed. $100-$200. One of 20 on Arches paper, for France. $250-$350. Author's first book. (See following entry.)

BOYLE, Kay. *Wedding Day and Other Stories*. Decorated boards, cloth spine. New York, (1930). First American edition (of the author's first book, retitled). In dust jacket. $40-$60.

BOYLE, Kay. *The White Horses of Vienna*. Cloth. New York, 1936. First edition. In dust jacket. $50-$60.

"BOZ." See Dickens, Charles. Also see *Sketches by "Boz."*

"BOZ." *Master Humphrey's Clock*. 88 weekly parts, white wrappers. London, 1840-41. (By Charles Dickens.) First edition. $800-$1,000. Also, $650 (A, 1972). Second edition: 20 monthly parts in 19, green wrappers. $300-$500. Third edition: 3 vols., brown cloth. (First book edition, issued under Dickens' name, which see.)

"BOZ." *Memoirs of Joseph Grimaldi*. Edited by "Boz." Illustrated by George Cruikshank. 2 vols., pink cloth. London, 1838 (Edited and written in part by Charles Dickens.) First edition, first issue, with no border around last plate. $150-$200. Second issue, crude border around plate. $75-$100.

"BOZ." *Oliver Twist; or, The Parish Boy's Progress*. Illustrated by George Cruikshank. 3 vols., brown cloth. London, 1838. (By Charles Dickens.) First edition, first issue, with "Fireside" plate, Vol. 3. $600-$800. Also, worn, $360 (A, 1974). (Eckel reports one copy that sold for $650.) Second issue, with "Rose Maylie and Oliver" replacing "Fireside" plate. $100-$150. (For second edition, sometimes called third issue, 1839, with Dickens on title page, and for first octavo edition, in parts and in book form, see author entries under *Oliver Twist* and *The Adventures of Oliver Twist*.)

"BOZ." *The Strange Gentleman: A Comic Burletta*. Printed buff wrappers, London, 1837. (By Charles Dickens.) First edition. $250 and up. Facsimile edition: (London, 1871). $75.

BRACKENRIDGE, H.M. See *Strictures on a Voyage to South America, etc.*

BRACKENRIDGE, H.M. *A Eulogy, on the Lives and Characters of John Adams & Thomas Jefferson*. 18 pp., plain wrappers. Pensacola, Fla., 1826. First edition. $350.

BRACKENRIDGE. H.M. *Journal of a Voyage up the Missouri*. Printed boards. Baltimore, 1815. First edition (actually second appearance of the journal, which first appeared in author's *Views of Louisiana*, which see). $300-$500. Baltimore, 1816 (cover date 1815). Boards. Second edition. $150-$200.

BRACKENRIDGE, H.M. *Views of Louisiana; Together with a Journal of a Voyage up the Missouri River, in 1814*. Boards, or leather. Pittsburgh, 1814. First edition. $1,000-$1,250. Baltimore, 1817. Boards. (Containing only *Views* and not the *Journal*.) $200-$250.

BRACKENRIDGE, Hugh Henry. *Gazette Publications*. Leather. Carlisle, Pa., 1806. First edition. $200-$250.

BRADBURY, John. *Travels in the Interior of America*. Boards. Liverpool, 1817. First edition, with errata slip. $1,000-$1,500. London, 1819. Folding map. Boards. Second edition. $750-$1,000.

BRADBURY, Ray. *Dandelion Wine*. Yellow cloth. Garden City, 1957. First edition. In dust jacket. $85-$100.

BRADBURY, Ray. *Dark Carnival*. Black cloth. Sauk City, Wis., 1947. Arkham House. First edition. In dust jacket. $175-$250. Author's first book.

BRADBURY, Ray. *Fahrenheit 451*. Cloth. New York, (1953). First trade edition. In dust jacket. $40-$50. Another issue: Asbestos boards. One of 200 signed. Issued without dust jacket. $150-$200. (Note: Also issued in a Ballantine paperback. $20-$25.)

BRADBURY, Ray. *The Golden Apples of the Sun*. Cloth. Garden City, 1953. First edition. In dust jacket. $50.

BRADBURY, Ray. *The Illustrated Man*. Tan cloth. Garden City, 1951. First edition. In dust jacket. $35-$45.

BRADBURY, Ray. *The Martian Chronicles*. Cloth. Garden City, 1950. First edition. In dust jacket. $60-$80. New York, no date. Limited Editions Club. $150-$200.

BRADBURY, Ray. *A Medicine for Melancholy*. Cloth. Garden City, 1959. First edition. In dust jacket. $40-$50.

BRADBURY, Ray. *The Silver Locusts*. Cloth. London, 1951. First English edition (of *The Martian Chronicles*). In dust jacket. $60-$80.

BRADBURY, Ray. *Switch on the Night*. Cloth. New York, 1955. First edition. In dust jacket. $50.

BRADFORD, Roark. *How Come Christmas*. Boards, paper label. New York, 1930. First edition. $75-$85.

BRADLEY, James. *The Confederate Mail Carrier*. 15 plates. Cloth. Mexico, Mo., 1894. First edition. $150-$200.

BRADLEY, Joshua. *Accounts of Religious Revivals in Many Parts of the United States from 1815 to 1818*. Calf. Albany, N.Y., 1819. First edition. $50-$60.

BRADLEY, William Aspenwall. *The Etching of Figures*. Half vellum. Marlborough-on-Hudson. N.Y., 1915. Dard Hunter paper and printing. One of 250. $150-$200.

BRADY, William. *Glimpses of Texas*. Folding map in color. Stiff wrappers. Houston, 1871. First edition. $200-$300.

BRAINE, John. *Room at the Top*. Cloth, London, 1957. First edition. In dust jacket. $25-$35.

BRAITHWAITE, William S. *Lyrics of Life and Love*. Cloth. Boston, 1904. First edition. $100-$125. Author's first book.

BRAITHWAITE, William S. (editor). *Anthology of Magazine Verse for 1913*. Wrappers or boards. Cambridge, Mass., (1913). First edition. $50. (First of the famous Braithwaite anthologies.)

BRAITHWAITE, William S. (editor). *Anthology of Magazine Verse for 1923*. Boards and cloth. Boston, 1923. First edition. One of 245 signed by Braithwaite. $40-$50.

BRAMAH, Ernest. *English Farming and Why I Turned it Up*. Cloth. London, 1894. (By Ernest Bramah Smith.) First edition. Issued without dust jacket. $100. Author's first book.

BRAMAH, Ernest. *The Wallet of Kai Lung*. Light-green cloth. London, (1900). (By Ernest Bramah Smith.) First English edition, first issue, measuring 1½ inches thick. $35-$50.

BRAMAN, D.E.E. *Information About Texas*. Cloth. Philadelphia, 1857. First edition. $300-$400. Philadelphia, 1858. Cloth. $75-$100.

BRANGWYN, Frank. *The Etched Work of Frank Brangwyn*. Half cloth. London, 1908. Limited edition on large paper. $100-$150.

BRANGWYN, Frank. *The Historical Paintings in the Great Hall of the Worshipful Company of Skinners*. London, 1909. One of 525. $75-$100. Another issue: One of 25 on vellum. $200-$250.

BRANGWYN, Frank, and Sparrow, Walter Shaw. *A Book of Bridges*. Half vellum. London, 1916. One of 75 on large paper, signed by Brangwyn. $125-$200.

BRATT, John. *Trails of Yesterday*. Portrait frontispiece and plates. Pictorial cloth. Lincoln, Neb., 1921. First edition. $60-$80.

BRAUTIGAN, Richard. *Four New Poets*. Wrappers. San Francisco, (1957). Inferno Press. First edition. $20-$25. First book appearance of Brautigan, with three other poets.

BRAUTIGAN, Richard. *The Galilee Hitch-Hiker*. Wrappers. San Francisco, 1958. $35-$50.

BRAUTIGAN, Richard. *Lay the Marble Tea*. Printed wrappers. San Francisco, 1959. First edition. $40-$60.

BRAUTIGAN, Richard. *The Octopus Frontier*. Printed wrappers. San Francisco, 1960. First edition. $40-$50.

BRAUTIGAN, Richard. *The Pill Versus the Springhill Mine Disaster*. Tan boards, brown cloth spine. San Francisco, (1968). First edition. One of 50 signed. $75-$100.

BRAUTIGAN, Richard. *Please Plant This Book*. Wrappers, with eight seed packets enclosed. Santa Barbara, 1968. $20-$25.

BRAUTIGAN, Richard. *In Watermelon Sugar*. Blue boards, black cloth spine. San Francisco, 1968. First edition. One of 50 signed. $75-$100.

*BRAVO (The): A Venetian Story*. 3 vols., boards, paper labels. London, 1831. (By James Fenimore Cooper.) First edition. $100-$150. Philadelphia, 1831. 2 vols., boards, paper labels. First American edition. $150-$200.

BRAYTON, Matthew. *The Indian Captive*. 68 pp., printed green wrappers, or boards. Cleveland. 1860. First edition. Wrappers: $450-$650. Boards: $250-$400. Also, $225 (A, 1954). Fostoria, Ohio, 1896. Boards. Second edition. $75-$100.

BRAZER, Esther Stevens. *Early American Decoration*. 34 color plates. Cloth. Springfield, Mass., (1947). $50. Springfield, (1950). $40.

*BREAD-WINNERS (The)*. Cloth. New York, 1884. (By John Hay.) First edition. $35-$50.

BRETON, Nicholas. *The Twelve Moneths and Christmas Day*. Boards. London, 1927, Golden Cockerel Press. One of 500. $125-$200. New York, 1951. One of 100, signed by Bruce Rogers. $75.

BREWSTER, Sir David. *A Treatise on the Kaleidoscope*. 7 plates. Cloth. Edinburgh, 1819. First edition. $200-$250.

BRICE, Wallace. *A History of Fort Wayne.* 7 plates. Cloth. Fort Wayne, Ind., 1868. First edition. $50-$75.

BRIDGENS, Richard. *Furniture, with Candelabra and Interior Decoration.* 60 full-page color plates. Folio, boards. London, 1838. $350-$450.

BRIDGES, Robert. *Eros and Psyche, A Poem.* Woodcuts from drawings by Edward Burne-Jones. White pigskin. Newtown, Wales, 1935. Gregynog Press. One of 300. In buckram case. $600-$750. Another issue: One of 15 specially bound by George Fisher. $1,250-$1,500.

BRIDGES, Robert. *The Growth of Love.* Boards and parchment. Oxford, 1890. Daniel Press. One of 100. $75-$100. Portland, Me., 1894. Mosher Press. Wrappers over boards. One of 40. $50

BRIDGES, Robert. *The Influence of the Audience.* Wrappers. Garden City, 1926. One of 100. Boxed. $50-$75.

BRIDGES, Robert. *Poems.* Cloth. London, 1873. First edition. $150-$200. Author's first book (suppressed by him in 1878).

BRIDGES, Robert. *Poems Written in the Year MCMXIII.* Blue printed boards and cloth. Chelsea (London), 1914. Ashendene Press. First edition. One of 85 with initials in red and blue. Boxed. $600-$850.

BRIDGES, Robert. *The Tapestry.* Boards. (London), 1925. First edition. One of 150. Boxed. $100-$150.

BRIDGES, Robert. *The Testament of Beauty.* Buckram. Oxford, 1929. First published edition. One of 50 signed. In dust jacket. $150-$200. Another issue: One of 200, unsigned. $75-$100. Trade edition: Boards. $10-$25. New York, 1929. One of 250. $35. (Note: In 1961 a privately printed, 1927-29 "trial issue" of 5 unbound parts was sold at auction in London for $252.)

BRIDWELL, J.W. (compiler). *The Life and Adventures of Robert McKimie.* 56 pp., pictorial wrappers. Hillsboro, Ohio, 1878. First edition. $750-$1,000.

*BRIEF Description of Western Texas (A).* Pictorial wrappers. San Antonio, 1873. (By W.G. Kingsbury.) First edition. $575-$750.

*BRIEF History of Christ's Hospital (A).* Boards, paper label. London, 1820. (By Charles Lamb.) First edition. $200-$300.

BRIFFAULT, Robert. *The Mothers.* 3 vols., cloth. New York, 1927. First edition. $100.

BRIGGS, L. Vernon. *Arizona and New Mexico, 1882; California, 1886; Mexico, 1891.* Portraits. Cloth. (Boston, 1932). First edition. $100-$150.

BRIGGS, L. Vernon. *History of Shipbuilding on North River, Plymouth County, Massachusetts.* 57 illustrations. Cloth. Boston, 1889. First edition. $100-$125.

BRIGHAM, Clarence S. *Paul Revere's Engravings.* 77 plates (some in color). Cloth. Worcester, Mass., 1954. First edition. In dust jacket. $75-$100.

BRILLAT-SAVARIN, J.A. *The Physiology of Taste.* Introduction by Arthur Machen. Portrait, other illustrations. Boards. London, 1925. One of 750. $50-$75. New York, 1949. Limited Editions Club. Translated by M.F.K. Fisher. Half leather. Boxed. $75-$100.

BRINNIN, John Malcolm. *The Garden is Political.* Cloth. New York, 1942. First edition. In dust jacket. $30-$40. Author's first book.

BRISBIN, James S. *The Beef Bonanza.* 8 plates. Pictorial cloth. Philadelphia, 1881. First edition. $150-$200.

*BRITISH Military Library (The).* 47 maps, plans and plates, 29 color plates of military costume, 10 leaves of music. 2 vols., morocco. London, 1799-1801. $275-$300.

BRITTON, Wiley. *Memoirs of the Rebellion on the Border, 1863.* Cloth. Chicago, 1882. First edition. $25-$30.

BRODIE, Walter. *Pitcairn's Island and The Islanders in 1850*. 4 plates. Cloth, paper label. London, 1851. First edition. $100-$150. London, 1851. Second edition. $50-$60.

BROMFIELD, Louis. *Awake and Rehearse*. Boards. New York, (1929). First edition. One of 500 signed. In dust jacket. Boxed. $40-$60.

BROMFIELD, Louis. *The Green Bay Tree*. Cloth. New York, 1924. First edition. In dust jacket. $40-$60. Author's first book.

BRONK, William. *Light and Dark*. Wrappers. (Ashland), 1956. First editon. $35. Author's first book.

BRONTË, Anne. See Bell, Acton; Bell, Currer.

BRONTË, Anne. *Self-Communion*. 2 facsimiles. Boards. London, 1900. First edition. One of 30. $75-$125.

BRONTË, Charlotte. See Bell, Currer.

BRONTË, Emily. See Bell, Ellis.

BRONTË, The Rev. Patrick. *Cottage Poems*. Blue boards. Halifax, 1811. First edition. $150-$200.

BRONTË, The Rev. P(atrick). *The Rural Minstrel*. Blue-gray boards. Halifax, 1813. First edition. $75-$100.

BROOKE, Arthur De Capell. *Travels Through Sweden, Norway, and Finmark, to the North Cape*. Map, 21 plates (2 colored). Calf, or boards and calf. London, (1823). First edition. $400-$500. London, 1831. Half calf. Second edition. $200-$300.

BROOKE, Arthur De Capell. *A Winter in Lapland and Sweden*. Calf, or boards and calf. London, 1826. First edition. $400-$500. London, 1827. Second edition. $200-$300.

BROOKE, H. K. *Annals of the Revolution*. Boards. Philadelphia, (1848). First edition. $100-$125.

BROOKE, L. *Johnny Crowe's Garden*. Illustrated by the author. Boards. London, 1903. First edition. $300-$350.

BROOKE, Rupert. *Collected Poems*. Portrait. Cloth, paper labels. New York, 1915. First edition. $75-$100. (Of the first edition, 100 copies were especially bound for members of the Woodberry Society. Value: $400-$500.) London, 1919. Riccardi Press. One of 13 on vellum. $800-$1,000.

BROOKE, Rupert. *John Webster and the Elizabethan Drama*. Cloth. New York, 1916. First edition. In dust jacket. $100-$150.

BROOKE, Rupert. *Lithuania: A Drama in One Act*. Pictorial brown wrappers. Chicago, 1915. Chicago Little Theatre. First edition. $100-$150.

BROOKE, Rupert. *1914 and Other Poems*. Portrait frontispiece. Dark blue cloth, paper label. London, 1915. First edition. In dust jacket. $75-$100. New York, 1915. American copyright edition: 87 copies, folded sheets. $75-$100. (A few were specially bound in morocco. Value: $350-$400, possibly more.)

BROOKE, Rupert. *"1914": Five Sonnets*. Printed wrappers. London, 1915. First edition. In printed envelope. $50.

BROOKE, Rupert. *The Old Vicarage, Grantchester*. Woodcut. Gray wrappers. London, 1916. First edition. $25-$35.

BROOKE, Rupert. *Poems*. Dark blue cloth, paper label. London, 1911. First edition. $125-$150. Author's first book of verse. (100 copies.)

*BROOKS-Bryce Anglo American Prize Essays—1927*. Illustrated. Boards, paper cover label. New York, (1927). First edition. $125. (Contains James Agee's first book appearance.)

BROOKS, Bryant B. *Memoirs of Bryant B. Brooks.* Plates. Cloth. Glendale, Calif., 1939. First edition. One of 150. $50-$75.

BROOKS, Gwendolyn. *Annie Allen.* Cloth. New York, (1949). First edition. In dust jacket. $50-$75.

BROOKS, Gwendolyn. *The Bean Eaters.* Cloth. New York, (1960). First edition. In dust jacket. $60-$80.

BROOKS, Gwendolyn. *Bronzeville Boys and Girls.* New York, (1956). First edition. In dust jacket. $20-$25.

BROOKS, Gwendolyn. *Family Pictures.* Wrappers. Detroit, (1970). First edition. $25.

BROOKS, Gwendolyn. *Maud Martha.* Cloth. New York, 1953. First edition. In dust jacket. $50-$60.

BROOKS, Gwendolyn. *Report from Part One.* Unbound advance copy. Detroit, (1972). (First page is publisher's blurb.) $25-$30.

BROOKS, Gwendolyn. *A Street in Bronzeville.* Cloth. New York, 1945. First edition. In dust jacket. $100-$125. Author's first book.

*BROTHERS (The): A Tale of the Fronde.* 2 vols., cloth, paper labels. New York, 1835. (By Henry William Herbert.) First edition, first issue, in brown cloth. $200-$250. Author's first book.

BROUGHTON, William Robert. *A Voyage of Discovery to the North Pacific Ocean.* 9 plates and maps (7 folding). Half calf. London, 1804. First edition. $2,000-$2,250.

BROUILLET, J.B.A. *Authentic Account of the Murder of Dr. Whitman and Other Missionaries.* 108 pp., wrappers. Portland, 1869. Second edition of *Protestantism in Oregon* (see item following). $1,000 and up.

BROUILLET, J.B.A. *Protestantism in Oregon: Account of the Murder of Dr. Whitman, and the Ungrateful Calumnies of H.H. Spalding, Protestant Missionary.* Wrappers. New York, 1853. First edition. $3,000 and up.

BROWER, Jacob V. *Memoirs of Explorations in the Basin of the Mississippi.* Maps. 8 vols., cloth. St. Paul, Minn., 1898-1904. One of 300. $400-$500.

BROWN, Bob. *Demonics.* Wrappers. Cagnes-sur-Mer, France, 1931. First edition. $250-$300.

BROWN, Bob. *Readies for Bob Brown's Machine.* Wrappers. Cagnes-sur-Mer, France, 1931. First edition. $300-$400.

BROWN, Charles Brockden. See *Monroe's Embassy.*

BROWN, Charles Brockden. *Arthur Mervyn: A Tale.* 3 vols., boards. London, 1803. First English edition. $150-$200. (Note: The first edition was issued anonymously in America in 1799-1800. See entry under *Arthur Mervyn*.)

BROWN, Charles Brockden. *Carwin, the Biloquist, and Other American Tales and Pieces.* Boards. London, 1822. First English edition (of "Memoirs of Carwin, etc.," from William Dunlap's *The Life of Charles Brockden Brown*, which see). $300-$350.

BROWN, Fredric. *The Fabulous Clipjoint.* Blue cloth. New York, 1947. First edition. In dust jacket. $35-$50. Author's first book.

BROWN, Isaac V. *Memoirs of the Rev. Robert Finley, D.D.* Calf. New Brunswick, N.J., 1819. First edition. $27.50.

BROWN, J. Cabell. *Calabazas, or Amusing Recollections of an Arizona "City."* Illustrated. Printed wrappers. San Francisco, 1892. First edition. $150-$250.

BROWN, J. Willard. *The Signal Corps, U.S.A., in the War of the Rebellion.* Cloth. Boston, 1896. $100-$150.

BROWN, James S. *California Gold: An Authentic History of the First Find*. Portrait frontispiece. 20 pp., printed wrappers. Oakland, 1894. First edition. One of 55. $200-$300.

BROWN, James S. *Life of a Pioneer*. Portrait. 2 plates. Cloth. Salt Lake City, 1900. First edition. $100-$150.

BROWN, Jesse, and Willard, A.M. *The Black Hills Trails*. Numerous illustrations. Cloth. Rapid City, S.D., 1924. First edition. $75-$100.

BROWN, John. *Rab and His Friends*. Pictorial wrappers. Boston, 1859. First American edition. $35-$40.

BROWN, John Henry. *History of Dallas County from 1837 to 1887*. 114 pp., wrappers. Dallas, 1887. First edition. $150-$250.

BROWN, John Henry. *History of Texas, 1685-1892*. 25 plates. 2 vols., cloth. St. Louis, (1892-93). First edition. $200-$250.

BROWN, John Henry. *Indian Wars and Pioneers of Texas*. Plates. Cloth. Austin, Tex., (1896). First edition. $300-$400.

BROWN, John Henry. *Political History of Oregon*. Vol. 1. (All published.) Illustrated, folding map. Cloth. Portland, Ore., 1892. First edition. $350-$400.

BROWN, John H(enry). *Reminiscences and Incidents, of "The Early Days" of San Francisco*. Folding frontispiece plan. Cloth. San Francisco, (1886). First edition. $500-$600. San Francisco, (1933). Grabhorn printing. Half cloth. One of 500. $65-$85. Another issue: One of 25 in morocco, with additional reproductions, etc. $175-$225.

BROWN, John Henry, and Speer, W.S. *The Encyclopedia of the New West*. Calf. Marshall, Tex., 1881. First edition. $300-$500.

BROWN, John P. *Old Frontiers: The Story of the Cherokee Indians*. Cloth. Kingsport, Tenn., 1938. First edition. $50-$60.

BROWN, Joseph M. *Astyanax: An Epic Romance of Llion, Atlantis, and Amaraca*. Illustrated. Cloth. New York, 1907. First edition. $75-$100.

BROWN, Paul. *Aintree*. Illustrated. Pictorial cloth. New York, 1930. Derrydale Press. First edition. One of 850. $75-$125. Another issue: One of 50 large paper copies with an initialed drawing by Brown. $500-$750. Also $550 (A, 1977).

BROWN, Paul. *Spills and Thrills*. Illustrated. Cloth. New York, 1933. First edition. One of 750 signed. In dust jacket. $75-$100.

BROWN, Samuel J. *In Captivity: The Experience, Privations and Dangers of Sam'l J. Brown, etc*. Text in 2 columns. Illustrated. Full leather. Mankato, Minn., (1896). First edition. $500-$600.

BROWN, Samuel R. *The Western Gazetteer, or Emigrant's Directory*. Sheep. Auburn, N.Y., 1817. First edition, first issue, with 3-line errata slip. $200-$300. Second issue, with 4-line errata. $125-$200. Third issue, with advertisements. $100-$150.

BROWN, William C. *The Sheepeater Campaign in Idaho*. Folding map. 32 pp., wrappers. Boise, 1926. First edition. One of 50. $100-$125.

BROWN, William H. *The Early History of the State of Illinois*. 16 pp., printed wrappers. Chicago, 1840. First edition. $1,000-$1,250.

BROWN, William Robinson. *The Horse of the Desert*. Illustrated. Cloth. New York, 1929. Derrydale Press. One of 750. In dust jacket. $200-$300. Another issue: One of 75 signed. $500-$600.

BROWNE, J. Ross. *Adventures in the Apache Country*. Illustrated by the author. Cloth. New York, 1869. First edition. $150-$250.

BROWNE, J. Ross. *Report of the Debates in the Convention of California on the Formation of the State Constitution*. Cloth. Washington, 1850. First edition. $125-$150.

BROWNE, J. Ross. *Report . . . on the Late Indian War in Oregon and Washington Territory.* Half leather. Washington, 1858. First edition. $75-$100.

BROWNE, Thomas A. See Boldrewood, Rolf.

BROWNE, Sir Thomas. *Hydriotaphia: Urn Burial.* Waltham Saint Lawrence, 1923. Golden Cockerel Press. One of 115. $200-$300.

BROWNE, Sir Thomas. *Religio Medici.* Waltham Saint Lawrence, 1923. Golden Cockerel Press. One of 115. $150-$300. New York, 1939. Limited Editions Club. John Henry Nash printing. Boxed. $50-$60.

BROWNE, Sir Thomas. *Urn Burial and The Garden of Cyprus.* Edited by John Carter. 30 hand-colored drawings by Paul Nash. Folio, vellum and morocco. London, 1932. Curwen Press. One of 215. In slipcase. $1,000-$1,500.

BROWNING, Elizabeth Barrett. See B., E.B.; Barrett, Elizabeth B.; Barrett, Elizabeth Barrett. Also see *An Essay on Mind; Prometheus Bound.*

BROWNING, Elizabeth Barrett. *Aurora Leigh.* Cloth. London, 1857. First edition. $100-$150.

BROWNING, Elizabeth Barrett. *Casa Guidi Windows: A Poem.* Green cloth. London, 1851. First edition. $100-$150.

BROWNING, Elizabeth Barrett. *The Enchantress and Other Poems.* Printed wrappers. London, 1913. First edition. One of 30. $150-$175.

BROWNING, Elizabeth Barrett. *Leila, A Tale.* Printed wrappers. London, 1913. First edition. One of 30. $150-$175.

BROWNING, Elizabeth Barrett. *Poems.* 2 vols., brown cloth. London, 1850. ("New Edition.") Second edition, first issue, with single address in imprint, (and containing first book appearance of "Sonnets from the Portuguese"; see B., E.B., entry and author-title entry below). $500-$750.

BROWNING, Elizabeth Barrett. *Poems Before Congress.* Red cloth. London, 1860. First edition, with 32-page publisher's catalogue dated February, 1860. $100-$200.

BROWNING, Elizabeth Barrett. *Sonnets from the Portuguese.* (Note: For the first appearance of the sonnets, see *Poems* under "Elizabeth Barrett Browning" entry; for the faked Thomas J. Wise first edition, see B., E.B., entry. The following entries are all reprinted versions of the original work.) (Boston), 1896. Copeland & Day. Hand-colored illustrations. Wrappers over boards. $150. London, 1887 (date 1889 on cover). Ballantyne Press. Morocco. One of 8 on vellum. $400-$500. London, 1897. Illustrated. Wrappers. (No copies in original wrappers noted.) (East Aurora, 1898). Roycrofters. Half cloth. One of 480. $25-$35. Chicago, (1899). One of 15. $75-$100. New Rochelle, 1900. Doves Press [*sic*]. One of 485. $50-$60. Another issue: One of 60 on vellum. $60-$80. (Boston), 1902. One of 250. $50-$75. London, 1906. Vellum. One of a few printed in red and black on vellum. $75-$100. London, (1909). Buckram. One of 500. In dust jacket. $75-$100. London, 1914. Riccardi Press. Vellum. One of 12 on vellum. $1,200-$1,500. Montagnola, 1925. Morocco. One of 225. $150-$200. San Francisco, 1925-27. 2 vols., half vellum (including facsimile volume). One of 250. $50-$60. San Francisco, 1931. 2 vols. One of 250. $50-$60. New York, 1948. Limited Editions Club. Cloth. Boxed. $50-$60.

BROWNING, Robert. See Barrett, Elizabeth, and Browning, Robert. Also see *Pauline: A Fragment of a Confession.*

BROWNING, Robert. *Aristophanes' Apology.* Green cloth. London, 1875. First edition, with ad leaf at end. $50-$75.

BROWNING, Robert. *Asolando.* Red cloth. London, 1890. First edition. $100-$150.

BROWNING, Robert. *Balaustion's Adventure.* Beveled red-brown cloth. London, 1871. First edition. $75-$100.

BROWNING, Robert. *Bells and Pomegranates.* 8 parts, printed wrappers. London,

1841-46. First edition, with half title for second part. $1,000 and up. (A set with three parts inscribed by Browning to an uncle brought $2,750 at auction in 1974. Another, with one number inscribed by the author, sold for $425 at auction in 1972.) First book edition (parts bound in one volume, cloth, with the half title to the second part). $350-$500.

BROWNING, Robert. *Christmas Eve and Easter Day: A Poem.* Cloth. London, 1850. First edition. $75-$125.

BROWNING, Robert. *Dramatic Romances and Lyrics.* Illustrated. Morocco. London, 1899. Ballantyne Press. One of 10 on vellum. $1,000-$1,250. Also, $481 (A, 1975). Another issue: Buckram. One of 210. $75-$100.

BROWNING, Robert. *Dramatis Personae.* Red cloth. London, 1864. First edition. $125-$150. (London, 1910). Doves Press. Vellum. One of 250 printed in red and black. $600-$850.

BROWNING, Robert. *An Essay on Percy Bysshe Shelley.* Edited by W.T. Harden. Sheets printed on vellum, unbound, in buckram folder and slipcase. (London), 1888. One of 4 (3?) printed on vellum. $400-$500.

BROWNING, Robert. *Fifine at the Fair.* Dark-brown cloth. London, 1872. First edition. $75-$100.

BROWNING, Robert. *Men and Women.* 2 vols., green cloth. London, 1855. First edition, first binding. $200-$250. London, 1908. Doves Press. 2 vols., vellum. One of 262 printed in red and black. $600-$750. In a special Doves binding of morocco. $1,000-$1,250.

BROWNING, Robert. *Pacchiarotto and How He Worked in Distemper: With Other Poems.* Beveled gray cloth. London, 1876. First edition, with ad leaf at end. $75-$100.

BROWNING, Robert. *Paracelsus.* Drab boards, paper label. London, 1835. First edition, first issue, with 8 pages of ads at front dated Dec. 1, 1842. $750-$1,000. Author's first acknowledged book.

BROWNING, Robert. *The Pied Piper of Hamelin.* 35 colored illustrations by Kate Greenaway. Pictorial boards. London, (1888). First edition. In dust jacket. $250-$350. London, 1934. Illustrated by Arthur Rackham. Limp vellum. De luxe edition. $400-$500.

BROWNING, Robert. *The Ring and the Book.* 4 vols., green cloth. London, 1868-69. First edition, first binding, with spines of first 2 volumes in Arabic numerals and of next 2 in Roman numerals. $300-$400. New York, 1949. Limited Editions Club. 2 vols., boards and morocco. Boxed. $60-$80.

BROWNING, Robert. *Some Poems.* Frontispiece in color. Boards. London, 1904. Eragny Press. One of 226. In dust jacket. $250-$350.

BROWNING, Robert. *Sordello.* Boards, paper label. London, 1840. First edition, first issue, in boards (later issue being cloth). $400-$500.

BROWNING, Robert. *Strafford: An Historical Tragedy.* Stiff gray wrappers, paper label on front. London, 1837. First edition. $500-$600.

BRUFF, J. Goldsborough. *Gold Rush: The Journals, Drawings and Other Papers of J. Goldsborough Bruff.* Edited by Georgia W. Read and Ruth Gaines. 21 plates. 2 vols., boards. New York, 1944. First edition. (1,158 printed.) $100-$150. New York, 1949. Illustrated. 2 vols. in one, cloth. (Abridged.) In dust jacket. $15-$25.

BRUFFEY, George A. *Eighty-one Years in the West.* Portrait. 152 pp., wrappers. Butte, 1925. First edition. $50-$60.

BRUMBAUGH, Gaius Marcus. *Genealogy of the Brumbaugh Families.* Illustrated. Cloth. New York, (1913). One of 1,000. $40-$50.

BRUNEFILLE, G.E. *Topo.* Illustrated by Kate Greenaway. Cloth. London, 1880. (By Gertrude Elizabeth Cambell.) First edition. $75-$100.

BRUNSON, Alfred. *A Western Pioneer.* 2 vols., cloth. Cincinnati, 1872 and 1879. First edition. $75-$100. (Note: A difficult set to bring together.)

BRUNSON, Edward. *Profits in Sheep and Cattle in Central and Western Kansas*. 16 pp., wrappers. Kansas City, 1883. First edition. $150-$175.

BRYANT, Edwin. *What I Saw in California*. Cloth. New York, 1848. First edition. $250-$350. New York, 1848. Cloth. Second edition. $150-$200. Santa Ana, Calif., 1936. Half morocco. $50-$75.

BRYANT, Gilbert Ernest. *The Chelsea Porcelain Toys*. 63 plates, 47 in color. Cloth. London, 1925. One of 650 signed. In dust jacket. $200-$250.

BRYANT, John Howard. *Poems*. Cloth. New York, 1855. First edition. $50-$60.

BRYANT, Wilbur F. *The Blood of Abel*. Cloth. Hastings, Neb., 1887. First edition. $200-$250. Lacking front free end paper, $100 (A, 1969).

BRYANT, William Cullen. *The Embargo; or, Sketches of the Times: A Satire*. (Cover title.) Self-wrappers (stitched); also plain slate blue or marbled paper wrappers. Boston, 1809. Second edition. Wrappers: $600 and up. Stitched: $500 and up. (For first edition, see title entry, *The Embargo*.)

BRYANT, William Cullen. *The Fountain and Other Poems*. Boards; or cloth, label on spine; or, cloth with gold stamping on front cover. New York, 1842. First edition. (No priority on bindings, according to Blanck.) $150-$200.

BRYANT, William Cullen. *Hymns*. Brown-orange or blue cloth. (New York, 1864). First edition, first state, with reading "Dwells on Thy works in deep delight" in second line of fourth stanza on page 9. $100-$150.

BRYANT, William Cullen. *Poems*. Brown or grayish printed boards (375 copies?—Blanck), or printed brown wrappers (200 copies?—Blanck). Cambridge, Mass., 1821. First edition. Boards: $1,250 and up. Wrappers: $1,500 and up. New York, 1832. Second edition. Boards and blue cloth. $200-$300. New York, 1836. Third edition. $100-$150. New York, 1947. Limited Editions Club. Illustrated by Thomas Nason. Leather. Boxed. $40-$60.

BRYANT, William Cullen. *Thirty Poems*. Brown cloth. New York, 1864. First edition, first state, wove paper, line 5 from bottom of page 213 reading "veielo." $75-$150. Second state, laid paper, reading "vuielo" on page 213. $50-$75.

BRYANT, William Cullen. *Unpublished Poems*. Illustrated. Boards. Boston, 1907. Bibliophile Society. One of 470 on vellum. Boxed. $75-$85.

BRYCE, James. *The American Commonwealth*. 3 vols., cloth. London, 1888. First edition, first issue, with the chapter in Vol. 3 on the Tweed Ring, later suppressed. $250-$350. Second issue, with Tweed Ring matter omitted. $150-$200.

BRYHER, Winifred. *The Lament for Adonis*. Translated from the Greek. Wrappers. London, 1918. First edition. $300-$350. Also, $250 (A, 1977). Author's first book.

BUCHAN, John. *The Marquis of Montrose*. Plates, maps, plans. Cloth. London, 1913. First edition. $100-$125.

BUCHAN, John. *Pilgrim Fathers*. Wrappers. Oxford, 1898. First edition. $100-$125.

BUCHAN, John. *Poems—Scots and English*. Blue cloth and boards. London, 1917. One of 50 signed. $75-$150.

BUCHAN, John. *Sir Quixote of the Moors*. Cloth. London, 1895. First edition, first issue, with full title on spine. $100-$150. New York, 1895. Cloth. First American edition. $30-$40.

BUCHAN, John. *The Thirty-Nine Steps*. Blue cloth. Edinburgh, 1915. First edition. In dust jacket. $200-$250.

BUCHANAN, Robert. *The Devil's Case*. Cloth. London, (1896). First edition. $75-$100.

BUCHANAN, Robert. *The Fleshly School of Poetry*. Pink or violet pictorial wrappers. London, 1872. First edition. $150-$175.

BUCHANAN, Robertson. *Practical and Descriptive Essays on the Economy of Fuel, and Management of Heat.* 2 plates. Boards. Glasgow, 1810. First edition. $300-$400. Also, $225 (A, 1977).

BUCHANAN, Robertson. *A Practical Treatise on Propelling Vessels by Steam.* 17 plates, one folding. Boards. Glasgow, 1816. First edition. $400-$500.

BUCK, Irving A. *Cleburne and His Command.* Plates. Cloth. New York, 1908. First edition. $50-$75.

BUCK, Pearl S. (translator). *All Men Are Brothers.* Translated from the Chinese of Shui Hu Chuan. 2 vols. New York, (1933). First edition. $35-$50. New York, 1948. Limited Editions Club. Edited by Lin Yutang. Illustrated by Miguel Covarrubias. 2 vols., stiff wrappers, Chinese silk paper, tied with thongs. Boxed. $100.

BUCK, Pearl S. *East Wind: West Wind.* Cloth. New York, (1930). First edition. In dust jacket. $35-$40.

BUCK, Pearl S. *The Good Earth.* Tan cloth. New York, (1931). First edition, first issue, with "flees" for "fleas" in line 17 of page 100, with "John Day Publishing Company" on copyright page, and with top edges stained brown. In brown dust jacket. $75-$100. Later issue, green top edges, in dust jacket. $25-$30. Advance issue, for review: Printed wrappers. $100.

BUCK, Pearl S. *Sons.* Cloth. New York, (1932). First edition. One of 371 de luxe copies, signed. In dust jacket. Boxed. $75-$100.

BUCKINGHAM, Nash. *De Shootinest Gent'man and Other Tales.* Edited by Col. Harold P. Sheldon. Illustrated. Cloth. New York, (1934). Derrydale Press. First edition. One of 950. $400-$500.

BUCKINGHAM, Nash. *Mark Right!* Illustrated. Cloth. New York, (1936). Derrydale Press. One of 1,250. $175-$250.

BUCKINGHAM, Nash. *Ole Miss.* Edited by Paul A. Curtis. Illustrated. Leatherette. New York, (1937). Derrydale Press. One of 1,250. $150-$225.

BUCKLEY, Francis. *English Baluster Stemmed Glasses of the 17th and 18th Centuries.* 18 plates. Buckram. Edinburgh, 1912. $100-$150.

BUCKLEY, Francis. *Old London Drinking Glasses.* 14 plates. Buckram. Edinburgh, 1913. $100-$150.

BUCKLEY, Wilfred. *Diamond Engraved Glasses of the 16th Century.* 33 plates. Boards. London, 1929. One of 250. $100-$125.

BUDGE, Sir E. A. Wallis. *Amulets and Superstitions.* 22 plates, 300 other illustrations. Cloth. London, 1930. $75-$85.

BUDGE, Sir E. A. Wallis. *The Gods of the Egyptians, or Studies in Egyptian Mythology.* 98 color plates. 2 vols., pictorial cloth. London, 1904. $150-$200.

BUECHNER, Frederick. *A Long Day's Dying.* Cloth. New York, 1950. First edition. In dust jacket. $40-$50. Author's first book.

BUEL, J.W. *Life and Marvelous Adventures of Wild Bill, the Scout.* Frontispiece and plate. 93 pp., pictorial wrappers. Chicago, 1880. First edition, presumed first issue, with cover dated 1880. $600-$800.

BUFFUM, E. Gould. *Six Months in the Gold Mines.* Printed wrappers, or cloth. Philadelphia, 1850. First edition. Wrappers: $300-$400. Cloth: $200-$300.

BUKOWSKI, Charles. *At Terror Street and Agony Way.* Cloth. Los Angeles, 1968. Black Sparrow Press. First edition. One of 75 signed by the author with an original illustration by the author. $85-$125.

BUKOWSKI, Charles. *Cold Dogs in the Courtyard.* Wrappers. Literary Times and Cyfoeth Publications, 1965. First edition. One of 500. $50-$60.

BUKOWSKI, Charles. *Crucifix in a Deathhand*. Pictorial wrappers. New Orleans, 1962, Loujon Press. First edition, limited and signed. $50-$75.

BUKOWSKI, Charles. *The Curtains are Waving, etc.* Printed wrappers. (Los Angeles), 1967. First edition. One of 125 signed. $85-$125.

BUKOWSKI, Charles. *The Days Run Away Like Wild Horses Over the Hills.* Boards. Los Angeles, 1969. First edition. One of 250 signed. $35.

BULFINCH, Thomas. *The Age of Chivalry*. 6 illustrations. Brown cloth. Boston, 1859. First edition. $150.

BULFINCH, Thomas. *The Age of Fable*. Brown cloth. Boston, 1855. First edition, first state, with names of both printer and stereotyper on copyright page. $150-$200. New York, 1956. Limited Editions Club. Illustrated by Joe Mugnaini. Cloth. Boxed. $60-$70.

BULLEN, A.H. *A Collection of Old English Plays*. 7 vols., boards, parchment spines. London, 1882-90. One of 150. $250-$350.

BULLEN, Frank T. *The Cruise of the "Cachalot."* Folding map and plates. Blue cloth. London, 1898. First edition. $150-$200. Author's first book.

BULLER, Sir Walter Lawry. *A History of the Birds of New Zealand*. 35 hand-colored plates. Cloth. London, 1873. First edition. $1,250-$1,750. London, 1887-88. 48 colored plates, 2 plain plates. 13 parts in 8, wrappers. $2,000-$2,500. London, 1888. 2 vols., half morocco. Second edition. $1,250-$1,500.

BULLOCK, William. *Six Months Residence and Travels in Mexico*. 2 folding plans, folding view, 11 other views, 4 colored aquatint plates. Boards and cloth. London, 1824. First edition. $350-$450.

BULWER-LYTTON, Edward. See Caxton, Pisistratus. Also see *The Coming Race; Falkland; The Last Days of Pompeii; Pelham; Rienzi.*

BULWER-LYTTON, Edward. *Ismael; an Oriental Tale*. Boards. London, 1820. First edition. $300-$400. Author's first book.

BUNNER, H.C. *A Woman of Honor*. Cloth. Boston, 1883. First edition. $40-$50. Author's first book.

BUNTING, Basil. *Briggflatts*. Black cloth. London, (1966). One of 100 in cloth. In dust jacket. $80-$100.

BUNTING, Basil. *Collected Poems*. Cloth. London, (1968). First edition. One of 150 signed. In dust jacket. $40-$50.

BUNTING, Basil. *Descant on Rawthey's Madrigal: Conversations with Basil Bunting*. Boards. Kentucky, (1968). One of 25 signed by Bunting and Jonathan Williams. In dust jacket. $75-$100.

BUNTING, Basil. *First Book of Odes*. Boards. London, no date. One of 175. $50-$60.

BUNTING, Basil. *Loquitur*. Full morocco. London, (1965). First edition. One of 26 signed. In dust jacket. $100-$125.

BUNTING, Basil. *Redimiculum Matellarum*. Wrappers. Milan, 1930. First edition. $750-$1,000. Author's first book.

BUNTING, Basil. *Two Poems*. Wrappers. California, 1967. First edition. One of 30 signed (of an edition of 250). $75.

BUNYAN, John. *The Pilgrim's Progress*. Portrait frontispiece. Full brown morocco, gilt London, 1849. Chiswick Press. $150-$200. London, 1928. Cresset Press. 10 wood engravings. Black parchment. One of 195. $350-$600. New York, 1941. Limited Editions Club. 29 William Blake illustrations in color. One of 1,500. Boxed. $100-$150.

BURGESS, Anthony. *A Clockwork Orange*. Cloth. London, 1962. First edition. In dust jacket. $50-$75.

BURGESS, Gelett. *Are You a Bromide?* Boards, paper label on front cover. New York, 1906. First edition. In dust jacket. $75-$100.

BURGESS, Gelett. *Goops and How to Be Them.* 90 drawings by the author. Red cloth. New York, (1900). First edition. $250-$300. London, 1900. Illustrated by the author. Pictorial cloth. First English edition. Lightly soiled, $200.

BURGESS, Gelett. *Le Petit Journal des Refusées: Number 1.* (All published.) Wrappers. San Francisco, 1896. First edition. (Printed on wallpaper.) $100 and up.

BURGESS, Gelett. *The Nonsense Almanack for 1900.* Wrappers. New York, (1899). First edition. $75-$100.

BURGESS, Gelett. *The Purple Cow!* Illustrated. 8 leaves. (San Francisco, 1895). First edition, first state of first printing (printed on both sides of leaf) on rough China paper. $300-$400. Second state (printed on one side of leaf only). $150-$200. Author's first book.

BURKE, Edmund. *Correspondence of Edmund Burke and William Windham.* Edited by J.P. Gilson. Half morocco. Cambridge, 1910. Limited edition (fewer than 100 issued). $100-$150.

BURGESS, Thornton Waldo. *Old Mother Wind.* Illustrated. Pictorial tan cloth. Boston, (1910). First edition. $150-$175. Author's first book for children.

BURKE, John. *Dreams and Derisions.* Illustrated by Rockwell Kent. Half morocco. (New York), 1927. (By Ralph Pulitzer.) First edition. One of 100 (of an edition of 300) signed by Kent. Boxed. $400-$500.

BURKE, Kenneth. *The White Oxen and Other Stories.* Cloth. New York, 1924. First edition. In dust jacket. $50-$60. Author's first book.

BURKE, Thomas. *Limehouse Nights.* Terra-cotta cloth. London, 1916. First edition. $40-$50. New York, 1926. Illustrated. Cloth. $35.

BURKE, W.S. (compiler). *Directory of the City of Council Bluffs and Emigrants' Guide to the Gold Regions of the West.* Folding map. 32 pp., plus ads, patterned cloth. Council Bluffs, Iowa, 1866. First edition. $1,250-$1,500. Also, $950 (A, 1968).

BURNETT, Frances Hodgson. *The Drury Lane Boys' Club.* 78 pp., blue wrappers. Washington, 1892. First edition. One of 800. $100-$150.

BURNETT, Frances Hodgson. *Editha's Burglar.* Illustrated by Henry Sandham. Pictorial brown cloth. Boston, 1888. First edition, first state, with "I thought I heard something" under frontispiece. $50-$75. Second state, with name only under frontispiece. $40-$50.

BURNETT, Frances Hodgson. *Little Lord Fauntleroy.* Illustrated by Reginald B. Birch. Pictorial gray-green (blue) or tan cloth. New York, 1886. First edition, first issue, with DeVinne Press imprint at end. $200-$300. London, 1886. Pictorial cloth. First English edition, with copyright page dated November 9, 1886. $75-$100.

BURNETT, Frances Hodgson. *The Secret Garden.* Illustrated. Cloth, pictorial label. New York, (1911). First edition. $100-$150. Another issue: with no illustrations. (Blanck knew of no priority.) $50-$75.

BURNETT, Peter H. *Recollections and Opinions of an Old Pioneer.* Cloth. New York, 1880. First edition. $150-$175.

BURNETT, W.R. *Little Caesar.* Blue cloth. New York, 1929. First edition. In dust jacket. $40-$50. Author's first book.

BURNEY, Fanny (Frances). *Evelina.* 16 full-page illustrations by Arthur Rackham. Cloth. London, 1898. $75-$150.

BURNEY, Frances. See D'Arblay, Madame.

BURNEY, James. *A Chronological History of the Discoveries in the South Sea or Pacific*

*Ocean.* Maps, charts, plates. 5 vols., contemporary boards and leather. London, 1803-17. First edition. Large paper issue: $2,500-$3,500. Ordinary issue: $1,500-$2,500.

BURNEY, James. *History of the Buccaneers of America.* 3 maps (2 folding). Contemporary three-quarters morocco. London, 1816. First separate edition. Large paper issue: $350-$450. Ordinary issue: $250-$300.

BURNHAM, Daniel H., and Bennett, Edward H. *Plan of Chicago.* Illustrated. Leather and/ or cloth. Chicago, 1909. First edition. One of 1,650 copies. $300-$350. Another issue: Full vellum. $500-$600. (100 copies are said to have been issued thus. There was also an unknown number of copies bound in plain black linen wrappers. I once found five in a lot of architectural books.)

BURNS, John Horne. *The Gallery.* Cloth. New York, (1947). First edition. In dust jacket. $50. Author's first book.

BURNS, Robert. *Poems Ascribed to Robert Burns.* Boards. Glasgow, 1801. First edition. $150-$200.

BURNS, Robert. *Tam O'Shanter.* Illustrated, colored by hand. Stiff vellum. London, 1902. Essex House Press. One of 150. $200.

BURPEE, Lawrence J. *The Search for the Western Sea.* 6 maps, 51 plates. Cloth. London, 1908. First edition. $150-$200. New York, 1908. Cloth. First American edition. $100-$150. Toronto, (1908). Cloth. First Canadian edition. $100-$150. New York, 1936. Maps and plates. 2 vols., cloth. In dust jackets. $50-$75.

BURR, Aaron. *The Private Journal of Aaron Burr.* Edited by W. K. Bixby. Portraits. 2 vols., half cloth. Rochester, 1903. One of 250 signed by Bixby. $150-$200.

BURROUGHS, Edgar Rice. *At the Earth's Core.* Illustrated. Cloth. Chicago, 1922. First edition. In dust jacket. $150-$250.

BURROUGHS, Edgar Rice. *Back to the Stone Age.* Cloth. Tarzana, Calif., (1937). First edition. In dust jacket. $75-$100.

BURROUGHS, Edgar Rice. *The Beasts of Tarzan.* Illustrated. Olive cloth. Chicago, 1916. First edition. $150-$175.

BURROUGHS, Edgar Rice, *The Chessmen of Mars.* Illustrated. Red cloth. Chicago, 1922. First edition. $100-$135.

BURROUGHS, Edgar Rice. *The Eternal Lover.* Cloth. Chicago, 1925. First edition. $100-$135.

BURROUGHS, Edgar Rice. *A Fighting Man of Mars.* Frontispiece. Red cloth. New York, (1931). First edition, with Metropolitan Books imprint. $75-$150.

BURROUGHS, Edgar Rice. *I Am a Barbarian.* Illustrated. Cloth. Tarzana, (1967). First edition. In dust jacket. $25.

BURROUGHS, Edgar Rice. *Jungle Tales of Tarzan.* Illustrated. Cloth. Chicago, 1919. First edition. In dust jacket. $200-$250.

BURROUGHS, Edgar Rice. *The Master Mind of Mars.* Cloth. Chicago, 1928. First edition. In dust jacket. $100-$135.

BURROUGHS, Edgar Rice. *The Mucker.* Cloth. Chicago, 1921. First edition. In dust jacket. $250-$300.

BURROUGHS, Edgar Rice. *A Princess of Mars.* Illustrated. Cloth. Chicago, 1917. First edition. $150-$200.

BURROUGHS, Edgar Rice. *The Son of Tarzan.* Illustrated. Cloth. Chicago, 1917. First edition. In dust jacket. $150-$200. Lacking jacket, $75-$100.

BURROUGHS, Edgar Rice. *Tarzan and the Golden Lion.* Illustrated. Gold cloth. Chicago, 1933. First edition. $75-$100.

BURROUGHS, Edgar Rice. *Tarzan and the Jewels of Opar.* Illustrated, Dark-green cloth. Chicago, 1918. First edition. In dust jacket. $150-$250.

BURROUGHS, Edgar Rice. *Tarzan and the Leopard Men.* Cloth. Tarzana, (1935). First edition. In dust jacket. $75-$85.

BURROUGHS, Edgar Rice. *Tarzan at the Earth's Core.* Cloth. New York, (1930). Metropolitan Books. First edition. In dust jacket. $75-$100.

BURROUGHS, Edgar Rice. *Tarzan, Lord of the Jungle.* Illustrated. Cloth. Chicago, 1928. First edition. In dust jacket. $100-$125.

BURROUGHS, Edgar Rice. *Tarzan of the Apes.* Frontispiece. Red cloth. Chicago, 1914. First edition, first issue, with acorn device at foot of spine. In dust jacket. $2,000 and up. Also, $2,500 (A, 1977). Later, no acorn on spine. In dust jacket. $800-$1,200. (Burroughs specialists now question this long-established issue point, but the collector should try to have copies of each issue to be on the safe side.) Another issue: Advance review copy in pictorial wrappers. $1,000 and up. Author's first book. London, (1917). Orange-colored cloth. First English edition, with ads dated Autumn. In dust jacket. $150-$250.

BURROUGHS, Edgar Rice. *Tarzan the Untamed.* Illustrated. Cloth. Chicago, 1920. First edition. In dust jacket. $150-$200.

BURROUGHS, Edgar Rice. *Tarzan Triumphant.* Illustrated by Stanley Burroughs. Cloth. Tarzana, (1932). First edition. In dust jacket. $75-$100.

BURROUGHS, Edgar Rice. *Thuvia, Maid of Mars.* Illustrated. Cloth. Chicago, 1920. First edition. In dust jacket. $150-$200.

BURROUGHS, Edgar Rice. *The Warlord of Mars.* Frontispiece. Red cloth. Chicago, 1919. First edition. In dust jacket. $150-$200.

BURROUGHS, John. *Notes on Walt Whitman as Poet and Person.* Cloth, or blue wrappers. New York, 1867. First edition, first issue, leaves trimmed to 6 9/16 inches tall. Cloth: $100-$150. Wrappers: $75-$150. Later, 1867, clothbound, leaves 7¼ inches tall: $35-$40.

BURROUGHS, John. *Wake-Robin.* Green or terra-cotta cloth. New York, 1871. First edition. $75-$100.

BURROUGHS, John. *Winter Sunshine.* Cloth. New York, 1876. First edition. $40-$50.

BURROUGHS, William. See Lee, William.

BURROUGHS, William. *The Naked Lunch.* Green wrappers. Paris, (1959). Olympia Press. First edition, first binding. Without dust jacket. $65-$85. Later: Decorated wrappers. In dust jacket. $50-$75.

BURROUGHS, William. *The Soft Machine.* Printed wrappers. Paris, (1961). Traveller's Companion. First edition. In dust jacket. $35.

BURROUGHS, William. *The Ticket That Exploded.* Wrappers. Paris, (1962). Olympia Press. First edition. In dust jacket. $35.

BURROUGHS, William. *Time.* Illustrated by Brian Gysin. Wrappers. New York, 1965. First edition. One of 100 signed. $35-$45.

BURSON, William. *A Race for Liberty: or, My Capture, Imprisonment and Escape.* Cloth. Wellsville, 1867. $35-$40.

BURTON, Alfred. *The Adventures of Johnny Newcome in the Navy.* 16 colored plates by Rowlandson. Cloth. London, 1818. (By John Mitford.) First edition. $100-$150. (See John Mitford entry for third edition.)

BURTON, Harley True. *A History of the JA Ranch.* Portrait, map. Cloth. Austin, 1928. First edition. $250-$400.

BURTON, Maria Amparo. *The Squatter and the Don.* Cloth. San Francisco, 1885. First edition. $30-$40.

BURTON, Sir Richard F. *The City of the Saints and Across the Rocky Mountains to California.* 7 plates, folding map, folding plan. Cloth. London, 1861. First edition. $300-$400.

BURTON, Sir Richard F. *Falconry in the Valley of the Indus.* Frontispiece, other plates. Cloth. London, 1852. First edition $300-$350.

BURTON, Sir Richard F. *First Footsteps in East Africa; or, an Exploration of Harar.* With 2 maps and 4 colored plates. Cloth. London, 1856. First edition, first issue, with 24 pp. of ads dated March, 1856. $350-$450.

BURTON, Sir Richard F. *Goa, and the Blue Mountains.* Folding map, plates. Cloth. London, 1851. $200-$250.

BURTON, Sir Richard F. *The Gold-Mines of Midian and the Ruined Midianite Cities.* Folding map. Cloth. London, 1878. First edition. $200-$250.

BURTON, Sir Richard F. *The Lake Regions of Central Africa.* Folding map, 12 colored plates. 2 vols., cloth. London, 1860. First edition. $400-$600.

BURTON, Sir Richard F. *The Land of Midian (Revisited).* Folding map. 16 plates, 6 colored, 2 vols., cloth. London, 1879. First edition, first issue, with ads dated "9.78" $400-$500.

BURTON, Sir Richard F. *Personal Narrative of a Pilgrimage to El-Medinah and Meccah.* 16 plates (5 colored), 3 folding maps. 3 vols., cloth. London, 1855-56. First edition. $500-$750.

BURTON, Sir Richard F. *Vikram and the Vampire, or Tales of Hindu Devilry.* Illustrated, Pictorial cloth. London, 1870. First edition, first issue (black cloth). $150-$175.

BURTON, Sir Richard F. (translator). *The Book of the Thousand Nights and a Night.* (Arabian Nights). Illustrated by Valenti Angelo. 6 vols., boards, cowhide spines. New York, 1934. Limited Editions Club. Boxed. $150. Another Limited Editions Club edition: New York, 1954. Illustrated in color by Arthur Szyk. 4 vols. Boxed. $175-$200.

BURTON, Sir Richard F. (translator). *The Kasidah.* Illustrated by Valenti Angelo. Full leather. New York, 1937. Limited Editions Club. Boxed. $50-$60. See B., F.

BURTON, Robert. *The Anatomy of Melancholy.* Illustrated by E. McKnight Kauffer. 2 vols., half vellum and boards. London, 1925. Nonesuch Press. One of 750. $200-$250. Another issue: 2 vols. in one. One of 40 on vellum. $400-$500.

BURTON, W. *Josiah Wedgwood and His Pottery.* 32 color plates, 84 in black and white. Cloth. London, 1922. Limited Edition. In dust jacket. $150-$175.

BUTCHER, S. D. *S. D. Butcher's Pioneer History of Custer Country.* Illustrated. Cloth, or leather. Broken Bow, Neb., 1901. First edition. $100-$150.

BUTLER, Arthur G. *Lepidoptera Exotica.* 64 plates, 63 colored and one plain. Cloth. London, 1874. 64 plates, 63 colored and one plain. Cloth. London, 1874. First edition. $500-$750.

BUTLER, Arthur G. *Beautiful Foreign Finches and Their Treatment in Captivity.* 60 colored plates by F. W. Frohawk. Cloth. London, 1904. $150-$175.

BUTLER, Arthur G. *Foreign Finches in Captivity.* 60 hand-colored plates. Cloth. London. 1894. First edition. $400-$500. London, 1899. Illustrated with chromolithographs. Cloth. Second edition. $150-$175.

BUTLER, Ellis Parker. See *Pigs Is Pigs.*

BUTLER, Mann. *A History of the Commonwealth of Kentucky.* Portrait. Leather. Louisville, 1834. First edition. $200-$250.

BUTLER, Samuel. See *Erewhon.*

BUTLER, Samuel. *The Authoress of the Odyssey.* Maps and illustrations. Red cloth. London, 1897. First edition. $75-$100.

BUTLER, Samuel. *Erewhon Revisited Twenty Years Later.* Red cloth. London, 1901. First edition, with errata slip in preface. $150-$200. Lacking errata slip, $100-$150.

BUTLER, Samuel. *A First Year in Canterbury Settlement.* Folding map. Red cloth. London, 1863. First edition, with 32 pages of ads and light-brown end papers. $250-$300. Author's first book.

BUTLER, Samuel. *Life and Habit.* Brown cloth. London, 1878. First edition, with brown end papers. $50-$75.

BUTLER, Samuel. *The Note-Books of Samuel Butler.* Edited by H. F. Jones. Cloth. London, 1912. First edition. $50-$75.

BUTLER, Samuel. *Seven Sonnets and A Psalm of Montreal.* Unbound, or printed wrappers. Cambridge, 1904. First edition. In wrappers: $300-$400. Value in unbound state:? (Note: Lord Esher's copy, in printed wrappers and with a specially made folding case with his bookplate, brought $420 at auction in 1967.)

BUTLER, Samuel. *The Way of All Flesh.* Red cloth, gilt, top edges gilt. London, 1903. First edition. $300-$400. Also, $200 (A, 1974). New York, 1936. Limited Editions Club. 2 vols., leather. Boxed. $75-$100.

BUTTERFIELD, C. W. *An Historical Account of the Expedition Against Sandusky.* Portrait. Cloth. Cincinnati, 1873. First edition. $100-$150.

BUTTERFIELD, C. W. *History of the Discovery of the Northwest.* Cloth. Cincinnati, 1881. First edition. $150-$200.

BUTTERFIELD, C. W. *History of the Girtys.* Cloth. Cincinnati, 1890. First edition. $100-$150.

BUTTERFIELD, C. W. *History of Seneca County, Ohio.* Cloth. Sandusky, Ohio, 1848. First edition. $100-$150.

BUTTERWORTH, Benjamin J. *The Growth of Industrial Art.* 200 full-page plates. Folio, cloth. Washington, 1888. First edition. $200-$300. Washington, 1892. $150-$200.

BUTTERWORTH, Hezekiah. *Zig-Zag Journeys in Europe.* Boards. Boston, 1880. First edition. $50-$75.

BUTTS, Harriet N. Greene. *Bertha and Willie.* Printed wrappers. Hopedale, Mass., (about 1858). $25-$30.

BUTTS, Harriet N. Greene. *The Little Angel.* Woodcuts. Printed wrappers. Hopedale, (about 1852-58). $25-$30.

BUTTS, Harriet N. Greene. *"Out of Work."* Printed wrappers. Hopedale, (about 1858). $25-$30.

BUTTS, Harriet N. Greene. *"Playing Soldier."* Illustrated. Printed wrappers. Hopedale, (about 1852-58). $25-$30.

BUTTS, Mary. *Armed with Madness.* Drawings by Jean Cocteau. Blue cloth. London, 1928. First edition. One of 100. $225-$275.

BUTTS, Mary. *Ashe of Rings.* Wrappers. (Paris, 1925). First edition. Contact Editions. $75-$100. London, 1933. Cloth. First English edition. $40-$50.

BUTTS, Mary. *The Crystal Cabinet.* Cloth. London, (1937). First edition. $85-$150.

BUTTS, Mary. *Imaginary Letters.* Illustrated by Jean Cocteau. Cloth, paper label. Paris, 1928. $75-$85. Another issue: Boards. One of 250 numbered copies, with original copperplate engravings by Cocteau. $100-$150.

BUTTS, Mary. *The Macedonian.* Boards. London, 1933. First edition. $125-$150.

BUTTS, Mary. *Scenes From the Life of Cleopatra.* Cloth. London, (1935). First edition. In dust jacket. $175-$200.

BUTTS, Mary. *Several Occasions*. Cloth. London, (1932). First edition. In dust jacket. $85-$125.

BUTTS, Mary. *Speed the Plow and Other Stories*. Yellow cloth. London, 1923. First edition. $85. Author's first book.

BUXTON FORMAN, H. *Elizabeth Barrett Browning and Her Scarcer Books*. White boards. London, 1896. One of 30. $150-$175.

BYERS, William N., and Kellom, John H. *A Hand Book to the Gold Fields of Nebraska and Kansas*. Map. Blue pictorial printed wrappers. Chicago, 1859. First edition. $5,000-$6,000. Also, $3,700 (A, 1968).

BYNNER, Witter. See Morgan, Emanuel, and Knish, Anne.

BYNNER, Witter. *The New World*. Frontispiece. Decorated boards. San Francisco, 1919. One of 350. $35-$50.

BYNNER, Witter. *An Ode to Harvard and Other Poems*. Cloth, or leather. Boston, 1907. First edition. Cloth. $35-$50. Author's first book.

BYNNER, Witter. *The Persistence of Poetry*. Full red buckram. San Francisco, 1929. Book Club of California. One of 325 signed. Boxed. $75.

BYRD, Richard E. *Little America*. 74 maps and plates. Half vellum. New York, 1930. First edition. One of 1,000 signed. Boxed. $65-$100.

BYRD, Richard E. *Skyward*. 58 maps and plates. Boards. New York, 1928. First edition. One of 500 signed. $100.

BYRD, William (of Westover). *The Writings of "Colonel William Byrd of Westover in Virginia, Esqr."* Edited by John Spencer Bassett. Half vellum. New York, 1901. One of 500. $75-$100.

BYRNE, B. M. *Florida and Texas: A Series of Letters Comparing the Soil, Climate, and Productions of These States*. 40 pp., wrappers. Ocala, Fla., 1866. Third edition (of *Letters on the Climate, etc.*; see below). $250-$350.

BYRNE, B. M. *Letters on the Climate, Soils, and Productions of Florida*. 28 pp., wrappers. Jacksonville, 1851. Second edition. $300-$400. (Note: The first edition, for which I locate no reliable price data, was published in Ralston, Pa., according to Howes, who gives no date.)

BYRNE, Donn. *Brother Saul*. Brown batik boards, vellum spine. New York, (1927). First American edition. One of 500 signed. $40-$60.

BYRNE, Donn. *Crusade*. Japan vellum and cloth. Boston, 1928. First American edition. One of 365 signed. Boxed. $50-$60.

BYRNE, Donn. *Destiny Bay*. Half vellum. Boston, 1928. First edition with "Published September, 1928" on copyright page. $40-$60.

BYRNE, Donn. *Field of Honor*. Brown batik boards, vellum spine. New York, (1929). One of 500 large paper copies, signed by Dorothea Donn-Byrne (issued after the first trade edition). $40-$60.

BYRNE, Donn. *The Foolish Matrons*. Green cloth. New York, (1920). First edition, first issue, with "I-U" on copyright page. $50-$60.

BYRNE, Donn. *Messer Marco Polo*. Illustrated by C. B. Falls. Rust-colored cloth. New York, 1921. First edition, first printing, with conjugate of pages 145-146 used as terminal lining paper and with perfect type in the word "of" in the last line of page 10 and "forgettng" for "forgetting" in the third line of page 39. In dust jacket. $80-$125.

BYRNE, Donn. *Stories Without Women*. Frontispiece. Red ribbed cloth. New York, 1915. First edition. $100-$125. Author's first book.

BYRNE, Donn. *The Strangers' Banquet.* Cloth. New York, (1919). First edition, with "M-T" on copyright page. In dust jacket. $35-$40.

BYRON, George Gordon Noel, Lord. See Hobhouse, J.C.; Hornem, Horace. Also see *The Age of Bronze; Beppo; The Curse of Minerva; Don Juan; English Bards and Scotch Reviewers; Fugitive Pieces; Lara, a Tale; Monody on the Death of the Right Honorable R. B. Sheridan; Ode to Napoleon Buonaparte; Poems on Various Occasions; The Siege of Corinth.*

BYRON, George Gordon Noel, Lord. *The Bride of Abydos.* 72 pp., drab wrappers. London, 1813. First edition, first issue, with errata slip and with only 20 lines on page 47. $250 and up. Second issue, without errata slip and with 22 lines on page 47. $200 and up.

BYRON, George Gordon Noel, Lord. *Childe Harold's Pilgrimage: Canto the Third.* 79 pp., plain wrappers. London, 1816. First edition. (See note in preceding entry.)

BYRON, George Gordon Noel, Lord. *Childe Harold's Pilgrimage: Canto the Fourth.* Drab boards, white label. London, 1818. First edition, first issue, with 6-line errata list on page 236 and with page 155 ending with "the impressions of," etc. (See preceding entries.)

BYRON, George Gordon Noel, Lord. *Childe Harold's Pilgrimage: A Romaunt.* (Containing Cantos I and II.) Drab boards, white spine label. London, 1812. First edition, first issue; with "Written beneath a Picture of J-V-D" on page 189 ("of J-V-D" omitted later). (Note: The three volumes of *Childe Harold's Pilgrimage* are almost always offered for sale as a set, although there are exceptions. They are listed separately here for bibliographical identification. Fine sets in boards and wrappers as issued are rare, and the last major offerings were in the 1940's, when prices as high as $225 and $300 were realized at auction. The retail value of a complete set in original bindings and in fine condition has not been tested in today's market, so far as I have determined. My own estimate: $5,000 and up. The listings of the three volumes, and their varying condition, in the auction records are too extensive to record here. Consult the annual volumes—not the 5-year indexes—of *American Book-Prices Current* for help with particular problems.)

BYRON, George Gordon Noel, Lord. *The Corsair: A Tale.* Plain drab wrappers. London, 1814. First edition, first issue, with 100 pages. $600-$800, possibly more. Second issue, 108 pages. $500 and up.

BYRON, George Gordon Noel, Lord. *The Deformed Transformed.* Drab wrappers. London, 1824. First edition. $300-$400, possibly more.

BYRON, George Gordon Noel, Lord. *Fare Thee Well! A Poem.* (No regular title page.) 4 pp. No place, (1816). First edition. $6,000 at auction in London in 1972. (Only a few copies known.)

BYRON, George Gordon Noel, Lord. *The Giaour: A Fragment of a Turkish Tale.* 41 pp., drab wrappers. London, 1813. First edition, on Whatman paper watermarked 1809-10. $500 and up.

BYRON, George Gordon Noel, Lord. *Hebrew Melodies.* Wrappers. London, 1815. First edition, first issue, with ad for *Jacqueline* on reverse of signature E4. $500 and up. Also, $225 (A, 1970). Second issue, without *Jacqueline* ad. $200 and up.

BYRON, George Gordon Noel, Lord. *Hours of Idleness.* Drab boards. Newark, England, 1807. First edition, first issue, with line 2 of page 22 reading "Those tissues of fancy, etc." Second issue, with line 2 of page 22 reading "Those tissues of falsehood, etc." Either issue, $1,000 and up, possibly more. Also, a worn copy in half calf, $375 (A, 1974).

BYRON, George Gordon Noel, Lord. *The Island, or Christian and His Comrades.* Plain drab wrappers. London, 1823. First edition, with paper watermarked 1822. $1,000 and up. Also, $700 (A, 1974).

BYRON, George Gordon Noel. Lord. *The Lament of Tasso.* 19 pp., stitched, without wrappers. London, 1817. First edition. $500 and up.

BYRON, George Gordon Noel, Lord. *Letter to [John Murray] on the Rev. W. L. Bowles'*

*Strictures on the Life of Pope.* 55 pp., drab wrappers. London, 1821. First edition, first issue, without 1819 watermark on 4 leaves before ads. $500 and up. Second issue, with the watermark. Rebound in morocco, original covers preserved, $168 (A, 1968).

BYRON, George Gordon Noel, Lord. *Manfred, a Dramatic Poem.* 80 pp., drab wrappers, without lettering or labels. London, 1817. First edition, first issue, without quotation on title page and with printer's imprint in 2 lines on back of title page. $500 and up. Second issue, with printer's imprint in one line. $150-$200. Third issue, with Hamlet quotation on title page. $100-$150. London, 1929. Fanfrolico Press. Full vellum. One of 30 on vellum. $300-$400. Another issue: Half parchment. One of 550. $50-$75.

BYRON, George Gordon Noel, Lord. *Marino Faliero, Doge of Venice.* Drab boards. London, 1821. First edition, first issue, with speech on page 151 beginning "What crimes?" $500 and up. Also, $200 (A, 1975). Second issue, with speech on page 151 beginning "His Crimes!" $300 and up.

BYRON, George Gordon Noel, Lord. *Mazeppa: A Poem.* Plain drab wrappers. London, 1819. First edition, first issue, with imprint on page 70. $300-$350. Second issue, with imprint on back of page 71. $150-$200.

BYRON, George Gordon Noel, Lord. *The Parliamentary Speeches of Lord Byron.* Drab wrappers. London, 1824. First edition. $750 and up. Also, $250 (A, 1970).

BYRON, George Gordon Noel, Lord. *Poems.* Boards, or wrappers (?). London, 1816. First edition, first issue, with leaf of "Notes" and 2 ad leaves. $400-$600. Also, "wrappers" (original?), $77 (A, 1976).

BYRON, George Gordon Noel, Lord. *The Prisoner of Chillon, and Other Poems.* Drab wrappers. London, 1816. First edition, first issue, with recto of signature E8 blank. $500 and up. (London, 1865). Day & Son. 20 plates. $100-$150. Also, spine defective, $150 (A, 1974).

BYRON, George Gordon Noel, Lord. *Sardanapalus, The Two Foscari, Cain.* Boards, paper label on spine. London, 1821. First edition, with 10 pages of ads at front. $500-$750. Also, "rubbed," $90 (A, 1975).

BYRON, George Gordon Noel, Lord. *Werner: A Tragedy.* Plain drab wrappers. London, 1823. First edition, first issue, with ad for this book on page 188. $500-$750. Second issue, without ad for this book. $300 and up. Also, $100 (A, 1971).

# C

C.3.3. *The Ballad of Reading Gaol.* Cinnamon-colored cloth, vellum spine. London. (1898). (By Oscar Wilde.) First edition. One of 30 on Japanese vellum. $1,000-$1,250. Also, presentation copy. $850 (A, 1973). Another issue: Two toned cloth. One of 800. In plain dust jacket. $600-$800. Lacking jacket, $300-$450. London, 1898. Cloth. Second edition. $35-$50. London, 1898. Cloth. Third edition (bearing Wilde's name). One of 99 signed. $200-$250. London, 1899. Cloth. Pirated edition. $50. London, (1925). Woodcuts by Hans Masereel. Half morocco. One of 50. $85-$100. New York, 1937. Limited Editions Club. Calf. Boxed. $80-$100.

CABALLERIA Y COLLELL, Juan. *History of the City of Santa Barbara from Its Discovery to Our Own Days.* Translated by Edmund Burke. Plate, facsimile. 111 pp., wrappers. Santa Barbara, 1892. First edition. $150-$200.

CABELL, James Branch. *Ballades from the Hidden Way.* Boards. New York, 1928. First edition. One of 839 signed. $75-$100. Another issue: One of 8 on gray paper. $150-$200. Also, inscribed $200 (A,1975).

CABELL, James Branch. *Branchiana.* Green cloth. Richmond, Va., (1907). First edition. $400-$500. (147 copies issued). According to Nelson Bond, a Cabell bibliographer, there were 10 copies in red, not green, cloth. His valuation: $1,000.

CABELL, James Branch. *Chivalry.* Illustrated by Howard Pyle and others. Red cloth. New York, 1909. First edition. In printed glassine dust jacket. Boxed. $75-125.

CABELL, James Branch. *The Eagle's Shadow.* Red cloth. New York, 1904. First edition, first state, with dedication "M. L. P. B." and frontispiece of seated figure. $150-$200. Author's first book.

CABELL, James Branch. *Gallantry.* Illustrated in color by Howard Pyle. Decorated cloth, gilt top. New York, 1907. First edition, first binding, silver-gray cloth, stamped with white, silver, and gold lettering. In printed glassine dust jacket. Boxed. $75-100.

CABELL, (James) Branch. *Jurgen.* Reddish-brown cloth. New York, 1919. First edition, first state, with line rules on page 144 intact. In dust jacket. $200 and up. Lacking jacket, $50 and up. London, 1921. Illustrated by Frank C. Pape. Cloth. First English edition. $40-$60. London, 1949. Golden Cockerel Press. Half morocco. One of 500. $150. Another issue: One of 100 specially bound and with an extra engraving. $300-$400.

CABELL, James Branch. *The Line of Love.* Illustrated in color by Howard Pyle. Decorated green cloth, pictorial label. New York, 1905. First edition, first state, binding stamped with white and gold lettering. In glassine dust jacket. $75-150.

CABELL, James Branch. *The Majors and Their Marriages.* Wrappers or cloth. Richmond. (1915). First edition. Either issue: $500 and up.

CABELL, James Branch. *The Music from Behind the Moon.* 8 engravings. Boards. New York, 1926. First edition. In glassine dust jacket and slipcase. $50-$75.

CABELL, (James) Branch. *The Rivet in Grandfather's Neck.* Cloth. New York, 1915. First edition. In dust jacket. Boxed. $50.

CABELL, (James) Branch. *Sonnets from Antan.* Half cloth. New York, 1929. Grabhorn printing. First edition. One of 718 signed. $100-$125.

CABELL, James Branch. *The Way of Ecben.* Boards. New York, 1929. First edition. One of 850 on large paper, signed. In glassine dust jacket. Boxed. $75-$100.

CABEZA DE VACA, Álvar Núñez. *The Narrative of Álvar Núñez Cabeza de Vaca*. Translated by Buckingham Smith. 8 maps. Cloth. Washington, 1851. One of 110. $500-$850. New York, 1871. Three-quarters morocco. One of 100. $250-$350. (For another issue, under another title, see following entry.)

CABEZA DE VACA, Álvar Núñez. *Relation . . . of What Befel the Armament in the Indias Whither Pamphilo de Narvaez Went for Governor, etc.* Hand decorations in color by Valenti Angelo. Boards. San Francisco, 1929. Grabhorn printing. One of 300. Boxed. $250-$300.

*CABINET of Natural History and American Rural Sports (The)*. 3 vols., half calf. Philadelphia, 1830-32-33. First book edition. (Published by J. and T. Doughty. Includes 29 monthly parts [dated 1830 to 1834]; 57 plates, 54 colored.) $2,000-$4,000. Vols. 1 and 2 only, lacking 9 plates, $800 (A,1975). (Sets in parts are excessively rare.)

*CABINET-MAKER'S Assistant (The); A Series of Original Designs for Modern Furniture.* Plates. Folio, half calf. Glasgow, 1853. (By P. Thompson.) $100-$125.

CABLE, George W. *The Creoles of Louisiana*. Illustrated. Maroon pictorial cloth. New York, 1884. First edition. $50-$75.

CABLE, George W. *The Grandissimes*. Cloth. New York, 1880. First edition. $30-$40. New York, 1899. Illustrated. Vellum. One of 204. $50.

CABLE, George W. *Old Creole Days*. Decorated red, brown, or blue cloth. New York, 1879. First edition, first state, with no ads at back. $200-$250. Second state with ads. $100 and up. Author's first book. New York, 1897. Vellum. One of 204. $50-$75. New York, 1943. Limited Editions Club. Boxed. $50-$60.

CABLE, George W. *The Southern Struggle for Pure Government*. Wrappers. Boston, 1890. First edition. $75-$100.

CABLE, George W. *Strange True Stories of Louisiana*. Illustrated. Pictorial cloth, paper label. New York, 1889. First edition. $50-$60.

CAESAR, Julius. *Commentaries*. Translated by Somerset de Chair. Woodcuts by Clifford Webb. Buckram. London, 1951. Golden Cockerel Press. One of 320. $150-$175. Another issue: One of 70 specially bound. $600-$800.

CAIN, James. *The Postman Always Rings Twice*. Cloth. New York. 1934. First edition. In dust jacket. $25-$35.

CAIN, James M. *Love's Lovely Counterfeit*. Cloth. New York, 1942. First edition. In dust jacket. $25-$35.

CAIN, James M. *Our Government*. Cloth. New York, 1930. First edition. In dust jacket. $25-$30. Author's first book.

CAIN, James M. *Serenade*. Black cloth. New York, 1937. First edition. In dust jacket. $25-$35.

*CALAVAR: or, The Knight of the Conquest*. 2 vols., purple cloth, printed paper labels. Philadelphia, 1834. (By Robert Montgomery Bird.) First edition. $200-$250. Author's first book. Philadelphia, 1847. 2 vols., printed wrappers. Revised edition. $100-$150.

CALDWELL, Erskine. *American Earth*. Brown cloth. New York, 1931. First edition, with code letter "A" on copyright page. In dust jacket. $25-$35.

CALDWELL, Erskine. *The Bastard*. Illustrated. Cloth. New York, (1929). First edition. One of 200 signed (in an edition of 1,100 numbered copies). $150-$300. Also, $200 (A,1975). Author's first book.

CALDWELL, Erskine. *God's Little Acre*. Black cloth. New York, 1933. First edition. In dust jacket. $50-$75.

CALDWELL, Erskine. *Journeyman*. Red buckram, paper band. New York, 1935. First edition. One of 1,475. In glassine dust jacket. Boxed. $40-$50.

CALDWELL, Erskine. *Kneel to the Rising Sun and Other Stories.* Reddish-brown buckram, labels, top edges gilt. New York, 1935. First edition. One of 300 signed. Boxed. $35-$50. Trade edition: Cloth. In dust jacket. $15-$20.

CALDWELL, Erskine. *Mama's Little Girl.* 2 drawings by Alfred Morang. Printed wrappers. Mount Vernon, Me., 1932. One of 75. $100-$200.

CALDWELL, Erskine. *A Message for Genevieve.* Drawing by Alfred Morang. Printed wrappers. Mount Vernon, 1933. First edition. One of 100 signed. $75-$150.

CALDWELL, Erskine, *Poor Fool.* Illustrated. Blue buckram. New York, 1930. First edition. One of 1,000. $75-$125.

CALDWELL, Erskine. *Southways.* Gray-blue cloth. New York, 1938. First edition. In dust jacket. $30-$40.

CALDWELL, Erskine. *Tenant Farmer.* Green wrappers. New York, (1935). First edition. $75.

CALDWELL, Erskine. *Tobacco Road.* Cloth. New York, 1932. First edition, with code letter "A" on copyright page. In dust jacket. $60-$80.

CALDWELL, Erskine. *We Are the Living.* Cloth. New York, 1933. One of 250 signed. In glassine dust jacket. Boxed. $50-$60.

CALDWELL, Erskine, and Bourke-White, Margaret. *Say, Is This the U.S.A.* Illustrated. Cloth. New York, (1941). First edition. In dust jacket. $75.

CALDWELL, J. A. *History of Belmont and Jefferson Counties, Ohio.* Half leather. Wheeling, Ohio, 1880. $100-$200.

CALDWELL, J. F. J. *History of a Brigade of South Carolinians.* Cloth. Philadelphia, 1866. First edition. $125-$150.

CALHOUN, James S. *Official Correspondence of James S. Calhoun While Indian Agent at Santa Fe.* Illustrated, 4 maps. Cloth. Washington, 1915. First edition. $75-$100.

*CALIFORNIA Illustrated.* By a Returned Californian. 48 plates. Cloth. New York, 1852. (By J.M. Letts.) First edition, first issue, anonymous. $150-$200. Later issue, same year, author named: $100-150.

*CALIFORNIA Sketches, with Recollections of the Gold Mines.* Half leather. Albany, 1850. (By Leonard Kip.) First edition. $750.

CALISHER, Hortense. *In the Absence of Angels.* Cloth. Boston, 1951. First edition. In dust jacket. $50-$75. Author's first book.

CALL, Richard Ellsworth. *The Life and Writings of Rafinesque.* 2 plates, 3 facsimiles. 227 pp., wrappers. Louisville, 1895. First edition. $100-$150.

CALLAGHAN, Morley. *No Man's Meat.* Boards and cloth, paper label. Paris, 1931. First edition. One of 525 signed. In tissue dust jacket. Boxed. $100-$150. Also, $75 (A, 1975).

CALLAGHAN, Morley. *Strange Fugitive.* Cloth. New York, 1928. First edition. In dust jacket. $50-$60.

CALVERT, Frederick. *The Isle of Wight Illustrated.* Sepia lithograph frontispiece, colored map, 20 colored acquatint plates. Cloth. London, 1846. $350-$500.

·CALVERT, George C. *A Defence of the Dilettante.* San Francisco, 1919. Grabhorn printing. One of 200. $277 (A, 1974).

*CAMBRIDGE History of British Foreign Policy, 1783-1919.* Edited by Sir A. W. Ward and G. P. Gooch. 3 vols., cloth. London, 1922-23. $150-$200.

CAMERON, Julia M. *Victorian Photographs of Famous Men and Fair Women.* Boards and vellum. London, 1926. First edition. One of 450. $300-$450. New York, 1926. Boards and cloth. First American edition. One of 250. $250-$400. (Note: Contains an introduction by Virginia Woolf.)

CAMPBELL, Alexander, and Owen, Robert. *Debate on the Evidence of Christianity*. 2 vols. in one, calf. Bethany, Va., 1829. First edition. $100-$135.

CAMPBELL, Alexander, and Rice, N. L. *A Debate . . . on the Action, Subject, Design and Administration of Christian Baptism*. Boards. Lexington, Ky., 1844. First edition. $75-$125.

CAMPBELL, Archibald. *A Voyage Around the World*. Illustrated, map in color. Boards. Edinburgh, 1816. First edition. $500-$600. Another issue: 2 vols., calf. $300-$350.

CAMPBELL, J. *Idaho and Montana Gold Regions*. Map. Half morocco. Chicago, 1865. Second edition. $2,000-$2,500.

CAMPBELL, J. L. *The Great Agricultural & Mineral West*. Folding ad leaf and map. Printed wrappers. Chicago, 1866. "Third Annual Edition." (Second revised edition). $2,000-$2,500.

CAMPBELL, Patrick. *Travels in the Interior Inhabited Parts of North America*. 3 plates. Cloth. Toronto, 1937. First American edition. One of 550. $100-$150.

CAMPBELL, Roy. *Adamastor: Poems*. Cloth. London, 1930. First edition. One of 90 signed. $150-$200. Trade edition: In dust jacket. $25-$30. Capetown, 1950. New illustrated edition. $40-$60.

CAMPBELL, Roy. *Broken Record*. Cloth. London, 1934. First edition. In dust jacket. $35. Another issue: Vellum. One of 50 signed. $150-$200. Also, $103 (A, 1974).

CAMPBELL, Roy. *Choosing a Mast*. Illustrated by Barnett Freedman. Boards. London, 1931. First edition. One of 300 signed. $50-$75.

CAMPBELL, Roy. *The Flaming Terrapin*. Boards, cloth spine, paper label. London. 1924. First edition. In dust jacket. $50-$75. Author's first book.

CAMPBELL, Roy. *Flowering Reeds: Poems*. Cloth. London, 1933. First edition. One of 69 signed. $100-$150. Trade edition: Cloth. In dust jacket. $20-$30.

CAMPBELL, Roy. *The Georgiad*. Boards and cloth. London, 1931. Alcuin Press. One of 150 signed. $75-$100. Another issue: Vellum. One of 20 on goatskin parchment paper, signed. $200.

CAMPBELL, Roy. *The Gum Trees*. Illustrated by David Jones. Boards. London, 1930. First edition. One of 400 signed. $75-$100.

CAMPBELL, Roy. *Mithraic Emblems*. Cloth. London, 1936. First edition. One of 30 signed. $300-$400.

CAMPBELL, Roy. *Poems*. Decorated boards and morocco. Paris. 1930. Hours Press. First edition. One of 200 signed. $100-$150.

CAMPBELL, Roy. *Pomegranates*. Illustrated by James Boswell. Cloth. London, 1932. First edition. One of 99 signed. In glassine dust jacket. $100-$200.

CAMPBELL, Roy. *The Wayzgoose: A South African Satire*. Brown cloth. London, 1928. First edition. $25-$35.

CAMPE, M. *Polar Scenes*. Woodcut illustrations. Contemporary boards and leather. New York, (before 1827). $100.

CAMUS, Albert. *The Fall*. Folio, boards. (Kentfield, Calif., 1966.) Allen Press. One of 140. $325-$350.

CANFIELD, Chauncey L. (editor). *The Diary of a Forty-Niner*. Colored map. Pictorial boards. San Francisco, 1906. First edition. $35-$50.

CANNON, George Q. *Writings from the "Western Standard," Published in San Francisco.* Full morocco. Liverpool, 1864. First edition. $25-$35.

CANNON, J. P. *Inside of Rebeldom: The Daily Life of a Private in the Confederate Army.* Cloth. Washington, 1900. $125.

CANOVA, Andrew P. *Life and Adventures in South Florida.* 4 plates. Printed light-green wrappers. Palatka, Fla., 1885. First edition. $200-$250.

CAPOTE, Truman. *Breakfast at Tiffany's.* Yellow cloth. New York, (1958). First edition. In dust jacket. $35-$50.

CAPOTE, Truman. *A Christmas Memory.* Cloth. New York, (1966). First edition. One of 600 signed. Boxed. $75-$100.

CAPOTE, Truman. *In Cold Blood.* Black cloth. New York, (1965). First edition, first printing. One of 500 signed. In glassine dust jacket. Boxed. $75-$100. Trade edition: Cloth. In dust jacket. $25-$35. Advance copy, in wrappers: $75-$125.

CAPOTE, Truman. *The Grass Harp: A Play.* Boards. New York, (1952). First edition. In dust jacket. $60-$70.

CAPOTE, Truman. *Local Color.* Illustrated. Boards and cloth. New York, (1950). First edition. In dust jacket. $75-$125. London, (1950). Red leather. First English edition. One of 200. $100-$150.

CAPOTE, Truman. *Observations.* Photographs by Avedon. Folio, boards. New York, (1959). First edition. Boxed. $100-$150.

CAPOTE, Truman. *Other Voices, Other Rooms.* Cloth. New York, (1948). First edition. In dust jacket. $100-$125. Author's first book.

CAPOTE, Truman. *The Thanksgiving Visitor.* Cloth. New York, (1968). First edition. One of 300 signed. Boxed. $75-$100.

CAPOTE, Truman. *A Tree of Night and Other Stories.* Cloth. New York, (1949). First edition. In dust jacket. $50-$60.

CAPRON, Elisha S. *History of California.* Colored map. Cloth. Boston, 1854. First edition. $75-$100.

*CAPT. SMITH and Princess Pocahontas: An Indian Tale.* Boards. Philadelphia, 1805. (By John Davis.) First edition, first issue, with undated copyright notice. $2,000.

CARELESS, John. *The Old English 'Squire: A Poem in Ten Cantos.* 24 colored plates. Cloth. London, 1821. (By William A. Chatto.) First edition. $300. Another issue: Large paper. $400-$450.

CAREY, C. H. *History of Oregon.* Maps. Cloth. Chicago, 1922. Author's edition. $50-$75.

CAREY, David. *Life in Paris.* Illustrated by George Cruikshank. Full leather. London, 1822. First edition. $350-$500.

*CARL Werner, An Imaginative Story.* 2 vols., cloth. New York, 1838. (By William Gilmore Simms.) First edition. $200-$250.

CARLETON, William M. *Fax: A Campaign Poem.* Illustrated. Printed wrappers. Chicago, 1868. First edition. $500. Author's first book.

CARLISLE, Bill. *Bill Carlisle, Lone Bandit: An Autobiography.* Charles M. Russell illustrations. Fabrikoid. Pasadena, (1946). De luxe limited edition, signed. In dust jacket. $75-$100.

CARLSON, Anton J. *The Control of Hunger in Health and Disease.* Cloth. Chicago, (1916). First edition. $100-$150.

CARLTON, Robert. *The New Purchase: or, Seven and a Half Years in the Far West.* 2 vols., boards. New York, 1843. (By Baynard R. Hall.) First edition. $100-$150.

CARLYLE, Thomas. See *Sartor Resartus.*

CARLYLE, Thomas. *The French Revolution.* 3 vols., boards and cloth. London, 1837. First edition, first issue, with 2 pages of ads at end of Vol. 2. $350-$450. London, 1910. Illustrated. 2 vols., half vellum. One of 150 on large paper. $150-$200. New York, 1956. Limited Editions Club. Boxed. $85-$100.

CARLYLE, Thomas. *Occasional Discourse on the Nigger Question.* Wrappers. London, 1853. First edition. $200-$300.

CARLYLE, Thomas. *On Heroes, Hero-Worship, & the Heroic in History: Six Lectures.* Purple cloth. London, 1841. First edition. $200-$250. Also, rebound in morocco by the Doves Bindery (dated 1893), $375 (A, 1976).

CARLYLE, Thomas. *Past and Present.* Cloth. London, 1843. First edition. $100-$125.

CARLYLE, Thomas. *Shooting Niagara: and After?* Printed green wrappers. London, 1867. First edition. $100-$150.

CARMAN, Bliss. See Carmen [sic], Bliss; Lighthall, William D.

CARMAN, Bliss. *The Gate of Peace: A Poem.* Boards and cloth. New York, 1907. One of 112 signed. $75-$100. (Note: All except 24 destroyed by fire, says Johnson.)

CARMAN, Bliss. *Poems.* 2 vols., half leather. New York, 1904. First edition. One of 500 signed. $100-$150. Boston, 1905. 2 vols., boards. One of 500 signed. $100-$150.

CARMAN, Bliss. *The Vengeance of Noel Brassard.* Boards and cloth. Cambridge, 1919 (actually 1899). First edition, with misdated title page reading "MDCCCCXIX." $100-$150.

CARMAN, Bliss, and Hovey, Richard. *Songs from Vagabondia.* Boards. Boston, 1894. First edition. Limited Edition. $50-$60.

CARMEN, Bliss. *Low Tide on Grand Pre.* 13 pp., wrappers. Toronto, (1889? 1890?). (By Bliss Carman.) First edition (pirated). $150-$200. Author's first book, with his name misspelled. New York, 1893. Lavender cloth. First United States edition. $50.

CARNEVALI, Emanuel. *A Hurried Man.* Wrappers. Paris, (1925). Contact Editions. First edition. $125-$150.

*CAROLINE Tracy: The Spring Street Milliner's Apprentice.* Illustrated. Half leather. New York, 1849. First edition. $50-$75.

CARR, Alice. *North Italian Folk.* Hand-colored illustrations by Randolph Caldecott. Boards. London, 1878. First edition. One of 250. $150-$200.

CARR, John. *Early Times in Middle Tennessee.* Cloth. Nashville, 1857. First edition. $150-$200.

CARR, John. *Pioneer Days in California.* Portrait. Cloth. Eureka, Calif., 1891. First edition. $100-$125. Also, $60 (A, 1976).

CARR, Spencer. *A Brief Sketch of La Crosse, Wisconsin.* 28 pp., sewed. La Crosse, 1854. First edition. $250-$300. Also, $130 (A, 1967).

CARRINGTON, Mrs. Henry B. See *Ab-Sa-Ra-Ka, Home of the Crows.*

CARRINGTON, John Bodman, and Hughes, George Ravensworth. *The Plate of the Worshipful Company of Goldsmiths.* Illustrated. Red cloth. Oxford, 1926. $75-$100.

CARROLL, H. Bailey. *The Texan Santa Fe Trail.* Illustrated. Cloth. Canyon, Tex., 1951. Boxed. $75-$100.

CARROLL, H. Bailey, and Haggard, J. V. (translators). *Three New Mexico Chronicles.* Cloth. Albuquerque, 1942. $50-$75.

CARROLL, Lewis. See Dodgson, Charles L.; Spavery.

CARROLL, Lewis. *Alice's Adventures in Wonderland.* 42 illustrations by John Tenniel. Red cloth. London, 1865. (By Charles L. Dodgson.) First edition (suppressed by the author). Very rare in original binding. Modern sales records range from $2,464 for a copy "badly worn, leaves stained, etc.," (A, 1961) and $2,375 (A, 1971), for a worn and repaired copy, to $11,760 (A, 1965) and $16,000 (A, 1962) for presentation copies inscribed by the author. The rebound Jerome Kern copy brought $10,000 in 1929. (Because of the extreme rarity of the original edition, the collecting fraternity in general has come to accept the New York edition of 1866—the first American edition—as the "first edition," which it, in fact, is, since it consists of the sheets of the suppressed London first edition with a new title page displaying the New York imprint of its publisher, Appleton.) New York, 1866. Red cloth. First American edition (and *second issue* of the first edition). $800-$1,000. Also, worn and with front free end paper loose, $350 (A, 1974); $700 (A, 1970). London, 1866. Red cloth. Second edition (and first published English edition). $1,000 and up. Also, "soiled," $750 (A, 1975). (Princess Beatrice's vellum-bound copy was sold for $784 at auction in 1959 and for $2,160 when re-offered in 1969.) Boston, 1869. Green cloth. First edition printed in America. $300-$400. London, 1907. Illustrated by Arthur Rackham. Cloth. One of 1,130 signed by Rackham. $400-$500. Also, with an original Rackham watercolor, $1,300 (A, 1974). New York, (1907). Half cloth. One of 550. $300-$400. London, 1914. Tenniel illustrations. Vellum. One of 12 copies on vellum. $1,250-$1,500. Ordinary issue: One of 1,000. $75-$100. New York, 1932. Limited Editions Club. Signed by Alice Hargreaves, the original "Alice." $500-$650. New York, 1969. Salvador Dali illustrations. Folio, loose signatures in folder and leather-backed case. Limited edition, signed by Dali. $800-$1,200.

CARROLL, Lewis. *Alice's Adventures Under Ground.* 37 illustrations by the author. Red cloth, gilt edges. London, 1886. (By Charles L. Dodgson.) First edition. $100-$150. (Note: This is a facsimile of the original manuscript from which *Alice's Adventures in Wonderland* was developed.)

CARROLL, Lewis. *Feeding the Mind.* Gray boards and cloth. London, 1907. (By Charles L. Dodgson.) First edition. $40-$60.

CARROLL, Lewis. *The Game of Logic.* With envelope containing 9 counters and board diagram. Cloth. London, 1886. (By Charles L. Dodgson.) First (private) edition. $750-$1,000. Only a few copies known. London, 1887. Second edition. $100-$200. (Listed incorrectly in many auction records as the first edition.)

CARROLL, Lewis. *The Hunting of the Snark.* Illustrated by Henry Holiday. Pictorial cloth, gilt edges. London, 1876. (By Charles L. Dodgson.) First edition. In dust jacket. $250. Lacking jacket, $100-$150. Presentation copy: Red and gold cloth. With leaflet "An Easter Greeting to Every Child who Loves 'Alice.'" $425 (A, 1974).

CARROLL, Lewis. *Phantasmagoria and Other Poems.* Blue cloth. London, 1869. (By Charles L. Dodgson.) First edition. $200-$300.

CARROLL, Lewis. *Rhyme? and Reason?* Illustrated by A. B. Frost and Henry Holiday. Green cloth. London, 1883. (By Charles L. Dodgson.) First edition. $100-$150.

CARROLL, Lewis. *Sylvie and Bruno.* Illustrated by Harry Furniss. Cloth. London, 1889. (By Charles L. Dodgson.) First edition. In dust jacket. $100-$125. Lacking jacket, $65-$85.

CARROLL, Lewis. *Sylvie and Bruno Concluded.* Illustrated by Harry Furniss. Cloth. London, 1893. (By Charles L. Dodgson.) First edition. $65-$85. (Note: This title and the preceding one frequently are sold as a set. Most recent auction record for a set: $140 in the 1976 season.)

CARROLL, Lewis. *A Tangled Tale.* Illustrated by A. B. Frost. Pictorial cloth. London, 1885. (By Charles L. Dodgson.) First edition. $75-$125.

CARROLL, Lewis. *Three Sunsets and Other Poems.* Frontispiece and other illustrations. Cloth. London, 1898. First edition. $100-$150.

CARROLL, Lewis. *Through the Looking-Glass, and What Alice Found There.* 50 illustrations by John Tenniel. Red cloth. London, 1872. (By Charles L. Dodgson.) First edition, first issue, with "wade" on page 21. $300-$400. Boston, 1872. Cloth. First American edition. $60-$80. New York, 1931. Cheshire House. Cloth. $50. New York, 1935. Limited Editions Club. Signed by Alice Hargreaves. Boxed, $400-$500. Mount Vernon, N.Y., 1935. Illustrated. Leather. $50-$75.

CARRUTH, (Fred) Hayden. *The Voyage of the Rattletrap*. Illustrated by H. M. Wilder. Pictorial cloth. New York, 1897. First edition. $35-$50.

CARRYL, Charles E. *Davy and the Goblin*. Illustrated. Pictorial brown cloth. Boston, 1886. First edition, first issue, with "Korea" misspelled in terminal ad. $150-$200. Second issue, error corrected. $100.

CARSON, Christopher. See Grant, Blanche C.

CARSON, James H. *Early Recollections of the Mines, and a Description of the Great Tulare Valley*. Folding map. 64 pp., printed wrappers (with cover title reading "*Second Edition. Life in California, etc.*"). Stockton, Calif., 1852. First edition (in book form; earlier appearance was in the San Joaquin *Republican*). $2,000 and up. Also, spine repaired, $1,500 (A, 1968); lacking maps, $475 (A, 1973 and 1954). Oakland, 1950. 2 maps. One of 750. Reprint edition. $50. (See next entry.)

CARSON, James H. *Life in California*. Map. Cloth. Tarrytown, N.Y., 1931. (Reprint of *Early Recollections of the Mines*.) $50.

CARSTARPHEN, J. E. *My Trip to California in '49*. 8 pp., wrappers. (Louisiana, Mo., 1914.) Limited edition. $75-$150.

CARTER, John, and Pollard, Graham. *An Enquiry into the Nature of Certain 19th Century Pamphlets*. 4 plates. Cloth. London, 1934. First edition. In dust jacket. $100-$125.

CARTER, Robert G. *Massacre of Salt Creek Prairie and the Cow-boy's Verdict*. 48 pp., wrappers. Washington, 1919. First edition. $300.

CARTER, Robert G. *The Old Sergeant's Story: Winning the West from the Indians and Badmen in 1870 to 1876*. Portrait, plates. Cloth. New York, 1926. First edition. $75-$150.

CARTER, Robert G. *On the Border with Mackenzie*. 3 portraits. Cloth. Washington, (1935). First edition. $400-$500.

CARTER, Robert G. *On the Trail of Deserters*. Printed wrappers. Washington, 1920. One of 250. $150-$200.

CARTER, Robert G. *Pursuit of Kicking Bird: A Compaign in the Texas "Bad Lands."* 44 pp., wrappers. Washington, 1920. First edition. (100 copies printed.) $250-$325.

CARTER, Susannah. *The Frugal Housewife: or, Complete Woman Cook*. Illustrated. Boards. Philadelphia, 1802. $150-$200.

CARTER, W. A. *History of Fannin County, Texas*. Cloth. Bonham, Tex., 1885. First edition. $850-$1,000.

CARTIER-BRESSON, Henri. *The Decisive Moment*. Illustrated. Boards. New York, (1955). First edition. In dust jacket. With pamphlet of captions laid in. $200-$250. Also, $150 (A, 1976).

CARTIER-BRESSON, Henri. *The Europeans*. Boards. New York, (1955). First edition. $150. Also, $85 (A, 1974).

CARTIER-BRESSON, Henri. *The People of Moscow*. Cloth. New York, 1955. First edition. In dust jacket. $100-$150.

CARUTHERS, W. A. See *The Kentuckian in New-York*.

CARY, Joyce. *An American Visitor*. Cloth. London, 1933. First edition. In dust jacket. $100-$125.

CARY, Joyce. *The Horse's Mouth*. Cloth. London, (1944). First edition. In dust jacket.

$50-$75. (London), 1957. Marbled boards, vellum spine, leather label. One of 1,500 containing a discarded chapter from the novel. $75-$100.

CASEMENT, Roger. *Some Poems of Roger Casement.* Portrait. Gray printed wrappers. Dublin, 1918. First edition. $100.

CASENDER, Don Pedro. *The Lost Virgin of the South.* Cloth. Tallahassee, 1831. (By Michael Smith.) First edition. $500 and up. Courtland, Ala., 1833. Cloth. Second edition. $250 and up.

CASKODEN, Edwin. *When Knighthood Was in Flower.* Pictorial cloth. Indianapolis, 1898. (By Charles Major.) First edition, first issue, with 1897 copyright and no notice of reprints on copyright page. $60-$75.

CASLER, John. *Four Years in the Stonewall Brigade.* Folding facsimile. Cloth. Guthrie, Okla., 1893. First edition. $75-$100.

CASS, Lewis. *Substance of a Speech Delivered by Hon. Lewis Cass, of Michigan . . . on the Ratification of the Oregon Treaty.* 16 pp., sewed. Detroit, 1846. $75-$100.

CASTANEDA, Carlos. *The Teachings of Don Juan/A Yaqui Way of Knowledge.* Cloth. Berkeley, 1968. First edition. In dust jacket. $50. Author's first book.

CASTENADA, Carlos E. *Our Catholic Heritage in Texas, 1519-1810.* 5 vols., cloth. Austin, 1936-42. First edition. $750-$1,000.

*CASTLE Dismal; or, the Bachelor's Christmas.* Boards. New York, 1844. (By William Gilmore Simms.) First edition. $100-$150.

*CASTLE Rackrent; An Hibernian Tale.* Boards. London, 1800. (By Maria Edgeworth.) First edition. $250-$350.

CASTLEMAN, Alfred L. *Army of the Potomac: Behind the Scenes.* Cloth. Milwaukee, 1863. First edition. $75.

CASTLEMAN, John B. *Active Service.* Plates. Cloth. Louisville, 1917. $35-$40.

CASTLEMON, H. C. (Harry). *Frank on the Lower Mississippi.* Illustrated. Cloth. Cincinnati, 1867. (By Charles Austin Fosdick.) First edition. $40-$45.

CASTLEMON, Harry. *Guy Harris, the Runaway.* Printed wrappers. New York, 1887. (By Charles Austin Fosdick.) First edition, first issue. $50-$60.

CASTLEMON, Harry. *The Sportsman's Club Among the Trappers.* Plates. Cloth. Philadelphia, 1874. (By Charles Austin Fosdick.) First edition. $25-$30.

*CAT Morgan's Apology.* Broadside. New Haven, 1953. (By T. S. Eliot.) First edition. One of 30 printed by Eliot's bibliographer, Donald Gallup. $750 and up.

CATES, Cliff D. *Pioneer History of Wise County, Texas.* Illustrated. Stiff wrappers. Decatur, Tex., 1907. First edition. $200-$300.

CATHASAIGH, P. O. (editor). *The Story of the Irish Citizen Army.* Printed gray wrappers. Dublin, 1919. (By Sean O'Casey.) First edition. $100-$150. Author's first book.

CATHER, Willa. See McClure, S. S.; Milmine, Georgine. Also see *The Sombrero.*

CATHER, Willa. *Alexander's Bridge.* Blue, purple, and other colors of cloth. Boston, 1912. First edition, first issue, with "Willa S. Cather" on spine (later "Willa Cather") and with title and author's name in box on front cover and half title before title page. $100-$150. Another issue (?): "Willa S. Cather" on spine but title only in box on cover. $75-$100. Later issue, with half title after title page: $50. London, 1912. Brown cloth. First English edition (erroneously titled *Alexander's Bridges*). In dust jacket. $125.

CATHER, Willa. *April Twilights.* Brown boards, paper labels. Boston, 1903. First edition. Issued without dust jacket. $600-$800. Also, $600 (A, 1977). Author's first book. New

York, 1923. Boards and parchment. First revised edition. One of 450 signed. Boxed. $150.

CATHER, Willa. *Death Comes for the Archbishop.* Green cloth. New York, 1927. First edition. In dust jacket. $35-$60. Another issue: Boards and cloth. One of 175 signed. Boxed. $150-$200. One of 50 on vellum, signed. Boxed. $400-$550. London, 1927. Black cloth. First English edition. In dust jacket. $50-$60. New York, 1929. Illustrated by Harold von Schmidt. Vellum. One of 170 signed. Boxed. $150-$175.

CATHER, Willa. *A Lost Lady.* Cloth. New York, 1923. First edition, first issue, in green cloth (later tan). In dust jacket. $50-$60. Another issue: Boards and cloth. One of 20 lettered A to T, signed. In glassine dust jacket. Boxed. $350-$450. One of 200 numbered copies (same issue). $100-$150. Advance issue: Printed wrappers. $400.

CATHER, Willa. *Lucy Gayheart.* Cloth. New York, 1935. First edition, first printing (so stated). In dust jacket. $15-$25. Another issue: Buckram. One of 749 signed. In dust jacket. Boxed. $85-$125.

CATHER, Willa. *My Antonia.* Illustrated by W. T. Benda. Brown cloth. Boston, 1918. First edition, first issue, with illustrations on glazed paper inserted. In dust jacket. $300-$400. Also, $200 (A, 1975). Lacking jacket, $100-$200. London, 1919. Cloth. First English edition. In dust jacket. $50-$100.

CATHER, Willa. *My Mortal Enemy.* Boards and cloth. New York, 1926. First edition. In dust jacket. Boxed. $15-$25. Another issue: Boards and cloth. One of 220 signed. Boxed. $75-$100.

CATHER, Willa. *Not Under Forty.* Cloth. New York, 1936. First edition, first printing (so stated). In dust jacket. $15-$25. Another issue: One of 333 large paper copies on vellum, signed. Boxed. $125-$150.

CATHER, Willa. *The Novels and Stories of Willa Cather.* 13 vols., two-toned cloth. Boston, 1937-41. Autograph edition. One of 950 signed. $500-$750. Also, $400 and $325 (A, 1967).

CATHER, Willa. *O Pioneers!* Colored frontispiece by Clarence Underwood. Cloth. Boston. 1913. First edition, first issue, either tan or cream ribbed cloth (later, brown) and with last page of text on tipped-in leaf. In dust jacket. $200-$250. Lacking jacket, $100-$150. Second issue (brown cloth). In dust jacket. $50-$75.

CATHER, Willa. *Obscure Destinies.* Green cloth. New York, 1932. First edition. In dust jacket. $30-$40. Another issue: Vellum and boards. One of 260 on vellum, signed. $150-$250.

CATHER, Willa. *One of Ours.* Cloth. New York, 1932. First edition. In dust jacket. $50-$75. Another issue: Boards. One of 35 on vellum, signed. Boxed. $300-$400. Another issue: One of 310 on handmade paper, signed. Boxed. $150-$200. Second printing (of trade edition): Boards ("For bookseller friends.") $35-$50.

CATHER, Willa. *The Professor's House.* Orange and blue cloth. New York, 1925. First edition. In dust jacket. $25-$35. Another issue: Buckram and boards. One of 40 on vellum (of an issue of 225), signed. $300-$400. One of 185 (of this issue), signed. $150-$200.

CATHER, Willa. *Sapphira and the Slave Girl.* Cloth. New York, 1940. First edition (so stated). In dust jacket. $15-$25. (Note: Trade binding of this is often faded under the dust jacket. The faded copies are worth less—$7.50-$10.) Another issue: Half buckram. One of 520 signed. In dust jacket. $75-$100.

CATHER, Willa. *Shadows on the Rock.* Green cloth. New York, 1931. First edition, advance issue, mislabeled "Second edition" on copyright page. In dust jacket. $35-$50. Regular trade edition ("First edition" on copyright page): In dust jacket. $15-$25. Another issue: Marbled boards, leather label. One of 619 signed. In dust jacket. Boxed. $100-$150. Another issue: Full orange vellum. One of 199 on vellum, signed. In dust jacket. Boxed. $200-$250.

CATHER, Willa. *The Song of the Lark.* Blue cloth. Boston, 1915. First edition, first issue, with boxed ads on copyright page. In dust jacket. $150-$250. Lacking jacket, $75 and up.

CATHER, Willa. *The Troll Garden.* Crimson cloth. New York, 1905. First edition, first issue, with "McClure Phillips & Co." at foot of spine. $200-$300. (If with dust jacket, much more.)

CATHER, Willa. *Youth and the Bright Medusa.* Cloth. New York, 1920. First edition. In dust jacket. $35-$50. Another issue: One of 25 signed. $250-$350.

CATHER, Willa, and Canfield, Dorothy. *The Fear That Walks by Noonday.* Boards, paper label. New York, 1931. First edition. One of 30. $750-$1,000. Also, $650 (A, 1977). (Note: This first appeared in *The Sombrero,* which see under title entry.)

CATHERWOOD, Frederick. *Views of Ancient Monuments in Central America, Chiapas, and Yucatan.* Colored title page, engraved map, 25 lithographs. Folio, half morocco. London, 1844. First edition. $4,000-$5,000. Also, $2,750 (A, 1970). New York, 1844. First American edition. Equally valuable. Barre, Mass., 1965. One of 500 facsimile copies. $300-$400.

CATHERWOOD, Mrs. Mary Hartwell. *Spanish Peggy.* Red cloth. Chicago, 1899. First edition. $25-$35.

*CATHOLIC Anthology, 1914-1915 (The).* Edited by Ezra Pound. Gray boards. London, 1915. First edition. $300-$400. Also, $300 (A, 1977). (Note: Includes T. S. Eliot's "The Love Song of J. Alfred Prufrock" and four other poems.)

CATLIN, George. *Letters and Notes on the Manners, Customs, and Conditions of the North American Indians.* 2 maps (one folding), one chart, 309 illustrations. 2 vols., cloth, paper labels. London, 1841. First edition, first issue, with "Frederick" for "Zedekiah." on page 104. $750-$1,000. Also; $400 (A, 1972). Second issue. $600-$750. London, 1841. 2 vols., cloth. Second edition. $400-$500. New York, 1841. 2 vols., cloth. First American edition. $400-$500. (Note: Many other later editions, some with plates colored by hand, titles altered, etc. See American and British auction records.)

CATLIN, George. *O-Kee-Pa, a Religious Ceremony.* 13 colored lithographs. Cloth. London, 1867. First edition. $1,500-$2,000. Also, $900 (A, 1972).

CATLIN, George. *North American Indian Portfolio.* 25 colored plates mounted on cardboard; text in cloth-backed wrappers. Large folio, morocco-backed cloth portfolio. London, 1844. First edition. $15,000 and up. Also, $10,000 (A, 1972). (Copies with plates missing bring less, of course. See auction records.) London, (1845?). Second edition. 31 colored plates. $12,500 (Chicago, 1970.) Facsimile of 1844 edition. One of 1,000. $100. One of 26 (of this edition). $250 and up.

CATO. *Cato's Moral Distichs.* Facsimile of 1735 Philadelphia edition printed by Benjamin Franklin; with an original leaf bound in. Cloth. San Francisco, 1939. One of 250. $100-$150.

CATON, John Dean. *The Last of the Illinois, and a Sketch of the Pottawatomies.* 36 pp., wrappers. Chicago, 1870. First edition. $75-$100.

*CATTLE Raising in South Dakota.* 32 pp., wrappers. (Forest City, 1904.) $100-$125.

CAVALCANTI, Guido. *Rime.* (In English and Italian.) Edited by Ezra Pound. 40 plates. Stiff red printed wrappers. Genova, Italy, (1932). First edition. $100-$150.

CAVE, Roderick. *The Private Press.* Illustrated. Cloth. London, (1971). First edition. In dust jacket. $50.

CAVENDISH, George. *Life of Thomas Wolsey, Cardinal Archbishop of York.* Edited by F. S. Ellis. Limp vellum with ties. London, 1893. Kelmscott Press. One of 250. $300-$400.

CAXTON, Pisistratus. *What Will He Do with It?* 4 vols., cloth. Edinburgh, (1859). (By Edward Bulwer-Lytton.) First edition. $150-$200.

CAXTON, William. *The History of Reynard the Foxe.* Vellum. London, 1892. Kelmscott Press. One of 300. $500-$750. Another issue: One of 10 on vellum. $1,500-$1,750. Also. $1,096 (A, 1972).

*CELEBRATION of the 73d Anniversary of the Declaration of Independence . . . on Board the Barque "Hannah Sprague," etc.* 16 pp., wrappers. New York, 1849. First edition. $75-$150.

CELIZ, Fray Francisco. *Diary of the Alarcon Expedition into Texas, 1718-1719.* Translated by Fritz L. Hoffman. 10 plates. Cloth. Los Angeles, 1935. One of 600. $75-$150.

CELLINI, Benvenuto. *The Autobiography of Benvenuto Cellini.* Translated by John Addington Symonds. Illustrated by Salvador Dali. Blue cloth, gilt top. Garden City. 1946. One of 1,000 signed by Dali. Boxed. $100-$150.

CENDRARS, Blaise. *Panama, or The Adventures of My Seven Uncles.* Translated from the French and illustrated by John Dos Passos. Pictorial wrappers. New York, 1931. First edition. One of 300 signed by Cendrars and Dos Passos. Boxed. $75-$125. Also, $50 (A, 1975).

CERRUTI, Henry. *Ramblings in California.* Boards and cloth. Berkeley, 1954. One of 500. $40-$50.

CERVANTES, Miguel de. *Don Quixote.* (Note: Because this seventeenth-century classic has gone into innumerable editions, the following listings are limited to a few representative selections. See the British and American auction records for more extensive records.)

CERVANTES, Miguel de. *El Ingenioso Hidalgo Don Quixote de la Mancha.* Facsimile of the first and second parts, Madrid, 1605 and 1615. 2 vols., vellum with ties. (New York), no date. Hispanic Society of America. One of 100. Boxed. $200-$300. Another edition: New York, 1932. 2 vols., cloth. One of 100. $75-$100.

CERVANTES, Miguel de. *The History of Don Quixote of the Mancha.* P. A. Motteux's translation revised anew (1743). 21 illustrations by E. McKnight Kauffer. 2 vols., morocco. London, 1930. Nonesuch Press. $150-$200.

CERVANTES, Miguel de. *The History of the Valorous and Wittie Knight-Errant, Don Quixote of the Mancha.* Thomas Shelton translation. Woodcut initials and borders by Louise Powell. 2 vols., pigskin. London, 1927-28. Ashendene Press. One of 225. $1,500-$1,800. Another issue: One of 22 on vellum. $4,000-$6,000.

CERVANTES, Miguel de. *The History of the Valorous and Witty Knight-Errant, Don Quixote of the Mancha.* Thomas Shelton translation. Daniel Vierge illustrations. 4 vols., boards. New York, 1906-07. One of 140. $350-$400. Also, $160. (A, 1975).

CERWIN, Herbert (compiler). *Famous Recipes by Famous People.* Illustrated. Wrappers. Del Monte, Calif., (1936). First edition. (Issued by Hotel Del Monte.) $100-$125, (Includes contributions by Gertrude Stein, John Steinbeck, and others.)

CHADWICK, Henry. *The Game of Base Ball: How to Learn It, How to Play It, and How to Teach It.* Cloth. New York, (1868). First edition, with rules for 1868. $75-$100.

CHADWICK, Hector M. and N. K. *The Growth of Literature.* 3 vols., cloth. Cambridge, 1932-40. $95.

CHAGALL, Marc (illustrator). *Drawings for the Bible.* (French issue: *Dessins pour la Bible.*) Text by Gaston Bachelard. Boards. New York (and Paris), 1960. (Constituting *Verve, No. 37/38.*) $2,000-$2,500. Also, auction records ranging up to $850 (1976).

CHAGALL, Marc (illustrator). *Illustrations for the Bible.* Edited by Jean Wahl. Translated by Samuel Beckett from the Paris title of the same year *(Eaux-fortes pour la Bible).* 29 lithographs (17 in color), 105 plates. Pictorial boards in color. New York (or Paris), 1956. First edition. In dust jacket. $2,000-$2500. Also, "spine defective," $750 (A, 1976). The French edition (which constituted *Verve, No. 33/34)* had auction records in 1975 of as high as $900 and $895; in 1974 a copy with a signed Chagall drawing made $1,300 at auction. Another issue: Paris, 1956. Wrappers. One of 275 signed by the artist. $4,000 (A, 1971).

CHAGALL, Marc (illustrator). *The Jerusalem Windows.* (French: *Vitraux pour Jérusalem.*) Text by Jean Leymarie. Cloth. New York (or Monte Carlo), 1962. In dust jacket.

$150-$200. Also, a 1963 French edition, one of 270 signed by Chagall and Leymarie, $946 (A, 1974).

CHAGALL, Marc (illustrator). *The Story of the Exodus.* 24 colored lithographs, Bible text. Folio, unbound signatures, in stiff white wrappers. Paris-New York, 1966. First edition. One of 25 on Arches paper, signed by Chagall. Boxed. $3,900 (U.S. catalogue, 1970) and $5,290 (Swiss catalogue, 1970). Also, $2,800 (A, 1970); $4,133.33 (A, Switzerland, 1969).

CHAHTA-IMA. *La Nouvelle Atala ou La Fille de L'Esprit.* Printed wrappers. Nouvelle-Orléans (New Orleans), 1879. First edition. $100-$150. (Note: Contains a contribution by Lafcadio Hearn—his first book appearance.)

*CHAINBEARER (The), or, The Littlepage Manuscripts.* 3 vols., tan boards. London, 1845. (By James Fenimore Cooper.) First edition. $200-$300. New York, 1845. 2 vols., wrappers. $200-$300. (Note: Name is misspelled "Fennimore" on front cover.)

CHAMBERS, Andrew Jackson. *Recollections.* 40 pp., stapled. No place, (1947). First edition. $75-$100. (More common than once believed.)

CHAMBERS, Robert W. *The King in Yellow.* Chicago, 1895. First edition. Green cloth with lizard design (preferred binding, perhaps earliest). $100-$110.

CHAMISSO, Adelbert von. *A Sojourn at San Francisco Bay 1816.* 8 plates. Half cloth. San Francisco, 1936. Grabhorn printing. One of 250. $75.

CHAMISSO, Adelbert von. *The Wonderful History of Peter Schlemihl.* 6 illustrations. Printed wrappers. London, 1843. First edition. $250-$300. Corner chipped from front wrapper, rebacked, $175.

CHANDLER, Raymond. *The Big Sleep.* Cloth. New York, 1939. First edition. In dust jacket. $250-$350. Author's first book.

CHANDLER, Raymond. *Farewell, My Lovely.* Brown cloth. New York, 1940. First edition. In dust jacket. $75-$150.

CHANDLER, Raymond. *The Long Good-Bye.* Boards. London, 1953. First edition. In dust jacket. $50-$75.

CHANDLER, Raymond. *Red Wind.* Cloth. Cleveland, (1946). First edition. In dust jacket. $40-$50.

CHANNING. William Ellery (1780-1842). *The Duties of Children.* Wrappers. Boston, 1807. First edition. $100-$150.

CHANNING, William Ellery (1780-1842). *A Sermon Delivered at the Ordination of the Rev. Jared Sparks, etc.* Stitched. Boston, 1819. First edition. $75-$100.

CHANNING, William Ellery (1818-1901). *John Brown, and The Heroes of Harper's Ferry: A Poem.* Green cloth. Boston, 1886. First edition. $75-$150.

*CHANTICLEER: A Bibliography of The Golden Cockerel Press.* Waltham Saint Lawrence, 1936. One of 300. $150-$200.

CHANUTE, Octave. *Progress in Flying Machines.* 85 illustrations. Cloth. New York, (1894). First edition. $75-$100.

CHAPELLE, Howard I. *The Baltimore Clipper.* Illustrated. Cloth (leatherette). Salem, Mass., 1930. $100-$125. Another issue: Marbled boards. One of 97. $150-$200.

CHARLEVOIX, Pierre F. X. *Journal of a Voyage to North America.* Folding map. 2 vols., boards and cloth. Chicago, 1923. Caxton Club. First American edition. $150-$200.

CHARSLEY, Fanny Anne. *The Wild Flowers Around Melbourne.* 13 color plates. Folio, blue cloth. London, 1867. $250-$300.

*CHARTER of Dartmouth College (The).* Stitched. Hanover, N.H., 1815. $100.

*CHARTERED Surveyor (The), His Training and His Work.* Foreword by the Rt. Hon. Winston Churchill. Boards and cloth. London, (1932). First edition. $75-$100.

CHASE, Charles M. *The Editor's Run in New Mexico and Colorado.* Illustrated. Pictorial wrappers. Lyndon, Vt.. 1882. First edition. $200-$300.

CHASE, Owen (and others). *Narratives of the Wreck of the Whale Ship "Essex."* 12 wood engravings by Robert Gibbings. Cloth. London, 1935. Golden Cockerel Press. One of 275. $250-$300.

CHATTERTON, E. Keble. *Ship-Models.* Edited by Geoffrey Holme. 142 plates, many in color. Buckram. London, 1923. One of 1,000. $200-$250.

CHATTERTON, E. Keble. *Steamship Models.* 128 plates, some in color. Buckram. London, 1924. One of 1,000 signed. $100-$150.

CHATTO, William A. See Careless, John.

CHAUCER, Geoffrey. (Note: The editions of Chaucer, like those of the Bible, Shakespeare, and other classic universal works are too numerous to permit a complete listing here. Following are a few outstanding representative items.)

CHAUCER, Geoffrey. *The Canterbury Tales.* Colored plates by W. Russell Flint. 3 vols., limp vellum, silk ties. London, 1913. Riccardi Press. One of 500. $300-$350. Also, one of 12 on vellum, and with extra plates in cloth portfolio. $1,500-$2,000. New York, 1930. Illustrated by Rockwell Kent. 2 vols., pigskin. One of 75 signed. $800-$1,000. Another issue: Cloth. One of 924 signed. $200-$225. Waltham Saint Lawrence, 1929-31. Golden Cockerel Press. Eric Gill engravings. 4 vols., folio, boards, morocco spine. One of 485. $1,500-$2,000. Another issue: One of 15 on vellum. Boxed. $4,000 or more. New York, 1946. Limited Editions Club. Illustrated by Arthur Szyk. Half pigskin. Boxed. $100-$125.

CHAUCER, Geoffrey. *The Ellesmere Chaucer. (The Canterbury Tales.)* Facsimile, including 71 pages illuminated in gold and colors. 2 vols., folio, half morocco. Manchester, England, 1911. $750-$1,000.

CHAUCER, Geoffrey. *Troilus and Criseyde.* Edited by Arundell del Re. 5 full-page illustrations, 5 half-page decorations, and engraved title page by Eric Gill. Folio, boards and morocco. Waltham Saint Lawrence, 1927. Golden Cockerel Press. One of 225. $2,000-$2,250.

CHAUCER, Geoffrey. *Works.* Woodcut illustrations, borders, and initials. Folio, boards. London, 1896. Kelmscott Press. One of 425. $8,500-$10,000. Also, $7,500 (A, 1977); $5,000 (A, 1975); $7,000 and $6,536 (A, 1974). Another issue: White blind-stamped pigskin, in wooden box with brass hinges and clasps, by the Doves Bindery. One of 46. $10,000-$15,000. Also, $8,256 (A,1977); $8,944 (A,1975).

CHAYEVSKY, Paddy. *Television Plays.* Cloth. New York, 1955. First edition. In dust jacket. $25-$30.

CHEEVER, John. *The Enormous Radio and Other Stories.* Cloth. New York, 1953. First edition. In dust jacket. $40-$60.

CHEEVER, John. *Homage to Shakespeare.* 15 pp., blue buckram. Stevenson, Conn., (1968). First edition. One of 150 signed. In dust jacket. $100-$125.

CHEEVER, John. *The Wapshot Chronicle.* Cloth. New York, (1957). First edition. In dust jacket. $40-$50.

CHEEVER, John. *The Way Some People Live.* Cloth. New York, (1943). First edition. In dust jacket. $100-$150. Author's first book.

CHERRY-GARRARD, Apsley. *The Worst Journey in the World: Antarctic, 1910-1913.* Maps and panoramas, color plates. 2 vols., boards, paper labels. London, 1922. First edition. $150-$200.

CHESTERTON, G. K. *The Ballad of the White Horse.* Half cloth. London, (1928). First edition. One of 100. In dust jacket. $75-$100.

CHESTERTON, G.K. *Charles Dickens Fifty Years After.* Wrappers. No place, 1920. One of 25. $100.

CHESTERTON, G.K. *Chaucer.* Cloth. London, 1932. First edition. In dust jacket. $30-$40.

CHESTERTON, G.K. *Collected Poems.* Boards and parchment. London, 1927. One of 350 signed. $50-$60.

CHESTERTON, G.K. *The Father Brown Stories.* Calf. London, 1929. First edition. $100-$150.

CHESTERTON, G. K. *Grey-Beards at Play: Rhymes and Sketches.* Boards and buckram. London, 1900. First edition. $100-$125. Author's first book.

CHESTERTON, G. K. *The Innocence of Father Brown.* Illustrated by S. S. Lucas. Red cloth. London, 1911. First edition. In dust jacket. $75-$100.

CHESTERTON, G. K. *Manalive.* Color frontispiece. Cloth. London, (1912). First edition. In dust jacket. $75-$100.

CHESTERTON, G. K. *The Sword of Wood.* Boards. London, 1928. First edition. One of 530 signed. In dust jacket. $35-$50.

CHESTERTON, G. K. *The Wild Knight and Other Poems.* Half vellum. London, 1900. First edition. $40-$50.

CHESNUTT, Charles W. *Frederick Douglass.* Limp leather. Boston, 1899. First edition. $75-$100.

CHESNUTT, Charles W. *The Wife of His Youth and Other Stories.* Cloth. Boston,1899. First edition. $75-$100.

*CHICAGO: A Strangers' and Tourists' Guide to the City of Chicago.* Illustrated, including 4 folding plates and a folding map. Cloth. Chicago, 1866. First edition. $100-$125.

*CHICAGO Illustrated.* (Cover title.) 52 tinted lithograph views. Text by James W. Sheahan. Oblong folio, morocco. (Chicago, 1866-67.) Jevne and Almini, publishers. First edition, second issue $4,000-$5,000. (The original issue was in 13 parts and is now very rare. Probable value: $10,000 and up—if one should be offered for sale.) New York, 1952. 12 plates. Portfolio. Reprint edition. $150-$250.

CHILD, Andrew. *Overland Route to California.* Full leather. Milwaukee, 1852. First edition. $5,000-$7,500.

CHILD, Lydia Maria. See *The Frugal Housewife; Hobomok.*

*CHILDREN in Prison and Other Cruelties of Prison Life.* 16pp., wired wrappers. London, (1898). (By Oscar Wilde.) First edition. $200-$225.

*CHILDREN of the Chapel (The): A Tale.* By the Author of "Mark Dennis." Red cloth. London, 1864. (By Algernon C. Swinburne.) First edition, first issue, with "Joseph Masters" in imprint (later,"J. Masters & Co."). $75-$100.

*CHILD'S Book About Whales (The).* Woodcuts. 16 pp., printed wrappers. Concord, N.H. 1843. $100-$150.

*CHILD'S Botany (The).* Boards. Boston, 1828. (By Samuel Griswold Goodrich.) First edition. $45-$50.

CHILDS, C. G. (engraver). *Views in Philadelphia and Its Vicinity.* Engraved title page, plan, 24 engraved views. Cloth or boards. Philadelphia, 1827-(30). First edition. $600-$1,000.

CHITTENDEN, Hiram M. *The American Fur Trade of the Far West.* Folding map, plan, 3 facsimiles, 6 plates. 3 vols., green cloth. New York, 1902. First edition. $200-$300. New York, 1936. Plates. 2 vols., cloth. Boxed. $75-$100.

CHITTENDEN, Hiram M. *History of Early Steamboat Navigation on the Missouri River.* 16 plates. 2 vols., cloth. New York, 1903. One of 950. $75-$100.

CHITTENDEN, Hiram M. (editor). *Life, Letters and Travels of Father Jean-Pierre de Smet.* Map, 3 plates, 3 facsimiles. 4 vols., cloth. New York, 1905. First edition. $300-$400.

CHIVERS, Thomas Holley. *Conrad and Eudora.* Cloth, or leather (?). Philadelphia, 1834. First edition. $100-$150.

CHIVERS, Thomas Holley. *Eonchs of Ruby: A Gift of Love.* printed white boards. New York, 1851. First edition. $125-$150.

CHIVERS, Thomas Holley. *The Lost Pleiad and Other Poems.* Printed tan wrappers. New York, 1845. First edition. $100-$150.

CHIVERS, Thomas Holley. *Memoralia.* Boards and cloth. Philadelphia, 1853. First edition. $50-$60.

CHIVERS, Thomas Holley. *Nacoochee: or, The Beautiful Star.* Cloth. New York, 1837. First edition. $150-$200.

CHIVERS, Thomas Holley. *The Path of Sorrow.* Blue boards, purple cloth, paper label. Franklin, T(enn.), 1832. First edition. $400-$500. Author's first book.

CHIVERS, Thomas Holley. *Search After Truth.* Printed tan wrappers. New York, 1848. First edition. $100-$150.

*CHRISTIANISM: Or Belief and Unbelief Reconciled.* 59 pp., cloth, paper label. No place, (1832). (By Leigh Hunt.) First edition. (75 printed.) $250-$350.

*CHRISTMAS Gift from Fairy-Land (A).* Cloth. New York, (1838). (By James Kirke Paulding.) First edition, second (?) issue. $150-$200. (Note: This was also published under the title *A Gift from Fairy-Land.)*

*CHRONICLES of the City of Gotham.* Half cloth. New York, 1830. (By James Kirke Paulding.) First edition. $100-$150.

CHURCHILL, Winston (American novelist). *The Celebrity.* Cloth. New York, 1898. First edition. $25-$30. Author's first book.

CHURCHILL, Sir Winston S. See *The Chartered Surveyor.*

CHURCHILL, Sir Winston S. *Addresses Delivered in the Year 1940, etc.* Cloth. San Francisco, 1940. Grabhorn Press. One of 250. $150.

CHURCHILL, Sir Winston S. *Arms and the Covenant: Speeches.* Compiled by Randolph S. Churchill. Frontispiece. Buckram. London, 1938. First edition. In dust jacket. $125-$150.

CHURCHILL, Sir Winston S. *Beating the Invader.* 2 pp., unbound (as issued). (London, 1941.) $50-$75.

CHURCHILL, Sir Winston S. *Great Contemporaries.* Illustrated. Cloth. London, 1937. First edition. In dust jacket. $75-$100.

CHURCHILL, Sir Winston S. *Ian Hamilton's March.* Portrait, maps, plans. Red cloth. London, 1900. First edition. $200-$250. New York, 1900. First American edition. $100.

CHURCHILL, Sir Winston S. *India: Speeches.* Orange wrappers. London, (1931). First edition. In dust jacket. $150-$300. Second impression: Green wrappers. $75-$125.

CHURCHILL, Sir Winston S. *Liberalism and the Social Problem.* Cloth. London, 1909. First edition. $200-$300.

CHURCHILL, Sir Winston S. *London to Ladysmith via Pretoria.* Maps and plans. Fawn-colored cloth. London, 1900. First edition. $100-$150. New York, 1900. Buckram. First American edition. $75-$100.

CHURCHILL, Sir Winston S. *Lord Randolph Churchill.* Frontispieces, plates. 2 vols., cloth. London, 1906. First edition $100-$125.

CHURCHILL, Sir Winston S. *Marlborough: His Life and Times.* Plates, facsimiles, maps, plans. 4 vols., morocco, gilt tops. London, (1933-38). First edition. One of 155 signed. $1,000-$1,400. Also, $600 (A,1974). Trade edition: 4 vols., cloth. In dust jackets. $125-$150.

CHURCHILL, Sir Winston S. *My African Journey.* Maps and plates. Pictorial red cloth. London, 1908. First edition $150-$200.

CHURCHILL, Sir Winston S. *My Early Life.* Portraits, maps, plates. Cloth. London, 1930. First edition. $150-$175. New York, 1930. Illustrated. Cloth. First American edition. $75-$100.

CHURCHILL, Sir Winston S. *The People's Rights.* Pictorial wrappers, or cloth. London, (1909). First edition, first issue, with index. Either binding: $300-$400. Second issue. $100-150.

CHURCHILL, Sir Winston S. *The River War.* Portraits, colored maps, folding illustrations. 2 vols., pictorial cloth. London, 1899. First edition. $500-$600.

CHURCHILL, Sir Winston S. *Savrola: A Tale of the Revolution in Aurania.* Cloth. New York, 1900. First edition. $600-$750. London, 1900. Cloth. First English edition $200-250.

CHURCHILL, Sir Winston S. *Secret Session Speeches.* Cloth. London, (1946). First edition. In dust jacket. $30-$40. (Some copies especially bound in leather and inscribed.)

CHURCHILL, Sir Winston S. *Step by Step, 1936-1939.* Green cloth. London, 1939. First edition. $100-$200.

CHURCHILL, Sir Winston S. *The Story of the Malakand Field Force.* Portrait and 5 maps and plans. Cloth. London, 1898. First edition, first issue, with errata slip preceding first map. $600-$800.

CHURCHILL, Sir Winston S. *Thoughts and Adventures.* Cloth. London, (1932). First edition. $100-$125.

CHURCHILL, Sir Winston S. *The World Crisis.* Maps, plans, other illustrations. 6 vols., cloth. London, 1923-31. First edition. $250-$300.

CHURCHILL, Sir Winston S., and Martindale, C. C., S. J. *Charles IXth, Duke of Marlborough, K. G.* Wrappers. London, 1934. First edition. $80-$125.

CINCINNATUS. *Travels on the Western Slope of the Mexican Cordillera.* Engraved title page. Cloth. San Francisco, 1857. (By Marvin T. Wheat.) First edition. $200-$300.

CINDERELLA. Retold by C. S. Evans. Frontispiece in color and numerous silhouette illustrations by Arthur Rackham. Half cloth. London, 1919. One of 525 signed by the artist. In dust jacket. $250-$350. Another issue: Half vellum: One of 325 on vellum, signed by Rackham, with an extra plate. $400-$500, possibly more.

CINDERELLA, or The Little Glass Slipper. 11 woodcuts. 30 pp., pictorial orange wrappers. Cooperstown, N.Y., 1839. (By Charles Perrault.) $50-$60. New York, (about 1880). Illustrations, 10 pp., of text. Colored pictorial boards. McLoughlin toy book. $50-$75.

CLAIBORNE, John Herbert. *Seventy-five Years in Old Virginia.* Cloth. New York, 1905. $50-$60.

CLAPPE, Louise A. K. S. *California in 1851 (in 1852): The Dame Shirley Letters.* 2 vols. San Francisco, 1933. Grabhorn printing. One of 500. $150-$200.

CLARK, Charles E. *Prince and Boatswain: Sea Tales from the Recollection of Rear-Admiral Charles E. Clark.* Blue cloth. Greenfield, Mass., (about 1915). (Edited by John P. Marquand and James M. Morgan.) First edition. $35-$50. Marquand's first book appearance.

CLARK, Charles M. *A Trip to Pike's Peak.* Frontispiece, 18 woodcuts. Cloth. Chicago, 1861. First edition. $600-$850.

CLARK, Daniel. *Proofs of the Corruption of Gen. James Wilkinson, and of His Connexion with Aaron Burr.* Boards. Philadelphia, 1809. First edition. $500.

CLARK, Daniel M. *The Southern Calculator, or Compendious Arithmetic.* Boards. Lagrange, Ga., 1844. $50-$60.

CLARK, John A. *Gleanings by the Way.* Cloth. Philadelphia, 1842. First edition. $200-$300.

CLARK, Roland. *Gunner's Dawn.* Illustrated, including signed frontispiece. Leatherette. New York, 1937. Derrydale Press. First edition. One of 950. Boxed. $100-$150. Another issue: One of 50 signed, with signed engravings. $1,500-2,000. Also, $1,500 (A, 1977).

CLARK, Roland. *Pot Luck.* Illustrated, including signed frontispiece etching. Half leather. West Hartford, Vt., (1945). First edition. One of 150. $200-$250. Another issue: Cloth. One of 460 signed. Boxed. $100-$150.

CLARK, Roland. *Roland Clark's Etchings.* Illustrated, with a signed frontispiece etching. Folio, cloth. New York, (1938). Derrydale Press. First edition. One of 800. Boxed. $350-$550. Another issue: Half morocco. One of 50 (presentation) with 2 signed etchings. $3,500 (A, 1977).

CLARK, Walter (editor). *Histories of the Several Regiments and Battalions from North Carolina in the Great War, 1861-1865.* Plates. 5 vols., cloth. Raleigh. 1901. $225.

CLARK, Walter Van Tilburg. *Christmas Comes to Hjalsen.* Pictorial wrappers. Reno, 1930. First edition. In original mailing envelope. $300-$350. Author's first book.

CLARKE, A. B. *Travels in Mexico and California.* Printed wrappers. Boston, 1852. First edition. $750-$1,000.

CLARKE, Arthur C. *Childhood's End.* Cloth. New York, (1953). First edition. In dust jacket. $60-$75.

CLARKE, Arthur C. *Earthlight.* Cloth. New York, (1955). First edition. In dust jacket. $50-$60.

CLARKE, Lewis. *Narrative of the Sufferings of Lewis Clarke During a Captivity of More Than Twenty-five Years.* Portrait. Wrappers. Boston, 1845. First edition. $100-$150.

CLARKE, Rebecca S. See May, Sophie.

*CLASS Poem.* Printed wrappers. (Cambridge, Mass.), 1838. (By James Russell Lowell.) First edition. $200-$300. Author's first published work.

*CLASS Poem. 1915.* 4 pp. (New Haven), 1915. (By Archibald MacLeish.) $2,500 (A, 1977). Author's first separately published work.

CLAY, John. *My Life on the Range.* Illustrated. Cloth. Chicago (1924). First edition $120-$175.

CLAYTON, W(illiam). *The Latter-Day Saints' Emigrants' Guide.* 24 pp., plain wrappers. St. Louis, 1848. First edition. $3,500-$5,000.

CLEMENS, Samuel Langhorne, See Twain, Mark. Also see *Date 1601; What Is Man?*

CLEVELAND, Richard J. *A Narrative of Voyages and Commercial Enterprises.* 2 vols., cloth. Cambridge, Mass., 1841. First edition. $350.

*CLOCKMAKER (The); or the Sayings and Doings of Samuel Slick of Slickville.* Cloth, paper label. Halifax, 1836. (By Thomas Chandler Haliburton.) First edition. $150-$250. Also, $100 (A,1968). Philadelphia, 1836. Boards. First United States edition. $100-$150.

CLUM, Woodworth. *Apache Agent: The Story of John P. Clum.* Illustrated, including frontispiece in color of Geronimo. Cloth. Boston, 1936. First edition. In dust jacket. $35-50.

CLUTTERBUCK, Captain. *The Monastery.* 3 vols., boards, paper labels. Edinburgh, 1820. (By Sir Walter Scott.) First edition. $100-$150.

CLYMER, W.B.S., and Green, Charles R. *Robert Frost: A Bibliography.* Cloth. Amherst, 1937. One of 500 (of an edition of 650). $75. Another issue: One of 150 signed. $100-$150.

COATES, Robert M. *The Eater of Darkness.* Wrappers, paper labels. (Paris, 1926.) Contact Editions. $300-$350. Also, worn, $200 (A, 1977).

COATSWORTH, Elizabeth. *The Cat Who Went to Heaven..* Illustrated by Lynd Ward. Cloth. New York, 1930. First edition. In dust jacket. $40-$50.

COBB, Irvin S. *Back Home.* Illustrated. Cloth. New York, (1912). First edition, first printing, with "Plimpton Press" slug on copyright page, and first binding, with publisher's name in 3 lines on spine. $50-$60. Author's first book.

COBB, Irvin S. *Old Judge Priest.* Cloth. New York, (1916). First edition, first issue, with square-diamond insignia on title page. In dust jacket. $40-$60.

COBB, Irvin S. *Piano Jim and the Impotent Pumpkin Vine, "Charley Russell's Best Story—to My Way of Thinking."* 24 pp., wrappers. No place, 1947. One of 100. $75-$100.

COBBETT, William, *Rural Rides.* Woodcut map. Boards and cloth. London, 1830. First edition. $200-$250. London, 1930. Edited by G. D. H. and Margaret Cole. Illustrated. 3 vols., boards. $150-$200.

COBDEN-SANDERSON, T. J. *Amantium Irae: Letters to Two Friends, 1864-1867.* Frontispiece portrait. Limp vellum. Hammersmith (London), 1914. Doves Press. One of 150. $200-$250. In a Doves binding of morocco. $800-$1,200.

COBDEN-SANDERSON, T. J. *The City Metropolitan.* London, 1911. Doves Press. Limited edition. $100-$125.

COBDEN-SANDERSON, T. J. *The City Planned.* London, 1912. Doves Press. Limited edition. $75-$100.

COBDEN-SANDERSON, T. J. *Credo.* London, 1908. Doves Press. One of 250. $200-$250. In a morocco binding by the Doves Bindery, $180 (A,1976).

COBDEN-SANDERSON, T. J. *The Ideal Book or Book Beautiful.* London, 1900. Doves Press. One of 300. $200-$250.

COCKERELL, S. C. (editor). *Laudes Beatae Mariae Virginis.* Printed in red, black, and blue. Boards and linen. London, 1896. Kelmscott Press. One of 250. $300-$450.

COCKERELL, S. C. (editor). *Some German Woodcuts of the 15th Century.* 35 reproductions. Boards and linen. London, 1897. Kelmscott Press. One of 225. $300-$400.

COCTEAU, Jean. *Orphée.* Translated by Carl Wildman. Frontispiece by Pablo Picasso. Boards. London, 1933. First edition in English. One of 100 signed by Cocteau and Picasso. $650.

COFFIN, Charles C. *The Boys of '76.* Illustrated. Pictorial cloth. New York, 1887. First edition. $60-$75.

COFFIN, Joshua. *A Sketch of the History of Newbury, Newburyport, and West Newbury.* Map, tables. Cloth. Boston, 1845. $50-$75.

COFFINBERRY, Andrew. *The Forest Rangers.* Cloth. Columbus, 1842. First edition. $150.

COHN, Albert M. *George Cruikshank: A Catalogue Raisonné.* Illustrated. Brown cloth. London, 1924. First edition. One of 500. $200-$250.

COHN, David L. *New Orleans and Its Living Past.* Illustrated. Cloth. Boston, 1941. Limited, signed edition. $50-$60.

COHN, Louis Henry. *A Bibliography of the Works of Ernest Hemingway.* Illustrated. Cloth. New York, 1931. First edition. One of 500. $100-$125. (Colophon calls for 5 lettered copies; there were none.)

COKE, Henry J. *A Ride Over the Rocky Mountains to Oregon and California.* Portrait. Cloth. London, 1852. First edition. $150-$250.

COKE, Richard. *Inaugural Address.* 14 pp., wrappers. Austin, 1874. $100-$125.

COKE, Richard. *Message to the 14th Legislature.* 14 pp., sewed, Austin, 1874. $35-$50. Same, to 15th Legislature, 1st session: Houston, 1876. 68 pp., sewed. $35-$50.

COLBERT, E. *Chicago: Historical and Statistical Sketch of the Garden City.* 120 pp., wrappers. Chicago, 1868. First edition. $75-$100.

COLE, Emma. *Life and Sufferings.* Plates. 36 pp., wrappers. Boston, 1844. $150.

COLERIDGE, Samuel T. See *Lyrical Ballads.*

COLERIDGE, Samuel T. *Aids to Reflection.* Drab boards, paper label. London, 1825. First edition. $75-$100.

COLERIDGE, Samuel T. *Biographia Literaria.* 2 vols., green or blue boards, paper labels. London, 1817. First edition. $300-$400.

COLERIDGE, Samuel T. *Christabel: Kubla Khan, A Vision: The Pains of Sleep.* Plain drab wrappers, or boards. London, 1816. First edition, first issue, with 4 pages of February ads at back, and with a half title. $800-$1,200. Also, $700 (A, 1975). London, 1904. Eragny Press. Colored frontispiece. Boards. One of 236. In dust jacket. $350-$500.

COLERIDGE, Samuel T. *Confessions of an Inquiring Spirit.* Cloth, paper label. London, 1840. First edition. $75-$100. Boston, 1841. Cloth, paper label. $40.

COLERIDGE, Samuel T. *Hints Towards the Formation of a More Comprehensive Theory of Life.* Boards. London, 1817. First edition. $100-$125.

COLERIDGE, Samuel T. *A Lay Sermon.* Printed wrappers. London, 1817. First edition. $300-$350. Also, a rebacked copy, $155 (A, 1975).

COLERIDGE, Samuel T. *Notes, Theological, Political, and Miscellaneous.* Cloth. London, 1853. First edition. $75-$100.

COLERIDGE, Samuel T. *Osorio: A Tragedy.* Boards, paper label. London, 1873. First edition. One of 50 large paper copies. $200-$300.

COLERIDGE, Samuel T. *Poems Chosen Out of the Works of Samuel Taylor Coleridge.* Printed with "Golden" type in red and black. Woodcut borders and initial letters. Vellum. London, 1896. Kelmscott Press. One of 300. $500-$750.

COLERIDGE, Samuel Taylor. *Remorse: A Tragedy in Five Acts.* Stitched. London, 1813. First edition. $600-$800.

COLERIDGE, Samuel T. *The Rime of the Ancient Mariner.* Illustrated by Gustave Doré. Cloth. New York, 1877. $100-$125. London, 1899. Vale Press. Illustrated by Charles Ricketts. Boards. One of 210. $125-$150. London, 1903. Essex House. Frontispiece. Vellum. One of 150 on vellum. $150-$250. London, 1910. Illustrated by Willy Pogany. Stiff vellum. One of 25 on vellum, signed by Pogany. In cloth wrapper and slipcase. $300-$400. Another issue: One of 525 signed by Pogany. $100-$150. Bristol, England, 1929. 10 engravings by David Jones. Canvas. One of 60 with extra set of engravings, signed by the artist. $800-$1,000. Another issue: Boards and cloth. One of 470 signed by Jones. $300-$600. Oxford, 1930. Boards and cloth, designed by Bruce Rogers. One of 750. $75-$100. Los Angeles, (1964). Tamarind Workshop. Colored lithographs. Printed wrappers. One of 45. $1,000 and up.

COLERIDGE, Samuel T. *Selected Poems.* Vellum. London, 1935. Nonesuch Press. One of 500. $125-$150.

COLERIDGE, Samuel T. *Sibylline Leaves: A Collection of Poems.* Drab boards, paper label. London, 1817. First edition, with errata leaf. $400-$500.

COLERIDGE, Samuel T. *Specimens of the Table Talk of the Late Samuel Taylor Coleridge.* Frontispiece. 2 vols., boards with labels. London, 1835. First edition. $150-$200.

COLERIDGE, Samuel T. *The Statesman's Manual; or the Bible the Best Guide to Political Skill and Foresight.* Blue-green printed wrappers. London, 1816. First edition. $500 and up.

COLERIDGE, Samuel T. *Zapolya.* Wrappers. London, 1817. First edition. $150-$200.

*COLLECTION of Familiar Quotations (A).* Brown cloth. Cambridge, Mass., 1855. (By John Bartlett.) First edition. $150-$200.

COLLIER, John Payne. *A Bibliographical and Critical Account of the Rarest Books in the English Language.* 2 vols., half cloth. London, 1865. First edition. $150-$200. New York, 1866. 4 vols., cloth. First American edition. One of 75 on large paper. $100-$200.

COLLIER, John Payne. *Memoirs of Edward Alleyn.* Cloth. London, 1841. First edition. $50-$75.

COLLINS, Charles. *Collins' History and Directory of the Black Hills.* 91 pp., printed yellow wrappers. Central City, Dakota Territory, 1878. First edition. $2,000-$2,500. Also, $1,200 (A,1968).

COLLINS, Charles (compiler). *Collins' Omaha Directory.* Printed boards. (Omaha, 1866.) First edition. $500-$600. Also, $325 (A,1968).

COLLINS, David. *An Account of the English Colony in New South Wales.* 2 maps, 32 plates. Leather or boards. London, 1804. Second edition. $200-$300.

COLLINS, Dennis. *The Indians' Last Fight; or, the Dull Knife Raid.* 8 plates. Cloth. (Girard, Kan., about 1915.) First edition. $150-$200.

COLLINS, John S. *Across the Plains in '64.* Pictorial cloth. Omaha, 1904. First edition. $75-$100.

COLLINS, Mrs. Nat. *The Cattle Queen of Montana.* Compiled by Charles Wallace. Illustrated. Stiff wrappers. St. James, Minn., 1894. First edition. $1,000 and up. Spokane, (about 1898-1902). Plates. Pictorial wrappers. $150-$200.

COLLINS, Lieut. R. M. *Chapters from the Unwritten History of the War Between the States.* Cloth. St. Louis, 1893. First edition. $200-$300.

COLLINS, Wilkie. *After Dark.* 2 vols, cloth. London, 1856. First edition. $300-$400.

COLLINS, Wilkie, *Antonina.* 3 vols., cloth. London, 1850. First edition. $250-$350. Author's first novel.

COLLINS, Wilkie. *Armadale.* Illustrated. 2 vols., decorated brown cloth. London, 1866. First edition. $150-$200. New York, 1866. Illustrated. Cloth. $75-$100.

COLLINS, Wilkie, *The Dead Secret.* 2 vols., cloth. London, 1857. First edition. $150-$200.

COLLINS, Wilkie. *The Evil Genius.* 3 vols, cloth. London, 1886. First edition. $200-$300.

COLLINS, Wilkie. *The Frozen Deep: A Drama.* Printed wrappers. No place, 1866. First printing. One of a few copies privately printed. $400-$500. London, 1874. 2 vols., cloth. First published edition (*The Frozen Deep and Other Tales*). $100-$150.

COLLINS, Wilkie. *The Law and the Lady.* 3 vols., cloth. London, 1875. First edition. $250-$350. New York, 1875. Illustrated. Wrappers. First American edition. $150-$200.

COLLINS, Wilkie. *The Legacy of Cain.* 3 vols., cloth. London, 1889. First edition. $150-$175.

COLLINS, Wilkie. *Memoirs of the Life of William Collins, R. A.* 2 vols., cloth. London, 1848. First edition. $150-$200. Author's first book.

COLLINS, Wilkie. *Miss Gwilt, A Drama in Five Acts.* Wrappers. No place, 1875. First edition. $250-$350. (Altered from the novel *Armadale.*)

COLLINS, Wilkie. *Mr. Wray's Cash-Box.* Frontispiece. Cloth. London, 1852. First edition. $100-$125.

COLLINS, Wilkie. *The Moonstone: A Romance.* 3 vols., purple cloth. London, 1868. First edition, first issue, with half titles, with misprint "treachesrouly" on page 129 of Vol. 2, and with ads in Vols. 2 and 3. $600-$800. Also, $288 (A, 1967); presentation copy, inscribed by Collins $2,500 (A, 1963). Play version: Privately printed, 1877. Unbound as issued. $250-$300. New York, 1959. Limited Editions Club. Cloth. Boxed. $50-$60.

COLLINS, Wilkie. *No Name.* 3 vols., red cloth. London, 1862. First edition. $200-$250. Boston, 1863. Cloth. First American edition. $150-$200.

COLLINS, Wilkie. *The Woman in White.* Illustrated by John McLenan. Brown cloth. New York, 1860. First edition, first issue, with the woman on spine in white. $200-$250. London, 1860. 3 vols., cloth. First English edition (published a month after the first American edition), first issue, with ads at end of Vol. 3 dated August 1, 1860. $500-$600. New York, 1964. Limited Editions Club. Boards. Boxed. $40-$45.

COLMAN, George, the Younger. See Mathers, John.

COLMAN, Sir Jeremiah. *The Noble Game of Cricket.* 105 plates, 33 colored. Buckram. London, 1941. One of 150. In dust jacket. $200-$250.

COLT, Miriam Davis. *Went to Kansas.* Cloth. Watertown, N.Y., 1862. First edition. $100-$150.

COLTON, Calvin. *Tour of the American Lakes.* Boards. London, 1853. First edition. $150.

COLTON, J. H. (publisher). See *The State of Indiana Delineated.*

COLTON, J. H. (publisher). *Particulars of Routes, Distances, Fares, etc.* 12 pp. (11 of text). (Caption title.) Accompanying Colton's Map of the United States . . . and a Plan of the Gold Region. Map folded into brown cloth covers, with printed paper label; text attached to inside of front cover. New York, 1849. First edition, first issue, with "longitude West from Greenwich" at top of map. $400-$700.

COLTON, Walter. *Three Years in California.* Map, 6 portraits, 6 plates, folding facsimile. Black cloth. New York, 1850. First edition. $100-$150.

COLUM, Padriac. *Creatures.* Illustrated. Boards. New York, 1937. First edition. One of 300. In dust jacket. $35-$75.

*COLUMBIA Verse: 1897-1924.* Boards and cloth. New York, 1924. First edition. $75-$100. (Note: Poems by Louis Zukofsky and others.)

COLUMBUS, Christopher. *The Voyages of Christopher Columbus: Being the Journals, etc.* Translated by Cecil Jane. 5 maps. Half vellum. London, 1930. One of 1,050. $75-$100.

COMBE, William. See: Doctor Syntax; Quiz. Also see *The English Dance of Death; The Dance of Life; The Tour of Doctor Prosody; A History of Madeira; Journal of Sentimental Travels, etc.; The History of Johnny Quae Genus.*

COMBS, Leslie. *Narrative of the Life of Gen. Leslie Combs.* (Cover title.) 23 pp., plus errata leaf. Wrappers. (New York, 1852). First edition. $250. Another issue: (Washington), 1852. 20 pp., printed wrappers. Rebound in cloth, $130 (A, 1967—the Streeter copy, with no mention of first edition).

*COMING Race (The).* Scarlet-orange cloth, blocked in black and gold. Edinburgh, (1871). (By Edward Bulwer-Lytton.) First edition. $35-50.

*COMMERCIAL Tourist (The); or, Gentleman Traveller: A Satirical Poem.* 5 colored plates by I.R. Cruikshank. Boards with label. London, 1822. (By Charles William Hempel.) First edition. $200-$250.

COMPTON-BURNETT, Ivy. *Dolores.* Cloth. Edinburgh & London, 1911. First edition. $600-$800. Author's first book, suppressed by her.

COMPTON-BURNETT, Ivy. *Pastors and Masters.* Cloth. London, 1925. First edition. In dust jacket. $50-$75.

CONARD, Howard Louis. *"Uncle Dick" Wootton, the Pioneer Frontiersman of the Rocky Mountain Region.* Portrait, 31 plates. Decorated cloth. Chicago, 1890. First edition. $150-$300.

CONCLIN, George. *Conclin's New River Guide, or a Gazeteer of All the Towns on the Western Waters.* 44 full-page route maps. 128 pp., wrappers. Cincinnati, 1850. $100-$150. Cincinnati, 1853. $75-$100.

*CONFEDERATE Receipt Book.* Wrappers. Richmond, 1863. First edition. $200-$350.

*CONFESSION; or, The Blind Heart.* 2 vols., cloth. Philadelphia, 1841. (By William Gilmore Simms.) First edition. $100-$125.

*CONFESSIONS of an English Opium-Eater.* Boards, paper label. London, 1822. (By Thomas De Quincey.) First edition, first issue, with ad leaf at end. $1,000-$1,500. Also, $516 (A, 1976); $550 (A, 1971). Second issue, lacking ad leaf: Boards. $750-$1,000. Also, covers loose, $600 (A, 1974). Philadelphia, 1823. Boards, paper label. First American edition. $100-$200. London, 1885. Morocco. One of 50 large paper copies. $150-$200. New York, 1930. Limited Editions Club. Boards. Boxed. $40-$60.

*CONFESSIONS of Harry Lorrequer (The).* Illustrated by Phiz. 11 parts, pictorial pink wrappers. Dublin, 1839. (By Charles Lever.) First edition. $250-$300. Another issue: Cloth. First edition in book form. $100-$125. Author's first book.

CONGREVE, William. *The Complete Works of William Congreve.* Edited by Montague Summers, 4 vols., boards and cloth. London, 1923. Nonesuch Press. One of 825. $150-$200. Another issue: Boards and vellum. One of 75 on handmade paper. $300-$400.

CONNELLEY, William E. *Quantrill and the Border Wars.* Illustrated. Red buckram. Cedar Rapids, Iowa, 1910. First edition. $50-$75.

CONNELLEY, William E. *The War with Mexico, 1846-47: Doniphan's Expedition.* 2 maps, illustrations. Cloth. Topeka, 1907. First edition. $50-$60.

CONNELLEY, William E. *Wild Bill and His Era.* 12 plates. Cloth. New York, 1933. First edition. In dust jacket. $35-$50.

CONNELLY, Marc. *The Green Pastures.* Illustrated in color by Robert Edmond Jones. Green boards. New York, 1930. One of 550 signed. Boxed. $50-$75. Some signed copies issued in morocco: $75-$125.

CONNETT, Eugene V. (editor). *Upland Game Bird Shooting in America.* Illustrated, including color plates. Pictorial cloth. New York, 1930. Derrydale Press. First edition. One of 850. $400-$500. Another issue: Brown morocco. One of 75 with 6 original signed etchings. $2,000-$2,250. Also, $1,800 (A, 1977).

CONNICK, Charles J. *Adventures in Light and Color.* Color plates and collotype plates. Buckram. New York, (1937). First edition. De luxe issue, with 42 plates in color, 48 in collotype. $125-$150. Trade issue: 36 colored plates. Cloth. $75-$100. London, 1937. 36 color plates, 48 in collotype. Cloth. First English edition. $75-$100. (Note: The first edition contains the first printing of Robert Frost's poem "Unless I Call It a Pewter Tray.")

CONNOLLY, A. P. *A Thrilling Narrative of the Minnesota Massacre and the Sioux War of 1862-1863.* Illustrated. Cloth. Chicago, (1896). First edition. $100-$125.

CONNOLLY, Cyril. See Palinurus.

CONNOLLY, Cyril. *The Rock Pool.* Wrappers. Paris, (1936). Obelisk Press. First edition. $250-$350. Author's first book.

CONRAD, Joseph. See anonymous entry *The Nigger of the "Narcissus." Preface.* (Under N.)

CONRAD, Joseph. *"Admiralty Paper."* Facsimile plate. Blue wrappers. (New York, 1925.) First edition. One of 93. $175-$225.

CONRAD, Joseph. *Almayer's Folly: A Story of an Eastern River.* Dark-green cloth. London, 1895. First edition, first issue, with first "e" missing in "generosity" in the second line from last on page 110. $500-$600. "Colonial" edition, same place and date, $300-$400. New York, 1895. Cloth. First American edition. $100-$150. Author's first book.

CONRAD, Joseph. *The Arrow of Gold: A Story Between Two Notes.* Dark-blue cloth. Garden City, 1919. First edition, first issue, with the reading "credentials and apparently" in line 16 of page 5. In dust jacket. $200-$300. Second issue ("credentials and who"): In dust jacket. $150-$200. London, (1919). Dark-green cloth. First English edition, first issue, with running head intact on page 67. In dust jacket. $50-$75. Second issue, with "A" missing in "Arrow" in headline on page 67. In dust jacket. $25-$30.

CONRAD, Joseph. *The Black Mate.* Green cloth. (Edinburgh), 1922. First edition. One of 50. $300-$400. Also, $210 (A, 1968).

CONRAD, Joseph. *Chance: A Tale in Two Parts.* Sage-green cloth. London, (1913). First edition, first issue, with "First published in 1913" on verso of title page. In dust jacket. $1,500-$2,000. Also, with a letter from Thomas J. Wise laid in, $1,700 (A, 1977). Second issue, with tipped in title page bearing 1914 date on verso: $50-$75. Garden City, 1913. Dark blue cloth. First American edition. One of 150 issued for copyright purposes. $100-$150. New York, 1914. Cloth. First published American edition. In dust jacket. $25-$35.

CONRAD, Joseph. *The Children of the Sea.* Mottled blue-gray cloth. New York, 1897. First edition (of the book published in England as *The Nigger of the "Narcissus").* $200-$300.

CONRAD, Joseph. *The Dover Patrol.* Light-blue wrappers. Canterbury, 1922. First edition, first issue, without title page. One of 75. $150-$200.

CONRAD, Joseph. *Joseph Conrad's Letters to His Wife.* Limp imitation leather. London, 1927. First edition. One of 220 signed by Jessie Conrad. $100-$150.

CONRAD, Joseph. *Last Essays.* Green cloth. London, 1926. First edition. $50-$75.

CONRAD, Joseph. *Laughing Anne: A Play.* Full vellum, gilt top, uncut. London, 1923. First edition. One of 200 signed. Boxed. $200-$225.

CONRAD, Joseph. *Letters from Joseph Conrad to Richard Curle.* Boards and cloth. New York, 1928. First edition. One of 850. $40-$50. Another issue: Black cloth. One of 9 on green paper. $250.

CONRAD, Joseph. *Life and Letters.* 2 vols., dark blue cloth. London, 1927. First edition. $75-$100. Garden City, 1927. Illustrated. First American edition. In dust jacket, $40-$60.

CONRAD, Joseph. *Lord Jim.* Gray-green cloth. Edinburgh, 1900. First edition. $100-$125.

CONRAD, Joseph. *The Mirror of the Sea: Memories and Impressions.* Light green cloth. London, (1906). First edition, with 40 pages of ads dated August, 1906. $100-$135. New York, 1906. Blue cloth. First American edition. In dust jacket. $40-$50.

CONRAD, Joseph. *The Nigger of the "Narcissus."* Gray cloth. London, 1898. First published English edition (of *The Children of the Sea).* $200-$250. (A copyright issue of about 7 copies was published in London, 1897, in wrappers. An inscribed copy of this book sold for $4,900 in 1928.) New York, 1965. Limited Editions Club. Boxed. $50.

CONRAD, Joseph. *Nostromo: A Tale of the Seaboard.* Bright-blue cloth. London, 1904. First edition, first issue, with 7 preliminary leaves and 478 pages of text. $100-$150. Second issue, with 8 preliminary leaves and 480 pages of text: $50-$80. New York, 1904. Green cloth. First American edition. $35. New York, 1961, Limited Editions Club, Boxed. $50.

CONRAD, Joseph. *Notes by Joseph Conrad in a Set of His First Editions in the Possession of Richard Curle.* Buckram, paper label. London, 1925. First edition. One of 100 signed by Curle. $75-$100.

CONRAD, Joseph. *Notes on Life and Letters.* Green cloth. London, 1921. First edition, first issue, with "S" and "A" missing from the word "Sea" in "Tales of the Sea" in table of contents. One of 33 privately printed. In dust jacket. $200-$350. Lacking jacket, $75. Also, presentation copy, $280 (A, 1968). First trade edition, with same errors in contents page: In dust jacket. $75-$85. Second issue, with "S" and "A" put in by hand press: In dust jacket. $35-$50. Third issue, page reprinted: In dust jacket. $25.

CONRAD, Joseph. *Notes on My Books.* Boards, parchment spine, paper labels. London, 1921. First English edition. One of 250 signed. In dust jacket. $200-$300.

CONRAD, Joseph. *One Day More: A Play in One Act.* Buckram and boards. London, 1919. Beaumont Press. One of 250. $150-$175. Another issue: One of 24 on Japan vellum, signed. $500-$600. Also, $336 (A, 1969). Garden City, 1920. Boards and parchment. One of 377 signed. $200-225.

CONRAD, Joseph. *An Outcast of the Islands.* Dark-green cloth, top edges gilt. London, 1896. First edition, first issue, with "this" for "there" in fourth line from last on page 26 and "absolution" for "ablution" in line 12 of page 110. $100-$125.

CONRAD, Joseph. *The Point of Honor: A Military Tale.* Illustrated by Dan Sayre Groesbeck. Decorated cloth. New York, 1908. First edition. In dust jacket. $100-$125.

CONRAD, Joseph. *The Rescue: A Romance of the Shallows.* Dark-blue cloth. Garden City, 1920. First edition. In dust jacket. $75-$100. London, 1920. Flexible red cloth (text differing from other editions). First English edition, first issue. One of 40 privately printed advance copies. $150-$200. London, 1920. Green cloth. First published English edition. In dust jacket. $50-$60.

CONRAD, Joseph. *The Rover.* Green cloth. London, (1923). First edition. In dust jacket. $50-$75. Garden City, 1923. Boards. First American edition. One of 377 signed. In dust jacket. Boxed. $100-$150. Trade edition: Cloth. In dust jacket. $35-$50.

CONRAD, Joseph. *The Secret Agent: A Drama in Three Acts.* Portrait frontispiece. Boards and parchment. London, 1923. First edition. One of 1,000 signed. $150-$200. Trade edition: Cloth. First issue, with misprint on page 117 and with 40 pages of ads at end. In dust jacket. $100-$135.

CONRAD, Joseph. *The Secret Agent: A Simple Tale.* Red cloth. London, (1907). First edition, with September ads at end. $150-$175.

CONRAD, Joseph. *A Set of Six.* Blue cloth. London, (1908). First edition, first issue, with ads dated February, 1908. $100-$150. Second issue, with ads dated June, 1908: $85-$125.

CONRAD, Joseph. *The Shadow-Line: A Confession.* Pale-green cloth. London, (1917). First edition, first issue, with 18 pages of ads at end. In dust jacket. $150-$175.

CONRAD, Joseph. *Some Reminiscences.* Yellow wrappers. New York, 1908. First edition (advance issue for copyright purposes). One of about 6 copies. $1,000 and up. London, 1912. Dark-blue cloth. First published edition. In dust jacket. $75-$125.

CONRAD, Joseph. *Suspense.* Boards. Garden City, 1925. First edition. One of 377. In dust jacket. $100-$135. London, 1925. Dark-red cloth. First English edition. In dust jacket. $50-$75.

CONRAD, Joseph. *Tales of Hearsay.* Dark-green cloth. London, (1925). First edition. In dust jacket. $60-$80. Garden City, 1925. Dark-blue cloth. First American edition. In dust jacket. $35.

CONRAD, Joseph. *Tales of Unrest.* Dark-green cloth. London, 1898. First edition, first issue, with all edges untrimmed. $100-$150. New York, 1898. Decorated brown cloth. First American edition. $75-$100.

CONRAD, Joseph. *'Twixt Land and Sea Tales.* Olive-green cloth. London, 1912. First edition, first issue, with misprint "Secret" instead of "Seven" on front cover. In dust jacket. $600-$800. Second issue, with "Seven" stamped over erased word "Secret": In dust jacket. $150-$175.

CONRAD, Joseph. *Typhoon.* Illustrated. Dark-green cloth. New York, 1902. First edition, first issue, with 4 pages of ads. In dust jacket. $150-$200. London, 1903. Dark-gray cloth. First English edition, first issue, with windmill device and without "Reserved for the Colonies only" on verso of half title. In dust jacket. $100-$125.

CONRAD, Joseph. *Under Western Eyes.* Red cloth. London, (1911). First edition, first issue, with ads dated September, 1911. In dust jacket. $75-$100.

CONRAD, Joseph. *Victory: An Island Tale.* Dark blue cloth. Garden City, 1915. First edition. In dust jacket. $200-$225. London, (1915). Red cloth, with 35 pages of ads at back and "Author's Note," which is not in the American edition. First English edition. In dust jacket. $150-$200.

CONRAD, Joseph. *Within the Tides: Tales.* Sage-green cloth. London, 1915. First edition. In dust jacket. $75-$125.

CONRAD Joseph. *Youth: A Narrative and Two Other Stories.* Light-green cloth. Edinburgh, 1902. First edition, first issue, with ads dated "10/02" at end. In dust jacket. $200-$250.

CONRAD, Joseph, and Hueffer, Ford M. *The Inheritors: An Extravagant Story.* Pictorial yellow cloth. New York, 1901. First edition, first issue, with the dedication leaf reading "To Boys and Christina." Only a few copies known. Up to $1,000. Also, $425 (A, 1962). First published edition, with a corrected dedication, on a stub: "To Borys and Christina": $75-$125. London, 1901. Yellow cloth. First English edition, first issue, without dedication leaf. $70-$85.

CONRAD, Joseph, and Hueffer, Ford M. *Romance: A Novel.* Bright-blue cloth. London, 1903. First edition, with 8 pages of ads at end. In dust jacket. $200-$250. New York, 1904. Cloth. First American edition. In dust jacket. $75-$100.

CONRAD, Capt. Thomas Nelson. *The Rebel Scout.* Cloth. Washington, 1904. First edition. $75-$100.

CONROY. Jack. *The Disinherited.* Cloth. (New York, 1933.) First edition. In dust jacket. $75-$100. Author's first book.

CONSIDERANT, Victor. *European Colonization in Texas.* 38 pp., wrappers. New York, 1855. First edition. $350-$750.

CONSTABLE, Henry. *Poems and Sonnets.* Woodcut border, ornamental woodcut initials. White pigskin. London, 1897. One of 210. $100-$150.

*CONSTITUTION and Laws of the Muskogee Nation.* Sheep. St. Louis, 1880. $200-$250.

*CONSTITUTION and Playing Rules of the International Baseball Association . . . and Championship Record for 1877.* 77 pp., wrappers. Jamaica Plain, Mass., 1878. $100-$150.

*CONSTITUTION and Rules of Business of the Essex Western Emigration Co.* 8 pp., wrappers. Lawrence, 1856. $125-$150.

*CONSTITUTION of the Republic of Mexico and the State of Coahuila and Texas (The).* Half calf. New York, 1832. $1,000-$1,500.

*CONSTITUTION of the U.S.A. . . . . Also, an Act to Establish a Territorial Government for Utah.* 48 pp., sewed. Salt Lake City, 1852. $750-$1,000.

*CONTACT Collection of Contemporary Writers.* Wrappers. (Paris, 1925.) Contact Editions.

One of 300. $300-$400. (Contains work by Ernest Hemingway, James Joyce, Ezra Pound, Gertrude Stein, William Carlos Williams, and others.)

*CONTESTACIONES Habidas entre el Supremo Gobierno Mexicano, etc.* 36 pp., printed wrappers. Mexico, 1847. First edition, first issue, with horn of plenty at foot of last page. $125-$175. Second issue, with Herrera letter on last page. $75-$100.

*CONVERSATIONS on the Mackinaw and Green-Bay Indian Missions.* Boards, Boston, 1821. (By Elizabeth Sanders.) First edition. $35.

CONWAY, Moncure D. *Barons of the Potomack and Rappahannock.* Illustrated. Boards. New York, 1892. Grolier Club. First edition. One of 360. $40-$50.

COOK, David J. *Hands Up, or 20 Years of Detective Life in the Mountains and on the Plains.* 32 plates. Wrappers. Denver, 1882. First edition. $250-$300. Cloth, same date, later issue: $200-$250. Denver, 1897. Second edition, enlarged, with *20 Years* changed to *35 Years* in title. $50-$60.

COOK, James H. *Fifty Years on the Old Frontier.* Plates. Cloth. New Haven, 1923. First edition. In dust jacket. $35-$50.

COOK, John R. *The Border and the Buffalo.* Plates. Pictorial cloth. Topeka, 1907. First edition. $40-$60.

COOKE, Giles B. *Just Before and After Lee Surrendered to Grant.* 8 pp., wrappers. (Houston, 1922.) First edition. $50-$60. With printing errors corrected in ink, $35.

COOKE, John (editor). *The Dublin Book of Irish Verse.* Dark-green limp leather. Dublin, 1909. First edition. $50. Another issue: Cloth. $25-$35. (Note: Contains three poems by James Joyce.)

COOKE, John Esten. See Effingham, C. Also see *Leather Stocking and Silk; The Life of Stonewall Jackson.*

COOKE, John Esten. *A Life of General Robert E. Lee.* Cloth. New York, 1871. First edition. $25-$35.

COOKE, John Esten. *Surry of Eagle's Nest.* Illustrated by Winslow Homer. Cloth. New York, 1866. First edition, with Bunce and Huntington imprint. $50-$75.

COOKE, Philip St. George. *The Conquest of New Mexico and California.* Folding map. Cloth. New York, 1878. First edition. $150-$250.

COOKE, Philip St. George. *Scenes and Adventures in the Army.* Cloth. Philadelphia, 1857. First edition. $150-$175.

COON, James Churchill. *Log of the Cruise of 1889 D.T.S.C., New Smyrna to Lake Worth, East Coast of Florida.* 119 pp., printed wrappers. Lake Helen, Fla., 1889. First edition. $100.

COOPER, J. W. *Game Fowls, Their Origin and History.* Colored lithographs. Pictorial green cloth, gilt. West Chester, Pa., (1869). $50-$75.

COOPER, James Fenimore. See Morgan, Jane. Also see *The Bee-Hunter; The Borderes; The Bravo; The Chainbearer; The Deerslayer; The Headsman; The Heidenmauer; Home as Found; The Last of the Mohicans; Lionel Lincoln; The Monikins; The Pathfinder; The Pilot; The Pioneers; The Prairie; Precaution; Ravensnest; The Red Rover; The Redskins; Satanstoe; The Spy; The Two Admirals; The Water Witch; The Wept of Wish Ton-Wish; The Wing-and-Wing; Wyandotte.*

COOPER, James Fenimore. *The Battle of Lake Erie.* Printed wrappers. Cooperstown, N.Y., 1843. First edition. $50-$75.

COOPER, James Fenimore. *The History of the Navy of the United States of America.* Maps. 2 vols., cloth. Philadelphia, 1839. First edition. $125-$175. London, 1839. 2 vols., cloth. First English edition. $75-$125. Paris, 1839. 2 vols. in one, half leather. $75-$100.

COOPER, James Fenimore. *The Jack O'Lantern.* 3 vols., drab brown boards, purple cloth, paper spine labels. London, 1842. First edition (of the novel issued anonymously in America as *The Wing-and-Wing,* which see as title entry). $100-$150.

COOPER, James Fenimore. *Lives of Distinguished American Naval Officers.* 2 vols., cloth, or 2 vols., printed blue wrappers. Philadelphia, 1846. First edition. Cloth: $75-$100. Wrappers: $150-$200.

COOPER, James Fenimore. *Notions of the Americans.* 2 vols., boards, paper labels. London, 1828. First edition. $75-$100. Philadelphia, 1828. 2 vols., boards, paper labels. First American edition. $50-$75.

COOPER, Lane (editor). *A Concordance to the Poems of William Wordsworth.* Cloth. London, 1911. First edition. $100-$125.

COOPER, Thomas. *On Irritation and Insanity.* 2 portraits. Boards. London, 1833. $35-$40.

COOVER, Robert. *The Origin of the Brunists.* Wrappers. New York, (1966). First edition, advance copy. $75-$100. Regular edition: Boards. In dust jacket. $50. Author's first book.

COPLAND, Robert (translator). *The History of Helyas Knight of the Swan.* Illustrated. Pigskin. New York, 1901. Grolier Club. One of 325. $85-$110.

COPPARD, A. E. *Adam and Eve and Pinch Me.* White buckram. Waltham Saint Lawrence, 1921. Golden Cockerel Press. First edition. One of 160 (from an edition of 550). $40-$50. Another issue: Orange boards. One of 340. $50-$85. New York, 1922. Boards and cloth. First American edition. $15-$20.

COPPARD, A. E. *The Black Dog.* Boards and cloth. London, 1923. First edition. $25.

COPPARD, A. E. *Cherry Ripe: Poems.* Illustrated. Full purple and green morocco. (Monmouthshire, England), 1935. Tintern Press. One of 10 signed. $100-$150. Another issue: One of 150. $50-$60.

COPPARD, A. E. *Pink Furniture.* Illustrated. Vellum. London, 1930. First edition. One of 260 signed. In dust jacket. $50-$60.

COPPARD, A. E. *Silver Circus.* Full vellum. (London, 1928). First edition. One of 125 signed. $35.

COPPARD, A. E. *Yokohama Garland and Other Poems.* Boards and buckram. Philadelphia, (1926). Centaur Press. First edition. One of 500 signed. Boxed. $60-$80.

CORELLI, Marie. *Barabbas.* 3 vols.. cloth. London, (1893). First edition. $75-$125.

CORELLI, Marie. *The Mighty Atom.* Cloth. London, 1896. First edition. $35-$50.

CORELLI, Marie. *Ziska: The Problem of a Wicked Soul.* Cloth. Bristol, England, 1897. First edition. $40-$50.

CORNER, William. *San Antonio de Bexar.* Map, 16 plates. Cloth. San Antonio, 1890. First edition. $60-$80.

CORNFORD, Frances. *Autumn Midnight.* Woodcuts by Eric Gill. Wrappers. London, 1923. First edition. $60-$80.

CORNWALL, Bruce. *Life Sketch of Pierre Barlow Cornwall.* 6 portraits. Boards. San Francisco, 1906. First edition. $35-$50.

CORRILL, John. *A Brief History of the Church of Christ of Latter Day Saints.* 50 pp., sewed. St. Louis, 1839. First edition. $5,000 and up.

CORSO, Gregory. *Ankh.* Oblong, magenta wrappers. New York, 1971. First edition. One of 100 signed. $35-$50.

CORSO, Gregory. *Bomb.* Wrappers. San Francisco, (1958). City Lights. First edition. $35-$50.

CORSO, Gregory. *Gasoline.* Wrappers. San Francisco, (1958). City Lights Books. First edition. $35-$50.

CORSO, Gregory. *10 Times a Poem.* Flexible pictorial boards. No place, 1971. First edition. One of 20 signed, with holograph poem on colophon page. $100-$125.

CORSO, Gregory. *The Vestal Lady on Brattle and Other Poems.* Printed wrappers. Cambridge, Mass., 1955. First edition. $150-$200. Author's first book. (250 copies.)

*CORVO, 1860-1960: A Collection of Essays by Various Hands.* Edited by Cecil Woolf and Brocard Sewell. Aylesford, England, 1961. First edition. One of 300 signed. In glassine dust jacket. $35-$50.

CORVO, Baron (Frederick William Rolfe). See Rolfe, Fr. Also see *Tarcissus.*

CORVO, Baron. *The Desire and Pursuit of the Whole.* Veridian (dark green) cloth. London, (1934). (By Frederick William Rolfe.) First edition, first binding. In dust jacket. $125-$150.

CORVO, Baron. *In His Own Image.* Blue-gray cloth. London. 1901. (By Frederick William Rolfe.) First edition, with ad leaf. In dust jacket. $150-$250. Variant issue: Red cloth, with "Bodley Head" imprint on spine, instead of "John Lane." $237 in a 1975 catalogue.

CORVO, Baron. *Letters to Grant Richards.* Boards. (Hurst, England, 1952.) (By Frederick William Rolfe.) Peacocks Press. First edition. One of 200. $100-$200.

CORVO, Baron. *Stories Toto Told Me.* Printed green wrappers. London, 1898. (By Frederick William Rolfe.) First edition. No. 6 of the Bodley Booklets. $250-$350, possibly more. Also, $250 (A, 1977).

CORVO, Baron. *Chronicles of the House of Borgia.* 10 plates. Pictorial red buckram. London, 1901. (By Frederick William Rolfe.) First edition. $200-$250. New York, 1901. Dark red or black cloth. First American edition. $150-$200.

COSSLEY-BATT, Jill L. *The Last of the California Rangers.* Illustrated. Three-quarters green morocco. New York, 1928. First edition. One of 200 signed. $35-$50. Trade edition: Cloth. In dust jacket. $15-$20.

COSTANSO, Miguel. *The Spanish Occupation of California.* Portraits, folding maps. Boards. San Francisco, 1934. One of 550. In slipcase. $75-$100.

COUES, Elliott (editor). *New Light on the Early History of the Greater Northwest.* Frontispiece, facsimile, 3 maps in pocket of Vol. 3. 3 vols., cloth. New York, 1897. One of 1,000. $200-$250. Another issue: Half vellum. One of 100 on large paper. $300-$400.

COULTER, E. Merton, *Travels in the Confederate States: A Bibliography.* Cloth. Norman, Okla., 1948. First edition. In dust jacket. $35-$50.

*COUNT Julian; or, the Last Days of the Goth.* Cloth. Baltimore, 1845. (By William Gilmore Simms.) First edition. $100-$150.

*COUNT Julian: A Tragedy.* Boards, printed label. London, 1812. (By Walter Savage Landor.) First edition. $250-$300. Also, $130 (A, 1976).

COURSEY, O. W. *"Wild Bill" (James Butler Hickok).* Illustrated. Cloth. Mitchell, S.D., (1924). First edition. $30-$50.

COURTAULD, George. *Address to Those Who May Be Disposed to Remove to the United States of America.* 40 pp., wrappers. Sudbury, 1820. First edition. $1,250.

COUTS, Cave J. *From San Diego to the Colorado in 1849.* 3 maps on 2 sheets. Boards. Los Angeles, 1932. First edition. $75-$100.

COUTS, Joseph. *A Practical Guide for the Tailor's Cutting Room.* 13 colored plates, 14 uncolored. Half morocco. London, (1848). $80.

COWAN, Robert E. *A Bibliography of the History of California and the Pacific West,*

*1510-1906.* Boards and linen. San Francisco, 1914. First edition. One of 250. Boxed. $150-$250. San Francisco, 1933. 3 vols., boards and cloth. $200-$250.

COWARD, Noel. *"I'll Leave It to You."* Wrappers. London, 1920. First edition. $50-$75. Author's first book (?).

COWLEY, Malcolm. *Blue Juniata: Poems.* Cloth. New York, 1929. First edition. $75-$100.

COWLEY, Malcolm. *Racine.* Wrappers. Paris, 1923. First edition. $100-$150. Author's first book.

COX, Isaac. *The Annals of Trinity County.* Half cloth. San Francisco, 1940. John Henry Nash printing. One of 350. Boxed. $35-$50.

COX, James. *Historical and Biographical Record of the Cattle Industry and the Cattlemen of Texas and Adjacent Territory.* Colored frontispiece, other illustrations. Decorated leather. St. Louis, 1895. First edition. $3,000-$4,000, possibly more. Spine restored, $2,250. New York, 1959. 2 vols., half leather. Boxed. One of 500. $100-$150.

COX, Nicholas. *The Gentleman's Recreation.* London, 1928. Cresset Press. One of 600. $75-$100. Another issue: One of 50. $100-$125.

COX, Palmer. *The Brownies Around the World.* Illustrated. Cloth. New York, (1894). First edition. $100-$125.

COX, Palmer. *The Brownies at Home.* Pictorial boards. New York, (1893). First edition. In dust jacket. $100-$125.

COX, Palmer. *The Brownies: Their Book.* Green glazed pictorial boards. New York, (1887). First edition, first issue, with DeVinne Press seal immediately below copyright notice. In dust jacket. $500-$750. Second issue, with seal about 2½ inches from bottom of page. In dust jacket. $400-$500.

COX, Palmer. *Queer People with Wings and Stings and Their Kweer Kapers.* Pictorial boards. Philadelphia, (1888). First edition. $80-$125.

COX, Palmer. *Queerie Queers with Hands, Wings and Claws.* Pictorial boards. Buffalo, ("about 1887"). First edition. $100-$150.

COX, Ross. *Adventures on the Columbia River.* 2 vols., boards. London, 1831. First edition. $500-$750. New York, 1832. Cloth or boards. First American edition. $350-$500.

COX, Sandford C. *Recollections of the Early Settlement of the Wabash Valley.* Cloth. Lafayette, Ind., 1860. First edition. $60-$80.

COXE, Louis O. *The Sea Faring and Other Poems.* Cloth. New York, (1947). First edition. In dust jacket. $40-$50. Author's first book.

COY, Owen C. *Pictorial History of California.* 261 photographs. Cloth. Berkeley, 1925. $75-$85.

COYNER, David H. *The Lost Trappers.* Cloth. Cincinnati, 1847. First edition. $300-$400. Cincinnati, 1850. Cloth. Second edition. $150-$200.

COZZENS, Frederick S. *Acadia.* 2 plates. Cloth. New York, 1859. First edition. $50.

COZZENS, James Gould. *Cock Pit.* Cloth. New York, 1928. First edition. In dust jacket. $75-$100.

COZZENS, James Gould. *Confusion.* Cloth. Boston, 1924. First edition. In dust jacket. $125-$150. Author's first book.

CRABBE, George. *The Borough: A Poem.* Boards, printed label. London, 1810. First edition. $100-$150.

CRABBE, George, *Tales of the Hall.* 2 vols., Boards. London, 1819. First edition. $100-$150.

CRAIG, John R. *Ranching with Lords and Commons.* 17 plates. Pictorial cloth. Toronto, (1903). First edition. $200-$300.

CRAKES, Sylvester. *Five Years a Captive Among the Black-Feet Indians.* 6 plates. Cloth. Columbus, Ohio, 1858. First edition. $300-$350.

CRANCH, Christopher Pearse. *Giant Hunting: or, Little Jacket's Adventures.* Illustrated. Pictorial cloth. Boston, 1860. $75-$100.

CRANCH, Christopher Pearse. *Kobboltozo.* Illustrated. Cloth. Boston, 1857. First edition. $75-$100.

CRANCH, Christopher Pearse. *The Last of the Huggermuggers.* Illustrated. Cloth. Boston, 1856. First edition. $75-$100.

CRANE, Hart. See *The Pagan Anthology.*

CRANE, Hart. *The Bridge.* 3 photographs by Walker Evans. Stiff printed wrappers. Paris, 1930. Black Sun Press. First edition. One of 200, (weighing 19¼ ounces each). In glassine dust jacket. Boxed. $750-$1,000. Also, $750 (A, 1977). Also, 20 (or 25?) copies not for sale, on thin paper and weighing 15¼ ounces each. $750-$1,000. Another issue: One of 50 on Japan vellum; signed. In glassine dust jacket and slipcase. $2,000-$2,500. Also, $1,800 (A, 1977). Also, 8 lettered copies on vellum, signed by the poet. $3,500-$5,000. New York, 1930. Cloth. First American edition. In dust jacket. $400-$500.

CRANE, Hart. *The Collected Poems of Hart Crane.* Edited by Waldo Frank. Portrait frontispiece. Red cloth. New York, (1933). First edition, first issue, with flat spine and imprint of "Liveright Inc., Publishers." In dust jacket. $75-$100. Second issue, with rounded spine and imprint of "Liveright Publishing Corporation": In dust jacket. $35-$50. Another issue: Brown cloth. One of 50 "for friends." $285-$350. Also, soiled and worn, $175 (A, 1977).

CRANE, Hart. *Two Letters.* Leaflet, 4 pp. Brooklyn Heights, 1934. First edition. One of 50. $300-$350. Also, $225 (A, 1977).

CRANE, Hart. *Voyages.* Illustrated by Leonard Baskin. Oblong, wrappers in board folder. New York, 1957. First edition. One of 975. $200-$300.

CRANE, Hart. *White Buildings.* Foreword by Allen Tate. Boards, cloth spine. (New York), 1926. First edition, first issue, with Tate's first name misspelled "Allan." In dust jacket. $1,000-$1,250. Second issue, with tipped-in title page, Tate's name spelled correctly: In dust jacket. $300-$400. Lacking jacket, $150-$200. Author's first book.

CRANE, Stephen. See Smith, Johnston. Also see *The Lanthorn Book; Pike County Puzzle.*

CRANE, Stephen. *Active Service.* Light-green cloth. New York, (1899). First edition. In dust jacket. $125-$175. London, 1899. Cloth. First English edition. $50-$60.

CRANE, Stephen. *The Black Riders and Other Lines.* Yellow cloth or gray decorated boards. Boston, 1895. First edition. (500 copies.) $285-$350. Also, $175 (A, 1977); $230 (A, 1968). Another issue: Plain boards, paper label. One of 50 printed in green ink on vellum. No copies noted for sale in recent years. Estimated value: $750-$1,000. (Note: Johnson reports three copies of this issue were said to have been bound in full vellum.)

CRANE, Stephen. *George's Mother.* Tan cloth. New York, 1896. First edition. $50-$75. London, 1896. Cloth. $40-$60.

CRANE, Stephen. *Great Battles of the World.* Illustrated by John Sloan. Red cloth. Philadelphia, 1901. First edition. $60-$80. London, 1901. Cloth. $40-$60.

CRANE, Stephen. *Last Words.* Red cloth. London, 1902. First edition. $150-$200.

CRANE, Stephen. *Legends.* 4 pp., printed buff wrappers. Ysleta, Tex., 1942. First edition. One of 45. $125-$150.

CRANE, Stephen. *The Little Regiment and Other Episodes of the American Civil War.* Cream-yellow buckram. New York, 1896. First edition, first state, with 6 pages of ads at the back, the first page headed "Gilbert Parker's Best Books." In dust jacket. $300-$350.

CRANE, Stephen. *A Lost Poem.* Wrappers. New York, (1932). First edition. One of 100. $40-$50.

CRANE, Stephen. *Maggie: A Girl of the Streets.* Cream-yellow buckram. New York, 1896. Second (revised) edition, first state, with title page printed in capital and lower case Roman type, according to Blanck. $150-$200. Also, $90 (A, 1975); $65 (A, 1972). (For first edition, see Johnston Smith, *Maggie: A Girl of the Streets.)*

CRANE, Stephen. *The Monster and Other Stories.* Illustrated. Red cloth. New York, 1899. First edition. In dust jacket. $150-$200. London, 1901. Revised edition, with four stories added. $75-$100. (No American edition of this revision recorded.)

CRANE, Stephen. *The Open Boat and Other Tales of Adventure.* Dark-green pictorial cloth. New York, 1898. First American edition. In dust jacket. $300-$350. Also, $170 (A, 1976). London, 1898. First English edition, with nine added stories. $100-$125.

CRANE, Stephen. *The Red Badge of Courage.* Cream-yellow buckram. New York, 1895. First edition, first state, with perfect type in the last line on page 225. In dust jacket. $1,000 and up. Lacking jacket, $500-$750. New York, 1896. Cloth. $75-$100. New York, (1931). Grabhorn printing. Illustrated by Valenti Angelo. Boards. One of 980. $100-$150. New York, 1944. Limited Editions Club. Illustrated. Embossed morocco. Boxed. $85-$125.

CRANE, Stephen. *The Third Violet.* Cream-yellow buckram. New York, 1897. First edition. In dust jacket. $100-$150.

CRANE, Stephen. *War Is Kind.* Illustrated by Will Bradley, Pictorial gray boards. New York, 1899. First edition. $350-$400. Also, $300 (A, 1977).

CRANE, Stephen. *Whilomville Stories.* Illustrated by Peter Newell. Light-green cloth. New York, 1900. First edition. $75-$100. London, 1910. Blue cloth. First English edition. $50-$60.

CRANE, Stephen. *Wounds in the Rain.* Cloth. London, 1900. First edition. $100-$150. New York, (1900). Cloth. First American edition. $75-$100.

CRANE, Walter. *The Bases of Design.* Blue-gray cloth. London, 1898. First edition. $75-$100.

CRANE, Walter. *Flora's Feast.* Illustrated by the author. Boards. London, 1889. First edition. $100-$125.

CRANE, Walter. *Of the Decorative Illustration of Books Old and New.* Illustrated. Cloth. London, 1896. First edition. One of 130. $100-$125. London, (1921). In dust jacket. $25-$35.

CRANE, Walter. *Renascence: A Book of Verse.* 39 designs by Crane. Boards, vellum spine. London, 1891. Chiswick Press. One of 100 large paper copies. $150. Another issue: One of 44 on vellum, signed. $200. Trade edition: $40-$50.

CRANE, Walter. *Slate and Pencil-Vania.* Illustrated. Pictorial half cloth. London, 1885. First edition. $75-$100.

CRANE, Walter. *Valentine and Orson.* 8 color illustrations. Printed wrappers. (London, about 1870-73). Sixpence Toy Book. $75-$100.

CRANFORD. By the author of "Mary Barton," "Ruth," etc. Green cloth. London, 1853. (By Elizabeth C. Gaskell.) First edition. $250-$350.

CRAPSLEY, Adelaide. *Verse.* Cloth. Rochester, N.Y., 1915. First edition. $60-$75.

CRARY, Mary. *The Daughters of the Stars.* Illustrated by Edmund Dulac. Green cloth, vellum spine. London, 1939. One of 500 signed by the author and the artist. In dust jacket. $300-$400.

CRAWFORD, Isabell C. *The Tapestry of Time.* Blue cloth. Boston, 1927. First edition. In dust jacket. $75-$100.

CRAWFORD, Lewis F. *Rekindling Camp Fires.* Illustrated. Half leather. Bismarck, N.D., 1926. First edition. One of 100 signed. Boxed. $85-$125. Trade edition: Cloth. In dust jacket. $40-$60.

CRAWFORD, Lucy. *The History of the White Mountains.* Cloth. Portland, Me., 1846. First edition. $50-$60.

CRAWSHAY, Richard. *The Birds of Tierra del Fuego.* 21 color plates by J. G. Keulemans, 23 photographic views, map. Half morocco. London, 1907. One of 300. $300-$400.

CRAYON, Geoffrey. *The Alhambra.* 2 vols., drab boards, printed spine label. London, 1832. (By Washington Irving.) First edition. $150-$200. Philadelphia, 1832. Anonymously published ("By the Author of 'The Sketch-Book' "). 2 vols., boards and cloth, paper spine label. First American edition. $150-$200.

CRAYON, Geoffrey. *Bracebridge Hall, or The Humourists.* 2 vols., drab brown boards, paper label. New York, 1822. (By Washington Irving.) First edition. $750-$1,000. Also, repaired copy, $225 (A, 1975). London, 1822. Boards, paper label. First English edition (simultaneous with the American?), text ending on page 403, Vol. 2. $100-$150. New York, 1896. Surrey Edition. Arthur Rackham illustrations. 2 vols., pictorial cloth. $125-$150.

CRAYON, Geoffrey. *The Sketch Book of Geoffrey Crayon, Gent.* 7 parts, wrappers. New York, 1819-20. (By Washington Irving.) First edition. Parts 1 through 5 dated 1819, parts 6 and 8 dated 1820. Rarely offered in original wrappers. Rebound in 2 vols, calf. $550 in a 1974 catalogue. (Note: Second editions so identified on wrappers. Like *Salmagundi,* this is a complicated work to identify, and it exists in many variations. See Blanck, *A Bibliography of American Literature.*)

CRAYON, Geoffrey. *Tales of a Traveller.* 2 vols., boards and cloth, paper label. London, 1824. (By Washington Irving.) First edition. $75-$100. Philadelphia, 1824. 4 parts, wrappers. First American edition, first issue, with "H. C. Cary" (instead of Carey) on title page. $100-$150.

*CREEK Treaty Correspondence Preliminary to the Treaty of Aug. 7, 1856.* Boards. Washington, 1856. $150-$200.

*CREEK Treaty, Passed in Congress, Feb. 1901.* 11 pp., wrappers. Muskogee, Okla., 1901. $150-$200.

CREELEY, Robert. *About Women.* 5 pp., large square folio, unbound. Los Angeles, 1966. Limited extra issue of an introduction (3 poems) for a book of John Altoon lithographs. $50-$60.

CREELEY, Robert. *All That Is Lovely in Men.* Drawings by Dan Rice. Pictorial wrappers. Asheville, 1955. Jargon No. 10. First edition. One of 200 signed by Creeley and Rice. $50-$75.

CREELEY, Robert. *The Charm.* Leather-backed cloth. (Mt. Horeb, Wis.), 1967. Perishable Press. First edition. One of 250 signed. $40-$50. San Francisco, 1969. Boards and cloth. One of 100 signed. $35.

CREELEY, Robert. *5 Numbers.* Wrappers. (New York, 1968.) First edition. One of 150 manuscript facsimile copies, signed. $25-$30.

CREELEY, Robert. *For Love, Poems 1950-1960.* Cloth. New York, (1962). First edition. In dust jacket. $25-$30.

CREELEY, Robert. *The Gold Diggers.* Wrappers. (Mallorca), 1954. Divers Press. First edition. $85-$100. New York, (1965). First American edition. $25.

CREELEY, Robert. *If You.* Illustrated by Fielding Dawson. 14 unsewn leaves in wrappers. San Francisco, 1956. One of 200. $50-$75.

CREELEY, Robert. *The Immoral Proposition.* Wrappers. Baden, Germany, 1953. First edition. One of 200. $125-$150.

CREELEY, Robert. *The Kind of Act Of.* Wrappers. (Palma), 1953. Divers Press. First edition. $200-$250.

CREELEY, Robert. *Le Fou.* Frontispiece. Decorated wrappers. Columbus, Ohio, 1952. First edition. $175-$250. Author's first book.

CREELEY, Robert. *Numbers.* Wrappers. Stuttgart, 1968. Limited signed edition. In slipcase. $40-$50.

CREELEY, Robert. *Poems, 1950-1965.* Vellum and boards. London, (1966 ). First edition. One of 100 signed. In slipcase. $75-$100. New York, 1967. First American edition (with added poems). In dust jacket. $25-$30.

CREELEY, Robert. *A Sight.* Drawings by Ron Kitaj. Large portfolio, silk-screened facsimiles of handwritten poems. London, (1967). First edition. $100-$120.

CREELEY, Robert. *The Whip.* Wrappers. (Mallorca, 1957.) First edition. $40-$50. Another issue: Boards. $80-$100.

CREMONY, John C. *Life Among the Apaches.* Cloth. San Francisco, 1869. First edition. $200-$250.

CREUZBAUR, Robert (compiler). *Route from the Gulf of Mexico and the Lower Mississippi Valley to California and the Pacific Ocean.* 5 maps in pocket. 40 pp., cloth. New York, 1849. First edition. $4,000-$5,000. (A Texas dealer sold a copy in 1976 for $4,000.)

CREVEL, René. *Mr. Knife, Miss Fork.* Translated by Kay Boyle. Illustrated by Max Ernst. Cloth. Paris, 1931. Black Sun Press. One of 200. $1,000-$2,000. Another issue: One of 50 specially bound, signed by Crevel and Ernst. $2,500-$3,000.

CREYTON, Paul. *Martin Merivale; His X Mark.* Cloth. Boston, 1854. (By John Townsend Trowbridge.) First edition, first state, with Creyton, not Trowbridge, on spine and stereotyper's slug on copyright page. $50-$75. (Second state has Trowbridge on spine.)

CREYTON, Paul. *Paul Creyton's Great Romance!! Kate the Accomplice; or, the Preacher and the Burglar.* Pictorial pink wrappers. Boston, (1849). (By John Townsend Trowbridge.) First edition, with 1849 cover date. $1,000 and up. Author's first book.

CRICHTON, The Rev. *The Festival of Flora.* Hand-colored plates. Half leather and boards. London, 1818. Second edition. $225. Also, $160 (A, 1974).

*CRITERION (The): A Quarterly Review.* Vol. I, No. 1. Wrappers. London, October, 1922. First edition. This magazine contains the first appearance in print of T. S. Eliot's poem "The Waste Land." $400 (A, 1977).

CROAKER, Croaker & Co., and Croaker, Jun. *Poems.* 36 pp. Printed tan wrappers. New York, 1819. (By Joseph Rodman Drake and Fitz-Greene Halleck.) First edition. $500 and up. First book by each author. (Note: Reissued: *The Croakers.* Green cloth. New York, 1860. One of 250. $50.)

CROCKET, George L. *Two Centuries in East Texas.* Dallas, (about 1932). First edition. $150-$200.

CROCKETT, David. *An Account of Col. Crockett's Tour to the North and Down East.* Cloth. Philadelphia, 1835. (By Augustin S. Clayton?) First edition. $100-$150.

CROCKETT, David. *A Narrative of the Life of Col. David Crockett.* Written by Himself. Cloth. Philadelphia, 1834. First edition, with 22 pages of ads at end. $200-$250.

*CROMWELL: An Historical Novel.* 2 vols., brown cloth, paper labels, New York, 1838. (By Henry William Herbert.) First edition, first issue, with 12 pages of ads. $75-$125.

CROSBY, Caresse. *Crosses of Gold: A Book of Verse.* Hand-colored illustrations. Green parchment. Paris, 1925. First edition. One of 100. $150-$250. Author's first book.

CROSBY, Caresse. *Painted Shores.* Illustrated with 3 watercolors. Wrappers. Paris, 1927. First edition. One of 222 on Arches paper. $100-$150.

CROSBY, Caresse, *Poems for Harry Crosby.* Frontispiece. Boards and cloth. Paris, 1931. Black Sun Press. First edition. One of 44. $100-$150.

CROSBY, Harry. *Chariot of the Sun.* Introduction by D.H. Lawrence. Wrappers. Paris, 1931. Black Sun Press. One of 500. $75.

CROSBY, Harry. *Sleeping Together: Poems.* Wrappers. Paris, 1931. Black Sun Press. One of 500. $75-$100.

CROSBY, Harry. *Torchbearer.* Notes by Ezra Pound. Wrappers. Paris, 1931. Black Sun Press. One of 500. $75.

CROSBY, Harry. *Transit of Venus.* Printed wrappers. Paris, 1928. Black Sun Press. First edition. One of 44. $100-$150. Paris, 1929. Wrappers. Second edition. One of 200. In glassine dust jacket. Boxed. $50-$60. Paris, 1931. Preface by T.S. Eliot. One of 500. In glassine jacket. $75-$100.

CROSBY, Sylvester S. *The Early Coins of America.* 12 parts in 11, wrappers. Boston, 1873-75. $300-$400. Boston, 1878. 10 plates. Morocco. $50-$75.

*CROTCHET Castle.* By the Author of *Headlong Hall.* Boards, paper label, London, 1831. (By Thomas Love Peacock.) First edition. $200-$250.

CROTHERS, Samuel McCord. *Miss Muffet's Christmas Party.* Pictorial vellum wrappers. St. Paul, (1892). First edition. $50-$60. Author's first book.

CROTTY, D. G. *Four Years Campaigning in the Army of the Potomac.* Half morocco. Grand Rapids, 1894. First edition. $75-$85.

CROWDER, Henry; Beckett, Samuel; Aldington, Richard; and others. *Henry-Music.* Pictorial boards. Paris, 1930. Hours Press. First edition. One of 100 signed by Crowder. (Includes poems by the authors set to music by Crowder, a black musician.) $1,500 and up. Also, with an inscription to Augustus John, $1,700 (A, 1977).

CROWLEY, Aleister. See Therion, The Master. Also see *Aceldama.*

CROWLEY, Aleister. *Ahab and Other Poems.* Wrappers. London, 1903. $100-$150. Another issue: Vellum. Printed on vellum. $200-$300.

CROWLEY, Aleister. *Magick.* 4 vols., red wrappers. Paris, 1929. $100-$150.

CROWLEY, Aleister. *Moonchild: A Prologue.* Cloth. London, 1929. First edition. $60-$80.

CROWLEY, Aleister. *Olla: An Anthology of Sixty Years of Song.* Cloth. London, (1946). First edition. One of 500. In dust jacket. $150-$175.

CROWLEY, Aleister. *Songs of the Spirit.* Cloth. London, 1898. First edition. One of 50. $100-$150.

CROWLEY, Aleister. *The Soul of Osiris.* Boards, cloth spine, paper label. London, 1901. First edition. $100-$125.

CRUIKSHANK, George. See *The Humourist; More Hints on Etiquette.*

CRUIKSHANK, Percy. *Hints to Emigrants, or, Incidents in the Emigration of John Smith.* 9 full-page etchings. Pictorial wrappers. London, (about 1830). $75.

*CRYSTAL Age (A).* Black or red cloth. London, 1887. (By W. H. Hudson.) First edition, with 32 pages of ads at end. $200-$250.

CUFFE, Paul. *Narrative of the Life and Adventures of Paul Cuffe, a Pequot Indian.* Wrappers. New York, 1839. $175-$225.

*CUISINE Créole (La).* Pictorial cloth. New York, (1885). (Compiled by Lafcadio Hearn.) First edition, first issue, brown cloth, with "Brûlot" (in the ninth line of introduction) instead of "Brûlot." $500-$600. Also, "binding defective," $325 (A, 1974). New Orleans, 1922. Cloth. Second edition. $50-$60.

CULLEN, Countee. *The Ballad of the Brown Girl.* Cloth and boards, paper label. New York, 1927. First edition. One of 500. $60-$80.

CULLEN, Countee. *The Black Christ and Other Poems.* Decorations by Charles Cullen. Boards and cloth. New York, 1929. First edition. One of 128 signed. $125-$150. Trade edition. In dust jacket. $40-$60.

CULLEN, Countee. *Color.* Drawings by Charles Cullen. Boards and cloth. New York, 1925. First edition. In dust jacket. $50-$75. Author's first book.

CULLEN, Countee (editor). *Caroling Dusk.* Cloth. New York, 1927. First edition. In dust jacket. $60-$80.

CUMING, F. *Sketches of a Tour to the Western Country.* Leather. Pittsburgh, 1810. First edition. $300-$400.

CUMINGS, Samuel. *The Western Pilot.* Printed boards. Cincinnati, 1825. $600-$1,000. Cincinnati, 1829. $400.

CUMMINGS, E. E. See *Eight Harvard Poets.*

CUMMINGS, E. E. (No title.) Illustrated by the author. New York, 1930. First edition. One of 491 signed. $185-$200.

CUMMINGS, E. E. Green gold-flecked boards. New York, 1925. First edition. One of 111 on Vidalon paper, signed. Boxed. $150-$200. Another issue: One of 222 on rag paper, signed. Boxed. $60-$80.

CUMMINGS, E. E. *Anthropos: The Future of Art.* Half cloth. (New York, 1944.) First edition. One of 222. In cloth dust jacket. Boxed. $150-$200.

CUMMINGS. E. E. *Christmas Tree.* Green decorated boards. New York, 1928. First edition. In glassine dust jacket. $300-$350. Also, $275 (A, 1977).

CUMMINGS, E. E. *Ciopw.* Cloth. New York, 1931. First edition. One of 391 signed. $400-$500. Also, $300 (A, 1975).

CUMMINGS, E. E. *Eimi.* Yellow cloth. (New York, 1933.) First edition. One of 1,381 signed. In tissue dust jacket. $150-$200. New York, (1958). Boards and cloth. Third edition. One of 26 lettered and signed. In glassine jacket. $200-$300.

CUMMINGS, E. E. *The Enormous Room.* Tan buckram. New York, (1922). First edition. With or without fifth word ("shit") of last line on page 219 inked out. In dust jacket. $300-$400. Also $250 (A, 1971). Signed, $425 (A, 1977). Author's first book.

CUMMINGS, E. E. *Fairy Tales.* Illustrated. Cloth. New York, 1950. First edition. In dust jacket. $40-$50.

CUMMINGS. E. E. *50 Poems.* Cloth. New York, (1940). First edition. One of 150 signed. In glassine dust jacket. Boxed. $150-$200.

CUMMINGS. E. E. *Him.* Decorated boards, vellum spine and corners. New York, 1927. First edition. One of 160 signed. Boxed. $150-$175. First trade edition: $15-$20.

CUMMINGS, E. E. *I: Six Nonlectures.* Cloth. Cambridge, Mass., 1953. First edition. One of 350 signed. In dust jacket. $100-$125. Trade edition: Cloth. In dust jacket. $20-$25.

CUMMINGS, E. E. *is 5.* Gold-flecked orange boards, cloth spine. New York, 1926. First edition. In dust jacket. $75-$100. Another issue: Black boards. One of 77 signed. Boxed. $250-$300. Also, $275 (A, 1977).

CUMMINGS, E. E. *A Miscellany.* Cloth. New York, 1958. First edition. One of 75 signed. $150-$175.

CUMMINGS, E. E. *95 Poems.* Cloth. New York, (1958). First edition. One of 300 signed. In glassine dust jacket. Boxed. $100-$175.

CUMMINGS, E. E. *No Thanks*. Oblong, dark-blue cloth. (New York, 1935.) First edition. One of 90 on handmade paper, signed. In dust jacket. Boxed. $175-$225. Another issue: Morocco. One of 9 on Japan vellum, signed. With a manuscript page. $1,000-$1,500. Also, $1,300 (A, 1977). Another issue: First trade edition. One of 900 on Riccardi Japan paper. $50-$75.

CUMMINGS, E. E. *Santa Claus*. Frontispiece. Cloth. New York, (1946). First edition. One of 250 signed. In glassine jacket. $75. Trade edition: $20-$30.

CUMMINGS, E. E. *Tom: A Ballet*. Frontispiece by Ben Shahn. Cloth. (Santa Fe, 1935.) Arrow Edition. In dust jacket. $50-$75.

CUMMINGS, E. E. *Tulips and Chimneys*. Boards and cloth. New York, 1923. First edition. In dust jacket. $100-$150. Mount Vernon, N.Y., 1937. Boards, vellum spine. One of 481. In dust jacket. $50-$60. (Of this edition, there were supposed to be 148 signed by the author, but the sheets were lost between printer and binder.)

CUMMINGS. E. E. *W* [*Viva: Seventy New Poems*]. Folio, buckram and boards. New York, 1931. First edition. One of 95 signed. In glassine dust jacket. $200-$250. Trade edition. In silver dust jacket. $50-$75.

CUMMINGS. E. E. *XLI Poems*. Cloth, gilt label. New York, 1925. First edition. $75-$85.

CUMMINGS, Ray. *The Girl in the Golden Atom*. Gold cloth. New York, 1923. First edition. In dust jacket. $50-$75.

CUMMINS, Ella Sterling. *The Story of the Files: A Review of California Writers and Literature*. Illustrated. Decorated boards or cloth. (San Francisco), 1893. $50-$75.

CUMMINS, Mrs. Sarah J. W. *Autobiography and Reminiscences*. Portrait. Printed wrappers. (La Grande, Ore., 1914.) First edition. $35-$50. Reprint edition: (Walla Walla, Wash., 1914). $25-$30.

CUNARD, Nancy. *Black Man and White Ladyship: An Anniversary*. 10 pp., red wrappers. (Toulon), 1931. First edition. $125-$150.

CUNARD, Nancy. *G M: Memories of George Moore*. Boards. London, 1956. First edition. In dust jacket. $25-$30.

CUNARD, Nancy (editor). *Negro: Anthology*. Illustrated, including colored folding map. Brown buckram. London, 1934. First edition. $1,000-$1,500.

CUNARD, Nancy. *Parallax*. Boards. London, 1925. First edition. $75-$100.

CUNDALL, Joseph. See Percy, Stephen.

CUNNINGHAM, Eugene. *Triggernometry: A Gallery of Gunfighters*. 21 plates. Pictorial cloth. New York, 1934. First edition. In dust jacket. $50-$75.

CUNNINGHAME GRAHAM, R. B. See Graham.

CURLEY, Edwin A. *Nebraska: Its Advantages, Resources and Drawbacks*. Illustrated. Cloth. London, 1875. First edition. $75-$150.

*CURSE of Minerva (The)*. 25 pp., dark-brown glazed wrappers. London, 1812. (By George Gordon Noel, Lord Byron.) First edition. $2,500 and up.

CURTIS, Edward S. *The North American Indian*. Preface by Theodore Roosevelt. More than 1,500 plates. 20 quarto vols., half morocco, and 20 half morocco portfolios of plates. Cambridge, Mass., 1907-30. First edition. One of 500 sets (about half this number actually issued). Signed by Curtis and Roosevelt (some by Curtis only). At auction: $60,500 and $60,000 at separate sales in 1977; $60,000 in 1976; $32,000 in 1975; $31,000 in 1974.

CURTIS, George William. *See Nile Notes of a Howadji; The Potiphar Papers*.

CURTISS, Daniel S. *Western Portraiture, and Emigrants' Guide.* Illustrated. Cloth. New York, 1852. First edition. $100-$125.

CUSHMAN, H. B. *A History of the Choctaw, Chickasaw and Natchez Indians.* Greenville, Tex., 1899. First edition. $200-$250.

CUSHMAN, Henry Wyles. *A Historical and Biographical Genealogy of the Cushmans.* Illustrated. Cloth. Boston, 1855. $50-$60.

CUSTER, Elizabeth B. *"Boots and Saddles," or Life in Dakota with General Custer.* Portrait and map. Pictorial cloth. New York, 1885. First edition. $35.

CUSTER, George A. *My Life on the Plains.* 8 illustrations. Cloth. New York, 1874. First edition. $75-$125.

CUTBUSH, James. *The American Artist's Manual.* 39 plates. 2 vols., cloth. Philadelphia, 1814. $175-$200.

CUTTS, James M. *The Conquest of California and New Mexico.* Map, 3 plans. Cloth. Philadelphia, 1847. First edition. $150-$200.

CYNWAL, William. *In Defence of Woman.* 10 colored engravings. Full blue morocco. London, (1956). Golden Cockerel Press. One of 100. $75-$85. Another issue: Buckram. One of 500. $25-$35.

# D

D., B., and M., W. G. *Rumpel Stiltskin.* By B. D. and W. G. M. Edited by Michael Sadleir. Boards. London, 1952. (By Benjamin Disraeli and [William] George Meredith.) Roxburghe Club. One of 66. $150-$250.

D., H. *Collected Poems.* Cloth. New York, 1925. (By Hilda Doolittle.) First edition. $75-$100.

D., H. *Hedylus.* Decorated boards and cloth. Stratford-on-Avon (Oxford), 1928. (By Hilda Doolittle.) First edition. One of 775. In dust jacket. $100-$150.

D., H. *Hippolytus Temporizes.* Decorated boards and cloth. Boston, 1927. (By Hilda Doolittle.) First edition. One of 550. Boxed. $100-$125.

D., H. *Hymen.* Pale green wrappers. New York, 1921. (By Hilda Doolittle.) First American edition. $100-$200.

D., H. *Kora and Ka.* Printed wrappers. (Dijon, 1934.) (By Hilda Doolittle.) One of 100. $300-$350.

D., H. *Palimpsest.* Wrappers. Paris, 1926. Contact Editions. (By Hilda Doolittle.) First edition. $200-$250. Boston, 1926. Decorated boards and cloth. First American edition. One of 700. In dust jacket. $50-$75.

D., H. *Red Roses for Bronze.* Printed wrappers. New York, 1929. (By Hilda Doolittle.) First edition. $65-$85.

D., H. *Sea Garden: Imagist Poems.* Printed wrappers over boards. London, 1916. (By Hilda Doolittle.) $200-$300. Also, $150 (A, 1977). Boston, 1917. Green wrappers. First American edition. $100-$150.

D., H. *The Tribute and Circe—Two Poems.* Cloth. Cleveland, 1917. (By Hilda Doolittle.) First edition. One of 50. $150-$200.

D., H. *The Walls Do Not Fall.* Cloth. New York, 1944. (By Hilda Doolittle.) First edition. In dust jacket. $50-$75.

D., H. (translator). *Choruses from Iphigeneia in Aulis.* Translated from the Greek of Euripides. Wrappers. Cleveland, 1916. (By Hilda Doolittle.) First edition. $675 (A, 1977). Author's first book. (40 copies printed.)

DAHL, Roald. *Some Time Never.* Cloth. New York, 1948. First edition. $25-$30.

DAHLBERG, Edward. *Bottom Dogs.* Introduction by D. H. Lawrence. Cloth. London, (1929). First edition. One of 520. In dust jacket. $150-$200. Trade edition: In dust jacket. $40-$60. New York, 1930. First American edition. In dust jacket. $50-$75. Author's first book.

DAHLBERG, Edward. *The Confessions of Edward Dahlberg.* Illustrated. Cloth. New York. (1971), First edition. One of 200 signed. Boxed. $45-$50.

DAHLBERG, Edward. *Do These Bones Live?* Red cloth. New York, (1941). First edition. In dust jacket. $25-$30.

DAHLBERG, Edward. *From Flushing to Calvary.* New York, (1932). First edition. In dust jacket. $40-$60.

DAHLBERG, Edward. *Kentucky Blue Grass Henry Smith.* Drawings by Augustus Peck. Orange boards, blue cloth spine. Cleveland, 1932. First edition. One of 10 signed. In dust jacket. $600-$750. One of 85 numbered copies (not signed). In dust jacket. $100-$150. (Note: There are copies without the drawings. Value: $250-$300.)

DAHLBERG, Edward. *The Sorrows of Priapus.* Illustrated by Ben Shahn. Printed white boards. (New York, 1957.) Thistle Press. First edition. One of 150 signed by author and artist. Extra signed lithographs laid in. In glassine dust jacket. Boxed. $250-$300.

DALE, Edward Everett. *The Range Cattle Industry.* Plates. Cloth. Norman, Okla., 1930. First edition. One of 500. $125-$175.

DALE, Harrison Clifford (editor). *The Ashley-Smith Explorations.* 2 maps, 3 plates. Cloth. Cleveland, 1918. First edition. One of 750. $50-$80. Glendale, Calif., 1941. Cloth. Revised edition. One of 750. $30-$35.

DALI, Salvador. *Hidden Faces.* Cloth. New York, 1944. First edition. In dust jacket. $25-$30.

DALI, Salvador. *The Secret Life of Salvador Dali.* Illustrated. Cloth, pictorial labels. New York, 1942. First American edition. One of 119 copies with an original Dali drawing.In dust jacket. Boxed. $400-$600, possibly more. Also, $575 (A, 1975). Trade edition. Cloth. In dust jacket. $75-125.

*DALTON Brothers and Their Astounding Career of Crime (The).* By an Eye Witness. Pictorial wrappers. Chicago. 1892. First edition. $150.

DALTON, Emmett. *When the Daltons Rode.* Portrait and plates. Pictorial cloth. Garden City, 1931. First edition (so stated). In dust jacket. $50-$60.

DAMON, S. Foster. *William Blake: His Philosophy and Symbols.* Boards. Boston, 1924. First American edition. $50.

DAMON, Samuel C. *A Journey to Lower Oregon and Upper California, 1848-49.* Half cloth. San Francisco, 1927. Grabhorn printing. One of 250. $100-$150.

DAMPIER, William. *A New Voyage Round the World.* 4 maps, portrait. Half vellum. London, 1927. One of 975. $60-$80.

*DAMSEL of Darien (The).* 2 vols., boards or wrappers, paper spine labels. Philadelphia, 1839. (By William Gilmore Simms.) First edition, first issue, with errata slip before the first page of text in first volume. $100-$150.

DANA, Charles A. *The United States Illustrated.* (Prospectus.) Wrappers. New York, (1853). $50-$100.

DANA, Edmund. *Geographical Sketches on the Western Country; Designed for Emigrants and Settlers.* Boards. Cincinnati, 1819. First edition. $300-$400.

DANA, J. G., and Thomas, R. S. *A Report of the Trial of Jereboam O. Beauchamp.* 153 pp., wrappers. Frankfort, Ky., (1826). First edition. $500.

DANA, Richard Henry, Jr. See *Two Years Before the Mast.*

DANA, Richard Henry. Jr. *To Cuba and Back: A Vacation Voyage.* Brown cloth. Boston, 1859. First edition. $25-$35.

*DANCE of Life (The).* Frontispiece. Engraved title, 24 plates by Thomas Rowlandson. Boards, or cloth. London, 1817. (By William Combe.) First edition. $400-$500.

DANIEL, John W. *Character of Stonewall Jackson.* Cloth. Lynchburg, Va., 1868. First edition. $35-$50.

DANIELS, Jonathan. *Thomas Wolfe: October Recollections.* Cloth. Columbia, S.C., (1961). First edition. One of 750 signed. In dust jacket. $35-$50.

DANIELS, William M. *A Correct Account of the Murder of Generals Joseph and Hyrum*

*Smith, at Carthage, on the 27th Day of June, 1844.* 24 pp., wrappers. Nauvoo, Ill., 1845. First edition, first issue, without plates. $2,500-$3,500. Second issue, with two woodcut engravings added. $2,000 or more. Rebound in morocco, paper covers bound in, $1,100 (A, 1966).

DANTE ALIGHIERI. *La Divina Commedia, or The Divine Vision of Dante Alighieri.* In Italian and English. Illustrated. Orange vellum. London, 1928. Nonesuch Press. One of 1,475. $300-$400. (As *The Comedy of Dante Alighieri:*) San Francisco, 1958. 3 vols. Grabhorn printing. One of 300. $150-$200.

DA PONTE, Lorenzo. See *The Memoirs of Lorenzo Da Ponte.*

D'ARBLAY, Madame. *Memoirs of Doctor Burney.* (Arranged by his daughter, Madame D'Arblay.) 3 vols., boards. London, 1832. (By Frances Burney.) First edition. $200-$300.

DARBY, William. *The Emigrant's Guide to the Western and Southwestern States and Territories.* 3 maps, 2 tables. Leather. New York, 1818. First edition. $200-$300.

DARBY, William. *A Geographical Description of the State of Louisiana.* Map. Leather. Philadelphia, 1816. First edition. $200-$250. New York, 1817. Second edition, with 2 maps and large folding map in separate folder. $200-$300.

DARBY, William. *A Tour from the City of New-York, to Detroit, in the Michigan Territory.* 3 folding maps (one in some copies). Boards and calf. New York, 1819. First edition. $200-$250.

DARLINGTON, Mary Carson (editor). *Fort Pitt and Letters from the Frontier.* 3 maps, 3 plates. Cloth. Pittsburgh, 1892. First edition. One of 100 large paper copies. $100-$150. Ordinary issue: One of 200. $75-$100.

DARLINGTON, William M. (editor). *Christopher Gist's Journals.* 7 maps. Cloth. Pittsburgh, 1893. First edition. One of 100. $100-125.

*DARTMOUTH Verse, 1925.* (Portland, Me.), 1925. Mosher Press. One of 500. (Note: Contains an introduction by Robert Frost.) $75-$85.

DARWIN, Charles. *The Descent of Man.* Illustrated. 2 vols., green cloth. London, 1871. First edition, first issue, with errata on back of title page in Vol. 2 and with ads in each volume dated January. $500-$875. New York, 1871. 2 vols., cloth. First American edition. $100-$200.

DARWIN, Charles. *The Expression of the Emotions in Man and Animals.* Plates. Cloth. London, 1872. First edition. $400-$500.

DARWIN, Charles. *On the Origin of Species by Means of Natural Selection.* Green cloth. London, 1859. First edition, with ads at end dated June. $4,000-$5,000. Also, "hinges split," $2,000 (A, 1976). New York, 1860. Cloth. First American edition. $500-$650. New York, 1963. Limited Editions Club. Illustrated. Leather. Boxed. $150-$200.

DARWIN, Charles. *The Voyage of H.M.S. Beagle.* Illustrated by Robert Gibbings. Folio, decorated sailcloth. New York, 1956. Limited Editions Club. One of 1,500 signed by Gibbings. Boxed. $125-$150.

DASHIELL, Alfred (editor). *Editor's Choice.* Cloth. New York, (1935). First edition. In dust jacket. $35-$50. (Includes first book appearances of stories by Faulkner, Hemingway, and Wolfe.)

*DATE 1601. Conversation as It Was by the Social Fireside, in the Times of the Tudors.* 7 single leaves, with title on front of first leaf, unbound. (West Point, N.Y., 1882.) (By Samuel Langhorne Clemens.) First authorized edition. $500-$750. Also, $380 (A, 1968). Another edition: (Bangor, Me., 1894.) Calf. $150-$200. Also, $70 (A, 1968). San Francisco, 1925. Grabhorn printing. One of 100. $150-$200. (Note: There have been numerous pirated printings of this *sub rosa* item, including at least two unauthorized 1880 printings. See BAL.)

DAUBENY, Charles. *Journal of a Tour Through the United States and Canada . . . 1837-1838.* Folding map. Cloth. Oxford. 1843. First edition. One of 100. $300.

DAVENPORT, Cyril. *English Embroidered Bookbindings.* Cloth. London, 1899. $125-$150. Another issue: One of 50. $250-$350.

DAVENPORT, Cyril. *Roger Payne: English Bookbinder of the Eighteenth Century.* Chicago, 1929. Caxton Club. One of 250. $300-$500.

DAVENPORT, Cyril. *Royal English Bookbindings.* Frontispiece, 7 other color plates, 27 other illustrations. Cloth. London, 1896. $125-$150.

DAVENPORT, Cyril. *Samuel Mearne, Binder to King Charles II.* Chicago, 1929. Caxton Club. First edition. One of 250. $300-$450.

DAVENPORT, Homer. *My Quest of the Arab Horse.* Cloth. New York, 1909. First edition. $100-$125.

DAVIDSON, Donald. *Lee In the Mountains and Other Poems.* Cloth. Boston, 1938. First edition. In dust jacket. $50-$75.

DAVIDSON, Donald. *An Outland Piper.* Boards. Boston, 1924. First edition. $100-$125. Author's first book.

DAVIDSON, Donald. *The Tall Men.* Boards, cloth spine, label. Boston, 1927. First edition. $50-$60.

DAVIDSON, Gordon Charles. *The North West Company.* 5 folding maps. Cloth. Berkeley, 1918. First edition. $75-$100.

DAVIDSON, James Wood. *The Living Writers of the South.* Cloth. New York, 1869. First edition. $75-$100. (Note: Contains two poems constituting first book appearance of Joel Chandler Harris.)

DAVIES, W. H. *The Autobiography of a Super-Tramp.* Preface by Bernard Shaw. Buckram. London, 1908. First edition. $60-$75.

DAVIES, W. H. *The Lover's Song Book.* Marbled boards and cloth. Newtown, 1933. Gregynog Press. First edition. One of 250 signed. $150-$250. Another issue: Morocco. One of 18 bound by George Fisher. $600-$850.

DAVIES, W. H. *Selected Poems.* Portrait. Green morocco. Newtown, Wales, 1928. Gregynog Press. One of a few (from an edition of 310) specially bound by the Gregynog Bindery. $1,000-$1,250. Ordinary issue: Marbled boards and buckram. $150-$200.

DAVIES, W. H. *The Soul's Destroyer, and Other Poems.* Buff printed wrappers. (London, 1905.) First edition. $75-$125. Author's first book.

DA VINCI, Leonardo. *Thoughts on Art and Life.* Cloth. Boston, 1906. One of 303. $25-$30.

DAVIS, Duke. *Flashlights from Mountain and Plain.* Illustrated by Charles M. Russell. Cloth. Bound Brook, N.J., 1911. First edition. $50-$75.

DAVIS, Edmund. W. *Salmon-Fishing on the Grand Cascapedia.* Half vellum. (New York), 1904. First edition. One of 100. $300-$400.

DAVIS, Ellis A. *Commercial Encyclopedia of the Pacific Southwest.* Cloth. Oakland, 1915. $100-$150.

DAVIS, H. S. (compiler). *Reminiscences of Gen. William Larimer.* Plates, Folding table. Morocco. Lancaster, Pa., 1918. First edition. $200-$300.

DAVIS, Hubert. *The Symbolic Drawings . . . for "An American Tragedy."* Foreword by Theodore Dreiser. 20 drawings. Folio, gold and silver boards, cloth spine. (New York, 1930.) One of 525 signed by Dreiser and Davis. $125-$150. (Some copies were never signed.)

DAVIS, John. See *Walter Kennedy: An American Tale.*

DAVIS, Paris M. *An Authentick History of the Late War Between the United States and Great Britain.* Calf. Ithaca, 1829. First edition. $35-$50.

DAVIS, Rebecca Harding. *Kent Hampden.* Cloth. New York, 1892. First edition. $35.

DAVIS, Rebecca Harding. *Margret Howth: A Story of To-Day.* Cloth. Boston, 1862. First edition. $50-$75. Author's first book.

DAVIS, Richard Harding. *Adventures of My Freshman.* Wrappers. Bethlehem, Pa., (1883). First edition. $150-$250.

DAVIS, Richard Harding. *Cuba in War Time.* Illustrated by Frederic Remington. Boards. New York, 1897. First edition. $75-$100.

DAVIS, Richard Harding. *Dr. Jameson's Raiders vs. the Johannesburg Reformers.* Wrappers. New York, 1897. First edition. $50-$75.

DAVIS, Richard Harding. *Gallegher and Other Stories.* Yellow wrappers. New York, 1891. First edition, first issue. $115. Later, cloth.

DAVIS, Richard Harding. *The West From a Car-Window.* Illustrated by Frederic Remington. Cloth. New York, 1894. First edition. $40-$50.

DAVIS, William Heath. *Sixty Years in California.* Cloth. San Francisco, 1889. First edition. $200-$250. San Francisco, 1929. 44 maps and plates. Half morocco. Second edition. One of 2,000 (with title changed to *Seventy-five Years in California*). $75-$100. Another issue: Argonaut Edition. One of 100, with added plates and a page of the author's manuscript. $150. San Francisco, 1967. Illustrated. Cloth. In dust jacket. $30-$40.

DAVIS, William J. (editor). *The Partisan Rangers of the Confederate States Army.* 65 plates. Cloth. Louisville, 1904. (By Adam R. Johnson.) First edition. $100-$150.

DAVIS, William W. H. *El Gringo; or New Mexico and Her People.* Frontispiece. Cloth. New York, 1857. First edition. $100-$150.

DAVIS, William W. H. *The Fries Rebellion.* 10 plates. Cloth. Doylestown, Pa., 1899. First edition. $50.

DAVIS, William W. H. *The Spanish Conquest of New Mexico: 1527-1703.* Folding map, plate. Cloth. Doylestown, 1869. First edition. $100-$150.

DAVISON, Lawrence H. *Movements in European History.* Brown cloth. London, 1921. (By D. H. Lawrence.) First edition, first binding. $100-$150. Second binding, light blue cloth. $60-$80.

DAVY, Sir Humphrey. *On the Safety Lamp for Coal Miners.* Folding plate. Boards. London, 1818. First edition. $400-$600. Also, $375 (A, 1977).

*DAVY Crockett; or, The Lion-Hearted Hunter.* 96 pp., wrappers. New York, (about 1875). $100-$125.

*DAVY Crockett's Almanac, of Wild Sports in the West.* Pictorial wrappers. Nashville, (1835 to 1841). Depending on condition, the Nashville almanacs for these years are worth individually from $500 to $1,000 each, possibly more. Other Crockett Almanacs with Boston and Philadelphia imprints through the 1830's and into the 1850's bring $100 to $500 at retail. Also, at auction: Nashville, 1835-41, 7 vols., together with Boston edition for 1842, $2,450 (1962).

DAWSON, Charles C. *A Collection of Family Records.* Illustrated. Cloth. Albany, 1874. First edition. $45-$50.

DAWSON, Lionel. *Sport in War.* Illustrated by Lionel Edwards. Half leather. London, 1936. First edition. One of 75 signed. $150-$200.

DAWSON, Moses. *A Historical Narrative of the Civil and Military Services of Maj.-Gen. William Henry Harrison.* Boards. Cincinnati, 1824. First edition, first issue, with 15-line errata slip. $400-$600. Later issue, with 24-line errata slip: $300-$400.

DAWSON, Nicholas. *California in '41. Texas in '51. Memoirs.* Frontispiece. Cloth. (Austin, Tex., about 1910.) First edition. $500-$800. Inscribed copies, up to $1,000.

DAWSON, Nicholas. *Narrative of Nicholas "Cheyenne" Dawson.* Half cloth. San Francisco, 1933. Grabhorn Press. One of 500. In dust jacket. $75-$100.

DAWSON, Simon J. *Report on the Exploration of the Country Between Lake Superior and the Red River Settlement and the Assiniboine and Saskatchewan.* Illustrated, folding maps. 45 pp., half leather and cloth. Toronto, 1859. First edition. $200-$300.

DAWSON, Thomas F., and Skiff., F.J.V. *The Ute War: A History of the White River Massacre, etc.* 184 pp., printed wrappers, with ads. Denver, 1879. First edition. $2,000. Later issue, without ads, $1,000-$1,500.

DAWSON, William Leon. *The Birds of California.* Illustrated. 4 vols., folio cloth. San Diego, 1923. $300-$400. Another issue: Half leather. One of 350. $300-$400. Another issue: One of 100 signed. $400-$500. Later, a "Student's Edition," 3 vols., cloth. $100 and up.

DAWSON, William Leon. *The Birds of Ohio.* Illustrated. 2 vols., cloth. Columbus, Ohio, 1903. $75-$100.

DAWSON, William Leon, and Bowles, John H. *The Birds of Washington.* 2 vols., boards. Seattle, 1909. First edition. One of 200 signed. $150-$200. Another issue: "Edition De Luxe." One of 85. $300.

DAY, Clarence. *Life with Father.* Cloth. New York, 1935. First edition. In dust jacket. $25-$35.

DAY, Clarence. *Life with Mother.* Boards and cloth. New York, 1937. First edition. One of 750. $75-$125.

DAY, Sherman. *Report of the Committee on Internal Improvements, on the Use of the Camels on the Plains, May 30, 1885.* 11 pp., unbound. (Sacramento), 1885. $40-$45.

DAY-LEWIS, C. *Beechen Vigil & Other Poems.* Wrappers. London, (1925). First edition. $250-$300. Author's first book.

DAY-LEWIS, C. *Country Comets.* Boards. London, 1928. First edition. Boxed. $35-$40.

DAY-LEWIS, C. *The Magnetic Mountain.* London, 1933. First edition. One of 100 signed. In dust jacket. $100-$125. Trade edition. In dust jacket. $20-$25.

DAY-LEWIS, C. *Noah and the Waters.* Cloth. London, 1936. Hogarth Press. First edition. One of 100 signed. In dust jacket. $100-$125. Trade edition: in dust jacket. $20-$25.

DAY-LEWIS, C. (translator). *The Graveyard by the Sea.* (With title page for Paul Valéry's *Le Cimetière Marin* as right-hand page beside the title page for Day-Lewis's translation.) Marbled wrappers. London, (1945—actually 1947). First edition. One of 500. In fawn envelope. $200-$225.

DEAN, Bashford. *Catalogue of European Daggers.* 85 plates. Half cloth. New York, 1929. One of 900. $85-$100.

DEARBORN, Henry. *The Revolutionary War Journals of Henry Dearborn, 1775-1783.* 6 plates. Cloth. Chicago, 1939. Caxton Club. One of 350. Boxed. $100-$125.

DEARDEN, Robert R., Jr., and Watson, Douglas S. *An Original Leaf from the Revolution and an Essay Concerning It.* San Francisco, 1930. Grabhorn printing. One of 515 with leaf from 1782 Bible. $200-$400. Another issue: One of 50 with 2 leaves. $500-$600. Another issue: One of 15 with 2 leaves plus a leaf from the Benjamin Franklin printing of the "Confession of Faith." $800-$1,000.

DEBAR, J. H. *The West Virginia Handbook and Immigrant's Guide.* Folding map. Cloth. Parkersburg, W. Va., 1870. First edition. $100-$150.

DE BARTHE, Joe. *The Life and Adventures of Frank Grouard, Chief of Scouts.* Frontispiece, 67 plates. Pictorial cloth. St. Joseph, Mo., (1894). First edition. $150-$250.

DEBOUCHEL, Victor. *Histoire de la Louisiane.* Boards. Nouvelle-Orléans, 1841. First edition. $200-$350.

DECALVES, Don Alonso (pseudonym). *New Travels to the Westward.* 48 pp., sewed. Greenwich, Mass., 1805. $75-$85.

DE CAMP, L. Sprague. *Demons and Dinosaurs.* Cloth. Sauk City, Wis., 1970. Arkham House. First edition. In dust jacket. $65.

DE CHAIR, Somerset. *The Golden Carpet.* Frontispiece. Half morocco. London, 1943. Golden Cockerel Press. One of 470. $100-$150. Another issue: One of 30 specially bound and inscribed. $300-$400.

DE CHAIR, Somerset. *The Silver Crescent.* Photographs. Half morocco. London, 1943. Golden Cockerel Press. One of 470. $100-$150. Another issue: Full morocco. One of 30 specially bound and inscribed. $300-$400.

DE CHAIR, Somerset. *The Story of a Lifetime.* Engravings by Clifford Webb. Full sheep. Waltham Saint Lawrence. 1954. Golden Cockerel Press. One of 100 signed. Boxed. $100-$150. Another issue: One of 10 signed. $300-$400.

*DECLARATION of the Immediate Cause Which Induce and Justify the Secession of South Carolina from the Federal Union, and the Ordinance of Secession.* Wrappers, Charleston, 1860. First edition, first issue, with misprinted "Cause" for "Causes." $300-$350.

DE CORDOVA, J. *Texas: Her Resources and Her Public Men.* Tables. Cloth. Philadelphia, 1858. First edition, first issue, without index. $350-$500.

DE CORDOVA, J. *The Texas Immigrant and Traveller's Guide Book.* Cloth. Austin, 1856. First edition. $350-$600, possibly more.

*DEERSLAYER (The); or, The First War-Path.* By the Author of "The Last of the Mohicans." 2 vols., purple cloth, paper labels on spine. Philadelphia, 1841. (By James Fenimore Cooper.) First edition. $300-$400.

DEFOE, Daniel. *The Life and Strange Surprising Adventures of Robinson Crusoe.* New York, 1930. Limited Editions Club. Boxed. $125-$150. (Also see, *The Life, and Most Surprising Adventures* title entry.)

DEFOE, Daniel. *The Life and Surprising Adventures of Robinson Crusoe.* 54 pp., wrappers. New York, (1864). First Beadle Dime Classic edition, first issue, with publisher's address as 118 William Street. $35-$45.

DEFOE, Daniel. *A Tour Thro' London About the Year 1725.* Edited by Sir Mayson Beeton and E. B. Chancellor. Folio, cloth. London, 1929. One of 350. $200-$225. Another issue: Paneled calf. $50-$75.

DE FOREST, John W. *Miss Ravenel's Conversion from Secession to Loyalty.* Cloth. New York, 1867. First edition. $50-$60.

DE FOREST, John. W. *Playing the Mischief.* 185 pp., wrappers. New York, 1875. First edition. $35-$40. New York, 1876. Second printing. $25.

DE GIVRY, G. *Witchcraft, Magic and Alchemy.* Translated by J. C. Locke. 366 illustrations, 10 color plates. Cloth. London, (1931). In dust jacket. $150-$200.

DE GOURMONT, Remy. *The Natural Philosophy of Love.* Translated by Ezra Pound. Boards. New York (1922). First edition. In dust jacket. $75. London, 1926. Boards and cloth. First English edition. One of 1,500. In dust jacket. $35-$50.

DE GOUY, L.P. *The Derrydale Cook Book of Fish and Game.* 2 vols., buckram. New York, (1937). One of 1,250. In slipcase. $150-$175.

DE GRESS, J. O. *Regulations to Be Observed Under an Act to Establish and Maintain a System of Public Free Schools in Texas.* 7 pp., wrappers. Galveston, 1873. $50-$75.

DE HASS, Wills. *History of the Early Settlement and Indian Wars of Western Virginia.* 4 plates, folding facsimile. Decorated cloth. Wheeling, W. Va., 1851. First edition. $200-$250.

DEHN, Paul. *Quake, Quake, Quake: A Leaden-Treasury of English Verse.* Illustrated by Edward Gorey. Cloth. New York, 1961. First edition. In dust jacket. $75-$100.

DELAFAYE-BREHIER, Julie. *New Tales for Girls.* Illustrated. Printed boards. Boston, 1825 (cover date). $25-$30.

DELAFIELD, John, Jr. *An Inquiry into the Origin of the Antiquities of America.* 11 plates, including 18-foot-long folding tissue-paper plate. Cloth. New York, 1839. First edition. $100-$150. Cincinnati, 1839. $25-$35.

DE LA MARE, Walter. See Ramal, Walter.

DE LA MARE, Walter. *Behold, This Dreamer.* Colored frontispiece. Parchment. London, 1939. First edition. One of 50 signed. $125-$150.

DE LA MARE, Walter. *Broomsticks and Other Tales.* Wood engravings. Half cloth, leather label on spine. London, 1925. First edition. One of 278 signed. In dust jacket. $100-$125.

DE LA MARE, Walter, *The Captive and Other Poems.* Boards. New York, 1928. Bowling Green Press. First edition. One of 600 signed. $40-$60.

DE LA MARE, Walter. *The Connoisseur and Other Stories.* Boards. London, 1926. First edition. One of 250 signed. In dust jacket. $50-$75.

DE LA MARE, Walter. *Crossings: A Fairy Play.* Decorated boards. (London, 1921.) Beaumont Press. First edition. One of 264. Boxed. $50-$75. Another issue: Vellum. One of 56 signed. Boxed. $100-$125. Also, there were apparently 13 copies especially on vellum for presentation. One of 3 such, signed by C. W. Beaumont, was sold at auction in the 1975 season for $150.

DE LA MARE, Walter. *Desert Islands and Robinson Crusoe.* Engravings by Rex Whistler. Cloth. London, 1930. One of 650 signed. In dust jacket. $75-$100. First trade edition: Cloth. In dust jacket. $10-$15.

DE LA MARE, Walter. *Ding Dong Bell.* Boards. London, 1924. First edition. One of 300 signed. In dust jacket. $65-$75.

DE LA MARE, Walter. *Down-Adown-Derry.* Illustrated by Dorothy P. Lathrop. Blue cloth. London, 1922. First edition. In dust jacket. $50-$100.

DE LA MARE, Walter. *Henry Brocken.* Cloth. London, 1904. First edition, first issue, without gilt on top edges. In dust jacket. $200-$250.

DE LA MARE, Walter. *Lipset, Lispett and Vaine.* Woodcut decorations. Limp vellum. London, 1923. One of 200 signed. Boxed. $40-$75.

DE LA MARE, Walter. *The Listeners, and Other Poems.* Cloth. London, 1912. First edition. In dust jacket. $50-$60.

DE LA MARE, Walter. *The Lord Fish.* Illustrated by Rex Whistler. Parchment. London, (1933). First edition. One of 60 signed. In dust jacket. Boxed. $85-$125.

DE LA MARE, Walter. *Memoirs of a Midget.* Boards. London, (1921). First edition, first issue, with "Copyright 1921" on verso of title page. One of 210 signed. Boxed. $100-$150. Trade edition: Blue cloth. In dust jacket. $75-$85.

DE LA MARE, Walter. *On the Edge: Short Stories.* Illustrated. Pink cloth. London, 1930. First edition. One of 300 signed. In dust jacket. $50-$85.

DE LA MARE, Walter. *Peacock Pie: A Book of Rhymes.* Illustrated in color. Boards and cloth. London, 1924. One of 250 signed. In dust jacket. $75-$100.

DE LA MARE, Walter. *Poems.* Cloth. London, 1906. First edition. In dust jacket. $50-$60.

DE LA MARE, Walter. *Poems, 1901 to 1918*, 2 vols., boards and linen, leather labels. London, 1920. First edition. One of 210 signed. $100-$125.

DE LA MARE, Walter. *The Riddle and Other Stories*. Cream cloth. London, (1923). First edition. One of 310. In dust jacket. $50-$60. Another issue: "Author's edition." One of 25 for presentation. $100-$125.

DE LA MARE, Walter. *Seven Short Stories*. Colored illustrations. Boards. London, 1931. First edition. One of 170 signed. Boxed. $75-$100.

DE LA MARE, Walter. *Songs of Childhood*. Colored plates. Vellum and boards. London, 1923. One of 310 signed. In dust jacket. $100-$125. (Published earlier under his pen name, Walter Ramal, which see.)

DE LA MARE, Walter. *The Sunken Garden and Other Poems*. Boards and linen. (London), 1917. Beaumont Press. First edition. One of 230 signed. Boxed. $35-$50. Another issue: Vellum. One of 20 on Japan paper, signed. Boxed. $75-$100.

DE LA MARE, Walter. *This Year: Next Year*. Colored illustrations. Decorated cloth. London, 1937. First edition. One of 100 signed. In dust jacket. $75-$100.

DE LA MARE, Walter. *Two Tales*. Vellum and boards. London, 1925. First edition. One of 250 signed. Boxed. $50.

DE LA MARE, Walter. *The Three Mulla-Mulgars*. Green cloth. London, 1910. First edition, first issue, with errata slip. In dust jacket. $200-$250. London, (1924). Boards. One of 250 signed. $150-$200.

DE LA MARE, Walter. *The Veil and Other Poems*. Boards. London, 1921. First edition. One of 250 signed. In dust jacket. $50.

DELAND, Margaret. *Florida Days*. Pictorial tan cloth. Boston 1889. First edition. $25-$30.

DELAND, Margaret. *Old Chester Tales*. Illustrated by Howard Pyle. Cloth. New York, 1889. First edition, first issue, with "Chelsea" for "Chester" on page 5. $40-$60.

DELAND, Margaret. *The Old Garden and Other Verses*. White cloth and flowered cloth. Boston, 1886. First edition. $50. Author's first book. Boston, 1894. Illustrated by Walter Crane. Cloth. $150-$175.

DELANO, Alonzo. See *Pen-Knife Sketches*.

DELANO, Alonzo. *Life on the Plains and Among the Diggings*. Frontispiece and 3 plates. Cloth. Auburn, N.Y., 1854. First edition, first issue, with page 219 misnumbered 119 and with no mention of number of thousands printed. $350-$600.

DELANO, Alonzo. *Pen-Knife Sketches, or Chips of the Old Block*. Colored illustrations. Decorated boards. San Francisco, 1934. Grabhorn Press. One of 550. $50-$60. (For anonymous edition, see title entry.)

DELANO, Amasa. *A Narrative of Voyages and Travels, in the Northern and Southern Hemispheres*. 2 portraits, folding map, errata leaf. Boards, paper label. Boston, 1817. First edition. $300-$500.

DELANO, Judah. *Washington (D.C.) Directory*. Calf. Washington, 1822. First edition. $500 and up.

DELANO, Reuben. *Wanderings and Adventures of Reuben Delano*. 3 plates. 102 pp., wrappers. Worcester, Mass. 1846. First edition. $150.

DE LA SALLE, Nicolas. See La Salle, Nicolas de.

DELAY, Peter J. *History of Yuba and Sutter Counties, California*. Illustrated. Three quarters leather. Los Angeles, 1924. $100-$150.

DE LINCY, A. J. V. Le Roux. *Researches Concerning Jean Grolier, His Life and His Library*. Color plates. Full leather. New York, 1907. $200-$300.

DELL, Floyd. *Women as World Builders.* Cloth. Chicago, 1913. First edition. In dust jacket. $50-$75. Author's first book.

*DEMOCRACY: An American Novel.* White cloth, printed red end papers. New York, 1880. (By Henry Adams.) First edition. No. 112 in "Leisure Hour Series." Probable first issue with March 31, 1880, in last line on front pasted-down end paper. $200-$400. Also, $120 (A, 1975). Probable second issue, dated April 15, $100-$150.

DE MORGAN, William. *It Never Can Happen Again.* Portrait. 2 vols., cloth. London, 1909. First edition. $40-$50.

DE MORGAN, William. *Joseph Vance.* Light green cloth. London, 1906. First edition. $40-$60. Author's first book.

*DEMOS: A Story of English Socialism.* 3 vols, brown cloth. London, 1886. (By George Gissing.) First edition. $300-$500. Also, $300 (A, 1970).

DENBY, Edwin. *In Public, In Private: Poems.* Illustrated. Gray cloth. Prairie City, Ill., (1948). First edition. In dust jacket. $150-$200.

DENISON, Jesse. *First Annual Report to the Stockholders of the Providence Western Land Company.* 8 pp., wrappers. Providence, 1857. $75.

DENNY, Arthur A. *Pioneer Days on Puget Sound.* Cloth. Seattle, 1888. First edition, with errata slip. $100-$125. Seattle, 1908. One of 850. $30-$50.

DENTON, Sherman F. *As Nature Shows Them: Moths and Butterflies of the United States East of the Rocky Mountains.* 56 colored plates. 2 vols., half leather. Boston, (1900). One of 500. $500-$600. Also, $412 (A, 1974).

DEPONS, François. *Travels in Parts of South America, During the Years 1801-1804.* Folding map and plan. Contemporary boards. London, 1806. $300-$400.

DEPONS, François. *A Voyage to the Eastern Part of Terra Firma.* Translated by an American Gentleman. 3 vols., boards (none located) or contemporary leather. New York, 1806. (Translated by Washington Irving, Peter Irving, and George Caines.) First American edition (and first in English). In leather: $200-$300.

*DEPREDATIONS and Massacre by the Snake River Indians.* 16 pp., sewed. (Washington), 1861. $100-$125.

DE QUILLE, Dan. *History of the Big Bonanza.* Illustrated. Decorated cloth. Hartford, 1876. (By William Wright.) First edition, first issue, without plate No. 44. $75-$100.

DE QUILLE, Dan. *A History of the Comstock Silver Lode and Mines.* Printed wrappers. Virginia City, Nev., 1889. (By William Wright.) First edition. $100-$150.

DE QUINCEY, Thomas. See *Confessions of an English Opium Eater; Klosterhiem, or, The Masque.*

DE QUINCEY, Thomas. *The Logic of Political Economy.* Cloth, paper label. Edinburgh, 1844. First edition. $100-$150.

DE RICCI, Seymour. *A Bibliography of Shelley's Letters Published and Unpublished.* Cloth. London, 1927. $50-$75.

DE RICCI, Seymour. *The Book Collector's Guide.* Green cloth. Philadelphia, 1921. First edition. $50-$75.

DERLETH, August. *Dark of the Moon.* Cloth. Sauk City, Wis., 1947. First edition. In dust jacket. $40-$60.

DERLETH, August. *In Re: Sherlock Holmes.* Cloth. Sauk City, 1945. First edition. In dust jacket. $40-$50.

DERLETH, August. *The Memoirs of Solar Pons.* Foreword by Ellery Queen. Cloth. Sauk City, 1951. First edition. One of 2,038. In dust jacket. $65.

DERLETH, August. *The Return of Solar Pons.* Cloth. Sauk City, 1958. First edition. In dust jacket. $40-$50.

DERLETH, August. *Someone in the Dark.* Cloth. (Sauk City), 1941. Arkham House. First edition, first issue, 17.6 cm. tall. In dust jacket. $175-$200. Later: Falsely issued "first edition," a facsimile, bound with a headband (not on the first binding) and 18.35 cm. tall. (Some say Derleth issued it, but I have seen a note from Derleth blaming a "sly friend.") In jacket. $100-$125.

DE ROOS, Fred F. *Personal Narrative of Travels in the United States and Canada in 1826.* 14 plates and plans. Boards. London, 1827. First edition, $200-$300. Second edition, same date. 14 lithographs, 2 maps. Boards. $100-$150.

DERRY, Derry down. *A Book of Nonsense.* Illustrated. Oblong, printed wrappers. London (1846). (By Edward Lear.) First edition. One of 175. $2,000 and up. Author's first book for children.

DESCENDANT (The). Decorated cloth. New York, 1897. (By Ellen Glasgow.) First edition, first printing, with single imprint on title page, and first binding, with author's name omitted from spine. $50-$75. Author's first book.

DESCRIPTION of Central Iowa (A), with Especial Reference to Polk County and Des Moines, the State Capital. 32 pp., stitched. Des Moines, 1858. $350-$500.

DESCRIPTION of Tremont House (A), with Architectural Illustrations. Boards. Boston 1830. (By William G. Eliot.) First edition. $35-$50.

DESCRIPTIVE Account of the City of Peoria (A). 32 pp., wrappers. Peoria, 1859. $100-$125.

DESCRIPTIVE and Priced Catalogue of Books, Pamphlets, and Maps (A), etc. (Thomas Wayne Norris catalogue.) Patterned boards and red cloth. Oakland, 1948. Holmes Book Co.—Grabhorn. One of 500. $100-$150.

DESCRIPTIVE Bibliography of the Books Printed at the Ashendene Press, 1895-1935. 15 collotype plates, 10 of bindings; 2 photogravures, and numerous specimen pages, initial letters, woodcuts, etc. Cowhide. London, (1935). One of 390. Boxed. $750-$1,000.

DESCRIPTIVE Catalogue of the Marine Collection to Be Found at India House (A). 35 plates, 11 hand-colored. Half leather. New York, 1935. (By Carl C. Cutler.) One of 1,000. $200-$250.

DESCRIPTIVE, Historical, Commercial, Agricultural, and Other Important Information Relative to the City of San Diego, California. 22 photographs. 51 pp., wrappers. (San Diego), 1874. $750-$850.

DESCRIPTIVE Scenes for Children. 14 pp., sewed. Boston, (1828). $50-$60.

DE SHIELDS, J. T. *Border Wars of Texas.* Cloth. Tioga, Tex., 1912. First edition. $100-$150.

DE SHIELDS, J. T. *Cynthia Ann Parker.* Frontispiece, 3 portraits. Pictorial cloth. St. Louis, 1886. First edition. $100-$150.

DES IMAGISTES: An Anthology. Cloth. New York, 1914. (Edited by Ezra Pound.) First edition. $150-$200. London, 1914. Boards. First English edition. $75-$100. (Note: Includes poems by Pound and James Joyce.)

DE SMET, Pierre-Jean. *Letters and Sketches.* Illustrations, folding leaf, "The Catholic Ladder." Cloth. Philadelphia, 1843. First edition, first issue, with 352 (not 344) pages. $500-$750. Also, $380 (A, 1976).

DE SMET, Pierre-Jean. *Oregon Missions and Travels over the Rocky Mountains.* Folding map, 12 plates. Cloth. New York, 1847. First edition. $200-$250.

DE SMET, Pierre-Jean. *Western Missions and Missionaries.* Cloth. New York, 1863. First edition. $100-$150.

DE SOTO, Hernando. *The Discovery of Florida.* Translated by Buckingham Smith. Decorations in color by Mallette Dean. Folio, half cloth. San Francisco, 1946. Grabhorn Press. One of 280. $100-$200.

DE TONTY, Henri. *Relation of Henri de Tonty Concerning the Explorations of La Salle.* Text in French and English. Half vellum. Chicago, 1898. Caxton Club. One of 194. $200-$250.

*DESPERATE Remedies: A Novel.* 3 vols., red cloth. London, 1871. (By Thomas Hardy.) First edition. $750-$1,000. (A copy sold for $7,800 at the peak of Hardy's popularity.) Author's first book (500 printed). New York, 1874. Yellow cloth. First American edition, with "Author's Edition" on copyright page. $75-$100.

*DESTINY; or The Chief's Daughter.* 3 vols. boards. Edinburgh, 1831. (By Susan Edmonstone Ferrier.) First edition. $150-$200.

DEUTSCH, Babette. *Banners.* Boards, paper label. New York, (1919). First edition. In dust jacket. $75-$100. Author's first book.

DEUTSCH, Babette. *A Brittle Heaven.* Blue cloth. New York, (1926). First edition. In dust jacket. $40-$50.

DEUTSCH, Babette. *Fire for the Light.* Cloth. New York, (1930). First edition. In dust jacket. $50-$60.

DE VINNE, Theodore L. *Aldus Pius Manutius.* Boards and cloth. With original leaf from *Hypnerotomachia Poliphili.* Printed by Aldus in 1499. San Francisco, 1924. Grabhorn printing. One of 250. $300-$400. Also, $225 (A, 1974).

DE VINNE, Theodore L. *The Invention of Printing.* Half morocco. New York, 1876. First edition. $100-$125. New York, 1878. Cloth. Second edition. $75-$100.

DE VINNE, Theodore L. *Title Pages as Seen by a Printer.* Illustrated. Half calf. New York, 1901. Grolier Club. One of 340. $125-$150.

DE VOTO, Bernard. *Across the Wide Missouri.* 81 plates, some in color. Cloth. Boston, 1947. First edition. One of 265. Boxed. $75-$100. Trade edition: Cloth. In dust jacket. $25-$35. New York, no date. Book Collectors Society edition. One of 100. $50-$75.

DE VRIES, David. P. *Voyages from Holland to America, 1632-1644.* Cloth. New York, 1853. One of 125. $75-$100.

DE VRIES, Peter. *But Who Wakes the Bugler.* Illustrated by Charles Addams. Cloth. Boston, 1940. First edition. In dust jacket. $40-$50. Author's first book.

DE WITT, David Miller. *The Judicial Murder of Mary E. Surratt.* Cloth. Baltimore, 1895. First edition. $75-$150.

DE WOLFF, J. H. *Pawnee Bill (Maj. Gordon W. Lillie): His Experience and Adventures on the Western Plains.* Illustrated. Pictorial boards. No place, 1902. First edition. $75-$150.

DEXTER, A. Hersey. *Early Days in California.* Pictorial cloth. (Denver), 1886. First edition. $200-$250.

DEXTER, F. Theodore. *Forty-Two Years' Scrapbook of Rare Ancient Firearms.* Cloth. Los Angeles, (1954). Limited edition. $40-$50.

DÍAZ DEL CASTILLO, Bernal. *The Discovery and Conquest of Mexico, 1517-1521.* Translated by A. P. Maudslay. Illustrated by Miguel Covarrubias. Leather. New York, 1942. Limited Editions Club. Boxed. $150-$175.

DÍAZ DEL CASTILLO, Bernal. *The True History of the Conquest of Mexico.* Translated by Maurice Keatinge. Map, errata leaf. Contemporary half leather. London, 1800. First English edition. $200-$300.

DIBDIN, Thomas Frognall. Note: The following listings of the famous bibliographer's work record mainly rebound copies of such volumes that have appeared recently in the auction records and in catalogues of book dealers. They are intended only to indicate price ranges within which these books may likely be obtained.

DIBDIN, Thomas Frognall. *Aedes Althorpianae.* Illustrated. 2 vols., boards. London, 1822. First edition. $150-$250. (Note: This work consists of the fifth and sixth volumes of a 7-volume set usually listed as *Bibliotheca Spenceriana,* which see in entry following.) Another issue: Large paper, bound in full leather. One of 55. $400-$500.

DIBDIN, Thomas Frognall. *The Bibliographical Decameron.* Illustrated. 3 vols., morocco, London, 1817. First edition. Large paper issue: One of 50 copies. $575 (A, 1971). Ordinary issue: Boards. $200-$300 at retail.

DIBDIN, Thomas Frognall. *The Bibliomania; or Book Madness.* Contemporary calf. London, 1809. First edition. $300-$400. London, 1811. 2 vols., morocco. Second edition. $100-$150. Large paper issue: One of 18. $200-$300. Other issues in 2 vols.-in-one format, half leather: $75-$100. London, 1842. Calf. Third edition. $100-$150. London, 1876. Half morocco. Large paper edition, limited. $150-$200. Boston, 1903. Bibliophile Society. 4 vols., boards. One of 483. $100-$150.

DIBDIN, Thomas Frognall. *Bibliotheca Spenceriana.* 7 vols., contemporary leather. London, 1814-15, 1822 and 1823. (4 vols., 1814-15, *Books Printed in the XV Century;* 2 vols., 1822, *Aedes Althorpianae;* one vol., 1823, *Catalogue of Books . . . Formerly in the Library of the Duke de Cassano Serra.)* First editions. $600-$800.

DICKENS, Charles. Note: It is only necessary to examine the major book auction records of the last few years to understand the price advances in the Dickens market. Almost every set of Dickens parts and virtually all the book editions to come to market are defective and/or rebound. Gather ye Dickens while ye may.

DICKENS, Charles. See "Boz." Also see *Sketches by "Boz"; The Loving Ballad of Lord Bateman; More Hints on Etiquette.*

DICKENS, Charles. *The Adventures of Oliver Twist.* 24 illustrations by George Cruikshank. 10 monthly parts, green wrappers. London, 1846. "New edition." (Actually third edition, as stated in preliminary pages, and sometimes called first octavo edition; for earlier editions see *Oliver Twist* under "Boz" and Dickens.) Recent price range at retail: $600-$800; in January, 1931, a set brought $1,400 at auction in New York. Also, worn, $160 (A, 1976); $172 (A, 1973); some stains and repairs, $350 (A, 1970). Another set of parts, bound and with the original wrappers bound in, sold at a London auction in 1976 for $619. London, 1846. Slate-colored cloth. Third edition (in book form). $300-$400, possibly more.

DICKENS, Charles. *American Notes for General Circulation.* 2 vols., brown cloth. London, 1842. First edition, first issue, with second page of "Contents to Volume I" numbered XVI. $300-$400. Also, $175 (A, 1975).

DICKENS, Charles. *The Battle of Life: A Love Story.* Engraved title page and frontispiece by Maclise. Cloth. London, 1846. First edition, first issue, imprint on engraved title page in 3 lines, with "A Love Story" printed. $350-$400. Second issue, with imprint in 3 lines and "A Love Story" engraved on a scroll. $200-$300.

DICKENS, Charles. *Bleak House.* Illustrated by H. K. Browne. 20 parts in 19, blue pictorial wrappers. London, 1852-53. First edition. $600-$800. Defective copies for less. London, 1853. Green cloth. First book edition. $200-$300. Also, worn, $175 (A, 1974).

DICKENS, Charles. *A Child's History of England.* Frontispiece. 3 vols., reddish cloth. London, 1852-53-54. First edition, with title pages dated. $200-$350.

DICKENS, Charles. *The Chimes.* 13 illustrations. Engraved title page. Bright-red cloth. London, 1845. First edition, first issue, with imprint as part of engraved title. $250-$300. New York, 1931. Limited Editions Club. Illustrated by Arthur Rackham. Cloth. Boxed. $350-$450.

DICKENS, Charles. *A Christmas Carol.* 4 colored plates and 4 woodcuts by John Leech. Brown cloth. London, 1843. First published edition, first issue, with "Stave I" (not "Stave One") on first text page and with red and blue title page and green end papers. $1,000-$1,500. Also, $625 (A, 1974)—the famous Robert Hoe copy. Worn sets retail in the range of $200-$300 and up. Second issue, with "Stave I," red and blue title page, and yellow end papers. $250-$350 and up. Third issue, with "Stave One," red and blue title page, and yellow end papers. $250-$350 and up. Trial issue: London, 1844. (Richard Gimbel's "first state.") Title page in red and green, with green or yellow end papers. $500-$750. Also, $375 (A, 1967), $322 (A, 1962). Philadelphia, 1844. Yellow cloth. First American edition. $200 and up. London, (1915). Illustrated in color by Arthur Rackham. Pictorial vellum. Large paper edition. One of 525. $500-$600. Boston, 1934. Limited Editions Club. Boards and cloth. Boxed. $100-$150. San Francisco, 1950. Grabhorn printing. One of 250. $100-$125.

DICKENS, Charles. *The Complete Works of Charles Dickens.* Edited by Arthur Waugh, Hugh Walpole, Walter Dexter, and Thomas Halton. Illustrated. 23 vols, buckram (each vol. a different color), leather labels, gilt, with an original engraved steel plate. London, 1937-38. Nonesuch Press. One of 877 sets. $2,500-$3,000. Also, $1,478 (A, 1976).

DICKENS, Charles. *The Cricket on the Hearth.* Illustrated. Crimson cloth. London, 1846. First edition. $150-$250. New York, 1846. Wrappers. First American edition. $100-$150. New York, 1933. Limited Editions Club. Cloth. Boxed. $60-$80.

DICKENS, Charles. *Dombey and Son.* Illustrated by H.K. Browne. 20 parts in 19, green pictorial wrappers. London, 1846-47-48. First edition, with 12-line errata slip in Part V. $500-$600 and up. New York, 1846-48. 20 parts in 19 wrappers. First American edition. $300 and up. London, 1848. Dark-green cloth. First book edition. $100-$150. New York, 1957. Limited Editions Club. 2 vols., buckram. Boxed. $40-$50.

DICKENS, Charles. *Great Expectations.* 3 vols. purple cloth. London, 1861. First edition, first issue, with ads dated May, 1861. $5,500 (A, 1974)—the famous Jerome Kern-Barton Currie copy, which sold in 1929 for $3,500, a price unsurpassed until the William E. Stockhausen sale in New York City on November 19, 1974. Copies less fine ranged up to $1,100 at auction in the 1960's and 1970's. New York, 1937. Limited Editions Club. Cloth. Boxed. $40-$60.

DICKENS, Charles. *Hard Times, for These Times.* Green cloth. London, 1854. First edition. $200-$250.

DICKENS, Charles. *The Life and Adventures of Martin Chuzzlewit.* Illustrated by Phiz. 20 parts in 19, green wrappers. London, 1844. First edition, first issue, with "£" sign after "100" in reward notice on engraved title page. $600-$800 or more. Also, $550 (A, 1971). London, 1844. Prussian blue cloth (later, brown cloth). First book edition, first issue. $250-$350.

DICKENS, Charles. *The Life and Adventures of Nicholas Nickleby.* Frontispiece portrait by Maclise, illustrations by Phiz. 20 parts in 19, green pictorial wrappers. London, 1838-39. First edition, first issue, with "vister" for "sister" in line 17, page 123, part IV. $600-$800 or more. London, 1839. Cloth. First book edition. $150-$250 and up .

DICKENS, Charles. *Little Dorrit.* Illustrated by H. K. Browne. 20 parts in 19. blue wrappers London, 1855-57. First edition, first issue, with errata slip in Part XVI and uncorrected errors in Part XV. $600-$800 or more. London, 1857. Green cloth. First book edition, first issue. $200 and up.

DICKENS, Charles. *Master Humphrey's Clock.* Illustrated by George Cattermole and H. K. Browne, 3 vols., brown cloth. London, 1840-41. First book edition. $100-$150. (See entry under "Boz" for editions in parts.)

DICKENS, Charles. *Mr. Nightingale's Diary.* Green or brown cloth, gilt. Boston, 1877. First American edition. $100-$150. (Note: This book was published originally as an anonymous pamphlet in London in 1851. The Dickens bibliographer John C. Eckel reports only "three known copies traceable." Estimated value: $1,000 and up.)

DICKENS, Charles. *The Mystery of Edwin Drood.* 12 illustrations by S. L. Fildes. 6 parts, green pictorial wrappers. London, 1870. First edition. $400-$500. London, 1870. Green cloth. First book edition. $100-$125. Boston, 1870. Wrappers. First American edition. $150-$200. Brattleboro, Vt., 1873. Cloth. "Completed by the Spirit-Pen of Dickens, Through a Medium." (By Thomas P. James.) First edition in this form. $27.50-$50.

DICKENS, Charles. *Oliver Twist.* 3 vols., brown cloth. London, 1839. Second edition (or third issue of the 1838 original, which see under "Boz" entry). With Dickens on title page instead of "Boz." $100-$150. (For third, or first octavo, edition, see Dickens, *The Adventures of Oliver Twist.*)

DICKENS, Charles. *Our Mutual Friend.* Illustrations by Marcus Stone. 20 parts in 19, green pictorial wrappers. London 1864-65. First edition. $400-$700. London, 1865. 2 vols., brown cloth. First book edition. $200-$250.

DICKENS, Charles. *The Personal History of David Copperfield.* Illustrated by H. K. Browne. 20 parts in 19, green pictorial wrappers. London, 1849-50. First edition. $1,500-$2,000. Also, $1,000 (A, 1974); $550 (A, 1972); $600 (A, 1971). London, 1850. Dark-green cloth. First book edition, first state, with engraved title page dated 1850. $400-$600.

DICKENS, Charles. *Pictures from Italy.* Illustrations on wood by Samuel Palmer. Dark-blue cloth. London, 1846. First edition, first issue, with pages 5 and 270 unnumbered and with 2 pages of ads. $100-$200.

DICKENS, Charles. *The Posthumous Papers of the Pickwick Club.* Illustrated by R. Seymour and Phiz. 20 parts in 19, green wrappers. London, 1836-37. First edition. The most difficult of all of Dickens' works to obtain in collector's condition and therefore impossible to evaluate without close examination. Literally hundreds of "points" must be met for a "perfect Pickwick," as is evidenced in John C. Eckel's bibliographical notes covering 42 pages in *The First Editions of Charles Dickens.* The Jerome Kern copy (once owned by Dr. R. T. Jupp) brought $28,000 at auction in 1939. The highest auction price in recent times was $4,250, achieved in New York in 1974 and twice on separate sets at the same sale in London in 1971. In 1965 the Louis Silver copy sold for $2,800. London, 1837. Green cloth. First book edition, first issue, with the name "Tony Veller" on the signboard on the engraved title page. $300-$400 or more. Philadelphia, 1836-37. 5 vols., boards. First American edition. $300 and up. New York, 1933. Limited Editions Club. 2 vols., cloth. Boxed. $50-$60.

DICKENS, Charles. *A Tale of Two Cities.* Illustrated by H. K. Browne. 8 parts in 7, blue wrappers. London, 1859. First edition, first issue, with page 213 misnumbered "113" $2,500-$4,000. A very fine set was offered in a 1977 catalogue at $3,750. London, 1859. Red or green (scarcer) cloth. First book edition, first state, with dated engraved title page. $1,500 and up. Also, $1,100 (A. 1974)

DICKENS, Charles. *The Uncommercial Traveller.* Lilac cloth. London, 1861. First edition, with ads dated December, 1860, at end. $300-$400.

DICKENS, Charles. *The Village Coquettes: A Comic Opera.* Gray boards, or unstitched, unopened sheets. London, 1836. First edition. Very rare in original boards. In sheets: $300 and up.

DICKENSON, Jonathan. See Dickinson, Jonathan.

DICKENSON, Luella. *Reminiscences of a Trip Across the Plains in 1846.* Pictorial cloth. San Francisco, 1904. First edition. $400-$500.

DICKERSON, Philip J. *History of the Osage Nation.* Illustrations and map. 144 pp., pictorial wrappers. (Pawhuska, Okla., 1906.) First edition. $75-$100.

DICKEY, James. *Buckdancer's Choice.* Cloth. Middletown, (1965). First edition. In dust jacket. $40-$50.

DICKEY, James. *The Eye-Beaters, Blood, Victory, Madness, Buckhead and Mercy.* Cloth. Garden City, 1970. First edition. One of 250 signed. Boxed. $40-$50.

DICKEY, James. *The Suspect in Poetry.* Boards or wrappers. (Madison, Minn.), 1964. First edition. Dust jacket. $25-$35.

DICKEY, James. *Two Poems of the Air.* Calligraphic text. Decorated boards. Portland, (1964). Oblong, decorated boards. First edition. One of 300 signed by the poet and the calligrapher, Monica Moseley Pincus. In slipcase. $95.

DICKINS, James. *1861 to 1865, by an Old Johnnie: Personal Recollections and Experiences of the Confederate Army.* Cloth. Cincinnati, 1897. First edition. $75-$100.

DICKINSON, Emily. *Further Poems of Emily Dickinson.* Edited by Martha Dickinson Bianchi and Alfred Leete Hampson. Green cloth. Boston, 1929. First edition. One of 465 on large paper. In dust jacket. $100-$125. Trade edition: Cloth. In dust jacket. $15-$20.

DICKINSON, Emily. *Letters of Emily Dickinson.* Edited by Mabel Loomis Todd. 2 vols., green cloth. Boston, 1894. First edition, first binding, with Roberts Brothers imprint on spine. In dust jacket. $200-$225. Second printing: 2 vols., brown cloth. $75-$100.

DICKINSON, Emily. *Poems.* Edited by Mabel Loomis Todd and T. W. Higginson. White and gray cloth. Boston, 1890. First edition. $600-$750. Also, $550 (A, 1977). Author's first book. London, 1891. Cloth. First English edition. $350-$400. New York, 1952. Limited Editions Club. Morocco. Boxed. $70-$80.

DICKINSON, Emily. *Poems: Second Series.* Edited by T. W. Higginson and Mabel Loomis Todd. Gray or gray-green cloth, or white cloth with green spine. Boston, 1891. First edition with white silk ribbon page marker. $150-$200. Some special copies issued in decorated boards, calf spine: $300-$350.

DICKINSON, Emily. *Poems: Third Series.* Edited by Mabel Loomis Todd. Gray, green, or white and green cloth. Boston, 1896. First edition, first binding, with Roberts Brothers imprint on spine. $300.

DICKINSON, Emily. *The Single Hound: Poems of a Lifetime.* Boards and cloth. Boston, 1914. First edition, with "Published, September, 1914," on copyright page. In dust jacket. $300-$400. Lacking jacket. $150-$200. Boston, 1915. Boards and cloth. Second edition. In dust jacket. $75-$125.

DICKINSON, Emily. *Unpublished Poems.* Edited by Martha Dickinson Bianchi and Alfred Leete Hampson. Green cloth, pink label on spine. Boston, 1935. First edition. One of 525 de luxe copies. Boxed. $100-$125. Boston, 1936. Green cloth. First trade edition. In dust jacket. $35-$45.

DICKINSON, Henry C. *Diary of Henry C. Dickinson.* Plates. Cloth. Denver, (about 1889). First edition. One of 225. $50.

DICKINSON, Jonathan. *Narrative of a Shipwreck in the Gulf of Florida.* Leather. Stanford, N.Y., 1803. (By Jonathan Dickenson.) $150-$200. Burlington, N.J., 1811. Leather. $150-$200. Salem, Ohio, 1826. *(The Shipwreck and Dreadful Sufferings of Robert Barrow.)* Half calf. $150-$200. (Note: These are variant titles of reprintings of Dickenson's *God's Protecting Providence,* first published in Philadelphia in 1699, of which only 4 perfect copies are known.)

DIDIMUS, H. *New Orleans as I Found It.* Double columns, 125 pp., wrappers. New York, 1845. (By Edward H. Durrell.) First edition. $200-$350.

DIDION, Joan. *Run River.* Cloth. New York, (1963). First edition. In dust jacket. $75-$100. Author's first book.

DIEHL, Edith. *Bookbinding: Its Background and Technique.* Illustrated. 2 vols., cloth. New York, 1946. First edition. $125-$150.

DIENST, Alex. *The Navy of the Republic of Texas, 1835-1845.* Blue leather (presentation binding). Temple, Tex., (1909). First edition. $500-$750. Also in cloth: $250-$300.

DIETZ, August. *The Postal Service of the Confederate States of America.* 2 color plates. Half leather. Richmond, 1929. First edition. $75-$100.

DIGBY, Sir Kenelm. *Poems from Sir Kenelm Digby's Papers in the Possession of Henry A. Bright.* 2 portraits, facsimile. Half morocco. London, 1877. Roxburghe Club. One of 80. $150-$250.

DILLON, George. *The Flowering Stone.* Cloth. New York, 1931. First edition. In dust jacket. $25-$30.

DIMSDALE, Thomas J. *The Vigilantes of Montana.* 228 pp., printed wrappers. Virginia City, Mont., 1866. First edition. $1,500-$2,000. Also, half leather, original wrappers preserved, $750 (A, 1968); lacking back cover and spine, $475 (A, 1963); rebound in cloth, printed label, $250 (A, 1960), half morocco and lacking ads, $275 (A, 1959). Virginia City, 1882. 241 pp., printed wrappers. Second edition. $200-$215. Cloth, $150. Helena, Mont., (1915). 26 plates and 4 facsimiles. Third edition. $30-$40. Helena, 1915. Fourth edition. $27.50.

DINSMOOR, Robert. *Incidental Poems.* Boards and cloth, paper label. Haverhill, Mass., 1828. First edition. $100. (Note: Contains first appearance of John G. Whittier's poems in a book.)

DIOMEDI, Alexander. *Sketches of Modern Indian Life.* 79 pp., wrappers. (Woodstock, Md., 1894?) First edition. $100-$125.

DI PRIMA, Diane. *New Mexico Poems.* Wrappers. (New York, 1968.) First edition. One of 50 signed. $30-$35.

DI PRIMA Diane. *This Kind of Bird Flies Backward.* Introduction by Lawrence Ferlinghetti. Illustrated. Wrappers. (New York, 1958.) First edition. $40-$60. Author's first book.

*DIRECTORY of the City of Mineral Point for the Year 1859.* Map. 64 pp., sewed. Mineral Point, Wis., 1859. $200-$250.

*DIRECTORY of Newark for 1835-6.* Half leather. Newark, N.J., 1835. First edition. $500 and up.

*DISCARDS (The).* By Old Wolf. 22 pp., wrappers. (Yakima, Wash.?), 1920. (By Lucullus V. McWhorter.) $75-$100.

*DISCOURSE on the Aborigines of the Valley of the Ohio (A).* Folding map. 51 pp., sewed. Cincinnati, 1838. (By William Henry Harrison.) First edition. $75-$150.

*DISIECTA Membra.* 54 pp., red wrappers. London, 1915. (By Norman Douglas.) First edition. One of 100. $200.

DISNEY, Walt. *The Golden Touch.* Cloth. London, 1935. First edition. $75-$100.

DISNEY, Walt. *Honest John and Giddy.* Cloth. New York, (1940). First edition. In dust jacket. $50-$65.

DISNEY, Walt. *Little Red Riding Hood and the Big Bad Wolf.* Illustrated. Boards. Philadelphia, (1934). First edition. $50-$60.

DISNEY, Walt. *Mickey Mouse.* Illustrated: Pictorial boards. Racine, Wis., (1933). A "Big Little Book." $50-$75.

DISNEY, Walt. *Mickey Mouse Story Book.* Illustrated. Pictorial boards. Philadelphia, (1931). First edition. $75-$100.

DISNEY, Walt. *The Pop-Up Minnie Mouse.* Illustrated, with 3 double page pop-up cutouts. Pictorial boards. New York, (1933). $50.

DISNEY, Walt. *Stories from Walt Disney's Fantasia.* Illustrated. Boards. (New York, 1940.) First edition. In dust jacket. $75-$100.

DISRAELI, Benjamin. See D., B., and M., W. G. Also see *Henrietta Temple; The Letters of Runnymede; The Tragedy of Count Alarcos; Vivian Grey; The Young Duke.*

DISRAELI, Benjamin. *Sybil, or The Two Nations.* 3 vols, half cloth. London, 1845. First edition. $60-$75.

DISRAELI, Benjamin. *The Voyage of Capt. Popanilla.* Boards, printed label. London, 1828. First edition. $200-$250.

DISTURNELL, John. *The Influence of Climate in North and South America.* Cloth. New York, 1867. First edition. $50-$75.

DISTURNELL, John (publisher). *Disturnell's Guide Through the Middle, Northern, and Eastern States*. Map of New York City, folding map. Cloth. New York, June, 1847. First edition. $75.

DISTURNELL, John (publisher). *The Emigrant's Guide to New Mexico, California, and Oregon*. Folding map. 46 pp., brown cloth. New York, 1849. First edition, first issue, with map published by Disturnell and dated 1849. $500-$800. Also, $325 (A, 1968). Second edition, same date: Wrappers. With 1849 Disturnell map including "Col. Hays' Route." $600-$800. Also, $500 (A, 1968). New York, 1850. Cloth. $140 (A, 1971); spine gone, covers detached, $250 (A, 1968). (Note: Howes cites an 1849 edition with "map published by Colton." Colton Storm's catalogue of the Graff collection calls the Disturnell map "preferable.")

DISTURNELL, John (publisher). *The Great Lakes or Inland Seas of America*. Cloth. New York, 1868. $100.

DISTURNELL, John (publisher). *The Upper Lakes of North America: A Guide*. Cloth. New York, 1857. First edition. $75.

*DIX Ans sur la Côte du Pacifique par un Missionaire Canadien*. 100 pp., wrappers. Quebec, 1873 (By François X. Blanchet.) First edition. $75-$125.

DIX, John Ross. See Jones, J. Wesley.

DIXON, Richard W. *Odes and Eclogues*. Wrappers. Oxford, 1884. Daniel Press. One of 100. $175-$200.

DIXON, Sam Houston. *The Heroes of San Jacinto*. Illustrated. Cloth. Houston, 1932. $75-$125.

DIXON, Sam Houston, *The Poets and Poetry of Texas*. Cloth. Austin, 1885. $150-$250.

DOBIE, J. Frank. *Apache Gold and Yaqui Silver*. Illustrated by Tom Lea. Buckram. Boston. 1939. First (Sierra Madre) edition. One of 265 signed by author and artist. Boxed. $600-$1,000. Trade edition: Cloth. In dust jacket. $40-$50.

DOBIE, J. Frank. *Carl Sandburg and Saint Peter at the Gate*. Boards. Austin, 1966. One of 750. Boxed. $85-$125.

DOBIE, J. Frank. *Coronado's Children*. Maps, illustrated. Cloth. Dallas, (1930). First edition, first issue, without the word "clean" in dedication. In dust jacket. $100-$150.

DOBIE, J. Frank. *Cow People*. Full leather, including variant binding with hair on it. Boston, (1964). First edition. One of 75 de luxe copies. $500-$1,000. Trade edition: Cloth. In dust jacket. $20-$25.

DOBIE, J. Frank. *The First Cattle in Texas and the Southwest*. Stapled. Austin, 1939. First edition. $75-$125.

DOBIE, J. Frank. *The Flavor of Texas*. Illustrated. Cloth. Dallas, 1936. First edition. $100-$200.

DOBIE, J. Frank. *Folklore of the Southwest*. 16 pp., wrappers. No place, 1924. First edition. $100-$150.

DOBIE, J. Frank. *Guide to Life and Literature of the Southwest*. Illustrated. Wrappers. Austin, 1943. First edition. $35-$50.

DOBIE, J. Frank, *John C. Duval, First Texas Man of Letters*. Cloth. Dallas, 1939. First edition. One of 1,000. $100-$200.

DOBIE, J. Frank. *Legends of Texas*. Wrappers. Austin, 1924. First edition. $85-$150. Austin, 1924. Cloth. Second edition. $35-$50.

DOBIE, J. Frank. *The Longhorns*. 16 plates by Tom Lea. Rawhide. Boston. 1941. First edition. One of 265 signed. Boxed. $1,000-$1,750. Trade edition: Pictorial cloth. In dust jacket. $35.

DOBIE, J. Frank. *The Mustangs.* Illustrated. Leather. Boston, (1952). First edition. One of 100 with original drawing. Boxed. $1,500-$2,500. Trade edition: Cloth. In dust jacket. $35-$50.

DOBIE, J. Frank, and others (editors). *Mustangs and Cow Horses.* Cloth. Austin, 1940. First edition. $100-$200.

DOBIE, J. Frank. *Tales of the Mustang.* Morocco. Dallas, 1936. Book Club of Texas. Boxed. $400-$750.

DOBIE, J. Frank. *A Vaquero of the Brush Country.* Boards and cloth. Dallas, 1929. First edition, first issue, with "Rio Grande River" (in error) on end-sheet maps. In dust jacket. $75-$100. Author's first commercially published (trade) book.

DOBIE, J. Frank. *The Voice of the Coyote.* Illustrated. Cloth. Boston, 1949. First edition. In dust jacket. $35.

DOBSON, Austin. *Horace Walpole, A Memoir.* Illustrated by Percy and Leon Moran. Boards. New York, 1890. One of 50 on Japan paper. $60-$75.

DOBSON, Austin. *Three Unpublished Poems.* 6 leaves, brown wrappers. Winchester, England, 1930. First edition. $38.40.

DOBSON, Austin. *Vignettes in Rhyme.* Cloth. London, 1873. First edition. $75-$125. Author's first book.

DOCTOROW, E.L. *Welcome to Hard Times.* Cloth. New York, 1960. First edition. In dust jacket. $50. Author's first book.

*DOCUMENTOS Relativos al Piadoso Fondo de Misiones para Conversión y Civilización de las Numerosas Tribus Barbaras de la Antiua y Neuva California.* 60 pp., bound with 8 pp. *Esposición a la Comisión, etc.* Mexico, 1845. $300-$500.

DODDRIDGE, Joseph. *Notes, on the Settlement and Indian Wars, of the Western Parts of Virginia and Pennsylvania, etc.* Calf. Wellsburgh, Va., 1824. First edition. $300-$400. Rebound in calf, $200.

DODGE, Grenville M. *Biographical Sketch of James Bridger, Mountaineer, Trapper and Guide.* 2 plates. 10 leaves, wrappers. Kansas City, (1905). First edition, without preface. $50-$75. New York, 1905. 3 plates, one folding. 17 pp., wrappers. $35-$50.

DODGE, Grenville M. *How We Built the Union Pacific Railway.* 30 plates. Printed wrappers. Council Bluffs, Iowa, (1908?). First edition, first issue, without printer's name on page before title page. $100-$150. Second issue. $50-$100. Another edition: (New York, 1910 or 1908?) $35-$50.

DODGE, Grenville M. *Union Pacific Railroad, Report of G. M. Dodge, Chief Engineer, to the Board of Directors on a Branch Line from the Union Pacific Railroad to Idaho, Montana, Oregon, and Puget's Sound.* Large folding map. 13 pp., wrappers. Washington, 1868. First edition. $200-$300.

DODGE, J. R. *Red Men of the Ohio Valley.* Illustrated. Cloth. Springfield, Ohio, 1859. First edition. $50-$75. Springfield, 1860. Second edition. $50.

DODGE, M. E. *Hans Brinker; or, The Silver Skates.* Frontispiece, 3 plates. Cloth. New York, 1866. (By Mary Mapes Dodge.) First edition. $250-$350. New York, 1876. Cloth. With a new postscript by the author. $35-$50.

DODGE, M. E. *The Irvington Stories.* Frontispiece. 4 plates. Cloth. New York, 1865. (By Mary Mapes Dodge.) First edition. $50-$75. Author's first book.

DODGE, Mary Mapes. See Dodge, M.E.

DODGE, Mary Mapes. *Donald and Dorothy.* Illustrated. Cloth. Boston, 1883. First American edition. $40-$50.

DODGE, Orvil. *Pioneer History of Coos and Curry Counties, Oregon.* Illustrated. Cloth. Salem, Ore., 1898. First edition. $50-$75.

DODGE, Richard Irving. See *A Living Issue.*

DODGE, Richard Irving. *The Black Hills.* 14 tinted plates, folding map. Cloth. New York, 1876. First edition. $75-$100.

DODGE, Richard Irving. *Our Wild Indians.* Illustrated. Cloth. Hartford, 1882. First edition. $50-$75.

DODGE, Richard Irving. *The Plains of the Great West and Their Inhabitants.* Illustrated, folding map. Cloth. New York, 1877. First edition. $75-$100.

DODGE, Theodore A. *Riders of Many Lands.* 19 illustrations by Frederic Remington. Cloth. New York, 1894. First edition. $50-$75.

DODGE, William Sumner. *Oration: "Liberty, Her Struggles, Perils and Triumphs."* 30 pp., wrappers. San Francisco, 1868. First edition. $20-$25.

DODGE, William Sumner. *A Waif of the War; or, The History of the 75th Illinois Infantry.* Cloth. Chicago, 1866. $100-$125.

DODGSON, Campbell (editor). *An Iconography of the Engravings of Stephen Gooden.* Illustrated. Buckram. London, 1944. One of 500. $75. Another issue: Buckram, vellum spine, with original proof frontispiece (etching) signed by Gooden. One of 160. Boxed. $150-$175.

DODGSON, Charles L. See Carroll, Lewis; Spavery. Also see *An Index to "In Memoriam."*

DODGSON, Charles L. *Lawn Tennis Tournaments.* 10 pp., sewed, without wrappers. London, 1883. First edition. $150-$250.

DODGSON, Charles L. *Euclid and His Modern Rivals.* Charts and diagrams. Red cloth. London, 1879. First edition. $50-$75.

DODSON, W. C. (editor). *Campaigns of Wheeler and His Cavalry, 1862-1865.* Cloth. Atlanta, 1899. First edition. $75-$100.

DOLBEN, Digby Mackworth. *The Poems of Digby Mackworth Dolben.* Edited by Robert Bridges. Portrait, plates. Boards, cloth spine, paper label. London, 1911. First edition. $75-$100.

*DOMESTIC Cookery: The Experienced American Housekeeper.* Calf. New York, 1823. $75.

*DOMESTIC Manners of the Americans.* 24 plates. 2 vols., cloth, paper labels. London, 1832. (By Frances Trollope.) First edition. $100-$150. New York, 1832. Cloth. First American edition. $100-$150.

DONAN, P. *Gold Fields of Baker County, Eastern Oregon.* Folding map. 36 pp., wrappers. Portland, (1898). First edition. $35-$40.

*DON Juan.* 6 vols., boards, paper labels (*Don Juan,* 1819, followed by books of same title containing Cantos II, IV, and V; VI, VII, and VIII; IX, X, and XI; XII, XIII, and XIV; XV and XVI). London, 1819-21-23-23-23-24. (By George Gordon Noel, Lord Byron.) First editions. $1,000 and up. (Note: A complete set of the first editions, accompanied by the second edition of Cantos I-II, brought $700 at a New York auction in 1974.)

DONLEAVY, J. P. *The Ginger Man.* Green wrappers. Paris, (1955). First edition. $75-$85. Author's first book.

DONNE, John. *Complete Poetry and Selected Prose.* Edited by John Hayward. Blue morocco. London, 1919. Nonesuch Press. One of 675. Boxed. $75-$100. Another issue: Thin paper edition. $150-$200.

DONNE, John. *Love Poems.* Portrait. Vellum. London, 1923. Nonesuch Press. Limited edition on handmade paper. $100-$150. Another issue: Boards, vellum spine. One of 1,250. $75-$100.

DONNE, John. *Poems.* 2 vols., New York, 1895. Grolier Club. One of 380. $75-$100.

DONOHO, M. H. *Circle-dot, a True Story of Cowboy Life 40 Years Ago.* Frontispiece. Cloth. Topeka, 1907. First edition. $50-$60.

DOOLITTLE, Hilda. See D., H.; Helforth, John.

*DOOMED City (The).* Folding map. 54 pp., wrappers. Detroit, 1871. (By Charles H. Mackintosh.) $25-$35.

DORING, Ernest N. *How Many Strads?* Illustrated. Red cloth. Chicago, 1945. First edition, first printing. One of 1,400. Boxed. $100-$150. Inscribed, $200.

DORMAN, Caroline. *Wild Flowers of Louisiana.* Illustrated. Cloth. New York, 1934. $35-$50.

DORN, Edward. *Gunslinger: Books I and II.* 2 vols., cloth. Los Angeles, 1968-69. Black Sparrow Press. First editions, Limited and signed. $60-$75. Also issued in suede bindings.

DORN, Edward. *The Shoshoneans.* Photographs. Oblong, cloth. New York, 1966. First edition. In dust jacket. $50-$75.

DORN, Edward. *What I See in the Maximus Poems.* Wrappers. (Ventura, Calif.), 1960. First edition. $75-$100. Author's first book.

DOS PASSOS, John. See Cendrars, Blaise.

DOS PASSOS, John. *Airways, Inc.* Blue boards and cloth. New York, (1928). First edition. In dust jacket. $50-$60.

DOS PASSOS, John. *The Bitter Drink.* (San Francisco, 1939.) Grabhorn Press. One of 35. $150-$250.

DOS PASSOS, John. *Facing the Chair: Story of the Americanization of Two Foreignborn Workmen.* Wrappers. Boston, 1927. First edition. $50-$75.

DOS PASSOS, John. *Ford and Hearst.* San Francisco, 1940. Grabhorn Press. One of 35. $100-$150.

DOS PASSOS, John. *The 42nd Parallel.* Decorated orange boards and cloth. New York, 1930. First edition. In dust jacket. $50-$60.

DOS PASSOS, John. *Most Likely to Succeed.* Cloth. New York, (1954). First edition. One of 1,000 signed. In dust jacket. $50-$60.

DOS PASSOS, John. *1919.* Orange-red cloth. New York, (1932). First edition (so stated). In dust jacket. $40-$50.

DOS PASSOS, John. *Number One.* Gray and pink cloth. Boston, 1943. First edition. In dust jacket. $35-$50.

DOS PASSOS, John. *One Man's Initiation—1917.* Pale-blue cloth. London, (1920). First edition, first issue, with broken type on page 35. In dust jacket. $250-$300. Author's first book. New York, 1922. Red cloth, paper label. First American edition. One of 500 from English sheets. In dust jacket. $75-$100.

DOS PASSOS, John. *Orient Express.* Illustrated in color by the author. Cloth. New York, 1927. First edition. In dust jacket. $35-$50.

DOS PASSOS, John. *A Pushcart at the Curb.* Pictorial boards and cloth, paper label. New York, (1922). First edition, first state, with "GHD" insignia on copyright page. In dust jacket. $35-$50.

DOS PASSOS, John. *Rosinante to the Road Again.* Yellow boards and cloth, paper labels. New York, (1922). First edition, first state, with "GHD" on copyright page. In dust jacket. $35-$50.

DOS PASSOS, John. *Three Soldiers.* Black cloth. New York, (1921). First edition, first state, with "signing" for "singing" on page 213. In dust jacket. $75-$100. Lacking jacket. $35-$50. Advance copy: Tan wrappers. $275 (A, 1977).

DOS PASSOS, John. *U.S.A. (The 42nd Parallel, 1919, The Big Money).* Illustrated by Reginald Marsh. 3 vols., buckram. Boston, 1946. First illustrated edition. One of 365 signed. Boxed. $100-$125. Trade edition: 3 vols., cloth. $35-$50.

DOS PASSOS, John. *The Villages Are the Heart of Spain.* Cloth. Chicago, (1937). First edition, limited and numbered. $50-$60.

DOUGHTY, William. *The Physical Geography of the North Pacific Ocean and Peculiarities of Its Circulation.* 27 pp., wrappers. Augusta, Ga., 1867. First edition. $75-$200.

DOUGHTY, Charles M. *Travels in Arabia Deserta.* Illustrated, folding map in pocket. 2 vols., cloth. Cambridge, 1888. First edition. $300-$500. London, 1921. 2 vols., cloth. In dust jackets. $75-$125. New York, 1923. Introduction by T.E. Lawrence. 2 vols. $75-$100. New York, 1953. Limited Editions Club. Boxed. $40-$50.

DOUGLAS, Lord Alfred. *The City of the Soul.* Vellum boards. London, 1899. First edition. $50-$75.

DOUGLAS, Lord Alfred. *In Excelsis.* Cloth. London, 1924. First edition. One of 100 signed. In dust jacket. $40-$60.

DOUGLAS, Lord Alfred. *My Friendship with Oscar Wilde.* Boards and cloth. New York, 1932. $30-$40.

DOUGLAS, Lord Alfred. *Oscar Wilde and Myself.* Cloth. London, 1914. First edition. In dust jacket. $35-$50.

DOUGLAS, Lord Alfred. *Poèmes.* Text in English and French. Portrait frontispiece. Wrappers. Paris, 1896. First edition. One of 20 on Hollande paper. (Usually inscribed.) $150-$200. Ordinary issue: $25. Author's first book.

DOUGLAS, C. L. *Cattle Kings of Texas.* Illustrated. Cloth. Dallas, (1939). First edition. $75-$150. Second edition, same date: Rawhide. Limited. $150-$300.

DOUGLAS, C. L. *Famous Texas Feuds.* Illustrated. Decorated cloth and leather. Dallas, (1936). First edition. In dust jacket. $75-$125.

DOUGLAS, C. L. *The Gentlemen in White Hats.* Illustrated. Cloth. Dallas, (1934). First edition. In dust jacket. $75-$125.

DOUGLAS, David. *Journal Kept by David Douglas During His Travels in North America 1823-27.* Portrait. Cloth. London, 1914. First edition. One of 500. $125-$150.

DOUGLAS, George. *The House with the Green Shutters.* Cloth. London, 1901. (By George Douglas Brown.) First edition. $50-$60.

DOUGLAS, James. *The Gold Fields of Canada.* 18 pp., wrappers. Quebec, 1863. $100-$150.

DOUGLAS, Norman. See Bey, Pilaff; Douglass, G. Norman; McDonald, Edward D.; Normyx. Also see *The Blue Grotto and Its Literature; Disiecta Membra; Index; Some Antiquarian Notes; Three Monographs.*

DOUGLAS, Norman. *Alone.* Red cloth. London, 1921. First edition, first issue, with Postscript on page 140 and erratum slip facing page 156. In dust jacket. $35-$50.

DOUGLAS, Norman. *The Angel of Manfredonia.* Boards and cloth. San Francisco, 1929. One of 225 signed. $75-$125.

DOUGLAS, Norman. *Birds and Beasts of the Greek Anthology.* Frontispiece. Blue boards, paper label. (Florence, Italy), 1927. First edition. One of 500 signed. In dust jacket. $75-$125.

DOUGLAS, Norman. *Capri: Materials for a Description of the Island.* Illustrated. Boards and cloth, leather label. Florence, 1930. First edition. One of 500 signed. $75-$150. Another issue: Blue cloth. De Luxe issue. One of 103 signed. $200-$300.

DOUGLAS, Norman. *D. H. Lawrence and Maurice Magnus.* Portrait frontispiece. Tan wrappers. (Florence), 1924 (actually, 1925). First edition, with pink printed price slip tipped in. $50-$60.

DOUGLAS, Norman. *Experiments.* Boards, paper label. (Florence), 1925. First edition. One of 300 signed. In dust jacket. $75-$100. London, 1925. One of 300 signed. $50-$75.

DOUGLAS, Norman. *Fountains in the Sand.* Illustrated. Blue cloth, blocked in white. London, (1912). First edition, first state of binding; first issue, with 16 plates. $75-$100.

DOUGLAS, Norman. *How About Europe?* Decorated boards. (Florence), 1929. First edition. One of 550 signed. In dust jacket. $75-$100. London, 1930. Orange cloth. In dust jacket. $25-$30.

DOUGLAS, Norman. *In the Beginning.* Printed boards, leather label. (Florence), 1927. First edition. One of 700 signed. In dust jacket. $75-$125. New York, (1928). Boards. First American edition. In dust jacket. $35-$50.

DOUGLAS, Norman. *Late Harvest.* Brown cloth. London, 1946. First edition. In dust jacket. $35-$50.

DOUGLAS, Norman. *London Street Games.* Buckram. London, (1916). St. Catherine Press. First edition. One of 500. $75-$125. London, (1931). Boards and cloth. Second edition. One of 110 signed. $100-$150. Trade issue: $25-$30.

DOUGLAS, Norman. *Looking Back: An Autobiographical Excursion.* Illustrated. 2 vols., boards and buckram. London, 1933. First edition. One of 535 signed. In dust jacket. $100-$150. New York, 1933. Brown cloth. First American edition. In dust jacket. $20-$25.

DOUGLAS, Norman. *Nerinda (1901).* Orange boards. Florence, 1929. First edition. One of 475 signed. In dust jacket. Boxed. $85-$125.

DOUGLAS, Norman. *Old Calabria.* Brown buckram. London, (1915). First edition, first issue, with white end papers. In dust jacket. $50-$75. Boston, 1915. Light-green cloth. First American edition. In dust jacket. $50.

DOUGLAS, Norman. *One Day.* Portraits. Full scarlet leather. Chapelle-Reanville, France, 1929. Hours Press. First edition. One of 200 on Rives paper, signed. $150-$250. Another issue: Boards. One of 300. $75-$125.

DOUGLAS, Norman. *Paneros.* Gold cloth and boards, leather label. Florence, (1930). First edition. One of 250 signed. In dust jacket. Boxed. $150-$200. London, 1931. Boards and cloth. First English edition. One of 650. In dust jacket. $75-$125. New York, 1932. Illustrated. Vellum. First American edition. One of 750. Boxed. $40-$60.

DOUGLAS, Norman. *Siren Land.* Frontispiece portrait, plates and map. Cloth. London, 1911. First edition. $150-$200. New York, (1923). "New and revised edition." In dust jacket. $40-$50.

DOUGLAS, Norman. *Some Limericks.* Gold-colored linen. (Florence), 1928. First edition. One of 110 signed. $250-$300. (Florence), 1929. Wrappers. $75-$100. Another issue: Buckram. $75-$100. (Chicago, about 1928-30?). Buckram. First American edition. $75-$100. Second impression. $50-$60. Boston, 1942. Boards and leather. "4th Continental Edition." Boxed. $50.

DOUGLAS, Norman. *South Wind.* Brown cloth. London, (1917). First edition. $150-$200. London, 1922. Cloth. One of 150 on blue paper, signed. $150-$225. New York, 1928. Illustrated by Valenti Angelo. One of 250 signed by Douglas. Boxed. $75-$125. Chicago, 1929. Illustrated. 2 vols., buckram. In dust jacket. Boxed. $65-$85. Another issue: 2

vols., in one, half blue morocco. One of 40 signed. $150-$200. New York, 1932. Limited Editions Club. Cloth. Boxed. $40-$50.

DOUGLAS, Norman. *Summer Islands: Ischia and Ponza.* Blue cloth. London, (1931). First edition. One of 500. In dust jacket. $60-$80. First American edition: (New York), 1931. The Colophon. Illustrated. Cloth. One of 550 signed. Boxed. $35-$50.

DOUGLAS, Norman. *They Went.* Lavender cloth. London, 1920. First edition. In dust jacket. $40-$60. New York, 1921. Cloth. In dust jacket. $15-$20.

DOUGLAS, Norman. *Together.* Illustrated. Cloth. London, 1923. First edition. One of 275 on handmade paper, signed. In dust jacket. Boxed. $75-$100. Trade edition: Cloth. In dust jacket. $35-$50.

DOUGLASS, G. Norman. *Contribution to an Avifauna of Baden.* 12 pp., without covers. (London?,1894.) (By Norman Douglas.) First edition. $125.

DOUGLASS, G. Norman. *On the Darwinian Hypothesis of Sexual Selection.* 16 pp., wrappers. London, 1895. (By Norman Douglas.) First edition. $150-$250.

DOUGLASS, G. Norman. *On the Herpetology of the Grand Duchy of Baden.* 64 pp., pale gray-blue wrappers. London, 1894. (By Norman Douglas.) First edition. $125-$200.

DOUGLASS, G. Norman. *Report on the Pumice Stone Industry of the Lipari Islands.* 8 pp. London, 1895. (By Norman Douglas.) First edition. One of 125. $200-$250. (France), 1928. Hours Press. Second edition. One of 80. Inscribed, $103 (A,1975).

DOVES PRESS BIBLE. (A general term.) See *The English Bible.*

DOW, George Francis. *The Arts and Crafts in New England.* Illustrated. Half cloth. Topsfield, Mass., 1927. First edition. $75-$100.

DOW, George Francis. *The Sailing Ships of New England: Series Three.* Illustrated. Cloth. Salem, 1928. First edition. In dust jacket. $50-$60.

DOW, George Francis. *Slave Ships and Slaving.* Illustrated. Buckram. Salem, 1923. $75-$100. Another issue: Half cloth. Large paper. One of 97. $150-$200. Salem, 1927. Buckram. In dust jacket. $100-$125.

DOW, George Francis. *Whale Ships and Whaling.* Illustrated. Buckram. Salem, 1925. First edition. One of 950. $100-$150. Another issue: Half cloth. Large paper. One of 97. $150-$250.

DOW, George Francis, and Edmonds, John H. *The Pirates of the New England Coast.* 29 plates. Cloth. Salem, 1923. First edition. In dust jacket. $75-$100. Another issue: Large paper. One of 84. $100-$150. New York, 1968. New edition. $27.50.

DOW, Lorenzo. *The Life and Travels of Lorenzo Dow.* Half calf. Hartford, 1804. First edition. $300-$400.

DOWDEN, Edward. *A Woman's Reliquary.* Boards, cloth spine. Dundrum, Ireland, 1913. Cuala Press. One of 300. $50-$60.

DOWNEY, Fairfax. *Indian-Fighting Army.* Illustrated. Cloth. New York, 1941. First edition. In dust jacket. $50-$75. New York, 1944. Cloth. In dust jacket. $25-$30.

DOWNFALL and Death of King Oedipus (The). 2 parts, blue wrappers, or (later) bound together in blue wrappers. (Guildford, England, 1880-81.) (By Edward FitzGerald.) First edition. Bound together. $50-$75, possibly more. (No copies noted singly in parts in many years.)

DOWNIE, William. *Hunting for Gold: Personal Experiences in the Early Days on the Pacific Coast.* Frontispiece. Half morocco or cloth. San Francisco, 1893. First edition. $100-$125.

DOWNING, Andrew Jackson. *The Architecture of Country Houses.* Illustrated. Pictorial cloth. New York, 1850. First edition. $150-$200.

DOWNING, Andrew Jackson. *The Fruits and Fruit Trees of America.* 69 hand-colored plates. Half morocco. New York, 1850. $500-$750. Also, rubbed, $482 (A, 1975).

DOWSON, Ernest. *Decorations: In Verse and Prose.* Vellum. London, 1899. First edition. $75-$125.

DOWSON, Ernest. *The Pierrot of the Minute.* Illustrated by Aubrey Beardsley. Cloth. London, 1897. First edition. One of 300 on handmade paper. $150-$200. Another issue: One of 30 on Japan paper. $300-$400. New York, 1923. Grolier Club. One of 300 designed by Bruce Rogers. $100-$150.

DOWSON, Ernest. *The Poems of Ernest Dowson.* Illustrated by Aubrey Beardsley. Cloth. London, 1905. First edition. In dust jacket. $50-$75.

DOWSON, Ernest. *Verses.* Vellum. Cover decorations by Aubrey Beardsley. London, 1896. First edition. One of 30 on Japan paper. $250-$350. Another issue: One of 300 on handmade paper. $100-$150.

DOYLE, A. Conan. See *Beeton's Christmas Annual; Dreamland and Ghostland.*

DOYLE, A. Conan. *The Adventures of Sherlock Holmes.* Illustrated by Sidney Paget. Light-blue cloth. London, 1892. First edition, first binding, lacking lettering on street sign. $300-$450. (Note: A notorious book for cracked hinges. If so defective, value drops to $200-$275 or so.) Later binding, $200-$275.

DOYLE, A. Conan. *The Case-Book of Sherlock Holmes.* Red cloth. London, (1927). First edition. $75-$125.

DOYLE, A. Conan. *The Doings of Raffles Haw.* Cloth. London, 1892. First edition, first binding, smooth blue cloth. $50-$75.

DOYLE, A. Conan. *The Firm of Girdlestone.* Dark red-brown cloth, black lettering. London. 1890. First edition. $40-$60.

DOYLE, A. Conan. *The Great Shadow.* Pictorial wrappers. Bristol, England, 1892. First edition. $150-$200. Also, in cloth. $100-$125.

DOYLE, A. Conan. *The Great Shadow and Beyond the City.* Illustrated. Tan cloth. Bristol, England, (1893). First edition. $50-$75.

DOYLE, A. Conan. *His Last Bow.* Red cloth. London, 1917. First edition. $100-$150. New York, 1917. Cloth. First American edition. $30-$40.

DOYLE, A. Conan. *The History of Spiritualism.* 2 vols., cloth. New York, (1926). $50-$60.

DOYLE, A. Conan. *The Hound of the Baskervilles.* Illustrated by Sidney Paget. Decorated red cloth. London, 1902. First edition. $250-$300.

DOYLE, A. Conan. *The Land of Mist.* Cloth. London, (1926). First edition. In dust jacket. $40-$60.

DOYLE, A. Conan. *The Maracot Deep and Other Stories.* Cloth. London, (1929). First edition. In dust jacket. $75-$100.

DOYLE, A. Conan. *The Memoirs of Sherlock Holmes.* Illustrated by Sidney Paget. Blue cloth, gold letters. London, 1894. First edition. $250-$300, possibly more. New York, 1894. Blue cloth. First American edition. $250-$300. (Suppressed by Doyle.)

DOYLE, A. Conan. *Micah Clarke.* Blue cloth. London, 1889. First edition. $50-$75. New York, 1894. Cloth. First American edition. $35.

DOYLE, A. Conan. *My Friend the Murderer.* Wrappers. New York, (1893). First edition. $100-$125. (Suppressed by Doyle.)

DOYLE, A. Conan. *The Refugees: A Tale of Two Continents.* 3 vols., green cloth. London, 1893. First edition. $200-$250. New York, 1893. Illustrated. Cloth. First American edition. $20.

DOYLE, A. Conan. *The Return of Sherlock Holmes.* Cloth. London, 1905. First edition. $250-$300.

DOYLE, A. Conan. *Round the Red Lamp.* Red cloth. London, 1894. First edition. $50-$75.

DOYLE, A. Conan. *The Sign of Four.* Frontispiece. Dark-red cloth. London, 1890. First edition, first issue, with "Spencer Blackett's Standard Library" on spine. $300-$500. Second issue, dated 1890, with Griffith, Farren imprint on spine. $125-$150.

DOYLE, A. Conan. *The Speckled Band.* Stage diagrams. Printed brown wrappers. London, 1912. First edition. $100-$150.

DOYLE, A. Conan. *The Stark Munro Letters.* Frontispiece and vignette title page. Dark-green or blue cloth. London, 1895. First edition. $100-$125. New York, 1895. Red cloth. First American edition. $25.

DOYLE, A. Conan. *A Study in Scarlet.* Illustrated. White wrappers. London, 1888. First edition in book form, first issue, with "younger" correctly spelled in preface. $2,000 and up. Rebound, title page repaired, $875 (purchased from my company in 1973 by the late David A. Randall, curator of Indiana University's Lilly Library for the library's great detective story exhibition). (For actual first edition, see *Beeton's Christmas Annual.*)

DOYLE, A. Conan. *Through the Magic Door.* Cloth. London, 1907. First edition. $40-$50.

DOYLE, A. Conan. *Uncle Bernac.* Red cloth. London, 1897. First published edition. $35. New York, 1897. Red cloth. First American edition. $20.

DOYLE, A. Conan. *The Valley of Fear.* Frontispiece. Red cloth. London, 1915. First edition. $50. New York, (1919). Illustrated by Arthur I. Keller. Red cloth. First American edition. $25.

DOYLE, A. Conan. *The White Company.* 3 vols., dark-red cloth. London, 1891. First edition. $250-$300.

DOYLE, A. Conan, and Barrie, James M. *Jane Annie: Or the Good Conduct Prize.* Wrappers. London, 1893. First edition. $185.

DOYLE, John T. *In the International Arbitral Court of The Hague: The Case of the Pious Fund of California.* 106 pp., unbound. San Francisco, 1906. $100-$150.

DOYLE, John T. *On Behalf of the Roman Catholic Church of Upper California. Points in Reply Submitted by Messrs. Doyle and Doyle of Counsel for the Prelates.* 8 pp., self-wrappers. No place, (1902). $50-$100. Another edition: (Menlo Park, Calif.,1902.) 11 pp., wrappers. $50-$100.

DOYLE, John T. *The Pious Fund Case.* 67 pp., unbound. San Francisco, 1904 (?). $100-$150.

*DRAFT of a Constitution Published Under the Direction of a Committee of Citizens of Colorado.* Denver, 1875. $150-$300.

DRAGO, Harry Sinclair. *Wild, Woolly & Wicked.* Illustrated by Nick Eggenhofer. Cloth. New York, 1960. First edition. One of 250 signed. $75-$125. Trade edition. In dust jacket. $25.

*DRAGOON Campaigns to the Rocky Mountains.* By a Dragoon. Blue cloth. New York, 1836. (By James Hildreth.) First edition. $300-$400.

DRAKE, Benjamin. *The Great Indian Chief of the West.* Illustrated. Cloth. Cincinnati, 1856. Reprint edition of *The Life and Adventures of Black Hawk.* $50-$60.

DRAKE, Benjamin. *The Life and Adventures of Black Hawk.* Portrait and plates. Cloth. Cincinnati, 1838. First edition. $150-$175.

DRAKE, Benjamin. *Life of Tecumseh, and His Brother the Prophet.* Cloth. Cincinnati, 1841. First edition. $35-$50. Cincinnati, 1852. Reprint edition. $25.

DRAKE, Benjamin. *Tales and Sketches of the Queen City.* Cloth. Cincinnati, 1838. First edition. $75-$100.

DRAKE, Benjamin, and Mansfield, E. D. *Cincinnati in 1826.* 2 plates. Leather. Cincinnati, 1827. First edition. $100-$150.

DRAKE, Daniel. *An Account of Epidemic Cholera, as It Appeared in Cincinnati.* 46 pp., wrappers. Cincinnati, 1832. First edition. $200-$300.

DRAKE, Daniel. *Natural and Statistical View, or Picture of Cincinnati and the Miami Country.* 2 folding maps. Printed boards. Cincinnati, 1815. First edition. $300-$600.

DRAKE, Daniel. *Pioneer Life in Kentucky: A Series of Reminiscential Letters from Daniel Drake, M. D., of Cincinnati to His Children.* Portrait. Cloth. Cincinnati, 1870. First edition. $100-$125.

DRAKE, Daniel. *A Practical Treatise on the History, Prevention, and Treatment of Epidemic Cholera.* Cloth, paper spine label. Cincinnati, 1832. First edition. $300-$400, possibly more.

DRAKE, Daniel. *A Systematic Treatise, Historical, Etiological, and Practical, on the Principal Diseases of the Interior Valley of North America.* Maps and plates. Full leather. Cincinnati, 1850. First edition. $400-$500.

DRAKE, Daniel, and Wright, Guy W. (editors). *The Western Medical and Physical Journal, Original and Eclectic.* Vol. 1. Leather. Cincinnati, 1827-28. $125-$150.

DRAKE, Joseph Rodman. See Croaker.

DRAKE, Joseph Rodman. *The Culprit Fay and Other Poems.* Frontispiece, vignette title page. Blue or purple cloth. New York, 1835. First edition. $100-$150. (Also bound in full morocco.) New York, 1936. Cloth. $50-$60.

DRAKE, Joseph Rodman, and Halleck, Fitz-Greene. *The Croakers.* Green cloth. New York, 1860. One of 250. $50-$75. (See Croaker for first edition.)

DRAKE, Leah Bodine. *A Hornbook for Witches.* Cloth. Sauk City, Wis. 1950. First edition. In dust jacket. $350-$550.

DRAKE, Morgan. *Lake Superior Railroad: Letter to the Hon. Lewis Cass.* 24 pp., wrappers. Pontiac, 1853. $200-$300.

DRANNAN, Capt. William F. *Thirty-one Years on the Plains and in the Mountains.* Illustrated. Cloth. Chicago, 1899. First edition. $50-$75.

DRAPER, John William. *Human Physiology.* Illustrated. Cloth. New York, 1856. First edition. $100-$125.

DRAPER, John William. *A Treatise on the Forces Which Produce the Organization of Plants.* 4 plates. Cloth. New York, 1844. First edition. $100-$150.

DRAYSON, Capt. Alfred W. *Sporting Scenes Amongst the Kaffirs of South Africa.* 8 colored plates by Harrison Weir. Cloth. London, 1858. First edition. $100-$150.

DRAYTON, John. *Memoirs of the American Revolution.* Portrait, 2 maps. 2 vols., cloth. Charleston, 1821. First edition. $350-$500. Also, rebound in half leather, boxed, $180 (A, 1976).

DRAYTON, John. *A View of South-Carolina.* 2 maps, 2 tables, 3 plates. Boards. Charleston, 1802. First edition. $650-$800. Rebound in half leather, $500.

DRAYTON, Michael. *Poems.* Edited by J. Payne Collier. Half morocco. London, 1856. Roxburghe Club. $100-$150.

*DREAM Drops, or Stories from Fairy Land.* By a Dreamer. Wrappers, or cloth. Boston, (1887). (By Amy Lowell.) First edition. Wrappers (151 copies): $1,000 and up. Cloth (99 copies): $800 and up. Also, $900 (A,1977). Author's first book.

*DREAM of Gerontius (The).* Wrappers. London, 1866. (By John Henry, Cardinal Newman.) First edition, printed dedication "J. H. N. " $750-$1,000.

*DREAMLAND and Ghostland: An Original Collection of Tales and Warnings.* 3 vols., pictorial red cloth. London, (1887). First edition, first binding (red cloth). $500-$600. Also, $325 (A,1970). (Note: Contains 6 stories by A. Conan Doyle.)

DREISER, Theodore. See Davis, Hubert.

DREISER, Theodore. *An American Tragedy.* 2 vols., black cloth, white end papers. New York, 1925. First edition, first issue, with Boni & Liveright imprint. In dust jackets. Boxed. $75-$100. Another (later) issue: 2 vols., blue boards and cloth. First limited edition. One of 795 signed. In dust jackets. Boxed. $125-$200. New York, 1954. Limited Editions Club. Boxed. $60-$80.

DREISER, Theodore. *A Book About Myself.* Ribbed red cloth, white end papers. New York (1922). First edition. In dust jacket. $25-$35.

DREISER, Theodore. *The Carnegie Works at Pittsburgh.* Decorations by Martha Colley. Boards, paper label. Chelsea, (New York, 1927). First edition. One of 150. In dust jacket. $50-$75. Another issue: Cloth. One of 27 on Marlowe Antique paper with a manuscript sheet in a special pocket at back of the book. In dust jacket. $150-$200.

DREISER, Theodore. *Chains: Lesser Novels and Stories.* Decorated boards and cloth. New York, 1927. First edition. One of 440 signed. Boxed. $125-$175. Trade edition: Dark-blue cloth. In dust jacket. $20-$25.

DREISER, Theodore. *The Color of a Great City.* Illustrated. Black cloth, white end papers. New York, (1923). First edition. In dust jacket. $75-$100.

DREISER, Theodore. *Dawn: A History of Myself.* Boards and cloth. New York, (1931). First edition. One of 275 signed. Boxed. $75-$125. Trade edition: Red and black cloth. In dust jacket. $30-$40.

DREISER, Theodore. *Epitaph: A Poem.* Illustrated by Robert Fawcett. Full leather, New York, (1929). Heron Press. First edition. One of 200 on Van Gelder paper, signed. Boxed. $125-$175. Another issue: Silk. One of 200 on Keijyo Kami paper, signed. $100-$150. Another: Cloth. One of 700, signed. Boxed $35-$50.

DREISER, Theodore. *The Financier.* Mottled light-blue cloth. New York, 1912. First edition, first issue, with "Published October, 1912" and code letter "K-M" on copyright page. In dust jacket. $50-$75.

DREISER, Theodore. *Free, and Other Stories.* Slate-blue cloth. New York, 1918. First edition. In dust jacket. $40-$60.

DREISER, Theodore. *A Gallery of Women.* 2 vols., boards and vellum. New York, 1929. First edition. One of 560 signed. In dust jackets. Boxed. $125-$150. Trade edition: 2 vols., brown cloth. In dust jackets. Boxed. $35-$45.

DREISER, Theodore. *The "Genius."* Ribbed red cloth, white end papers. New York, 1915. First edition, first issue, 1¾ inches thick, and with page 497 so numbered. In dust jacket. $100-$125. Second issue, 1½ inches thick, no number on page 497. In dust jacket. $50-$75.

DREISER, Theodore. *The Hand of the Potter.* Light-green boards and cloth, paper label. New York, 1918. First edition, first issue, with natural linen spine (second issue is blue). In dust jacket. $75-$100. Second issue: $50-$75.

DREISER, Theodore. *Hey, Rub-A-Dub-Dub!* Dark-blue cloth. New York, 1920. First edition. In dust jacket. $40-$60.

DREISER, Theodore. *A Hoosier Holiday.* Illustrated. Light-green boards and dark-green cloth. New York, 1916. First edition, first issue, with page 173 as an integral leaf. In dust jacket. $50-$75.

DREISER, Theodore. *Jennie Gerhardt.* Frontispiece. Mottled light-blue cloth. New York,

1911. First edition, first issue, with "is" for "it" in line 30 of page 22. In dust jacket. $75-$125. Second issue, text corrected. $50-$75.

DREISER, Theodore. *Moods, Cadenced and Declaimed*. Marbled boards and cloth, white end papers. New York, 1926. First edition. One of 550 signed. Boxed. $50-$75. New York, 1928. Cloth. First trade edition (with new material). In dust jacket. $40-$45.

DREISER, Theodore. *My City*. Colored etchings by Max Pollak. Folio, boards and cloth. New York, (1929). First edition. One of 275. $125-$175.

DREISER, Theodore. *Plays of the Natural and the Supernatural*. Light-green boards, linen spine, green end papers. New York, 1916. First edition. With 4-page note, "The Anaesthetic Revelation," tipped in at back. In dust jacket. $125-$150.

DREISER, Theodore. *The Seven Arts: Life, Art and America*. 28 pp., cream wrappers. New York, 1917. First edition. $40-$75.

DREISER, Theodore. *Sister Carrie*. Dark-red cloth, white end papers. New York, 1900. First edition. $750-$1,000. Also, $800 (A,1977). (I have never seen this in dust jacket. If such a copy exists, the value should be $1,000 and up.) Author's first book. New York, 1907. Colored frontispiece. Cloth. First illustrated edition. $75-$100. New York, 1939. Limited Editions Club. Cloth. Boxed. $85-$100.

DREISER, Theodore. *The Titan*. Mottled light-blue cloth. New York, 1914. First edition. In dust jacket. $40-$60.

DREISER, Theodore. *Tragic America*. Gray cloth. New York, (1931). First published edition. In dust jacket. $50-$60. (Note: There also exist a few copies—6 or 12?—of a suppressed prepublication issue bound for the author's private use. Value: $250 and up?)

DREISER, Theodore. *A Traveler at Forty*. Illustrated by W. Glackens. Red cloth. New York, 1913. First edition. In dust jacket. $40-$50.

DREISER, Theodore. *Twelve Men*. Blue cloth. New York, 1919. First edition. In dust jacket. $40-$50.

DREW, C. S. *Communication . . . of the Origin and Early Prosecution of the Indian War in Oregon*. 48 pp., sewed. Washington, 1860. First edition. $100-$125.

DRIGGS, George W. *Opening of the Mississippi; or Two Years' Campaigning in the Southwest*. Cloth. Madison, Wis., 1864. First edition. $150-$200.

DRINKWATER, John. *Abraham Lincoln*. Scarlet or purple wrappers, printed label on spine. London, 1918. First edition, with pen-and-ink correction of misprint on page (5). In dust jacket. $50-$75. Another issue: Red boards. In dust jacket. $25-$35.

DRINKWATER, John. *A Book for Bookmen*. Buckram. London, 1926. First edition. One of 50 signed. $50-$75. Also, $43 (A,1976).

DRINKWATER, John. *Loyalties*. Illustrated. Vellum and boards. (London), 1918. Beaumont Press. First edition. One of 30 on Japan vellum, signed. $150-$200. Another issue: Boards and cloth. One of 200. $75-$125. Also, $69 (A,1976).

DRINKWATER, John, *Persephone*. Cloth. (New York, 1926.) First edition. One of 550 signed. $50-$75. Also, $35 (A,1976).

DRINKWATER, John. *Persuasion: Twelve Sonnets*. Wrappers. London, 1921. First edition. One of 50 signed. $75-$100.

DRINKWATER, John. *Poems*. Cloth. Birmingham, England, 1903. First edition. $100-$150. Author's first book.

DRINKWATER, John. *Rupert Brooke: An Essay*. Boards. London, 1916. First edition. One of 115. $75-$125.

DRINKWATER, John. *Tides: A Book of Poems*. Boards and cloth. (London),1917. Beaumont Press. First edition. One of 250. $50-$75. Another issue: One of 20 signed. $100-$125.

DRINKWATER, John, and Rutherston, Albert. *Claud Lovat Fraser: A Story of His Life.* Portrait frontispiece by Rutherston, 39 Fraser illustrations, 20 in color. Cloth. London, 1923. One of 450 signed. $75-$125. Also, $77 (A, 1974).

DRIPS, Joseph H. *Three Years Among the Indians in Dakota.* 139 pp., wrappers. Kimball, S. D., 1894. First edition. $600-$700.

DRUMHELLER, "Uncle Dan." *"Uncle Dan" Drumheller Tells Thrills of Western Trails in 1854.* Portraits. Cloth. Spokane, 1925. First edition. $60-$75.

DRURY, Dru. *Illustrations of Exotic Entomology.* Edited by J.O. Westwood. 150 hand-colored plates. 3 vols., half leather. London, 1837. $350-$500. Also, $344 (A, 1976 and 1975).

DRURY, the Rev. P. Sheldon (editor). *The Startling and Thrilling Narrative of the Dark and Terrible Deeds of Henry Madison, and His Associate and Accomplice Miss Ellen Stevens, Who Was Executed by the Vigilance Committee of San Francisco, on the 20th September Last.* Illustrated. 36 pp., pictorial wrappers. Cincinnati, (1857). First edition. $200-$300. Philadelphia, 1865. $100-$150.

DRYDEN, John. See *Satyr to His Muse; The Works of Virgil.*

DRYDEN, John. *Alexander's Feast.* Vellum. London, 1904. Essex House. One of 140 on vellum. $150-$200.

DRYDEN, John. *All for Love.* 2 vols., folio, half vellum. San Francisco, 1929. John Henry Nash printing. One of 250. $75-$100.

DRYDEN, John. *Dramatic Works.* Edited by Montague Summers. 6 vols., buckram and marbled boards. London, 1931-32. Nonesuch Press. $300-$350. Another issue: One of 50 sets on Van Gelder paper. $400-$650.

DRYDEN, John. *Of Dramatick Poesie. An Essay, 1668. Preceded by a Dialogue on Poetic Drama by T. S. Eliot.* Marbled boards, cloth spine. London, 1928. First edition. One of 580. In dust jacket. Boxed. $75-$100. Another issue: Boards and vellum. One of 55 signed by Eliot. In dust jacket. Boxed. $250-$350. Also, $300 (A, 1977).

DRYDEN, John. *Songs and Poems.* Illustrated. Half cloth. Waltham Saint Lawrence, England, 1957. Golden Cockerel Press. One of 400 (of an edition of 500). $150-$200. Another issue: Specially bound in morocco. One of 100, with a duplicate set of plates. $400-$450.

DRYSDALE, Isabel. *Scenes in Georgia.* Frontispiece. 83 pp., boards and cloth, paper label. Philadelphia (1827). First edition. $50-$60.

*DUBLIN Book of Irish Verse (The).* See Cooke, John (editor).

DU BOIS, John. *Campaigns in the West, 1856-61: The Journal and Letters of Col. John Du Bois with Pencil Sketches by Joseph Heger.* Plates, folding map. Boards and leather. Tucson, 1949. Grabhorn Press. First edition. One of 300 signed. $125-$200.

DU BOIS, John Witherspoon. *Life and Times of William Lowndes Yancey.* 9 plates. Cloth. Birmingham, Ala., 1892. First edition. $75-$85.

DU BOIS, W. E. Burghardt. *The Gift of Black Folk in the Making of America.* Cloth. Boston, 1924. First edition. In dust jacket. $75-$125.

DU BOIS, W. E. Burghardt. *The Souls of Black Folk.* Cloth. Chicago, 1903. First edition. In dust jacket. $300-$500.

DU CHAILLU, Paul. *Stories of the Gorilla Country.* Woodcuts. Pictorial cloth. New York, 1868. First edition. $150-$175.

DUER, John K. (editor). *The Nautilus: A Collection of Select Nautical Tales and Sea Stories.* 48 pp., plain wrappers. New York, 1843, First edition. $35-$50.

DUERER, Albrecht, *Of the Just Shaping of Letters*. New York, 1917. Grolier Club. One of 215. $150-$175.

DUFF, E. Gordon. *Early English Printing*. Illustrated. Folio, half morocco. London, 1896. One of 300. $100-$125.

DUFF, E. Gordon. *Fifteenth Century English Books*. Facsimile plates. Boards and cloth. Oxford, 1917. $100-$125.

DUFF, E. Gordon. *William Caxton*. Boards and cloth. Chicago, 1905. Caxton Club. One of 145 with an original leaf from Chaucer's *Canterbury Tales* of 1478. $1,000-$1,250. Also, $700 (A, 1974). Another issue: One of 107 without the leaf. $150-$200.

DUFLOT DE MOFRAS, Eugene. *Exploration du Territoire de l'Oregon*. Illustrated. 2 vols., leather; plus atlas, folio, cloth. Paris, 1844. First edition. $3,500-$7,500. Also, the atlas volume alone, $1,200 (A, 1974).

DUFLOT DE MOFRAS, Eugene. *Travels on the Pacific Coast*. Translated by Marguerite E. Wilbur. 2 folding maps, 8 plates. 2 vols., half leather. Santa Ana, 1937. $150-$175. Also, $100 (A, 1972).

DUFY, Raoul. *Madrigaux*. 25 hand-colored illustrations. Loose sheets in paper folder and slipcase. Paris, (1960). One of 200. $150-$200.

DU HAYS, Charles. *The Percheron Horse*. Full-page plates. Vellum. No place (Gillis Press), 1886. $75-$100, possibly more.

DUKE, Basil W. *History of Morgan's Cavalry*. Portrait. Cloth. Cincinnati, 1867. First edition. $75-$125. New York, 1906. 9 maps, 4 portraits. Cloth. Revised edition. $50-$60.

DUKE, Basil W. *Reminiscences*. Cloth. Garden City, 1911. First edition. $50-$60.

DULAC, Edmund. *Sinbad the Sailor and Other Stories from the Arabian Nights*. Illustrated by Dulac. Vellum. London, no date. One of 500 signed. $500-$600.

DU MAURIER, George. *Peter Ibbetson*. Edited and illustrated by George Du Maurier. 2 vols., gray cloth. London, 1892. First English edition, probable first issue, with brown lettering. $100-$125. Second issue, lettered in black. $60-$100. (Mixed sets sometimes occur and were probably so issued at the time.) New York, 1963. Limited Editions Club. Boards. Boxed. $35-$50.

DU MAURIER, George. *Trilby*. 3 vols., gray cloth. London, 1894. First edition. $75-$100. New York, 1894. Tan pictorial cloth. First American edition. $20-$25. London, 1895. Illustrated. Half vellum. One of 250 signed. $75-$100. New York, 1895. Vellum. One of 250 signed. $75-$100.

*DUN COW (The): An Hyper-Satyrical Dialogue in Verse*. 12 leaves, blue wrappers. London, 1808. (By Walter Savage Landor.) First edition. $1,000 and up? Also, half calf, $648 (A, 1969).

DUNBAR, Paul (Laurence). *Oak and Ivy*. Blue cloth. Dayton, Ohio, 1893. (By Paul Laurence Dunbar.) First edition. $150-$200. Also, $170 (A, 1973). Author's first book.

DUNBAR, Paul Lawrence. *L'il Gal*. Photographs by Leigh Richmond Miner. Pictorial green cloth. New York, 1904. (By Paul Laurence Dunbar.) First edition. $40-$60. Also, $35 (A, 1976).

DUNBAR, Paul Lawrence. *Lyrics of Lowly Life*. Cloth. New York, 1908. (By Paul Laurence Dunbar.) First edition. $50-$60. Also, $35 (A, 1976).

DUNBAR, Paul Lawrence. *Majors and Minors: Poems*. Frontispiece portrait. Cloth. (Toledo, 1895.) (By Paul Laurence Dunbar.) First edition, probable first binding, with beveled edges. $60-$80.

DUNBAR, Paul Lawrence. *Poems of Cabin and Field*. Illustrated. Pictorial cloth. New York, 1899. (By Paul Laurence Dunbar.) First edition. $50.

DUNBAR, Paul Lawrence. *The Uncalled.* Cloth. New York, 1898. (By Paul Laurence Dunbar.) First edition. $75.

DUNCAN, Andrew. *The Edinburgh New Dispensatory.* 6 plates. Contemporary calf. Edinburgh, 1803. First edition. $50-$100. Edinburgh, 1804. Calf. Second edition. $25-$50.

DUNCAN, Isadora. *Art of the Dance.* Illustrated. Half cloth. New York, 1928. Limited edition. $125-$150.

DUNCAN, Isadora. *My Life.* Illustrated. Cloth, leather label. New York, 1927. One of 650. $50-$75.

DUNCAN, John M. *Travels Through Part of the United States and Canada in 1818 and 1819.* 14 maps and plates. 2 vols., calf. Glasgow, 1823. First edition. $300-$600. New York, 1823. 2 vols., half calf. First American edition. $100-$175.

DUNCAN, L. Wallace. *History of Montgomery County, Kansas.* Half leather. Iola, Kan., 1903. First edition. $100-$150.

DUNCAN, L. Wallace. *History of Wilson and Neosho Counties, Kansas.* Half leather. Fort Scott, Kan., 1902. First edition. $100-$150.

DUNCAN, Robert. See *Epilogos.*

DUNCAN, Robert. *A Book of Resemblances.* Illustrated by Jess (Collins). Cloth. New Haven, 1966. First edition. One of 203 signed. $75-$125.

DUNCAN, Robert. *Caesar's Gate: Poems, 1949-1950.* Illustrated by Jess (Collins). Wrappers. (Mallorca), 1955. Divers Press. First edition. One of 200. $100-$125. Another issue: One of 13 signed. $250-$350.

DUNCAN, Robert. *Derivations.* Cloth. London, (1968). Fulcrum Press. First edition. One of 162 signed. In dust jacket. $75-$100.

DUNCAN, Robert. *Faust Foutu.* Wrappers. (Stinson Beach, Calif., 1959). First complete edition. One of 50 signed and including a special color drawing by the author. $100-$125. Also, 700 unsigned. $25-$35.

DUNCAN, Robert. *The First Decade.* Cloth. (London, 1968.) Fulcrum Press. First edition. One of 150 signed. In dust jacket. $50-$60. Trade edition: $15-$25.

DUNCAN, Robert. *Heavenly City, Earthly City.* Illustrated by Mary Fabilli. White boards. (Berkeley), 1947. First edition. In dust jacket. $75-$100. (There were also fewer than 100 specially prepared presentation copies. Value: $450 at auction in 1977.) Author's first book.

DUNCAN, Robert. *Letters.* Illustrated. Decorated wrappers. (Highlands, N. C. 1958.) First edition. One of 450. $40-$50. Another issue: Boards and calf. One of 60 signed, with an original drawing by Duncan on end papers. $250. Also, $110 (A, 1975).

DUNCAN, Robert. *Medieval Scenes.* Wrappers. San Francisco, (1950). First edition. One of 250 signed. $130-$150.

DUNCAN, Robert. *Six Prose Pieces.* Boards. (Mt. Horeb, or Madison (?), Wis.), 1966. First edition. One of 70. In dust jacket. $225-$250. (Some copies signed by the poet.)

DUNCAN, Robert. *A Selection of 65 Drawings.* Cloth portfolio. Los Angeles, 1970. First edition. One of 300 signed. Boxed. $50-$75.

DUNDASS, Samuel. *Journal of Samuel Rutherford Dundass.* 60 pp., wrappers. Steubenville, Ohio, 1857. First edition. $1,500-$2,000, possibly more.

DUNIWAY, Mrs. Abigail J. *Captain Gray's Company; or, Crossing the Plains and Living in Oregon.* Cloth. Portland, 1859. First edition. $1,500-$3,000.

DUNLAP, William. *Diary: Memoirs of a Dramatist.* 3 vols., buckram. New York, 1931. One of 100. $125.

DUNLAP, William. *The Life of Charles Brockden Brown.* Frontispiece. 2 vols., blue-gray boards, gray-green spine. Philadelphia, 1815. First edition. $200-$300. Also, $160 (A, 1972). (Note: Contains first printing of "Memoirs of Carwin" and other Brown items; see Brown entry.)

DUNLAP, William. *A History of the American Theatre.* Purple muslin, paper spine label. New York, 1832. First edition. $75-$150. London, 1833. 2 vols., half calf. First English edition. $50.

DUNLAP, William. *A History of the New Netherlands.* Illustrated, including 2 folding maps. 2 vols., boards and cloth, or cloth. New York, 1839 (and 1840). First edition, with errata leaf. $100-$150.

DUNLAP, William. *History of the Rise and Progress of the Arts of Design in the United States.* 2 vols., green boards and cloth. New York, 1834. First edition. $200-$250. Boston, 1918. Plates. 3 vols., cloth. $100-$150.

DUNLAP, William. *Memoirs of the Life of George Frederick Cooke.* Frontispieces. 2 vols, boards. New York, 1813. First edition. $100-$150.

DUNLAP, William. *A Narrative of the Events Which Followed Bonaparte's Campaign, etc.* Frontispiece. 5 plates. Leather. Hartford, 1814. First edition. $100-$150.

DUNN, Jacob Piatt. *Massacres of the Mountains.* Folding map and illustrations. Pictorial cloth. New York, 1886. First edition. $100-$150.

DUNN, John. *History of the Oregon Territory and British North-American Fur Trade.* Folding map. Cloth. London, 1844. First edition. $450-$800, possibly more.

DUNN, John. *The Oregon Territory and the British North American Fur Trade.* Wrappers. Philadelphia, 1845. First American edition (of *History of the Oregon Territory, etc.*). $300-$400.

DUNNE, Finley Peter. See *Mr. Dooley in Peace and in War.*

DUNNE, Finley Peter. *Mr. Dooley at His Best.* Half cloth. New York, 1938. One of 520, with a page of the original manuscript. $75-$100. Also, $45 (A, 1976).

DUNSANY, Lord. *The Book of Wonder.* Illustrated by Sidney H. Sime. Cloth. London, 1912. In dust jacket. $100-$125.

DUNSANY, Lord. *The Chronicles of Rodriguez.* Frontispiece. Light-brown cloth, vellum spine, leather label. London, 1922. One of 500 signed. $125-$150.

DUNSANY, Lord. *The Compromise of the King of the Golden Isles.* Illustrated by T. M. Cleland. Gold boards and cloth. New York, 1924. Grolier Club. One of 300. $125-$150.

DUNSANY, Lord. *Five Plays.* Illustrated. Cloth. London, 1914. First edition. $50-$75.

DUNSANY, Lord. *The Gods of Pegana.* Boards and cloth. London, 1905. First edition. In dust jacket. $100-$125.

DUNSANY, Lord. *A Journey.* Dark-blue boards. London, (1944). First edition. One of 250 initialed by the author. Boxed. $100-$110.

DUNSANY, Lord. *The King of Elfland's Daughter.* Frontispiece. Orange cloth, vellum spine, leather label. London, (1924). One of 250 signed. In dust jacket. $100-$150. Also, $112 (A, 1975).

DUNSANY, Lord. *Selections from the Writings of Lord Dunsany.* Edited and with introduction by William Butler Yeats. Boards and linen. Churchtown, Dundrum, Ireland, 1912. Cuala Press. One of 250. $75-$150.

DUNSANY, Lord. *Time and the Gods.* Illustrated by Sidney Sime. Cloth. London, 1906. First edition. $75-$135. London, (1922). Illustrated. Orange cloth, vellum spine, leather label. One of 250 signed. In dust jacket. $75-$100.

DUNTHORNE, Gordon. *Flower and Fruit Prints of the 18th and Early 19th Centuries.* Illustrated. Folio, cloth. Washington, 1938. One of 750, with folding plate listing subscribers. Boxed. $250-$350. Lacking the subscriber plate, $200-$250.

DUNTON, John. *Letters Written from New-England.* Half morocco. Boston, 1867. Prince Society. One of 150. $50-$75.

DU PONCEAU, M. *Mémoire au Sujet des Prétentions du Gouvernement des États Unis sur l'Alluvion du Fleuve Mississippi, etc.* Nouvelle-Orléans, 1808. Half calf. First edition. $500-$750.

DuPONT, Samuel F. *Extracts from Private Journal-Letters of Capt. S. F. DuPont.* Three-quarters morocco. Wilmington, Del., 1885. First edition. $850-$1,000. (Note: Fewer than 50 copies printed.)

DuPONT, Samuel F. *Official Dispatches and Letters of Rear Admiral DuPont, 1846-48; and 1861-63.* Half leather. Wilmington, 1883. First edition. $300-$350.

DURRELL, Lawrence. See Norden, Charles; Peeslake, Gaffer; Royidis, Emmanuel. Also see *The Fifth Antiquarian Book Fair.*

DURRELL, Lawrence. *The Alexandria Quartet.* Buckram. London, (1962). First collected edition of *Justine, Balthazar, Mountolive, and Clea.* One of 500 signed. Boxed. $200-$300. New York (1962). Marbled boards. First American edition. One of 199 signed. Boxed. $150-$250. (Note: The four individual titles in their original trade editions, offered together, all mint in dust jackets, brought $325 at auction in October, 1977. Offered in dealer catalogues at $250 and up in 1978.)

DURRELL, Lawrence. *Balthazar.* Cloth. London, 1958. First edition. In dust jacket. $40-$60.

DURRELL, Lawrence. *Beccafico.* Translated and edited by F. J. Temple. Wrappers. La Licorne, 1963. First edition. One of 150 signed. $80-$125.

DURRELL, Lawrence. *Bitter Lemons.* Illustrated. Cloth. London, 1957. First edition. In dust jacket. $40-$60.

DURRELL, Lawrence. *The Black Book: An Agon.* Wrappers. Paris, (1938). Obelisk Press. First edition. $400-$600.

DURRELL, Lawrence. *Clea.* Cloth. London, (1960). First edition. In dust jacket. $40-$60.

DURRELL, Lawrence. *Deus Loci.* Printed blue-gray wrappers. Ischia, Italy, 1950. First edition. One of 200 signed. $150-$175. Also, $125 (A, 1977).

DURRELL, Lawrence. *In Arcadia.* Music by Wallace Southam. Wrappers. London, 1968. Turret Books. First edition. One of 100 signed. $100-$150.

DURRELL, Lawrence. *Justine.* Cloth. London, 1957. First edition. In dust jacket. $75-$100.

DURRELL, Lawrence. *La Descente du Styx.* Translated by F. J. Temple. Wrappers. (Paris, 1964.) First edition. One of 250 signed. $75-$150.

DURRELL, Lawrence. *Mountolive.* Cloth. London, 1958. First edition. In dust jacket. $50-$60.

DURRELL, Lawrence. *Nothing Is Lost, Sweet Self.* Music by Wallace Southam. Pictorial wrappers. (London, 1967.) Turret Books. First edition. One of 100 signed. $35-$50.

DURRELL, Lawrence. *On Seeming to Presume.* Cloth. London, (1948). In dust jacket. $25-$35.

DURRELL, Lawrence. *On the Suchness of the Old Boy.* Illustrated by Sappho Durrell. London, 1972. One of 226 signed. $100-$125.

DURRELL, Lawrence. *The Parthenon.* Wrappers. (Rhodes, 1945 or 1946.) First edition. One of 25. $150-$200. Also, inscribed, $550 (A, 1977).

DURRELL, Lawrence. *Pied Piper of Lovers.* Cloth. London, 1935. First edition. $1,100 in a 1978 catalogue. Author's first novel; exceedingly scarce.

DURRELL, Lawrence. *A Private Country: Poems.* Gray cloth. London, (1943). First edition. $50-$60.

DURRELL, Lawrence. *Private Drafts.* Illustrated. Very small, pictorial wrappers (Nicosia, Cyprus), 1955. Proodos Press. One of 100 signed. $200-$250. Also, $225 (A, 1977).

DURRELL, Lawrence. *Prospero's Cell.* Illustrated. Cloth, London, (1945). First edition. In dust jacket. $40-$50.

DURRELL, Lawrence. *Quaint Fragment.* Portrait. Blue wrappers, or rose-red boards and cloth. (London), 1931. Cecil Press. First edition. $5,000 and up. Of two known copies, one in rose-red boards, spine worn, was catalogued by a New York bookseller (about 1963) at $750. This copy was sold at the Jonathan Goodwin auction in October, 1977, for $3,500. According to the Goodwin sale catalogue, there is an unbound copy at the University of California in Los Angeles. Author's first book.

DURRELL, Lawrence. *Sappho: A Play in Verse.* Cloth. London, (1950). First edition. In dust jacket. $40-$50.

DURRELL, Lawrence. *Six Poems, from the Greek of Sekilianos and Seferis.* Pictorial wrappers. Rhodes, 1946. First edition. Limited (50?) $300-$350. Also, a presentation copy, signed, $650 (A, 1977).

DURRELL, Lawrence. *Ten Poems.* Cloth. London, 1932. Caduceus Press. First edition. One of 12. $500 and up.

DURRELL, Lawrence. *Zero and Asylum in the Snow.* Wrappers. Rhodes, 1946. First edition. $100-$150. Berkeley, 1947. White boards. First American edition. In dust jacket. $50-$60.

DUSTIN, Fred. *The Custer Tragedy.* 3 folding maps in pocket. Cloth. Ann Arbor, 1939. First edition. One of 200. $400-$450.

*DUTCHMAN'S Fireside (The).* 2 vols., cloth. New York, 1831. (By James Kirke Paulding.) First edition, first issue, with date of May, 1831, in ad on back cover of Vol. 1. $150-$200.

DUVAL, Elizabeth W. *T. E. Lawrence: a Bibliography.* Boards. New York, (1938). First edition. One of 500. $75-$100.

DUVAL, John C. *The Adventures of Big-Foot Wallace.* 8 plates. Green cloth. Philadelphia, 1871. First edition. $500-$750.

DUVAL, John C. *Early Times in Texas.* Cloth. Austin, 1892. First edition. $150-$250.

DUVAL, K. D., and Smith, Sydney Goodsir (editors). *Hugh MacDiarmid: a Festschrift.* Cloth. Edinburgh, (1962). First edition. One of 50 with holograph poem signed by MacDiarmid tipped in. In dust jacket. $75-$125.

DWIGGINS, W. A. *Towards a Reform of the Paper Currency.* Boards and cloth. New York, 1932. Limited Editions Club. One of 452 signed. In dust jacket. Boxed. $200-$250. Also, $150 (A, 1976).

DWIGHT, Timothy. *A Discourse on Some Events of the Last Century.* Printed gray-blue wrappers. New Haven, 1801. First edition. $150-$200.

DWIGHT, Timothy. *The Psalms of David, Imitated in the Language of the New Testament.* Leather. Hartford, 1801. First edition. $100-$150.

DWIGHT, Timothy. *Travels in New-England and New York.* 3 maps. 4 vols., boards. New Haven, 1821-22. First edition, with errata slip in last volume. $300-$400.

DWINELLE, John W. *The Colonial History of the City of San Francisco.* Map. Printed wrappers. San Francisco, 1863. First edition. $600. Also, $300 (A, 1968). San Francisco, 1866. Map, 3 plates. Third edition, second issue, with inserted slip "No. CLXXI-Bis" and 7 pages of addenda. $750-$850. Also, $300 (A, 1968); $500 (A, 1960).

DYER, Mrs. D. B. *"Fort Reno," or Picturesque "Cheyenne and Arrapahoe Army Life," Before the Opening of Oklahoma.* 10 plates. Cloth. New York, 1896. First edition. $75-$200.

DYER, Frederick H. *A Compendium of the War of the Rebellion.* Cloth. Des Moines, 1908. First edition. $75-$100.

DYKES, W. R. *The Genus Iris.* 48 colored plates. Folio, cloth. Cambridge, 1913. First edition. $300-$400. Also, $275 (A, 1976). Another issue: Half morocco. $400-$600. Also, $425 (A, 1977); $450 (A, 1976).

*DYLLIA Nova Quinque Heroum atque Heroidum.* 2 parts in one, boards. Oxford, 1815. (By Walter Savage Landor.) First edition. $300-$400. Also, $192 (A, 1968).

# E

E., A. *By Still Waters, Lyrical Poems Old and New.* Boards. Dundrum, Ireland. 1906. Dun Emer Press. (By George W. Russell.) First edition. (200 copies issued.) In tissue dust jacket. $75-$85.

E., A. *Collected Poems.* Cloth. London, 1913. (By George W. Russell.) First edition. In dust jacket. $35-$50. London, 1928. Signed copy, $58 (A, 1975).

E., A. *The Dublin Strike.* (Caption title.) 8 pp., self-wrappers. (London, 1913.) (By George W. Russell.) First edition. $50-$75.

E., A. *Gods of War, with Other Poems.* Brown wrappers. Dublin, 1915. (By George W. Russell.) First edition. $30-$40.

E., A. *The Hero in Man.* (Cover title.) Printed wrappers. (Orpheus Press, 1909.) (By George W. Russell.) First edition. $35-$50.

E., A. *Homeward Songs by the Way.* Wrappers. Dublin, 1894. (By George W. Russell.) First edition. $150-$175. Author's first book.

E., A. *Midsummer Eve.* Boards. New York, 1928. (By George W. Russell.) First edition. One of 450 signed. In dust jacket. $60.

E., A. *The Nuts of Knowledge.* Boards, linen spine. (Dundrum, 1903.) Dun Emer Press. (By George W. Russell.) First edition. (200 copies issued.) In tissue dust jacket. $65-$85.

E., A. *Salutation: A Poem on the Irish Rebellion of 1916.* Wrappers. London, 1917. (By George W. Russell.) First edition. One of 25 signed. $150-$200. Also, $94.60 (A, 1971).

E., A. *Some Passages from the Letters of A. E. to W. B. Yeats.* Boards, linen spine. Dublin, 1936. Cuala Press. (By George W. Russell.) One of 300. In tissue dust jacket. $75-$100.

EARLE, Ferdinand (editor). *The Lyric Year.* Cloth. New York, 1912. First edition, first state, with "careful gentlemen" for "polite gentleman" in line 13 of page 25. In dust jacket. $75-$100. (Contains first appearance of Edna St. Vincent Millay's "Renascence.")

EARLE, Thomas (compiler). *The Life, Travels and Opinions of Benjamin Lundy.* Colored folding map. Cloth. Philadelphia, 1847. First edition. $500-$650.

EARLY, Gen. Jubal A. *Autobiographical Sketch and Narrative of the War Between the States.* Cloth. Philadelphia, 1912. First edition. $100-$125.

EARLY, Lieut. Gen. Jubal A. *A Memoir of the Last Year of the War for Independence in the Confederate States of America.* Toronto, 1866. First edition. $150-$200. Lynchburg, 1867. First United States edition. $150-$200. Also, disbound, $45 (A, 1976).

EASTAWAY, Edward. *Poems.* Portrait frontispiece. Gray boards, paper label. London, 1917. (By Edward Thomas.) First edition. $75-$100.

EASTLAKE, William. *The Bronc People.* Boards. New York, (1958). First edition. In dust jacket. $35-$50.

EASTLAKE, William. *Go In Beauty.* Cloth. New York, (1956). First edition. In dust jacket. $100-$125. Author's first book.

EASTMAN, Mary H. *The American Aboriginal Portfolio.* Engraved title page; 26 plates. Cloth. Philadelphia. (1853). First edition. $300-$500.

EASTON, John. *A Narrative of the Causes Which Led to Phillip's Indian War.* Map. Cloth. Albany, 1858. First edition. $60-$75.

EATON, Daniel Cady. *The Ferns of North America.* 2 vols., cloth. Salem, Mass., and Boston, 1880. First edition. $150-$250.

EATON, Rachel Caroline. *John Ross and the Cherokee Indians.* Cloth. Menasha, Wis., 1914. First edition. $150-$250.

EBERHART, Richard. *A Bravery of Earth.* Cloth. London, 1930. First edition. In dust jacket. $200-$250. Author's first book.

EBERHART, Richard. *Brotherhood of Men.* Wrappers. (Pawlet, Vt., 1949.) Banyan Press. First edition. One of 26 signed. $150-$175.

EBERHART, Richard. *Collected Verse Plays.* Boards and cloth. Chapel Hill, (1962). First edition. One of 100 signed. In glassine dust jacket. $100-$125.

EBERHART, Richard. *Thirty-one Sonnets.* Cloth. New York, (1967). First edition. One of 99 signed. Boxed. $75-$100. Also, $55 (A, 1976).

*ECCLESIASTES-LLYFR y Pregeth-Wr.* Woodcut vignette on title page, full page woodcut. Printed in red and black. Blue morocco, gilt. Newtown, Wales, 1927. Greynog Press. One of 223. $100-$150. Also, $68.80 (A, 1975). Another issue: One of 25 specially bound. In slipcase. $800-$1,000. Also, $550 (A, 1973).

*ECCLESIASTICUS.* See *The Wisdom of Jesus, Son of Sirach.*

*ECHO, The.* Marbled boards and leather. (New York, 1807.) (By Richard Alsop, Lemuel Hopkins, Theodore Dwight, etc.) First edition. $75-$100.

*ECHOES. By Two Writers.* Printed wrappers. Light brown wrappers. (Lahore, India, 1884.) (By Rudyard Kipling, with eight poems credited to his sister Beatrice.) First edition, printed at the Civil and Military Gazette Press. $600-$800. Also, inscribed by Kipling, lacking backstrip, $1,800 (A, 1975); $400 (A, 1972); inscribed by Kipling, $2,300 (A, 1971).

ECKENRODE, Hamilton J. *The Revolution in Virginia.* Cloth. Boston, 1916. First edition. $50-$60.

ECKSTEIN, John. *Picturesque View of the Diamond Rock.* 16 plates, 14 hand-colored. Oblong, folio, half morocco. London, 1805. Rebound copy, $1,150.

EDDINGTON, Arthur Stanley. *Stellar Movements and the Structure of the Universe.* Illustrated. Cloth. London, 1914. First edition. $125-$150. Author's first book.

EDDINGTON, Arthur Stanley. *The Internal Constitution of the Stars.* Cloth. Cambridge, 1926. First edition. $150-$200.

EDDISON, E. R. *The Worm Ouroboros.* Illustrated by Keith Henderson. Cloth. London, (1922). First edition. In dust jacket. $100-$150. Author's first book. New York, 1926. Illustrated. Cloth. First American edition. In dust jacket. $50-$75.

EDDY, Mary Baker. See Glover, Mary Baker.

EDE, Charles (editor). *The Art of the Book.* Illustrated. Cloth. London, (1951). First edition. Boxed. $35-$50.

EDE, Harold Stanley. *A Life of Gaudier-Brzeska.* Numerous plates (some colored), other illustrations. Cloth. London, 1930. One of 350. In dust jacket. Boxed. $250-$350. Also, lacking jacket, $112 (A, 1976).

EDELMAN, George W. *Guide to the Value of California Gold.* Disbound. Philadelphia, 1850. First edition. $1,000-$2,000.

EDGAR, Patrick Nisbett. *The American Race-Turf Register*. Vol. 1. (All published.) New York, 1833. First edition. $125-$150.

EDGEWORTH, Maria. See *Castle Rackrent; The Modern Griselda*.

EDMONDS, Walter D. *Rome Haul*. Cloth. Boston, 1929. First (presentation) edition, with "Published February, 1929" on copyright page. One of 1,001. In dust jacket. $50-$60. Trade edition: In dust jacket. $15-$25. Author's first book.

EDMONSTON, Catherine Devereux. *The Journal of Catherine Devereux Edmonston, 1860-1866*. Edited by Margaret Mackay Jones. Cloth. (Mebane, N.C.?), no date. $75-$85.

*EDWARD Lear on My Shelves*. Illustrated. Folio, boards, buckram spine, paper label. (Munich), 1933. (By William B. Osgood Field.) Bremer Press. First edition. One of 155. $300-$450. Also, $400 (A, 1972).

EDWARD, David B. *The History of Texas*. Folding map in color. Cloth. Cincinnati, 1836. First edition. $400-$650.

EDWARD VIII. *Farewell Speech of King Edward the Eighth Broadcast from Windsor Castle, December MCMXXXVI*. With 6-page note by William Saroyan. Large, decorated linen, white leather spine. San Francisco, 1938. Grabhorn Press. One of 200. $100-$150. Also, $75 (A, 1972).

EDWARDS, Billy. *Gladiators of the Prize Ring, or Pugilists of America*. Folio, cloth. Chicago, (1895). $100-$200.

*EDWARDS Chicago Directory (The)*. 40 pp., boards. Chicago, 1871. "Fire edition." $75-$150.

EDWARDS, E. I. *Desert Voices: A Descriptive Bibliography*. Illustrated. Tan buckram. Los Angeles, 1958. First edition. One of 500. In dust jacket. $75-$100. Also, $50 (A, 1975).

EDWARDS, E. I. *The Valley Whose Name Is Death*. Map. Cloth. Pasadena, 1940. First edition. $50-$75.

EDWARDS, Frank S. *A Campaign in New Mexico with Col. Doniphan*. Folding map. 184 pp., wrappers (cover date 1848), and cloth. Philadelphia, 1847. First edition. Wrappers: $500-$600. Cloth: $300-$400.

EDWARDS, J. C. *Speech in Relation to the Territory in Dispute Between the State of Missouri and the United States, etc.* 20 pp., sewed. Washington, 1843. $100-$175.

EDWARDS, John N. *Noted Guerrillas*. Frontispiece, 15 plates. Cloth. St. Louis, 1877. First edition. $75-$100.

EDWARDS, John N. *Shelby and His Men, or The War in the West*. Portrait, folding map. Cloth. Cincinnati, 1867. First edition. $75-$100. Also, rebacked and with map torn, $35 (A, 1975).

EDWARDS, John N. *Shelby's Expedition to Mexico*. Cloth. Kansas City, 1872. First edition. $75-$125.

EDWARDS, Jonathan. *Marcus Whitman*. Portraits. 48 pp. Spokane, 1892. First edition. $50-$75.

EDWARDS, Jonathan (1703-58). *Some Thoughts Concerning the Present Revival of Religion in New-England*. Calf. Lexington, Ky., 1803. $75.

EDWARDS, Philip Leget. *California in 1837*. Wrappers. Sacramento, 1890. First edition. $100-$150.

EDWARDS, Philip Leget. *The Diary of Philip Leget Edwards: The Great Cattle Drive from California to Oregon in 1837*. Boards. San Francisco, 1932. Grabhorn Press. One of 500. In dust jacket. $75. (This reprints *California in 1837*.)

EDWARDS, Philip Leget. *Sketch of the Oregon Territory; or, Emigrant's Guide.* 20 pp. Liberty, Mo., 1842. First edition. $5,000 estimated value. (Only one copy known.)

EDWARDS, Samuel E. *The Ohio Hunter.* Portrait. Cloth. Battle Creek, 1866. First edition. $500-$750.

EDWARDS, W. F. (publisher). *W. F. Edwards' Tourists' Guide and Directory of the Truckee Basin.* Illustrated. Cloth. Truckee, Calif., 1883. First edition. $125-$200.

EDWARDS, Weldon. *Memoir of Nathaniel Macon, of North Carolina.* 22 pp., wrappers. Raleigh, 1862. $100-$150.

EFFINGHAM, C. *The Virginia Comedians.* 2 vols., wrappers, or cloth. New York, 1854. (By John Esten Cooke.) First edition, first issue, with "earsed" for "erased" in line 3, page 249, Vol. 2. Wrappers (cover date 1855): $100-$150. Cloth: $50-$75.

EGAN, Pierce. See *Real Life in London.*

EGAN, Pierce. *Sporting Anecdotes.* 16 engraved plates, advertisement leaf at end. Morocco. London, 1804. First edition. $150-$250. London, 1825. Plates, including 3 in color. Morocco. $150-$350. Also, text soiled, binding rubbed, $72 (A, 1975).

EGE, Ralph. *Pioneers of Old Hopewell.* Portrait. Cloth. Hopewell, N.J., 1908. $50-$75.

EGGLESTON, Edward. *Among the Elgin Watch-Makers.* (Cover title.) Illustrated. 8 pp., wrappers. Chicago, (1873?). First edition. $100 or more.

EGGLESTON, Edward. *The Book of Queer Stories, and Stories Told on a Cellar Door.* Cloth. Chicago, 1871. First edition. $125-$150. Also, $80 (A, 1972).

EGGLESTON, Edward. *The Circuit Rider.* Decorated cloth. New York, 1874. First edition, first state, without the word "illustrated" on title page. $30-$45.

EGGLESTON, Edward. *The Hoosier School-Boy.* Illustrated by George D. Bush. Pictorial cloth. New York, 1883. First edition, first issue, with "Cousin Sukey" frontispiece and first chapter ending on page 16. $75-$100.

EGGLESTON, Edward. *The Hoosier Schoolmaster.* Illustrated by Frank Beard. Brown or terra-cotta cloth. New York, (1871). First edition, first state, with line 3 of page 71 reading "was out" (not "is out"). $150-$200. Also, with a piece torn from one end paper, $110 (A, 1974).

EGGLESTON, Edward. *The Manual: A Practical Guide to the Sunday-School Work.* Cloth. Chicago, 1869. First edition, first issue, with A. Zeese imprint. $100-$150. Author's first book.

EGGLESTON, Edward. *Mr. Blake's Walking-Stick.* Frontispiece and one plate. Light-gray wrappers. Chicago, 1870. First edition. $250-$300.

EGGLESTON, George Cary. *How to Educate Yourself: With or Without Masters.* Cloth. New York, 1872. First edition, first issue, with "ready in September" over ads at back. $75. Author's first book.

EGLE, William H. *History of Dauphine and Lebanon Counties (Pennsylvania).* Cloth. Philadelphia, 1883. $75-$100.

EGLE, William H. *An Illustrated History of the Commonwealth of Pennsylvania.* Cloth. Harrisburg, 1876. First edition. $40-$60.

EGLINTON, John. *Irish Literary Portraits.* Boards and cloth. London, 1935. (By William C. Magee). First edition. $40-$50.

EGLINTON, John. *Some Essays and Passages.* Selected by William Butler Yeats. Boards, linen spine. Dundrum, Ireland, 1905. (By William C. Magee.) Dun Emer Press. One of 200. $75-$100.

*EIGHT Harvard Poets.* Boards and cloth. New York, 1917. First edition. In glassine dust jacket. $100-$125. Also, $75 (A, 1973). (Note: Contains poems by E. E. Cummings, John Dos Passos, and others.)

*1862 Trip to the West (An)*. 10 plates. Full limp leather. Pawtucket, R.I., (1926). (By Lyman B. Goff.) First edition. $600-$1,000.

EIGNER, Larry. *Look at the Park*. Mimeographed printed wrappers. No place, no date. First edition $75-$100. Author's first book.

*El Gabilan*. Pictorial cloth. Salinas, Calif., 1919. Salinas High School Year Book, with 3 contributions by John Steinbeck, his first appearance in print. $500 and up. Also, ends of spine frayed, $1,000 (A, 1977).

ELIA; *Essays Which Have Appeared Under That Signature in the London Magazine*. Boards. London, 1823. (By Charles Lamb.) First edition, first issue, without Waterloo Place address in title page imprint. $500 and up. London, 1823. Boards. Second issue. $100-$150.

ELIA . . . *Second Series*. Boards, paper label. Philadelphia, 1828. First edition. (By Charles Lamb.) $100-$150.

ELIOT, George. See Strauss, Dr. David Friedrich.

ELIOT, George. *Adam Bede*. 3 vols., brown or salmon-colored (orange) cloth. Edinburgh, 1859. (By Mary Ann Evans).First edition. $1,500-$2,000.

ELIOT, George. *Daniel Deronda*. 8 parts, wrappers. Edinburgh, 1876. First edition, with erratum slip in Part 3. $200-$400. Book edition: 4 vols., cloth. $200 and up.

ELIOT, George. *Felix Holt, the Radical*. 3 vols., cloth. Edinburgh, 1866. (By Mary Ann Evans.) First edition. $400 and up. Also, $150 (A, 1974); $130 (A, 1973).

ELIOT, George. *Middlemarch: A Study of Provincial Life*. 8 parts, pictorial wrappers. Edinburgh, 1871. (By Mary Ann Evans.) First edition. $1,500 and up. Also, $1,100 (A, 1974). Edinburgh, 1871-72. 4 vols., cloth. First book edition. $400-$600.

ELIOT, George. *The Mill on the Floss*. 3 vols., salmon-colored cloth. Edinburgh, 1860. (By Mary Ann Evans.) First edition. $500-$650. Also, $425 (A, 1974).

ELIOT, George. *Romola*. 3 vols., green cloth. London, 1863. (By Mary Ann Evans.) First edition, first issue, with 2 pages of ads at end of Vol. 2. $500-$650. Also, $450 (A, 1974).

ELIOT, George. *Scenes of Clerical Life*. 2 vols., maroon cloth. Edinburgh, 1858. (By Mary Ann Evans.) First edition. $650-$800. Also, $1,700 (A, 1977)—a "superb" copy. Author's first book.

ELIOT, George. *Silas Marner: The Weaver of Raveloe*. Cloth. Edinburgh, 1861. (By Mary Ann Evans.) First edition. $450-$600. Also, $350 (A, 1974).

ELIOT, T. S. See Ridler, Anne; Perse, St. John; Dryden, John. Also see *Cat Morgan's Apology; The Catholic Anthology; The Criterion; Ezra Pound: His Metric and Poetry; Harvard Class Day 1910*.

ELIOT, T. S. *After Strange Gods: A Primer of Modern Heresy*. Black cloth. London, (1934). First edition. In dust jacket. $75-$85. New York, (1934). Red cloth. First American edition. In dust jacket. $35-$50.

ELIOT, T. S. *Animula*. Illustrated. Yellow wrappers. (London, 1929.) Ariel Poems, No. 23. First edition. $35-$50. London, 1929. Yellow boards. Large paper issue. One of 400 signed. $100-$150.

ELIOT, T. S. *Ara Vus Prec* (with spine reading *Ara Vos Prec*). Black boards and cloth, paper label (London, 1920.) Ovid Press. First edition. One of 30 signed. $1,000-$1,250. Also, $900 (A, 1977). Another issue: One of 220 numbered (but not signed) copies. $400-$600. (Note: There were also 4 presentation copies printed on Japan vellum. The correct title is *Ara Vos Prec*. Gallup has a note on binding variants, but I find it confusing.)

ELIOT, T. S. *Ash-Wednesday*. Blue cloth. New York and London, 1930. Fountain Press. First edition. One of 600 signed (200 for England, 400 for the United States). In cellophane dust jacket. Boxed. $300-$450. Also, $250 (A, 1977); lacking dust jacket, $200 (A, 1976). London, 1930. Brown cloth. First English trade edition. In green dust jacket. $50-$75. New York, 1930. Black cloth. First American trade edition. In glassine dust jacket. $35-$50.

ELIOT, T. S. *Charles Whibley: A Memoir*. Gray wrappers. (London), 1931. English Association Pamphlet No. 80. First edition. $75-$100. (Note: Of the edition of "probably" 4,000, says Donald Gallup in *T. S. Eliot: A Bibliography*, about 2,055 were issued without wrappers by the English Association and were reissued with other pamphlets for members.)

ELIOT, T. S. *The Classics and the Man of Letters*. Blue wrappers. London, 1942. First edition, first state, with "t" of "the" on title page correctly printed. $60-$80.

ELIOT, T.S. *The Cocktail Party*. Green cloth. London, (1950). First edition, with or without misprint "here" for "her" in first line of page 29. (Gallup gives no priority to copies with the misprint.) In dust jacket. $85-$100.

ELIOT, T.S. *Collected Poems, 1909-1935*. Advance proof in printed paper covers. London, (1936). First edition. $250-$400. (Note: Text and typography differ from first published edition.) London, (1936). Blue cloth. First published edition. In dust jacket. $100-$150. New York, (1936). Blue cloth. First American edition. In dust jacket. $75-$100.

ELIOT, T.S. *Dante*. Gray boards. London, (1929). First edition. In dust jacket. $50-$75. Another issue: Blue-green boards. One of 125 signed. $200-$250. Also, spine faded, $125 (A, 1977).

ELIOT, T.S. *The Dry Salvages*. Blue wrappers. London, (1941). First edition. $50-$60.

ELIOT, T.S. *East Coker: A Poem*. 8 pp., wire-stitched, unbound. (London), 1940. Reprint from the Easter number of *The New English Weekly*. 500 copies printed. "Second" edition. $50-$75. London, (1940). Yellow wrappers. First Faber & Faber edition. $40-$60. (Note: The first appearance of this poem was in a 4-page supplement to *The New English Weekly*, Easter, 1940. A copy of this supplement brought $50 at auction in 1969.)

ELIOT, T.S. *El Canto de Amor de J. Alfred Prufrock*. Wrappers (with sheets laid in). Mexico, 1938. One of 50. $100-$150.

ELIOT, T.S. *Elizabethan Essays*. Gray cloth. London, (1934). First edition, first issue, with misprint in series note on half title, "No. 21" (later copies have series note correctly printed "No. 24"). $100-$125.

ELIOT, T.S. *The Family Reunion*. Wrappers. London, (1939). "Proof copy," so imprinted on front cover. Signed on cover by Eliot. In dust jacket. $100 and up. London, (1939). Gray cloth. First edition. In dust jacket. $75-$100. New York, (1939). Black cloth. First American edition. In dust jacket. $30-$40.

ELIOT, T.S. *For Lancelot Andrewes*. Blue cloth, paper label. London, (1928). First edition. In dust jacket. $50-$75. Garden City, 1929. Purple-brown cloth. First American edition. In dust jacket. $30-$40.

ELIOT, T.S. *Four Quartets*. Black cloth. New York, (1943). First edition, first impression, with "First American edition" on copyright page. One of only 788 copies of an original impression of 4,165, 3,377 of which were destroyed because of incorrect margins. In dust jacket. $400-$600. Second impression, without the edition note on copyright page and without code designations in brackets used in subsequent impressions. In dust jacket. $150-$200. London, (1944). Tan cloth. First English edition. $25-$35. London, (1960). Marbled boards and white parchment spine. One of 290 signed. Boxed. $600-$650. Also, $600 (A, 1977).

ELIOT, T.S. *From Poe to Valéry*. Dark-blue boards. New York, (1948). First edition. One of 1,500. In original green paper mailing envelope. $100. Without envelope, $60-$80. Washington, 1949. White wrappers with cover title. One of 1,000. $30-$50.

ELIOT, T.S. *The Frontiers of Criticism*. 20 pp., wrappers. (Minneapolis, 1956.) First edition. $60-$80.

ELIOT, T.S. *Homage to John Dryden*. Stiff off-white wrappers. London, 1924. Hogarth Press. First edition. $100-$125.

ELIOT, T.S. *Journey of the Magi*. Wrappers. New York, 1927. First American edition. One of 27 printed to obtain American copyright. $1,000-$1,250. Also, $1,000 (A, 1977). (Only 12 were released for sale.) London, 1927. Wrappers. First edition. $75-$125.

ELIOT, T.S. *John Dryden: The Poet, the Dramatist, the Critic*. Frontispiece in color. Marbled boards and cloth. New York, 1932. First edition. One of 110 signed. In cellophane dust jacket. $300-$350. Also, $300 (A, 1977). Trade edition: Mulberry boards. In white dust jacket. $50-$75.

ELIOT, T.S. *Marina*. Illustrated. Blue wrappers. (London 1930.) Ariel Poems No. 29. First edition. $35-$50. London, 1930. Blue boards. Large paper issue. One of 400 signed. $125-$150.

ELIOT, T.S. *Notes Towards the Definition of Culture* . Cloth. London, (1948). First edition. In dust jacket. $75-$100. (Note: There were also 18 copies bound with "a" for "the" in the title on the spine, but none was placed on sale, according to Eliot's bibliographer Donald Gallup. A copy was sold at auction in October, 1977, for $425.) New York, (1949). Black cloth. First American edition. In dust jacket. $25-$35.

ELIOT, T.S. *Old Possum's Book of Practical Cats*. Yellow cloth. London, (1939). First edition. In dust jacket. $75-$125. New York, (1939). Gray cloth, First American edition. In dust jacket. $30-$35.

ELIOT, T.S. *Poems*. Decorated wrappers, white paper label. Richmond, England, 1919. Hogarth Press. First edition, first issue, with "capitaux" for "chapitaux" in line 11, page (13). $800-$1,000. Also, $800 (A, 1977). New York, 1920. Tan boards. First American edition (of *Ara Vos Prec*). (Note: this also includes the contents of the 1919 first edition of *Poems*.) In yellow dust jacket. $200-$250. Later: Brown dust jacket. $125 (A, 1977).

ELIOT, T.S. *Poems, 1909-1925*. Blue cloth, white paper spine label. London, 1925. First edition. In cream-colored dust jacket. $100-$150. Another issue: White linen, gilt. One of 85 signed (actually issued in 1926). In glassine dust jacket. $350-$400. Also, $317 (A, 1975). New York, (1932). Blue cloth, gilt. First American edition. In cream-colored dust jacket. $50-$75.

ELIOT, T.S. *A Practical Possum*. Wrappers. Cambridge, Mass., 1947. First edition. One of 80. $500 and up. Also, $500 (A, 1977).

ELIOT, T.S. *Prufrock and Other Observations*. 40 pp., buff printed wrappers. London, 1917. First edition. $1,000-$1,500. Also, a review copy with printed slip and one word in Eliot's hand. $2,500 (A, 1977). Author's first book.

ELIOT, T.S. *Religious Drama: Medieval and Modern*. Red cloth. New York, 1954. First edition. One of 300 signed. In glassine dust jacket. $150-$200. Also, $90 (A, 1975). (Note: There were also 26 lettered copies issued for presentation.)

ELIOT, T.S. *The Rock*. Heavy gray wrappers. London, (1934). First edition. (The paperbound issue was sold at the theatre in advance of the book's hardbound publication.) $75-$100.

ELIOT, T.S. *The Sacred Wood*. Blue cloth. London, (1920). First edition, first issue, with publisher's name at foot of spine measuring 3 mm. and without ads. In first issue dust jacket, without the sub-title on front. $150-$250. Also, $100. (A, 1977).

ELIOT, T.S. *Selected Essays, 1917-1932*. Blue vellum. London, (1932). First edition (English issue). One of 115 signed. In cellophane dust jacket. $350-$450. Also, $400 (A, 1977). First trade edition: Red cloth. In dust jacket. $50. New York, (1932). First trade edition (American issue). In dust jacket. $50.

ELIOT, T.S. *Shakespeare and the Stoicism of Seneca*. (Cover title.) Gray wrappers. London, 1927. First edition. $100-$135.

ELIOT, T.S. *A Song for Simeon*. Illustrated. White boards, gilt. London, 1928. Large paper signed edition. One of 500 signed. $100-$150. Also, $100 (A, 1971).

ELIOT, T.S. *Sweeney Agonistes*. Blue boards. London, (1932). First edition. In dust jacket. $75-$100.

ELIOT, T.S. *Thoughts After Lambeth*. Brown wrappers. London, (1931). First edition. $100-$125. Another (simultaneous) issue: Gray cloth. In glassine dust jacket. (300 published.) $150-$250.

ELIOT, T.S. *T.S. Eliot: The Complete Poems and Plays*. Blue-green cloth. New York, (1952). First edition. In dust jacket. $50-$60.

ELIOT, T.S. *Triumphal March*. Illustrated by E. McKnight Kauffer. Boards. London, 1931. First edition. One of 300 signed. $100-$150.

ELIOT, T.S. *Two Poems*. Wrappers, paper label. (Cambridge), 1935. First edition. One of 22 copies. $87.50 (A, 1972)—for a "proof copy." Another issue: One of 5 on vellum, signed. $600-$800. Also, $413 (A, 1975).

ELIOT, T.S. *The Undergraduate Poems of T.S. Eliot*. Printed gray wrappers. Cambridge, Mass., (1949). First edition. One of about 1,000. $100-$125. Also, $60 (A, 1972).

ELIOT, T.S. *The Use of Poetry and the Use of Criticism*. Red cloth. London, (1933). First edition. In dust jacket. $50-$75.

ELIOT, T.S. *The Waste Land*. Flexible black cloth, gilt. New York, 1922. First edition, first issue, with the flexible binding, the word "mountain" correctly spelled in line 339 of page 41, and the limitation numbers stamped in type 5 mm. high. One of 1,000 (of which about 500 were issued thus, according to Donald Gallup, Eliot's bibliographer). In salmon-colored dust jacket. $1,000-$1,250. Second state, flexible black cloth, with dropped "a" in "mountain." (The remaining copies of the first impression—about 500 being in this state.) In dust jacket. $500-$750. New York, (1923?). Black cloth. Second edition (so identified in colophon, but actually a second impression from the first edition type). In dust jacket. $200-$300. Richmond, 1923. Hogarth Press. Blue marbled boards, paper label. First English edition, first issue, with border of asterisks on the label. $400-$600. Also, $350 (A, 1977). Later, no asterisks, $200-$250. London, (1962). Marbled boards, white parchment spine. One of 300 signed. Boxed. $500-$550. Also, $500 (A, 1977).

ELIOT, T. S. *What Is a Classic?* Green wrappers. London, (1945). First edition. One of 500. $150-$175. First trade edition: Blue cloth. In dust jacket. $20-$30.

ELIOT, T.S. *Words for Music*. 4 pp., wrappers. (Bryn Mawr), 1934 (actually 1935). First edition. One of 20 (so stated, but actually more, according to Donald Gallup). $300 and up.

ELIZABETH *Bennet; or, Pride and Prejudice: A Novel*. 2 vols., boards and linen, paper label. Philadelphia, 1832. (By Jane Austen.) First American edition of *Pride and Prejudice*. $400-$500. Also, loose in binding, $130 (A, 1975).

ELKUS, Richard J. *Alamos*. Foreword by Barnaby Conrad. Half suede and cloth. San Francisco, 1965. Grabhorn Press. One of 487. $100-$150.

ELLICOTT, Andrew. *The Journal of Andrew Ellicott*. 14 maps and plates. Calf. Philadelphia, 1803. First edition, with errata leaf. $750-$1,000. Also, two different defective copies, $400 (A, 1975); $400 (1972). Philadelphia, 1814. Half leather. Second edition. $300-$400.

ELLIN, Stanley. *Mystery Stories*. Cloth. New York, 1956. First edition. In dust jacket. $50.

ELLIOT, D.G. *A Monograph of the Tetraoninae, or Family of the Grouse*. 27 color plates. 5 parts in 4, boards. New York, (1864)-65. First edition. $5,000-$6,000. Also, $3,750 (A, 1977). Also, in a folio half morocco binding. $3,750 (A, 1977); $6,536 (A, 1976). (Note: See the British and American auction records for several other Elliot monographs on birds, all of which are extremely valuable for their color plates.)

ELLIOT, D.G. *The New and Heretofore Unfigured Species of the Birds of North America*. 72 hand-colored plates. 2 vols., half morocco. New York, (1866-69). First edition. $7,000-$10,000. Also, stained, $5,504 (A, 1976); $6,500 (A, 1972).

ELLIOT, W.J. *The Spurs*. Plates and map. Cloth. (Spur, Tex., 1939.) First edition. $75-$100.

ELLIOTT, The Rev. Charles. *Indian Missionary Reminiscences*. Boards. New York, 1835. First edition. $75.

ELLIOTT, David Stewart. *Last Raid of the Daltons*. Illustrated. 72 pp., wrappers. Coffeyville, Kan., 1892. First edition. $350-$500. Coffeyville, 1892 (actually 1954). 60 pp. Second edition. (Fascimile, abridged.) $25-$50.

ELLIOTT, John, and Johnson, Samuel, Jr. *A Selected Pronouncing and Accented Dictionary*. Oblong, boards. Hartford, 1800. $75-$100.

ELLIOTT, W.W. *History of Arizona Territory*. Map and plates. Half cloth. San Francisco, 1884. First edition. $750-$1,000.

ELLIS, Edward S. See *On the Plains*.

ELLIS, Edward S. *The Life and Adventures of Col. David Crockett*. Half leather. New York, 1861. First edition. $60-$75.

ELLIS, Edward S. *The Life and Times of Christopher Carson*. Wrappers. New York, (1861). First edition. $80-$125.

ELLIS, Frederick S. *A Lexical Concordance to the Poetical Works of Percy Bysshe Shelley*. Half morocco. London, 1892. First edition. $125-$150.

ELLIS, Frederick S. (editor). *Psalmi Penitentiales*. Woodcut designs and initials. Boards and linen. London. 1894. Kelmscott Press. One of 300. $150-$300. Another issue: One of 12 on vellum. $1,000-$1,200.

ELLIS, Frederick S. (editor). *The Romance of Syr Ysambrace*. Printed in black and red. Woodcut borders and designs by E. Burne-Jones. Boards and linen. London, 1897. Kelmscott Press. One of 350. $250-$350.

ELLIS, Frederick S. (editor), and Caxton, William, and Morris, William (translators). *The Book of the Order of Chivalry (L'Ordre de Chevalerie)*. Printed in black and red. Woodcut by E. Burne-Jones. Vellum with ties. London, 1893. Kelmscott Press. One of 225. $400-$600. Also, $380 (A, 1976).

ELLIS, George F. *Bell Ranch As I Knew It*. Illustrated. Half cloth and fabrikoid. Kansas City, (1973). First edition. One of 250 with a signed print. Boxed. $75. Trade edition: In dust jacket. $15.

ELLIS, Havelock. *Kanga Creek: An Australian Idyll*. Waltham Saint Lawrence, 1922. Golden Cockerel Press. One of 29 on handmade paper. $200-$250.

ELLIS, Havelock. *Marriage Today and To-Morrow*. San Francisco, 1929. Grabhorn printing. One of 500 signed. $75.

ELLIS, William. *The American Mission in the Sandwich Islands*. Boards. Honolulu, 1866. First edition. $200-$250.

ELLIS, William. *Polynesian Researches, During a Residence of Nearly Six Years in the South Sea Islands*. 10 plates and maps, 16 woodcuts. 2 vols., half calf and marbled boards. London, 1829. First edition. $300-$400. Also, rebound in 4 vols., modern cloth, some dampstaining, $77 (A, 1975).

ELLIS, William Turner. *Memories: My 72 Years in the Romantic County of Yuba, California*. Boards and cloth. Eugene, Ore., 1939. John Henry Nash printing. In dust jacket. $50-$75.

ELLISON, Harlan (editor). *Dangerous Visions*. Garden City, 1967. First edition. In dust jacket. $75-$100.

ELLISON, Ralph. *Invisible Man*. Cloth. New York, (1952). First edition. In dust jacket. $85-$100. Author's first book.

ELLSWORTH, Henry W. *Valley of the Upper Wabash, Indiana.* Folding map, 3 folding lithographs. Stiff wrappers. New York, 1838. First edition. $150-$200.

ELLSWORTH, Lincoln. *The Last Wild Buffalo Hunt.* 32 pp., cloth. New York, 1916. First edition. $50-$75.

ELMER, Jonathan. *An Eulogium on the Character of Gen. George Washington.* 25 pp., half leather. Trenton, N.J., 1800. $400-$600.

ELMORE, James B. *Love Among the Mistletoe, and Poems.* Cloth. Alamo, Ind., 1899. First edition. $35-$50.

ELMSLIE, Kenward. *Pavilions.* Wrappers. New York, 1961. First edition. One of 300. $40-$60.

ELTON, R.H. *Jackson Almanac, 1836.* 36 pp., wrappers. (New York, 1835.) $50-$75.

ELWOOD, Louie B. *Queen Califia's Land.* San Francisco, 1940. Grabhorn Press. One of 325. $50-$60.

ÉLUARD, Paul. *Le Dur Désir de Dürer.* Frontispiece in color and 25 designs by Marc Chagall. Text in French. Folio, sheets in printed wrappers and board slipcase. Paris, (1946). Trianon Press. One of 330 on Rives paper, signed by author and artist. $450-$600. Philadelphia and London, (1950). Trianon Press. Translated by Stephen Spender and Frances Cornford. Colored frontispiece and black and white illustrations. Printed wrappers. First edition of the English translation. One of 1,500. $75-$125.

ELZAS, Barnett A. *The Jews of South Carolina from the Earliest Period to the Present Day.* 11 plates. Cloth. Philadelphia, 1905. $100-$125.

*EMBARGO (The), or Sketches of the Times; A Satire. By a Youth of Thirteen.* (Cover title.) 12 pp., self-wrappers (stitched). Boston, 1808. (By William Cullen Bryant.) First edition. $1,000 and up. (For second edition, see author and title.)

EMERSON, Charles L. *Rise and Progress of Minnesota Territory.* 64 pp., pictorial printed wrappers. St. Paul, 1855. First edition. $600-$800, possibly more.

EMERSON, Joseph. *Female Education.* 40 pp., plain wrappers. Boston, 1822. First edition. $75-$100.

EMERSON, Lucy. *The New-England Cookery.* Boards. Montpelier, Vt., 1808. First edition. $250-$300. Also, $117.60 (A, 1965).

EMERSON, Ralph Waldo. See *Nature.*

EMERSON, Ralph Waldo. *An Address Delivered Before the Senior Class in Divinity College, Cambridge . . . 15 July, 1838.* 31 pp., blue wrappers. Boston, 1838. First edition. $150-$200. Also, foxed, $80 (A, 1974).

EMERSON, Ralph Waldo. *An Address Delivered in the Court-House in Concord, Massachusetts, on 1st August, 1844, on the Anniversary of the Emancipation of the Negroes in the British West Indies.* 34 pp., tan wrappers. Boston, 1844. First edition. $150. (Also issued stitched, without wrappers.)

EMERSON, Ralph Waldo. *The American Scholar.* ("An Oration Delivered Before the Phi Beta Kappa Society.") 26 pp., wrappers or unlettered cloth. Boston, 1837. First edition. Wrappers: $500-$750. (Very rare.) Cloth: $250-$350.

EMERSON, Ralph Waldo. *The Conduct of Life.* Cloth. Boston, 1860. First edition, first issue, without signature mark "1" and with ads dated December, 1860. $75-$100.

EMERSON, Ralph Waldo. *English Traits.* Cloth. Boston, 1856. First edition. $75-$100.

EMERSON, Ralph Waldo. *Essays.* Cloth. Boston, 1841. First edition, first binding, without "First Series" on spine. $300-$400. London, 1906. Vellum. Doves Press. One of 300. $400-$500. Another issue: One of 25 printed on vellum. $3,500-$4,000. Also, $2,600 (A, 1974). New York, 1934. Limited Editions Club. Boards. Boxed. $50-$60.

EMERSON, Ralph Waldo. *Essays: Second Series*. Cloth. Boston, 1844. First edition, probable first binding, with "2D Series" on spine. $150-$200.

EMERSON, Ralph Waldo. *A Historical Discourse, Delivered Before the Citizens of Concord, 12th September, 1835*. 52 pp., blue wrappers. Concord, 1835. First edition. $150-$250.

EMERSON, Ralph Waldo. *The Journals of Ralph Waldo Emerson*. 10 vols., green cloth. Boston, 1909-14. First edition. $100. Another issue: Tan linen. One of 600 on large paper. $300-$400.

EMERSON, Ralph Waldo. *Lectures and Biographical Sketches*. Cloth. Boston, 1884. First edition. $35-$50.

EMERSON, Ralph Waldo. *Letters and Social Aims*. Cloth. Boston, 1876. First edition. $75-$100. Also, inscribed copies, $350 and $175 (A, 1975).

EMERSON, Ralph Waldo. *May-Day and Other Pieces*. White cloth. Boston, 1867. First edition, first issue, with "flowers" for "hours" on page 184. $50-$75. (Also issued in other colors of cloth.) London, 1867. Cloth. First English edition. $50-$75.

EMERSON, Ralph Waldo. *The Method of Nature*. 30 pp., printed tan wrappers. Boston, 1841. First edition. $100-$150. Also, $90 (A, 1974).

EMERSON, Ralph Waldo. *An Oration Delivered Before the Literary Societies of Dartmouth College, July 24, 1838*. Wrappers. Boston, 1838. First edition. $75-$100.

EMERSON, Ralph Waldo. *Poems*. Green cloth. London, 1847. First edition, first issue, with "Chapman Brothers" on foot of spine and ads dated Nov. 16, 1846. $150-$200. Also, worn, $120 (A, 1974). Boston, 1847. Yellow boards, paper label. First American edition, first issue, with 4 pages of ads dated Jan. 1, 1847. $500-$600. Also, $425 (A, 1968). Another (later?) copy, without the ads, $200 (A, 1974). New York, 1945. Limited Editions Club. Full leather. Boxed. $35-$50.

EMERSON, Ralph Waldo. *Representative Men*. Black or brown cloth. Boston, 1850. First edition, first issue, with hourglass design on front and back covers. $75-$100. London, 1850. Dark-brown cloth. First English edition (possibly issued simultaneously with the American edition, according to Blanck). $50-$75.

EMERSON, Ralph Waldo. *Society and Solitude*. Green cloth. Boston, 1870. First edition. $75-$100.

*EMILY Parker, or Impulse, Not Principle*. Frontispiece. Buff boards. Boston, 1827. (By Lydia Maria Child.) First edition. $150-$175.

*EMMA*. By the Author of "Pride and Prejudice," etc. 3 vols., blue or brown paper boards, drab paper spine, paper labels. London, 1816. (By Jane Austen.) First edition. $4,000 and up. Also, rubbed, hinge of Vol. II cracked, $2,750 (A, 1974). Rebound copies, $1,000 and up at retail. New York, 1964. Limited Editions Club. Illustrated in color by Fritz Kredel. Buckram. Boxed. $75-$85.

EMMART, Emily Walcott (translator). *The Badianus Manuscript*. By Martinus de la Cruz. 118 colored plates. Cloth. Baltimore, 1940. $100-$150.

EMMONS, George T. *The Emmons Journal*. 11 pp., wrappers. Eugene, Ore., (1925). $75-$100.

EMMONS, Dr. (Richard). *Tecumseh: Or, The Battle of the Thames*. 36 pp., wrappers. New York, 1836. $60-$80.

EMMONS, Samuel Franklin. *Atlas to Accompany a Monograph on the Geology and Mining Industry of Leadville, Colorado*. 35 single and double leaves, charts, etc., some in color. Large atlas, paper covers, unbound. Washington, 1883. $150-$200.

EMORY, William H. *Notes of a Military Reconnaissance*. 68 plates, 6 maps and plans. Cloth. Washington, 1848. House version. First edition. $150-$250. Another issue: Same place and date, Senate version. $150-$250.

ENGELS, Frederick. *Socialism, Utopian, and Scientific*. Red cloth. London, 1892. First edition in English. $150-$200.

ENGLE, Paul. *Worn Earth*. Boards. New Haven, 1932. First edition. In dust jacket. $40-$60. Author's first book.

ENGLEHARDT, Zephyrin. *The Franciscans in Arizona*. Map, plates. 236 pp., wrappers. Harbor Springs, Mich., 1899. First edition. $50-$75.

ENGELHARDT, Zephyrin. *The Franciscans in California*. Illustrated. Wrappers. Harbor Springs, 1897. First edition. $50-$75.

*ENGLISH Bards and Scotch Reviewers*. 54 pp., drab printed boards. London, (1809). (By George Gordon Noel, Lord Byron.) First edition, first issue, without preface. $800 and up. Also, $350 (A, 1972). Later issue, with preface: $200-$300.

*ENGLISH Bible (The)*. 5 vols., folio, vellum. London, 1903-05. Doves Press. One of 500. $2,000-$3,000. (Auction prices for fine copies have been averaging above $1,250 for several years as of spring, 1978.) In special bindings by the Doves Bindery, $5,000 and up. Auction example: $6,200 (1975).

*ENGLISH Dance of Death (The)*. Frontispiece, engraved title and 74 color plates by Thomas Rowlandson. 24 parts, wrappers. London, 1814-16. (By William Combe.) First edition. $1,000 and up. London, 1814 (or 1815)-16. 2 vols., cloth. First book edition. $750 and up. Also, rebound in morocco, $500 (A, 1975).

ENGLISH, William B. *Rosina Meadows, the Village Maid*. Wrappers. Boston, 1863. First edition. $100-$125.

*ENSIGN and Thayer's Traveller's Guide Through the States of Ohio, Michigan, Indiana, Illinois, Missouri, Iowa and Wisconsin*. (Variant titles.) Folding colored map. Leather. New York, 1850. $100-$150. Buffalo, 1853. $50-$75. New York, 1853. $50-$75. New York, 1854. $50-$75.

*EPILOGOS*. (Cover title.) Printed red wrappers. (Los Angeles, 1967.) (By Robert Duncan.) First edition. One of 100 signed, and with an original Duncan drawing (from an edition of 115). $175 (A, 1977).

*EPIPSYCHIDION: Verses, etc*. Drab wrappers. London, 1821. (By Percy Bysshe Shelley.) First edition. $2,000 and up. Auction record: spine missing, "only known copy in wrappers," $1,400 (1945). Rebound in morocco, $950 (A, 1962). Montagnola, Italy, 1923. Vellum. One of 222. $300-$400. Also, $275 (A, 1976).

*EPITOME of Electricity and Galvanism (An)*. By Two Gentlemen of Philadelphia. Boards. Philadelphia, 1809. (By Jacob Green and Ebenezer Hazard.) First edition. $150-$200.

EPPES, Susan Bradford. *Through Some Eventful Years*. Cloth. Macon, Ga., 1926. $50-$60.

EPSTEIN, Jacob. *Epstein: An Autobiography*. Illustrated. Leatherette. London, 1955. One of 195 signed. In dust jacket. $100-$150.

EPSTEIN, Jacob. *Let There Be Sculpture*. Frontispiece, 47 illustrations. Vellum. (London, 1940.) One of 100 signed. Boxed. $150-$175.

EPSTEIN, Jacob. *Seventy-Five Drawings*. Oblong, vellum. London, 1929. One of 220 signed. $150-$250.

*EREWHON, or Over the Range*. Brown cloth. London, 1872. First edition. (By Samuel Butler.) $150-$300. Newtown, Wales, 1932. Gregynog Press. Illustrated. Sheep. One of 275 on Japan vellum. $100-$150. Another issue: One of 25 specially bound in morocco by George Fisher. $600-$850. New York, 1934. Limited Editions Club. Introduction by Aldous Huxley, Illustrated by Rockwell Kent. Cloth. Boxed. $25-$50.

ERWIN, Milo. *The History of Williamson County, Illinois*. Cloth. Marion, Ill., 1876. First edition. $100-$150.

ESCANDON, Manuel, and Rascon, José. *Observaciónes que los Actuales Terceros Pos-*

*sedores de los Bienes que Pertenecieron al Fondo Piadoso de Californias, etc.* 12 pp., wrappers. Mexico, 1845. $150-$250.

ESHLEMAN, Clayton. *Mexico & North.* Wrappers. (Tokyo, 1961.) First edition. Signed by the author. $35. Author's first book.

ESPEJO, Antonio de. *New Mexico: Otherwise the Voiage of Anthony Espeio, Who in the Yeare 1583, With His Company, Discovered a Lande of 15 Provinces, etc.* Boards. (Lancaster. 1928.) First edition. One of 200. $150-$200.

*ESSAY on Mind (An), with Other Poems.* Blue-gray boards, white label on spine. London, 1826. (By Elizabeth Barrett Browning.) First edition, first issue, with the reading "found" in line 15, page 75. $825-$1,000. Also, rebacked, $325 (A, 1974).

*ESSAYS from Poor Robert the Scribe.* Boards, leather spine. Doylestown, Pa., 1815. (By Charles Miner.) First edition. $150-$200.

*ESSAYS of Howard on Domestic Economy.* Contemporary calf. New York, 1820. (By Mordecai Manuel Noah.) First edition. $80-$125.

ESSE, James. *Hunger: A Dublin Story.* Printed wrappers. Dublin, 1918. (By James Stephens.) First edition. $30-$40.

ESSHOM, Frank. *Pioneers and Prominent Men of Utah.* Cloth. Salt Lake City, 1913. $40-$65.

ESTAVA, José María. *La Campaña de la Mision.* Boards and cloth. Xalapa-Enriquez, Mexico, 1894. First edition. $150-$200.

ESTIENNE, Henri. *The Frankfort Book Fair.* Chicago, 1911. Caxton Club. One of 300. $100-$150

ETHELL, Henry C. *The Rise and Progress of Civilization in the Hairy Nation and the History of Davis County.* Cloth. Bloomfield, Iowa, 1883. First edition. $150.

*ETHNOLOGIC Dictionary of the Navajo Language (An).* By the Franciscan Fathers. 536 pp., wrappers. St. Michaels, Ariz., 1910. One of 200 on Japan vellum. $350-$500.

ETZENHOUSER, R. *From Palmyra, New York, 1830, to Independence, Missouri, 1894.* 444 pp., wrappers. Independence, 1894. First edition. $75-$100.

*EUGENE Aram: A Tale.* 3 vols., boards, paper labels. London, 1832. (By Edward Bulwer-Lytton.) First edition. $75-$125.

*EULOGY on the Life of Gen. George Washington (An).* Wrappers. Newburyport, Mass., 1800. (By Robert Treat Paine, Jr.) First edition. $100-$125.

*EUPHRANOR: A Dialogue on Youth.* Green cloth. London, 1851. (By Edward FitzGerald.) $150-$200. London, 1885. Green cloth, or stitched, without ads at end. Second edition. $75-$100. (Note: A few copies were bound for presentation, appendix canceled, corrections made in FitzGerald's hand.) Another edition: (Guildford, 1882.) (With subtitle *A May-Day Conversation at Cambridge* instead of *A Dialogue on Youth.*) Half leather and green boards. Third edition. One of 50 (not so stated). $50-$75.

EURIPIDES. *The Plays of Euripides.* Translated by Gilbert Murray. Illustrated. 2 vols., folio, red buckram. Newtown, Wales, 1931. Gregynog Press. One of 500. $350-$450. Another issue: Folio, 2 vols. in one, morocco. One of 25 specially bound by George Fisher. $2,000-$2,250.

*EVANGELICAL Hymns.* 24 pp., stitched. Greenwich, Mass., 1807. First edition. $75-$100.

EVANS, Augusta Jane. *St. Elmo.* Cloth. New York, 1867. (By Augusta Jane Evans Wilson.) First edition. $100-$200.

EVANS, Elwood. *Puget Sound: Its Past, Present and Future.* 16 pp., wrappers. Olympia, Wash., 1869. First edition. $200-$300.

EVANS, Elwood. *Washington Territory.* 51 pp., wrappers. Olympia, 1877. First edition. $175-$300.

EVANS, Estwick. *A Pedestrious Tour, of 4,000 Miles, Through the Western States and Territories.* Portrait. Boards. Concord, N.H., 1819. First edition. $600-$750.

EVELYN, John. *Memoirs, Illustrative of the Life and Writings of John Evelyn, Esq., F.R.S.* Edited by William Bray. Folding pedigree, 8 plates. 2 vols., calf. London (Bath), 1818. First edition. $400-$500. Also, rebacked, $240 (A, 1976).

*EVENINGS in New England.* By an American Lady. Brown boards. Boston, 1824. (By Lydia Maria Child.) First edition. $75-$125.

*EVENTFUL Lives of Helen and Charlotte Lenoxa (The), the Twin Sisters of Philadelphia.* Wrappers. Memphis, 1853. First edition, first issue, with date 1852 on cover. $100.

*EVENTS in Indian History, Beginning with an Account of the Origin of the American Indians, etc.* 8 plates. Sheepskin. Lancaster, Pa., 1841. (By James Wimer). First edition. $150-$200. Also, binding broken, $45 (A, 1976). Lancaster, 1843. Second edition. $100-$125.

EVERETT, Edward, *A Defence of Christianity.* Boards, paper label. Boston, 1814. First edition. $75-$100. Author's first book.

EVERETT, Edward. *An Oration Delivered on the Battlefield of Gettysburg, etc.* 48 pp., cloth wrappers. New York, 1863. $1,000-$1,250. Includes one of the early book appearances of Abraham Lincoln's Gettysburg Address. See: Lincoln, Abraham.

EVERETT, Horace. *Regulating the Indian Department.* Folding map. 133 pp., sewed. (Washington, 1934.) $50-$75.

EVERSON, William. See Antonius, Brother.

EVERSON, Bill (William). *These Are the Ravens.* (Cover title.) 11 pp., stapled self-wrappers. San Leandro, Calif., 1935. First edition. $150-$200. Author's first book.

EVERSON, William. *The Blowing of the Seed.* Green or brown flowered boards, leather spine. New Haven, 1966. First edition. One of 218 signed. $75-$125.

EVERSON, William. *In the Fictive Wish.* Cloth. (Berkeley, 1967.) Oyez Press. One of 220 signed. In plain dust jacket. $75-$125.

EVERSON, William. *Poems: MCMXLII.* Self-wrappers. (Waldport, Ore., 1945.) One of 500. $50-$75.

EVERSON, William. *The Residual Years.* Illustrated by the author. Wrappers. (Waldport, 1944.) First edition. One of 330 signed. $100. (New York, 1948.) Boards. One of 1,000. In dust jacket. $35-$50. (This edition, published by New Directions, is a collection of four prior works. It was reissued in hardback and in wrappers in 1968.)

EVERSON, William. *Single Source: The Early Poems of William Everson.* Introduction by Robert Duncan. Boards. Berkeley, (1966). First edition, first state, with misspelling "language." One of 25 signed. $100-$125. Trade issue (1,000 copies), first state. In dust jacket. $25-$35.

EVERSON, William. *The Springing of the Blade.* Decorated cloth. (Reno, 1968.) First edition. One of 180 signed. (Issued without dust jacket.) $75-$100.

EVERSON, William. *There Will be a Harvest.* Woodcut on title page. 4 pp., on 8 pp., French-fold. (Berkeley, 1960.) First edition. One of 200. $50-$75.

EVERSON, William. *Triptych for the Living.* Wrappers. (Oakland), 1951. First edition. One of 200 (actually fewer than 100). $250-$300. Also, $140 (A, 1973).

EVERSON, William. *X War Elegies.* Illustrated. Wrappers. Waldport, 1943. First edition, first state, wrappers lettered in black and yellow. $100-$135. Waldport, 1944. Expanded edition (retitled *War Elegies*). One of 975. $85. Signed copy, $100.

EVERSON, William. *The Year's Declension.* Boards. Berkeley, 1961. First edition. One of 100 signed. $100-$125.

EVERTS, Truman C. *Thirty-Seven Days of Peril.* San Francisco, 1923. Grabhorn printing. One of 375. $50.

EVERTS and Kirk. *The Official State Atlas of Nebraska.* Plates, 207 colored maps. Half calf. Philadelphia, 1885. $300-$600.

*EVIDENCE Concerning Projected Railways Across the Sierra Nevada Mountains.* Calf. Carson City, Nev., 1865. $750-$1,000, possibly more.

*EVIL of Intoxicating Liquor (The), and the Remedy.* 24 pp., sewed. Park Hill, Okla., 1844. $75-$100.

EVJEN, John O. *Scandinavian Immigrants in New York, 1630-1674.* Illustrated. Cloth. Minneapolis, 1916. First edition. $75-$125.

EWALD, Johannes. *The Death of Balder.* Translated by George Borrow. Cloth, paper label. London, 1899 (actually 1892). One of 250. $100-$150.

EWELL, Thomas T. *A History of Hood County, Texas.* Cloth. Granbury, Tex., 1895. First edition. $500-$800.

*EXAMINATION and Review of a Pamphlet, etc.* Stitched. Washington, 1837. $200.

*EXAMINATION of the President's Reply to the New Haven Remonstrance (An).* 69 pp., wrappers. New York, 1801. (By William Coleman.) First edition. $75-$100.

*EXETER Book of Old English Poetry (The).* Folio, buckram. London. 1933. $75-$80.

*EXPOSICIÓN del Ministro de Hacienda.* (Cover title.) 11 pp., wrappers. Mexico, 1836. $200-$300.

*EXTRACTS from the Autobiography of Calvin Coolidge.* Miniature book. Blue calf. Kingsport, Tenn., 1930. $35-$50.

EYE WITNESS (An). *Satan in Search of a Wife.* 4 full-page woodcuts and 2 vignettes by George Cruikshank. Pink wrappers. London, 1831. (By Charles Lamb.) First edition. $300-$500.

*EZRA Pound: His Metric and Poetry.* Portrait frontispiece by Gaudier-Brzeska. Rose paper boards, lettered in gold on front cover. New York, 1917 (actually 1918). (By T.S. Eliot.) First edition. In plain buff dust jacket. $300-$400. Also, $170 (A, 1973). Lacking jacket, $200-$250.

# F

F., M. T. *My Chinese Marriage.* By M.T.F. Green boards and cloth. New York, 1921. (By Mai Taim Fran king, although long attributed to Katherine Anne Porter as ghost-writer.) First edition. $100-$125. (Note: The late John S. Van E. Kohn, New York bookseller, once told me he had seen a letter in which Miss Porter denied authorship of the book and said that she only typed it.)

*FABLE for Critics (A).* Cloth, or boards. New York, (18)48. (By James Russell Lowell.) First edition, first state, without "A Vocal and Musical Medley" on title page and with pages 63 and 64 misnumbered. $100-$150. Also, "spotted," $75 (A, 1975).

*FABLES of Esope (The).* Translated out of the Frensshe into Englysshe by William Caxton. 37 engravings on wood by Agnes Miller Parker. Sheepskin. Newtown, Wales, 1931. Gregynog Press. One of 250. $250-$350.

*FACSIMILES of Royal, Historical, Literary, and Other Autographs in the Department of MSS., British Museum.* Edited by George F. Warner. 150 plates. 5 parts, folio, sewed. London, 1899. $100.

*FACTS Concerning the City of San Diego, the Great Southwestern Sea-port of the United States, with a Map Showing the City and Its Surroundings.* 14 pp., wrappers. San Diego, (1888). $200-$300.

*FACTS Respecting Indian Administration in the Northwest (The).* 74 pp., wrappers. (Victoria?, 1886.) $75-$100.

FAHEY, Herbert. *Early Printing in California.* Illustrated. Cloth. San Francisco, 1956. Grabhorn Press. One of 400. $200-$250.

FAIRBANKS, George R. *Early History of Florida.* 82 pp., sewed. St. Augustine, 1857. First edition. $200-$350.

FAIRBANKS, George R. *The Spaniards in Florida.* 120 pp., wrappers. Jacksonville, 1868. First edition. $150-$300.

FAIRCHILD, T.B. *A History of the Town of Cuyahoga Falls, Summit County.* 39 pp., cloth. Cleveland, 1876. $100-$200.

FAIRFIELD, Asa Merrill. *Fairfield's Pioneer History of Lassen County, California.* 4 plates, folding map. Pictorial cloth. San Francisco, (1916). First edition. $100-$150.

*FAIRY Book (The).* Frontispiece and 81 woodcuts by Joseph A. Adams. Brown cloth. New York, 1837. First edition. $35-$50.

*FAIRY Garland (A).* 12 colored illustrations by Edmund Dulac. Half vellum. London, (1928). First edition. One of 1,000 signed by the artist. $150-$300.

*FAITH Gartney's Girlhood.* Cloth. Boston, 1863. (By Mrs. A.D.T. Whitney.) First edition. $50-$75.

*FAITHFUL Picture (A), of the Political Situation in New Orleans.* 38 pp. (New Orleans) 1807. (By Edward James Workman.) (Also attributed to Edward Livingston.) $400-$500. Boston, 1808. 48 pp. $300.

FALCONER, Thomas. *Letters and Notes on the Texan Santa Fe Expedition, 1841-42.* Edited by F.W. Hodge. Portrait. Half cloth. New York, 1930. $100-$150.

FALCONER, Thomas. *On the Discovery of the Mississippi, and On the South-Western, Oregon, and North-Western Boundary of the United States.* Folding map, errata leaf. Cloth. London, 1844. First edition, first issue, with the map (later absent). $500-$750. Rebound in leather, $250-$500.

FALCONER, William. *A New Universal Dictionary of the Marine.* 35 full-page and folding plates. Half calf, leather label. London, 1815. $300-$400.

*FALKLAND.* Boards. London, 1827. (By Edward Bulwer-Lytton.) First edition. $150-$200. Author's first novel.

*FALKNER: A Novel.* 3 vols., cloth, paper labels. London, 1837. (By Mary Wollstonecraft Shelley.) First edition. $200-$300.

FALKNER, J. Meade. *The Lost Stradivarius.* Cloth. London, 1895. First edition. $60-$80.

FANNIE, Cousin (translator). *Red Beard's Stories for Children.* Silhouette illustrations. Boards, yellow label. Boston, 1856. $30-$40.

*FANNY.* 49 pp., printed gray wrappers. New York, 1819. (By Fitz-Greene Halleck.) First edition. $150-$200. Author's first separate book. (Note: There also exists a pirated 1819 edition, 67 pp.)

*FANSHAWE; A Tale.* Brown or buff boards, purple cloth spine, paper labels. Boston, 1828. (By Nathaniel Hawthorne.) First edition. $4,000-$5,000, possibly more. Also, $4,000 (A, 1975).

*FARM Yard Story.* 12 pp. with pull-out color illustrations. Glazed printed green boards. Boston, 1865. L. Prang & Co. $50-$60.

FARNHAM, S.B. *The New York and Idaho Gold Mining Co.* Folding map. 23 pp., wrappers. New York, 1864. $175-$300.

FARNHAM, Thomas J. *History of Oregon Territory.* Frontispiece map. Cloth. New York, 1844. First edition. $300-$400.

FARNHAM, Thomas J. *Travels in the Californias.* Map and plates. Cloth. New York, 1844. First edition, second (or clothbound) issue. $750-$850. Also, $300 (A, 1968). (Note: The first edition was issued first in 4 paperbound parts, which are rare in fine condition.)

FARNHAM, Thomas J. *Travels in the Great Western Prairies.* Cloth, leather label. Poughkeepsie, 1841. First edition. $750-$850. Ploughkeepsie (sic), 1843. Tan boards, lavender cloth. $300-$350.

FARQUHARSON, Martha. *Elsie Dinsmore.* Red cloth. New York, 1867. (By Martha Finley.) First edition, with publisher's address misprinted "605" for 506 Broadway on title page. $150-$175.

FARRELL, James T. *Calico Shoes and Other Stories.* Blue cloth. New York, (1934). First edition. In dust jacket. $35-$50.

FARRELL, James T. *Gas-House McGinty.* Cloth. New York, 1933. First edition. In dust jacket. $50-$75.

FARRELL, James T. *Guillotine Party.* Green cloth. New York, (1935). First edition. In dust jacket. $40-$50.

FARRELL, James T. *Judgment Day.* Cloth. New York, 1935. First edition, with "thay" for "they" in third line of page 218. In dust jacket. $40-$50.

FARRELL, James T. *A Misunderstanding.* Cloth. New York, 1949. One of 300 signed. $50-$60.

FARRELL, James T. *Young Lonigan: A Boyhood in Chicago Streets.* Cloth. New York, 1932. First edition. In dust jacket. $150-$175. Also, $105 (A, 1975). Author's first book.

FARRELL, James T. *The Young Manhood of Studs Lonigan*. Brown cloth. New York, (1934). First edition, with errata slip listing eight typographical errors, among them "Connolly" for "Connell" in line 18 of page 88. In dust jacket. $85-$100.

FAST, Edward G. *Catalogue of Antiquities and Curiosities Collected in the Territory of Alaska*. 32 pp., wrappers. (New York), 1869. $45-$50.

FAULKNER, J.P. *Eighteen Months on a Greenland Whaler*. Portrait. Cloth. New York, 1878. $35-$50.

FAULKNER, William. See Dashiell, Alfred; Massey, Linton; Petersen, Carl.

FAULKNER, William. *Absalom, Absalom!* Folding map at end. Printed paper boards, cloth spine. New York, 1936. First edition. One of 300 signed. $600-$800. Also, $500 (A, (1977); $650 (A, 1975). First trade edition: Cloth. In dust jacket. $100-$200. London, (1936). Buff cloth. First English edition. In dust jacket. $200-$250.

FAULKNER, William. *As I Lay Dying*. Beige cloth. New York. (1930). First edition, first issue, with dropped "I" on page 11 and top edges stained brown. In dust jacket. $500-$800. Also, $275 (A, 1977); $475 (A, 1975); $300 (A, 1974). (Note: In this book the preferred binding state has all the lettering complete and undamaged. See the Massey and Petersen bibliographies.) Second issue, with "I" correctly positioned. In dust jacket. $150-$200.

FAULKNER, William. *Big Woods*. Green cloth. New York, (1955). First edition, first printing. In dust jacket. $50-$75. Also, $40 (A, 1975).

FAULKNER, William. *Collected Stories of William Faulkner*. Gray cloth. New York, (1950). First edition. In dust jacket. $50-$60.

FAULKNER, William. *Descende Moïse*. Wrappers. Paris, 1955. First French translation of *Go Down, Moses*. One of 76 on velin (paper). $75.

FAULKNER, William. *Doctor Martino and Other Stories*. Red and black cloth. New York, 1934. First edition. One of 360 signed. In acetate jacket. Boxed. $500-$750. Also, $325 (A, 1977); $650 (A, 1975); $275 (A, 1974). Trade edition: Blue cloth. In dust jacket. $200 and up. Also, $275 (A, 1974). London, 1934. Brick-red cloth. First English edition. In dust jacket. $40-$50.

FAULKNER, William. *A Fable*. Blue buckram. (New York, 1954.) First edition, first printing. One of 1,000 signed. In tissue dust jacket. Boxed. $350-$450. Also, $275 and $325 (A, 1975). Trade edition: Maroon cloth. In dust jacket. $35-$50.

FAULKNER, William. *Go Down, Moses and Other Stories*. Salmon-colored boards, red cloth spine. New York, (1942). First edition, first printing. One of 100 signed. $3,500-$4,000. Also, $3,750 (A, 1977); $3,000 (A, 1975). Trade edition: Cloth (in various colors). In dust jacket. $150-$175. London, 1942. Cloth. First English edition. In dust jacket. $25.

FAULKNER, William. *A Green Bough*. Wood engravings by Lynd Ward. Tan cloth, paper labels. New York, 1933. First edition. One of 360 signed. $400-$500. Also, $375 (A, 1977); $250 (A, 1974). Trade edition: Green cloth. In dust jacket. $100-$150.

FAULKNER, William. *The Hamlet*. Green cloth and boards. New York, 1940. First edition, first printing. One of 250 signed. In cellophane dust jacket. Boxed. $750-$1,000, possibly more. Also, $750 (A, 1977); $850 (A, 1975); $750 (A, 1974). Trade edition: Black cloth. In dust jacket. $200-$250. Also, $200 (A, 1974).

FAULKNER, William. *Histoires Diverses*. Wrappers. Paris, (1967). First French edition. One of 42. $75. (No corresponding title in English.)

FAULKNER, William. *Idyll in the Desert*. Red marbled boards, paper label. New York, 1931. First edition. One of 400 signed. In glassine dust jacket. $500-$600. Also, $425 (A, 1975); $400 (A, 1974). Lacking jacket, $400 (A, 1977).

FAULKNER, William. *Intruder in the Dust*. Black cloth. New York, (1948). First edition, first printing. In dust jacket. $50-$75. London, 1949. Blue cloth. First English edition. In dust jacket. $25.

FAULKNER, William. *Jealousy and Episode*. Cloth. Minneapolis, 1955. First edition. One of 500. $100-$125.

FAULKNER, William. *Knight's Gambit*. Red cloth. New York, (1949). First edition. In dust jacket. $50-$75.

FAULKNER, William. *Light in August*. Beige buckram. (New York, 1932.) First edition, first printing. In dust jacket and glassine wrapper. $200-$250. Also, $170 (A, 1975).

FAULKNER, William. *The Mansion*. Black cloth. New York, (1959). First edition. One of 500 signed. In acetate dust jacket. $250-$300. Also, $200 (A, 1977); $225 (A, 1975). First trade edition: Blue cloth. In dust jacket. $25-$40. Also, a set of advance galley proofs, $550 (A, 1977).

FAULKNER, William. *The Marble Faun*. Mottled green boards, printed labels. Boston, (1924). First edition. (About 500 copies issued.) In dust jacket. $5,000-$6,000. Also, inscribed twice by Faulkner, $6,250 (A, 1977).

FAULKNER, William. *The Marionettes*. Unopened sheets. (Charlottesville, 1975.) First edition. One of 100. Boxed. $135-$150.

FAULKNER, William. *Mirrors of Chartres Street*. Illustrated. Tan cloth. (Minneapolis, 1953.) First edition. One of 1,000. In dust jacket. $50-$60.

FAULKNER, William. *Miss Zilphia Gant*. Brownish red cloth. (Dallas), 1932. Book Club of Texas. First edition. One of 300. In glassine dust jacket. $600-$750. Also, $650 (A, 1977); $550 (A, 1974).

FAULKNER, William. *Mosquitoes*. Blue cloth. New York, 1927. First edition. In first-issue dust jacket, with mosquito design. $1,000-$1,250. Also $1,000 (A, 1975).

FAULKNER, William. *Moustiques*. Wrappers. Paris, 1948. First French edition of *Mosquitoes*. One of 50 on velin (paper). $100-$150. Another issue: One of 150 on Alfa paper. $75-$100.

FAULKNER, William. *New Orleans Sketches*. Edited by Carvel Collins. Brown boards. New Brunswick, N.J., 1958. First American edition, first printing (so stated). In dust jacket. $40-$60.

FAULKNER, William. *Notes on a Horsethief*. Decorations by Elizabeth Calvert. Decorated green cloth. Greenville, Miss., 1950. First edition. One of 950 (of 975) signed. In cellophane dust jacket. $350-$400. Also, $250 (A, 1977). One of 25 copies marked "for presentation" and signed. $400-$500.

FAULKNER, William. *The Portable Faulkner*. Edited by Malcolm Cowley. Cloth. New York, 1946. First edition. In dust jacket. $40-$60.

FAULKNER, William. *Pylon*. Folding facsimile. Half blue cloth and silver boards. New York, 1935. First edition. One of 310 signed. Boxed. $500-$600. Also, $425 (A, 1977); $450 (A, 1975). Trade edition: Blue cloth, with black band. In dust jacket. $100-$135.

FAULKNER, William. *The Reivers: A Reminiscence*. Maroon cloth. New York, (1962). First edition, first printing. One of 500 signed. In acetate dust jacket. $300-$400. Also, $300 (A, 1975). Trade edition: Red cloth. In dust jacket. $25-$30.

FAULKNER, William. *Requiem for a Nun*. Half black cloth, marbled boards. New York, (1951). First edition. One of 750 signed. In acetate dust jacket. $300-$350. Also $300 (A, 1977); $275 (A, 1975). Trade edition: Green and black cloth. In dust jacket. $35-$50. Play version: New York, (1959). Adapted by Ruth Ford. Gray boards. First edition, first printing. In dust jacket. $35-$50.

FAULKNER, William. *Salmagundi*. Tan wrappers. Milwaukee, 1932. Casanova Press. First edition, first state, with bottom edges untrimmed. One of the first 26 copies of a total edition of 525. Boxed. $750 and up. Also, $750 (A, 1977). Other copies from the 525-copy run, boxed, $500-$600. (Note: Includes a poem by Ernest Hemingway, listed on title page.)

FAULKNER, William. *Sanctuaire.* Preface by André Malraux. Wrappers. Paris, (1933). First French edition of *Sanctuary.* One of 150 on Alfa paper. $50-$60.

FAULKNER, William. *Sanctuary.* Magenta boards and gray cloth. New York, (1931). First edition, first printing, with "First Published, 1931" on copyright page. In dust jacket. $600-$800. Also, $650 (A, 1975); $375 (A, 1974). London, 1931. Red cloth. First English edition. In dust jacket. $25-$35.

FAULKNER, William. *Sartoris.* Black cloth. New York, (1929). First edition. In dust jacket. $300-$550. Also, $150 (A, 1977); $400 (A, 1975); $300 (A, 1974).

FAULKNER, William. *Scheckige Mustangs.* 44 lithographs. Folio, decorated boards. Stuttgart, Germany, 1965. Illustrated edition of "Spotted Horses." One of 50 with an extra set of plates signed by the artist, Gunter Böhmer. Boxed. $150-$250.

FAULKNER, William. *Soldiers' Pay.* Blue cloth. New York, 1926. First edition. In dust jacket. $1,750-$2,000. Also, in jacket and signed by Faulkner, $4,250 (A, 1977). Lacking jacket, $250 and up. London, 1930. Green cloth. First English edition. In dust jacket. $75-$150. Author's first novel.

FAULKNER, William. *The Sound and the Fury.* Black, white, and gray patterned boards, white cloth spine. New York, (1929). First edition, first printing, with "First Published 1929" on copyright page. In dust jacket. $750-$1,000. Also, $850 (A, 1977); $425 (A, 1975); $325 (A, 1974). London, 1931. Black cloth. First English edition. In dust jacket. $75-$100.

FAULKNER, William. *These 13.* Tan and red cloth. New York, (1931). First edition. One of 299 signed. $400-$550. Also, $300 (A, 1977); $375 (A, 1974)—a poor copy. Trade edition: Blue and gray cloth. In dust jacket. $250-$300. Also, $225 (A, 1974). London, 1933. Blue cloth. First English edition. In dust jacket. $50-$75.

FAULKNER, William. *This Earth.* Illustrated by Albert Heckman. 8 pp., stiff tan wrappers. New York, 1932. First edition. (1,000 copies.) In plain white envelope. $100-$135.

FAULKNER, William. *The Town.* Tan cloth, top edges red. New York, (1957). First edition, first printing. One of 450 signed. In acetate dust jacket. $300-$400. Also, $300 (A, 1977); $250 (A, 1975). Trade edition: Red cloth. In dust jacket. $25-$40. London, 1958. Red boards. First English edition. In dust jacket. $15-$25.

FAULKNER, William. *The Unvanquished.* Illustrated by Edward Shenton. Boards and red cloth. New York, (1938). First edition, first printing. One of 250 signed. $500-$750. Also, $350 (A, 1977). Trade edition: Gray cloth. In dust jacket. $75-$100.

FAULKNER, William. *The Wild Palms.* Red cloth and boards. New York, (1939). First edition, first printing. One of 250 signed. In glassine dust jacket. $500-$550. Also, $425 (A, 1977). Trade edition: Tan cloth. In dust jacket. $75-$100. Advance issue: Green wrappers. $200 (A, 1977).

FAULKNER, William. *William Faulkner's Speech of Acceptance Upon the Award of the Nobel Prize for Literature.* Beige wrappers. (New York, 1951.) First separate edition, first printing. One of 1,500 by the Spiral Press. $35. Second printing. One of 2,500. $25. Third printing. One of 3,500. $15.

FAULKNER, William (editor). *Sherwood Anderson & Other Famous Creoles.* Drawings by William Spratling. Green boards, paper label. New Orleans, 1926. First edition. One of about 50 hand-tinted copies (of an issue of 250 numbered copies, from a 400-copy edition). With "W. Spratling" on front end paper. $750 and up. Other copies, $400-$600. Also, worn, $550 (A, 1977). Unnumbered copies, $150-$250 at retail.

FAUX, W. *Memorable Days in America.* Half leather. London, 1823. First edition. $200-$250.

FEARING, Kenneth. *Angel Arms.* Boards. New York, 1929. First edition. In dust jacket. $50-$75. Author's first book.

*FEAST of the Poets (The).* By the Editor of the Examiner. Boards, paper label. London, 1814. (By Leigh Hunt.) First edition. $200-$250.

FEATHERSTONHAUGH, George W. *A Canoe Voyage Up the Minnay Sotor.* 2 folding maps, 2 plates. 2 vols., cloth. London, 1947. First edition. $350.

FEININGER, Andreas. *Feininger on Photography.* Illustrated. Cloth. New York, (1949). First edition. In dust jacket. $40-$50.

FELLOWS-JOHNSTON, Annie. *The Little Colonel.* Green cloth. Boston, 1896. First edition. $50-$60.

FENOLLOSA, Ernest F. *Certain Noble Plays of Japan.* From manuscripts of Fenollosa, chosen and finished by Ezra Pound. Introduction by W.B. Yeats. Boards, linen spine. Churchtown, Dundrum, Ireland, 1916. Cuala Press. One of 350. $150-$200.

FENOLLOSA, Ernest F. *The Chinese Written Character as a Medium for Poetry.* Foreword by Ezra Pound. Black cloth, parchment spine. London, (1936). First edition. In dust jacket. $100-$125. New York, (1936). Green boards. First American edition. In dust jacket. $50-$60.

FERBER, Edna. *American Beauty.* Cloth. Garden City, 1931. First edition. One of 200 signed. In dust jacket. $50-$60.

FERBER, Edna. *Dawn O'Hara: The Girl Who Laughed.* Colored frontispiece. Cloth. New York, (1911). First edition. In dust jacket. $50-$60. Author's first book.

FERBER, Edna. *A Peculiar Treasure.* Boards and cloth. New York, 1939. First edition. One of 351 signed. In dust jacket. Boxed. $40-$50.

FERBER, Edna. *Saratoga Trunk.* Blue buckram. New York, 1941. First edition. One of 526 signed. In dust jacket. $75-$100. Also, $90 (A, 1975). Trade edition: Cloth. In dust jacket. $15.

FERBER, Edna. *Show Boat.* Green boards, white vellum spine. Garden City, 1926. First edition. One of 201 signed. Boxed. $75-$100. Another issue: Decorated boards (presentation copies, not signed). One of 1,000. $25. Trade edition: Yellow cloth. In dust jacket. $10-$12.50.

FERBER, Edna. *So Big.* Cloth. Garden City, 1924. First edition. In dust jacket. $25-$35.

FERLINGHETTI, Lawrence. *Pictures of the Gone World.* Stiff black printed wrappers, and boards. San Francisco, (1955). Wrappers, with wraparound label (500 copies): $35-$50. Another issue: Hard covers. One of 25 signed. $75-$125.

FERLINGHETTI, Lawrence. *The Secret Meaning of Things.* Cloth. (New York, 1968.) First edition. One of 150 signed. Boxed. $35-$50. Trade edition: In dust jacket. $15. Also issued later in wrappers.

FERNÁNDEZ DE SAN SALVADOR, Augustin. *Los Jesuitas Quitados y Restituidos al Mundo. Historia de la Antigua California.* Cloth or leather. Mexico, 1861. First edition. $100-$200.

FERRIER, Susan Edmonstone. See *Destiny, or, The Chief's Daughter: Marriage.*

FERRINI, VINCENT. *No Smoke.* Red cloth, cover and spine labels. Portland, Me., 1941. First edition. $25. Author's first book.

FEUCHTWANGER, Dr. Lewis. *A Treatise on Gems.* Cloth. New York, 1838. $50.

FICKE, Arthur Davison. See Morgan, Emanuel, and Knish, Anne.

FIDFADDY, Frederick Augustus. *The Adventures of Uncle Sam in Search After His Lost Honor.* Boards. Middletown, Conn., 1816. First edition. $75-$100.

FIELD, Eugene. *Culture's Garland.* Cloth, or printed gray wrappers. Boston, 1887. First edition. Wrappers: $35-$50. Another issue: Wrappers, leaves untrimmed. One of 6 (or 12?). Inscribed, $250. Blue cloth: $50.

FIELD, Eugene. *Florence Bardsley's Story.* Green cloth. Chicago, 1897. First edition. One of 25 on Japan vellum. $75-$100. Also, $60 (A, 1975). Another issue: One of 150 on paper. $25-$35.

FIELD, Eugene. *The Holy Cross and Other Tales*. Vellum. Cambridge, (Mass.), and Chicago, 1893. First edition. One of 20 on vellum, signed by the publisher. $100-$150. Another issue: Blue cloth. One of 110 on paper, signed by the publisher. $75-$100. Trade edition: Cloth, $40-$50.

FIELD, Eugene. *The House*. Boards. New York, 1896. First edition. One of 150 large paper copies. $75-$100. Also $60 (A, 1975).

FIELD, Eugene. *How One Friar Met the Devil and Two Pursued Him*. Boards. Chicago, (1900). First edition. One of 300. $75-$100. Also, $50 (A, 1975).

FIELD, Eugene. *A Little Book of Tribune Verse*. Cloth. Denver, 1901. First edition. One of 750. $50-$75.

FIELD, Eugene. *A Little Book of Western Verse*. Blue-gray boards and cloth. Chicago, 1889. First edition. One of 250 large paper copies. $75-$100. Also, $60 (A, 1976). New York, 1890. Cloth. First trade edition. $25. (Note: The first appearance of "Little Boy Blue.")

FIELD, Eugene. *The Love Affairs of a Bibliomaniac*. Frontispiece. Blue cloth. New York, 1896. First edition, first issue, with 8 titles listed. $50-$60. Another issue: Half vellum. One of 150 on Holland paper. $75-$100.

FIELD, Eugene. *Love-Songs of Childhood*. Vellum. New York, 1894. First edition. One of 106 on Van Gelder paper. $50-$75. Another issue: One of 15 on Japan vellum. $150-$200. Trade edition: Blue cloth. $15-$25.

FIELD, Eugene. *Poems of Childhood*. 9 color plates by Maxfield Parrish. Cloth. New York, 1904. First edition. $50-$75.

FIELD, Eugene. *Second Book of Tales*. Half vellum. Chicago. 1896. First edition. One of 150. $35-$50.

FIELD, Eugene. *Second Book of Verse*. Boards, leather label. Chicago, 1892. First edition. One of 300. In dust jacket. $75. Another issue: One of 12 with manuscript poems. $200 and up.

FIELD, Eugene. *Sharps and Flats*. 2 vols., blue cloth. New York, 1900. First edition. $30-$40. New York, 1901. 2 vols., half vellum. One of 150. $50-$75.

FIELD, Eugene. *The Stars: A Slumber Story*. Boards. New York, 1901. First edition. $50-$75.

FIELD, Eugene. *The Symbol and the Saint*. Wrappers. (Chicago), 1886. First edition. $300-$400.

FIELD, Eugene. *The Temptation of Friar Gonsol*. Vellum. Washington, 1900. One of 300 on paper. $35-$75. Another issue: One of 10 on vellum. $100-$150. Also, $80 (A, 1976). (Note: This is another edition of *How One Friar Met the Devil and Two Pursued Him*.)

FIELD, Eugene. *Tribune Primer*. Gray-blue wrappers. (Denver, 1881.) First edition. $2,000 (1970 catalogue). Author's first book.

FIELD, Eugene. *With Trumpet and Drum*. Boards. New York, 1892. First edition. One of 250. $50-$60. Another issue: One of 12 on vellum. $150-$200. Trade edition: Cloth. $15-$20.

FIELD, Rachel. *Hitty: Her First Hundred Years*. Illustrated by Dorothy P. Lathrop. Decorated cloth, paper label. New York, 1929. First edition. In dust jacket. $75-$100.

FIELD, Rachel. *Rise Up, Jennie Smith*. Wrappers. New York, (1918). First edition. $25. Author's first book.

FIELD, Stephen J. *Personal Reminiscences of Early Days in California*. Red cloth. (San

Francisco, 1880?) First edition. $75-$100. Second edition: (Washington, 1893.) Half morocco. $100-$150.

FIELD, William B. Osgood. See *Edward Lear on My Shelves; John Leech on My Shelves*.

FIELDING, Henry. *A Journey from this World to the Next*. San Francisco, 1930. Grabhorn Press. One of 500. $40-$50.

FIELDING, T.H. *A Picturesque Description of the River Wye*. 12 colored aquatint plates. Boards. London, 1841. $300-$400.

FIELDING, T.H., and Walton, J. *A Picturesque Tour of the English Lakes*. Color vignette and 48 colored aquatint plates. Cloth. London, 1821. $1,000-$1,250. Large paper issue: $1,250-$1,750.

*FIFTH Antiquarian Book Fair (The): A Handlist of Exhibitors Introduced by Lawrence Durrell*. 12 pp., stapled, wrappers. London, 1962. One of 10 on green paper, signed. $400 and up.

FIGUEROA, José. *The Manifesto*. (Translated from the original as published in Monterey in 1835.) Printed wrappers. San Francisco, 1855. First edition in English. $500-$750. Also, $350 (A, 1968).

FILISOLA, Gen. Vicente. *Evacuation of Texas*. 68 pp., half leather. Columbia, Tex., 1837. First edition in English (of item following). $2,500-$4,000, possibly more. (Sometimes called "the first real book published in Texas.")

FILISOLA, Gen. Vicente. *Representación dirigida al Supremo Gobierno por el General Vicente Filisola, en Defensa de Su Honor y Aclaración de Sus Operaciones como General en Gefe del Ejército sobre Tejas*. 82 pp., wrappers. Mexico, 1836. First edition. $1,500-$2,500.

FILLEY, William. *Life and Adventures of William Filley*. 7 plates and half-page cut. 96 pp., wrappers. Chicago, 1867. Printed by Fergus. First edition. $1,000-$1,500, possibly more. Another edition, same place and date: 112 pp., wrappers. Printed by Filley & Ballard. Second edition, $400-$600.

FINLAY, John. *Journal Kept by Hugh Finlay, Surveyor of Post Roads*. Leather and cloth. Brooklyn, 1867. One of 150. $75-$100. Also, $55 (A, 1974).

FINLEY, Ernest L. (editor). *History of Sonoma County*. (California.) Morocco. Santa Rosa, 1937. First edition. $75-$100.

FINLEY, James B. *History of the Wyandott Mission at Upper Sandusky, Ohio*. Calf. Cincinnati, 1840. First edition. $150-$200.

FINN, Huck. See Twain, Mark, *Tom Sawyer Abroad*.

FINNEY, Charles G. *The Circus of Doctor Lao*. Cloth. New York, 1935. First edition. In dust jacket. $75-$100. Author's first book.

FINNEY & Davis (publishers). *Biographical and Statistical History of the City of Oshkosh*. 76 pp., half leather. Oshkosh, 1867. First edition. $75-$100.

FIRBANK, Arthur Ronald. *Odette D'Antrevernes*. Pink or blue-gray wrappers. London, 1905. First edition. $150-$175. Also, about 10 sets of unbound signatures were made for presentation. A signed copy sold at auction for $650 in October, 1977. Author's first book.

FIRBANK, Ronald. *Concerning the Eccentricities of Cardinal Pirelli*. Cloth. London, 1926. First edition. In dust jacket. $75-$100.

FIRBANK, Ronald. *Odette: A Fairy Tale for Weary People*. Illustrated. Wrappers. London, 1916. First separate edition. $65.

FIRBANK, Ronald. *Prancing Nigger*. Introduction by Carl Van Vechten. New York, (1924). First edition. In dust jacket. $35-$50.

FIRBANK, Ronald. *Santal.* Wrappers. London, 1921. First edition. In glassine dust jacket. $135. Also, $52 (A, 1975).

FIRBANK, Ronald. *Sorrow in Sunlight.* Cloth. London, 1925. First English edition (of *Prancing Nigger).* One of 1,000. In dust jacket. $50.

*FIRST Annual Report of the Directors of the Central Mining Co.* 13 pp., wrappers. Detroit, 1855. $75-$100.

*FIRST Annual Review of Pierce County.* (Winconsin.) 48 pp., wrappers. Prescott, Wis., 1855. $100-$125.

*FIRST Catalogues and Circulars of the Botanical Garden of Transylvania University at Lexington in Kentucky, for the Year 1824.* 24 pp., sewed. Lexington, 1824. (By C.S. Rafinesque.) $150-$250.

*FIRST Published Life of Abraham Lincoln (The).* (Reprint of John Locke Scripps biography.) Half vellum. (Detroit, 1970.) Cranbrook Press. One of 245. $50-$75.

*FIRST Settlement and Early History of Palmyra, Wayne County; New York (The).* 10 pp., printed wrappers. Palmyra, 1858. $100-$150.

*FIRST Settlers of New England (The), or, Conquest of the Pequods, Narragansets and Pokanokets.* By a Lady of Massachusetts. Boards. Boston, (1829). (By Lydia Maria Child.) First edition, first issue, with undated title page. $75-$100.

FISH, Daniel. *Lincoln Bibliography.* Red cloth. New York, (1906). One of 75 signed. Boxed. $35-$50.

FISH, H.C. *The Voice of Our Brother's Blood: Its Source and Its Summons.* 16 pp., sewed. Newark, 1856. First edition. $100-$150.

FISHER, George. *Memorials of George Fisher, etc.* Cloth. Houston, 1840. First edition. $500-$1,000, possibly more.

FISHER, Harry C. *The Mutt and Jeff Cartoons.* Oblong folio, pictorial boards and cloth. Boston, 1910. First edition. $40-$50. First Mutt and Jeff book.

FISHER, John, Bishop of Rochester. *A Mornynge Remembraunce.* Frontispiece by C.R. Ashbee. Vellum. London, 1906. Essex House Press. One of 125. $50-$60. Another issue: One of 7 on vellum. $150-$200.

FISHER, O.C. *It Occurred in Kimble.* Illustrated. Pictorial cloth. Houston, 1937. First edition. One of 500. $100-$200.

FISHER, Richard S. *Indiana: Its Geography, Statistics, County Topography.* Large folding map in color. Cloth. New York, 1852. First edition. $150-$175.

FISHER, Rudolph. *The Walls of Jericho.* Decorated cloth. New York, 1928. First edition. $35.

FISHER, Vardis. *April: A Fable of Love.* Morocco. Caldwell, Idaho, and Garden City, 1937. First edition. One of 50 signed. $50-$75. Trade edition: Cloth. In dust jacket. $10-$15.

FISHER, Vardis. *Children of God, an American Epic.* Leather. Caldwell, 1939. First edition. One of 100 signed. $50-$75. New York, 1939. Cloth. First trade edition. In dust jacket. $25-$40.

FISHER, Vardis. *City of Illusion.* Cloth. New York, (1941). First edition. In dust jacket. $20-$25. Caldwell, 1941. One of 1,000. $35-$50. Another issue: Morocco. One of 100 signed. $75-$100.

FISHER, Vardis. *Dark Bridwell.* Cloth. Boston, 1931. First edition. In dust jacket. $25.

FISHER, Vardis. *Forgive Us Our Virtues.* Morocco. Caldwell, 1938. First edition. One of 75 signed. $75-$100. Also, $32 (A, 1969). Trade edition: Cloth. In dust jacket. $10-$15.

FISHER, Vardis. *A Goat for Azazel*. Cloth. Denver, (1956). First edition. One of 200 signed. $25-$35.

FISHER, Vardis. *In Tragic Life*. Cloth. Caldwell, 1932. First edition. In dust jacket. $35-$50. Another issue: Leather. One of 25 signed. $100. Garden City, 1932. Cloth. In dust jacket. $10-$15.

FISHER, Vardis. *Jesus Came Again*. Cloth. Denver, (1956). First edition. One of 200 signed. $25-$35.

FISHER, Vardis. *My Holy Satan*. Cloth. Denver, (1958). First edition. One of 200 signed. $25.

FISHER, Vardis. *The Neurotic Nightingale*. Cloth. (Milwaukee, 1935.) First edition. One of 300 signed. $50-$75. One of 25 unsigned (for review). $25.

FISHER, Vardis. *No Villain Need Be*. Cloth. Caldwell, 1936. First edition (so stated). In dust jacket. $25. Another issue: One of 75 in full leather, signed. $50-$75. Garden City, 1936. In dust jacket. $10-$15.

FISHER, Vardis. *Odyssey of a Hero*. Half cloth. Philadelphia, 1937. First edition. One of 50 signed. $75-$100. Trade edition: Cloth. $10-$15.

FISHER, Vardis. *Passions Spin the Plot*. Cloth. Caldwell, 1933. First edition, first state, with 1933 date (suppressed). In dust jacket. $100-$125. Also, $55 (A, 1963). Caldwell, 1934. Second state (dated 1934). In dust jacket. $25-$35. Another issue: Morocco. One of 75 signed. $50-$75.

FISHER, Vardis. *Peace Like a River*. Cloth. Denver, (1957). First edition. One of 200 signed. $25-$35.

FISHER, Vardis. *Sonnets to an Imaginary Madonna*. Boards, pink paper labels. New York, 1927. First edition. In dust jacket. $75-$125. Author's first book.

FISHER, Vardis. *Toilers of the Hills*. Cloth. Boston, 1928. First edition. In dust jacket. $25-$35.

FISHER, Vardis. *We Are Betrayed*. Cloth. Caldwell, (1935). First edition (so stated). In dust jacket. $25. Another issue: Morocco. One of 75 signed. $50-$75. Garden City, 1935. Cloth. In dust jacket. $10-$15.

FISHER, William (compiler). *An Interesting Account of the Voyages and Travels of Captains Lewis and Clark*. 2 portraits. Calf. Baltimore, 1812. First edition. $200-$350. Baltimore, 1813. 2 portraits, 4 (sometimes 3) plates. Calf. $100-$250.

FISK, Capt. James L. *Expedition from Fort Abercrombie to Fort Benton*. (Caption title.) House Exec. Doc. No. 80. 36 pp., sewed. (Washington, 1863.) First edition. $35-$50.

FITE, Emerson D., and Freeman, Archibald (editors). *A Book of Old Maps Delineating American History*. 74 maps in facsimile, colored frontispiece. Folio, cloth. Cambridge, Mass., 1926. First edition. In dust jacket. $200-$250.

FITHIAN, Philip Vickers. *Journal and Letters, 1767-1774*. 8 plates. Cloth. Princeton, 1900. First edition. $50-$75.

FITTS, Dudley. *Two Poems*. Wrappers. No place, (1932). First edition. One of 100 signed. $35-$50.

FITZ GERALD, Edward. See Aeschylus. Also see *The Downfall and Death of King Oedipus; Euphranor; The Mighty Magician; Polonius; Readings in Crabbe's "Tales of the Hall"; Rubaiyat of Omar Khayyam; Salaman and Absal; The Two Generals*.

FITZ GERALD, Edward. *Letters and Literary Remains of Edward FitzGerald*. Edited by William Aldis Wright. Frontispiece plates. 3 vols., cloth. London, 1889. First edition. $75-$125. London, 1902-03. 7 vols., cloth. One of 775. $100-$150.

FITZ GERALD, Edward. *Letters of Edward FitzGerald.* Frontispiece. 2 vols., cloth. London, 1894. First edition. $30-$40.

FITZ GERALD, Edward. *Letters of Edward FitzGerald to Fanny Kemble, 1871-1883.* Edited by William Aldis Wright. Frontispiece portrait. Cloth. London, 1895. First edition. $30-$50.

FITZ GERALD, Edward (translator). *Six Dramas of Calderon.* Watered crimson cloth. London, 1853. First edition. $50-$75.

FITZGERALD, F. Scott. See *A Book of Princeton Verse II.*

FITZGERALD, F. Scott. *All the Sad Young Men.* Dark-green cloth. New York, 1926. First edition, first printing, with Scribner seal on copyright page and perfect type on page 248. In dust jacket. $400-$500. Also, $300 (A, 1974); jacket worn, $225 (A, 1977).

FITZGERALD, F. Scott. *The Beautiful and Damned.* Dark-green cloth. New York, 1922. First edition, first issue, with no ads at back and with "Published March, 1922" on copyright page. In first-issue dust jacket with title in solid black. $1,000-$1,250. In second-issue jacket, title in outline lettering. $600-$850. Also, $600 (A, 1977). Toronto, 1922. Cloth. First Canadian edition. In dust jacket. $75.

FITZGERALD, F. Scott. *The Crack-Up.* Edited by Edmund Wilson. Patterned boards and cloth, paper label. (New York, 1945.) New Directions. First edition, first printing, with title page in red and black. In dust jacket. $50-$75.

FITZGERALD, F. Scott. *Flappers and Philosophers.* Cloth. New York, 1920. First edition, first printing, with "Published September, 1920" and publisher's seal on copyright page. In dust jacket. $450-$500. Also, in frayed jacket, $375 (A, 1977).

FITZGERALD, F. Scott. *The Great Gatsby.* Dark-green cloth. New York, 1925. First edition, first issue, with "sick in tired" in line 9 of page 205. First-issue dust jacket, with lower-case "J" on back panel and with flaps listing books by Fitzgerald and Lardner $850-$1,250. In second issue dust jacket, with "Perilously Near a Masterpiece" on back of jacket. $350-$500.

FITZGERALD, F. Scott. *The Mystery of the Raymond Mortgage.* 12 pp., wrappers. New York, 1960. First edition. One of 750. $200-$225.

FITZGERALD, F. Scott. *Tales of the Jazz Age.* Dark-green cloth. New York, 1922. First edition, first issue, with "Published September, 1922" and Scribner seal on copyright page. In dust jacket. $350-$450.

FITZGERALD, F. Scott. *Taps at Reveille.* Green cloth. New York, 1935. First edition, with Scribner "A" on copyright page. In dust jacket. $600-$750. Also, $550 and $425 (A, 1977 and 1974).

FITZGERALD, F. Scott. *Tender Is the Night.* Dark-green cloth. New York, 1934. First edition, first issue, with Scribner "A" and seal on copyright page. In dust jacket. $400-$600.

FITZGERALD, F. Scott. *This Side of Paradise.* Dark-green cloth. New York, 1920. First edition, first printing, with "Published April, 1920" and publisher's seal on copyright page. In dust jacket. $500-$600. Third issue: with the author's "apology" leaf, signed, $650. Author's first novel.

FITZGERALD, F. Scott. *Thoughtbook of Francis Scott Key Fitzgerald.* Introduction by John R. Kuehl. White boards. Princeton, 1965. First edition. One of 300 copies. In glassine dust jacket. $50-$100.

FITZGERALD, F. Scott. *The Vegetable.* Dark-green cloth. New York, 1923. First edition, first printing, with "Published April, 1923" and publisher's seal on copyright page. In dust jacket. $300-$450.

FITZGERALD, F. Scott, and others. *The Evil Eye: A Musical Comedy in Two Acts.* Boards and cloth. (Cincinnati, New York, & London, 1915.) First edition. $1,000-$1,400.

FITZGERALD, F. Scott, and others. *Fie! Fie! Fi-Fi! A Musical Comedy in Two Acts.*

Boards and cloth. (Cincinnati, New York & London, 1914.) First edition. $750-$1,000. Also, $650 (A, 1977).

FITZGERALD, F. Scott, and others. *Safety First: A Musical Comedy in Two Acts.* Boards and cloth. Cincinnati, New York & London, (1916). First edition. $1,000-$1,500. Also, $1,000 (A, 1977).

FITZGERALD, Robert. *Poems.* Orange cloth. New York, 1935. $50-$75. Author's first book.

FITZGERALD, Zelda. *Save Me the Waltz.* Green cloth. New York, 1932. First edition. In dust jacket. $300-$400. Also, $300 (A, 1977).

FITZHUGH, George. *Cannibals All! Or, Slaves Without Masters.* Cloth. Richmond, Va., 1857. First edition. $150-$250.

*FIVE Young American Poets.* Tan cloth. Norfolk, Conn., 1944. New Directions. First edition. In dust jacket. $35-$50. (Note: Contains work by Tennessee Williams and others.)

FLAUBERT, Gustave. *Herodias.* Half cloth. London, (1901). Eragny Press. $100-$150.

FLECKER, James Elroy. *The Golden Journey to Samarkand.* Dark-blue cloth. London, 1913. First edition. $35-$50. Another issue: Boards. One of 50 signed. $100.

FLEMING, Alexander. *Penicillin.* Cloth. London, 1946. First edition. $100-$150.

FLEMING, C.B. *Early History of Hopkins County, Texas.* Cloth. No place, 1902. $200-$300, possibly more.

FLEMING, Sandford. *Memorial of the People of Red River to the British and Canadian Governments.* 7 pp., printed front paper cover. Quebec, 1863. $500-$600.

FLEMING, Walter L. *Documentary History of Reconstruction.* 9 facsimiles. 2 vols., half calf. Cleveland, 1906-07. First edition. $85-$150. (Occasionally available more cheaply; John H. Jenkins thinks "there is a remainder lot floating around out there.")

FLETCHER, Charles H. *Jefferson County, Iowa, Centennial History.* 35 pp., printed wrappers. Fairfield, Iowa, 1876. $75-$100.

FLETCHER, John Gould. *Fire and Wine.* Cloth. London, (May, 1913). First edition. $150-$175. Author's first book.

FLETCHER, John Gould. *Irradiations: Sand and Spray.* Green wrappers. Boston, 1915. First edition. $50-$75.

FLETCHER, John Gould. *Japanese Prints.* Cloth. Boston, 1918. Four Seas Press. First edition. $75-$85.

FLETCHER, John Gould. *Preludes and Symphonies.* Cloth, paper label. New York, 1930. First edition. In dust jacket. $50-$60.

FLETCHER, John Gould. *XXIV Elegies.* Cloth. Santa Fe, (1935). First edition. One of 400 signed. $80-$100.

FLETCHER, W. A. *A Rebel Private, Front and Rear.* Portrait. Cloth. Beaumont, Tex., 1908. First edition. $300-$500.

FLEURY, Claude. *A Short Catechism, Containing a Summary of Sacred History, and Christian Doctrine.* Calf. Detroit, 1812. $1,250-$1,500.

FLICKINGER, Robert E. *Pioneer History of Pocahontas County, Iowa.* Cloth. Fonda, Iowa, 1904. First edition. $75-$85.

FLINDERS, Matthew. *Narrative of His Voyage in the Schooner Francis.* Engravings by John Buckland Wright. Cloth. Waltham Saint Lawrence, 1946. Golden Cockerel Press. One of 750. $280.

FLINT, Micah P. *The Hunter and Other Poems.* Boards. Boston, 1826. First edition. $80-$100.

FLINT, Timothy. *A Condensed Geography and History of the Western States, or the Mississippi Valley.* 2 vols., tan boards, paper labels. Cincinnati, 1828. First edition. $250-$350.

FLINT, Timothy. *Indian Wars of the West.* Calf, or half leather. Cincinnati, 1833. $200-$300.

FLINT, Timothy. *Lectures Upon Natural History.* Cloth. Boston, 1833. First edition. $125-$250.

FLINT, Timothy. *Recollections of the Last Ten Years.* Tan boards, paper label. Boston, 1826. First edition. $300-$500.

FLINT, W. Russell. *Breakfast in Perigord.* Illustrated. Half morocco. London, 1968. One of 525 signed by Flint. Boxed. $175-$225.

FLINT, W. Russell. *Drawings.* 134 plates. Half morocco. London, 1950. One of 125 signed by Flint, with an original drawing in folder at end. Boxed. $600 and up. Another issue: One of 500. $150-$200. Trade issue: Cloth. In dust jacket. $60-$100.

FLINT, W. Russell. *Minxes Admonished or Beauty Reproved.* Illustrated, including color. Morocco and boards. (London), 1955. Golden Cockerel Press. Boxed. $200-$225.

*FLORENCE Farr, Bernard Shaw, and W. B. Yeats: Letters.* Edited by Clifford Bax. Boards, cloth spine. Dublin, 1941. Cuala Press. First edition. One of 500. $100-$150.

*FLOURE (The) and The Leafe, & the Boke of Cupide, God of Love, or the Cuckow and the Nightingale.* 2 large woodcut initial words from the Kelmscott Chaucer. Printed in black and red. Boards and linen. (Hammersmith, London, 1896.) Kelmscott Press. One of 300. $350-$450. Another issue: One of 10 on vellum. $1,250-$1,500.

FLOWER, Richard. *Letters from Illinois, 1810-1821.* 76 pp., half morocco. London, 1822. First edition. $300-$500.

FLOWER, Robin (translator). *Love's Bitter-Sweet.* Boards and linen. Dublin, 1925. Cuala Press. One of 500. In dust jacket. $50-$75.

FOLEY, P. K. *American Authors, 1795-1895: A Bibliography.* Cloth. Boston, 1897. One of 500. $50-$60. One of 75. $75-$100.

FOOTE, Henry Stuart. *Texas and the Texans.* 2 vols., cloth. Philadelphia, 1841. First edition. $350-$500.

FORBES, Alexander. *California: A History.* 10 lithographs, map colored in outline. Cloth. London, 1839. First edition, with errata slip. $350-$450. San Francisco, 1919. Map, 10 plates. One of 250 signed by the publisher. $80-$100. San Francisco, 1937. John Henry Nash printing. Marbled boards. One of 650. In dust jacket. $50-$60. San Francisco, 1939. $35-$50.

FORBES, Edwin. *Life Studies of the Great Army.* 40 plates. Half morocco. (New York), 1876. First edition. $250-$300. Also, rubbed and rebacked, $180 (A, 1976).

FORBES, Edwin. *Thirty Years After: An Artist's Story of the Great War.* 80 full-page plates, 20 portraits. 4 vols., folio, cloth. New York, (1890). First edition. $150. Another issue: 2 vols., cloth. $50-$75.

FORBES, Sir. James. *Oriental Memoirs.* 21 colored plates, other illustrations. 4 vols., contemporary full red morocco. London, 1813. First edition. $500-$750. London, 1834-35. 3 vols. (including atlas), half morocco. $250-$350.

FORBES, James Grant. *Sketches, Historical and Topographical, of the Floridas.* Map (not in all copies). Boards, paper label. New York, 1821. First edition. With the map. $350-$500.

FORBUSH, Edward Howe. *Birds of Massachusetts and Other New England States.* Color illustrations by L. A. Fuertes. 3 vols., cloth. (Boston), 1925-27-29. $200-$300. Also, $150 (A, 1975).

FORD, Charles Henri. *The Garden of Disorder and Other Poems.* Boards and cloth. London, (1938). First edition. One of 30 signed. In dust jacket. $150-$175.

FORD, Charles Henri. *A Pamphlet of Sonnets.* Drawing by Pavel Tchelitchew. Printed wrappers. Majorca, 1936. First edition. One of 50 signed by Ford and Tchelitchew. $75-$125.

FORD, Charles Henri, and Tyler, Parker. *The Young and Evil.* Wrappers. Paris, (1933). First edition. $75-$100.

FORD, Ford Madox. See Conrad, Joseph, and Hueffer, Ford Madox. (Note: Ford changed his name from Hueffer to Ford in 1919.) Also see *The Imagist Anthology.*

FORD, Ford Madox. *Joseph Conrad: A Personal Remembrance.* Frontispiece, 2 other plates. Green cloth. London, 1924. First edition. In dust jacket. $50-$60.

FORD, Ford Madox. *Last Post.* Cloth. London, (1928). First English edition. In dust jacket. $100.

FORD, Ford Madox. *Mr. Bosphorus and the Muses.* Illustrated by Paul Nash. Half cloth. London, (1923). First edition. One of 70. In dust jacket. $250-$350. Ordinary issue: In dust jacket. $50-$75.

FORD, Ford Madox. *New Poems.* Cloth. New York, 1927. One of 325 signed. In glassine dust jacket. $135.

FORD, Ford Madox. *New York Is Not America.* Cloth. London, 1927. First edition. In dust jacket. $75-$100. (New York, 1927.) First American edition. In dust jacket. $25-$35.

FORD, Ford Madox. *No More Parades.* Cloth. London, (1925). First edition. In dust jacket. $50-$75.

FORD, Ford Madox. *Vive le Roy.* Cloth. London, (1937). First edition. In dust jacket. $50-$75.

FORD, Ford Madox Hueffer. *Women & Men.* Wrappers. Paris, 1923. Three Mountains Press. First edition. One of 300. $250-$300.

FORD, Henry Chapman. *Etchings of the Franciscan Missions of California.* 24 matted plates, unbound, 28 pp. of text, stitched, in half morocco portfolio. New York, 1883. Imperial edition. One of 50 signed by the artist. $2,000 and up.

FORD, Paul Leicester. *Franklin Bibliography.* Half leather. Brooklyn, 1889. First edition. One of 500. $75-$100.

FORD, Paul Leicester. *The Great K. & A. Robbery.* Pictorial cloth. New York, 1897. First edition, first issue, without "Train" before "Robbery" on title page. $75-$100.

FORD, Paul Leicester. *The Honorable Peter Stirling and What People Thought of Him.* Red cloth. New York, 1894. First edition, first state, with "Sterling" for "Stirling" on front cover. $75-$150.

FORD, Thomas. *A History of Illinois.* Cloth. Chicago, 1854. First edition, first issue, with "1814" (instead of "1818") in the extended title. $75-$100.

FORD, Thomas. *Message of the Governor . . . the Disturbances in Hancock County.* 21 pp., disbound. Springfield, Ill., 1844. $450. (On the Mormon disorders in Illinois.)

FORD, Webster. *Songs and Sonnets.* Cloth. Chicago, 1910. (By Edgar Lee Masters.) First edition. $100-$125.

*FORE and Aft: or, Leaves from the Life of an Old Sailor.* By "Webfoot." Illustrated. Cloth. Boston, 1871. (By W. D. Phelps.) First edition. $100-$150.

FOREMAN, Grant. *Advancing the Frontier*. Maps. Cloth. Norman, Okla., 1933. First edition. In dust jacket. $75-$100.

FOREMAN, Grant. *Indian Removal*. Cloth. Norman, 1932. First edition. In dust jacket. $100-$150.

FOREMAN, Grant. *Indians and Pioneers*. Map, 8 plates. Cloth. New Haven, 1930. First edition. In dust jacket. $75-$100.

FOREMAN, Grant. *Pioneer Days in the Early Southwest*. Folding map. Cloth. Cleveland, 1926. First edition. $100-$150.

FOREMAN, Grant (editor). *Indian Justice*. Cloth. Harlow, Okla., 1934. (By John Payne.) First edition. In dust jacket. $75-$100.

*FOREST and Stream Fables*. Sewed. New York, (1886). (By Rowland Evans Robinson.) First edition. $150. Author's first published work.

FORESTER, Frank. See Forrester, Frank; Herbert, Henry William; Herbert, W. H.

FORESTER, Frank. *American Game in Its Seasons*. Illustrated by the author. Cloth. New York, 1853. (By Henry William Herbert.) First edition. $100-$125.

FORESTER, Frank. *The Complete Manual for Young Sportsmen*. Illustrated by the author. Cloth. New York, 1856. (By Henry William Herbert.) First edition. $100-$150.

FORESTER, Frank. *The Deerstalkers*. Printed wrappers. Philadelphia, 1849. (By Henry William Herbert.) First edition. $500-$600.

FORESTER, Frank. *Field Sports in the United States, and the British Provinces of America*. 2 vols., green cloth. London, 1848. (By Henry William Herbert.) First edition, first issue, with "Provinces of America" on title page (changed later to "Provinces of North America"). $100-$150. New York, 1849. 2 vols., green cloth. First American edition, first issue, with "Ruffed Grouse" frontispiece. (Issued as *Frank Forester's Field Sports of the United States, etc.*) $100-$150.

FORESTER, Frank. *Frank Forester and His Friends*. 3 vols., salmon cloth. London, 1849. (By Henry William Herbert.) First edition. $100-$150.

FORESTER, Frank. *Frank Forester's Fish and Fishing of the United States and British Provinces of North America*. Illustrated by the author. Blue cloth. London, 1849. (By Henry William Herbert.) First English edition. (Note: Possibly issued simultaneously with the American first edition, according to Blanck.) $100-$150. New York, 1850 (actually 1849). Blue cloth. First American edition. $100-$125. New York, 1850. Second American edition, with bound sheets of the *Supplement* of 1850 bound in. (See Forester, *Supplement*.) $75-$100.

FORESTER, Frank. *Frank Forester's Fugitive Sporting Sketches*. Edited by Will Wildwood (Fred E. Pond). Cloth or wrappers. Westfield, Wis., 1879. (By Henry William Herbert.) First edition. Wrappers: $150-$250. Cloth: $100-$150.

FORESTER, Frank. *Frank Forester's Horse and Horsemanship of the United States and British Provinces of North America*. Plates, pedigree tables. 2 vols., purple cloth. New York, 1857. (By Henry William Herbert.) First edition. $100-$150.

FORESTER, Frank. *Hints to Horse-Keepers*. Frontispiece, 23 plates. Cloth. New York, 1859. (By Henry William Herbert.) First edition. $75-$125.

FORESTER, Frank. *The Hitchcock Edition of Frank Forester*. 4 vols., cloth. New York, 1930. (By Henry William Herbert.) Derrydale Press. First edition. $150-$200.

FORESTER, Frank. *My Shooting Box*. Frontispiece, 2 plates. Cloth. Philadelphia, 1846. (By Henry William Herbert.) First edition, first state, with ads dated May, 1845, on page 180 and "mattter" for "matter" in last line of page 35. $400-$450. Also, in morocco, $130 (A, 1971); $220 (A, 1962).

FORESTER, Frank. *Supplement to Frank Forester's Fish and Fishing*. Frontispiece. Cloth. New York, 1850. (By Henry William Herbert.) First edition. $75-$100.

FORESTER, Frank. *Trouting Along the Catasauqua.* Boards. New York, 1927. (By Henry William Herbert.) First edition. One of 423. In dust jacket. $150-$200.

FORESTER, Frank. *The Warwick Woodlands.* Printed tan-yellow wrappers. Philadelphia, 1845. (By Henry William Herbert.) First edition. $1,000 and up. Rebound, $500 and up. New York, 1851. Illustrated. Cloth, or printed wrappers. Second edition. Wrappers: $300-$500. Cloth: $75-$100. New York, 1934. Derrydale Press. Leatherette. $100-$150.

FORESTER, Harry. *Ocean Jottings from England to British Columbia.* Cloth. Vancouver, 1891. $75-$100.

FORNEY, Col. John W. *What I Saw in Texas.* (Cover title.) Map and plates. 92 pp., pictorial wrappers. Philadelphia, (1872). First edition. $250-$350. Second edition. $200-$300.

FORREST, Lieut. Col. Charles R. *A Picturesque Tour Along the Rivers Ganges and Jumna, in India.* 24 colored plates, colored vignettes. Cloth, or leather. London, 1824. First edition. $750-$1,000, possibly more. Also, rubbed and rebacked, $654 (A, 1975).

FORRESTER, Frank. *Fishing with Hook and Line.* Printed wrappers. New York, (1858). (By Henry William Herbert.) First edition, with Brother Jonathan imprint. $1,000 and up. Also, $900 (A, 1962)—"one of two known copies."

FORSTER, E. M. *Abinger Harvest.* Plain brown printed wrappers. London, (1936). First edition. Advance proof copy, including "A Flood in the Office," later eliminated. $300-$400. Also, $125 (A, 1972). First published edition, first issue, with "A Flood in the Office" included: Cloth. In dust jacket. $100-$150.

FORSTER, E. M. *Alexandria: A History and a Guide.* Folding map in pocket at rear. Boards. Alexandria, Egypt, 1922. First edition. $150-$225. Alexandria, 1938. Boards. Second edition. One of 250 signed. $100-$150. Also, $52 (A, 1975); $100 (A, 1970); $120 (A, 1969).

FORSTER, E. M. *Anonymity: An Enquiry.* Illustrated boards. London, 1925. Hogarth Press. First edition. $50-$60.

FORSTER, E. M. *Aspects of the Novel.* Dark-red cloth. London, 1927. First edition. In dust jacket. $75-$100.

FORSTER, E. M. *The Celestial Omnibus and Other Stories.* Brown cloth. London, 1911. First edition. $50-$60.

FORSTER, E. M. *Desmond McCarthy.* Gray wrappers. Stanford, 1952. First edition. One of 72. $100.

FORSTER, E. M. *The Eternal Moment and Other Stories.* Red cloth. London, 1928. First edition. In dust jacket. $60-$80.

FORSTER, E. M. *Goldsworthy Lowes Dickinson.* Plain wrappers. London, 1934. First edition. Advance proof copy. $60. First published edition: Cloth. In dust jacket. $25.

FORSTER, E. M. *The Government of Egypt.* Wrappers, paper label. London, (1920.) (Official recommendations of a Labour committee, 1919.) First edition. $75-$100. Also, $70 (A, 1972); $62 (A, 1971).

FORSTER, E. M. *Goldsworthy Lowes Dickinson.* Plain wrappers. London, 1934. First edition. Advance proof copy. $60. First published edition: Cloth. In dust jacket. $25.

FORSTER, E. M. *Howard's End.* Cloth. London, 1910. First edition. In dust jacket. $75-$100.

FORSTER, E. M. *The Longest Journey.* Cloth. London, 1907. First edition. In dust jacket. $75-$100.

FORSTER, E. M. *A Passage to India.* Red cloth. London, 1924. First edition. In dust jacket. $300-$400. Without jacket, $100-$200, possibly more. Another issue: Boards and cloth. One of 200 signed. In slipcase. $500-$600. Also, $450 (A, 1974).

FORSTER, E. M. *Pharos and Pharillon.* Boards. Richmond, England, 1923. Hogarth Press.

First edition. $100-$125. New York, 1923. Orange cloth. First American edition. In dust jacket. $25-$35.

FORSTER, E. M. *A Room with a View.* Cloth. London, 1908. First edition. In dust jacket. $40-$50.

FORSTER, E. M. *Sinclair Lewis Interprets America.* (Cover title.) 10 pp. stapled, self-wrappers. (Cambridge, Mass., 1932.) First edition. One of 100. $65-$85.

FORSTER, E. M. *The Story of the Siren.* Wrappers. Richmond, 1920. Hogarth Press. First edition. (500 copies printed.) $200-$250.

FORSTER, E. M. *Where Angels Fear to Tread.* Cloth. Edinburgh, 1905. First edition, first issue, with this title not mentioned in ads at back. In dust jacket. $200-$300. Second issue, with title in ads. Lacking jacket, $120 (A, 1972). Author's first book. New York, 1920. Black cloth. First American edition. In dust jacket. $35-$50.

FORSYTH, James W., and Grant, F. D. *Report of an Expedition up the Yellowstone River, Made in 1875.* Folding map. 17 pp., wrappers. Washington, 1875. $100-$200.

*FORT Braddock Letters.* Boards and calf. Worcester, Mass., 1827. (By John G. C. Brainard.) $50-$75.

FORT, Charles. *The Book of the Damned.* Cloth. New York, 1919. First edition. In dust jacket. $75-$100.

FORT, Charles. *Lo!* Cloth. Illustrated by Alexander King. New York, (1931). First edition. In dust jacket. $35-$50.

FORT, Charles. *The Outcast Manufacturers.* Cloth. New York, 1909. First edition. $75-$100. Author's first book.

*FORTUNES of Colonel Torlogh O'Brien (The).* 10 monthly parts, wrappers. Dublin, 1847. (By Joseph Sheridan Le Fanu.) First edition. $200-$250. First book edition: Cloth. $100.

*FORTUNES of Nigel (The).* 3 vols., boards, paper labels. Edinburgh, 1822. (By Sir Walter Scott.) First edition. $150-$250. Also, $175 (A, 1974).

*FORTUNES of Perkin Warbeck (The).* 3 vols., boards, cloth spine, printed labels. London, 1830. (By Mary Wollstonecraft Shelley.) First edition. $150-$250.

FOSS, Sam Walter. *The Song of the Library Staff.* Illustrated by Merle Johnson. Stapled. New York, 1906. First edition. $30-$40.

FOSTER, Charles. *The Gold Placers of California.* Map. Printed wrappers. Akron, Ohio, 1849. First edition. $3,000 and up. Also, $1,750 (A, 1968).

FOSTER, The Rev. G. L. *The Past of Ypsilanti.* 48 pp., printed wrappers. Detroit, 1857. First edition. $100-$125.

FOSTER, George G. (editor). *The Gold Regions of California.* Frontispiece map. Printed wrappers. New York, 1848. $300-$500. London, (1849). $100-$150.

FOSTER, George G. *New-York by Gaslight.* Wrappers. New York, 1850. First edition. $35-$50.

FOSTER, Isaac. *The Foster Family, California Pioneers.* Illustrated. Cloth. (Santa Barbara, 1925.) $100-$150.

FOSTER, James S. *Advantages of Dakota Territory.* 51 pp., wrappers. Yankton, 1873. First edition. $1,000-$1,500.

FOSTER, James S. *Outlines of History of the Territory of Dakota and Emigrant's Guide to the Free Lands of the Northwest.* Folding map. 127 pp., wrappers. Yankton, 1870. First edition. $2,500 and up. Also, $950 (A, 1968).

FOSTER, Myles Birket. *A Day in a Child's Life.* Illustrated by Kate Greenaway. Glazed boards and cloth. (London), no date. First edition. $150.

FOUNTAIN, Albert J. *Bureau of Immigration of the Territory of New Mexico: Report of Dona Ana County.* 34 pp., wrappers. Santa Fe, 1882. $150-$175.

FOUQUÉ, F. H. K. de La Motte. *Undine.* Illustrated in color by Arthur Rackham. Vellum with ties. London, 1909. Limited edition, signed. $300-$350. New York, 1930. Limited Editions Club. Boxed. $30-$40.

*FOUR Gospels of the Lord Jesus Christ (The).* Decorations by Eric Gill. Half pigskin. Waltham Saint Lawrence, 1931. Golden Cockerel Press. One of 500. In slipcase. $1,400-$1,750. Another issue: One of 12 on vellum. $29,000 and $12,000 (A, 1977).

*FOURTEENTH Anniversary of the Society of California Pioneers.* Wrappers. San Francisco, 1864. $100-$125.

FOWLES, John. *The Collector.* Boards. Boston, (1963). First American edition. In dust jacket. $35. Author's first novel.

FOX, John, Jr. *A Cumberland Vendetta and Other Stories.* Illustrated. Cloth. New York, 1896. First edition. $40-$50. Author's first book.

FOX, John, Jr. *The Little Shepherd of Kingdom Come.* Illustrated by F. C. Yohn. Smooth red cloth, paper label. New York, 1903. First edition, first issue, with "laugh" for "lap" in line 14, page 61. One of 100 signed by Fox and Yohn. $50-$60. Trade edition: Ribbed red cloth. $25. New York, 1931. Illustrated by N. C. Wyeth. Half vellum. One of 512 signed by Wyeth. $300-$400.

FOX, John, Jr. *The Trail of the Lonesome Pine.* Red cloth. New York, 1908. First edition, first state, with Scribner seal on copyright page. $35.

FOX, Lady Mary. *Account of an Expedition to the Interior of New Holland.* Contemporary leather. London, 1837. First edition. $300.

*FRA Luca de Pacioli of Borgo San Sepolcro.* Portrait, plates. Boards, vellum spine. New York, 1933. Grolier Club. One of 390. $300-$400. Also, $325 (A, 1975).

*FRANCE, Its King, Court, and Government.* By an American. Cloth. New York, 1840. (By Lewis Cass.) First edition. $50-$75.

FRANCHERE, Gabriel. *Narrative of a Voyage to the Northwest Coast of America, etc.* 3 plates. Cloth. New York, 1854. First edition in English. $250-$300.

FRANCHERE, Gabriel. *Relation d'un Voyage à la Côte du Nord-Ouest de l'Amérique Septentrionale, dans les Années 1810-1814.* Contemporary calf. Montreal, 1820. First edition. $1,000-$5,000.

FRANCIS, Grant R. *Old English Drinking Glasses.* 72 plates. Buckram. London, 1926. In dust jacket. $100-$125.

FRANCIS of Assisi, St. *I Fioretti del Glorioso Poverello di Cristo S. Francesco di Assisi.* 54 woodcuts. Vellum. London, 1922. Ashendene Press. One of 240. $350-$450.

FRANCIS of Assisi, St. *Laudes Creaturarum.* London, 1910. Doves Press. One of 250. $250-$300.

FRANCIS of Assisi, St. *Un Mazzetto Scelto di Certi Fioretti del Glorioso Poverello di Cristo San Francesco di Assisi insieme col Cantico al sole del Medesimo.* 11 woodcuts. Folio, boards. London, 1904. Ashendene Press. One of 125 on paper. $400-$525. Another issue: One of 25 on vellum. $1,200-$1,500.

*FRANCIS Parkman.* 4 pp., leaflet. (Boston, 1894.) (By Oliver Wendell Holmes.) First edition. (About 50 to 77 printed.) $100-$150.

*FRANK Fairleigh; or Scenes from the Life of a Private Pupil.* Illustrated by George Cruikshank. 15 parts, blue-green wrappers. London, 1850. (By Frank E. Smedley.) First edition, first issue, with dated title page. $150-$200. Backs of three wrappers incorrect, two inserts lacking, $100. Another issue: Cloth. $35-$50.

*FRANKENSTEIN; or The Modern Prometheus.* 3 vols., boards, paper labels. London,

1818.(By Mary Wollstonecraft Shelley.) First edition. $3,000 and up. Also, rebound in half leather, lacking half titles, some ad leaves, and with one leaf torn, $722 (A, 1975). New York, 1934. Limited Editions Club. Boxed. $40-$50.

FRANKS, David. *The New-York Directory.* 82 pp., cloth. New York, 1786. First edition. $4,000-$6,000. Also $1,100 (A, 1969). (Note: There is an earlier auction record of $2,500.) New York, 1909. Folding map. Printed wrappers. Reprint. $75-$100.

FRAZER, Sir James George. *Totemism.* Cloth. Edinburgh, 1887. First edition. $75-$100. Author's first book.

FREDERIC, Harold. *The Damnation of Theron Ware.* Dark-green cloth. Chicago, 1896. First edition. $50-$125.

FREDERIC, Harold. *The Deserter and Other Stories.* Cloth. Boston, (1898). First edition. $60-$70.

FREDERIC, Harold. *In the Valley.* 16 plates by Howard Pyle. Cloth. New York, 1890. First edition. $75-$125.

FREDERIC, Harold. *Seth's Brother's Wife.* Tan cloth. New York, 1887. First edition, first issue, with 1886 copyright and no ads. $100-$135. Author's first book.

FREDERICK, J. George (editor). *Artists' and Writers' Chap Book.* Wrappers. (New York), 1933. First edition. $30-$50.

FREDERICK, J. V. *Ben Holladay, the Stagecoach King.* Folding map. Cloth. Glendale, Calif., 1940. First edition. $50-$75. Also, $65 (A, 1971).

*FREE-and-Easy Songbook (The).* Plates. Davy Crockett portrait on title page. Cloth. Philadelphia, 1834. $200-$300.

FREEMAN, George D. *Midnight and Noonday.* Printed boards and cloth. Caldwell, Kan., 1890. First edition. $150-$200. Also, $125 (A, 1968). Caldwell, 1892. Red cloth. Second edition. $50-$60.

FREEMAN, James W. See *Prose and Poetry of the Live Stock Industry.*

FREMAUX, Leon J. *New Orleans Characters.* 17 color plates. Folio, cloth and morocco. (New Orleans), 1876. First edition. $400-$600.

FRÉMONT, John Charles. *Geographical Memoir Upon Upper California.* Senate Misc. Doc. No. 148. Folding map (not in all copies). 67 pp., wrappers. Washington, 1848, First edition, with map. $150-$300.

FRÉMONT, John Charles. *Narrative of the Exploring Expedition ot the Rocky Mountains, in the Year 1842, etc.* Folding map by Rufus B. Sage, 2 plates. Cloth. Syracuse, 1847. (First publication of the famous Sage map.) $750-$1,000.

FRÉMONT, John Charles. *Oregon and California: The Exploring Expedition to the Rocky Mountains, Oregon and California.* 2 portraits, 2 plates. Cloth. Buffalo, 1849. $75. (One of several reprints of *Report of the Exploring Expedition.)*

FRÉMONT, John Charles. *Report of the Exploring Expedition to the Rocky Mountains in the Year 1842.* Senate edition. 22 plates, 5 maps, one folding. Cloth. Washington, 1845. First edition. $300. (House edition, same date.)

FRÉMONT, John Charles. *Report on an Exploration of the Country Lying Between the Missouri and the Rocky Mountains, etc.* Senate Doc. 243. 6 plates, folding map. Wrappers. Washington, 1843. First edition. $200-$300.

FRENCH, Capt. W. J. *Wild Jim, the Texas Cowboy and Saddle King.* Portrait. 76 pp., wrappers. Antioch, Ill., 1890. First edition. $400-$600.

FRENCH, William. *Some Recollections of a Western Ranchman.* Gray cloth. London, (1927). First edition. $150-$250. New York, (1928). First American edition. In dust jacket. $250-$300.

FREUD, Sigmund. *Totem and Taboo.* Cloth. New York, 1918. First edition in English. $100-$175.

FREYTAS, Father Nicholas de. *The Expedition of Don Diego Dionisio de Penaloza, from Santa Fe to the River Mischipi and Quiviha in 1662.* Edited by John G. Shea. Boards. (New York), 1882. $100-$200.

FRIEDMAN. I. I. *The Lucky Number.* Cloth. Chicago, 1896. First edition. $50-$75. Author's first book.

FRIEDMAN, I. K. *The Radical.* Cloth. New York, 1907. First edition. In dust jacket. $50-$75.

FRINK, F. W. *A Record of Rice County, Minnesota, in 1868.* 24 pp., wrappers. Faribault, Minn., 1868. First edition. $100-$200. Faribault, 1871. Second edition. $75-$85.

FRINK, Margaret A. *Journal of the Adventures of a Party of California Gold-Seekers.* 2 frontispieces. Cloth. (Oakland, 1897.) First edition. $400-$600.

FROISSART, Sir John. *Chronicles of England, France, Spain, and the Adjoining Countries.* Translated by Thomas Johnes. Illustrations illuminated in gold and colors by H. Noel Humphreys. 2 vols., half red morocco. London, 1852. $150-$200.

*FROM Ocean to Ocean in a Winton.* Illustrated. 36 pp., wrappers. Cleveland, 1903. Winton Motor Carriage Co. $30-$50.

FROST, A. B. *A Book of Drawings.* Illustrated. Folio, boards. New York, 1904. First edition. $75-$100.

FROST, A. B. *Sports and Games in the Open.* 53 color plates. Folio, pictorial cloth portfolio. New York, 1899. First edition. $250-$350.

FROST, John. *History of the State of California.* Contemporary morocco. Auburn, Calif., 1850. First edition. $100-$200.

FROST, Robert. See Robinson, Edwin Arlington, Schreiber, Georges. Also see *Dartmouth Verse, 1925; Poems of Child Labor.*

FROST, Robert. *Away!* Wood engravings by Stefan Martin. Pictorial wrappers. New York, 1958. First edition. One of 185 with Al Edwards imprint. $50-$60.

FROST, Robert. *A Boy's Will.* Bronze, or brown, pebbled cloth, lettered in gilt. London, 1913. First edition, first state, (in 2 variant bindings—the bronze and brown), with all edges untrimmed. $850-$1,200. Also, $950 (A, 1972); $700 (A, 1968). (Special note concerning other later copies: This book offers a classic example of bibliographical confusion—some call it nitpicking—and controversy, which is what makes book collecting a matter of unending fascination for dedicated collectors. The bibliographers are still sorting out the unresolved mysteries of this book in its various forms. Hence any 1913 copy is a "must" for the collector. Following are three additional "states" of the book as defined by authorities on Frost books.) Second state, (first issue, second binding), white, or cream, parchment (vellum), stamped in red. Value: $600 and up. Third state, (second issue, third binding), buff (cream) printed wrappers, with horizontal rule at top of the "A" in title. Value: $450 and up. Also, soiled, $150 (A, 1977). Fourth state, (second issue, fourth binding?), wrappers, plain "A." Value: $250 and up. Same issue: One of 135 signed by Frost. $300 and up. Also, $200 (A, 1977). Author's first book. New York, 1915. Cloth. First American edition, first issue, with "aind" for "and" in last line of page 14. In dust jacket. $100-$150. Second issue, spelling error corrected. In dust jacket. $35-$50.

FROST, Robert. *Collected Poems.* Tan buckram. New York, 1930. Random House. First collected edition. One of 1,000 signed. In dust jacket. $100-$125. Trade issue, later: New York, (1930). Holt. Portrait. Cloth. First edition (so stated). $50-$60. New York, 1939. Title page woodcut. Decorated cloth. In dust jacket. $35-$50. New York, 1949. Cloth. In dust jacket. $35-$50.

FROST, Robert. *Complete Poems.* Cloth. New York, 1949. Holt. First edition. One of 500 signed. In dust jacket. $200-$250.

FROST, Robert. *The Complete Poems of Robert Frost.* Illustrated. 2 vols., blue-gray cloth. New York, 1950. Limited Editions Club. One of 1,500 signed. Boxed. $300.

FROST, Robert. *A Considerable Speck.* Folio, self-wrappers. No place, (1939). First edition. One of fewer than 100 on Dard Hunter paper, printed by the junior Dard Hunter. $400-$500. Also, $375 (A, 1977).

FROST, Robert. *The Cow's in the Corn.* Decorated boards, spine label. Gaylordsville, N.Y., 1929. Slide Mountain Press. First edition. One of 91 signed. With or without errata slip. $400-$500. Also, $275 (A, 1977); $275 (A, 1969), $325 (A, 1968).

FROST, Robert. *A Further Range.* Tan cloth. New York, (1936). First edition. One of 803 signed. In slipcase. $75-$125. Trade issue, later: Red cloth. First edition (so stated). (4,100 printed.) In dust jacket. $15-$20.

FROST, Robert. *The Gold Hesperidee.* 8 pp., wrappers. (Cortland, N.Y., 1935.) Bibliophile Press. First edition, first issue, with "A" on copyright page and with next to last line on page 7 unturned (second issue has the line turned and carried over). $100-$150. Second issue. $75-$100.

FROST, Robert. *Greece.* Self-wrappers. Chicago, (1948). Black Rose Press. First edition. One of 47. In mailing envelope. $300-$350. Also, $250 (A, 1977).

FROST, Robert. *Hard Not to Be King.* Cloth. New York, 1951. First edition. One of 300 signed. $75-$150.

FROST, Robert. *In the Clearing.* Buckram, New York, (1962). First edition. One of 1,500 signed. Boxed. $75-$125. Trade issue: Cloth. In dust jacket. $20-$25.

FROST, Robert. *The Lone Striker.* Printed wrappers in envelope. (New York, 1933.) First edition. No. 8 in the "Borzoi Chap Books." $40-$50.

FROST, Robert. *The Lovely Shall Be Choosers.* 6 pp., printed brown wrappers. New York, 1929. First edition. One of 475. $100-$125.

FROST, Robert. *A Masque of Mercy.* Half cloth. New York, (1947). First edition. One of 751 signed. Boxed. $75-$100. Trade issue: Blue cloth. In dust jacket. $15.

FROST, Robert. *A Masque of Reason.* Half cloth. New York, (1948). First edition. One of 800 signed. Boxed. $75-$100. Trade issue: Blue cloth. In dust jacket. $15.

FROST, Robert. *Mountain Interval.* Blue cloth. New York, (1916). First edition, first issue, with verses 6 and 7, page 88, repeated. In dust jacket. $75-$125. New York, 1921. Bust portrait. Boards. Second edition. In dust jacket. $20-$25.

FROST, Robert. *Neither Out Far nor in Deep.* Wrappers. (Christmas token.) (New York), 1935. First edition. Spiral Press. $35-$50.

FROST, Robert. *New Hampshire: A Poem with Notes and Grace Notes.* Woodcuts. Dark-green boards and cloth. New York, 1923. First trade edition. In dust jacket. $35-$50. Another issue: One of 350 signed. In glassine dust jacket. Boxed. $200-$250. Also, jacket and box worn, $150 (A, 1977). London, 1924. Boards. First English edition. $30-$40. Hanover, N.H., 1955. New Dresden Press. Buckram and boards. First separate edition of title poem. One of 750 signed. $50-$75.

FROST, Robert. *North of Boston.* Green buckram. London, (1914). First edition, first state, gold lettering on front cover and spine, blind-stamped rule all around front cover. In dust jacket. $800-$1,000 and up. Also, writing on flyleaf, $700 (A, 1969); $850 (A, 1968); inscribed, $1,050 (A, 1968); lacking jacket, spine dull, inscribed by Frost, $650 (A, 1977). Second state, lettered in blind on front. $400-$500. Also, no jacket, spine faded, inscribed, $375 (A, 1977). Third state, blue cloth, black lettering. $300-$400. Also, $196 (A, 1964). Fourth state, green cloth, blind rule at top and bottom of front cover. $300-$400. Fifth state, leaves 5⅜ by 7¾ inches. $200. Also, $140 (A, 1971). Other binding variants also noted, with A-range in the 1960's and 1970's up to $300. Also, inscribed copies in all bindings at higher prices than noted here. (Frost signed a great many books!) New York, 1914. Brown boards, cloth back. First American edition, made up of English sheets with a new title page tipped in on a stub. In dust jacket. $200-$300. New York, 1915. Linen. Second American edition (first to be printed in America). In dust jacket. $100-$150.

FROST, Robert. *Our Hold on the Planet.* Wrappers. (Christmas token.) (Various places, 1940.) First edition. $35-$40.

FROST, Robert. *Selected Poems.* Green decorated boards and cloth. New York, 1923. First edition, with "March, 1923" on copyright page. In dust jacket. $75-$100. London, (1923). Cloth. First English edition. In dust jacket. $35-$50.

FROST, Robert. *Steeple Bush.* Blue boards and cloth. New York, 1947. First edition. One of 751 signed. Boxed. $75-$125. Trade issue: Cloth. In dust jacket. $30-$40.

FROST, Robert. *Three Poems.* Wrappers. Hanover, N.H., (1935). First edition. (125 copies printed.) $150-$200.

FROST, Robert. *To a Young Wretch.* Wrappers. (Christman token.) (Various places, 1937.) First edition. $75-$100. Also, $62.80 (A, 1968).

FROST, Robert. *Triple Plate.* Wrappers. (Christmas token.) (Eight varying places, 1939.) First edition. $50-$60.

FROST, Robert. *Robert Frost: Two Letters Written on His Undergraduate Days at Dartmouth College in 1892.* Wrappers, paper label, stapled. Hanover, 1931. First edition. (10 copies printed.) $3,000 and up. Also, loose in wrappers, $2,600 (A, 1977); inscribed, $3,750 (A, 1975).

FROST, Robert. *Two Tramps in Mud Time.* Wrappers. (Christmas token.) (Various places, 1934.) First edition. $50-$60.

FROST, Robert. *A Way Out.* Salmon-colored boards, cloth spine. New York, 1929. Harbor Press. First edition. One of 485 signed. In glassine dust jacket. $100-$150.

FROST, Robert. *West-Running Brook.* Green boards and cloth. New York, (1928). First (trade) edition. In dust jacket, $40-$60. Another issue: 4 plates signed by J.J. Lankes. Boards. One of 1,000 signed. Without "First Edition" on copyright page. In glassine jacket. Boxed. $125-$150.

FROST, Robert. *A Witness Tree.* Portrait. Decorated boards and cloth. New York, 1942. First edition. One of 735 signed. Boxed. $100-$125. Trade issue: Blue cloth. In dust jacket. $25-$35.

*FRUGAL Housewife (The).* By the Author of *Hobomok.* Boards. Boston, 1829. (By Lydia Maria Child.) First edition. $100-$150.

FRY, Frederick. *Fry's Traveler's Guide, and Descriptive Journal of the Great North Western Territories.* Cloth. Cincinnati, 1865. First edition. $500-$600.

FRY, James B. *Army Sacrifices.* Cloth. New York, 1879. First edition. $100-$150.

FRY, Roger. *Giovanni Bellini.* Illustrated. Boards and cloth. London, 1899. First edition. $75-$100. Author's first book.

*FUGITIVE Pieces.* 66 pp., green-gray wrappers. No place, (1806). (By George Gordon Noel, Lord Byron.) First edition. Price: In the thousands. All except four copies were destroyed, according to De Ricci. London, 1886. Vellum. Facsimile edition. One of 100. $75-$100. Another issue: One of 7 on Japan paper. $200-$250.

*FUGITIVES, An Anthology of Verse.* Decorated paper boards, cloth back. New York, (1928). First edition. $75-$125.

FULKERSON, H. S. *Random Recollections of Early Days in Mississippi.* Printed wrappers. Vicksburg, 1885. First edition. $300-$500. Cloth: $200.

FULLER, C. L. *Pocket Map and Descriptive Outline History of the Black Hills of Dakota and Wyoming.* Folding map. 56 pp., stiff wrappers. Rapid City, 1887. First edition. $600-$850.

FULLER, Emeline. *Left by the Indians*. (Cover title.) Portrait. 41 pp., printed wrappers. (Mt. Vernon, Iowa, 1892.) First edition. $150-$200. New York, 1936. Facsimile reprint. $10-$15.

FULLER, Henry Blake. See Page, Stanton.

FULLER, Henry Blake. *Bertram Cope's Year*. Cloth. Chicago, 1919. First edition. $75-$150. Also, $100 (A, 1975).

FULLER, Henry Blake. *The Cliff-Dwellers*. Cloth. New York, 1893. First edition, first issue, with author's name on front cover as "Henry Fuller." $50. (Later, "Henry B. Fuller.")

FULLER, S. Margaret. *Woman in the 19th Century*. Wrappers or cloth. New York, 1845. First edition. $75-$100.

FULLMER, John S. *Assassination of Joseph and Hyrum Smith, the Prophet and the Patriarch of the Church of Jesus Christ of Latter-day Saints*. 40 pp., half leather. Liverpool, 1855. First edition. $200-$300.

FULMORE, Z. T. *The History and Geography of Texas as Told in County Names*. Cloth. (Austin, 1915.) First edition. $75-$200.

FULTON, A. R. *The Red Men of Iowa*. 26 plates. Cloth. Des Moines, 1882. First edition. $100-$200.

FULTON, Robert. *Torpedo War, and Submarine Explosions*. 5 plates. Cloth. New York, 1810. First edition. $1,250-$1,500. Also, ex-library copy, $1,000 (A, 1977).

FUNKHOUSER, W. D. *Wild Life in Kentucky*. Cloth. Frankfort, 1925. $75-$85.

FURBER, George C. *The Twelve Months Volunteer*. Cloth. Cincinnati, 1848. First edition. $150-$200.

# G

GADDIS, William. *The Recognitions*. Cloth. New York, (1955). First edition. In dust jacket. $100-$125. Advance copy: Wrappers. $250-$300. Author's first book.

GAG, Wanda. *Millions of Cats*. Boards. New York, 1928. First trade edition. In dust jacket. $100-$125. Another issue. One of 250 signed and with a signed engraving. Boxed. $300.

GAGE, Thomas. *The Correspondence of Thomas Gage*. Edited by Clarence Edwin Carter. 2 vols., boards. New Haven, 1931-33. First edition. $100.

GAINE, Hugh. *The Journals of Hugh Gaine, Printer*. Edited by Paul Leicester Ford. Plates. 2 vols., boards. New York, 1902. First edition. One of 350. $75-$100. Another issue: Cloth. One of 30 printed on Japan paper. $150-$175.

GAINES, Ernest J. *Catherine Carmier*. Cloth. New York, 1964. First edition. In dust jacket. $75. Author's first book.

GALE, George. *Upper Mississippi*. Frontispiece, maps, plates. Cloth. Chicago, 1867. First edition. $80-$100.

GALLAHER, James. *The Western Sketch-Book*. Plates. Cloth. Boston, 1850. First edition. $100-$200.

GALLATIN, Albert. *Considerations on the Currency and Banking System of the United States*. Wrappers. Philadelphia, 1831. First edition. $100-$125.

GALLATIN, Albert. *Letters of Albert Gallatin on the Oregon Question*. Stitched. Washington, 1846. First edition. $60-$75.

GALLATIN, Albert Eugene. *Art and the Great War*. Illustrated. Folio, full morocco. New York, 1919. First edition. One of 100, signed. Boxed. $150-$200. Also, $125 (A, 1974). Trade edition: Half cloth. $50-$75.

GALLATIN, Albert Eugene. *Portraits of Whistler*. 40 illustrations. Boards. New York, 1918. First edition. One of 250. Boxed. $75-$125. Trade edition: Half cloth. $50-$75.

GALLICO, Paul. *The Snow Goose*. Illustrated by Peter Scott, including 4 color plates. Morocco. London, 1946. One of 750 signed. $60-$125. Trade edition: In dust jacket. $35-$50.

GALSWORTHY, John. See Sinjohn, John.

GALSWORTHY, John. *Awakening*. Illustrated. Boards. London, (1920). First edition. In dust jacket. $35.

GALSWORTHY, John. *Caravan*. Green cloth. London, 1925. First edition. In dust jacket. $20-$25. Another (later) issue: Limp leather. One of 265 signed. $40-$50.

GALSWORTHY. John. *The Country House*. Green cloth. London, 1907. First edition, with publisher's windmill stamp in lower right corner of back cover. $35-$50.

GALSWORTHY, John. *The Dark Flower*. Dark-red cloth. London, 1913. First edition, first issue, with 22 pages of ads at end. In dust jacket. $50-$60.

GALSWORTHY, John. *The Forsyte Saga*. Folding genealogical table. Green cloth. London, 1922. First edition, first issue, with genealogical table pulling out to the right. In dust jacket. $100-$150. Another issue: Green limp leather. One of 275 signed. $150-$200.

GALSWORTHY, John. *The Full Moon: A Play in Three Acts.* Green wrappers. London, 1915. First edition, first issue, without the listing of cast on back leaf. $50.

GALSWORTHY, John. *The Inn of Tranquility.* Green buckram. London, 1912. First edition. In dust jacket. $20-$25.

GALSWORTHY, John. *The Island Pharisees.* Green cloth. London, 1904. First edition, first (unpublished) issue, with no mention of this title in publisher's list. $500 and up? No recent auction records, no copies noted in dealer catalogues. Also, $1,375 (A, 1930). First published edition. $35-$50. New York, 1904. Blue cloth. First American edition (750 made from English sheets). $25-$35.

GALSWORTHY, John. *The Land: A Plea.* Woodcut. 24 pp., sewed. London, (1918). First edition. One of 35. $50.

GALSWORTHY, John. *The Man of Property.* Green cloth. London, 1906. First edition, first issue, with broken bar of music on page 200. $100-$150.

GALSWORTHY, John. *A Modern Comedy.* Folding table. Full limp vellum. London, 1929. First edition. One of 1,030 signed. $60-$80. Trade edition: Cloth. In dust jacket. $10.

GALSWORTHY, John. *The Plays of John Galsworthy.* Green cloth. London, 1939. First edition. One of 1,275 signed. $50-$60.

GALSWORTHY, John. *The Silver Spoon.* Cloth. London, (1926). First edition. One of 265 signed. $40-$60. Trade edition: Cloth. In dust jacket. $15.

GALSWORTHY, John. *Swan Song.* Blue buckram. London, (1928). First edition. One of 525 signed. $35-$50. Trade edition: Cloth. In dust jacket. $15.

GALSWORTHY, John. *The White Monkey.* Cloth. London, 1924. First edition. In dust jacket. $10. London (1926). Buckram. One of 265 signed. $40-$60.

GALT, John. See Balwhidder, The Rev. Micah. Also see *The Provost; Ringan Gilhaize; The Steam-Boat.*

GALT, John. *The Bachelor's Wife.* Boards. Edinburgh, 1824. First edition. $100-$150.

GALT, John. *Lawrie Todd.* 3 vols., cloth. London, 1830. First edition. $150-$200. New York, 1830. 2 vols. in one, boards. First American edition. $100-$150.

GALTON, Francis. *Finger Prints.* Cloth. London, 1892. First edition. $200-$300. Also, rebound in calf, dampstained, $146 (A, 1976).

GALTON, Francis. *Hereditary Genius.* Folding table. Cloth. London, 1869. First edition. $350-$500.

*GAMEKEEPER at Home (The).* Cloth. London, 1878. (By Richard Jefferies.) First edition. $75-$100. London, 1880. $50-$60.

GANCONAGH. *John Sherman and Dhoya.* Gray cloth, lettered in blue; also in yellow wrappers, lettered in black. London, (1891). (By William Butler Yeats.) First edition. Cloth: $350-$500. Also, $312 (A, 1968). Wrappers: $250-$350. (Note: The cloth issue is scarcer than the one in wrappers. Most copies offered in recent years have been in poor condition.)

GANNETT, William C. *The House Beautiful.* With designs by Frank Lloyd Wright. Folio, half leather. River Forest, Ill., Winter, 1896-97. One of 90 signed by Wright and William Winslow, the publisher (Auvergne Press). $2,500 and up. (Note: Gannett's text first appeared in a pamphlet of 24 pages in Boston in 1895. The original spelled his name correctly.)

GANOE, W. A. *History of the United States Army.* Cloth. New York, 1924. First edition. $25-$35.

GANTT, E. W. *Address to the People of Arkansas.* 24 pp., sewed. Little Rock, 1863. First edition. $100-$125.

GARCES, Francisco. *On the Trail of the Spanish Pioneer.* Translated by Elliott Coues. Illustrated. 2 vols . cloth. New York, 1900. First edition. One of 950. $75-$100.

GARCÍA y CUBAS, Antonio. *Atlas Geografíco, Estadistico e Histórico de la República Mexicana.* 33 double-page maps in color. Folio, boards. Mexico, 1858. One of 300. $750-$1,500.

GARD, Wayne. *Along the Early Trails of the Southwest.* Illustrated. Half leather. Austin, 1969. First edition. One of 250 signed and with an extra set of color plates. $100-$200.

GARD, Wayne. *Sam Bass.* Illustrated. Cloth. Boston, 1936. First edition. In dust jacket. $75-$100.

GARDEN, Alexander. *Anecdotes of the Revolutionary War in America.* First Series. Boards. Charleston, 1822. First edition. $100-$150. Charleston, 1828. Boards. Second Series. First edition. $75-$100. Together. First and Second Series, fine copies: $350.

GARDINER, Abigail. *History of the Spirit Lake Massacre and the Captivity of Miss Abbie Gardner.* Portrait. Cloth. Des Moines, 1885. First edition. $50-$75.

GARDNER, Alexander: See *Photographic Sketch Book of the War.*

GARDNER, John. *Grendel.* Illustrated. Cloth. New York, 1971. First edition. In dust jacket. $35-$50.

GARDNER, John. *The Resurrection.* Cloth. (New York, 1966.) First edition. In dust jacket. $200-$250. Author's first book.

GARDNER, John. *The Wreckage of Agathon.* Cloth. New York, (1970). First edition. In dust jacket. $25-$35.

GARDNER, Ralph D. *Horatio Alger; or, The American Hero Era.* Illustrated. Cloth. Mendota, Ill., (1964). First edition. In dust jacket. $65-$75. Also, $40 (A, 1976).

GARLAND, Hamlin. *The Book of the American Indian.* Colored frontispiece and 34 plates by Frederic Remington. Folio, boards and cloth. New York, 1923. First edition (so stated). In dust jacket. $150-$250. Also, $150 (A, 1975).

GARLAND, Hamlin. *Cavanagh, Forest Ranger.* Frontispiece. Cloth. New York, 1910. First edition, with "Published March, 1910" on copyright page. $30-$40.

GARLAND, Hamlin. *The Light of the Star.* Frontispiece. Cloth. New York, 1904. First edition, with "Published May, 1904" on copyright page. $30-$40.

GARLAND, Hamlin. *Main-Travelled Roads.* Gray printed wrappers. Boston, 1891. First edition, first issue, with "Arena Library" at top and "First Thousand" at bottom of front cover. $100-$150. Another issue: Blue or gray cloth. $50-$75.

GARLAND, Hamlin. *A Member of the Third House.* Wrappers. Chicago, (1892). First edition. $35-$50. Another issue: Cloth. $25.

GARLAND, Hamlin. *The Mystery of the Buried Crosses.* Cloth. New York, 1939. First edition (so indicated on copyright page). $35-$50.

GARLAND, Hamlin. *A Pioneer Mother.* Wrappers. Chicago, 1922. First edition. One of 500. $35-$50. Another issue: Boards. One of 25. $50-$60.

GARLAND, Hamlin. *Prairie Songs.* Illustrated. Cloth. Cambridge, Mass., and Chicago, 1893. First edition. One of 110 de luxe copies. $150-$200. Trade edition: $40-$50.

GARLAND, Hamlin. *A Son of the Middle Border.* Cloth. New York, 1917. First edition. Limited, signed issue. $75-$125. Trade edition: In dust jacket. $25-$35.

GARLAND, Hamlin. *Under the Wheel: A Modern Play in Six Scenes.* Wrappers. Boston, 1890. First edition. $75-$100. Author's first book.

GARLAND, James. *Letter of James Garland to His Constituents.* 31 pp., sewed. (Washington, 1840.) $25.

GARMAN, K. E. *Moving-Picture Circus.* Illustrated. Movable book with 8 specially cut leaves on stiff cardboard. Chicago, 1909. $50-$75.

GARNEAU, Joseph, Jr. *Nebraska: Her Resources, Advantages and Development.* (Cover title.) 24 pp., printed wrappers. Omaha, 1893. First edition. $100-$200.

GARNER, James W. *Reconstruction in Mississippi.* Cloth. New York, 1901. First edition. $100-$150.

GARNETT, David. *The Grasshoppers Come.* Illustrated. Yellow buckram. London, 1931. First edition. One of 200 signed. $50-$60.

GARNETT, Richard. *The Twilight of the Gods and Other Tales.* Cloth. London, 1888. First edition. $40-$50.

GARRARD, Lewis H. *Wah-To-Yah, and the Taos Trail.* Decorated cloth. Cincinnati, 1850. First edition, first issue, with page 269 misnumbered 26. $600-$800. San Francisco, 1936. Grabhorn Press. Boards. One of 550. $65-$100.

GARRETT, Edmund H. (editor). *Victorian Songs.* Illustrated by Garrett. Vellum, gilt. Boston, 1895. First edition. One of 225. In parchment dust jacket. $50-$75.

GARRETT, Pat F. *The Authentic Life of Billy, The Kid.* Frontispiece and 5 plates. 137 pp., pictorial blue wrappers. Santa Fe, 1882. First edition, with ad inside back wrapper. $800-$1,000, possibly more.

GARVER, Will L. *Brother of the Third Degree.* Cloth. Boston, 1894. First edition. $40-$50.

GARVIE, James. *Abraham Lincoln toni kin, qa Aesop tawoyake kin. (Life of Abraham Lincoln and Aesop's Fables.)* 17 pp., printed wrappers. Santee [Indian] Agency, Neb., 1893. $150-$250.

GASCOYNE, David. *Poems 1937-1942.* Color illustrations. Pictorial boards. (London, 1943.) PL Editions. First edition. In dust jacket. $75-$100.

GASKELL, Elizabeth C. See *Cranford; Mary Barton; North and South.*

GASKELL, Elizabeth C. *The Life of Charlotte Brontë.* 2 vols., cloth. London, 1857. First edition. $100-$150.

GASKELL, Elizabeth C. *Sylvia's Lovers.* 3 vols., cloth. London, 1863. First edition. $100-$150.

GASS, Patrick. *Gass's Journal of the Lewis and Clark Expedition.* Edited by James K. Hosmer. Illustrated. Cloth. Chicago. 1904. $40-$50. Another issue: One of 75 on large paper. $100-$125.

GASS, Patrick. *A Journal of the Voyages and Travels of a Corps of Discovery, Under the Command of Capt. Lewis and Capt. Clark, etc.* Boards and leather. Pittsburgh, 1807. First edition. $600-$800. London, 1808. First English edition. $300-$350. Philadelphia, 1810. Calf. Second edition (without plates). $300-$350. Philadelphia, 1810. 6 plates added. Calf. Second illustrated edition (actually third edition). $300-$350. Paris, 1810. Map. Wrappers. First French edition. $350-$500. Philadelphia, 1812. 6 plates, folding map. Calf. Fourth edition. $350-$400. 75 on large paper. $100-$125.

GASS, William H. *Omensetter's Luck.* Cloth. (New York, 1966.) First edition. In dust jacket. $40-$50. Author's first book.

GASS, William H. *Willie Masters' Lonesome Wife.* Illustrated. Black cloth. (Evanston, 1968.) First edition. One of 100 (possibly more?) signed. $75-$85. Also, 300 copies, unsigned. $25. Also in wrappers. $7.50-$10.

GAUGUIN, Paul. *Intimate Journals.* Translated by Van Wyck Brooks. 27 illustrations by

Gauguin. Boards. New York, 1921. First edition in English. One of 999. $75-$100. London, 1923. 24 plates. Cloth. One of 530. $50-$75.

GAUGUIN, Paul. *Letters to Edouard Vollard and André Fontainas.* 10 woodcuts. Boards and cloth. San Francisco, 1943. Grabhorn Press. One of 250. $300-$400.

GAUTIER, Théophile. *One of Cleopatra's Nights.* Translated by Lafcadio Hearn. Cloth. New York, 1892. First American edition. $50-$75.

GAY, Frederick A. *For Gratuitous Distribution: Sketches of California.* (Cover title.) 16 pp., printed wrappers. (New York, 1848.) First edition. $250-$350.

GAYERRE (Gayarre?), Charles. *A Sketch of Gen. Jackson: By Himself.* 21 pp., printed wrappers. New Orleans, 1857. First edition. $150-$200.

GELBER, Jack. *The Connection.* Pictorial wrappers. New York, (1960). First edition. $30-$40.

*GEM (A): "The City of the Plains." Abilene: The Centre of the "Golden Belt."* Woodcuts. 64 pp., printed wrappers. Burlington, Iowa, 1887. First edition. $75-$100.

*GEM of the Rockies! (The): Manitou Springs.* Plates and tables. 23 pp., printed wrappers. Manitou Springs, Colo., (about 1885). First edition. $75-$100.

*GENERAL and Statistical Description of Pierce County (Wisconsin).* 9 pp., sewed. (Prescott, Wis., 1854.) First edition. $100-$150.

*GENERAL Instructions to Deputy Surveyors.* Folding diagram. 25 pp., sewed. Little Rock, 1837. First edition. $100-$150.

*GENERAL Orders Affecting the Volunteer Force: Adjutant General's Office, 1863.* Cloth. Washington, 1864. (Contains Lincoln presidential orders, including Emancipation Proclamation.) $150-$200.

*GENERAL Orders Affecting the Volunteer Force: Adjutant General's Office, 1864.* Cloth. Washington, 1865. (Contains Lincoln presidential orders.) $150-$200.

GENÊT, Edmond Charles. *Memorial on the Upward Forces of Fluids.* Folding table, 6 plates. Printed brown boards. Albany, 1825. First edition. $1,250-$1,500, possibly more.

*GENIUS of Oblivion (The), and Other Poems.* By a Lady of New-Hampshire. Gray boards, paper label on spine. Concord, N.H., 1823. (By Sarah Josepha Hale.) First edition. $100-$200. Author's first book.

GENTHE, Arnold. *Impressions of Old New Orleans: A Book of Pictures.* Foreword by Grace King. Green boards and cloth. New York, (1926). First edition, with Doran monogram on copyright page. $125-$175.

*GEOLOGICAL Survey of Texas: First Annual Report.* Austin, 1890. $100-$125. Austin, 1891. Second report. $100. Austin, 1892. Third report. $100.

GEORGE, Henry. *Our Land and Land Policy, National and State.* Folding map in black and red. 48 pp., printed wrappers. San Francisco, 1871. First edition. $300-$350. Author's first book (?).

GEORGE, Henry. *Progress and Poverty.* Green or blue cloth. San Francisco, 1879. "Author's Edition." First edition, first issue, with the slip asking that no reviews be printed. $300-$400. Second issue, without the slip referring to reviews. $200-$250.

*GEORGE Mason, The Young Backwoodsman.* Tan boards, paper label. Boston, 1829. (By Timothy Flint.) First edition. $100-$150.

*GEORGE Pierce Baker, A Memorial.* Batik boards, paper label. New York, 1929. First edition. Large paper copy signed by all the contributors, including Eugene O'Neill. (A few copies only were issued.) $75-$100.

*GEORGIA Scenes, Characters, Incidents, etc., in the First Half Century of the Republic.* By a Native Georgian. Brown boards, cloth back, paper labels. Augusta, Ga., 1835. (By Augustus Baldwin Longstreet.) First edition. $400-$600. Author's first book. New York, 1840. Illustrated. Cloth. Second edition. $150-$200.

GERARD Manley Hopkins. By the Kenyon Critics. Cloth. New York, (1945). First edition. In dust jacket. $50-$60.

GERHARD, Fred. Illinois As It Is. Map. Frontispiece, 3 folding maps. Cloth. Chicago, 1857. First edition. $150-$200.

GERNSBACK, Hugo. Ralph 124C41: A Romance of the Year 2660. Illustrated. Blue cloth. Boston, 1925. First edition. In dust jacket. $150-$200.

GERSHWIN, George. George Gershwin's Song-Book. Illustrated by Alajolov. Portrait, song reproductions. Full blue morocco. New York, 1932. One of 300 signed by Gershwin and Alajolov. $1,000-$1,250. Also, a copy marked "Review," $1,300 (A, 1977).

GERSHWIN, George. Porgy and Bess. Frontispiece in color. Morocco. New York, 1935. First edition. One of 250 signed by Gershwin, DuBose Heyward, and others. $400-$450. Also, $400 (A, 1975).

GERSTAECKER, Friedrich. California Gold Mines. Foreword by Joseph A. Sullivan. Folding map, illustrations. Pictorial boards. Oakland, 1946. One of 500 signed by Sullivan. $75-$100.

GERSTAECKER, Friedrich. Scenes of Life in California. San Francisco, 1942. Grabhorn Press. One of 500. $100-$125.

GESNER, Abraham. A Practical Treatise on Coal, Petroleum, and Other Distilled Oils. Illustrated. Cloth. New York, 1861. First edition. $350-$400.

GETTING a Wrong Start: A Truthful Autobiography. Terra-cotta cloth. New York, 1915. (By Emerson Hough.) First edition, with "Published March, 1915" on copyright page. $35-$50.

GHIRARDELLI, Ynez. The Artist H. Daumier. San Francisco, 1940. Grabhorn Press. One of 250. $150-$200.

GIBBINGS, Robert. Over the Reefs. Illustrated by the author. Morocco. London, 1948. First edition. One of 100 signed. $75-$100.

GIBBINGS, Robert. The Wood Engravings of Robert Gibbings. Illustrated. Boards. London, (1959). First edition. In acetate dust jacket. $30-$50.

GIBRAN, Kahlil. Twenty Drawings. Illustrated. Boards. New York, 1919. First edition. $30-$50.

GIBSON, Charles Dana. Americans. Illustrated. Oblong folio, cloth. New York, 1900. First edition. One of 250 signed. $75-$100.

GIBSON, Charles Dana. Drawings. Plates. Oblong folio, boards and cloth. New York, 1897. First edition. $75-$100.

GIBSON, Charles Dana. Eighty Drawings, Including the Weaker Sex. Oblong folio, cloth. New York, 1903. First edition. One of 250 signed. $75-$100.

GIBSON, Charles Dana. The Gibson Book. Illustrated. 2 vols., oblong folio, boards. New York, 1906. First edition. In dust jacket. $100-$125. New York, 1907. $75-$100.

GIBSON, Charles Dana. London, As Seen by Gibson. Illustrated. Oblong folio, cloth. New York, 1897. First edition. $50-$85.

GIBSON, Wilfrid W. Home: A Book of Poems. Woodcut. Boards and vellum. London, 1920. Beaumont Press. First edition. One of 35 on vellum, signed. $150-$200.

GIDDINGS, Marsh. First Annual Message to the Legislative Assembly of the Territory of New Mexico. 54 pp., printed wrappers. Santa Fe, 1871. First edition. $125-$175.

GIDE, André. *If It Die . . . An Autobiography.* Translated by Dorothy Bussy. Silk binding. New York, (1935). First edition. One of 100 signed. Boxed. $35-$50.

GIDE, André. *Montaigne: An Essay in Two Parts.* Cloth. London, 1929. One of 800 signed. In dust jacket. $50-$75.

GIDE, André. *Oscar Wilde.* Notes, etc., by Stuart Mason. 5 illustrations. Half parchment and cloth. Oxford, 1905. One of 50 signed by Mason. $40-$50.

GIDNEY, Eleazer. *A Treatise on the Structure, etc., of the Human Teeth.* Cloth. Utica, 1824. First edition. $75-$100.

GILBERT, Ann (Taylor), and Taylor, Jane. *Hymns for Infant Minds.* Printed wrappers. Newburyport, Mass., 1814. $100-$125.

GILBERT, Benjamin. *A Narrative of the Captivity and Sufferings of Benjamin Gilbert and His Family.* (Edited by William Walton.) Leather. Philadelphia, 1848. Third edition. $50.

GILBERT, Paul T., and Bryson, Charles L. *Chicago and Its Makers.* Illustrated. Buckram. Chicago, 1929. First edition. $75-$100. Another issue: Full morocco. One of 2,000. $150-$300. Also, $250 (A, 1973).

GILBERT, William. *On the Magnet, Magnetick Bodies, etc.* Woodcuts. Folio, limp vellum, silk ties. London, 1900. One of 250. $100-$125. (Note: Issued for the Gilbert Club along with S. P. Thompson's *Notes on the De Magnete of Dr. William Gilbert,* London, 1901. Together, $150-$200.)

GILBERT, W. S. *The "Bab" Ballads: Much Sound and Little Sense.* Illustrated by the author. Green cloth. London, 1869. First edition, first issue, with Hotten imprint on title page. $150-$175. Also, $80 (A, 1974).

GILBERT, W. S. *Fifty "Bab" Ballads.* Green cloth. London, (1876). First edition. $40-$60.

GILBERT, W. S. *Iolanthe and Other Operas.* Illustrated by W. R. Flint. Half morocco. London, 1910. First edition. $75-$100.

GILBERT, W. S. *The Mikado.* Illustrated. Cloth. London, 1928. In dust jacket. $50-$75.

GILBERT, W. S. *More "Bab" Ballads.* Green cloth. London, (1873). First edition. $40-$50.

GILBERT, W. S. *A New and Original Extravaganza Entitled Dulcamara; or, The Little Duck and the Great Quack.* Illustration. Orange wrappers. London, 1866. First edition. $500 and up. Author's first published work.

GILBERT, W. S. *Songs of a Savoyard.* Illustrated by the author. Cloth. London, (1890). First edition. $100-$125. (Note: Dated title page indicates second edition.)

GILCHRIST, Alexander. *Life of William Blake.* Illustrated. 2 vols., cloth. London, 1863. First edition. $100-$150. London, 1880. Blue cloth. Second edition. $100-$125.

GILDER, Richard Watson. *The New Day.* Cloth. New York, 1876. First edition. $25-$35.

GILES, William B. *Political Miscellanies.* Calf. (Virginia, 1830.) $65-$85.

GILHAM, William B. *Manual of Instruction for the Volunteers and Militia of the Confederate States.* Folding charts. Cloth. Richmond, 1861. $250-$500. (Note: This general price range applies for any edition of this wartime manual.)

GILHESPY, F. Brayshaw. *Crown Derby Porcelain.* Plates. Cloth. Leigh-on-Sea, England, 1951. One of 600, signed. In dust jacket. $150-$200.

GILHESPY, F. Brayshaw. *Derby Porcelain.* 77 plates, 13 in color. Buckram. London, 1961. In dust jacket. $35-$50.

GILL, Eric. *Art-Nonsense and Other Essays.* Half calf. London, 1929. First edition. One of 100 signed. $125-$175. Trade edition: Cloth. In dust jacket. $30-$40.

GILL, Eric. *Clothes.* 10 wood engravings by the author. Boards, leather spine. London, 1931. One of 160 signed. $100-$150.

GILL, Eric. *Clothing Without Cloth: An Essay on the Nude.* 4 wood engravings by the author. Cloth. London, 1931. Golden Cockerel Press. One of 500. $100-$200.

GILL, Eric. *An Essay on Typography.* Illustrated. Cloth. (London, 1931.) One of 500, signed. In dust jacket. $75-$100.

GILL, Eric. *From the Jerusalem Diary.* Illustrated. Half cloth. (London), 1953. First edition. One of 300. $80-$100.

GILL, Eric (illustrator). See *The Four Gospels of the Lord Jesus Christ.*

GILLELAND, J. C. *The Ohio and Mississippi Pilot.* 16 maps. Calf, or boards and calf. Pittsburgh, 1820. First edition. $1,000 and up. Also, covers worn, text foxed and stained, $700 (A, 1967).

GILLELEN, F. M. L. *The Oil Regions of Pennsylvania.* 17 maps (one folding), frontispiece, 3 other plates. 67 pp., wrappers. Pittsburgh, (1865?). First edition. $500-$750, possibly more.

GILLETT, James B. *Six Years with the Texas Rangers.* 8 plates. Cloth. Austin, (1921). First edition. $50-$85. New Haven, 1925. Cloth. $25-$30.

GILMOR, Harry. *Four Years in the Saddle.* Cloth. New York, 1866. First American edition. $40-$60.

GINSBERG, Allen. *Empty Mirror: Early Poems.* Introduction by William Carlos Williams. Decorated wrappers. New York, (1961). Totem Press. First edition. $35-$45.

GINSBERG, Allen. *Howl for Carl Solomon.* First edition. (see next entry.)

GINSBERG, Allen. *Howl and Other Poems.* Introduction by William Carlos Williams. Printed wrappers. San Francisco, (1956). First edition. $250-$300. (Note: *Howl* appeared originally as *Howl for Carl Solomon,* 17 pages mimeographed and stapled at San Francisco State College in 1955. Value: $1,000 and up. Also, an inscribed and corrected copy, $1,400 at auction in October, 1977.)

GINSBERG, Allen. *Kaddish: A Dramatic Mass.* Mimeographed, leatherette. New York, (about 1965). One of 18. $100-$150.

GINSBERG, Allen. *Kaddish and Other Poems.* Wrappers. (San Francisco 1961.) First edition. $50-$75.

GINSBERG, Allen. *Siesta in Xbalba and Return to the States.* Self-wrappers, stapled. Near Icy Cape, Alaska, July, 1956. First edition. One of about 56 copies mimeographed. $1,000-$1,500. Author's first book.

GINSBERG, Allen. *T. V. Baby Poems.* Boards. (London, 1967.) Cape Goliard Press. First edition. One of 100 signed. In dust jacket. $50-$65. Trade edition: Wrappers. $7.50.

GINSBERG, Allen. *Wales—A Visitation July 29, 1967.* Boards. London, 1968. Cape Goliard Press. First edition. One of 100 signed, with author's recording of poem. In dust jacket. $50-$60.

*GINX'S Baby: His Birth and Other Misfortunes.* Cloth. London, 1870. (By John Edward Jenkins.) First edition. $50. Author's first book.

GIRARD, Just. *Adventures of a French Captain, at Present a Planter in Texas.* Boards or cloth. New York, 1878. (By Just Jean Etienne Roy.) $150-$300.

GIRAUD, J. P., Jr. *The Birds of Long Island.* Plate. Cloth. New York, 1844. First edition. $100-$200. Also, rubbed, $160 (A, 1974).

GISSING, George. See *Demos: A Story of English Socialism.*

GISSING, George. *Born in Exile.* 3 vols., slate-gray cloth. London, 1892. First edition. $150-$300.

GISSING, George. *By the Ionian Sea: Notes of a Ramble in Southern Italy.* Illustrated in color and black and white. White cloth. London, 1901. First edition. $75-$100.

GISSING, George. *Charles Dickens: A Critical Study.* Dark-red cloth. London, 1898. First edition. $50-$75.

GISSING, George. *Denzil Quarrier.* Olive cloth. London, 1892. First edition. $100-$125.

GISSING, George. *The Emancipated.* 3 vols., boards and cloth. London, 1890. First edition. $175-$225.

GISSING, George. *Eve's Ransom.* Red cloth. London, 1895. First edition, with 16 pages of ads for Autumn, 1894. $75-$100.

GISSING, George. *The House of Cobwebs and Other Stories.* Blue cloth. London, 1906. First edition. $40-$60.

GISSING, George. *In the Year of Jubilee.* 3 vols., blue cloth. London, 1894. First edition. $200-$250.

GISSING, George. *Isabel Clarendon.* 2 vols., green cloth. London, 1886. First edition. $200-$250.

GISSING, George. *A Life's Morning.* 3 vols., light-blue cloth. London, 1888. First edition. $150-$200.

GISSING, George. *The Nether World.* 3 vols., light-blue or green cloth. London, 1889. First edition. $200-$250.

GISSING, George. *New Grub Street.* 3 vols., dark-green cloth. London, 1891. First edition. $500-$750. Also, $300 (A, 1972). Second edition, same date. $100-$150.

GISSING, George. *The Odd Women.* 3 vols., blue cloth. London, 1893. First edition. $150-$200.

GISSING, George. *Our Friend the Charlatan.* Illustrated. Cloth. London, 1901. First edition. $50-$85.

GISSING, George. *The Private Papers of Henry Ryecroft.* Green cloth. Westminster, England, 1903. First edition, with three ad leaves. $125-$250. New York, 1903. Cloth. First American edition. $75-$100. Portland, Me., 1921. Boards. One of 25 on Japan vellum. $100-$125. Another issue: One of 700. $25-$35. New York, 1927. Purple cloth. In dust jacket. $40-$60.

GISSING, George. *Thyrza.* 3 vols., dark-red cloth. London, 1887. First edition. $200-$250. Also, rubbed, hinges weak, $72 (A, 1975).

GISSING, George. *The Town Traveller.* Light-red cloth. London, 1898. First edition, with ads dated April, 1898. $75-$150.

GISSING, George. *The Unclassed.* 3 vols., blue cloth. London, 1884. First edition. $150-$250.

GISSING, George. *Veranilda: A Romance.* Red cloth. London, 1904. First edition, with 16 pages of ads at back. In dust jacket. $150-$250.

GISSING, George. *Will Warburton: A Romance of Real Life.* Red cloth. London, 1905. First edition, with 16 pages of ads at back. $100-$150.

GISSING, George. *Workers in the Dawn.* 3 vols., light-brown cloth. London, 1880. First edition, with black end papers. $750-$1,000. Author's first book. (Note: The auction record for this book is $1,550, established in 1928.)

GISSING, George. *A Yorkshire Lass*. Boards, paper label. New York, 1928. First edition. One of 93. $50-$75.

GIST, Christopher. *Christopher Gist's Journals*. 7 maps. Cloth. Pittsburgh, 1893. First edition. One of 10 on large paper. $200-$225.

GLASGOW, Ellen. See *The Descendant*.

GLASGOW, Ellen. *Phases of an Inferior Planet*. Brown cloth. New York, 1898. First edition , with erratum slip. $25-$35.

GLASS, E. L. N. *History of the Tenth Cavalry, 1866-1921*. Illustrated. Cloth. Tucson, 1921. First edition. $75-$100.

*GLEANINGS from the Inside History of the Bonanzas*. 40 pp., printed wrappers. (San Francisco, 1878.) First edition. $125.

GLEESON, William. *History of the Catholic Church in California*. 4 maps and plans, 9 plates. 2 vols., cloth. San Francisco, 1871-72. First edition. $300. San Francisco, 1872. 2 vols. in one. Second edition. $125.

GLEN, Duncan (editor). *Poems Addressed to Hugh MacDiarmid and Presented to Him on His 75th Birthday*. Frontispiece, other illustrations. Boards and leather. (Preston, Lancashire, England, 1967.) One of 50 signed by all the contributors, etc. $150 and up. Another issue: One of 350 signed by editor and illustrator. $100 and up. (Note: MacDiarmid is the pen name of C. M. Grieve.)

GLENN, Allen. *History of Cass County (Missouri)*. Cloth. Topeka, 1917. First edition. $100-$150, possibly more.

GLISAN, R. *Journal of Army Life*. Folding table, 21 plates. Cloth. San Francisco, 1874. First edition. $60-$80.

GLOVER, Mary Baker. *Science and Health, With Key to the Scriptures*. Black cloth. Boston, 1875. (By Mary Baker Eddy.) First edition, first issue, with errata slip and without index. $1,250-$1,500. Lynn, Mass., 1878. Second edition. $300-$500. Lynn, 1881. 2 vols., cloth. Third edition. $200-$300. Lynn, 1882. 2 vols., cloth. $150-$200. Boston, (1941). One of 1,000. $400-$500. Also, $325 (A, 1971).

*GOBIERNO Independiente de Mexico*. Wrappers. Mexico, 1882. $500 and up.

GODDARD, Paul B., and Parker, Joseph E. *The Anatomy, Physiology and Pathology of the Human Teeth*. Illustrated. Half calf. Philadelphia, 1844. First edition. $75-$100. New York, 1854. $35-$50.

GODDARD, R. H. *A Method of Reading Extreme Altitudes*. 10 plates. Wrappers. Washington, 1919. First edition. $1,500. Front cover torn, $1,350 (1977 catalogue).

GODWIN, William. *Deloraine*. 3 vols., boards. London, 1833. First edition. $100-$150. Another set, one cover loose, name cut from title of first volume, other defects, $60-$75.

GODWIN, William. *Essay on Sepulchres*. Engraved frontispiece. Boards, paper label. London, 1809. First edition. $150-$200.

GODWIN, William. *Fleetwood: or, The New Man of Feeling*. 3 vols., boards. London, 1805. First edition. $100-$150.

GODWIN, William. *Mandeville: A Tale of the 17th Century in England*. 3 vols., boards London, 1817. First edition. $400-$500. Also, $325 (A, 1970).

GODWIN, William. *Of Population . . . An Answer to Mr. Malthus' Essay*. Boards. London, 1820. First edition. $350-$450.

GOETHE, Johann Wolfgang von. *Faust*. Translated into English rhyme by Robert Talbot. Contemporary calf. London, 1835. First edition of this translation. $75-$80. Lowell, Mass., 1840. Translated by A. Hayward. Cloth. First American edition. $100-$150. First part only of *Faust (Erster Teil)*: (London), 1906. Doves Press. One of 300. $400-$500. Another issue: Full vellum. One of 25 on vellum. $1,500-$2,000. Also, $850 (A, 1974). This edition, as a set, with the second part of *Faust, Zweiter Teil*, issued by the press in 1910 in 250 copies: $600-$800. In Doves Bindery bindings: $1,000 and up. London, 1908. 31 color plates by Will Pogany. Full vellum. One of 250 signed by Pogany. $200-$300. London, (1925). Illustrated by Harry Clarke. Half vellum. In dust jacket. One of 1,000 signed by Clarke. $250-$325. New York, (about 1925). One of 1,000 signed. $150-$250.

GOETHE, Johann Wolgang von. *Torquato Tasso: ein Schauspiel.* Printed in red and black. Vellum. London, 1913. Doves Press. One of 200. $400-$600. Another issue. One of 12 on vellum. $1,200-$1,500.

GOGARTY, Oliver St. John. *Elbow Room.* Boards, linen spine. Dublin, 1939. Cuala Press. One of 450. In dust jacket. $75-$100.

GOGARTY, Oliver St. John. *An Offering of Swans.* Introduction by William Butler Yeats. Boards and cloth, paper label. Dublin, 1923. Cuala Press. First edition. One of 300. In dust jacket. $75-$100.

GOGARTY, Oliver St. John. *Wild Apples.* Preface by William Butler Yeats. Boards and linen. Dublin, 1928. Cuala Press. One of 250. In dust jacket. $75-$85. Another issue: One of 50. $200. (Note: Wade's bibliography records only a 250-copy Cuala Press edition of 1930.)

*GOLD, Silver, Lead, and Copper Mines of Arizona.* 40 pp., printed wrappers. (Philadelphia, 1867.) First edition. $500.

GOLDING, William. *Lord of the Flies.* Red cloth. London, (1954). First edition. In dust jacket. $100-$125. Author's first book. New York, (1954). First American edition. In dust jacket. $50-$75.

GOLDSBOROUGH, Charles W. *The United States' Naval Chronicle.* Vol. 1. (All published.) Pictorial boards. Washington City, 1824. First edition, with errata slip pasted on last page. $150-$250.

GOLDSCHMIDT, E. P. *The Printed Book of the Renaissance.* 7 plates. Cloth. Cambridge, 1930. One of 750. $150-$200.

GOLDSMITH, Oliver. *The Vicar of Wakefield.* 12 color illustrations and some in black and white by Arthur Rackham. Parchment. London, (1929). One of 575 signed by the artist. Boxed. $400-$600. London, 1903. Caradoc Press. One of 14 on vellum. $600-$800. Another issue: One of 360. $100-$125.

GOLL, Yvan. *Jean Sans Terre (Landless John).* Preface by Allen Tate. Translated by William Carlos Williams and others. Illustrated. Folio, boards. San Francisco, 1944. Grabhorn Press. One of 175. $200-$250.

GOOD, P. P. *The Family Flora and Materia Medica Botanica.* 96 colored plates. 2 vols., cloth. Elizabethtown, N. J., and Cambridge, Mass., (1845-54). $500-$600. New York, 1845. 48 colored plates. 2 vols., cloth. $300-$400.

GOOD, P. P. *A Materia Medica Animalia.* 24 color plates. Cloth. Cambridge, Mass., 1853. $100-$150.

GOODMAN, Paul. *Stop-light: 5 Dance Poems.* Cloth. Harrington Park, N. J., 1941. First edition. In dust jacket. $50-$60.

GOODMAN, Paul. *Ten Lyric Poems.* Wrappers. (New York, 1934.) First edition. $30-$40. Author's first book.

GOODRICH, Samuel G. See Parley, Peter. Also see *The Vagabond.*

GOODWIN, H. C. *Pioneer History; or Cortland County and the Border Wars of New York.* 3 portraits. Cloth. New York, 1859. First edition. $75-$100.

GOODWIN, Mrs. L. S. *The Gambler's Fate: A Story of California.* Woodcuts. 50 pp., pictorial wrappers. Boston, 1864. First edition. $80-$100.

GOODYEAR, W. A. *The Coal Mines of the Western Coast of the United States.* Cloth. San Francisco, 1877. First edition. $85-$150.

GOOKIN, Frederick W. *Daniel Gookin, 1612-1687.* 10 plates. Cloth. Chicago, 1912. First edition. One of 202. $85-$125.

GORDON, Alexander. *An Historical and Practical Treatise Upon Elemental Locomotion, by Means of Steam Carriages on Common Roads.* 14 plates. Gray boards. London, 1832. First edition. $200-$350. London, 1834. (Retitled *A Treatise, etc.)* $200-$250.

GORDON, Caroline. *Aleck Maury, Sportsman.* Green cloth. New York, 1934. First edition, first binding. In dust jacket. $100-$125.

GORDON, Caroline. *The Forest of the South.* Cloth. New York, 1945. First edition. In dust jacket. $35-$50.

GORDON, Caroline. *Penhally.* Cloth. New York, 1931. First edition. In dust jacket. $75-$100. Author's first book.

GORDON, J. E. H. *A Practical Treatise on Electric Lighting.* 23 plates, other illustrations. Cloth. London, 1884. First edition. $200.

GORDON, M. L. *Experiences in the Civil War.* Edited by Donald Gordon. Illustrated. Cloth. Boston, 1922. First edition. $40-$50.

GORDON, Samuel. *Recollections of Old Milestown, Montana.* 19 plates. 42 pp., Miles City, Mont., 1918. First edition. $100-$150.

GOREY, Edward. See: Dehn, Paul; Moore. Merrill; Weary, Ogdred.

GOREY, Edward. *Amphigorey.* Cloth. New York, 1972. First edition. One of 50 signed. Boxed. With original watercolor. $400-$600. Trade edition: In dust jacket. $25-$30.

GOREY, Edward. *The Bug Book.* Wrappers. New York, (1959). First edition. $100-$150. New York, 1960. Boards. In dust jacket. $75-$100.

GOREY, Edward. *The Doubtful Guest.* Illustrated. Boards. Garden City, 1957. First edition. In dust jacket. $75-$85. London, 1958. Boards. In dust jacket. $60-$80.

GOREY, Edward. *The Gilded Bat.* Boards. New York, (1966). First edition. In dust jacket. $40-$60.

GOREY, Edward. *The Iron Tonic.* Decorated wrappers. New York, 1969. Albondocani Press. One of 200 signed. First edition. $100-$150.

GOREY, Edward. *The Listing Attic.* Illustrated. Boards. New York, 1954. First edition. In dust jacket. $100-$125.

GOREY, Edward. *The Object Lesson.* Decorated paper boards. New York, 1958. First edition. In dust jacket. $75-$100. (London, 1958.) First English edition. In dust jacket. $75.

GOREY, Edward. *The Sopping Thursday.* Cloth. New York, 1970. One of 26 copies, lettered, signed and in slipcase, with original unpublished drawing. $350-$450. Another issue: Wrappers. One of 300 signed. $35-$50.

GOREY, Edward. *The Unstrung Harp.* Illustrated by the author. Decorated boards. New York, (1953). First edition. In dust jacket. $75-$100. Author's first book.

GOREY, Edward. *The Vinegar Works.* Three volumes comprising the following titles: *The Gashlycrumb Tinies; The Insect God; The West Wing.* Boards. New York, 1963. In decorated slipcase. $75-$125.

GORHAM, George C. *The Story of the Attempted Assassination of Justice Field.* Half leather. No place, (about 1893). First edition. $35-$40.

GORIN, Franklin. *The Times of Long Ago.* Cloth. Louisville, 1929. First edition. $35-$50.

GORMAN, Herbert. *James Joyce*. Cloth. New York, 1924. First edition. In dust jacket. $40-$50. (Note: Contains new material by Joyce.)

GORRELL, J. R. *A Trip to Alaska*. 40 pp., printed green wrappers. Newton, Iowa, 1905. First edition. $100-$200.

GOSNELL, Harpur Allen (editor). *Before the Mast in the Clippers*. Composed of the Diaries of Charles A. Abbey. Illustrated. Boards. New York, 1937. Derrydale Press. First edition. One of 950. $75-$125.

GOTHEIN, M. L. *A History of Garden Art*. Illustrated. 2 vols., cloth. London, (1928). First edition. In dust jacket. $100-$150.

GOUDY, Frederic W. *A Half Century of Type Design and Typography*. Illustrated. 2 vols., cloth. New York, 1946. First edition. One of 300. $75-$125.

GOUDY, Frederic W. *Typologia: Studies in Type Design and Type-Making*. Illustrated. Half morocco. Berkeley, 1940. First edition. One of 300 signed. Boxed. $125-$200. Trade edition: Cloth. $50-$100.

*GOUDY Gaudeamus: In Celebration of the Dinner Given Frederic W. Goudy, etc.* Folding title page by Bruce Rogers. Marbled boards and cloth. (New York), 1939. One of 195. $50-$100.

GOUGE, William M. *The Fiscal History of Texas*. Cloth. Philadelphia, 1852. First edition. $100-$200.

GOULD, E. W. *Fifty Years on the Mississippi*. Frontispiece. Pictorial cloth. St. Louis, 1889. First edition. $100-$125.

GOULD, John. *The Birds of Asia*. Edited by R. B. Sharpe. 530 hand-colored lithographed plates. 7 vols., folio, half (or full) morocco. London, 1850-83. $35,200 (A, 1977). (Compare: $18,000 at auction in 1972; $16,800 in 1968.)

GOULD, John. *The Birds of Australia*. 681 hand-colored lithographed plates. 8 vols., folio morocco (including supplement volume). London, 1840-69. $37,400 (A, 1977). (Compare: $18,750 at auction in 1972; $16,250 in 1971.)

GOULD, John. *The Birds of Great Britain*. 367 hand-colored lithographed plates. 5 vols., half morocco. London, 1862-73. $13,760 and $12,000 (A, 1977). (Compare: $11,250 at auction in 1972; $8,000 in 1971.)

GOULD, John. *Birds of New Guinea and the Adjacent Papuan Islands*. 320 hand-colored lithographed plates. 5 vols., folio half morocco. London, 1875-88. $26,000 (A, 1977). (Compare: $12,500 at auction in 1970.)

GOULDING, F. R. *Marooner's Island*. Frontispiece. Cloth. Philadelphia, 1869. First edition. $75-$100.

GOULDING, F. R. *Robert and Harold; or, The Young Marooners on the Florida Coast*. Cloth. Philadelphia, 1852. First edition. $200-$300.

GOULDING, F. R. *The Young Marooners on the Florida Coast*. 6 engraved plates. Decorated red cloth. London, 1853. First English edition (of *Robert and Harold; or, The Young Marooners on the Florida Coast*). $200 and up. Philadelphia, 1867. 10 plates. Cloth. New and enlarged edition (of *Robert and Harold*). First printing, with 1866 copyright. $50-$75.

GOVE, Capt. Jesse A. *The Utah Expedition, 1857-58*. Edited by Otis G. Hammond. 5 plates. Half cloth. Concord, N. H., 1928. First edition. $35-$50. Another issue: One of 50 on large paper. $100-$125.

GRABHORN, Edwin. *Figure Prints of Old Japan*. 52 reproductions. Boards. San Francisco, 1959. Grabhorn printing. Book Club of California. One of 400. In dust jacket. $250-$300.

GRABHORN, Edwin. *The Fine Art of Printing*. Stiff wrappers. (San Francisco), 1933. Grabhorn printing. One of 50 for the Roxburghe Club. $100-$150.

GRABHORN, Edwin. *Landscape Prints of Old Japan.* 52 full-color plates. Boards. San Francisco, 1960. Grabhorn printing. Book Club of California. One of 450. $300-$400.

GRABHORN, Jane Bissell (editor). *A California Gold Rush Miscellany.* Colored plates, folding map. Folio, boards. (San Francisco), 1934. Grabhorn printing. First edition. One of 550. $50-$75.

GRABHORN, Robert. *A Short Account of the Life and Work of Wynkyn de Worde.* San Francisco, 1949. Grabhorn Press. One of 375. $200-$300.

*GRACE Darling.* 4 pp. (foolscap folded to form pamphlet). Carlisle, England, (1843). (By William Wordsworth.) First edition. $75-$150. Also, $90 (A, 1974). (Note: An unauthorized, undated reprint bearing a Newcastle imprint also exists.)

GRACIE, Archibald. *The Truth About Chickamauga.* Plates, folding maps. Cloth. Boston, 1911. First edition. $40-$50.

GRAHAM, G. A. *The Irish Wolfhound.* Cloth. Dursley, Ireland, 1885. First edition. $8,000-$12,000. Also, see Hogan, Edmund, and Graham for reprint edition of 1939.

GRAHAM, J. D. *A Lunar Tidal Wave in Lake Michigan.* 3 plates. Wrappers. Chicago, 1860. First edition. $75-$125.

GRAHAM, Maria. *Journal of a Residence in Chile During the Year 1822 and a Voyage from Chile to Brazil in 1823.* 14 colored plates. Half calf. London, 1824. First edition. $400-$500.

GRAHAM, R. B. Cunninghame. *The District of Menteith.* Illustrated, including an original etching by Sir D. Y. Cameron. Folio, half calf. Stirling [Scotland], 1930. One of 250 signed. In dust jacket. Boxed. $200-$250.

GRAHAM, R. B. Cunninghame. *Notes on the District of Menteith.* Printed gray wrappers. London, 1895. First edition, first issue. $75-$100.

GRAHAM, Tom. *Hike and the Aeroplane.* Colored illustrations by Arthur Hutchins. Decorated cloth. New York, (1912). (By Sinclair Lewis.) First edition, first issue, with "August, 1912" on copyright page. In dust jacket. $600-$750. Lacking jacket, $400-$500. Also, $425 (A, 1976); $350 (A, 1975). Sinclair Lewis' first book.

GRAHAM, W. A. *The Custer Myth.* Cloth. Harrisburg, (1953). First edition. In dust jacket. $50-$75.

GRAHAM, W. A. *Major Reno Vindicated.* 30 pp., wrappers. Hollywood, 1935. First edition. $75-$100.

GRAHAM, W. A. (editor). *The Official Record of a Court of Inquiry Convened . . . By Request of Major Marcus A. Reno to Investigate His Conduct at the Battle of the Little Big Horn, etc.* Multigraphed, 2 vols., folio, cloth. Pacific Palisades, Calif., 1951. One of 125. $350-$500.

GRAHAME, Kenneth. *Dream Days.* Cloth. New York, 1899 (actually 1898). First edition, first issue, with 15 pages of ads at end dated 1898. $75-$125. London and New York, (1902). Illustrated by Maxfield Parrish. $75-$125. London, (1930). Illustrated by Ernest H. Shepard. Boards and vellum. One of 275 signed. Boxed. $200-$250.

GRAHAME, Kenneth. *The Golden Age.* Cloth. London, 1895. First edition. $100-$175. London, 1900 (actually 1899). Illustrated by Maxfield Parrish. Cloth. $50-$75. London, (1928). Illustrated by Ernest H. Shepard. Boards and vellum. One of 275 signed. $150-$200. Trade edition: In dust jacket. $40-$50.

GRAHAME, Kenneth. *Pagan Papers.* Title page designed by Aubrey Beardsley. Cloth. London, 1894. First edition. One of 450. $100-$125. Author's first book.

GRAHAME, Kenneth. *The Wind in the Willows.* Frontispiece by Graham Robertson. Pictorial cloth. London, (1908). First edition. In dust jacket. $1,000-$3,500. Also, $3,500 (A, 1977)—a remarkably fine copy. Lacking jacket but relatively fine, $500 and up. New

York, 1908. Cloth. First American edition. $100-$150. London, (1931). Illustrated by Ernest H. Shepard. Map. Gray boards and cloth. One of 200 signed. In dust jacket. Boxed.
$400-$600. Also, $353 (A, 1976). New York, 1940. Limited Editions Club. Edited by A.
A. Milne. Illustrated by Arthur Rackham. Boards and cloth. Boxed. $350-$500. London,
1951. Illustrated by Rackham. Full white calf. One of 500. Boxed. $500-$600. London,
(1964). Illustrated by Rackham. Calf. $150-$200.

*GRAND Jury Report, and the Evidence Taken by Them in Reference to the Great Riot in New
Orleans, July 30, 1866.* 17 pp., sewed. New Orleans, 1866. $125-$200.

GRANT, Arthur H. *The Grant Family.* Cloth. Poughkeepsie, 1878. $35-$50.

GRANT, Blanche C. (editor). *Kit Carson's Own Story.* Plates. 138 pp., wrappers. Taos,
1926. First edition. $50-$60.

GRANT, Robert. *Jack Hall, or The School Days of an American Boy.* Illustrated by F. G.
Attwood. Pictorial cloth. Boston, 1888. First edition. $35-$50.

GRANT, U. S. *General Orders, No. 67.* (Announcing the death of Lincoln and the succession of Johnson.) Sewed. Washington, 1865. $100-$125.

GRANT, U. S. *General Orders, No. 74.* 43 pp., sewed. Washington, 1868. $100.

GRANT, U. S. *Message Communicating the Report and Journal of Proceedings of the Commission Appointed to Obtain Concessions from the Sioux Indians.* 90 pp., sewed. Washington, 1876. $100-$125.

GRANT, U. S. *Personal Memoirs.* 2 vols., three-quarters leather. New York, 1885-86. First
edition. Large paper issue. $100-$135. Trade edition: Cloth. $25-$50.

GRANVILLE, Austyn. *The Fallen Race.* Cloth. Chicago, 1892. First edition. $75-$100.

GRAVES, H. A. *Andrew Jackson Potter, the Noted Parson of the Texan Frontier.* Portrait.
Cloth. Nashville, 1881. First edition. $300-$500. Nashville, 1882. Second edition.
$150-$300. Nashville, 1883. Third edition. $100-$150. Nashville, 1888. $75-$100.

GRAVES, H. A. (compiler). *Reminiscences and Events of Rev. John Wesley De Vilbiss.*
Cloth. Galveston, 1886. First edition. $150-$300.

GRAVES, Richard S. *Oklahoma Outlaws.* Illustrated. 131 pp., pictorial red wrappers.
(Oklahoma City, 1915.) First edition. $50-$75.

GRAVES, Robert. See Riding, Laura (and Graves).

GRAVES, Robert. *Adam's Rib.* Wood engravings by James Metcalf. Brick-red cloth. (London, 1955.) Trianon Press. First edition. One of 250 signed. In dust jacket. $125-$175.
One of 26 (A to Z). $200-$250. Trade edition: Cloth. In dust jacket. $10.

GRAVES, Robert. *Beyond Giving: Poems.* Wrappers. (London), 1969. First edition. One of
536 signed. $60-$80.

GRAVES, Robert. *But It Still Goes On.* Bright-green cloth. London, (1930). First edition,
first state, with reference to "The Child She Bare" on page 157. In dust jacket. $75-$100.
Second state, corrected page 157 tipped in. In dust jacket. $25.

GRAVES, Robert. *Colophon to Love Respelt.* Printed wrappers. (London), 1967. First edition. One of 350 signed. In dust jacket. $50-$75.

GRAVES, Robert. *Country Sentiment.* Light-blue boards. London, (1920). First edition. In
dust jacket. $100-$150.

GRAVES, Robert. *The English Ballad.* Cloth. London, 1927. First edition. $40-$50.

GRAVES, Robert. *Fairies and Fusiliers.* Wine-red cloth. London, (1917). First edition. In
dust jacket. $100-$150. Second impression: (London, 1919.) Bright-red cloth. $75-$100.

GRAVES, Robert. *The Feather Bed.* Decorated pink boards. Richmond (England), 1923. Hogarth Press. One of 250 signed. $200-$250.

GRAVES, Robert. *Goliath and David.* Wrappers. (London, 1916.) First edition. (200 copies printed.) $375-$500.

GRAVES, Robert. *Good-bye to All That: An Autobiography.* Illustrated. Salmon-pink cloth. London, (1929). First edition, first state, with poem by Siegfried Sassoon on pages 341-43. In dust jacket. $250-$300. Lacking jacket, $100-$150. Second state, with Sassoon poem removed and erratum slip at 398-99. In dust jacket. $85-$125. New York, (1930). Red cloth. First American edition. In dust jacket. $40-$50.

GRAVES, Robert. *Impenetrability or the Proper Habit of English.* Light-blue boards. London, 1926. Hogarth Press. First edition. $60-$85.

GRAVES, Robert. *John Kemp's Wager: A Ballad Opera.* White boards. Oxford, 1925. First edition. $75-$100. Another issue: Boards, parchment spine. One of 100 signed. In dust jacket. $200-$300.

GRAVES, Robert. *Lars Porsena, or The Future of Swearing and Improper Language.* Plum-colored boards, paper labels. London, (1927). First edition, with 16 pages of ads. $50-$75. New York, (1927). Blue or olive-green cloth. First American edition. In dust jacket. $35.

GRAVES, Robert. *Lawrence and the Arabs.* Illustrated. Mustard-colored (orange) cloth. London, (1927). First edition. In dust jacket. $50-$60.

GRAVES, Robert. *Love Respelt.* Illuminated by Aemilia Laracuen. Cloth. London, (1965). First edition. One of 250 signed. In dust jacket. $60-$80. One of 30 out of series copies. $35-$50. (There were also 18 copies reprinted and lettered A to R, according to Fred H. Higginson.)

GRAVES, Robert. *Love Respelt Again.* Cloth. Garden City, (1969). First American edition. One of 1,000 signed. In dust jacket. $60-$85.

GRAVES, Robert. *Mammon and the Black Goddess.* Wrappers. London, 1965. Proof copy (so imprinted on cover). $35-$50. (Note: The published edition, bound in gray cloth, with dust jacket is not scarce and is of nominal value.)

GRAVES, Robert. *Man Does, Woman Is.* Buff linen, blue cloth spine. London, 1964. First edition. One of 175 signed. In glassine dust jacket. $100-$125. Another issue: One of 26 (A to Z). $200-$225. Trade edition: Cloth. In dust jacket. $10-$20.

GRAVES, Robert. *Mrs. Fisher, or The Future of Humour.* Plum-colored boards, paper labels. London, 1928. First edition. In dust jacket. $50-$75.

GRAVES, Robert. *Mock Beggar Hall.* Gray pictorial boards. London, 1924. Hogarth Press. First edition. $100-$125.

GRAVES, Robert. *The More Deserving Cases.* Portrait. Red morocco. (Marlborough, England), 1962. Marlborough College Press. First edition. One of 400 signed. $75-$125. Another issue: Blue buckram. One of 350 signed. $75-$125.

GRAVES, Robert. *My Head! My Head!* Decorated red cloth, black spine. London, 1925. First edition. $60-$80.

GRAVES, Robert. *On English Poetry.* Cream-colored boards and cloth, paper label. New York, 1922. First edition, first issue, with misprints "that" for "than that" on page 33 and "have" for "how" on page 145. In dust jacket. $75-$100. London, (1922). Bright yellow cloth. First English edition, first issue (with misprints), first binding. In dust jacket. $50-$75. Second state binding, buff boards. $40-$60.

GRAVES, Robert. *Over the Brazier.* Pictorial gray wrappers. London, 1916. Poetry Bookshop. First edition. $600-$750. Also, $350 (A, 1977). Author's first book. London, (1920). Gray boards, blue cloth spine. Second edition. In dust jacket. $200-$300. Lacking jacket, $75-$100.

GRAVES, Robert. *The Pier-Glass.* Portrait. Yellow decorated boards. London, (1921). First edition. One of 500. In dust jacket. $75-$100. New York, 1921. Boards. First American edition. In dust jacket. $35-$50.

GRAVES, Robert. *Poems 1953.* Bright-green boards, white cloth spine. London, (1953). First edition. One of 250 signed. In dust jacket. $75-$100. Trade edition: Sea-green cloth. In dust jacket. $15-$20.

GRAVES, Robert. *Poems (1914-1927).* White boards, parchment spine. London, 1927. One of 115 signed. In dust jacket. $300-$400.

GRAVES, Robert. *Poems (1914-1926).* Slick white cloth with black cobbled design. London, 1927. First edition. In dust jacket. $150-$200.

GRAVES, Robert. *Poems 1929.* Yellow-green cloth. London, 1929. Seizin Press. First edition. One of 225 signed. $100-$200.

GRAVES, Robert. *Poems, 1926-1930.* Maroon cloth, paper labels. London, (1931). First edition. In dust jacket. $75-$85.

GRAVES, Robert. *Poetic Unreason and Other Studies.* Dark-blue cloth, paper label. (London, 1925.) First edition. In dust jacket. $75-$100.

GRAVES, Robert. *The Real David Copperfield.* Blue cloth. London, (1933). First edition. In dust jacket. $40-$50.

GRAVES, Robert. *Seventeen Poems Missing from "Love Respelt."* Wrappers over boards. (London), 1966. First edition. One of 330 signed. $50-$75.

GRAVES, Robert. *The Shout.* Decorated gray boards. London, 1929. First edition. One of 530 signed. In dust jacket. $85-$125.

GRAVES, Robert. *T. E. Lawrence to His Biographer, Robert Graves.* Buff cloth. New York, 1938. First edition. One of 500 signed by Graves (issued with Liddell Hart's book of the same title) with Doubleday imprint. Boxed (with the Liddell Hart book). $250. Also, $150 (A, 1971). London, (1939). Red cloth. First English edition. One of 500 signed by Graves. In dust jacket. Issued boxed as a set with the Liddell Hart book. $250.

GRAVES, Robert. *Ten Poems More.* Boards and green morocco. Paris, 1930. Hours Press. First edition, with misprints on pages 7, 10, and 15. One of 200 signed. In transparent dust jacket. $100-$150.

GRAVES, Robert. *To Whom Else?* Pictorial boards and cloth. Deya, Mallorca, 1931. Seizin Press. First edition. One of 200 signed. In dust jacket. $100-$150.

GRAVES, Robert. *Treasure Box.* Light-blue wrappers. (London, 1919.) First edition. One of 200. $300-$400. (Most copies sold are signed.)

GRAVES, Robert. *Welchman's Hose.* Wood engravings by Paul Nash. Decorated boards and cloth. London, 1925. First edition. One of 525. In transparent dust jacket. $100-$200.

GRAVES, Robert *Whipperginny.* Decorated magenta boards. London, (1923). First edition. In dust jacket. $50-$100. New York, 1923. Boards. First American edition. In dust jacket. $50-$75.

GRAVES, Robert, and Lindsay, Jack (editors). *Loving Mad Tom: Bedlamite Verses of the 16th and 17th Centuries.* Illustrated. Boards and vellum. London, (1927). Fanfrolico Press. First edition. One of 375. $100-$150.

GRAVES, W. W. *Annals of Osage Mission.* Illustrated. Cloth. St. Paul, Kan., 1935. First edition. $100-$200.

GRAY, Asa. *Elements of Botany.* Half leather. New York, 1836. First edition. $350-$400.

GRAY, David. *The Sporting Works of David Gray.* Illustrated. 3 vols., cloth. New York, 1929. Derrydale Press. First edition. One of 750. Boxed. $85-$125.

GRAY, Henry. *Anatomy, Descriptive and Surgical.* Cloth. London, 1858. First edition. $750-$1,000. Philadelphia, 1859. Illustrated, including color. Calf. $100-$150.

GRAY, John W. *The Life of Joseph Bishop.* Cloth. Nashville, 1858. First edition. $100-$125.

GRAYDON, Alexander. *Memoirs of a Life, Chiefly Passed in Pennsylvania, Within the Last 60 Years.* Cloth. Harrisburg, 1811. First edition, with errata leaf. $100-$125. Edinburgh, 1822. Boards and cloth. First English edition. $50-$60.

*GREAT Eastern Gold Mining Co. (The).* Map. 7 pp., wrappers. New York, 1880. $150-$200.

*GREAT Steam-Duck (The) . . . An Invention for Aerial Navigation.* By a Member of the LLBB. 32 pp. Louisville, 1841. First edition. $1,500 and up.

*GREAT Trans-Continental Railroad Guide.* Wrappers. Chicago, 1869. First edition. $200-$250.

*GREAT Western Almanac for 1848.* Wrappers. Philadelphia, (1847). First edition. $300-$350.

GREAVES, Richard. *Brewster's Millions.* Red cloth. Chicago, 1903. (By George Barr McCutcheon.) First edition. $25-$35.

GRECE, Charles F. *Facts and Observations Respecting Canada, and the United States of America.* Contemporary leather. London, 1819. First edition. $200-$350.

GREELEY, Horace. *An Overland Journey from New York to San Francisco.* Cloth. New York, 1860. First edition. $75-$150.

GREEN, Anna Katharine. *The Circular Study.* Red cloth. New York, 1900. First edition. In dust jacket. $75-$100. Lacking jacket, $40-$60.

GREEN, Anna Katharine. *The Leavenworth Case: A Lawyer's Story.* Plate. Terra-cotta cloth. New York, 1878. First edition. $400-$500.

GREEN, Ben K. *The Color of Horses.* Illustrated in color. Half cloth and fabrikoid. Flagstaff, Ariz., (1974). First edition. One of 150 signed. Boxed. $125-$150. Trade edition. In dust jacket. $25-$30.

GREEN, Ben K. *The Last Trail Drive Through Downtown Dallas.* Illustrated. Half leather. Flagstaff, (1971). First edition. One of 100 signed and with a Joe Beeler drawing in ink and watercolor. Boxed. $350-$400. Trade edition: Cloth. In dust jacket. $25.

GREEN, Ben K. *A Thousand Miles of Mustangin'.* Illustrated. Half cloth. Flagstaff, (1972). First edition. One of 150 signed. Boxed. $75-$100. Trade edition: Cloth. $35.

GREEN, Ben K. *Wild Cow Tales.* Illustrated. Cloth. New York, 1969. First edition. In dust jacket. $35.

GREEN, Henry. *Back.* Cloth. London, 1950. (By Henry Vincent Yorke.) First edition. In dust jacket. $40-$50.

GREEN, Henry. *Blindness.* Cloth. New York, (1926). (By Henry Vincent Yorke.) First American edition. In dust jacket. $75-$100. Author's first book.

GREEN, Jonathan S. *Journal of a Tour on the Northwest Coast of America in the Year 1829.* Edited by Edward Eberstadt. Boards, paper label. New York, 1915. First edition. One of 150. $200-$250. (Note: There were also 10 copies on Japan vellum, and they are of course more valuable.)

*GREEN Mountain Boys (The).* 2 vols., boards, paper labels. Montpelier, Vt., 1839. (By Daniel Pierce Thompson.) First edition, first issue, with publisher's name misspelled "Waltton" in copyright notices of Vol 2. $300-$400, possibly more.

GREEN, Mowbray A. *The Eighteenth Century Architecture of Bath.* Plates and plans. Buckram. Bath, England, 1904. One of 500. $75-$125.

GREEN, Thomas. *The Universal Herbal, or Botanical, Medical and Agricultural Dictionary.* Colored plates. 2 vols., contemporary half calf, gilt paneled spines. Liverpool, (1816-20). First edition. $500-$700. Also, $447 (A, 1975).

GREEN, Thomas J. *Journal of the Texian Expedition Against Mier.* 11 plates, 2 plans. Cloth, New York 1845. First edition. $150-$200.

GREEN, Thomas M. *The Spanish Conspiracy.* Cloth. Cincinnati, 1891. First edition. $100-$125.

GREENAN, Edith. *Of Una Jeffers.* 5 photographic illustrations. Cloth. Los Angeles, 1939. One of 250. In dust jacket. $100-$150.

GREENAWAY, Kate. See Harte, Bret; Mavor, William; Taylor, Jane and Ann.

GREENAWAY, Kate. *A Apple Pie.* Colored illustrations. Oblong, half cloth. London, (1886). First edition. In dust jacket. $150-$200. Lacking jacket, $75-$150.

GREENAWAY, Kate. *Almanacks.* Illustrated in color by the author. Pictorial boards, wrappers, or cloth. London, (1883-95 and 1897, with no *Almanack* issued in 1896). First editions. Complete sets in fine condition and with dust jackets, where required, are worth $1,500 to $2,000, possibly more, depending on condition. Individual years retail in the $80-$100 range, if in fine condition; less if not fine.

GREENAWAY, Kate. *Kate Greenaway's Alphabet.* Colored illustrations. Pictorial boards. London, (1885?). First edition, first issue. $85-$100. Second issue: Wrappers. $40-$60.

GREENAWAY, Kate. *Kate Greenaway's Birthday Book for Children.* Verses by Mrs. Sale Barker. 382 illustrations (12 plates in color). Pictorial boards. London, (1880). First edition. $75-$100. (Sometimes catalogued or listed in the auction records under Mrs. Barker's name.)

GREENAWAY, Kate. *Kate Greenaway's Book of Games.* Colored plates. Pictorial boards. London, (1889). $75-$100.

GREENAWAY, Kate. *Kate Greenaway Pictures.* Portrait frontispiece, 20 pictures in color. Cloth. London, 1921. In dust jacket. $100-$125.

GREENAWAY, Kate. *Marigold Garden.* Illustrated in color by the author. Pictorial boards and cloth. (London, 1885.) First edition. $100-$125.

GREENAWAY, Kate. *Under the Window: Pictures and Rhymes for Children.* Colored illustrations. Pictorial boards. London, (1878). First edition, first issue, with printer's imprint on back of title page and with reading "End of Contents" at foot of page 14. In dust jacket. $100-$150.

GREENAWAY, Kate (illustrator). *Dame Wiggins of Lee and Her Seven Wonderful Cats.* Edited by John Ruskin. 22 woodcuts. Gray cloth. London, (1885). First edition with the Greenaway illustrations. $75-$100.

GREENAWAY, Kate (illustrator). *A Day in a Child's Life.* Music by Myles B. Foster. Color illustrations. Pictorial boards in color. London, (1881). First edition. $100-$125.

GREENAWAY, Kate (illustrator). *Language of Flowers.* Colored illustrations. Boards. London, (1884). First edition. $75-$150.

GREENAWAY, Kate (illustrator). *The "Little Folks" Painting Book.* Stories and verses by George Weatherly. Pictorial wrappers. London, (1879). First edition. $100-$125.

GREENAWAY, Kate (illustrator). *Mother Goose or The Old Nursery Rhymes.* Illustrated in color by Kate Greenaway. Various colors of cloth, or wrappers. London, (1881). First edition. Cloth: In dust jacket. $100-$150. Inscribed copies, $200 and up. Wrappers: Approximately the same values if not defective.

GREENAWAY, Kate, and Crane, Walter. *The Quiver of Love.* Colored illustrations. Cloth. (London, 1876.) Marcus Ward & Co. First edition. $200-$250, possibly more if in fine condition.

GREENBURG, Dan W. *Sixty Years: A Brief Review. The Cattle Industry in Wyoming, etc.*
Illustrated. 73 pp., pictorial wrappers. Cheyenne, 1932. First edition (so stated).
$175-$200.

GREENE, Graham. See Bey, Pilaff.

GREENE, Graham. *Babbling April: Collected Poems.* Boards. Oxford, 1925. First edition.
In dust jacket. $400-$600. Also, with review slip, $550 (A, 1977). Lacking jacket,
$200-$300. Also, $155 (A, 1976). Author's first book.

GREENE, Graham. *The Bear Fell Free.* Cloth. (London, 1935.) First edition. One of 285
signed. In dust jacket. $150-$200.

GREENE, Graham. *Brighton Rock.* Red cloth. London, (1938). First edition. In dust jacket.
$100-$150.

GREENE, Graham. *Confidential Agent.* Cloth. London, 1939. First edition. In dust jacket.
$50-$60.

GREENE, Graham. *A Gun for Sale.* Cloth. London, (1936). First edition. In dust jacket.
$75-$125.

GREENE, Graham. *It's a Battlefield.* Black cloth. London, (1934). First edition. In dust
jacket. $100-$150.

GREENE, Graham. *The Lawless Roads.* Cloth. London, 1939. First edition. In dust jacket.
$35-$50.

GREENE, Graham. *L'Homme et Lui-Même.* Wrappers. Paris, (1947). First French translation of *The Man Within.* One of 10 copies marked "H. [ors] C. [ommerce]." $50-$75.

GREENE, Graham. *The Man Within.* Cloth. London, (1929). First edition. In dust jacket.
$150-$175. Garden City, 1929. Green cloth. First American edition. In dust jacket.
$75-$100.

GREENE, Graham. *May We Borrow Your Husband?* Decorated boards. London, (1967).
First edition. One of 500 signed. $75-$100.

GREENE, Graham. *The Name of Action.* Cloth. London, (1930). First edition. In dust jacket. $75-$100.

GREENE, Graham. *The Power and the Glory.* Cloth. London, 1940. First edition. In dust
jacket. $75-$125.

GREENE, Graham. *Rumour at Nightfall.* Red cloth. London, 1931. First edition. In dust
jacket. $100-$125.

GREENE, Graham. *Stamboul Train.* Cloth. London, (1932). First edition. In dust jacket.
$50-$75.

GREENE, Graham. *The Third Man.* New York, 1950. First American edition. In dust jacket. $35-$50.

GREENE, Max. *The Kanzas Region.* 2 maps. Printed wrappers, or cloth. New York, 1856.
First edition. Wrappers: $125-$150. Cloth: $100-$125.

GREENE, Talbot. *American Nights' Entertainment.* Purple cloth. Jonesborough, Tenn.,
1860. First edition. $75-$100.

GREENEWALT, Crawford H. *Hummingbirds.* Color plates. Morocco. Garden City,
(1960). First edition. One of 500, signed. $400-$500. Trade edition: Cloth. In dust jacket.
$200-$250.

GREENHOW, Robert. *The Geography of Oregon and California.* Folding map. Wrappers.
Boston, 1845. Later edition of his *Memoir.* $150-$200. Also, $170 (A, 1972).

GREENHOW, Robert. *The History of Oregon and California.* Map. Calf. Boston, 1844. Enlarged edition of his *Memoir.* $125-$150. Boston, 1845. Wrappers. "Second edition." $100-$125.

GREENHOW, Robert. *Memoir, Historical and Political.* Folding map. Sewed. Washington, 1840. First edition. $100-$125. (Senate Document 174.)

GREER, James K. *Bois d'Arc to Barb'd Wire.* Plates, maps. Pictorial cloth. Dallas, 1936. First edition. In dust jacket. $80-$100.

GREER, James K. *Colonel Jack Hays: Texas Frontier Leader and California Builder.* Illustrated. Cloth. New York, 1952. First edition. In dust jacket. $75-$100.

GREER, James K. (editor). *A Texas Ranger and Frontiersman.* Illustrated. Cloth. Dallas, 1932. First edition. In dust jacket. $50-$75.

GREGG, Alexander. *History of the Old Cheraws.* 4 maps, illustrated. Cloth. New York, 1867. First edition. $50-$75.

GREGG, Asa. *Personal Recollections of the Early Settlement of Wapsinonoc Township and the Murder of Atwood by the Indians.* Tables. Dark purple wrappers. West Liberty, Iowa, (about 1875-1880). First edition. $750-$1,000.

GREGG, Josiah. *Commerce of the Prairies.* 2 maps (one folding), 6 plates. 2 vols., brown pictorial cloth. New York, 1844. First edition, first issue, with only New York in imprint. $1,000-$1,500. Second issue, with imprint "New York and London." $600-$800. (Note: There were also issued in 1844 a small number of first edition copies in black cloth, gilt, with gilt edges, for presentation by the author. Value: $1,500-$2,000.) New York, 1845. 2 vols., cloth. Second edition. $200-$300.

GREGOIRE, H. *An Enquiry Concerning the Intellectual and Moral Faculties, and Literature of Negroes.* Translated by D. B. Warden. Boards. Brooklyn, 1810. First American edition. $350.

GREGORY, Isabella Augusta Persse, Lady. *A Book of Saints and Wonders.* Boards and linen. Dundrum, Ireland, 1906. Dun Emer Press. One of 200. $75-$125.

GREGORY, Isabella Augusta Persse, Lady. *Coole.* Boards and linen. Dublin, 1931. Cuala Press. One of 250. In tissue dust jacket. $75-$125.

GREGORY, Isabella Augusta Persse, Lady. *The Kiltartan Poetry Book.* Boards and linen. Dundrum, Ireland, 1918. Cuala Press. One of 400. $50-$100.

GREGORY, Isabella Augusta Persse, Lady. *My First Play.* Boards and cloth. London, 1930. First edition. One of 530 signed. In dust jacket. $40-$60.

GREGORY, John. *Industrial Resources of Wisconsin.* Cloth. Milwaukee, 1855. First complete edition. $300-$350.

GREGORY, Samuel. *History of Mexico; with An Account of the Texan Revolution.* Map (not in all copies). 100 pp., pictorial wrappers. Boston, 1847. First edition. $150-$200. Issue without map, $100-$125.

GREGORY, Thomas Jefferson, and others. *History of Solano and Napa Counties, California.* Illustrated. Maps. Three-quarters leather. Los Angeles, 1912. $100-$125.

GREVILLE, Charles C. F. *The Greville Memoirs.* Edited by Lytton Strachey and Roger Fulford. Frontispieces. 8 vols., buckram. London, 1938. One of 630. $350-$450.

GREVILLE, Fulke, Lord Brooke. *Caelica.* Edited by Una Ellis-Fermor. Boards and leather. Newtown, Wales, 1936. Gregynog Press. One of 225. $125-$150. Another issue: Blue morocco, specially decorated by the Gregynog bindery. $500-$750.

GREVILLE, Fulke, Lord Brooke. *The Life of the Renowned Sir Philip Sidney.* Portrait. Limp vellum, silk ties. Bedford Park, Chiswick, England, 1906. One of 11 on vellum. $500 and up.

GREY, Zane. *Betty Zane.* Illustrated by the author. Cloth. New York, (1903). First edition. $100-$150. Also, with a cancelled check laid in, $70 (A, 1975). Author's first book.

GREY, Zane. *The Day of the Beast.* Cloth. New York, (1922). First edition. In dust jacket. $25-$35.

GREY, Zane. *The Last of the Plainsmen.* Cloth. New York, 1908. First edition. In dust jacket. $60-$80.

GREY, Zane. *Riders of the Purple Sage.* Illustrated. Cloth. New York, 1912. First edition, with "Published January 1912" on copyright page. In dust jacket. $75-$100.

GREY, Zane. *Tales of Fishes.* Half morocco. New York, (1919). First edition. Signed copy, $110 (A, 1975). Note: Other Zane Grey fishing titles, all in half morocco, were sold at auction in the 1975 season, all at $110 each, as follows: *Tales of Fishing Virgin Seas.* New York, 1925; *Tales of Fresh-Water-Fishing.* New York, 1928; *Tales of Lonely Trails.* New York, (1922); *Tales of Southern Rivers.* New York, (1924); *Tales of Swordfish and Tuna.* New York, 1927; *Tales of Tahitian Waters.* New York, 1931 (in dust jacket, with binding scratched); *Tales of the Angler's El Dorado, New Zealand.* New York, 1926.

GREY, Zane. *Tappan's Burro.* Cloth. New York, (1923). First edition. In dust jacket. $35-$50.

*GREYSLAER: A Romance of the Mohawk.* 2 vols., cloth, paper labels on spines. New York, 1840. (By Charles Fenno Hoffman.) First edition, with errata slip in first volume. $100-$150. Also, $80 (A, 1973).

GRIEVE, C. M. See: Glen, Duncan; MacDiarmid, Hugh; Mc'Diarmid, Hugh.

GRIEVE, Maud. *A Modern Herbal.* 96 plates. 2 vols., cloth. London, (1931). First edition. In dust jackets. $150-$200. New York, 1931. 2 vols., cloth. $180 (A, 1971).

GRIFFITH, George. *A Honeymoon in Space.* Illustrated. Pictorial cloth. London, 1901. First edition. $100-$125.

GRIFFITH, Thomas. *Sketches of the Early History of Maryland.* Frontispiece. Calf. Baltimore, 1821. First edition. $75-$100.

GRIFFITHS, D., Jr. *Two Years' Residence in the New Settlements of Ohio.* Frontispiece. Cloth. London, 1835. First edition. $600-$750.

GRILE, Dod. *Cobwebs: Being the Fables of Zambri, the Parsee.* Illustrated. Heavy pictorial printed wrappers, or boards. (London, about 1884.) "Fun" Office. (By Ambrose Bierce.) Reprint edition of *Cobwebs from an Empty Skull* (see entry following). $75-$100.

GRILE, Dod. *Cobwebs from an Empty Skull.* Illustrated. Blue cloth. London, 1874. (By Ambrose Bierce.) First edition. $100-$150.

GRILE, Dod. *The Fiend's Delight.* Purple-brown cloth. London, (1872). (By Ambrose Bierce.) First edition. $150-$200. Author's first book. New York, 1873. Brown or purple-brown cloth. First American edition, without publisher's ads. $25-$35.

GRILE, Dod. *Nuggets and Dust Panned Out in California.* Yellow pictorial wrappers. London, (1873). (By Ambrose Bierce.) First edition. $125-$150.

GRIMALDI, Joseph. See "Boz."

GRIMM, Jacob L. K. and W. K. *The Fairy Tales of the Brothers Grimm.* Translated by Mrs. Edgar Lucas. Illustrated with color plates by Arthur Rackham. Vellum. London, 1909. One of 750 signed by Rackham. $400-$500. Trade edition: Cloth. $150-$200.

GRIMM, Jacob L. K. and W. K. *Little Brother and Little Sister.* Color plates by Arthur Rackham. Cloth. London, (1917). One of 525 signed by Rackham, with an extra plate. $500-$700. Trade edition: Cloth. $150-$200.

GRIMM, Jacob L. K. and W. K. *Six Fairy Tales.* Illustrated by David Hockney. Folio, calf.

London, 1970. Petersburg Press. One of 575 (Edition D), with folder of signed illustrations. $1,250-$1,500.

GRINNELL, George Bird. *American Game-Bird Shooting.* Illustrated. Cloth. New York, (1910). First edition. $75-$100.

GRINNELL, George Bird. *The Cheyenne Indians: Their History and Way of Life.* Illustrated. 2 vols., cloth. New Haven, 1923. First edition. $75-$100.

GRINNELL, George Bird. *The Fighting Cheyennes.* Maps. Cloth. New York, 1915. First edition. In dust jacket. $65-$100.

GRINNELL, George Bird. *The Indians of Today.* Illustrated. Folio, pictorial cloth. Chicago, 1900. First edition. $100-$125. London, (1900). Retitled *The North American Indians, etc.* $100.

GRINNELL, George Bird. *Two Great Scouts and Their Pawnee Battalion.* Map, illustrations. Cloth. Cleveland, 1928. First edition. $65-$75.

GRINNELL, Joseph. *Gold Hunting in Alaska.* Illustrated. Red boards and green cloth. Elgin, Ill., (1901). First edition. $75-$100.

GRINNELL, Joseph, and others. *Animal Life in the Yosemite.* Illustrations (some in color). Cloth. Berkeley, 1924. $50-$75.

GRINNELL, Joseph, and others. *The Game Birds of California.* 16 color plates, other illustrations. Cloth. Berkeley, 1918. $75-$100.

GRINNELL, Joseph, and others. *Vertebrate Natural History of a Section of Northern California Through the Lassen Peak Region.* Folding colored map. Cloth. Berkeley, 1930. $50-$75.

GRISWOLD, David D. *Statistics of Chicago, Ills., Together with a Business Advertiser, and Mercantile Directory for July, 1843.* 24 pp., printed wrappers. (Chicago), 1843. First edition. $800-$1,000. Also, $500 (A, 1967).

GRISWOLD, N. W. *Beauties of California.* 18 color plates. Wrappers. San Francisco, 1883. First edition. $150-$175.

GRISWOLD, Rufus W. *The Republican Court.* Morocco. New York, 1856. First edition. $50-$75. Also, $55 (A, 1972).

GRISWOLD, W. M. *A Descriptive List of Novels and Tales Dealing with American Country Life.* 52 pp., stiched. Cambridge, Mass., 1890. First edition. $50-$75.

GRISWOLD, Wayne. *Kansas Her Resources and Developments.* Illustrated. Printed wrappers. Cincinnati, 1871. First edition. $50-$60.

GRONOW, Rees Howell. *The Reminiscences and Recollections of Captain Gronow.* Illustrated. 2 vols., cloth. London, 1889. One of 875. $100-$125.

GROOS, J. J. *Report of the General Land Office.* 21 pp., wrappers. Houston, 1874. $100-$125. Houston, 1876. 27 pp., wrappers. $100.

GROSART, A. B. (editor). *Occasional Issues of Unique and Very Rare Books.* 17 vols., half morocco. London, 1875-81. "Limited to a small number of copies." $1,000 and up.

GROSSMITH, George. *The Diary of a Nobody.* Illustrated by Weedon Grossmith. Light-brown cloth. Bristol, England, (1892). First edition. $50-$75.

GROSZ, George. *Ecce Homo.* Illustrated. Boards. New York, 1965. First American edition. In dust jacket. $35-$50.

GROSZ, George. *George Grosz: Twelve Reproductions from His Original Lithographs.* Wrappers. Chicago, 1921. First edition. $100-$150.

*GROUPED Thoughts and Scattered Fancies.* Cloth. Richmond, Va., 1845. (By William Gilmore Simms.) First edition. $200-$250.

GROVER, La Fayette (editor). *The Oregon Archives.* Printed yellow wrappers. Salem, 1853 (actually 1854). First edition. $750-$1,000. Also, $400 (A, 1969).

*GRYLL Grange.* By the Author of *Headlong Hall.* Cloth. London, 1861. (By Thomas Love Peacock.) First edition, with 4 pages of ads at end. $200-$250.

GUÉRIN, Maurice de. *The Centaur.* Translated by George B. Ives. Boards (Montague, Mass.), 1915. One of 135. Bruce Rogers typography. $400-$500. Rebound in full morocco. Presentation copy, signed by Rogers. $700.

*GUIDE, Gazetteer and Directory of Nebraska Railroads.* Folding map, 6 plates. 210 pp., wrappers. Omaha, 1872. (By J.M. Wolfe.) First edition. $250-$350.

*GUIDE for Emigrants to Minnesota (A).* By a Tourist. Map. 16 pp., printed blue wrappers. St. Paul, 1857. First edition. $200-$300.

GUILD, Jo. C. *Old Times in Tennessee.* Green cloth. Nashville, 1878. First edition. $150-$200. Also, $100 (A, 1967).

GUINEY, Louise Imogen. *Songs at the Start.* Half morocco. Boston, 1884. First edition. $35-$40. (Also issued in cloth.) Author's first book.

GUNN, Donald. *History of Manitoba from the Earliest Settlement to 1835.* Portrait. Cloth. Ottawa, 1880. First edition. $100-$125.

GUNN, Douglas. *San Diego: Climate, Resources, Topography, Production, etc.* 40 pp., plus 16 pp. of ads, printed wrappers. San Diego, 1886. Fourth edition (first 1886 edition). $400.

GUNN, Otis B. *New Map and Hand-Book of Kansas and the Gold-Mines.* Large map in color, folding into back cloth covers, and accompanied by text pamphlet *(Gunn's Map and Hand-Book, etc.),* bound in salmon-colored printed wrappers. Pittsburgh, 1859. First edition. $3,000-$3,500.

GUNN, Thom. *The Explorers.* Printed wrappers. Devon, England, (1969). First edition. (100 copies issued.) One of 64 plain copies. $30-$50. Also, 20 with a poem in the author's hand, $50; 10 copies with three holograph poems, $75-$100; 6 copies with 19 poems written out, $100-$150.

GUNN, Thom. *A Geography.* Wrappers. Iowa City, 1966. First edition, signed. One of 220. $30-$50.

GUNNISON, John W. *The Mormons; or, Latter-Day Saints, in the Valley of the Great Salt Lake.* Illustrated. Dark-blue cloth. Philadelphia, 1852. First edition $100-$200.

GUNSAULUS, Helen C. *The Clarence Buckingham Collection of Japanese Prints: The Primitives.* Plates. Folio, cloth. Chicago, (1955). One of 500. $150-$200. Also, $130 (A, 1974).

GUNTER, Archibald Clavering. *Mr. Barnes of New York.* Cloth, or wrappers. New York, 1887. First edition, first issue, with perfect type in copyright notice. Wrappers: $125. Cloth: $100.

*GUY MANNERING; or, The Astrologer.* 3 vols., boards. Edinburgh, 1815. (By Sir Walter Scott.) First edition. $200-$300.

*GUY Rivers: A Tale of Georgia.* 2 vols., cloth, paper labels. New York, 1834. (By William Gilmore Simms.) First edition. $300-$400. Also, flyleaves torn, $140 (A, 1974).

GUYER, I. D. *History of Chicago.* Illustrated. Cloth. Chicago, 1862. First edition. $200-$250. Also, $120 (A, 1975).

# H

H., H. (translator). *Bathmendi: A Persian Tale*. Translated from the French of Florian. Printed wrappers. Boston, 1867. (Translated by Helen Hunt Jackson.) $150. First publication by the translator.

H., H. *A Century of Dishonor*. Cloth. New York, 1881. (By Helen Hunt Jackson.) First edition. $75-$100.

H., H. *Verses*. Cloth. Boston, 1870. (By Helen Hunt Jackson.) First edition. $50-$75. Author's first book.

HABBERTON, John. See *Helen's Babies; Other People's Children*.

HABERLY, Loyd. *Almost a Minister: A Romance of the Oregon Hopyards*. Illustrated in color by the author. Patterned paper cover, leather spine. (St. Louis, 1942.) Mound City Press. One of 375. $35-$50.

HABERLY, Loyd. *Anne Boleyn, and Other Poems*. Printed in red and black on handmade paper. Niger morocco. Newtown, Wales, 1934. Gregynog Press. One of 300. $100-$150. Another issue: One of 15 (from the edition) elaborately bound. $600-$800.

HABERLY, Loyd. *The Antiquary: A Poem*. Morocco. Long Crendon, England, 1933. Seven Acres Press. One of 100 signed. $100-$150.

HABERLY, Loyd. *Artemis: A Forest Tale*. Illustrated in color by Haberly. Full green morocco. (St. Louis, 1942.) Mound City Press. One of 240. $75-$150.

HABERLY, Loyd. *The Boy and the Bird: An Oregon Idyll*. Woodcuts. Full green morocco. Long Crendon, 1932. Seven Acres Press. One of 155 signed. $100-$150.

HABERLY, Loyd. *The City of the Sainted King and Other Poems*. Full orange-red morocco. (Cambridge, Mass.), 1939. One of 200. $75-$125.

HABERLY, Loyd. *The Keeper of the Doves*. Morocco. Long Crendon, 1933. Seven Acres Press. One of 100 signed. $100-$125.

HABERLY, Loyd. *Medieval English Paving Tiles*. Half morocco. Oxford, 1937. One of 425. $100-$150. Also, $95 (A, 1976).

HABERLY, Loyd. *Poems*. Dark-blue morocco. Long Crendon, 1930. Seven Acres Press. One of 120. $100-$150.

HACKETT, James. *Narrative of the Expedition Which Sailed from England in 1817, to Join the South American Patriots*. Boards. London, 1818. First edition. $150-$250.

HAEBLER, Konrad. *The Early Printers of Spain and Portugal*. Frontispiece and facsimiles. Wrappers. London, 1897 (actually 1896). $100-$150. (Also noted in cloth and half morocco.)

HAFEN, LeRoy R. (editor). *The Mountain Men and the Fur Trade of the Far West*. Illustrated. 10 vols., cloth. Glendale, Calif., 1965-72. In plain dust jackets. $350-$475.

HAFEN, LeRoy R. *The Overland Mail, 1849-1869*. Map, 7 plates. Cloth. Cleveland, 1926. First edition. $60-$80.

HAFEN, LeRoy R. *Overland Routes to the Gold Fields*. 7 plates, folding map. Cloth. Glendale, 1942. First edition. $50-$60.

HAFEN, LeRoy R. and Ann W. *The Old Spanish Trail*. Plates and maps. Cloth. Glendale, 1954. First edition. $25-$35.

HAFEN, LeRoy R. and Ann W. (editors). *The Far West and the Rockies, 1820-75*. Illustrated. 15 vols., green cloth. Glendale, 1954-61. $350-$450. Also, $270 (A, 1968).

HAFEN, LeRoy R., and Ghent, W. J. *Broken Hand: The Life Story of Thomas Fitzpatrick, Chief of the Mountain Men*. Map, 8 plates. Cloth-backed boards. Denver, 1931. First edition. One of 100 large paper copies, signed. $250-$300. Another issue: Cloth. One of 500. In dust jacket. $100-$150.

HAFEN, LeRoy R., and Young, Francis Marion. *Fort Laramie and the Pageant of the West, 1834-1890*. Illustrated. Cloth. Glendale, 1938. First edition. $50-$60.

HAFEN, Mary Ann. *Recollections of a Handcart Pioneer of 1860*. Plates. Cloth. Denver, 1938. First edition. $35-$50.

HAGGARD, H. Rider. *Allan Quatermain*. Frontispiece, 19 plates. Cloth. London, 1887. First edition. $90-$125. Another issue: Half brown morocco. One of 112 on large paper. $150-$200.

HAGGARD, H. Rider. *Allan's Wife and Other Tales*. Illustrated. Half leather. London, 1889. First edition, first issue, with Spencer Blackett imprint on spine. One of 100 on large paper. $50. Trade edition: Cloth. $15-$25.

HAGGARD, H. Rider. *Ayesha: The Return of She*. Illustrated. Cloth. London, 1905. First edition. $75-$100. New York, 1905. Red cloth. First American edition. $15.

HAGGARD, H. Rider. *Cetywayo and His White Neighbours*. Green cloth. London, 1882. First edition.(750 copies.) $200-$250. Author's first book

HAGGARD, H. Rider. *Cleopatra*. Illustrated. Half leather. London, 1889. First edition. One of 57 on large paper. $100-$150. Trade edition: Cloth. $35-$50.

HAGGARD, H. Rider. *Colonel Quaritch, V. C.: A Tale of Country Life*. 3 vols., red cloth. London, 1888. First edition. $150-$200.

HAGGARD, H. Rider. *Dawn*. 3 vols., olive-green cloth. London, 1884. First edition. $400-$500. Also, inscribed copy, worn, $1,100 (A, 1975). Author's first novel.

HAGGARD, H. Rider. *Heart of the World*. Dark-blue or black cloth. London, 1896. First edition. $75-$100.

HAGGARD, H. Rider. *Jess*. Red cloth, London, 1887. First edition. $60-$85.

HAGGARD, H. Rider. *King Solomon's Mines*. Folding colored frontispiece, map. Bright-red cloth. London, 1885. First edition, first issue, with the word "Bamamgwato" in line 14, page 10, and "wrod" for "word" in note on page 307. $100-$150.

HAGGARD, H. Rider. *Maiwa's Revenge*. Black cloth. London, 1888. First edition. $50-$75.

HAGGARD, H. Rider. *Mr. Meeson's Will*. Cloth. London, 1888. First edition. $50-$75.

HAGGARD, H. Rider. *Montezuma's Daughter*. Dark-blue cloth. London, 1893. First edition. $50-$60.

HAGGARD, H. Rider. *Pearl Maiden*. Cloth. London, 1903. First edition. $65-$85.

HAGGARD, H. Rider. *She: A History of Adventure*. Printed wrappers. New York, 1886. First edition. $100-$150. London, 1887. Illustrated. Blue cloth. First English edition, first issue, with "Godness me" in line 38, page 269, etc. $200-$250.

HAGGARD, H. Rider. *Stella Fregelius: A Tale of Three Destinies*. Dark-blue cloth. London, 1904. First edition. $75-$85.

HAGGARD, H. Rider. *The Witch's Head*. 3 vols., cloth. London, 1885. First edition. $200-$300.

HAINES, Elijah M. *The American Indian*. Half morocco. Chicago, 1888. First edition. $75-$100. Also, worn, $24 (A, 1974).

HAINES, Elijah M. *Historical and Statistical Sketches of Lake County, State of Illinois*. Folding frontispiece. 112 pp., printed wrappers. Waukegan, Ill., 1852. First edition. $250-$300.

HAIR, James T. (publisher). *Gazetteer of Madison County, Illinois* . Cloth. Alton, Ill., 1866. First edition. $100-$125.

HAKES, Harlo. *Landmarks of Steuben County, New York*. Cloth. Syracuse, 1896. First edition. $75-$100.

HAKEWILL, James. *A Picturesque Tour of the Island of Jamaica*. 21 colored aquatint plates. Half leather. London, 1825. First edition. $4,500-$5,000.

HAKEWILL, James. *A Picturesque Tour of Italy*. 63 plates, 36 hand-colored. Folio, half morocco. London, 1820. $250-$350.

HALBERT, Henry S., and Ball, Timothy H. *The Creek War of 1813 and 1814*. Portraits, folding map (not in all copies). Cloth. Chicago, 1895. First edition. $100-$125.

HALE, Edward Everett. See *The Man Without a Country*.

HALE, Edward Everett. *Kanzas and Nebraska*. Folding map. Blue or red cloth. Boston, 1854. First edition. $50-$65.

HALE, Edward Everett. *A Tract for the Day: How to Conquer Texas Before Texas Conquers Us*. 16 pp., self-wrappers. Boston, 1845. First edition. $150-$300, possibly more.

HALE, John. *California as It Is*. Boards. San Francisco, 1954. Grabhorn Press. One of 150. $100-$125.

HALE, Lucretia P. *Last of the Peterkins*. 4 plates. Red cloth. Boston, 1886. First edition. $50.

HALE, Lucretia P. *The Peterkin Papers*. Illustrated by F. G. Attwood. Green cloth. Boston, 1880. First edition. $250.

HALE, Sarah Josepha. See *The Genius of Oblivion*.

HALE, Sarah Josepha. *Northwood: A Tale of New England*. 2 vols., buff boards and rose-colored muslin. Boston, 1827. First edition. $75-$100.

HALE, Sarah Josepha (editor). *The Countries of Europe, and the Manners and Customs of Its Various Nations*. Illustrated. Printed wrappers. New York, (about 1842). First edition. $75-$100.

HALE, Sarah Josepha (editor). *The Good Little Boy's Book*. Printed flexible boards. New York, (about 1848). First edition. $50-$75.

HALE, Sarah Josepha Buell (editor). *Happy Changes; or Pride and Its Consequences*. Printed flexible boards. New York, (about 1842). First edition. $50-$60.

HALE, Will. *Twenty-four Years a Cowboy and Ranchman in Southern Texas and Old Mexico*. 268 pp., stiff purplish-blue wrappers. Hedrick (Headrick), Oklahoma Territory, (1905). (By William Hale Stone.) First edition. $4,000-$5,000. (Note: Only four copies known—two in the Library of Congress, one in the University of Oklahoma Library, and one in private hands. The latter, worn and somewhat soiled, was sold to a private collector for $3,600 by my company in 1974.)

HALEY, J. Evetts. *Charles Goodnight, Cowman and Plainsman*. Illustrated by Harold Bugbee. Cloth. Boston, 1936. First edition, with dated title page. In dust jacket. $75-$100.

HALEY, J. Evetts. *Charles Schriener, General Merchandise: The Story of a Country Store.* Illustrated by Harold Bugbee. Cloth. Austin, 1944. First edition. $75-$100. Limited edition: $400-$500.

HALEY, J. Evetts. *Fort Concho on the Texas Frontier.* Illustrated by Harold Bugbee. Cloth. San Angelo, 1952. First edition. One of 185 signed. Boxed. $250-$300. Trade edition: Cloth. In dust jacket. $75-$100.

HALEY, J. Evetts. *The Heraldry of the Range.* Illustrated by Harold Bugbee. Cloth. Canyon, Tex., 1949. First edition. In dust jacket. $250-$300.

HALEY, J. Evetts. *Jeff Milton: A Good Man with a Gun.* Illustrated by Harold Bugbee. Cloth. Norman, Okla., 1948. First edition. In dust jacket. $50-$75.

HALEY, J. Evetts. *Life on the Texas Range.* Photographs by Erwin E. Smith. Pictorial cloth. Austin, 1952. First edition. Boxed. $75-$100.

HALEY, J. Evetts. *The XIT Ranch of Texas.* 2 maps, 30 plates. Cloth. Chicago, 1929. First edition. $250-$300. Author's first book.

HALIBURTON, Thomas Chandler. See *The Clockmaker.*

HALL, Basil. *The Great Polyglot Bibles.* Folio, loose in wrappers. San Francisco, 1966. One of 400. Boxed. $175-$200.

HALL, Capt. Basil. *Forty Etchings, from Sketches made with the Camera Lucida, in North America, in 1827 and 1828.* Folding map, 20 plates. Printed boards. Edinburgh, 1829. First edition. $500-$600. Also, stained, rebacked, $375 (A, 1975). Edinburgh, 1830. Boards. Fourth edition. $300-$400.

HALL, Capt. Basil. *Travels in North America.* Colored folding map, folding table. 3 vols., half calf. Edinburgh, 1829. First edition. $200-$300. Philadelphia, 1829. Illustrated. 2 vols., boards. First American edition. $100-$150.

HALL, Bert L. *Roundup Years.* Illustrated. Pictorial cloth. (Pierre, S.D., 1954.) First edition. $50-$60.

HALL, Carroll D. (editor). *Donner Miscellany.* Boards. San Francisco, 1947. Book Club of California. (Printed by the Allen Press.) One of 350. $100-$150.

HALL, Edward H. *The Great West.* Map. 89 pp., printed wrappers. New York, 1864. First edition. $150-$200. New York, 1865. Map. 198 pp., pictorial wrappers. $150-$200. New York, 1870. Boards. $75-$125.

HALL, Francis. *Travels in Canada and the United States in 1816 and 1817.* Folding map. Boards and calf. London, 1818. First edition. $200-$225. Boston, 1818. Boards. First American edition. $100-$150. London, 1819. Second edition. $100-$125.

HALL, Frederic. *The History of San Jose and Surroundings.* Plates, map. Cloth. San Francisco, 1871. First edition. $125-$150.

HALL, Frederick. *Letters From the East and From the West.* Cloth. Washington, (1840). First edition. $50-$60. Baltimore, 1840. Cloth. $50.

HALL, George Eli. *A Balloon Ascension at Midnight.* Illustrated by Gordon Ross. Boards. San Francisco, 1902. One of 30 on vellum, signed. $125-$150.

HALL, Henry (editor). *The Tribune Book of Open-Air Sports.* Illustrated. Pictorial cloth. New York, 1887. First edition. $100-$150. (Note: The first book composed on the linotype machine.)

HALL, J. *Sonora: Travels and Adventures in Sonora.* Cloth. Chicago, 1881. First edition. $1,250 and up. Also, worn and shaken, $700 (A, 1966).

HALL, James. *The Harpe's Head: A Legend of Kentucky.* Wrappers, or cloth. Philadelphia, 1833. First edition. Wrappers: $150-$200. Cloth: $100-$125. Also, $75 (A, 1967).

HALL, James. *Legends of the West*. Boards and muslin. Philadelphia, 1832. First edition. $50-$75. Philadelphia, 1833. Cloth. Second edition. $25-$35. Cincinnati, 1869. Cloth. $25.

HALL, James. *Letters from the West*. Boards. London, 1828. First edition. $100-$150.

HALL, James. *Notes on the Western States*. Cloth. Philadelphia, 1838. Later edition of *Statistics of the West*. $50-$60.

HALL, James. *The Romance of Western History*. Frontispiece. Cloth. Cincinnati, 1857. First edition. $50-$60.

HALL, James. *Sketches of History, Life, and Manners in the West*. Vol. 1. (All published.) Brown cloth. Cincinnati, 1834. First edition. $75-$100. Philadelphia, 1835. 2 vols., cloth. First complete edition. $100-$125.

HALL, James. *Statistics of the West*. Cloth. Cincinnati, 1836. First edition, first printing, purple cloth. $100-$150. Second printing, slate-colored cloth. $75-$100. Cincinnati, 1837. Cloth. $35.

HALL, James (editor). *The Western Souvenir: A Christmas and New Year's Gift for 1839*. Illustrated. Silk. Cincinnati, (1828). First edition. $150-$300.

HALL, James Norman. See Nordhoff, Charles B. (For *Mutiny on the Bounty*.)

HALL, James Norman. *Kitchener's Mob*. Portrait. Cloth. Boston, 1916. First edition. In dust jacket. $25-$35. Author's first book.

HALL, James Norman, and Nordhoff, Charles B. *The Lafayette Flying Corps*. Illustrated, including colored plates. 2 vols, blue cloth. Boston, 1920. First edition. In dust jackets. $300-$450.

HALL, Manly P. *An Encyclopedic Outline of Masonic, Cabbalistic and Rosicrucian Symbolical Philosophy*. Colored plates, text illustrations. Folio boards and vellum. San Francisco, 1928. John Henry Nash printing. One of 550 signed. Boxed. $450-$550.

HALL, Manly P. *The Secret Teaching of All Ages*. Illustrated. Half morocco. Los Angeles, 1975. "Golden Anniversary Edition" of *An Encyclopedic Outline* (see above entry). One of 550 signed. $100.

HALL, Marshall. *New Memoir on the Nervous System*. 5 plates. Boards. London, 1843. First edition. $200-$300.

HALL, Marshall. *Principles of the Theory and Practice of Medicine*. Sheep. Boston, 1839. First American edition. $50-$75. (Note: Contains new material by Oliver Wendell Holmes.)

HALL, Marguerite Radclyffe. *The Forgotten Island*. Black cloth. London, 1915. First edition. In dust jacket. $150-$200.

HALL, (Marguerite) Radclyffe. *The Master of the House*. Buckram, vellum spine. London, (1932). First edition. One of 172 signed. $175-$200. Trade edition: Cloth. In dust jacket. $50-$60. New York, (1932). First American edition. In dust jacket, $25.

HALL, Marguerite Radclyffe. *Poems of the Past and Present*. Green cloth. London, 1910. First edition. In dust jacket. $150-$200.

HALL, Marguerite Radclyffe. *A Sheaf of Verses*. Pink cloth. London, 1908. First edition. $175-$225.

HALL, (Marguerite) Radclyffe. *The Well of Loneliness*. Black cloth. London, (1928). First edition, first issue, with "whip" for "whips" on page 50, line 3. In dust jacket. $125-$150. Paris, (1928). Edited by Havelock Ellis. Black cloth. $50-$75. New York, 1928. Boards and cloth. First American edition. In dust jacket. $50-$75. New York, 1929. 2 vols., half cloth. One of 225 signed. Boxed. $150-$175.

HALL, Samuel R. *Lectures to Female Teachers on School-Keeping*. Boards. Boston, 1832. First edition. $50-$100.

HALL, Samuel R. *Lectures on School-Keeping*. Boards and cloth. Boston, 1829. First edition. $150-$200.

HALLAS, Richard. *You Play the Black and the Red Comes Up*. Red cloth. New York, 1938. (By Eric Knight.) First edition. In dust jacket. $50.

HALLECK, Fitz-Greene. See Croaker. Also see *Alnwick Castle; Fanny*.

HALLENBECK, Cleve. *The Journal of Fray Marcos de Niza*. Illustrated. Cloth. Dallas, 1949. First edition. In dust jacket. Boxed. $100-$125.

HALLEY, William. *Centennial Year Book of Description of the Contra Costa Under Spanish, Mexican, and American Rule*. Illustrated. Cloth. Oakland, 1876. $75-$150.

HALSEY, R. T. H. *Pictures of Early New York on Dark Blue Staffordshire Pottery*. 155 illustrations, mostly in color. Cloth. New York, 1899. First edition. One of 286 on handmade paper. $100-$150. Another issue: One of 30 on vellum. $200-$300.

HALSTEAD, Murat. *The Caucuses of 1860*. Cloth. Columbus, Ohio, 1860. First edition. $75-$100.

HAMBLETON, Chalkley J. *A Gold Hunter's Experience*. Green cloth. Chicago, 1898. First edition. $150-$250.

HAMERTON, Philip G. *Etching and Etchers*. Illustrated. Half morocco. London, 1868. First edition. $250-$350. London, 1880. Third edition. (With a Whistler etching.) $500-$600.

HAMILTON, Dr. Alexander. *Hamilton's Itinerarium*. Map. Half leather. St. Louis, 1907. One of 487. Boxed. $125-$150.

HAMILTON, Gail. *Gala-Days*. Cloth. Boston, 1863. (By Mary Abigail Dodge.) First edition. $50-$65.

HAMILTON, H. W. *Rural Sketches of Minnesota*. 40 pp., printed wrappers. Milan, Ohio, 1850. First edition. $500 and up. Also, $325 (A, 1974).

HAMILTON, John P. *Travels Through the Interior Provinces of Colombia*. Map, 7 plates. 2 vols., calf. London, 1827. First edition. $150-$200.

HAMILTON, W. T. *My Sixty Years on the Plains*. Edited by E. T. Sieber. 8 plates (6 by Charles M. Russell). Cloth. New York, 1905. First edition. $75-$100.

HAMILTON, The Rev. William, and Irvin, the Rev. S. M. *An Ioway Grammar*. Wrappers. (Wolf Creek, Neb.), 1848. Ioway and Sac Mission Press. First edition. $1,000-$1,250.

HAMMER, William J. *Radium, and Other Radio-Active Substances*. Illustrated. Cloth. New York, 1903. First edition. $250-$350.

HAMMETT, Dashiell. *The Dain Curse*. Cloth. New York, 1929. First edition. In dust jacket. $50-$200.

HAMMETT, Dashiell. *The Glass Key*. Light-green cloth. New York, 1931. First edition. In dust jacket. $300-$350.

HAMMETT, Dashiell. *The Maltese Falcon*. Gray cloth. New York, 1930. First edition. In dust jacket. $300-$500. (One dealer we know got $700 for a copy!)

HAMMETT, Dashiell. *Red Harvest*. Cloth. New York, 1929. First edition. In dust jacket. $50-$75. Author's first book.

HAMMETT, Dashiell. *The Thin Man*. Green cloth. New York, 1934. First edition. In first issue (red) dust jacket. $125-$150. In second issue (green) dust jacket. $100-$125. (Note: The "seep" for "sleep" misprint, page 209, once believed by bibliographers to be a first-issue point, is no longer valid, since it appeared through several printings, according to the detective fiction authority Otto Penzler. The prime *Thin Man* is one with the red jacket, most experts agree.)

HAMMOND, John Martin. *Colonial Mansions of Maryland and Delaware*. 65 plates. Cloth. Philadelphia, 1914. First edition. Limited. $100-$125.

HANCOCK, R. R. *Hancock's Diary: or, a History of the 2d Tennessee Confederate Cavalry*. 2 plates. Cloth. Nashville, 1887. First edition. $125-$150.

*HANDBOOK for Boys*. Dark olive khaki cloth, either flexible or hardbound. New York, 1911. First edition of the first official Boy Scouts of America Handbook. $100-$150.

*HANDBOOK for Scout Masters: Boy Scouts of America*. Cloth. New York, (1914). First edition. In original khaki Scout case. $50-$75. (Note: The first *Handbook for Scout Masters*.)

*HAND Book of Monterey and Vicinity (The)*. 152 pp., printed wrappers. Monterey, 1875. $100-$150.

*HAND-Book of Ness County, the Banner County of Western Kansas*. 36 pp., wrappers. Chicago, 1887. $175-$225.

*HANDLEY Cross: or, Mr. Jorrocks's Hunt*. 17 color plates and numerous woodcuts by John Leech. 17 parts in pictorial wrappers. London, 1853-54. (By Robert Smith Surtees.) First illustrated edition. With all the ads and slips and with the words "with the aid of the illustrious Leech" in the preface. $300-$600. London, 1854. Cloth. First illustrated book edition. $150-$200.

*HANDLEY Cross; or, The Spa Hunt*. 3 vols., boards and cloth. London, 1843. (By Robert Smith Surtees.) First edition. $75-$125.

HANNA, Charles A. *The Wilderness Trail*. Maps and illustrations. 2 vols., cloth. New York, 1911. First edition. One of 1,000. In dust jackets. Boxed. $125-$150.

HANNOVER, Emil. *Pottery and Porcelain: A Handbook for Collectors*. Illustrated. 3 vols., cloth. London, 1925. First edition. $250-$300, possibly more.

HANSON, George A. *Old Kent: The Eastern Shore of Maryland*. Cloth. Baltimore, 1876. First edition. $50-$75.

*HARBINGER (The): A May-Gift*. Cloth, paper spine label. Boston, 1833. First edition. $40-$60. (Note: Contains 17 poems by Oliver Wendell Holmes.)

HARDEE, William J. *Rifle and Light Infantry Tactics*. 2 vols., or 2 vols. in one, half leather. Memphis, 1861. $175-$200. (Other editions in the same year in Richmond and Philadelphia.)

HARDIN, John Wesley. *The Life of John Wesley Hardin*. Portrait, other illustrations. 144 pp., printed wrappers. Seguin, Tex., 1896. First edition, first issue, with portrait of Hardin's brother mislabeled "John." $35-$50. Second issue, with the Hardin portrait tipped in. $25-$35. (A more common book than once supposed.)

HARDIN, Mrs. Philomelia Ann Maria Antoinette. *Everybody's Cook and Receipt Book*. Printed boards. Cleveland, 1842. First edition. $50-$75.

HARDING, George L. *D. B. Updike and the Merrymount Press*. Stiff wrappers. San Francisco, 1943. Roxburghe Club. One of 150. $75-$125.

HARDING, George L. *Don Augustin V. Zamorano: Statesman, Soldier, Craftsman, and California's First Printer*. Illustrated. Cloth. Los Angeles, 1934. First edition. In dust jacket. $100-$150.

HARDY, John. *A Collection of Sacred Hymns, Adapted to the Faith and Views of the Church of Jesus Christ of Latter Day Saints*. 160 pp., full calf. Boston, 1843. First edition. $2,000.

HARDY, Joseph. *A Picturesque and Descriptive Tour in the Mountains of the High Pyrenees*. Map, 24 hand-colored plates. Cloth. London, 1825. First edition. $300-$400.

HARDY, Thomas. See Henniker, Florence. Also see *Desperate Remedies; Under the Greenwood Tree.*

HARDY, Thomas. *"And There Was a Great Calm."* Wrappers. London, 1920. Chiswick Press. First edition. One of 25 initialed by Florence Emily Hardy. $25-$35.

HARDY, Thomas. *Before Marching and After.* Wrappers. (London, 1915.) First edition. One of 25. $25.

HARDY, Thomas. *A Changed Man.* Frontispiece and map. Green cloth. London, 1913. First edition. In dust jacket. $75-$125. New York, 1913. Blue cloth. First American edition. $25-$35.

HARDY, Thomas. *Compassion: An Ode.* 6 pp., printed wrappers. (Dorchester, England, 1924.) First edition. One of 25 signed by Hardy. $35-$50. Another issue (?): 10 pp., printed wrappers. "Printed for A. J. A. Symons." One of 50 signed by Symons. $61.60 (A, 1966).

HARDY, Thomas. *The Convergence of the Twain.* Blue boards, paper label on front cover. London, 1912. First edition. One of 10 signed by the printers. $75-$100.

HARDY, Thomas. *A Defence of "Jude the Obscure."* Wrappers. Edinburgh, 1928. First edition. One of 30. $100-$150.

HARDY, Thomas. *Domicilium.* Wrappers. (London, 1916.) First edition. One of 25. $100-$150.

HARDY, Thomas. *The Duke's Reappearance.* Boards. New York, 1927. One of 89. $50-$75.

HARDY, Thomas. *The Dynasts: A Drama of the Napoleonic Wars.* 3 vols., green cloth. London, 1903-06-08. First edition, first issue (of Vol. 1, with date 1903 on title page). In dust jackets. $750 and up. Also, $450 (A, 1974). Presentation set (so blind-stamped on title pages). $450. Also, $175 (A, 1968). London, 1904-06-08. Second issue (of Vol. 1). $50-$100. London, 1910. Portrait. Cloth. First one-volume edition. In dust jacket. $25. London, 1927. Portrait etching, signed by Francis Dodd. 3 vols., half vellum. One of 525 signed by Hardy. In dust jackets. $450-$500.

HARDY, Thomas. *The Dynasts: Prologue and Epilogue.* Wrappers. (London, 1914.) First edition. One of 12. $75-$100.

HARDY, Thomas. *Far from the Madding Crowd.* 12 illustrations by H. Patterson. 2 vols., pictorial green cloth. London, 1874. First English edition, first issue, with "Sacrament" in first line of page 2, Vol. 1. $1,000 and up. Also, $2,600 (A, 1977)—a "superb" copy. (Copies in ordinary worn condition bring much lower prices at retail.) New York, 1958. Limited Editions Club. Illustrated. Half leather. Boxed. $35-$50.

HARDY, Thomas. *Fellow-Townsmen.* Wrappers. New York, (1880). First edition. George Munro, publisher. $75-$100.

HARDY, Thomas. *A Group of Noble Dames.* Light-brown cloth. (London, 1891.) First edition, first issue, with yellow end papers. $60-$80. Second issue, white end papers. $35-$50. New York, 1891. Brown cloth. First American edition. $25.

HARDY, Thomas. *The Hand of Ethelberta.* 11 illustrations by George Du Maurier. 2 vols., terra-cotta cloth. London, 1876. First edition, first issue, with "two or three individuals" instead of "five or six individuals" in caption facing page 146 in Vol. 1. $250-$400. Also, hinges cracked, $200 (A, 1975).

HARDY, Thomas. *Human Shows: Far Phantasies; Songs and Trifles.* Green cloth. London. 1925. First edition. In dust jacket. $60-$100.

HARDY, Thomas. *An Indiscretion in the Life of an Heiress.* Vellum. (London), 1934. First edition. One of 100. $100-$150.

HARDY, Thomas. *Jezreel: The Master and the Leaves.* Wrappers. London, 1919. First edition. One of 25 initialed by Florence Emily Hardy. $125-$150.

HARDY, Thomas. *Jude the Obscure*. Map, etching by H. Macbeth-Raeburn. Green cloth. (London, 1896). First edition, first issue, with Osgood's name on title page and spine. $150-$200. New York, 1969. Limited Editions Club. Boxed. $80-$100.

HARDY, Thomas. *A Laodicean; or, The Castle of the De Stancys*. 3 vols., slate-colored cloth. London, 1881. First English edition, first issue, without the word "or" on half title of Vol. 1. $200-$250. Second issue, with the word "or" on half title of Vol. 1. $150-$200. New York, (1881). Wrappers (without title page but with cover title only). First edition. $150-$250.

HARDY, Thomas. *Late Lyrics and Earlier*. Green cloth. London, 1922. First edition. In dust jacket. $50-$75.

HARDY, Thomas. *Life's Little Ironies*. Green cloth. London, (1894). First edition. $70-$80. New York, 1894. Green cloth. First American edition. $25.

HARDY, Thomas. *The Mayor of Casterbridge*. 2 vols., blue cloth. London, 1886. First edition. $250-$400. New York, 1886. Wrappers. First American edition. $75-$100. New York, 1964. Limited Editions Club. Illustrated. Half morocco. Boxed. $50-$60.

HARDY, Thomas. *Moments of Vision and Miscellaneous Verses*. Green cloth. London, 1917. First edition. In dust jacket. $75-$125.

HARDY, Thomas. *No Bell-Ringing*. Wrappers. Dorchester, England, 1925. First edition. One of 25. $75-$100.

HARDY, Thomas. *Notes on "The Dynasts."* Printed wrappers. Edinburgh, 1929. First edition. One of 20. $100-$150.

HARDY, Thomas. *Old Mrs. Chundle*. Boards and cloth. New York, 1929. First edition. One of 742. $40-$60.

HARDY, Thomas. *A Pair of Blue Eyes*. 3 vols., green or maroon cloth, yellow end papers. London, 1873. First edition, first issue, with "c" dropped or missing from the word "clouds" in last line on page 5 of Vol. 2. $250-$300.

HARDY, Thomas. *Poems of the Past and the Present*. White (cream) or dark-green cloth. (London, 1902.) First edition. $75-$100.

HARDY, Thomas. *The Return of the Native*. Frontispiece map. 3 vols., brown cloth. London, 1878. First edition, first binding, with double blind rule on back cover. $1,200-$1,500. Also, $1,200 (A, 1974). New York, 1878. Cream-colored cloth. First American edition. $60-$80. London, 1929. Illustrated by Clare Leighton. Batik boards, vellum spine. One of 1,500 signed by the artist. Boxed. $75-$100.

HARDY, Thomas. *Satires of Circumstances*. Green cloth. London, 1914. First edition. In dust jacket. $75-$100.

HARDY, Thomas. *Selected Poems*. Photogravure portrait on title page. Blue cloth. London, 1916. First edition. $85. London, 1921. Riccardi Press. Woodcut engravings, including title page, by William Nicholson. Vellum. One of 100. In dust jacket. $150-$200. Another issue: Limp vellum with ties. One of 14 on vellum, signed by author and artist. $800-$1,000. Another issue: Half cloth. One of 1,025. $75-$85.

HARDY, Thomas. *Some Romano-British Relics Found at Max Gate*. Printed wrappers. Dorchester, 1890. First edition. $100-$125.

HARDY, Thomas. *Song of the Soldiers*. 4 pp., wrappers. Hove, England, 1914. First edition. $50-$60.

HARDY, Thomas. *Souvenir Programme: Wessex Scenes from "The Dynasts."* Illustrated. Limp boards. (Dorchester, 1916.) One of 12 signed. $100 and up.

HARDY, Thomas. *Tess of the D'Urbervilles*. 3 vols., brownish-orange cloth. (London, 1891.) First edition, first issue, with "Chapter XXV" for "Chapter XXXV" and with "road" for "load" on page 198, Vol. 3. $600-$800. Also, $550 (A, 1975). (London, 1892.)

Second issue, with corrections. $250-$300. London, 1926. 41 wood engravings by Vivien Gribble, folding map. Marbled boards, vellum spine. One of 325 signed. In dust jacket. $200-$300.

HARDY, Thomas. *The Three Wayfarers*. Half cloth. New York, 1930. One of 542. In dust jacket. $75-$100.

HARDY, Thomas. *Time's Laughingstocks and Other Verses*. Green cloth. London, 1909. First edition. $75-$100.

HARDY, Thomas. *The Trumpet-Major*. 3 vols., decorated red cloth. London, 1880. First edition. $400-$600. Also, $375 (A, 1974). Second issue, green cloth. $150-$300. New York, 1880. Pictorial cloth. First American edition. $150-$250.

HARDY, Thomas. *Two on a Tower: A Romance*. 3 vols., green cloth. London, 1882. First edition. $200-$275. New York, 1882. Decorated yellow cloth. First American edition. $100-$125.

HARDY, Thomas. *The Two Hardys*. Unbound. (London?), 1927. One of 50. $100-$150.

HARDY, Thomas. *The Well-Beloved*. Etching, map. Ribbed dark-green cloth. London, (1897). First edition, first issue, with Osgood's name on title page and spine. $75-$100.

HARDY, Thomas. *Wessex Poems and Other Verses*. 30 illustrations by the author. Dark green, blue, or white cloth. (London, 1898.) First edition. $100-$125. London, 1908. Illustrated. Cloth. $25.

HARDY, Thomas. *Wessex Tales, Strange, Lively and Commonplace*. 2 vols., green cloth. London, 1888. First edition. $300-$350.

HARDY, Thomas. *Winter Night in Woodland*. 6 pp., wrappers. (London, 1925.) First edition. One of 25. $100-$150.

HARDY, Thomas. *Winter Words in Various Moods and Metres*. Olive-green cloth. London, 1928. First edition. In dust jacket. $75-$100. Also, $40 (A, 1975). New York, 1928. Green cloth. First American edition. In dust jacket. $35-$50.

HARDY, Thomas. *The Woodlanders*. 3 vols., smooth dark-green cloth. London, 1887. First edition, first binding, first issue, with ad leaf at end of Vol. 1. $400-$500. Also, $275 and $240 (A, 1975); $292 (A, 1973). Second binding, pebbled dark-green cloth. $300-$350.

HARDY, Thomas. *Yuletide in a Younger World*. Wrappers. New York, 1927. First American edition. One of 27 issued to obtain copyright. $250-$350. Also, $200 (A, 1977).

HARDY, Thomas; Lorne, the Marquis of, and Alexander, Mrs. *Three Notable Stories*. Gray cloth. London, 1890. First edition. $75-$100.

HARE, George H. *Guide to San Jose and Vicinity*. 2 maps. 85 pp., wrappers. San Jose, 1872. First edition. $150-$175.

HARFORD, Henry. *Fan: The Story of a Young Girl's Life*. 3 vols., sage-green cloth. London, 1892. (By W. H. Hudson.) First edition. $1,500-$2,000.

HARGRAVE, Catherine Perry. *A History of Playing Cards*. Illustrated. Cloth. Boston, 1930. First edition. In dust jacket. $200-$250.

HARLAN, Jacob Wright. *California, '46 to '88*. Portrait frontispiece. Cloth. San Francisco, 1888. First edition. $100-$125.

HARLOW, Alvin F. *Old Towpaths*. Illustrated. Cloth. New York, 1926. First edition. $75-$125.

HARLOW, Alvin F. *Old Waybills*. Illustrated. Cloth. New York, 1934. First edition. In dust jacket. $75-$125.

HARLOW, Neal. *The Maps of San Francisco Bay*. Folio, half leather. San Francisco, 1950. Grabhorn Press. One of 375. $400-$500.

HARMAN, S. W. *Hell on the Border.* Portrait, map. Stiff printed green wrappers. Fort Smith, Ark., (1898). First edition. $400-$500. Later: Cloth. $300-$350.

HARMON, Daniel Williams. *A Journal of Voyages and Travels in the Interiour* (sic) *of North America.* Portrait, folding map. Calf. Andover, Mass., 1820. First edition, first issue, with map placed opposite title page and with no errata slip. $300-$500.

*HAROLD the Dauntless.* Boards. Edinburgh, 1817. (By Sir Walter Scott.) First edition. $75-$150.

HARPER, Henry H. *A Journey in Southeastern Mexico.* Boards. Boston, 1910. First edition. $35-$50.

HARRINGTON, Kate. *In Memoriam: Maymie, April 6th, 1869.* 60 pp., cloth. Keokuk, Iowa, 1870. First edition. $75.

HARRINGTON, Kate. *Old Settlers' Poem.* 17 pp., printed wrappers. Keokuk, 1874. $75-$100.

HARRIS, Albert W. *The Blood of the Arab.* Cloth. Chicago, 1941. First edition. $50-$75.

HARRIS, Chapin A. *The Dental Art.* Cloth. Baltimore, 1839. First edition. $150-$200.

HARRIS, Chapin A. *A Dictionary of Dental Science.* Calf. Philadelphia, 1849. First edition. $75-$100.

HARRIS, Dean. *By Path and Trail.* Illustrated. Cloth. Chicago, 1908. $25.

HARRIS, Frank. *Elder Conklin and Other Stories.* Cloth. New York, 1894. First edition. $35-$50. Author's first book. London, 1895. Green cloth. First English edition. $25-$35.

HARRIS, Frank. *Joan La Romee: A Drama.* Cloth. London, (1927). Fortune Press. First edition. One of 350 signed. In dust jacket. $50-$75.

HARRIS, Frank. *La Vie d'Oscar Wilde.* 2 vols., printed wrappers. Paris, 1928. One of 110. $100-$125.

HARRIS, Frank. *A Mad Love.* 70 pp., printed wrappers. New York, 1920. $35-$50.

HARRIS, Frank. *The Man Shakespeare and His Tragic Life Story.* Boards and vellum. London, 1909. First edition. One of 150 on large paper, signed $50-$75. Trade edition: Green cloth. $20-$25.

HARRIS, Frank. *Oscar Wilde: His Life and Confessions.* 2 vols., half morocco. New York, 1916. First edition. Japan paper issue. In dust jackets. Boxed. $100-$150.

HARRIS, Frank. *Stories of Jesus the Christ.* Wrappers. New York, 1919. Pearson's 25¢ Library. First edition. $40-$50. (Note: Includes a Shaw contribution.)

HARRIS, George Washington. See Spavery.

HARRIS, Henry. *California's Medical Story.* Half morocco. San Francisco, 1932. Grabhorn Press. One of 200. $75-$125.

HARRIS, Joel Chandler. See Davidson, James Wood.

HARRIS, Joel Chandler. *Daddy Jake the Runaway.* Illustrated. Pictorial cream-colored glazed boards. New York, (1889). First edition. $100-$150.

HARRIS, Joel Chandler. *Free Joe and Other Georgian Sketches.* Pictorial red cloth. New York, 1887. First edition. $100-$150. Also, $119 (A, 1976).

HARRIS, Joel Chandler. *Nights with Uncle Remus.* Illustrated. Pictorial gray cloth. Boston, 1883. First edition. $75-$100.

HARRIS, Joel Chandler. *Plantation Pageants.* Illustrated. Cloth. Boston, 1899. First edition. $50-$65.

HARRIS, Joel Chandler. *Tales of the Home Folks in Peace and War.* Illustrated. Cloth. Boston, 1898. First edition. In dust jacket. $75-$100.

HARRIS, Joel Chandler. *The Tar-Baby and Other Rhymes of Uncle Remus.* Cloth. New York, 1904. First edition. In dust jacket. $100-$150.

HARRIS, Joel Chandler. *Uncle Remus and His Legends of the Old Plantation.* Olive-green cloth. London, 1881. First English edition of *Uncle Remus: His Songs and His Sayings.* $150-$200.

HARRIS, Joel Chandler. *Uncle Remus: His Songs and His Sayings.* Illustrated by Frederick S. Church and James S. Moser. Pictorial blue cloth. New York, 1881. First edition, first issue, with "presumptive" for "presumptuous" in last line, page 9, and with no mention of this book in ads at back. $350-$400. Author's first book. Second issue, with "presumptuous" in last line, page 9. $50-$60. (For first English edition, see preceding entry.) New York, 1895. Illustrated by A. B. Frost. Vellum. One of 250 signed. $80-$125. Trade edition: Red buckram. $15-$25. New York, 1920. Edited by Thomas Nelson Page. Illustrated. Pictorial cloth. $75-$125. Mount Vernon, N.Y., (1937). Morocco. One of 50. $35-$50. New York, 1957. Limited Editions Club. Illustrated. Pictorial cloth. Boxed. $100.

HARRIS, Mark. *Trumpet to the World.* Yellow cloth. New York, (1946). First edition. In dust jacket. $35. Author's first book.

HARRIS, Sarah Hollister. *An Unwritten Chapter of Salt Lake, 1851-1901.* Cloth. New York. 1901. First edition. $200-$250.

HARRIS, Thaddeus Mason. *The Journal of a Tour into the Territory Northwest of the Alleghany Mountains.* 4 maps (3 folding) and a folding plate. Marbled boards, paper spine and paper label. Boston, 1805. First edition. $125-$250.

HARRIS, Thomas Lake. *A Lyric of the Golden Age.* Cloth. New York, 1856. First edition. $50-$60.

HARRIS, Thomas M. *Assassination of Lincoln.* Illustrated. Pictorial cloth. Boston, (1892). First edition. $35-$50.

HARRIS, W. B. *Pioneer Life in California.* 98 pp., pictorial wrappers. Stockton, 1884. First edition. $250.

HARRIS, William Charles. *The Fishes of North America That Are Captured on Hook and Line.* Vol. 1. (All published.) Folio, half leather. New York, 1898. First edition. $75-$100.

HARRIS, William R. *The Catholic Church in Utah.* Map, 25 plates. Cloth. Salt Lake City, (1909). First edition. $50. (Also issued in 2 vols.)

HARRISON, E. J. *The Thrilling, Startling and Wonderful Narrative of Lieutenant Harrison.* Illustration in text. 30 pp., printed buff wrappers. Cincinnati, 1848. First edition. $1,000 and up. (Note: Three copies known.)

HARRISON, Fairfax. *Virginia Land Grants.* Cloth. Richmond, 1925. First edition. $35-$50.

HARRISON, William Henry. *A Discourse on the Aborigines of the Valley of the Ohio.* Folding map. 51 pp., wrappers. Cincinnati, 1838. First edition. $75-$100. Presentation copy with manuscript corrections by Harrison, $750.

HART, Charles Henry, and Biddle, Edward. *Memoirs of the Life and Works of Jean Antoine Houdon.* 33 full-page plates. Cloth. Philadelphia, 1911. One of 250. $75-$100.

HART, George. *The Violin: Its Famous Makers and Their Imitators.* Illustrated. Cloth. London, 1875. First edition. $100-$150. Boston, 1884. Cloth. $50-$60.

HART, John A., and others. *History of Pioneer Days in Texas and Oklahoma.* 12 plates. 249 pp., cloth. (Guthrie, Okla., 1906.) First edition. $150-$200. Second edition: (Guthrie, 1909?) 271 pp., cloth. $75.

HART, John A., and others. *Pioneer Days in the Southwest.* 12 plates. 320 pp., cloth. Guthrie, 1909. Enlarged edition of *History of Pioneer Days, etc.* $40-$50. Another issue: 16 plates. $40-$50.

HART, Joseph C. *The Romance of Yachting.* Cloth. New York, 1848. First edition. $75-$125.

HARTE, Bret. See *Oration, Poem, and Speeches; Outcroppings.*

HARTE, Bret. *The Argonauts of North Liberty.* Cloth. Boston, 1888. First edition. $75-$100. Toronto, (1888). Wrappers. $30-$40.

HARTE, Bret. *Bret Harte's Heathen Chinee.* Yellow wrappers. London (about 1881). $125.

HARTE, Bret. *Condensed Novels and Other Papers.* Illustrated by Frank Bellew. Violet cloth. New York, 1867. First edition. $100-$125. Also, spine faded, $70 (A, 1974). Author's first book.

HARTE, Bret. *Dickens in Camp.* Half cloth. San Francisco, 1922. Grabhorn printing. One of 350. $40-$60.

HARTE, Bret. "*Excelsior.*" (Cover title.) 16 pp., oblong, blue wrappers. Five Points, N.Y., (1877). First edition, first issue, with Donaldson imprint. $75-$100. Later issue, without Donaldson imprint: $35-$50. (Also issued in cloth.)

HARTE, Bret. *Gabriel Conroy.* Illustrated. Mauve cloth. Hartford, 1876. First American edition, first binding. $150-$200. London, (1876). 3 vols., cloth. First edition. $100-$150. Also, rubbed, $65 (A, 1971).

HARTE, Bret. *The Lost Galleon and Other Tales.* Cloth. San Francisco, 1867. First edition. $125-$200. Author's first book of verse.

HARTE, Bret. *The Luck of Roaring Camp and Other Sketches.* Green or terra-cotta cloth. Boston, 1870. First edition, first issue, without the story "Brown of Calaveras." $300-$400. Second issue: Brown cloth. $100-$200. Boston, 1870. Second edition. $100-$150. San Francisco, 1916. John Henry Nash printing. Half cloth. One of 260. $75-$100. San Francisco, 1948. Grabhorn Press. Folio, half cloth. One of 300. $75-$85.

HARTE, Bret. *Mliss: An Idyl of Red-Mountain.* Printed wrappers. New York, (1873). (Pirated edition of the story, which originally appeared in *The Luck of Roaring Camp.* Contains 50 additional chapters by R. G. Densmore.) First edition, first issue, with Harte's name on the title page and front cover. $1,000 and up. Part of spine missing, $500. Also, A-record: $900 (1945). Second issue, with Harte's name removed and with page 34 a cancel leaf. $400-$500. San Francisco, 1948. Grabhorn Press. Half cloth. One of 300. $65-$100.

HARTE, Bret. *The Pliocene Skull.* Illustrated by E. M. Schaeffer. 9 leaves, flexible purple boards and cloth. (Washington, 1871?). First edition, presumed first issue. $150-$250. Presumed second issue: 10 leaves, flexible boards, with drawing of miner on front cover. $75-$100. (Note: Blanck questions this long-accepted sequence but doesn't say why. The first issue has an auction record of $170, set in 1944.)

HARTE, Bret. *Poems.* Green cloth. Boston, 1871. First edition, first issue, with Fields, Osgood monogram on title page and "S.T.K." for "T.S.K." on page 136. $75-$100.

HARTE, Bret. *The Queen of the Pirate Isle.* 28 color illustrations by Kate Greenaway. Decorated cloth. London, (1886). First edition, first issue, bound in unbleached linen, with green end papers, gilt edges. $150-$200. Boston, 1887 (actually 1886). Illustrated. Cloth. First American edition. $75-$125.

HARTE, Bret. *San Francisco in 1866.* San Francisco, 1951. Grabhorn Press. One of 400. $75-$100.

HARTE, Bret. *The Story of Enriquez.* Boards. San Francisco, 1924. Grabhorn Press. First edition. One of 100. $75-$100.

HARTE, Bret. *Tales of the Argonauts, and Other Sketches*. Cloth. Boston, 1875. First edition. $40-$65.

HARTE, Bret. *Tales of the Gold Rush*. Illustrated. Cloth. New York, 1944. Limited Editions Club. First edition. Boxed. $50-$60.

HARTE, Bret. *Tennessee's Partner*. Boards and vellum. San Francisco, 1907. First edition. $40-$60.

HARTE, Bret. *The Wild West*. Hand-colored illustrations. Burlap. Paris, (1930). Harrison of Paris. First edition. One of 36 on vellum. Boxed. $100-$150. Another issue: One of 840. $50-$60.

HARTE, Bret, and Bellows, the Rev. Henry W. *Fourteenth Anniversary of the Society of California Pioneers. Oration: By Rev. Henry W. Bellows. Poem: By Frank Bret Harte, Esq.* Printed wrappers. San Francisco, 1864. First edition. $150-$250.

HARTE, Bret, and Twain, Mark. *Sketches of the Sixties*. Boards and cloth. San Francisco, 1926. First edition. One of 250. In dust jacket. $75-$100.

HARTLEY, L. P. *The Go-Between*. Red cloth. London, 1953. First edition. In dust jacket. $35-$50.

HARTLEY, Marsden. *Twenty-Five Poems*. Wrappers. (Paris, 1923,) First edition. $100-$125.

HARTLEY, Oliver C. *Digest of the Laws of Texas*. Buckram. Philadelphia, 1850. $150-$200.

HARTSHORNE, Albert. *Old English Glasses*. Color frontispiece, plates, numerous drawings. Folio, vellum and cloth. London, 1897. $75-$150.

HARTZENBUSCH, Juan Eugenio. *The Lovers of Teruel*. Translated by Henry Thomas. Morocco. Newtown, Wales, 1938. Gregynog Press. One of 175. $250-$300. Another issue: One of 20 specially bound in morocco by George Fisher. $400-$600.

*HARVARD Class Day 1910*. (Cover title.) Illustrated. 17 leaves, stiff cream wrappers, red cord ties. (Cambridge, Mass.), 1910. $600-$900. Also, $600 (A, 1977). (Note: Includes a class ode by T. S. Eliot, his first contribution to a book.)

*HARVARD Lyrics*. Cloth. Boston, 1899. First edition. Includes "Vita Mea," the first published work of Wallace Stevens. $250 (A, 1977).

*HARVEY BELDEN: or a True Narrative of Strange Adventures*. Cloth. Cincinnati, 1848. (By Nathaniel A. Ware.) First edition. $50-$75.

HARVEY, George. *Scenes of the Primitive Forest of America*. 4 hand-colored plates. Folio, boards. New York, 1841. With London imprint on binding. $3,000-$4,000. Also, $2,400 (A, 1969).

HARVEY, Henry. *History of the Shawnee Indians*. Illustrated. Cloth. Cincinnati, 1855. First edition, first issue, without portrait. $125-$200.

HARVEY, William. *The Anatomical Exercises*. Edited by Geoffrey Keynes. Drawing by Stephen Gooden. Full morocco. London, (1928). Nonesuch Press. One of 1,450. $150-$200.

*HASHEESH Eater (The)*. Cloth. New York, 1857. (By Fitz-Hugh Ludlow.) First edition. $50-$75. Also, $40 (A, 1976). Author's first book.

HASKELL, Burnette G. *Kaweah, a Co-operative Commonwealth*. 16 pp., wrappers. San Francisco, 1887. First edition. $100-$150.

HASKINS, C. W. *The Argonauts of California*. Cloth. New York, 1890. First edition. $150-$200. Also, hinges cracked, $95 (A, 1976).

HASTAIN, E. *Township Plats of the Creek Nation*. Full limp morocco. Muskogee, Okla., 1910. $150-$250.

HASTINGS, Lansford W. *The Emigrant's Guide to Oregon and California.* 152 pp., wrappers, or printed boards. Cincinnati, 1845. First edition. $10,000 and up. Rebound in calf and boards, $6,500. Also, in boards, covers "cracked," $4,000 (A, 1968); rebound in leather, $4,700 (A, 1959); rebound in facsimile wrappers, $4,000 (A, 1963).

HASTINGS, Lansford W. *A New History of Oregon and California.* Frontspiece. Half cloth. Cincinnati, 1849. (One of several later printings of his *Emigrants' Guide.*) $300-$350. Also, $225 (A, 1973).

HASTINGS, Sally. *Poems, on Different Subjects. To Which Is Added a Descriptive Account of a Family Tour to the West, in the Year 1800.* Leather. Lancaster, Pa., 1808. First edition. $200-$250.

HASWELL, Anthony (editor). *Memoirs and Adventures of Capt. Matthew Phelps.* Leather. Bennington, Vt., 1802. First edition. $400-$500.

HATFIELD, Edwin F. *History of Elizabeth, New Jersey.* 8 plates. Morocco. New York, 1868. First edition. $75-$125.

HATTERAS, Owen. *Pistols for Two.* Pink wrappers. New York, 1917. (By H. L. Mencken and George Jean Nathan.) First edition. $75-$85.

HAUPT, Herman. *Reminiscences.* Cloth. Milwaukee, 1901. First edition. Limited and signed. $75-$100.

HAVEN, Charles T., and Belden, Frank A. *History of the Colt Revolver.* Illustrated. Cloth. New York, 1940. First edition. Boxed. $50-$75. Another issue: Morocco. Signed. Boxed. $100-$200. New York, (about 1960). Cloth. $25-$35.

*HAWBUCK Grange; or, The Sporting Adventures of Thomas Scott, Esq.* 8 illustrations by Phiz. Blind-stamped pictorial red cloth. London, 1847. (By Robert Smith Surtees.) First edition, with 32-page catalogue dated April, 1847, bound in at end. $100-$150.

HAWES, Charles Boardman. *The Dark Frigate.* Illustrated by A. L. Ripley. Pictorial cloth. Boston, (1923). First edition. In dust jacket. $50.

HAWES, William Post. *Sporting Scenes and Sundry Sketches.* Edited by Frank Forester. Illustrated. 2 vols., cloth. New York, 1842. First edition. $75-$125.

HAWKER, Peter. *Instructions to Young Sportsmen.* Boards. London, 1814. First edition. $350-$500. Also, $350 (A, 1975). London, 1816. Second edition. $100-$150. London, 1824. Third edition. $50-$100. Philadelphia, 1846. Cloth. First American edition. $50-$100.

HAWKER, The Rev. Robert S. *The Cornish Ballads and Other Poems.* Green cloth. London, 1869. First edition. $100-$125.

HAWKER,The Rev. Robert S. *The Quest of the Sangraal: Chant the First.* Cloth. Exeter, England, 1864. First edition. Printed on vellum. $500. Also, $325 (A, 1970).

HAWKES, J. C. B., Jr. *Fiasco Hall.* Wrappers. Cambridge, Mass., 1943. (By John Hawkes.) First edition. (150 copies printed.) $250-$350. Also, $225 (A, 1977). Author's first book. (60 copies reportedly destroyed, according to the bibliographer Gary M. Lepper.)

HAWKES, John. *The Cannibal.* Gray Cloth.(Norfolk, Conn., 1949.) New Directions. First edition, first binding. In dust jacket. $75-$100.

HAWKES, John. *Lunar Landscapes.* Cloth. (New York, 1969.) New Directions. First edition. One of 150 signed. Boxed. $50-$60. Trade edition: In dust jacket. $20-$25.

HAWKES, John. *Second Skin.* Cloth. (New York, 1964.) New Directions. First edition. One of 100 signed. In slipcase. $50-$75. Trade edition: In dust jacket. $10-$15.

HAWKINS, Alfred. *Hawkins's Picture of Quebec; with Historical Recollections.* 14 plates. Boards. Quebec, 1834. First edition. $200-$250.

HAWKS *of Hawk-Hollow (The)*. 2 vols., purple cloth, paper labels. Philadelphia, 1835. (By Robert Montgomery Bird.) First edition. $150-$250. Also, cloth faded, $80 (A, 1974).

HAWLEY, A. T. *The Climate, Resources, and Advantages of Humboldt County*, 42 pp., wrappers. Eureka, Calif., 1879. First edition. $450-$500.

HAWLEY, A. T. *The Present Condition, Growth, Progress and Advantages of Los Angeles City and County, Southern California*. Map. 144 pp., printed wrappers. Los Angeles, 1876. First edition. $400-$600. Also, $300 (A, 1968).

HAWLEY, R. D. *The Hawley Collection of Violins*. Half cloth. Chicago, 1904. Limited edition. $150-$250.

HAWLEY, W. A. *The Early Days of Santa Barbara*. 5 plates. 105 pp., printed wrappers. New York, 1910. First edition. $100-$150.

HAWLEY, Walter A. *Oriental Rugs: Antique and Modern*. Plates. Half morocco. New York, 1913. $150-$200. New York, 1922. $150. New York, 1937. Cloth. $100-$125.

HAWLEY, Zerah. *A Journal of a Tour Through Connecticut, Massachusetts, New York, etc.* Boards. New Haven, 1822. First edition. $400-$500. Also, $250 (A, 1967); rebound in half morocco, $180 (A, 1966).

HAWTHORNE, Nathaniel. See *Fanshawe; Peter Parley's Universal History; The Sister Years*.

HAWTHORNE, Nathaniel. *Biographical Stories for Children*. Cloth, Boston, 1842. First edition. $75-$100.

HAWTHORNE, Nathaniel. *The Blithedale Romance*. 2 vols., cloth. London, 1852. First edition. $150-$200. Boston, 1852. Tan cloth. First American edition, with 4 pages of ads at end. $75-$125.

HAWTHORNE, Nathaniel. *The Celestial Rail-Road*. 32 pp., buff wrappers. Boston, 1843. First edition and first separate printing. $1,250 and up. Also, foxed, covers mended, $950 (A, 1974). (Note: No priority established for two imprints—Wilder or Fish—both excessively rare.)

HAWTHORNE, Nathaniel. *Doctor Grimshawe's Secret*. Edited by Julian Hawthorne. Pictorial cloth. Boston, 1883. First edition. $100-$150. Large paper issue, same date but later: One of 250 numbered copies; some signed by the editor. $100-$125.

HAWTHORNE, Nathaniel. *Famous Old People, Being the Second Epoch of Grandfather's Chair*. Cloth, paper label. Boston, 1841. First edition. $150-$200.

HAWTHORNE, Nathaniel. *The Gentle Boy: A Thrice-Told Tale*. Engraved frontispiece. Wrappers. Boston, 1839. First edition. $450.

HAWTHORNE, Nathaniel. *Grandfather's Chair: A History*. Cloth, paper label. Boston, 1841. First edition. $150-$175.

HAWTHORNE, Nathaniel. *The House of the Seven Gables*. Brown cloth. Boston, 1851. First edition, presumed first binding, with roman ampersand in spine imprint and March ads. $400-$500. Also, a stained copy, $300 (A, 1974).

HAWTHORNE, Nathaniel. *Liberty Tree, with the Last Word of Grandfather's Chair*. Green cloth, paper label. Boston, 1841. First edition, first issue, with second line of page 24 ending "in a Con-". $100-$150.

HAWTHORNE, Nathaniel. *Life of Franklin Pierce*. Frontispiece. Printed wrappers, or cloth. Boston, 1852. First edition. Wrappers: $150-$200. Cloth: $100-$150.

HAWTHORNE, Nathaniel. *Love Letters of Nathaniel Hawthorne*. Portrait. 2 vols., boards and vellum. Chicago, 1907. First edition. One of 67. $150.

HAWTHORNE, Nathaniel. *The Marble Faun: or, The Romance of Monte Beni*. 2 vols., brown cloth. Boston, 1860. First American edition, first issue, without "Conclusion" at end. $250-$400. Also, $200 (A, 1974). Second issue, with "Conclusion." $100-$150. (For first English edition, which may have preceded the American, see Hawthorne, *Transformation.*)

HAWTHORNE, Nathaniel. *Mosses from an Old Manse.* 2 vols., wrappers, or one volume, cloth. New York, 1846. First edition. Wrappers: $750 and up. One-volume issue: $200-$300.

HAWTHORNE, Nathaniel. *Our Old Home.* Brown cloth. Boston, 1863. First edition, first state, with ad on page 399. $75-$125. London, 1863. 2 vols., cloth. First English edition. $50-$75. (Note: Blanck thinks this was issued simultaneously with the American first.)

HAWTHORNE, Nathaniel. *Passages from the American Note-Books.* 2 vols., green cloth. Boston, 1868. First edition, with spine reading "Ticknor & Co." (Later, "Fields, Osgood & Co.") $150-$250.

HAWTHORNE, Nathaniel. *The Scarlet Letter.* Brown cloth. Boston, 1850. First edition, first issue, with "reduplicate" in line 20 of page 21; "characterss" in line 5 of page 41, and "catechism" in line 29 of page 132. $750-$850. Also, $650 (A, 1975). Boston, 1850. Cloth. Second edition. $150-$200. New York, 1892. Cloth. Illustrated by F.O.C. Darley. $100-$125. New York, 1908. Grolier Club. Illustrated. Boards. One of 300. $100-$125. New York, (1915). Illustrated by Hugh Thomson. $75-$100. New York, 1928. Grabhorn Press. Colored woodblocks by Valenti Angelo. Half morocco. One of 980. In dust jacket. $100-$125. New York, 1941. Limited Editions Club. Illustrated by Henry Varnum Poor. Leather. Boxed. $60-$85.

HAWTHORNE, Nathaniel. *The Snow-Image and Other Twice-Told Tales.* Brown cloth. Boston, 1852. First edition. $100-$125. London, 1851. Cloth. First English edition. (Issued simultaneously with American first edition, Blanck suggests. Titled *The Snow-Image, and Other Tales.*) $50-$60.

HAWTHORNE, Nathaniel. *Tanglewood Tales, for Girls and Boys.* Decorated cloth. Boston, 1853. First American edition. $150-$250. London, 1853. Green cloth. First edition (preceding the American edition by a few days). $100-$125. London, (1918). Illustrated by Edmund Dulac. Half vellum. One of 500 signed by Dulac. $300-$350.

HAWTHORNE, Nathaniel. *Transformation.* 3 vols., old rose cloth. London, 1860. First English edition of *The Marble Faun,* which see. $100-$150. (Note: Possibly preceded the American first edition, says Blanck.)

HAWTHORNE, Nathaniel. *True Stories from History and Biography.* Cloth. Boston, 1851. First edition, first issue, with verso of title page imprinted "Cambridge: Printed by Bolles and Houghton." $75-$100.

HAWTHORNE, Nathaniel. *Twice-Told Tales.* Brownish cloth. Boston, 1837. First edition. $1,000-$1,250. Also, a rubbed copy, $650 (A, 1974); $1,250 (A, 1960)—for a copy "in unusually fine condition . . . lettering on backstrip in brilliant gilt." Retail values for copies in very good condition range up to $600 and more. New York, 1966. Limited Editions Club. Colored illustrations by Valenti Angelo. Blue cloth. Boxed. $40-$50.

HAWTHORNE, Nathaniel. *A Wonder-Book for Girls and Boys.* Frontispiece, 6 plates. Purple or green cloth. Boston, 1852. First edition, first issue, with gilt decorations covering only top third of spine and with no ads. $400-$600. Also, $250 and (rubbed) $350 (A, 1974). London, 1852. 8 engravings. Decorated blue cloth. First English edition. $150-$200. London, 1893. Illustrated by Walter Crane. Decorated cloth. $75-$125. Cambridge, Mass., 1893. Crane illustrations. Vellum. One of 250. $100-$150. London, (1922). Illustrated by Arthur Rackham. White buckram. One of 600 signed by the artist. Boxed. $350-$450.

HAWTHORNE, Nathaniel (editor). *Journal of an African Cruiser.* Cloth. New York, 1845. (By Horatio Bridge.) First edition. $100-$150.

HAY, John. See *The Bread-Winners.*

HAY, John. *Jim Bludso of the Prairie Belle, and Little Breeches.* Illustrated by S. Eytinge,

Jr. 23 pp., printed orange wrappers. Boston, 1871. First edition. $75-$100. Author's first book.

HAY, John. *Letters of John Hay and Extracts from Diary.* 3 vols., cloth, paper labels. Washington, 1908. First edition. $250-$350. Also, $130 (A, 1975).

HAYDEN, Ferdinand V. *Geological and Geographical Atlas of Colorado.* 20 double-page maps, mostly colored. Three-quarters morocco. (Washington), 1877. $100-$150. Washington, 1881. $75-$100.

HAYDEN, Ferdinand V. *Sun Pictures of Rocky Mountain Scenery.* 30 mounted photographs. Half morocco. New York, 1870. First edition. $1,750-$2,000, possibly more.

HAYDEN Ferdinand V. *The Yellowstone National Park.* 2 maps. Illustrated in color by Thomas Moran. Folio, half morocco portfolio. Boston, 1876. First edition. $3,000-$4,000. Also, $2,400 (A, 1973).

HAYMOND, Creed. *The Central Pacific Railroad.* 181 pp., wrappers. Washington, (about 1888). First edition. $75-$125.

HAYMOND, Henry. *History of Harrison County, West Virginia.* Cloth. Morgantown, W. Va., (1910). First edition. $75-$100.

HAYWARD, John (compiler). *English Poetry: An Illustrated Catalogue of First and Early Editions Exhibited by the National Book League, 1947.* Facsimiles. Buckram. Cambridge, 1950. One of 550. In dust jacket. $150-$175. Another issue: One of 50. In dust jacket. $250-$300.

HAYWOOD, John. *The Civil and Political History of the State of Tennessee.* Calf. Knoxville, 1823. First edition, with tipped-in copyright slip and inserted printed slip. $400-$500. Also, $300 (A, 1969).

HAYWOOD, John. *The Natural and Aboriginal History of Tennessee.* Leather. Nashville, 1823. First edition, with errata leaf. $500-$600. Also, $350 (A, 1969); in morocco, $450 (A, 1967).

HAZEL, Harry. *The Flying Artillerist.* 3 full-page woodcuts. 92 pp., wrappers. New York, 1853. (By Justin Jones.) First edition. $100-$150.

HAZEL, Harry. *The Flying Yankee, or the Cruise of the Clipper.* Wrappers. New York, (1853). (By Justin Jones.) First edition. $75-$100. Also, $47 (A, 1974).

HAZEL, Harry. *Old Put; or, The Days of Seventy-Six.* 104 pp., sewed. New York, (1852). (By Justin Jones.) First edition. $75-$100.

HAZEL, Harry. *The Rebel and the Rover.* Wrappers. Philadelphia, (about 1855). (By Justin Jones.) $75-$100.

HAZEL, Harry. *The West Point Cadet.* Illustrated. 100 pp., printed wrappers. Boston, 1845. (By Justin Jones.) First edition. $100-$125.

HAZEN, Gen. W. B. *A Narrative of Military Service.* Map, illustrations. Cloth. Boston, 1885. $25-$35.

HAZEN, Gen. W. B. *Our Barren Lands.* 53 pp., printed blue wrappers. Cincinnati, 1875. First edition. $300-$350. Also, rebound in cloth, $225 (A, 1968).

HAZEN, Gen. W. B. *Some Corrections of "Life on the Plains."* (Cover title.) 18 pp., wrappers. St. Paul, 1875. First edition. $750-$1,000.

HAZLITT, William. *Characters of Shakespear's plays.* Boards, paper label. London, 1817. First edition. $150-$250.

HAZLITT, William. *Conversations of James Northcote, Esq., R.A.* Portrait. Boards, paper label. London, 1830. First edition. $75-$100.

HAZLITT, William. *Lectures on the English Poets*. Boards, paper label. London, 1818. First edition, with 4 pages of ads at end dated May 1, 1818. $150-$200.

HAZLITT, William. *Political Essays, with Sketches of Public Characters*. Boards, paper label. London, 1819. First edition. $75-$100.

HEADLEY, John W. *Confederate Operations in Canada and New York*. Portraits. Cloth. New York, 1906. First edition. $85-$100.

*HEADLONG Hall*. Boards. London, 1816. (By Thomas Love Peacock.) First edition. $200-$300.

*HEADSMAN (The)*. 3 vols., tan boards, or rose-colored cloth. London, 1833. (By James Fenimore Cooper.) First edition. $250-$350. Also, in boards, worn, $100 (A, 1970). Philadelphia, 1833. 2 vols., blue boards. First American edition. $200-$250.

HEAL, Ambrose. *London Tradesmen's Cards of the 19th Century*. Illustrated. Half vellum. London, 1925. (100 copies printed at the Curwen Press.) $150-$175.

HEAP, Gwinn Harris. *Central Route to the Pacific*. Folding map (not in all copies), 13 tinted plates. Cloth. Phildelphia, 1854. First edition, first issue, with Plate IV lacking a plate or page number. $400-$500.

HEARN, Lafcadio. See Bisland, Elizabeth; Gautier, Théophile; Chahta-Ima. Also, see *La Cuisine Créole; Historical Sketch-Book and Guide to New Orleans*.

HEARN, Lafcadio. *Chita: A Memory of Last Island*. Salmon-colored cloth. New York, 1889. First edition. In dust jacket. $150-$250. Lacking jacket, $50-$75, possibly more.

HEARN, Lafcadio. *Editorials from the Kobe Chronicle*. (Cover title.) Printed white wrappers. (New York, 1913.) First edition. One of 100, with an addenda slip tipped in. $200-$300. Also, $180 (A, 1976).

HEARN, Lafcadio. *Gleanings in Buddha-Fields*. Blue cloth. Boston, 1897. First edition. $75-$100.

HEARN, Lafcadio. *Glimpses of Unfamiliar Japan*. Illustrated. 2 vols., black or olive cloth. Boston, 1894. First edition. In dust jackets. $150-$200.

HEARN, Lafcadio. *"Gombo Zhebes"; Little Dictionary of Creole Proverbs*. Pictorial cloth. New York, 1885. First edition. $100-$125.

HEARN, Lafcadio. *In Ghostly Japan*. Illustrated. Pictorial blue cloth. Boston, 1899. First edition. $50-$60.

HEARN, Lafcadio. *Insects and Greek Poetry*. Printed blue boards. New York, 1926. First edition. One of 550. In glassine dust jacket. $50-$60.

HEARN, Lafcadio. *Japan: An Attempt at Interpretation*. Colored frontispiece. Tan cloth. New York, 1904. First edition. In dust jacket. $75-$100. Lacking jacket, $35-$50.

HEARN, Lafcadio. *Japanese Fairy Tales*. 5 vols., wrappers. Tokyo, (1898-1903). First editions. *(The Boy Who Drew Cats, The Goblin Spider, The Old Woman Who Lost Her Dumpling, The Fountain of Youth, Chin Chin Kobakama.)* $400-$500 for complete sets. (Note: Blanck calls the bibliographical problems connected with these little woodblock books "insoluble." However, they have frequently been at auction in various forms, including large paper and crepe paper states.)

HEARN, Lafcadio. *The Japanese Letters of Lafcadio Hearn*. Edited by Elizabeth Bisland. Green cloth. Boston, 1910. First edition. One of 200 large paper copies. $75-$100.

HEARN, Lafcadio. *A Japanese Miscellany*. Illustrated. Pictorial green cloth. Boston, 1901. First edition. (Copies with or without "October, 1901" on copyright page are acceptable first editions, Blanck seems to suggest.) In dust jacket. $75-$85.

HEARN, Lafcadio. *Kokoro*. Green cloth. Boston, 1896. First edition. $50-$60.

HEARN, Lafcadio. *Kotto*. Illustrated. Pictorial olive cloth. New York, 1902. First edition, presumed first state, with background of title page upside down, artist's monogram in upper right corner. In dust jacket. $75-$100.

HEARN, Lafcadio. *Kwaidan*. Illustrated. Pictorial cloth. Boston, 1904. First edition. In dust jacket. $50-$75. New York, 1932. Limited Editions Club. Color plates. Printed silk binding. In silk wraparound case. $100-$135.

HEARN, Lafcadio. *Leaves from the Diary of an Impressionist*. Facsimile Hearn letter. Blue boards. Boston, 1911. First edition. One of 575. $75-$85.

HEARN, Lafcadio. *Lectures on Tennyson*. Cloth. Tokyo, (1941). First edition. One of 500. In dust jacket. $150-$200. Also, $160 (A, 1976).

HEARN, Lafcadio. *The Romance of the Milky Way*. Cloth. Boston, 1905. First edition. In dust jacket. $40-$60.

HEARN, Lafcadio. *Shadowings*. Illustrated. Pictorial blue cloth. Boston, 1900. First edition. In dust jacket. $75-$100.

HEARN, Lafcadio. *Some Chinese Ghosts*. Pictorial rose-colored cloth. Boston, 1887. First edition. $150-$175. (Also in red and other colors of cloth.)

HEARN, Lafcadio. *Some New Letters and Writings*. Cloth. Tokyo, 1925. First edition. In dust jacket. $100-$150.

HEARN, Lafcadio. *Stray Leaves from Strange Literature*. Blue cloth. Boston, 1884. First edition, first issue, with JR. O. & CO. imprint on spine. $100-$150. Author's first book.

HEARN, Lafcadio. *Two Years in the French West Indies*. Illustrated. Decorated olive cloth. New York, 1890. First edition. $75-$100.

HEARN, Lafcadio. *Youma*. Frontispiece. Cloth, paper labels. New York, 1890. First edition, first binding, white calico with blue design. $75-$100.

*HEART of the West (The): An American Story*. By an Illinoian. Brown cloth. Chicago, 1871. First edition. $75-$100. (Note: The author's real name remains a mystery.)

HEART, Capt. Jonathan. *Journal*. Edited by C.W. Butterfield. 94 pp., tan printed wrappers. Albany, N. Y., 1885. First edition. One of 150. $75-$150.

HEARTMAN, Charles F. *The New-England Primer*. Facsimiles. Boards. New York, 1915. First edition. One of 265. $75-$100. New York, 1934. Cloth. One of 300. $30-$35.

HEARTMAN, Charles F., and Canny, James R. *A Bibliography of the First Printings of Edgar Allan Poe*. Cloth. Hattiesburg, Miss., 1940. First edition. $75-$100.

HEARTMAN, Charles F., and Rede, Kenneth. *A Bibliographical Checklist of the First Editions of Edgar Allan Poe*. 3 vols., boards. Metuchen, N.J., 1932. Limited to 240, 202, and 100. $75-$100.

HEBARD, Grace R. *Sacajawea*. Plates and maps. Cloth. Glendale, Calif., 1933. First edition. One of 750. $75-$100.

HEBARD, Grace R. *Washakie*. 7 maps, 16 plates. Cloth. Cleveland, 1930. First edition. $50-$75.

HEBARD, Grace R., and Brininstool, E. A. *The Bozeman Trail*. Plates, 2 folding maps. 2 vols., cloth. Cleveland, 1922. First edition. $100-$150. Glendale, Calif., 1960. 2 vols. in one, cloth. $40-$60.

HEBISON, W. C. *Early Days in Texas and Rains County*. 50 pp., wrappers. Emory, Tex., 1917. First edition. $125-$250, possibly more.

HECHT, Anthony. *Aesopic: Twenty-Four Couplets*. Thomas Bewick illustrations. Boards. Northampton, (1968). Gehenna Press. One of 50 signed by Leonard Baskin, with an extra set of plates. $150-$250. Also, $85 (A, 1974).

HECHT, Anthony. *The Seven Deadly Sins*. Illustrated by Leonard Baskin. Oblong, stiff wrappers. Northampton, Mass., 1958. First edition. One of 300 signed by author and artist. $150-$250. Also, $90 (A, 1971).

HECHT, Anthony. *A Summoning of Stones*. Cloth. New York, (1954). First edition. In dust jacket. $40-$60. Author's first book.

HECHT, Ben. *The Bewitched Tailor*. Drawing by George Grosz. 8 pp., printed wrappers. New York, 1941. First edition. One of 875 signed by author and artist. $75-$100.

HECHT, Ben. *A Book of Miracles*. Cloth. New York, 1939. First edition. In dust jacket. $25. Also, advance copy in wrappers, $35 (A, 1976).

HECHT, Ben. *Christmas Eve: A Morality Play*. Vellum. (New York), 1928. First edition. One of 111 signed. $75-$100. Also, $50 (A, 1976).

HECHT, Ben. *Fantazius Mallare*. Illustrated by Wallace Smith. Cloth. Chicago, 1922. First edition. One of 2,000. In dust jacket. $40-$50.

HECHT, Ben. *A Jew in Love*. Cloth. New York, (1931). First edition. One of 150 signed. Boxed. $50-$75. Trade edition: First issue, with no indication of second printing. (Suppressed.) $50 and up. (Note: Only a small quantity issued.)

HECHT, Ben. *The Kingdom of Evil*. Illustrated. Black cloth. Chicago, 1924. One of 2,000. In dust jacket. $35.

HECHT, Ben. *A Thousand and One Afternoons in Chicago*. Illustrated. Boards. Chicago, (1922). First edition. In dust jacket. $50-$75.

HECHT, Ben, and Bodenheim, Maxwell. *Cutie, a Warm Mama*. Orange cloth or orange boards and cloth. Chicago, 1924. (By Ben Hecht alone.) First edition. One of 200 (probably a spurious limitation). In dust jacket. $50-$65.

HECHT, Ben, and Fowler, Gene. *The Great Magoo*. Illustrated. Cloth. New York, (1933). First edition. In dust jacket. $75-$100. Also, $35 (A, 1976).

HECKENDORN & Wilson. *Miners and Business Men's Directory*. (For Tuolumne, Calif.) 104 pp., printed wrappers. Columbia, Calif., 1856. First edition. $1,500-$2,500. Also, $950 (A, 1968); $1,100 (A, 1959).

HECKEWELDER, John. *An Account of the History, Manners, and Customs of the Indian Nations*. Calf. Philadelphia, 1818. First edition. $100-$150. Philadelphia, 1819. Second edition. $75-$85.

HECKEWELDER, John. *A Narrative of the Mission of the United Brethren Among the Delaware and Mohegan Indians*. Portrait and errata slip. Boards. Philadelphia, 1820. First edition. $150-$250. Cleveland, 1907. 3 maps, 5 plates. Three-quarters leather. One of 160 on large paper. $150-$175. Also, $100 (A, 1975).

HEGAN, Alice Caldwell. *Mrs. Wiggs of the Cabbage Patch*. Olive-green cloth. New York, 1901. First edition, first issue, with gold sky on cover. $50-$60.

*HEIDENMAUER (The); or The Benedictines*. By the Author of "The Pilot." 3 vols., green or tan boards. London, 1832. (By James Fenimore Cooper.) First edition. $150-$200. Philadelphia, 1832. 2 vols., gray-blue boards. First American edition. $100-$150.

HEINLEIN, Robert A. *Double Star*. Cloth. Garden City, 1956. First edition. In dust jacket. $60-$75.

HEINLEIN, Robert A. *The Rolling Stones*. Cloth. New York, (1952). First edition. In dust jacket. $40-$50.

HEINLEIN, Robert A. *Starman Jones*. Cloth. New York, (1953). First edition. In dust jacket. $40-$50.

HEINLEIN, Robert A. *Starship Troopers*. Cloth. New York, (1959). First edition. In dust jacket. $85.

HEINLEIN, Robert A. *Stranger in a Strange Land*. Cloth. New York, (1961). First edition. In dust jacket. $75.

HEINLEIN, Robert A. *Time for the Stars*. Cloth. New York, (1956). First edition. In dust jacket. $40-$50.

*HELEN'S Tower*. Title page and 6 leaves. Pink wrappers. Clandeboye, Canada, 1861. First published edition. $50. (Note: Contains a leaf of verse by Alfred, Lord Tennyson.)

HELFORTH, John. *Nights*. Printed wrappers. (Dijon, France, 1955.) (By Hilda Doolittle). One of 100. $200-$250.

HELLER, Elinor, and Magee, David. *Bibliography of the Grabhorn Press, 1915-1940*. Illustrated. Boards and calf. San Francisco, 1940. One of 210. (Also, note: *Bibliography . . . from 1940 to 1956*. San Francisco, 1957. [By Dorothy and David Magee.] One of 225. Boards. $500-$750, possibly more.)

HELLER, Joseph. *Catch-22*. Cloth. New York, 1961. First edition. In dust jacket. $100-$150. Author's first book.

HELLER, Joseph. *Something Happened*. Cloth. New York, 1974. First edition. One of 350. signed. Boxed. $100-$125. Trade edition: Cloth. In dust jacket. $15-$20.

HELPER, Hinton R. *The Land of Gold*. Cloth. Baltimore, 1855. First edition. $100-$125.

HEMANS, Felicia. *The League of the Alps, The Siege of Valencia, The Vespers of Palermo, and Other Poems*. Boards, paper label. Boston, 1826. First edition. $50.

HEMANS, Felicia. *Poems*. Boards. Liverpool, 1808. First edition. $80-$150.

HEMINGWAY, Ernest. See Bahr, Jerome; Cohn, Louis Henry; Dashiell, Alfred; Faulkner, William, *Salmagundi*; North, Joseph; Paul, Elliot; Schreiber, Georges. Also see *Kiki's Memoirs; Somebody Had to Do Something; Tabula; Senior Tabula*.

HEMINGWAY, Ernest. *Across the River and into the Trees*. Cloth. New York, 1950. First American edition, first issue, with "A" on copyright page. In dust jacket. $35-$50. (Note: First dust jacket lettered yellow; later, orange.) London, (1950). Green cloth. First edition (preceding the American first by 3 days). In dust jacket. $35-$50.

HEMINGWAY, Ernest. *Cinquante Mille Dollars*. Wrappers. Paris, 1928. First French edition (of *Fifty Grand*). One of 110 large paper copies. $500 and up. Also, $650 (A, 1977).

HEMINGWAY, Ernest. *Death in the Afternoon*. Frontispiece and photographs. Black cloth. New York, 1932. First edition, first issue, with "A" on copyright page. In dust jacket. $150-$250. Also, $225 (A, 1974). London, (1932). Illustrated. Orange cloth. First English edition. In dust jacket. $50-$75.

HEMINGWAY, Ernest. *A Farewell to Arms*. Black cloth, gold paper labels, New York, 1929. First edition, first state, without the notice that "none of the characters in this book is a living person." In dust jacket. $400-$550. $300 and $375 (A, 1977). Second state. In dust jacket. $350-$500. Another issue: Light blue-green boards, vellum spine and corners, black leather label. One of 510 signed. In glassine dust jacket. Boxed. $600-$800. Also, $600 (A, 1977); $650 and $500 (A, 1974). London, (1929). Cloth. First English edition. In dust jacket. $100-$150. Another issue: Advance copy in wrappers. $250-$350. New York, 1948. Illustrated by Daniel Rasmusson. Cloth. First illustrated edition. $100-$125.

HEMINGWAY, Ernest. *Fiesta*. Blue cloth. London, (1927). First English edition of *The Sun Also Rises*. In dust jacket. $300-$450. Also, in soiled jacket, $375 (A, 1977).

HEMINGWAY, Ernest. *The Fifth Column and the First Forty-nine Stories*. Red cloth. New York, 1938. First edition, first printing, with "A" on copyright page. In dust jacket. $100-$150. (Also, 30 advance dummy copies for salesmen, with title page *The First 48*. A copy in a temporary dust jacket brought $1,600 at auction in October, 1977.)

HEMINGWAY, Ernest. *For Whom the Bell Tolls*. Beige cloth. New York, 1940. First edition, first printing, with "A" on copyright page. In first state dust jacket without photographer's name ("Arnold") under author's picture. $150-$250. Also, $175 (A, 1977). (There were also 15 presentation copies in advance of publication, all presumably signed by Hemingway. Value: $1,500 and up? Additionally there were 30 dummy copies for salesmen, with 6 pages of text, in advance of publication. A copy sold for $2,000 at auction in October, 1977.) New York, 1942. Limited Editions Club. Cloth. Boxed. $100-$125.

HEMINGWAY, Ernest. *God Rest You Merry Gentlemen*. Red cloth. New York, 1933. First edition. One of 300. In glassine dust jacket. $300-$400.

HEMINGWAY, Ernest. *Green Hills of Africa*. Light green cloth. New York, 1935. First edition, first issue, with "A" on copyright page. In dust jacket. Without fading of spine cloth (usually encountered), $150-$200. In dust jacket but with faded spine, $75-$125. London, 1935. Cloth. First English edition. In dust jacket. $75-$85.

HEMINGWAY, Ernest. *In Our Time*. Frontispiece portrait by Henry Strater. Decorated tan boards. Paris, 1924. Three Mountains Press. First edition. One of 170. $2,500-$3,000. Also, $2,750 (A, 1977). New York, 1925. Black cloth. First American edition. In dust jacket. $500-$750. Also, $450 (A, 1977). London, 1926. Cloth. First English edition. In dust jacket. $400-$450. Also, $350 (A, 1977). New York, 1930. Introduction by Edmund Wilson. Cloth. In dust jacket. $75-$100.

HEMINGWAY, Ernest. *Introduction to Kiki of Montparnasse*. (Cover title.) 8 pp., printed white self-wrappers. New York, 1929. First edition. One of 25 for copyright, published by Edward W. Titus. $1,000 (A, 1977).

HEMINGWAY, Ernest. *L'Adieu aux Armes*. Wrappers. Paris, 1931. First French translation of *A Farewell to Arms*. One of 180. $100-$200.

HEMINGWAY, Ernest. *Men Without Women*. Black cloth, gold labels. New York, 1927. First edition, first state, weighing 15 or 15½ ounces. In dust jacket. $400-$500. Also, $325 (A, 1977).

HEMINGWAY, Ernest. *Nouvelles et Récits*. Colored plates. Decorated cloth. Paris, 1963. First edition. $100-$125.

HEMINGWAY, Ernest. *The Old Man and the Sea*. Folio, wrappers. *Life* magazine printing of the novel. First edition. Vol. 33, No. 9. Sept. 1, 1952. $10-$15. Uncorrected advance galley proofs of this printing, $200 and up. New York, 1952. Black buckram. First edition, presentation issue (preceding trade edition). One of 30. In tissue dust jacket. $1,300 (A, 1977). Trade edition: Blue cloth. In dust jacket. $35-$50. New York, (1960). Illustrated by C. F. Tunnicliffe and R. Sheppard. Cloth. First illustrated edition. In dust jacket. $25-$35.

HEMINGWAY, Ernest. *Paris Est Une Fête*. Printed wrappers. Paris, 1964. First French translation of *A Moveable Feast*. One of 112 on velin. $75-$100.

HEMINGWAY, Ernest. *Siesta*. Cloth. London, (1927). First English edition (of *The Sun Also Rises*). In dust jacket. $250-$400. Also, $375 (A, 1977).

HEMINGWAY, Ernest. *The Spanish Earth*. Illustrated. Pictorial tan cloth. Cleveland, 1938. First edition, first issue, with pictorial end papers showing a large FAI banner. One of 50 or 100 copies of a limited edition of 1,000. In dust jacket. $400-$450. Also, $450 (A, 1977); $225 (A, 1976).

HEMINGWAY, Ernest. *The Sun Also Rises*. Black cloth, gold labels. New York, 1926. First edition, first state, with "stoppped" for "stopped" on page 181, line 26. In dust jacket. $800-$1,200. Also, $1,000 (A, 1977). See *Fiesta* for first English edition.

HEMINGWAY, Ernest. *Three Stories & Ten Poems*. Gray-blue wrappers. (Paris, 1923). Contact Publishing Co. First edition. One of 300. $1,500-$2,000. Also, $1,400 (A, 1971). Author's first book.

HEMINGWAY, Ernest. *To Have and Have Not*. Black cloth. New York, 1937. First edition, first issue, with "A" on copyright page. In dust jacket. $75-$100. London, 1937. Blue cloth. First English edition. In dust jacket. $60-$75.

HEMINGWAY, Ernest. *Today Is Friday*. (Caption title; no title page.) 8 pp., white wrappers (with Jean Cocteau drawing). (Englewood, N.J., 1926.) First edition. One of 300. In printed envelope. $400-$600. Also, $400 (A, 1977).

HEMINGWAY, Ernest. *The Torrents of Spring*. Dark green cloth. New York, 1926. First edition. In dust jacket. $200-$300. Paris, 1932. White wrappers. In glassine dust jacket. $200-$300. London, (1933). First English edition. In dust jacket. $150-$250. Also, $250 (A, 1977). Advance copy: Wrappers. Repaired, $350 (A, 1977).

HEMINGWAY, Ernest. *Two Christmas Tales*. Blue wrappers. (Berkeley), 1959. Hart Press. One of 150. $185-$275.

HEMINGWAY, Ernest. *Winner Take Nothing*. Black cloth, gold paper labels. New York, 1933. First edition, with "A" on copyright page. In dust jacket. $150-$200. (There were also 30 dummy copies for salesmen, title page reading *Stories [Title to Be Determined]*. A copy sold at auction in October, 1977, for $1,800.)

HEMINGWAY, Ernest (editor). *Men at War: The Best War Stories of All Time*. Black cloth. New York, (1942). First edition. In dust jacket. $50-$75.

HENDERSON, Robert W. *Early American Sport: A Chronological Check-List*. Cloth. New York, 1937. Grolier Club. $100-$125.

HENKLE, Moses. *Gospel of Nicodemus, the Believing Jew*. 40 pp., sewed. Columbus, Ohio, 1826. First edition. $75-$100.

HENKLE, Moses. *Last Wills and Testaments of Thirteen Patriarchs, and Gospel of Nicodemus, the Believing Jew*. 67 pp., sewed. Urbana, Ohio, 1827. $75-$100.

HENLEY, William Ernest. *A Book of Verses*. Stiff printed wrappers. London, 1888. First edition. $75-$85.

HENLEY, William Ernest. *Hawthorn and Lavender with Other Verses*. Boards. London, 1901. One of 20. $75-$125.

HENLEY, William Ernest. *London Types*. 12 colored illustrations by William Nicholson. Vellum, London, 1898. First edition. $150-$250. Another issue: Cloth. $150-$200.

HENLEY, William Ernest. *Small Letters*. Frontispiece. Wrappers. (London), 1933. First edition. One of 60. $75-$100.

HENLEY, William Ernest. *A Song of Speed*. Printed wrappers, or cloth. London, 1903. First edition. $75-$100.

HENLEY, William Ernest. *The Song of the Sword and Other Verses*. Green cloth. London, 1892. First edition. $75-$100.

HENLEY, William Ernest (editor). *Lyra Heroica: A Book of Verse for Boys*. Boards. London, 1892. One of 100 on large paper. $100-$125.

HENNEPIN, Father Louis. *A Description of Louisiana*. Translated by John G. Shea. Cloth. New York, 1880. One of 250. $100-$150.

HENNIKER, Florence. *In Scarlet and Grey: Stories of Soldiers and Others*. Pictorial title page. Red cloth. London, 1896. First edition. $75-$100. (Note: Contains "The Spectre of the Real," by Thomas Hardy and Florence Henniker.)

*HENRIETTA Temple: A Love Story*. 3 vols., cloth. London, 1837. (By Benjamin Disraeli.) First edition. $300-$400.

HENRY, Alexander (the younger), and Thompson, David. See: Coues, Elliott (editor).

HENRY, Alexander. *Travels and Adventures in Canada and the Indian Territories*. Boards. New York, 1809. First edition, first issue, without the portrait by Maverick. $500-$600. Also, $475 (A, 1974). (Note: Howes says the second issue with the portrait is preferred by collectors, but recent sales do not indicate that this is the case.) Boston, 1901. Cloth. One of 700. $100-$125.

HENRY, Edward Richard. *Classification and Use of Fingerprints.* 11 plates, 3 folding. Cloth. London, 1900. First edition. $250-$300.

HENRY, John Joseph. *An Accurate and Interesting Account of the Hardships and Sufferings of That Band of Heroes, Who Traversed the Wilderness in the Campaign Against Quebec in 1775.* Boards, or leather. Lancaster, Pa., 1812. First edition. $200-$250. (Note: Most copies I have seen are heavily foxed and browned internally.)

HENRY, John Joseph. *Campaign Against Quebec.* Sheep. Watertown, N.Y. 1844. Revised edition of *An Accurate and Interesting Account, etc.* $50-$75.

HENRY, O. See *The O. Henry Calendar.*

HENRY, O. *Cabbages and Kings.* Pictorial black cloth. New York, 1904. (By William Sidney, later spelled Sydney, Porter.) First edition, first issue, with "McClure, Phillips & Co." on spine. In dust jacket. $300-$400. Also, $350 (A, 1974). Lacking jacket, $100 and up. Author's first book.

HENRY, O. *The Four Million.* Red cloth. New York, 1906. (By William Sidney Porter.) First edition. In dust jacket. $50-$75.

HENRY, O. *The Gentle Grafter.* Illustrated. Red cloth. New York, 1908. (By William Sidney Porter.) First edition. In dust jacket. $30-$35.

HENRY, O. *The Gift of the Magi.* Illustrated by Stephen Gooden. Half morocco. London, (1939). (By William Sidney Porter.) First edition. One of 105 signed. $75-$125. Another issue: Boards. In dust jacket. $35-$50.

HENRY, O. *Heart of the West.* Pictorial brown cloth. New York, 1907. (By William Sidney Porter.) First edition. In dust jacket. $200-$300. Lacking jacket, $75-$100.

HENRY, O. *The Hiding of Black Bill.* Pictorial wrappers. New York, (about 1913?). (By William Sidney Porter.) First edition. $50-$100.

HENRY, O. *Let Me Feel Your Pulse.* Illustrated. Cloth. New York, 1910. (By William Sidney Porter.) First edition, with October copyright notice. In dust jacket. $75-$85.

HENRY, O. *O. Henry Encore: Stories and Illustrations.* Edited by Mary Harrell. Leatherette. Dallas, (1936). (By William Sidney Porter.) First edition. (One of 5 issued for copyright purposes?) $250 and up. Also, $100 (A, 1965).

HENRY, O. *Roads of Destiny.* Red cloth. New York, 1909. (By William Sidney Porter.) First edition, first state, with "h" missing in line 6 on page 9. In dust jacket. $50-$75. Lacking jacket, $30-$40.

HENRY, O. *Rolling Stones.* Illustrated. Cloth. Garden City, 1912. (By William Sidney Porter.) First edition. In dust jacket. $60-$80. Lacking jacket, $25-$35.

HENRY, O. *Sixes and Sevens.* Red cloth. Garden City, 1911. (By William Sidney Porter.) First edition. In dust jacket. $50-$75. Lacking jacket, $20-$25.

HENRY, O. *The Stories of O. Henry.* Illustrated. New York, 1965. Limited Editions Club. Boxed. $50-$65.

HENRY, O. *The Trimmed Lamp.* Frontispiece by Alice Barber Stephens. Red cloth. New York, 1907. (By William Sidney Porter.) First edition, with "Published April, 1907" on copyright page. In dust jacket. $75-$125. Lacking jacket, $25-$30.

HENRY, O. *The Voice of the City.* Red cloth. New York, 1908. (By William Sidney Porter.) First edition, first binding, with McClure imprint on spine. In dust jacket. $100. New York, 1935. Limited Editions Club. Buckram. Boxed. $150-$175.

HENRY, O. *Waifs and Strays: 12 Stories.* Cloth. Garden City, 1917. (By William Sidney Porter.) First edition. One of 200. $75-$100. Also, $40 (A, 1975).

HENRY, O. *Whirligigs.* Red cloth. New York, 1910. (By William Sidney Porter.) First edition, with "Published September, 1910" on copyright page. In dust jacket. $75-$125. Lacking jacket, $25-$30.

HENRY, Samuel J. *Foxhunting Is Different*. Illustrated. Pictorial cloth. New York (1938). Derrydale Press. First edition. One of 950. $75-$100.

HENTY, G. A. *All But Lost*. 3 vols., cloth. London, 1869. First edition. $1,000-$1,500.

HENTY, G. A. *At Agincourt*. Illustrated. Cloth. London, 1897. First edition, first issue, with no mention of this title in ads at end. $25-$35.

HENTY, G. A. *In the Heart of the Rockies*. Pictorial green cloth. New York, 1894. First edition. $40-$60.

HENTY, G. A. *A March on London*. 8 plates. Cloth. London, 1898 (actually 1897). First edition. $75-$100.

HENTY, G. A. *The March to Coomassie*. Cloth. London, 1874. First edition. $250-$350.

HENTY, G. A. *The Queen's Cup*. 3 vols., cloth. London, 1897. First edition, first issue, with ads dated Nov., 1896. $1,000 and up. Also, $850 (A, 1972).

HENTY, G. A. *St. Bartholomew's Eve*. Cloth. London, 1894. First English edition. $50-$75.

HENTY, G. A. *Search for a Secret*. 3 vols., cloth. London, 1867. First edition. $1,500-$2,000. Also, $1,625 (A, 1972).

HENTY, G. A. *The Tiger of Mysore*. Map, 12 plates. Cloth. London, 1896 (actually 1895). $50-$75. New York, 1895. Blue cloth. First American edition. $35-$50.

HENTY, G. A., and others. *Brains and Bravery*. 8 plates by Arthur Rackham. Cloth. London, 1903. First edition. $200-$300.

HENTY, G. A., and others. *Camps and Quarters*. Original printed wrappers. New York, 1889. First edition. $1,000 and up. Also, $950 (A, 1972).

HERBERT, Edward, Lord. *The Autobiography of Edward, Lord Herbert of Cherbury*. Wood engravings by H. W. Bray. Folio, buckram. Newtown, Wales, 1928. Gregynog Press. One of 300. $200-$350. Another issue: One of 25 specially bound in morocco. $1,250-$1,500.

HERBERT, Frank. *Dune*. Cloth. Philadelphia, (1965). First edition. In dust jacket. $75-$110.

HERBERT, George. *The Temple*. Portrait frontispiece. Cloth. London, 1927. Nonesuch Press. $75-$100.

HERBERT, George. *Poems*. Edited by H. W. Davies. Illustrated. Marbled boards and cloth. Newtown, 1923. Gregynog Press. One of 300. $150-$200. Another issue: One of 43 specially bound in morocco. $800-$1,000.

HERBERT, H. W. See Herbert, W. H.

HERBERT, Henry William. See Forester, Frank; Forrester, Frank; Hawes, William Post; Herbert, W. H. Also see *The Brothers; Cromwell*.

HERBERT, Henry William. *Marmaduke Wyvil*. Drab boards, paper label. London, 1843. First edition. $200-$300. New York, (1843). Printed wrappers. First American edition. $200-$300.

HERBERT, Henry William. *The Quorndon Hounds*. Frontispiece, 3 plates. Cloth. Philadelphia, 1852. First edition. $150-$350.

HERBERT, Henry William. *Ruth Whalley; or, The Fair Puritan*. Printed wrappers (dated 1845 on front). Boston, (1844). First edition. $250 and up. Boston, 1845. (Cover title.) Pinkish tan wrappers. Second edition, first state of wrappers, with author's name as "Wm. Henry" instead of "Henry William." $100-$150.

HERBERT, Henry William. *The Village Inn.* Wrappers. New York, 1843. First edition. $250 and up.

HERBERT, J. A. *Illuminated Manuscripts.* Color frontispiece, 50 other plates. Cloth. London, 1911. First edition. $75-$125.

HERBERT, Sir William. *Croftus, sive de Hibernia Liber.* Printed from a manuscript at Powis castle. 2 genealogical tables. Half morocco. London, 1887. Roxburghe Club. $200-$250. Another issue: Printed on vellum. $400-$450.

HERBERT, W. H. *Ringwood the Rover: A Tale of Florida.* Printed wrappers. Philadelphia, 1843. (By Henry William Herbert.) First edition. $400-$500. Second edition, with "H. W. Herbert" as author. $150-$200.

HERFORD, Oliver. *An Alphabet of Celebrities.* Illustrated. Cloth. Boston, 1899. First edition. $30-$50.

HERGESHEIMER, Joseph. *Balisand.* Boards and cloth. New York, 1924. First edition. One of 175 signed. Boxed. $35-$40.

HERGESHEIMER, Joseph. *The Bright Shawl.* Boards and vellum. New York, 1922. First edition, with "Published, October, 1922" on copyright page. One of 225 signed. $25.

HERGESHEIMER, Joseph. *Cytherea.* Red buckram. New York, 1922. First edition. One of 270 signed. In dust jacket. $25. Presentation copies: 100 in boards. $35.

HERGESHEIMER, Joseph. *The Happy End.* Buckram. New York, 1919. First edition. One of 60 large paper copies, signed. In dust jacket. $35-$50.

HERGESHEIMER, Joseph. *Java Head.* Cloth. New York, 1919. First edition. One of 100. $40-$50.

HERGESHEIMER, Joseph. *The Lay Anthony.* Cloth. New York, 1914. First edition. In dust jacket. $35-$50. Author's first book.

HERGESHEIMER, Joseph. *The Limestone Tree.* Buckram. New York, 1931. First edition. One of 225 signed. In dust jacket. Boxed. $25.

HERGESHEIMER, Joseph. *The Party Dress.* Limp orange vellum. New York, 1930. First edition. One of 60 on Japan vellum, signed. $50-$60.

HERGESHEIMER, Joseph. *The Presbyterian Child.* Half morocco. New York, 1923. First edition. One of 950, signed. $35-$50.

HERGESHEIMER, Joseph. *Quiet Cities.* Cloth. New York, 1928. First edition. One of 210 signed. In dust jacket. $25.

HERGESHEIMER, Joseph. *San Cristóbal de la Habana.* Boards and cloth. New York, 1920. First edition. One of 100 signed. Boxed. $40-$45.

HERGESHEIMER, Joseph. *Swords and Roses.* Decorated boards. New York, 1929. First edition. One of 225 signed. In dust jacket. $30-$45. Trade edition: Gray cloth. In dust jacket. $10.

HERGESHEIMER, Joseph. *The Three Black Pennys.* Brown cloth. New York, 1917. First edition, first issue, with medallion on half title about 2 inches from bottom of page. In dust jacket. $30-$35. New York, 1930. Illustrated. Vellum. One of 170 signed. Boxed. $50-$60.

HERGESHEIMER, Joseph. *Tropical Winter.* Cloth. New York, 1933. First edition. One of 210 signed. In dust jacket. $40-$50. Trade edition: Black cloth. In dust jacket. $10.

HERGESHEIMER, Joseph. *Wild Oranges.* Orange boards and cloth. New York, 1918. One of 85. In dust jacket. $40-$50.

HERMAN, William. *The Dance of Death.* Brown or green cloth. (San Francisco, 1877.) (By

Ambrose Bierce.) First edition. $100 and up. San Francisco, 1877. Red or blue cloth. Second edition, with dated title page. $35-$40.

HERNDON, William H., and Weik, Jesse W. *Herndon's Lincoln: The True Story of a Great Life.* 63 plates. 3 vols., blue cloth. Chicago, (1889). First edition. $200-$300. Also, $150 (A, 1970); $425 [sic] (A, 1969). Chicago, 1890. 3 vols., cloth. Second edition. $50-$75.

HERNE, Peregrine (pseudonym). *Perils and Pleasures of a Hunter's Life; or the Romance of Hunting.* Colored frontispiece and plates. Cloth. Boston, 1854. First edition. $50-$75. Boston, 1856. 12 woodcut plates. Half leather. $35. New York, 1857. Plates. Cloth. $25.

HERODOTUS. See *The History of Herodotus.*

HERRICK, Robert. *One Hundred and Eleven Poems.* Illustrated by W. Russell Flint. Sheepskin. London, 1955. Golden Cockerel Press. One of 105 copies issued with 8 extra plates signed by Flint. In slipcase. $1,000-$1,200. Another issue: Cloth, parchment spine. One of 550. Boxed. $200-$300.

HERRICK, Robert. *Poems.* Woodcut title page. Vellum. (London, 1895.) Kelmscott Press. One of 250. $650-$850.

HERRICK, Robert. *Selections from the Poetry of Robert Herrick.* Illustrated. Cloth. Boston, 1882. First edition. $75-$100.

HERRING, John Frederick. *Portraits of the Winning Horses of the Great St. Leger Stakes.* 10 colored plates. Large folio, leather-backed boards. Doncaster, England, (1824). First edition, first state, with Sheardown & Son imprint on all plates. $4,000-$5,000. Also, $2,660 (A, 1965). Another edition: (London, 1929.) 15 colored plates. Large folio, leather-backed boards. With a colored proof of "Tarrarre" plate. $3,000 and up. Also, $1,456 (A, 1961).

HERRINGTON, W. D. *The Deserter's Daughter.* 27 pp., wrappers. Raleigh, 1865. First edition. $50-$75.

HERSCHEL, Sir John F. W. *Results of Astronomical Observations Made During the Years 1834-38 at the Cape of Good Hope.* 18 full-page and folding engraved plates. Cloth. London, 1847. First edition. $250-$300.

HERSEY, John. *The Wall.* Illustrated. Cloth. New York, 1957. Limited Editions Club. Boxed. $50-$65.

HERTZ, John. *Racing Memoirs.* Mounted photographic plates, some in color. Half morocco. Chicago, 1954. $100-$150

HESTON, James Franklin. *Moral and Political Truth.* Calf. Philadelphia, 1811. First edition. $40-$50.

HEWITSON, William. *Illustrations of New Species of Exotic Butterflies.* 300 plates. 5 vols., half morocco. London, (1856)-76. $1,500 and up. Also, a worn copy, $950 (A, 1976).

HEWITT, Edward R. *Secrets of the Salmon.* Half cloth. New York, 1922. One of 780. $35-$50.

HEWITT, Graily. *Lettering for Students and Craftsmen.* Illustrated. White buckram. London, 1930. One of 380 signed. $100-$125.

HEWITT, Graily. *The Pen & Type-Design.* Illustrated. Full red morocco. London, 1928. First Edition Club. One of 250. $175-$200. Another issue: Boards and cloth. $75-$100.

HEWITT, Randall H. *Across the Plains and Over the Divide.* Folding map, portrait, 58 plates. Pictorial cloth. New York, (1906). First edition. $85-$125.

HEWITT, Randall H. *Notes By the Way: Memoranda of a Journey Across the Plains, from Dundee, Ill., to Olympia, W. T. May 7 to November 3, 1862.* 58 pp., printed wrappers. Olympia, Wash., 1863. First edition. $3,000 and up.

HEWLETT, Maurice. *A Masque of Dead Florentines.* Illustrated. Oblong, tan buckram. London, 1895. First edition. $25-$35.

HEWLETT, Maurice. *Quattrocentisteria.* Illuminated by Valenti Angelo. Folio, half vellum. New York, 1927. One of 175. $75-$85.

HEWLETT, Maurice. *The Song of the Plow.* Frontispiece. Boards. London, (1916). First edition. One of 100 signed. $50-$60.

HEYWARD, Du Bose. *Brass Ankle.* Cloth. New York, (1931). First edition. One of 100 signed. Boxed. $50-$60.

HEYWARD, Du Bose. *The Half-Pint Flask.* Boards and cloth. New York, 1929. First edition. One of 175 signed. In dust jacket. $40-$65.

HEYWARD, Du Bose. *Porgy.* Black cloth. New York, (1925). First edition, first issue, with gold-stamped binding and publisher's monogram on copyright page. In dust jacket. $40-$50. (For *Porgy & Bess*, the musical, see Gershwin, George.)

HEYWARD, Du Bose. *Skylines and Horizons.* Cloth. New York, 1924. First edition. In dust jacket. $25-$35.

HIGBEE, Elias, and Thompson, R. B. *The Petition of the Latter-Day Saints.* 13 pp., sewed. Washington, 1840. First edition. $100-$200.

HIGGINBOTHAM, Harlow Niles. *The Making of a Merchant and Other Papers.* Cloth. Wausau, Wis., (1900). Philosopher Press. First edition. One of 100. $50-$60.

HIGGINS, F. R. *Arable Holdings: Poems.* Boards and linen. Dublin, 1933. Cuala Press. One of 300. In tissue dust jacket. $50-$60.

HIGGINS, George. *"The King of Counties": Miami County.* 32 pp., wrappers. Paola, Kan., 1877. First edition. $100-$125.

HIGGINS, Godfrey. *Anacalypsis, an Attempt to Draw Aside the Veil of the Saitic Isis.* 6 engraved plates. 2 vols., cloth. London, 1836. First edition, with errata slip. $100-$150.

HIGGINSON, Thomas Wentworth. *The Birthday in Fairy-land: A Story for Children.* Printed wrappers. Boston, 1850. First edition. $50-$75.

HILDEBRAND, Samuel S. *Autobiography.* Illustrated. Cloth. Jefferson City, Mo., 1870. First edition. $75-$100.

HILDRETH, Richard. *The History of Banks.* Boards. Boston, 1837. First edition. $100-$175.

HILDRETH, Samuel P. *Biographical and Historical Memoirs of the Early Pioneer Settlers of Ohio.* 6 plates. Cloth. Cincinnati, 1852. First edition. $75-$100.

HILDRETH, Samuel P. *Genealogical and Biographical Sketches of the Hildreth Family.* Cloth. Marietta, Ohio, 1840. $75-$125.

HILDRETH, Samuel P. *Memoirs of the Early Pioneer Settlers of Ohio.* Leather. Cincinnati, 1854. Later reprint of *Biographical and Historical Memoirs.* $50-$60.

HILDRETH, Samuel P. *Pioneer History.* Folding map, 8 plates. Half leather. Cincinnati, 1848. First edition. $100-$150.

HILL, George F. *A Corpus of Italian Medals of the Renaissance Before Cellini.* 201 full-page plates. 2 vols., folio, buckram. London, 1930. $250-$300.

HILL, W. H.; A. F.; and A. E. *Antonio Stradivari, His Life and Work.* Illustrated. Morocco. London, 1902. First edition. One of 100. $300-$400. London, 1909. Second edition. $75-$100.

HILL, W. H.; A. F.; and A. E. *The Violin-Makers of the Guarnieri Family.* Plates. Half vellum. London, 1931. One of 200. $300-$400.

HILLARD, Elias B. *The Last Men of the Revolution.* 12 plates, 6 colored; facsimiles (in some copies). Half morocco. Hartford, 1864. First edition. $400-$600.

HILLS, Chester. *The Builder's Guide.* 70 plates. 2 vols. in one, folio, boards. Hartford, 1834. First edition. $200-$300. Hartford, 1846. 50 plates. $150-$200.

HILLS, Sir John. *Points of a Racehorse.* Illustrated. Folio, cloth. London, 1903. $100-$150.

HILLS, John Waller. *History of Fly-Fishing for Trout.* Half cloth. London, 1921. One of 50 signed. $100-$125.

HILLS, John Waller. *A Summer on the Test.* 12 plates by N. Wilkinson. Calf. London, (1924). One of 300 signed. $150-$200. Another issue: 12 signed etchings by N. Wilkinson. Half parchment. London, (about 1925). One of 25. $250-$350.

HILLYER, Robert. *Sonnets and Other Lyrics.* Boards. Cambridge, Mass., 1917. First edition. In dust jacket. $35-$40. Author's first book.

HILTON, A. *Oklahoma and Indian Territory Along the Frisco.* Illustrated, 2 folding maps. 91 pp., wrappers. St. Louis, 1905. $100-$200.

HIMES, Chester. *Cast the First Stone.* Cloth. New York, (1952). First edition. In dust jacket. $30-$40.

HIMES, Chester B. *If He Hollers Let Him Go.* Cloth. New York, 1947. First edition. In dust jacket. $40-$50. Author's first book.

HIMES, Chester. *Pinktoes.* Wrappers. Paris, (1961). Olympia Pres.. First edition. $25-$40.

HIMES, Chester. *The Third Generation.* Cloth. New York, (1954). First edition. In dust jacket. $50-$75.

HIMSELF. See *Sheppard Lee.*

HIND, Henry Youle. *Narrative of the Canadian Red River Exploring Expedition of 1857, etc.* Plates (some colored), folding maps, charts. 2 vols., brown cloth. London, 1860. $600-$800.

HIND, Henry Youle. *North-West Territory.* Folding maps and plans. Cloth. Toronto, 1859. First edition. $200-$300.

HIND, Henry Youle. *A Sketch of an Overland Route to British Columbia.* Folding map. Dark-green flexible cloth, paper label on front cover. Toronto, 1862. First edition, with errata slip. $1,000, possibly more.

HINKLE, James. F. *Early Days of a Cowboy on the Pecos.* Illustrated. 35 pp., pictorial wrappers. Roswell, N.M., 1937. First edition. $400-$500.

HINMAN, Wilbur F. *The Story of the Sherman Brigade.* Morocco. (Alliance, Ohio), 1897. $35-$50.

HINTON, Richard J. *The Hand-Book of Arizona.* 4 maps, 16 plates. Cloth. San Francisco, 1878. First edition. $100-$125.

*HINTS Towards Forming the Character of a Young Princess.* 2 vols., boards. London, 1805. (By Hannah More.) First edition. $150-$200.

HIPKINS, A. J., and Gibb, William. *Musical Instruments: Historic, Rare, and Unique.* 50 color plates. Half leather. London, 1888. One of 1,040. $250-$350, possibly more.

HIRSHBERG, Dr. L. K. *What You Ought to Know About Your Baby.* Cloth. New York, 1910. First edition. In dust jacket. $150-$200. (Note: Written in collaboration with H. L. Mencken.)

*HISTORIA Cristiana de la California.* Boards and calf. Mexico, 1864. (By El Domingo.) $150-$200.

*HISTORICAL and Descriptive Review of the Industries of Tacoma, 1887.* 108 pp., unbound. Los Angeles, 1887. $100-$150.

*HISTORICAL and Descriptive Review of the Industries of Walla Walla.* 112 pp., wrappers. No place, 1891. $150-$175.

*HISTORICAL and Scientific Sketches of Michigan.* Cloth. Detroit, 1834. First edition. $200-$250.

*HISTORICAL Sketch Book and Guide to New Orleans and Environs.* Plates, folding map. Pictorial wrappers. New York, 1885. (By Lafcadio Hearn and others.) First edition, first issue, with spelling "Bizoin" (instead of "Bisoin") at head of title page. $200-$300. Also, $180 (A, 1976).

*HISTORICAL War Map (The).* Folding maps, plus maps in text. 56 pp., printed boards. Indianapolis, 1862. Asher & Co. $100-$150.

*HISTORY of Alameda County, California.* Portraits. Cloth. Oakland, 1883. (By J. P. Munro-Fraser.) First edition. $150-$200.

*HISTORY of Amador County, California.* Full leather. Oakland, 1881. First edition. $150-$300.

*HISTORY of the Arkansas Valley, Colorado.* Illustrated. Half leather. Chicago, 1881. $125-$150.

*HISTORY of Beasts and Birds.* 25 woodcuts. 30 pp., miniature book, 3⅞ x 2½ inches. Orange wrappers. Cooperstown, N.Y., 1838. $75-$100.

*HISTORY of the Bible.* Illustrated. 256 pp., miniature book. (2 x 1 5/16 inches). Sheep, gilt spine. Sandy-Hill, N.Y., 1925. $100-$125.

*HISTORY of the Bible.* Woodcuts. 192 pp., miniature book, 2 ⅙ x 1 ¾ inches. Calf. Bridgeport, Conn., 1831. $100-$125.

*HISTORY of Black Hawk County, Iowa.* Illustrated. Half leather. Chicago, 1868. $125-$150.

*HISTORY of the Brooklyn and Long Island Fair, Feb. 22, 1864.* Leather. Brooklyn, 1864. $75-$100.

*HISTORY of the City of Denver, Arapahoe County, and Colorado.* Illustrated. Half morocco. Chicago, 1880. First edition. $100-$125.

*HISTORY of the Counties of Woodbury and Plymouth, Iowa.* Half leather. Chicago, 1890-91. $100-$150.

*HISTORY of Crawford and Richland Counties, Wisconsin.* Cloth. Springfield, Ill., 1884. (By C. W. Butterfield and George A. Ogle.) First edition. $100-$125.

*HISTORY of Dearborn and Ohio Counties, Indiana, from Their Earliest Settlement, etc.* Cloth. Chicago, 1885. First edition. $100-$150.

*HISTORY of Floyd County, Iowa.* Half leather. Chicago, 1882. $100-$125.

*HISTORY of Franklin, Jefferson, Washington, Crawford and Gasconade Counties, Missouri.* Illustrated. Half leather. Chicago, 1888. $100-$150.

*HISTORY of Franklin and Pickaway Counties, Ohio.* Illustrated. Half leather. No place, 1880. $100-$125.

*HISTORY of Godefrey of Boloyne (The).* Vellum with ties. London, 1893. Kelmscott Press. One of 300. $500-$600. Also, $450 (A, 1976).

*HISTORY of the Great Lakes.* Plates, 5 double-page maps. 2 vols., cloth. Chicago, 1899. (Edited by John B. Mansfield.) First edition. $100-$125.

*HISTORY of Henry Esmond (The).* 3 vols., brown cloth, paper labels. London, 1852. (By William Makepeace Thackeray.) First edition, with 16 pages of ads dated September. $150-$250.

*HISTORY of Herodotus of Halicarnassus (The).* Translation of G. Rawlinson, revised by A. W. Lawrence. 9 wood engravings, maps. Vellum and cloth. London, 1935. Nonesuch Press. In dust jacket. $250-$350.

*HISTORY of Idaho Territory.* 2 maps, 69 plates, 2 facsimiles. Half morocco. San Francisco, 1884. First edition. $250-$350.

*HISTORY of the Indian Wars with the First White Settlers of the United States (A).* Leather. Montpelier, Vt., 1812. (By Daniel C. Sanders.) First edition. $200-$250. Also, worn, $100 (A, 1967). Rochester, 1828. Boards. Second edition. (Chapter 27 omitted.) $75-$100.

*HISTORY of Jasper County, Missouri.* Illustrated. Half leather. Des Moines, 1883. $100-$125.

*HISTORY of Jo Daviess County, Illinois.* Illustrated. Half leather. Chicago, 1878. $100-$125.

*HISTORY of Johnny Quae Genus (The).* 24 colored plates by Thomas Rowlandson. 8 parts, wrappers. London, 1822. (By William Combe.) First edition. $200-$300. London, 1822. Boards. First book edition. $400-$500.

*HISTORY of the Late War in the Western Country.* Boards. Lexington, Ky., 1816. (By Robert B. McAfee.) First edition, with the "extra" printed leaf (of Gen. Winchester's criticism) at end. $400-$500. Bowling Green, Ohio, (1919). Cloth. One of 300. $50-$75.

*HISTORY of Lawrence County, Pennsylvania.* Half morocco. Philadelphia, 1877. First edition. $125-$150.

*HISTORY of Los Angeles County, California.* Colored folding map, 113 lithographs. Morocco and boards. Oakland, 1880. First edition. $450 and up.

*HISTORY of Madeira (A).* 27 colored plates. Boards or cloth. London, 1821. (By William Combe.) First edition. $250-$400.

*HISTORY of Marin County, California.* Frontispiece, 35 portraits. Full sheep. San Francisco, 1880. (By J. P. Munro-Fraser.) First edition. $350-$450.

*HISTORY of Mendocino County, California.* Portraits. Sheep. San Francisco, 1880. $300-$400.

*HISTORY of Mercer County, Pennsylvania.* Half morocco. Philadelphia, 1877. First edition. $100-$125.

*HISTORY of Milam, Williamson, Bastrop, Travis, Lee and Burleson Counties, Texas.* Half leather. Chicago, 1893. $300-$450.

*HISTORY of Montana, 1739-1885.* Folding map, plates. Half morocco. Chicago, 1885. (Edited by Michael A. Leeson.) First edition. $300-$350.

*HISTORY of Napa and Lake Counties, California.* Illustrated. Full sheep. San Francisco, 1881. First edition $300-$400.

*HISTORY of Nevada.* 116 plates. Half morocco. Oakland, 1881. (Edited by Myron Angel.) First edition. $250-$300.

*HISTORY of Nevada County, California.* Illustrated. Oblong folio, cloth, leather spine. Oakland, 1880. (By Frank L. Wells.) First edition. $350-$450. Also, badly worn, $300 (A, 1974).

*HISTORY of Ontario County, New York.* Half leather. Philadelphia, 1876. $100-$125.

*HISTORY of Pike County, Illinois.* Half leather. Chicago, 1880. $125-$150.

*HISTORY of Pike County, Missouri.* Half leather. Des Moines, 1883. $150-$175.

*HISTORY of Sangamon County, Illinois.* Illustrated. Half leather. Chicago, 1881. $100-$125.

*HISTORY of San Joaquin County, California.* Illustrated. Oblong folio, leather. Oakland, 1879. (By Frank T. Gilbert.) First edition. $400-$450. Also, worn, $300 (A, 1974).

*HISTORY of San Luis Obispo County, California.* Portraits and scenes. Half leather. Oakland, 1883. (By Myron Angel.) First edition. $300-$400.

*HISTORY of Santa Barbara and Ventura Counties, California.* Half leather. Oakland, 1883. (By Jesse D. Mason.) $150-$200.

*HISTORY of a Six Weeks' Tour Through a Part of France, Switzerland, Germany, and Holland.* Boards, green cloth spine, paper label. London, 1817. (By Percy Bysshe Shelley.) First edition. $400-$500.

*HISTORY of Sonoma County, California.* Illustrated. Three-quarters leather. San Francisco, 1880. First edition. $150-$200.

*HISTORY of the Steam-Boat Case (A), Lately Discussed by Counsel Before the Legislature of New Jersey.* 48 pp., unbound. Trenton, N.J., 1815. $175-$225.

*HISTORY of Texas (A), or The Emigrant's Guide to the New Republic, by a Resident Emigrant.* Frontispiece (colored in some copies). Cloth. New York, 1844. (Edited by A. B. Lawrence and C. J. Stille.) Third edition of *Texas in 1840.* With color plate, $200-$300. With plate not colored, $150-$200.

*HISTORY of Tioga County, Pennsylvania.* Cloth. No place, 1897. $100-$125.

*HISTORY of Wabasha County, Minnesota.* Compiled by Franklyn Curtiss-Wedge and others. Cloth. Winona, Minn., 1920. $50.

*HISTORY of Walworth County, Wisconsin.* Illustrated. Half leather. Chicago, 1882. $100-$125.

*HISTORY of Waukesha County, Wisconsin.* Illustrated. Half leather. Chicago, 1880. $100-$125.

*HISTORY of Wayne County, New York.* Illustrated. Half leather. Philadelphia, 1877. $75-$100.

HITTELL, John S. *The Commerce and Industries of the Pacific Coast of North America.* Folding colored map, plates. Cloth. San Francisco, 1882. First edition. $125-$150.

HITTELL, John S. *A History of the City of San Francisco.* Cloth. San Francisco, 1878. First edition. $125-$150.

HITTELL, John S. *The Resources of Vallejo.* Folding map. Printed wrappers. (Vallejo, Calif., 1869.) First edition. $300-$400.

HITTELL, John S. *Yosemite: Its Wonders and Its Beauties.* 20 mounted photographic views by "Helios." Green cloth. San Francisco, 1868. First edition. $1,250. Also, $650 (A, 1973). (Note: The plates are by the pioneer photographer Eadweard Muybridge, and the book is much sought for by collectors in both the Americana and photographic fields.)

HITTELL, Theodore H. (editor). *Adventures of James Capen Adams, Mountaineer and Grizzly Bear Hunter, of California.* 12 wood engravings. Cloth. San Francisco, 1860. First edition. $100-$150. Boston, 1861. 12 plates. Cloth. $50-$75.

HOARE, Sarah. *Poems on Conchology and Botany.* 5 hand-colored plates. Cloth, paper label. London, 1831. First edition. $75-$100.

HOBBS, G. A. *Bilbo, Brewer, and Bribery in Mississippi Politics.* Cloth. (Memphis), 1917. First edition. $50.

HOBBS, James. *Wild Life in the Far West.* 20 plates, colored frontispiece. Cloth. Hartford, 1872. First edition. $100-$150. Hartford, 1873. Second edition. $80-$100. Hartford, 1874. $50. Hartford, 1875. $35.

HOBHOUSE, J. C. (compiler). *Imitations and Translations from the Ancient and Modern Classics.* Pink boards. London, 1809. First edition. $100-$150. (Note: Contains nine new poems by Lord Byron.)

*HOBOMOK, a Tale of Early Times.* Boards. Boston, 1824. (By Lydia Maria Child.) First edition. $150-$200. Author's first book.

HOBSON, G. D. *English Binding Before 1500.* 55 plates, other illustrations. Folio, buckram. Cambridge, 1929. First edition. One of 500. In dust jacket. $125-$150.

HOBSON, G. D. *Maioli, Canevari and Others.* 6 plates in color, 58 in black and white. Brown morocco. London, 1926. First edition. One of 25. $500-$600. Another issue: Cloth. $125-$175. Boston, 1926. Cloth. First American edition. $100-$150.

HOBSON, G. D. *Thirty Bindings.* 30 plates (some in color). Folio, cloth. London, 1926. First Edition Club. One of 600. $100-$200.

HOBSON, R. L. *A Catalogue of Chinese Pottery and Porcelain in the Collection of Sir Percival David.* 180 plates, mostly in color. Folio, linen. London, 1934. First edition. In portfolio box. $1,000-$1,500. Another issue: Silk boards. One of 30 on vellum, signed by Hobson. Boxed. $1,500-$2,000.

HOBSON, R. L. *Chinese Art.* 100 color plates. Cloth. London, 1927. First edition. $100-$200. New York, 1927. First American edition. $100-$200.

HODGE, Frederick W. *Handbook of American Indians North of Mexico.* Map. 2 vols., cloth. Washington, 1907-10. First edition. $100-$150. Washington, 1912. 2 vols. $75-$100. New York, 1959. $35-$50.

HODGE, Gene Meany. *The Kachinas Are Coming.* 18 color plates. Cloth. Los Angeles, 1936. $75-$125.

HODGES, M. C. *The Mestico; or, The War-path and Its Incidents.* 204 pp., printed wrappers. New York, 1850. First edition, with author identified on cover as "W. C. Hodges." $200-$250, possibly more.

HODGSON, Adam. *Letters from North America.* Map, plate. 2 vols., boards. London, 1824. First English edition of *Remarks During a Journey, etc.* With 2 errata slips. $200-$250.

HODGSON, Adam. *Remarks During a Journey Through North America in the Years 1819-21.* Leather. New York, 1823. First (pirated) edition. $75-$100.

HODGSON, J. E. *The History of Aeronautics in Great Britain.* Colored frontispiece, 150 plates, some colored. Buckram. Oxford, 1924. First edition. One of 1,000. $150-$200.

HODGSON, Joseph. *The Alabama Manual and Statistical Register for 1869.* Printed boards. Montgomery, 1869. First edition. $125-$150.

HODGSON, Joseph. *The Cradle of the Confederacy.* Cloth. Mobile, 1876. First edition. $125-$150.

HODGSON, Ralph. *The Last Blackbird and Other Lines.* Cloth. London, 1907. First edition, first issue, edges uncut. $50-$75. wide. $150-$200.

HODGSON, William Hope. *The Boats of the 'Glen Carrig.'* Cloth. London, 1907. First edition. $200-$250.

HODGSON, William Hope. *The House on the Borderland and Other Novels.* Cloth. Sauk City, Wis., 1946. First American edition. In dust jacket. $200-$225.

HODGSON, Mrs. Willoughby. *Old English China.* 16 colored plates and 64 illustrations from photographs. Cloth. Lodnon, 1913. First edition. $100-$150.

HOFER, A.F. *Grape Growing.* 32 pp., wrappers. McGregor Iowa. 1878. First edition. $100.

HOFFMAN, Charles Fenno. See *Greyslaer; A Winter in the West.*

HOFFMAN, Charles Fenno. *The Pioneers of New York.* 55 pp., printed on tan wrappers. New York, 1848. First edition, with seal on front cover 1⅜ inches wide. $150-$200.

HOFFMAN, Charles Fenno. *Wild Scenes in the Forest and Prairie.* 2 vols., boards, paper label on spine. London, 1839. First edition. $150-$200. New York, 1843. 2 vols., boards. First American edition. $150-$200.

HOGAN, Edmund. *The Irish Wolfdog.* Illustrated. Blue cloth. Dublin , 1897. First edition. $5,000 and up. (Most copies were destroyed by fire.)

HOGAN, Edmund, and Graham, Capt. (G.A.). *The Irish Wolfdog and The Irish Wolfhound.* Illustrated. Blue cloth. Dublin, 1939. $200-$300. (Reprints of the earlier Hogan and Graham works.)

HOGG, Robert, and Bull, H. G. (editors). *The Herefordshire Pomona, Containing Original Figures and Descriptions of the Most Esteemed Kinds of Apples and Pears.* 77 colored plates, 3 plain plates. 2 vols., wrappers. London, 1876-85. First edition. $1,000 and up. Rebound in morocco and in cloth, $500-$800. In morocco, $620 (A, 1975).

HOLBROOK, John Edwards. *Ichthyology of South Carolina.* Vol. 1 (All published.) 28 colored plates. Three-quarters morocco. Charleston, 1860. First edition. $750-$1,000. Also, $550 (A, 1975).

HOLDEN, W. C. *Alkali Trails.* Maps, illustrations. Cloth. Dallas, (1930). First edition. $75-$85.

HOLDEN, W. C. *Rollie Burns; or, An Account of the Ranching Industry on the South Plains.* Maps, illustrations. Pictorial cloth. Dallas, (1932). First edition, first issue, tan cloth. $75-$100. Second issue, green cloth, without frontispiece. $50-$75.

HOLDEN, W. C. *The Spur Ranch.* Cloth. Boston, (1934). First edition. $100-$200.

HOLDER, Charles F. *All About Pasadena and Its Vicinity.* Wrappers. Boston, 1889. First edition. $75-$100.

HOLDER, Charles F. *The Channel Islands of California.* Cloth. Chicago, 1910. First edition. $75-$100. Second edition, same date. $50.

HOLDING, C. B. *Green Bluff: A Temperance Story.* Cloth. St. Louis, 1874. First edition. $50.

*HOLKHAM Bible-Picture Book (The).* Facsimile of the fourteenth-century manuscript. Folio, half morocco, or vellum. London, 1954. (Edited by W. O. Hassall.) $75-$100. Another issue: One of 100 in full morocco, signed. $150-$200.

HOLLEY, Mary Austin. *Texas: Observations, Historical, Geographical and Descriptive.* Folding map. Cloth. Baltimore, 1833. First edition. $1,250-$1,500, possibly more. Lexington, Ky., 1836. Map in color. Cloth. Second edition (but an essentially different and re-written book, the first having been designed to encourage emigration, the second to encourage U.S. recognition). $750-$1,000.

HOLLIDAY, George H. *On the Plains in '65.* Illustrated. 97 pp., printed wrappers. No place, 1883. First edition. $600-$750.

HOLLINGSWORTH, John McHenry. *Journal.* Frontispiece in color. Half buckram. San Francisco, 1923. First edition. One of 300. $85-$100.

HOLLISTER, Ovando J. *History of the First Regiment of Colorado Volunteers.* 178 pp., printed wrappers. Denver, 1863. First edition. $2,000-$2,500.

HOLLISTER, Ovando J. *The Silver Mines of Colorado.* 87 pp., printed wrappers. Central City, 1867. First edition. $500-$600. Also, $350 (A, 1968). Springfield, Mass., 1867. Cloth. Enlarged edition (retitled *The Mines of Colorado*). $75-$100. Also, $42 (A, 1972).

HOLLISTER, Uriah S. *The Navajo and His Blanket.* 10 color plates, other illustrations. Cloth. Denver, 1903. First edition. $100-$175.

HOLMES, John Clellon. *Go.* Cloth. New York, 1952. First edition, first issue, with "A" on copyright page. In dust jacket. $75-$100. Author's first book.

HOLMES, Mrs. Mary J. *Cousin Maude, and Rosamond.* Cloth. New York, 1860. First edition. $50-$60.

HOLMES, Mary J. *Tempest and Sunshine; or, Life in Kentucky.* Gray cloth. New York, 1854. First edition. $50-$75.

HOLMES, Oliver Wendell. See Hall, Marshall. Also see *The Autocrat of the Breakfast-Table; Francis Parkman; The Harbinger; The Poet at the Breakfast-Table; Songs of the Class of MDCCCXXIX.*

HOLMES, Oliver Wendell. *Astraea: The Balance of Illusions. A Poem.* Yellow boards. Boston, 1850. First edition, first printing, with ampersand in printer's imprint on copyright page set above the line. $75-$100. (Also issued in rough reddish-brown cloth.)

HOLMES, Oliver Wendell. *The Benefactors of the Medical School of Harvard University.* Tan wrappers. Boston, 1850. First edition. $50-$75.

HOLMES, Oliver Wendell. *Border Lines of Knowledge in Some Provinces of Medical Science.* Cloth. Boston, 1862. First edition, with Ticknor & Co. imprint on spine. $50-$60.

HOLMES, Oliver Wendell. *Boylston Prize Dissertations for the Years 1836 and 1837.* Folding colored map of New England. Cloth. Boston, 1838. First edition. $40-$60.

HOLMES, Oliver Wendell. *The Claims of Dentistry.* Tan wrappers. Boston, 1872. First edition. $75-$125. Also, loose in wrappers, $60 (A, 1975).

HOLMES, Oliver Wendell. *The Contagiousness of Puerperal Fever.* (Caption title.) 28 pp., printed buff wrappers. (Boston, 1843 or 1844?) First edition. $500 and up.

HOLMES, Oliver Wendell. *Currents and Counter-Currents in Medical Science: An Address . . . Before the Massachusetts Medical Society.* Printed salmon-colored wrappers. Boston, 1860. First edition. $75-$100.

HOLMES, Oliver Wendell. *Currents and Counter-Currents in Medical Science. With Other Address and Essays.* Cloth. Boston, 1861. First edition, first issue, with triple-ruled blind-stamped frame enclosing "T & F" initials on cover. $40-$60. Also, inscribed, $80 (A, 1976).

HOLMES, Oliver Wendell. *Elsie. Venner: A Romance of Destiny.* 2 vols., brown cloth. Boston, 1861. First edition, "probable" first printing, with ads dated January, 1861. $75-$100. With February ads, $50-$75.

HOLMES, Oliver Wendell. *The Guardian Angel.* 2 vols., plum-colored cloth. London, 1867. First edition. $35. Boston, 1867. Cloth. First American edition. $25.

HOLMES, Oliver Wendell. *Homoeopathy, and Its Kindred Delusions.* Tan boards, paper label. Boston, 1842. First edition. $50-$75.

HOLMES, Oliver Wendell. *Humorous Poems.* Portrait frontispiece. Printed wrappers, or cloth. Boston, 1865. First edition. Wrappers: $75-$100. Cloth: $50-$75.

HOLMES, Oliver Wendell. *John Lothrop Motley: A Memoir.* Portrait. Cloth. Boston, 1879. First American edition. $35. Another issue: Beveled cloth, gilt top. One of 516 on large paper. $50-$75. (Note: An English copyright edition, dated London, 1878, bound in brown cloth, preceded the American edition.)

HOLMES, Oliver Wendell. *Mechanism in Thought and Morals.* Cloth. Boston, 1871. First edition. $75-$100.

HOLMES, Oliver Wendell. *A Mortal Antipathy*. Green cloth. Boston, 1885. First edition, first issue, with *Elsie Venner* listed at $1.50 in ad opposite title page. $35-$40.

HOLMES, Oliver Wendell. *Oration Delivered Before the City Authorities of Boston, on the Fourth of July, 1863*. Printed salmon-colored wrappers. Boston, 1863. First trade edition. $40-$50. Another issue, "Private Copy": Boston, 1863. Leather or cloth. One of about 12. Inscribed by Holmes. $100 and up.

HOLMES, Oliver Wendell. *Over the Teacups*. Olive-green cloth. Boston, 1891. First edition, first state, with no price for this book on ad leaf facing title page. $100-$125. Also, "later issue, no advts.," $45 (A, 1968).

HOLMES, Oliver Wendell. *A Poem . . . Delivered at the Dedication of the Pittsfield Cemetery, Sept. 9, 1850*. 8 pp., drab wrappers. (Pittsfield, Mass., 1850.) First edition. $30-$40.

HOLMES, Oliver Wendell. *Poems*. Decorated cloth, paper label. Boston, 1836. First edition, with Boston imprint only. $150-$250. Also, $60 (A, 1974). Later 1836 issue: Boston and New York imprint. $100-$150. Boston, 1849. Boards, or cloth. "New and Enlarged Edition." $50-$75.

HOLMES, Oliver Wendell. *The Position and Prospects of the Medical Student*. Printed tan wrappers. Boston, 1844. First edition. $100-$125.

HOLMES, Oliver Wendell. *The Professor at the Breakfast-Table*. Cloth. Boston, 1860. First edition. $40-$50. Another issue: Beveled cloth, edges gilt. Large paper. $75-$100. London, 1860. Cloth. First English edition. $25.

HOLMES, Oliver Wendell. *Puerperal Fever, as a Private Pestilence*. Wrappers or cloth. Boston, 1855. First edition (under this title). In wrappers: $3,500. (This is a recent catalogue price. Rebound copies have sold at auction recently at $200 and $70. No copies in original cloth noted.)

HOLMES, Oliver Wendell. *Teaching from the Chair and at the Bedside*. Printed gray wrappers. Boston, 1867. First edition. $100-$150.

HOLMES, Oliver Wendell. *Urania: A Rhymed Lesson*. Printed blue wrappers. Boston, 1846. First edition. $50-$75.

HOLMES, Oliver Wendell. *Valedictory Address . . . Harvard University, March 10th, 1858*. Wrappers. Boston, 1858. First edition. $75-$100.

HOLMES, Justice Oliver Wendell. *The Common Law*. Cloth. Boston, 1881. First edition. $250-$400. Also, $190. (A, 1974). Author's first book.

HOLMES, Roberta E. *The Southern Mines of California*. Plates and maps. Boards. San Francisco, 1930. Grabhorn Press. One of 250. $85-$100.

*HOLY BIBLE*. Folio, red cloth. Cleveland, 1949. One of 975 designed by Bruce Rogers. $300-$400. Another issue: One of 20 with a decorative headpiece for each book. $600-$800.

*HOME As Found*. By the Author of *Homeward Bound*. 2 vols., cloth, or boards and cloth, with paper spine labels. Philadelphia, 1838. (By James Fenimore Cooper.) First edition, first printing, with a note in Vol. 1 about the paper used in the book. $150-$200.

HOMER, *The Homeric Hymn to Aphrodite*. Translated by F. L. Lucas. 10 wood engravings. Full red morocco. London, 1948. Golden Cockerel Press. One of 100 (from an edition of 750) specially bound, signed by Lucas. Boxed. $300-$350. Another issue: Half morocco. One of 650. $75-$100.

HOMER. *The Odyssey of Homer*. Translated by T. E. Shaw (T. E. Lawrence, of Arabia). With 25 large rondels in gold and black. Small folio, black morocco. (London), 1932. First edition. One of 530 designed by Bruce Rogers. Boxed. $750-$1,000. Note: A few copies were signed by Lawrence, "T. E. Shaw," and Rogers and bring $2,000-$3,000. Also, $1,500 (A, 1976). New York, 1932. Morocco (11 copies); calf (about 23 copies). First American edition (for copyright purposes). A copy in morocco was sold at a New

York auction in October, 1977, for $1,200. Boston, 1929. Translated by George H. Palmer. Illustrated by N. C. Wyeth. Cloth. $75-$125. Another issue: One of 550 signed. With an extra set of color plates. $200-$300.

*HOMES in Texas on the Line of the International and Great Northern Railroad.* 79 pp., wrappers. (Chicago, 1879.) (By N. W. Hunter.) First edition. $150-$250.

HONIG, Louis O. *The Pathfinder of the West: James Bridger.* Illustrated. Leatherette. Kansas City, 1951. Limited, signed edition. $40-$50.

HONIG, Louis O. *Westport, Gateway to the Early West.* Illustrated. Cloth. North Kansas City, 1950. One of 525 signed. $50-$75.

*HONORED in Verse: The Tributes of a Galaxy of American Poets.* (On the Death of President Garfield.) 9 pp., wrappers. Boston, 1881. $75.

HOOD, Thomas. *Humorous Poems.* Illustrated. Cloth. London, 1893. First edition. $35-$50.

HOOD, Thomas. *Miss Kilmansegg and Her Precious Leg: A Golden Legend.* Illustrated. Boards. (Camden, 1904.) Essex House Press. One of 200. $75-$100.

HOOKER, W. A. *The Horn Silver Mine: Report.* (Cover title.) 5 tinted views, colored map. 32 pp., wrappers. New York, 1879. $150-$175.

HOOPER, Johnson J. *Dog and Gun: A Few Loose Chapters on Shooting.* 105 pp., printed wrappers (woodcut on front). New York, 1856. First edition, published by A. O. Moore, with dated title page. $100-$150.

HOOVER, Herbert C. *Fishing for Fun.* Illustrated. Cloth. New York, (1963). First edition. One of 200 signed. Boxed. $100.

HOOVER, Herbert C. *A Remedy for Disappearing Game Fish.* Woodcuts. Marbled boards and cloth. New York, 1930. First edition. One of 990 signed. Boxed. $75-$100.

HOOVER, Herbert C., and Hoover, Lou Henry (translators). *De Re Metallica.* From the Latin of Georgius Agricola. Illustrated. Parchment boards. London, 1912. First English edition. $200-$250. Signed by Hoover, and sometimes by Mrs. Hoover, $300-$400.

HOPE, Anthony. *The Dolly Dialogues.* 4 plates by Arthur Rackham. Cloth. London, 1894. (By A. H. Hawkins.) First edition, first issue, with "Dolly" as running headband on lefthand pages. $100-$150. (Also issued in wrappers.)

HOPE, Anthony. *The Prisoner of Zenda.* Dark-red cloth. London, (1894). (By A. H. Hawkins.) First edition, first issue, with list of 17 (not 18) titles on page 311. $100-$150.

HOPKINS, Gerard Manley. *Poems.* Edited by Robert Bridges. 2 portraits, 2 double-page facsimiles. Blue-gray boards and linen. London, (1918). First edition. In dust jacket. $200-$250.

HOPKINS, Gerard Manley. *Selected Poems.* London, 1954. Nonesuch Press. One of 1,100. $75-$100.

HOPKINS, Gerard T. *A Mission to the Indians, from the Indian Committee of Baltimore Yearly Meeting, to Fort Wayne in 1804.* Edited by Martha E. Tyson. 198 pp., wrappers. Philadelphia, 1862. First edition. $150-$200.

HOPKINS, Harry C. *History of San Diego: Its Pueblo Lands and Water.* Cloth. San Diego, (1929). $60-$80.

HOPKINS, T. M. *Reminiscences of Col. John Ketcham, of Monroe County, Indiana, by His Pastor, Rev. T. M. Hopkins.* 22 pp., printed wrappers. Bloomington, Ind., 1866. First edition. $300-$350.

HOPPE, E. O. (photographer). See King, Richard.

HOPWOOD, Avery. See Rinehart, Mary Roberts.

HORBLIT, Harrison D. *One Hundred Books Famous in Science.* New York, 1964. Grolier Club. One of 1,000. $200-$225.

HORN, Hosea B. *Horn's Overland Guide.* Folding map. Cloth. New York, 1852. First edition, first issue, 78 pp. $400-$500. Second issue, same date, 83 pp., cloth. $250-$300. New York, (1853). Map (different from that in original edition). Cloth. $200-$250.

HORN, Stanley F. *Invisible Empire.* Illustrated. Cloth. Boston, 1948. First edition. In dust jacket. $50-$75.

HORN, Tom. *Life of Tom Horn, Government Scout and Interpreter.* 13 illustrations. Cloth. Denver, (1904). First edition. $50-$75. Another issue: Printed wrappers ("less scarce," says Ramon F. Adams). $35-$50.

HORNEM, Horace, Esq. *Waltz: An Apostrophic Hymn.* 27 pp., wrappers. London, 1813. (By George Gordon Noel, Lord Byron.) First edition. $5,000 and up. Also, $5,250 (A, 1977). Rebound in full morocco, $4,000. Also, unbound, uncut, some repairs to margins and corners, $3,920 (A, 1965)—the Louis H. Silver copy; rebound in half calf, $1,176 (A, 1960).

*HORSE-SHOE Robinson.* 2 vols., purple cloth, paper labels on spines. Philadelphia, 1835. (By John Pendleton Kennedy.) First edition. $200-$250.

HORT, Lieut. Col. *The Horse Guards.* 12 colored lithographs. Cloth. London, 1850. (By John Josiah Hort.) Second edition. $100-$150.

HORT, Lieut. Col. *Penelope Wedgebone: The Supposed Heiress.* 8 colored etchings by Alfred Ashley. Calf. London, (about 1850). (By John Josiah Hort.) $100-$125.

HORTON, George. *War & Mammon.* Wrappers. Wausau, Wis., 1900. Philosopher Press. First edition. $40-$50.

HOSACK, David. *Essays on Various Subjects of Medical Science.* 3 vols., half leather. New York, 1824-30. First edition. $300.

HOSHOUR, Samuel Klinefelter. See Altisonant, Lorenzo.

HOSMER, Hezekiah L. *Early History of the Maumee Valley.* 70 pp., printed wrappers. Toledo, Ohio, 1858. First edition. $250-$300.

HOSMER, Hezekiah L. *Montana: An Address . . . Before the Travellers' Club, New York City, January, 1866.* (Cover title.) 23 pp., printed wrappers. New York, 1866. First edition. $750-$850.

HOSMER, Hezekiah L. *Report of the Committee on Foreign Correspondence of the Grand Lodge of Montana, at Its Seventh Annual Communication.* 55 pp., wrappers. Helena, 1872. $150-$250.

HOSMER, John Allen. *A Trip to the States, by the Way of the Yellowstone and Missouri.* Cloth, or tan printed boards. Virginia City, Mont., 1867. First edition. $3,000 and up. Also, last leaf torn away, $800 (A, 1968)—the Streeter copy, in cloth. (Note: The Graff copy at the Newberry Library is in boards.)

HOUDINI, Harry. *The Right Way to Do Wrong: An Exposé of Successful Criminals.* Wrappers. Boston, 1906. (By Ehrich Weiss.) First edition. $75-$100. Author's first book.

HOUGH, Emerson. See *Getting a Wrong Start.*

HOUGH, Emerson. *The Covered Wagon.* Frontispiece. Cloth. New York, 1922. First edition, first issue, with "(1)" below last line of text. In dust jacket. $50-$75. Lacking jacket, $35-$50.

HOUGH, Emerson. *The King of Gee Whiz.* Illustrated. Pictorial cloth. Indianapolis, (1906). First edition, first issue, with last word on page 26 "Banjo." In dust jacket. $75-$100.

HOUGH, Emerson. *The Mississippi Bubble.* Cloth. Indianapolis, (1902). First edition, first issue, with "April" on copyright page and "Hough" on spine (not "Emerson Hough"). In dust jacket. $75-$100. Lacking jacket, $25-$35.

HOUGH, Emerson. *The Singing Mouse Stories.* Cloth. New York, 1895. First edition. $50-$75. Author's first book.

HOUGH, Emerson. *The Story of the Cowboy.* Illustrated. Decorated cloth. New York, 1897. First edition. $50-$60.

HOUGH, Emerson. *The Story of the Outlaw.* Illustrated. Boards. New York, 1907. First edition, first state, with printer's rule at top of page v. $35-$50.

HOUGH, Emerson. *The Way to the West.* Cloth. Indianapolis, (1903). First edition. $35-$50. Also, $25 (A, 1972).

HOUGH, Franklin B. *History of Jefferson County, New York.* Half leather. Albany, 1854. First edition. $100-$150.

HOUGH, Franklin B. *A History of Lewis County . . . New York.* Illustrated. Half leather. Albany, 1860. First edition. $75-$125.

HOUGH, Franklin B. *History of St. Lawrence and Franklin Counties, New York.* Illustrated. Half leather. Albany, 1853. $100-$150.

HOUGH, Franklin B. *Washingtonia.* Plates, folding map. 2 vols., half morocco. Roxbury, Mass., 1865. First edition. One of 91. $75-$100. Another issue: Wrappers. One of 200 on large paper. $75-$125. Also, $70 (A, 1976).

HOUGH, Romeyn B. *The American Woods.* Mounted specimens. 2 vols., leather-covered cases, silver clasps. Lowville, N.Y., 1888-91. $300-$400, possibly more. Lowville, 1893-1910. 300 plates, 12 text pamphlets. In 12 cases. $400-$600, possibly more.

HOUGHTON, Jacob. *The Mineral Region of Lake Superior.* 2 maps on one folding sheet. Cloth. Buffalo, 1846. First edition. $100-$125.

HOUSE, Homer D. *Wild Flowers of New York.* Illustrated in color. 2 vols., cloth. Albany, 1918. First edition. $75-$100. Albany, 1923. 2 vols., cloth. $50-$75.

HOUSMAN, A. E. *Fragment of a Greek Tragedy.* Printed wrappers. Cambridge, 1921. First edition. $75-$100.

HOUSMAN, A. E. *Last Poems.* Dark-blue buckram. London, 1922. First edition, first issue, with comma and semicolon missing after "love" and "rain," respectively, on page 52. In dust jacket. $50-$75.

HOUSMAN, A. E. *More Poems.* Portrait. Morocco and cloth. London, (1936). First edition. One of 379. In dust jacket. $40-$50. Another issue: Cloth. First trade edition. In dust jacket. $20.

HOUSMAN, A. E. *A Shropshire Lad.* Gray-blue boards, vellum spine, paper label, London, 1896. First edition, first state, with the word "Shropshire" on the label exactly 33 millimeters wide. $800-$1,000. Also, covers faded and worn, $425 (A, 1977). (Only 350 copies.) New York, 1897. Boards, vellum spine. First American edition. $500-$750. (Only 150 copies.) Philadelphia, (1902). Henry Altemus, publisher. Cloth. First edition to be printed in America. $250-$350. London, 1914. Vellum. One of 12 on vellum. $750-$1,000. New York, (1935). Heritage Press. Illustrated by Edward A. Wilson. Calf. Boxed. $75.

HOUSMAN, Laurence. *Followers of St. Francis.* Cloth. London, 1923. First edition. In dust jacket. $35-$50.

HOUSMAN, Laurence. *Stories from the Arabian Nights.* Mounted color plates by Edmund Dulac. Cloth. London, (1907). $100-$125. Another issue: Vellum with silk ties. One of 350 signed. $300-$350.

HOUSTON, Sam. *Speech of . . . Exposing the Malfeasance and Corruption of John

*Charles Watrous, Judge of the Federal Court of Texas, and His Confederates.* Frontispiece. New York, 1860. $150-$250.

HOUSTOUN, Mrs. Matilda C. *Texas and the Gulf of Mexico.* 10 plates. 2 vols., cloth. London, 1844. First edition. $300-$350. Philadelphia, 1845. Frontispiece of Santa Anna. Wrappers. First American edition. $100-$150.

HOVEY, Richard. *Poems.* Printed wrappers, or cloth. Washington, 1880. First edition. Wrappers: $200-$300. Cloth: $100-$150. Author's first book. Inscribed copy offered by dealer for $400 in 1972.

*HOW the Buffalo Lost His Crown.* Illustrated by Charles M. Russell. 44 pp., oblong, brown cloth. (New York, 1894.) (By John H. Beacom.) First edition. $1,000 and up.

*HOW to Win in Wall Street.* By a Successful Operator. Cloth. New York, 1881. (By Joaquin Miller.) First edition. $35-$50.

HOW, George E., and Howe, Jane P. *English and Scottish Silver Spoons.* Photographs. 3 vols., cloth. London, 1952-57. First edition. One of 550. In dust jackets. $400-$500.

HOWARD, B. B. *The Charter and Ordinances of the City of Galena.* Half calf. Galena, Ill., 1853. $150-$250.

HOWARD, Benjamin C. *A Report of the Decisions of the Supreme Court . . . in the Case of Dred Scott vs. John F. A. Sandford.* Wrappers. New York, 1857. $100-$150. (The Dred Scott Decision.)

HOWARD, H. R. See *The Life and Adventures of Joseph T. Hare.*

HOWARD, H. R. (editor). *The History of Virgil A. Stewart, and His Adventures in Capturing and Exposing the "Great Western Land Pirate" (John A. Murrell) and His Gang.* Cloth. New York, 1836. First edition. $200-$250. Howard's first book. New York, 1837 Illustrated. Cloth. $75.

HOWARD, James Q. *The Life of Abraham Lincoln.* 102 p., wrappers. Columbus, Ohio, 1860. First edition, first issue, buff paper covers, 8 unnumbered pages of ads. $100-$150.

HOWARD, Jas. H. W. *Bond and Free.* Frontispiece portrait. Cloth. Harrisburg, 1886. First edition, first issue, with portrait opposite title page. $150-$200.

HOWARD, McHenry. *Recollections of a Maryland Confederate Soldier.* Folding map, plates. Cloth. Baltimore, 1914. First edition. $150-$200.

HOWARD, Oliver Otis. *Account of Gen. Howard's Mission to the Apaches and Navajos.* 12 pp., wrappers. No place, no date. $75-$100.

HOWARD, Oliver Otis. *My Life and Experiences Among Our Hostile Indians.* Illustrated. Cloth. Hartford, (1907). First edition. $75-$100.

HOWARD, Oliver Otis. *Nez Perce Joseph.* 2 portraits and 2 maps. Cloth. Boston, 1881. First edition. $150-$200.

HOWARD, Robert E. *Always Comes Evening.* Cloth. Sauk City, Wis., 1957. First edition. In dust jacket. $250-$300.

HOWARD, Robert E. *Skull-Face and Others.* Cloth. Sauk City, 1946. First edition. In dust jacket. $250-$350.

HOWARD, William. *Narrative of a Journey to the Summit of Mont Blanc.* Boards. Baltimore, 1821. First edition. $75.

HOWBERT, Irving. *The Indians of the Pike's Peak Region.* 4 plates. Cloth. New York, 1914. First edition. $50-$60.

HOWBERT, Irving. *Memories of a Lifetime in the Pike's Peak Region.* Frontispiece. Cloth. New York, 1925. Enlarged edition of preceding title. $35.

HOWE, E. D. *History of Mormonism.* Frontispiece. Cloth. Painesville, Ohio, 1840. Second edition of *Mormonism Unvailed* [sic]. $350-$400 .

HOWE, E. D. *Mormonism Unvailed* [sic]. Frontispiece. Cloth. Painesville, 1834. First edition. $1,500-$2,000.

HOWE, E. W. *The Story of a Country Town.* Illustrated by W. L. Wells. Decorated cloth. Atchison, Kan., 1883. First edition, first issue, with "D. Caldwell, Manufacturer. Atchison, Kan." rubber-stamped inside front cover and no lettering at foot of spine. $75-$125. Author's first book.

HOWE, Henry. *Historical Collections of the Great West.* 2 vols. in one, cloth. Cincinnati, 1851. First edition. $50-$100. Cincinnati, 1852. $35-$50. (Also bound in leather and half leather; numerous other later editions.)

HOWE, Henry. *Historical Collections of Ohio.* Map, woodcuts. Cloth. Cincinnati, 1847. First edition. $75-$100. Cincinnati, 1848. $40-$50. Cincinnati, 1875. $40-$50. Columbus, 1889. 3 vols. in 2, cloth. $60. (Also bound in leather and half leather; numerous other editions.)

HOWE, Henry. *Historical Collections of Virginia.* Map, illustrations, engraved title page. Cloth. Charleston, S.C., 1845. First edition. $100-$125. (Also bound in leather and half leather; numerous other later editions.)

HOWE, John. *Howe's Almanac for the Year of Our Lord, 1804.* Wrappers. Greenwich, Mass., (1803). $100-$150.

HOWE, John. *A Journal Kept by Mr. John Howe, While He Was Employed as a British Spy, During the Revolutionary War.* 44 pp., wrappers. Concord, N.H., 1827. First edition. $500-$650. Also, a rebound copy, $350 (A, 1972).

HOWE, Mark A. De Wolfe. *Rari Nantes: Being Verses and a Song.* Wrappers. Boston, 1893. First edition. One of 80. $50. Author's first book.

HOWE, Octavius T. *The Argonauts of '49.* Illustrated. Half cloth. Cambridge, Mass., 1923. First edition. In dust jacket. $75-$100.

HOWE, Octavius T., and Matthews, Frederick C. *American Clipper Ships, 1833-58.* 114 plates. 2 vols.: Vol. 1, marbled boards; Vol. 2, cloth. Salem, 1926-27. First edition. $150-$200.

HOWELLS, William Dean. See *Poems of Two Friends.*

HOWELLS, William Dean. *A Boy's Town.* Frontispiece and 22 plates. Cloth. New York, 1890. First edition, first state, without illustration on page 44. $40-$60.

HOWELLS, William Dean. *A Chance Acquaintance.* Cloth. Boston, 1873. First edition. $25-$35.

HOWELLS, William Dean. *A Hazard of New Fortunes.* Illustrated. Wrappers. New York, 1890. First edition, first state. $500-$600. Also, $425 (A, 1977). (Cloth copies were later.)

HOWELLS, William Dean. *A Little Girl Among the Old Masters.* 54 plates. Oblong, cloth. Boston, 1884. First edition. $35-$50.

HOWELLS, William Dean. *My Mark Twain.* Illustrated. Sage-colored cloth. New York, 1910. First edition. $50-$60.

HOWELLS, William Dean. *Niagara Revisited.* Colored illustrations, colored title page. 12 pp., decorated buff boards. Chicago, (about 1884). First edition, with or without 16 pages of ads at end. $150-$175.

HOWELLS, William Dean. *Poems.* Cloth. Boston, 1873. First edition. $100-$150.

HOWELLS, William Dean. *The Rise of Silas Lapham.* Blue or brown cloth. Boston, 1885. First edition, first issue, with "Mr. Howells's Latest Works" in boxed ad facing title page and with unbroken type in the word "sojourner" at bottom of page 176. $125-$150. New York, 1961. Limited Editions Club. Illustrated. Buckram. Boxed. $35.

HOWELLS, William Dean. *Suburban Sketches*. Illustrated by A. Hoppin. Decorated brown cloth. Boston, 1871. First edition. $100 and up? (No records of this book for sale in my research.) Boston, 1872. Revised and enlarged edition. $25-$35. Author's first book of fiction.

HOWELLS, William Dean. *Venetian Life*. 18 aquatints. 2 vols., vellum. Cambridge, Mass., 1892. One of 250 on vellum. $50. (Note: One of many later editions of a book first published in New York in 1866.)

HOWELLS, William Dean, and Hayes, J.L. *Lives and Speeches of Abraham Lincoln and Hannibal Hamlin*. 96 pp., printed buff wrappers. Columbus, Ohio, 1860. First edition, first issue, with pages 95-96 blank. $1,000 and up (?). Excessively rare: Blanck locates one copy, rebound; Howes locates two copies in libraries; we know of another privately held. Second issue, engraving of Republican Wigwam, Chicago, on page 96. $1,000 and up. Also, spine chipped, hinges cracked, $800 (A, 1974). Howes does not mention this issue; Blanck locates two imperfect copies. Another issue: Wigwam on page 95. Howes locates five. Second edition, same date. 2 portraits. 74 pp., cloth. First issue, without period after "0" in imprint. $100 and up. Later issues, same date, with period. $50 and up.

HOWELLS, William Dean; Twain, Mark; and others. *The Niagara Book*. Cloth, or printed wrappers. Buffalo, 1893. First edition, first printing, with no ads at end, page 226 blank, and copyright notice in 3 lines. $200-$250.

HOWES, Wright (compiler). *U.S.-iana*. Blue buckram. New York, 1954. First edition. $75-$100. New York, 1962. Buckram. Second edition. $100-$125.

HOWISON, John. *Sketches of Upper Canada*. Edinburgh, 1821. First edition. $150. Edinburgh, 1822. Second edition. $100-$125. Edinburgh, 1825. Third edition. $75-$100.

HOWITT, Samuel. *The British Sportsman*. 72 plates. Oblong, half morocco. London, no date (but with plates dated 1798-1800). First edition (?). $1,000 and up. Also, one plate missing, covers rubbed, $860 (A, 1974). London, 1812. Frontispiece, 71 plates. Morocco. (Often listed in records as the first edition.) $1,000 and up. Also, $722 (A, 1975).

HOWLAND, S.A. *Steamboat Disasters and Railroad Accidents in the United States*. Illustrated. Sheep. Worcester, Mass., 1840. First edition. $75-$100.

HOWLEY, James P. *The Beothucks or Red Indians of Newfoundland*. Plates. Cloth. Cambridge, Mass., 1915. First edition. $150-$200. Also, spine defective, 100 (A, 1972).

HRDLICKA, Ales. *The Anthropology of Florida*. Cloth. DeLand, 1922. First edition. $75-$100.

HUBBARD, Elbert. *A Message to Garcia*. Suede. East Aurora, N.Y., 1899. First edition. One of 1,000. $35 and up. (Note: The limitation is listed variously as 1,000, 925, 28, which indicates special issues not traced in my researches.)

HUBBARD, Gurdon Saltonstall. *Incidents in the Life of Gurdon Saltonstall Hubbard*. Edited by Henry E. Hamilton. Frontispiece. Cloth. (Chicago), 1888. First edition. $100-$150. Also, $75 (A, 1976).

HUBBARD, John Niles. *Sketches of Border Adventures, in the Life and Times of Maj. Moses Van Campen*. Leather. Bath, N.Y., 1841. $350-$500.

HUBBARD, Robert. *Historical Sketches of Roswell Franklin and Family*. Half leather. Dansville, N.Y., 1839. First edition. $325. Also, $175 (A, 1974).

HUDSON, Derek. *Arthur Rackham: His Life and Work*. Color plates. Cloth. London, 1960. First edition. In dust jacket. $100-$150. New York, (1960). First American edition. In dust jacket. $100-$150.

*HUDSON River Portfolio*. See Wall, W.G.

HUDSON, Stephen. *Celeste and Other Sketches*. Wood engravings. Decorated cloth. (London), 1930. (By Sydney Schiff.) First edition. One of 50 on Japan vellum, signed, with an extra set of engravings. Boxed. $100-$135.

HUDSON, W.H. See Harford, Henry; Sclater, P.L., and Hudson, W.H. Also see *A Crystal Age*.

HUDSON, W.H. *Birds in a Village*. Chocolate-colored buckram. London, 1893. First edition. $100-$150.

HUDSON, W.H. *Birds in London*. Illustrated. Cloth. London, 1898. First edition. $100-$125.

HUDSON, W.H. *British Birds*. 8 color plates. Cloth. London, 1895. First edition. $150-$175.

HUDSON, W.H. *El Ombu*. Light-green cloth, or wrappers. London, 1902. First edition. Cloth: $100-$125. Wrappers: $150-$175.

HUDSON, W.H. *Far Away and Long Ago*. Dark-green cloth. London, 1918. First edition. In dust jacket. $150-$175. London, 1931. Vellum. One of 110. $150-$250. New York, 1943. Limited Editions Club. Illustrated. Half leather. Boxed. $75-$100.

HUDSON, W.H. *Green Mansions*. Light-green cloth. London, 1904. First edition, first issue, without publisher's design on back cover. $200-$300. Second issue. $150-$200. London, 1926. Illustrated. One of 165. $75-$100. New York, 1935. Limited Editions Club. Illustrated. Boards. Boxed. $65-$75. New York, 1944. Frontispiece and 9 color plates. Boards and cloth. Boxed. $85-$100.

HUDSON, W.H. *Idle Days in Patagonia*. Illustrated. Crimson buckram. London, 1893. First edition, with 2 ad leaves at end and "Chapman & Hall" on cover. One of 1,750. $50-$75.

HUDSON, W.H. *A Little Boy Lost*. Illustrated. Dull yellow buckram. London, 1905. First edition. $100-$150.

HUDSON, W.H. *Lost British Birds*. Illustrated. 32 pp., light-green wrappers. (London, 1894.) First edition. $75-$100. (Note: Reprints are dated 1894 on the cover.)

HUDSON, W.H. *The Naturalist in La Plata*. Illustrated. Dark-green cloth. London, 1892. First edition, with ads dated April, 1892, at end. $75-$100.

HUDSON, W.H. *The Purple Land That England Lost*. 2 vols., light-blue cloth. London, 1885. First edition, first issue, with October ads in second volume. $500-$750. Later issue: Purple cloth. $300-$350. Author's first book. Second edition: Retitled *The Purple Land*. Boards. London, 1929. $50-$60.

HUEFFER, Ford Madox. See Conrad, Joseph, and Hueffer, Ford Madox. Also see Ford, Ford Madox (for books published after 1919, when he changed his name).

HUEFFER, Ford H. Madox. *The Brown Owl*. Boards and cloth. London, 1892 (actually 1891). First edition. $350-$400. Author's first book.

HUEFFER, Ford Madox. *Between St. Dennis and St. George*. Cloth. London, 1915. (By Ford Madox Ford.) First edition. $50-$75.

HUEFFER, Ford Madox. *The Fifth Queen*. Cloth. London, 1906. (By Ford Madox Ford.) First edition. $35-$50.

HUEFFER, Ford Madox. *On Heaven*. Cloth. London, 1918. (By Ford Madox Ford.) First edition. $50-$60.

HUEFFER, Ford Madox. *The Queen Who Flew*. Illustrated. Vellum. London, 1894. (By Ford Madox Ford.) First edition. One of 25 signed. $200-$300. Trade issue: Decorated cloth. $50.

HUEFFER, Ford Madox. *Songs from London*. Wrappers. London, 1910. (By Ford Madox Ford.) First edition. $75-$100.

HUGHES, John T. *California: Its History, Population, Climate, Soil, Productions, and Harbors*. 105 pp., printed wrappers. Cincinnati, 1848. First edition. $200-$250.

HUGHES, John T. *Doniphan's Expedition, Containing an Account of the Conquest of New Mexico*. Frontispiece. 144 pp., printed wrappers. Cincinnati, 1847. First edition, first issue, lacking words "cheap edition" on the covers. $2,500-$3,500. Cincinnati, 1848. Wrappers. Second edition. $250-$300. Cincinnati, 1848. Cloth. Third edition. With map. $100-$125. Cincinnati, no date. Fourth edition. $75-$100. Topeka, 1907. $35.

HUGHES, Langston. *The Panther and the Lash*. Cloth. New York, 1967. First edition. In dust jacket. $25-$35.

HUGHES, Langston. *I Wonder as I Wander*. Cloth. New York, (1956). First edition. In dust jacket. $35-$45.

HUGHES, Langston. *The Weary Blues*. Boards. New York, 1926. First edition. In dust jacket. $75-$100. Author's first book.

HUGHES, Richard. *Gipsy-Night and Other Poems*. Portrait. Boards. (Waltham Saint Lawrence), 1922. Golden Cockerel Press. First edition. One of 750. $50-$60. Chicago, 1922. Portrait. Boards and cloth. One of 63 signed, with a special proof of portrait. $150.

HUGHES, Richard. *A High Wind in Jamaica*. Boards and cloth. London, 1929. First complete English edition. One of 150 signed. $150-$185. Trade edition: Green cloth. In dust jacket. $60-$80. (Note: The first edition was published in New York as *The Innocent Voyage*.)

HUGHES, Richard. *The Innocent Voyage*. Decorated blue boards and blue linen. New York, 1929. First edition. In dust jacket. $40-$50. New York, 1944. Limited Editions Club. Leather. Boxed. $75-$100. (Published in England as *A High Wind in Jamaica*.)

HUGHES, Richard. *The Sisters' Tragedy*. Wrappers. Oxford, 1922. First edition. $90. Author's first book.

HUGHES, Richard. *The Spider's Palace*. Illustrated. Boards and cloth. London, 1931. One of 110 signed. In dust jacket. $50-$60.

HUGHES, Richard B. *Pioneer Years in the Black Hills*. Edited by Agnes Wright Spring. Illustrated. Cloth. Glendale, Calif., 1957. First edition. $35-$50.

HUGHES, Ted. (Note: This poet's habit of inscribing books and providing manuscript copies of poems to be sold with his books makes an accurate record of his book values extremely difficult. The entries that follow are therefore tentative and conditional.)

HUGHES, Ted. *The Burning of the Brothel*. Woodcuts in color. Printed wrappers. (London, 1966.) Turret Books. First edition. One of 300. $50-$75. One of 75 (of the edition of 300) signed by Hughes. $100-$150.

HUGHES, Ted. *Crow*. Cloth. London, 1970. First edition. In dust jacket. $35. With a signed poem in author's hand, $75-$100. London, (1973). 12 drawings by Leonard Baskin. Cloth. One of 400 signed. $90.

HUGHES, Ted. *Eat Crow*. Illustrated by Leonard Baskin. Black leather. London, 1971. One of 150 signed. Boxed. $125.

HUGHES, Ted. *A Few Crows*. Illustrated. Imitation leather. Exeter, 1970. First edition. One of 150. $50-$65.

HUGHES, Ted. *The Hawk in the Rain*. Cloth. London, (1957). First edition. In dust jacket. $50-$65. New York. (1957). In dust jacket. $25.

HUGHES, Ted. *Pike*. Folio, broadside. Northampton, Mass., 1959. Gehenna Press. $50-$75.

HUGHES, Ted. *Prometheus on His Crag*. Illustrated. Purple morocco. London, 1973. One of 160 signed, with a signed Leonard Baskin drawing. Boxed. $135.

HUGHĘS, Ted. *Recklings*. Cloth. London, (1966). Turret Books. One of 150 signed. In dust jacket. $100-$125.

HUGHES, Thomas. See *Tom Brown at Oxford; Tom Brown's School Days*.

HUGO, Victor. *Toilers of the Sea*. 3 vols., pebbled green cloth. London, 1866. First edition in English. $100-$150.

HULANISKI, F.J. (editor). *History of Contra Costa County, California*. Illustrated. Half morocco. Berkeley, 1917. First edition. $75-$100.

HULME, F. Edward. *Suggestions in Floral Design*. 52 colored plates. Folio, cloth. London, (about 1880). $150-$200.

HULTON, Paul, and Quinn, David Beers. *The American Drawings of John White, 1577-1590*. Frontispiece, 160 plates, 76 in color. 2 vols., folio, red buckram. London, 1964. First edition. $500-$750. Also, $375 (A, 1974).

HUMANITAS (pseudonym). *Hints for the Consideration of the Friends of Slavery*. 32 pp., half leather. Lexington, Ky., 1805. First edition. $2,000.

HUMFREVILLE, J. Lee. *Twenty Years Among Our Savage Indians*. 250 engravings. Cloth. Hartford, 1897. First edition. $75-$125.

*HUMOURIST (The)*. 40 colored etchings, including vignette title pages by George Cruikshank. 4 vols., pink boards. London, 1819-20. (By George Cruikshank.) First edition, first issue, without "Vol. 1" on title page and with all plates dated 1819. $500-$750. Second issue, dated 1819-22: 4 vols., boards. $800-$1,200, possibly more. London, 1892. 4 vols., half morocco. One of 70 on large paper. $350-$450, possibly more.

HUMPHREY, William. *The Last Husband and Other Stories*. Cloth. New York, 1953. First edition. In dust jacket. $35. Author's first book.

HUMPHREYS, Arthur L. *Old Decorative Maps and Charts*. Illustrated. Buckram. London, 1926. One of 1,500. In dust jacket. $100-$150. Another issue: Half vellum. De luxe edition. One of 100 with separate mounted plates. $200-$300.

HUMPHREYS, Henry Noel. *The Illuminated Books of the Middle Ages*. 39 colored plates, one plain plate. Folio, half calf. London, 1844-49. First edition. $500-$600.

HUMPHRIES, Sydney. *Oriental Carpets, Runners and Rugs*. Illustrated. Folio, cloth. London, 1910. $100-$150.

HUNEKER, James. *Painted Veils*. Blue boards, vellum spine. New York, (1920). First edition, on watermarked paper. One of 1,200 signed. $50-$60.

HUNT, George M. *Early Days Upon the Plains of Texas*. Portrait. Cloth. Lubbock, (1919). First edition. $200-$300.

HUNT, J. *An Adventure on a Frozen Lake: A Tale of the Canadian Rebellion of 1837-8*. 46 pp., wrappers. Cincinnati, 1853. $175-$225.

HUNT, J.H.L. *Juvenilia; or, A Collection of Poems*. Frontispiece. Boards, paper label. London, 1801. First edition. $500-$600. Leigh Hunt's first book.

HUNT, James H. *A History of the Mormon War*. Cloth. St. Louis, 1844. First edition. $150-$250.

HUNT, James H. *Mormonism: Embracing the Origin, Rise and Progress of the Sect*. Cloth. St. Louis, 1844. Expanded edition of the foregoing title. With errata leaf. $300-$350.

HUNT, John. *Gazetteer of the Border and Southern States*. Folding map in color. Cloth. Pittsburgh, 1863. First edition. $75-$100.

HUNT, Leigh. See Hunt, J.H.L. Also, see *Christianism; The Feast of the Poets; Sir Ralph Esher.*

HUNT, Leigh. *The Autobiography of Leigh Hunt.* Portraits. 3 vols., cloth. London, 1850. First edition. $200-$250.

HUNT, Leigh. *Captain Sword and Captain Pen: A Poem.* Illustrated. Cloth. London, 1835. First edition. $50.

HUNT, Leigh. *The Correspondence of Leigh Hunt.* Edited by His Eldest Son. Portrait. 2 vols., tan cloth. London, 1862. First edition. $125-$135.

HUNT, Leigh. *The Descent of Liberty: A Mask.* London, 1815. First edition. $100-$150.

HUNT, Leigh. *Foliage; or Poems Original and Translated.* Blue boards, label. London, 1818. First edition. $125-$200. Also, $95 (A, 1974).

HUNT, Leigh. *Imagination and Fancy.* Cloth. London, 1844. First edition. $75-$100.

HUNT, Leigh. *A Jar of Honey from Mount Hybla.* Engraved title page. Illustrated. Glazed boards. London, 1848. First edition, first binding. $250-$300. (Later issue is plain cloth.)

HUNT, Leigh. *Lord Byron and Some of His Contemporaries.* Illustrated. Boards and cloth. London, 1828. First edition. $125-$175. Second edition, same date. $75-$100.

HUNT, Leigh. *Men, Women and Books.* Portrait, 2 vols., orange cloth. London, 1847. First edition. $150-$200.

HUNT, Leigh. *The Palfrey.* 6 woodcuts. Cloth. London, 1842. First edition. $100-$150.

HUNT, Leigh. *The Poetical Works of Leigh Hunt.* Pink boards, printed label. London, 1832. First edition. $100-$125.

HUNT, Leigh. *Stories from the Italian Poets.* 2 vols., dark-blue cloth. London, 1846. First edition, with December ads. $125-$150.

HUNT, Leigh. *The Story of Rimini: A Poem.* Boards, white paper back-label. London, 1816. First edition, with half title. $100-$125.

HUNT, Leigh. *The Town: Its Memorable Characters and Events.* 2 vols., orange cloth. London, 1848. First edition, with ads at end dated January. $50-$75. (Note: Apparently a favorite book of many collectors for rebinding with extra illustrations. Prices of such extra-illustrated books vary widely and depend not only on the quality of the illustrations but the binding as well.)

HUNT, Leigh. *Ultra-Crepidarius: A Satire on William Gifford.* Wrappers. London, 1823. First edition. $250-$350.

HUNT, Lynn Bogue. *An Artist's Game Bag.* 4 color plates, other illustrations. Full leatherette. New York, 1936. Derrydale Press. First edition, limited. $200-$300. Trade issue: Cloth. $50-$75.

HUNT, Richard S., and Randel, Jesse F. *Guide to the Republic of Texas.* Folding map. 63 pp., cloth. New York, 1839. First edition. $750-$850, possibly more.

HUNT, Richard S., and Randel, Jesse F. *A New Guide to Texas.* Folding map. 62 pp., cloth. New York, 1845. Second edition of preceding title. $600-$850. New York, 1846 (sic). With map dated 1848. $350.

HUNT, Rev. T. Dwight. *Address Delivered Before the New England Society of San Francisco, at the American Theatre.* 20 pp., sewed. San Francisco, 1853. $100-$150.

HUNT, T. Dwight. *The Past and Present of the Sandwich Islands.* Cloth. San Francisco, 1853. First edition. $250.

HUNTER, Alexander. *Johnny Reb and Billy Yank.* Illustrated. Cloth. New York, 1905. First edition. $35-$50.

HUNTER, Dard. (Note of caution: The recent and current market in the papermaking books of this authority has shown extremely wide swings in prices at auction, in many cases exceeding the prices of books readily available in retail book shops. A prime example is the entry that follows—recorded in the last edition of this *Handbook* as "$1,000 and up.")

HUNTER, Dard. *Chinese Ceremonial Paper.* Photographs and paper specimens. Boards and morocco. Chillicothe, Ohio, 1937. First edition. One of 125 signed. Boxed. $4,200 (A, 1975); $700 (A, 1974).

HUNTER, Dard. *The Literature of Papermaking, 1390-1800.* Illustrated. Folio, folding sheets in half canvas folder. (Chillicothe, 1925.) One of 190 signed. $1,500-$2,000. Also, $1,500 (A, 1977).

HUNTER, Dard. *Massachusetts Institute of Technology: Dard Hunter Paper Museum.* Frontispiece photograph. Printed wrappers with woodcut on front. (Cambridge, Mass., 1939.) $250.

HUNTER, Dard. *My Life with Paper.* 58 illustrations, including specimens. Cloth. New York, 1958. First edition. $50-$75.

HUNTER, Dard. *Old Papermaking.* Illustrated. Folio, boards. Chillicothe, 1923. One of 200 signed. $1,250 (A, 1975); $700 (A, 1974); $800 (A, 1973).

HUNTER, Dard. *Old Papermaking in China and Japan.* 31 paper specimens, 11 wood engravings in color, other illustrations and photographs. Folio, linen portfolio. Chillicothe, 1932. One of 200 signed. $1,000 and up.

HUNTER, Dard. *Papermaking by Hand in America.* Frontispiece in color, facsimiles tipped in. Boards and linen. Also morocco. (Chillicothe, 1950.) Mountain House Press. First edition. One of 210 signed. Boxed. $4,000-6,000. Also, $2,900 (A, 1977).

HUNTER, Dard. *Papermaking by Hand in India.* 27 paper specimens, 85 photographs. India print cloth and calf. New York, 1939. One of 375 signed. In slipcase. $1,500 and up. Also, $1,600 (A, 1975); $425 (A, 1973).

HUNTER, Dard. *Paper-Making in the Classroom.* 46 plates. Cloth. Peoria, (1931). $100-$200.

HUNTER, Dard. *Papermaking in Indo-China.* Reproductions. Decorated boards and morocco. (Chillicothe), 1947. Mountain House Press. One of 182 on handmade paper. $1,000 and up.

HUNTER, Dard. A. *Papermaking Pilgrimage to Japan, Korea and China.* Photographs and paper specimens. Boards and morocco. New York, 1936. First edition. One of 370 signed. Boxed. $1,500-$2,000. Also, $2,000 (A, 1975).

HUNTER, Dard. *Papermaking Through Eighteen Centuries.* Illustrated. Buckram. New York, 1930. First edition. In dust jacket. $250-$500. Also, $400 (A, 1975); $100 (A, 1972).

HUNTER, Dard. *Primitive Papermaking.* Illustrated. Folding sheets in buckram portfolio, with ties. Chillicothe, 1937. First edition. One of 200. $1,500-$2,000. Also, $1,700 (A, 1975); $550 (A, 1973).

HUNTER, Dard, and others. *Five on Paper.* Illustrated. Morocco. North Hills, Pa., 1963. Bird & Bull Press. One of 169. $250-$350.

HUNTER, Dard, Jr. *A Specimen of Type.* Specimens and illustrations. 12 pp., folio, gray-blue wrappers, paper label. Cambridge, Mass., 1940. One of 100 signed. $250-$350.

HUNTER, George. *Reminiscences of an Old Timer.* 16 plates. Pictorial cloth. San Francisco, 1887. First edition. $80-$100. Battle Creek, 1888. Cloth. Third edition. $50.

HUNTER, J. Marvin (compiler). *The Trail Drivers of Texas.* Illustrated. 2 vols., pictorial cloth. (San Antonio, 1920-23.) First edition. $125-$150. Limited, signed issue: One of 100. $400-$600. Second edition: 2 vols., cloth. (San Antonio, 1924.) $100. Nashville,

1925. 2 vols. in one, cloth. In dust jacket. $50-$75. New York, 1963. 2 vols., half morocco. Boxed. $50-$75.

HUNTER, J. Marvin, and Rose, Noah H. *The Album of Gun-Fighters*. Illustrated. Pictorial cloth. (Bandera, Tex., 1951.) First edition. In dust jacket. $50-$75. Limited edition, with signed slip. $150-$200.

HUNTER, John D. *Manners and Customs of Several Indian Tribes Located West of the Mississippi*. Plain boards, paper label. Philadelphia, 1823. First edition. $175-$200.

HUNTER, John D. *Memoirs of a Captivity Among the Indians of North America*. Boards. London, 1823. First English edition of *Manners and Customs* (see preceding entry). $200-$225. London, 1824. Boards. Third edition. $100-$150.

HUNTER, William S., Jr. *Hunter's Ottawa Scenery*. 14 plates. Folio, cloth. Ottawa, 1855. First edition. $500-$750.

HUNTER, William S., Jr. *Hunter's Panoramic Guide from Niagara Falls to Quebec*. Engraved title, folding panoramic chart. Pictorial cloth. Boston, 1857. $50-$100. Montreal, 1860. $40-$50.

*HUNTERS of Kentucky (The)*. 100 pp., wrappers. New York, 1847. (By Benjamin Bilson.) First edition. $150-$200. (Piracy of James O. Pattie's *Personal Narrative.)*

HUNTINGTON, D.B. *Vocabulary of the Utah and Sho-Sho-Ne, or Snake Dialects, with Indian Legends and Traditions*. 32 pp., stitched. Salt Lake City, 1872. $125-$150.

HURST, Samuel H. *Journal-History of the 73d Ohio Volunteer Infantry*. Cloth. Chillicothe, Ohio, 1866. First edition. $50-$75.

HURSTON, Zora Neale. *Mules and Men*. Illustrated by Miguel Covarrubias. Cloth. Philadelphia, 1935. First edition. In dust jacket. $75.

HURSTON, Zora Neale. *Seraph on the Suwanee*. Wrappers. New York, 1948. First edition. Publisher's advance copy with blurb on front wrapper. $75-$100. Regular trade edition: In jacket. $25-$30.

HURSTON, Zora Neale. *Tell My Horse*. Cloth. Philadelphia, 1938. First edition. In dust jacket. $35.

HUSTON, John. *Frankie and Johnny*. Illustrated by Miguel Covarrubias. Cloth. New York, 1930. First edition. In dust jacket. $50.

HUTCHINGS, James M. *Scenes of Wonder and Curiosity in California*. Illustrated. Decorated cloth. San Francisco, (1860). First edition. $100-$125. San Francisco, 1861. Second edition (or issue). $75-$100. New York, 1870. Green cloth. $50-$75. New York, 1872. Cloth. $75-$100. London, 1865. First English edition. $75-$100.

HUTCHINS, Thomas. *A Topographical Description of Virginia, Pennsylvania, Maryland and North Carolina*. Folding map, 2 plans, 2 facsimiles. Cloth. Cleveland, 1904. One of 20 on handmade paper. $75-$100. One of 240 others. $25-$35.

HUXLEY, Aldous. See *Jonah*.

HUXLEY, Aldous. *Antic Hay*. Yellow cloth, yellow stained top. London, 1923. First edition. In dust jacket. $25-$35.

HUXLEY, Aldous. *Apennine*. Boards and cloth, paper label. Gaylordsville, N.Y., 1930. First edition. One of 91 signed. In slipcase. $150-$200.

HUXLEY, Aldous. *Arabia Infelix and Other Poems*. Boards and cloth. New York, 1929. Fountain Press. First edition. One of 692 signed. $100-$135.

HUXLEY, Aldous. *Beyond the Mexique Bay*. Illustrated. Boards and cloth. London, 1934. First edition. One of 210 signed. $150-$200. Trade edition: Orange cloth. In dust jacket. $50-$60.

HUXLEY, Aldous. *Brave New World*. Buckram, leather label. London, 1932. First edition. One of 324 signed. $350-$400. Trade edition: Blue cloth. In dust jacket. $150-$200. New York, 1974. Limited Editions Club. Boxed. $50-$60.

HUXLEY, Aldous. *Brief Candles*. Black cloth. New York, 1930. Fountain Press. First American edition. One of 842 signed. $75-$125. Trade edition: Cloth. In dust jacket. $40-$50. London, 1930. Red cloth. First edition. In dust jacket. $40-$50.

HUXLEY, Aldous. *The Burning Wheel*. Woodcut decorations. Yellow wrappers, paper label. Oxford, 1916. First edition. $500-$600. Also, $425 (A, 1977). Author's first book.

HUXLEY, Aldous. *The Cicadas and Other Poems*. Boards and cloth. London, 1931. One of 160 signed. In dust jacket. $100-$135. Trade edition: Brown cloth. In dust jacket. $35-$50.

HUXLEY, Aldous. *Crome Yellow*. Yellow cloth, top stained green. London, 1921. First edition. In dust jacket. $100.

HUXLEY, Aldous. *The Defeat of Youth and Other Poems*. Without title page. Decorated stiff wrappers. (Oxford, 1918.) First edition. Limited edition. $100-$125.

HUXLEY, Aldous. *Do What You Will*. Half cloth. London, 1929. First edition. One of 260 signed. $80-$135. Trade edition: Tan cloth. In dust jacket. $40-$50.

HUXLEY, Aldous. *Ends and Means*. Half cloth. London, 1937. First edition. One of 160 signed. $100-$150. Trade edition: Cloth. In dust jacket. $30-$40.

HUXLEY, Aldous. *Essays New and Old*. Boards and buckram. London, 1926. Florence Press. First edition. One of 650 signed. In dust jacket. $100-$135.

HUXLEY, Aldous. *Eyeless in Gaza*. Decorated boards and brown buckram. London, 1936. One of 200 signed. $150-$250. Trade edition: Tan cloth. In dust jacket. $35-$45.

HUXLEY, Aldous. *Holy Face and Other Essays*. Colored illustrations. Buckram. London, 1929. First edition. One of 300. Boxed $125-$135.

HUXLEY, Aldous. *Leda*. Half cloth. London, 1920. First edition. One of 160 signed. $100-$150. Trade edition: Red cloth, with top stained red. In dust jacket. $30-$50. Garden City, 1929. Cloth. One of 364 (361?) signed. Boxed. $75-$100.

HUXLEY, Aldous. *Little Mexican and Other Stories*. Red cloth, top stained red. London, 1924. First edition. In dust jacket. $35-$50.

HUXLEY, Aldous. *The Most Agreeable Vice*. Small self-wrappers. Los Angeles, 1938. First edition. One of 500. $75.

HUXLEY, Aldous. *Mortal Coils*. Blue cloth, top stained blue. London, 1922. First edition. In dust jacket. $40-$60.

HUXLEY, Aldous. *Music at Night and Other Essays*. Boards and buckram. New York, 1931. Fountain Press. First edition. One of 842 signed. $75-$100.

HUXLEY, Aldous. *The Olive Tree and Other Essays*. Green buckram. London, 1936. First edition. One of 160 signed. $100-$150.

HUXLEY, Aldous. *On the Margin*. Blue-green cloth, top stained blue. London, 1923. First edition, with page vi numbered v in error. In dust jacket. $100-$125.

HUXLEY, Aldous. *Point Counter Point*. Green buckram. London, 1928. First edition. One of 256 signed. $200-$250. Trade edition: Orange cloth. In dust jacket. $50-$75.

HUXLEY, Aldous. *Prisons*. Piranesi plates. Wrappers and cloth-backed board folder. (Paris), 1949. Trianon Press. One of 212 signed. $250-$300.

HUXLEY, Aldous. *Proper Studies*. Boards and cloth. London, 1927. First edition. One of 250 signed. $60-$80.

HUXLEY, Aldous. *Selected Poems*. Decorated boards. Oxford, 1925. First edition. $60-$80.

HUXLEY, Aldous. *Texts and Pretexts*. Decorated boards and buckram. London, 1932. First edition. One of 214 signed. $100-$125.

HUXLEY, Aldous. *Vulgarity in Literature*. Boards and buckram. London, 1930. First edition. One of 260 signed. $100-$150. Trade edition: Decorated boards. $30-$40.

HUXLEY, Aldous. *Wheels*. Decorated boards and cloth. Oxford, 1917. First edition. $75-$100.

HUXLEY, Aldous. *The World of Light*. Boards and buckram. London, 1931. First edition. One of 160 signed. $100-$150.

HUXLEY, Aldous (editor). *An Encyclopedia of Pacifism*. Wrappers. London, (1937). First edition. $75-$100.

HUXLEY, Aldous, and Gilbert, Stuart. *Joyce the Artificer*. Wrappers. (London), 1952. First edition. One of 90. $150-$250.

HUXLEY, T.H. *Evidence as to Man's Place in Nature*. Illustrated. Cloth. London, 1863. First edition. $250-$350.

HYDE, Douglas (translator). *The Love Songs of Connacht*. Boards and linen. Dundrum, Ireland, 1904. Dun Emer Press. One of 300. $75-$100.

HYDE, George E. *The Early Blackfeet and Their Neighbors*. 45 pp., wrappers. Denver, 1933. One of 75. $100-$125.

HYDE, George E. *The Pawnee Indians*. 2 vols., printed wrappers. Denver, 1934. One of 100. First edition. $100-$125.

HYDE, George E. *Red Cloud's Folk*. Cloth. Norman, Okla., 1937. First edition. In dust jacket. $50-$75.

HYDE, George E. *Rangers and Regulars*. 47 pp., wrappers. Denver, 1933. One of 50. $85-$125.

HYDE, S.C. *Historical Sketch of Lyon County, Iowa*. Map. 40 pp., wrappers. Le Mars, Iowa, 1872. First edition. $85-$100.

*HYMNS and Prayers for Use at the Marriage of Michael Hornby and Nicolette Ward at St. Margaret's Church*. 16 pp., blue wrappers. Westminster (London), 1928. Ashendene Press. $100-$125.

*HYMNS for Infant Minds*. Wrappers. Boston, 1814. (By Ann and Jane Taylor.) $40-$50.

HYNE, C.J. Cutcliffe. *Honour of Thieves: A Novel*. Cloth. London, 1895. First edition. $35-$50.

*HYPERION: A Romance*. By the author of "Outre-Mer." 2 vols., tan boards, paper labels, white end papers. New York, 1839. (By Henry Wadsworth Longfellow.) First edition, first binding. $500-$600. Also, brown end papers (later), $350 (A, 1975).

# I

IBN KHALLIKAN. *Biographical Dictionary.* Translated from the Arabic by Baron Mac Guckin de Slane. 4 vols., cloth. New York, 1961. $150-$200.

IBSEN, Henrik. *Peer Gynt: A Dramatic Poem.* Illustrated in color by Arthur Rackham. Full white vellum. London, (1936). One of 460 signed by Rackham. Boxed. $400-$500. Trade edition: Cloth. In dust jacket. $150-$200. Philadelphia, (1936). First American trade edition. $150-$200. New York, 1955. Limited Editions Club. Illustrated. Pictorial boards. Boxed. $50-$60.

*IDAHO: A Guide in Word and Picture.* Illustrated. Pictorial cloth. Caldwell, 1937. First edition. In dust jacket. $75-$85. (Note: Edited by Vardis Fisher.)

IDE, Simeon. *The Conquest of California: A Biography of William B. Ide.* Illustrations, map. Boards and cloth. Oakland, 1944. Grabhorn Press. One of 500. In dust jacket. $50-$65.

IDE, William Brown. *A Biographical Sketch of the Life of William B. Ide . . . And . . . Account of the Virtual Conquest of California, etc.* Half leather and cloth. (Claremont, N.H., 1880.) (By Simeon Ide.) First edition. $750-$1,000. (80 copies issued.) Another edition: Printed wrappers. (Claremont, 1885?). $500-$600, possibly more.

IDE, William Brown. *Who Conquered California?* Printed boards and cloth. Claremont, N. H., (1880? 1885?). (By Simeon Ide.) First edition. $250-$350.

*IDEAL Husband (An).* By the Author of *Lady Windermere's Fan.* Lavender cloth. London, 1899. (By Oscar Wilde.) First edition. Large paper tissue: One of 100. $300-$350. Signed issue: Vellum. One of 12 on vellum. $750-$1,000. Trade issue: One of 1,000. Light brownish-red linen. $75-$150.

*IDLE Man (The).* 6 parts, wrappers. New York, 1821-22. (Edited by Richard Henry Dana, Sr.) $150-$200. (Note: Contains new poems by William Cullen Bryant.)

*IDLENESS and Industry Exemplified, in the History of James Preston and Ivy Lawrence.* Boards and calf. Philadelphia, 1803. (By Maria Edgeworth.) First American edition. $150-$175.

*I KUNSTITUSHUN i Micha i nan vlhpisa Chickasha, Okla i nan apesa yvt apesa tokmak oke.* ("Chickasaw People, Their Constitution and Their Law 1857-59. 1867-68. 1870-72.") Translated from English to Chickasaw by Allen Wright. Cloth. Chickasha, Okla., 1872. First edition. $400-$500.

*ILLINOIS Central Railroad Company (The), Offers Over 2,000,000 Acres, etc.* 64 pp., sewed. New York, 1856. (By John Wilson.) First edition. $100-$125.

*ILLINOIS in 1837; A Sketch.* Folding colored map. Boards and cloth. Philadelphia, 1837. (By S. Augustus Mitchell?) First edition, first issue, with "animals" misspelled "animalas" on title page. $65-$100. Second issue, error corrected. $50-$75. Philadelphia, 1838. (Title changed to *Illinois in 1837 & 8.*) $40-$50.

*ILLUSTRATED Album of Biography of Pope and Stevens Counties, Minnesota.* Half leather. Chicago, 1888. $75-$100.

*ILLUSTRATED Atlas and History of Yolo County, California (The).* 50 plates, map in color. Atlas folio, cloth. San Francisco, 1879. First edition. $350.

*ILLUSTRATED Historical Atlas of the State of Indiana.* Half leather. Chicago, 1876. $100-$150.

*ILLUSTRATED History of Los Angeles County (An).* Illustrated. Full morocco. Chicago, 1889. First edition. $250-$300.

*ILLUSTRATED History of San Joaquin County (An).* Full leather. Chicago, 1890. $200-$250.

*IMAGINARY Conversations of Literary Men and Statesmen.* 2 vols., boards, paper labels. London, 1824. (By Walter Savage Landor.) First edition. $150-$200. (Note: Three other volumes of the *Conversations* subsequently appeared.) New York, 1936. Limited Editions Club. Linen. Boxed. $30.

*IMAGIST Anthology (The).* Edited by Ford Madox Ford and Glenn Hughes. Cloth. New York, 1930. First edition. One of 1,000. $85-$100. London, 1930. Yellow cloth. First English edition. $75-$85.

*IMPARTIAL Appeal (An) to the Reason, Interest, and Patriotism of the People of Illinois, on the Injurious Effects of Slave Labour.* 16 pp., disbound. (Philadelphia?), 1824. (By Morris Birkbeck.) $2,000 and up. Also, $1,700 (A, 1967). (Note: Only four copies known.)

*IMPARTIAL Inquirer (The).* 96 pp., stitched, or in leather binding. Boston, 1811. (By John Lowell.) First edition. $50-$75.

*IMPORTANCE of Being Earnest (The).* By the Author of *Lady Windermere's Fan.* Reddish-brown linen. London, 1899. (By Oscar Wilde.) First edition. $150-$200. Another issue: One of 100 on large paper, signed. $750-$1,000. Also, $800 (A, 1977). Another issue: Vellum. One of 12 on Japan paper, signed. $1,000 and up. Also, copy No. 2, inscribed by Wilde to Edward Strongman, $2,950 in a 1974 catalogue. New York, 1956. 2 vols., decorated boards. Limited edition. Boxed. $75-$125.

*IN a Good Cause: A Collection of Stories, Poems, and Illustrations.* Decorated vellum boards. London, 1885. First edition. $50-$60. (Note: Contains first appearance of an Oscar Wilde poem, "Le Jardin des Tuileries.")

*INCHIQUIN, The Jesuit's Letters, During a Late Residence in the U. S. A.* Leather. New York, 1810. (By Charles J. Ingersoll.) First edition. $75-$85.

*INCIDENTAL Numbers.* Boards. London, 1912. (By Elinor Wylie.) First edition. One of 65. $3,500-$5,000. Also, $1,300 (A, 1976); $3,750 (A, 1974). Author's first book.

*INCIDENTS of Border Life.* 5 plates. Half calf. Chambersburg, Pa., 1839. (By Joseph Pritts.) First edition, first issue, with only 491 pages. $75-$100. Second issue, 6 plates, 507 pages. $50-$75. Lancaster, Pa., 1841. $35-$50.

*INDEX.* 20 pp., red wrappers. London, 1915. (By Norman Douglas.) First edition. One of 100. $75-$100. (Note: The index is to nine Capri monographs by Douglas.)

*INDEX to "In Memoriam" (An).* Dark-brown or purple cloth. London, 1862. (By Charles L. Dodgson.) First edition, first issue, without ads. $75-$100.

*INDIAN Council in the Valley of the Walla-Walla, 1855 (The).* 32 pp., pale blue printed wrappers. San Francisco, 1855. (By Lawrence Kip.) First edition. $750-$1,000. Rebound in calf, $750. Eugene, Ore., 1897. $50-$60.

*INDIAN Missions (The), in the United States of America, etc.* 34 pp., plain blue wrappers. Philadelphia, 1841. First edition. $1,500 and up. Also, $1,100 (A, 1967). (This Jesuit report includes two letters of Pierre Jean De Smet.)

*INDIAN Summer.* Stitched paper wrappers. (Madison, Wis., 1912.) (By William Ellery Leonard.) First edition. $35-$50.

*INDIANS (The): Or Narratives of Massacres and Depredations, etc.* By a Descendant of the Huguenots. 79 pp., calf. Rondout, N.Y., 1846. (By Johannes H. Bevier.) First edition. $100.

*INDUSTRIAL Prodigy of the New Southwest (The).* Illustrated. 157 pp., wrappers. Muskogee, Indian Territory, (about 1902). $75-$100.

*INFIDEL (The); or The Fall of Mexico.* 2 vols., purple cloth, paper labels. Philadelphia, 1835. (By Robert Montgomery Bird.) First edition. $200-$300.

INGELOW, Jean. *The High Tide.* Wrappers. Boston, 1864. First edition. $50-$60.

INGERSOLL, Ernest. *An Island in the Air.* Cloth. New York, 1905. First edition. In dust jacket. $40-$60.

INGERSOLL, Luther A. *Century Annals of San Bernardino County.* (1769 to 1904). Portraits and views. Full morocco. Los Angeles, 1904. First edition. $100-$150.

INGERSOLL, Robert G. *The Gods and Other Lectures.* Cloth. Peoria, 1874. First edition, first binding, lettered title on spine. $50-$60.

INGERSOLL, Robert G. *An Oration Delivered . . . at Rouse's Hall, Peoria, Ill., at the Unveiling of a Statue of Humboldt, September 14th, 1869.* Wrappers. Peoria, 1869. First edition. Author's first published work. $75-$100.

INGOLDSBY, Thomas. *The Ingoldsby Legends, or Mirth and Marvels.* Etchings by George Cruikshank and John Leech. 3 vols., brown cloth. London, 1840-42-47. First edition, with misprint "topot" on page 350 of Vol. 3 and blank page 236 in Vol. 1. (By Richard Harris Barham.) $300-$450. London, 1898. Illustrated by Arthur Rackham. Green cloth. $100-$150. London, 1907. Illustrated by Rackham. White vellum. One of 560 signed by Rackham. $400-$500. Ordinary issue: Cloth. $150. (Several other Rackham editions in cloth: 1909, 1914, 1920, 1929, etc.)

INGRAHAM, Joseph Holt. See *The South-West.*

INGRAHAM, Joseph Holt. *Pierce Fenning, or, The Lugger's Chase.* Illustrated. 95 pp., stitched. Boston, 1846. First edition. $100-$125.

INGRAHAM, Joseph Holt (editor). *The Prince of the House of David.* Illustrated. Cloth. New York, 1855. First edition. $75-$100.

*INHERITANCE (The).* 3 vols., boards. Edinburgh, 1824. (By Susan Edmonstone Ferrier.) First edition, with half titles. $200-$250.

*IN MEMORIAM.* Dark-purple cloth. London, 1850. (By Alfred, Lord Tennyson.) First edition, first issue, with "baseness" for "bareness" in line 3, page 198. $150-$200. London, 1900. Vale Press. Cloth. One of 330. $50-$75. London, 1914. Riccardi Press. Vellum with silk ties. One of 12 on vellum. $1,000. Also, $624 (A, 1971). London, 1933. Nonesuch Press. Limp vellum. $100-$150. Another issue: Boards. One of 2,000. $40-$50.

*IN MEMORIAM: Harry Elkins Widener.* Morocco. No place, 1912. (By Dr. A. S. W. Rosenbach.) $75-$100.

*IN PRINCIPIO.* (The first chapter of Genesis.) Full morocco, by the Doves Bindery. London, (1911). Doves Press. One of 200. $250-$350.

INMAN, Col. Henry. *The Old Santa Fe Trail.* Frontispiece, 8 plates by Frederic Remington, folding map. Cloth. New York, 1897. First edition. $100-$125.

INMAN, Col. Henry. *Stories of the Old Santa Fe Trail.* Pictorial cloth. Kansas City, 1881. First edition. $50-$75. Author's first book.

INMAN, Col. Henry (editor). *Buffalo Jones' 40 Years of Adventure.* 43 plates. Pictorial cloth. Topeka, 1899. First edition. $60-$100.

INMAN, Col. Henry, and Cody, William F. *The Great Salt Lake Trail.* Map, 8 plates. Pictorial buckram. New York, 1898. First edition, first binding, blue (later brown). $50-$75.

*INSTRUCTION for Heavy Artillery . . . for the Use of the Army of the United States.* 39 plates, tables, charts. Cloth. Charleston, 1862. $350-$400.

*IRENE the Missionary.* Green or brown cloth. Boston, 1879. (By John W. DeForest.) First edition. $50-$60.

IRON, Ralph. *The Story of an African Farm.* 2 vols., cloth. London, 1883. (By Olive Schreiner.) First edition. $300-$350. Uganda (New York), 1961. Limited Editions Club. Illustrated by Paul Hogarth. Cloth. Boxed. $50-$60.

IRVIN, S. M. *Sophie Ruberti.* (Cover title.) 8 pp., sewed. Highland, Kan., 1865. Frst edition. $150.

IRVING, John Treat, Jr. *The Hawk Chief: A Tale of the Indian Country.* 2 vols., cloth. Philadelphia, 1837. First edition. $200-$250.

IRVING, John Treat, Jr. *The Hunters of the Prairie, or the Hawk Chief.* 2 vols., boards and cloth. London, 1837. First English edition of *The Hawk Chief.* $150-$250.

IRVING, John Treat, Jr. *Indian Sketches, Taken During an Expedition to the Pawnee Tribes.* 2 vols., boards, or cloth. Philadelphia, 1835. First edition. $250-$350. London, 1835. 2 vols., boards. First English edition. $100-$150.

IRVING, Washington. See Agapida, Fray Antonio; Crayon, Geoffrey; Depons, Francois; Knickerbocker, Diedrich; Langstaff, Launcelot; Oldstyle, Jonathan. Also see *Abbotsford; Biography of James Lawrence; Legends of the Conquest of Spain; A Tour of the Prairies.*

IRVING, Washington. *Adventures of Captain Bonneville.* 3 vols., boards, paper label. London, 1837. First edition. $200-$300. (For first American edition, see *The Rocky Mountains.)*

IRVING, Washington. *Astoria, or Anecdotes of an Enterprise Beyond the Rocky Mountains.* Folding map. 2 vols., blue cloth. Philadelphia, 1836. First edition, first state, with copyright notice on back of first title page and garbled footnote on page 239 of Vol. 2. $400-$600. Also, with some defects, $200 (A, 1974). London, 1836. 3 vols., gray boards, paper spine labels. First English edition. $500-$600. Also, $500 (A, 1974).

IRVING, Washington. *Biography and Poetical Remains of the Late Margeret Miller Davidson.* Black cloth. Philadelphia, 1841. First edition. $40-$60.

IRVING, Washington. *Chronicles of Wolfert's Roost.* Tan cloth. Edinburgh (London), 1855. First edition, first issue, with *Constable's Miscellany* listed as "In the Press . . . Volume V" (later reading, "Volume VII"). $150-$250. (For first American edition, see Irving, *Wolfert's Roost.)*

IRVING, Washington. *A History of the Life and Voyages of Christopher Columbus.* 2 folding maps. 4 vols., boards, paper labels. London, 1828. First edition. (Blanck thinks all copies issued by Murray under this date are acceptable first editions regardless of variations.) $200-$300. New York, 1828. Folding map. 3 vols., boards, paper labels. First American edition. $100-$150.

IRVING, Washington. *The Legend of Sleepy Hollow.* Illustrated in color by Arthur Rackham. Cloth. London, (1928). $100-$125. Another issue: Vellum. One of 375 signed by Rackham. $400-$600. Also, $500 (A, 1976).

IRVING, Washington. *The Life of George Washington.* 5 vols., cloth. New York, 1855-59. First edition, with dates as follows: Vols. 1 and 2, 1855; 3, 1856; 4, 1857, and 5, 1859. $100-$150. Another issue: Large paper edition (Vol. 2 dated 1856). One of 110 copies. $300-$350. (Note: See Blanck's detailed description for the complicated publishing history of this book.)

IRVING, Washington. *The Rocky Mountains.* "Digested from the Journal of Captain B. L. E. Bonneville . . . by Washington Irving." 2 folding maps. 2 vols., blue cloth, printed labels. Philadelphia, 1837. First American edition, first issue, with no ads and 2 blank flyleaves at each end. $150-$300. (For first edition, see Irving, *Adventures of Captain Bonneville.)*

IRVING, Washington. *Voyages and Discoveries of the Companions of Columbus.* Cloth. London, 1831. First edition. $100-$150. Philadelphia, 1831. Boards and cloth, paper label. First American edition. $75-$100.

IRVING, Washington. *Wolfert's Roost and Other Papers.* Frontispiece. Slate-green cloth. New York, 1855. First American edition, first issue, with frontispiece and vignette title page on a stub. $75-$100. (For first edition, see Irving, *Chronicles of Wolfert's Roost.*)

ISELIN, Isaac. *Journal of a Trading Voyage Around the World, 1805-1808.* (New York, about 1897.) First edition. (100 copies printed.) $350-$400.

ISHERWOOD, Christopher. See Auden, W. H., and Isherwood, Christopher; Baudelaire, Charles.

ISHERWOOD, Christopher. *All the Conspirators.* Cloth. London, 1928. First edition. In dust jacket. $100-$135. Author's first novel.

ISHERWOOD, Christopher. *The Berlin Stories: The Last of Mr. Norris. Goodbye to Berlin.* Cloth. (Norfolk, Conn.), 1945. New Directions. First edition. In dust jacket. $35-$50.

ISHERWOOD, Christopher. *Goodbye to Berlin.* Cloth. London, 1939. Hogarth Press. First edition. In dust jacket. $135-$150.

ISHERWOOD, Christopher. *Lions and Shadows: An Education in the Twenties.* Portrait frontispiece. Cloth. London, 1938. First edition, first issue. In dust jacket. $75-$100. Norfolk, (1947). New Directions. Blue cloth. First American edition. In dust jacket. $35.

ISHERWOOD, Christopher. *The Memorial: Portrait of a Family.* Cloth. London, 1932. Hogarth Press. First edition. In dust jacket. $80-$100. Norfolk, (about 1946). New Directions. Cloth. First American edition. In dust jacket. $25.

ISHERWOOD, Christopher. *Mr. Norris Changes Trains.* Cloth. London, 1935. Hogarth Press. In dust jacket. $125-$175.

ISHERWOOD, Christopher. *Prater Violet.* Gray cloth. New York, (1945). First edition. In dust jacket. $40-$50. London, (1946). First English edition. In dust jacket. $25.

ISHERWOOD, Christopher. *Sally Bowles.* Cloth. London, 1937. First edition. In dust jacket. $75-$85.

ISHERWOOD, Christopher. *The World in the Evening.* Cloth. London, (1954). First edition. In dust jacket. $30-$40. New York, (1954). Cloth. First American edition. In dust jacket. $25.

*IVANHOE: A Romance.* 3 vols., boards. Edinburgh, 1820. (By Sir Walter Scott.) First edition. $750 and up. Also, spine of second volume defective, $650 (A, 1974). New York, 1951. Limited Editions Club. Illustrated. 2 vols., pictorial cloth. Boxed. $40-$50.

IVES, Joseph C. *Report Upon the Colorado River of the West.* 3 folding maps, 31 plates. Cloth. Washington, 1861. First edition, Senate issue. $200-$250.

IVINS, Virginia W. *Pen Pictures of Early Western Days.* Plates. Cloth. (Keokuk, Iowa), 1905. First edition. $50. Second edition: (Keokuk), 1908. $35.

# J

JACKSON, A. P., and Cole, E. C. *Oklahoma! Politically and Topographically Described.* Map (not in all copies). Kansas City, (1885). First edition. $75-$100.

JACKSON, A. W. *Barbariana: or Scenery, Climate, Soils and Social Conditions of Santa Barbara City and County.* 48 pp., printed wrappers. San Francisco. 1888. $100-$125.

JACKSON, Andrew. *Message from the President of the United States, in Compliance with a Resolution of the Senate Concerning the Fur Trade and Inland Trade to Mexico.* 86 pp., unbound. (Washington, 1832.) Senate Doc. 90. First edition. $250-$350.

JACKSON, Andrew. *To the Citizens of Pennsylvania.* 12 pp., wrappers. (Washington, 1834.) $50-$75.

JACKSON, Charles James. *An Illustrated History of English Plate, Ecclesiastical and Secular.* Colored frontispiece, 76 photogravure plates, 1,500 other illustrations. 2 vols., half morocco. London, 1911. First edition. $250-$350.

JACKSON, Mrs. F. Nevill. *Toys of Other Days.* 9 color plates, 273 plain illustrations. Full vellum. London, 1908. One of 50. $200-$250. Aother issue: Morocco. One of 150. $150-$200. Ordinary issue: Cloth. $75-$100.

JACKSON, George. *Sixty Years in Texas.* Plates. Cloth. (Dallas, 1908.) First edition, first issue, with 322 pages. $100-$150.

JACKSON, Helen Hunt. See H. H. Also see *Mercy Philbrick's Choice.*

JACKSON, Helen Hunt. *The Procession of Flowers in Colorado.* Illustrated. Cloth. Boston, 1886. First edition. One of 100. $150-$200.

JACKSON, Helen Hunt. *Ramona.* Decorated cloth. Boston, 1884. First edition. $150-$200. Also, front cover stained, $90 (A, 1973). Los Angeles, 1959. Limited Editions Club. Introduction by J. Frank Dobie. Cloth. Boxed. $125-$175.

JACKSON, Holbrook. *The Anatomy of Bibliomania.* 2 vols., cloth. London, 1930. Soncino Press. First edition. One of 1,000. $100-$150. Another issue: Morocco. One of 48 signed. $200-$250. New York, 1931. 2 vols., cloth. First American edition. $50-$60. New York, 1950. Cloth. In dust jacket. $20.

JACKSON, Holbrook. *The Fear of Books.* Full black morocco. London, 1932. First edition. One of 40 (of an edition of 2,048), signed. $200-$250. Trade edition: Buckram (2,008 copies). $35-$50.

JACKSON, Shirley. *The Lottery.* Cloth. New York, 1949. First edition. In dust jacket. $35-$50.

JACKSON, Shirley. *The Road Through the Wall.* Cloth. New York, 1948. First edition. In dust jacket. $75-$100. Author's first book.

JACOB, J. G. *The Life and Times of Patrick Gass.* 4 plates. Cloth. Wellsburg, Va., 1859. First edition. $200-$250.

JACOBS, W. W. *Many Cargoes.* Cloth. London, 1896. First edition. $35-$50. Author's first book.

JAEGER, Benedict, and Preston, H. C. *The Life of North American Insects.* Cloth. Providence, 1854. First edition. $50-$75.

JAMES, Edwin (editor). *Account of an Expedition from Pittsburg to the Rocky Mountains.* 2 maps, 8 plates. 3 vols. (including atlas), boards and leather, paper labels. Philadelphia, 1822-23. First edition. $1,200-$1,500. Also, rebacked, $950 (A, 1975); in modern half leather, $550 (A, 1972). London, 1823. 3 vols., boards. First English edition. $300-$400.

JAMES, Edwin (editor). *A Narrative of the Captivity and Adventures of John Tanner.* Frontispiece portrait. Tan boards, purple cloth, paper label. New York, 1830. First edition. $400-$500.

JAMES, Frank. *The Only True History of the Life of Frank James. Written by Himself.* (Cover title.) Illustrated. 134 pp., wrappers. (Pine Bluff, Ark., 1926.) First edition. $75-$100. (Note: Ramon F. Adams calls this a "brazen" and "worthless" fake.)

JAMES, Fred. *The Klondike Goldfields and How to Get There.* Map. 68 pp., tan wrappers. London, 1897. First edition. $300-$350. Also, $180 (A, 1969).

JAMES, Henry. See Besant, Walter.

JAMES, Henry. *The Ambassadors.* Red cloth. London, 1903. First edition. $75-$125. New York, 1903. Gray-blue boards, with blue linen dust jacket. First American edition, first issue, with "Published November, 1903" on copyright page. $75-$125. New York, 1963. Limited Editions Club. Illustrated. Boards. Boxed. $50-$60.

JAMES, Henry. *The American.* Cloth. Boston, 1877. First edition, first binding, with Osgood imprint on spine. $125-$150.

JAMES, Henry. *The American Scene.* Maroon buckram. London, 1907. First edition. $50-$60. New York, 1907. Blue cloth. First American edition. $35.

JAMES, Henry. *The Aspern Papers: Louisa Pallant: The Modern Warning.* 2 vols., blue cloth. London, 1888. First edition. $100-$125.

JAMES, Henry. *The Awkward Age.* Brown cloth. New York, 1899. First edition, first issue, with sans-serif "p" in spine imprint. $75-$100. London, 1899. Light-blue cloth. First English edition (possibly simultaneous with the New York edition). $150-$175.

JAMES, Henry. *The Better Sort.* Rose-colored cloth. New York, 1903. First edition, with "Published, February, 1903" on copyright page. $50-$60. London, 1903. Red cloth. First English edition (simultaneous with the American first). $50-$60.

JAMES, Henry. *The Bostonians.* 3 vols., blue cloth. London, 1886. First edition. $250 and up. London, 1886. First one-volume edition. $75-$100.

JAMES, Henry. *A Bundle of Letters.* Stiff printed wrappers. Boston, (1880). First edition, Blanck's state A, with comma after "Jr." on front cover. $75-$100.

JAMES, Henry. *Confidence.* 2 vols., cloth. London, 1880. First edition. $75-$100. Boston, 1880. Brick-colored cloth (one volume). First American edition, first issue, with Houghton, Osgood imprint on spine. $150-$225.

JAMES, Henry. *Daisy Miller: A Study.* Printed tan or gray wrappers, or green cloth. New York, 1879. First edition. Wrappers: $100-$150. Cloth: $100-$125. New York, 1969. Limited Editions Club. Boxed. $40-$50.

JAMES, Henry. *Daisy Miller and An International Episode.* Vellum. New York, 1892. First edition. $35-$50. Trade edition: Cloth. $25.

JAMES, Henry. *The Diary of a Man of Fifty, and a Bundle of Letters.* Tan wrappers, or green cloth. New York, 1880. First edition. Wrappers: $75. Cloth: $35-$50.

JAMES, Henry. *Embarrassments.* Blue cloth. London, 1896. First published edition, first issue, with 4 irises on front of binding. $50-$75. New York, 1896. Maroon cloth. First American edition. $35-$50.

JAMES, Henry. *English Hours.* Illustrated by Joseph Pennell. Gray cloth. London, 1905. First edition. $50. Second binding, half buckram. $30. Boston, 1905. Cloth, or half morocco. First American edition. $25. Another issue: Boards and linen. One of 421 on large paper. $60-75.

JAMES, Henry. *Essays in London and Elsewhere.* Salmon-colored cloth. London, 1893. First edition. $50-$60. New York, 1893. Blue cloth. First American edition. $40-$50.

JAMES, Henry. *The Europeans: A Sketch.* 2 vols., blue cloth. London, 1878. First edition. $250-$300. Boston, 1879. Cloth (in one volume). First American edition. $75-$125.

JAMES, Henry. *The Golden Bowl.* 2 vols., tan cloth. New York, 1904. First edition, with "Published, November, 1904" on copyright page. $75-$100.

JAMES, Henry. *An International Episode.* Gray wrappers, or flexible green cloth. New York, 1879. First edition, first state, with "blue" for "beth" in the first line of page 45. Wrappers: $175-$250. Cloth: $100-$125.

JAMES, Henry. *Italian Hours.* Plates (some colored). Green buckram. London, 1909. First edition. In dust jacket. $100-$125. Boston, 1909. Terra-cotta cloth. First American edition, with "Published November 1909" on copyright page. In dust jacket. $50-$75.

JAMES, Henry. *The Ivory Tower.* Edited by Percy Lubbock. Portrait. Blue cloth. London, (1917). First edition. $60-$75. New York, 1917. Greenish-brown cloth. First American edition, with "Published October, 1917" on copyright page. In dust jacket. $40-$50.

JAMES, Henry. *The Letters of Henry James.* Edited by Percy Lubbock. 2 portrait frontispieces and facsimile. 2 vols., blue cloth. London, 1920. First edition. In dust jackets. $50-$60. New York, 1920. 2 vols., greenish-black cloth. First American edition. In dust jackets. $40-$50. Lacking jackets, $25-$30.

JAMES, Henry. *Letters of Henry James to Walter Berry.* Printed vellum wrappers. Paris, 1928. Black Sun Press. First edition. One of 16 on Japan vellum, each with an original letter. $400 and up. Another issue: One of 100 on Van Gelder paper. $200.

JAMES, Henry. *A Little Tour in France.* Cloth. Boston, 1885. First edition. $50-$60. Cambridge (Mass.), 1900. Illustrated by Joseph Pennell. Boards and cloth. One of 250 large paper copies. $75-$100. Trade edition: (With Boston imprint, not Cambridge.) Cloth. $25. London, 1900. Half vellum. One of 150 on vellum. $100-$125.

JAMES, Henry. *The Madonna of the Future and Other Tales.* 2 vols., blue cloth. London, 1879. First edition. $150-$200.

JAMES, Henry. *"A Most Unholy Trade."* Printed wrapper over flexible boards. (Cambridge, Mass.), 1923. Scarab Press. First edition. One of 100. $150-$200.

JAMES, Henry. *Notes of a Son and Brother.* Frontispiece, 5 plates. Greenish-brown cloth. New York, 1914. First edition. In dust jacket. $50-$75. London, 1914. Cloth. First English edition. In dust jacket. $40.

JAMES, Henry. *Notes and Reviews.* Half leather and cloth. Cambridge, Mass., 1921. First edition. One of 30 on vellum. $150-$175.

JAMES, Henry. *The Other House.* 2 vols., blue cloth. London, 1896. First English edition $100-$150. New York, 1896. Red cloth (one volume). First American edition (published simultaneously with the London edition?). $100.

JAMES, Henry. *The Outcry.* Cloth. London, (1911). First edition. In dust jacket. $100-$150. New York, 1911. Greenish-brown cloth. First American edition, with "Published September, 1911" on copyright page. In dust jacket. $50-$100.

JAMES, Henry. *A Passionate Pilgrim, and Other Tales.* Cloth. Boston, 1875. First edition, first binding, with "J.R. Osgood & Co." on spine. $250-$300. Author's first book.

JAMES, Henry. *The Portrait of a Lady.* 3 vols., blue or dark-green cloth. London, 1881. First edition. $500-$600. Boston, 1882. Cloth. First American edition $60-$75. New York, 1967. Limited Editions Club. Colored plates. Marbled boards and cloth. Boxed. $50-$60.

JAMES, Henry. *Portraits of Places*. Blue-green cloth. London, 1883. First edition, first binding, with "M" in Macmillan larger than other letters. $70-$80. Boston, 1884. Cloth. First American edition. $35-$50.

JAMES, Henry. *The Princess Casamassima*. 3 vols., blue cloth. London, 1886. First edition. $500-$600. Also, $375 (A, 1975). London [ sic ], 1886. Blue-green cloth (in one volume). First American edition. $75-$125. London, 1887. First British one-volume edition (same as the preceding but with 1887 title page). $75-$100.

JAMES, Henry. *Refugees in Chelsea*. Boards. London, 1920. First edition. Ashendene Press. (50 copies printed.) $500-$600.

JAMES, Henry. *The Reverberator*. 2 vols., cloth. London, 1888. First edition. $200-$250. London, 1888. First American edition (one volume). Blue cloth. $100. Second English edition (one volume), same date: $75.

JAMES, Henry. *Roderick Hudson*. Cloth. Boston, 1876. First edition, first binding, with Osgood imprint on spine. $100-$150. Later binding: Houghton Mifflin imprint on spine. $50-$75. Author's first novel.

JAMES, Henry. *The Sense of the Past*. Edited by Percy Lubbock. Portrait. Blue cloth. London, (1917). First edition. In dust jacket. $50-$60. New York, 1917. Greenish-brown cloth. First American edition, with "Published October, 1917" on copyright page. In dust jacket. $40-$50.

JAMES, Henry. *The Siege of London*. Cloth. Boston, 1883. First edition, with Osgood imprint on spine. $75-$100.

JAMES, Henry. *A Small Boy and Others*. Greenish-brown cloth. New York, 1913. First edition, first issue, with 11-line publisher's ad. In dust jacket. $50-$60. London, 1913. Blue cloth. First English edition (possibly simultaneous with New York edition). In dust jacket. $50.

JAMES, Henry. *The Soft Side*. Maroon buckram. New York, 1900. First edition. $50. London, 1900. Red cloth. First English edition (possibly simultaneous with the New York first). $50.

JAMES, Henry. *The Spoils of Poynton*. Blue cloth. London, 1897. First (?) edition. $125-$175. Boston, 1897. Cloth. First American edition. (Blanck thinks this may have been simultaneous with the English first.) $125-$175.

JAMES, Henry. *Stories Revived*. 3 vols., cloth. London, 1885. First edition, first binding, blue cloth. $150-$175.

JAMES, Henry. *Transatlantic Sketches*. Brown cloth. Boston, 1875. First edition, first binding, with Osgood imprint on spine. $125-$150.

JAMES, Henry. *The Turn of the Screw*. Illustrated. Half morocco. London, 1940. Hand and Flower Press. One of 200. $100-$150. New York, 1949. Limited Editions Club. Illustrated. Buckram. Boxed. $35-$40.

JAMES, Henry. *Views and Reviews*. Vellum, leather spine. Boston, 1908. First edition. One of 160. $100-$135. Trade edition: Olive cloth. $40-$50.

JAMES, Henry. *Washington Square*. Dark olive-green cloth. New York, 1881. First edition. $50-$60. New York, 1971. Limited Editions Club. Boxed. $30-$40.

JAMES, Henry. *Washington Square: The Pension Beaurepas: A Bundle of Letters*. 2 vols., cloth. London, 1881. First edition. $125-$175.

JAMES, Henry. *Watch and Ward*. Cloth. Boston, 1878. First edition, first printing, with blank leaf after page 219. $50-$75.

JAMES, Henry. *What Maisie Knew*. Blue cloth. London, 1898 (actually 1897). First edition. $75-$110. Chicago, 1894. Slate-colored cloth. First American edition. $50-$60.

JAMES, Henry. *The Wheel of Time*. Decorated gray-green cloth. New York, 1893. First edition. $40-$60.

JAMES, Henry. *William Wetmore Story and His Friends.* Frontispiece. 2 vols., green cloth. Edinburgh, 1903. First British edition. $50-$60. Boston, 1903. 2 vols., green cloth. First American edition (issued simultanously with the Edinburgh edition). $50-$60.

JAMES, Henry. *The Wings of the Dove.* 2 vols., red cloth. New York, 1902. First edition, with "Published, August, 1902" on copyright page. $60-$90. London, 1902. First English edition. $50-$60.

JAMES, Jesse, Jr. *Jesse James, My Father.* 4 portraits. White printed wrappers. Kansas City, Mo., 1899. (Ghostwritten by A. B. Macdonald?) First edition. $150-$200. Cleveland, (1906). Reprint edition. $20-$25.

JAMES, M. R. *Ghost Stories of An Antiquary.* Cloth. London, 1904. First edition. In dust jacket. $200-$250. Lacking jacket, $135-$175.

JAMES, Philip. *Children's Books of Yesterday.* Edited by G. Geoffrey Holme. Cloth. London, 1933. First edition. In dust jacket. $80-$100.

JAMES, Thomas. *Three Years Among the Indians and Mexicans.* 130 pp., plain wrappers. Waterloo, Ill., 1846. First edition. $6,000-$8,000. Also, waterstained and rebacked, $4,100 (A, 1963); rebound in boards, defective, $1,500 (A, 1968); new covers supplied, $2,600 (A, 1954). St. Louis, 1916. 12 plates. Half cloth. Second edition. One of 365. $85-$100.

JAMES, W. S. *Cow-boy Life in Texas.* 34 plates. Pictorial cloth. Chicago, (1893). First edition. $75-$125. Chicago, (1898). 27 plates. Cloth. $30-$40.

JAMES, Will. *All in the Day's Riding.* Cloth. New York, 1933. First edition. In dust jacket. $40-$50.

JAMES, Will. *Cowboys North and South.* Illustrated by the author. Buckram. New York, 1924. First edition. In dust jacket. $65-$75. Author's first book.

JAMES, Will. *Lone Cowboy: My Life Story.* Illustrated. Cloth, leather label. New York, 1930. First edition. One of 250 with an original drawing. $400-$750. Also, $400 (A, 1974); $150 (A, 1975). Trade edition: Green cloth. In dust jacket. $35-$50.

JAMES, Will. *Smoky the Cowhorse.* Illustrated by the author. Cloth. New York, 1926. First edition. In dust jacket. $50-$75.

JAMES, William. *The Principles of Psychology.* 2 vols., cloth. New York, 1890. First edition. $150-$200. London (1890). Cloth. First English edition. $75-$100.

JAMES, William F., and McMurry, George H. *History of San Jose, California.* Cloth. San Jose, 1933. First edition. $60-$80.

JAMESON, Anna Brownell. *The Beauties of the Court of King Charles II.* 21 hand-colored engraved portraits on India paper. Calf. London, 1833. $150-$250.

JANSON, Charles William. *The Stranger in America.* Engraved title page, plan of Philadelphia, 9 (sometimes 10) aquatint plates. Boards and calf. London, 1807. First edition. $600-$800. Also, $302 (A, 1969). Plates (10) hand-colored, $928 in a 1975 British catalogue. Philadelphia, 1807. Boards and calf. First American edition. $200-$300.

JANVIER, Thomas A. *The Aztec Treasure-House.* Illustrated by Frederic Remington. Decorated cloth, New York, 1890. First edition. $100-$150.

JARRELL, Randall. *Blood for a Stranger.* Cloth. New York, (1942). First edition. In dust jacket. $125-$150. Author's first book.

JARRELL, Randall. *Little Friend, Little Friend.* Cloth. New York, 1945. First edition. In dust jacket. $100-$110.

JARRELL, Randall. *Losses.* Cloth. New York, (1948). First edition. In dust jacket. $75-$100.

JARRELL, Randall. *The Seven-League Crutches.* Cloth. New York, (1951). First edition. In dust jacket. $50.

JEFFERIES, Richard. See *The Gamekeeper at Home.*

JEFFERIES, Richard. *Amaryllis at the Fair.* Cloth. London, 1887. First edition. $75-$100.

JEFFERIES, Richard. *Bevis: The Story of a Boy.* 3 vols., cloth. London, 1882. First edition. $200-$250.

JEFFERIES, Richard. *Greene Ferne Farm.* Green cloth. London, 1880. First edition. $150-$200.

JEFFRIES, Richard. *Jack Brass, Emperor of England.* 12 pp., tan wrappers. London, 1873. First edition. $350-$400.

JEFFERIES, Richard. *The Open Air.* Printed cloth. London, 1885. First edition. $75-$100.

JEFFERIES, Richard. *Restless Human Hearts.* 3 vols., cloth. London, 1875. First edition. $175-$225.

JEFFERS, Robinson. See Powell, Lawrence Clark; Sterling, George; *Continent's End.*

JEFFERS, Robinson. *Apology for Bad Dreams.* 16 pp., wrappers. Paris, 1930. First edition. One of 30 designed by Ward Ritchie. $200-$225.

JEFFERS, Robinson. *An Artist.* Frontispiece. Introduction by Benjamin De Casseres. 16 pp., wrappers. (Austin, 1928). First edition. One of 96 (actually 196). $150-$250. (Printed by John S. Mayfield; most copies destroyed or damaged by fire.)

JEFFERS, Robinson. *Be Angry at the Sun.* Marbled boards and cloth. New York, (1941). First edition. One of 100 signed. In glassine dust jacket. Boxed. $400-$450. Trade edition: Cloth. In dust jacket. $35-$50.

JEFFERS, Robinson. *The Beaks of Eagles.* Folio, 3 leaves, printed yellow wrappers. San Francisco, 1936. Grabhorn Press. First edition. $200-$250.

JEFFERS, Robinson. *Californians.* Blue cloth. New York, 1916. First edition. In dust jacket. $300-$400. Lacking jacket, $150-$200. "Advance Copy, For Review Only" (perforation so stamped on title page). In dust jacket. $350-$500. Author's first commercially published book. Cayucos, 1971. Boards and cloth. Introduction by William Everson. One of 50 (of an edition of 500) signed by Everson. $75.

JEFFERS, Robinson. *Cawdor and Other Poems.* Buckram. New York, 1928. First edition. One of 375 on large paper, signed. In dust jacket. Boxed. $200-$250. Lacking jacket, $150-$200. Trade edition: Boards and cloth. In dust jacket. $50-$75. London, 1929. Hogarth Press. Boards. First English edition. $50-$60.

JEFFERS, Robinson. *Dear Judas and Other Poems.* Boards and cloth. New York, 1929. First edition (preceding the limited edition). In dust jacket. $60-$80. Also, in dust jacket. $40 (A, 1970). Limited edition, same date: Boards, vellum spine. One of 375 signed. In glassine dust jacket. Boxed. $125-$175. From the same issue: One of 25 lettered copies. $250-$275. London, 1930. Hogarth Press. Boards. First English edition. $50-$60.

JEFFERS, Robinson. *De Rerum Virtute.* Decorated boards, linen spine, leather label. (San Francisco, 1953.) Grabhorn Press. First edition. One of 30. In plain purple dust jacket. $650-$850.

JEFFERS, Robinson. *Descent to the Dead.* Boards and vellum. New York, (1931). First edition. One of 500 (actually 550) signed. Boxed. $150-$225. (No trade edition issued.)

JEFFERS, Robinson. *The Double Axe and Other Poems.* Blue cloth. New York, 1948. First edition. In dust jacket. $35-$50. Also, a few copies (?) with an inserted leaf before title page, signed by Jeffers. $265 in a 1978 catalogue.

JEFFERS, Robinson. *Flagons and Apples.* (By John Robinson Jeffers.) Cinnamon boards, linen spine, paper label. Los Angeles, 1912. First edition. (500 copies.) $600-$750. Author's first book.

JEFFERS, Robinson. *Give Your Heart to the Hawks.* Marbled boards and calf. New York,

1933. First edition. One of 200 signed. $175-$225. Trade edition: Brown cloth. In dust jacket. $40-$60.

JEFFERS, Robinson. *Hope Is Not for the Wise.* Folio, 4 pp., printed wrappers. (San Mateo), 1937. Quercus Press. First edition. One of 24. $600-$800.

JEFFERS, Robinson. *The House-Dog's Grave—Haig's Grave.* Morocco. (San Mateo, 1939.) Quercus Press. One of 30. $500-$700.

JEFFERS, Robinson. *Hungerfield.* Foreward by Frederick Mortimer Clapp. 19 pp., boards, linen spine, morocco label. (San Francisco), 1952. Grabhorn Press. First edition. One of 30. $600-$700. New York, (1954). Boards and cloth. First trade edition. In dust jacket. $40-$50.

JEFFERS, Robinson. *The Loving Shepherdess.* 9 etchings by Jean Kellogg. Boards. New York, 1956. First edition. One of 115. Boxed. $400-$450.

JEFFERS, Robinson. *Medea.* Boards and cloth. New York, (1946). First edition, first issue, with word "least" omitted on page 99. In dust jacket. $75-$100. Second issue, corrected. In dust jacket. $30-$40.

JEFFERS, Robinson. *Natural Music.* Folio, leaflet. San Mateo, 1947. Quercus Press. First edition. Presentation copies, inscribed by Jeffers. $500-$750.

JEFFERS, Robinson. *The Ocean's Tribute.* 4 pp., folio broadside. San Francisco, 1958. Grabhorn Press. First edition. $85-$100.

JEFFERS, Robinson. *A Poem.* Single sheet, French-folded. (San Mateo), 1937. Quercus Press. First edition. One of 10. $500-$600.

JEFFERS, Robinson. *Poems.* Portrait. Buckram, paper label. San Francisco, 1928. Book Club of California. First edition. One of 310. Boxed. $200-$225. Also, 10 "printer's copies" in half red morocco, signed. $500 and up.

JEFFERS, Robinson. *Poetry, Gongorism and a Thousand Years.* 12 pp., decorated boards. (Los Angeles), 1949. Ward Ritchie Press. First edition. One of 200. $200-$250.

JEFFERS, Robinson. *Return: An Unpublished Poem.* 4 pp., wrappers over flexible boards. San Francisco, 1934. Grabhorn Press. One of 250. $100-$150. Another issue: One of 3 on vellum. $800-$1,000.

JEFFERS, Robinson. *Roan Stallion, Tamar, and Other Poems.* Purple boards, black cloth spine. New York, 1925. First edition. In dust jacket. $75-$100. Another (later) issue, same date: Marbled boards, Author's Presentation Edition. One of 12. $300. Also, $75 (A, 1966). New York, 1926. Second edition (or printing). $35-$45. London, 1928. Hogarth Press. Boards. First English edition. $50-$60. New York, 1935. First Modern Library Edition. Flexible cloth. In dust jacket. $25. (Note: Contains a new introduction by Jeffers.)

JEFFERS, Robinson. *Rock and Hawk.* (Signed or inscribed as a Christmas token.) New Haven, 1934. First edition. One of 20. $300-$400.

JEFFERS, Robinson. *Solstice and Other Poems.* Patterned boards and buckram. New York, 1935. Grabhorn printing. One of 320, signed. In gray dust jacket. $200-$250. Trade edition: New York, (1935). Green cloth. In dust jacket. $35-$50.

JEFFERS, Robinson. *Stars.* 8 pp., black boards, white paper label. (Pasadena), 1930. Flame Press. One of 72, with errata leaf. (All except 6 copies were destroyed because of a typographical error.) $1,500-$2,000. Also, $1,000 (A, 1977); $1,500 (A, 1973). Second edition, same date. Printed blue wrappers. One of 110. $200-$250, possibly more.

JEFFERS, Robinson. *Such Counsels You Gave to Me.* Illustrated by Fritz Eichenberg. Patterned boards and morocco. New York, (1937). Spiral Press. First edition. One of 300 signed. In dust jacket. Boxed. $150-$200. Trade edition: Cloth. In dust jacket. $40-$60.

JEFFERS, Robinson. *Tamar and Other Poems.* Cloth. New York, (1924). First edition. (500 copies.) In plain gray dust jacket. $400-$450.

JEFFERS, Robinson. *Themes in My Poems*. Woodcuts by Mallette Dean. 46 pp., decorated boards, cloth spine, label. San Francisco, 1956. Book Club of California. First edition. One of 350. In plain brown dust jacket. $150-$175.

JEFFERS, Robinson. *Thurso's Landing and Other Poems*. Buckram. New York, (1932). First edition. One of 200 signed. In cellophane dust jacket. Boxed. $250-$300. Also, one of 15 out of series copies, $150 (A, 1974). Trade edition: Boards and cloth. In dust jacket. $50-$75.

JEFFERS, Robinson. *Two Consolations*. 6 leaves, rose or gray boards. (San Mateo), 1940. Quercus Press. First edition. One of 250. $150-$200.

JEFFERS, Robinson. *The Women at Point Sur*. Boards and cloth. New York, 1927. First edition (preceding the limited edition). In dust jacket. $50-$75. Limited edition: New York, (1927). Silver on black boards and vellum. One of 265 signed. In glassine dust jacket. Boxed. $150-$200. Also, $110 (A, 1975); $100 (A, 1974).

JEFFERS, Una. *Visits to Ireland: Travel Diaries of Una Jeffers*. Foreword by Robinson Jeffers. Boards and cloth. Los Angeles, 1954. Ward Ritchie Press. First edition. One of 300. Boxed. $50-$75.

JEFFERSON, H. E. *Oklahoma: The Beautiful Land*. 202 pp., printed wrappers. Chicago, 1889. First edition. $500 and up.

JEFFERSON, Thomas. *An Appendix to the Notes on Virginia Relative to the Murder of Logan's Family*. 58 pp., sewed. Philadelphia, 1800. First edition. $150-$200.

JEFFERSON, Thomas. *A Manual of Parliamentary Practice for the Use of the Senate of the United States*. Calf. Washington, 1801. First edition. $200-$300.

JEFFERSON, Thomas. *Message from the President of the United States, Communicating Discoveries Made in Exploring the Missouri, Red River, and Washita by Capts. Lewis and Clark, Dr. Sibley, and Mr. Dunbar, etc.* 2 folding tables, map (in some copies). 171 pp., unbound. Washington, 1806. "Printed by Order of the Senate." First edition. With map. $5,000-$6,000. Without map, up to $3,000, possibly more.

JEFFERSON, Thomas. *Notes on the State of Virginia*. Leather. Baltimore, 1800. $100-$150. Boston, 1801. Folding map. Leather. $150-$300. (Note: There are numerous 19th Century editions; ones with the map are more valuable. For the first, anonymous publication, Paris, 1782—actually 1785—and other 18th-century editions, see the book auction records.)

JEFFREY, J. K. See *The Territory of Wyoming*.

JENKINS, John H. *Cracker Barrel Chronicles: A Bibliography of Texas Town and Country Histories*. Full tan leather. Austin, 1965. First edition. One of 15 signed. Boxed. $150.

JENKS, Ira C. *Trial of David F. Mayberry, for the Murder of Andrew Alger*. (Cover title.) 48 pp., wrappers. Janesville, Wis., 1855. First edition. $250-$300.

JENKS, J. W. P. *(With the Compliments of J. W. P. Jenks:) Hunting in Florida in 1874.* (Cover title; caption title for text is *Hunting in Florida*.) Folding map of Everglades. 70 pp., printed buff wrappers. (Providence, R.I., 1884?). First (?) edition. $300-$400. Also, $175 (A, 1969).

JENNINGS, A. *Through the Shadows with O. Henry*. Illustrated. Pictorial cloth. New York, (1921). First edition. In dust jacket. $50-$75.

JENNINGS, N. A. *A Texas Ranger*. Tan pictorial cloth. New York, 1899. First edition. $200-$250.

JEREMIAH. See *The Lamentations of Jeremiah*.

JEROME, Chauncey. *History of the American Clock Business for the Past 60 Years*. Printed wrappers. New Haven, 1860. First edition. $150-$200.

JEROME, Jerome K. *Three Men in a Boat*. Illustrated. Light-blue cloth. Bristol, England,

1889. First edition, first issue, with title page reading as follows: "Bristol/J. W. Arrowsmith, Quay Street/London/Simpkin, Marshall & Co., 4 Stationer's Hall Court/ (rule) 1889/All rights reserved/." $75-$100.

JERROLD, Douglas. *A Man Made of Money.* 12 plates by John Leech. 6 parts, pictorial wrappers, and cloth. London, 1849. First edition. In parts: $200 and up. Cloth: $100-$150.

JERROLD, Douglas. *Mrs. Caudle's Curtain Lectures.* Cloth. London, 1866. First edition. $75-$100.

*JESSE James: The Life and Daring Adventures of This Bold Highwayman and Bank Robber.* Pictorial wrappers. Philadelphia, (about 1882). (Anonymous.) First edition. $75-$125.

JEWETT, Sarah Orne. *Betty Leicester.* Decorated cloth. Boston, 1890. First edition, early state, with this book last in ad opposite title page. $50-$75.

JEWETT, Sarah Orne. *The Country of the Pointed Firs.* Cloth. Boston, 1896. First edition. $100-$125.

JEWETT, Sarah Orne. *Deephaven.* Cloth. Boston, 1877. First edition, first issue, with the reading "was" in line 16, page 65. (Later reading, "so.") $50-$60. Author's first book.

JEWITT, Charles. *Temperance Toy.* Hand-colored engravings. 16 pp., printed wrappers. Boston, 1840. $50-$75.

JEWITT, John R. *Journal, Kept at Nootka Sound.* 48 pp., stitched. Boston, 1807. First edition. $3,000-$3,500. Also, $2,200 (A, 1969). Boston, 1931. Frontispiece. Half cloth. $35-$50.

JEWITT, John R. *Narrative of the Sufferings and Adventures of John R. Jewitt.* Edited by Richard Alsop. 2 plates. Calf. Middletown, 1815. First edition, first issue, with Loomis & Richards imprint. $500-$700. Second issue, Seth Richards imprint. $400-$500. New York, (about 1815). $150-$250.

*JOAQUIN (The Claude Duval of California); or The Marauder of the Mines.* 160 pp., pictorial wrappers. New York, (1865—actually later, in the 1870's). (By Henry L. Williams.) First edition. $175-$250. New York, 1888. Decorated cloth. Second edition. $100-$125.

JOCKNICK, Sidney. *Early Days on the Western Slope of Colorado.* 25 plates. Cloth. Denver, 1913. First edition. $150-$200.

JOHL, Janet. *More About Dolls.* Illustrated. Cloth. New York, 1946. First edition. In dust jacket. $100-$110.

JOHL, Janet. *Still More About Dolls.* Illustrated. Cloth. New York, 1950. First edition. In dust jacket. $75-$125.

JOHL, Janet. *Your Dolls and Mine.* Illustrated. Cloth. New York, 1952. First edition. In dust jacket. $75-$100.

*JOHN Bull in America; or, The New Munchausen.* Boards, or cloth. New York, 1825. (By James Kirke Paulding.) First edition. $100-$150.

*JOHN Halifax, Gentleman.* 3 vols., brown cloth. London, 1856. (By Dinah M. Craik.) First edition, first issue, with 3 pages of ads at end of Vol. 1, one page at end of Vol. 2, and 2 pages at end of Vol. 3. $600-$800.

*JOHN Leech on My Shelves.* Illustrated. Boards and buckram. (Munich), 1930. (By William B. Osgood Field.) Bremer Press. One of 155. Boxed. $200-$250.

*JOHN Marr and Other Sailors.* 103 pp., printed yellow wrappers. New York, 1888. (By Herman Melville.) First edition. One of 25. $1,000 and up. Also, $850 (A, 1948)—"Believed to be Melville's copy, with some corrections in his hand." Princeton, 1922. Half cloth. One of 175. $60-$100.

JOHN, W. D. *Swansea Porcelain.* 20 color illustrations, others in black and white. Buckram. London, 1958. First edition. $100-$125.

*JOHN Woodvil: A Tragedy.* Plain pink or blue boards. London, 1802. (By Charles Lamb.) First edition. $500-$650.

JOHNSON, Benj. F. (of Boone). *"The Old Swimmin'-Hole" and 'Leven More Poems.* Wrappers. Indianapolis, 1883. (By James Whitcomb Riley.) First edition. $150-$250. Also, $95 (A, 1976); $150 (A, 1973). (Note: There exists a 1909 facsimile, which lacks the "W" in "William" on page 41. Value: about $10.)

JOHNSON, Crisfield (compiler). *The History of Cuyahoga County, Ohio.* Double column pages. Half morocco. Cleveland, 1879. First edition. $85-$125.

JOHNSON, Don Carlos. *A Brief History of Springville, Utah.* Wrappers. Springville, 1900. First edition, with errata slip. $50-$75.

JOHNSON, Edwin F. *Railroad to the Pacific, Northern Route.* 3 maps, 8 plates. Boards and calf. New York, 1854. Second (actually first) edition. $200-$300.

JOHNSON, Frank M. *Forest, Lake and River.* Portrait, colored frontispiece. 2 vols., bound in suede. Boston, 1902. One of 350. $200-$250.

JOHNSON, Harrison. *Johnson's History of Nebraska.* Frontispiece, other illustrations; folding map in color. Blue cloth. Omaha, 1880. First edition. $125-$150.

JOHNSON, Henry L. *Gutenberg and the Book of Books.* Illustrated. Folio, buckram. New York, 1932. One of 750. In slipcase. $85-$125.

JOHNSON, James Weldon. *Along This Way.* Cloth. New York, 1933. First edition. In dust jacket. $50-$60.

JOHNSON, James Weldon. *Fifty Years and Other Poems.* Half cloth. Boston, (1917). First edition. One of 110 on Japan vellum, signed. $150-$175.

JOHNSON, James Weldon. *God's Trombones.* Illustrated. Cloth. New York, 1922. First edition. In dust jacket. $60-$80.

JOHNSON, James Weldon. *Saint Peter Relates an Incident of the Resurrection Day.* Folio, black boards, gilt. New York, 1930. One of 200 signed. Boxed. $100-$150.

JOHNSON, James Weldon (editor). *The Second Book of Negro Spirituals.* Cloth. New York, 1926. First edition. $50-$75.

JOHNSON, Lionel. *The Art of Thomas Hardy.* Portrait. Boards. London, 1894. First edition. One of 150. $75-$100. Ordinary issue: Cloth. $30-$50.

JOHNSON, Lionel. *Poems.* Boards. London, 1895. First edition. One of 750. $75-$100. Another issue: One of 25, signed. $175-$225.

JOHNSON, Lionel. *Twenty One Poems.* Selected by William Butler Yeats. Boards and linen. Dundrum, Ireland, 1904. Dun Emer Press. One of 220. $75-$100.

JOHNSON, Overton, and Winter, William H. *Route Across the Rocky Mountains, etc.* Cloth-backed boards. Lafayette, Ind., 1846. First edition. $1,500-$2,000, possibly more. Also, $650 (A, 1971); $1,000 and $700 (A, 1968).

JOHNSON, Owen. *The Tennessee Shad.* 8 plates by F. R. Gruger. Pictorial cloth. New York, 1911. First edition. In dust jacket. $175-$250. Lacking jacket, $75-$100.

JOHNSON, Owen. *The Varmint.* Cloth. New York, 1910. First edition. $75-$100. Boston, 1930. Illustrated. Morocco. Limited edition. $50-$60.

JOHNSON, Rossiter. *Phaeton Rogers: A Novel of Boy Life.* Illustrated. Decorated cloth. New York, 1881. First edition. $150-$200.

JOHNSON, Rossiter (editor). *A History of the World's Columbian Expedition.* 4 vols., cloth. New York, 1897-98. First edition. $100-$150.

JOHNSON, Samuel. *A Diary of a Journey into North Wales.* Edited by R. Duppa. Plates. Boards. London, 1816. First edition. $150-$200.

JOHNSON, Samuel. *A Journey to the Western Islands of Scotland.* Half calf, marbled boards. Baltimore, 1810. First American edition. $100-$150.

JOHNSON, Sid S. *Some Biographies of Old Settlers.* (Vol. 1—all published.) Cloth. Tyler, Tex., 1900. First edition. $150-$250.

JOHNSON, Sidney S. *Texans Who Wore the Gray.* Illustrated. Cloth. Tyler, (about 1907). First edition. $100-$200.

JOHNSON, Mrs. Susannah. *A Narrative of the Captivity of Mrs. Johnson.* Boards and sheep. Windsor, Vt., 1807. Second edition. $250-$300.

JOHNSON, Theodore T. *Sights in the Gold Region, and Scenes by the Way.* Cloth. New York, 1849. First edition. $200-$250. New York, 1850. Folding map, 7 plates (2 colored). Cloth. Second edition. $150-$200.

JOHNSTON, Carrier Polk, and McGlumphy, W. H. S. *History of Clinton and Caldwell Counties, Missouri.* Half leather. Topeka, 1923. $75-$125.

JOHNSTON, Charles. *A Narrative of the Incidents Attending the Capture, Detention, and Ransom of, etc.* Boards. New York, 1827. First edition. $200-$225. Also, $125 (A, 1975).

JOHNSTON, George. *The History of Cecil County, Maryland.* Folding map. Cloth. Elkton, Md., 1881. First edition. $100-$125.

JOHNSTON, George. *The Poetry and Poets of Cecil County, Maryland.* Cloth. Elkton, 1887. First edition. $50.

JOHNSTON, Lieut. Col. J. E. and others. *Reports of the Secretary of War, with Reconnaissances of Routes from San Antonio to El Paso, etc.* 2 folding maps, 72 plates. Cloth. Washington, 1850. First edition. $150-$300.

JOHNSTON, Mary. *To Have and to Hold.* Illustrated by Howard Pyle and others. Red buckram, paper label. Boston, 1900. First edition. One of 250. $100-$125. Trade edition: Cloth. $25-$30.

JOHNSTON, William G. *Experiences of a Forty-niner.* Portrait, 13 plates. Cloth. Pittsburgh, 1892. First edition. (With later, separately issued, folding map and an extra portrait.) $450-$500.

JOHONNOT, Jackson. *The Remarkable Adventures of Jackson Johonnot.* 24 pp., stitched. Greenfield, Mass., 1816. First edition. $125-$150.

JOINVILLE, John, Lord of. *The History of Saint Louis, King Louis of France.* Illustrated. Dark maroon morocco. Newtown, Wales, 1937. Gregynog Press. One of 200. In slipcase. $800-$1,200.

JOLAS, Eugene. *Secession in Astropolis.* Wrappers. Paris, 1929. Black Sun Press. One of 100. In slipcase. $80-$125.

JOLAS, Maria (editor). *A James Joyce Yearbook.* Wrappers. Paris, 1949. Transition Press. First edition. In dust jacket. $50-$60. (Note: Contains a section, "Ad Writer," attributed to Joyce.)

*JONAH: Christmas, 1917.* Wrappers. Oxford, 1917. Holywell Press. (By Aldous Huxley.) First edition. One of 50. (Most were inscribed for presentation.) $1,000 and up. Also, an inscribed copy, $1,400 (A, 1977).

JONES, A. D. *Illinois and the West.* Folding map. Cloth. Boston, 1838. First edition. $100-$150.

JONES, Anson B. *Memoranda and Official Correspondence Relating to the Republic of Texas, Its History and Annexation.* Portrait. Cloth. New York, 1859. First edition. $150-$200. Chicago, (1966). Map, facsimile letter. Leather. One of 150. Boxed. $75.

JONES, Charles Colcock. *Religious Instruction of the Negroes in the United States*. Cloth. Savannah, 1842. First edition. $150-$200.

JONES, Charles, C., Jr. *Antiquities of the Southern Indians*. 30 plates. Cloth. New York, 1873. First edition. $75-$100.

JONES, Charles C., Jr. *Biographical Sketches of the Delegates from Georgia to the Continental Congress*. Cloth. Boston, 1891. $50.

JONES, Charles C., Jr. *The Dead Towns of Georgia*. Maps. Cloth. Savannah, 1878. First edition. $100.

JONES, Charles C., Jr. *Historical Sketch of the Chatham Artillery*. 3 maps. Half leather. Albany, 1867. First edition. $125.

JONES, Charles C., Jr. *The History of Georgia*. 19 maps and plates. 2 vols., cloth. Boston, 1883. First edition. $150-$250.

JONES, Charles C., Jr. *The History of Savannah, Georgia*. 21 portraits. Half leather. Syracuse, 1890. First edition. $150-$225.

JONES, Charles C., Jr. *The Siege of Savannah in December, 1864*. 184 pp., wrappers. Albany, 1874. First edition. $75-$125. Another issue: One of 10 on large paper. $250-$300.

JONES, Charles C., Jr. (editor). *The Siege of Savannah in 1779*. Map, index (not in all copies). Wrappers. Albany, 1874. First edition. One of 100. With the index: $100-$125. Without index: $75-$100.

JONES, Charles Jess. See Inman, Col. Henry.

JONES, D. W. *Forty Years Among the Indians*. Cloth. Salt Lake City, 1890. First edition, with portrait (not in all copies). $75.

JONES, David. *The Anathemata*. Cloth. London, (1952). First edition. In dust jacket. $75.

JONES, David. *In Parenthesis*. Illustrated by the author. Cloth. London, 1937. First edition. In dust jacket. $75-$100. Author's first book. London, (1961). Introduction by T. S. Eliot. Blue cloth. One of 70 signed by Jones and Eliot. In plastic dust jacket. $300-$400. Also, $325 (A, 1977)—listed incorrectly in catalogue of the Jonathan Goodwin sale as "first edition." Trade edition: In jacket. $25. New York, (1962). Tan cloth. First American edition. In dust jacket. $20.

JONES, David. *A Journal of Two Visits Made to Some Nations of Indians on the West Side of the River Ohio, in the Years 1772 and 1773*. Wrappers. New York, 1865. Second edition. One of 200. $100-$150. One of 50 on large paper. $200-$250. (Note: A first edition of David Jones' journal, Burlington, N.J., 1774, brought $5,250 at auction on May 4, 1966.)

JONES, David. *The Trilane's Visitation*. Cloth. (London, 1969). First edition. One of 150, signed. $75.

JONES, E. Alfred. *The Old Silver of American Churches*. 145 plates. Folio, buckram. Letchworth, England, 1913. One of 506. $300-$400.

JONES, E. Alfred. *Old Silver of Europe and America*. 96 plates. Cloth. London, 1928. First edition. $75-$100.

JONES, Edith Newbold. *Verses*. Wrappers. Newport, R.I., 1878. (By Edith Wharton.) First edition. $500-$750. Also, half morocco, original front cover bound in, $165 (A, 1947). Author's first book.

JONES, Gwyn. *The Green Island*. Woodcuts by John Petts. Green and gray morocco. London, 1946. Golden Cockerel Press. One of 100. $75-$100. Ordinary issue: One of 400. $40-$60.

JONES, James. *From Here to Eternity*. Black cloth. New York, 1951. First edition, with "A" on copyright page. Presentation edition, signed. In dust jacket. $200-$300. Trade edition: Cloth. In dust jacket. $75-$85. Author's first book.

JONES, James. *The Thin Red Line.* Cloth. New York, (1962). First edition, first issue, with "A" on copyright page. In dust jacket. $30-$40.

JONES, Jonathan H. *A Condensed History of the Apache and Comanche Indian Tribes.* Illustrated. Cloth. San Antonio, 1899. First edition. '$400-$600. (Note: Better known by its cover title, *Indianology*.)

JONES, J. Wesley (Written by John Ross Dix). *Amusing and Thrilling Adventures of a California Artist, while Daguerreotyping a Continent, etc.* Illustrated, including 4 woodcuts in text. 92 pp., pictorial wrappers. Boston, 1854. (By George Spencer Phillips.) First edition. $2,500-$3,000. (Note: Five years ago this was an inexpensive book, but it has risen sharply in value through its rediscovery as an early item in the history of photography.)

JONES, Justin. See Hazel, Harry.

JONES, Owen. *The Grammar of Ornament.* 100 colored lithographs, engraved title page (illuminated), woodcuts. Half morocco. London, 1856. First edition. $400-$500. London, (1865). 112 plates. Cloth. $100-$150. London, 1868. 112 plates. Cloth. $150-$200. London, 1910. Cloth. $200-$250.

JONES, Adj. Gen. R. *General Orders, No. 16, Reporting General Court Martial Convened at Fort Kearney, Oregon Route, for Offense Committed There.* 11 pp., sewed. Washington, 1851. $100-$150.

JONES, Samuel. *Pittsburgh in the Year Eighteen-Hundred and Twenty-six.* Frontispiece. Boards. Pittsburgh, 1826. First edition. $1,000 and up.

JONES, T. Gwynn. *Detholiad o' Ganiadau: Collected Poems of T. Gwynn Jones.* Wood engravings by R. A. Maynard. Buckram. Newtown, Wales, 1926. Gregynog Press. One of 474. $75-$100. Another issue: Blue morocco. One of 26 specially bound. $400-$500, possibly more.

JONES, Thomas A. *J.Wilkes Booth.* Illustrated. Cloth. Chicago, 1893. First edition. $50-$75.

JONES, William Carey. *Land Titles in California.* 55 pp., wrappers. San Francisco, 1852. First edition. $500-$600. Also, rebound in morocco, $275 (A, 1968).

JONES, William Carey. *Letters in Review of Attorney General Black's Report to the President of the U. S., on the Land Titles of California.* 31 pp., wrappers. San Francisco, 1860. $125-$175.

JONES, William Carey. *The "Pueblo Question" Solved.* 36 pp., sewed. San Francisco, 1860. First edition. $150-$250.

JONES, William Carey. *Report on the Subject of Land Titles in California,* 60 pp., wrappers. Washington, 1850. First edition. $200-$300.

JONG, Erica. *Fruits and Vegetables, Poems.* Cloth. New York, (1971). First edition. In dust jacket. $35-$50. Author's first book.

JONSON, Ben. *A Croppe of Kisses: Selected Lyrics.* Edited by John Wallis. Folio, morocco and buckram. London, 1937. Golden Cockerel Press. One of 250. $100-$150. Another issue: One of 50 specially bound in morocco. $300-$350.

JONSON, Ben. *The Masque of Queenes.* Illustrated by Inigo Jones. Folio, red vellum. London, 1930. One of 350. Boxed. $75-$100.

JONSON, Ben. *Songs: A Selection.* Colored frontispiece. Boards. London, 1906. Eragny Press. One of 175. In dust jacket. $350-$450.

JONSON, Ben. *Volpone: or The Foxe.* Illustrated by Aubrey Beardsley. Decorated cloth. New York, 1898. One of 1,000. $150-$200. Another issue: Vellum. One of 100 on vellum. $350-$450. New York, 1952. Limited Editions Club. Illustrated. Cloth. Boxed. $80-$100.

JORDAN, Thomas, and Pryor, J. P. *The Campaigns of Lieut.-Gen. N. B. Forrest.* 6 maps, 6 plates. Cloth. New Orleans, 1868. First edition. $100-$125.

*JORROCK'S Jaunts and Jollities*. 12 illustrations by Phiz. Decorated cloth. London, 1838. (By Robert Smith Surtees.) First edition. $300-$400. Philadelphia, 1838. 2 vols., half cloth. First American edition. $100-$200. London, 1843. 15 color plates by Henry Alken. Green cloth. Second edition, first state, with 8 pages of ads and printer's imprint at end. $500-$600. Second edition, later state, with ads announcing a new edition of *The Life of John Mytton.* $400-$500. London, 1869. 16 colored Alken plates. Cloth. Third edition. $150-$250. (Many other 19th Century editions. See auction records.) New York, 1932. Limited Editions Club. Boxed. $40-$50.

*JOURNAL Historique de l'Éstablissement des Français à la Louisiane.* Three-quarters morocco. Nouvelle-Orléans, 1831. (By Bernard de la Harpe). First edition. $350-$400.

*JOURNAL of the Convention to Form a Constitution for the State of Wisconsin: Begun and Held at Madison on the 5th Day of October, 1846.* Boards and calf. Madison, 1847. First edition. $150-$200.

*JOURNAL of an Excursion Made by the Corps of Cadets. etc., Under Capt. Partridge.* Marbled wrappers. Concord, N. H., 1822. $75-$100.

*JOURNAL of the Expedition of Dragoons Under the Command of Col. Henry Dodge to the Rocky Mountains During the Summer of 1835.* 2 folding maps. Wrappers, or cloth. (Washington, 1836.) (By Lt. G. P. Kingsbury.) First edition. Wrappers: $250-$350. Cloth: $150-$175. (See also Nolie Mumey entry.)

*JOURNAL of the Hartford Union Mining and Trading Company.* 88 pp., wrappers. On board the Henry Lee, 1849. (By George G. Webster, or John Linville Hall, who printed it?) First edition. $3,000 and up. Second edition (with title revised to *Around the Horn in '49: Journal, etc.*): (Wethersfield, Conn., or Hartford, 1898.) Cloth. $150-$200. San Francisco, 1928. Book Club of California. Half cloth. One of 250 printed by the Grabhorns. $75-$100.

*JOURNAL of the Proceedings of a Convention of Physicians, of Ohio, Held in Columbus, Jan. 5, 1835.* Daniel Drake, Chairman. 30 pp., wrappers. Cincinnati, 1835. (Main report by Drake.) $150-$175.

*JOURNAL of the Senate of South Carolina, Being the Session of 1863.* 190 pp., unbound. Columbia, 1863. $40-$60.

*JOURNAL of Sentimental Travels in the Southern Provinces of France.* 18 colored plates by Thomas Rowlandson. Boards, morocco, or cloth (remainder). London, 1821. (By William Combe.) First edition. $350-$450.

*JOURNAL of a Tour Around Hawaii, the Largest of the Sandwich Islands.* 3 plates, folding map. Boards and cloth. Boston, 1825. (By William Ellis.) First edition. $250 and up.

*JOURNAL of a Tour from Boston to Savannah, etc. (A).* Cloth. Cambridge, Mass., 1849. (By Daniel Nason.) First edition. $75-$125.

JOUTEL, Henri. *A Journal of the Last Voyage Perform'd by Monsr. de la Sale, to the Gulph of Mexico.* Folding map in pocket. Boards. Chicago, 1896. Caxton Club. One of 206. Boxed. $150-$250. Also, $160 (A, 1975). Another issue: One of 3. $300-$400.

JOYCE, James. See Gorman, Herbert; Jolas, Maria; Skeffington, F. J. C., and Joyce, James A. Also see *Des Imagistes; The Dublin Book of Irish Verse; The Venture*

JOYCE, James. *Anna Livia Plurabelle.* Edited by Padraic Colum. Cloth. New York, 1928. First edition. One of 850 signed. $400-$500. Also, $300 (A, 1975). One of 50 on green paper (from the 850-copy edition). $700 (A, 1977). Chicago, (1935). With music by Hazel Felman. Folio, printed wrappers. One of 350. $50-$75.

JOYCE, James. *Chamber Music.* Cloth (in three or more variant bindings). London, (1907). First edition. $750-$1,000. Also, "exceptionally fine," $1,900 (A, 1977). Boston, (1918). Cloth. First (unauthorized) American edition. $100-$150. New York, 1918. Cloth. First American edition. In dust jacket. $200-$300. London, 1918. Wrappers. Second English edition. $100-$150. New York, 1923. Black boards. $35-$50. London, 1923. Cloth. $35.

JOYCE, James, *Collected Poems*. Frontispiece portrait. Decorated boards. New York, 1936. Black Sun Press. First edition. One of 750. In glassine dust jacket. $250-$350. Another issue: One of 50 on vellum, signed. In tissue dust jacket. Boxed. $750-$1,250. Another issue: One of 3 lettered and signed copies, $3,750 (A, 1977). New York, 1937. Cloth. First trade edition. In dust jacket. $50-$75.

JOYCE, James. *Dubliners*. Red cloth. London, 1914. First edition. In dust jacket. $1,000-$1,500. Also, $1,400 (A, 1977). New York, 1916. Cloth. First American edition (from the English sheets). In dust jacket. $200-$250. New York, 1917. First edition from American sheets. In dust jacket. $150-$200. London, 1922. Egoist Press. In dust jacket. $100-$125. Also, signed by Joyce in 1936, $264 (A, 1973).

JOYCE, James, *Epiphanies*. Boards and cloth. (Buffalo), 1956. First edition. One of 550. In plain white dust jacket. $100-$150.

JOYCE, James. *Exiles*. Green boards and cloth. London, 1918. First edition. $300-$400. Also, presentation copy, signed, $1,300 (A, 1977). New York, 1918. Boards and buckram. First American edition. In dust jacket. $200-$225. New York, 1951. Half cloth. One of 1,900. In dust jacket. $100-$125.

JOYCE, James. *Finnegans Wake*. Buckram. London, 1939. First edition. One of 425 on large paper, signed. Boxed. $1,200-$1,500. Also, $1,300 (A, 1978); $1,200 and $900 (A, 1975); $1,000 (A, 1970); London, (1939). Cloth. First trade edition. In dust jacket. $150-$300. New York, 1939. Black cloth. First American edition. In dust jacket. $100-$150. Paris, 1962. Wrappers. First French translation. One of 67 on vellum. $100-$125.

JOYCE, James. *Gas from a Burner*. Long folio broadside. Flushing (Trieste), 1912. Signed by Sylvia Beach. $5,500 (A, 1977). Later edition: Dublin, 1922. $728 (A, 1966).

JOYCE, James. *Haveth Childers Everywhere: Fragment from Work in Progress*. Stiff printed wrappers. Paris, 1930. First edition. One of 500 on Vidalon paper. In glassine dust jacket. Boxed. $400-$500. Also 75 "Writer's Copies." $500-$750. Another issue: One of 100 on Japan vellum, signed. Boxed. $750-$1,000. Another issue: One of 10 on vellum, signed. In glassine dust jacket. Boxed. $1,500-$2,000. Also, $2,200 (A, 1977). London, (1931). Yellow wrappers printed in red. First English edition. $250-$350.

JOYCE, James. *The Holy Office*. Broadside. (Pola, Austria-Hungary, 1904 or 1905?) First edition. $2,000 and up. Also, $2,100 (A, 1977). (Fewer than 100 printed. So far as can be established, the author's first separately published work.)

JOYCE, James. *Ibsen's New Drama*. Foolscap, boards, paper label. London, (1930). First edition. One of 40. $750-$1,000. Also, $1,100 (A, 1977).

JOYCE, James. *James Clarence Mangan*. Foolscap, boards, paper label. London, (1930). First edition. One of 40. $750-$1,000. Also, $1,000 (A, 1977).

JOYCE, James. *The Joyce Book*. Blue silk. London, (1933). First edition. One of 500 in printed envelope. $1,000-$1,250. Also, $1,100 (A, 1977).

JOYCE, James. *The Mime of Mick, Nick, and the Maggies*. Designs in color by Lucia Joyce. Stiff white wrappers. Boxed. The Hague, Netherlands, 1934. First edition. One of 1,029. Boxed. $250-$300. One of 29 copies from the edition signed by Joyce and his daughter. $3,000 and up. Also, $3,250 (A, 1977).

JOYCE, James. *Pomes Penyeach*. Boards. Paris, 1926. First edition, with errata slip. $100-$125. Another issue: One of 13 on handmade paper. $400-$500. Paris, 1932. Oblong folio sheets on Japan paper, illuminated by Lucia Joyce. Green silk folder. One of 25 signed. $2,500 and up. Also, $2,600 (A, 1977). Paris and London, 1932. First English edition. $150-$200. London, (1933). First edition printed in England. $150-$200.

JOYCE, James. *A Portrait of the Artist as a Young Man*. Blue cloth. New York, 1916. First edition. In dust jacket. $600-$800. Also, $800 (A, 1977). London, (1917). Green cloth. First English edition (from American sheets.) In dust jacket. $100-$125. London, 1918.

First English edition printed in England. In dust jacket. $100-$125. London, 1924. Revised edition. In dust jacket. $75-$100. New York, 1968. Limited Editions Club. Illustrated. Half leather. Boxed. $150-$200.

JOYCE, James. *Stephen Hero.* Cloth. London, 1944. First edition. In dust jacket. $100-$150. New York, (1944). Green boards and cloth. First American edition. In dust jacket. $40-$60.

JOYCE, James. *Storiella as She Is Syung.* Flexible orange vellum. (London, 1937.) Corvinus Press. One of 176. Boxed. $1,000-$1,250. Also, $1,200 (A, 1977). One of 25 (of the 176) signed by Joyce. Boxed. $2,000 and up. Also, $2,000 (A, 1977).

JOYCE, James. *Tales Told of Shem and Shaun: Three Fragments from Work in Progress.* Portrait by Brancusi. Wrappers. Paris, 1929. Black Sun Press. First edition. One of 500 on Van Gelder paper. In glassine dust jacket. Boxed. $250-$420. Another issue: One of 100 on vellum, signed (plus 50 not-for-sale copies). Boxed. $1,250-$1,500. Also, $1,000 and $900. (A, 1977). London, (1932). Boards. First English edition (retitled *Two Tales of Shem and Shaun*). In dust jacket. $75-$85.

JOYCE, James. *Two Essays.* See Skeffington.

JOYCE, James. *Ulysses.* Printed blue wrappers. Paris, 1922. First edition. One of 100 on Dutch handmade paper, signed. $10,000 and up. Also, $10,000 (A, 1977); $8,000 (A, 1975). Another issue: One of 150 on Verge d'Arches paper. $3,000-$4,500. Also, worn and torn, $2,600 (A, 1977); $1,300 (A, 1968). Another issue: One of 740 on handmade paper. $1,500 and up. Also, $1,800 (A, 1977); $1,300 (A, 1974). (Various later printings of the Paris edition appeared through the 1920's.) London, 1922. Egoist Press. Wrappers. First English edition (printed in France), with errata slip and 4-page leaflet of press notices. One of 2,000. $1,000 and up. Also, $850 (A, 1977); $864 (A, 1970). London, 1923. Full red morocco (with limitation notice of 500 in gold on covers). Second English edition (printed in France). One of "at least three" surviving confiscation by British customs agents. $4,000 (A, 1977)—Jonathan Goodwin's copy. Paris, 1927. Blue wrappers. First American edition, unauthorized Samuel Roth piracy. $300-$400. Paris, 1929. Wrappers. First French translation (as *Ulysse*). One of 10 on Van Gelder paper. $2,000 and up. Also, $1,600 (A, 1968). Another issue: One of 25 on Holland paper. $1,500. Another issue: One of 875 on Alfa paper. $250 and up. Hamburg, (1932). Odyssey Press. 2 vols., printed wrappers. First Odyssey Press edition. (One of 25 signed?) $1,750 and up. Also, $1,500 (A, 1968). Ordinary copies: $100-$300. (New York, 1934.) First authorized American edition. Cream-colored cloth. In dust jacket. $75-$100. Also, signed by Joyce, $130 (A, 1968). New York, 1935. Limited Editions Club. Illustrated by Henri Matisse. Pictorial buckram. One of 250 signed by Joyce and Matisse. $1,500-$2,500. Also, $1,900 (A, 1977). Another issue: One of 1,250 signed only by Matisse. $800-$1,000. Also, $900 (A, 1977); $950 (A, 1976). (Six signed proofs of the Matisse etchings for this book were issued in an edition of 150 in canvas portfolios. A set sold in October, 1977, in New York for $3,250.) London, 1936. Green buckram. First English edition to be printed in England. One of 900. In dust jacket. $400-$500. Another issue: Vellum. One of 100 signed. Boxed. $3,000 and up. Also, $2,250 (A, 1977).

JUDD, A. N. *Campaigning Against the Sioux.* Plate, other illustrations. 45 pp., pictorial wrappers. (Watsonville, Calif., 1906.) First edition. $700 and up. Rebound in cloth, covers bound in, $600. Watsonville, 1909. Wrappers. Second edition. $300-$400. Also, $250 (A, 1968).

JUDD, Cyril. *Outpost Mars.* Cloth. New York, (1952). (By C. M. Kornbluth and Judith Merrill.) First edition. In dust jacket. $40-$50.

JUDD, Silas. *A Sketch of the Life and Voyages of Capt. Alvah Judd Dewey.* Boards and cloth. Chittenango, N. Y., 1838. First edition. $350-$450.

*JUDGES and Criminals: Shadows of the Past.* 100 pp. San Francisco, 1858. (By Dr. Henry M. Gray?) First edition. $750-$1,000. (Note: Only 2 copies known, according to Wright Howes.)

*JUDITH.* 4 mounted color plates by W. Russell Flint, with an extra set of plates in folder. Vellum. London, 1928. First edition. One of 100 signed by Flint. Boxed. $200-$275. Another issue: 4 color plates. Boards. One of 875. Boxed. $35-$50.

*JUSTICE and Expediency; or Slavery Considered with a View to Its Rightful and Effectual Remedy, Abolition.* Stitched without covers. Haverhill, Mass. 1833. (By John Greenleaf Whittier.) First edition. $450-$500.

*JUVENILE Lyre.* Boards and leather. Boston, 1936. (By Lowell Mason and E. Ives, Jr.) $75-$100.

# K

*KA Euanelio a Mataio.* (Together with *Marako and Ioane.*) Gospels of Matthew, Mark and John in Hawaiian. 3 vols., sewed. Rochester, N.Y., 1828-29. $350-$400.

KABOTIE, Red. *Designs from the Ancient Mimbrenos, with Hopi Interpretation.* Illustrated, including color. Half cloth. San Francisco, 1949. Grabhorn Press. One of 250. $295.

KAIN, Saul. *The Daffodil Murderer.* Yellow (orange) wrappers printed in red. (London), 1913. (By Siegfried Sassoon.) First edition. $150-$200. Presentation copy, signed, $500; soiled copy, $295 (British catalogue, 1977).

KANE, Elisha Kent. *Arctic Explorations.* Plates, 2 folding maps. 2 vols., pictorial cloth. Philadelphia, 1856. First edition. $100-$125.

KANE, Elizabeth D. See *Twelve Mormon Homes Visited, etc.*

KANE, Paul. *Wanderings of an Artist Among the Indians of North America.* Folding map, 8 colored plates, woodcuts. Cloth. London, 1859. First edition. $750-$1,000.

KANE, Thomas Leiper. *The Mormons.* 84 pp., printed wrappers. Philadelphia, 1850. First edition. $250-$300. Second edition, same date. 92 pp., wrappers. $100.

KANE, Thomas Leiper. *The Private Papers of . . . A Friend of the Mormons.* Portrait. Boards and cloth. San Francisco, 1937. Grabhorn Press. $75-$85.

KANT, Immanuel. *Critick of Pure Reason.* Green cloth, paper label. London, 1838. First edition in English. $750 and up. Spine repaired, $500.

KANTOR, MacKinlay. *Andersonville.* Cloth. Cleveland, (1955). First edition. In dust jacket. $25. Limited, signed edition. Boxed. $50-$60.

KANTOR, MacKinlay. *Spirit Lake.* Cloth. Cleveland, (1961). First edition. In dust jacket. $25.

*KATHERINE Walton; or, The Rebel of Dorchester.* Cloth. Philadelphia, 1851. (By William Gilmore Simms.) First edition. $200-$250.

KAVANAGH, Patrick. *The Great Hunger.* Boards and linen. Dublin, 1942. Cuala Press. One of 250. In dust jacket. $50-$75.

KAYE-SMITH, Sheila. *Little England.* Cloth. London, (1918). First edition. In dust jacket. $35-$50.

KAYE-SMITH, Sheila. *The Tramping Methodist.* Cloth. London, 1908. First edition. In dust jacket. $100-$150. Author's first book.

KEATING, William H. (compiler). *Narrative of an Expedition to the Source of St. Peter's River, Lake Winnepeek, etc.* Folding map, 15 plates. 2 vols., boards. Philadelphia, 1824. First edition. $300-$350. London, 1825. Maps, plates, tables. 2 vols., boards. First English edition. $200-$250.

KEATS, John. *Endymion: A Poetic Romance.* Drab buff boards, printed paper label on spine. London, 1818. First edition, first issue, with one line of errata (not 5) and 2 (not 5) ad leaves at end. $2,500-$3,500. Also, "worn, hinges split," $2,000 (A, 1974). Second issue, with 5-line errata. $2,000 and up. London, (1947). Golden Cockerel Press. Wood engravings. Buckram and vellum. One of 400. $300-$400. Another issue: Vellum. One of 100 specially bound. $500-$650.

KEATS, John. *John Keats' Unpublished Poem to His Sister Fanny, 1818.* Facsimile. Vellum-backed cloth. Boston, 1909. Bibliophile Society. First edition. One of 489 on vellum. $35.

KEATS, John. *Lamia, Isabella, The Eve of St. Agnes, and Other Poems.* Boards, paper label; or calf. London, 1820. First edition, with half title and 8 pages of ads at end. Boards: $7,500 and up. Also, rubbed, hinge cracked, $5,200 (A, 1974); worn, $2,500 (A, 1972). Waltham Saint Lawrence, England, 1928. Golden Cockerel Press. Woodcuts by Robert Gibbings. Sharkskin and cloth. One of 500. $250-$300. Another issue: One of 15 on vellum. In sharkskin binding by Sangorski & Sutcliffe. $1,500-$1,750.

KEATS, John. *Letters of John Keats to Fanny Brawne, Written in the Years 1819 and 1820.* Edited by Harry Buxton Forman. Etched frontispiece and facsimile. Cloth. London, 1878. First edition. One of 50. $150-$250.

KEATS, John. *Life, Letters, and Literary Remains of John Keats.* Edited by Richard Monckton Milnes. Engraved portrait and facsimile. 2 vols., cloth. London, 1848. First edition. $250-$300.

KEATS, John. *Odes, Sonnets and Lyrics.* Portrait frontispiece. Wrappers. Oxford, 1895. Daniel Press. One of 250. $200-$250.

KEATS, John. *Poems.* Woodcut vignette of Spenser on title page. Boards, paper label on spine. London, 1817. First edition. $10,000 and up. Also, some leaves loose, $4,320 (A, 1965); rebound in morocco, $2,000 (A, 1974); rebound in calf, lacking blank leaf, half title loose, $1,540 (A, 1965). (A copy in boards, inscribed by the poet, was sold at auction in New York in November, 1975, for $15,000.) London, 1894. Kelmscott Press. Vellum. One of 300. $750-$1,000. London, 1898. Vale Press. 2 vols., cloth. One of 210. $200-$250. London, 1914. Doves Press. (As *Selected Poems.*) Edited by T.J. Cobden-Sanderson. Vellum. One of 200. $400-$500. Some copies in morocco by the Doves Bindery. $1,000 and up. London, 1915. Florence Press. 2 vols., limp vellum with ties. One of 250. $100. New York, 1966. Limited Editions Club. Boards and leather. Boxed. $100.

KEATS, John. *Poetical Works.* Printed in double columns within ruled borders. Yellow wrappers. London, 1840. First complete collected edition. $500-$750.

KEATS, John. (*Selected Poems.*) See *Poems.*

KEATS, John. *Three Essays.* Stiff wrappers. London, (1889). Chiswick Press. First edition. One of 50. Boxed. $125-$150.

KEDDIE, James, Jr. *The Second Cab.* 95 pp., wrappers. Boston, 1947. First edition. One of 300. $75-$85.

*KEEP Cool.* 2 vols., boards. Baltimore, 1817. (By John Neal.) First edition. $200-$250. Author's first book.

KEES, Weldon. *Collected Poems.* Boards and leather. Iowa City, 1960. Stone Wall Press. First edition. One of 180 (200?). $100-$125.

KEES, Weldon. *The Last Man.* Boards and cloth. San Francisco, 1943. First edition. One of 300. (Published without dust jacket.) $60-$80.

KEET, Alfred Ernest. *Stephen Crane: In Memoriam.* Light orange wrappers. New York, no date. First edition. One of 50. $40-$50.

KEITH, Elmer. *Six Guns by Keith.* Illustrated. Full padded calf. Harrisburg, (1955). First edition. One of 100 signed. Boxed. $100-$125.

KEITH, G.M. *A Voyage to South America and the Cape of Good Hope.* Boards. London, 1819. First edition, first issue, printed by Phillips. $250-$300. London, 1819. Revised edition, printed by Vogel. With list of subscribers. $250-$300.

KELEHER, William A. *The Fabulous Frontier.* 11 plates. Cloth. Santa Fe, (1945). First edition. One of 500. In dust jacket. $100-$125.

KELEHER, William A. *The Maxwell Land Grant*. Illustrated. Pictorial cloth. Santa Fe, (1942). First edition. In dust jacket. $100-$110.

KELLER, David H. *The Devil and the Doctor*. Cloth. New York, (1940). First edition. In dust jacket. $50-$60.

KELLER, George. *A Trip Across the Plains*. 58 pp., printed wrappers. (Masillon, Ohio, 1851.) First edition. $4,500. Also, $2,500 (A, 1968).

KELLEY, Edith Summers. *Weeds*. Cloth. New York, (1923). First edition. In dust jacket. $75-$100. Author's first book.

KELLEY, Hall J. *General Circular to All Persons of Good Character Who Wish to Emigrate to the Oregon Territory*. 28 pp., printed wrappers. Charlestown, Mass., 1831. First edition. $600. Also, $230 (A, 1972); $325 (A, 1969).

KELLEY, Hall J. *A Geographical Sketch of That Part of North America Called Oregon*. Folding map. 80 pp., printed wrappers. Boston, 1830. First edition. $1,250 and up. Also, $700 (A, 1969).

KELLEY, Hall J. *History of Colonization of the Oregon Territory*. 12 pp., sewed. Worcester, Mass., 1850. First edition. $1,000 and up. Also, leaves pinned together with a contemporary straight pin, $550 (A, 1969).

KELLEY, Hall J. *A History of the Settlement of Oregon and the Interior of Upper California*. 128 pp., printed wrappers. Springfield, Mass., 1868. First edition. $5,000 and up. Another edition (date and place unknown) in facsimile: $125.

KELLEY, Hall J. *A Narrative of Events and Difficulties in the Colonization of Oregon and the Settlement of California*. 92 pp., printed wrappers. Boston, 1852. First edition. $2,000.

KELLEY, Joseph (Bunco). *Thirteen Years in the Oregon Penitentiary*. Illustrated. 142 pp., stiff wrappers. Portland, 1908. First edition. $50-$75.

KELLEY, William Melvin. *A Different Drummer*. Cloth. Garden City, 1962. First edition. In dust jacket. $50-$75. Author's first book.

KELLOGG, H.S. *Life of Mrs. Fmily J. Harwood*. Illustrated. Decorated cloth. Albuquerque, 1903. First edition. $125. (Note: Yes, "Fmily" is what it says.)

KELLY, Charles. *Old Greenwood: The Story of Cable Greenwood, Trapper, Pathfinder and Early Pioneer of the West*. Illustrated. Cloth. Salt Lake City, 1936. First edition. One of 350. In dust jacket. $75-$85.

KELLY, Charles. *The Outlaw Trail: A History of Butch Cassidy and His Wild Bunch*. Illustrated. Pictorial cloth (leatherette). Salt Lake City, 1938. First edition. $75-$100. New York, 1959. Pictorial cloth. In dust jacket. $25.

KELLY, Charles. *Salt Desert Trails*. Illustrated. Cloth (leatherette). Salt Lake City, 1930. First edition. $50-$75.

KELLY, Charles (editor). See Lee, John D.

KELLY, Charles, and Birney, Hoffman, *Holy Murder*. Illustrated. Cloth. New York, (1934). First edition. In dust jacket. $35-$50.

KELLY, Charles, and Howe, Maurice L. *Miles Goodyear, First Citizen of Utah*. Illustrated. Cloth. Salt Lake City, 1937. First edition. One of 350. In dust jacket. $75-$85.

KELLY, George Fox. *Land Frauds of California*. 36 pp., wrappers. (Santa Clara?), 1864. First edition. $500 and up. Also, defective, $350 (A, 1968).

KELLY, Jonathan F. *The Humors of Falconbridge*. Cloth. Philadelphia, 1856. First edition. $35-$50.

KELLY, L.V. *The Range Men: The Story of the Ranchers and Indians of Alberta*. Illustrated. Pictorial cloth. Toronto, 1913. First edition. $300-$350.

KELLY, Robert. *Armed Descent*. Wrappers. (New York, 1961.) Hawk's Well Press. First edition. $35-$50. Author's first book.

KELLY, Robert. *Her Body Against Time*. Cloth, or wrappers. Mexico City, 1963. First edition. Cloth (about 50 copies). $35-$50. Wrappers: $10.

KELLY, Robert. *Sonnets*. Illustrated in color by the author. Boards, paper labels. Los Angeles, 1968. First edition. One of 65 signed, with an original drawing and/or a holograph poem. $35-$50. Another issue: One of 10 bound in leather, with the added material. Another issue: Wrappers. One of 245 signed. (No prices noted on these two items.)

KELLY, William. *An Excursion to California over the Prairie, Rocky Mountains, and Great Sierra Nevada*. 2 vols., cloth. London, 1851. First edition $150-$200.

*KEMPTON-Wace Letters (The)*. Green decorated cloth. New York, 1903. (By Jack London and Anna Strunsky.) First edition. $75-$100. Reprint edition, same date: Authors named on title page. $50-$60.

*KENDAL and Windermere Railway. Two Letters Reprinted from the Morning Post*. Sewed. London, (1844). (By William Wordsworth.) First edition, with Whittaker imprint. $300-$500. Kendal, England, (1845). 24 pp., single sheet folded. Revised edition, with Branthwaite imprint. $200-$225.

KENDALL, George Wilkins. *Narrative of the Texan Santa Fe Expedition*. 5 plates, folding map. 2 vols., cloth. New York, 1844. First edition. $200-$350. London, 1844. Map, 5 plates. 2 vols., cloth. First English edition. $100-$150. New York, 1856. 2 vols., cloth. Seventh edition, with two extra chapters and part of Falconer's diary. $600-$750. (Note: A classic example of a book which is more valuable in a later edition than in the first edition.)

KENDALL, George Wilkins. *The War Between the United States and Mexico*. Map, 12 colored plates by Carl Nebel. Folio, cloth. New York, 1841. First edition. $1,500-$2,500, possibly more.

KENDALL, Joseph. *A Landsman's Voyage to California*. Portrait. Marbled boards. San Francisco, 1935. One of 200. $50-$60.

KENDERDINE, T.S. *A California Tramp and Later Footprints*. 39 views. Pictorial cloth. Newtown, Pa., 1888. First edition. $100-$150.

*KENILWORTH*. 3 vols., boards. Edinburgh, 1821. (By Sir Walter Scott.) First edition. $500-$600.

KENNEDY, Edward G. *The Etched Work of Whistler*. 6 vols. (text vol. and half cloth plate folders). New York, 1910. First edition. Grolier Club. One of 402. $1,500-$2,000.

KENNEDY, James Harrison. *A History of the City of Cleveland*. Cloth. Cleveland, 1896. $75-$100.

KENNEDY, John F. *Inaugural Address*. Portrait. Vellum. Los Angeles, 1965. One of 1,000. $75-$100.

KENNEDY, John F. *Profiles in Courage*. Cloth. New York, (1956). First edition (so stated). In dust jacket. $75-$100. (Signed and/or inscribed copies bring considerably more.) New York, 1961. Cloth. "Inaugural Edition." In dust jacket. Signed by the President, $300 (A, 1976).

KENNEDY, John F. *Why England Slept*. Cloth. New York, 1940. First edition. In dust jacket. $150-$300. London, (1940). Red cloth. First English edition, with ads dated 1940. In dust jacket. $150-$200.

KENNEDY, John F. (editor). *As We Remember Joe*. Portrait frontispiece, photographs. Red cloth. (Cambridge, Mass., 1945.) First edition. In glassine dust jacket. $1,350-$1,600. (Signed and/or inscribed copies bring considerably more.)

KENNEDY, John Pendleton. See Secondthoughts, Solomon. Also see *Horse-Shoe Robinson; Rob of the Bowl; Swallow Barn*.

KENNEDY, John Pendleton, *Memoirs of the Life of William Wirt*. Frontispiece. 2 vols., black cloth. Philadelphia, 1849. First edition. $75-$100.

KENNEDY, Margaret. *The Constant Nymph*. Cloth. London, 1924. First edition, first issue, with ads on verso of half title. In dust jacket. $35-$40.

KENNEDY, Margaret. *The Ladies of Lyndon*. Cloth. London, (1923). First edition. In dust jacket. $35.

KENNEDY, Pendleton. See *The Blackwater Chronicle*.

KENNEDY, W. S. *The Plan of Union: or a History of the Churches of the Western Reserve*. Cloth, Hudson, Ohio, 1856. First edition. $35-$50.

KENNEDY, William. *Texas: Its Geography, Natural History, and Topography*. 118 pp., wrappers. New York, 1844. First edition. $200-$250. (Reprint in part of *Texas: The Rise, Progress, etc.*)

KENNEDY, William. *Texas: The Rise, Progress and Prospects of the Republic of Texas*. Maps, charts. 2 vols., cloth. London, 1841. First edition. $500-$600. Another issue: 2 vols. in one, cloth. $400-$500. Second edition, same date: $300-$400. Fort Worth, 1925. Maps. Cloth. $35.

KENT, Henry W. (compiler). *Bibliographical Notes on One Hundred Books Famous in English Literature*. Half vellum. New York, 1903. Grolier Club. One of 305. $300-$450. (Issued as a supplement to the Grolier Club title of 1902, *One Hundred Books Famous in English Literature*, which was also limited to 305 copies. This title contains an introduction by George E. Woodberry and is usually available in the $100-$150 price range. Together, the two books are currently valued in the $400-$600 range.)

KENT, Rockwell. *A Birthday Book*. Illustrated by the author. Pictorial cloth (silk). New York, 1931. First edition. One of 1,850, signed. $75-$100. (Note: This book has a 1975 auction record of $225 at the Los Angeles branch of Sotheby Parke Bernet. The top auction record elsewhere is $40, as of 1976.)

KENT, Rockwell. *The Bookplates and Marks of Rockwell Kent*. 85 plates. Decorated cloth. New York, 1929. First edition. One of 1,250, signed. In dust jacket. $100-$125.

KENT, Rockwell. *Forty Drawings . . . to Illustrate the Works of William Shakespeare*. Portfolio of drawings. (Garden City, 1936.) First edition. One of 1,000. Boxed. $200-$250.

KENT, Rockwell. *Greenland Journal*. Illustrated. Cloth. New York, (1962). First edition. With a set of 6 lithographs, one signed. Boxed. $150-$250.

KENT, Rockwell. *How I Make a Wood Cut*. Illustrated. Cloth. Pasadena, 1934. First edition. One of 1,000. $75-$100.

KENT, Rockwell. *It's Me O Lord*. Illustrated. Cloth. New York, (1955). In dust jacket. $60-$75.

KENT, Rockwell. *Later Bookplates & Marks of Rockwell Kent*. Illustrated. Cloth. New York, 1937. First edition. One of 1,250, signed. In dust jacket. $85-$110.

KENT, Rockwell. *N. by E.* Illustrated. Pictorial silvered blue buckram. New York, 1930. First edition. One of 900 signed. Boxed. $100-$150. Another issue: Linen, with an extra page, for presentation. One of 100. Boxed. $150-$200. Trade edition: Cloth. In dust jacket. $25-$30.

KENT, Rockwell. *Northern Christmas*. Illustrated. Pictorial boards. New York, (1941). First edition. $50.

KENT, Rockwell. *Salamina*. Illustrated. Blue cloth. New York, 1935. First edition (so stated). In dust jacket. $40-$45.

KENT, Rockwell. *To Thee! A Toast in Celebration of a Century*. Boards. Manitowoc, Wis., (1946). First edition. $35.

KENT, Rockwell. *Voyaging Southward from the Strait of Magellan.* Tan buckram. New York, 1924. First edition. In dust jacket. $75-$100. Another issue: Blue boards. One of 110 signed, with an extra signed woodcut. $200-$250.

KENT, Rockwell. *Wilderness: A Journal of Quiet Adventure in Alaska.* 69 illustrations. Gray linen. New York, 1920. First edition, first binding. In dust jacket. $100-$150. Second binding, tan pictorial boards. $75-$100. Author's first book.

KENT, Rockwell (editor). *World-Famous Paintings.* 100 color plates. Brown cloth. New York, (1939). First edition, first binding, with color print of "The Laughing Cavalier" on front cover. $35-$50.

KENTUCKIAN in *New-York (The)*. By a Virginian. 2 vols., cloth. New York, 1834. (By W. A. Caruthers.) First edition. $150-$200.

KENYON, Frederic G. *Ancient Books and Modern Discoveries.* Half vellum. Chicago, 1927. Caxton Club. First edition. One of 350. In dust jacket. Boxed. $150-$225. Also, $100 (A, 1976); $120 (A, 1974).

KENYON, William Asbury. *Miscellaneous Poems.* Cloth. Chicago, 1845. First edition. $300-$400. Also, $190 (A, 1967).

KER, Henry. *Travels Through the Western Interior of the United States.* Half leather. Elizabethtown, N.J., 1816. First edition. $150-$200.

KERCHEVAL, Samuel. *A History of the Valley of Virginia.* Leather. Winchester, Va., 1833. First edition. $100-$150. Woodstock, Va., 1850. $50.

KEROUAC, Jack. *The Dharma Bums.* Cloth. New York, 1958. First edition. In dust jacket. $50.

KEROUAC, Jack. *Doctor Sax.* Beige cloth, brown spine. New York, (1959). First edition. One of 30 signed. $200-$550 (latter price in a 1978 catalogue). Trade edition: Cloth. In dust jacket. $75-$200 (in the same catalogue). Wrappers: $10-$15.

KEROUAC, Jack. *Excerpts from Visions of Cody.* Boards and cloth. (New York, 1959.) New Directions. First edition. One of 750 copies signed (of an edition of 805). In acetate dust jacket. $150-$175.

KEROUAC, Jack. *Mexico City Blues.* Boards and cloth. New York, (1959). First edition. One of 30 signed. $150-$200. Trade edition: Cloth. $35-$40. Wrappers: $10-$15.

KEROUAC, Jack. *On the Road.* Cloth. New York, 1957. First edition. In dust jacket. $100-$150. Another copy, with extra white promotional dust jacket, $750 in a 1978 catalogue.

KEROUAC, Jack. *A Pun for Al Gelpi.* Broadside, oblong. (Cambridge, Mass., 1966.) First edition. One of 100 signed. $75-$125.

KEROUAC, Jack. *The Subterraneans.* Boards and cloth. New York, (1958). First edition. One of 100. $300.

KEROUAC, John (Jack). *The Town and the City.* Cloth. New York, (1950). First edition. In dust jacket. $150-$200. Advance review copy in wrappers: $600 in a 1978 catalogue. Author's first book.

KEROUAC, Jack. *Visions of Cody.* Introduction by Allen Ginsberg. Cloth. (New York, 1972.) First edition. In dust jacket. $25.

KEROUAC, Jack. *Visions of Gerard.* Illustrated. Cloth. New York, (1963). First edition. In dust jacket. $50.

KERR, Hugh. *A Poetical Description of Texas, etc.* Cloth. New York, 1838. First edition. $600-$1,000.

KESEY, Ken. *One Flew Over the Cuckoo's Nest.* Cloth. New York, (1962). First edition. In dust jacket. $50-$75. Author's first book.

288 RUSSELL HAWES KETTELL

KETTELL, Russell Hawes. *The Pine Furniture of Early New England.* 229 full-page reproductions and 55 working drawings. Linen. Garden City, 1929. First edition, limited.
$75-$100.

KETTELL, Samuel. *Specimens of American Poetry, with Critical and Biographical Notices.* 3 vols., boards, paper labels. Boston, 1829. First edition. $100-$250.

KEWEN, Edward John Cage. *Idealina.* Cloth. San Francisco, 1843. First edition. $50-$60.

KEWEN, Edward John Cage. *Oration and Poem Before the Society of California Pioneers.*
Wrappers. San Francisco, 1854. First edition. $50-$60.

KEYES, Daniel. *Flowers for Algernon.* Cloth. New York, (1966). First edition. In dust jacket. $40-$50.

KEYNES, Geoffrey. *A Bibliography of Sir Thomas Browne.* Illustrated. Buckram. Cambridge, England, 1924. First edition. One of 750 signed. In dust jacket. $50-$75.

KEYNES, Geoffrey. *A Bibliography of William Blake.* Illustrated. Half blue leather. New
York, 1921. Grolier Club. One of 250. $400-$500. New York, 1969. Cloth. $60-$75.

KEYNES, Geoffrey. *A Bibliography of William Hazlitt.* Illustrated. Boards. London, 1931.
Nonesuch Press. One of 750. $75-$100.

KEYNES, Geoffrey. *A Bibliography of the Works of Dr. John Donne.* Cloth. Cambridge,
1914. First edition. One of 300. $75-$100. Cambridge, 1932. Second edition. One of 350.
$75-$100. Cambridge, 1958. Third edition. One of 750. In dust jacket. $100-$125.

KEYNES, Geoffrey. *A Bibliography of the Writings of William Harvey, M. D.* Illustrated.
Buckram. Cambridge, 1928. First edition. One of 300. $75-$100. Cambridge, 1953. Second edition. One of 750. $100-$125.

KEYNES, Geoffrey. *Jane Austen: A Bibliography.* Illustrated. Boards. London, 1929.
Nonesuch Press. One of 875. $75-$100.

KEYNES, Geoffrey. *John Evelyn: A Study in Bibliophily,.* Illustrated. Cloth. Cambridge,
1937. First edition. One of 300. In dust jacket. $75-$100. New York, 1937. One of 130.
$100-$150.

KEYNES, Geoffrey. *John Ray: A Bibliography.* Illustrated. Boards. London, 1951. First
edition. One of 650. In dust jacket. $80-$100.

KEYNES, Geoffrey, *William Pickering: Publisher.* Illustrated. Cloth. London, 1924. Chiswick Press. First edition. One of 350. $75-$100.

KEYNES, Geoffrey, and Wolfe, Edwin, II. *William Blake's Illuminated Books: A Census.* 8
plates. Cloth. New York, 1953. Grolier Club. First edition. One of 400. $100-$125.

KEYNES, John Maynard. *The Economic Consequences of the Peace.* Cloth. London, 1919.
First edition. In dust jacket. $150-$250.

KEYNES, John Maynard. *The General Theory of Employment, Interest, and Money.* Cloth.
London, 1936. First edition. In dust jacket. $150.

KHERDIAN, David. *On the Death of My Father and Other Poems.* Introduction by William
Saroyan. Cloth. Fresno, (1970). First edition. One of 26 signed by the poet and Saroyan.
In dust jacket. $75-$100.

KIDD, J. H. *Personal Recollections of a Cavalryman with Custer's Michigan Cavalry Brigade in the Civil War.* Cloth. Ionia, Mich., 1908. First edition. $100-$175.

KIDDER, A. V. *An Introduction to the Study of Southwestern Archaeology.* 50 plates.
Cloth. New Haven, 1924. First edition. $50-$60.

*KIKI'S Memoirs.* Translated by Samuel Putnam. Introduction by Ernest Hemingway. Illustrated. Wrappers. Paris, 1930. First edition, with glassine wrapper and imprinted band
around book. $150-$200.

KILBOURN, John. *Columbian Geography.* Leather. Chillicothe, Ohio, 1815. First edition. $200-$300.

KILBOURN, John. *The Ohio Gazetteer, or Topographical Dictionary.* Boards, or calf. Columbus, 1816. First edition. $100-$150. Second edition, same date. $50-$75.

KILBOURNE, E. W. *Strictures on Dr. I. Galland's Pamphlet, Entitled "Villainy Exposed," with Some Account of His transactions in Lands of the Sac and Fox Reservation, etc., in Lee County, Iowa.* 24 pp., sewed. Fort Madison, Iowa, 1850. First edition. $200-$250.

KILBOURNE, Payne K. *History and Antiquities of the Name and Family of Kilbourne.* 3 plates. Cloth. New Haven, 1856. First edition. $40-$50.

KILMER, Joyce. *Summer of Love.* Cloth, gilt top. New York, 1911. First edition, first issue, with the Baker & Taylor imprint at foot of spine (later Doubleday, Page & Co.). In dust jacket. $100-$150. Author's first book. Another (preliminary) issue: Trial binding of unlettered red cloth. $150-$200. Second issue (Doubleday, Page). In dust jacket. $30-$40.

KILMER, Joyce. *Trees and Other Poems.* Boards, paper labels. New York, (1914). First edition, first state, without "Printed in U.S.A." on copyright page. In dust jacket. $75-$100.

KIMBALL, Fiske. *The Creation of the Rococo.* 274 illustrations. Buckram and boards. Philadelphia, 1943. In dust jacket. $75-$100.

KIMBALL, Fiske. *Domestic Architecture of the American Colonies and of the Early Republic.* Illustrated. Cloth. New York, 1922. First edition. In dust jacket. $100.

KIMBALL, Fiske. *Mr. Samuel McIntire, Carver, the Architect of Salem.* Illustrated. Cloth. Portland, Me., 1940. One of 675. In dust jacket. $150-$200.

KIMBALL, Fiske. *Thomas Jefferson, Architect.* Illustrated. Cloth. Boston, 1916. First edition. One of 350. In dust jacket. $200-$300.

KIMBALL, Heber C. *The Journal of Heber C. Kimball.* Edited by R. B. Thompson. 60 pp., printed wrappers. Nauvoo, Ill., 1840. First edition. $1,000-$1,250.

*KING and Queen of Hearts (The).* 15 plain or colored illustrations. Printed wrappers. London, 1805. (By Charles Lamb.) First edition, early (earliest?) printing, undated cover, name of "Hodgkins" misspelled on cover. $1,500 and up. Also, $1,000 (A, 1947, the Jerome Kern copy—"the only copy known" with wrapper dated 1805). Various cover dates have been noted on copies sold at auction over the years—1806, 1808, 1809, etc. Auction prices, 1941-77: $250, $800, $700 (dated 1806, yellow wrappers, illustrations hand-colored), $182 (brown wrappers, spine defective).

KING, Alexander. *Gospel of the Goat.* 30 plates. Folio, boards and morocco. Chicago, 1928. One of 100. $100-$125.

KING, C. W. *Antique Gems and Rings.* Illustrated. 2 vols., cloth. London, 1872. First edition. $75-$125.

KING, C. W. *Handbook of Engraved Gems.* Illustrated. Cloth. London, 1866. First edition. $100-$125.

KING, C. W. *The Natural History of Gems or Decorative Stones.* Illustrated. Cloth. London, 1867. First edition. $200-$250.

KING, Charles. *Cadet Days.* Illustrated. Pictorial cloth. New York, 1894. First edition. $25-$35.

KING, Charles. *Campaigning with Crook.* 9 plates. Cloth. New York, 1890. First edition. $35-$50.

KING, Charles. *The Fifth Cavalry in the Sioux War of 1876: Campaigning with Crook.* 134 pp., printed wrappers. Milwaukee, 1880. First edition. $250-$300.

KING, Frank M. *Longhorn Trail Drivers*. Illustrated. Cloth. (Los Angeles, 1940.) First edition. One of 400 signed. $100-$125.

KING, Frank M. *Wranglin' the Past*. Portrait. Leatherette. (Los Angeles, 1935.) First edition. One of 300 signed. $100-$125.

*KING Glumpus: An Interlude in One Act*. 3 hand-colored plates by William Makepeace Thackeray. Yellow wrappers. London, 1857. (By John Barrow.) First edition. $500-$1,000, possibly more.

KING, Richard. *Narrative of a Journey to the Shores of the Arctic Ocean, in 1833, 1834, and 1835*. Plates, maps. 2 vols., boards. London, 1836. First edition. $200-$300.

KING, Richard, and Hoppe, E. O. *The Book of Fair Women*. Text by King, photographs by Hoppe. Cloth. London, 1922. First edition. In dust jacket. $75-$125.

KING, W. Ross. *The Sportsman and Naturalist in Canada*. 6 color plates, other illustrations. Cloth. London, 1866. First edition. $200-$250.

KING, William. *Chelsea Porcelain*. 171 illustrations (7 colored). Buckram. London, 1922. $80-$100. Another issue: Pigskin. One of 75 signed. $100-$150. Another issue: One of 13 on vellum. $200-$250.

KINGLAKE, A. W. *Eothen, or Traces of Travel Brought Home from the East*. Frontispiece in color, colored plate. Boards and cloth. London, 1844. First edition. $200-$250.

KINGMAN, John. *Letters, Written by John Kingman, While on a Tour to Illinois and Wisconsin, in the Summer of 1838*. 48 pp., printed wrappers. Hingham, Mass., 1842. First edition. $1,000-$1,250. Also, $550 (A, 1967).

KINGSLEY, Charles. *At Last: A Christmas in the West Indies*. Illustrated. 2 vols., cloth. London, 1871. First edition. $100-$125.

KINGSLEY, Charles. *The Heroes; or, Greek Fairy Tales for My Children*. 8 illustrations by the author. Pink decorated cloth. Cambridge, 1856 (actually, 1855). First edition. $75-$100. London, 1912. Riccardi Press. Illustrated by W. Russell Flint. Vellum. One of 500. In dust jacket. $200-$250. Another issue: One of 12 on vellum, with a duplicate set of plates. $400-$500.

KINGSLEY, Charles, *The Water-Babies*. Illustrated. Cloth. London, 1863. First edition, first issue, with "L'Envoi" leaf. $400-$500. Without the leaf, $200-$300. London, 1909. 42 colored plates by Warwick Goble. Vellum. One of 260. $100-$150.

KINGSLEY, Charles. *Westward Ho!* 3 vols., blue cloth. Cambridge, 1855. First edition, with 16 pages of ads at end of Vol. 3 dated February, 1855. $400-$500. New York, 1947. Limited Editions Club. Illustrated. 2 vols., boards. Boxed. $60-$80.

KINGSLEY, Henry. *Austin Elliot*. 2 vols., blue cloth. London, 1863. First edition, with 2 ad leaves in Vol. 1 and 16 pages of ads in Vol. 2. $100-$200.

KINGSLEY, Henry. *The Recollections of Geoffrey Hamlyn*. 3 vols., blue cloth. Cambridge, 1859. First edition. $100-$150. Author's first book. Boston, 1849. Cloth. First American edition. $30-$40.

KINGSLEY, Henry. *Valentin: A French Boy's Story of Sedan*. 2 vols., brick-red rough cloth. London, 1872. First edition. $75-$100.

KINNELL, Galway. *What a Kingdom It Was*. Boards. Boston, 1960. First edition. In dust jacket. $75-$100. Author's first book.

KINNELL, Galway (translator). *Bitter Victory*. By René Hardy. Cloth. Garden City, 1956. First edition. In dust jacket. $40-$65. Kinnell's first book appearance.

KINO, Eusebio F. *Historical Memoir of Primeria Alta*. Edited by Herbert Eugene Bolton. 7 maps, plates. 2 vols., cloth. Cleveland, 1919. One of 750. In dust jackets. $150-$200. Berkeley, 1948. Illustrated. 2 vols. in one, cloth. $60.

KINZIE, Mrs. Juliette A. See *Narrative of the Massacre at Chicago.*

KINZIE, Mrs. Juliette A. *Wau-Bun, the "Early Day" in the North-West.* 6 plates. Pictorial cloth. New York, 1856. First edition. $100-$125. London, 1856. First English edition. $50-$65. Chicago, 1901. Caxton Club. Illustrated. Cloth. $50-$75.

KIP, Lawrence. See *The Indian Council in the Valley of the Walla Walla.*

KIP, Lawrence. *Army Life on the Pacific.* Cloth. New York, 1859. First edition. $50-$75.

KIPLING, Rudyard. See *Echoes; Quartette.*

KIPLING, Rudyard. *Barrack-Room Ballads and Other Verses.* Red cloth. London, 1892. First English edition. One of 225 on large paper. $125-$150. Another issue: Buckram and vellum. One of 30 on vellum. $250-$300. (For first American edition, see Kipling, *Departmental Ditties.*).

KIPLING, Rudyard. *The Benefactors.* Boards and cloth. New York, 1930. First edition. One of 91 copies. Pirated edition. $30.

KIPLING, Rudyard. *"Captains Courageous": A Story of the Grand Banks.* 22 illustrations. Blue cloth, gilt edges. London, 1897. First English edition. In dust jacket. $300-$400. Lacking jacket, $200. (Note: A few copies were issued in paper covers in 1896 for copyright purposes.)

KIPLING, Rudyard. *The City of Dreadful Night and Other Places.* Gray-green pictorial wrappers. Allahabad, 1891. No. 14 of Wheeler's Indian Library. First published (and second Indian) edition. $600-$800. Also, $275 (A, 1974); $400 (A, 1973); $375 (A, 1970). Allahabad and London, (1891). Wrappers. First English edition. $150-$200.

KIPLING, Rudyard. *The City of Dreadful Night and Other Sketches.* Sewed, without cover. Allahabad, India, 1890. First (suppressed) edition. $5,000 and up. Also, in contemporary brown cloth, $2,200 (A, 1942). (Note: The only known copy.)

KIPLING, Rudyard. *Collected Verse.* Red cloth. New York, 1907. First edition, first issue, without index. $35. New York, 1910. Color illustrations. Half vellum. First illustrated edition. One of 125 signed. $50-$75. London, 1912. Limp vellum. One of 100 signed. $100-$150. Another issue: One of 500. $40-$50.

KIPLING, Rudyard. *The Courting of Dinah Shadd.* Blue wrappers. New York, 1890. First authorized edition. No. 680 in Harper's Franklin Square Library. $35-$50. (Note: The pirated Hurst clothbound edition, New York, 1890, is considered the genuine first edition. A copy brought $210 at auction in 1930.)

KIPLING, Rudyard. *Departmental Ditties and Other Verses.* Pictorial tan wrappers. Lahore, India, 1886. First edition. (Issued in the form of a government envelope.) $600-$750. Calcutta, India, 1886. Printed boards. Second edition. $35-$50. New York, (1890). Red cloth. First American edition, first issue, with "Lovell" at foot of spine. $200. Also, $150 (A, 1976). (Note: This also constitutes the first American edition of *Barrack-Room Ballads.*) London, 1897. Illustrated. Vellum and cloth. First English (and first illustrated) edition. One of 150 on large paper. $75-$100.

KIPLING, Rudyard. *The Feet of the Young Men.* Illustrated with photographs. Brown boards and vellum. Garden City, 1920. First edition. One of 377 signed by the author. $100-$125.

KIPLING, Rudyard. *The Female of the Species.* Oblong, boards. Garden City, 1912. First edition. $25-$35. (Note: There also exists an earlier broadside printing, New York, about 1911. A copy brought $120 at auction in 1960.)

KIPLING, Rudyard. *The Five Nations.* Limp vellum. London, 1903. First edition. One of 30 on vellum. $100-$125. Another issue: Boards. One of 200 large paper copies. $75-$100. Trade edition: Cloth. $15-$20.

KIPLING, Rudyard. *In Black and White.* Gray-green pictorial wrappers. Allahabad, (1888). First edition. No. 3 of the Indian Railway Library. $300-$400. Also, $375 (A, 1974). Allahabad and London, (1890). Gray-green wrappers. First English edition. $50-$75.

KIPLING, Rudyard. *The Jungle Book* [and] *The Second Jungle Book.* Illustrated. 2 vols., blue pictorial cloth. London, 1894-95. First editions. In dust jackets. $400-$600. New York, 1968. Limited Editions Club. (*The Jungle Books.*) $50-$75.

KIPLING, Rudyard. *Just So Stories for Little Children.* Illustrated by the author. Decorated red cloth. London, 1902. First edition. In dust jacket. $400-$500. Lacking jacket, $150.

KIPLING, Rudyard. *Kim.* Illustrated by J. K. Kipling. Green cloth. New York, 1901. First edition, first issue, with rhymed chapter headings for Chapters 8 and 13 only. In dust jacket. $150-$200. London, 1901. Red cloth. First English edition. In dust jacket. $200-$300. Also, $210 (A, 1974). (Note: There also exists a single proof copy of the English first, dated 1900 on title page. It brought $800 at auction in 1942.) Paris, 1930. Illustrated. 2 vols, sheets in board folders. $75-$100. New York, 1962. Limited Editions Club. Cloth. Boxed. $40-$50.

KIPLING, Rudyard. *Letters of Marque.* Red and blue cloth. Allahabad, 1891. First (suppressed) edition. $228. (Note: A "trial" copy, unbound, brought $260 at auction in 1942.) London, 1891. Gray-green pictorial wrappers. First English edition, with "Vol. I" notation. (One of 3 known copies.) $1,000 (A, 1942).

KIPLING, Rudyard. *Letters to the Family.* Light-blue wrappers. Toronto, 1908. First edition. $75-$100.

KIPLING, Rudyard. *The Light That Failed.* Blue cloth. London, 1891. First English edition. $50-$60. (Note: A few paperbound copies dated 1890 were issued for copyright purposes.)

KIPLING, Rudyard. *On Dry-Cow Fishing as a Fine Art.* Vignette. Decorated boards. Cleveland, 1926. Rowfant Club. First edition. One of 176. Boxed. $125-$150.

KIPLING, Rudyard. *Pan in Vermont.* Stiff dark-gray wrappers. London, 1902. First edition. $125.

KIPLING, Rudyard. *The Phantom 'Rickshaw and Other Tales.* Gray-green pictorial wrappers. Allahabad, (1889). No. 5 of the Indian Railway Library. First edition, first binding, with apostrophe before the word "Rickshaw" on front cover. $600-$750. Also, $600 (A, 1974). Second issue, without apostrophe. $100-$150. London, (1890). First English edition. $35-$50.

KIPLING, Rudyard. *Plain Tales from the Hills.* Olive-green pictorial cloth. Calcutta, 1888. First edition, first issue, with ads dated December, 1887. $200-$225. (Note: A few copies exist with front cover blank.)

KIPLING, Rudyard. *Poems, 1886-1929.* 3 vols., red morocco. London, 1929. First edition. One of 525 signed. In dust jackets. $400-$500. Garden City, 1930. 3 vols., vellum boards. One of 537 signed. $400-$500.

KIPLING, Rudyard. *Puck of Pook's Hill.* Red cloth. London, 1906. First edition. $50. New York, 1906. 4 color plates by Arthur Rackham. Pictorial cloth. First illustrated edition. $75-$100. (I have owned two variant bindings of this edition, the differences—in height design—not mentioned by either the Kipling or Rackham bibliographers. Either binding is an acceptable first edition.)

KIPLING, Rudyard. *Schoolboy Lyrics.* Brown printed or plain white wrappers. Lahore, 1881. First edition, first issue, plain white wrappers. $4,000-$5,000. Also, $4,300 (A, 1975).

KIPLING, Rudyard. *Sea and Sussex from Rudyard Kipling's Verse.* 24 color plates by Donald Maxwell. Boards and vellum. London, 1926. One of 500 signed. In dust jacket. Boxed. $85-$110. Garden City, 1926. One of 150 signed. $150-$200.

KIPLING, Rudyard. *Soldier Tales.* Illustrated. Blue cloth. London, 1896. First edition. In dust jacket. $50-$75.

KIPLING, Rudyard. *Soldiers Three.* Pictorial wrappers. Allahabad, 1888. First edition, first state, without cross-hatching on barrack doors on the cover. $400-$600. Second issue, with the cross-hatching. $150-$200.

KIPLING, Rudyard. *A Song of the English*. Illustrated by W. Heath Robinson. Full white vellum. London, (1909). First edition. One of 500 signed by the artist. Boxed. $75-$125.

KIPLING, Rudyard. *Stalky and Co.* Cloth. London, 1899. First edition. $40-$50.

KIPLING, Rudyard. *The Story of the Gadsbys*. Gray-green pictorial wrappers. Allahabad, (1888). No. 2 of the Indian Railway Library. First edition. $200-$400.

KIPLING, Rudyard. *A Tour of Inspection*. Boards. New York, 1928. First edition. One of 93. $100-$125.

KIPLING, Rudyard. *Under the Deodars*. Wrappers. Allahabad, (1888). No. 4 of the Indian Railway Library. First edition, first state of wrappers, without shading around "No. 4" and "One Rupee." $300-$400. Later, with shading on wrappers. $200-$250.

KIPLING, Rudyard. *Verse: Inclusive Edition, 1885-1918*. 3 vols., vellum. London, 1919. First edition. One of 100 signed. $200-$250. Trade issue: Red cloth. $50-$60. Garden City, 1919. Boards. One of 250 signed. $75-$125.

KIPLING, Rudyard. *Wee Willie Winkie and Other Child Stories*. Gray-green pictorial wrappers. Allahabad, (1888). No. 6 of the Indian Railway Library. First edition, first issue, with periods after "A" and "H" on cover. $400-$500.

KIPLING, Rudyard. *White Horses*. Lilac-colored printed wrappers. London, 1897. First edition (a Thomas J. Wise forgery). $250-$300.

KIPLING, Rudyard. *The White Man's Burden*. Lilac-colored printed wrappers. London, 1899. First English edition (a Thomas J. Wise forgery). $300-$400. (Note: There also exists a true first edition, for copyright, issued in 10 copies, gray wrappers, in New York in 1899. A copy inscribed by Kipling sold for $500 in 1942.)

KIPLING, Rudyard. *With the Night Mail*. Color plates. Cloth. New York, 1909. First edition. $40-$50.

KIPLING, Rudyard. *With Number Three, Surgical & Medical, and New Poems*. Printed wrappers. Santiago de Chile, 1900. First edition. $275. (Livingston says most of the 400 copies were pulped.)

KIRSTEIN, Lincoln. *Low Ceiling*. Cloth. New York, 1935. First edition. In dust jacket. $35-$50.

KIZER, Carolyn. *The Ungrateful Garden*. Cloth. Bloomington, (1961). First edition. In dust jacket. $60-$75. Author's first book.

*KLONDYKE Mines and the Golden Valley of the Yukon (The)*. 24 pp., self-wrappers. No place, 1897. $100-$150.

*KLOSTERHEIM: or the Masque*. By the English Opium Eater. Boards, paper label. Edinburgh, 1832. (By Thomas De Quincey.) First edition. $100-$150.

KNEEDLER, H. S. *The Coast Country of Texas*. 76 pp., wrappers. Cincinnati, 1896. First edition. $100-$125.

KNICKERBOCKER, Diedrich. *A History of New York, from the Beginning of the World to the End of the Dutch Dynasty*. Engraved plate. 2 vols., blue boards. New York, 1809. (By Washington Irving.) First edition, first state, with 268 pp. in Vol. 1. $1,000 and up. London, 1839. Illustrated by George Cruikshank. $50-$85. New York, 1867. 2 vols., full morocco. Author's revised edition. $100-$150. New York, 1900. Illustrated by Maxfield Parrish. Boards and cloth. $100-$150. Other Parrish editions in 1903 and 1915, comparably priced.

KNIGHT, Dr. (John), and Slover, John. *Indian Atrocities*. 96 pp., plain yellow boards, cloth spine, Nashville, 1843. First edition. $2,000 and up. Also, $1,500 (A, 1967). Cincinnati, 1867. Printed wrappers. One of 500. $100-$125.

KNIGHT, Sarah K., and Buckingham, The Rev. Mr. (Thomas). *The Journals of Madam Knight and Rev. Mr. Buckingham*. Boards. New York, 1825. First edition. $75-$100.

KNIGHT, William Allen. *The Song of Our Syrian Guest.* 14 pp., green leatherette. Boston, (1903). First edition, first issue, with announcement of *The Love Watch* for "early in 1904" on next to last page. $35.

KNISH, Anne. See Morgan, Emanuel, and Knish, Anne.

*KNOEPFEL's Schoharie Cave.* 2 folding woodcuts. 16 pp., wrappers. New York, 1853. First edition. $50-$75.

KNOX, Dudley W. *Naval Sketches of the War in California.* 28 colored drawings by William H. Meyers. Introduction by Franklin D. Roosevelt. Boards, white leather spine. New York, 1939. Grabhorn printing. One of 1,000. $200-$300.

KOCH, Frederick H. (editor). *Carolina Folk-Plays, Second Series.* Cloth. New York, 1924. First edition, with dated title page. In dust jacket. $100-$150. Also, signed by Koch, $150 (A, 1977). (Note: Contains "The Return of Buck Gavin," Thomas Wolfe's first appearance in a book.)

KOHL, J. G. *Kitchi-Gami: Wanderings Round Lake Superior.* Illustrated. Half calf. London, 1860. First edition in English. $150-$250.

*KONINGSMARKE, the Long Finne: A Story of the New World.* 2 vols., boards. New York, 1823. (By James Kirke Paulding.) First edition. $75-$100.

KOOP, Albert J. *Early Chinese Bronzes.* 110 plates (3 colored). Cloth. London. 1924. $75-$100. Another issue: Calf. One of 40 on China paper, signed. $150-$200. New York, 1924. Cloth. First American edition. In dust jacket. $50-$75.

KOOPS, Matthias. *Historical Account of the Substances Which Have Been Used to Describe Events . . . from the Earliest Date to the Invention of Paper.* Printed on paper made of straw alone. Morocco. London, 1800. First edition. $250-$350. London, 1801. Boards and cloth. Second edition. $150-$200.

KOREN, Elizabeth. *Fra Pioneertiden.* Illustrated. Cloth. Decorah, Iowa, 1914. First edition. $75-$100.

KOSEWITZ, W. F. von. *Eccentric Tales, from the German.* 20 hand-colored etched plates by George Cruikshank from sketches by Alfred Crowquill. Cloth. London, 1827. First edition. $100-$150.

KOSINSKI, Jerzy. *The Painted Bird.* Cloth. Boston, 1965. First edition. In dust jacket. $125-$150. Author's first book.

KOTZEBUE, Otto Von. *A New Voyage Round the World, 1823-26.* 3 maps and 2 plates. 2 vols., boards, paper labels. London, 1830. First edition in English. $350-$500.

KOTZEBUE, Otto Von. *A Voyage of Discovery, Into the South Sea and Beering's Straits.* Colored plates, engraved folding charts. 3 vols., brown boards, paper labels. London, 1821. First edition in English. $1,250-$1,500.

KRAKEL, Dean F. *The Saga of Tom Horn.* Illustrated. Cloth. (Laramie, 1954.) First edition (suppressed). In dust jacket. $100-$125. Second edition, with text on page 13 and 54 revised. $50-$60.

KRAKEL, Dean F. *South Platte Country.* Illustrated. Pictorial wrappers. Laramie, 1954. First edition. $40-$60.

KREYMBORG, Alfred, *Selected Poems, 1912-1944.* Cloth. New York, 1945. First edition. One of 250 signed. Boxed. $35-$40.

KREYMBORG, Alfred (editor). *Others: An Anthology of the New Verse.* Boards. New York, 1917. First edition. $60-$75.

KROEBER, Alfred L. *Handbook of the Indians of California.* Folding map, 10 other maps, 73 plates on 38 sheets. Cloth. Washington, 1925. First edition. $75-$100.

KRUSENTERN, A. J. von. *Voyage Round the World in the Years 1803, 1804, 1805, and*

*1806*. 2 color plates, folding map. 2 vols., calf. London, 1813. First edition in English. $1,500-$2,000.

KUNITZ, Stanley J. *Intellectual Things*. Cloth. Garden City, 1928. First edition. In dust jacket. $50-$75. Author's first book.

KUNZ, George Frederick. *The Curious Lore of Precious Stones*. 86 illustrations (6 in color). Pictorial cloth. Philadelphia, (1913). First edition. $100-$150.

KUNZ, George Frederick. *Gems and Precious Stones of North America*. 8 colored plates, other illustrations. Cloth. New York, 1890. First edition, with errata slip. $85-$100.

KUNZ, George Frederick. *Ivory and the Elephant in Art, in Archaeology, and in Science*. Illustrated. Cloth. Garden City, 1916. First edition. $150-$200.

KUNZ, George Frederick. *The Magic of Jewels and Charms*. Illustrated, including color. Pictorial cloth. Philadelphia, (1915). $50-$75.

KUNZ, George Frederick. *Rings for the Finger*. Illustrated. Cloth. Philadelphia, 1917. First edition. $75-$100.

KUNZ, George Frederick, and Stevenson, Charles Hugh. *The Book of the Pearl*. Illustrated, including color plates. Pale-blue cloth. New York, 1908. First edition. $100-$150. London, 1908. First English edition. $100-$150.

KUTTNER, Henry, and Moore, C. L. *No Boundaries*. Cloth. New York, (1955). First edition. In dust jacket. $50-$60.

KUYKENDALL, Judge W. L. *Frontier Days*. Portrait. Cloth. (Denver?), 1917. First edition. In dust jacket. $35-$50.

# L

L., E. V. *Sparks from a Flint: Odd Rhymes for Odd Times.* Cloth. London, 1890. (By E. V. Lucas?) First edition. $50-$75. Lucas' first book?

LABOULAYE, Édouard. *Laboulaye's Fairy Book.* Translated by Mary L. Booth. Cloth. New York, 1867. First edition. $35-$50.

LA BREE, Ben (editor). *The Confederate Soldier in the Civil War, 1861-1865.* Illustrated. Folio, cloth. Louisville, 1895. First edition. $200-$300.

LA CROIX, Arda. *Billy the Kid.* Illustrated. Wrappers. New York, 1907. First edition. $100-$150.

*LADIES Almanack . . . Written and Illustrated by a Lady of Fashion.* Pictorial wrappers. Paris, 1928. (By Djuna Barnes.) First edition. One of 1,000. Issued with glassine wraparound. $225-$250. Another issue: Vellum. One of 40 with hand-colored plates. $1,000 and up. Also, $850 (A, 1977).

*LADY Audley's Secret.* 3 vols., blue cloth. London, 1862. (By Mary E. Braddon.) First edition. $3,000-$4,000. Also, $2,240 (A, 1965).

*LAFITTE: The Pirate of the Gulf.* 2 vols., cloth. New York, 1836. (By Joseph Holt Ingraham.) First edition. $250-$300.

LA FONTAINE, Jean de. *The Fables of Jean de la Fontaine.* Translated into English verse by Edward Marsh. 26 engravings on copper by Stephen Gooden. 2 vols., vellum. London, 1931. One of 525 signed by the translator and artist. $200-$350. (Also, see Marianne Moore entry for her translation.)

LA FRENTZ, F. W. *Cowboy Stuff.* Illustrated. Boards. New York, 1927. First edition, first issue, with 49 plates. One of 500. $200-$250. Second issue, 50 plates. $200.

*LA GUERRA de Tejas sin Máscara.* 20 pp., stitched. Mexico, 1845. $300-$400.

LAMANTIA, Philip. *Erotic Poems.* White boards. (Berkeley), 1946. First edition. $30-$35. Author's first book.

LAMANTIA, Philip. *Touch of the Marvelous.* Boards. (Berkeley), 1966. First edition. One of 50 signed. $30-$40. Another issue: Wrappers (1,450 copies). $7.50-$10.

LAMB, Charles. See An Eye Witness. Also see *The Adventures of Ulysses; Beauty and the Beast; Elia; John Woodvil; The King and Queen of Hearts; The Last Essays of Elia; Mr. H.; Mrs. Leicester's School; The New Year's Feast on His Coming of Age; Poetry for Children.*

LAMB, Charles. *Album Verses, with a Few Others.* Cloth-backed boards, paper label. London, 1830. First edition. $400-$500.

LAMB, Charles, *The Child Angel, a Dream.* Printed in red and black. Vellum. London, 1910. One of 12 on vellum. $200-$300.

LAMB, Charles. *Elia and the Last Essays of Elia.* Woodcut portrait. 2 vols., buckram. Newtown, Wales, 1929. Gregynog Press. One of 285. In slipcase. $300-$350. Another issue: One of 25 specially bound in morocco. $600-$650. (For first editions of the *Elia* books, see title entries.)

LAMB, Charles. *The Letters of Charles Lamb, to Which Are Added Those of His Sister Mary Lamb.* Edited by E. V. Lucas. 3 vols., cloth. (London, 1935.) First edition. In dust jackets. $75-$100.

LAMB, Charles. *Specimens of English Dramatic Poets, Who Lived About the Time of Shakespeare: with Notes.* Gray boards. London, 1808. First edition. $150-$200.

LAMB, Charles. *Tales from Shakespeare.* 20 plates by William Mulready. 2 vols., boards. London, 1807. First edition, first issue, with imprint on back of page 235. $2,000-$3,000. (Auction values for rebound copies have ranged in the 1970's to $700 and more.) Second issue, back of page 235 blank. $2,000 and up. London, 1909. Arthur Rackham color plates. Buckram with ties. One of 750 large paper copies, signed by Rackham. $400-$600. Another issue: Ordinary copies, in cloth: $100-$150. (Note: Mary Lamb collaborated in writing this book.)

LAMB, Charles. *The Works of Charles Lamb.* 2 vols., cloth-backed boards, paper labels. London, 1818. First edition, first issue, with ads at end dated "June, 1818." $500-$600. London, 1903. Edited by William Macdonald. 12 vols. $250-$350. London, 1903-05. (*Works* of Charles and Mary Lamb.) 7 vols. $100-$150.

LAMBOURNE, Alfred. *An Old Sketch-Book Dedicated to the Memory of My Father.* 18 plates. 53 pp., plates. 78 pp., atlas folio, half morocco and tan cloth. Boston, (1892). First edition. $350-$450.

LAMBOURNE, Alfred. *The Old Journey: Reminiscences of Pioneer Days.* 18 plates. 53 pp., yellow and buff cloth. (Salt Lake City, 1897.) "Jubilee Edition" (of *An Old Sketch-book*). $50-$60.

LAMBOURNE, Alfred. *Scenic Utah: Pen and Pencil.* 20 plates. White cloth, black leather spine. New York, 1891. First edition. $50-$75.

*L'ÂME PÉNITENTE, ou Le Nouveau Pensez-y-Bien; Considération sur les Vérités Éter-nelles, etc.* Unbound, uncut. Detroit, 1809. (Barthelemi Baudrand, editor.) $1,500 and up. Also, $1,100 (A, 1967). In calf binding, uncut, $750 (1956 catalogue); no other copies noted.

*LAMENTATIONS of Jeremiah (The).* Folio, morocco. Newtown, Wales, 1933. Gregynog Press. One of 250. $350-$450.

LAMON, Ward H. *The Life of Abraham Lincoln.* Plates and facsimiles. Green or rust-col-ored cloth. Boston, 1872. First edition. $125-$150.

LANCASTER, Joseph. *The British System of Education.* 5 plates, frontispiece. Cloth. Georgetown, 1812. First edition. $50-$75.

LANCASTER, Robert A., Jr. *Historic Virginia Homes and Churches.* Illustrated. Cloth. Philadelphia, 1915. First edition. $75-$100. Philadelphia, 1917. $50-$65.

LANDOR, Walter Savage. See *Count Julian: A Tragedy; The Dun Cow; Idyllia Nova Quinque; Imaginary Conversations; Pericles and Aspasia; Poems from the Arabic and Persian; Poetry by the Author of Gebir; Popery, British and Foreign; Simonidea.*

LANDOR, Walter Savage. *Andrea of Hungary, and Giovanna of Naples.* Boards, paper la-bel; or purple cloth. London, 1839. First edition. $50-$60.

LANDOR, Walter Savage. *Dry Sticks, Fagoted.* Dark-green cloth. Edinburgh, 1858. First edition. $75-$100.

LANDOR, Walter Savage. *Epicurus, Leontion, and Ternissa.* Woodcut border, initial, and ornaments. Pigskin. London, 1896. Vale Press. One of 210. $150 and up.

LANDOR, Walter Savage. *Gebir, Count Julian, and Other Poems.* Boards, cloth spine, la-bel. London, 1831. First edition. $150 and up.

LANDOR, Walter Savage. *Heroic Idyls, with Additional Poems.* Cloth. London, 1863. First edition. $35-$50.

LANDOR, Walter Savage. *The Last Fruit off an Old Tree*. Purple cloth. London, 1853. First edition, with 8 pages of ads. $50-$75.

LANDOR, Walter Savage. *A Modern Greek Idyl*. Green printed wrappers. London, 1917. First edition. One of 30. $100 and up.

LANDOR, Walter Savage. *A Poet's Dream*. Orange-colored wrappers. Edinburgh, 1928. One of 35, with a manuscript note in Thomas J. Wise's hand. $100 and up. Also, $36 (A, 1967).

LANDOR, Walter Savage. *To Elizabeth Barrett Browning and Other Verses*. Green printed wrappers. London, 1917. First edition. One of 30. $100 and up.

LANE, Lydia Spencer. *I Married a Soldier*. Cloth. Philadelphia, 1893. First edition. $75-$85.

LANE, Walter P. *Adventures and Recollections of Gen. Walter P. Lane*. Portrait. 114 pp., wrappers. Marshall, Tex., 1887. First edition. $800-$1,200.

LANG, Andrew. *Ballads and Lyrics of Old France, with Other Poems*. White cloth. London, 1872. First edition. $35. Author's first book.

LANG, Andrew. *The Blue Fairy Book*. Illustrated. Boards. London, 1889. First edition. $100-$150. New York, (about 1897). McLoughlin. Pictorial boards. $50-$75.

LANG, Andrew. *The Blue Poetry Book*. Illustrated. Boards. London, 1891. First edition. One of 150. $125-$150. Trade edition: $15-$20.

LANG, Andrew. *The Gold of Fairnilee*. Illustrated. Cloth. Bristol, England, (1888). First edition. $75-$100. New York, 1888. First American edition. $35-$50.

LANG, Andrew. *The Green Fairy Book*. Illustrated. Boards. London, 1892. First edition. One of 150. $100-$125. Trade edition: $25-$30.

LANG, Andrew. *Old French Title Pages*. Boards. San Francisco, 1924. Grabhorn printing. One of 260. $50-$75.

LANG, Andrew. *The Olive Fairy Book*. Illustrated. Decorated cloth. London, 1907. First trade edition. $40-$60. New York, 1907. Cloth. First American edition. $35-$50.

LANG, Andrew. *Prince Charles Edward*. Illustrated. Half morocco. London, 1900. First edition. One of 350. $75-$100. Another issue: Morocco, extra. $100-$150.

LANG, Andrew. *The Princess Nobody*. Illustrated. Half cloth. London, (1884). First edition. $75-$100.

LANG, Andrew. *The Red Fairy Book*. Illustrated. Gray and white boards. London, 1890. First edition. One of 113 on large paper. $100-$150.

LANG, Andrew. *The True Story Book*. Illustrated. Boards. London, 1893. First edition. One of 150. $100-$150. Trade edition: Cloth. $20-$25.

LANG, Andrew. *XXII Ballades in Blue China*. Full vellum. London, 1880. First edition. $150-$200. Another copy, morocco. $200-$250.

LANG, H. O. (editor). *History of the Willamette Valley*. 6 plates, facsimile, errata leaf. Calf. Portland, Ore., 1885. First edition. $75-$100.

LANG, William W. *A Paper on the Resources and Capabilities of Texas*. 19 pp., wrappers. (New York), 1881. First edition. $50-$75. Second edition, same date, 31 pp. $35-$50.

LANG, William W. *The Relative Increase of Population and Production*. 8 pp., sewed. New York, 1881. $50.

LANGFORD, Nathaniel Pitt. *Diary of the Washburn Expedition to the Yellowstone . . . in 1870*. 122 pp., cloth. No place, 1905. Inscribed and signed, $175.

LANGFORD, Nathaniel Pitt. *Vigilante Days and Ways.* 15 plates. 2 vols., pictorial cloth. Boston, 1890. First edition. $100-$150.

LANGLEY, Henry G. *The San Francisco Directory for the Year 1858.* Boards. San Francisco, 1858. $300-$350.

LANGSDORFF, George H. von. *Narrative of the Rezanov Voyage to Nueva California, 1806* . Map, plates. Half cloth. San Francisco, 1927. One of 260. $100-$150.

LANGSDORFF, George H. von. *Voyages and Travels in Various Parts of the World During 1803-7.* Maps and plates. 2 vols. boards, or cloth. London, 1813-14. First English edition. $1,500. Carlisle, Pa., 1817. Folding plate. 2 vols. in one, sheepskin. First American edition (abridged). $350-$400.

LANGSTAFF, Launcelot, and others. *Salmagundi; or, The Whim-Whams and Opinions of Launcelot Langstaff, Esq., and Others.* 2 vols., wrappers, or 20 parts, wrappers. New York, 1807-08. (By Washington Irving, William Irving, and James Kirke Paulding.) First edition. $15,000 and up. Also, a set in mixed states and with defects, $11,000 (A, 1971). Most items offered are mixed sets of the parts bound in one or two volumes. Examples: 20 parts (two of them first issue), bound in 2 vols., boards, $1,700 (A, 1974), and 20 parts, (16 of them first issue), bound in 2 vols., calf, $2,000 (A, 1963). Most sets sell at much lower prices. An extremely complicated work, existing in numerous states and difficult to identify. See Blanck, *A Bibliography of American Literature.*

LANGSTON, Mrs. George. *History of Eastland County, Texas.* Illustrated. Cloth. Dallas, 1904. First edition. $175-$300.

LANGWORTHY, Franklin. *Scenery of the Plains, Mountains and Mines.* Cloth. Ogdensburgh, N.Y., 1855. First edition. $200-$225.

LANGWORTHY, Lucius H. *Dubuque: Its History, Mines, Indian Legends.* 82 pp., printed green wrappers. Dubuque, Iowa, (1855). First edition. $300-$400. Cloth, $200.

LANIER, Sidney. *The Boy's Mabinogion.* Illustrated by Alfred Fredericks. Decorated cloth. New York, 1881. First edition. $100-$125. Also, rubbed, $35 (A, 1976).

LANIER, Sidney. *Florida: Its Scenery, Climate, and History.* Illustrated. Cloth. Philadelphia, 1876. First edition, with dated title page. $75-$100.

LANIER, Sidney. *Tiger-Lilies.* Cloth. New York, 1867. First edition, first state, with title page on a stub. $100-$150. Second state, title page an integral leaf. $75-$100. Author's first book.

LANMAN, Charles. *Adventures in the Wilds of the United States and British American Provinces.* 12 plates. 2 vols., cloth. Philadelphia, 1856. Second edition. $200-$300.

LANMAN, Charles. *Adventures of an Angler in Canada.* Frontispiece. Half leather. London, 1848. First edition. $150-$175.

LANMAN, Charles. *Haw-Ho-Noo, or Records of a Tourist.* Cloth. Philadelphia, 1850. First edition. $150-$200.

LANMAN, Charles. *A Summer in the Wilderness.* Cloth. New York, 1847. First edition. $75-$100.

LANMAN, Charles. *A Tour to the River Saguenay.* Wrappers. Philadelphia, 1848. First edition. $100-$150.

LANMAN, James H. *History of Michigan.* Folding map. Cloth. New York, 1839. First edition. $75-$125.

*LANTHORN Book (The).* Half brown leather and green cloth. New York, (1898). (By Stephen Crane and others.) First edition. One of 125. $150-$175. Another issue: One of 12 signed by Crane and others. $250-$300.

LAPHAM, I. A. *A Geographical and Topographical Description of Wisconsin.* Folding map (with 1844 copyright). Cloth. Milwaukee, 1844. First edition. $200-$300. (Note: First bound book printed in Wisconsin.)

LAPHAM, I. A. *Wisconsin*. Colored map (dated 1845). Cloth. Milwaukee, 1846. Second edition (of *A Geographical and Topographical Description of Wisconsin*). $150-$200. Later issue, with map dated 1847, $65 (A, 1976).

*LARA, a Tale. Jacqueline, a Tale*. Drab boards, paper label. London, 1814. (By George Gordon Noel, Lord Byron.) First edition, with 4 pages of ads. $300-$500.

*LARAMIE, Hahn's Peak and Pacific Railway System: The Direct Gateway to Southern Wyoming, Northern Colorado, and Eastern Utah*. 110 illustrations. Oblong folio, wrappers. No place, no date (about 1910). $125-$200.

LARCOM, Lucy. *Similitudes*. Cloth. Boston, 1854. First edition. $35-$50. Author's first book.

LARDNER, Ring W. *Bib Ballads*. Illustrated by Fontaine Fox. Decorated brown cloth. Chicago, (1915). First edition. Boxed. $150-$200. Author's first book (500 printed).

LARDNER, Ring W. *The Big Town*. Green cloth. Indianapolis, (1921). First edition. In dust jacket. $35-$50.

LARDNER, Ring W. *Gullible's Travels*. Indianapolis, (1917). First edition. In dust jacket. $75-$100.

LARDNER, Ring W. *How to Write Short Stories (with Samples)*. Green cloth. New York, 1924. First edition, first issue, with Scribner seal on copyright page. In dust jacket. $50-$60. Also, inscribed, $75 (A, 1967).

LARDNER, Ring W. *The Love Nest and Other Stories*. Green cloth. New York, 1926. First edition, with Scribner seal. In dust jacket. $50.

LARDNER, Ring W. *My 4 Weeks in France*. Cloth. Indianapolis, (1918). First edition. In dust jacket. $35.

LARDNER, Ring W. *Regular Fellows I Have Met*. Green flexible suede. Chicago, 1919. First edition, $250-$350, possibly more.

LARDNER, Ring W. *Round Up*. Green cloth. New York, 1929. First edition, with Scribner seal. In dust jacket. $25.

LARDNER, Ring W. *Stop Me If You've Heard This One*. Boards. New York, 1929. First edition. $75-$100.

LARDNER, Ring W. *Treat 'Em Rough: Letters from Jack the Kaiser Killer*. Illustrated. Green boards, paper labels. Indianapolis, (1918). First edition, first printing, without the poem "TO R.W.L." on page 6. In dust jacket. $50-$75. Second printing, with the poem. In dust jacket. $25-$35.

LARDNER, Ring W. *What of It?* Green cloth. New York, 1925. First edition, first issue, with pages 191, 201, 200. In dust jacket. $75. Second issue, pages 191 to 201 corrected by cancel leaf. In jacket. $35.

LARDNER, Ring W. *You Know Me Al*. Brown cloth. New York, (1916). First edition. In dust jacket. $35-$50.

LARDNER, Ring W., and Kaufman, George S. *June Moon*. Mauve cloth. New York, 1930. First edition, with "A" on copyright page. In dust jacket. $25-$35.

LARIMER, Mrs. Sarah L. *The Capture and Escape; or, Life Among the Sioux*. 5 plates. Cloth. Philadelphia, 1870. First edition. $50-$75. Philadelphia, 1871. $25-$35.

LARKIN, Thomas O., and others. *California in 1846*. Half cloth. San Francisco, 1935. Grabhorn Press. One of 550. $50-$60.

LAROQUE, François A. *Journal of François A. Laroque from the Assiniboine to the Yellowstone, 1805*. 82 pp., printed wrappers. Ottawa, 1910. First edition. $75-$100.

LARPENTEUR, Charles. *Forty Years a Fur Trader of the Upper Mississippi*. 12 illustrations, 6 maps. 2 vols., blue cloth. New York, 1898. First edition. $75-$100.

LA SALLE, Charles E. *Colonel Crocket, the Texas Trailer*. 84 pp., pictorial wrappers. New York, no date (1871). $100-$150.

LA SALLE, Nicolas de. *Relation of the Discovery of the Mississippi River*. French and English texts. Boards and vellum. Chicago, 1898. Caxton Club. First edition in English. One of 269. $200-$225.

LA SALLE, René Robert Cavelier. *Relation of the Discoveries and Voyages of Cavelier de La Salle*. English and French texts. Half vellum. Chicago, 1901. Caxton Club. One of 227. $250-$300. Also, $150 (A, 1975).

LA SHELLE, Kirke. *Poker Rubaiyat*. 12 full-page woodcuts in color by Frank Holme. Colored wrappers. (Phoenix, 1903.) Bandar-Log Press. One of 254. $250-$350.

*LAST Days of Pompeii (The)*. 3 vols., boards. London, 1834. (By Edward Bulwer-Lytton.) First edition, with errata slips in each volume. $300-$400. New York, 1956. Limited Editions Club. Illustrated. Cloth. Boxed. $35-$50.

*LAST Essays of Elia (The)*. Boards, paper label. London, 1833. (By Charles Lamb.) First English edition (second edition of the Second Series of Elia essays, the first edition having been published in Philadelphia 5 years before; see *Elia* entry). $750-$1,000.

*LAST Man (The)*. 3 vols., boards. London, 1826. (By Mary Wollstonecraft Shelley.) First edition, with ad leaf at end of Vol. 1. $500-$600.

*LAST of the Mohicans (The)*. By the Author of "The Pioneers." 2 vols., tan boards, paper labels. Philadelphia, 1826. (By James Fenimore Cooper.) First edition, first issue, with page 89 misnumbered 93 in first volume. $3,000-$4,000. London, 1826. 3 vols., boards. First English edition. $750-$1,000. New York, 1932. Limited Editions Club. Illustrated. Half buckram. Boxed. $40-$50. Also, $75 (A, 1974)—in Los Angeles.

LATOUR, A. Lacarrière. *Historical Memoir of the War in West Florida and Louisiana in 1814-15*. With an atlas. 2 vols., boards. Philadelphia, 1816. First edition. $1,000-$1,500. Also, 2 vols., contemporary calf, rebacked, $425 (A, 1967); spine "perished," lacking atlas, $175 (A, 1968); atlas plates bound in, $160 (A, 1970).

LAUFER, Berthold. *Paper and Printing in Ancient China*. Chicago, 1931. Caxton Club. One of 250. $150-$175.

LAUGHTON, L. D. Carr. *Old Ship Figure-Heads and Sterns*. 8 colored plates, 48 in monochrome. With 2 portfolios of plates, one a duplicate set of the colored plates and an unpublished plate, matted, the other a series of 8 engraved plates, matted, similar, and apparently unpublished. Three-quarters pigskin. London, 1925. One of 100. $300-$400. Ordinary issue: Cloth. In dust jacket. $100-$150.

LAURENS, Henry. *The Army Correspondence of Col. John Laurens in the Years 1777-8*. Three-quarters calf. New York, 1867. Bradford Club. One of 75. $100-$150.

LAVATER, J. C. *Le Lavater Portatif, ou Précis de l'Art de Connaître les Hommes par les Traits du Visage*. 33 colored portraits. Wrappers. London, 1811. $200-$300.

*LA VERDAD Desnuda sobre la Guerra de Tejas, O sea contestación al Folleto Titulado; La Guerra de Tejas sin Mascara*. 43 pp., sewed. Mexico, 1845. $300-$450.

LAW, John. *Address Delivered before the Vincennes Historical and Antiquarian Society*. Folding map. 48 pp., wrappers. Louisville, 1839. First edition. $100-$150. Also, $80 (A, 1967).

LAW, John. *Colonial History of Vincennes*. Cloth. Vincennes, Ind., 1858. $50-$75.

*LAW of Descent and Distribution Governing Lands of the Creek Nation, as Held by C. W. Raymond, Judge of the U.S. Court for the Indian Territory*. 14 pp., printed wrappers. No place, 1903. Democrat Printing Co. $200-$300.

LAWRENCE, Ada, and Gelder, Stuart. *Young Lorenzo: Early Life of D.H. Lawrence*. Illustrated. Vellum. Florence, (1932). First edition. One of 740 (or 750). In dust jacket. $100-$125.

LAWRENCE, D.H. See Davison, Lawrence H.; Verga, Giovanni.

LAWRENCE, D.H. *Amores: Poems.* Cloth. London, (1916). First edition, first issue, with 16 pages of ads at end. In dust jacket. $200-$300. Lacking jacket, $100-$150. Later issue, without the 16 ad pages. In dust jacket. $50-$75.

LAWRENCE, D. H. *Apocalypse.* Photographic frontispiece. Boards, leather label. Florence, Italy, 1931. First edition. One of 750. In dust jacket. $125-$150. London, (1932). Frontispiece. Cloth. First English edition. In dust jacket. $50-$75.

LAWRENCE, D.H. *Assorted Articles.* Red cloth. London, 1930. First edition. In dust jacket. $40-$50.

LAWRENCE, D.H. *Bay: A Book of Poems.* Hand-colored illustrations. Decorated boards. (Westminster, 1919). Beaumont Press. First edition. One of 30 on Japan vellum, signed. $750-$1,000. Also, $500 (A, 1975); $624 (A, 1971); $672 (A, 1969). (Note: There were also 3 extra copies of this issue for presentation. Value: $1,500 and up.) Another issue: One of 50 on cartridge paper. $500-$750. Another issue: One of 120 on handmade paper. $350-$400.

LAWRENCE, D.H. *Birds, Beasts and Flowers.* Pink buckram, paper label. New York, 1923. First edition. In dust jacket. $250-$350. London, 1923. Boards and cloth. First English edition. In dust jacket. $60-$80. London, 1930. Cresset Press. 12 engravings. Vellum-backed boards. First illustrated edition. $200-$250. Another issue: Cloth-backed boards. $85-$125. Another issue: Full pigskin. One of 30, with an extra suite of 7 of the plates. Boxed. $500-$600.

LAWRENCE, D.H. *Collected Poems.* 2 vols., boards, parchment spines. London, 1928. One of 100 signed. In dust jacket. $500-$600. New York, (1929). 2 vols., brown cloth. First American edition. Boxed. $80-$100.

LAWRENCE , D. H. *David: A Play.* Tan cloth. London, (1926). First edition. One of 500. In dust jacket. $75-$125.

LAWRENCE, D. H. *England, My England and Other Stories.* Blue-gray cloth. New York, 1922. First edition. In dust jacket. $100-$150. London, 1924. Brown cloth. First English edition. In dust jacket. $75-$85.

LAWRENCE, D. H. *The Escaped Cock.* Color frontispiece by Lawrence. White wrappers. Paris, 1929. Black Sun Press. First edition. One of 450 on Van Gelder paper. In glassine dust jacket. Boxed. $300-$350. Another issue: One of 50 on vellum. $500-$750. Also, $650 (A, 1977). (Note: Published later in England as *The Man Who Died.*)

LAWRENCE, D. H. *Etruscan Places.* 20 plates. Cloth. London, 1932. First edition. In dust jacket. $100-$125.

LAWRENCE, D. H. *Fantasia of the Unconscious.* Blue ribbed cloth. New York, 1922. First edition. In dust jacket. $75-$100. London, 1923. First English edition. In dust jacket. $50-$80.

LAWRENCE, D. H. *Fire and Other Poems.* Introduction by Robinson Jeffers. Linen. (San Francisco), 1940. Grabhorn Press. First edition. One of 300. In plain tan dust jacket. $200-$300.

LAWRENCE, D. H. *Glad Ghosts.* Wrappers. London, 1926. First edition. One of 500. $75-$100.

LAWRENCE, D. H. *Kangaroo.* Brown cloth. London, (1923). First edition. In dust jacket. $50-$75. New York, 1923. Blue cloth. First American edition. In dust jacket. $25-$30. Paris, (1933). Wrappers. One of 67. $30-$40.

LAWRENCE, D. H. *Lady Chatterley's Lover.* Mulberry boards, paper spine label. (Florence, Italy), 1928. First edition. One of 1,000 signed. In plain dust jacket. $750-$1,000. Also, $650 (A, 1977). Paris, (1950). Color plates, text drawings. Loose leaves in wrappers. One of 100 on velin. In cloth case. $300 and up. (A New York dealer offered a copy with an autograph letter, signed, laid in at $1,350 in 1971.)

LAWRENCE, D. H. *The Ladybird, etc.* Brown cloth. London, (1923). First edition (of a book published later in America as *The Captain's Doll*). In dust jacket. $50-$75.

LAWRENCE, D. H. *Last Poems.* Edited by Richard Aldington and G. Orioli. Frontispiece in color. Boards, paper label. Florence, 1932. First edition. One of 750. In dust jacket. $150-$200. London, 1933. Boards and cloth. First English edition. In dust jacket. $50-$75. New York, 1933. Blue-green cloth. First American edition. In dust jacket. $35-$50.

LAWRENCE, D.H. *The Letters of D.H. Lawrence.* Edited by Aldous Huxley. Plates. Vellum. London, (1932). First edition. One of 525. In slipcase. $150-$200. Trade issue: Cloth. In dust jacket. $35-$50. Second edition, same date. Cloth. In dust jacket. $25-$30.

LAWRENCE, D. H. *Look! We Have Come Through!* Bright-red cloth. London, 1917. First edition. In dust jacket. $150-$250. New York, 1919. Cloth. First American edition. In dust jacket. $25.

LAWRENCE, D. H. *The Lost Girl.* Brown cloth. London, no date (1920). First edition, first issue, with pages 256 and 268 not tipped in and with page 268 reading "whether she noticed anything in the bedrooms, in the beds." In dust jacket. $300-$350. Second issue, pages 256 and 268 tipped in. In dust jacket. $100-$125. New York, 1921. Cloth. First American edition. In dust jacket. $50-$75.

LAWRENCE, D. H. *Love Among the Haystacks.* Cloth. London, 1930. Nonesuch Press. One of 1,600. In dust jacket. $60-$85.

LAWRENCE, D. H. *Love Poems and Others.* Dark-blue cloth. London, 1913. First edition, first binding, smooth blue buckram. In dust jacket. $300-$500.

LAWRENCE, D. H. *The Lovely Lady.* Cloth. London, 1933. First edition. In dust jacket. $50-$60.

LAWRENCE, D. H. *The Man Who Died.* Buckram. London, 1931. First English edition (of a book first published in Paris, 1929, as *The Escaped Cock*). One of 2,000. In dust jacket. $50-$75. Trade edition: Cloth. In dust jacket. $20.

LAWRENCE, D. H. *Mornings in Mexico.* Cloth. London, 1927. First edition. In dust jacket. $100-$125.

LAWRENCE, D. H. *My Skirmish with Jolly Roger.* Boards. New York, 1929. First edition. One of 600. In tissue dust jacket. $35-$50.

LAWRENCE, D. H. *Nettles.* Red wrappers. London, 1930. First edition. $50-$75.

LAWRENCE, D. H. *New Poems.* Gray wrappers. London, 1918. First edition. One of 500. $75-$150. New York, 1920. Boards, paper labels. First American edition. $25-$35.

LAWRENCE, D. H. *An Original Poem.* Printed wrappers. (England), 1934. First edition. (150 printed). $200-$250.

LAWRENCE, D. H. *The Paintings of D. H. Lawrence.* 26 colored plates. Folio, half morocco and green cloth. London (1929). Mandrake Press. First edition. One of 500. $300-$450. Another issue: One of 10 on Japan paper. $750-$1,000.

LAWRENCE, D. H. *Pansies.* Boards and cloth. London, (1929). First edition. In dust jacket. $100-$150. Limited issue: Boards. One of 250 signed. In dust jacket. $300-$400. Another (later) edition, same place and date: White wrappers. "Definitive and Complete Edition." Portrait frontispiece. One of 500 signed. In glassine dust jacket. Boxed. $200-$250. Another issue: Limp leather. One of 50. $600-$750. Also, $500 (A, 1977). Another issue: Pink wrappers. (Not signed.) $60-$85. New York, 1929. First American edition. In dust jacket. $25-$30.

LAWRENCE, D. H. *The Plumed Serpent.* Brown cloth. London, (1926). First edition. In dust jacket. $75-$85. New York, 1926. Cloth. In dust jacket. $25-$35.

LAWRENCE, D. H. *A Prelude*. Cloth, leather spine. Surrey, England, 1949. Merle Press. First edition. One of 100. $100-$125.

LAWRENCE, D. H. *The Prussian Officer and Other Stories*. Blue cloth. London, (1914). First edition, first variant, with 20 pages of ads at back. In dust jacket. $200-$300. Second issue, with 16 pages of ads. In dust jacket. $100-$150. New York, 1914. Cloth. In dust jacket. $30.

LAWRENCE, D. H. *Psychoanalysis and the Unconscious*. Gray boards. New York, 1921. First edition. In dust jacket. $60-$80.

LAWRENCE, D. H. *The Rainbow*. Blue-green cloth. London, (1915). First edition, with ads dated "Autumn, 1914." In dust jacket. $2,000-$2,500. Also, $2,200 (A, 1977). Lacking jacket. $400-$600. New York, 1916. Cloth. First American edition. In dust jacket. $150-$200. Stockholm, 1942. Printed yellow wrappers. Pirated edition. $40-$60.

LAWRENCE, D. H. *Rawdon's Roof*. Decorated boards. London, 1928. First edition. One of 530 signed. In dust jacket. $150-$200.

LAWRENCE, D. H. *Reflections on the Death of a Porcupine and Other Essays*. Marbled boards, canvas spine. Philadelphia, 1925. Centaur Press. First edition. One of 925. Boxed. $75-$100.

LAWRENCE, D. H. *St. Mawr*. (With "The Princess.") Brown cloth. London, (1925). First edition. In dust jacket. $40-$60. New York, 1925. Cloth. First separate edition (without "The Princess"). In dust jacket. $30-$35.

LAWRENCE, D. H. *Sea and Sardinia*. 8 colored plates. Boards and cloth. New York, 1921. First edition. In dust jacket. $100-$125. London, 1923. Cloth. First English edition. In dust jacket. $50-$75.

LAWRENCE, D. H. *Sons and Lovers*. Dark-blue cloth. London, (1913). First edition, first issue, without date on title page. In dust jacket. $1,000, possibly more. Second state, with dated title page tipped in. In dust jacket. $500-$750. Also. $650 (A, 1977). New York, 1913. Purple cloth. First American edition. In dust jacket. $50-$100.

LAWRENCE, D. H. *Studies in Classic American Literature*. Blue cloth. New York, 1923. First edition. In dust jacket. $100-$150.

LAWRENCE, D. H. *Sun*. Marbled wrappers. London, 1926. First edition. One of 100. $500-$750. Paris, 1928. Black Sun Press. Wrappers. First unexpurgated edition. One of 150. $350-$450. Another issue: One of 15 on vellum. In glassine dust jacket. Boxed. $750-$1,000. London, 1928. Boards and cloth. In dust jacket. $50-$75. (Note: There also exists a spurious edition, dated 1929, boards and cloth. $35.)

LAWRENCE, D. H. *Tortoises*. Pictorial boards. New York, 1921. First edition. In dust jacket. $100-$200.

LAWRENCE, D. H. *Touch and Go*. Flexible orange boards, paper labels. London, 1920. First edition. In dust jacket. $75-$100. New York, 1920. Orange boards. First American edition. In dust jacket. $50-$60.

LAWRENCE, D. H. *The Trespasser*. Dark-blue cloth. London, 1912. First edition, with 20 pages of ads at end. $350-$500.

LAWRENCE, D. H. *Twilight in Italy*. Blue cloth. London, (1916). First edition. In dust jacket. $300-$400. Also, $275 (A, 1975).

LAWRENCE, D. H. *The Virgin and the Gipsy*. White boards, paper label. Florence, 1930. First edition. One of 810. In dust jacket. Boxed. $100-$150. London, (1930). Cloth. First English edition. In dust jacket. $40-$60.

LAWRENCE, D. H. *The White Peacock*. Blue cloth. New York, 1911. First edition, first issue, with integral title page and 1910 copyright date. $8,500-$10,000. Also, $3,250. (A, 1972). Variant (second) issue, with a tipped-in title page and 1911 copyright date. $1,250-$1,500. Also, $1,100 (A, 1977). London, 1911. Dark blue-green cloth. First English edition, first issue, with publisher's windmill device on back cover and with page 227 not tipped in. $500-$600. Second issue, with page 227 tipped in. $400-$500. Author's first book.

LAWRENCE, D. H. *The Widowing of Mrs. Holroyd*. Red cloth. New York, 1914. First edition. In dust jacket. $200-$300. London, 1914. Cloth. First English edition. In dust jacket. $50-$75.

LAWRENCE, D. H. *The Woman Who Rode Away*. Brown cloth. London, (1928). First edition. In dust jacket. $100-$150.

LAWRENCE, D. H. *Women in Love*. Dark-blue cloth. New York, 1920. First edition. One of about 18 to 25 (of an edition of 1,250) signed on the title page by Lawrence. In dust jacket. $1,500-$2,000. Also, without jacket, $1,500 (A, 1977). Unsigned copies of the limited issue: In dust jacket. $400-$600. Trade edition: Blue cloth. In dust jacket. $35-$50. Another issue: New York, 1920 (actually 1922). Brown boards. One of 50 signed. $400-$600. Also, $130 (A, 1972). (There were also 50 copies from the same sheets issued in England.) London, (1921). Brown cloth. First English trade edition. In dust jacket. $100-$125.

LAWRENCE, D. H. (translator). *The Story of Dr. Manente*. By A. F. Grazzini. Frontispiece, 2 plates. Parchment boards. Florence, (1929). First edition. One of 200 signed by Lawrence. $200-$300. Another issue: One of 1,000. In dust jacket. $50-$75.

LAWRENCE, Frieda. *"Not I, But the Wind."* Boards and cloth. Santa Fe, N.M., 1934. First edition. One of 1,000 signed. In dust jacket. $100-$150. London, 1935. Cloth. First English edition. In dust jacket. $40-$50.

*LAWRENCE of Arabia*. (Two essays: "The Artist in War and Letters," by B. H. Liddell Hart, and "Himself," by Ronald Storrs.) Boards and cloth. (London, 1936.) Corvinus Press. First edition. One of 25 on Barcham Green "Boswell" paper (of an edition of 128, signed). $400 and up. Another issue: One of 70. $288 (A, 1972). Another: One of 12 on hand-made paper, printed for Storrs. $384 (A, 1973).

LAWRENCE, Richard Hoe (compiler). *History of the Society of Iconophiles of the City of New York*. Reproductions of 119 plates. Boards and morocco. New York, 1930. First edition. One of 186. $75-$100.

LAWRENCE, T. E. See Graves, Robert; Homer; Shaw, T. E. Also see *The Seven Pillars of Wisdom*.

LAWRENCE, T. E. *Crusader Castles*. Portraits and facsimilies, 2 maps in envelopes. 2 vols., half red morocco. London, 1936. Golden Cockerel Press. First edition. One of 1,000. $500-$750.

LAWRENCE, T. E. *The Diary of T. E. Lawrence*. Illustrated. Boards and morocco. London, 1937. Corvinus Press. First edition. One of 203. $400-$500. Another issue: Morocco. One of 30 on Canute paper. Boxed. $1,500 and up. Also, $1,400 (A, 1977). Another: Limp vellum. One of 40 on Medway paper. Boxed. $1,000 and up. Also, $728 (A, 1972).

LAWRENCE, T. E. *Eight Letters*. Edited by H. Granville-Barker. Wrappers. London, 1939. First edition. One of 50. $750-$1,000.

LAWRENCE, T. E. *An Essay on Flecker*. Buckram. London, 1937. Corvinus Press. First edition. One of 30. $600-$800. New York, 1937. Printed wrappers. First American edition. One of about 50 for copyright purposes. $1,400 (A, 1977).

LAWRENCE, T. E. *Letter to His Mother*. Plates. Boards. London, 1936. Corvinus Press. First edition. One of 24. $750-$1,000.

LAWRENCE, T. E. *Letters*. Edited by David Garnett. Maps and plates. Buckram. London, 1938. First edition. In dust jacket. $50-$100.

LAWRENCE, T. E. *Letters from T. E. Shaw to Bruce Rogers* [and] *More Letters to Bruce Rogers*. 2 vols., limp buckram. No place, 1933-36. First editions. Limited to 200 and 300, respectively. $800-$1,000.

LAWRENCE, T. E. *Men in Print.* Half morocco. London, 1940. Golden Cockerel Press. First edition. One of 500. $250-$350. Another issue: Morocco. One of 30 specially bound with supplement. Boxed. $600-$1,000. Also, $500 (A, 1977).

LAWRENCE, T. E. *Minorities.* Edited by J. M. Wilson. Preface by C. Day-Lewis. Frontispiece portrait. Half calf, leather label. London, 1971. One of 125 signed by Day-Lewis. In glassine dust jacket. $85-$100.

LAWRENCE, T. E. *The Mint: A Day-book of the R.A.F. Depot Between August and December, 1922.* Leather and blue cloth. London, (1955). First published edition. One of 2,000. Boxed. $100-$200. Trade edition: Cloth. In dust jacket. $50-$60.

LAWRENCE, T. E. *Revolt in the Desert.* Frontispiece, map, and portraits. Buckram. London, 1927. First edition. In dust jacket. $35-$50. Another issue: Half morocco. One of 315 on large paper. $200-$300. New York, 1927. Illustrated. Cloth. First American edition. In dust jacket. $25. Another issue: Buckram. One of 250. $75-$100.

LAWRENCE, T. E. *Secret Despatches from Arabia.* Portrait frontispiece. Morocco and cloth. London, (1939). Golden Cockerel Press. First edition. One of 1,000. $300-$350. Another issue: White pigskin. One of 30 with part of the manuscript of *The Seven Pillars of Wisdom.* $700-$800.

LAWRENCE, T. E. *Seven Pillars of Wisdom.* 66 plates, other illustrations, 4 folding maps. Full leather. (London), 1926. First edition, inscribed "Complete" and signed "T.E.S." (for T. E. Shaw, Lawrence's adopted name). $5,000 and up. Also, $5,500 (A, 1974); $4,000 (A, 1975). Ordinary edition: One of 500. $400-$500. (For first American copyright edition, one of only two copies, with no author named, see title entry.) London, (1935). Buckram and leather. First published edition. One of 750. In dust jacket. Boxed. $200-$250. Trade edition: Buckram. In dust jacket. $35-$50. Garden City, 1935. Buckram and leather. First published American edition. Limited. In dust jacket. Boxed. $100. Trade edition: Cloth. In dust jacket. $25-$35.

LAWRENCE, T. E. *Shaw-Ede: T. E. Lawrence's Letters to H. S. Ede.* 7 pp. of facsimiles. Morocco. London, 1942. Golden Cockerel Press. One of 500. $250-$350. Another issue: One of 30 specially bound. $600-$800.

LAWRENCE, W. J. *The Elizabethan Playhouse and Other Studies.* 30 plates. 2 vols., boards and cloth. Stratford-on-Avon, England, 1912-13. Shakespeare Head Press. One of 760. $100-$150.

*LAWS and Decrees of the State of Coahuila and Texas, in Spanish and English.* Calf. Houston, 1839. $500-$750.

*LAWS and Regulations of Union District, Clear Creek County, C.T.* 19 pp., printed wrappers. Central, C. T. (Colorado Territory), 1864. $600-$750. Also, $350 (A, 1968).

*LAWS for the Better Government of California.* 68 pp. San Francisco. 1848. Only two copies known of this first English book printed in California. $5,000 or more (?).

*LAWS of the Cherokee Nation.* Cloth. Tahlequah, Indian Territory, 1852. $500-$600.

*LAWS of the Choctaw Nation, Made and Enacted by the General Council from 1886 to 1890.* (In English and Choctaw.) Cloth. Atoka, Indian Territory, 1890. One of 250. $200-$400.

*LAWS OF Gregory District, February 18 & 20, 1860.* (Cover title.) 12 pp., prir.ted wrappers. Denver, 1860. $1,000-$1,250. Also, $600 (A, 1968).

*LAWS of the Territory of Kansas, Passed at the 2d Session of the General Legislative Assembly.* Cloth. Lecompton, (1857). $125-$150.

*LAWS of the Territory of Louisiana (The).* Sheep. St. Louis, 1808 (actually 1809). $10,000 and up. Also, $8,000 (A, 1967).

*LAWS of the Territory of New Mexico.* 71 pp., wrappers. Santa Fe, N.M., 1862. $250-$300.

*LAWS of the Town of San Francisco (The).* 8 pp., wrappers(?). San Francisco, 1847. First edition. $1,000 and up. Also, an imperfect copy (lacking pages 5-8) in board binder, $1,000 (A, 1968).

*LAWS Relating to Internal Improvement in the State of Michigan.* 16 pp., sewed. Detroit, 1837. $75-$100.

*LAWYERS and Legislators, or Notes on the American Mining Companies.* Half calf. London, 1825. (By Benjamin Disraeli.) First edition. $150 and up.

LAY, William, and Hussey, Cyrus M. *A Narrative of the Mutiny on Board the Ship Globe of Nantucket.* Calf. New-London, Conn., 1828. First American edition. $250-$300.

LAYARD, Georges. *George Cruikshank's Portraits of Himself.* Illustrated. Vellum and cloth. London, 1897. First edition. One of 250 large paper copies signed by Layard. $150-$200.

LAYNE, J. Gregg. *Annals of Los Angeles.* Plates. Cloth. San Francisco, 1935. First edition. $50-$75.

LAZARUS, Emma. *Poems and Translations.* Cloth. New York, 1867. First edition. $100 and up. Author's first book.

LAZARUS, Emma. *Songs of a Semite.* Cloth. New York, 1882. First edition. $100-$150.

LEA, Albert M. *Notes on the Wisconsin Territory.* Folding map. 53 pp., printed boards. Philadelphia, 1836. First edition. $1,000-$1,250. Another issue: Wrappers. $1,000-$1,250.

LEA, Homer, *The Vermilion Pencil.* Cloth. New York, 1908. First edition. In dust jacket. $50.

LEA, Pryor. *An Outline of the Central Transit, in a Series of Six Letters to Hon. John Hemphill.* 32 pp., printed wrappers. Galveston, 1859. First edition. $75-$150.

LEA, Tom. *Calendar of the Twelve Travelers Through the Pass of the North.* Illustrated. Folio, cloth. El Paso, Tex., 1946. Carl Hertzog printing. First edition. One of 365 signed. In dust jacket. $500-$750.

LEA, Tom. *The King Ranch.* Illustrated by the author. 2 vols., buckram. Boston, (1957). First edition. Boxed. $50. Another issue: Limited "Private Edition," printed on paper watermarked with running "W" brand. 2 vols., decorated crash linen. Boxed. $500-$800.

LEA, Tom. *Randado.* Illustrated. Stiff wrappers. (El Paso, 1941). Carl Hertzog printing. First edition. One of 100 signed. $500-$1,000.

LEACH, A. J. *Early Day Stories: The Overland Trail, etc.* 7 plates. Brown cloth. (Norfolk, Neb., 1916.) First edition. In dust jacket. $50-$75.

LEACOCK, Stephen. *Canada: The Foundations of Its Future.* 31 full-page illustrations. Morocco. Montreal, 1941. First edition. $125-$150.

LEACOCK, Stephen. *Literary Lapses: A Book of Sketches.* Half linen, green boards, spine label. Montreal, 1910. First edition. In dust jacket. $50-$75. Author's first book of humor (preceded by a 1906 political work).

LEACOCK, Stephen. *Nonsense Novels.* Cloth. London, 1911. First edition. In dust jacket. $35-$50. New York, 1911. Cloth. First American edition. In dust jacket. $35. Montreal, 1911. Green cloth. First Canadian edition. In dust jacket. $40-$60. London, 1921. Illustrated by John Kettlewell, including 8 color plates. Cloth. First illustrated edition. In dust jacket. $50-$60.

LEACOCK, Stephen. *Sunshine Sketches of a Little Town.* Colored frontispiece. Cloth. London, 1912. First edition. In dust jacket. $40-$60.

LEADBEATER, Mary. *Cottage Dialogues Among the Irish Peasantry.* Edited by Maria Edgeworth. Illustrated. 2 vols., boards, paper labels. London, 1811, and Dublin, 1813. First editions. $180.

*LEADVILLE Chronicle Annual.* 40 pp., wrappers. Leadville, Colo., 1881. $150-$200.

*LEADVILLE, Colorado: The Most Wonderful Mining Camp in the World.* 44 pp., printed wrappers. Colorado Springs, 1879. (By John L. Loomis.) $300-$350. Also, $175 (A, 1968).

LEAF, Munro. *The Story of Ferdinand.* Illustrated by Robert Lawson. Pink decorated boards, cloth spine. New York, 1936. First edition. In dust jacket. $200-$225.

LEAF, Munro. *Wee Gillis.* Illustrated by Robert Lawson. Burlap, paper labels. New York, 1938. First edition. One of 525 signed. Boxed. $150. Trade edition: Boards. In dust jacket. $65.

LEAR, Edward. See Derry, Derry down.

LEAR, Edward. *A Book of Nonsense.* Illustrated. Oblong, stiff wrappers. London, 1861. Second (and enlarged) edition. $250 and up. (For first edition, see entry under Lear's pen name Derry down Derry.)

LEAR, Edward. *Calico Pie.* Illustrated by the author. Glazed boards. London, no date. First edition. $100-$150.

LEAR, Edward. *Illustrated Excursions in Italy.* Map, 30 plates. 2 vols., folio, cloth. London, 1846. First edition. $600-$800.

LEAR, Edward. *Illustrations of the Family Psittacidae, or Parrots.* 42 hand-colored plates. Folio, half morocco. London, 1830-32. First edition. $6,000-$8,000. Also, $5,000 (A, 1976).

LEAR, Edward. *Journal of a Landscape Painter in Corsica.* Illustrated. Cloth. London, 1870. First edition. $300-$400.

LEAR, Edward. *Journals of a Landscape Painter in Albania.* Map. Illustrated in color. Cloth. London, 1851. First edition. $300-$500.

LEAR, Edward. *Journals of a Landscape Painter in Southern Calabria.* 2 maps. Illustrated. Cloth. London, 1852. First edition. $300-$500.

LEAR, Edward. *Laughable Lyrics.* Illustrated. Cloth. London, 1877. First edition. $100-$200.

LEAR, Edward. *More Nonsense, Pictures, Rhymes, Botany, etc.* Illustrated. Boards and linen. London, 1872 (actually 1874). First edition. $250-$300.

LEAR, Edward. *Nonsense Songs, Stories, Botany, and Alphabets.* Illustrated. Boards and cloth. London, 1871. First edition: $250-$350. Boston, 1871. Illustrated. Boards. First American edition. $150-$200.

LEAR, Edward. *Views in Rome and Its Environs.* Illustrated (plates in sepia). Folio, half morocco. London, 1841. First edition. $600-$800. Plates hand-colored, $800-$1,000, possibly more.

LEAR, Edward. *Views in the Seven Ionian Islands.* Illustrated. Folio, cloth. London, 1863. First edition. $2,000 and up.

LEAR, P. G. and L. O. *The Strange and Striking Adventures of Four Authors in Search of a Character.* 24 pp., light-purple wrappers, purple label on front cover. London, 1926. (By Charles Kenneth Scott-Moncrief.) One of 350 signed. $100-$150.

*LEATHER Stocking and Silk.* Cloth. New York, 1854. (By John Esten Cooke.) First edition. $75-$125. Author's first book.

*LEAVES from Margaret Smith's Journal.* Cloth, or wrappers. Boston, 1849. (By John Greenleaf Whittier.) First edition. Wrappers: $100-$125. Cloth: $50-$75.

*LEAVES of Grass.* Portrait frontispiece on plain paper. Dark-green cloth, gilt- and blind-stamped, marbled end papers. Brooklyn, 1855. (By Walt Whitman.) First edition, first issue, without ads or reviews: first binding, gilt lettering and borders on both covers. $10,000 and up. Prices at auction through the 1960's and 1970's for copies in from good to fine condition have ranged up to $9,000 (1969). (Note: This exceptionally fine copy, owned by the late Thomas Winthrop Streeter, was the same copy, formerly the property of the late Arthur Swann, New York collector and auction gallery executive, sold for $3,700 in 1960 at the auction of the Swann library.) Worn copies have been occasionally available at retail prices ranging from $2,000 to $5,000. Second issue, plain yellow end papers, no gold on back cover, $2,000 and up. Third issue, same as second but with ads or press notices bound in. $1,000 and up.Brooklyn, 1856. Cloth. Second edition, with ad leaf of Fowler & Wells, the publisher, at back of the book. $1,000 and up. Rebacked, $500. Boston, "Year '85 of the States" (1860-61). Third edition, first issue, with "George C. Rand & Avery" on copyright page, portrait on tinted paper, orange-colored (or brick-red) cloth. $150-$300. Second issue, same date, has portrait on white paper. Same value. Third issue (first pirated issue), without the Rand & Avery notice. $100 and up. New York, 1867. Half morocco or cloth. Fourth edition, with "Ed'n 1867" stamped on back in gold. (Several variant issues, for which see Wells and Goldsmith, *A Concise Bibliography of the Works of Whitman*.) $200 and up. Washington, 1871. Wrappers, or half morocco. Fifth edition. $200 and up. Later in 1871: *Leaves of Grass, Passage to India.* Green wrappers. $50-$100. Camden, 1876. Half cream-colored calf and marbled boards. Sixth edition. "Author's Edition," signed. $600-$800. Also, rubbed, $300 (A, 1974). (For variants, see Wells and Goldsmith, cited above.) Boston, 1881-82. Yellow cloth. Seventh edition, first issue (very rare), with "Third edition" on title page (suppressed). $400-$500, possibly more. Second issue, without "Third Edition" on title page. $150 and up. (Note: A presentation copy to A. C. Swinburne sold for $1,200 in London in 1968.) Camden, 1882. Dark-green cloth. "Author's Edition," signed. $600 and up. Also, $300 (A, 1974). Philadelphia, 1882. Yellow cloth. "First Philadelphia edition," with Whitman's name on cover. $200 and up. Philadelphia, 1884. Yellow cloth. Seventh edition, later issue, with McKay imprint. $200 and up. Philadelphia, 1889. Limp black morocco. One of 300 signed. 70th Birthday Edition. $500 and up. Philadelphia, 1891-92. First issue, brown wrappers. $800-$1,000, possibly more. Also, worn, $600 (A, 1971). Later issue: Dark-green cloth or gray wrappers. $500 and up. Portland, Me., 1919. Mosher Press. Cloth. One of 400. $100 and up. There were also several other issues of this edition: Boards (250 copies), $100 and up; (100 copies), $150 and up; (50 copies on vellum), $200 and up. New York, 1930. Grabhorn printing. 37 woodcuts. Leather-backed mahogany boards. One of 300. $750-$1,000. Also, $500 (A, 1977). New York, (1933). Cloth. Introduction by Sherwood Anderson. $50. New York, 1942. Limited Editions Club. Edward Weston photographs. 2 vols., boards. $600-$800. Mount Vernon, N.Y., (1943). Peter Pauper Press. Half morocco. One of 1,100. $100 and up.

*LEAVES of Grass Imprints: American and European Criticisms of "Leaves of Grass."* 64 pp., printed brown wrappers. Boston, 1860. First edition. $400 and up. Also, stained, $200 (A, 1974).

LEBRIJA, Joaquin, and Berrera, Ignacio. *Análisis e Impugnacion del Proyectó de le Sobre Arbitrios para la Guerra de Tejas.* 31 pp., sewed. Mexico, 1841. $200-$400.

LECKENBY, Charles H. (compiler). *The Tread of Pioneers.* Illustrated. Cloth. Steamboat Springs, Colo., (1945). First edition. $75-$100.

LE CONTE, Joseph. *A Journal of Ramblings Through the High Sierras of California.* 9 mounted photos. Blue cloth. San Francisco, 1875. First edition. $1,000-$1,250. (Only a few copies printed.)

LE DUC, W. G. *Minnesota Year Book and Traveller's Guide for 1851.* Folding map. Boards, leather spine. St. Paul, (1851). First year of issue. $200-$250. Other issues: For 1852, with frontispiece plate. $100. For 1853, folding map. $50-$100.

LEDYARD, John. See *The Adventures of a Yankee.*

LEE, Andrew. *The Indifferent Children.* Cloth. New York, (1947). (By Louis Auchincloss.) First edition. In dust jacket. $40-$50. Author's first book.

LEE, Harper. *To Kill a Mockingbird.* Wrappers. Philadelphia, (1960). First edition. Advance reading copy. $75-$125. Trade edition: Cloth. In dust jacket. $50-$75.

LEE, Maj. Henry, Jr. *The Campaign of 1781 in the Carolinas.* Calf. Philadelphia, 1824. First edition. $175-$250.

LEE, John D. *J. D. Lee's Bekjendelse.* 36 pp., wrappers. Salt Lake City, 1877. $100-$125.

LEE, John D. *The Journals of John D. Lee, 1846-47 and 1859.* Edited by Charles Kelly. Cloth. Salt Lake City, 1938. First edition. One of 250. In dust jacket, $75-$100.

LEE, L. P. (editor). *History of the Spirit Lake Massacre!* (Cover title.) Illustrated. 48 pp., pictorial wrappers. New Britain, Conn., 1857. First edition. $75-$100.

LEE, Nelson. *Three Years Among the Camanches.* 2 plates (including portrait-title page). Wrappers, or cloth. Albany, N.Y., 1859. First edition. Wrappers: $1,500-$2,000. Cloth: $750-$1,000.

LEE, Susan P. *Memoirs of William Nelson Pendleton.* Portrait. Cloth. Philadelphia, 1893. First edition. $75-$100.

LEE, William, *Junkie.* (And) Helbrant, Maurice, *Narcotic Agent.* Back-to-back in pictorial wrappers. New York, (1953). Ace Books. First edition. $50-$75. (*Junkie* is by William Burroughs. Burroughs' first book.)

*LEE Trial (The)! An Exposé of the Mountain Meadows Massacre.* 64 pp., printed wrappers. Salt Lake City, 1875. First edition. $850-$1,000. Also, $400 (A, 1968).

LEECH, John. *Follies of the Year.* 21 hand-colored plates. Oblong, leather-backed cloth. London (1864). First collected edition. $250-$400. London (about 1865). $150-$200.

LEECH, John. *Hunting: Sports and Pastimes.* Illustrated. 2 vols., elephant folio, boards. London, 1865. First edition. $400-$500.

LEECH, John. *Mr. Briggs and His Doings: Fishing.* 12 color plates. Oblong, wrappers. London, (1860). First edition. $600-$750.

LEECH, John. *Portraits of Children of the Nobility.* Illustrated. Cloth. London, 1841. First edition. $150-$200.

LEECH, John. *The Rising Generation.* 12 color plates. Folio, boards and morocco. London, (1848). First edition. $250-$400.

LEEPER, David Rohrer. *The Argonauts of Forty-nine.* Illustrated. Cloth. South Bend, 1894. First edition. $75-$100.

LEESE, Jacob P. *Historical Outline of Lower California.* 46 pp., printed wrappers. New York, 1865. First edition. $150-$175.

LE FANU, Joseph Sheridan. See *The Fortunes of Colonel Torlogh O'Brien.*

LE FANU, Joseph Sheridan. *All in the Dark.* 2 vols., cloth. London, 1866. First edition. $250-$350.

LE FANU, Joseph Sheridan. *Checkmate.* 3 vols., cloth. London, 1871. First edition. $350-$450.

LE FANU, Joseph Sheridan. *Chronicles of Golden Friars.* 3 vols., cloth. London, 1871. First edition. $300-$400.

LE FANU, Joseph Sheridan. *Ghost Stories and Tales of Mystery.* Illustrated by "Phiz." Cloth. Dublin, 1851. First edition. $350-$500.

LE FANU, Joseph Sheridan. *Green Tea and Other Ghost Stories.* Cloth. Sauk City, Wis., 1945. First edition. In dust jacket. $85-$125.

LE FANU, Joseph Sheridan. *Guy Deverell.* 3 vols., cloth. London, 1865. First edition. $600-$750.

LE FANU, Joseph Sheridan. *Haunted Lives.* 3 vols., cloth. London, 1868. First edition. $500-$600.

LE FANU, Joseph Sheridan. *The House by the Churchyard.* 3 vols., cloth. London, 1863. First edition. $400-$650. Second edition, same date. 3 vols. in one, cloth. $150-$200.

LE FANU, Joseph Sheridan. *In a Glass Darkly.* 3 vols., cloth. London, 1872. First edition. $400-$500.

LE FANU, Joseph Sheridan. *The Purcell Papers.* 3 vols., blue-black cloth. London, 1880. First edition. $300-$450.

LE FANU, Joseph Sheridan. *The Rose and the Key.* 3 vols., cloth. London, 1871. First edition. $250-$350.

LE FANU, Joseph Sheridan. *Wylder's Hand.* 3 vols., cloth. London, 1864. First edition. $350-$500.

LE FANU, Joseph Sheridan. *The Wyvern Mystery.* 3 vols., cloth. London, 1869. First edition. $400-$500.

LEFÈVRE, Raoul. *The Recuyell of the Historyes of Troye.* Translated by William Caxton. Edited by H. Halliday Sparling. Woodcut title, borders, and initials. 3 vols. in two, folio, limp vellum with ties. London, 1892. Kelmscott Press. One of 300. $500-$600.

LE GALLIENNE, Richard. *The Book-Bills of Narcissus.* Wrappers. Derby, England, 1891. First edition. One of 50 on large paper. $75-$100. Ordinary issue: $40-$60.

LE GALLIENNE, Richard. *English Poems.* Boards. London, 1892. First edition. $25. Another issue: One of 25 on Japan paper. $75-$100.

LE GALLIENNE, Richard. *Limited Editions: A Prose Fancy.* Wrappers. London, 1893. One of 100 signed. Boxed. $75-$125.

LE GALLIENNE, Richard. *My Ladies' Sonnets.* Boards. (Liverpool), 1887. First edition. One of 250 signed. $100-$200. Ordinary issue: $35-$50. Author's first book.

LE GALLIENNE, Richard. *The Quest of the Golden Girl.* Green cloth. Cambridge, 1896. First edition. $40-$50.

LE GALLIENNE, Richard. *Robert Louis Stevenson: An Elegy, and Other Poems, Mostly Personal.* Cloth. London, 1895. First edition. One of 500. $40-$50. Another issue: One of 75 on large paper. $50-$75.

LE GALLIENNE, Richard. *The Romance of Perfume.* Illustrated. Boards. London, 1928. First edition. $100-$125.

*LEGENDS of the Conquest of Spain.* By the Author of "The Sketch-Book." Green cloth, paper label. Philadelphia, 1835. (By Washington Irving.) First edition. $100-$250.

LEGGETT, Mortimer Dormer. *A Dream of a Modest Prophet.* Green cloth. Philadelphia, 1890. First edition. $50-$75.

*LEGION Book (The).* Edited by H. Cotton Minchin. Stephen Gooden copperplate of "Mounted Soldier" (self-portrait) on title page, numerous other illustrations, including 9 color plates. Full white pigskin, gilt- and blind-stamped. London, 1929. One of 100 signed by authors and artists, by Edward, Prince of Wales, and by 5 prime ministers. (Gift book published for the Prince of Wales.) $400-$500.

LEGLER, Henry E. *Of Much Love and Some Knowledge of Books.* Chicago, (1912). Caxton Club. One of 354. $75-$125.

LE GUIN, Ursula. *A Wizard of Earthsea.* Cloth. Berkeley, (1968). First edition. In dust jacket. $100-$150.

LEHMANN, John. *A Garden Revisited and Other Poems.* Cloth. London, 1931. Hogarth Press. First edition. In dust jacket. $60-$75.

LEIBER, Fritz, Jr. *Night's Black Agents.* Cloth. Sauk City. 1947. Arkham House. First edition. In dust jacket. $50-$75. Author's first book.

LEIGH, William R. *The Western Pony.* 6 color plates, with an extra signed plate laid in. Cloth. New York, (1933). First edition. One of 100. In dust jacket. $400-$600. Also, $230 (A, 1974).

LEINSTER, Murray. *Sidewise in Time*. Cloth. Chicago, 1950. (By Will F. Jenkins.) First edition. In dust jacket. $40-$50.

LELAND, Charles Godfrey. *Meister Karl's Sketch-Book*. Cloth. Philadelphia, 1855. First edition. $40-$50. Author's first book.

LELAND, Charles Godfrey. *The Union Pacific Railway*. 95 pp., printed wrappers. Philadelphia, 1867. First edition. $75-$125.

LEONARD, H.L.W. *Oregon Territory*. 88 pp., printed blue or buff wrappers. Cleveland, 1846. First edition. $2,500-$3,000. Also, $1,300 (A, 1969). (Note: Only 3 copies known.)

LEONARD, Irving (translator). *The Mercurio Volante of Don Carlos De Siguenza y Gongora*. Boards. Los Angeles, 1932. One of 665. In dust jacket. $75-$100.

LEONARD, William Ellery. See *Indian Summer*.

LEONARD, William Ellery. *Aesop and Hyssop*. Decorated gray cloth. Chicago, 1912. First edition. $40-$50.

LEONARD, William Ellery. *Glory of the Morning*. Brown printed wrappers. Madison, Wis., 1912. First edition. $50-$100.

LEONARD, William Ellery. *The Lynching Bee and Other Poems*. Green cloth. New York, 1920. First edition. In dust jacket. $40-$50.

LEONARD, William Ellery. *A Son of Earth: Collected Poems*. Portrait frontispiece. Cream boards, paper label. New York, 1928. First edition. One of 35 lettered copies, signed. $50-$100.

LEONARD, William Ellery. *Two Lives*. Cloth. New York, 1925. First published edition. One of 150 signed. $50-$75.

LEONARD, William Ellery (translator). *The Tale of Beowulf*. Illustrated by Rockwell Kent. Folio, cloth. New York, 1932. First edition. One of 950. $150-$250.

LEONARD, Zenas. *Narrative of the Adventures of Zenas Leonard*. 87 pp., wrappers. Clearfield, Pa., 1839. First edition. $10,000-$12,000. Also, rebound in three-quarters leather and marbled boards, $6,250 (A, 1968); in morocco, tears in 5 leaves repaired, $5,500 (A, 1966); in half morocco, title page repaired, $5,000 (A, 1964). Cleveland, 1904. Illustrated. Cloth. One of 520. $40-$60.

LEROUX, Gaston. *The Phantom of the Opera*. Illustrated in color. Cloth. Indianapolis, 1911. First edition. In dust jacket. $50-$75.

*LES ORNEMENS de la Mémoire, ou les Traits Brillans des Poètes François les Plus Célèbres*. Boards. Detroit, 1811. (By Pons Augustin Alletz.) First edition, first issue, with "k" instead of "x" in name of printer, A. Coxshaw. $500-$600.

LESSING, Doris. *The Grass Is Singing*. Cloth. London, (1950). First edition. In dust jacket. $50-$60.

LESSING, Doris. *Martha Quest*. Cloth. London, (1952). First edition. In dust jacket. $40-$50.

LESTER, John C., and Wilson, D. L. *Ku Klux Klan: Its Origin, Growth and Disbandment*. 117 pp., wrappers. Nashville, 1884. First edition. $150-$200.

*LETTER from the Secretary of State, Accompanying Certain Laws of the North-western and Indian Territories of the United States, etc.* 53 pp., sewed. (Washington), 1802. $125-$150.

*LETTER of Amerigo Vespucci (The), Describing His Four Voyages to the New World*. Hand-colored map and illustrations by Valenti Angelo. Vellum. San Francisco, 1926. Grabhorn Press. One of 250. Boxed. $150-$250. Also, $150 (A, 1973).

*LETTER of J.C. Frémont to the Editors of the National Intelligencer, Communicating Some*

*General Results of a Recent Winter Expedition Across the Rocky Mountains, etc.* 7 pp., binder's cloth. (Washington, 1854). $100-$200.

*LETTERS from the South.* 2 vols., printed boards. New York, 1817. (By James Kirke Paulding.) First edition. $100-$150.

*LETTERS of Edward, Prince of Wales, 1304-1305.* Edited by Hilda Johnstone. Frontispiece. Half leather. London, 1931. Roxburghe Club. $75-$125.

*LETTERS of Runnymede (The).* Cloth. London, 1836. (By Benjamin Disraeli.) First edition. $100-$150.

LETTS J.M. See *California Illustrated; A Pictorial View of California.*

LEVER, Charles. See Lorrequer, Harry. Also See *The Confessions of Harry Lorrequer.*

LEVER, Charles. *Davenport Dunn, or The Man of the Day.* Illustrated by H.K. Browne ("Phiz"). 20 parts in 21, wrappers. London, 1857-59. First edition. $100-$150.

LEVER, Charles. *The Knight of Gwynne: A Tale of the Time of the Union.* Frontispiece, title page and 38 plates by "Phiz." 20 parts in 19, wrappers. London, 1846-47. $150-$250.

LEVER, Charles. *Luttrell of Aaran.* Illustrated. 16 parts in 15, pictorial wrappers. London, 1863-65. First edition. $100-$150.

LEVER, Charles. *The O'Donoghue: A Tale of Ireland.* 13 parts in 11, wrappers. Dublin, 1845. First edition. $150-$250.

LEVER, Charles. *One of Them.* Illustrated by "Phiz." 15 parts in 14, pictorial wrappers. London, 1861. First edition. $150-$250.

LEVER, Charles. *Roland Cashel.* 20 parts in 19, wrappers. London, 1848-49. First edition. $150-$250. London, 1850. Cloth. First book edition. $40-$60.

LEVER, Charles. *Sir Brook Fossbrooke.* 3 vols., blue cloth. Edinburgh. 1866. First edition, first binding, with publisher's imprint on spine. $150-$200.

LEVERTOFF (LEVERTOV), Denise. *The Double Image.* Cloth. London, 1946. Cresset Press. First edition. In dust jacket. $150-$200. Author's first book.

LEVERTOV, Denise. *The Cold Spring and Other Poems.* Boards. (New York), 1968 (1969?). New Directions. First edition. One of 100 on Shagun paper, signed. In dust jacket. Another issue: One of 8 lettered (instead of numbered) and signed. Each issue: $60-$80.

LEVERTOV, Denise. *Here and Now.* Wrappers. San Francisco, (1957). $45.

LEVERTOV, Denise. *In the Night: A Story.* Wrappers. New York, 1968. Albondocani Press. One of 150 signed. $35-$50.

LEVERTOV, Denise. *Overland to the Islands.* Decorated wrappers. Highlands, N.C., 1958. First edition. One of 450. In dust jacket. $40-$50. Highlands, 1964. Deluxe edition. One of 50 signed. $75-$100.

LEVERTOV, Denise. *Three Poems.* Stiff wrappers. Mt. Horeb, Wis., 1968. Perishable Press. One of 250. $50-$75.

LEVERTOV, Denise. *With Eyes at the Back of Our Heads.* Cloth. (New York, 1959). New Directions. First edition. In dust jacket. $35-$50.

LEVY, Daniel. *Les Français en Californie.* 373 pp., wrappers. San Francisco, 1884. First edition. $150-$200. San Francisco, 1885. Second edition. $100-$125.

LEVY, Julien. *Surrealism.* 64 illustrations. Pictorial boards. New York, 1936. Black Sun Press. First edition. In dust jacket. $100-$150.

LEWIS, Alfred Henry. *The Apaches of New York.* Frontispiece and 10 plates. Red cloth. New York, (1912). First edition. In dust jacket. $40-$50.

LEWIS, Alfred Henry. *The Black Lion Inn.* Frontispiece and 15 plates by Frederic Remington and others. Tan cloth. New York, 1903. First edition, with "Published, May, 1903" on copyright page. In dust jacket. $100-$150. Lacking jacket, $35-$50.

LEWIS, Alfred Henry. *Richard Croker.* Frontispiece and 15 plates. Green cloth. New York, 1901. First edition, first issue, with transposed lines in last paragraph of page 26. $40-$50.

LEWIS, Alfred Henry. *Wolfville.* Frontispiece and 11 plates by Frederic Remington. Cloth. New York, (1897). First edition, first issue, with "Moore" in perfect type in line 18, page 19. $150-$200. Also, $70 (A, 1974); $120 (A, 1973). (Later printings so identified.) Author's first book.

LEWIS, Alfred Henry. *Wolfville Days.* Frontispiece by Frederic Remington. Red cloth. New York, (1902). First edition. $100-$150.

LEWIS, Elisha J. *The American Sportsman.* Illustrated. Cloth. Philadelphia, 1855. $75-$100. Philadelphia, 1857. $50-$60.

LEWIS, Elisha J. *Hints to Sportsmen.* Cloth. Philadelphia, 1851. First edition. $75-$100.

LEWIS, H. *Das Illustrirte Mississippithal.* Engraved title page, frontispiece, 78 other color plates (one folding). Boards. Düsseldorf, Germany, (1854-1857). First edition. $10,000-$15,000.

LEWIS, J.O. *The Aboriginal Port Folio.* 72 colored portraits. 3 advertisements leaves (constituting, with title leaf, all the text). 10 parts, wrappers. Philadelphia, 1836 (actually 1835). First edition. $15,000-$20,000. (A cash sale for $15,000 took place at the 1976 New York International Rare Book Fair.) Incomplete sets are infrequently offered, as, for example, a set of 53 of the plates catalogued late in 1977 by one dealer at $4,500. Howes says that "ordinary" copies have 72 plates, while some have 77 and a few 80.

LEWIS, John Frederick. *Sketches of Spain and Spanish Character.* Lithograph title page and 25 tinted plates. Folio, half morocco. London, (1836). First edition. $400-$600.

LEWIS, Matthew Gregory. See *Tales of Terror.*

LEWIS, Matthew Gregory. *The Isle of Devils.* Marbled boards and gray cloth. London, 1912. Second edition. One of 20 on large paper. $50-$75.

LEWIS, Matthew Gregory. *Journal of a West India Proprietor in the Island of Jamaica.* Cloth. London, 1834. First edition. $150-$250.

LEWIS, Matthew Gregory. *The Life and Correspondence of Matthew Gregory Lewis.* Illustrated. 2 vols., boards. London, 1839. First edition. $100-$150.

LEWIS, Matthew Gregory. *The Monk.* Engraved title page, 5 color plates. Morocco. London, 1826. $200 and up. Another edition: No place, no date (privately printed). Portrait. 2 vols., half morocco. One of 300. $100 and up. (A number of other reprintings have been made.) (Note: Since this handbook is limited to nineteenth- and twentieth-century books, the anonymous 3-volume 1796 London first edition of Lewis' Gothic tale is not included in the detailed listings. A Chicago dealer a few years ago catalogued the 3-volume set in contemporary calf at $650, while a London dealer offered another at $182. A spurious 1796 edition sometimes appears for sale. It bears a Waterford, Ireland, imprint, but, as noted in the A. Edward Newton sale catalogue, "As usual with copies bearing the above imprint the paper is watermarked 1818.")

LEWIS, Matthew Gregory. *Poems.* Boards, paper label, London, 1812. First edition. $100-$150.

LEWIS, Matthew Gregory. *Romantic Tales.* 4 vols., boards. London, 1808. First edition. $250-$350.

LEWIS, Matthew Gregory. *Rosario, or The Female Monk.* Half calf. Chicago, 1891. $50-$100.

LEWIS, Matthew Gregory. *Tales of Wonder*. 2 vols., boards. London, 1801. First edition. $150-$250. Another issue: 2 vols. in one, on large paper. $200-$300. Rebound, $100 and up. (Note: Comparable values also apply to the Dublin 2-volume edition of 1801.)

LEWIS, Matthew Gregory (translator). *The Bravo of Venice*. (From the German of J.D. Zschokke.) Boards. London, 1805. First edition. $200-$300.

LEWIS, Meriwether, and Clark, William. *History of the Expedition Under the Command of Captains Lewis and Clark, etc.* Prepared for the Press by Paul Allen (actually by Nicholas Biddle). Folding map and 5 charts. 2 vols., printed boards. Philadelphia, 1814. First edition. $10,000 (A, 1973)—a badly worn copy; $35,000 (A, 1967)—the exceptionally fine Thomas Winthrop Streeter copy. Previously the highest auction price recorded for this book was $5,200 (1963), earlier prices having ranged from $1,000 to $3,500 (1966) for copies in original binding. Copies rebound in leather: $4,000-$5,000, possibly more. London, 1814. First English edition. (See Lewis and Clark entry under *Travels to the Source of the Missouri River.*) New York, 1842. Folding map. 2 vols., calf. Abridged edition. $200 and up. New York, 1893. Edited by E. Coues. Map. 4 vols., boards and cloth. $200-$250. Chicago, 1902. Edited by James K. Hosmer. 2 vols., cloth. $50-$75. Chicago, 1905. Edited by Hosmer. Cloth. $40-$60.

LEWIS, Meriwether, and Clark, William. *Original Journals of the Lewis and Clark Expedition, 1804-1806*. Edited by Reuben Gold Thwaites. 8 vols., cloth, including atlas of maps and plates. New York, 1904-05. First edition. $600-$800. Another issue: 7 vols. in 14, plus atlas, boards. One of 50 sets on Japan paper. $5,500 (A, 1977). Another issue: One of 200 sets on Van Gelder paper. $800 (A, 1977). New York, 1959. 8 vols., cloth. Facsimile of 1904-05 edition. $150-$200. Another issue: One of 15. $400-$500. Also, $250 (A, 1977). New York, 1962. 2 vols. Limited Editions Club. $100-$120.

LEWIS, Meriwether, and Clark, William. *Travels to the Source of the Missouri River and Across the American Continent to the Pacific Ocean*. Edited by Thomas Rees. Folding map and 5 charts. Boards and calf. London, 1814. First English edition of *History of the Expedition, etc.* $800-$1,200. London, 1815. 6 maps. 3 vols., boards and calf. Second English edition. $300-$450.

LEWIS, Oscar. *Hearn and His Biographers*. Facsimiles. Boards and cloth in portfolio. San Francisco, 1930. Westgate Press (Grabhorn printing). First edition. One of 350. $75-$150.

LEWIS, Oscar. *The Origin of the Celebrated Jumping Frog of Calaveras County*. Decorations by Valenti Angelo. Boards. San Francisco, 1931. Grabhorn Press. One of 250. $125-$175.

LEWIS, Sinclair. See Graham, Tom .

LEWIS, Sinclair. *Arrowsmith*. Blue boards and buckram. New York, (1925). First edition. One of 500 signed. In glassine dust jacket. Boxed. $200-$250. First trade edition: Cloth. Marked "Second printing" (first trade edition) on copyright page. In dust jacket. $30-$40

LEWIS, Sinclair. *Babbitt*. Blue cloth. New York, (1922). First edition, first state, with "Purdy" for "Lyte" in line 4, page 49. In dust jacket. $80-$100. London, no date. Purple cloth. First English edition. In dust jacket. $35-$50.

LEWIS, Sinclair. *Cheap and Contented Labor*. Illustrated. 32 pp., pictorial blue wrappers. (New York), 1929. First edition, first state, without quotation marks in front of "Dodsworth" on title page. $40-$60. Later, error corrected. $35-$45.

LEWIS, Sinclair. *Elmer Gantry*. Blue cloth. New York, (1927). First edition, first binding (20,000 copies) with "G" on spine resembling "C" (reading "Elmer Cantry"). In dust jacket. $60-$85. Later binding, corrected. $25-$30.

LEWIS, Sinclair. *Free Air*. Decorated blue cloth. New York, 1919. First edition. In dust jacket. $50-$75.

LEWIS, Sinclair. *The Innocents*. Cloth. New York, (1917). First edition, with "F-R" on copyright page. In dust jacket. $150-$200.

LEWIS, Sinclair. *The Job*. Green cloth. New York, (1917). First edition, with "B-P" on copyright page. In dust jacket. $50-$75.

LEWIS, Sinclair. *Keep Out of the Kitchen*. Printed boards. (New York), 1929. First edition. (Advertising promotion piece for the story in Cosmopolitan magazine.) $650 (A, 1977). (Note: A California dealer catalogued a copy in 1975 at $75.)

LEWIS, Sinclair. *Kingsblood Royal*. Reddish-brown buckram. New York, (1947). First edition. One of 1,050 signed. Boxed. $50-$60.

LEWIS, Sinclair. *Launcelot*. 4 pp., decorated wrappers. (New York, 1932.) First edition in book form. One of 100. $100 and up. (First published in *The Yale Literary Review*.)

LEWIS, Sinclair. *Main Street*. Dark blue cloth. New York, 1920. First edition, first issue, with perfect folio on page 54. In dust jacket. $150-$200. New York, 1937. Limited Editions Club. Grant Wood illustrations. Cloth. Boxed. $100-$125.

LEWIS, Sinclair. *The Man Who Knew Coolidge*. Blue cloth. New York, (1928). First edition. In dust jacket. $40-$50.

LEWIS, Sinclair. *Our Mr. Wrenn*. Cloth. New York, 1914. First edition, with "M-N" on copyright page. In dust jacket. $150-$200. Also, $120 (A, 1971). Another issue: "Advance Copy—Not Published" stamped on title page. $175. Author's second book and the first under his own name. (For actual first book, see entry under Graham, Tom.)

LEWIS, Sinclair. *The Trail of the Hawk*. Blue cloth. New York, (1915). First edition, with "H-P" on copyright page. In dust jacket. $75-$125. Advance copy: Red cloth wrappers, printed spine label. $700 (A, 1977).

LEWIS, W.S., and Phillips, P.C. (editors). *The Journal of John Work*. Map. Illustrations. Cloth. Cleveland, 1923. First edition. $100-$135.

LEWIS, Wyndham. *The Apes of God*. Illustrated by the author. Cream-colored buckram. London, 1930. First edition. One of 750 signed. In dust jacket. $150-$175. New York, 1932. Cloth. First edition. In dust jacket. $25-$35.

LEWIS, Wyndham. *The Art of Being Ruled*. Cloth. London, 1926. First edition. In dust jacket. $75-$100.

LEWIS, Wyndham. *Blasting and Bombardiering: Autobiography 1914-1926*. Illustrated. Cloth. London, 1937. First edition. In dust jacket. $60-$80.

LEWIS, Wyndham. *The Caliph's Design*. Marbled stiff wrappers. London, 1919. The Egoist, Ltd. First edition. $100-$125.

LEWIS, Wyndham. *The Childermass: Section I*. (All published.) Yellow buckram. London, 1928. First edition. One of 225 signed. In dust jacket. $200-$300. Trade edition: Cloth. In dust jacket. $60-$80.

LEWIS, Wyndham. *The Diabolical Principle and The Dithyrambic Spectator*. Cloth. London, 1931. First edition. In dust jacket. $60-$80.

LEWIS, Wyndham. *Doom of Youth*. Cloth. London, 1932. First edition (withdrawn). In dust jacket. $75-$100.

LEWIS, Wyndham. *The Enemy*. Nos. 1-3. (All published). Illustrated. Pictorial wrappers. London, 1927-29. $100-$150.

LEWIS, Wyndham. *Enemy Pamphlets: No. 1*. Wrappers. London, (1930). $50-$75.

LEWIS, Wyndham. *The Enemy of the Stars*. Illustrated by the author. Pictorial boards and cloth. London, 1932. First edition. In dust jacket. $75-$100.

LEWIS, Wyndham. *Hitler*. Cloth. London, 1931. First edition. $125-$200.

LEWIS, Wyndham. *The Ideal Giant*. Boards and cloth. London, (1917). First edition. One of 50. $200-$300. Author's first written work, a collection of stories.

LEWIS, Wyndham. *Left Wings Over Europe, or, How to Make a War About Nothing.* Cloth. London, 1936. First edition. In dust jacket. $50-$75.

LEWIS, Wyndham. *[16 Illustrations for "Timon of Athens.]* London, (1914). Limited edition (Plates loose in folder). $750-$1,000. Author's first book.

LEWIS, Wyndham. *Tarr.* Cloth. London, 1918. The Egoist, Ltd. First edition. In dust jacket. $100-$150.

LEWIS, Wyndham. *Thirty Personalities and A Self-Portrait.* 31 plates, loose in buckram and board portfolio. London, 1932. First edition. One of 200 signed. $200-$250.

LEWIS, Wyndham. *Time and Western Man.* Cloth. London, 1927. First edition. In dust jacket. $75-$100.

LEWIS, Wyndham. *The Tyro.* Nos. 1 and 2. (All published.) Illustrated. Wrappers. London, 1921-22. $200-$250.

LEWIS, Wyndham. *The Wild Body: A Soldier of Humour and Other Stories.* Decorated boards, cloth spine. London, 1927. First edition. One of 79 signed. In dust jacket. $150-$200.

*LEY y Reglamento Aprobado de la Junta Directiva y Económica del Fondo Piadoso de Californias.* 20 pp., calf. Mexico, 1833. $250 and up.

LHOMOND, M. *Elements of French Grammar.* Cloth, paper label. Portland (Brunswick), Me., 1830. (Translated anonymously by Henry Wadsworth Longfellow; Longfellow's first book.) First edition. The only copy noted for sale in many years was a repaired copy, rebound in morocco, sold at auction in 1960 for $200.

LHOMOND, M. *French Exercises.* Purple cloth, paper label. Portland (Brunswick), Me., 1830. (Translated anonymously by Henry Wadsworth Longfellow.) First edition. Rebound in morocco, $100 (A, 1960). (Note: Johnson says that this book and Lhomond's *Elements of French Grammar* were bound as one volume later in 1830 and that the combined book edition of 1831 was "the first book to bear Longfellow's name on the title page.")

*LIBER Amoris: or, The New Pygmalion.* Pink boards, green cloth spine, paper label on side. London, 1823. (By William Hazlitt.) First edition. $100 and up. London, 1894. Illustrated. Buckram. One of 500. $50-$75.

*LIBER Scriptorum: The First Book of the Authors Club.* Full morocco. New York, 1893. First edition. One of 251 signed by contributors. $300-$350. *Liber Scriptorum: The Second Book, etc.* New York, 1921. Morocco. One of 251. $100-$150.

LIEBLING, A.J. *Back Where I Came From.* Orange-tan cloth. New York, (1938). First edition. In dust jacket. $50-$75. Author's first book.

LIEBLING, A.J. *Chicago: The Second City.* Illustrated by Steinberg. Pictorial boards. New York, 1952. First edition. In dust jacket. $30-$40.

LIEBLING, A.J. *The Telephone Booth Indian.* Gray cloth. Garden City, 1942. First edition. In dust jacket. $75-$100.

*LIFE.* (Magazine.) Vol. 1, No. 1. November 23, 1936. First issue of the modern Life. $75-$100. (We have tried in general to rule out magazines of general interest in this book, but so many inquiries have been received that the first issue of the modern picture magazine Life is being included here as an exception.)

*LIFE Among the Indians.* Woodcut plates. 80 pp., colored pictorial wrappers. (New Haven, about 1870.) (By Healy & Bigelow.) Kickapoo Indian medicine promotion pamphlet. $100 and up. (Also, see *Life and Scenes, etc.*)

*LIFE and Adventures of Broncho John: His Second Trip up the Trail, by Himself.* (Cover title.) Illustrated. 32 pp., pictorial wrappers. (Valparaiso, Ind., 1908.) (By John H. Sullivan.) $125-$150.

*LIFE and Adventures of Calamity Jane.* By Herself. Portrait. 8 pp., wrappers. Livingston, Mont., (1896). First edition. $300-$400.

*LIFE and Adventures of Charles Anderson Chester, the Notorious Leader of the Phila-delphia "Killers."* Wrappers. Philadelphia, 1850. First edition. $75-$100.

*LIFE and Adventures of John Nicol, Mariner (The).* Illustrated by Gordon Grant. White canvas, leather labels. New York, 1936. Limited edition. With an original signed drawing by Grant. $50-$75. London, (1937). Cloth. $50-$60.

*LIFE and Adventures (The) of Joseph T. Hare, the Bold Robber and Highwayman.* 16 engravings. Pictorial wrappers. New York, 1847. (By H.R. Howard.) First edition. $100-$150.

*LIFE and Adventures of Robert Voorhis, the Hermit of Massachusetts.* Portrait. Wrappers. Providence, 1829. First edition, first issue, with "Voorhis" in the title. $275-$350.

*LIFE, and Most Surprising Adventures of Robinson Crusoe of York, Mariner, etc. (The).* Boards. Philadelphia, 1803. (By Daniel Defoe.) $150-$200. (Also, see Defoe entries.)

*LIFE and Scenes Among the Kickapoo Indians: Their Manners, Habits and Customs.* Portrait, other illustrations. 175 pp., printed wrappers. New Haven, (1839). $100-$125. Also, see *Life Among the Indians.)*

*LIFE and Travels of Josiah Mooso (The).* Portrait. Cloth. Winfield, Kan., 1888. First edition. $150-$200.

*LIFE and Writings of Maj. Jack Downing of Downingville (The), Away Down East in the State of Maine.* Boards. Boston, 1833. (By Seba Smith.) First edition. $150-$200.

*LIFE for a Life (A).* By the Author of "John Halifax, Gentleman," etc. 3 vols., cloth. London, 1859. (By Dinah Maria Mulock.) First edition. $200-$250.

*LIFE in California, etc.* By an American, 9 plates. Cloth, New York, 1846. (By Alfred Robinson.) First edition. $300-$400. San Francisco, 1897. Cloth. $75-$100. San Francisco, 1925. Cloth. One of 250. $75-$100.

*LIFE in a Man-of-War, etc.* By a Fore-Top-Man. Brown cloth. Philadelphia, 1841. (By Henry J. Mercier.) First edition. $100-$150.

*LIFE in the New World; or Sketches of American Society.* Cloth. New York, (1844). (By Karl Postl.) First edition. $100-$125.

*LIFE of Joaquin Murieta the Brigand Chief of California (The).* 7 full-page plates. Pictorial wrappers (dated 1861). San Francisco. 1859. (By John R. Ridge.) Second ("spurious") edition. $2,500-$3,000. Also, $1,400 (A, 1968).

*LIFE of Major-General Harrison (The).* Portrait, plates. Printed boards. Philadelphia, 1840. First edition. $75-$100.

*LIFE of MA-KA-TAI-ME-SHE-KIA-KIAK or Black Hawk.* Tan boards and cloth. Cincinnati, 1833. (J. B. Patterson, editor.) First edition. $200-$250. Boston, 1834. Pale-green boards. $75-$100. Oquawka, Ill., 1882. Cloth. $75-$100.

*LIFE of Saint David (The).* Edited by Ernest Rhys. Colored wood engravings. Red morocco. Newtown, Wales, 1927. Gregynog Press. One of 150. $600-$800. Another issue: One of 25 specially bound by George Fisher. $1,200-$1,500.

*LIFE of Saint George (The).* Engraved frontispiece and title page by I. de B. Lockyer. Marbled boards. London, no date (modern). One of 21 on vellum. $100 and up.

*LIFE of Stonewall Jackson (The).* By a Virginian. Printed wrappers. Richmond, 1863. (By John Esten Cooke.) First edition, with Ayres & Wade imprint. $100-$175.

*LIFE, Speeches and Public Services of Abram [sic] Lincoln, Together with a Sketch of the Life of Hannibal Hamlin (The).* Portrait. 117 pp., pictorial wrappers. New York, 1860. Wigwam Edition. $150 and up.

LIGHTHALL, William D. (editor). *Songs of the Great Dominion.* Cloth. London, 1889. (By Bliss Carman.) First edition. $50-$60.

*LILY and the Totem (The); or, the Huguenots in Florida.* Cloth. New York, 1850. (By William Gilmore Simms.) First edition. $100-$150.

LIN, Frank. *What Dreams May Come.* Cloth, or wrappers. Chicago, (1888). (By Gertrude Atherton.) First edition. Wrappers: $200-$300. Also, $140 (A, 1975). Cloth: $75-$100. London, 1889. First English edition. $50. Author's first book.

LINCOLN, Abraham. *The Life and Public Services of General Zachary Taylor.* Marbled boards. Boston, 1922. First edition. One of 435. $75-$100.

LINCOLN, Abraham, and Douglas, Stephen A. *Political Debates.* Brown rippled, or tan, cloth. Columbus, Ohio, 1860. First edition, first issue, with no ads, no rule on copyright page, and with a "2" at foot of page 17. $150 and up. (Note: Second and later editions of this work differ in various minor details, the principal distinguishing point being the "2" at page 13, instead of 17. For a detailed discussion, see Ernest J. Wessen's pamphlet, *Debates of Lincoln and Douglas: A Bibliographical Discussion,* New York, 1946.)

LINCOLN, Abraham, and Everett, Edward. *The Gettysburg Solemnities: Dedication of the National Cemetery at Gettysburg, Pennsylvania, November 19, 1863, etc.* (Cover title.) 16 pp., printed pamphlet. Wahington, (1863). First known printing in pamphlet form of the Gettysburg Address. $15,000 (A, 1967). Also, see Everett, Edward.

LINCOLN, Mrs. D. A. *Frozen Dainties.* 32·pp., wrappers. Nashua, N.H., 1889. First edition. $75-$100.

LINCOLN, Mrs. D. A. *Mrs. Lincoln's Boston Cook Book.* Marbled boards, cloth spine and corners. Boston, 1884. First edition. $850-$1,250.

LINCOLN, Joe. *Cape Cod Ballads and Other Verse.* Drawings by E. W. Kemble. Decorated yellow cloth. Trenton, N.J., 1902. (By Joseph C. Lincoln.) First edition. $75-$100. In dust jacket. Author's first book.

LINCOLN, Joseph C. *Cape Cod Yesterdays.* 12 mounted plates. Cloth. Boston, 1935. Large paper Chatham edition. One of 1,075 signed. $75-$100.

LINCOLN, Joseph C. *Cap'n Eri.* Cloth. New York, 1904. First edition. $50-$75.

LINDBERGH, Charles A. *The Spirit of St. Louis.* Cloth. New York, 1953. First edition. Limited and signed "Presentation Edition." In dust jacket. $50-$75. Trade edition: In dust jacket. $20-$25.

LINDBERGH, Charles A. *"We": The Famous Flier's Own Story of His Life and His Trans-Atlantic Flight.* Illustrated. Half vellum. New York, 1927. Author's autograph edition. One of 1,000 signed. Boxed. $125-$300. Trade edition: Blue cloth. In dust jacket. $20-$25.

LINDLEY, John. *Pomologia Britannica; or Figures and Descriptions of the Most Important Varieties of Fruit Cultivated in Great Britain.* 152 colored plates. 3 vols., half brown morocco. London, 1841. First edition. $2,000-$2,500.

LINDLEY, John. *Rosarum Monographia: Or, a Botanical History of Roses.* One plain and 18 colored plates. Boards. London, 1820. First edition. $600-$1,000. London, 1830. Second edition. $500-$750.

LINDSAY, Jack. See Graves, Robert, and Lindsay, Jack.

LINDSAY, Jack. *Storm at Sea.* Illustrated. Half morocco. London, 1935. One of 250 signed. $75-$100.

LINDSAY, Norman. *Etchings.* Cloth. London, 1927. One of 129. $250-$400. Another issue: Buckram, vellum spine. One of 31 signed, with a signed etching by Lindsay. $500-$750.

LINDSAY, Norman. *A Homage to Sappho.* Illustrated by Jack Lindsay. Vellum. London, 1928. Fanfrolico Press. One of 70, signed. $350-$450.

LINDSAY, Vachel. *Collected Poems*. Half cloth. New York, 1923. First edition. One of 400 signed. $100-$150. Trade edition: Cloth. In dust jacket. $30-$50. New York, 1925. Illustrated by Lindsay. Pictorial boards. First illustrated edition. One of 350, signed. Boxed $75-$100. Trade edition: Blue cloth. In dust jacket. $40-$50.

LINDSAY, Vachel. *The Congo and Other Poems*. Pictorial cloth. New York, 1914. First edition. In dust jacket. $75-$125.

LINDSAY, Vachel. *General William Booth Enters into Heaven and Other Poems*. Red cloth. New York, 1913. First edition. In dust jacket. $75-$100. Author's first book.

LINDSAY, Vachel. *The Golden Book of Springfield*. Boards. New York, 1920. First edition. In dust jacket. $50-$75.

LINDSAY, Vachel. *The Golden Whales of California, and Other Rhymes in the American Language*. Reddish-brown decorated cloth. New York, 1920. First edition. In dust jacket. $50-$75.

LINDSAY, Vachel. *A Handy Guide for Beggars*. Cloth. New York, 1916. First edition. In dust jacket. $40-$60.

LINDSAY, Vachel. *A Memorial of Lincoln Called The Heroes of Time*. 12 pp., stitched wrappers. (Springfield, Ill.), 1910. First edition. $200-$300.

LINDSAY, Vachel. *Proclamation of the Gospel of Beauty*. Broadside. (Springfield, 1912.) First edition. $200-$300.

LINDSAY, Vachel. *Rhymes To Be Traded For Bread*. 12 pp., self-wrappers. (Springfield, 1912.) $250-$350.

LINDSAY, Vachel. *The Soul of the City Receives the Gift of the Holy Spirit*. Illustrated by the author. Wrappers. (Springfield, 1913.) First edition. $200-$350.

LINDSAY, Vachel. *The Tramp's Excuse and Other Poems*. (Cover title.) Decorations by the author. Printed wrappers with cord tie. (Springfield, 1909.) First edition. $1,000-$1,200. (Note: Both Merle Johnson and the auction records incorrectly—and persistently—list the place of publication as Springfield, Ohio. It is Springfield, Ill.)

LINDSAY, Vachel. *The Wedding of the Rose and the Lotus*. Illustrated stiff printed leaflet poem. 3 pp. (Springfield, 1912.) First edition. $200-$400.

LINDSAY, William S. *History of Merchant Shipping and Ancient Commerce*. 3 maps, 3 plates, numerous other illustrations. 4 vols., cloth. London, 1874-76. $250-$350.

LINDSEY, Charles. *The Prairies of the Western States*. 100 pp., wrappers. Toronto, 1860. First edition. $200-$250.

LINDSLEY, John Berrien. *The Military Annals of Tennessee*. 2 plates. Cloth. Nashville, 1886. First edition. $100-$150.

*LINES on Leaving the Bedford St. Schoolhouse*. 4 pp., plain wrappers. (Boston, 1880.) (By George Santayana.) First edition. $600-$800. Author's first published work.

LINFORTH, James (editor). *Route from Liverpool to Great Salt Valley*. Folding map and 30 full-page plates. 120 pp., plus "Notice to Subscribers." 15 paperbound parts. Liverpool, July, 1854, to September, 1855. $5,000 and up. Liverpool, 1855. Boards. First edition in book form. With map partly colored by hand. $600-$850.

*LINGUAL Exercises for Advanced Vocabularians*. By the Author of "Recreations." Cloth. Cambridge, 1925. (By Siegfried Sassoon.) First edition. One of 90. $300-$400.

LINKLATER, Eric. *Position at Noon*. Beige buckram. London, (1958). First edition. One of 250 signed. In dust jacket. $75-$100.

LINN, John Blair (1777-1804). *Valerian: A Narrative Poem*. Portrait and silhouette. Boards. Philadelphia, 1805. First edition. $100 and up. (Note: Contains Charles Brockden Brown's sketch of Linn, his brother-in-law.)

LINN, John Blair (1831-1899). *Annals of Buffalo Valley, Pennsylvania.* Illustrated. Cloth. Harrisburg, 1877. First edition. $50-$75.

LINN, John J. *Reminiscences of Fifty Years in Texas.* Illustrated. Cloth. New York, 1883. First edition, with errata slip. $100-$150.

LINSLEY, Daniel C. *Morgan Horses.* Illustrated. Cloth. New York, 1857. First edition. $85-$125. New York, 1860. Cloth. $35-$50.

LINTON, William James. *The Masters of Wood-Engraving.* 196 plates (165 mounted), colored frontispiece. Cloth. London, 1889. First edition. One of 600, signed. $300-$500. New Haven, 1889. First American edition. One of 500. $200-$250. Another issue: One of 100, signed. $300-$500.

*LIONEL Lincoln: or, The Leaguer of Boston.* By the Author of *The Pioneers.* 2 vols., drab boards, paper labels. New York, 1825-1824. (By James Fenimore Cooper.) First edition. (Vol. 2 is dated 1824.) $250-$400.

LIPSCOMB, George. *The History and Antiquities of the County of Buckingham.* Numerous maps, plates and woodcuts. 4 vols., half leather. London, 1847. First edition. $500-$600. Another issue: Large paper. $750 and up.

L'ISLE-ADAM, Villiers de. *Axel.* Translated by H.P.R. Finberg. Preface by W.B. Yeats. Illustrated by T. Sturge Moore. White cloth. London, 1925. One of 500. $80-$100.

LITCH, Josiah. *The Probability of the Second Coming of Christ About A.D. 1843.* Cloth. Boston, 1838. First edition. $100.

LITTELL, William. *Festoons of Fancy.* Mottled calf. Louisville, Ky., 1814. First edition. $2,000 (A,1967).

LITTELL, William. *Principles of Law & Equity, etc.* 101 pp., plus errata page, half leather. (Frankfort, Ky.?), 1808. First edition, with errata slip. $100 and up.

LITTLE, James A. *Biographical Sketch of Feramorz Little.* Morocco. Salt Lake City, 1890. First edition. $50-$60.

LITTLE, James A. *From Kirtland to Salt Lake City.* Illustrated. Cloth. Salt Lake City, 1890. First edition. $75-$100.

LITTLE, James A. *Jacob Hamblin: A Narrative of Personal Experiences as a Frontiersman, Missionary to the Indians, and Explorer.* Cloth. Salt Lake City, 1881. First edition. $50-$60.

LITTLE, James A. *What I Saw on the Old Santa Fe Trail.* Frontispiece. 127 pp., printed wrappers. Plainfield, Ind., (1904). First edition. $100-$150.

*LITTLE Lucy: or, The Careless Child Reformed.* 33 pp., printed wrappers. Cambridge, Mass., 1820. First edition. $65.

LITTLEHEART, Oleta. *The Lure of the Indian Country.* Moccasin-skin binding. Sulphur, Okla., 1908. First edition. Signed presentation copy, $40.

*LIVING Issue (A).* 37 pp., wrappers. (Suppressed portion of Dodge's *Our Wild Indians.*) Washington, 1882. (By Richard Irving Dodge.) $200-$250.

LIVINGSTON, Edward. *An Answer to Mr. Jefferson's Justification of His Conduct in the Case of the New-Orleans Batture.* 2 folding maps. Half leather. Philadelphia, 1813. First edition. $2,500. Also, $1,300 (A, 1967).

LIVINGSTON, Luther S. *Franklin and His Press at Passy.* Illustrated. Boards and cloth. New York, 1914. Grolier Club. First edition. One of 300. $150-250.

*LIVRE d'Esther (Le).* Illustrated in color by Arthur Szyk. Wrappers. Paris, (1925). One of 175 on Japan vellum, with an extra set of plates in black and white. In slipcase. $200. One of 30, with extra plates and an original watercolor, signed and dated by Szyk. $300-$350. (Note: Usually in the auction records under "Bible" entries.)

LIZARS, John. *A System of Anatomical Plates of the Body, with Descriptions and Observations.* Text volume, plus folio atlas of 101 colored plates. Leather. Edinburgh, (1822-26). First edition. $400-$600.

LLEWELLYN, Richard. *How Green Was My Valley.* Yellow buckram, leather label. London, (1939). First edition. One of 200 signed. In slipcase. $50-$75.

LLOYD, James T. *Steamboat Directory, and Disasters on the Western Waters.* Cloth. Cincinnati, 1856. First edition, first issue, with 326 pp. $150-$250. (Second issue has 331 pp.; valued a little less by purists.)

LLOYD, Robert. *The Actor.* With an Essay by Edmund Blunden. Illustrated. Boards and vellum. London, 1926. One of 60 on vellum, signed by Blunden. $75-$100.

*LOAN Exhibition of 18th and Early 19th Century Furniture, Glass, etc.* Cloth. New York, 1929. (Girl Scouts' Loan Exhibition catalogue.) $200-$300. Also, $100 (A, 1975); $175 (A,1974).

LOCKWOOD, Frank C. *The Apache Indians.* Cloth. New York, 1938. First edition. In dust jacket. $50-$60.

LOCKWOOD, Frank C. *Arizona Characters.* Illustrated. Pictorial cloth. Los Angeles, 1928. First edition. In dust jacket. $60-$75.

LOCKWOOD, Frank C. *Pioneer Days in Arizona.* Illustrated. Cloth. New York, 1932. First edition. In dust jacket. $50-$75.

LOCKWOOD, Luke Vincent. *The Pendleton Collection.* 102 full-page plates. Morocco. Providence, 1904. One of 160 on Japan vellum, signed. $200-$300, possibly more.

LOFTING, Hugh. *Doctor Dolittle's Post Office.* Cloth. New York, (1923). First edition. In dust jacket. $25-$35.

LOFTING, Hugh. *The Story of Doctor Dolittle.* Illustrated by the author. Decorated orange-colored cloth, pictorial paper label. New York, 1920. First American edition. In dust jacket. $100-$150.

*LOG of the Cruise of Schooner Julius Webb, Which Sailed from Norwich, Ct., on July 23, 1858, etc.* 40 pp., wrappers. Worcester, Mass., 1858. (By A.B.R. Sprague.) First edition. $100 and up.

LOGUE, Christopher. *The Girls.* Half leather. London, 1969. One of 26, signed. $85.

LOMAS, Thomas J. *Recollections of a Busy Life.* Portraits. Folded sheets, unbound. (Cresco, Iowa, 1923.) First edition. $100 and up. (Copies in binding are worth roughly the same.)

LONDON, Charmian. *The Book of Jack London.* Illustrated. 2 vols., blue cloth. London, 1921. First edition. In dust jackets. $50-$75. New York, 1921. 2 vols., cloth. First American edition. In dust jackets. $50-$75.

LONDON, Jack. See *The Kempton-Wace Letters.*

LONDON, Jack. *The Abysmal Brute.* Frontispiece. Olive-green cloth, stamped in yellow and dark green. New York, 1913. First edition, first binding, first issue, with "Published, May, 1913" on copyright page. In dust jacket. $150-$200. Lacking jacket, $100-$125. Later, binding stamped in black. In dust jacket. $75-$100. Toronto, 1913. First Canadian edition. In dust jacket. $200-$250. (Unrecorded in the bibliographies of London.)

LONDON, Jack. *The Acorn Planter.* Red cloth. New York, 1916. First edition. In dust jacket. $200 and up. Lacking jacket, $100-$150, possibly more.

LONDON, Jack. *Adventure.* Dark-blue or red pictorial cloth. New York, 1911. First edition. In dust jacket. $100-$150. Lacking jacket, $35-$50. (Note: Red cloth is said to be scarcer and may be worth a premium.)

LONDON, Jack. *Before Adam.* Illustrated by Charles Livingston Bull. Tan pictorial buckram. New York, 1907. First edition. In dust jacket. $200 and up. Lacking jacket, $40-$50.

LONDON, Jack. *Burning Daylight.* Frontispiece. Blue and yellow pictorial cloth. New York, 1910. First edition, first printing, with blank leaf after ads. In dust jacket. $100-$150. Lacking jacket, $40-$60.

LONDON, Jack. *The Call of the Wild.* Illustrated by Philip R. Goodwin and Charles Livingston Bull. Green pictorial cloth. New York, 1903. First edition, first issue, with vertically ribbed cloth. In dust jacket. $200-$250. Lacking jacket, $100-$150. London, 1903. Decorated blue cloth. First English edition. In dust jacket. $150-$200. New York, 1960. Limited Editions Club. Cloth. Boxed. $80-$100.

LONDON, Jack. *Children of the Frost.* Illustrated by Raphael M. Bray. Green pictorial cloth. New York, 1902. First edition. In dust jacket. $100-$125. Lacking jacket, $50-$75.

LONDON, Jack. *The Cruise of the Dazzler.* Frontispiece. Cream-colored cloth. New York, 1902. First edition, first issue, with "Published October, 1902" on copyright page. In dust jacket. $500-$750. Lacking jacket, $250-$400.

LONDON, Jack. *The Cruise of the Snark.* Frontispiece in color. Blue cloth, colored print on front cover. New York, 1911. First edition. In dust jacket. $150-$200. Lacking jacket, $50-$75.

LONDON, Jack. *A Daughter of the Snows.* Illustrated in color by F.C. Yohn. Red pictorial cloth. Philadelphia, 1902. First edition. In dust jacket. $150-$200. Lacking jacket, $75-$85. London, 1904. Red cloth. First English edition. Lacking jacket, $25.

LONDON, Jack. *The Dream of Debs.* Pictorial wrappers. Chicago, no date (1912?) First edition, first issue, with ad for Gustavus Myers book on back cover. $100-$150. Second (?) issue, ad headed "Books by Jack London" on back. $50-$60. Later, back cover headed "Study Socialism." $25-$35.

LONDON, Jack. *The Faith of Men and Other Stories.* Cloth. New York, 1904. First edition. In dust jacket. $100-$150. Lacking jacket, $50-$75.

LONDON, Jack. *The God of His Father and Other Stories.* Dark-blue decorated cloth. New York, 1901. First edition. In dust jacket. $150-$200. Lacking jacket, $75-$100.

LONDON, Jack. *Hearts of Three.* Cloth. New York, 1920. First American edition. In dust jacket. $150-$200. Lacking jacket, $60-$80.

LONDON, Jack. *The House of Pride.* Pictorial light-green cloth. New York, 1912. First edition. In dust jacket. $150-$200. Lacking jacket, $50-$75.

LONDON, Jack. *The Human Drift.* Frontispiece portrait of London. Reddish-brown cloth. New York, 1917. First edition. In dust jacket. $300-$350. Lacking jacket. $225 (in a 1978 catalogue).

LONDON, Jack. *The Iron Heel.* Blue pictorial cloth. New York, 1908. First edition. In dust jacket. $150-$200. Lacking jacket, $75-$100. Another issue: New York, (1908). Wilshire imprint. In dust jacket. $100-$150. Lacking jacket, $50-$75.

LONDON, Jack. *The Jacket.* Cloth. London, (1915). First edition, with "Published 1915" on back of title page. In dust jacket. $150-$200. (See *The Star Rover* for first American edition.)

LONDON, Jack. *John Barleycorn.* Illustrated by H. I. Dunn. Dark-green (black) cloth. New York, 1913. First edition, first printing, with one blank leaf following page 243. In dust jacket. $100-$150. Lacking jacket, $50-$65. Later, with no blank after page 243, lacking jacket, rubbed, $30 (in 1977 catalogue).

LONDON, Jack. *The Little Lady of the Big House.* Frontispiece in color. Blue decorated cloth. New York, 1916. First edition. In dust jacket. $100-$150. Lacking jacket, $45-$75.

LONDON, Jack. *Love of Life.* Cloth. New York, 1907. First edition. In dust jacket. $125-$175. Lacking jacket, $50-$100.

LONDON, Jack. *Martin Eden.* Frontispiece. Dark-blue cloth. New York, 1909. First published edition. In dust jacket. $75-$100. Lacking jacket, $75-$85.

LONDON, Jack. *Michael, Brother of Jerry.* Red cloth. New York, 1917. First edition. In dust jacket. $100-$150. Lacking jacket, $50-$75.

LONDON, Jack. *The Mutiny of the Elsinore.* Cloth. New York, 1914. First edition. In dust jacket. $125-$150. Lacking jacket, $50-$75.

LONDON, Jack. *On the Makaloa Mat.* Decorated light-blue cloth. New York, 1919. First edition. In dust jacket. $100-$150. Lacking jacket, $40-$60.

LONDON, Jack. *Revolution.* Printed wrappers. Chicago, (1909). First edition. $150 and up. (Note: This pamphlet occurs in two states: Blanck's A-state, with ad "A Socialist Success," and B-state, with ad "Pocket Library of Socialism." Priority uncertain.)

LONDON, Jack. *Revolution and Other Essays.* Dark-blue or light-tan cloth. New York, 1910. First edition. In dust jacket. $200-$225. Lacking jacket, $75-$125.

LONDON, Jack. *The Road.* Frontispiece. Gray cloth. New York, 1907. First edition. In dust jacket. $150-$200. Lacking jacket, $80-$100.

LONDON, Jack. *The Scarlet Plague.* Cloth. New York, 1915. First published edition. In dust jacket. $100-$150. Lacking jacket, $50-$65.

LONDON, Jack. *Scorn of Women.* Cloth. New York, 1906. First edition. In dust jacket. $300-$400. Lacking jacket. $150-$250.

LONDON, Jack. *The Sea-Wolf.* Illustrated by W.J. Aylward. Blue cloth. New York, 1904. First edition, first issue, with spine lettered in gold. In dust jacket. $200-$250. Lacking jacket, $75-$125. Later, spine lettered in white. In dust jacket. $75-$100. New York, 1961. Limited Editions Club. Cloth. Boxed. $50-$65.

LONDON, Jack. *Smoke Bellew.* Illustrated by P.J. Monahan. Blue-gray pictorial cloth. New York, 1912. First edition. In dust jacket. $75-$125. Lacking jacket, $25-$35.

LONDON, Jack. *The Son of the Sun.* Illustrated by A.O. Fischer. Light-blue pictorial cloth. Garden City, 1912. First edition. In dust jacket. $100-$150. Lacking jacket, $30-$50.

LONDON, Jack. *The Son of the Wolf.* Frontispiece. Slate-colored cloth, stamped in silver, or green cloth. Boston, 1900. First edition, first printing, with flyleaf at back; favored first binding in slate-colored cloth. In dust jacket. $200-$250. Lacking jacket, $85-$100. Author's first book. (Note: Hensley C. Woodbridge, John London, and George H. Tweney, in *Jack London: A Bibliography*, Georgetown, Calif., 1966, question the long-accepted slate-colored binding as the first. They also note two states of that binding and conclude that either of these as well as two varying green bindings must be considered as firsts; in other words, they say a collector must own all four to be sure he has a correct first edition. A fine bit of hairsplitting for the avid collector to chew over. See Blanck for further comments.)

LONDON, Jack. *The Star Rover.* Frontispiece in color. Blue cloth. New York, 1915. First American edition. In dust jacket. $250. (For first edition, see *The Jacket.*)

LONDON, Jack. *The Strength of the Strong.* Pictorial wrappers. Chicago, (1911). First edition, first issue, with Kinzie Street address in ads. $100-$150. Second issue, with Ohio Street in ads. $50-$75.

LONDON, Jack. *The Strength of the Strong and Other Pieces.* Frontispiece. Light-blue decorated cloth. New York, 1914. First edition. In dust jacket. $75-$100. Lacking jacket, $40-$60.

LONDON, Jack. *Tales of the Fish Patrol.* Illustrated by George Varian. Decorated cloth. New York, 1905. First edition. In dust jacket. $150-$200. Lacking jacket, $50-$75.

LONDON, Jack. *War of the Classes.* Dark-red cloth. New York, 1905. First edition. In dust jacket. $150-$200. Lacking jacket, $75-$100.

LONDON, Jack. *When God Laughs and Other Stories.* Illustrated. Dark olive-green pictorial cloth. New York, 1911. First edition. In dust jacket. $150-$200. Lacking jacket, $75-$100.

LONDON, Jack. *White Fang.* Illustrated, including colored frontispiece. Gray cloth. New York, 1906. First edition, first issue, without tipped-in title page and with no plates missing (they often are). In dust jacket. $150-$200. Lacking jacket, $30-$50. London, (1907). Dark-gray pictorial cloth. First English edition. $50-$75. New York, 1973. Limited Editions Club. $40-$50.

LONDON, Jack. *Wonder of Woman: A "Smoke Bellew" Story.* Printed wrappers. New York, (1912). First edition. $150-$250.

*LONE Star Guide Descriptive of Countries on the Line of the International and Great Northern Railroad of Texas (The).* Folding map and table, plates. 32 pp., wrappers. St. Louis, (about 1877). (By H.M. Hoxie.) $150-$300.

LONG, Frank Belknap. *The Hounds of Tindalos.* Black cloth. Sauk City, 1946. First edition. In dust jacket. $60-$80. Author's first book.

*LONG Island Atlas.* Cloth. New York, 1873. Published by Beers, Comstock & Cline. $300-$350.

LONG, Stephen H. *Voyage in a Six-Oared Skiff to the Falls of St. Anthony in 1817.* Map. Cloth. Philadelphia, 1860. First edition. $100-$125.

LONGFELLOW, Henry Wadsworth. See M. Lhomond's *Elements of French Grammar* (Longfellow's first book) and *French Exercises.* Also see *Hyperion; Manuel de Proverbes Dramatiques; Novelas Españolas; Outre-Mer.*

LONGFELLOW, Henry W. *Ballads and Other Poems.* Boards, paper label. Cambridge, Mass., 1842. First edition, first issue, with small "t" in "teacher" in last line of page 88 and with quotation marks at end of line 1, page 34. $250-$350.

LONGFELLOW, Henry W. *The Belfry of Bruges and Other Poems.* White wrappers. Cambridge, 1846. First edition, first state, with date 1845 on front cover and 1846 on title page. $250-$300. (Note: There were also some copies issued in boards.)

LONGFELLOW, Henry Wadsworth. *The Courtship of Miles Standish.* 135 pp., drab printed wrappers, imprinted "Author's Protected Edition." London, 1858. First edition, first printing. $400-$500. Later, cloth, 227 pp. Second printing. $350. Boston, 1858. Brown cloth. First American edition, first printing, with "treacherous" for "ruddy" in third line of page 124. $250-$300. Another issue: Purple "gift" binding. $250-$350.

LONGFELLOW, Henry Wadsworth. *Evangeline: A Tale of Acadie.* Brown or yellow boards, paper label. Boston, 1847. First edition, first printing, with line 1, page 61, reading "Long," not "Lo." $400-$500. Also, spine restored, $225 (A, 1975); rebound, original boards preserved, $225 (A, 1968). "Lo" issue: $150-$250.

LONGFELLOW, Henry Wadsworth. *From My Arm-Chair.* Leaflet, 2 leaves. (Cambridge, 1879.) First published edition, with reading "is wrought" in line 3 of 11th stanza. $150-$250. (Note: In a proof printing noted by Blanck the reading "are wrought" occurs.)

LONGFELLOW, Henry Wadsworth. *The Golden Legend.* Cloth. Boston, 1851. First edition. $300-$400. London, 1851. Cloth. First English edition. $50-$60.

LONGFELLOW, Henry Wadsworth. *Poems on Slavery.* 31 pp., printed yellow wrappers. Cambridge, 1842. First edition. $250-$350. Also, $225 (A, 1974). Cambridge, Mass., 1842. Second edition. $35-$50.

LONGFELLOW, Henry Wadsworth. *The Seaside and the Fireside.* Cloth or boards. Boston, 1850. First edition. $100-$150. Another (later) issue: Large paper. $75-$100.

LONGFELLOW, Henry Wadsworth. *The Song of Hiawatha.* Green cloth, or printed tan wrappers. London, 1855. First edition, with ads dated March. $500-$600. (No copies noted recently in wrappers.) Boston, 1855. Brown cloth. First American edition, first print-ing, with November ads and "dove" for "dived" in line 7 of page 96. $150-$200. Another issue: Blue or red "gift" bindings. $150-$200. Boston, 1856. Blue cloth. Large paper edi-tion. $75-$100. Boston, 1891. Illustrated by Frederic Remington. Vellum. One of 250. $250-$350. Another issue: Cloth or suede. Unnumbered. $100-$125.

LONGFELLOW, Henry Wadsworth. *The Spanish Student: A Play in Three Acts*. Yellow boards, paper label. Cambridge, 1843. First edition. $75-$100.

LONGFELLOW, Henry Wadsworth. *Syllabus de la Grammaire Italienne*. Cloth. Boston, 1832. First edition, first state, with "la traite" for "le traite" in line 13 of advertisement and rule under "Bowdoin College" on title page. $150-$200.

LONGFELLOW, Henry Wadsworth. *Tales of a Wayside Inn*. Cloth. Boston, 1863. First edition, first state of ads on page 11, with "Nearly ready" for this book, which is not priced. $150-$200.

LONGFELLOW, Henry Wadsworth. *"There Was a Little Girl."* Boards. New York, (1883). First edition. $75-$100. (Note: Blanck and others have questioned Longfellow's authorship of this nursery poem.)

LONGFELLOW, Henry Wadsworth. *Voices of the Night*. Tan or drab boards, paper label. Cambridge, 1839. First edition, first state, with line 10 on page 78 reading "His, Hector's arm" instead of "The arm of Hector." $400-$500. (Note: Fewer than 10 copies known, according to the late David A. Randall, curator of the Lilly Library at Indiana Universi-ty.) Second state. $100-$150. Author's first book of poetry.

LONGFELLOW, Henry Wadsworth (translator). *Coplas de Don Jorge Manrique*. Cloth, paper spine label. Boston, 1833. First edition. $100-$125.

LONGSTREET, Augustus Baldwin. See *Georgia Scenes, Characters, Incidents, etc.*

LONGSTREET, James. *From Manassas to Appomattox*. 44 maps and plates, 2 leaves of facsimiles. Cloth. Philadelphia, 1896. First edition. $75-$100.

LONGUS. *Les Amours Pastorales de Daphnis et Chloé*. Translated by J. Amyot. 151 litho-graphs by Pierre Bonnard. Morocco. Paris, 1902. One of 40 on Chine paper. $15,000-$20,000. Also, $17,500-plus (A, 1974); $8,160 (A, 1969). Another issue: One of 200. $5,000 and up. Also, $4,000 (A, 1971). London, 1933 (actually 1934). Ashendene Press. Woodcuts by Gwendolen Raverat. Half vellum. One of 290. $600-$750. Another issue: Morocco. One of 20 on vellum. $5,000 and up. Also, $3,798 (A, 1975). (Note: For numerous other editions of this classic, see the book auction records.)

LOOMIS, Chester A. *A Journey on Horseback Through the Great West, in 1825*. 27 pp., printed wrappers. Bath, N.Y., (1820's). First edition. $200-$250.

LOOS, Anita. *"Gentlemen Prefer Blondes."* Illustrated. Cloth. New York, 1925. First edi-tion, first issue, with "Divine" for Devine" on contents page. In dust jacket. $40-$60. Author's first book.

LORANT, Stefan (editor). *The New World: The First Pictures of America*. Illustrated. Cloth. New York, (1946). In dust jacket. Boxed. $50-$60.

LORIMER, George Horace. *Letters from a Self-Made Merchant to His Son*. 36 pp., wrap-pers. Philadelphia, 1901. First edition. $75-$100. Boston, 1902. Cloth. First (complete) edition. $35.

LORING, Rosamond B. *Decorated Book Papers*. Illustrated. Boards and cloth. Cambridge, 1942. First edition. In dust jacket. One of 250. $125-$150.

LORREQUER, Harry (pseudonym for Charles Lever). See *The Confessions of Harry Lorrequer*.

LORREQUER, Harry. *Charles O'Malley, the Irish Dragoon*. Illustrated by H.K. Browne ("Phiz"). 22 parts in 21, printed pink pictorial wrappers. Dublin, 1841. (By Charles Lev-er.) First edition. $200-$300. Dublin, 1841. First edition in book form. $100-$150. Lon-don, 1897. 16 plates by Arthur Rackham. Cloth. $150-$300.

LOTHROP, Amy. *Dollars and Cents.* 2 vols., purple cloth. New York, 1852. (By Anna Bartlett Warner.) First edition. $75-$100.

LOTHROP, Harriet M.S. See Sidney, Margaret.

LOUDON, Archibald. *A Selection of Some of the Most Interesting Narratives, of Outrages, Committed by the Indians, in Their Wars, with the White People.* 2 vols., leather. Carlisle, Pa., 1808-11. First edition. $2,000-$2,500. Also, $1,500 (A, 1967).

LOUDON, Mrs. Jane. *British Wild Flowers.* 60 hand-colored plates. Cloth. London, 1846. First edition. $600-$750 and up. Rebound copies, a little less. Also, second edition, no date, $300 (A, 1975). (Note: A number of later editions—1849, 1855, 1859, etc.—are all worth about as much as the original.)

LOUDON, Mrs. Jane. *The Ladies' Flower Garden of Ornamental Annuals.* 48 colored plates. Cloth. London, 1840. First edition. $600-$750 and up. Rebound, a little less. (Note: Editions following in 1842, 1844, and 1849 are about as valuable as the original. Mrs. Loudon also produced four other books in this series: *Ornamental Bulbous Plants.* London, 1841. 58 colored plates. Cloth. $500-$750. Also, $485 (A, 1975). *Ornamental Greenhouse Plants.* London, 1848. 75 colored plates. Cloth. $600-$750 and up. Also, $506 (A, 1975). Rebound, a little less. *Ornamental Perennials.* 96 colored plates. 2 vols., cloth. London, 1843-44. $700-$800 and up. As with Mrs. Loudon's wild flower book, the later editions of this color plate series sometimes bring almost as much as the originals. A complete set of the *Ornamentals* is currently worth $2,500-$3,500 at retail, depending on binding and condition.)

LOUGHBOROUGH, John. *The Pacific Telegraph and Railway.* 2 folding maps. 80 pp., unbound. St. Louis, 1849. First edition. $1,000 and up. Another issue: Printed wrappers. $1,000 and up.

LOUGHEED, Victor. *Vehicles of the Air.* Illustrated. Cloth. Chicago, (1909). First edition. $50-$100.

LOVE, Annie Carpenter. *History of Navarro County.* Cloth. Dallas, 1933. One of 100, signed. $75.

LOVE, Nat. *The Life and Adventures of Nat Love.* Plates. Pictorial cloth. Los Angeles, 1907. First edition. $100-$150.

LOVE, Robertus. *The Rise and Fall of Jesse James.* Frontispiece. Cloth. New York, 1926. First edition. $35-$50.

LOVECRAFT, H.P. *Beyond the Wall of Sleep.* Cloth. Sauk City, Wis., 1943. First edition. One of 1,217. In dust jacket. $300-$400.

LOVECRAFT, H.P. *The Case of Charles Dexter Ward.* Cloth. London, 1951. First edition. In dust jacket. $50.

LOVECRAFT, H.P. *The Cats of Ulthar.* 16 pp., wrappers. Cassia, Fla., 1935. First edition. One of 2,035. In dust jacket. $100-$150.

LOVECRAFT, H.P. *Collected Poems.* Illustrated. Black cloth. Sauk City, 1963. First edition. In dust jacket. $50-$60.

LOVECRAFT, H.P. *The Haunter of the Dark.* Introduction by August Derleth. London, 1951. First edition. In dust jacket. $65.

LOVECRAFT, H.P., *Marginalia.* Illustrated. Black cloth. Sauk City, 1944. First edition. One of 2,035. In dust jacket. $150-$175.

LOVECRAFT, H.P., *The Outsider and Others.* Cloth. Sauk City, 1939. First edition. One of 1,268. In dust jacket. $400-$500. (Note: This is the first book published by August Derleth's Arkham House.)

LOVECRAFT, H.P. *The Shadow Over Innsmouth.* Illustrated. Cloth. Everett, Pa., 1936. First edition, with errata sheet. In dust jacket. $500-$750. (Earliest copies—about 10— were issued without errata sheet. This is Lovecraft's first published book.)

LOVECRAFT, H.P. *The Shunned House.* 59 pp., unbound, folded signatures. Athol, Mass., 1928. First edition, first issue. $1,000 and up. (As late as the 1960's these were still available from August Derleth, the publisher of Lovecraft's principal fantasy books, at $17.50.) Later copies, bound in wrappers by R.H. Barlow, a Lovecraft associate. One of 10. $1,000 and up. Special Arkham House issue by Derleth: One of about 100, trimmed and bound in black cloth about 1961. Issued without dust jacket. $850-$1,000. (A copy, crudely bound in boards and canvas, was in the Jonathan Goodwin sale, Part 2, in 1977 but was withdrawn.) Author's first (unpublished) book (about 250 copies in all.)

LOVECRAFT, H.P. *Something About Cats and Other Pieces.* Edited by August Derleth. Cloth. Sauk City, 1949. First edition. One of 2,995. In dust jacket. $75-$85.

LOVECRAFT, H.P., and Derleth, August. *The Lurker at the Threshold.* Cloth. Sauk City, 1945. First edition. One of 3,041. In dust jacket. $50-$75.

LOVECRAFT, H.P. *Supernatural Horror in Literature.* Black or (later?) red cloth. New York, 1945. First edition. Black cloth: (Issued without dust jacket.) $50-$75. Red cloth: (Without jacket.) $35-$75.

LOVECRAFT, H.P., and others. *The Shuttered Room and Other Pieces.* Illustrated. Black cloth. Sauk City, 1959. First edition. One of 2,500. In dust jacket. $75-$100.

LOVECRAFT, H.P., and Derleth, August. *The Survivor and Others.* Cloth. Sauk City, 1957. First edition. In dust jacket. $50-$75.

LOVEDAY, John. *Diary of a Tour in 1732 Through Parts of England, Wales, Ireland and Scotland.* Half morocco. London, 1890. Roxburghe Club. $150-$200.

LOVER, Samuel. *Handy Andy: A Tale of Irish Life.* Illustrated by the author. 12 parts, printed wrappers. London, January-December, 1842. First edition. $200-$250. London, 1842. Green cloth. First edition in book form. $40-$50.

*LOVING Ballad of Lord Bateman (The).* Preface by Charles Dickens. Illustrated by George Cruikshank. Green cloth. London, 1839. (By William Makepeace Thackeray, though sometimes ascribed to Dickens, or to both Thackeray—for the ballad—and Dickens, or to Cruikshank.) First edition, first issue, with the word "wine" in fifth stanza. $300-$400.

LOWE, C. Bruce. *Breeding Racehorses by the Figure System.* Edited by William Allison. Illustrated. Cloth. London, 1895. First edition. $100-$150.

LOWELL, Amy. See *Dream Drops; Some Imagist Poets.*

LOWELL, Amy. *A Dome of Many-Colored Glass.* Boards, cloth spine, paper labels. Boston, 1912. First edition. In dust jacket. $75-$150. Author's first book aside from *Dream Drops.*

LOWELL, Amy. *The Madonna of Carthagena.* Wrappers. No place, 1927. First edition. One of 50. $100-$150.

LOWELL, Amy. *What's O'Clock.* Gray-blue boards and cloth. Boston, 1925. First edition. In dust jacket. $50-$75.

LOWELL, James Russell. See Wilbur, Homer. Also see *Class Poem; A Fable for Critics.*

LOWELL, James Russell. *Among My Books.* Cloth. Boston, 1870. First edition. $35-$50.

LOWELL, James Russell. *Among My Books: Second Series.* Cloth. Boston, 1876. First edition, first state, with 1875 copyright date and "Belles-Letters" on title page. $50-$60.

LOWELL, James Russell. *Conversations on Some of the Old Poets.* Cloth, wrappers, or boards. Cambridge, Mass., 1845. First edition. $100-$125.

LOWELL, James Russell. *Heartsease and Rue.* Boards and cloth. Boston, 1888. First edition. $100-$125.

LOWELL, James Russell. *Ode Recited at the Commemoration of the Living and Dead Sol-*

*diers of Harvard University, July 21, 1865.* Gray boards, paper label. Cambridge, 1865. First edition. One of 50. $1,000-$1,250.

LOWELL, James Russell. *On Democracy.* 15 pp., wrappers. Birmingham, England (1884). First edition, first state, privately printed and without price at top of first leaf. $100-$150. Second state (first published edition), with price. $50-$75.

LOWELL, James Russell. *Poems.* Boards, paper label. Cambridge, 1844. First edition. $50-$75.

LOWELL, James Russell. *Poems.* 2 vols., boards or cloth. Boston, 1849. First edition. $75-$100.

LOWELL, James Russell. *Poems: Second Series.* Boards or cloth. Cambridge, 1848. First edition. $75-$100.

LOWELL, James Russell. *The President's Policy.* Wrappers. (Philadelphia, 1864.) First edition, first state, with "crises" spelled "crisises" in first line of text. $100-$150.

LOWELL, James Russell. *Under the Willows and Other Poems.* Cloth. Boston, 1869. First edition, first issue, with errata slip at page 286 and first word in line 7 of page 224 reading "Thy." $100-$150.

LOWELL, James Russell. *The Vision of Sir Launfal.* Printed glazed yellow boards. Cambridge, 1848. First edition. $150-$200.

LOWELL, James Russell. *A Year's Life.* Boards, paper label. Boston, 1841. First edition, with errata slip. $150-$200. Author's first book (preceded by *Class Poem* pamphlet).

LOWELL, Robert. *Fall 1961.* Broadside. Milford, N.H., 1965. First edition. One of 115 signed. $100-$175.

LOWELL, Robert. *For the Union Dead.* Green cloth. New York, (1964). First edition, first printing (so stated). In dust jacket. $25-$30. London, 1965. First English edition. In dust jacket. $15-$20.

LOWELL, Robert. *4 by Robert Lowell.* Illustrated by Robert Scott. Decorated wrappers, stitched. (Cambridge, Mass., 1969). One of 126 copies, signed by Lowell. Accompanied by four broadsides, one for each poem. $195-$250.

LOWELL, Robert. *Land of Unlikeness.* Printed boards. (Cummington, Mass.), 1944. First edition. One of 250. $1,500. Another issue: One of 26 signed. $3,000-$4,000. Author's first book.

LOWELL, Robert. *Life Studies.* Cloth. London, (1959). First edition. In dust jacket. $40-$60. New York, 1959. First American edition. In dust jacket. $50-$75.

LOWELL, Robert. *Lord Weary's Castle.* Black cloth. New York, (1946). First edition. In dust jacket. $145.

LOWELL, Robert. *The Mills of the Kavanaughs.* Cloth. New York, (1951). First edition. In dust jacket. $100-$125.

LOWELL, Robert. *R.F.K. 1925-1968.* Broadside. (Cambridge, Mass., 1969.) One of 50 signed. $150-$175.

LOWELL Robert (translator). *Poesie di Montale.* Stiff printed wrappers. Bologna, Italy, (1960). First edition. One of 550. $50-$75.

LOWELL, Robert (translator). *The Voyage and Other Versions of Poems by Baudelaire.* Illustrated by Sidney Nolan. Folio, blue and purple beveled cloth. London, (1968). First edition. One of 210 signed by Lowell and the illustrator. Boxed. $150-$200.

LOWMAN, Al (compiler). *This Bitterly Beautiful Land: A Texas Commonplace Book.* Woodcuts. Folio, boards. Austin, 1972. First edition. One of 275 signed. $450-$550.

LOWRY, Malcolm. *Under the Volcano*. Cloth. New York, (1947). First edition. In dust jacket. $150-$200. Author's first book.

LOWRY, Robert. *Hutton Street*. Pictorial wrappers. Cincinnati, 1940. First edition. $50-$100. Author's first book.

LOWRY, Robert. *The Journey Out*. Stiff wrappers. (Bari, Italy, 1945.) First edition, signed. $100-$125.

LOWRY, Walter. *Tumult at Dusk*. Folding map. Parchment boards. San Francisco, 1963. Grabhorn Press. One of 100. In plastic slipcase. $125-$150.

LOY, Mina. *Lunar Baedeker*. Printed wrappers. (Paris, 1923.) First edition. $75-$125.

LOY, Mina, *Lunar Baedeker & Time Tables*. Cloth. Highlands, N.C. 1958. First edition. Jargon 23. One of 50 signed "author's copies." In acetate dust jacket. $100-$125. (Note: Contains an introduction by William Carlos Williams and others.)

LUBBOCK, Basil. *Adventures by Sea from the Art of Old Time*. 115 plates, including 22 in color. Buckram. London, 1925. First edition. One of 1,750. $50-$60.

LUBBOCK, Basil. *The Last of the Windjammers*. Illustrated. 2 vols., cloth. Boston, 1927. First edition. In dust jackets. $100-$150. Lacking jackets. $75-$100.

LUBBOCK, Basil, and Spurling, John. *Sail: The Romance of the Clipper Ship*. 78 full-page color plates. 3 vols., cloth. London, 1927-30-36. First edition. One of 1,000. In dust jackets. $750-$1,000.

LUBBOCK, F. R. *In Memoriam: Jefferson Davis*. 59 pp., half morocco. Austin, 1891. First edition. $200-$250. Presentation copy, signed, $550.

LUCAS, E. V. See L., E. V.

LUCAS, E. V. *The Book of Shops*. Illustrated in color. Oblong folio, boards and cloth. London, (1899). $50-$75.

LUCAS, E. V. *Playtime and Company*. Illustrated by Ernest H. Shepard. Vellum. London, (1925). One of 15 signed by author and artist. $200-$225. Another issue: Boards and cloth. One of 100 signed. In dust jacket. $75-$100.

LUCAS, Thomas J. *Camp Life and Sport in South Africa*. Illustrated. Cloth. London, 1878. $200-$300.

LUCAS, Thomas J. *Pen and Pencil Reminiscences of a Campaign in South Africa*. 21 colored plates. London, (1861). $250-$350.

LUCAS, Victoria. *The Bell Jar*. Cloth. London, 1963. (By Sylvia Plath.) First edition. In dust jacket. $200-$400, possibly more. London, 1964. Contemporary Fiction Edition. In dust jacket. $25.

LUCE, Edward S. *Keoghe, Comanche and Custer*. Illustrated. Cloth. (St. Louis), 1939. Limited, signed edition. In dust jacket. $125-$150.

*LUCERNE: Its Homes, Climate, Mineral Resources, etc.* 37 pp., printed wrappers. Los Angeles, 1888. (By Theron Nichols.) First edition. $100-$125.

LUCRETIUS CARUS, Titus. *De Rerum Natura Libri Sex*. Printed in red and black, with initial letters in blue and one in gold. Boards, vellum spine. London, 1913. Ashendene Press. One of 85 on handmade paper. $1,250-$1,500.

LUDLOW, Fitz-Hugh. See *The Hasheesh Eater*.

LUDLOW, N.M. *Dramatic Life as I Found It*. Cloth. St. Louis, 1880. First edition. $75-$100.

LUHAN, Mabel Dodge. *Taos and Its Artists*. Illustrated. Red cloth. New York, 1947. First edition. In dust jacket. $150-$200.

# MARCHING MEN

### BY
### SHERWOOD ANDERSON
AUTHOR OF "WINDY McPHERSON'S SON"

NEW YORK: JOHN LANE COMPANY
LONDON: JOHN LANE, THE BODLEY HEAD
TORONTO: S. B. GUNDY ∴ ∴ MCMXVII

---

"URBS IN HORTO."

# HISTORY

OF

# CHICAGO.

FROM THE

## EARLIEST PERIOD TO THE PRESENT TIME.

IN THREE VOLUMES.

VOLUME I.—ENDING WITH THE YEAR 1857.

BY A. T. ANDREAS.

CHICAGO:
A. T. ANDREAS, PUBLISHER.
1884

---

# SENSE

AND

# SENSIBILITY:

## A NOVEL.

*IN THREE VOLUMES.*

## BY A LADY.

VOL. I.

**London:**
PRINTED FOR THE AUTHOR,
*By C. Roworth, Bell-yard, Temple-bar,*
AND PUBLISHED BY T. EGERTON, WHITEHALL.
1811.

---

# A TRIP TO
# CALIFORNIA IN 1853

## BY WASHINGTON BAILEY

Recollections of a gold seeking trip
by ox train across the plains and
mountains by an old Illinois pioneer

LeRoy Journal Printing Company
1915

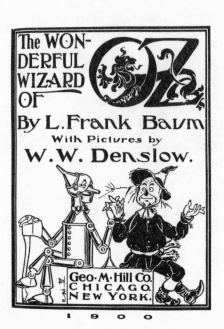

The WON-
DERFUL
WIZARD
OF **Oz**

By L. Frank Baum

With Pictures by
W. W. Denslow.

Geo·M·Hill Co.
CHICAGO.
NEW YORK.

1 9 0 0

---

DARK
CARNIVAL

*By*
RAY BRADBURY

ARKHAM HOUSE   •   SAUK CITY, WIS.
1947

---

*The Bean Eaters*

▲▲▲▲▲▲▲▲▲▲▲▲▲▲▲▲▲▲▲▲▲▲▲▲▲▲▲▲▲▲▲▲▲▲▲▲▲▲▲▲▲▲▲

GWENDOLYN BROOKS

*Harper & Brothers, Publishers   New York*

---

LIFE AND MARVELOUS ADVENTURES

OF

# WILD BILL,

## THE SCOUT.

BEING A TRUE AND EXACT HISTORY OF ALL THE
SANGUINARY COMBATS AND HAIR-BREADTH
ESCAPES OF THE MOST FAMOUS SCOUT
AND SPY AMERICA EVER PRODUCED.

BY
J. W. BUEL,
OF THE ST. LOUIS PRESS.

*ILLUSTRATED.*

CHICAGO:
BELFORD, CLARKE & CO.
1880.

# ARMED WITH MADNESS

*by*
MARY BUTTS

*

With drawings by JEAN COCTEAU

*

*LONDON*
WISHART & COMPANY

1928

---

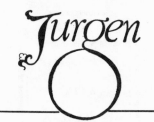

A Comedy of Justice

By
JAMES BRANCH CABELL

*"Of JURGEN eke they maken mencioun,*
*That of an old wyf gat his youthe agoon,*
*And gat himselfe a shirte as bright as fyre*
*Wherein to jape, yet gat not his desire*
*In any countrie ne condicioun."*

NEW YORK
ROBERT M. McBRIDE & CO.
1919

---

# APRIL
# TWILIGHTS
POEMS BY

*Willa Sibert Cather*

Boston: Richard G. Badger
The Gorham Press: 1903

---

# MY ANTONIA

BY

WILLA SIBERT CATHER

*Optima dies . . . prima fugit*
VIRGIL

**WITH ILLUSTRATIONS BY**
W. T. BENDA

BOSTON AND NEW YORK
HOUGHTON MIFFLIN COMPANY
The Riverside Press Cambridge
1918

raymond
chandler

*the*

*big*

*sleep*

*NEW YORK · ALFRED · A · KNOPF*

1939

---

THE

LATTER-DAY SAINTS'

EMIGRANTS' GUIDE:

BEING A

TABLE OF DISTANCES,

SHOWING ALL THE

SPRINGS, CREEKS, RIVERS, HILLS, MOUNTAINS,
CAMPING PLACES, AND ALL OTHER NOTABLE PLACES,

FROM COUNCIL BLUFFS,

TO THE

VALLEY OF THE GREAT SALT LAKE.

ALSO, THE

LATITUDES, LONGITUDES AND ALTITUDES
OF THE PROMINENT POINTS ON THE ROUTE.

TOGETHER WITH REMARKS ON THE NATURE OF THE LAND,
TIMBER, GRASS, &c.

THE WHOLE ROUTE HAVING BEEN CAREFULLY MEASURED BY A ROADOME-
TER, AND THE DISTANCE FROM POINT TO POINT, IN
ENGLISH MILES, ACCURATELY SHOWN.

BY W. CLAYTON.

ST. LOUIS:
MO. REPUBLICAN STEAM POWER PRESS—CHAMBERS & KNAPP.
1848.

---

ALMAYER'S FOLLY

A Story of an
Eastern River

BY

Joseph Conrad

Qui de nous n'a eu sa terre
promise, son jour d'extase et
sa fin en exil?—AMIEL.

*LONDON*

T. FISHER UNWIN

PATERNOSTER SQUARE

MDCCCXCV

---

THE SPY;

A TALE OF

THE NEUTRAL GROUND.

" Breathes there a man with soul so dead
Who never to himself hath said,
This is my own, my native land.—"

BY

THE AUTHOR OF "PRECAUTION.

IN TWO VOLUMES.

VOL. I.

NEW-YORK:
WILEY & HALSTED, 3, WALL-STREET

Wm. Grattan, Printer.

1821.

by E. E. Cummings

is

5

NEW YORK
BONI & LIVERIGHT
1926

---

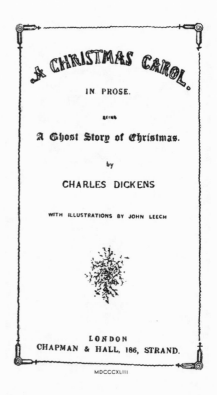

A CHRISTMAS CAROL.

IN PROSE.

BEING

A Ghost Story of Christmas.

by

CHARLES DICKENS

WITH ILLUSTRATIONS BY JOHN LEECH

LONDON
CHAPMAN & HALL, 186, STRAND.

MDCCCXLIII

---

THE SIGN OF FOUR

BY

A. CONAN DOYLE

AUTHOR OF
MICAH CLARKE,' 'THE FIRM OF GIRDLESTONE,' 'THE CAPTAIN
OF THE POLESTAR,' ETC., ETC.

LONDON
SPENCER BLACKETT
MILTON HOUSE, 35, ST. BRIDE STREET, E.C
1890
[All rights reserved]

---

YOUNG
LONIGAN

A Boyhood in Chicago Streets

by

JAMES T. FARRELL

Introduction by
FREDERIC M. THRASHER
Associate Professor of Education, New York University
Author of "The Gang"

NEW YORK
THE VANGUARD PRESS
1932

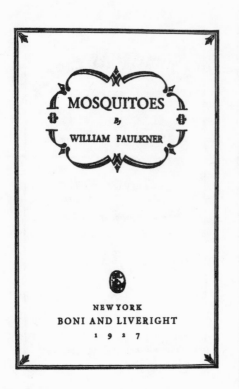

MOSQUITOES

By

WILLIAM FAULKNER

NEW YORK
BONI AND LIVERIGHT
1 9 2 7

---

# A GREEN BOUGH

## BY WILLIAM FAULKNER

NEW YORK · NINETEEN THIRTY-THREE
HARRISON SMITH AND ROBERT HAAS

---

# THE GREAT GATSBY

BY

F. SCOTT FITZGERALD

Then wear the gold hat, if that will move her;
If you can bounce high, bounce for her too,
Till she cry "Lover, gold-hatted, high-bouncing lover,
I must have you!"
—THOMAS PARKE D'INVILLIERS.

NEW YORK
CHARLES SCRIBNER'S SONS
1925

---

THE

# WARWICK WOODLANDS,

OR

## THINGS AS THEY WERE THERE,

### TEN YEARS AGO,

## BY FRANK FORESTER.

HENRY WILLIAM HERBERT,

AUTHOR OF "CROMWELL," "MARMADUKE WYVIL," "ROBE CAS-
TLETON," "RINGWOOD THE ROVER," "GUARICA," "THE
BROTHERS," &c. &c.

PHILADELPHIA:
G. B. ZIEBER & CO.
1845.

Price 50 Cents.

# MLISS.

## AN IDYL OF RED·MOUNTAIN.

A STORY OF CALIFORNIA IN 1863.

BY BRET HARTE,

Author of "Condensed Novels," "Heathen Chinee," "Luck of Roaring Camp,"
"Mrs. Skaggs's Husbands," Etc., Etc.

NEW YORK:
ROBERT M. DE WITT, PUBLISHER,
No. 33 ROSE STREET,
(Between Duane and Frankfort Streets.)

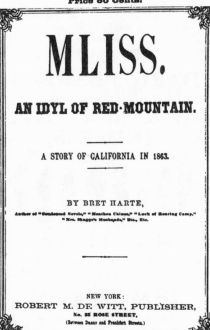

---

# FANSHAWE,

## A TALE.

"Wilt thou go on with me !"—Southey.

—◦§◦—

BOSTON:
MARSH & CAPEN, 362 WASHINGTON STREET.
PRESS OF PUTNAM AND HUNT.
1828.

---

# DEATH IN THE AFTERNOON

By
Ernest Hemingway

CHARLES SCRIBNER'S SONS
NEW YORK · LONDON
1932

NARRATIVE
OF THE
TRAGICAL DEATH
OF MR.

# DARIUS BARBER,

AND HIS
SEVEN CHILDREN,
WHO WERE INHUMANLY BUTCHERED BY THE

# INDIANS,

IN CAMDEN COUNTY, GEORGIA, JANUARY 26, 1813.

To which is added an account of the Captivity and Sufferings of MRS. BARBER, who was carried away a
Captive by the SAVAGES, and from whom she for-
tunately made her escape six weeks afterwards.

☞ It may be a gratification to the reader, to learn that
the said tribe of SAVAGES have been since exter-
minated by the Brave and Intrepid

## GEN. JACKSON,

And the Troops under his command.

BOSTON—Printed for DAVID HAZEN—Price 2d.

---

# Flagons and Apples

## By John Robinson Jeffers

Los Angeles, U.S.A.
Grafton Publishing Company
—1912—

---

# OUR EXAGMINATION
# ROUND HIS FACTIFICATION
# FOR INCAMINATION
# OF WORK IN PROGRESS

BY

SAMUEL BECKETT, MARCEL BRION, FRANK BUDGEN,
STUART GILBERT, EUGENE JOLAS, VICTOR LLONA,
ROBERT McALMON, THOMAS McGREEVY,
ELLIOT PAUL, JOHN RODKER, ROBERT SAGE,
WILLIAM CARLOS WILLIAMS.

*with*

*LETTERS OF PROTEST*
BY
G. V. L. SLINGSBY AND VLADIMIR DIXON.

SHAKESPEARE AND COMPANY
SYLVIA BEACH
12, RUE DE L'ODÉON — PARIS
M CM XX IX

---

# WHY
# ENGLAND
# SLEPT

---

*JOHN F. KENNEDY*

*NEW YORK · 1940*

WILFRED FUNK, INC.

JOHN KEROUAC

# THE
# TOWN
# &
# THE
# CITY

HARCOURT, BRACE AND COMPANY
NEW YORK

# THE RAINBOW

BY
## D. H. LAWRENCE
AUTHOR OF "SONS AND LOVERS"

NEW YORK
B. W. HUEBSCH
MCMXVI

# MORNINGS IN
# MEXICO

By
## D. H. LAWRENCE

LONDON:
MARTIN SECKER
1927

THE

# ARGONAUTS OF 'FORTY-NINE

SOME RECOLLECTIONS OF THE PLAINS AND THE DIGGINGS

BY

DAVID ROHRER LEEPER

ILLUSTRATED
By O. MARION ELBEL, FROM SELECTIONS AND SUGGESTIONS
BY THE AUTHOR

"Golden days, remembered days,
The days of 'Forty-Nine"

SOUTH BEND, INDIANA
J. B. STOLL & COMPANY, PRINTERS
1894

# THE SHUNNED HOUSE

BY

H. P. LOVECRAFT

With a Preface by Frank Belknap Long, Jr.

••••••••••

ATHOL, MASS.
Published by W. Paul Cook
The Recluse Press
1928

# IN A GERMAN PENSION

BY

KATHERINE ·MANSFIELD

LONDON
STEPHEN SWIFT & CO. LTD
10          John Street,          Adelphi

---

THE

# Banditti of the Plains

— OR THE —

Cattlemen's Invasion of Wyoming in 1892

———

[THE CROWNING INFAMY OF THE AGES.]

———

By A. S. MERCER.

# RENASCENCE
AND
## OTHER POEMS

BY

EDNA ST. VINCENT MILLAY

NEW YORK
MITCHELL KENNERLEY
MCMXVII

THE

# BARK COVERED HOUSE,

OR

BACK IN THE WOODS AGAIN ;

BEING A GRAPHIC AND THRILLING DESCRIPTION OF REAL
PIONEER LIFE IN THE

## WILDERNESS OF MICHIGAN.

(ILLUSTRATED.)

BY WILLIAM NOWLIN, ESQ.

———

DETROIT:
PRINTED FOR THE AUTHOR.
1876.

---

*American Dramatists Series*

# THIRST

*And Other One Act Plays by*

## EUGENE G. O'NEILL

ARTI et VERITATI

## BOSTON: THE GORHAM PRESS
TORONTO: THE COPP CLARK CO., LIMITED

---

# NINETEEN
# EIGHTY-FOUR

*A Novel*

BY

## GEORGE ORWELL

LONDON
## SECKER & WARBURG
1949

---

THE

## OREGON TRAIL

SKETCHES

OF

PRAIRIE AND ROCKY-MOUNTAIN LIFE

BY

FRANCIS PARKMAN

Illustrated by Frederic Remington

BOSTON
LITTLE, BROWN, AND COMPANY
1892

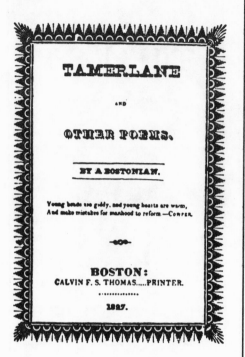

TAMERLANE

and

OTHER POEMS.

BY A BOSTONIAN.

Young heads are giddy, and young hearts are warm,
And make mistakes for manhood to reform —COWPER.

BOSTON:
CALVIN F. S. THOMAS.....PRINTER.

1827.

# SUNDOWN
# LEFLARE

*Written and Illustrated by*
## FREDERIC REMINGTON

### NEW YORK AND LONDON
### HARPER & BROTHERS PUBLISHERS
### 1899

The Children of the Night

*A Book of Poems*

BY

EDWIN ARLINGTON ROBINSON

BOSTON
RICHARD G. BADGER & COMPANY
M DCCC XCVII

## CHICAGO POEMS

By

CARL SANDBURG

NEW YORK
HENRY HOLT AND COMPANY
'1916

✢ In ✢ Reckless ✢ Ecstasy ✢
Charles A. Sandburg

"I had better bring this poor, pallid epistle to a close. My vocabulary is rampant to-night—the tide of expression foams, the combers glitter with speech-stuff, but the spindrift is no account. Here comes another! and it lashes this letter to its close."—*From a letter.*

"These things are as they will be, whatever I mean by that. I am like Keats at least in this, that the roaring of the wind is my wife, and the stars thru the window panes are my children. As for posterity, I say with the Hibernian, 'What has it ever done for us?'"—*From a letter.*

Asgard Press:
Galesburg, Illinois,
1904

---

# QUEEN MAB;

A

## PHILOSOPHICAL POEM:

### WITH NOTES.

BY

### PERCY BYSSHE SHELLEY.

ECRASEZ L'INFAME!
*Correspondance de Voltaire.*

Avia Pieridum peragro loca, nullius ante
Trita solo ; juvat integros accedere fonteis ;
Atque haurire : juratque novos docerpere flores.
\* \* \* \* \* \*
Unde prius nulli velarint tempora musæ.
Primum quod magnis doceo de rebus ; et arctis
Religionum animos nodis exsolvere pergo.
*Lucret.* lib. iv.

Δος πω γῦ, καὶ κοσμον κινησω.
*Archimedes.*

### LONDON:

PRINTED BY P. B. SHELLEY,
23, Chapel Street, Grosvenor Square.

## 1813.

---

# A TEXAS COW BOY

OR,

## FIFTEEN YEARS

ON THE

### Hurricane Deck of a Spanish Pony.

TAKEN FROM REAL LIFE

BY

### CHAS. A. SIRINGO,

AN OLD STOVE UP "COW PUNCHER," WHO HAS SPENT
NEARLY TWENTY YEARS ON THE GREAT
WESTERN CATTLE RANGES.

M. UMBDENSTOCK & CO., Publishers,
Chicago, Illinois.
1885.

---

# THREE LIVES

STORIES OF THE GOOD
ANNA, MELANCTHA AND
THE GENTLE LENA

BY

### GERTRUDE STEIN

### THE GRAFTON PRESS

NEW YORK                    MCMIX

# Harmonium
### *by* Wallace Stevens

New York **Alfred · A · Knopf** Mcmxxiii

---

# The Man
# With The Blue Guitar
### *& other poems*

*WALLACE STEVENS*

NEW YORK : *ALFRED A. KNOPF* : LONDON

1937

---

## STRANGE CASE

OF

## DR. JEKYLL AND MR HYDE

BY

ROBERT LOUIS STEVENSON

LONDON
LONGMANS, GREEN, AND C.O.
1886

---

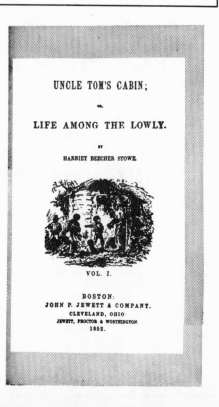

UNCLE TOM'S CABIN;

OR,

LIFE AMONG THE LOWLY.

BY
HARRIET BEECHER STOWE.

VOL. I.

BOSTON:
JOHN P. JEWETT & COMPANY.
CLEVELAND, OHIO:
JEWETT, PROCTOR & WORTHINGTON.
1852.

A Novel without a Hero.

BY

WILLIAM MAKEPEACE THACKERAY.

LONDON ;
BRADBURY & EVANS, BOUVERIE STREET
1848

# WALDEN;

## OR,

# LIFE IN THE WOODS.

By HENRY D. THOREAU,

AUTHOR OF "A WEEK ON THE CONCORD AND MERRIMACK RIVERS."

I do not propose to write an ode to dejection, but to brag as lustily as chanticleer in the
morning, standing on his roost, if only to wake my neighbors up. — Page 92.

BOSTON:
TICKNOR AND FIELDS.
M DCCC LIV.

# LIFE, ADVENTURES

AND

# CAPTURE

OF

# TIBURCIO VASQUEZ.

## The Great California Bandit and Murderer.

By Maj. BEN. C. TRUMAN.
Editor of Los Angeles Star.

PRINTED AT
LOS ANGELES STAR OFFICE,
1874.

# LIFE ON THE MISSISSIPPI

BY

MARK TWAIN

AUTHOR OF "THE INNOCENTS ABROAD," "ROUGHING IT,"
"THE PRINCE AND THE PAUPER," ETC.

WITH MORE THAN 300 ILLUSTRATIONS

*Mississippi Steamboat of Fifty Years Ago.*

[SOLD BY SUBSCRIPTION ONLY.]

BOSTON
JAMES R. OSGOOD AND COMPANY
1883

# SNOW-BOUND.

## A WINTER IDYL.

BY

JOHN GREENLEAF WHITTIER.

BOSTON:
TICKNOR AND FIELDS.
1866.

---

# AMERICAN BLUES

Five Short Plays
by Tennessee Williams

 ★

ACTING EDITION · PRICE 85 CENTS

★

DRAMATISTS
PLAY SERVICE
INC.

---

# JOURNAL

OF

# JOHN WOOD,

AS KEPT BY HIM WHILE TRAVELING FROM CINCINNATI TO THE
GOLD DIGGINGS IN

# CALIFORNIA,

IN THE SPRING AND SUMMER OF 1850,

CONTAINING AN ACCURATE ACCOUNT OF THE
OCCURRANCES, TRANSACTIONS AND
CIRCUMSTANCES DAILY.

Also, an Account of each Tribe of Indians, Description
of the Country passed through each day,
Quality of Soil, &c., &c.,

TOGETHER WITH A TABLE OF DISTANCES

FROM MISSOURI TO OREGON, EMIGRANT'S ROUTE, &c , &c.

CHILLICOTHE:
PRESS OF ADDISON BOOKWALTER.
1852.

---

# LOUIS ZUKOFSKY

# "A"

# 1–12

with an essay on Poetry by the author
and a final note by William Carlos Williams

ORIGIN PRESS 1959

*LUKE Darrell, the Chicago Newsboy.* Cloth. Chicago, 1865. First edition. $100-$150.

LUKE, L.D. *Adventures and Travels in the New Wonder Land of Yellowstone Park.* Cloth. Utica, 1886. $75-$100.

LUMPKIN, Wilson. *The Removal of the Cherokee Indians from Georgia.* 2 portraits. 2 vols., cloth. Wormsloe, Ga., 1907. First edition. One of 500. $75-$100.

LUTTIG, John C. *Journal of a Fur-Trading Expedition on the Upper Missouri.* Map, 4 plates. Boards and cloth. St. Louis, 1920. First edition. One of 365. $100-$125.

LYELL, Charles. *Principles of Geology.* Maps and plates. 3 vols., leather. London, 1930-32-33. First edition. $750-$1,000.

LYELL, James P.R. *Early Book Illustrations in Spain.* Colored frontispiece, 247 other illustrations. Cloth. London, 1926. One of 500. $150-$200.

LYKKEJAEGER, Hans. *The Luck of a Wandering Dane.* Boards. Philadelphia, 1855. (By Andrew M. Smith.) First edition. $300-$350.

LYMAN, Albert. *Journal of a Voyage to California, and Life in the Gold Diggings.* Frontispiece. Pictorial wrappers, or cloth. Hartford, 1852. First edition. Wrappers: $1,000-$1,500. Cloth: $500-$600.

LYMINGTON, Lord. *Spring Song of Iscariot.* Wrappers. Paris, 1929. Black Sun Press. One of 125 on Van Gelder paper. $75-$85. Another issue: One of 25 on Japan paper. $100-$125.

LYNCH, Bohun. *The Prize Ring.* Illustrated. Boards. London, 1925. First edition. One of 750. $100-$150.

LYON, Irving Whitall. *The Colonial Furniture of New England.* Plates. Cloth. Boston, 1891. First edition. $75-$100. Boston, 1925. Cloth. Third edition. One of 515. $50-$75.

LYRE, Pinchbeck. *Poems.* Boards. (London, 1931.) (By Siegfried Sassoon.) First edition. In glassine dust jacket. $50-$75.

*LYRICAL Ballads with Other Poems.* 2 vols., drab boards. London, 1800. (By William Wordsworth and Samuel Taylor Coleridge.) Second edition (so designated on the first volume alone). $1,500-$2,500. London, 1802. 2 vols., boards. Third edition. $200-$400. possibly more. London, 1805. 2 vols, boards. Fourth edition. $200 and up. (Note: The first edition, first issue, 1798, with a Bristol—instead of London—imprint on the title page, is an extremely rare book, of which no complete copy in original pink boards has appeared in many years.)

LYTLE, Andrew. *Bedford Forrest and His Critter Company.* Cloth. New York, 1931. First edition. In dust jacket. $75-$100.

LYTLE, Andrew. *The Long Night.* Cloth. Indianapolis, (1936). First edition. In dust jacket. $50-$75.

LYTTON, Lord (Edward Bulwer). See Bulwer-Lytton, Edward.

# M

MABINOGION (The): *A New Translation from the White Book of Rhydderch and the Red Book of Hergest.* By Gwyn Jones and Thomas Jones. Woodcut title page and other illustrations by Dorothea Braby. Folio, half morocco. London, 1948. Golden Cockerel Press. One of 475. $400-$600. Another issue: One of 75 specially bound. $1,000-$1,250.

McADAM, R. W. *Chickasaws and Choctaws.* Comprising the Treaties of 1855 and 1866. 67 pp., wrappers. Ardmore, Okla., 1891. First edition. $300-$350.

McAFEE, Robert B. See *History of the Late War in the Western Country.*

McALMON, Robert. *Being Geniuses Together.* Blue cloth. London, (1938). First edition. $500. (A, 1977).

McALMON, Robert. *A Companion Volume.* Gray wrappers. (Paris, 1923.) Contact Editions. First edition. $250-$350.

McALMON, Robert. *Distinguished Air (Grim Fairy Tales).* Vellum. Paris, 1925. Contact Editions. First edition. One of 115 copies. $450-$500. Also, $400 (A, 1977).

McALMON, Robert. *Explorations.* Cloth. London, 1921. Egoist Press. First edition. $200-$300. Author's first book.

McALMON, Robert. *A Hasty Bunch.* Wrappers. (Paris, 1922.) Contact Editions. First edition. $400-$450. Also, $375 (A, 1977). Worn, $150 in a 1978 catalogue.

McALMON, Robert. *North America, Continent of Conjecture.* Wrappers. (Paris, 1929). Contact Editions. First edition. One of 310. In glassine dust jacket. $150-$250.

McALMON, Robert. *Not Alone Lost.* Cloth. Norfolk, Conn., (1937). New Directions. In dust jacket. $50-$75.

McALMON, Robert. *Post-Adolescence.* Wrappers. (Paris, 1923.) Contact Editions. First edition. In glassine dust jacket. $250-$350. Worn, $100 in a 1978 catalogue.

McALMON, Robert. *The Portrait of a Generation.* Stiff wrappers. (Paris, 1926.) Contact Editions. First edition. One of 200. $250-$350. One of 10 (from this edition). Vellum. Signed. $475 (A, 1977).

McALMON, Robert. *Village: As It Happened Through a Fifteen Year Period.* Wrappers. (Paris, 1924.) Contact Editions. First edition. $250-$350.

MACARIA: *or, Altars of Sacrifice.* 183 pp., wrappers. Richmond, 1864. (By Augusta Jane Evans Wilson.) First edition. $350-$500.

MacARTHUR, Douglas. *Military Demolitions.* Printed wrappers. Fort Leavenworth, Kan., 1909. $75.

MACARTHUR, James. *New South Wales: Its Present State and Future Prospects.* Colored map. Cloth. London, 1837. (Written by Edward Edwards from Macarthur's notes.) $300-$400.

MACAULAY, Rose. *Catchwords and Claptrap.* Printed boards. London, 1926. Hogarth Press. First edition. $40-$60.

MACAULAY, Rose. *63 Days: The Story of the Warsaw Rising.* Stiff wrappers. (London), 1945. First edition. $35.

MACAULAY, Thomas Babington. *Evening: A Poem*. Wrappers. Cambridge, 1821. First edition. $150-$250.

MACAULAY, Thomas Babington. *Lays of Ancient Rome*. Brown cloth. London, 1842. First edition. $100-$150.

MACAULAY, Thomas Babington. *Pompeii*. Wrappers. (Cambridge, 1819.) $200-$250.

MacBETH, George. *A Form of Words*. Cloth. Oxford, 1954. First edition. One of 150. $135. Author's first book.

MacCABE, Julius P. Bolivar. *Directory of the City of Detroit*. Printed boards. Detroit, 1837. First edition. $500-$600.

MacCABE, Julius P. Bolivar. *Directory of the City of Milwaukee*. Full leather. Milwaukee, 1847. First edition. $150-$200.

MacCABE, Julius P. Bolivar. *Directory of Cleveland and Ohio City, for the Years 1837-1838*. Printed boards. Cleveland, 1837. First edition. $800-$1,000.

McCAIN, Charles W. *History of the S.S. "Beaver."* Illustrated. Blue cloth. Vancouver, 1894. First edition. $100-$125.

McCALL, George A. *Letters from the Frontiers*. Cloth. Philadelphia, 1868. First edition. $100-$150.

McCALL, Hugh. *The History of Georgia*. 2 vols., boards. Savannah, 1811-16. First edition. $400-$500.

McCALLA, William L. *Adventures in Texas*. Black cloth. Philadelphia, 1841. First edition. $500-$750.

McCARTHY, Mary. *The Company She Keeps*. Cloth (New York), 1942. First edition. In dust jacket. $40-$50. Author's first book.

McCARTHY, Mary. *The Oasis*. Cloth. New York, (1949). First edition. In dust jacket. $25-$35.

McCARTHY, Mary. *Venice Observed*. Illustrated. Cloth. New York, (1956). First edition. In dust jacket. $35-$50.

McCLELLAN, Henry B. *The Life and Campaigns of Maj. Gen. J.E.B. Stuart*. Portrait, 7 maps. Cloth. Boston, 1885. First edition. $80-$100.

McCLELLAND, Nancy. *Duncan Phyfe*. Illustrated. Cloth. New York, (1939). Limited, signed edition. Boxed. $150-$200.

McCLELLAND, Nancy. *Historic Wallpapers*. Illustrated, including color plates. Half cloth. Philadelphia, 1924. First edition, limited. $150-$250. Ordinary issue: $100-$150.

McCLINTOCK, John S. *Pioneer Days in the Black Hills*. Edited by Edward Senn. Illustrated. Cloth. Deadwood, (1939). First edition. $100-$125.

McCLINTOCK, Walter. *Old Indian Trails*. 28 plates, including 4 in color. Pictorial cloth. Boston, 1923. First edition. $50-$75. London, 1923. First English edition. $50-$75.

McCLINTOCK, Walter. *The Old North Trail*. Folding map, 9 color plates. Cloth. London, 1910. First edition. $75-$125.

M'CLUNG, John A. *Sketches of Western Adventure*. Boards, linen spine. Maysville, Ky., 1832. First edition. $750-$1,000. Also, rebound in half calf, browned and foxed, $650 (A, 1967). Philadelphia, 1832. Second edition. $300-$400.

McCLURE, J.B. *Edison and His Inventions*. Illustrated. Cloth. Chicago, 1879. First edition, first state, with no reviews of his book in the ads and with "With copious illustrations" in one line on title page. $75-$100. (Note: Contains Joel Chandler Harris' "Uncle Remus and the Phonograph.")

McCLURE, Michael. *The Beard*. Folio, pictorial wrappers. (Berkeley, 1965.) First edition. One of 330. $50-$75. (San Francisco), 1967. Coyote Press. Wrappers. $10. Another issue: One of 40, signed. $30-$40.

McCLURE, Michael. *The Cherub*. Full leather. Los Angeles, 1970. Black Sparrow Press. One of 26, signed, with a drawing by the author. $75-$100. Another issue: Boards. One of 250, signed. $25-$35.

McCLURE, Michael. *Dark Brown*. Boards and leather. San Francisco, 1961. One of 25 on Japan paper, signed. $75-$100. Another issue: Wrappers. $15-$20.

McCLURE, Michael. *Ghost Tantras*. Cloth. San Francisco, (1964). First edition. One of 20, signed. $50. Another issue: Wrappers. $15-$20.

McCLURE, Michael. *Hail Thee Who Play*. Printed yellow boards and cloth. Los Angeles, 1968. Black Sparrow Press. First edition. One of 75 signed, with a drawing by the author. In dust jacket. $50-$75. Another issue: Printed wrappers. One of 250, signed. $30-$35.

McCLURE, Michael. *Hymns to St. Geryon and Other Poems*. Decorated wrappers. San Francisco, 1959. First edition. $25.

McCLURE, Michael. *Little Odes & The Raptors*. Blue linen. Los Angeles, 1969. First edition. One of 200, signed. $25. Another issue: Leather. One of 26, signed, with a drawing by the author. $50-$75. Ordinary issue: Wrappers. $10-$15.

McCLURE, Michael. *Love Lion Book*. Wrappers. San Francisco, 1966. First edition. $10. Later: Boards. One of 40, signed. $30-$50.

McCLURE, Michael. *Muscled Apple Swift*. Decorated wrappers. (Topango, Calif., 1968.) First edition. One of 63, signed. $75-$85. Ordinary issue (87 copies): $20-$30.

McCLURE, Michael. *Passage*. Wrappers. Big Sur, Calif., 1956. Jargon 20. First edition. One of 200. $200-$225. Author's first book.

McCLURE, Michael. *Plane Pomes*. Stiff wrappers. New York, 1969. One of 100, signed. $35. Another issue: One of 26, signed and lettered. $50.

McCLURE, Michael. *Poisoned Wheat*. Red cloth. San Francisco, 1965. First edition. One of 24, signed. In dust jacket. $100. Ordinary issue: Wrappers. $15-$20.

McCLURE, Michael. *The Sermons of Jean Harlow & The Curses of Billy the Kid*. Wrappers. San Francisco, 1968. First edition. $15. Later (about 1970), boards. One of 50, signed. $30-$40.

McCLURE, Michael. *Thirteen Mad Sonnets*. Illustrated. Stiff wrappers. Milan, Italy, (1964). One of 299. $30-$40.

McCLURE, S.S. *My Autobiography*. Red cloth. New York, (1914). (Ghost-written by Willa Cather.) First edition, first issue, with "May, 1914" on copyright page. In dust jacket. $150-$200.

McCOLLUM, William. *California As I Saw It*. 72 pp., wrappers. Buffalo, 1850. First edition. $7,500. Lacking back wrapper, $6,500.

McCONKEY, Mrs. Harriet E. (Bishop). *Dakota War Whoop; or, Indian Massacres and War in Minnesota*. 6 portraits. Cloth. St. Paul, 1863. First edition. $100-$150.

McCONNELL, H.H. *Five Years a Cavalryman*. Text on pink paper. Cloth. Jacksboro, Tex., 1889. First edition. $150-$200.

McCONNELL, Joseph Carroll. *The West Texas Frontier*. Cloth. Jacksboro, 1933. First edition, $100-$150.

McCONNELL, W.J. *Early History of Idaho*. 2 plates. Cloth. Caldwell, 1913. First edition. In dust jacket. $75-$100.

McCOOK, Henry C. *American Spiders and Their Spinningwork*. Portrait, 35 hand-colored plates. 3 vols., cloth. London, 1889-93. First edition. "Author's Edition." One of 250. $500-$750. Philadelphia, 1889-93. 3 vols., cloth. First American edition. One of 750. $400-$500.

McCORISON, Marcus A. *Vermont Imprints, 1778-1820: A Check List.* Cloth. Worcester, 1963. First edition. In dust jacket. $50-$70. With 1968 and 1973 supplements. $100-$150.

McCORKLE, John, and Barton, O.S. *Three Years with Quantrell.* 11 plates. Maroon wrappers. Armstrong, Mo., (1914). First edition. $200-$300.

McCORMICK, Richard C. *Arizona: Its Resources and Prospects.* Folding map. 22 pp., buff printed wrappers. New York, 1865. First edition. $100-$150.

McCORMICK, S.J. *Almanac for the Year 1864; Containing Useful Information Relative to the Population, Progress and Resources of Oregon, Washington and Idaho.* 56 pp., wrappers. Portland, (1863). $200 and up.

McCOY, Horace. *No Pockets in a Shroud.* Tan cloth. London, (1937). First edition. In dust jacket. $75-$100.

McCOY, Horace. *They Shoot Horses, Don't They?* Tan cloth. New York, 1935. First edition. In dust jacket. $75-$100. London, (1935). Cloth. In dust jacket. $50-$60. Author's first book.

McCOY, Isaac. *History of Baptist Indian Missions.* Cloth. Washington, 1840. First edition. $150-$175.

McCOY, Isaac. *Remarks on the Practicability of Indian Reform.* 47 pp., wrappers. Boston. 1827. First edition. $200-$300. New York, 1829. Half leather. Second edition. $75-$100.

McCOY, Isaac. *Remove Indians Westward.* (Caption title.) 48 pp., sewed. (Washington), 1829. First edition. $100-$150.

McCOY, Joseph G. *Historic Sketches of the Cattle Trade of the West and Southwest.* Portraits and plates. Pictorial brown cloth. Kansas City, 1874. First edition. $750-$1,250.

McCRACKEN, Harold. *The Charles M. Russell Book.* Illustrated, including color plates. Leather. Garden City, 1957. First edition. One of 250, signed. Boxed. $600-$750. Trade edition: Buckram. In dust jacket. $50-$60.

McCRACKEN, Harold. *The Frank Tenney Johnson Book.* Illustrated, including color plates, by Johnson. Garden City, 1974. First edition. One of 350, signed, with an extra color plate. Boxed. $200-$250.

McCRACKEN, Harold. *The Frederic Remington Book.* Illustrated. Leather. Garden City, 1966. First edition. One of 500, signed. Boxed. $350-$425.

McCRACKEN, Harold. *Frederic Remington's Own West.* Illustrated. Calf. New York, 1960. First edition. One of 167, signed. Boxed. $300-$450.

McCRACKEN, Harold. *George Catlin and the Old Frontier.* Illustrated, including colored plates. Decorated leather. New York, 1959. One of 250, with extra color plate tipped in at front. Boxed. $300-$400. Trade edition: Cloth. In dust jacket. $35-$50.

M'CREERY, John. *A Selection, from the Ancient Music of Ireland, Arranged for the Flute or Violin.* Boards. Petersburgh, Va., 1824. First edition. $100 and up.

McCULLERS, Carson. *The Ballad of the Sad Cafe.* Cloth. Boston, 1951. First edition. In dust jacket. $35-$50.

McCULLERS, Carson. *The Heart Is a Lonely Hunter.* Cloth. Boston, 1940. First edition. In dust jacket. $125-$150. Author's first book.

McCULLERS, Carson. *Reflections in a Golden Eye.* Cloth. Boston, 1941. First edition. In dust jacket. $75-$100.

McCUTCHEON, George Barr. See Greaves, Richard.

McCUTCHEON, George Barr. *Brood House: A Play in Four Acts.* Boards. New York, 1910. First edition. One of 75. $75-$85.

McCUTCHEON, George Barr. *A Fool and His Money.* Cloth. New York, 1913. First edition. One of 50, signed. In dust jacket. $75-$85.

McCUTCHEON, George Barr. *Graustark.* Pictorial cloth. Chicago, 1901. First edition, first issue, with "Noble" instead of "Lorry" in line 6 of page 150. $50-$75. Author's first book.

McCUTCHEON, George Barr. *Kindling and Ashes.* Boards. New York, 1926. First edition. One of 25, signed. $75-$100. Trade edition: Cloth. In dust jacket. $20-$30.

McCUTCHEON, George Barr. *One Score and Ten.* Boards. New York, 1919. First edition. One of 30, signed. $75-$100.

McCUTCHEON, George Barr. *Viola Gwyn.* Boards and parchment. New York, 1922. First edition. One of 50 signed. $75-$125.

McCUTCHEON, John T. *Bird Center.* Illustrated. Pictorial boards and cloth. Chicago, 1904. First edition. $40-$60.

McDANIELD, H.F., and Taylor, N.A. *The Coming Empire; or, 2,000 miles in Texas on Horseback.* Cloth. New York, (1877). First edition. $60-$100.

MacDIARMID, Hugh. See Duval, K.D.; Glen, Duncan; Grieve, C.M. (Note: The following listings under MacDiarmid's name include books with title pages reading "M'Diarmid" and "Mc'Diarmid.")

MacDIARMID, Hugh. *Cunninghame Graham: A Centenary Study.* Cloth. Glasgow, (1952). (By C.M. Grieve.) First edition. In dust jacket. $35-$50.

MacDIARMID, Hugh. *Direadh I, II, III.* Boards and leather. Frenich, Foss, England, 1974. First edition. One of 200, signed. Boxed. $100-$150.

MacDIARMID, Hugh. *A Drunk Man Looks at the Thistle.* Cloth. Edinburgh. 1926. (By C.M. Grieve.) First edition. In dust jacket. $75-$100.

MacDIARMID, Hugh. *The Fire of the Spirit.* Blue wrappers. Glasgow, 1965. (By C.M. Grieve.) One of 50, signed. $90-$100. Another issue: Wrappers. One of 350. $25.

MacDIARMID, Hugh. *First Hymn to Lenin and Other Poems.* Portrait frontispiece. Half black morocco and boards. London, (1931). (By C.M. Grieve.) Unicorn Press. First edition. One of 50, signed. $200-$300. Another issue: Red and black buckram. One of 450. Boxed. $100-$150.

MacDIARMID, Hugh. *The Kind of Poetry I Want.* Boards and vellum. Edinburgh, 1961. (By C.M. Grieve.) First edition. One of 300, signed. Boxed. $200-$235. Another issue: One of 500. Boxed. $60-$75.

MacDIARMID, Hugh. *O Wha's Been Here Afore Me, Lass.* 4 pp., folded. No place, 1931. Blue Moon Press. (By C.M. Grieve.) First edition. One of 100, signed. $90-$100.

MacDIARMID, Hugh. *Penny Wheep.* Blue cloth. (Edinburgh), 1926. (By C.M. Grieve.) First edition. In dust jacket. $90-$100.

MacDIARMID, Hugh. *Poems to Paintings by William Johnstone, 1933.* Wrappers. Edinburgh, 1963. (By C.M. Grieve.) First edition. One of 100, signed. $55-$100.

MacDIARMID, Hugh. *Poetry Like the Hawthorn. From In Memoriam James Joyce.* Stiff yellow wrappers. Hemel Hempstead, England, 1962. (By C.M. Grieve.) First edition. One of 25, signed (from an issue of 150). $50-$75. Unsigned, $25-$35.

MacDIARMID, Hugh. *Sangschaw.* Cloth. (Edinburgh), 1925. (By C.M. Grieve.) First edition. In dust jacket. $100-$150, possibly more. Poet's first book of verse.

MacDIARMID, Hugh. *Scots Unbound and Other Poems.* Frontispiece. Cloth. Stirling, Scotland, 1932. (By C.M. Grieve.) First edition. One of 350, signed. $100-$125.

MacDIARMID, Hugh. *Second Hymn to Lenin and Other Poems*. Frontispiece. Cloth. London, 1935. (By C.M. Grieve.) First edition. In dust jacket. $75-$100.

MacDIARMID, Hugh. *Stony Limits and Other Poems*. Cloth. London, 1934. (By C.M. Grieve.) First edition. $100-$150.

MacDIARMID, Hugh. *Sydney Goodsir Smith*. Buckram, leather label. Edinburgh, 1963. (By C.M. Grieve.) First edition. One of 35 specially bound and signed by the author. $125-$150. Another issue: Wrappers. One of 100. $60-$80.

MacDIARMID, Hugh. *To Circumjack Cencrastus, or The Curly Snake*. Wrappers, or cloth. Edinburgh, 1930. (By C.M. Grieve.) First edition. Wrappers: $50. Cloth. In dust jacket. $35-$50. Another issue: Blue morocco extra. Binding signed by Arthur Currie. $250 and up.

MacDIARMID, Hugh. *The Uncanny Scot*. Edited by Kenneth Buthlay. Buckram. (London, 1968.) (By C.M. Grieve.) First edition. One of 40 signed by Grieve. In dust jacket. $85-$100.

MacDIARMID, Hugh, *When the Rat-Race Is Over*. Gray wrappers. London, 1962. (By C.M. Grieve.) First edition. One of 40, signed. $75-$100.

MacDIARMID, Hugh. *Whuchulls: A Poem*. Wrappers. London, 1966. (By C.M. Grieve.) One of 100. $50-$75.

MacDIARMID, Hugh (editor). *The Voice of Scotland*. Vol. XIX, No. 3. Loose leaves, printed one side only, in cloth case. (Edinburgh, 1961.) (C.M. Grieve, editor.) Proof copies of an unpublished issue of this Scottish quarterly. (Only a few copies were run off for the editor.) $200 and up.

MacDONAGH, Donagh. *Veterans and Other Poems*. Boards and linen. Dublin, 1941. Cuala Press. First edition. One of 270. In dust jacket. $50-$60.

MacDONALD, George. *At the Back of the North Wind*. Illustrated by Arthur Hughes. Cloth. London, 1871. First edition. $400-$600.

MacDONALD, George. *Dealings with the Fairies*. Illustrated by Arthur Hughes. Cloth. London, 1867. First edition. $350-$450.

MacDONALD, George. *Phantastes*. Cloth. London, 1858. First edition, with 16 pages of ads at end. $175-$250. London, 1912. Cloth. $50-$75.

MacDONALD, George. *The Princess and the Goblin*. Illustrated by Arthur Hughes. Cloth. London, 1897. First edition. $200-$350.

MacDONALD, George. *Within and Without: A Dramatic Poem*. Cloth. London, 1855. First edition. $150-$250. Author's first book.

MacDONALD, Hugh. *John Dryden: A Bibliography*. Portrait. Cloth. Oxford, 1939. First edition. In dust jacket. $75-$100.

MacDONALD, James. *Food from the Far West*. Decorated cloth. London, 1878. First edition. $125-$150. New York, (1878). Cloth. First American edition. $100-$125.

McDONALD, Archibald. *Peace River: A Canoe Voyage from Hudson's Bay to Pacific, by the Late George Simpson . . . in 1828*. Edited by Malcolm McLeod. Folding map. 119 pp., printed wrappers. Ottawa, 1872. First edition, with errata. $450-$500.

McDONALD, Edward D. *A Bibliography of the Writings of Norman Douglas*. Cloth. Philadelphia, 1927. First edition. One of 100, signed by McDonald and Douglas. In dust jacket. $100-$125. Ordinary issue. In dust jacket. $35-$50.

McDONALD, Frank V. (editor). *Notes Preparatory to a Biography of Richard Hayes McDonald*. Vol. 1. (All published.) Illustrated. Brown cloth. Cambridge, Mass., 1881. First edition. One of 150. $300-$400. Also, $225 (A, 1973).

McDONALD, John. *Biographical Sketches of Gen. Nathaniel Massie, Gen. Duncan McArthur, Capt. William Wells, and Gen. Simon Kenton*. Calf. Cincinnati, 1838. First edition. $150-$200.

M'DONELL, Alexander. *A Narrative of Transactions in the Red River Country.* Folding map. Boards. London, 1819. First edition. $1,250-$1,500.

MACDOUGALL, William. *The Red River Rebellion.* 68 pp., wrappers. Toronto, 1870. First edition. $100-$150.

McEACHRAN, D. *Notes of a Trip to Bow River North-West Territories.* Cloth (not original). Montreal, 1881. First edition. $150-$175.

McELROY, Joseph. *A Smuggler's Bible.* Cloth. New York, (1964). First edition. In dust jacket. $50. Author's first book.

MacFALL, Haldane. *Aubrey Beardsley, the Man and His Work.* Illustrated. Cloth. New York, 1927. First edition. In dust jacket. $50-$75. Another issue: One of 300, signed. In dust jacket. $75-$125. New York, 1928. Cloth. In dust jacket. $35-$50. London, (1928). Boards. First English edition. In dust jacket. $50-$60. Another issue: One of 100, with 6 extra illustrations. In dust jacket. $75-$125.

MacFALL, Haldane. *The Book of Lovat.* Half cloth. London, 1923. First edition. One of 150, signed. In dust jacket. $100-$125. Ordinary issue: In dust jacket. $30-$40.

MacFALL, Haldane. *The Splendid Wayfaring.* Cloth. London, 1913. First edition. In dust jacket. $100-$150.

MacFALL, Haldane. *The Wooings of Jezebel Pettyfer.* Pictorial cloth. London, 1898. First edition, first issue, with portrait of Jezebel on front cover. $125-$150. Also, $75 (A, 1975).

McFADDEN, William S. *Corvallis to Crescent City, California, in 1874.* Mimeographed, 44 pp., wrappers. (WPA.) No place, (1937). $35-$50.

McFEE, William. *Aliens.* Cloth. London, 1914. First edition, first state, with ads dated 1915. In dust jacket. $40-$60. New York, 1916. Cloth. First American edition. In dust jacket. $25.

McFEE, William. *Casuals of the Sea.* Frontispiece in color. Cloth. London, 1916. First edition. In dust jacket. $125-$150. Also, $75 (A, 1975).

McFEE, William. *The Harbourmaster.* Boards and cloth. Garden City, 1931. First edition. One of 377 signed. Boxed. $40-$60. Garden City, 1932. Cloth. First trade edition. In dust jacket. $25.

McFEE, William. *Iron Men and Wooden Ships.* Woodcuts by Edward A. Wilson. Folio, boards. New York, 1924. First edition. One of 200, signed. Boxed. $75-$100.

McFEE, William. *Letters from an Ocean Tramp.* Colored frontispiece. Blue cloth. London, 1908. First edition, first state, with "Cassell & Co." at foot of spine. $150-$175. Author's first book.

McFEE, William. *The Reflections of Marsyas.* Boards. Gaylordsville, N.Y., 1933. Slide Mountain Press. One of 300, signed. In glassine dust jacket. $40-$50.

McFEE, William. *A Six-Hour Shift.* Boards, vellum spine. Garden City, 1920. First edition. One of 377, signed. In dust jacket. $40-$60.

McGAW, James F. *Philip Seymour, or, Pioneer Life in Richland County, Ohio.* 2 plates. Cloth. Mansfield, Ohio, 1858. First edition. $200-$250.

McGEE, Joseph H. *Story of the Grand River Country, 1821-1905.* Portrait. Brown printed wrappers. (Gallatin, Mo., 1909.) First edition. $100-$150.

McGILLYCUDDY, Julia B. *McGillycuddy Agent: A Biography of Dr. Valentine T. McGillicuddy.* Illustrated. Pictorial cloth. Stanford, (1941). First edition. In dust jacket. $40-$55.

McGLASHAN, C.F. *History of the Donner Party: A Tragedy of the Sierras.* Cloth. Truckee, Calif. (1879). First edition. $500-$600. San Francisco, 1880. Illustrated. Cloth. Second edition. $300-$350.

McGOWAN, Edward. *Narrative of Edward McGowan.* Illustrated. Pictorial wrappers. San Francisco, 1857. First edition. $600-$800. San Francisco, 1917. (As *Narrative of Ned McGowan.*) Boards. One of 200. $35-$50.

McGREEVY, Thomas. *Poems.* Cloth. London, 1934. First edition. In dust jacket. $35-$50.

McGUANE, Thomas. *The Sporting Club.* Cloth. New York, (1968). First edition. In dust jacket. $30-$40. Author's first book.

MACHEN, Arthur. See Siluriensis, Leolinus

MACHEN, Arthur. *Bridles and Spurs.* Green boards and cloth. Cleveland, 1951. Grabhorn printing for the Rowfant Club. One of 178. Boxed. $50.

MACHEN, Arthur. *The Canning Wonder.* Boards and vellum. London, 1925. One of 130, signed. In dust jacket. $40-$50. Trade edition: Cloth. In dust jacket. $15-$20.

MACHEN, Arthur. *The Chronicle of Clemendy.* Frontispiece. Half vellum. Carbonnek, Wales, 1888. First edition. One of 250. Boxed. $75-$100. Carbonnek, 1923. (Printed in U.S.A.) Blue boards, parchment spine. One of 1,050, signed. $25-$30.

MACHEN, Arthur. *The Cosy Room and Other Stories.* Pink cloth. London, (1936). First edition. In dust jacket. $60-$80.

MACHEN, Arthur. *Dog and Duck.* Illustrated. Batik boards and cloth. London, 1924. First edition. One of 150 (of an edition of 900), signed. In dust jacket. $25.

MACHEN, Arthur. *Dreads and Drolls.* Boards, parchment spine. London, 1926. First edition. One of 100, signed. In dust jacket. $30-$40.

MACHEN, Arthur. *Fantastic Tales.* Frontispiece, 8 plates. Boards. Carbonnek, 1890. First edition. One of 500. $40-$50. Carbonnek, 1923. (Printed in U.S.A.) One of 50, signed. In dust jacket. $100-$150.

MACHEN, Arthur. *Far Off Things.* Boards. London, (1922). First edition. One of 100, signed. In dust jacket. $50-$60. Trade edition, later: Green cloth. In dust jacket. $20.

MACHEN, Arthur. *The Great God Pan and the Inmost Light.* Pictorial blue cloth. London, 1894. First edition. $40-$60.

MACHEN, Arthur. *The Hill of Dreams.* Frontispiece. Dark-red buckram. London, 1907. First edition, with "E. Grant Richards" at bottom of spine. In dust jacket. $75.

MACHEN, Arthur. *The House of Souls.* Frontispiece. Pictorial light-gray buckram. London, 1906. First edition. In dust jacket. $50-$75. Lacking jacket, $40.

MACHEN, Arthur. *Notes and Queries.* Green buckram, paper label. London, 1926. First edition. One of 265 signed. In dust jacket. $40-$60. Trade edition: Cloth. In dust jacket. $20.

MACHEN, Arthur. *Ornaments in Jade.* Cloth. New York, 1924. First edition. One of 1,000, signed. In dust jacket. Boxed. $25-$50.

MACHEN, Arthur. *The Shining Pyramid.* Edited by Vincent Starrett. Illustrated. Black cloth. Chicago, 1923. One of 875. In dust jacket. $50-$60. London, 1925. Blue cloth. First English edition. One of 250, signed. In dust jacket. $75-$85. Trade edition: Cloth. In dust jacket. $20-$25.

MACHEN, Arthur. *Strange Roads and With the Gods in Spring.* Cloth. London, 1923. First edition. In dust jacket. $25-$35. London, 1924. Half vellum. One of 300, signed. $50-$75.

MACHEN, Arthur. *Things Near and Far.* Boards. London, (1923). First edition. One of 100, signed. In dust jacket. $75-$100. Trade edition: Cloth. In dust jacket. $25.

MACHEN, Arthur. *The Three Impostors.* Blue cloth. London, 1895. First edition. $40-$60.

MACHEN, Arthur (editor). *One Hundred Merrie and Delightsome Stories.* (Translated by

Robert B. Douglas.) Illustrated. 2 vols., cloth. Carbonnek, 1924. (Printed in U.S.A.) First edition. In dust jackets. $75-$100.

McILVAINE, William, Jr. *Sketches of Scenery and Notes of Personal Adventure, in California and Mexico.* 16 plates, including engraved title page. Purplish cloth. Philadelphia, 1850. First edition. $750-$1,000. San Francisco, 1951. Folio, half cloth. One of 400. $100-$150.

McINTIRE, Jim. *Early Days in Texas: A Trip to Hell and Heaven.* 16 plates, pictorial cloth. Kansas City, Mo., (1902). First edition. $200-$400, possibly more.

MACK, Effie. *Nevada: A History of the State.* Map, facsimiles. Glendale, Calif., 1936. First edition. One of 250, signed. $75-$100.

MACK, Solomon. *A Narraitive* [sic] *of the Life of Solomon Mack.* 48 pp., wrappers. Windsor, (Conn.?), no date (1810-12?). First edition. $300-$400.

MACKAIL, J. W. *The Life of William Morris.* 22 illustrations. 2 vols., cloth. London, 1899. First edition. $50-$75. Also, rebound in morocco by Douglas Cockerell, $375 (A, 1975). London, 1901. Half morocco. $50-$60.

MACKAIL, J. W. *William Morris: An Address.* Vellum. London, 1901. Doves Press. First edition. One of 300. $200-$350. Another issue: Morocco. Specially bound by the Doves Bindery. Boxed. $1,000-$1,500. Also, $672 (A, 1969). One of 15 on vellum. $1,000 and up. London, 1902. Boards, vellum spine. $100 and up.

MACKAY, Charles. *Memoirs of Extraordinary Popular Delusions and the Madness of Crowds.* 5 portraits. 3 vols., gray cloth. London, 1841. First edition. $125-$150.

MACKAY, Charles. *The Mormons: Their Progress and Present Condition.* 10 parts, wrappers. London, 1851. First edition. $300-$350. London, 1851. Cloth. First book edition. $50-$65.

MACKAY, Malcolm S. *Cow-Range and Hunting Trail.* 38 illustrations. Cloth. New York, 1925. First edition. In dust jacket. $60-$100.

McKAY, Claude. *Banjo.* Decorated boards and cloth. New York, 1929. First edition. In dust jacket. $75-$100.

McKAY, Claude. *Gingertown.* Cloth. New York, 1932. First edition. In dust jacket. $50-$75.

McKAY, Claude. *Harlem Shadows: The Poems of Claude McKay.* Boards and cloth, paper label. New York, (1922). First edition. In dust jacket. $100-$150.

McKAY, Claude. *A Long Way from Home.* Green cloth. New York, (1937). First edition. In dust jacket. $35-$50.

McKAY, Claude. *Songs of Jamaica.* Wrappers over boards. Kingston, 1912. First edition. $600-$800. Author's first book.

McKAY, Claude. *Spring in New Hampshire and Other Poems.* Wrappers. London, 1920. First edition. $250-$300.

McKAY, Richard C. *Some Famous Sailing Ships.* 10 color plates, 48 illustrations. Boards and cloth. New York, 1928. One of 250. $75-$100. New York, (1934). One of 200, signed. Boxed. $75.

McKAY, Richard C. *South Street: A Maritime History of New York.* 48 illustrations. Two-tone cloth. New York, (1934). One of 200, signed. Boxed. $75.

McKAY, Robert H. *Little Pills.* 3 plates. Khaki cloth. Pittsburg, Kan., 1918. First edition. $75-$100.

McKAY, William, and Roberts, W. *John Hoppner, R. A.* Illustrated. Cloth. London, 1909. $100-$125. London, 1909-14. 2 vols., buckram (including supplement). $150-$175.

MACKAYE, Percy. *Johnny Crimson: A Legend of Hollis Hall.* Cover design by Eric Pape. Wrappers. Boston, 1895. First edition. $75. Author's first book.

MACKAYE, Percy. *Saint Louis: A Civic Masque.* Boards, paper label. New York, 1914. First edition. One of 300, signed. $35-$50.

McKEE, James Cooper. *Narrative of the Surrender of a Command of U. S. Forces at Fort Fillmore, N.M., in July A.D. 1861.* (Cover title.) 30 pp., printed self-wrappers. New York, 1881. Second edition. $125-$150. (The rare first edition appeared in Prescott, Arizona Territory, in 1878. Estimated value: $1,000 and up.)

McKEE, Dr. W. H. *The Territory of New Mexico, and Its Resources.* Map. 12 pp., printed wrappers. New York, 1866. First edition. $2,000-$2,500. Also, $1,200 (A, 1966).

MACKENNA, F. Severne. *Worcester Porcelain.* Frontispiece in color, 80 plates. Buckram. Leigh-on-Sea, 1950. One of 500, signed. In dust jacket. $100-$150.

McKENNEY, Thomas L. *Sketches of a Tour to the Lakes.* 29 full-page engravings, some in color. Boards, paper label. Baltimore, 1827. First edition. $300-$400.

M'KENNEY, Thomas L., and Hall, James. *History of the Indian Tribes of North America.* Map. 120 colored plates and list of subscribers. 3 vols., folio, cloth, or half leather. Philadelphia, 1836-38-44. First edition. $10,000 and up. Also, $6,500 (A, 1972). (Note: Also issued in 20 paperbound parts—very rare. A complete set was catalogued by a San Francisco book shop at $19,500 in December, 1974.) Philadelphia, 1837-42-44. 3 vols., folio. Second edition. Up to $10,000, possibly more. Philadelphia, 1838-42-44. 3 vols., folio. Third edition. Up to $10,000, possibly more. Several other folio editions in reprint through the 1840s are worth up to $10,000, possibly more, in fine condition. Philadelphia, 1848-49-50. 3 vols., octavo, leather. First octavo edition. $4,000-$5,000. Other editions, octavo, at auction: Philadelphia, 1854. 3 vols., $1,300 (1975); Philadelphia, 1855. 3 vols., bindings rubbed, $1,900 (A, 1977): Philadelphia, 1872-74-& no date. 3 vols., including atlas folio. $4,400 (1975). A modern edition: Edinburgh, 1933-34. 3 vols., blue cloth. In dust jackets. Boxed. $250-$350.

MACKENZIE, Alexander. *Voyages from Montreal, on the River St. Lawrence, Through the Continent of North America.* Frontispiece, 3 folding maps. Boards and cloth. London, 1801. First edition. $1,500-$1,750. London, 1802. 2 vols., boards. Second edition. $500-$750. New York, 1802. Folding map. Boards. First American edition. $400-$600. Philadelphia, 1802. 2 vols., boards. $400-$500. (Note: Imperfect copies of all these editions, rebound and with defects of various kinds, appear frequently at auction and in the catalogues of dealers and, as usual, are acceptable substitutes for all but the most demanding collectors.)

MACKENZIE, Compton. *Extraordinary Women.* Cloth. London, 1928. First edition. One of 100, signed. In dust jacket. $85-$125.

MACKENZIE, Compton. *Poems.* Gray wrappers. Oxford, 1907. First edition. $50-$65.

MACKENZIE, James. *Angina Pectoris.* Illustrated. Cloth. London, (1923). First edition. $150-$200.

McKIM, Randolph H. *A Soldier's Recollections: Leaves from the Diary of a Young Confederate.* Cloth. New York, 1911. First edition. $60-$80.

McKINSTRY, George H., Jr. *Thrilling and Tragic Journal Written by George H. McKinstry Jr., While on a Journey to California in 1846-47.* Broadside folded to book size, printed paper covers. West Hoboken, (1920). First edition. One of 65. $75-$100.

McKNIGHT, Charles. *Old Fort Duquesne: or, Captain Jack, the Scout.* Cloth. Pittsburgh, 1873. First edition. $40-$60.

McKNIGHT, George S. *California 49er: Travels from Perrysburg to California.* (Cover title.) 27 pp., printed red wrappers. Perrysburg, Ohio, 1903. First edition. $150-$200.

McKUEN, Rod. *And Autumn Came.* Cloth. New York, (1954). First edition. In dust jacket. $75-$100. Author's first book.

McLAUGHLIN, James. *My Friend the Indian.* Illustrated. Cloth. Boston, 1910. First edition. $35-$50.

McLEOD, Donald. *History of Wiskonsan, from Its First Discovery to the Present Period.* 4 plates, folding map. Cloth. Buffalo, 1846. First edition. $250-$300. (Note: Wright Howes says some copies have plates and no map and others map and no plates.)

MacLEISH, Archibald. See *Class Poem,* 1915.

MacLEISH, Archibald. *Air Raid.* Cloth. New York, 1948. First edition. In dust jacket. $40-$50.

MacLEISH, Archibald. *America Was Promises.* Cloth. New York, 1939. First edition. In dust jacket. $25.

MacLEISH, Archibald. *American Letters for Gerald Murphy.* Half leather and cloth. Arroyo Grande, 1935. First edition. One of 150. $200. Another, covers dusty. $75.

MacLEISH, Archibald. *Conquistador.* Folding map. Cloth. Boston, 1932. First edition. In dust jacket. $50-$65.

MacLEISH, Archibald. *Einstein.* Printed wrappers. Paris, 1929. Black Sun Press. First edition. One of 100 on Van Gelder paper. Boxed. $75-$100. One of 50 on vellum, signed. Boxed. $250-$350. Also, $225 (A, 1977).

MacLEISH, Archibald. *The Fall of the City.* Boards. New York, 1937. First edition. In dust jacket. $30-$40.

MacLEISH, Archibald. *Frescoes for Mr. Rockefeller's City.* Wrappers. New York, 1933. First edition. $30-$35.

MacLEISH, Archibald. *The Happy Marriage and Other Poems.* Boards, paper label. Boston, 1924. First edition. In dust jacket. $50-$60.

MacLEISH, Archibald. *Land of the Free.* Illustrated with photographs. Linen. New York, (1938). First edition. In dust jacket. $75-$85.

MacLEISH, Archibald. *New Found Land.* Wrappers. Paris, 1930. Black Sun Press. First edition. One of 100 numbered copies (of an edition of 135). Boxed. $75-$100. One of 35 on vellum, signed. Boxed. $125-$150. One of 10 of the vellum copies initialed by Harry Crosby. $200-$250. Boston, 1930. (Printed in Paris.) First American edition. $35.

MacLEISH, Archibald. *Nobodaddy.* Black cloth. Cambridge, Mass., 1926. First edition. One of 700. In dust jacket. $35-$40. Another issue: One of 50 on large paper. In dust jacket. $125-$150.

MacLEISH, Archibald. *Poems, 1924-1933.* Cloth. Boston, 1933. First edition. In dust jacket. $50-$75.

MacLEISH, Archibald. *The Pot of Earth.* Gold decorated boards. Cambridge, 1925. First edition. One of 100 on handmade paper. In dust jacket. Boxed. $75-$100. Boston, 1925. Boards. Trade edition. In dust jacket. $25-$30.

MacLEISH, Archibald. *Public Speech: Poems.* Full calf. New York, (1936). First edition. One of 275 signed. In glassine dust jacket. Boxed. $50-$75. Trade edition: Blue cloth. First issue, with F & R monogram on copyright page. In dust jacket. $20-$25.

MacLEISH, Archibald. *Songs for Eve.* Cloth. Boston, 1954. First edition. In dust jacket. $25-$35.

MacLEISH, Archibald. *Songs for a Summer Day.* Wrappers. (New Haven), 1913. First edition. $150-$250. Author's first book.

MacLEISH, Archibald. *Streets in the Moon.* Decorated boards and cloth. Boston, 1926. First edition. One of 60 on handmade paper, signed. Boxed. $125-$135. Another issue: One of 540. $30-$35.

MacLEISH, Archibald. *Tower of Ivory.* Boards, paper labels. New Haven, 1917. First edition. In dust jacket. $200-$250. Also, $275 (A, 1977). Author's first hardbound book.

MacLEISH, Archibald, and others. *"What Is America's Foreign Policy?"* 12 pp., mimeographed. State Dept. press release. (Washington), 1945. $75-$100.

MacLOW, Jackson. *22 Light Poems.* Decorated cloth. Los Angeles, 1968. Black Sparrow Press. One of 125 signed. $35-$50. Another issue: Wrappers. One of 750. $15-$20.

McLUHAN, Herbert Marshall. *The Mechanical Bride.* Cloth. New York, (1951). First edition. In dust jacket. $40-$50. Author's first book.

McMASTER, S. W. *Sixty Years on the Upper Mississippi.* 300 pp., flexible wrappers. Rock Island, Ill., 1893 (printer's foreword dated Galena, Ill., 1895). First edition. $175-$200.

McMURRAY, W. J. *History of the 20th Tennessee Regiment Volunteer Infantry, C.S.A.* Cloth. Nashville, 1904. First edition. $50-$75.

McMURTRIE, Douglas C. *The Beginnings of Printing in Chicago.* Half cloth. Chicago, 1931. One of 160. $50.

McMURTRIE, Douglas C. *The Beginnings of Printing in Utah.* Half cloth. Chicago, 1931. One of 160. $50.

McMURTRIE, Douglas C. *Bibliography of Chicago Imprints.* 1835-50. Buckram. Chicago, 1944. One of 200. $35-$50.

McMURTRIE, Douglas C. *Early Printing in New Orleans, 1764-1810.* Illustrated. Half cloth. New Orleans, 1929. One of 410. $60-$80.

McMURTRIE, Douglas C. *Early Printing in Wisconsin.* Cloth. Seattle, 1931. $50-$75.

McMURTRIE, Douglas C. *Early Printing in Wyoming.* Cloth. Hattiesburg, Miss., 1943. $35.

McMURTRIE, Douglas C. *Eighteenth Century North Carolina Imprints, 1749-1800.* Facsimiles. Cloth. Chapel Hill, 1938. One of 200. In dust jacket. $25-$35.

McMURTRIE, Douglas C. *The First Printers of Chicago.* Half cloth. Chicago, 1927. One of 650. $25-$35. Another issue: One of 250. $50-$60.

McMURTRIE, Douglas C. *The Golden Book.* Illustrated. Half morocco. Chicago, 1927. First edition. One of 220 signed. $60-$80.

McMURTRIE, Douglas C. *A History of Printing in the United States.* Vol. II. (All published.) Cloth. New York, 1936. First edition. $75-$100. (Covers Middle and South Atlantic states.)

McMURTRIE, Douglas C. *The Invention of Printing.* Printed wrappers. Chicago, 1942. $50.

McMURTRIE, Douglas C. *Jotham Meeker: Pioneer Printer of Kansas.* Portrait and facsimiles. Cloth. Chicago, 1930. One of 650. $25-$35.

McMURTRIE, Douglas C., and Allen, Albert H. *Early Printing in Colorado.* Cloth. Denver, 1935. First edition. $75-$100.

McMURTRIE, Douglas C., and Eames, Wilberforce. *New York Printing.* 78 illustrations. Cloth. Chicago, 1928. $75-$100.

McMURTRIE, Henry. *Sketches of Louisville and Its Environs.* Map and table. Boards. Louisville, 1819. First edition. $200-$250.

McMURTRY, Larry. *Horseman, Pass By.* Boards and cloth. New York, (1961). First edition. In dust jacket. $125-$150. Author's first book.

McMURTRY, Larry. *In a Narrow Grave.* Cloth. Austin, 1968. Encino Press. First edition, first issue, with "skyscrappers" for "skyscrapers," page 105, and other errors. (Suppressed.) In dust jacket. $250 and up. Second issue, errors corrected: In jacket. $50-$75. Limited issue: Half leather. One of 250 signed. Boxed. $200-$225.

McMURTRY, Larry. *It's Always We Rambled: An Essay on Rodeo.* Boards. New York, 1974. First edition. One of 300, signed. (Issued without dust jacket.) $50-$75.

McMURTRY, Larry. *The Last Picture Show.* Tan cloth. New York, 1966. First edition. In dust jacket. $35-$50.

McMURTRY, Larry. *Leaving Cheyenne.* Cloth. New York, 1963. First edition. In dust jacket. $85-$110.

MacNEICE, Louis. *Autumn Journal.* Cloth. London, 1939. First edition. In dust jacket. $75-$100.

MacNEICE, Louis. *Blind Fireworks.* Cloth. London, 1929. First edition. In dust jacket. $125-$150. Author's first book.

MacNEICE, Louis. *The Earth Compels.* Cloth. London, 1939. First edition. In dust jacket. $50-$60.

MacNEICE, Louis. *The Last Ditch.* Boards, linen spine, paper label. Dublin, 1940. Cuala Press. First edition. One of 450. In tissue dust jacket. $100-$125.

MacNEICE, Louis. *Poems.* Cloth. London, 1935. First edition. In dust jacket. $50. Signed, $50-$75.

MacNEICE, Louis. *Poems.* Cloth. New York, (1937). First edition. (Same title as the 1935 book but not the same content.) In dust jacket. $40-$60.

MacNEICE, Louis. *Springboard.* Cloth. London, 1944. First edition. In dust jacket. $30-$40.

McNEIL, Samuel. *McNeils* [sic] *Travels in 1849, to, Through and from the Gold Regions.* 40 pp., plain wrappers. Columbus, Ohio, 1850. First edition. $5,000 and up. Also, $3,500 (A, 1968)—the Thomas W. Streeter copy, one of only 5 known.

MacNUTT, Francis A. *Bartholomew de Las Casas, His Life, Apostolate, and Writings.* Portrait. 2 vols., half cloth. Cleveland, 1909. First edition. In dust jackets. $75-$150.

MACOMB, David B. *Answer to Enquiries Relative to Middle Florida.* 5 unnumbered leaves. Tallahassee, 1827. First edition. $1,000 and up. Also, bound in modern cloth, $800 (A, 1967).

MACON, T. J. *Reminiscences of the 1st Company of Richmond Howitzers.* Cloth. Richmond, (about 1909). First edition. $100-$125.

MACQUOID, Percy. *The History of English Furniture.* Illustrated, including color plates. 4 vols., buckram. London, 1904-08. First edition. $250-$400.

MACQUOID, Percy, and Edwards, Ralph. *The Dictionary of English Furniture.* 43 color plates, about 3,000 other illustrations. 3 vols., folio, buckram. London, 1924-27. First edition. $500-$750. London, 1954. 3 vols., folio. buckram. $500-$600.

McSHEEHY, H. J. *A Hunt in the Rockies.* Frontispiece and photographs. 135 pp., printed red wrappers. Logansport, Ind., 1893. First edition. $300-$400, possibly more.

McWHORTER, Lucullus V. *The Border Settlers of Northwestern Virginia from 1768 to 1795.* Cloth. Hamilton, Ohio, 1915. First edition. $75-$85.

McWILLIAMS, John. *Recollections.* Portrait, Cloth. Princeton, (about 1919). First edition. $75-$100.

MACY, John (editor). *American Writers on American Literature.* Cloth. New York, 1931. First edition. In dust jacket. $40-$60.

MADARIAGA, Salvador de. *Don Quixote: An Introductory Essay in Psychology.* Boards and linen. Newtown, Wales, 1934. Gregynog Press. One of 250. $300.

MADDEN, Frederic W. *Coins of the Jews.* Illustrated. Folio, half leather. London, 1881. First edition. $150-$175. London, 1903. Second edition. $75-$100.

MADISON, James. *Communications from the American Ministers at Ghent.* 74 pp., sewed. Washington, 1814. First edition, with final signature "10." $50-$60.

MADISON, James. *Communications from the Plenipotentiaries of the U. S. Negotiating Peace with Great Britain.* 28 pp., sewed. Washington, 1814. $60-$75.

MADISON, James. *Message from the President of the United States.* 19 pp. Washington, 1813. $100-$125. (Note: Covers the captivity of Mrs. Crawley among the Creek Indians.)

MADISON, James. *Message from the President of the United States, Recommending an Immediate Declaration of War Against Great Britain.* 12 pp., sewed. Washington, 1812. $200-$300.

MADRID Y ORMAECHEA, German. *Historia Christiana de la California.* 5 plates. 238 pp., wrappers. Mexico, 1864. $300 and up.

MAGEE, David. *The Hundredth Book: A Bibliography of . . . The Book Club of California.* 18 reproductions, many in color. Folio, half cloth. San Francisco, 1958. Grabhorn printing. One of 400. In dust jacket. $200-$300.

MAGEE, Dorothy, and Magee, David. *Bibliography of the Grabhorn Press, 1940-1956.* Illustrated. Folio, half morocco. San Francisco, 1957. One of 225. $650-$850. See Heller, Elinor, and Magee, David.

*MAGNA Carta and Other Charters of English Liberties.* Tan pigskin. (London, 1938.) Guyon House Press. One of 250. $150-$200.

MAGOFFIN, Susan Shelby, *Down the Santa Fe Trail and into Mexico.* Edited by Stella M. Drumm. Map, plates. Cloth. New Haven, 1926. First edition. In dust jacket. $75-$125.

MAGOUN, F. Alexander. *The Frigate Constitution and Other Historic Ships.* Illustrated, including 16 folding plates. Buckram. Salem, 1928. One of 97 large paper copies. $150-$200. Ordinary issue: $75-$85.

MAGRUDER, Allan B. *Political, Commercial and Moral Reflections, on the Late Cession of Louisiana, to the United States.* Boards. Lexington, Ky., 1803. First edition. $3,000-$3,500. Also, $2,100 (A, 1967).

MAGUIRE, H. N. *The Coming Empire: A Complete and Reliable Treatise on the Black Hills, Yellowstone and Big Horn Regions.* 7 plates, folding map. Cloth. Sioux City, Iowa, 1878. First edition. $300-$400.

MAGUIRE, H. N. *The Lakeside Library: The People's Edition of the Black Hills and American Wonderland.* (Caption title.) Illustrations and map. 36 pp., stitched. Chicago, 1877. First edition. $300 and up. Also, $150 (A, 1968).

MAHAN, A. T. *The Influence of Sea Power upon History.* Illustrated. Cloth. Boston, 1890. First edition. $400-$600.

MAHAN, A. T. *The Navy in the Civil War.* Illustrated. Cloth. New York, 1883. First edition. $50-$75. Author's first book.

MAHAN, D. H. *An Elementary Course of Civil Engineering.* 176 wood engravings. Cloth. New York, 1846. $75 and up.

MAHAN, D. H. *An Elementary Treatise on Advanced-Guard, Out-Post and Detachment Service of Troops in the Presence of an Enemy.* Cloth. New Orleans, 1861. $100 and up.

MAHAN, D. H. *Summary of the Course of Permanent Fortification, etc.* Boards. West Point, 1850. First edition. $150 and up.

*MAID Marian.* Boards. London, 1822. (By Thomas Love Peacock.) First edition. $500-$600.

MAILER, Norman. *Barbary Shore.* Black cloth. New York, (1951). First edition with circled "R" on copyright page. In dust jacket. $40-$50.

MAILER, Norman. *Deaths for the Ladies and Other Disasters.* Printed wrappers. New York, (1962). First edition. $30-$40. Another issue: Cloth. In dust jacket. $25.

MAILER, Norman. *Gargoyle, Guignol, False Closet.* 4 pp., leaflet. Dublin, 1964. First edition. One of 100. $75-$100.

MAILER, Norman. *The Naked and the Dead.* Black boards. New York, (1948). First edition, with circled "R" on copyright page. In dust jacket. $200-$250. Author's first book. (Note: A hefty book bound in notoriously cheap fashion—paper over boards—thus rare in fine condition immediately after publication.) Same: advance copy in printed wrappers. $200 and up. Another, signed. $275 (in a 1977 catalogue). London, (1949). Full wine-colored morocco. First English edition. One of 240 bound for the Collector's Book Club. $50-$60. Another issue: One of 13. $162.40 (A, 1966).

MAILER, Norman. *The White Negro.* Wrappers. (San Francisco, 1957.) City Lights. First edition, first issue, with 35¢ price on front cover. $35-$40.

MAILLARD, N. Doran. *The History of the Republic of Texas, from the Discovery of the Country to the Present Time.* Folding map. Dark-blue cloth. London, 1842. First edition. $350-$600.

MAJOR, Charles. See Caskoden, Edwin.

MAJOR *Jones's Courtship; or Adventures of a Christmas Eve.* 61 pp., wrappers. Savannah, Ga., 1850. (By William Tappan Thompson.) First edition. $75-$150.

MAJOR *Jones's Sketches of Travel, Comprising the Scenes, Incidents, and Adventures in His Tour from Georgia to Canada.* Illustrated by F.O.C. Darley. Philadelphia, 1848. (By William Tappan Thompson.) First edition. $200-$250.

MAJORS, Alexander. *Seventy Years on the Frontier.* Frontispiece and plates. Blue pictorial cloth, or wrappers. Chicago, 1893. First edition. Wrappers: $75. Cloth: $50. Another edition: Denver, no date. Wrappers, without illustrations. $15-$25.

MALAMUD, Bernard. *The Natural.* Gray or red cloth. New York, (1952). First edition. In dust jacket. $60-$85. Author's first book. (Note: Red cloth has been called the first binding, a point disputed by a gray cloth copy seen with a review slip pasted in.)

MALAMUD, Bernard. *The Tenants.* Orange cloth. New York, (1971). First edition, first binding. One of 250, signed. In dust jacket. $35. Trade edition : In dust jacket. $15.

MALET, Capt. H. E. *Annals of the Road.* 10 colored plates, woodcuts. Cloth. London, 1876. First edition. $100-$150.

MALKIN, B. H. *A Father's Memoirs of His Child.* Folding map, 3 plates. Boards. London, 1806. First edition. $125-$175.

MALORY, Sir Thomas. *Le Morte D'Arthur.* Edited by H. O. Sommer and Andrew Lang. 3 vols., wrappers. London, 1889-91. $200 and up. London, (1893-94). Illustrated by Aubrey Beardsley, 12 parts, printed wrappers. One of 300 on Dutch handmade paper. $1,000-$1,500. Another issue: 3 vols., pictorial cloth. One of 300. $750-$1,000. Another issue: 2 vols., cloth. One of 1,500. $300-$500. London, 1909. Cloth. Second Beardsley edition. $200-$250. London, 1910-11. Riccardi Press. Illustrated in color by W. Russell Flint. 4 vols., limp vellum. One of 500. $400-$500. Another issue: Boards and cloth. $250-$300. London, 1913. Ashendene Press. Illustrated by Charles and Margaret Gore. Folio, full cowhide. One of 145. Boxed. $2,000-$2,500. Another issue: One of 8 on vellum. $3,500-$5,000. London, 1917. Illustrated by Arthur Rackham. Vellum. One of 500 signed by Rackham. $500-$750. Also, with an original watercolor, signed by Rackham on limitation page—$1,500-$1,750. Another issue: Cloth. $150-$200. London, 1927. Illustrated by Beardsley. Half vellum. One of 1,600. $200-$350. London, (1929). Illustrated by W. Russell Flint. Morocco. $400-$750. London, 1933. Shakespeare Head Press. Illustrated, 2 vols., morocco. One of 370. $300-$500. New York, 1936. Limited Editions Club. Illustrated by Robert Gibbings. 3 vols., boards and cloth. Boxed. $150-$200.

MALRAUX, André. *The Metamorphosis of the Gods.* Illustrated. Red morocco. Garden City, 1960. First American edition. One of 50, signed. Boxed. $150-$200. Trade edition: Cloth. In dust jacket. $30-$40.

MALRAUX, André. *The Psychology of Art.* Illustrated. 3 vols., cloth. (New York, 1949-50.) First American edition. In dust jackets. $200-$250.

MALRAUX, André. *The Voices of Silence.* Illustrated. Cloth. Garden City, 1953. First American edition. In dust jacket. Boxed. $60-$85.

MALRAUX, André. *The Walnut Trees of Altenburg.* Translated by A. W. Fielding. Cloth. London, 1952. First English edition. In dust jacket. $80-$100.

MALTHUS, Thomas Robert. *Definitions in Political Economy.* Boards. London, 1827. First edition. $300-$350.

MALTHUS, Thomas Robert. *An Essay on the Principle of Population.* Boards. London, 1803. Second edition. $200-$250. (Note: The anonymous first edition, London, 1798, boards, sells for $3,000 and up if in fine condition.) Washington, 1809. 2 vols., contemporary calf. First American edition. $250-$350.

MALTHUS, Thomas Robert. *An Inquiry into the Nature and Progress of Rent.* Boards. London, 1815. First edition. $350-$400.

MALTHUS, Thomas Robert. *Principles of Political Economy.* Boards. London, 1820. First edition. $500-$750. Boston, 1821. Boards. First American edition. $200-$300.

*MAN Without a Country (The).* 23 pp., terra-cotta wrappers. Boston, 1865. (By Edward Everett Hale.) First edition, first issue, without the publisher's printed yellow "Announcement" slip tipped in. $400-$500. Second issue, with the "Announcement" slip tipped in. $250-$350. New York, 1902. Vellum. "Birthday Edition." One of 80 on Japan paper. $100-$125. New York, 1936. Limited Editions Club. Boxed. $25-$35.

MANGAM, William D. *The Clarks: An American Phenomenon.* Cloth. New York, 1941. First edition. In dust jacket. $250.

*MANIFIESTO al Mundo. La Justicia y la Necesidad de la Independencia de la Nueva España.* 19 pp., sewed. Puebla, Mexico, 1821. (By Manuel Barcena.) First edition. $600-$800, possibly more.

MANLY, William Lewis. *Death Valley in '49.* 4 plates. Cloth. San Jose, 1894. First edition. $100-$135.

MANN, Thomas. *The Beloved Returns.* Boards. New York, 1940. First American edition. One of 395, signed. In dust jacket. Boxed. $85-$125.

MANN, Thomas. *Buddenbrooks, Verfall einer Familie.* 2 vols., half morocco. Berlin, 1901. First edition. $200-$300. Author's first book. London, 1924. Translated by H. T. Lowe-Porter. 2 vols., cloth. First edition in English. In dust jackets. $75-$85.

MANN, Thomas. *The Magic Mountain.* 2 vols., half vellum. New York, 1927. One of 200, signed. $250-$350. New York, 1962. Limited Editions Club. Illustrated. Half cloth. Boxed. $125-$150.

MANN, Thomas. *Nocturnes.* Lithographs by Lynd Ward. Pictorial cloth. New York, 1934. One of 1,000, signed. Boxed. $75-$85.

MANN, Thomas. *A Sketch of My Life.* White buckram. Paris, (1930). First edition. One of 695 on Van Gelder paper. $50-$60. Another issue: One of 75 on vellum. $150-$250.

MANNING, Wentworth. *Some History of Van Zandt County, Texas.* Vol. 1. (All published.) Illustrated. Maps. Cloth. Des Moines, (1919). First edition. $85-$125.

MANNING-SANDERS, Ruth. *Martha Wish-You-Ill.* 16 pp., wrappers. London, 1926. Hogarth Press. First edition. $35-$50.

MANSFIELD, Edward D. *Exposition of the Natural Position of Mackinaw City, and the Climate, Soil, and Commercial Elements of the Surrounding Country.* 2 maps. 47 pp., printed wrappers. Cincinnati, 1857. First edition. $200-$250.

MANSFIELD, Katherine. *The Aloe.* Buckram. London, 1930. First edition. One of 750. In dust jacket. $100-$135. New York, 1930. Boards. First American edition. One of 975. In dust jacket. Boxed. $60-$80.

MANSFIELD, Katherine. *Bliss and Other Stories.* Brick-red cloth. London, (1920). First edition, with page 13 numbered 3. In white dust jacket with author's portrait. $150-$175. New York, 1921. Cloth, paper label. First American edition. In dust jacket. $50-$60.

MANSFIELD Katherine. *The Doves' Nest and Other Stories.* Blue-gray cloth, blue spine lettering. London, (1923). First edition, first issue, with verso of title page blank. One of 25. In dust jacket. $300-$400. Second issue, with "First published June, 1923" on back of title page. In dust jacket. $100-$125.

MANSFIELD, Katherine. *The Garden Party and Other Stories.* Light-blue cloth, lettered in blue. London, (1922). First edition, first issue, with "sposition" for "position" in last line on page 103. In strawberry-colored dust jacket. One of 25. $400-$500. Also, $425 (A, 1975). Later binding state, orange (ocher) lettering. In dust jacket. $75-$85. London, (1939). Verona Press. 16 color lithographs by Marie Laurencin. Decorated cloth. One of 1,200. In dust jacket. Boxed. $300-$400.

MANSFIELD, Katherine. *In a German Pension.* Green cloth. London, (1911). First edition. In orange (ocher) dust jacket. $400-$500. Author's first book.

MANSFIELD, Katherine. *Je Ne Parle Pas Français.* Green wrappers. Hampstead, England, 1919 (actually 1918). Heron Press. First edition. One of 100. $400-$600.

MANSFIELD, Katherine. *The Journal of Katherine Mansfield.* Edited by J. Middleton Murry. Cloth. London, 1927. First edition. In dust jacket. $75-$100.

MANSFIELD, Katherine. *Poems.* Brown boards, red leather spine label. London, (1923). First edition. In cream-colored dust jacket. $125-$135.

MANSFIELD, Katherine. *Prelude.* Blue pictorial wrappers. Richmond, England, (1918). Hogarth Press. First edition, with or without design on covers by J. D. Fergusson. $200-$250. Another issue: Blue boards and linen. One of 300. $300-$350.

MANSFIELD, Katherine. *Something Childish and Other Stories.* Gray buckram. London, (1924). First edition, first issue, without "First published 1924" on verso of title page. In dust jacket. $125-$175. Second issue. In dust jacket. $40-$65.

MANSFIELD, Katherine. *To Stanislaw Wyspianski.* Printed wrappers. London, 1938. One of 100 printed for Bertram Rota. $100-$125.

*MANSFIELD Park: A Novel.* By the Author of *Sense and Sensibility* and *Pride and Prejudice.* 3 vols., blue boards, white paper labels. London, 1814. (By Jane Austen.) First edition, with Vols. 1 and 3 bearing Sidney imprint on back of half titles and Vol. 2 the Roworth imprint. $5,000-$7,500. Also, $4,250 (A, 1974). London, 1816. 3 vols., cloth. $500 and up.

*MANUAL of Military Surgery.* Prepared for the Use of the Confederate States Army. 30 lithograph plates. Cloth-backed wrappers. Richmond, 1863. (By John J. Chisholm.) First illustrated edition (?). $850.

*MANUEL de Proverbes Dramatiques.* 288 pp., cloth, printed spine label. Portland (Brunswick), Me. 1830. First edition. No record in modern times. First edition, second issue, with last page misnumbered 188. (Edited anonymously by Henry Wadsworth Longfellow.) Rebound in morocco, $80 (A, 1960). (Note: Blanck's *BAL* also describes a preliminary issue of the same edition with only 156 pages.)

*MAP of Texas with Parts of the Adjoining States.* 30 sections, folded into red leather covers.

Philadelphia, (1830). (Compiled by Stephen F. Austin.) First edition. $3,000-$4,000, possibly more.

*MARCH of the First (The).* (First Regiment of Colorado Volunteers.) 36 pp., stitched, plus 4 pp. of ads. Denver, 1863. First edition. $3,500. Also, $2,000 (A, 1968).

MARCLIFFE, Theophilus. *The Looking Glass: A True History of the Early Years of an Artist.* Boards. London, 1805. (By William Godwin.) First edition. $750-$1,000.

MARCUS Aurelius Antonius. *The Thoughts of the Emperor Marcus Aurelius.* Translated by George Long. Wrappers. London, 1897. Ashendene Press. One of 30. $1,500-$2,000. London, 1909. Illustrated by W. Russell Flint. Limp vellum with ties. One of 17 on vellum. $750-$1,000. Another issue: Vellum or half cloth. One of 500. $150-$250.

MARCY, Randolph B. *Exploration of the Red River of Louisana.* (Senate Exec. Doc. 54.) 65 plates, 2 maps, 2 vols., brown cloth and green cloth (atlas case). Washington, 1853. First edition. $100-$150. Washington, 1854. Second edition, printed by Tucker. $50. Washington, 1854. House version, printed by Nicholson. $50.

MARCY, Randolph B. *The Prairie Traveler: A Hand-Book for Overland Expeditions.* Map, frontispiece, 10 plates. Cloth. New York, 1859. First edition. $200-$250. London, 1863. Edited by R. F. Burton. Map. Half morocco. First English edition. $150-$200.

MARDERSTEIG, Hans. *Pastonchi: A Specimen of a New Letter for Use on the "Monotype."* Illustrated with plates and booklet inserts. Marbled boards and vellum. (London, 1928.) One of 200 on Fabriano paper, printed by Mardersteig. $100-$200.

MARIGNY, Bernard. *Réflexions sur la Campagne du Gen. Jackson en Louisiane en 1814-15.* 51 pp., wrappers. Nouvelle-Orléans, 1848. First edition. $200-$300.

*MARK Twain's Sketches.* See Twain, Mark.

*MARKET Harborough; or, How Mr. Sawyer Went to the Shires.* Cloth. London, 1861. (By George John Whyte-Melville.) First edition. $75-$100.

MARKHAM, Edwin. *The Man with the Hoe.* 4 pp., printed wrappers. San Francisco, 1899. First book edition. $150 and up. (Earlier, Jan. 15, 1899: Special supplement to San Francisco Sunday *Examiner*, containing first separate printing of the poem, 4 pp. $200 and up.) New York, 1899. Green cloth. Second edition, first issue, with "fruitless" for "milkless" in line 5, page 35. $40-$50.

MARKHAM, Edwin. *New Poems: Eighty Songs at Eighty.* Portrait. Boards and leather. Garden City, 1932. First edition (so stated). One of 100, signed. Boxed. $50-$75. Trade edition: Cloth. In dust jacket. $25.

MARKLAND, George. *Pteryplegia: The Art of Shoot-Flying.* Hand-colored plates by Robert Ball. Boards. New York, 1931. Derrydale Press. One of 200 signed by the artist. $150-$250. Another issue: Black and white plates. One of 300. $75-$100.

MARKS, B. *Small-Scale Farming in Central California.* 48 pp., printed wrappers. San Francisco, (1888). $100-$125.

MARKS, Elias, M.D. *The Aphorisms of Hipprocrates.* Boards, paper label. New York, 1818. First edition. $50-$60.

MARKS, M. R. *The Advantages and Resources of Orange County, Florida.* 2 maps. 16 pp., wrappers. Orlando, Fla. (1879). $100-$125.

MARLOWE, Christopher. *Edward the Second.* Hand-colored illustrations. Folio, vellum. London, 1929. Aquila Press. One of 40. $300-$350. Another issue: One of 500. $75-$100.

MARLOWE, Christopher. *The Famous Tragedy of the Rich Jew of Malta.* Engravings by Eric Ravilious. Cloth. London, 1933. Golden Hours Press. One of 250. $100-$150.

MARLOWE, Christopher, and Chapman, George. *Hero and Leander.* Illustrated. Vellum. London, 1894. Vale Press. One of 220. $400-$500. London, 1933. Illustrated by Lettice Sanford. Cloth. One of 206. $75-$100.

MARLY, Mary. *Out of the Dump.* Illustrated. Pictorial cloth. Chicago, 1909. First edition. $75.

MARQUAND, John P. See Clark, Charles E.

MARQUAND, John P. *The Late George Apley.* Green cloth. New York, 1937. First edition. In dust jacket. $25-$35.

MARQUAND, John P. *Ming Yellow.* Cloth. Boston, 1935. First edition. In dust jacket. $35-$50.

MARQUAND, John P. *Point of No Return.* Cloth. Boston, 1949. First edition. One of 600, signed. In dust jacket. $50-$65. Trade edition. In dust jacket. $20-$25.

MARQUAND, John P. *The Unspeakable Gentleman.* Cloth. New York, 1922. First edition, with Scribner seal on copyright page. In dust jacket. $50-$60. Another issue: Boards and cloth. Limited, signed, for booksellers. $75-$100. Author's first novel.

MARQUIS, Don. *Archy and Mehitabel.* Black cloth. Garden City, 1927. First edition, first printing. In dust jacket. $60-$75.

MARQUIS, Don. *Danny's Own Story.* Illustrated by E. W. Kemble. Cloth. Garden City, 1912. First edition. In dust jacket. $35. Author's first book.

MARQUIS, Don. *Dreams and Dust.* Cloth. New York, (1915). First edition. In dust jacket. $25-$35.

MARQUIS, Don. *How Hank Signed the Pledge in a Cistern.* Wrappers. New York, (about 1912). First edition. $40-$60.

MARQUIS, Don. *The Old Soak, and Hail and Farewell.* Boards and cloth. Garden City, 1921. First edition. In dust jacket. $25-$30.

MARQUIS, Thomas B. *Memoirs of a White Crow Indian (Thomas H. LeForge).* Illustrated. Pictorial yellow cloth. New York, (1928). First edition. In dust jacket. $35-$50. Lacking jacket, $25-$30. London, 1928. Illustrated. Pictorial cloth. First English edition. In dust jacket. $25-$35.

MARQUIS, Thomas B. *A Warrior Who Fought Custer.* Illustrated. Cloth. Minneapolis, 1931. First edition, first binding, with "Midwest" on spine. In dust jacket. $50-$60.

MARRANT, John. *A Narrative of the Life of John Marrant.* 48 pp., wrappers. Halifax, 1812. (Edited by William Aldridge.) $50. (Note: One of innumerable nineteenth-century reprints of a book first published in London in 1785. Howes calls it "one of the earliest written by an American Negro.")

*MARRIAGE: A Novel.* 3 vols., boards. Edinburgh, 1818. (By Susan Edmonstone Ferrier.) First edition. $500-$750. Also, $360 (A, 1968).

MARRIOTT, William. *A Collection of English Miracle-Plays or Mysteries.* Boards, paper labels. Basel, Switzerland, 1838. First edition. $50-$100.

MARRYAT, Frank. *Mountains and Molehills.* 18 woodcuts, 8 color plates. Salmon-colored cloth. London, 1855. (By Francis S. Marryat.) First edition. $400-$500. New York, 1855. Frontispiece. Pictorial cloth. First American edition. $150-$200.

MARRYAT, Frederick. See *Mr. Midshipman Easy; Olla Podrida; Percival Keene; Snarleyyow.*

MARRYAT, Frederick. *A Diary in America.* 6 vols., (Parts I and II, each 3 vols.), boards. London, 1839. First edition. $300-$400. Philadelphia, 1839-40. 3 vols., half cloth (2 vols., 1839, and 2d Series, 1 vol., 1840). First American edition. $100-$150. Paris, 1839-40. 2 folding maps. 2 vols., half leather. $100-$150.

MARRYAT, Frederick. *Jacob Faithful.* 3 vols, half cloth. London, 1834. First edition. $150-$250.

MARRYAT, Frederick. *The Little Savage.* Illustrated. 2 vols., green cloth. London, 1848-49. First edition. $150-$250.

MARRYAT, Frederick. *Masterman Ready.* Illustrated. 3 vols., cloth. London, 1841-42-42. First edition. $300-$400.

MARRYAT, Frederick. *The Mission.* Map, frontispiece. 2 vols., cloth. London, 1845. First edition, with 32 pages of ads in Vol. 1. $150-$200.

MARRYAT, Frederick. *Narrative of the Travels and Adventures of Monsieur Violet, in California, Sonora and Western Texas.* Map. 3 vols., cloth. London, 1843. First edition. $250-$350. Second edition: London, 1843. 3 vols., cloth. With map. Retitled: *The Travels and Romantic Adventures of Monsieur Violet, etc.* $200-$250.

MARRYAT, Frederick. *Poor Jack.* Illustrated. 12 parts, pictorial wrappers. London, 1840. First edition. $400-$500. London, 1840. Pictorial cloth. First book edition. $150-$200.

MARRYAT, Frederick. *The Privateer's Man.* 2 vols., cloth. London, 1846. First edition, with many ads in first volume. $150-$200.

MARRYAT, Frederick. *The Settlers in Canada.* 2 frontispieces. 2 vols., cloth. London, 1844. First edition. $150-$200.

MARSH, James B. *Four Years in the Rockies.* Portrait. Blue cloth. New Castle, Pa., 1884. First edition. $350-$400.

MARSH, John. *Hannah Hawkins, the Reformed Drunkard's Daughter.* Cloth. New York, 1844. First edition. $75-$100.

MARSH, W. Lockwood. *Aeronautical Prints and Drawings.* Illustrated, including color plates. Cloth. London, 1924. First edition. In dust jacket. $250-$350. Another issue: Pigskin. One of 100. $400-$500.

MARSHALL, Archibald. *The Honour of the Clintons.* Cloth. London, (1913). First edition. In dust jacket. $30-$35.

MARSHALL, Charles I. *History of Door County, Wisconsin.* Portrait. Boards and cloth. Sturgeon Bay, Wis., 1881. First edition. $100-$125.

MARSHALL, Humphrey. *The History of Kentucky.* Calf. Frankfort, 1812. First edition. $1,000-$1,250. Also, repaired, $500 (A, 1973). Frankfort, 1824. 2 vols., sheepskin. Second edition. $400-$500. Also, rubbed, $150 (A, 1972).

MARSHALL, Jabez P. *Memoirs of the Late Rev. Abraham Marshall.* Boards. Mount Zion, Ga., 1824. First edition. $75.

MARSHALL, John. *Opinion of the Supreme Court, etc. in the Case of Samuel Worcester Versus the State of Georgia.* 39 pp., sewed. Washington, 1832. First edition. $250-$300. Second edition, same date. 20 pp., half calf. $100-$150.

MARSHALL, L. G. *The Arabian Art of Taming and Training Wild and Vicious Horses.* 36 pp., wrappers. (Circleville, Ohio), 1857. $100-$125.

MARSHALL, Paule. *Brown Girl, Brownstones.* Cloth. New York, (1959). First edition. In dust jacket. $80-$100. Author's first book.

MARSHALL, William I. *Acquisition of Oregon, and the Long Suppressed Evidence About Marcus Whitman.* Portrait. 2 vols., green cloth. (Seattle), 1905. First edition. $150-$250. Portland, 1911. 2 vols., cloth. $100-$125.

*MARTIAL Achievements of Great Britain and Her Allies from 1799 to 1815 (The).* 52 colored plates. Half morocco. London, (1814-15). $2,000-$3,000.

MARTIN, Aaron. *An Attempt to Show the Inconsistency of Slave-Holding, with the Religion of the Gospel.* 16 pp., stitched. Lexington, Ky., 1807. First edition. $2,000-$2,500. Also, $1,200 (A, 1967).

*MARTIN Faber, the Story of a Criminal.* 2 vols., cloth. New York, 1837. (By William Gilmore Simms.) First edition. $300-$450.

MARTIN, Fredrik R. *The Miniature Painting and Painters of Persia, India and Turkey from the 8th to the 18th Century.* 271 collotype plates, 48 text illustrations, 5 plates in gold and colors by W. Griggs. 2 vols., folio, buckram. London, 1912. $500-$750, possibly more.

MARTINEAU, Harriet. *Feats on the Fjord.* Illustrated by Arthur Rackham. Cloth. London, 1899. First edition. $100-$150. London, (1911). Plates in color. Cloth. $100-$150.

MARTINEAU, Harriet. *How to Observe Morals and Manners.* Cloth. London, 1848. First edition. $100-$150.

MARTINEAU, Harriet. *Retrospect of Western Travel.* 2 vols., cloth. London, 1838. First edition. $250-$350. New York, 1838. 2 vols., half linen. First American edition. $150-$200.

MARTINEAU, Harriet. *Society in America.* 3 vols., cloth. London, 1837. First edition. $300-$400. New York, 1837. 2 vols., cloth. $100-$150.

MARTÍNEZ CARO, Ramón. *Verdadera Idea de la Primera Campaña de Tejas y Sucesos Ocurridos despues de la acción de San Jacinto.* Printed wrappers. Mexico, 1837. First edition. $1,000-$1,500.

MARVEL, Ik. *Dream Life.* Cloth. New York, 1851. (By Donald G. Mitchell.) First edition, first state, with stereotyper's slug on copyright page. $35-$50.

MARVEL, Ik. *Fresh Gleanings.* 2 vols., printed wrappers, or one vol., cloth. New York, 1847. (By Donald G. Mitchell.) First edition. Wrappers: $100-$150. Cloth: $30-$40.

MARVEL, Ik. *Looking Back at Boyhood.* 21 pp., wrappers. (Norwich, Conn.), June, 1906. (By Donald G. Mitchell.) First edition. $75-$100.

MARVEL, Ik. *The Reveries of a Bachelor.* Dark-blue cloth, or leather. New York, 1850. (By Donald G. Mitchell.) First edition, first printing, with last word, "sleep," on page 29 in perfect type. $75-$100.

MARVIN, Frederic R. *Yukon Overland: The Gold-Digger's Handbook.* Folding map, 18 plates. Printed orange wrappers. Cincinnati, 1898. First edition. $150-$200.

MARVY, Louis (and Thackeray, William Makepeace). *Sketches After English Landscape Painters.* With Short Notices by W. M. Thackeray. 20 color plates. Folio, cloth. London, (1850). First edition. $250-$350.

MARX, Groucho. *Beds.* Cloth. New York, 1930. First edition. In dust jacket. $50-$60.

MARX, Karl. *Capital.* 2 vols., red cloth. London, 1887. First edition in English (of the first volume of Marx's major work). $850. New York, 1889. Yellow cloth. First American edition. $400-$500.

*MARY BARTON: A Tale of Manchester Life.* 2 vols., mulberry cloth. London, 1848. (By Elizabeth C. Gaskell.) First edition. $250-$350. Author's first book.

MASEFIELD, John. *Ballads.* Printed wrappers. London, 1903. First edition. No. 13 of "The Vigo Cabinet Series." $65-$85.

MASEFIELD, John. *The Bird of Dawning.* 4 color plates. Buckram. London, 1933. First illustrated edition. One of 300, signed. Boxed. $40-$50.

MASEFIELD, John. *Collected Poems.* Portrait. Cream-colored cloth, leather label. London, 1923. First edition. One of 530, signed. Boxed. $50-$60.

MASEFIELD, John. *The Coming of Christ.* Boards and vellum. London, 1928. First edition. One of 275, signed. In dust jacket. $75-$100.

MASEFIELD, John. *The Hawbucks.* Boards, vellum spine. London, 1929. First edition. One of 275, signed. In dust jacket. $75-$100.

MASEFIELD, John. *John M. Synge: A Few Personal Recollections.* Boards and linen. Dundrum, Ireland, 1915. Cuala Press. First edition. One of 350. $75-$125. Signed by W. B. Yeats on colophon page, $165.

MASEFIELD, John. *Salt Water Ballads.* Blue buckram. London, 1902. First edition, first issue, with Grant Richards imprint on title page. One of 500. $400-$500. Also, $250 (A, 1976). Author's first book.

MASEFIELD, John. *Some Memories of W. B. Yeats.* Boards and linen. Dublin, 1940. Cuala Press. First edition. One of 370. In tissue dust jacket. $50-$85.

MASEFIELD, John. *Sonnets and Poems.* Blue cloth, paper labels. Lollingdon, England, 1916. First edition. In dust jacket. $65-$75.

MASEFIELD, John. *South and East.* Color plates. Vellum. London, 1929. One of 260, signed. Boxed. $50-$75.

MASEFIELD, John. *The Trial of Jesus.* Boards. London, 1925. First edition. One of 525, signed. $75-$85.

MASEFIELD, John. *The Wanderer of Liverpool.* Colored frontispiece, 4 diagrams (3 folding), other plates. Black cloth. London, 1930. First edition. One of 525, signed. Boxed. $75-$100. New York, 1930. Illustrated. Boards and cloth. One of 350, signed. Boxed. $50-$75.

MASON, Allen C. *Tacoma.* (Caption title.) 24 pp., wrappers. (Portland, 1888.) $100-$125.

MASON, Emily V. (editor). *The Southern Poems of the War.* Cloth. Baltimore, 1867. First edition. $50-$75.

MASON, The Rev. George. *Ode on the Loss of the Steamship Pacific.* 4 pp., printed wrappers. Nanaimo, B. C., 1875. $125-$150.

MASON, Z. H. *A General Description of Orange County, Florida.* Map. 56 pp., wrappers. Orlando. (1881). First edition. $250-$300.

MASON, Otis T. *Indian Basketry.* Illustrated, including color plates. 2 vols., pictorial buckram. New York, 1904. First edition. $300-$400.

MASON, Dr. Phillip. *A Legacy to My Children.* Portrait. Cloth. Connersville, Ind., 1868. $50.

*MASQUE of Poets (A).* Black cloth. Boston, 1878. First edition, first issue. $200-$250. Also, worn, $70 (A, 1974). Second issue, reddish brown or green cloth. In cloth "Red Line" box. One of 500. $125-$150. (Note: Contains work by Henry David Thoreau, as well as Emily Dickinson's first book appearance—the poem "Success"—and the only such appearance in her lifetime.)

MASSEY, Gerald. *A Book of the Beginnings.* 2 vols., cloth. London, 1881. First edition. $100-$125.

MASSEY, Gerald. *The Natural Genesis, or Second Part of a Book of the Beginnings.* 2 vols., cloth. London, 1883. First edition. $200-$225.

MASSEY, Linton R. (compiler). *William Faulkner: "Man Working," 1919-1962.* Illustrated. Cloth. Charlottesville, Va., 1968. First edition. Catalogue of the Faulkner collections at the University of Virginia. $50-$75.

MASSIE, J. Cam. *A Treatise on the Eclectic Southern Practice of Medicine.* Sheepskin. Philadelphia, 1854. First edition. $150-$200.

MASSON, L.F.R. *Les Bourgeois de la Compagnie du Nord-Ouest.* Folding map. 2 vols., green and orange wrappers. Quebec, 1889-90. First edition. $300-$350.

MASTERMAN, Walter S. *The Flying Beast.* Cloth. New York, (1932). First American edition. In dust jacket. $35-$45.

MASTERS, Edgar Lee. See Ford, Webster; Wallace, Dexter.

MASTERS, Edgar Lee. *Along the Illinois.* Cloth. Prairie City, Ill., 1942. First edition. $35-$50.

MASTERS, Edgar Lee. *A Book of Verses.* Gray boards. Chicago, 1898. First edition. $175-$250. Author's first book.

MASTERS, Edgar Lee. *Gettysburg, Manila, Acoma.* Cloth. New York, 1930. First edition. One of 375, signed. $65-$75.

MASTERS, Edgar Lee. *Godbey: A Dramatic Poem.* Boards and cloth. New York, 1931. First edition. One of 347, signed. Boxed. $60-$75.

MASTERS, Edgar Lee. *The Golden Fleece of California.* Woodcut illustrations. Cloth. Weston, Vt., (1936). First edition. One of 550, signed. In glassine dust jacket. Boxed. $50-$60. New York, (1936). Cloth. First trade edition. In dust jacket. $15-$20.

MASTERS, Edgar Lee. *The Leaves of the Tree.* Printed wrappers. Chicago, 1909. First edition. $75-$100.

MASTERS, Edgar Lee. *Lee: A Dramatic Poem.* Cloth. New York, 1926. First edition. One of 250, signed. $50-$60. Trade edition: Cloth. In dust jacket. $15-$20.

MASTERS, Edgar Lee. *Lincoln: The Man.* Illustrated. Half vellum and cloth. New York, 1931. First edition. One of 150, signed. $50-$75.

MASTERS, Edgar Lee. *Maximilian.* Wrappers, with paper labels, or boards. Boston, 1902. First edition. Wrappers: $200 (1976 catalogue). Boards: $75-$85.

MASTERS, Edgar Lee. *The New Spoon River.* Vellum and boards. New York, 1924. First edition. One of 360, signed. $85-$110.

MASTERS, Edgar Lee. *The New Star Chamber and Other Essays.* Boards. Chicago, 1904. First edition. $85-$125.

MASTERS, Edgar Lee. *The Serpent in the Wilderness.* Boards and cloth. New York, (1933). First edition. One of 400, signed. In glassine dust jacket. Boxed. $75-$85. One of 84 copies (of the same issue), with a page of the manuscript inserted, $200 and up.

MASTERS, Edgar Lee. *Spoon River Anthology.* Blue cloth. New York, 1915. First edition, first issue, measuring exactly 7/8 inches across top. In dust jacket. $400-$500. Lacking jacket, $250-$300. New York, 1942. Limited Editions Club. Illustrated. Buckram. Boxed. $80-$100.

MATHERS, E. Powys. *Procreant Hymn.* Engravings by Eric Gill. Buckram. Waltham St. Lawrence, England, 1916. Golden Cockerel Press. One of 200. $200-$300.

MATHERS, John, and A Solid Gentleman. *The History of Mr. John Decastro and His Brother Bat, Commonly Called Old Crab.* 4 vols., boards, paper labels. London, 1815. (By George Colman, the Younger.) First edition. $200 and up.

MATHESON, Richard. *Born of Man and Woman.* Cloth. Philadelphia, 1954. First edition. In dust jacket. $40-$50. Author's first book.

MATHESON, Richard. *A Stir of Echoes.* Cloth. Philadelphia, (1958). First edition. In dust jacket. $35.

MATHEWS, A.E. *Canyon City, Colorado, and Its Surroundings.* Map, 5 plates. Cloth. New York, 1870. First edition. $3,000-$3,500.

MATHEWS, A.E. *Pencil Sketches of Colorado.* 23 plates in color. Cloth. (New York), 1866. First edition. $4,000-$5,000. Facsimile reprint: (Denver, 1961.) Oblong folio, cloth. $50-$75.

MATHEWS, A.E. *Pencil Sketches of Montana.* 31 plates (4 folding). Cloth. New York, 1868. First edition. $3,000-$3,500.

MATHEWS, Alfred E. *Gems of Rocky Mountain Scenery.* 20 plates. Cloth. New York, 1869. First edition. $1,500-$1,750.

MATHEWS, Alfred E. *Interesting Narrative; Being a Journal of the Flight of Alfred E. Mathews, of Stark Co., Ohio, from the State of Texas, etc.* 34 pp., sewed. (New Philadelphia, Ohio), 1861. First edition. $1,000-$1,250.

MATHEWS, Edward J. *Crossing the Plains . . . in '59.* Cloth. No place, (1930?). First edition. $150 and up.

MATHEWS, Mrs. M.M. *Ten Years in Nevada.* Illustrated. Leather, or cloth. Buffalo, N.Y., 1880. First edition. $200-$250.

MATHIESSEN, Peter. *At Play in the Fields of the Lord.* Advance copy in wrappers. New York, (1965). First edition. $35.

MATSELL, George W. *Vocabulum; or, the Rogue's Lexicon.* Cloth. New York, (1859). First edition. $50-$75.

MATURIN, Charles Robert. See *Melmoth the Wanderer.*

MATURIN, Charles Robert. *Women; Or, Pour et Contre: A Tale.* 3 vols., boards. Edinburgh, 1818. First edition. $350-$450.

MAUGHAM, W. Somerset. *Ah King: Six Stories.* Blue cloth. London (1933). First edition. In dust jacket. $25-$30. Another issue: Buckram. One of 175, signed. Boxed. $150-$200. Garden City, 1933. Black cloth. First American edition. In dust jacket. $15-$20.

MAUGHAM, W. Somerset. *Ashenden, or The British Agent.* Blue-gray cloth. London, 1928. First edition. In dust jacket. $100-$150.

MAUGHAM, W. Somerset. *The Bishop's Apron.* Cloth. London, 1906. First edition. $100-$150.

MAUGHAM, W. Somerset. *The Book-Bag.* Portrait frontispiece. Half cloth and blue and white boards. Florence, Italy, 1932. First edition. One of 725, signed. In dust jacket. $125-$150.

MAUGHAM, W. Somerset. *Cakes and Ale.* Blue cloth. London, (1930). First edition, first issue, with "won" instead of "won't" in line 14 of page 147. In dust jacket. $40-$50. Second issue, corrected. In dust jacket. $25-$30. London, (1954). Decorations by Graham Sutherland. Boards and leather. One of 1,000, signed. Boxed. $250-$300.

MAUGHAM, W. Somerset. *The Casuarina Tree.* Cloth. London, 1926. First edition. In dust jacket. $50-$75.

MAUGHAM, W. Somerset. *Christmas Holiday.* Blue cloth. London, (1939). First edition. In dust jacket. $25-$30.

MAUGHAM, W. Somerset. *The Constant Wife.* Blue cloth. New York, 1926. First edition. In dust jacket. $50-$60. London, 1927. Black cloth. First English edition. In dust jacket. $35-$50.

MAUGHAM, W. Somerset. *Cosmopolitans: Very Short Stories.* Blue cloth. London, 1936. First edition. In dust jacket. $20-$25. Another issue: Red buckam. One of 175, signed. $100-$125.

MAUGHAM, W. Somerset. *Don Fernando.* Cloth. London, 1935. First edition. In dust jacket. $20-$25. Another issue: Buckram. One of 175, signed. Boxed. $85-$125. Garden City, 1935. Black cloth. First American edition. In dust jacket. $15-$20.

MAUGHAM, W. Somerset. *The Explorer.* Cloth. London, 1908 (actually 1907). First edition. $75-$100. New York, 1909. Illustrated. Cloth. First American and first illustrated edition. $40-$50.

MAUGHAM, W. Somerset. *The Hero.* Red cloth. London, 1901. First edition. $75-$100.

MAUGHAM, W. Somerset. *The Judgment Seat*. Frontispiece by Ulrica Hyde. Cloth. London, 1934. Centaur Press. First edition. One of 150, signed. In dust jacket. $100-$150.

MAUGHAM, W. Somerset. *The Land of the Blessed Virgin*. Boards. London, 1905. First edition, $100-$150.

MAUGHAM, W. Somerset. *The Letter: A Play in Three Acts*. Cloth. London, (1927). First edition. $100-$150. (Also issued in wrappers.)

MAUGHAM, W. Somerset. *Liza of Lambeth*. Decorated green cloth. London, 1897. First edition. $400-$600. Also, $240 (A, 1969). Author's first book. London, 1947. Vellum and boards. Jubilee Edition. One of 1,000, signed. In dust jacket. $100-$150.

MAUGHAM, W. Somerset. *The Magician*. Cloth. London, 1908. First edition. $50-$80.

MAUGHAM, W. Somerset. *The Making of a Saint*. Illustrated. Pictorial cloth. Boston, 1898. First edition, first issue, with "In Press" under this title in ads. $200-$250.

MAUGHAM, W. Somerset. *A Man of Honour*. Printed wrappers. London, 1903. Chapman & Hall. First edition. $750 and up. (Only 150 printed.)

MAUGHAM, W. Somerset. *The Merry-Go-Round*. Blue cloth. London, 1904. First edition. $40-$50.

MAUGHAM, W. Somerset. *Mrs. Craddock*. Cloth. London, 1902. First edition. $35-$50.

MAUGHAM, W. Somerset. *The Moon and Sixpence*. Sage-green cloth. London, (1919). First edition, first issue, with 4 pages of ads, including a list of 6 (not 7) novels by Eden Phillpotts. In dust jacket. $100-$150. Third issue, listing 7 Phillpotts novels. $25. New York, (1919). Tan cloth. First American edition, first state, with "Maughan" for "Maugham" on front cover and spine. In dust jacket. $100-$150.

MAUGHAM, W. Somerset. *My South Sea Island*. Wrappers. Chicago, 1936. First edition, first issue, with "Sommerset" on title page. $400-$500. Second issue, error corrected. One of 50. $200-$250.

MAUGHAM, W. Somerset. *The Narrow Corner*. Cloth. London, (1932). First edition. In dust jacket. $40-$50.

MAUGHAM, W. Somerset. *Of Human Bondage*. Green cloth. New York, (1915). First edition, first issue, with Doran imprint and misprint in line 4 of page 257. In dust jacket. $400-$600. London, (1915). Blue cloth. First English edition, first state, with ads at end. In dust jacket. $285-$400. Garden City, 1936. Illustrated by Schwabe. Buckram. First illustrated edition. One of 751, signed. In dust jacket. Boxed. $125-$150. New York, 1938. Limited Editions Club. Edited by Theodore Dreiser. Illustrated by John Sloan. 2 vols., cloth. Boxed. $300-$400.

MAUGHAM, W. Somerset. *Of Human Bondage; With Digression on the Art of Fiction*. Printed boards. (Washington), 1946. One of 500, signed. $75-$100.

MAUGHAM, W. Somerset. *On a Chinese Screen*. Boards and cloth. New York, (1922). First edition. In dust jacket. $35-$50. London, (1922). Black cloth. First English edition. In dust jacket. $25.

MAUGHAM, W. Somerset. *Orientations*. Cloth. London, 1899. First edition, first issue, with two-color title page and gilt top. $35-$50.

MAUGHAM, W. Somerset. *The Painted Veil*. Cloth. New York, 1925. First edition. In dust jacket. $35. Another issue: Boards. One of 250, signed. In dust jacket. $150-$200. London, (1925). Blue cloth. First English edition, first issue, with "Hong-Kong" (not "Tching-Yen" in line 15, page 16, etc. $400-$500.

MAUGHAM, W. Somerset. *Penelope: A Comedy*. Printed wrappers. London, 1912. First edition. $50-$60.

MAUGHAM, W. Somerset. *The Razor's Edge*. Buckram. Garden City, 1944. First edition. One of 750, signed. Boxed. $100-$135.

MAUGHAM, W. Somerset. *The Sacred Flame*. Black cloth, paper labels. New York, 1928. First edition, first issue, measuring 6 3/4 x 5 1/16 inches. In dust jacket. $50-$75. London, 1928 (actually 1929). First English edition (American sheets with new title page). In dust jacket. $35-$50.

MAUGHAM, W. Somerset. *Sheppy: A Play in Three Acts*. Brown cloth. London, 1933. First edition. In dust jacket. $40-$50. Another issue: Advance copy in plain brown wrappers. $100-$125.

MAUGHAM, W. Somerset. *Strictly Personal*. Buckram. Garden City, 1941. First edition. One of 515, signed. Boxed. $75-$100. Trade edition. In dust jacket. $25.

MAUGHAM, W. Somerset. *The Summing Up*. Black cloth. London, (1938). First edition. In dust jacket. $25-$35. Garden City, 1938. Black cloth. First American edition. In dust jacket. $25. New York, 1954. Buckram. One of 391, signed. Boxed. $150-$200.

MAUGHAM, W. Somerset. *The Trembling of a Leaf*. Cloth. London, (1921). First English edition. In dust jacket. $40-$50.

MAUGHAM, W. Somerset. *The Unconquered*. Cloth. New York, 1944. One of 300, signed. In dust jacket. $100-$125.

MAUGHAM, W. Somerset. *The Unknown*. Wrappers. London, 1920. First edition. $50-$75. Signed copy, $90.

MAUGHAM, E. Somerset. *The Vagrant Mood: Six Essays*. Boards and calf. London, (1952). First edition. One of 500, signed. In glassine dust jacket. Boxed. $100-$125. Garden City, 1953. Black cloth. First American edition. In dust jacket. $25.

MAUGHAM, W. Somerset. *A Writer's Notebook*. Blue buckram, vellum spine. London, (1949). First edition. One of 1,000, signed. Boxed. $80-$100. Trade edition. In first issue dust jacket listing "Maughamiana." $25. Garden City, 1949. Cloth. First American edition. One of 1,000, signed. Boxed. $80-$100. Trade edition: Cloth. In dust jacket. $20-$25.

MAULDIN, William Henry (Bill). *Star Spangled Banter*. Pictorial wrappers. San Antonio, 1941, First edition. The cartoonist's first book. $35-$50.

MAURELLE, Don Antonio. *Abstract of a Narrative of an Interesting Voyage from Manilla to San Blas, etc.* Calf. Boston, 1801. $300-$350.

MAUROIS, André. *Ariel: A Shelley Romance*. Wrappers. (London), 1935. Penguin Books. $100-$150. (First Penguin paperback.)

MAURY, M.F. *The Physical Geography of the Sea*. 12 plates. Cloth. New York, 1855. First edition. $450-$550.

MAVERICK, Samuel Augustus. *Notes on the Storming of Bexar in the Close of 1835*. Edited by F.C. Chabot. Illustrated. Cloth. San Antonio, 1942. One of 100 signed by Chabot. $200-$300.

MAVOR, William. *The English Spelling-Book*. Illustrated by Kate Greenaway. Pictorial boards. London, 1885 (actually 1884). First edition. $125-$150.

MAW, Henry Lister. *Journal of a Passage from the Pacific to the Atlantic*. Folding map. Boards. London, 1829. First edition. $250-$350.

MAWE, John. *Travels in the Interior of Brazil*. Map, 8 plates. Boards. London, 1812. First edition. $500-$600. London, 1821. Map, 5 color plates. Boards. Second edition. $300-$400. Philadelphia, 1816. Illustrated. Boards. $200-$300.

MAXIMILIAN, Prince of Wied. *Travels in Brazil*. 9 plates. Half leather. London, 1820. First English edition. $300-$400.

MAXIMILIAN, Prince of Wied. *Travels in the Interior of North America*. Translated by H.E. Lloyd. Folding map, 81 colored vignettes and plates. 2 vols., half morocco (text plus atlas folio volume). London, 1843-44. First edition. $20,000-$25,000. Also, with 3 plates stained, $15,096 (A, 1973); $13,000 (A, 1967). (The atlas volume alone, valued for the plates, is actually worth $10,000 to $15,000, possibly more.)

MAXWELL, William Audley. *Crossing the Plains: Days of '57*. Illustrated. Brown pictorial wrappers. (San Francisco, 1915.) First edition. $75-$100.

MAY, Robert L. *Rudolph the Red-Nosed Reindeer*. Illustrated by Denver Gillen. Pictorial wrappers. (Chicago), 1939. First edition. $75-$125. (Christmas give-away for Montgomery Ward.) Later edition: Evanston, no date. Miniature book bound in full leather for the Schori Press. Limited and signed by May and Ward Schori. $75-$100.

MAY, Sophie. *Dottie Dimple*. 3 woodcut plates by N. Brown. Decorated brown cloth. Boston, 1865. (By Rebecca S. Clarke.) First edition. $100-$125.

MAY, Sophie. *Little Prudy*. Cloth. Boston, 1865. (By Rebecca S. Clarke.) First edition. $75-$100.

MAYER, Luigi. *Views in the Ottoman Dominions*. 70 colored plates. 2 vols., folio, boards. London, 1810. $450-$550.

MAYER, Luigi. *Views in Palestine*. 48 full-page colored plates. 2 vols. in one, folio, half morocco. London, 1804-03. $500-$600.

MAYHEW, Augustus. *Paved with Gold*. Illustrated by Hablot K. Browne. 13 parts, wrappers. London, (1857-58). First edition. $300-$400. London, 1858. Cloth. First book edition. $100-$150.

MAYHEW, Experience. *Indian Narratives*. Frontispiece. Half leather and boards. Boston, (1829). First American edition. $150-$200.

MAYHEW, Henry. *London Characters*. Illustrated. Cloth. London, 1874. First edition. $100-$150.

MAYHEW, Henry. *London Labour and the London Poor*. 4 vols., cloth. London, 1861-62. $400-$500.

MAYNARD, Charles J. *Atlas of Plates from the Directory to the Birds of Eastern North America*. Wrappers. West Newton, Mass., 1905. $150-$200.

MAYNARD, Charles J. *The Birds of Eastern North America*. Wrappers. Newtonville, Mass., 1881. $150-$200. Newtonville, 1896. Cloth. $125-$150.

MAYNARD, Charles J. *The Butterflies of New England*. 8 hand-colored lithographs. Half morocco. Boston, 1886. First edition. $150-$175.

MAYNARD, Charles J. *The Eggs of North American Birds*. 9 parts, wrappers. Boston, (1890). $150-$200.

MAYNARD, G.W. *Report on the Property of the Alice Gold and Silver Mining Co., Butte*. Maps, plates, 28 pp., wrappers. New York, 1882. $100-150.

MAYO, Robert. *Political Sketches of Eight Years in Washington*. Cloth. Baltimore, 1839. First edition. $100-$200.

MAYO, W.S. (editor). *Kaloolah, or Journeyings to the Djebel Kumri: An Autobiography of Jonathan Romer*. Frontispiece and engraved title page by F.O.C. Darley. Pictorial cloth. New York, 1849. First edition. $100-$125.

MEAD, Peter B. *An Elementary Treatise on American Grape Culture and Wine Making*. Cloth. (New York), 1867. First edition. $40-$50.

MEADE, Gen. G.G. *Report of the Ashburn Murder*. 130 pp., printed wrappers. (Atlanta, about 1868.) With errata slip and leaf of explanation from Meade. $100.

MEANS, James. *Manflight*. 29 pp., printed wrappers. Boston, 1891. First edition. $150-$200.

MEANS, James. *The Problem of Manflight.* Diagrams. 20 pp., pictorial wrappers. Boston, 1894. $100-$150.

MEANY, Edmond S. *Origins of Washington Geographic Names.* Cloth. Seattle, 1923. $50.

MEEKE, Mrs. (Mary). *The Veiled Protectress; or, The Mysterious Mother.* 5 vols., contemporary half calf. London, 1819. First edition. $250.

MEEKER, Ezra. *Washington Territory West of the Cascade Mountains.* 52 pp., printed wrappers. Olympia, Wash., 1870. First edition. $350-$375.

MEIKLE, James. *Famous Clyde Yachts, 1880-87.* 31 colored aquatints, mounted as drawings, with tissue guards. Atlas folio, cloth. Glasgow, 1888. $150-$175.

MEINHOLD, William. *Sidonia the Sorceress.* Translated by Lady Wilde. Illustrated. Limp vellum with ties, London, 1893. Kelmscott Press. One of 300. $500-$750.

*MELINCOURT.* By the Author of *Headlong Hall.* 3 vols., boards. London, 1817. (By Thomas Love Peacock.) First edition. $300-$400.

MELINE, James F. *Two Thousand Miles on Horseback.* Map. Cloth. New York, 1867. First edition. $100-$150.

MELISH, John. *A Geographical Description of the United States.* 3 maps. Boards. Philadelphia, 1815. First edition. $150-$200. Philadelphia, 1816. 5 maps. Boards. Second edition. $75-$100. Philadelphia, 1818. 3 maps. Boards. Third edition. $50. Philadelphia, 1822. 12 maps. Boards. $50.

MELISH, John. *A Military and Topographical Atlas of the United States.* 8 maps and plans, 5 folding. Half leather. Philadelphia, 1813. First edition. $1,000-$1,250. Philadelphia, 1815. 12 maps and plans, 9 folding and colored in outline. Half leather. $750-$1,000, possibly more.

*MELLICHAMPE: A Legend of the Santee.* 2 vols., cloth, paper labels. New York, 1836. (By William Gilmore Simms.) First edition. $100-$150.

MELLICK, Andrew D. *The Story of an Old Farm.* Frontispiece. Cloth. Somerville, N.J., 1889. First edition. $75-$100.

*MELMOTH the Wanderer.* 4 vols., boards and cloth. Edinburgh, 1820. (By Charles Robert Maturin.) First edition, first binding (cloth is later). $500-$600. Edinburgh, 1821. 4 vols., boards. Second edition. $200-$300.

MELTZER, David. *The Dark Continent.* Brown cloth. (Berkeley), 1967. First edition. One of 31, signed. (Issued without dust jacket.) $40-$60.

MELTZER, David. *The Process.* Cloth. Berkeley, 1965. First edition. One of 25, signed. In dust jacket. $50-$60.

MELTZER, David. *Ragas.* Pictorial wrappers. (San Francisco, 1959.) First edition. $50-$60.

MELTZER, David. *Round the Poem Box.* Leather. Los Angeles, 1969. One of 26, signed, with an original illustration by the author. $75-$85. Another issue: One of 125, signed. $60-$80. Another issue: Wrappers. One of 300, signed. $20-$30.

MELTZER, David. *Yesod.* Cloth. London, (1969). One of 100, signed. In glassine dust jacket. $50-$60. Trade edition: Cloth. In dust jacket, $20. Also, in wrappers, $20-$25.

MELTZER, David, and Schenker, Donald. *Poems.* Glazed white wrappers, taped spine (as issued). (SanFrancisco, 1957.) First edition. One of 470. $40-$50. Another issue: Hardbound. One of 30, signed. $75-$85. First book for both poets.

MELVILLE, Herman. See *John Marr and Other Sailors; Timoleon.*

MELVILLE, Herman. *The Apple-Tree Table and Other Sketches.* Boards and cloth. Princeton, 1922. First edition. One of 175 on handmade paper. $25-$35. Trade edition: Cloth. $10.

MELVILLE, Herman. *Battle-Pieces and Aspects of the War.* Blue, green, or salmon-colored cloth. New York, 1866. First edition, first issue, with "hundred" misspelled "hnndred" in copyright notice. $600-$800. Also, spine rubbed, $450 (A, 1974). Second issue, error corrected. $400-$500. (Note: There was no English edition.)

MELVILLE, Herman. *Benito Cereno.* Illustrated in color by E. McKnight Kauffer. Folio, buckram. London, 1926. Nonesuch Press. One of 1,650. $75. (Note: See entry following under *Billy Budd.*).

MELVILLE, Herman, *Billy Budd and Other Prose Pieces.* Edited by Raymond W. Weaver. Cloth. London, 1924. First edition. One of 750. (Issued as part of the *Works.*) In dust jacket. $50-$75.

MELVILLE, Herman. *Billy Budd* [and] *Benito Cereno.* Illustrated. White sailcloth. New York, 1965. Limited Editions Club. Boxed. $50-$75.

MELVILLE, Herman. *Clarel: A Poem and Pilgrimage in the Holy Land.* 2 vols., brick-red or green cloth, chocolate end papers. New York, 1876. First edition. $500 and up.

MELVILLE, Herman. *The Confidence-Man.* Green or purple-brown cloth. New York, 1857. First edition, without half title. $400-$500. London, 1857. Yellow-brown cloth. First English edition, first issue, without "Roberts" in publisher's name below ads on recto of front free end paper. $150-$250.

MELVILLE, Herman. *The Encantadas (Las Encantadas).* Edited by Victor W. Von Hagen. Colored woodcuts by Mallette Dean. Pictorial boards and cloth. Burlingame, Calif., 1940. Grabhorn printing. One of 550. $50-$75.

MELVILLE, Herman. *Israel Potter.* Purple-brown or green cloth, yellow end papers. New York, 1855. First edition, without half title; first state, with perfect type in first line of page 113. $200-$300. Second state, imperfect type on page 113. $150-$200. London, 1855. Cloth. First English edition. $75-$100.

MELVILLE, Herman. *A Journal up the Straits, October 11, 1856-May, 1857.* Edited by Raymond W. Weaver. Portrait frontispiece. Marbled cloth. New York, 1935. First edition. One of 650. In dust jacket. $85-$125.

MELVILLE, Herman. *Mardi: and A Voyage Thither.* 3 vols., pale-green cloth, white end papers with blue designs. London, 1849. First edition, without half title in Vol. 1. $250-$350. New York, 1849. 2 vols., dark purple-brown or green muslin, or wrappers. First American edition, with 8 pages of ads at end of Vol. 2. Cloth: $400-$500. Wrappers: $600-$750, possibly more.

MELVILLE, Herman. *Moby-Dick; or, The Whale.* Slate-blue, black, brown, or scarlet cloth, orange or marbled end papers. New York, 1851. First American edition, with publisher's name blind-stamped at center of sides, 6 blank leaves at front and back. $4,000-$5,000, possibly more. Also, $2,800 (A, 1977); $4,250 (A, 1974); $1,000 (A, 1972); $850 (A, 1970); $1,000 (A, 1968); $2,500 (A, 1967). Chicago, 1930. Lakeside Press. Illustrated by Rockwell Kent. 3 vols., silver-decorated cloth. One of 1,000. In aluminum slipcase. $500-$600. Also, $375 (A, 1974); inscribed, $575 (A, 1975). New York, 1943. Limited Editions Club. Illustrated by Boardman Robinson. 2 vols., full morocco. Boxed. $150-$200.

MELVILLE, Herman. *Narrative of a Four Months' Residence Among the Natives of a Valley of the Marquesas Islands; or, A Peep at Polynesian Life.* Map. 2 parts, wrappers, or cloth (two parts bound as one). London, 1846. First edition (of the book published later that year in New York as *Typee*), first issue, with the reading "Pomarea" on page 19, line 1. Wrappers: $4,000-$5,000. Red cloth: First book edition. $3,000-$5,000. Also, $2,000 (A, 1974). Author's first book. Second issue, "Pomere." $2,000. London, 1847. Cloth. $200-$300.

MELVILLE, Herman. *Omoo: A Narrative of Adventures in the South Seas.* Map. 2 parts printed gray or brown wrappers, or cloth (in one volume). London, 1847. First edition. Wrappers: $2,000 and up. Red cloth: First book edition. $750-$1,000. Also, chipped, $475

(A, 1974). New York, 1847. Frontispiece map, one illustration. 2 parts, cream-white wrappers, or pictorial cloth (one volume). First American edition. Wrappers: $5,000 and up. Also, stained and worn, $2,250 (A, 1974). Cloth: First book edition. $750 and up. Also, $450 (A, 1975); faded and worn, $400 (A, 1974). New York, 1961. Limited Editions Club. Illustrated. White linen. Boxed. $50-$75.

MELVILLE, Herman. *The Piazza Tales*. Pale-blue cloth. New York, 1856. First edition, first issue, with yellow end papers. $300-$400. Later issue, blue end papers. $200-$300. London, 1856. Blue cloth. First English edition. $75-$125.

MELVILLE, Herman. *Pierre; or, The Ambiguities*. Gray cloth, or wrappers. New York, 1852. First edition, cloth, with 4 blank pages at front and back, no half title, gray-green end papers. $650-$750. Wrappers: $750 and up. London, 1852. Blue embossed cloth, yellow end papers. First English edition. $250 and up.

MELVILLE, Herman. *Poems*. Cloth. London, 1924. First edition. (Issued as part of the *Works*.) In dust jacket. $75.

MELVILLE, Herman. *Redburn: His First Voyage*. 2 vols., dark-blue cloth, white end papers with blue pattern. London, 1849. First edition. $1,500-$2,500. Also, $1,200 (A, 1974). New York, 1849. Purple-brown muslin, or wrappers. First American edition, first issue, with October ads. Cloth: $300-$400. Wrappers: $500 and up.

MELVILLE, Herman. *The Refugee*. Cloth. Philadelphia, (1865). First edition. $75. (Pirated edition of *Israel Potter*.)

MELVILLE, Herman. *Some Personal Letters*. Edited by Meade Minnigerode. Portrait, 2 facsimiles. Half linen. New York, 1922. First edition. In dust jacket. $75-$100.

MELVILLE, Herman. *Typee: A Peep at Polynesian Life*. Map frontispiece. 2 parts, thick fawn-colored printed wrappers. New York, 1846. First American edition (of *Narrative of a Four Months' Residence Among the Natives of a Valley of the Marquesas*). $1,500 and up. Another issue: Cloth (blue or brown), in one volume. First American book edition, with 4 pages of ads. $400-$500. Second issue, same date, with added story, "The Story of Toby." $150 and up. Author's first book. New York, 1847. Cloth. Revised edition, with 8 pages of ads. $50-$100. New York, 1935. Limited Editions Club. Illustrated. Printed boards. Boxed. $60-$80.

MELVILLE, Herman. *The Whale*. 3 vols., bright-blue and cream-colored cloth, pale-yellow end papers. London, 1851. First edition (of the book published later that year in New York as *Moby-Dick*) $15,000-$20,000. Also, $17,000 (A, 1974). Another copy, worn and soiled, $8,500 (in a 1977 catalogue).

MELVILLE, Herman. *White-Jacket: or, The World in a Man-of-War*. 2 vols., light-blue cloth, yellow end papers. London, 1850. First edition. $600-$750. New York, 1850. 2 parts, yellow wrappers, or one vol., purple-brown or blue-gray cloth, with 6 pages of ads. First American edition. Wrappers: $1,000 and up. Cloth (one volume); $600-$800. Also, worn $350 (A, 1974). London, 1853. 2 vols. in one, cloth. First English one-volume edition. $400-$500.

MELVILLE, Herman. *The Works of Herman Melville*. 16 vols., cloth. London, 1922-(24). ("Standard Edition.") First edition. One of 750. in dust jackets. $750-$1,000. (Also issued in full or half leather.)

*MEMOIRS of a Fox-Hunting Man*. Blue cloth. London, (1928). (By Siegfried Sassoon.) First edition, first issue, with rough trimmed fore-edges. In dust jacket. $35-$50. Another issue: Cloth. One of 260, signed. $150-$200. London, (1929). Illustrated by William Nicholson. Vellum. One of 300, signed. In dust jacket. Boxed. $100-$150.

*MEMOIRS of an Infantry Officer*. Blue cloth. London, (1930). (By Siegfried Sassoon.) First edition, first issue, with untrimmed edges. In dust jacket. $15-$25. Another issue: Blue cloth. One of 750, signed. $75-$100. London, 1931. Illustrated by Barnett Freedman. Parchment (or vellum) boards. One of 320, signed. In dust jacket. Boxed. $100-$125. Trade edition: Cloth. In dust jacket. $40-$60.

*MEMOIRS of the Life of the Late John Mytton, Esq*. 12 plates in color by John Alken. Cloth. London, 1835. (By C.J. Apperley.) First edition. $750-$1,000. London, 1837. 18

plates. Cloth. Second edition. $400-$600. London, 1851. 18 plates. Cloth. Third edition. $350-$400.

*MEMOIRS of Lorenzo Da Ponte (The).* 22 pp., stitched. New York, 1829. First American edition. $50-$60.

*MEMORANDA: Democratic Vistas.* Light-green wrappers. Washington, 1872. (By Walt Whitman.) First edition, first printing. $300-$400. (For later printing, Whitman identified as author on title page, see Whitman entry under this title.)

*MEMORIA sobre las Proporciones Naturales de las Provincias Internas Occidentales, Causas de que Han Provenido sus Atrasos, etc.* 62 pp., sewed. Mexico, 1822. $850-$1,000.

*MEMORIAL and Biographical History of Johnson and Hill Counties, Texas.* Illustrated. Leather. Chicago, 1892. First edition. $300-$350.

*MEMORIAL and Biographical History of McLennan, Falls, Bell and and Coryell Counties, Texas.* Half leather. Chicago, 1893. $350-$500.

*MEMORIAL to the Legislature of New York (A), Upon the Effects of the Passage of the Trade of the Western States Through the Welland and Oswego Canals.* 24 pp., sewed. Rochester, 1845, $75-$100.

*MEMORIAL to the President and Congress for the Admission of Wyoming Territory to the Union.* 75 pp., wrappers. Cheyenne, 1889. $125-$150.

MENCKEN, H.L. See Hatteras, Owen; Hirshberg, Dr. L.K.

MENCKEN, H.L. *The American Language.* Black cloth. New York, 1919. First edition. One of 1,500. In dust jacket. $35-$50. Another issue: One of 25, signed. In dust jacket, $750-$850.

MENCKEN, H.L. *The Artist.* Boards. Boston, 1912. First edition. In dust jacket. $75-$125.

MENCKEN, H.L. *Damn! A Book of Calumny.* Cloth. New York, 1918. First edition. In dust jacket. $100-$135.

MENCKEN, H.L. *George Bernard Shaw: His Plays.* Cloth. Boston, 1905. First edition. In dust jacket. $75-$85.

MENCKEN, H.L. *In Defense of Women.* Cloth. New York, 1918. First edition, first issue, with publisher's name mispelled "Ppilip." In dust jacket. $100-$125. Second issue, with name corrected. In dust jacket. $50-$75.

MENCKEN, H.L. *The Literary Capital of the United States.* Wrappers. Chicago, 1920. First edition. $75-$125.

MENCKEN, H.L. *A Little Book in C Major.* Cloth. New York, 1916. First edition. In dust jacket. $100-$125.

MENCKEN, H.L. *Menckeniana: A Schimpflexikon.* Vellum. New York, 1928. First edition. One of 80, signed. Boxed, $150-$200. Another issue: Red boards and cloth. One of 230, signed. Boxed. $100-$125. Trade edition: Cloth. In dust jacket. $25.

MENCKEN, H.L. *Notes on Democracy.* Cloth. New York, (1926). First edition. In dust jacket. $30-$35. Another issue: One of 200, signed. $80-$100. Another issue: One of 35 on vellum, signed. $200-$250.

MENCKEN, H.L. *The Philosophy of Friedrich Nietzsche.* Red cloth. Boston, 1908. First edition, first state, with "Friedrich" omitted on spine. In dust jacket. $60-$100.

MENCKEN, H.L. *Prejudices: First Series.* Cloth. New York, (1919). First edition. In dust jacket. $10-$15. Another issue: One of 50, signed. Boxed. $100 and up.

MENCKEN H.L. *Prejudices: Second Series.* Cloth. New York, (1920). First edition. In dust jacket. $10-$15. Another issue: One of a few large paper copies, signed. $100 and up.

MENCKEN, H.L. *Prejudices: Third Series*. Cloth. New York, (1922). First edition. In dust jacket. $30-$40. Another issue: One of 110, signed. Boxed. $80-$100.

MENCKEN, H.L. *Prejudices: Fourth Series*. Cloth. New York, (1924). First edition. In dust jacket. $30-$40. Another issue: One of 110, signed. Boxed. $80-$100.

MENCKEN, H.L. *Prejudices: Fifth Series*. Cloth. New York, (1926). First edition. In dust jacket. $30-$40. Another issue: One of 200, signed. Boxed. $60-$80.

MENCKEN, H.L. *Prejudices: Sixth Series*. Cloth. New York, (1927). First edition. In dust jacket. $30-$40. Another issue: One of 50 on vellum, signed. $100 and up. Another issue: One of 140 on rag paper, signed. $80-$100.

MENCKEN, H.L. *A Treatise on the Gods*. Cloth. New York, 1930. First edition (so stated). In dust jacket. $50-$75. Another issue: One of 375, signed. $75-$125.

MENCKEN, H.L. *Ventures into Verse*. Illustrated. Boards, paper label, or brown wrappers. Baltimore, 1903. First edition. Wrappers: $1,000-$2,000, possibly more. Also, inscribed by Mencken, $900 (A, 1969). Boards: $1,000 and up. Also, a presentation copy inscribed by Mencken, $3,250 (A, 1977). (About 100 copies believed printed in all; 45 noted are in boards, and presumably the rest were in wrappers.) Author's first book. Baltimore, (1960). Second edition (facsimile of the first edition). One of 250. $15-$20.

MENCKEN, H.L. (editor). *The Gist of Nietzsche*. Cloth. Boston, 1910. First edition. In dust jacket. $100-$125.

MENCKEN, H.L., and Nathan, George Jean. *Heliogabalus: A Buffoonery in 3 Acts*. Black cloth. New York, 1920. First edition. One of 2,000. In dust jacket. $35. Another issue: Vellum. One of 60 signed by the authors. $150-$200. Another issue: Wrappers. $25-$35.

MENCKEN, H.L.: Nathan, George Jean; and Wright, Willard Huntington. *Europe After 8:15*. 7 plates by Thomas Hart Benton. Decorated yellow cloth. New York, 1914. First edition, first binding, with blue stamping. In dust jacket. $80-$125.

MERA, H.P. *The Rain Bird: A Study in Pueblo Design*. Illustrated by Tom Lea. Wrappers. Santa Fe, 1937. First edition. In dust jacket. $100-$150.

*MERCEDES of Castile: Or, the Voyage to Cathay*. By the Author of *The Bravo*. 2 vols., cloth, paper labels. Philadelphia, 1840. (By James Fenimore Cooper.) First edition. $100-$150.

MERCER, A.S. *The Banditti of the Plains*. Illustrated. Map. Cloth. (Cheyenne, 1894.) First edition, $1,500-$2,000. Another edition: (Cheyenne, 1895.) Wrappers. With Mercer's manuscript notes, $250 (A, 1968). Sheridan, Wyo., 1930. Wrappers. $35-$50. San Francisco, 1935. Grabhorn Press. Illustrated. Half cloth. One of 1,000. $50-$75.

MERCER, A.S. *Washington Territory: The Great North-West*. 38 pp., printed wrappers. Utica, 1865. First edition. $500-$600. Also, rebound in cloth, $250 (A, 1973).

*MERCY Philbrick's Choice*. Black cloth. Boston, 1876. (By Helen Hunt Jackson.) First edition. $75-$85.

MEREDITH, George. *The Amazing Marriage*. 2 vols., green cloth. Westminster (London), 1895. First edition. $100-$150.

MEREDITH, George. *Beauchamp's Career*. 3 vols., green cloth. London, 1876. First edition. $250-$350.

MEREDITH, George. *Diana of the Crossways*. 3 vols., cloth. London, 1885. First complete book edition. $300-$350.

MEREDITH, George. *The Egoist*. 3 vols., cloth. London, 1879. First edition. $300-$600. Also, $550 (A, 1970). London, 1920. One of 30. ("Arranged for the Stage.") $100-$150.

MEREDITH, George. *Emilia in England*. 3 vols., purple cloth. London, 1864. First edition. $150-$300.

MEREDITH, George. *Farina*. Cloth. London, 1857. First edition. $100-$150.

MEREDITH, George. *Letters to Edward Clodd and Clement K. Shorter*. 39 pp., wrappers. London, 1913. One of 30. $100-$150.

MEREDITH, George. *Lord Ormont and His Aminta*. 3 vols., cloth. London, 1894. First edition. $50-$75.

MEREDITH, George. *Modern Love and Poems of the English Roadside*. Green cloth. London, 1862. First edition. $100-$150. Portland, Me., 1891. Heavy printed wrappers. First American edition. In dust jacket. $50-$75.

MEREDITH, George. *One of Our Conquerors*. 3 vols., blue cloth. London, 1891. First edition. $75-$125.

MEREDITH, George. *The Ordeal of Richard Feverel*. 3 vols., brown cloth. London, 1859. First edition. $200-$300.

MEREDITH, George. *Poems*. Green cloth. London, (1851). First edition. With half title and with errata slip at end. $250-$350. Author's first book.

MEREDITH, George. *A Reading of Earth*. Boards. London, 1888. First edition. $40-$50.

MEREDITH, George. *The Shaving of Shagpat*. Brown cloth. London, 1856. First edition. $100-$135. New York, 1955. Limited Editions Club. Illustrated. Boards and leather. Boxed. $25-$35.

MEREDITH, George. *The Tale of Chloe. The House on the Beach. The Case of General Ople and Lady Camper*. Boards and parchment. London, 1894. One of 250. $100-$150.

MEREDITH, George. *Vittoria*. 3 vols., purple or maroon cloth. London, 1867. First edition. $150-$200.

MEREDITH, William. *Love Letter from an Impossible Land*. Boards. New Haven, 1944. First edition. In dust jacket. $50-$75. Author's first book.

MERRICK, George B. *Old Times on the Upper Mississippi*. Illustrated. Blue cloth. Cleveland, 1909. First edition. $50-$75.

MERRICK, Leonard. *Conrad in Quest of His Youth: An Extravagance of Temperament*. Cloth. London, 1903. First edition. $75.

MERRILL, James. *The Black Swan and Other Poems*. Wrappers. Athens, 1946. First edition. One of 100. The poet's scarce second book. $250-$350.

MERRILL, James. *The Country of a Thousand Years of Peace*. Cloth. New York, 1959. First edition. In dust jacket. $35-$50.

MERRILL, James. *First Poems*. Cloth. New York, 1951. First edition. One of 990. In dust jacket. $100-$125. Author's first commercially published book.

MERRILL, James. *Jim's Book: A Collection of Poems and Short Stories*. (By James Ingram Merrill.) Maroon buckram and gray boards. New York, 1942. First edition. In glassine dust jacket. $1,000-$1,500, possibly more.

MERRILL, James. *1939: An American Woman Explores the Estate of Friends Who Have Fled France*. Broadside, with block print by Laurence Scott. (Cambridge, Mass.), 1965. One of 50 signed by the poet and the artist. $75-$125.

MERRILL, James. *The Seraglio*. Boards. New York, 1957. First edition. In dust jacket. $25.

MERRILL, James. *Short Stories*. Wrappers. Pawlet, Vt., 1954. Banyan Press. First edition. One of 210, signed. $300-$400.

MERRILL, James. *16. IX 65*. Broadside, illustrated by Laurence Scott. No place, no date

(Impressions Workshop, 1968.) One of 10 in horizontal layout, signed by the poet and the artist. $150. Another issue: Vertical layout. One of 100, also signed by both. $90-$100.

MERRILL, James. *Violent Pastoral.* Wrappers. (Cambridge, Mass., 1965.) First edition. One of 100, signed. $60-$85.

MERRILL, James. *The Yellow Pages.* Cloth. Cambridge, Mass., 1974. One of 50, signed. (Issued without dust jacket.) $50-$60. (There was a 1971 typescript facsimile of much of this poetry issued by Merrill in a 25-copy edition in St. Louis.)

MERRIMAN, Henry Seton. *From One Generation to Another.* 2 vols., pea-green cloth. London, 1892. (By High Stowell Scott.) First edition. $100.

MERRITT, Abraham. *Burn Witch Burn.* Cloth, New York, (1933). First edition. In dust jacket. $50-$75.

MERRITT, Abraham. *Creep, Shadow!* Cloth. Garden City, 1934. First edition. In dust jacket. $50-$75.

MERRITT, Abraham. *Dwellers in the Mirage.* Cloth. New York, (1932). First edition. In dust jacket. $50-$75.

MERRITT, Abraham. *The Face in the Abyss.* New York, (1931). First edition. In dust jacket. $75-$100.

MERRITT, Abraham. *The Moon Pool.* Pictorial wrappers, or cloth. New York, 1919. First edition. Wrappers: $50-$75. Cloth: In dust jacket. $50-$75. Author's first book.

MERRITT, Abraham. *The Ship of Ishtar.* Red-brown cloth, stamped in yellow. New York, 1926. First edition, first binding. In dust jacket. $100-$125.

*MERRY-MOUNT; a Romance of the Massachusetts Colony.* 2 vols., cloth. Boston, 1849. (By John Lothrop Motley.) First edition. $75-$100. Second edition, same date. $50. (Also issued as 2 vols. in one, cloth.)

*MERRY Tales of the Three Wise Men of Gotham (The).* Boards and cloth. New York, 1826. (By James Kirke Paulding.) First edition. $50-$100.

MERTON, Thomas. *Original Child Bomb.* Cloth. (New York, 1961.) New Directions. One of 500, signed. $75-$85. Trade edition: Boards. $15-$20.

MERTON, Thomas. *Thirty Poems.* Tan boards. Norfolk, (1944). First edition. In dust jacket. $35-$50. Wrappers: $20-$30. Author's first book.

MERTON, Thomas. *The Tower of Babel.* Woodcut illustrations. Folio, boards and vellum. (Norfolk), 1957. New Directions. First edition. One of 250, signed. Boxed. $200-$225.

MERTON, Thomas. *What Are These Wounds?* Cloth. Milwaukee, 1950. First edition. In dust jacket. $30-$40.

MERWIN, W.S. *The Dancing Bears.* Blue boards. New Haven, 1954. First edition. In dust jacket. $60-$80.

MERWIN, W.S. *A Mask for Janus.* Foreword by W.H. Auden. Blue boards. New Haven, 1952. First edition. In dust jacket. $75-$100. Author's first book.

MERWIN, W.S. *Three Poems.* Oblong, stiff wrappers. New York, 1968. One of 100, signed. $25-$30.

MERYMAN, Richard. *Andrew Wyeth.* Color plates. Oblong, two-tone buckram. Boston, 1968. First trade edition, first printing,. In dust jacket. $400-$500.

METCALF, Samuel L. *A Collection of Some of the Most Interesting Narratives of Indian Warfare in the West.* Portrait. Leather. Lexington, 1821. First edition. $350-$450.

METCALFE, John. *The Feasting Dead.* Black cloth. Sauk City, Wis., 1954. First edition. In dust jacket. $35-$45.

MEW, Charlotte. *The Farmer's Bride*. Pictorial wrappers. London, 1916. First edition. $35-$50. Author's first book.

MEW, Charlotte. *The Rambling Sailor*. Boards. London, 1919. First edition. In dust jacket. $25-$35.

*MEXICAN Treacheries and Cruelties*. Illustrated, 32 pp. pictorial wrappers. Boston, 1847. First edition. (By Lieut. G.N. Allen.) $75-$100. Boston, 1848. Second edition, $100-$150.

*MEXICO and the United States: An American View of the Mexican Question*. By a Citizen of California. 33 pp., printed wrappers. San Francisco, 1866. $100-$150.

*MEXICO in 1842 . . . to Which is Added, An Account of Texas and Yucatan, and of the Santa Fe Expedition*. Folding map. Cloth. New York, 1842. (By George F. Folsom or Charles J. Folsom?) First edition. $300-$500.

*MEXICO, su Evolución Social*. L. Justus Sierra, editor. 3 vols., folio, leather. Mexico, 1900-02. $300-$400.

MEYER, George. *Autobiography of George Meyer: Across the Plains with an Ox Team in 1849*. 2 portraits. Printed tan wrappers. Shenandoah, Iowa, 1908. First edition. $150-$200.

MEYERS, William H. *Journal of a Cruise to California and the Sandwich Islands*. Frontispiece, 10 color plates. Folio, half leather. San Francisco, 1955. Grabhorn Press. One of 400 for the Book Club of California. In dust jacket. $150-$175.

MEYERS, William H. *Naval Sketches of the War in California, 1846-1947*. Descriptive text by Dudley Know. Introduction by Franklin D. Roosevelt. Folio, half white leather. San Francisco, 1939. Grabhorn Press. One of 1,000. $150-$300.

MEYERS, William H. *Sketches of California and Hawaii*. Folio, cloth, paper label. (San Francisco), 1970. Book Club of California. One of 450. $150.

MEYNELL, Alice. *Essays*. Boards. London, 1914. First edition. One of 250 on orange paper. $25. Trade edition: Blue buckram. $10.

MEYNELL, Alice. *Other Poems*. White wrappers. (London, 1896.) One of 50 printed for Christmas cards. $75-$100.

MEYNELL, Alice. *Poems*. Brown cloth. London, 1893. First edition (under this title). One of 50, signed. $100-$125. (For actual first edition, see Thompson, A.C., *Preludes*.) London, 1913. Portrait. Blue boards and cloth. One of 250, signed. $35. Trade edition: Blue buckram. $10.

MEYNELL, Alice. *The Rhythm of Life and Other Essays*. Cloth. London, 1893. First edition. One of 50, signed. $35-$50. Trade edition: $10.

MEYNELL, Alice. *Ten Poems, 1913-1915*. Limp vellum. Westminster (London), 1915. First edition. One of 50. $200-$250.

MEYNELL, Francis. *Typography*. Illustrated, including color. Buckram. London, 1923. Pelican Press. $100-$150.

MEYRICK, Samuel R. *A Critical Inquiry into Antient Armour as It Existed in Europe, but Particularly in England from the Norman Conquest to the Reign of Charles II*. Illustrated, including hand-colored plates. 3 vols., folio, half morocco. London, 1824. First edition. $600-$850. London, 1842. 3 vols., half leather. Second edition. $750-$1,000.

MEYRICK, Samuel R., and Skelton, J. *Engraved Illustrations of Antient Arms and Armour, from the Collection of Llewelyn Meyrick*. 2 frontispieces, 2 engraved titles, 2 vignettes and 151 engraved plates. 2 vols., half morocco. London, 1830. $250-$350.

*MICHAEL Bonham: or, the Fall of Bexar*. By a Southron. Cloth. Richmond, 1852. (By William Gilmore Simms.) First edition. $300-$400.

MICHAUX, F.A. *Travels to the Westward of the Allegany Mountains*. Translated by B.

Lambert. Folding map. Boards. London, 1805. (Printed by Mawman.) First English edition. $250-$350. London, 1805. (Printed by Crosby.) Boards. Second English edition. $200. London, 1805. (Printed by Phillips.) Another translation. Third English edition. $100-$150.

*MIGHTY Magician (The)*. (Half title only): Bound with *Such Stuff as Dreams Are Made Of*. (Half title only.) The two plays apparently to have been published as *Two Dramas of Calderon* (but no title page known to exist). 132 pp., gray wrappers, with imprint at end: "John Childs & Son." Bungay, (1865). (By Edward Fitz Gerald.) First edition. $500-$750.

MIKESELL, Thomas (editor). *The History of Fulton County, Ohio*. Leather. Madison, Wis., 1905. First edition. $75-$100.

MILES, Gen. Nelson A. *Personal Recollections and Observations*. Illustrated by Frederic Remington and others. Pictorial cloth, leather, or half leather. Chicago, 1896. First edition, first issue, with caption under frontispiece reading "General Miles." $85-$125. Second issue, with rank under portrait as "Maj. Gen." $65-$75. Chicago, 1897. Second edition. With an added plate at end. $35-$50.

MILES, William. *Journal of the Sufferings and Hardships of Capt. Parker H. French's Overland Expedition to California*. 24 pp., printed wrappers. Chambersburg, Pa., 1851. First edition. $3,500-$3,750.

*MILITARY Commanders and Designating Flags of the United States Army, 1861-1865*. (Cover title.) Plates. Half leather. Philadelphia, 1887. $250 and up.

MILL, John Stuart. *Autobiography*. Green cloth. London, 1873. First edition, first issue, without errata. $75-$100.

MILL, John Stuart. *On Liberty*. Cloth. London, 1859. First edition. $250-$350.

MILL, John Stuart. *Principles of Political Economy*. 2 vols., cloth. London, 1848. First edition. $500-$750. London, 1849. 2 vols., cloth. Second edition. $200-$225. London, 1865. 2 vols., cloth. Sixth edition. $100-$125.

MILL, John Stuart. *The Subjection of Women*. Cloth. London, 1869. First edition. $100-$150.

MILLAY, Edna St. Vincent. See Boyd, Nancy; Earle, Ferdinand.

MILLAY, Edna St. Vincent. *Aria da Capo*. Cloth. New York, 1921. First edition. In dust jacket. $25-$35. (Note: *The Chapbook*, No. 14, London, August, 1920, is composed entirely of this work. Auction price, 1968: $15.)

MILLAY, Edna St. Vincent. *The Ballad of the Harp-Weaver*. Illustrated. Decorated wrappers. New York, 1922. First edition (so stated). $100. Presentation copy, signed, $175. Also, signed copies, $150 and $160 (A, 1966). Another issue: One of 5 on Japan vellum. $250.

MILLAY, Edna St. Vincent. *The Buck in the Snow and Other Poems*. Boards and cloth. New York, 1928. First edition (so stated). In dust jacket. $20-$25. Another issue: Full blue limp leather. $20-$25. Another issue: One of 479, signed. In glassine dust jacket. Boxed. $75-$100. Another issue: Boards and vellum. One of 36 on vellum, signed. In glassine dust jacket. Boxed. $150-$225.

MILLAY, Edna St. Vincent. *Collected Sonnets*. Blue cloth. New York, 1941. In dust jacket. $15-$20. Another issue: Full red limp leather. $25-$30.

MILLAY, Edna St. Vincent. *Conversation at Midnight*. Blue boards and cloth. New York, 1937. First edition (so stated). In dust jacket. $15-$20. Another issue: Full blue limp leather. Boxed. $25. Another issue: Boards and cloth. One of 579, signed. In glassine dust jacket. Boxed. $75-$100. Another issue: One of 36 on vellum, signed. In glassine dust jacket. Boxed. $100-$150.

MILLAY, Edna St. Vincent. *Fatal Interview: Sonnets*. Boards and cloth. New York, 1931. First edition (so stated), first issue, with top edges stained yellow. In dust jacket.

$20-$25. Another issue: One of 479, signed. In glassine dust jacket. Boxed. $50-$75. Another issue: One of 36 on vellum, signed. In glassine dust jacket. Boxed. $100-$150. Another issue: One of six exhibition copies, bound in marbled boards and cloth. $500-$600.

MILLAY, Edna St. Vincent. *A Few Figs from Thistles*. Wrappers. New York, 1920. First edition. $175-$200. New York, 1921. Green wrappers. Second edition, with added material. $25-$35.

MILLAY, Edna St. Vincent. *The Harp-Weaver and Other Poems*. Cloth. New York, 1923. First edition (so stated). In dust jacket. $50-$75. Also, inscribed. $120 (A, 1966).

MILLAY, Edna St. Vincent. *Huntsman, What Quarry?* Boards and cloth. New York, 1939. First edition (so stated). In dust jacket. $20-$25. Another issue: Full blue limp leather. Boxed. $25. Another issue: Boards and cloth. One of 551, signed. In glassine dust jacket. Boxed. $100-$125. Another issue: Boards and vellum. One of 36 on vellum. In glassine dust jacket. Boxed. $150-$200.

MILLAY, Edna St. Vincent. *Invocation to the Muses*. Sewed wrappers. New York, 1941. First edition. One of 60. $100-$150.

MILLAY, Edna St. Vincent. *The King's Henchman*. Boards and cloth. New York, 1927. First edition. In dust jacket. $25. Another issue: One of 158, signed. In glassine dust jacket. Boxed. $100-$125. Another issue: One of 31 on vellum, signed. $150-$200. Another issue: "Artist's Edition." One of 500, signed. $75-$100.

MILLAY, Edna St. Vincent. *The Lamp and the Bell*. Printed green wrappers. New York, 1921. First edition. $100-$150. Another (later) issue, same date: Boards. In dust jacket. $15-$25.

MILLAY, Edna St. Vincent. *Mine the Harvest*. Cloth. New York, (1954). First edition. In dust jacket. $25.

MILLAY, Edna St. Vincent. *Poems*. Cloth. London, 1923. First edition. In dust jacket. $125-$150. Also, signed by the author, $100 (A, 1968).

MILLAY, Edna St. Vincent. *Poems Selected for Young People*. Boards and cloth. New York, 1929. First edition (so stated). One of 1,050, signed. Boxed. $50-$75.

MILLAY, Edna St. Vincent. *The Princess Marries the Page*. Decorations by J. Paget Fredericks. Full blue leather. New York, 1932. First edition (so stated). Boxed. $25. Another issue: Boards and cloth. In dust jacket. $20-$25.

MILLAY, Edna St. Vincent. *Renascence: (A Poem)*. Plain wrappers, sewed. New York, 1924. First separate edition. (Printed by Frederic and Bertha Goudy.) Limited. $150-$200.

MILLAY, Edna St. Vincent. *Renascence and Other Poems*. Black cloth. New York, 1917. First edition, first issue, on Glaslan watermarked paper. In dust jacket. $350-$450. Another issue: White vellum paper boards. One of 15 (actually 17) on Japan vellum, signed. $5,500 (A, 1977). Author's first book.

MILLAY, Edna St. Vincent. *Second April*. Black cloth. New York, 1921. First edition, first state, on Glaslan watermarked paper. In dust jacket. $125-$200.

MILLAY, Edna St. Vincent. *Two Slatterns and a King*. Wrappers. Cincinnati, 1921. First edition. $60-$75.

MILLAY, Edna St. Vincent. *Wine from These Grapes*. Boards and cloth, or leather. New York, 1934. First edition (so stated). In dust jacket. $25. (Note: Also issued as part of a 2-vol. set with *Epitaph for the Race of Man*. One of 299 sets on paper, Vol. 1 of each set signed. $75-$100. Another issue: One of 36 on vellum, signed. $350-$500.)

MILLER, Andrew. *New States and Territories*. Folding map table. 32 pp., boards. (Keene, N.H., 1818.) First edition. $1,000-$1,500. Map table signed by author, $1,250. Also $1,200 (A, 1967). Another edition: (Keene), 1819. Folding table. 96 pp., boards. Second edition. $750-$1,000.

MILLER, Arthur. *After the Fall*. Light-brown buckram. New York, (1964). First edition. One of 999, signed. (500 for private distribution). Boxed. $50. Trade edition: Boards and cloth. In dust jacket. $20.

MILLER, Arthur. *All My Sons*. Cloth. New York, (1947). First edition. In dust jacket. $50-$75.

MILLER, Arthur. *Death of a Salesman*. Pictorial orange cloth. New York, 1949. First edition. In dust jacket. $75-$100.

MILLER, Arthur. *Situation Normal*. Yellow cloth. New York, (1944). First edition. In dust jacket. $75-$100. Author's first book.

MILLER, Benjamin S. *Ranch Life in Southern Kansas and the Indian Territory*. Frontispiece. 163 pp., printed wrappers. New York, 1896. First edition. $250-$350.

MILLER, E. *The History of Page County, from the Earliest Settlement in 1843 to 1876, etc.* Folding map. Limp black cloth. Clarinda, Iowa, 1876. First edition. $75-$100.

MILLER, Henry. *Account of a Tour of the California Missions, 1856*. Pencil drawings by Miller. 59 pp., boards. San Francisco, 1952. Grabhorn Press. One of 375. Boxed. $125-$165.

MILLER, Henry. *The Air-Conditioned Nightmare*. Gray cloth. (New York, 1945.) New Directions. First edition. In dust jacket. $50-$60.

MILLER, Henry. *Aller Retour New York*. Cloth. (New York), 1945. First American edition. One of 500. (Issued without dust jacket.) $80-$100.

MILLER, Henry. *The Amazing and Invariable Beauford De Laney*. Printed wrappers. (Yonkers), 1945. Alicat Book Shop. First edition. $35-$40.

MILLER, Henry. *Black Spring*. Pictorial wrappers. Paris, (1936). Obelisk Press. First edition, with yellow paper censorship band, "Cannot be bought in England and U.S.A." $500-$750. New York, (1963). Boards and cloth. First American edition. In dust jacket. $25.

MILLER, Henry. *The Books in My Life*. Cloth. (Norfolk, Conn., 1952). (Printed in Ireland) First edition. In dust jacket. $75-$85.

MILLER, Henry. *The Colossus of Maroussi*. Patterned blue boards and cloth. San Francisco, (1941). Colt Press. First edition. One of 100, signed. (Issued without dust jacket.) $100-$150. Another issue: Cloth, paper label. In dust jacket. $50.

MILLER, Henry. *The Cosmological Eye*. Tan cloth, with brown lettering and photograph of an eye inset on cover. Norfolk, (1939). New Directions. First edition. In dust jacket. First book under Miller's name to be published in the United States. $50-$75.

MILLER, Henry. *Un Etre Etoilique*. Wrappers. (London, 1937.) First edition. $300.

MILLER, Henry. *Hamlet*. Vol. 1 and 2 (the second with Michael Fraenkel). 2 vols., wrappers. (Santurce, Puerto Rico, 1939) and New York, (1941). First edition. $150-$200. (A combined edition with the title *The Michael Fraenkel-Henry Miller Correspondence Called Hamlet* was published in wrappers in London in 1962. Value: $50-$75.)

MILLER, Henry. *Into the Night Life*. Illustrated by Bezalel Schatz. Folio, cloth. (Berkeley, 1947.) First edition. One of 800 signed by the author and the artist. $750-$850. Boxed. $400-$700.

MILLER, Henry. *Maurizius Forever*. Colored drawings by Miller. Green boards. San Francisco. 1946. Colt Press. First edition. One of 500. Printed at the Grabhorn Press. In plain brown dust jacket. $75-$85.

MILLER, Henry. *Max and the White Phagocytes*. Thick tan wrappers. Paris, (1938). Obelisk Press. First edition. $400-$450.

MILLER, Henry. *Money and How It Gets That Way.* Tan wrappers. Paris, (1938). Booster Broadside No. 1. $250-$350. Also, a presentation copy, signed, $200 (A, 1977).

MILLER, Henry. *Murder the Murderer.* Printed wrappers. (Big Sur, Calif., 1944.) First edition. $35-$40.

MILLER, Henry. *Nexus.* Wrappers. Paris, (1960). Obelisk Press. First edition (?). $50-$75. ("Generally accepted as the true first edition," according to Robert A. Wilson, New York specialist dealer in modern literature.)

MILLER, Henry. *Order and Chaos Chez Hans Reichel.* Introduction by Lawrence Durrell. Leather-backed cloth. New Orleans, (1966). First edition. "Green Oasis edition." One of 11, signed. In dust jacket. Boxed. $150-$200. Another issue: "Crimson Oasis edition." One of 26, signed. In jacket and box. $150. Another issue: "Blue Oasis edition." One of 99, signed. In dust jacket. Boxed. $100-$125.

MILLER, Henry. *Plexus.* 2 vols., wrappers. Paris, (1953). First English language (and first authorized) edition. $75-$100. (Robert A. Wilson catalogued a French language edition, Paris, 1952, wrappers, in 1977, at $75 and reported it to be the true first edition.)

MILLER, Henry. *Quiet Days in Clichy.* Photographs by Brassai. Printed wrappers. Paris, (1965). Olympia Press. First edition. $150-$175.

MILLER, Henry. *Reflections on the Death of Mishima.* Pictorial boards. Santa Barbara, 1972. First edition. One of 200, signed. $50-$75.

MILLER, Henry. *Remember to Remember.* Cloth. (New York, 1947.) New Directions. First edition. In dust jacket. $75-$100.

MILLER, Henry. *Scenario (A Film with Sound).* Double-page frontispiece. Wrappers. Paris, 1937. One of 200, signed. $500-$750. Also, a copy with the frontispiece laid in loose and the book catalogued "as issued," $400 (A, 1977). (Note: Wilson in 1977 catalogued a rebound copy in yellow cloth, without frontispiece, at $200, and reported, "Lacks the frontispiece, as has every copy we have examined.")

MILLER, Henry. *Semblance of a Devoted Past.* Illustrated by Miller. Stiff wrappers. Berkeley, 1944. First edition. One of 1,150. $50-$60.

MILLER, Henry. *Sexus.* 2 vols., cloth. Paris, 1948. First edition. $100.

MILLER, Henry. *The Smile at the Foot of the Ladder.* Pictorial boards and cloth. New York, (1948). First edition. In dust jacket. $75-$100. (San Francisco), 1955. Greenwood Press. Printed wrappers. One of 500. In glassine dust jacket. $75-$100.

MILLER, Henry. *The Time of the Assassins: A Study of Rimbaud.* Half cloth and cut-out boards. New York, (1956). First edition. In acetate dust jacket. $25-$35.

MILLER, Henry. *Tropic of Cancer.* Preface by Anaïs Nin. Decorated wrappers. Paris, (1934). Obelisk Press. First edition, with "First published September 1934" on copyright page and with wrap-around band. $2,500 and up. Also, $2,000 (A, 1977). Author's first book. New York, 1940. Cloth. First (pirated) American edition. $75-$100. New York, (1961). Grove Press. Introduction by Karl Shapiro. Preface by Anaïs Nin. Patterned boards and cloth. One of 100, signed. First authorized American edition. (Issued without dust jacket.) $100-$125. Trade edition. Boards. In dust jacket. $15. Later in 1961, cloth, in jacket, $10.

MILLER, Henry. *Tropic of Capricorn.* Decorated wrappers. Paris, (1939). Obelisk Press. First edition, with price on spine and with errata slip. $550-$650. (Wilson reports a variant copy without price on spine.)

MILLER, Henry. *Tropique du Cancer.* Colored lithographs by Timar. Loose in pictorial wrappers. Paris, 1945. One of 51, with an extra set of plates and an original drawing $150-$200. Another issue: One of 750. $75-$100.

MILLER, Henry. *Watercolors, Drawings and His Essay "The Angel Is My Watermark!"* Illustrated. Small folio, cloth. London, 1962. First edition. With each of the 12 reproductions signed by Miller. $150-$200. New York, (1962). First American edition. In glassine dust jacket. $75-$85.

MILLER, Henry. *The Waters Reglitterized*. Portrait and plates. Pictorial wrappers. (San Jose), 1950. First edition. One of 1,000. $25-$35.

MILLER, Henry. *What Are You Going to Do About Alf?* Printed wrappers. Paris, 1935. First edition. $135-$150. Berkeley, (1944). Printed self-wrappers. One of 738. First American edition. $25-$30.

MILLER, Henry. *(The) Wisdom of the Heart*. Brown cloth. (New York, 1941.) New Directions. First edition. One of 1,500. In dust jacket. $20-$25.

MILLER, Henry. *The World of Sex*. Blue cloth. (Chicago, 1940.) One of 250. Boxed. $75-$100. Later: Blue cloth. (New York, 1940.) "One of 1,000." $40-$50.

MILLER, Henry; Hiler, Hilaire; and Saroyan, William. *Why Abstract?* Cloth. (New York, 1945.) New Directions. First edition. In dust jacket. $40-$60. London, (1948). Falcon Press. Cloth. Second edition. In dust jacket. $20-$25.

MILLER, Cincinnatus H. *Joaquin, et al.* Portland, Ore., 1869. (By Joaquin Miller.) First edition. $150.

MILLER, J.P., and Patterson John. *Nomination of President and Vice President of the United States*. (Caption title.) 12 pp. sewed. (Steubenville, Ohio, 1923.) $100-$150.

MILLER, Joaquin. See Miller, Cincinnatus H. Also see *How to Win in Wall Street; Specimens*.

MILLER, Joaquin. *'49, The Gold-Seeker of the Sierras*. Printed wrappers. New York, 1884. First edition. $75-$100. (Also issued in cloth, and in boards and cloth.)

MILLER, Joaquin. *An Illustrated History of Montana*. Illustrated. 2 vols., morocco. Chicago, 1894. First edition. $150-$175.

MILLER, Joaquin. *Life Amongst the Modocs: Unwritten History*. Cloth. London, 1873. First edition. $35-$50.

MILLER, Joaquin. *Memorie and Rime*. Printed tan wrappers. New York, 1884. First edition. $35-$50. Another issue: Cloth. $15-$20.

MILLER, Joaquin. *Overland in a Covered Wagon*. Edited by Sidney A. Firman. Illustrated. Cloth. New York, 1930. First edition, first printing, with "(1)" below last line of text. In dust jacket. $25-$35.

MILLER, Joaquin. *Pacific Poems*. Green cloth, gilt. London, 1871. First edition. ("Suppressed by the author and extremely scarce."—De Ricci.) $500-$750. Also, rubbed, $475 (A, 1971).

MILLER, Joaquin. *A Royal Highway of the World*. Illustrated. Cloth. Portland, 1932. First edition. One of 245. $35.

MILLER. Joaquin. *Songs of the Mexican Seas*. Cloth. Boston, 1877. First edition. $35-$50.

MILLER, Joaquin. *Songs of the Sierras*. Cloth. London, 1871. First edition. $35-$50. Boston, 1871. Cloth. First published American edition, first binding, with "R.B." at foot of spine. $35-$40.

MILLER, Joaquin. *Songs of the Sun-Lands*. Cloth. London, 1873. First edition. $35-$50. Another issue: Large paper. $50-$75.

MILLER, Joaquin. *Unwritten History: Life Among the Modocs*. Cloth. Hartford, 1874. First American edition (of *Life Amongst the Modocs*). $35.

MILLER, John F. *A Refutation of the Slander and Falsehoods Contained in a Pamphlet Entitled Sally Miller, etc.* 70 pp., wrappers. New Orleans, 1845. $150-$200.

MILLER, Lewis B. *Saddles and Lariats.* Illustrated. Pictorial cloth. Boston, 1912. First edition. $100-$125.

MILLER, Merle. *That Winter.* Cloth. New York, 1948. First edition. In dust jacket. $30-$40.

MILLER, Patrick. *The Green Ship.* 8 wood engravings by Eric Gill, with an extra set of the plates on Japan vellum. Full morocco. London, 1936. Golden Cockerel Press. One of 62. $400-$500. Another issue: Half morocco and boards. One of 138. $125-$150.

MILLER, Patrick. *Woman in Detail.* 5 illustrations by Mark Severin, with a duplicate set of the 5 plates and with 3 additional ones in a pocket at the end. Half morocco and boards. London, 1947. Golden Cockerel Press. One of 100, signed. $100-$150. Another issue: One of 450. $50-$60.

MILLER, T. L. *History of Hereford Cattle.* Illustrated. Pictorial cloth. Chillicothe, Mo., 1902. First edition. $75.

MILLER, Thomas. *Common Wayside Flowers.* Illustrated by Birket Foster. Decorated brown cloth. London, 1860. First edition. $40-$60.

MILLER, Walter M., Jr. *A Canticle for Leibowitz.* Cloth. Philadelphia, (1959). First edition. In dust jacket. $50-$60.

MILLER, William. *Evidence from Scripture and History of the Second Coming of Christ, About the Year 1843.* Boards. Troy, N.Y., 1838. First edition. $100-$125.

MILLS, Anson. *Big Horn Expedition.* Folding map. 15 pp., tan printed wrappers. No place, no date (1874?). First edition. $500-$600. Also, $250 (A, 1968).

MILLS, Robert. *Atlas of the State of South Carolina.* 29 double-page maps, colored by hand. Folio, half leather. Baltimore, (about 1826). First edition. (Issued to accompany Mills' *Statistics;* see item following). $750-$1,000.

MILLS, Robert. *Statistics of South Carolina.* Map (not in all copies). Boards. Charleston, 1826. First edition. $100-$150.

MILLS, Samuel J., and Daniel Smith. *Report of a Missionary Tour . . . . West of the Alleghany Mountains.* Wrappers. Andover, 1815. First edition. $150.

MILLS, William W. *Forty Years at El Paso, 1858-1898.* Frontispiece. Cloth. (Chicago, 1901.) (Printed at El Paso, Tex.) First edition. $150-$200. El Paso, 1962. Mesquite Edition. $200.

MILMINE, Georgine. *The Life of Mary Baker G. Eddy and the History of Christian Science.* Edited by Willa S. Cather. Illustrated. Cloth. New York, 1909. (Largely written by Miss Cather.) First edition. In dust jacket. $100-$150. London, 1909. Cloth. First English edition. $50.

MILNE, A. A. See Grahame, Kenneth; Shepard, Ernest H.

MILNE, A. A. *By Way of Introduction.* Cloth. London, (1929). First edition. In dust jacket. $25. New York, (1929). Decorated boards and cloth. First American edition. One of 166 on vellum, signed. Boxed. $75. Trade edition: Boards and cloth. In dust jacket. $15.

MILNE, A. A. *The Christopher Robin Story Book.* Illustrated by Ernest H. Shepard. Pictorial cloth. London, (1926). First edition. In dust jacket. $35-$50. New York, (1929). Pictorial boards and cloth. One of 350, signed. $200-$300.

MILNE, A. A. *A Gallery of Children.* 12 full-page illustrations in color by Saida. Folio, white buckram. London, 1925. First edition. One of 500, signed. $500-$750. Also, $425 (A, 1977).

MILNE, A. A. *The House at Pooh Corner.* Decorations by Ernest H. Shepard. Boards and buckram. London, (1928). First edition. One of 350, signed. In dust jacket. $400-$450. Another issue: Vellum. One of 20 on Japan paper, signed. $600-$750. Trade edition: Pink cloth. In dust jacket. $150. New York, (1928). Illustrated. Cloth. First American edition. One of 250, signed. $200-$300. Trade edition: Cloth. In dust jacket. $40-$50.

MILNE, A. A. *The Ivory Door.* Boards. London, 1929. First edition. In dust jacket. $25-$30.

MILNE, A. A. *Lovers in London.* Cloth. London, 1905. First edition. $75-$125. Author's first book.

MILNE, A. A. *Michael and Mary: A Play.* Green cloth. London, 1930. First edition. One of 260, signed. $50-$75.

MILNE, A. A. *Now We Are Six.* Illustrated by Ernest H. Shepard. Boards and cloth. London, (1927). First edition. One of 200, signed. In dust jacket. $300-$350. Inscribed by author and illustrator, $400. Another issue: Vellum. One of 20 on Japan paper, signed. $500-$600. Trade edition: Pictorial maroon cloth. In dust jacket. $125-$150.

MILNE, A. A. *The Red House Mystery.* Cloth. London, (1922). First edition. In dust jacket. $75-$85.

MILNE, A. A. *The Secret and Other Stories.* Red linen. New York, 1929. Fountain Press. First edition. One of 742, signed. In dust jacket. $50-$75.

MILNE, A. A. *Those Were the Days.* Decorated buckram. London, (1929). First edition. One of 250, signed. In dust jacket. $150-$175.

MILNE, A. A. *Toad of Toad Hall: A Play from Kenneth Grahame's Book "The Wind in the Willows."* Boards and buckram. London, (1929). First edition. One of 200, signed by Milne and Grahame. In dust jacket. $300-$400. Trade edition: Cloth. In dust jacket. $50-$60.

MILNE, A. A. *When I Was Very Young.* Illustrated by Ernest H. Shepard. Cloth. New York, 1930. Fountain Press. First edition. One of 842, signed. Boxed. $150-$175.

MILNE, A. A. *When We Were Very Young.* Illustrated by Ernest H. Shepard. Boards and cloth. London, (1924). First edition. One of 100, signed. In dust jacket. $400-$500. Trade edition, first issue: Pictorial blue cloth, plain end papers, page ix not numbered. In dust jacket. $275. Later copies, $150-$200. New York, (1924). Pictorial boards and cloth. First American edition. One of 100, signed. In dust jacket. $400-$500.

MILNE, A. A. *Winnie-the-Pooh.* Illustrated by Ernest H. Shepard. Boards and buckram. London, (1926). First edition. One of 350, signed. In dust jacket. $500-$600. Another issue: Vellum. One of 20 on vellum, signed. $900-$1,000. Trade edition. Pictorial green cloth. In dust jacket. $200. New York, (1926). Pictorial boards and cloth. First American edition. One of 200, signed. In dust jacket. $500-$600.

MILTON, John. *Areopagitica.* Blue boards. (London, 1903.) Eragny Press. First issue of this edition. One of 40 saved from a fire (out of an edition of 200 copies). $945. London, 1907. Doves Press. Limp vellum. One of 300. $300-$400. Another issue: One of 25 on vellum. $2,000-$2,500.

MILTON, John. *Comus.* Vellum. London, 1901. Essex House Press. One of 150 on vellum. $150. London, (1921). Illustrated in color by Arthur Rackham. Parchment. One of 550 signed by Rackham. $300-$400. Trade edition: Cloth. $150-$200. Newtown, Wales, 1931. Gregynog Press. Illustrated by Blair Hughes-Stanton. Boards and buckram. One of 250. $250-$350. Another issue: Morocco. One of 25 specially bound by George Fisher. $500-$600. London, 1937. Nonesuch Press. Illustrated. Boards. Boxed. $75-$100. New York, 1954. Limited Editions Club. Illustrated by Edmund Dulac. Boards. Boxed. $30-$40.

MILTON, John. *Four Poems: L'Allegro, Il Penseroso, Arcades, Lycidas.* Wood engravings by Blair Hughes-Stanton. Red morocco. Newtown, 1933. Gregynog Press. One of 250 on Japan vellum. $250-$300. Another issue: One of 14 specially bound by George Fisher. $750 and up.

MILTON, John. *Hymn on the Morning of Christ's Nativity.* Woodcut by Noel Rooke. 16

pp., folio, blue wrappers. (London), 1928. Ashendene Press. One of "about 220 copies." $400-$500.

MILTON, John. *Paradise Lost.* Woodcuts by Mary Groom. Half pigskin. London, 1937. Golden Cockerel Press. One of 200. $500-$750.

MILTON, John. *Paradise Lost and Miscellaneous Poems. Paradise Regain'd & Samson Agonistes.* Illustrated by William Blake. 2 vols., decorated boards and vellum-paper spine. London, 1926. Nonesuch Press. One of 1,450 on rag paper. $150 and up.

MILTON, John. *Paradise Lost* [and] *Paradise Regain'd.* Printed in red and black. 2 vols., vellum. London, 1902-05. Doves Press. One of 300. $800-$1,000. Another issue: 2 vols., vellum. One of 25 on vellum. $1,500-$2,500.

MILTON, John. *Paradise Lost* [and] *Paradise Regained.* Illustrated by D. Galanis. 2 vols., folio, pigskin. London, 1931. Cresset Press. One of 195. Boxed. $400-$500. Another issue: 2 vols., sharkskin. One of 10 on vellum. Boxed. $1,500-$2,500.

MILTON, John. *Poems in English.* 53 plates by William Blake. 2 vols., half vellum and brown boards. London, 1926. Nonesuch Press. One of 1,450 on Van Gelder paper. $200-$250. Another issue: 2 vols. in one, vellum. One of 90 on India paper. $400-$500.

*MINNESOTA Guide (The).* 94 pp., wrappers. St. Paul, 1869. (By J.F. Williams.) First edition. $75-$100.

*MIRIAM Coffin, or, The Whale Fisherman: A Tale.* 2 vols., cloth. New York, 1834. (By Joseph C. Hart.) First edition. $200-$250.

*MIROURE of Man's Salvacionne (The): a Fifteenth Century Translation into English of the "Speculum Salvationis."* With a facsimile page. Half morocco. London, 1888. $200-$250.

MIRRLEES, Hope. *Paris: A Poem.* Wrappers, paper label. Richmond, England, 1919. Hogarth Press. First edition. $100.

*MIRROR of Olden Time Border Life.* 13 plates (17 in some). Leather. Abingdon, Va., 1849. (By Joseph Pritts.) First edition. $150-$200.

*MISCELLANIES.* By the Author of *Letters on the Eastern States.* Boards. Boston, 1821. (By William Tudor.) First edition. $75-$100.

*MISFORTUNES of Elphin (The).* Boards. London, 1829. (By Thomas Love Peacock.) First edition. $300-$400. Newtown, Wales, 1928. Gregynog Press. Woodcuts. Buckram-backed cloth. One of 250. $150-$200. Another issue: Morroco. One of 25 bound by George Fisher. $1,000-$1,250.

*MR. DOOLEY in Peace and in War.* Green cloth. Boston, 1898. (By Finley Peter Dunne.) First edition. In dust jacket. $75-$100. Lacking jacket, $25-$35. Author's first book.

*MR. FACEY Romford's Hounds.* 24 color plates by John Leech and Phiz (H. K. Browne). 12 parts, pictorial wrappers. London, 1864-65. (By Robert Smith Surtees.) First edition, with first state wrappers of Part I reading "Mr. Facey Romford's Hounds" (second state and all subsequent parts read "Mr. Romford's Hounds"). $400-$500. London, 1865. Pictorial cloth. First book edition. $200-$250.

*MR. H., or Beware a Bad Name.* 36 pp., sewed, Philadelphia, 1813. (By Charles Lamb.) First edition. $1,500-$2,500.

*MR. MIDSHIPMAN Easy.* 3 vols., boards and cloth. London, 1836. (By Frederick Marryat.) First edition. $300-$400.

*MR. SPONGE'S Sporting Tour.* 13 color plates and 84 woodcuts by John Leech. 13 parts in 12, pictorial wrappers. London, 1852-53. (By Robert Smith Surtees.) First edition, first issue, with the dedication to Lord Elcho (second issue reading "Earl Elcho"). $350-$500. Second issue. $300-$400. London, 1853. Pictorial cloth. First edition, first issue, in book form. $100-$150.

*MRS. LEICESTER'S School: or, The History of Several Young Ladies, Related by Themselves.* Frontispiece by J. Hopwood. Boards. London, 1809. (By Charles and Mary Lamb.) First edition, first issue, with only one ad on last leaf. $1,000 and up. Also, rebound, $640 (A, 1976).

MITCHEL, Martin, *History of the County of Fond du Lac, Wisconsin.* 96 pp., printed yellow wrappers. Fond du Lac, 1854. First edition. $100-$125.

MITCHELL, Donald G. See Marvel, Ik.

MITCHELL, Donald G. *The Dignity of Learning: A Valedictory Oration.* Printed wrappers. New Haven, 1841. First edition. $50-$75.

MITCHELL, G.R. *The Pacific Gold Company of Gilpin County, Colorado.* 19 pp., wrappers. Boston, 1866. $125-$150.

MITCHELL, Isaac. *The Asylum; or, Alonzo and Melissa.* Frontispiece. 2 vols., calf. Poughkeepsie, 1811. First edition. $250 and up. Author's first (and only) book. (Note: Many later editions appeared with Daniel Jackson, Jr., as the author.)

MITCHELL, John D. *Lost Mines of the Great Southwest.* Cloth. (Phoenix, 1933.) First edition. $75-$100.

MITCHELL, Joseph. *The Missionary Pioneer.* Tan boards. New York, 1827. First edition. $300-$350.

MITCHELL, Margaret. *Gone with the Wind,* Gray cloth. New York, 1936. First edition, first issue, with "Published May, 1936" on copyright page and no note of other printings. In presumed first issue dust jacket. $400-$600, possibly more. (Note: Although the Macmillan Company has no clear cut records on the dust jacket printings for *Gone with the Wind,* an examination of several dozen dust-jacketed May copies in the collection of Herb Bridges of Sharpsburg, Ga., turned up two different issues of the jacket. The one that Bridges and I agree may be the first, and worth a little more than the other, bears on the back panel an advertisement headed "Macmillan Spring Novels" and listing *GWTW* far down in a list of 17 books. The ad on the other jacket is headed "New Macmillan Books" and has the Mitchell novel at the top of another list. Presumably Macmillan reprinted the jacket to give *GWTW* top billing in the ad—used interchangeably on jackets for other books—when the publishers realized they had a winner on their hands.)

MITCHELL, S. Augustus. See *Illinois in 1837.*

MITCHELL, S. Augustus (publisher). *Accompaniment to Mitchell's New Map of Texas, Oregon and California, with the Regions Adjoining.* 46 pp., text and large colored map, folding into leather covers. Philadelphia, 1846. First edition. $350-$400.

MITCHELL, S. Augustus (publisher). *Description of Oregon and California, Embracing An Account of the Gold Regions.* Folding map in color. Gold-stamped cloth. Philadelphia, 1849. First edition. $600-$800.

MITCHELL, S. Augustus. *Traveller's Guide Through the United States.* Folding map. 74 pp., leather. Philadelphia, (1836). First text edition under this title. $100-$125. New York, 1851. $50-$75.

MITCHELL, S. Weir. See S., E. W., and M., S. W. Also see *The Wonderful Stories of Fuz-Buz the Fly.*

MITCHELL, S. Weir. *Hugh Wynne, Free Quaker.* Illustrated by Howard Pyle. 2 vols., gray or light brown cloth. New York, 1897. First edition, first issue, with last word on page 54, Vol. 1, being "in" and line 16 on page 260, Vol. 2, reading "before us." $75-$85. Later issue, text corrected: 2 vols. gray boards, white cloth spines, paper labels. One of 60 large paper copies, signed, with separate plates by Howard Pyle laid in. $100-$150. (Note: A few copies of the first edition, first issue, exist with an 1869 title page—not published. One of these was sold at auction in the 1972-73 season for $1,400.)

MITCHELL, S. Weir. *Mr. Kris Kringle.* Boards and cloth. Philadelphia, 1893. First edition. $35-$50.

MITCHELL, S. Weir. *Researches upon the Venom of the Rattlesnake.* Folio, wrappers. Washington, 1861. $100-$150.

MITCHELL, S. Weir, and others. *Gunshot Wounds and Other Injuries of Nerves.* Wrappers. Philadelphia, 1864. $200-$225.

MITCHELL, W. H. *Geographical and Statistical History of the County of Olmstead.* 121 pp., printed wrappers. Rochester, Minn., (1866). First edition. $100-$125.

MITCHELL, W. H. *Geographical and Statistical Sketch of the Past and Present of Goodhue County.* 191 pp., wrappers. Minneapolis, 1869. First edition. $100-$125.

MITFORD, John. *The Adventures of Johnny Newcome in the Navy.* Color plates. Half calf. London, 1819. Second edition. $150-$200. London, 1823. Third edition. $75-$125. (See Alfred Burton entry for first edition.)

MITFORD, Mary Russell. *Our Village.* Boards, paper label. London, 1824. First edition. $200-$250. London, 1910. Illustrated by Hugh Thomson. Half leather. $35-$50.

MITFORD, Mary Russell. *Poems.* Boards. London, 1810. First edition, with leaf of "Alterations." $300-$400. Author's first book.

MIVART, St. George. *Dogs, Jackals, Wolves, and Foxes.* Illustrated, including 45 color plates. Cloth. London, 1890. First edition. $400-$500.

MIVART, St. George. *A Monograph of the Lories, or Brush-Tongued Parrots.* 61 colored plates and 4 colored maps. Cloth. London, 1896. First edition. $2,000-$2,500.

*MODERN Griselda (The).* Boards, London, 1805. (By Maria Edgeworth.) First edition. $100-$150.

MOELLHAUSEN, Baldwin. *Diary of a Journey from the Mississippi to the Coasts of the Pacific with a United States Government Expedition.* Translated by Mrs. Percy Sinnett. Illustrations, including color plates. Folding map. 2 vols., cloth. London, 1858. First edition. $400-$500.

MOELVILLE, A. F. Bertrand de. *The Costume of the Hereditary States of the House of Austria.* 50 colored engravings. Full contemporary morocco. London, 1804. First English edition. $400 and up.

MOFFETTE, Joseph F. *The Territories of Kansas and Nebraska.* 2 folding maps. Cloth. New York, 1855. First edition. $1,000-$1,250. New York, 1856. Second edition. $500.

MOKLER, A. J. *History of Natrona County, Wyoming.* Illustrated. Buckram. Chicago, 1923. First edition. $75-$100.

*MOLL Pitcher, a Poem.* Blue printed wrappers. Boston, 1832. (By John Greenleaf Whittier.) First edition. (Note: No copy in original wrappers has been noted at sale for many years. Estimated retail value: $1,500-$2,500. Rebound copies, $500 and up.) Philadelphia, 1840. *(Moll Pitcher, and the Minstrel Girl: Poems.)* Wrappers. $150-$200.

*MONASTERY (The).* 3 vols., boards, paper spines and labels. Edinburgh, 1820. (By Sir Walter Scott.) First edition. $100-$150.

MONETTE, John W. *History of the Discovery and Settlement of the Valley of the Mississippi.* 3 maps, 4 plans, 2 plates. Cloth. New York, 1846. First edition. $150-$225.

*MONIKINS (The): A Tale.* By the Author of "The Spy." 3 vols., drab tan boards. London, 1835. (By James Fenimore Cooper.) First edition. $150-$250. Philadelphia, 1835. 2 vols., boards. First American edition. $250-$350.

MONKS, William. *History of Southern Missouri and Northern Arkansas.* Cloth. West Plains, Mo., 1907. First edition. $100-$125.

*MONODY on the Death of the Right Honorable R. B. Sheridan.* 12 pp., wrappers. London, 1816. (By George Gordon Noel, Lord Byron.) First edition, first issue, with first line on page 11 beginning "To weep," etc. $1,000 and up. Very rare; no copies in wrappers for sale in many years. In contemporary calf binding, $84 (A, 1967). Second issue, line 1 on page 11 beginning "To mourn." $300-$500. In contemporary leather, $55 (A, 1971); $108 (A, 1969).

MONROE, Harriet. *The Columbian Ode.* Pictorial wrappers. Chicago, 1893. First (Souvenir) Edition. In original envelope. $50-$65.

MONROE, Harriet. *Valeria and Other Poems.* Vellum and cloth. Chicago, 1891. First edition. $50-$60. Author's first book. Chicago, 1892. Cloth. First published edition. $25.

MONROE, James. *The Memoir of James Monroe, Esq., Relating to His Unsettled Claims Upon the People and Government of the U.S.* 60 pp., sewed, Charlottesville, Va., 1828. $150-$175.

*MONROE'S Embassy, or the Conduct of the Government, in Relation to Our Claims to the Navigation of the Missisippi* [sic]. 57 pp., wrappers. Philadelphia, 1803. (By Charles Brockden Brown.) $300-$350. (Note: Signed at the end with the pseudonym Poplicola.)

*MONT Saint Michel and Chartres.* Blue cloth, leather label on spine. Washington, 1904. (By Henry Adams.) First edition. Privately printed. $400-$600. Inscribed by the author, $750. Washington, 1912. Revised and enlarged edition. $75-$125. Boston, 1913. Half brown cloth and tan boards. First published edition. $25. New York, 1957. Limited Editions Club. Cloth and leather. Boxed. $40-$60.

MONTAGUE, C. E. *A Hind Let Loose.* Cloth. London, (1910). First edition. In dust jacket. $35-$50. Author's first book.

MONTAGUE, C. E. *A Writer's Notes on His Trade.* Introduction by H. M. Tomlinson. Woodcut portrait. Buckram and boards. London, 1930. First edition. One of 700 signed by Tomlinson. $35-$50.

MONTAIGNE, Michel de. *Essays.* Translated by John Florio. 3 vols., folio, half cloth. Boston, 1902–04. One of 265 designed by Bruce Rogers and inscribed by him. In dust jackets and folding cases. $400-$450. London, 1931. Nonesuch Press. 2 vols., full morocco. Boxed. $100-$125.

*MONTANA, Its Climate, Industries and Resources.* Illustrated. 74 pp., wrappers. Helena, Mont., 1884. First edition. $150-$200.

*MONTANA. Territory. History and Business Directory 1879.* Map. 5 plates. Printed boards and leather. Helena, (1879). (By F. W. Warner.) First edition. $300-$600.

MONTGOMERY, Cora. *Eagle Pass; or, Life on the Border.* Stiff wrappers. New York, 1852. (By Mrs. William L. Cazneau.) First edition. $75-$100.

MONTULE, Eduard. *A Voyage to North America, and the West Indies, in 1821.* Folding and full-page plates. Printed wrappers. London, 1821. First edition in English. $200-$250.

MOODY, William Vaughn. *The Masque of Judgment.* Cloth. Boston, 1900. First edition. $35-$50. Another issue: Boards. One of 150. $50. Author's first book.

MOORCOCK, Michael. *The Stealer of Souls.* Cloth. London, 1963. First edition. In dust jacket. $35-$40.

MOORCOCK, Michael. *Stormbringer.* Cloth. London, (1965). First edition. In dust jacket. $25-$35.

MOORE, Sir Alan Hilary. *Sailing Ships of War, 1800-1860.* 90 full-page plates, 12 in color. Cloth. London, 1926. One of 1,500. $100-$150. Another issue: Half leather. One of 100. $250-$350.

MOORE, Brian. *The Lonely Passion of Judith Hearn.* Cloth. London, 1955. First edition. In dust jacket. $65. Boston, (1955). Boards. First American edition. In dust jacket. $25-$30.

MOORE, C. L. *Northwest of Earth.* Cloth. New York, (1954). First edition. In dust jacket. $40-$50.

MOORE, C. L. *Shambleau and Others*. Cloth. New York, (1953). First edition. In dust jacket. $40-$50.

MOORE, Clement C. See *A New Translation, etc.; The New York Book of Poetry; Observations upon Certain Passages in Mr. Jefferson's "Notes on Virginia."*

MOORE, Clement C. *Christmas Carol. The Visit of Saint Nicholas*. Broadside; text printed in blue. Philadelphia, (1842). $35-$50.

MOORE, Clement C. *The Night Before Christmas*. Color plates by W. W. Denslow. Pictorial boards. New York, 1902. $100-$150. Philadelphia, (1931). 4 color plates and text drawings by Arthur Rackham. Cloth. $250-$350. London, (1931). Vellum. One of 550. $500-$600. Trade edition. Boards. $150-$200.

MOORE. Clement, C. *Poems*. Brown boards. New York. 1844. First edition. $250-$300.

MOORE, Clement C. *A Visit from St. Nicholas*. Illustrated by F. O. C. Darley. Pictorial wrappers. New York, 1862. $75-$100.

MOORE, Edward. *We Moderns: Enigmas and Guesses*. Cloth. London, (1918). (By Edwin Muir.) First edition. In dust jacket. $100-$150. Muir's first book.

MOORE, Edward A. *The Story of a Cannoneer Under Stonewall Jackson*. Cloth. New York, 1907. First edition. $100-$150.

MOORE, George. *The Brook Kerith*. Half brown cloth, marbled sides. Edinburgh, 1916. First edition. $30-$50. Another issue: Parchment and boards. One of 250, signed. $75-$85. London, 1929. Illustrated by Stephen Gooden. Vellum. One of 375 signed by Moore and Gooden. $100-$150. New York, 1929. Illustrated by Gooden. Half vellum. One of 500. $100-$125.

MOORE, George. *Esther Waters*. Dark olive-green cloth. London, 1894. First edition, first issue, without floral ornament on front cover. $75-$125.

MOORE, George. *Flowers of Passion*. Black cloth. London, 1878. First edition, with 1877 copyright and errata slip. $300-$400.

MOORE, George. *Heloise and Abelard*. 2 vols., half vellum. London, 1921. First edition. One of 1,000, signed. In dust jackets. $35-$50. New York, 1921. 2 vols., boards. First American edition. One of 1,250. In dust jackets. $20-$35.

MOORE, George. *Literature at Nurse, or, Circulating Morals*. Self-wrappers, sewed. London, 1885. First edition. $400-$450.

MOORE, George. *The Making of an Immortal*. Boards. New York, 1927. Bowling Green Press. One of 15 on green paper, signed. $75-$100. One of 1,240 on white paper, signed. $20.

MOORE, George. *Memoirs of My Dead Life*. Blue-gray cloth. London, 1906. First edition. $75-$100. New York, 1920. Boards and parchment. One of 1,500 (not signed). In dust jacket. $25. London, 1921. Colored frontispiece and decorated title page. Boards and parchment. One of 1,030, signed. $35-$45.

MOORE, George. *A Modern Lover*. 3 vols., blue cloth. London, 1883. First edition. $450 and up.

MOORE, George. *A Mummer's Wife*. Cloth. London, 1885. First edition. $75-$100.

MOORE, George. *Pagan Poems*. Blue cloth. London, 1881. First edition. $400-$500. (Note: Moore removed the title page from most copies and complete copies are rare.)

MOORE, George. *Parnell and His Island*. Wrappers. London, 1887. First edition. $100.

MOORE, George. *Peronnik the Fool*. Cloth. London, 1926. Bruce Rogers printing. $25-$35. Chapelle-Reanville, France, 1928. Hours Press. Cloth. Revised edition. One of 200 signed. $100-$150. London, 1933. Engravings by Stephen Gooden. Full vellum. One of 525 signed by author and artist. $80-$100.

MOORE, George. *Spring Days*. Green cloth. London, 1888. First edition. $40-$50.

MOORE, George. *A Story-Teller's Holiday*. Half vellum. London, 1918. First edition. One of 1,000, signed. In dust jacket. $35-$50. New York, 1918. Cloth. First American edition. One of 1,250, signed. $25. New York, 1928. 2 vols., cloth. One of 1,250, signed. $15-$20.

MOORE, George. *Ulick and Soracha*. Engraved plate by Stephen Gooden. Buckram. London, 1926. Nonesuch Press. One of 1,250 on vellum, signed. In dust jacket. $40-$60.

MOORE, George. *Vain Fortune*. Illustrated. Buckram. London, (1890). First edition. One of 150. $15-$20.

MOORE, George, and Lopez, Bernard. *Martin Luther: A Tragedy in Five Acts*. Blue-gray cloth. London, 1879. First edition. $50-$60.

MOORE, H. Judge. *Scott's Campaign in Mexico*. Cloth. Charleston, 1849. First edition. $250-$350.

MOORE, Henry. *Heads, Figures and Ideas*. Illustrated. Boards and cloth. London, 1959. First edition. In dust jacket. $150-$175.

MOORE, Julia A. *The Sentimental Song Book*. 54 pp., wrappers. Grand Rapids, 1876. First edition. $100 and up.

MOORE, Marianne. *The Absentee: A Comedy in Four Acts*. Blue cloth. New York, 1962. First edition. One of 326 signed. In tissue dust jacket. $125-$150.

MOORE, Marianne. *Collected Poems*. Cloth. London, (1951). First edition, with or without errata slip. In dust jacket. $35-$50.

MOORE, Marianne. *Complete Poems*. Half buckram. New York, (1967). First edition, with or without errata slip. In dust jacket. $50-$60.

MOORE, Marianne. *Eight Poems*. 10 hand-colored drawings. Half cloth. New York, (1963). First edition. One of 195, signed. Boxed. $400-$500. Also, a copy with addendum slip and "With the Author's Compliments" slip, $500 (A, 1977).

MOORE, Marianne. *Le Mariage*. Translated by Jeffrey Kindley. Decorated wrappers. New York, 1965. First edition. One of 50. $50-$60.

MOORE, Marianne. *Marriage: Manikin No. 3*. 16 pp., light-blue pictorial wrappers. New York, (1923). First edition, with 4-page leaflet by Glenway Wescott laid in, as issued. $450-$550.

MOORE, Marianne. *Nevertheless*. Cloth. New York, (1944). First edition, first printing. In dust jacket. $50-$60.

MOORE, Marianne. *Observations*. Cloth-backed boards, paper label. New York, 1924. First edition. In dust jacket. $250-$300.

MOORE, Marianne. *The Pangolin and Other Verse*. Drawings by George Plank. Decorated boards, paper label. (London), 1936. First edition. One of 120. $500-$600. Also, $425 (A, 1977).

MOORE, Marianne. *Poems*. Decorated wrappers, paper label. London, 1921. Egoist Press. First edition. $200-$300. Author's first book.

MOORE, Marianne. *Predilections*. Cloth. New York, 1955. First edition. In dust jacket. $40-$50.

MOORE, Marianne. *Selected Poems*. Introduction by T. S. Eliot. Green or turquoise cloth. New York, 1935. First edition. In dust jacket. $60-$75. London, (1935). Red cloth (purple later). First English edition. In dust jacket. $40-$50.

MOORE, Marianne. *Silence*. Wrappers, paper label. (Cambridge, Mass., 1965.) First edition. One of 25. $100-$150.

MOORE, Marianne. *The Student.* Broadside. New York, 1965. First edition (of this reprint from *What Are Years*). One of 25. $40-$50.

MOORE, Marianne. *A Talisman.* Wrappers. (Cambridge, 1965.) First edition. One of 20. $100-$125.

MOORE, Marianne. *Tipoo's Tiger.* Printed wrappers. New York, 1967. First edition. One of 126 signed, and with correction in line 24 in author's hand. $200-$250.

MOORE, Marianne. *What are Years.* Cloth. New York, 1941. First edition, first printing. In dust jacket. $50-$60.

MOORE, Marianne (translator). *The Fables of La Fontaine.* Cloth. New York, 1954. One of 400, signed. Boxed. $100-$150. Trade edition: In dust jacket. $30-$40. New York, (1964). Cloth. Revised edition. In dust jacket. $20-$25.

MOORE, Marianne, and Wallace, David. *Letters from and to the Ford Motor Company.* Half cloth. New York, 1958. First edition. Boxed. $75-$100.

MOORE, Marinda B. (Mrs. M.B.) *The Dixie Primer, for the Little Folks.* Wrappers. Raleigh, 1863. Third edition. $70 (A, 1976).

MOORE, Marinda B. (Mrs. M.B.). *The Dixie Speller.* Boards. Raleigh, 1864. $150-$200.

MOORE, Marinda B. (Mrs. M. B.). *The Geographical Reader, for the Dixie Children.* 48 pp., boards. Raleigh, 1863. First edition. $100-$150.

MOORE, Marinda B. (Mrs. M. B.). *Primary Geography.* 6 colored double-spread maps. Cloth. Raleigh, 1864. Second edition. $220 (A, 1977).

MOORE, Merrill. *Record from a Sonnetorium.* Cartoons by Edward St. John Gorey. Cloth. New York, (1951). First edition. In dust jacket. $50-$60.

MOORE, S. S., and Jones, T. W. *The Traveller's Directory.* 38 maps on 22 leaves. 52 pp., contemporary calf. Philadelphia, 1802. First edition. $500-$750. Philadelphia, 1804. $500-$600.

MOORE, Thomas. *The Epicurean: A Tale.* Boards, paper label. London, 1827. First edition. $75.

MOORE, Thomas. *Fables for the Holy Alliance.* Boards. London, 1823. First edition. $100.

MOORE, Thomas. *Irish Melodies.* Boards. Dublin, 1820. First edition. $40-$60. London, 1821. Boards. First authorized edition. $150-$200. London, 1846. Half morocco. $200.

MOORE, Thomas. *Lalla Rookh, an Oriental Romance.* Boards. London, 1817. First edition. $100-$150.

MOORE, Thomas. *The Loves of the Angels: A Poem.* Boards. London, 1823. First edition. $75-$100.

MOORE, Thomas. *Lyrics and Satires.* Selected by Sean O'Faolain. 5 designs by Hilda Roberts. Boards and cloth. Dublin, 1929. Cuala Press. One of 130. In dust jacket. $75-$100.

MOORE, Thomas. *Paradise and the Peri.* Illuminated borders. Folio, leather, or cloth. (London, about 1860.) First edition. $75-$100.

MOORE, Thomas (translator). *The Odes of Anacreon.* Morocco. London, 1800. First edition. $50-$75.

MOORE, T. Sturge. *A Brief Account of the Origin of the Eragny Press.* Illustrated. Boards. London, 1903. Eragny Press. One of 235. $250-$350.

MOORE, T. Sturge. *The Little School: A Posy of Rhymes.* Woodcuts. Boards. London, 1905. Eragny Press. One of 185. In dust jacket. $100-$150. Another issue: Morocco. One of 10 on vellum. $400-$500.

MOORE, T. Sturge. *The Vinedresser and Other Poems.* Cloth. London, 1899. Unicorn Press. First edition. $75-$100. Author's first published book.

MORE, Hannah. See *Hints Towards Forming the Character of a Young Princess.*

MORE, Hannah. *Sacred Dramas, Chiefly Intended for Young Persons.* Calf. Boston, 1801. First American edition. $45-$50.

*MORE Hints on Etiquette.* Illustrated. Cloth. London, 1838. (By George Cruikshank or Charles Dickens?) First edition. $150-$250.

MORE, Sir Thomas. *Utopia.* Woodcut borders and initials, printed in black and red. Vellum with ties. London, 1893. Kelmscott Press. $400-$500. (London, 1906.) Ashendene Press. Boards and linen. One of 100. $1,000-$1,250. Another issue: Morocco. One of 20 on vellum. $5,000. Also $3,500 (A, 1970). Waltham Saint Lawrence, England, 1929. Golden Cockerel Press. Decorations by Eric Gill. Buckram. $100-$125. New York, 1934. Limited Editions Club. Woodcuts by Bruce Rogers. Vellum and boards. Boxed. $40-$50.

MORECAMP, Arthur. *The Live Boys; or, Charlie and Nasho in Texas.* Pictorial cloth. Boston, (1878). (By Thomas Pilgrim.) First edition. $100-$150. Author's first book.

MOREHEAD, James T. *Address in Commemoration of the First Settlement of Kentucky.* Printed wrappers. Frankfort, 1840. First edition. $100-$150.

MORFI, Juan Agustin. *History of Texas, 1673-1779.* Map, 4 plates. 2 vols., boards and cloth. Albuquerque, 1935. First edition. One of 500. $150-$300. New York, 1967. Facsimile edition. $50-$60.

MORGAN, Charles. *The Gunroom.* Cloth. London, 1919. First edition. $60-$80. Author's first novel.

MORGAN, Charles. *Sparkenbroke.* Morocco. London, 1936. First edition. One of 210, signed. $100-$125. Trade edition: Green cloth. In dust jacket. $20-$25.

MORGAN, Dale L. See Ashley, William H.

MORGAN, Dale L. *Jedediah Smith and the Opening of the West.* 20 plates. Cloth. Indianapolis, (1953). First edition. In dust jacket. $35-$50.

MORGAN, Dale L., and Wheat, Carl I. *Jedediah Smith and His Maps of the American West.* 7 folding maps. Cloth. San Francisco, 1954. First edition. One of 530. $250-$300.

MORGAN, Dick T. *Morgan's Manual of the U. S. Homestead and Townsite Laws.* Buff printed wrappers. Guthrie, Okla., 1893. First edition. $150-$300.

MORGAN, Emanuel. *Pins for Wings.* Illustrated by William Saphier. Boards. (New York, 1920.) (By Witter Bynner.) First edition. $100-$125.

MORGAN, Emanuel, and Knish, Anne. *Spectra: A Book of Poetic Experiments.* Boards. New York, 1916. (By Witter Bynner [Morgan] and Arthur Davison Ficke [Knish].) First edition. (Issued without dust jacket.) $75-$100.

MORGAN, Jane. *Tales for Fifteen.* Printed tan boards. New York, 1823. (By James Fenimore Cooper.) First edition. Extremely rare; no sales noted in any records consulted. Value: $1,000 and up?

MORGAN, John Hill, and Fielding, Mantle. *The Life Portraits of Washington and Their Replicas.* Illustrated. Folio, cloth. Philadelphia, (1931). First edition. One of 1,000. Another issue: Full morocco. One of 180, signed. $200-$300.

MORGAN, Lewis H. *The American Beaver and His Works.* Map, 23 plates. Cloth. Philadelphia, 1868. First edition. $100.

MORGAN, Lewis H. *Ancient Society.* Cloth. New York, 1877. First edition. $100-$150.

MORGAN, Lewis H. *The Indian Journals of Lewis Henry Morgan.* Illustrated, including color plates and maps. Oblong, cloth. Ann Arbor, Mich., (1959). In dust jacket. $35-$50.

MORGAN, Lewis H. *The League of the Ho-De'-No-Sau-Nee, or Iroquois.* 21 plates, map, table. Cloth. Rochester, 1851. First edition. $75-$100. Another issue: Maps and plates colored by hand. $200-$300. New York, 1922. Edited by H. H. M. Lloyd. 2 vols. in one, cloth. $50-$75.

MORGAN, Martha M. (editor). *A Trip Across the Plains in the Year 1849.* 31 pp., printed wrappers. San Francisco, 1864. First edition. $5,000-$6,000.

MORIER, James. See *Ayesha.*

MORISON, Stanley. *The Art of the Printer.* Illustrated. Cloth. London, 1925. In dust jacket. $125-$175. Paris, (1925). $100-$150.

MORISON, Stanley. *English Liturgical Books.* Green buckram. (Cambridge, 1942.) First edition. One of 21 bound (from an edition of 50). $150-$200. (Suppressed and reissued in 1943 in another format.)

MORISON, Stanley. *The English Newspaper.* Illustrated. Folio, cloth. Cambridge, 1932. First edition. In dust jacket. $200-$250.

MORISON, Stanley. *Four Centuries of Fine Printing.* Illustrated with 625 facsimiles. Folio, cloth. London, (1924). One of 390. $400-$500. Another issue: Morocco. One of 13 signed. $600-$750. London, (1949). 272 facsimile title pages. Calf. Second edition, revised. One of 200. $100-$200.

MORISON, Stanley, *Fra Luca de Pacioli of Borgo S. Sepolcro.* Boards, vellum spine. New York, 1933. First edition. One of 390. $400-$500. Another issue: One of 7 on large paper. $600-$750.

MORISON, Stanley. *Modern Fine Printing.* Facsimiles. Cloth. London, 1925. First edition. One of 650 in English. $300-$400.

MORISON, Stanley. *On Monotype Printers' Flowers.* Boards. London, 1924. $50-$75.

MORISON, Stanley. *On Type Faces.* Illustrated. Folio, half cloth. London, 1923. First edition. One of 750. In dust jacket. $150-$200.

MORISON, Stanley (editor). *A Newly Discovered Treatise on Classic Letter Design.* Facsimile reproduction. Vellum and boards. Paris, 1927. First edition. One of 350. Boxed. $350-$500.

MORISOT, Berthe. *The Correspondence of Berthe Morisot.* Illustrated. Cloth. London, 1957. First edition. In dust jacket. $50-$75.

MORLAND, T. H. *The Genealogy of the English Race-Horse.* Frontispiece. Boards. London, 1810. $75-$100.

MORLEY, C. D. *The Eighth Sin.* Printed pale blue-gray wrappers. Oxford, 1912. (By Christopher Morley.) First edition. One of 250. $450-$600. Also, presentation copy, inscribed, $600 (A, 1977). Author's first book.

MORLEY, Christopher. *The Haunted Bookshop.* Cloth. New York, 1919. First edition, first state, with page number at bottom of page 76 and perfect "Burroughs" above it. In dust jacket. $75-$100.

MORLEY, Christopher. *The Palette Knife.* Illustrated in color. Pictorial cloth. Chelsea, N.Y., 1929. First edition. One of 450, signed. $75.

MORLEY, Christopher. *Parnassus on Wheels.* Gray boards, tan cloth spine. Garden City, N.Y., 1917. First edition, first state, with space between the "Y" and "e" in "Years" in line 8, page 4. In dust jacket. $200-$400. Lacking jacket, $100-$150.

MORLEY, Christopher. *Paumanok.* Boards. Garden City, 1926. First edition. One of 107, signed. In dust jacket. $75.

MORLEY, Christopher. *Songs for a Little House.* Boards. New York, (1917). First edition, first state, with quotation from Southwell facing title page. $30-$40.

MORLEY, Christopher. *Where the Blue Begins.* Pictorial cream and blue marbled boards, blue cloth spine. Garden City, 1922. First edition. In dust jacket. $15-$25. London and New York, (1924). Illustrated, including color plates, by Arthur Rackham. Light-blue decorated cloth. First large paper edition. In dust jacket. $150-$200. Another issue: Green and blue boards. One of 100 signed by author and artist. In tissue dust jacket. Boxed. $500-$600. London and New York, (1925). First English edition. One of 175, signed. In dust jacket. Boxed. $500-$600. Trade edition. Cloth. $150-$200.

MORPHIS, J. M. *History of Texas.* Plates, folding map in color. Cloth. New York, 1874. First edition. $150-$200.

MORRELL, Benjamin. *Narrative of Four Voyages to the South Seas. North and South Pacific Ocean.* Portrait. Boards and cloth. New York, 1832. First edition. $300-$400.

MORRELL, Z. N. *Flowers and Fruits from the Wilderness; or 36 Years in Texas.* Cloth. Boston, 1872. First edition. $100-$200.

MORRIS, Eastin. *The Tennessee Gazetteer.* Printed boards, leather spine. Nashville, 1834. First edition. $1,000-$1,250.

MORRIS, William. *Child Christopher and Goldilind the Fair.* Woodcuts. 2 vols., decorated boards and cloth. London, 1895. Kelmscott Press. One of 600. $300-$350. Another issue: One of 12 printed on vellum. $850-$1,200.

MORRIS, William. *The Defence of Guenevere, and Other Poems.* Printed in black and red. Woodcut borders. Vellum with ties. London, 1892. Kelmscott Press. One of 300. $450-$600. London, 1904. Half vellum. De La More Press. $75-$100.

MORRIS, William. *A Dream of John Ball and A King's Lesson.* Woodcut borders and designs by Morris and E. Burne-Jones. Vellum with ties. London, 1892. Kelmscott Press. One of 300. $300-$400.

MORRIS, William. *The Earthly Paradise.* Woodcut title. 8 vols., vellum with ties. London, 1896-97. Kelmscott Press. One of 225. $1,000-$1,250.

MORRIS, William. *Gothic Architecture.* Blue boards. (London, 1893.) Kelmscott Press. One of 45 on vellum (of an edition of 1,545). $750. Ordinary copies, first issue, with "Eyk" for "Eyck" on page 45: $250.

MORRIS, William. *Guenevere.* 8 plates. Half cloth. London, 1930. Fanfrolico Press. One of 450. $100-$125.

MORRIS, William. *In Praise of My Lady.* Half leather. New York, 1928. Aries Press. One of 31. $100-$125.

MORRIS, William. *The Life and Death of Jason: A Poem.* Woodcut frontispiece, other decorations by E. Burne-Jones. Vellum with ties. London, 1895. Kelmscott Press. One of 200. $700-$850.

MORRIS, William. *Love Is Enough.* Woodcut borders and 2 illustrations by E. Burne-Jones. Vellum with ties. London, 1897. Kelmscott Press. One of 300. $450-$650.

MORRIS, William. *News from Nowhere.* Woodcut frontispiece, borders, and initials. Vellum with ties. London, 1892. Kelmscott Press. One of 300. $300-$400.

MORRIS, William. *Note by William Morris on His Aims in Founding the Kelmscott Press.* Woodcuts. Boards and cloth. London, 1898. Kelmscott Press. With errata slip. One of 525. $350-$400. (Note: The last book printed at the Kelmscott Press.)

MORRIS, William. *Printing: An Essay.* Boards. Park Ridge, Ill., 1903. First edition. Limited. $200-$300.

MORRIS, William. *The Roots of the Mountains.* Decorated cloth. London, 1890 (actually 1899). One of 250. First edition. $150-$200.

MORRIS, William *Sir Galahad: A Christmas Mystery.* Leather. London, 1858. First edition. $75-$100. (A Thomas J. Wise forgery.) New Rochelle, N.Y., 1902. Elston Press.

Half vellum. One of 80. $150-$200. (Chicago, 1904.) Blue Sky Press. Gray paper over blue cloth boards. One of 500 designed by Thomas Wood Stevens. $50-$75. Another issue: One of 25 on vellum. $100-$150.

MORRIS, William. *The Story of the Glittering Plain.* Woodcut title and borders. Illustrations by Walter Crane. Vellum with ties. London, 1891. Kelmscott Press. One of 200. Boxed. $800-$1,200. London, 1894. Vellum. One of 250. Boxed. $800-$1,200.

MORRIS, William. *The Story of Gunnlaug the Worm-tongue and Raven the Skald.* (All copies have spaces where initial capital letters were to have been printed at the beginning of each chapter.) Boards and cloth. London, 1891. Chiswick Press. One of 75. $175-$225.

MORRIS, William. *The Sundering Flood.* Woodcuts. Boards and cloth, London, 1897. Kelmscott Press. One of 300. $250-$300. (One of two, possibly more, on vellum, in a new binding of calf and oak boards, was offered by a London dealer at $6,250 in 1973.)

MORRIS, William. *Under an Elm-Tree.* Wrappers (?). Aberdeen, 1891. First edition. $75-$100. (Note: H. Buxton Forman forged wrappers for this pamphlet.)

MORRIS, William. *The Water of the Wondrous Isles.* Woodcut borders and initials. Vellum with ties. London, 1897. Klemscott Press. One of 250. $500-$600.

MORRIS, William. *The Well at the World's End.* 4 woodcuts and initial letters by E. Burne-Jones. Vellum with ties. London, 1896. Kelmscott Press. One of 350. $750-$1,000.

MORRIS, William. *The Wood Beyond the World.* Woodcut frontispiece, other illustrations. Vellum with ties. London, 1894. Kelmscott Press. First edition. One of 350. $600-$750.

MORRIS, William (translator). *Of the Friendship of Amis and Amile.* Woodcut title and borders. Full red morocco. London, 1894. Kelmscott Press. One of 500. $100-$200. Another issue: One of 15 on vellum. $1,000-$1,250.

MORRIS, William (translator). *The Tale of the Emperor Coustans and of Over the Sea.* 2 woodcut titles and borders. Boards and linen. (London, 1894.) Kelmscott Press. One of 525. $400-$600.

MORRIS, William, and Wyatt, A. J. (translators). *The Tale of Beowulf.* Woodcut title and borders. Vellum with ties. London, 1895. Kelmscott Press. One of 300. $500-$750.

MORRIS, Wright. *The Deep Sleep.* Cloth. New York, 1953. First edition. In dust jacket. $35-$50.

MORRIS, Wright. *The Field of Vision.* Cloth. New York, (1956). First edition. In first state (blue and black) dust jacket. $50.

MORRIS, Wright. *God's Country and My People.* Cloth. New York, (1958). First edition. In first state dust jacket with price "$7.95" (later changed to $10). $50-$60.

MORRIS, Wright. *The Home Place.* Illustrated. Cloth. New York, 1948. First edition. In dust jacket. $50-$60.

MORRIS, Wright, *The Inhabitants.* Illustrated with author's photographs. Cloth. New York, 1946. First edition. In dust jacket. $50-$60.

MORRIS, Wright. *Man and Boy.* Cloth. New York, 1951. First edition. In dust jacket. $35-$50.

MORRIS, Wright. *The Man Who Was There.* Cloth. New York, 1945. First edition. In dust jacket. $75-$100.

MORRIS, Wright. *My Uncle Dudley.* Cloth, paper label. New York, (1942). First edition. In dust jacket. $75-$100.

MORRIS, Wright. *The World in the Attic.* Cloth. New York, 1949. First edition, with the Scribner "A" on copyright page. In dust jacket. $40-$50.

MORRISON, Arthur. *The Dorrington Deed-Box.* Illustrated. Red cloth. London, (1896). First edition. $200-$250.

MORRISON, James. *Journal.* Illustrated by Robert Gibbings. Buckram. (London), 1935. Golden Cockerel Press. One of 125. $300.

MORRISON, Toni. *The Bluest Eye.* Cloth. New York, (1970). First edition. $25-$35. Author's first book.

MORSE, A. Reynolds. *Dali: A Study of His Life and Work.* Illustrated. Cloth. Greenwich, Conn., (1958). First American edition. In acetate dust jacket. $75.

MORSE, Edward S. *Catalogue of the Morse Collection of Japanese Pottery.* Frontispiece, 68 plates. Boards. Cambridge, Mass., 1901. First edition. $150-$200.

MORSE, Jedidiah. *A Report to the Secretary of War . . . on Indian Affairs.* Colored folding map. Boards. New Haven, 1822. First edition. $250-$350.

MORSE, John F., and Colville, Samuel. *Illustrated Historical Sketches of California.* No. 1 (all published). Frontispiece. Printed wrappers. Sacramento, 1854. First edition. $600-$800.

MOSKOWITZ, Sam. *The Immortal Storm: A History of Science-Fiction Fandom.* Spiralbound wrappers. Atlanta, 1951. First edition. One of 150. $150-$200.

MOSS, Howard. *The Toy Fair.* New York, 1954. First edition. In dust jacket. $30-$40.

MOSS, Howard. *The Wound and the Weather.* Cloth. New York, (1946). First edition. In dust jacket. $40-$50. Author's first book.

MOTLEY, Willard. *Knock on Any Door.* Gray cloth. New York, (1947). First edition. In dust jacket. $25-$35.

MOTT, Mrs. Mentor. *The Stones of Palestine.* 12 mounted photographs by Francis Bedford. Cloth. London, 1865. First edition. $300-$400.

MOWRY, Sylvester. *Memoir of the Proposed Territory of Arizona.* Map (not in all copies). 30 pp., printed wrappers. Washington, 1857. First edition. $2,000-$2,500.

MUIR, Edwin. See Moore, Edward.

MUIR, Edwin. *Chorus of the Newly Dead.* Wrappers, paper label. Richmond, England, 1926, Hogarth Press. First edition. $100-$125.

MUIR, Edwin. *First Poems.* Boards, printed label. London, 1925. First edition. $100-$150.

MUIR, Edwin. *Latitudes.* Cloth. New York, 1924. First edition. In dust jacket. $50-$75. London, 1926. Cloth. First English edition. In dust jacket. $50.

MUIR, Edward. *Six Poems.* Half cloth. Warlingham, England, 1932. Samson Press. First edition. One of 110. $100-$125.

MUIR, John. *The Mountains of California.* Cloth. New York, 1894. First edition. In dust jacket. $75-$100. Author's first book.

MUIR, Percy H. *English Children's Books, 1600-1900.* Illustrated, including color plates. Cloth. London, 1954. First edition. In dust jacket. $75-$100. New York, 1954. Illustrated. Blue cloth. First American edition. In dust jacket. $50-$75.

MUIR, Percy H. *Points, 1874-1930.* Illustrated. Parchment and boards. London, 1931. First edition. One of 500. $100-$135.

MUIR, Percy H. *Points, 1866-1934.* Illustrated. Parchment and boards. London, 1931. First edition. One of 750. $80-$125.

MULFORD, Clarence E. *Bar-20.* Illustrated by N. C. Wyeth and F.E. Schoonover. Pictorial cloth. New York, 1907. First edition, first issue, with the reading "Blazing Star" in the list of illustrations. In dust jacket. $50-$75. Author's first book.

MULFORD, Clarence E. *Bar-20 Days.* Illustrated by Maynard Dixon. Brown cloth. Chicago, 1911. First edition. In dust jacket. $50-$60.

MULLAN, John. *Miners' and Travelers' Guide to Oregon, etc.* Folding colored map. Cloth. New York, 1865. First edition. $300-$400.

MULLAN, John. *Report on the Construction of a Military Road from Fort Walla-Walla to Fort Benton.* 4 folding maps, 10 plates, 8 colored. Cloth. Washington, 1863. First edition. $150-$200.

MULLET, J. C. *A Five Years' Whaling Voyage.* 68 pp. Cleveland, 1859. First edition. $350-$500.

MULOCK, Dinah Maria (Mrs. Craik). See *The Adventures of a Brownie; John Halifax, Gentleman; A Life for a Life; The Ogilvies.*

MUMEY, Nolie, *Bloody Trails Along the Rio Grande.* Portrait, map. Cloth. Denver, 1938. Limited edition. In dust jacket. $35-$50.

MUMEY, Nolie. *Calamity Jane.* Folding map, illustrations, 2 pamphlets in envelope at end. Boards, pictorial label. Denver, 1950. One of 200, signed. $75.

MUMEY, Nolie. *Colorado Territorial Scrip.* Illustrated. Cloth. Boulder, 1966. First edition. One of 350, signed. $75-$100.

MUMEY, Nolie. *Creede: History of a Colorado Mining Town.* Illustrated. Half cloth. Denver, 1949. One of 500, signed. $85-$100.

MUMEY, Nolie. *History of the Early Settlements of Denver.* Map, 2 folding plates. Boards and vellum. Glendale, Calif., 1942. First edition. One of 500, signed. $50-$75.

MUMEY, Nolie. *James Pierson Beckwourth.* Folding map. Boards. Denver, 1957. First edition. One of 500. $75-$100.

MUMEY, Nolie. *John Williams Gunnison.* Colored portrait, plates, folding map. Boards. Denver, 1955. First edition. One of 500, signed. $75-$100.

MUMEY, Nolie. *The Life of Jim Baker.* Frontispieces, other illustrations, map. Boards. Denver, 1931. First edition. One of 250, signed. $200-$250.

MUMEY, Nolie. *March of the First Dragoons to the Rocky Mountains in 1835.* Errata slip, plates, folding map. Boards. Denver, 1957. First edition. One of 350, signed. $75-$100.

MUMEY, Nolie. *Nathan Addison Baker: Pioneer Journalist.* Illustrated. 4 folding facsimiles in cover pocket. Cloth. Denver, 1965. Limited edition. $35-$50.

MUMEY, Nolie. *Old Forts and Trading Posts of the West.* Vol. 1. (All published.) Cloth. Denver, 1956. First edition. One of 500. $50-$75.

MUMEY, Nolie. *Pioneer Denver, Including Scenes of Central City, Colorado City, and Nevada City.* Folding plate, other illustrations. Boards. Denver, 1948. First edition. One of 240, signed. $75-$100.

MUMEY, Nolie. *Poker Alice.* Illustrated, including folding map. Pictorial wrappers. Denver, 1951. First edition. One of 500, First issue: Map with New Mexico labeled as Nevada. In tissue dust jacket. $50-$75. Later, map corrected; $40-$60.

MUMEY, Nolie. *Rocky Mountain Dick (Richard W. Rock): Stories of His Adventures.* Illustrated. Cloth. Denver, 1953. One of 500, signed. $40-$50.

MUMEY, Nolie. *A Study of Rare Books.* Illustrated. Half cloth and boards. Denver, 1930. First edition. One of 1,000, signed. $100-$200.

MUMEY, Nolie. *The Teton Mountains.* Boards. Denver, 1947. First edition. One of 700. $75-$85.

MUMEY, Nolie (editor). *Edward Dunsha Steele: A Diary of His Journey from Lodi, Wisc., Across the Plains to Boulder, Colo., in 1859.* Half cloth. Boulder, 1960. One of 500. $50-$75.

MUNDY, Talbot. *Rung Ho!* Cloth. New York, 1914. First edition. In dust jacket. $50-$75. Author's first book.

MUNDY, Talbot. *Tros of Samothrace.* Cloth. New York, 1934. First edition. In dust jacket. $150.

MUMFORD, Lewis. *The Story of Utopias.* Cloth. New York, (1922). First edition. In dust jacket. $25. Author's first book.

MUNRO, H. H. See Saki.

MUNRO, Robert. *A Description of the Genessee Country, in the State of New-York.* Map. 16 pp., boards. New York, 1804. (By Charles Williamson.) First edition. $375-$450.

MUNROE, Kirk. *The Fur-Seal's Tooth.* Illustrated by W. A. Rogers. Pictorial cloth. New York, 1894. First edition. $35-$50.

MUNROE, Kirk. *Wakulla: A Story of Adventure in Florida.* Illustrated. Cloth. New York, 1886. First edition. $35-$50. Author's first book.

MUNTHE, Axel. *The Story of San Michele.* Cloth. London, (1929); First edition. With printed slip about distribution of profits. Boxed. $50-$65.

*MURDER by Deputy U. S. Marshal E. M. Thornton of E. M. Dalton Waylaid and Assassinated in Cold Blood.* 16 pp., wrappers. Salt Lake, 1886. $100-$200.

MURRAY, Charles A. *Travels in North America.* 2 plates. 2 vols., cloth. London, 1839. First edition. $200-$300. New York, 1839. 2 vols., cloth. First American edition. $100-$150.

MURRAY, Sir John, and Hjort, Dr. Johan. *The Depths of the Ocean.* 13 plates and folding maps, 575 text illustrations. Cloth. London, 1912. $35-$50.

MURRAY, Keith A. *The Modocs and Their War.* Unbound. Norman, Okla., (1959). First edition. Advance copies which escaped warehouse fire, $75-$125. Second printing, bound in cloth, same date. In dust jacket. $20-$25.

MURRAY, Lois L. *Incidents of Frontier Life.* 2 portraits. Cloth. Goshen, Ind., 1880. First edition. $125-$150.

*MY Darling's A. B. C.* Accordion sheet of 26 leaves with colored alphabet. Orange boards. Philadelphia. (about 1835-40). $100-$150.

MYER, Isaac. *Qabbalah.* Illustratged. Cloth. Philadelphia, 1888. One of 350. $150-$250.

MYERS, Frank, *Soldiering in Dakota.* Wrappers. Huron, S. D., 1888. First edition. $600-$750. Pierre, S. D., 1936. Wrappers. $35-$50.

MYERS, J. C. *Sketches on a Tour Through the Northern and Eastern States.* Contemporary sheepskin. Harrisonburg, Va., 1849. First edition. $150-$200.

MYRICK, Herbert. *Cache la Poudre: The Romance of a Tenderfoot in the Days of Custer.* Cloth. New York, 1904. First edition. In dust jacket. $50-$75. Another issue: Buckskin. One of 500 signed. $150-$200.

*MYSTERIES and Miseries of San Francisco (The).* By a Californian. Cloth. New York, (1853). First edition. Rebound in morocco and marbled boards, internally water-stained, $750. (Note: This is the Thomas W. Streeter copy, purchased for $175 in 1959 from my friend the late Paul Schopflin, and sold at auction in 1968 for $425. Mr. Streeter notes, "No other copy seems to be recorded," but Wright's *American Fiction, 1850-1875* lists a copy in the Library of Congress. Author unknown.)

*MYSTERIES of a Convent.* By a Noted Methodist Preacher. 112 pp., wrappers. Philadelphia, (1854). First edition. $75-$100.

*MYSTERIES of Mormonism (The): A Full Exposure of Its Secret Practices and Hidden Crimes.* By an Apostle's Wife. Wrappers. New York, 1882. $125-$150.

*MYSTERIOUS Marksman (The): or The Outlaws of New York.* Wrappers. Cincinnati. (about 1855). (By Emerson Bennett.) First edition. $300-$500.

# N

NABOKOFF, Vladimir. *Laughter in the Dark.* Cloth. Indianapolis, (1938). (By Vladimir Nabokov.) First edition. In the dust jacket. $100-$125. Author's first book to be issued in the United States. (Published in England as *Camera Obscura.*)

NABOKOFF-SIRIN, Vladimir. *Camera Obscura.* Translated by Winifred Roy. Cloth. London, (1936). (By Vladimir Nabokov.) First edition. In dust jacket. $100-$150. First novel by the author to be published in English. (See *Laughter in the Dark,* above.)

NABOKOFF-SIRIN, Vladimir. *Despair.* Cloth. London, (1937). (By Vladimir Nabokov.) First edition. In dust jacket. $150-$200.

NABOKOV, Vladimir. *Bend Sinister.* Cloth. New York, (1947). First edition. In dust jacket. $65-$85.

NABOKOV, Vladimir. *Conclusive Evidence: A Memoir.* Cloth. New York, (1951). First edition. In dust jacket. $40-$55.

NABOKOV, Vladimir. *The Eye.* Cloth. New York, 1966. Phaedra. First American edition. In dust jacket. $30-$40.

NABOKOV, Vladimir. *Laughter in the Dark.* Green cloth. Indianapolis (1938). First American edition (of *Camera Obscura*). In dust jacket. $50-$75.

NABOKOV, Vladimir. *Lolita.* 2 vols., wrappers. Paris, (1955). Olympia Press. First edition, first issue, with the price of 900 francs on back covers. $250-$300. Paris, (1958). Second printing. $35-$50.

NABOKOV, Vladimir. *Nikolai Gogol.* Tan cloth. Norfolk, Conn., (1944). First edition. In dust jacket. $35-$45.

NABOKOV, Vladimir. *Nine Stories.* Printed blue wrappers. New York, (1947). First edition. $75-$100.

NABOKOV, Vladimir. *Pale Fire.* Black cloth. New York, (1962). First edition, first impression. In dust jacket with "First Impression" imprint. $50-$75.

NABOKOV, Vladimir. *Poems.* Drawings by Robin Jacques. Cloth. Garden City, 1959. First edition. In dust jacket. $60-$75. London, (1861). Light-blue pebbled boards. First English edition. In dust jacket. $35-$50.

NABOKOV, Vladimir. *The Real Life of Sebastian Knight.* Rough cloth, paper labels. Norfolk, Conn., (1941). New Directions. First edition, first issue (with binding as described). In dust jacket. $75-$100. London, (1945). Cloth. First English edition. In dust jacket. $35-$50.

NABOKOV, Vladimir. *The Waltz Invention.* Cloth. (New York), 1966. Phaedra. First edition in English. In dust jacket. $40-$50.

NABOKOV, Vladimir (translator). *Three Russian Poets: Selections from Pushkin, Lermontov, and Tyutchev.* Stiff wrappers. Norfolk, (1944). New Directions. First edition. $35-$50.

NANSEN, Fridtjof. *Farthest North.* 127 maps and plates. 2 vols., pictorial cloth. London, 1897. First edition in English. $75.

NAPTON, William B. *Over the Santa Fe Trail, 1857.* 99 pp., pictorial wrappers. Kansas City, 1905. First edition. $100-$125.

*NARRATIVE and Report of the Causes and Circumstances of the Deplorable Conflagration at Richmond.* Sheepskin and oak boards. (Richmond, Va.?), 1812. First edition. $100-$200.

*NARRATIVE of the Adventures and Sufferings of Capt. Daniel D. Heustis (A).* Frontispiece. 168 pp., printed wrappers. Boston, 1847. First edition. $1,000-$1,250.

*NARRATIVE of Arthur Gordon Pym (The).* Blue or gray cloth, paper label on spine. New York, 1838. (By Edgar Allan Poe.) First edition. $400-$500. Also, $250 (A, 1974). Rebound, $100 and up. London, 1838. Cloth. First English edition. $400-$500. Also, $375 (A, 1974). New York, 1930. Limited Editions Club. Boards. Boxed. $40-$50.

*NARRATIVE of the Captivity and Providential Escape of Mrs. Jane Lewis.* (Cover title.) Woodcut plate. 24 pp., cloth. (New York), 1833. (By William P. Edwards?) First edition. $300. New York, 1834. Wrappers. $150.

*NARRATIVE of the Captivity and Sufferings of Ebenezer Fletcher of New-Ipswich (A).* 22 pp., stitched. Windsor, Vt., 1813. Second edition. $300. New-Ipswich, N.H., 1827. Fourth edition (so stated; it is actually the third edition). $150 and up. New-Ipswich, (about 1828). $75. (Note: There are only 3 known copies of the first edition, published in Amherst in 1798.)

*NARRATIVE of the Captivity and Sufferings of Mrs. Hannah Lewis.* 24 pp., including folding woodcut plate. Boston, 1817. (By William P. Edwards.) First edition. $200-$250. Another edition: (Identical main title except "Harriet" for "Hannah"): Boston, 1821. Half morocco. $100 (A, 1971).

*NARRATIVE of the Capture and Burning of Fort Massachusetts.* Boards. Albany, 1870. (By the Rev. John Norton.) One of 100. $75-$100. (Note: The first edition, Boston, 1748, is very rare.)

*NARRATIVE of the Capture and Providential Escape of Misses Frances and Almira Hall, etc.* Plate. 25 pp., printed wrappers. (St. Louis?), 1832. (By William P. Edwards?) First edition. $600-$850. Later: 26 pp., no place, no date (1833). Second edition. $200-$300.

*NARRATIVE of Dr. Livingston's Discoveries in Central Africa, from 1849 to 1856.* Folding woodcut map. Illustrated boards. London, 1857. First edition, with David Livingstone's name spelled "Livingston." $100 and up.

*NARRATIVE of the Extraordinary Life of John Conrad Shafford.* Frontispiece. 25 pp., wrappers. New York, 1840. First edition. $250 and up. New York, 1841. $110 (A, 1976.).

*NARRATIVE of the Facts and Circumstances Relating to the Kidnapping and Presumed Murder of William Morgan (A).* 36 pp., stitched. (Batavia, N.Y., 1827.) First edition. $100-$125.

*NARRATIVE of the Life and Adventures of Matthew Bunn.* 55 pp., sewed. Batavia, 1828. Seventh edition. $35.

*NARRATIVE of the Massacre at Chicago, August 15, 1812, and of Some Preceding Events.* Frontispiece map. 34 pp., printed wrappers. Chicago, 1844. (By Mrs. Juliette A. Kinzie.) First edition. $2,000-$2,500. Also, $1,850 (A, 1975).

*NARRATIVE of Occurrences (A), in the Indian Countries of North America.* Stiff printed wrappers. London, 1807. (By Samuel Hull Wilcocke?) $750-$1,000.

*NARRATIVE of Some of the Adventures, Dangers, and Sufferings of a Revolutionary Soldier (A).* Cloth. Hallowell, Me., 1830. (By James Sullivan Martin?) First edition. $100-$125.

*NARRATIVE of the Sufferings and Adventures of Capt. Charles H. Barnard (A).* Folding map, 6 plates. Boards. New York, 1829. First edition. $250-$300.

*NARRATIVE of the Sufferings of Massy Harbison.* 66 pp., leather. Pittsburgh, 1825. First edition. $400-$600. Pittsburgh, 1828. 98 pp., boards and linen. Second edition. $325. Beaver, Pa., 1836. Half cloth. Fourth edition. $75-$100.

*NARRATIVE of the Suppression by Col. Burr (A), of the "History of the Administration of John Adams."* Stitched. New York, 1802. (By James Cheetham.) First edition. $200-$300.

*NARRATIVE of the Tragical Death of Mr. Darius Barber and His Seven Children (A).* Frontispiece. 24 pp., wrappers. Boston, (about 1818) . First edition. Very rare; Howes says "4 perfect copies known." $750-$1,000.

NASBY, Petroleum V. *The Nasby Papers.* 64 pp., printed wrappers. Indianapolis, 1864. (By David Ross Locke.) First edition, first binding, with "Indianaolis" on front cover. $75-$100. Author's first book.

NASH, Ogden. *Hard Lines.* Illustrated by O. Soglow. Tan cloth. New York, 1931. First edition. In dust jacket. $75-$100. Author's first book.

NASH, Ogden. *Scrooge Rides Again.* Decorated wrappers. (Berkeley), 1960. First edition. (150 copies.) $50-$60.

NATHAN, George Jean. See Hatteras, Owen; Mencken, H.L., and Nathan, George Jean.

NATHAN, Robert. *The Concert.* Cloth. New York, 1940. First edition. One of 250, signed. $75-$125.

NATHAN, Robert. *One More Spring.* Illustrated. Decorated boards. Stamford, Conn., 1935. One of 750. Boxed. $50.

NATHAN, Robert. *Peter Kindred.* Cloth. New York, 1919. First edition. In dust jacket. $25-$35. Author's first book.

*NATIONAL Elgin Watch Company's Illustrated Almanac for 1875 (The).* Printed wrappers. Chicago, (1874). First edition. $75-$100. (Note: Includes "My Rococo Watch," by Louisa May Alcott.)

*NATURE.* Cloth. Boston, 1836. (By Ralph Waldo Emerson.) First edition, first state, with page 94 misnumbered 92. $350-$500. Also, $325 (A, 1974). Second state, error corrected. $75-$100. Emerson's first published book. New York, 1929. Boards. One of 250. In dust jacket. $150-$200.

*NAUTICAL Reminiscences.* By the Author of *A Mariner's Sketches.* Boards and cloth. Providence, 1832. (By Nathaniel Ames.) First edition. $50-$75.

*NAVAL Achievements of Great Britain and Her Allies from 1793 to 1817 (The).* 55 hand-colored plates. Half morocco. London, (1817). $4,000-$5,000.

*NAVAL Monument (The).* 25 plates. Errata slip. Calf. Boston, 1816. (By Abel Bowen.) First edition. $200-$250.

*NAVIGATOR (The).* Boards or wrappers. Pittsburgh, 1804. (By Zadok Cramer.) Fourth edition (of *The Ohio and Mississippi Navigator,* which see) and first edition with this title. The two copies known are in institutional libraries. Pittsburgh, 1806. 14 charts. 94 pp., plain wrappers. Fifth edition. Worn, $1,700 (A, 1967). Pittsburgh, 1808. Boards. Sixth edition. $230 (A, 1971); $325 (A, 1967). Pittsburgh, 1811. Boards. Seventh edition. Worn, $225 (A, 1975). Pittsburgh, 1814. Boards. Eighth edition. $150-$200. Pittsburgh, 1814. Boards. Ninth edition. $150-$200. Pittsburgh, 1818. Boards. Tenth edition. $100-$150. Pittsburgh, 1821. Boards. Eleventh edition. $75-$100. Pittsburgh, 1824. Boards. Twelfth edition. $50-$100.

NEAGOE, Peter (editor). *Americans Abroad.* Illustrated. Yellow cloth, tan cloth spine. The Hague, Netherlands, 1932. First edition. In dust jacket. $200-$300. Also, $200 (A, 1977). (Note: This anthology contains Henry Miller's first book appearance, as well as new material by William Carlos Williams and others.)

NEAL, John. See Adams, Will. Also see *Authorship: A Tale; Keep Cool; Seventy-Six.*

NEAL, John. *The Moose-Hunter; or, Life in the Maine Woods.* Wrappers. New York, (1864). First edition, first issue, with No. 73 announced on the inside of the front cover. $250-$300.

NEAL, John. *Rachel Dyer: A North American Story.* Boards and cloth. Portland, Me., 1828. First edition. $300-$400.

NEAL, Joseph Clay. *Peter Ploddy, and Other Oddities.* Boards. Philadelphia, 1844. First edition. $35-$50.

NECESSITY *of a Ship-Canal Between the East and West (The).* 45 pp., sewed. Chicago, 1863. (By J. W. Foster.) First edition. $150-$200.

NEESE, George M. *Three Years in the Confederate Horse Artillery.* Cloth. New York, 1911. First Edition. $75-$100.

NEIHARDT, John G. *Black Elk Speaks.* Illustrated, including color plates. Decorated cloth. New York, 1932. First edition. In dust jacket. $50-$60.

NEIHARDT, John G. *A Bundle of Myrrh.* Limp leather. (New York), MCMIII (1903). First edition. One of 5. $100 and up. New York, 1907. Boards and cloth. Revised edition. $25.

NEIHARDT, John G. *Collected Poems.* 2 vols., cloth. New York, 1926. First edition. One of 250 signed. In dust jackets. $50-$75.

NEIHARDT, John G. *The Divine Enchantment: A Mystical Poem.* Cloth. New York, 1900. First edition. $250. Author's first book.

NEIHARDT, John G. *The Lonesome Trail.* Frontispiece. Pictorial cloth. New York, 1907. First edition. $50.

NEIHARDT, John G. *The Song of Hugh Glass.* Cloth. New York, 1915. First edition. In dust jacket. $40-$50.

NEIHARDT, John G. *The Song of the Indian Wars.* Cloth. New York, 1925. First edition. One of 500, signed. In dust jacket. $75-$100. Trade edition: Cloth. In dust jacket. $30-$40.

NEIHARDT, John G. *The Song of Three Friends.* Cloth. New York, 1919. First edition. In dust jacket. $30-$50.

NEIHARDT, John G. *The Splendid Wayfaring.* Cloth. New York, 1920. First edition. In dust jacket. $40-$50.

NEIL, John B. *Biennial Message of the Governor of Idaho to the 11th Session of the Legislature of Idaho Territory.* 19 pp., wrappers. Boise City, Idaho, 1880. $125-$150.

NEMEROV, Howard. *The Homecoming Game.* Cloth. New York, 1957. First edition. In dust jacket. $40-$50.

NEMEROV, Howard. *The Image and the Law.* Black cloth. (New York, 1947.) First edition. In dust jacket. $75-$100. Author's first book.

NEMEROV, Howard. *The Painter Dreaming in the Scholar's House.* Oblong, stiff wrappers. New York, 1968. One of 126, signed. In dust jacket. $50-$60.

NERUDA, Pablo. *Bestiary/Bestiario.* Woodcuts by Antonio Frasconi. Folio, boards and cloth. New York, (1965). First edition. One of 300, signed, with a signed frontispiece woodcut. Boxed. $150-$175.

NERUDA, Pablo. *Heights of Macchu Picchu.* Boards. London, (1966). First English edition. In dust jacket. $20-$25.

NERUDA, Pablo. *We Are Many.* Translated by Alastair Reid. Boards. London, (1967). First edition in English. One of 100, signed. In dust jacket. $75-$125.

NESBIT, Edith. *Ballads and Lyrics of Socialism, 1883-1908.* Cloth. London, 1908. First edition. $40-$50.

NESBIT, Edith. *Wet Magic*. Cloth. London, (1913). First edition. $35-$40.

NEVILL, Ralph. *British Military Prints*. Plates, including color. London, 1909. First edition. $50-$65.

NEVILL, Ralph. *Old English Sporting Books*. Plates, including color. Buckram. London, 1924. First edition. One of 1,500. $150-$200.

NEVILL, Ralph. *Old English Sporting Prints and Their History*. 103 full-page plates, 47 in color. Buckram. London, 1923. First edition. One of 1,500. $100-$125.

*NEW BEDFORD and Fairhaven Signals*. Boards. New Bedford, Mass., 1834. $150-$200.

*NEW Country: Prose and Poetry*. Edited by Michael Roberts. Cloth. London, 1933. Hogarth Press. First edition. $40-$50. (Note: Contains first appearance of three W.H. Auden poems.)

*NEW Directions in Prose and Poetry*. (Vol. 1) Edited by James Laughlin IV. Boards or printed yellow and red wrappers. Norfolk, Conn., 1936. First edition. $65-$75. (Note: Includes new material by Ezra Pound, Wallace Stevens, E. E. Cummings, and others.) Other annuals in this series: 1937 edition (Vol. 2), boards, $50; 1938 (Vol. 3), boards, $35-$50; 1939 (Vol. 4), boards, $35-$50; 1940 (Vol. 5), cloth, $20-$25; 1941 (Vol. 6), cloth, $20-$25; 1942 (Vol. 7), cloth, $20-$25.

*NEW Empire (The): Oregon, Washington, Idaho*. Folding map. Wrappers. Portland, Ore., 1888. First edition. $75-$100.

*NEW ENGLAND Primer (The)*. Illustrated. 63 pp., boards and leather. Boston, printed for G. Smith, (about 1815-30). Boards chipped and broken, $35. Other editions: New England (Boston?), Printed for the Purchaser, (about 1800-12). Illustrated. 32 leaves, boards. $75. Walpole, N.H., 1814. Isaiah Thomas printing. 32 leaves, boards. $65. Middletown, Conn., 1829. Illustrated. 32 leaves, wallpaper wrappers. $65. Boston, (about 1815-30). Loring, publisher. 32 leaves, wrappers. $45.

*NEW Guide of the Conversation in Portuguese and English (The)*. Introduction by Mark Twain. Unbound sheets. Boston, 1883. First edition. $35-$50. (Note: Blanck does not list this but records a London paperback of 1884 by this title.)

*NEW Poets*. Spiral-bound stiff wrappers. Prairie City, Ill., 1941. Press of James A. Decker. First edition. $50-$75.

*NEW Ritual for "Sam" (A): Written by One Connected with the Cincinnati Times, and Dedicated to "Sam's" Numerous Friends*. Wrappers. Cincinnati, 1855. First edition. $50-$75.

*NEW SPAIN and the Anglo-American West: Contributions Presented to Herbert E. Bolton*. Portrait. 2 vols., cloth. (Los Angeles, 1932.) First edition. One of 500. Boxed. $150-$200.

*NEW TESTAMENT of Our Lord and Saviour Jesus Christ*. Translated into the Choctaw Language. Leather. New York, 1848. First edition. $150-$200. New York, 1854. Cloth. Second edition. $75-$100.

*NEW Texas Spelling Book (The)*. Pictorial boards. Houston, 1863. (By E. H. Cushing.) $1,000-$1,500.

*NEW Topographical Atlas of St. Lawrence County, New York*. Colored maps and plans. Cloth. Philadelphia, 1865. First edition. $300-$350.

*NEW Translation with Notes (A), of the Third Satire of Juvenal*. Marbled boards and cloth. New York, 1806. (By Clement C. Moore and John Duer.) First edition, with "Additional Errata" leaf. $100. Moore's first book appearance.

*NEW Year's Feast on His Coming of Age (The)*. Hand-colored woodcuts. Stiff wrappers. London, 1824. (By Charles Lamb.) First edition. $500 and up. Also, $370 (A, 1976).

*NEW YORK Book of Poetry (The)*. Engraved half title. Cloth. New York, 1837. (Edited anonymously by Charles Fenno Hoffman.) First edition. $125-$150. (Note: Contains first book appearance of Clement C. Moore's "A Visit from St. Nicholas.")

*NEW YORK and Oro-Fino Gold and Silver Mining Co. of Idaho.* 31 pp., wrappers. New York, 1865. First edition. $125-$150.

*NEW YORK Primer (The).* Woodcuts. 33 pp., blue pictorial wrappers. New York, 1818. $125-$150.

*NEW ZEALAND, Graphic and Descriptive.* Edited by W.T.L. Travers. Map, 25 colored lithographic views, 19 other views on 6 plates, wooduts in text. Folio, half cloth. London, 1877. $250-$350.

NEWBERRY, Clare Turlay. *Marshmallow.* Illustrated. Pictorial boards. New York, (1942). First edition, with duplicate illustration tipped in for framing. In dust jacket. $50.

NEWBERRY, J.S. *Report on the Properties of the Ramshorn Consolidated Silver Mining Company at Bay Horse, Idaho.* 16 pp., wrappers. New York, (1881). $125-$150.

NEWELL, Rev. Chester. *History of the Revolution in Texas.* Folding map. Cloth. New York, 1838. First edition. $400-$500.

NEWELL, Peter. See *Topsys & Turveys.*

NEWELL, Peter. *The Hole Book.* Illustrated in color by the author. Stapled blue cloth, pictorial cover label. New York, (1908). First edition, with "Published October 1908" below copyright notice. In dust jacket. $250. Lacking jacket, $75.

NEWELL, Peter. *Pictures and Rhymes.* 50 plates. Boards. New York, 1899. First edition. $50-$75.

NEWELL, Peter. *The Rocket Book.* 22 colored plates. Cloth. New York, (1912). First edition. $75-$100.

NEWELL, Peter. *A Shadow Show.* 36 color plates. Pictorial boards. New York, 1896. First edition. $75-$100.

NEWHALL, J. B. *The British Emigrants' "Hand Book."* (Cover title.) 99 pp., printed yellow wrappers. London, 1844. First edition. $750-$850.

NEWHALL, John B. *Sketches of Iowa.* Map in color. Cloth. New York, 1841. First edition. $350-$500.

NEWMAN, John Henry, Cardinal. See *The Dream of Gerontius; Verses on Various Occasions.*

NEWMAN, John Henry, Cardinal. *Apologia Pro Vita Sua.* 8 parts, printed wrappers. London, 1864. First edition. $600-$800. London, 1864. Cloth. First book edition. $150-$200.

NEWMAN, John Henry, Cardinal. *Discourses Addressed to Mixed Congregations.* Cloth. London, 1849. First edition. $40-$50.

NEWMAN, John Henry, Cardinal. *Lectures.* Cloth. London, 1837. First edition. $50.

NEWMAN, John Henry, Cardinal. *Lectures on Justification.* Cloth, paper label. London, 1838. First edition. $40-$50.

NEWMAN, John Henry, Cardinal, and others (editors). *Lyra Apostolica.* Purple cloth. Derby, England, 1836. First edition. $250.

NEWMARK, Harris. *Sixty Years in Southern California. 1853-1913.* 33 plates. Cloth. New York, 1916. First edition. $40-$60. Boston, 1930. Edited by M. H. and M. R. Newmark. 182 illustrations. Cloth. $50-$75.

NEWTON, A. Edward. *The Amenities of Book Collecting and Kindred Affections.* Illustrated. Half cloth. Boston, 1918. First edition, without index. In dust jacket. $50-$75. Author's first book.

NEWTON, A. Edward. *Derby Day and Other Adventures.* Illustrated. Cloth. Boston, 1934. First edition. In dust jacket. $15-$20. Another issue: Half cloth. One of 1,129, signed. Boxed. $40-$65.

NEWTON, A. Edward. *Doctor Johnson: A Play.* Illustrated. Boards. Boston, 1923. First edition. In dust jacket. $15. Another issue: One of 585, signed. $40-$65.

NEWTON, A. Edward. *End Papers.* Illustrated. Cloth. Boston, 1933. First edition. In dust jacket. $15. Another issue: Boards and cloth. One of 1,351, signed. Boxed. $50-$75.

NEWTON, A. Edward. *The Format of the English Novel.* Illustrated, including colored frontispiece. Cloth. Cleveland, 1928. First edition. One of 289. Boxed. $65-$75.

NEWTON, A. Edward. *The Greatest Book in the World.* Boards. Boston, (1925). First edition. In dust jacket. $15. Another issue: One of 470, signed. $50-$60.

NEWTON, A. Edward. *A Magnificent Farce and Other Diversions of a Book Collector.* Illustrated. Boards. Boston, (1921). First edition. In dust jacket. $15. Another issue: One of 265, signed. Boxed. $35-$45.

NEWTON, A. Edward. *Newton on Blackstone.* Cloth. Philadelphia, 1937. First edition. One of 2,000, signed. In dust jacket. $25.

NEWTON, A. Edward. *On Books and Business.* Boards. (New York), 1930. First edition. One of 325, signed. $25-$35.

NEWTON, A. Edward. *Rare Books, etc.* (Sale catalogue.) Illustrated. 3 vols., printed gray boards. New York, 1941. In dust jackets. $75-$100.

NEWTON, A. Edward. *This Book Collecting Game.* Illustrated. Half cloth. Boston, 1928. First edition. In dust jacket. $15. Another issue: One of 990, signed. $40-$50.

NEWTON, A. Edward. *A Tourist in Spite of Himself.* Cloth. Boston, 1930. First edition. In dust jacket. $15. Another issue: One of 525, signed. $30-$50.

NEWTON, J. H. (editor). *History of the Pan-handle . . . West Virginia.* Maps and plates. Cloth. Wheeling, W. Va., 1879. First edition. $75-$85.

NEWTON, J. H. (editor). *History of . . . Venango County, Pennsylvania.* 47 plates. Half leather. Columbus, Ohio, 1879. $100-$125.

NEWTON, James. *A Compleat Herbal.* 176 copper plates. Boards, printed label. London, 1802. $100-$150. London, 1805. $100-$150.

NEWTON, John F. *The Return to Nature.* Boards. London, 1811. First edition. $85-$100.

NICHOLS, Beach. *Atlas of Schuyler County, New York.* 21 maps in color, 31 leaves. Cloth. Philadelphia, 1874. $150-$250.

NICHOLSON, John. *The Martyrdom of Joseph Standing.* Cloth. Salt Lake City, 1886. First edition. $50-$60.

NICHOLSON, William. *Clever Bill.* Illustrated by the author. Pictorial boards. (New York, about 1926 or 1927.) First American edition. $125.

*NICK of the Woods, or The Jibbenainosay.* 2 vols., purple cloth, paper label. Philadelphia, 1837. (By Robert Montgomery Bird.) First edition. $400-$500.

NICOLL, Allardyce. *Stuart Masques and the Renaissance Stage.* 197 illustrations. Cloth. London, 1937. $40-$50.

NICOLLETT, Joseph Nicolas. *Report Intended to Illustrate a Map of the Hydrographical Basin of the Upper Missouri River.* Senate Doc. 237, 26th Congress, 2d session. Folding map. 170 pp., wrappers, or cloth. Washington, 1843. First edition. $300-$375. Washington, 1845. House Doc. 52. Smaller map. Sewed. $100-$150.

NICOLSON, Marjorie Hope. *Voyages to the Moon.* Cloth. New York, 1948. First edition. In dust jacket. $40-$50.

NIELSEN, Kay (illustrator). Books illustrated by this artist have risen sharply in value in recent years. I have located no reliable bibliography and thus advise the enthusiast to work with a specialist dealer in children's books or in illustrated books, since records are sparse and often incomplete. The Nielsen books are sometimes listed under the author's name and at others under the artist's name. Besides limited and trade editions in England, there are often corresponding issues in America, as well as many reprints. Most of the Nielsen books appear to have been undated, which adds further to the difficulties in establishing a reliable price range on the various titles. I list here only the best-known Nielsen title.

NIELSEN, Kay (illustrator). *East of the Sun and West of the Moon.* (By Peter Christen Asbjornsen and Jorgen I. Moe.) 25 color plates. Cloth. London, (1914). First edition. $800-$1,000. Another issue: Vellum. One of 500, signed. $1,000-$1,500. New York, no date. Cloth. First American trade edition. In dust jacket. $200-$300.

*NIGGER of the "Narcissus" (The) Preface.* Wire-stitched sheets. (Hythe, England, 1902). (By Joseph Conrad.) First edition. One of 100. Privately printed for Conrad, who had suppressed this preface in the first edition of his 1898 novel. (About 40 copies were accidentally destroyed.) $1,700 (A, 1977).

NIGHTINGALE, Florence. *Notes on Nursing.* Flexible cloth. London, (1859). First edition. $125-$200.

*NIGHTMARE Abbey.* Blue boards, paper spine, paper label. London, 1818. (By Thomas Love Peacock.) First edition. $400-$500.

*NILE Notes of a Howadji.* Cloth, or tan printed wrappers. New York, 1851. (By George William Curtis.) First edition. Wrappers: $100-$150. Cloth: $75. Author's first book.

NIMMO, Joseph, Jr. *Range and Ranch Cattle Traffic.* (Caption title.) 4 folding maps, 200 pp., wrappers. (Washington, 1884.) First edition. $1,500-$2,000.

NIMROD. *The Life of a Sportsman.* 36 colored plates by Alken. Cloth. London, 1842. (By C. J. Apperley.) First edition, first issue, in blue cloth. $1,500 and up. Also, much repaired, $900 (A, 1975). Second issue, red cloth. $1,000 and up.

NIMROD. *Remarks on the Condition of Hunters, the Choice of Horses, and their Management.* Half calf, leather label. London, 1831. (By C. J. Apperley.) First collected edition. $200-$300.

*NIMROD'S Hunting Tours.* 18 hand-colored plates. Grained calf. London, 1903. (By C. J. Apperley.) One of 500. $350-$450.

NIN, Anaïs. *D. H. Lawrence: An Unprofessional Study.* Facsimiles. Black cloth. Paris, 1932. First edition. One of 550. In dust jacket. $100-$150. Author's first book. Denver, (1964). Wrappers. First American edition. $30.

NIN, Anaïs. *The House of Incest.* Covered wrappers. Paris, (1936). First edition. One of 249. $100-$150. (New York, 1947.) Gemor Press. Illustrated by Ian Hugo. Folio, cloth. First American edition. One of 50, signed. $150-$175. Trade issue: Cloth. $20.

NIN, Anaïs. *Nuances.* Cloth. No place, (1970). Sans Souci Press. One of 99 signed. $100-$150.

NIN, Anaïs. *This Hunger.* 5 hand-colored woodcuts by Ian Hugo. Decorated boards. (New York, 1945.) Gemor Press. First edition. One of 50, signed. $250. Trade edition: One of 1,000. $50-$75.

NIN, Anaïs. *Unpublished Selections from the Diary of Anais Nin.* Wrappers. Athens, Ohio, (1968). First edition. One of 140, signed. $100-$150.

NIN, Anaïs. *The Winter of Artifice.* Wrappers. Paris, (1939). Obelisk Press. First edition. $100-$150. (New York, 1942.) Copper engravings by Ian Hugo. Pictorial boards. First American edition. One of 500. $50-$75. Denver, (1961). Cloth. $15-$20.

*NINA Balatka.* 2 vols., cloth. Edinburgh, 1867. (By Anthony Trollope.) First edition, first issue, with ad leaf inset in Vol. 1. $400-$600.

*NINETY-FIRST Psalm (The).* 4 leaves. Wood engravings. (London), 1944. Golden Cockerel Press. Boxed. $50-$75.

NOEL, Theophilus. *Autobiography and Reminiscences of Theophilus Noel*. Red cloth. Chicago, 1904. First edition. $75-$100.

*NONESUCH Century (The): An Appraisal, a Personal Note and a Bibliography of the First Hundred Books Issued by the Press, 1923-1934*. Illustrated. Buckram. London, 1936. One of 750. In dust jacket. $300-$350.

NORDEN, Charles. *Panic Spring*. Cloth. New York, (1937). (By Lawrence Durrell.) First edition. In dust jacket. $150-$250. Lacking jacket, $145 in a 1978 catalogue.

NORDHOFF, Charles B. See Hall, James Norman (for *The Lafayette Flying Corps*).

NORDHOFF, Charles B., and Hall, James Norman. *Mutiny on the Bounty*. Cloth. Boston, 1932. First edition, first issue, with plain end papers. In jacket. $35-$50. Later, printed end papers. $25. New York, 1947. Limited Editions Club. Boxed. $40-$50.

NORMYX. *Unprofessional Tales*. Pictorial white cloth. London, 1901. (By Norman Douglas and Elsa Fitzgibbon.) First edition. One of 750. $300-$350. Norman Douglas' first book, written in collaboration with his wife.

NORRIS, Frank. *Blix*. Tan pictorial cloth. New York, 1899. First edition. $40-$50.

NORRIS, Frank. *A Deal in Wheat and Other Stories of the New and Old West*. Illustrated by Frederic Remington and others. Red cloth. New York, 1903. First edition. $50-$75.

NORRIS, Frank. *A Man's Woman*. Red cloth. New York, 1900. First edition. $35-$50.

NORRIS, Frank. *McTeague: A Story of San Francisco*. Red cloth. New York, 1899. First edition, first issue, with "moment" as last word on page 106. $200-$350. San Francisco, 1941. Colt Press. Illustrated. Buckram and boards. One of 500. $40-$50.

NORRIS, Frank. *Moran of the Lady Letty*. Green cloth. New York, 1898. First edition. $75-$100.

NORRIS, Frank. *The Octopus*. Red cloth. New York, 1901. First edition. $50-$60.

NORRIS, Frank. *The Pit*. Red cloth. New York, 1903. First edition (so stated on copyright page). $30-$35. Another issue: Gray boards, paper label. Presentation edition. $60-$75.

NORRIS, Frank. *The Responsibilities of the Novelist and Other Literary Essays*. Green cloth. New York, 1903. First edition, first state, with untrimmed edges. $30-$40.

NORRIS, Frank. *Yvernelle: A Legend of Feudal France*. Illustrations, some in color. Cloth, or leather. Philadelphia, 1892 (actually 1891). First edition. $750-$1,000. Also, spine ends frayed, $600 (A, 1977). Author's first book.

NORRIS, J. W. *A Business Advertiser and General Directory of the City of Chicago for the Year 1845-6*. Folding plate. 156 pp., wrappers. Chicago, 1845. First edition. $1,500-$2,000. Also, rebound in cloth, $1,400 (A, 1975). (Note: The folding plate in this second Chicago city directory is believed to be the earliest view of Chicago as a city.)

NORRIS, J. W. *General Directory and Business Advertiser of the City of Chicago for the Year 1844*. 116 pp., printed wrappers. Chicago, 1844. First edition, first printing. $1,000-$1,500. Another issue: cloth, with binder's slip bound in. $1,000-$1,500. (Note: This is the first Chicago city directory.)

NORRIS, Thomas Wayne (book collection). *A Descriptive and Priced Catalogue . . . of California and the Far West*. Illustrated. Boards and cloth. Oakland, 1948. $100-$150.

*NORTH and South*. 2 vols., cloth. London, 1855. (By Elizabeth C. Gaskell.) First edition. $300-$400.

NORTH, Andrew. *Plague Ship*. Cloth. New York, (1956). (By Alice Mary Norton, whose main pseudonym is Andre Norton.) First edition. In dust jacket. $25-$35. (Another valuable North title: *Sargasso of Space*. New York, [1955]. First edition. In dust jacket. $25-$35.)

NORTH, Joseph. *Men in the Ranks: The Story of 12 Americans in Spain.* Foreword by Ernest Hemingway. Wrappers. New York, 1939. First edition. $40-$50.

NORTH, Thomas. *Five Years in Texas; or, What You Did Not Hear During the War.* Cloth. Cincinnati, 1870. First edition. $100-$150.

*NORTHANGER Abbey; and Persuasion.* By the Author of *Pride and Prejudice,* etc. 4 vols., blue-gray or pink boards and linen, white paper labels. London, 1818. (By Jane Austen.) First edition. $2,500-$3,000. Also, $1,800 (A, 1975).

*NORTHERN Route to Idaho (The).* Large folding map, 8 pp. of text. Cloth. St. Paul, (1864). (By D. D. Merrill.) $2,000-$3,000.

*NORTHERN Traveller (The).* 16 maps and 4 plates. Boards. New York, 1825. (By Theodore Dwight, Jr.) First edition. $125-$150. New York, 1826. Second edition. $75-$100.

*NORTH-WEST Coast of America, Being Results of Recent Ethnological Researches from the Collections of the Royal Museum at Berlin.* 15 plates, 5 in color. Half leather. New York, no date. $75-$100.

NORTON, Andre. *Star Man's Son, 2250 A.D.* Cloth. New York, (1952). (By Alice Mary Norton.) First edition. In dust jacket. $25-$35.

NORTON, Harry J. *Wonder-Land Illustrated; or, Horseback Rides Through the Yellowstone National Park.* Map, 18 plates. Pictorial wrappers. Virginia City, Mont., (1873). First edition. $100-$125.

NORTON, Mary. *The Borrowers.* Illustrated. Boards. New York, (1953). First American edition. In dust jacket. $40-$50.

*NOTES by Joseph Conrad, Written In a Set of His First Editions in the Possession of Richard Curle.* Cloth, paper label. London, 1925. One of 100 signed by Curle. Boxed. $75-$100.

*NOTES of a Journey Through France and Italy.* Boards, paper label. London, 1826. (By William Hazlitt.) First edition, first issue, with author's name omitted on title page. $150-$250. Second issue (corrected). $100-$150.

*NOTES on California and the Placers.* 2 plates (not in all copies). 128 pp., printed wrappers. New York, 1850. (By James Delavan.) First edition. $1,500-$2,000, possibly more.

*NOTHING to Do.* Frontispiece. Cloth. Boston, 1857. (By Horatio Alger, Jr.) First edition. $75-$100.

*NOTICE sur la Rivìere Rouge dans le Territoire de la Baie-d'Hudson.* 32 pp., wrappers. Montreal, 1843. (By Alexandre Taché?) First edition. $1,500-$1,750.

*NOTICES of Parkersburg, Virginia, As It Is in 1860.* Folding map, colored plate. 12 pp., printed wrappers. Baltimore, 1860. First edition. $75-$100.

*NOTICES of Sullivan's Campaign, or the Revolutionary Warfare in Western New-York.* Colored frontispiece (not in all copies). Cloth. Rochester, 1842. First edition. $100-$150.

NOTT, Manford A. *Across the Plains in '54.* 232 pp., wrappers. (San Francisco, about 1915.) "Second" (actually first) edition. $75-$100.

NOTT, Stanley Charles. *Chinese Jade Throughout the Ages.* 39 color illustrations, 182 in black and white. Cloth. London, 1936. In dust jacket. $100-$125.

NOVAK, Joseph. *The Future is Ours, Comrade.* Cloth. Garden City, 1960. (By Jerzy Kosinski.) First edition. In dust jacket. $50-$60. Kosinski's first book.

*NOVELAS Españolas.* Marbled boards. Portland, Me., 1830. First edition. (Edited anonymously by Henry Wadsworth Longfellow.) $100 and up.

NOWLIN, William. *The Bark Covered House.* 6 plates. Cloth. Detroit, 1876. First edition. $1,000-$1,250.

NOYES, Al J. *In the Land of Chinook: or, The Story of Blaine County.* 24 plates. Cloth. Helena, (1917). First edition. $50-$75.

NUTTALL, Thomas. *The Genera of North American Plants.* 2 vols. in one, boards. Philadelphia, 1818. First edition. $200-$300.

NUTTALL, Thomas. *Journal of Travels into the Arkansa Territory, During the Year 1819.* Folding map, 5 plates. Boards. Philadelphia, 1821. First edition. $650-$750.

NUTTALL, Zelia. *The Book of the Life of the Ancient Mexicans.* Part I. 90 pp. of color plates. Oblong, leather. Berkeley, 1903. $35-$50.

NUTTING, Wallace. *The Clock Book.* Cloth. Framingham, Mass., 1924. First edition. In dust jacket. $50. Garden City, 1935. Cloth. In dust jacket. $25.

NYE-STARR, Kate. *A Self-Sustaining Woman: or, The Experience of Seventy-Two Years.* Portrait. Red cloth. Chicago, 1888. First edition. $2,500-$3,000. Also, $1,600 (A, 1976). (Note: Until recently this was a little known book—the only copies located being the Newberry Library's Graff copy, one at Yale, and another which I found and sold about 1970. Since then I have heard of possibly two others—the 1976 copy at auction and one that passed through the hands of a Texas dealer who did not recognize its scarcity. Both Howes [ in *U.S.-iana*] and Charles P. Everitt [ in *Adventures of a Treasure Hunter*] give inaccurate titles: the latter reference also gives the date incorrectly as 1881.)

# O

*OAK Openings (The); or, The Bee-Hunter.* By the Author of *The Pioneers.* 2 vols., printed tan wrappers. New York, 1848. (By James Fenimore Cooper.) First American edition. $300-$400.

OAKES, William. *Scenery of the White Mountains.* 16 plates, sometimes colored, each with a leaf of text. Folio, cloth. Boston, (1848). First edition. Uncolored: $100-$125. Colored: $250-$300.

OAKLEY, Violet. *The Holy Experiment . . . Murals in the Governor's Reception Room at Harrisburg.* Elephant folio, full leather, copper clasps. (Harrisburg, Pa., 1922.) First edition. One of 500. $50-$75. Another issue: One of 250, signed. $100-$125.

OAKWOOD, Oliver. *Village Tales, or Recollections of By-past Times.* Cloth. Trenton, N.J., 1827. (By Stacy Gardner Potts.) First edition. $50-$75.

OATES, Joyce Carol. *Anonymous Sins & Other Poems.* Boards. Baton Rouge, (1969). First edition. In dust jacket. $25.

OATES, Joyce Carol. *By the North Gate.* Cloth. New York, (1963). First edition. In dust jacket. $50-$60. Author's first book.

OATES, Joyce Carol. *Cupid and Psyche.* Wrappers, paper label. New York, 1970. First edition. One of 200, signed. $50-$75.

OATES, Joyce Carol. *Them.* Cloth. New York, 1969. First edition. In dust jacket. $45-$65.

OATES, Joyce Carol. *The Wheel of Love.* Cloth. New York, 1970. First edition. In dust jacket. $25-$35.

OATES, Joyce Carol. *Women In Love and Other Poems.* Decorated wrappers. New York, 1968. First edition. One of 150, signed. $60-$70.

O'BEIRNE, H. F. *Leaders and Leading Men of the Indian Territory. Vol. 1, History of the Choctaws and Chickasaws.* 7 plates. Cloth. Chicago, 1891. First edition. $200-$300, possibly more.

O'BETJEMAN, Deirdre. *Some Immortal Hours: A Rhapsody of the Celtic Twilight.* 7 leaves, folio. London, 1962. (By John Betjeman.) One of 12 (of a total issue of 20) copies of a facsimile printing of the author's holograph manuscript, hand-colored and signed by Betjeman. $200-$300.

O'BRYAN, William. *A Narrative of Travels in the United States . . . and Advice to Emigrants and Travellers Going to That Interesting Country.* Portrait. Dark-blue cloth. London, 1836. First edition. $150-$300.

*OBSERVATIONS on the Wisconsin Territory.* Folding map. Cloth. Philadelphia, 1835. (By William Rudolph Smith.) First edition. $450-$600.

*OBSERVATIONS upon Certain Passages in Mr. Jefferson's "Notes on Virginia."* 32 pp., plain blue-gray wrappers. New York, 1804. (By Clement C. Moore?) First edition. $125-$150. If Moore wrote this, it is his first publication.

O'CASEY, Sean. *Drums Under the Window.* Cloth. London, 1945. First edition. In dust jacket. $30-$40.

O'CASEY, Sean. *The Plough and the Stars*. Portrait. Boards and cloth. London, 1926. First edition. In dust jacket. $50-$60.

O'CASEY, Sean. *Rose and Crown*. Cloth. London, 1952. First edition. In dust jacket. $30-$45.

O'CASEY, Sean. *The Silver Tassie*. Portrait. Boards and cloth. London, 1928. First edition. $35-$50.

O'CASEY, Sean. *Two Plays*. Cloth. London, 1926. First edition. In dust jacket. $50-$60.

O'CASEY, Sean. *Windfalls*. Cloth. London, 1934. First edition. In dust jacket. $30-$40.

O'CONNOR, Flannery. *A Good Man is Hard to Find*. Cloth. New York, 1955. First edition. In dust jacket. $35-$50.

O'CONNOR, Flannery. *The Violent Bear it Away*. Cloth. New York, (1960). First edition. In dust jacket. $50-$60.

O'CONNOR, Flannery. *Wise Blood*. Cloth. New York, (1952). First edition. In dust jacket. $75-$100. Author's first book.

O'CONNOR, Frank. *Lords and Commons*. Boards and linen. Dublin, 1938. Cuala Press. First edition. One of 250. In dust jacket. $100-$125.

O'CONNOR, Frank. *A Picture Book*. Illustrated by Elizabeth Rivers. Boards, linen spine. Dublin, 1943. Cuala Press. First edition. One of 480. In dust jacket. $75-$85.

O'CONNOR, Frank. *Three Old Brothers and Other Poems*. Boards. London, (1936). First edition. In dust jacket. $50-$60.

O'CONNOR, Frank. *Three Tales*. Boards, linen spine. Dublin, 1941. Cuala Press. One of 250. In dust jacket. $50-$75.

O'CONNOR, Frank. *The Wild Bird's Nest*. Boards and cloth. Dublin, 1932. Cuala Press. One of 250. $75-$85.

OCULUS. *The Home of the Badgers*. 36 pp., tan printed wrappers. Milwaukie [ *sic* ], 1845. (By Josiah B. Grinnell.) First edition. $1,500-$2,000. Also, $735 (A, 1959); rebound in modern morocco, $600 (A, 1967). (For second edition, see *Sketches of the West*.)

*ODE Performed in the Senate-House, Cambridge, on the Sixth of July, MDCCCXLVII at the First Commencement After the Installation of His Royal Highness the Prince Albert, Chancellor of the University*. 8 pp., printed wrappers. Cambridge, 1847. (By William Wordsworth.) First edition. $350-$500.

*ODE to Napoleon Buonaparte*. 16 pp., wrappers. London, 1814. (By George Gordon Noel, Lord Byron.) First edition. $750-$1,000, possibly more. Copies in bindings, $200 and up.

*ODES*. Gray wrappers. (London, 1868.) (By Coventry Patmore.) First edition. $200-$300.

ODETS, Clifford. *Golden Boy*. Brown cloth. New York, (1937). First edition. In dust jacket. $40-$50.

ODETS, Clifford. *Three Plays*. Brown cloth. New York, (1935). First edition. In dust jacket. $25-$30.

OEHLER, Andrew. *The Life, Adventures, and Unparalleled Sufferings of Andrew Oehler*. Leather. (Trenton, N. J.), 1811. First edition. $150-$250.

*OF the Just Shaping of Letters. From the Applied Geometry of Albrecht Dürer*. Translated by R. T. Nichol. Decorations by Bruce Rogers. Marbled boards. New York, 1917. One of 195. $75-$100.

O'FAOLAIN, Sean. *The Born Genius*. Green buckram. Detroit, 1936. One of 250, signed. Boxed. $35-$50.

O'FAOLAIN, Sean. *Midsummer Night Madness / & Other Stories.* Preface by Edward Garnett. Green cloth. London, (1932). First edition. In dust jacket. $145. Author's first book.

O'FAOLAIN, Sean. *A Nest of Simple Folk.* Green cloth. London, (1933). First edition. In dust jacket. $90.

O'FAOLAIN, Sean. *There's a Birdie in the Cage.* Green cloth. London, 1935. First separate edition. One of 285, signed. In dust jacket. $35.

*OFFICIAL Historical Atlas of Alameda County.* Folding maps, full-page views. Atlas folio, half leather. Oakland, 1878. First edition. $300-$350.

*OFFICIAL Record from the War Department of the Proceedings of the Court Martial Which Tried, and the Orders of Gen. Jackson for Shooting the Six Militia Men, etc.* 32 pp., sewed. Washington, 1828. First edition. $125-$150.

OFFICIAL *Report of the Trial of Laura D. Fair, for the Murder of Alex P. Critienden.* Frontispiece. Printed wrappers. San Francisco, 1871. First edition. $75-$100.

OFFICIAL *Reports of the Debates and Proceedings in the Constitutional Convention of the State of Nevada . . . July 4, 1864.* Sheepskin. San Francisco, 1866. $150-$300.

OFFUTT, Denton. *The Educated Horse.* Illustrated. Cloth. Washington, 1854. $50.

O'FLAHERTY, Liam. *The Assassin.* Cloth. London, (1928). First edition. One of 150, signed. $135-$200.

O'FLAHERTY, Liam. *The Black Soul.* Black cloth, paper label. London, (1924). First edition. In dust jacket. $90.

O'FLAHERTY, Liam. *The Child of God.* Wrappers. London, 1926. First edition. One of 100, signed. $100-$150. Another issue: One of 25, signed. $150-$250.

O'FLAHERTY, Liam. *Civil War.* Wrappers. London, 1925. First edition. One of 100, signed. $150-$175.

O'FLAHERTY, Liam. *Darkness: A Tragedy.* Portrait. Wrappers. London, 1926. First edition. One of 100, signed. $150-$200.

O'FLAHERTY, Liam. *The Ecstasy of Angus.* Green cloth. London, 1931. Chiswick Press. First edition. One of 365, signed. $75-$100.

O'FLAHERTY, Liam. *The Informer.* Cloth. London, (1925). First edition. In dust jacket. $150-$250.

O'FLAHERTY, Liam. *The Puritan.* Orange cloth. London, 1932. First edition. In dust jacket. $50-$75.

O'FLAHERTY, Liam. *Red Barbara and Other Stories.* Half cloth. New York, 1928. First edition. One of 600, signed. $75-$100.

O'FLAHERTY, Liam. *Return of the Brute.* Cloth. London, 1929. First edition. In dust jacket. $40-$50.

O'FLAHERTY, Liam. *Thy Neighbor's Wife.* Black cloth. London, (1923). First edition. In dust jacket. $145. Author's first book.

OGDEN, George W. *Letters from the West.* Boards. New Bedford, Mass., 1823. First edition. $600-$750.

*OGILIVIES (The).* 3 vols., cloth. London, 1849. (By Dinah Maria Mulock.) First edition. $100. Author's first novel.

O'HARA, Frank. *A City Winter and Other Poems.* Illustrated by Larry Rivers. Decorated wrappers. New York, 1951. First edition. One of 130. $350-$450. Another issue: Boards and cloth. One of 20 with an original drawing by Rivers. $350-$850. (Note: One copy offered for sale in a 1976 catalogue included the original drawing of O'Hara nude, used to illustrate the dust jacket, suppressed, for the poet's *Collected Poems*. It was priced at $1,325.) Author's first book.

O'HARA, Frank. *The Collected Poems of Frank O'Hara*. Cloth. New York, 1971. First edition. In suppressed dust jacket with a photograph of Larry Rivers' drawing of a nude O'Hara. $50-$75. In later jacket, $25-$35.

O'HARA, Frank. *In Memory of My Feelings*. Illustrated. Folio, printed sheets in folder and slipcase. New York, 1967. One of 2,500. $75-$100.

O'HARA, Frank. *Meditations in an Emergency*. Cloth. New York, (1957). One of 15, signed by the poet, each numbered and containing as frontispiece (loose) an original drawing by Grace Hartigan. In slipcase. $250-$300. Ordinary edition: $20-$25.

O'HARA, Frank. *Odes*. Silk-screen prints by Michael Goldberg. Folio, boards. New York, (1960). First edition. One of 225, signed by author and artist. In acetate dust jacket. $150-$200.

O'HARA, John. *And Other Stories*. Green cloth. New York, (1968). First edition. One of 300, signed. Boxed. $40-$50. Trade edition: Cloth. In dust jacket. $15.

O'HARA, John. *Appointment in Samarra*. Pictorial wrappers. New York, (1934). "Presentation Edition" (so imprinted on end paper), laid into dust jacket of published book. $400-$500. First trade edition: Black cloth. Errata slip laid in. In dust jacket. $300-$450. Also, $250 (A, 1977). Author's first book.

O'HARA, John. *Butterfield 8*. Black cloth. New York, (1935). First edition. In dust jacket. $100-$125.

O'HARA, John. *The Doctor's Son*. Black cloth. New York, (1935). First edition. In dust jacket. $40-$50.

O'HARA, John. *Hope of Heaven*. Cloth. New York, (1938). First edition. In dust jacket. $35-$50.

O'HARA, John. *The Instrument*. Brown cloth. New York, (1967). First edition. One of 300, signed. Boxed. $40-$50. Trade edition: Cloth. In dust jacket. $15.

O'HARA, John. *The Lockwood Concern*. Blue cloth. New York, (1965). First edition. One of 300, signed. Boxed. $40-$50. Trade edition: Cloth. In dust jacket. $15.

O'HARA, John. *Pal Joey*. Black cloth. New York, (1940). First edition. In dust jacket. $50-$60. Advance copy: Wrappers. $125.

O'HARA, John. *Ten North Frederick*. Cloth. New York, (1955). First edition. In dust jacket. $25-$30.

*O. HENRY Calendar. 1917 (The)*. Paper covers, cord tie. (New York, 1916.) $35.

*OLD Fashioned Mother Goose' [sic] Melodies (The)*. Pictures in color. Cloth. (New York), 1879. First edition. $50. (Note: Contains "There was a Little Girl," probably by Henry Wadsworth Longfellow.)

*OLD Soldier's History (The). Written by Himself*. 20 pp., printed wrappers. Haverhill, Mass., 1861. (By Charles Fairbanks?) First edition. $75.

OLDER, (Mr. and Mrs.) Fremont. *The Life of George Hearst, California Pioneer*. Vellum. San Francisco, 1923. John Henry Nash printing. First edition. $50-$75.

OLDHAM, Williamson S., and White, George W. *Digest of the General Statute Laws of the State of Texas*. Cloth. Austin, 1859. $150-$250.

OLDSTYLE, Jonathan. *Letters of Jonathan Oldstyle, Gent*. By the Author of *The Sketch-Book*. Brown wrappers. New York, 1824. (By Washington Irving.) First edition. $200-$300.

OLIPHANT, Laurence. *Minnesota and the Far West*. Folding map and 7 plates. Half leather. Edinburgh, 1855. First edition. $150-$200.

OLIVER, Chad. *Another Kind*. Cloth. New York, (1955). First edition. In dust jacket. $40-$50.

OLIVER, John W. (publisher). *Guide to the New Gold Region of Western Kansas and Nebraska*. Folding map. 32 pp., printed wrappers. New York, 1859. First edition. $5,000-$6,000.

*OLLA Podrida*. 3 vols., boards and cloth, or cloth. London, 1840. (By Frederick Marryat.) First edition. $150-$250.

OLLIVANT, Alfred. *Bob: Son of Battle*. Green decorated cloth. New York, 1898. First edition. 40-$60.

OLSEN, Tillie. *Tell Me a Riddle*. Cloth. Philadelphia, 1961. First edition. In dust jacket. $60-$75. Author's first book.

OLSON, Charles. *Call Me Ishmael*. Yellow cloth. (New York, 1947.) First edition. In dust jacket. $100-$125. Author's first book.

OLSON, Charles. *Human Universe and Other Essays*. Edited by Donald Allen. Woodcut by Robert LaVigne, photography by Kenneth Irby. Decorated boards, vellum spine. San Francisco, 1965. First edition. One of 250. $75-$100.

OLSON, Charles. *The Maximus Poems*. 1/10. Gray wrappers. Stuttgart, 1953. Jargon 7. First edition. One of 50, signed. In slipcase. $350-$400. Another issue: Blue wrappers. One of 300. $100-$150.

OLSON, Charles. *The Maximus Poems. 11/22* . Wrappers. Stuttgart, 1956. Jargon 9. First edition. One of 50, signed. $350-$400. Another issue: One of 300. $150-$200. New York, 1960. One of 26, signed. Boxed. $250-$300.

OLSON, Charles. *Mayan Letters*. Printed wrappers. Mallorca, 1953 (actually 1954). Divers Press. First Edition. One of 600. $75.

OLSON, Charles. *O'Ryan 12345678910*. Linen, vellum spine. San Francisco, (1965). First edition. One of 26, signed. $175.

OLSON, Charles. *Stocking Cap: A Story*. Printed white wrappers, tied. San Francisco, 1966. Grabhorn printing. First edition. One of 100. $50-$65.

OLSON, Charles. *'West.'* Boards. London, 1966. First edition. One of 25, signed. In dust jacket. $100-$175. Trade edition: Wrappers. $15.

OLSON, Charles. *Y & X*. Illustrated by Corrado Cagli. Printed wrappers. (Paris), 1948. Black Sun Press. First edition. One of 100. Boxed. $50-$75. Washington, 1950. Wrappers. Second edition. $10.

OMAR Khayyam. See *The Rose Garden of Omar Khayyam; Rubaiyat of Omar Khayyam*.

*ON English Prose Fiction as Rational Amusement*. (Caption title.) 44 pp., sewed. (London. late in 1869?) (By Anthony Trollope.) First edition. $750 and up. Also, $400 (A, 1970).

*ON the Plains; or, The Race for Life*. 62 pp., pictorial yellow wrappers. New York, (1863). (By Edward S. Ellis.) $300-$400. Also, rebound in cloth, $200 (A, 1968).

*ON the "White Pass" Pay-Roll*. By the President of the White Pass & Yukon Route. 15 plates. Dark-blue cloth. Chicago, 1908. (By S.H. Graves.) First edition. $300-$350.

ONDERDONK, James L. *Idaho: Facts and Statistics*. Wrappers. San Francisco, 1885. First edition. $150-$300.

*ONE Hundred Books Famous in English Literature*. See Kent, Henry W.

*ONE Hundred Influential American Books Printed Before 1900*. Illustrated. Boards and cloth. New York, 1947. Grolier Club. First edition. One of 600. $100-$125.

O'NEILL, Eugene. See Sanborn, Ralph; Shay, Frank. Also see *George Pierce Baker, a Memorial.*

O'NEILL, Eugene. *Ah, Wilderness!* Blue cloth. New York, 1933. First edition (so stated). In dust jacket. $25. Another (later) issue: Blue calf. One of 325, signed. In dust jacket. Boxed. $100-$150.

O'NEILL, Eugene. *All God's Chillun Got Wings, and Welded.* Buff boards and cloth. New York, (1924). First edition. In dust jacket. $75-$85.

O'NEILL, Eugene. *Anna Christie.* Yellow boards, or wrappers. London, (1923). First separate edition. Boards: In dust jacket. $75. Wrappers: $100. New York, 1930. 12 illustrations by Alexander King. Purple and red boards, black cloth spine. First illustrated (and first American) edition. One of 775. In dust jacket. Boxed. $75-$125.

O'NEILL, Eugene. *Before Breakfast.* Light blue-green wrappers. New York, 1916. First separate edition. $125-$150. (Second book appearance; for the first appearance see entry following under *Provincetown Plays: Third Series.*)

O'NEILL, Eugene. *Beyond the Horizon.* Brown boards and cloth. New York, (1920). First edition, probable first state, with capital letters on front cover 9/16 inch high. In dust jacket. $75-$100. Second issue. In dust jacket. $25.

O'NEILL, Eugene. *Days Without End.* Blue cloth. New York, (1934). First edition (so stated). In dust jacket. $40-$50. Another (later) issue: Morocco. One of 325, signed. $75-$125.

O'NEILL, Eugene. *Desire Under the Elms.* Pictorial black cloth. New York, 1925. First separate edition. In dust jacket. $35.

O'NEILL, Eugene. *Dynamo.* Green cloth. New York, 1929. First edition. In dust jacket. $25. Another (later) issue: Purple vellum. One of 775 signed. Boxed. $75-$125.

O'NEILL, Eugene. *The Emperor Jones: Diff'rent: The Straw.* Buff boards and cloth. New York, (1921). First edition, first issue, with plain (not mottled) boards. In dust jacket. $100-$125. Lacking jacket, $50-$60. Cincinnati, (1921). White wrappers. $100. New York, 1928. 8 illustrations in color by Alexander King. Boards and cloth. One of 775, signed. In dust jacket. Boxed. $135-$200.

O'NEILL, Eugene. *Gold.* Blue-green boards and cloth. New York, (1921). First edition (with 1920 copyright). In dust jacket. $75.

O'NEILL, Eugene. *The Great God Brown: The Fountain: The Moon of the Caribbees and Other Plays.* Green cloth. New York, 1926. First edition. In dust jacket. $60-$80. London, (1926). *(The Great God Brown.)* Bright-blue cloth. First English edition. In dust jacket. $50-$60.

O'NEILL, Eugene. *The Hairy Ape: Anna Christie: The First Man.* Buff boards and cloth. New York, (1922). First edition. In dust jacket. $100. London, (1923). *(The Hairy Ape and Other Plays.)* Bright-blue cloth. First English edition. In dust jacket. $40. New York, (1929). 9 illustrations in color by Alexander King. Boards. First separate and illustrated edition. One of 775, signed. In dust jacket. Boxed. $125-$150.

O'NEILL, Eugene. *The Iceman Cometh.* Blue cloth. New York, (1946). First edition. In dust jacket. $50-$60.

O'NEILL, Eugene. *Ile: A Play in One Act.* (Cover title.) 11 pp. of text from Smart Set, May, 1918, stapled into stiff cream-yellow wrappers. (New York, 1918?) First edition. $850.

O'NEILL, Eugene. *Lazarus Laughed.* Green cloth. New York, 1927. First edition. In dust jacket. $30. Another (later) issue: Vellum and boards. One of 775, signed. In dust jacket. Boxed. $75-$125.

O'NEILL, Eugene. *Long Day's Journey into Night.* Black and gray cloth. New Haven, 1956. First edition. In dust jacket. $25-$40.

O'NEILL, Eugene. *Marco Millions.* Green cloth. New York, 1927. First edition. In dust jacket. $30-$40. Another (later) issue: Vellum and boards. One of 450, signed. Boxed. $75-$110.

O'NEILL, Eugene. *The Moon of the Caribbees and Six Other Plays of the Sea*. Brown boards and cloth. New York, 1919. First edition, first state, 7/8 inch thick. In dust jacket. $75-$100. Second state, $50-$75. London, (1923). Bright-blue cloth. First English edition. In dust jacket. $30-$40.

O'NEILL, Eugene. *Mourning Becomes Electra*. Cloth. New York, 1931. First edition. (Issued simultaneously with Theatre Guild edition.) In dust jacket. $35-$40. Another (later) issue: Japan vellum. One of 550, signed. Boxed. $150-$200. Also, an advance copy, 3 vols., tan wrappers, $300 (A, 1977). London, (1932). Blue cloth. First English edition. In dust jacket. $30.

O'NEILL, Eugene. *Strange Interlude*. Green cloth. New York, 1928. First edition. In dust jacket. $25-$35. Another (later) issue: Vellum. One of 775, signed. Boxed. $125-$165. London, (1928). Blue cloth. First English edition. In dust jacket. $20.

O'NEILL, Eugene. *Thirst and Other One Act Plays*. Dark gray boards, tan cloth spine, paper labels. Boston, (1914). First edition. In dust jacket. $150-$250. Also, inscribed by the author, $800 (A, 1977). Author's first book.

O'NEILL, Eugene, and others. *The Provincetown Plays: First Series*. Printed light-blue wrappers. New York, 1916. First edition. $150-$175. (Note: Contains first book appearance of O'Neill's *Bound East for Cardiff*.)

O'NEILL, Eugene, and others. *The Provincetown Plays: Third Series*. Orange wrappers. New York, 1916. First edition. In green dust jacket. $125-$200. (Note: Contains first book appearance of O'Neill's *Before Breakfast*; see separate title entry.)

ONKEN, Otto: See Wells, William, and Onken, Otto.

*ONLY Authentic Life of Abraham Lincoln, Alias 'Old Abe,' a Son of the West*. (Cover title.) Illustrated. 16 pp., printed wrappers. No place, no date (1864?) $75-$100. Another edition: New York, (1864). $60.

*ONTWA, The Son of the Forest: A Poem*. Boards. New York, 1832. (By Henry Whiting.) First edition. $100-$150.

OPPEN, George. *Discreet Series*. Preface by Ezra Pound. Cloth. New York, 1934. First edition. In dust jacket. $100-$150.

OPPENHEIMER, Joel. *Acts*. Printed wrappers. Mt. Horeb, Wis., 1976. One of 112, signed. $45-$55.

*OPPOSITION of the South to the Development of Oregon and Washington Territory*. 8 pp., folded. (Washington, 1859.) $75-$100.

OPTIC, Oliver. *The Boat Club; or, The Bunkers of Rippleton*. Frontispiece, 3 plates. Slate-purple pictorial cloth. Boston, 1855. (By William T. Adams.) First edition. $200-$250. Another issue: Pictorial presentation binding. $300-$400. First Oliver Optic book.

*ORANGE County History Series*. 2 vols., folio, boards and cloth. (Santa Ana, Calif., 1931-32.) $100-$200.

*ORATION, Poem, and Speeches . . . June 5th, 1867*. Printed wrappers. San Francisco, 1867. $200 and up. (Note: Includes a poem by Bret Harte.)

ORBELIANI, Sulkhan-Saba. *The Book of Wisdom and Lies*. Translated by Oliver Waldorp. Woodcut title and borders. Vellum with ties. London, 1894. Kelmscott Press. One of 250. $350-$500.

ORCUTT, William Dana. *The Book in Italy*. Plates, including color. Folio, boards. New York, 1928. One of 750. In dust jacket. $100-$125. Trade edition: Cloth. In dust jacket. $15-$20. London, 1928. Half vellum. One of 750. In dust jacket. $125-$150.

ORCUTT, William Dana. *In Quest of the Perfect Book*. Plates, including color. Half vellum.

Boston, 1926. First edition. One of 365. In dust jacket. $50-$85. Trade edition: Cloth. In dust jacket. $20-$25.

ORCUTT, William Dana. *The Kingdom of Books*. Plates, including color. Half vellum. Boston, 1927. One of 475. Boxed. $75-$100. Trade edition: Cloth. In dust jacket. $20-$25.

ORCUTT, William Dana. *The Magic of the Book*. Illustrated. Half vellum. New York, 1930. First edition. One of 375. In dust jacket. $50-$75. Trade edition: Cloth. In dust jacket. $15-$20.

ORD, John Waller. *England: A Historical Poem*. 2 vols., contemporary cloth, paper labels. London, 1834. First edition. $100-$125.

*ORDER of the Governor in Council, for Further Regulating the Inland Navigation from the United States by the Port of St. Johns*. (Quebec, 1800.) $150-$175.

*ORDINANCES of the Town of Berkeley, Alameda County, California (The)*. 24 pp., wrappers. Berkeley, 1882. $100-$125.

*ORDINARY Evening in New Haven, (An)*. Wrappers. New Haven, 1949. First edition. Transactions of the Connecticut Academy of Arts and Sciences. $50-$75. (Contains an 11-page poem by Wallace Stevens written to mark a Sesquicentennial celebration.)

*OREGON: Agricultural, Stock Raising, Mineral Resources, Climate, etc.* (Published by U.P.R.R.) 68 pp., wrappers. Council Bluffs, Iowa, 1888. $75-$100.

O'REILLY, Bernard. *Greenland, the Adjacent Seas, and the North-West Passage*. 3 folding maps, 18 plates. Half cloth. London, 1818. First edition. $400-$500.

O'REILLY, Harrington. *Fifty Years on the Trail*. Illustrated by Paul Frenzeny. Pictorial cloth. London, 1889. First edition. $100-$125. London, 1890. Wrappers. Second edition. $50-$75. New York, 1889. Cloth. First American edition. $50.

*ORIGIN and Traditional History of the Wyandotts*. Cloth. Toronto, 1870. (By Peter D. Clarke.) First edition. $75-$100.

ORIOLI, G. *Adventures of a Bookseller*. Pictorial orange wrappers folded over blue paper. Florence, Italy, (1937). First edition. One of 2 on blue paper, signed. $250 and up. Another issue: One of 300, signed. $50-$75.

ORME, Edward. *Collection of British Field Sports*. Colored title page and 20 colored plates after Howitt. Oblong folio, half morocco. London, 1807-08. First edition. $12,000-$15,000. Guildford, England, 1955. 29 color plates. Facsimile. Folio, full crimson morocco. One of 20 with an original plate included. $1,000-$1,500. Ordinary issue: Half morocco. $400-$500.

*ORPHEUS in Diloeryum*. Wrappers. London, 1908. (By Siegfried Sassoon.) First edition, first issue, anonymously issued. $750-$1,000. Another (later) issue in the same year, bearing the author's name: Vellum and cloth. $200-$250. Special issue: One of 5 on handmade paper. $750 and up. Also, with a holograph note from Sassoon, $1,160 (A, 1975).

ORR, George. *The Possession of Louisiana by the French*. 44 pp., boards. London, 1803. First edition. $150-$200.

ORR, N.M. (compiler). *The City of Stockton*. 64 pp., printed wrappers. Stockton, Calif., 1874. First edition. $150-$175.

ORR and Ruggles. *San Joaquin County*. Map, plates. 130 pp., wrappers. Stockton, 1887. First edition. $150-$200.

ORTEGA, Luis. *California Hackamore (La Jáquima)*. 109 photographs, 29 sketches by Al Napoletano. Pictorial leather. (Sacramento, 1948.) First edition. $50-$75.

ORTON, Richard H. *Records of California Men in the War of the Rebellion, 1861-1867*. Cloth. Sacramento, 1890. First edition. $75-$100.

ORVIS, Charles F., and Cheny, A. Nelson (compilers). *Fishing with the Fly*. 15 color plates. Cloth. Manchester, Vt., 1883. First edition. $150-$250. Boston, 1892. Cloth. $50-$60.

ORWELL, George. *Animal Farm: A Fairy Story.* Dark green cloth. London, 1945. (By Eric Arthur Blair.) First edition. In presumed first dust jacket (with blue advertisement on verso). $250-$350. In presumed later jacket (red ad). $200-$300. New York, (1946). Cloth. First American edition. In dust jacket. $40-$60. Same: wrappers. Publisher's advance proof copy for review. $75-$100.

ORWELL, George, *Burmese Days.* Cloth. New York, 1934. (By Eric Arthur Blair.) First edition. In dust jacket. $150. London, 1935. Cloth. First English edition. In dust jacket. $125-$150. Author's first novel.

ORWELL, George. *A Clergyman's Daughter.* Cloth. London, 1935. (By Eric Arthur Blair.) First edition. In dust jacket. $100-$150.

ORWELL, George. *Down and Out in Paris and London.* Cloth. London, 1933. (By Eric Arthur Blair.) First edition. In dust jacket. $150-$200. New York, 1933. Cloth. First American edition. In dust jacket. $100-$150. Author's first book.

ORWELL, George. *Homage to Catalonia.* Cloth. London, 1938. (By Eric Arthur Blair.) First edition. In dust jacket. $100-$135. New York, 1952. Cloth. First American edition. In dust jacket. $20-$30.

ORWELL, George. *The Lion and the Unicorn.* Cloth. New York, 1941. (By Eric Arthur Blair.) First edition. In dust jacket. $30-$40. London, (1941). Cloth. First English edition. In dust jacket. $50-$60.

ORWELL, George. *Nineteen Eighty-four.* Green cloth. London, 1949. (By Eric Arthur Blair.) First edition. In dust jacket. $150-$200. New York, 1949. Gray cloth. First American edition. In red (first issue) dust jacket. $50-$60.

ORWELL, George. *Politics & the English Language.* Printed wrappers. (Evansville), 1947. (By Eric Arthur Blair.) First edition. $100.

ORWELL, George. *The Road to Wigan Pier.* Foreword by Victor Gollancz. Illustrated. Limp orange cloth wrappers. London, 1937. (By Eric Arthur Blair.) First edition, wrappers lettered "Left Book Club Edition." $50-$75. Trade Edition: Cloth. $25.

OSBORNE, Eric. *Victorian Detective Fiction.* Introduction by John Carter. Cloth. London, 1966. First edition. One of 500, signed by Carter and by Dorothy Glover and Graham Greene, whose collection is catalogued in the book. In dust jacket. $200-$300.

OSBOURNE, John. *Epitaph for George Dillon.* Cloth. London, (1958). First edition. In dust jacket. $25-$35.

OSBOURNE, John. *Inadmissible Evidence.* Cloth. London, (1965). First edition. In dust jacket. $30-$40.

OSBOURNE, John. *Luther.* Cloth. London, (1961). First edition. In dust jacket. $25-$35.

*OSCEOLA; or, Fact and Fiction: A Tale of the Seminole War.* By a Southerner. Illustrated. Cloth. New York, 1838. (By James Birchett Ransom.) First edition. $150-$175.

OSGOOD, Ernest Staples. *The Day of the Cattleman.* 14 plates and maps. Cloth. Minneapolis, 1929. First edition. In dust jacket. $85-$135.

OSGOOD, Frances S. *The Poetry of Flowers and Flowers of Poetry.* Half leather. New York, 1851. $50-$60.

O'SHAUGHNESSY, Arthur W.E. *An Epic of Women and Other Poems.* Pictorial title page, 2 plates. Purple cloth. London, 1870. First edition. $100-$150.

O'SHAUGHNESSY, Arthur W.E. *Music and Moonlight.* Cloth. London, 1874. First edition. $35-$50.

O'SHAUGHNESSY, Arthur W.E. *Songs of a Worker.* Cloth. London, 1881. First edition. $40-$50.

OSLER, Sir William. *Aequanimitas.* 10 pp., printed wrappers. Philadelphia, 1889. First edition. $100. London, 1904. First English edition. $25-$35.

OSLER, Sir William. *An Alabama Student and Other Biographical Essays*. Cloth. Oxford, England, 1908. First edition. $50-$75. New York, 1909. Cloth. Second edition. $30-$40.

OSLER, Sir William. *Aphasia and Associated Speech Problems*. Illustrated. Cloth. New York, 1920. $50-$60.

OSLER, Sir William. *The Cerebral Palsies of Children*. Cloth. Philadelphia, 1889. First edition. $100-$150.

OSLER, Sir William. *The Evolution of Modern Medicine*. Cloth. New Haven, 1921. First edition. $150-$200.

OSLER, Sir William. *Incunabula Medica: A Study of the Earliest Printed Medical Books, 1467-1480*. Illustrated. Boards and cloth. London, 1923. First edition. $300-$400.

OSLER, Sir William. *Lectures on the Diagnosis of Abdominal Tumors*. Cloth, or wrappers. New York, 1894. $75-$100. New York, 1895. Wrappers. $50. London, 1898. Cloth. $50.

OSLER, Sir William. *The Master-Word in Medicine*. Wrappers. Baltimore, 1903. $75-$100.

OSLER, Sir William. *On Chorea and Choreiform Affections*. Cloth. Philadelphia, 1894. First edition. $100-$150.

OSLER, Sir William. *The Principles and Practice of Medicine*. Cloth. New York, 1892. First edition. $300-$400. Edinburgh, 1894. Cloth. First English edition. $150 and up.

OSLER, Sir William. *Students' Notes*. Half cloth. Montreal, 1882. First edition. $100.

OSLER, Sir William (editor). *Bibliotheca Osleriana: A Catalogue of Books Illustrating the History of Medicine and Science*. Cloth. Oxford, 1929. First edition. $300-$400. Montreal, 1969. Cloth. $100 and up.

O'SULLIVAN, Timothy, and Bell, William. *Photographs Showing Landscapes, Geological, and Other Features*. (Wheeler Survey.) 60 mounted photos, printed title page. Folio, three-quarters leather. (Washington, 1875.) $10,000-$12,500. Also, $6,000 (A, 1971).

OTERO, Miguel Antonio. *My Life on the Frontier*. Illustrated. 2 vols., cloth. New York, 1935, and Albuquerque, 1939. First editions. (Vol. 1 limited to 750 signed; Vol. 2 limited to 400.) $100-$125. Trade editions (illustrations omitted in each): Cloth. Each, in dust jackets, $20-$30.

OTERO, Miguel Antonio. *The Real Billy the Kid*. Illustrated. Cloth. New York, 1936. First edition. In dust jacket. $50-$75.

OTIS, James. *Jenny Wren's Boarding-House*. Illustrated. Pictorial brown or blue cloth. Boston, (1893). (By James Otis Kaler.) First edition. $50-$60.

OTIS, James. *Toby Tyler or Ten Weeks with a Circus*. Illustrated by W.A. Rogers. Light brown, green, or orange cloth. New York, 1881. (By James Otis Kaler.) First edition. $100-$150.

OTWAY, Thomas. *The Complete Works of Thomas Otway*. Edited by Montague Summers. 3 vols., batik boards and vellum. London, 1926. Nonesuch Press. One of 90 on handmade paper. $250-$350. Another issue: 3 vols., boards, paper label. One of 1,250. $100-$125.

OUIDA. *Syrlin*. 3 vols., cloth. London, 1980. (By Marie Louise de la Ramée.) First edition. $300-$400.

OUIDA. *A Tale of a Toad*. Decorated cloth and morocco. London, 1939. Corvinus Press. (By Marie Louise de la Ramée.) One of 25. $150-$200.

OUIDA. *Under Two Flags*. 3 vols., cloth. London, 1867. (By Marie Louise de la Ramée.) First edition. $300-$400.

*OUR Friends the Coeur D'Aleine Indians*. 21 pp., wrappers. St. Ignatius Print., Mont., 1886. (By Lawrence B. Palladino.) $110-$125.

*OUR Great Indian War: The Miraculous Lives of Mustang Bill (Mr. William Rhodes Decker) and Miss Marion Fannin*. Illustrated. 78 pp., pictorial pale-green wrappers. Philadelphia, (1876?). $225-$250.

*OUR Kith & Kin, or, a History of the Harris Family, 1754-1895*. Cloth. (Philadelphia, 1895.) $50-$60.

*OUTCROPPINGS: Being Selections of California Verse*. Cloth. San Francisco, 1866. First edition, probable first issue, with "Staining" spelled "Sraining" on page 70 and with no ornament on page 102. $150-$200. (Note: Edited anonymously by Bret Harte.)

*OUTLINE Description of U.S. Military Posts and Stations in the Year 1871*. Cloth. Washington, 1872. $75-$100.

*OUTRE-MER: A Pilgrimage Beyond the Sea*. Nos. I and II. Marbled wrappers and blue wrappers. Boston, 1833 and 1834. (By Henry Wadsworth Longfellow.) First editions. $500 and up. (Note: A complicated title bibliographically; for example, there are at least three wrapper variants on No. I, while No. II may be in either wrappers or boards of various colors. For a full discussion, see BAL.) Also issued clothbound as 2 vols. in one. $200 and up.

OVID. *The Amores of P. Ovidius Naso*. Translated by E. Powys Mathers. 5 engravings on copper by T.E. Laboureur. Half morocco. Waltham Saint Lawrence, England, 1932. Golden Cockerel Press. One of 350. $150-$250.

OVID. *Shakespeare's Ovid: Being Arthur Golding's Translation of the Metamorphoses*. Edited by W.H.D. Rouse. With a type-facsimile of the original title page. Boards, linen spine. London, 1904. De La More Press. One of 350. $100-$150. Another issue: Morocco. One of 12 on vellum. $1,000-$1,500.

OWEN, John Pickard. *The Fair Haven*. By the Late John Pickard Owen. Edited by William Bickersteth Owen. Green cloth. London, 1873. (By Samuel Butler, of *Erewhon*.) First edition. $50-$75.

OWEN, Richard E., and Cox, E.T. *Report on the Mines of New Mexico*. (Cover title.) 59 pp., printed wrappers. Washington, 1865. First edition. $500-$600.

OWEN, Robert. See Campbell, Alexander.

OWEN, Robert. *A New View of Society*. 4 parts in one, boards. London, 1813-14. First edition. $500-$600. London, 1816. Boards. Second edition. $150-$200.

OWEN, Robert Dale. *A Brief Practical Treatise on the Construction and Management of Plank Roads*. Plate. Cloth. New Albany, Ind., 1850. First edition. $125-$150.

OWEN, Wilfred. *Poems*. Cloth, paper label. London, 1920. First edition. In dust jacket. $150-$200. Author's first book.

OWEN, Wilfred. *Thirteen Poems*. Drawings by Ben Shahn and Leonard Baskin. Folio, half morocco. Northampton, Mass., 1956. Gehenna Press. One of 400, signed by Baskin. $300-$400. Another issue: One of 35 specially bound and with a proof of portrait signed by both artists. $500-$600.

OWENS, Rochelle. *Not Be Essence That Cannot Be*. Stiff printed wrappers. New York, (1961). First edition. $30-$40. Author's first book.

# P

P., E. *Hugh Selwyn Mauberley*. Brown boards and cloth. (London), 1920. (By Ezra Pound.) Ovid Press. First edition. One of 165 unsigned copies from an edition of 200. $1,000-$1,500. Also, $1,300 (A, 1977). One of 15 on vellum, signed, bound in white parchment and one of 20 signed copies bound in brown cloth. Each: $2,000 and up.

PACKARD, Wellman, and Larison, G. *Early Emigration to California*. 2 portraits. 23 pp., printed wrappers. Bloomington, Ill., 1928. One of 30. $100-$150.

*PAGAN Anthology. (The)*. Boards, paper label. New York, (1918). First edition. $200-$250. Also, $225 (A, 1977). (Contains two poems by Hart Crane, constituting his first book appearance.)

PAGE, Stanton. *The Chevalier of Pensieri-Vani*. Cloth, or wrappers. Boston, (1890). (By Henry Blake Fuller.) First edition. Wrappers: $200-$250. Cloth: $100-$150. Author's first book.

PAGE, Thomas Nelson. *In Old Virginia*. Pictorial cloth. New York, 1887. First edition, first issue, with no advertisement for "Free Joe" on last page. $50.

PAGE, Thomas Nelson. *Two Little Confederates*. Illustrated. Blue cloth. New York, 1888. First edition, first printing, with 10 ad pages at back. $60-$80.

PAINE, Albert Bigelow. *Captain Bill McDonald, Texas Ranger*. Illustrated. Cloth. New York, 1909. First edition. $75-$100. Another issue: Morocco. $100-$125.

PAINE, Albert Bigelow. *Thomas Nast: His Period and His Pictures*. Illustrated. Cloth. New York, 1904. First edition. $35-$50.

PALEY, Grace. *The Little Disturbances of Man*. Cloth. Garden City, 1959. First edition. In dust jacket. $50-$75. Author's first book.

PALINURUS. *The Unquiet Grave: A Word Cycle*. Frontispiece and 3 collotype plates. Gray wrappers. London, 1944. (By Cyril Connolly.) Curwen Press. First edition. One of 1,000. In dust jacket. $75-$100. (Note: Copies in "original cloth" are also listed in the auction records.)

PALLADINO, Lawrence B. See *Our Friends the Coeur D'Aleine Indians*.

PALLADINO, Lawrence B. *Indian and White in the Northwest*. Illustrated. Cloth, or half leather. Baltimore, 1894. First edition. $150-$250. Lancaster, Pa., 1922. Revised edition. $25-$35.

PALLAS, P.S. *Travels Through the Southern Provinces of the Russian Empire*. Maps and plates. 2 vols., boards, paper labels. London, 1802-03. First English edition. $1,000-$1,500.

PALMER, H.E. *The Powder River Indian Expedition, 1865*. 59 pp., printed gray wrappers. Omaha, 1887. First edition. $300-$350.

PALMER, Harry. *Base Ball: The National Game of the Americans*. 69 pp., wrappers. Chicago, 1888. $100 and up.

PALMER, Joel. *Journal of Travels over the Rocky Mountains, to the Mouth of the Columbia River, etc*. Brown printed wrappers. Cincinnati, 1847. First edition, first issue, with date 1847 on paper cover not overprinted or changed, and with errata slip tipped in.

$1,500-$2,000. Second issue, with corrections made. $1,000. Cincinnati, 1852. Half leather. Second edition. $500-$750.

PALMER, William J. *Report of Surveys Across the Continent.* 3 maps and profile, 20 photographic plates. Wrappers. Philadelphia, 1869. First edition. $750-$1,000. Later issue: One map, no photos. $100-$150.

PALOU, Francisco. *The Expedition into California of the Venerable Padre Junipero Serra and His Companions in the Year 1769.* Translated by Douglas S. Watson. Half vellum. San Francisco, 1934. One of 400. In dust jacket. $75-$100.

PALOU, Francisco. *Historical Memoirs of New California.* 4 vols., cloth. Translated by Herbert Eugene Bolton. Berkeley, 1926. $200-$250.

PALOU, Francisco. *The Life of the Venerable Padre Junipero Serra..* Translated by the Rev. J. Adam. Cloth. San Francisco, 1884. First edition in English. $75-$100.

PALOU, Francisco. *Noticias de la Nueva California.* Illustrated. 4 vols., printed wrappers. San Francisco, 1874. One of 100. $1,000 and up.

PAPWORTH, John B. *Hints on Ornamental Gardening.* 28 hand-colored plates, sepia plate, woodcut plans. Boards. London, 1823. First edition. $500-$600.

PAPWORTH, John B. *Rural Residences.* 27 full-page hand-colored aquatint plates. Boards. London, 1818. First edition. $600-$750. London, 1832. Cloth. Second edition. $400-$500.

PAPWORTH, John B. *Select Views of London.* 76 colored aquatint plates, 5 folding. Boards. London, 1816. First book edition. $2,000-$2,500, possibly more.

PAREDES Y ARRILLAGA, Mariano. *Ultimas Communicaciones Entre el Gobierno Mexicano y el Enviada Estraordinario y Ministro Plenipotenciario Nombrado por el de los Estados Unidos.* 22 pp., wrappers. Mexico, 1846. $350-$500.

*PARK Hotel (The): Travelers' Guide for 1872, Containing a Brief History of the City of Madison and Its Attractions.* Illustrated. 128 pp., wrappers. Madison, Wis., 1872. $100-$125.

PARK, Robert Emory. *Sketch of the 12th Alabama Infantry.* Wrappers. Richmond, Va., 1906. First edition. $100-$125.

PARKER, A. A. *Trip to the West and Texas.* 2 plates. Cloth. Concord, N.H., 1835. First edition. $250-$300. Concord, 1836. Colored folding map and 3 plates. Cloth. Second edition. $300-$400. (Note: Howes reports 2 plates; my own copy came with 3. Howes says not all copies included the map; in such cases the value should be around $100 or less.)

PARKER, Aaron. *Forgotten Tragedies of Indian Warfare in Idaho.* 10 pp., double-column, wrappers. Grangeville, Idaho, 1925. $100-$125.

PARKER, Dorothy. *After Such Pleasures.* Buckram. New York, 1933. First edition. One of 250 signed. Boxed. $75-$100. Trade edition: Tan cloth. In dust jacket. $15-$20

PARKER, Dorothy. *Death and Taxes.* Half cloth. New York, 1931. First edition. One of 250 signed. $50-$60. New York, 1932. Black Sun Press. Printed wrappers. $20-$25.

PARKER, Dorothy. *Laments for the Living.* Cloth. New York, 1930. First edition. In dust jacket. $50-$60. New York, 1932. Black Sun Press. Printed wrappers. $20-$25.

PARKER, Dorothy. *Men I'm Not Married To.* Boards. Garden City, 1922. First edition (so stated). (Bound in, inverted and with separate title, *Women I'm Not Married To,* by Franklin P. Adams.) In dust jacket. $40-$60. Author's first book.

PARKER, Dorothy. *Not So Deep as a Well.* Illustrated by Valenti Angelo. Half buckram. New York, 1936. First edition. One of 485, signed. $50-$75. Trade edition: Cloth. In dust jacket. $15-$20.

PARKER, Dorothy. *Sunset Gun.* Boards and cloth. New York, 1928. First edition. One of 250, signed. Boxed. $75-$100. Trade edition: Boards. In dust jacket. $15-$20.

PARKER, Frank J. (editor). *Washington Territory! The Present and Prospective Future of the Upper Columbia Country.* 17 pp., printed wrappers. Walla Walla, Wash., 1881. First edition. $400-$500.

PARKER, Henry W. *How Oregon Was Saved to the U.S.* 10 pp., wrappers. New York, 1901. $35-$50.

PARKER, J. M. *An Aged Wanderer: A Life Sketch of . . . a Cowboy on the Western Plains in the Early Days.* 32 pp., wrappers. San Angelo, Tex., no date. First edition. $200-$250.

PARKER, John R. *The New Semaphoric Signal Book.* Hand-colored flags. Printed boards. Boston, 1836. $100-$125.

PARKER, John R. *The United States Telegraph Vocabulary.* 3 plates, one in color. Pictorial boards. Boston, 1832. First edition. $150-$175.

PARKER, Samuel. *Journal of an Exploring Tour Beyond the Rocky Mountains.* Folding map, plate. Cloth. Ithaca, 1838. First edition. $350-$450. Edinburgh, 1841. Half leather. $100. Auburn, N.Y., 1846. Cloth. $40-$50.

PARKER, Solomon. *Parker's American Citizen's Sure Guide.* Boards. Sag Harbor, N.Y., 1808. First edition. $150-$175.

PARKER, W.B. *Notes Taken During the Expedition Commanded by Capt. R.B. Marcy.* Cloth. Philadelphia, 1856. First edition. $250-$400, possibly more.

PARKER & Huyett. *The Illustrated Miners' Hand-Book and Guide to Pike's Peak.* 6 plates, 2 folding maps. Cloth. St. Louis, 1859. (By Nathan H. Parker and D.H. Huyett.) First edition. $5,000-$6,000.

PARKMAN, Francis. *The California and Oregon Trail.* One vol. in cloth, or 2 vols in printed wrappers. New York, 1849. First edition. Wrappers: $4,500 and up. (Note: The only set known in wrappers, one with the lower wrapper missing on Vol.1, was sold recently by a dealer of my acquaintance for $4,500. He had catalogued it a few years before at $3,750!) New York, 1849. Frontispiece and engraved title page. Cloth. First clothbound edition. $500-$600. (Note: See the Thomas W. Streeter sale catalogue for a note on the inconclusive bibliographical data on this book.)

PARKMAN, Francis. *History of the Conspiracy of Pontiac and the War of the North American Tribes.* 4 maps. Gray cloth. Boston, 1851. First edition. $100-$150.

PARKMAN, Francis. *The Old Regime in Canada.* Cloth. Boston, 1874. First edition. One of 75 on large paper. $100-$150.

PARKMAN, Francis. *The Oregon Trail.* Illustrated by Frederic Remington. Leather, or pictorial tan cloth. Boston, 1892. First edition. Leather: $250-$350. Cloth: $150-$250. New York, 1925. Illustrated by Remington and N.C. Wyeth. Half cloth. One of 975. $200-$225 New York, 1943. Limited Editions Club. $80-$100.

PARLEY, Peter. *Peter Parley's Universal History, on the Basis of Geography.* 2 vols., cloth. Boston, 1837. (By Nathaniel Hawthorne.) First edition. $1,000 and up. Also, rebound, $225 (A, 1976).

PARLEY, Peter. *The Tales of Peter Parley About America.* 32 (30?) engravings. Blue boards, red leather spine. Boston, 1827. (By Samuel G. Goodrich.) First edition. $3,000 and up. Also, badly worn, $2,750 (A, 1974). Author's first book.

PARMLY, Levi Spear. *A Practical Guide to the Management of the Teeth.* Boards. Philadelphia, 1819. First edition. $175-$200.

PARNELL, Thomas. *Poems.* Selected by Lennox Robinson. Boards and linen. Dublin, 1927. Cuala Press. One of 200. In dust jacket. $65-$85.

PARRY, William Edward. *Journal of a Second Voyage for the Discovery of a North-West Passage.* 39 plates, maps and charts. Cloth. London, 1824. First edition. $300-$500.

PARRY, William Edward. *Journal of a Voyage for the Discovery of a North-West Pass-*

*age . . . in the Years, 1819–20.* 20 plates and maps. Boards. London, 1821. First edition, with errata slip. $500-$750.

PARSONS, George Frederic. *The Life and Adventures of James W. Marshall.* Portrait frontispiece. Cloth. Sacramento, 1870. First edition. $100-$150. San Francisco, 1935. Grabhorn Press. Boards. $65-$85.

*PARTICULAR Account of the Dreadful Fire at Richmond, Dec. 26, 1811.* 48 pp., sewed. Baltimore, 1812. $75-$100.

*PARTISAN (The); A Tale of the Revolution.* 2 vols., cloth, paper labels. New York, 1835. (By William Gilmore Simms.) First edition. $200-$250.

*PASADENA as It Is Today from a Business Standpoint.* (Cover title.) 32 pp., printed wrappers. (Pasadena, 1886.) $150-$200.

*PASADENA, California, Illustrated.* Plates. 45 pp., pictorial wrappers. Pasadena, 1886. $100-$125.

*PASADENA, Los Angeles County, Southern California.* 36 pp., wrappers. Los Angeles, 1898. $100-$125.

PASQUIN, Peter. *A Day's Journal of a Sponge.* 6 hand-colored plates. Wrappers. London, 1824. (By M. Egerton.) $475-$550.

*PASSION-Flowers.* Cloth. Boston, 1854. (By Julia Ward Howe.) First edition. $50-$60. Author's first book.

PASTERNAK, Boris. *Doctor Zhivago.* Cloth, London, 1958. First edition in English. In dust jacket. $40-$50.

PASTERNAK, Boris. *Selected Poems.* Cloth. London, 1946. First edition. In dust jacket. $25-$35.

PATCHEN, Kenneth, *Before the Brave.* Red cloth. New York, (1936). First edition. In dust jacket. $75-$85.

PATCHEN, Kenneth. *The Dark Kingdom.* Wrappers, painted by the author. New York, (1942). First edition. One of 75, signed. Boxed. $100-$150. Trade edition: Cloth. In dust jacket. $20-$25.

PATCHEN, Kenneth. *Fables and Other Little Tales.* Boards and cloth, paper labels. Karlsruhe, Germany, 1953. First edition. One of 50 with covers hand-painted by Patchen, signed. $125-$200.

PATCHEN, Kenneth. *The Famous Boating Party.* Boards and cloth. (New York, 1954). First edition. One of 50 with covers hand-painted by Patchen and with limitation in Patchen's hand, signed. $150-$200.

PATCHEN, Kenneth. *First Will.* Cloth. (New York, 1948.) First edition. One of 126, signed. In dust jacket. $60-$80.

PATCHEN, Kenneth. *Glory Never Guesses.* Silk-screened poems on Japanese papers, some leaves hand-colored by Patchen, in portfolio wrappers. No place, no date (1955). First edition. One of 200. $150-$200.

PATCHEN, Kenneth. *Hurrah for Anything.* Illustrated. Boards. Highlands, N.C., 1957. First edition. One of 100. $150-$250.

PATCHEN, Kenneth. *The Journal of Albion Moonlight.* Boards and cloth. (Mount Vernon, N.Y., 1941.) First edition. One of 50, signed. Boxed. $150-$250.

PATCHEN, Kenneth. *Memoirs of a Shy Pornographer.* Cloth. New York, 1945. First edition. In dust jacket. $25-$35.

PATCHEN, Kenneth. *The Moment.* Hand-painted and -lettered by the author. Woven boards, vellum spine. No place, (1955). First edition. One of 47. $100-$150. Another edition: (Alhambra, Calif., 1960.) Folio, vellum and cloth. One of 42, signed. $150.

PATCHEN, Kenneth. *Orchards, Thrones and Caravans.* Boards. San Francisco, (1952). First edition. "Vellum edition." One of 170, signed. $75-$100. Another issue: Boards. One of 90. "Engraver's edition," with cover engraving by David Ruff, signed by Patchen and Ruff. $150-$200. Also, $130 (A, 1972).

PATCHEN, Kenneth. *Panels for the Walls of Heaven.* Boards. (Berkeley), 1946. First edition. One of 150 with covers hand-painted by author and with limitation notice in Patchen's hand, signed. $100-$150. Another issue: Boards, with different design. One of 150. $100-$150. Also, $50 (A, 1970). Another issue: Also different. One of 150. $100-$150.

PATCHEN, Kenneth. *Poem-Scapes.* Hand-painted boards. Highlands, 1958. First edition. One of 75, signed. $100-$150. Another (?) issue: One of 42 signed, and including a hand-written poem. $75-$150. Trade edition: Stiff wrappers. $7.50-$10.

PATCHEN, Kenneth. *Red Wine and Yellow Hair.* Boards and cloth. New York, (1949). First edition. One of 108 with covers hand-painted by author and with limitation notice in Patchen's hand, signed. $125. Another issue: One of 108 with different design on cover. $125. Trade edition: Cloth. In dust jacket. $25.

PATCHEN, Kenneth. *Sleepers Awake.* Red cloth. (New York, 1946.) First (black paper) edition. One of 148, signed. $50-$75. Another issue: White cloth, with original decoration on cover by the author. One of 75, signed. In dust jacket. $150-$200. Trade edition: Cloth. In dust jacket. $25.

PATCHEN, Kenneth. *A Surprise for the Bagpipe Players.* Silk-screened poems on Japanese papers, some leaves hand-colored by Patchen, in portfolio wrappers. No place, (1955). First edition. One of 200. $150-$200.

PATCHEN, Kenneth. *The Teeth of the Lion.* Wrappers. Norfolk, Conn., 1942. First edition. $25-$35.

PATCHEN, Kenneth. *To Say If You Love Someone.* Cloth. Prairie City, Ill., (1930). Press of James A. Decker. First edition. In dust jacket. $75-$100. Author's first book.

PATCHEN, Kenneth. *When We Were Here Together.* Boards. (New York, 1967.) First edition. One of 75 with hand-painted covers by author, signed. $100-$125.

PATER, Walter. *Appreciations, with An Essay on Style.* Cloth. London, 1889. First edition. $40-$50.

PATER, Walter. *Essays from "The Guardian."* Boards. London, 1896. Chiswick Press. First edition. One of 100. $50-$75.

PATER, Walter. *An Imaginary Portrait.* Wrappers. London, 1894. Daniel Press. One of 250. $65-$75.

PATER, Walter. *Imaginary Portraits.* Cloth. London, 1887. First edition. $40-$50.

PATER, Walter. *Marius the Epicurean.* 2 vols, cloth. London, 1885. First edition. $50-$75. Portland, Me., 1900. 2 vols., morocco. One of 450. $75-$100. Another issue: One of 35. In dust jackets. $100-$125. London, 1913. 2 vols., vellum. One of 12 on vellum. $750-$1,000. London, 1929. Illustrated by Thomas Mackenzie. 2 vols., half vellum. One of 325 signed by Mackenzie. $75-$125.

PATER, Walter. *Plato and Platonism: A Series of Lectures.* Cloth. New York, 1893. First American edition. One of 100. $75-$100.

PATER, Walter. *The Renaissance: Studies in Art and Poetry.* Illustrated. Limp wrappers. Portland, 1902. One of 35 on vellum. $150.

PATER, Walter. *Sebastian Van Storck.* 8 colored plates. Cloth. London, 1927. One of 1,050. $150-$200.

PATER, Walter. *Studies in the History of the Renaissance.* Dark-green cloth. London, 1873. First edition. $75-$100. Author's first book.

*PATHFINDER (The); or, The Inland Sea..* By the Author of *The Pioneers.* 3 vols., boards and cloth, paper labels. London, 1840. (By James Fenimore Cooper.) First edition.

$300-$350. Philadelphia, 1840. 2 vols., green or purple cloth, paper labels. First American edition, first issue, without copyright notice in Vol. 1 and with printer's imprint at about center of page 2. $400-$450. New York, 1965. Limited Editions Club. Buckram. Boxed. $40-$60.

PATMORE, Coventry. See *The Angel in the House; Odes.*

PATMORE, Coventry. *Faithful For Ever.* Cloth. London, 1860. First edition. $75-$100.

PATMORE, Coventry. *Poems.* Cloth. London, 1844. First edition. $100-$150. Author's first book.

PATMORE, Henry John. *Poems.* Vellum. Oxford, 1884. Daniel Press. One of 125. $200-$250.

PATTERSON, A.W. *History of the Backwoods; or, The Region of the Ohio.* Folding map. Cloth. Pittsburgh, 1843. First edition. $400-$500.

PATTERSON, Joseph Medill. *A Little Brother of the Rich.* Cloth. Chicago, 1908. First edition. In dust jacket. $100-$125.

PATTERSON, Lawson B. *Twelve Years in the Mines of California.* Cloth. Cambridge, Mass., 1862. First edition. $150-$175.

PATTERSON, Samuel. *Narrative of the Adventures and Sufferings of Samuel Patterson.* Boards. Rhode Island, 1817. First edition. $250-$300. Palmer, Mass., 1817. Contemporary sheep. Second edition. $175-$200. (Note: Ghostwritten by Ezekiel Terry.)

PATTIE, James O. *The Personal Narrative of James O. Pattie, of Kentucky.* Edited by Timothy Flint. 5 plates. Mottled calf. Cincinnati, 1831. First edition, first issue, published by John H. Wood. $8,500-$10,000, possibly more. Cincinnati, 1833. Second issue (reissue of the 1831 sheets with new title page). $1,200-$1,500.

PATTON, The Rev. W.W., and Isham, R.N. *U.S. Sanitary Commission, No. 38: Report on the Condition of Camps and Hospitals at Cairo . . . Paducah and St. Louis.* 12 pp., stitched. Chicago, 1861. First edition. $100-$150.

PAUL, Elliott, and Allen, Jay. *All the Brave.* Illustrated by Luis Quintinalla. Preface by Ernest Hemingway. Pictorial wrappers. New York, (1939). First edition. $40-$60.

PAUL, William. *The Rose Garden.* 15 color plates. Cloth. London, 1848. First edition. $175-$250.

PAULDING, Hiram. *Journal of a Cruise of the United States Schooner Dolphin.* Folding map. Cloth. New York, 1831. First edition. $400-$650.

PAULDING, James Kirke. See Langstaff, Launcelot. Also see *A Christmas Gift from Fairy-Land; Chronicles of the City of Gotham; The Dutchman's Fireside; John Bull in America; Letters from the South; The Merry Tales of the Three Wise Men of Gotham; A Sketch of Old England; Westward Ho!*

PAULDING, James Kirke. *The Backwoodsman: A Poem.* Boards. Philadelphia, 1818. First edition. $150-$200.

*PAULINE: A Fragment of a Confession.* Gray or brown boards, paper label. London, 1833. (By Robert Browning.) First edition. $16,000 (A, 1929—the Jerome Kern copy). Author's first book—and the rarest of them all. London, 1886. Edited by Thomas J. Wise. Boards. One of 400. $50-$75. Another issue: One of 25 on large paper. $150-$250.

PAULISON, C.M.K. *Arizona: The Wonderful Country.* 31 pp., printed wrappers. Tucson, 1881. First edition. $2,000-$3,000. Also, $1,800 (A, 1966).

PAYNE, John Howard. *Clari; or, The Maid of Milan; An Opera, in Three Acts.* Stitched, old paper wrappers. London, 1823. First edition. $500 and up. (Note: This work contains on page 8 the first printing of Payne's "Home! Sweet Home!")

PAYNE, John Howard, and Bishop, Henry R. *Home! Sweet Home! Sung by Miss M. Tree, in Clari.* 4 pp., folio, sheet music. London, (1823). First separate edition. $300 and up.

*PEACH Orchard (The).* Woodcuts. 24 pp., self-wrappers. Northampton, Mass., 1839. $100 and up.

*PEACH River: A Canoe Voyage from Hudson's Bay to the Pacific.* Folding map, errata slip. Printed wrappers. Ottawa, 1872. (By Archibald McDonald.) First edition. $450-$500.

PEACOCK, Francis. *Sketches Relative to the History and Theory, but More Especially to the Practice of Dancing.* Boards. Aberdeen, Scotland, 1805. First edition. $200-$300.

PEACOCK, Thomas Love. See *Crotchet Castle; Gryll Grange; Headlong Hall; Maid Marian; Melincourt; The Misfortunes of Elphin; Nightmare Abbey; Rhododaphne.*

PEACOCK, Thomas Love. *The Genius of the Thames.* Boards. London, 1810. First edition. $350-$450.

PEACOCK, Thomas Love. *Palmyra and Other Poems.* Frontispiece. Boards. London, 1806. First edition. $200-$250.

PEACOCK, Thomas Love. *The Philosophy of Melancholy: A Poem in Four Parts.* Boards. London, 1812. First edition. $200-$250.

PEAKE, Mervyn. *Captain Slaughterboard Drops Anchor.* Illustrated. 48 pp., cloth. London, 1939. First edition. In dust jacket. $150-$200. London, 1945. Color illustrations. Second edition. In dust jacket. $125-$150.

PEAKE, Mervyn. *Drawings.* Cloth. London, 1949. First edition. $25-$35.

PEAKE, Mervyn. *Titus Groan.* Cloth. London, 1946. First edition. In dust jacket. $65-$75.

PEARSE, James. *A Narrative of the Life of James Pearse.* Boards and leather. Rutland, Vt., 1825. First edition. $200-$250.

PEARSON, Edmund L. *The Voyage of the Hoppergrass.* Illustrated by Thomas Fogarty. Pictorial cloth. New York, 1913. First edition. In dust jacket. $50-$75.

PEARSON, Jonathan, and others. *The History of the Schenectady Patent.* 28 maps and plates. Albany, 1883. Second edition. One of 300. $50-$75. Another issue. One of 50 on large paper. $100-$125.

PEATTIE, Donald Culross. *An Almanac for Moderns.* Lynd Ward illustrations. Cloth. New York, (1935). First edition. In dust jacket. $35-$50. New York, 1938. Limited Editions Club. $50-$60.

PEATTIE, Donald Culross. *Audubon's America.* Color plates and other illustrations. Cloth. Boston, 1940. First edition. In dust jacket. $20-$25. Another issue: Limited edition, with an extra set of color plates. $75-$100.

PEATTIE, Donald Culross. *A Book of Hours.* Decorations by Lynd Ward. Buckram. New York, 1937. First edition. One of 550, signed. $75. Trade edition: Cloth. In dust jacket. $10.

PEATTIE, Elia W. *How Jacques Came into the Forest of Arden.* Illustrated. Boards. Chicago, (1901). Blue Sky Press. One of 25 on vellum. $50-$60. Another issue: Tan morocco. One of 3. Boxed. $100-$150.

PECK, George Wilbur. *Peck's Bad Boy and His Pa.* Wrappers, or cloth. Chicago, 1883. First edition, first issue, with the text ending on page 196, the last word in perfect type, and with the printer's rules on the copyright page ⅞ inch apart. Wrappers: $300-$400. Cloth: $200-$250. Later issues, same date, wrappers or cloth. $25-$35.

PECK, John M. *A Discourse in Reference to the Decease of the Late Governor of Illinois, Ninian Edwards.* 20 pp., printed wrappers. Rock Spring, Ill., 1834. First edition. $1,000-$1,250.

PECK, John M. *A Gazetteer of Illinois.* Cloth. Jacksonville, Ill., 1834. First edition. $100-$150. Philadelphia, 1837. Cloth, paper label. Second edition. $75-$100.

PECK, John M. *A Guide for Emigrants, Containing Sketches of Illinois, Missouri, and the Adjacent Parts.* Map. Cloth. Boston, 1831. First edition. $75-$125.

PECK, John M. *A New Guide for Emigrants to the West.* Map. Cloth. Boston, 1836. Enlarged edition. $75-$125.

PEEK, Peter V. *Inklings of Adventure in the Campaigns of the Florida Indian War.* (Cover title.) 72 pp., double columns, printed yellow wrappers. Schenectady, 1846. First edition. $4,500-$5,000. Schenectady, 1860. Pictorial wrappers. $350. (Note: Catalogued by a New York dealer in the 1950's as, "so far as we can trace, the only known copy." The same dealer had sold the first edition copy noted above in 1936.)

PEESLAKE, Gaffer. *Bromo Bombastes: A Fragment from a Laconic Drama.* Black boards, paper label. London, 1933. Caduceus Press. (By Lawrence Durrell.) First edition. One of 100. $2,000 and up. Also. binding marked, $1,600 (A, 1977).

PEET, Frederick T. *Civil War Letters and Documents of Frederick T. Peet.* Boards. Newport, R.I., 1915. First edition. One of 50. $75-$125.

PEET, Frederick T. *Personal Experiences in the Civil War.* Boards. New York, 1905. First edition. One of 50. $75-$125.

PEIRCE, A.C. *A Man from Corpus Christi.* Cloth. New York, 1894. First edition. $150-$250.

*PELAYO: A Story of the Goth.* 2 vols., cloth, paper labels. New York, 1838. (By William Gilmore Simms.) First edition. $200-$300, possibly more.

*PELHAM.* 3 vols., boards. London, 1828. (By Edward Bulwer-Lytton.) First edition, with ad leaf in Vol. 3. $200-$250.

*PEN Knife Sketches; Or, Chips of the Old Block.* 24 full-page illustrations. Wrappers. Sacramento, 1853. (By Alonzo Delano.) First edition. $500-$600. Second edition, same year: $300-$400. (For a modern reprint, see entry under author's name.)

PENDENNIS, Arthur (editor). *The Newcomes.* Illustrated by Richard Doyle. 23 parts in 24, yellow wrappers. London, 1853-55. (By William Makepeace Thackeray.) First edition. $1,000 and up for fine copies with all major bibliographical points. $500 and up for copies in mixed state, repaired, etc. London, 1854-55. 2 vols., cloth. First book edition. $75-$100. (Note: As with most 19th century publications in paperbound parts, *The Newcomes* is a complicated problem for collectors and requires the use of a bibliography to determine its degree of bibliographical correctness. Any set in good condition should be carefully examined for proper evaluation.)

PENDLETON, Nathanial Greene. *Military Posts—Council Bluffs to the Pacific Ocean.* (Caption title.) Folding map. Sewed. (Washington, 1843.) $75-$100.

PENN, William (pseudonym). *Essays on the Present Crisis in the Present Condition of the . . . Indians.* Stitched. Boston, 1829. (By Jeremiah Evarts.) First edition. $50-$75. Philadelphia, 1830. Stitched. $35-$40.

PENNELL, E. R., and Pennell, Joseph. *Our Philadelphia.* Boards. Philadelphia, 1914. First edition. One of 289, signed. With 10 extra lithographs. $150-$200. Trade edition: Cloth. $75-$100.

PENNELL, Joseph. *The Adventures of an Illustrator.* Illustrated. Half leather. Boston, 1925. Limited edition, signed. $150-$175. Trade edition: Cloth. $80-$100.

PENNELL, Joseph. *The Glory of New York.* 24 color reproductions. Folio, cloth. New York, 1926. One of 350 designed by Bruce Rogers. In dust jacket. Boxed. $150-$200.

PENROSE, Charles W. *"Mormon" Doctrine, Plain and Simple.* Cloth. Salt Lake City, 1882. First edition. $75-$100.

*PENTLAND Rising (The).* Green wrappers. Edinburgh, 1866. (By Robert Louis Stevenson.) First edition. $1,000 and up. Also, $700 (A, 1977). Stevenson's first book.

*"PEOPLE'S Reville" (The): Souvenir Hill City, Graham County, Kansas.* (Cover title.) 112 pp., wrappers. Topeka, 1906. $50-$60.

PEPPER, Capt. George W. *Personal Recollections of Sherman's Campaigns in Georgia and the Carolinas.* Cloth. Zanesville, Ohio, 1866. First edition. $150-$200.

PEPYS, Samuel. *Memoirs . . . Comprising His Diary from 1659 to 1669.* Edited by Richard, Lord Braybrooke. Portraits, views and facsimiles. 2 vols., boards, paper labels. London, 1825. First edition. $1,250-$1,500, possibly more. Also, foxed, hinges cracked, $950 (A, 1976). Another issue: One of 12 on thick paper, stamped "Presentation Copy." $550 (A, 1974)—in contemporary morocco. London, 1828. 5 vols., boards. Second (and first octavo) edition. $100-$150. New York, 1942. Limited Editions Club. Illustrated. 10 vols., pictorial boards and buckram. $125-$150. (Note: There have been numerous other editions of the Pepys diary, most of them multi-volume versions. See the British and American book auction records for detailed listings.)

PERCEVAL, Dean. *A Thousand Miles in a Canoe.* Printed wrappers. Bushnell, Ill., 1880. First edition. $1,250-$1,500.

*PERCIVAL Keene.* 3 vols., boards. London, 1842. (By Frederick Marryat.) First edition. $150-$200.

PERCY, Stephen. *Robin Hood and His Merry Foresters.* 8 full-page hand-colored illustrations. Cloth. New York, 1855. (By Joseph Cundall.) $100-$125.

PERCY, Walker. *The Moviegoer.* Cloth. New York, 1961. First edition. In dust jacket. $50. Author's first book.

PERELMAN, S. J. *Dawn Ginsbergh's Revenge.* Apple-green "plush" binding. (Second issue had silver cloth.) New York, (1929). First edition. In dust jacket. $125-$150. Second binding. In dust jacket. $75-$100. Author's first book.

PEREZ DE LUXAN, Diego. *Expedition into New Mexico Made by Antonio de Espejo, 1582-1583.* Translated by George Peter Hammond and Agapito Rey. Half vellum. Los Angeles, 1929. One of 500 copies. $250-$350.

*PERICLES and Aspasia.* 2 vols., drab boards, blue-green cloth, paper labels. London, 1836. (By Walter Savage Landor.) First edition. $200-$250. London, 1903. Half pigskin. One of 220. $40-$60. New York, 1903. Folio, boards. One of 210. $40-$60.

PERKINS, Charles Elliott. *The Pinto Horse.* Illustrated by Edward Borein. Pictorial boards. Santa Barbara, 1927. First edition. In dust jacket. $75-$100.

PERKINS, Lucy Fitch. *The Dutch Twins.* Illustrated by the author. Pictorial olive cloth. Boston, 1911. First edition, first issue, with blank end papers. $100-$150. Second issue: Green cloth, pictorial end papers. $50-$75.

PERKINS, P.D., and Perkins, Ione. *Lafcadio Hearn: A Bibliography.* 6 plates. Cloth. Boston, 1934. Boxed. $75-$100.

PERRAULT, Charles. *The Sleeping Beauty in the Wood.* Mounted photogravures of Gustave Doré drawings. Cloth. Philadelphia, 1863. $100.

PERRY, Oliver Hazard. *Hunting Expeditions of Oliver Hazard Perry.* 3 plates. Cloth. Cleveland, 1899. First edition. One of 100. $750-$1,000.

PERSE, St. J. *Anabasis.* French and English texts. Translated by T. S. Eliot. Blue-green cloth. London, 1930. (By Alexis St. Leger Leger.) First edition in English. In white dust jacket. $35-$50. Another issue: Green cloth. One of 350 signed by Eliot. In cellophane dust jacket. Boxed. $250-$300. Second trade issue: London, 1930 (actually 1937). Green cloth. In green dust jacket. $35-$50. New York, (1938). Black cloth. First American edition (second edition, revised). In dust jacket. $35-$50. New York, (1949). Gray cloth. Third edition, revised. In dust jacket. $30. London, (1959). Plum cloth. Revised. In gray dust jacket. $25-$35.

*PERSONAL Reminiscences of a Maryland Soldier.* Cloth. Baltimore, 1898. (By G. W. Booth.) First edition. $100-$150.

*PETER Parley's Universal History.* Maps and engravings. 2 vols., black cloth. Boston, 1837. (Compiled by Nathaniel Hawthorne and his sister Elizabeth.) First edition, with "Great Tree" design in gilt on covers. $1,000-$1,500, possibly more.

*PETER Pilgrim; or a Rambler's Recollections.* 2 vols., green or purple muslin, paper labels. Philadelphia, 1838. (By Robert Montgomery Bird.) First edition. $150-$200.

PETERS, DeWitt C. *Kit Carson's Life.* Illustrated. Cloth. Hartford, 1874. $75-$100. Hartford, 1875. Cloth. $25-$35. London, (about 1875). Cloth. $25-$35. (Note: This is an enlarged version of the title following.)

PETERS, DeWitt C. *The Life and Adventures of Kit Carson, the Nestor of the Rocky Mountains.* 10 plates. Cloth. New York, 1858. First edition. $75-$100. New York, 1859. Cloth. $35.

PETERS, Fred J. *Railroad, Indian and Pioneer Prints by N. Currier and Currier and Ives. Clipper Ship Prints. Sporting Prints.* Illustrated. 3 vols., cloth. New York, 1930. Limited edition. Boxed. $125-$200.

PETERS, Harry T. *America on Stone: A Chronicle of American Lithography.* 154 plates, 18 in color. Cloth. Garden City, 1931. First edition. One of 751. Boxed. $500-$750. Also, $500 and $425. (A, 1977).

PETERS, Harry T. *California on Stone.* 112 plates. Cloth. Garden City, 1935. First edition. One of 501. In dust jacket. Boxed. $400-$600. Also, $300 (A, 1977).

PETERS, Harry T. *Currier and Ives, Printmakers to the American People.* 300 reproductions (including color). 2 vols., cloth. Garden City, 1929-31. First edition. One of 510. Boxed. $600-$750. Garden City, 1942. Cloth. Special edition in one volume. In dust jacket. $35-$50.

PETERS, William E. *Ohio Lands and Their History.* Cloth. Athens, Ohio, 1930. Third edition. $25-$35.

PETERS, William E. *Ohio Lands and Their Subdivision.* Folding map in pocket. Cloth. (Athens), 1918. Second edition. $35.

PETERSEN, Carl. *Each in Its Ordered Place: A Faulkner Collector's Notebook.* Green morocco-grained cloth. Ann Arbor, (1975). First edition, first printing. (1,000 copies.) In dust jacket. $35-$50. Second printing (falsely identified on copyright page as "first printing"). Orange cloth, sepia end papers (instead of green as in true first printing); text on different paper from first printing, and with better clarity in illustrations. (400 printed.) Issued without dust jacket. $20-$25.

PETERSEN, William J. *Steamboating on the Upper Mississippi.* Decorated cloth. Iowa City, 1937. First edition. $60-$80.

*PETITION of the Latter-Day Saints, Commonly Known as Mormons (The).* (Caption title.) 13 pp., sewed. Washington, 1840. (By Elias Higbee, Robert B. Thompson, and others.) $100-$125.

PETTER, Rodolphe. *English-Cheyenne Dictionary.* Folio, full black calf. Kettle Falls, Wash., 1913-15. First edition. One of 100. $200-$225.

PHAIR, Charles. *Atlantic Salmon Fishing.* Edited by Richard C. Hunt. Illustrated. Folio, cloth. New York, (1937). Derrydale Press. One of 950. In dust jacket. $200-$300. Another issue: Half morocco. One of 40, signed, with portfolio of mounted flies. $4,500 (A, 1977).

PHELPS and Ensign (publishers). *Traveller's Guide Through the United States, Containing Stage, Steamboat, Canal and Rail-road Routes, with the Distances from Place to Place.* Folding map. Leather. New York, 1838. First edition. $100-$125. Other similar *Traveller's Guides*, same publishers: 1840, $100; 1850, $75; 1851, $100-$150.

PHELPS, Noah A. *A History of the Copper Mines and Newgate Prison, at Granby, Conn.* 34 pp., wrappers. Hartford, 1845. $100-$150.

PHILBY, H. St. J.B. *A Pilgrim in Arabia.* Portrait. Buckram, leather spine. London, 1943. Golden Cockerel Press. One of 350. $175-$225.

*PHILIP Dru, Administrator.* Cloth. New York, 1919. (By Col. E. M. House.) First edition. In dust jacket. Cloth. $75-$125.

PHILLIPS, D. L. *Letters from California.* Cloth. Springfield, Ill., 1877. First edition. $75-$100.

PHILLIPS, J. V. *Report on the Geology of the Mineral Districts Contiguous to the Iron Mountain Railroad.* 14 pp., printed wrappers. St. Louis, 1859. $75-$85.

PHILLIPS, Philip A. S. *Paul de Lamerie, Citizen and Goldsmith of London.* Illustrated. Folio, cloth. London, 1935. One of 250. $300-$450. London, 1968. Folio, cloth. In dust jacket. $75-$125.

PHILLIPS, Sir Richard. *Modern London.* Folding frontispiece, folding map, 31 colored plates of "Cries of London" with gray borders. Half calf. London, 1804. $500-$600. London, 1805. $500-$600.

PHILLPOTTS, Eden. *Children of the Mist.* Frontispiece. Blue cloth. London, 1898. First edition, first printing with the "8" present on page 48. $50-$75.

PHILLPOTTS, Eden. *A Dish of Apples.* Illustrations, including color, by Arthur Rackham. White cloth. London, (1921). One of 500, signed. $400-$500. Another issue: One of 55 on Batchelor's Kelmscott paper. $750-$1,000. Trade edition: Cloth. $80-$125.

PHILLPOTTS, Eden. *The Girl and the Faun.* Illustrated by Frank Brangwyn. Half vellum. London, 1916. One of 350, signed. $75-$125. Trade edition: $25-$35.

PHILLPOTTS, Eden. *My Adventure in the Flying Scotsman.* Colored cloth. London, 1888. First edition, first issue. $100-$200. Second issue: Stiff wrappers, or boards. $75-$100. Author's first book.

*PHOTOGRAPHIC Sketch Book of the War.* 100 gold-toned albumen prints, with leaf of text for each. 2 vols., oblong folio, morocco. Washington, (1865-66). (By Alexander Gardner.) First edition. $8,000-$12,000, possibly more.

PHYLOS the Tibetan. *An Earth Dweller's Return.* Illustrated. Cloth. Milwaukee, 1940. (By Frederick S. Oliver.) First edition. $50-$75.

PICKETT, Albert James. *History of Alabama, and Incidentally of Georgia and Mississippi.* Map, 3 plans, 8 plates. 2 vols., cloth. Charleston, 1851. First edition. $200-$300. Second edition, same place and date. $125-$200.

PICKETT, Albert James. *Invasion of the Territory of Alabama, by 1,000 Spaniards, Under Ferdinand de Soto, in 1540.* 41 pp., wrappers. Montgomery, 1849. First edition. $300-$350.

PICKTHALL, Marmaduke. *Said the Fisherman.* Cloth. London, 1903. First edition. $65-$85. Author's first book.

*PICTORIAL View of California (A).* By a Returned Californian. 48 plates. Cloth. New York, 1853. (By J. M. Letts.) Later edition of *California Illustrated.* $150-$200.

PIERCE, N. H., and Brown, Nugent E. (compilers). *The Free State of Menard.* Illustrated. Pictorial cloth. Menard, Tex., 1946. First edition. $35-$50.

PIERSON, B. T. *Directory of the City of Newark for 1838-9.* Printed boards. Newark, N.J., 1838. One of 500. $100 and up.

PIGAFETTA, Antonio. *Magellan's Voyage Around the World.* Translated by James A. Robertson. Portrait, maps, facsimiles. 3 vols., cloth. Cleveland, 1906. One of 350. $150-$200.

PIGMAN, Walter Griffith. *Journal.* Edited by Ulla Staley Fawkes. Boards. Mexico, Mo., 1942. First edition. One of 200. $35-$50.

*PIGS Is Pigs.* Decorated oyster-white wrappers. Chicago, 1905. Railways Appliances Company. (By Ellis Parker Butler.) First edition. $150 and up. (Note: Author's name appears only on decoration at first text page.).

PIKE, Albert. *Prose Sketches and Poems, Written in the Western Country.* Brown cloth, leather label. Boston, 1834. First edition. $1,000-$1,500.

*PIKE County Puzzle, Vol. 1, No. 1.* 4 pp. (Burlesque of country newspaper.) Camp Interlaken, Pa., 1894. (By Stephen Crane.) $150 and up.

PIKE, James. *The Scout and Ranger.* Portrait, 24 plates. Black cloth. Cincinnati, 1865. First edition, first issue, with errata leaf and uncorrected errors. $400-$600. Second issue, without errata leaf. $300-$350.

PIKE, Z. M. *An Account of Expeditions to the Sources of the Mississippi.* Portrait, 4 maps, 2 charts, 3 tables. 2 vols., boards. Philadelphia, 1810. First edition. $1,000-$1,500. Another issue: Maps in separate cloth atlas-folder. $2,500-$3,500.

PIKE, Z. M. *An Account of a Voyage up the Mississippi River.* Map. 68 pp., stiched, plain wrappers. (Washington, 1807?) (By Nicholas King from Pike's notes?) First edition. $1,500-$2,000. Also, $1,100 (A, 1967).

PIKE, Z. M. *Exploratory Travels Through the Western Territories of North America.* 2 maps. Boards. London, 1811. First English edition (of *An Account of Expeditions to the Sources of the Mississippi).* $800-$1,200.

PILCHER, Joshua. *Report on the Fur Trade and Inland Trade to Mexico.* Cloth. Washington, 1832. First edition. $150-$200.

PILGRIM, Thomas. See Morecamp, Arthur.

*PILOT (The): A Tale of the Sea.* By the Author of *The Pioneers.* 2 vols., blue boards, paper labels. New York, 1823. (By James Fenimore Cooper.) First edition. $150-$250. London, 1824. 3 vols., boards. First English edition. $100-$125. New York, 1968. Limited Editions Club. $35-$45.

*PILOT Knob. Mendota.* Map, portrait, and plates. 23 pp., pictorial wrappers. (St. Paul, 1887.) (By Gen. H. H. Sibley.) First edition. $100-$125.

PINDAR. *Odes of Victory.* Translated by C. J. Billson. 90 wood engravings by John Farleigh. 2 vols., limp vellum with ties, lettered in gold on front covers and spines. Stratford, England, 1928. Shakespeare Head Press. 2 vols., folio boards. One of 250. $150-$200. Stratford, 1930. Vellum. One of 7 on vellum. Boxed. $1,500-$2,250.

PINKERTON, A. F. *Jim Cummins: or, The Great Adams Express Robbery.* Illustrated. Pictorial cloth. Chicago, 1887. First edition. $75-$125.

PINKERTON, Allan. *The Detective and the Somnambulist.* Frontispiece. Cloth. Chicago, 1875. First edition, first state, with no mention of this book in ads. $75-$100.

PINKERTON, Allan. *The Expressman and the Detective.* Cloth. Chicago, 1874. First edition. $65-$85.

PINKERTON, Allan. *The Spy of the Rebellion.* Illustrated. Cloth. New York, 1883. First edition. $50-$60. Kansas City, 1883. Cloth. $35. Hartford, 1884. Cloth. $35. Hartford, 1885. Cloth. $35.

PINKERTON, Allan. *Tests on Passenger Conductors.* 35 pp., wrappers. Chicago, 1867. First edition. $150-$250. Author's first book.

PINKERTON, William A. *Train Robberies, Train Robbers, and "Hold-up" Men.* Illustrated. Wrappers. Chicago, 1907. First edition. $75-$100. (Note: Adams, in *Six-Guns and Saddle Leather,* lists an undated edition without locating place of publication.)

PINTER, Harold. *The Birthday Party and Other Plays.* Cloth. London, (1960). First edition. In dust jacket. $35-$45.

PINTER, Harold. *The Caretaker.* Cloth. London, (1960). First edition. In dust jacket. $30-$45.

PINTER, Harold. *Five Screen Plays.* Cloth. London, 1971. One of 150, signed. $50.

PINTER, Harold. *The Homecoming.* Cloth. London, (1965). First edition. In dust jacket. $45-$60.

PINTER, Harold. *No Man's Land.* Cloth. London, (1975). First edition. One of 150, signed. $30-$45.

PINTER, Harold. *Old Times.* Cloth. London, 1971. One of 150, signed. $50-$75.

PINTER, Harold. *Poems.* Half red morocco. London, 1968. First edition. One of 200, signed. With erratum. $50. London, (1971). Half leather. Second edition. One of 100, signed. In acetate dust jacket. $40-$60.

*PIONEERING on the Plains. Journey to Mexico in 1848. The Overland Trip to California.* (Cover title.) Illustrated. 119 pp., wrappers. (Kaukauna, Wis., 1924.) (By Alexander W. McCoy and others.) First edition. $150-$250.

*PIONEERS (The): or, The Sources of the Susquehanna: A Descriptive Tale.* By the Author of *Precaution.* 2 vols., tan boards, paper labels. New York, 1823. (By James Fenimore Cooper.) First edition, first issue, with E. B. Clayton imprint in Vol. 1 and with folio 329 at left side of page in Vol. 2. $300-$500. Second issue. $100-$150. London, 1823. 3 vols., boards. First English edition. $100-$150.

PIOZZI, Hester Lynch. *Piozzi Marginalia.* Edited by Percival Merritt. Boards and cloth. Cambridge, 1925. One of 75. $75-$100.

PITMAN, Benn (reporter). *The Assassination of President Lincoln and the Trial of the Conspirators.* Illustrated. Cloth. Cincinnati, 1865. First edition. $75-$100.

PITMAN, Benn (reporter). *The Trials for Treason at Indianapolis.* Illustrated. Cloth. Cincinnati, 1865. First edition. $75-$100.

*PITTSBURGH Business Directory.* Cloth, paper label. Pittsburgh, 1837. (By Isaac Harris.) With errata leaf. $125-$150.

"*PLAIN OR Ringlets?*" 13 colored plates. Other illustrations by John Leech. 13 parts in 12, wrappers. London, 1859-60. (By Robert Smith Surtees.) First edition. $400-$550. London, 1860. Pictorial cloth. First book edition. $150-$200.

*PLAIN Speaker (The): Opinions on Books, Men, and Things.* 2 vols., boards, paper labels. London, 1826. (By William Hazlitt.) First collected edition. $200-$300.

PLATH, Sylvia. See Lucas, Victoria. Also, see *A Winter Ship.*

PLATH, Sylvia. *Ariel.* Cloth. London, (1965). First edition. In dust jacket. $60-$85. New York, (1966). Cloth. First American edition. In dust jacket. $35.

PLATH, Sylvia. *The Colossus.* Cloth. London, (1960). First edition. In dust jacket. $100-$125. Author's first book (aside from the leaflet *A Winter Ship*). New York, 1962. Cloth. First American edition. In dust jacket. $50-$75.

PLATH, Sylvia. *Crystal Gazer and Other Poems.* Buckram and boards. London, 1971. Rainbow Press. One of 400 copies. In slipcase. $125-$150.

PLATH, Sylvia. *Fiesta Melons.* Cloth. Exeter, 1971. First edition. One of 150. In dust jacket. $50-$75.

PLATH, Sylvia. *Lyonnesse.* Leather and boards. London, 1971. Rainbow Press. First edition. One of 400. In slipcase. $75-$85.

PLATH, Sylvia. *Million Dollar Month.* Stiff wrappers. Frensham, England, (1971). First edition. One of 500. $35-$50.

PLATH, Sylvia. *Pursuit.* Drawings and an etching by Leonard Baskin. Morocco. (Cambridge), 1973. Rainbow Press. One of 100, with signed frontispiece by Baskin. Boxed. $175-$250.

PLATH, Sylvia. *Three Women: A Monologue for Three Voices.* Illustrated. White cloth. London, 1968. First edition. One of 150 numbered copies (of an edition of 185). $50-$75. Another issue: Boards and leather. One of 5 on handmade paper. $500-$750.

PLATH, Sylvia. *Uncollected Poems.* Facsimile. Wrappers. London, (1965). Turret Books. First edition. One of 150. $150-$200.

PLATH, Sylvia. *Wreath for a Bridal.* Stiff wrappers. Frensham, (1970). First edition. One of 100. In tissue dust jacket. $50-$75.

PLATO. *The Phaedo of Plato.* Translated by William Jowett. Title and initials in red. Buckram. Waltham Saint Lawrence, England, 1930. Golden Cockerel Press. With letter laid in calling attention to error of translator's name as William instead of Benjamin. $100-$125.

PLATT, P.L., and Slater, N. *The Travelers' Guide Across the Plains, upon the Overland Route to California.* Folding map. 64 pp., printed yellow wrappers. Chicago, 1852. First edition. $7,500 and up. (Note, reprinted from the second edition of this *Handbook:* Only one perfect copy is known—in the Newberry Library, Chicago—and the only other complete copy lacks part of the map. Both copies were found through my syndicated column "Gold in Your Attic," published from 1957 to 1971. The Streeter copy, the only one known prior to these discoveries, lacked the first 16 pages, including the title page, and the bibliographer Wright Howes had guessed—incorrectly in both instances—that it was published in "English Prairie, Ill.," as suggested by the map, in 1854. It was sold at the Streeter auction in 1968 for $1,800. Addendum, as of 1978: Another copy, condition not known to me, is said to have been found a few years ago, but I am not informed if this is true.) San Francisco, 1963. Edited by Dale Morgan. Illustrated. Black boards, orange cloth spine. Second edition. In acetate dust jacket. $50.

PLEASANTS, J. Hall, and Sill, Howard. *Maryland Silversmiths, 1715-1830.* Illustrated. Half cloth. Baltimore, 1930. One of 300. $250-$350.

PLEASANTS, W. J. *Twice Across the Plains, 1849-1856.* 10 plates, 2 portraits. Pictorial green cloth. San Francisco, 1906. First edition. $400-$600.

PLIMPTON, Florus B. *The Lost Child.* (Cover title.) 79 pp., wrappers. Cleveland, 1852. First edition. $200-$300.

PLOMER, William. *Address Given at the Memorial Service for Ian Fleming.* Black cloth, paper label. (London), 1962. First edition. In dust jacket. $50-$75.

PLOMER, William. *The Fivefold Screen.* Black cloth. London, 1932. First edition. One of 450, signed. In dust jacket. $30-$40.

PLOMER, William. *Sado.* Orange cloth. London, 1931. First edition. In dust jacket. $30-$40.

PLOMER, William. *Selected Poems.* Cloth. London, (1940). First edition. In dust jacket. $25.

PLOMER, William. *Turbott Wolfe.* Cloth. London, 1925. First edition. $60-$80.

PLUMBE, John, Jr. *Sketches of Iowa and Wisconsin.* Folding map on thin paper. 103 pp., printed wrappers. St. Louis, 1839. First edition. $2,250-$2,500.

POE, Edgar Allan. *See The Narrative of Arthur Gordon Pym; Tamerlane and Other Poems.*

POE, Edgar Allan, *Al Aaraaf, Tamerlane, and Minor Poems.* Blue or reddish-tan boards, ivory paper spine. Baltimore, 1829. First edition. (Some copies misdated 1820 on title page; a few also stitched, without covers.) $50,000 and up. Also, stitched, without covers, $40,000 (A, 1974); boards, $1,600 (A, 1954); $1,100 and $1,250 (A, 1947); stitched, $2,000 (A, 1954) and same copy, $3,100 (A, 1939); "first edition, early issue, bound with 5 others, half roan on marbled boards of circa 1840," $10,000 (A, 1968).

POE, Edgar Allan. *The Bells and Other Poems.* 28 color plates by Edmund Dulac. Folio, decorated vellum with silk ties. London, (about 1912). One of 750 large paper copies, signed by Dulac. $300-$400. Another issue, unsigned. $150-$200.

POE, Edgar Allan. *The Conchologist's First Book.* Illustrated. Printed pictorial boards, leather spine. Philadelphia, 1839. First edition, first state, with snail plates in color. $400 and up. Also, plates uncolored, $175 (A, 1974).

POE, Edgar Allan. *Edgar Allan Poe Letters Till Now Unpublished in the Valentine Museum, First edition.* One of 1,550. $50-$75.

POE, Edgar Allan. *Eureka: A Prose Poem.* Black cloth. New York, 1848. First edition, with 12 or 16 pages of ads at end. $400-$500, possibly more. Also, $225 (A, 1974).

POE, Edgar Allan. *The Fall of House of Usher.* Illustrated. Printed wrappers. Paris, 1928. Black Sun Press. One of 300. $100-$150. Aaastricht, Holland, 1930. Illustrated. Cloth. $100-$150.

POE, Edgar Allan. *Histoires Extraordinaires.* Par Edgar Poe. Translated by Charles Baudelaire. Wrappers. Paris, 1856. First edition in French of Poe's *Tales.* $400-$500. Paris, 1857. (As *Nouvelles Histoires Extraordinaires.*) Wrappers. $300-$400. Paris, 1927-28. Etchings. 4 vols., morocco. One of 10 on Hollande paper. $1,000-$1,250.

POE, Edgar Allan. *Histoires Grotesques et Sérieuses.* Translated by Charles Baudelaire. Half leather. Paris, 1865. $300-$400.

POE, Edgar Allan. *The Journal of Julius Rodman.* Colored illustrations. Half cloth and boards. San Francisco, 1947. Grabhorn printing. One of 500. $50-$75.

POE, Edgar Allan. *La Chute de la Maison Usher.* Translated by Charles Baudelaire. Illustrated. Three-quarters morocco. Paris, 1922. One of 72 on Japan paper. $400-$500, possibly more.

POE, Edgar Allan. *Mesmerism: "In Articulo Mortis."* 16 pp., stitched, without covers. London, 1846. First edition. $300-$600.

POE, Edgar Allan. *Murders in the Rue Morgue.* Facsimile of Drexel Institute manuscript. 2 water colors. Folio, half morocco. Philadelphia, (1895). $100-$150. Antibes, (1958). Allen Press. Boards. One of 150. $150-$175. Also see Poe, *The Prose Romances.*

POE, Edgar Allan. *Poems.* Pale-green cloth. New York, 1831. Second edition (so identified on title page, but actually the first edition). $10,000-$15,000. Also, stained, binding detached, $6,250 (A, 1966). London, 1881. Cloth. One of 50 on large paper. $150-$200. Brussels, 188. (sic.—actually 1888). Translated by Mallarmé. Illustrated by Manet. Wrappers. $750-$1,000. Brussels, 1897. Wrappers. One of 500. $200 and up. New York, 1943. Limited Editions Club. Boxed. $40-$50.

POE, Edgar Allan. *The Prose Romances of Edgar A. Poe, etc. Uniform Serial Edition . . . No. 1. Containing the Murders in the Rue Morgue, and The Man That Was Used Up.* 40 pp., wrappers. Philadelphia, 1843. First edition. $25,000-$50,000. Also, in facsimile wrappers, $20,000 (A, 1974); in (original?) wrappers, stained and torn, $20,000 (A, 1973). Also see Poe, *Murders in the Rue Morgue.*

POE, Edgar, Allan. *The Raven and Other Poems.* Printed wrappers, or cloth. New York, 1845. First edition, first issue, with "T. B. Smith, Stereotyper" on copyright page. $3,000-$4,000. Also, defective, $2,300 (A, 1974). London, 1846. Cloth. First English edition, with new title page tipped in over sheets of the American first. $600-$800. New York, 1884. Edited by E. C. Stedman. 26 plates by Gustave Doré. Folio, pictorial cloth. $100-$125. London, 1901. Vellum with ties. One of 50 on vellum. $100-$150. New York, 1906. Illustrated by Galen J. Perrett. Morocco. One of 26. $300-$400.

POE, Edgar Allan. *The Raven and Other Poems. (&) Tales.* 2 vols. in one, dark blue cloth. New York, 1845. First edition of each work in the one-volume format; first issue of *The Raven* (see preceding entry) and third issue of *Tales* (see entry following), without stereotyper's slug. $1,500-$2,000.

POE, Edgar Allan. *Some Letters of Edgar Allan Poe to E. H. N. Patterson of Oquawka, Illinois.* Edited by Eugene Field. Folio, cloth. Chicago, 1898. Caxton Club. One of 186. Boxed. $150-$200. (Note: Poe reportedly sent about five copies of his *Murders in the Rue Morgue* to this rural Illinois friend. They have never been found.)

POE, Edgar Allan. *Tales.* Printed buff wrappers, or cloth. New York, 1845. First edition, first state, with T. B. Smith and H. Ludwig slugs on copyright page, 12 pp. of ads at back. $3,500-$5,000. Later state, without Smith and Ludwig lines, rebound in morocco, $200 (A, 1972).

POE, Edgar Allan. *Tales of the Grotesque and Arabesque.* 2 vols., purplish cloth, paper labels. Philadelphia, 1840. First edition, first issue, with page 213 in Vol. 2 wrongly numbered 231. $7,500 and up. Also, rubbed, issue not stated, $1,500 (A, 1975). Second issue, page 213 correctly numbered. $2,500-$5,000. Also, $1,400 (A, 1974). Another issue: 2 vols. in one. Page 213 correctly numbered, 4 pages of ads bound in at end. $7,500 and up. Also, in contemporary leather, $5,000 (A, 1967). Chicago, 1930. Lakeside Press. Full morocco. One of 1,000. $150-$200.

POE, Edgar Allan. *Tales of Mystery and Imagination.* Illustrated by Harry Clarke. Pictorial vellum. London, 1919. One of 170 signed by Clarke. $350-$400. New York, 1936. Cloth. First American edition with the Clarke illustrations. In dust jacket. $150-$225. London, (1935). Illustrated by Arthur Rackham. Full pictorial vellum. One of 460 signed by Rackham. $450-$550. Philadelphia, (1935). First trade edition. In dust jacket. $150-$200. New York, 1941. Limited Editions Club. $50-$60.

POEMS. Wrappers. (London, 1906.) Chiswick Press. (By Siegfried Sassoon.) First edition. $500 and up. Also, inscribed, $2,743 (A, 1975). Author's first book. London, (1911). Wrappers. One of 35, signed. $500-$750.

POEMS and Ballads of Young Ireland. White cloth. Dublin, 1888. First edition. $250-$300. (Note: Contains four contributions by William Butler Yeats.)

POEMS by Two Brothers. Drab boards, paper label. London, (1827). (By Alfred, Charles and Frederick Tennyson.) First edition. $1,250-$1,500. Also, spine split, $1,000 (A, 1974). Alfred Tennyson's first book.

POEMS Chiefly in the Scottish Dialect. By a Native of Scotland. Contemporary calf. Washington, Pa., 1801. (By David Bruce.) First edition. $400-$500. (Note: Contains original material also by H. H. Brackenridge.)

POEMS from the Arabic and Persian. Sewed. Warwick, England, 1800. (By Walter Savage Landor.) First edition, first issue, with "Rivington" in imprint and 10 leaves only. $200-$250. Second issue, without "Rivington" in imprint, 12 leaves. $150-$200.

POEMS of Child Labor. Wrappers. New York, 1924. First edition. $75-$100. (Note: Published by the National Child Labor Committee; includes a poem by Robert Frost.)

POEMS of Two Friends. Brown cloth. Columbus, Ohio, 1860. (By William Dean Howells and John J. Piatt.) First edition. $400. Also, $275 (A, 1977). Howells' first book.

POEMS on Various Occasions. Gray-green boards, pink label lettered "Poems." Newark, (England), 1807. (By George Gordon Noel, Lord Byron.) First edition. $1,000 and up.

POET at the Breakfast-Table (The). Cloth. Boston, 1872. (By Oliver Wendell Holmes.) First edition, first state, with "Talle" for "Table" in the running head on page 9. $100-$150.

POETRY by the Author of "Gebir." 111 pp., sewed. Warwick, England, (1800). (By Walter Savage Landor.) First (suppressed) edition, with pages 65-111, later suppressed, intact. $500 and up. London, 1802. Blue wrappers. First published edition, first issue, with Sharpe's imprint stamped by hand on page 64, where the text ends. $200 and up.

*POETRY for Children, Entirely Original.* Illustrated. 2 vols., green boards, red leather spines. London, 1809. (By Charles and Mary Lamb.) First edition. $1,000 and up. (Note: A very rare book, with auction records of $2,200 in 1900, $3,300 in 1920, and $375 in 1941. A defective copy with title leaf in Vol. 2 from another copy brought $620 at auction in 1976, but no fine copies have appeared for sale in many years.) Boston, 1812. Marble-backed boards. First American edition. $250-$500.

*POET'S PACK (The), Of George Washington High School.* By Members of The Poetry Club and the Poetry Class, 1927-1931. Cloth. New York, 1932. Contains first four book-published poems by Delmore Schwartz. First edition. $50-$75.

POLK, James K. *Message of the President of the United States in Relation to the Indian Difficulties in Oregon . . . March 29, 1848.* (Caption title.) (Washington, 1848.) $50-$75.

POLLARD, Alfred W. *An Essay on Colophons.* Folio, half vellum. Chicago, 1905. Caxton Club. One of 252. Boxed. $150-$200.

POLLARD, Alfred W. *Fine Books.* 40 plates. Cloth. London, 1912. First edition. In dust jacket. $75-$100. New York, 1912. Plates. Cloth. First American edition. In dust jacket. $75-$100.

POLLARD, Alfred W. *Last Words on the History of the Title-Page.* Colored frontispiece and facsimiles. Folio, buckram. London, 1891. One of 260. $100-$125.

POLLARD, Alfred W. *Records of the English Bible.* Cloth. London, 1911. First edition. $100-$125.

POLLARD, Alfred W. *Shakespeare Folios and Quartos.* Illustrated. Boards. London, 1909. First edition. $150.

POLLARD, Edward A. *The First Year of the War.* 374 pp., printed wrappers. Richmond, 1862. First edition. $100-$150.

POLLARD, Edward A. *The Lost Cause.* Folding map in color. Cloth. New York, 1867. First edition. $40-$75.

POLLARD, Edward A. *Observations in the North.* 142 pp., wrappers. Richmond, 1865. First edition. $300-$400.

POLLARD, Edward A. *The Seven Days' Battles in Front of Richmond.* 45 pp., printed wrappers. Richmond, 1862. First edition. $350-$400.

POLLARD, Edward A. *The Southern Spy.* 103 pp., wrappers. Richmond, 1861. First edition. $150-$200.

POLLARD, Hugh B. C. *A History of Firearms.* Illustrated. Cloth. London, 1926. $125-$175. London, 1930. $100-$125. London, 1933. $100-$125.

POLLARD, Hugh B. C., and Barclay-Smith, Phyllis. *British and American Game-Birds.* Illustrated. Half leather. New York, 1939. Derrydale Press. First edition. One of 125. $250-$350. London, 1945. Half leather. $125.

POLLEY, J. B. *Hood's Texas Brigade.* 25 plates. Cloth. New York, 1910. First edition. $350-$450.

POLLEY, J. B. *A Soldier's Letters to Charming Nellie.* 16 plates. Cloth. New York, 1908. First edition. $200-$250.

*POLONIUS: A Collection of Wise Saws and Modern Instances.* Green cloth. London, 1852. (By Edward Fitz Gerald.) First edition. $100-$150.

POOLE, Ernest. *The Harbor.* New York, 1915. First edition. In dust jacket. $35-$50.

POOLE, Ernest. *Katharine Breshovsky: For Russia's Freedom.* Pictorial boards. Chicago, 1905. First edition. $75-$100. Author's first book.

POOR, M. C. *Denver, South Park and Pacific.* Illustrated, with map in pocket. Cloth. Denver, 1949. First edition. One of 1,000, signed. In dust jacket. $350-$400. (A passing note on the increased prices of books on railroading: I purchased a copy of this from a dealer's catalogue at $15 about 12 years ago.)

*POOR Sarah.* 18 pp., sewed. (Park Hill, Indian Territory, Oklahoma), 1943. Park Hill Mission Press. $100 and up. (Note: Originally this story of "a pious Indian woman" was a publication of the American Tract Society of New York.)

POORE, Ben Perley. *A Descriptive Catalogue of the Government Publications of the United States.* Cloth. Washington, 1885. $100-$125. New York, 1962. 2 vols., cloth. $100-$125.

POPE, Alexander. *The Rape of the Lock.* Illustrated by Aubrey Beardsley. Cloth. London, 1896. $150-$200.

POPE, Saxton. *Hunting with the Bow and Arrow.* Illustrated. Boards and cloth. (San Francisco, 1923.) First edition. $50-$60.

*POPERY, British and Foreign.* Printed wrappers. London, 1851. (By Walter Savage Landor.) First edition. $100-$150.

PORTALIS, Baron Roger (editor). *Researches Concerning Jean Grolier, His Life and His Library.* Illustrated. Three-quarters morocco. New York, 1907. Grolier Club. One of 300. Boxed. $200-$250.

PORTER, Edwin H. *The Fall River Tragedy.* Plates. Cloth. Fall River, Mass., 1893. First edition. $50-$60.

PORTER, Eleanor H. *Pollyanna.* Illustrated. Pink silk cloth. Boston, 1913. First edition. $200-$300. Also, $200 (A, 1976). Later, green cloth, $50-$75. London, 1913. Blue cloth, pictorial cover label. First English edition. $50-$75.

PORTER, Gene Stratton. *Birds of the Bible.* Illustrated. Pictorial cloth. Cincinnati, (1909). First edition. $75.

PORTER, Gene Stratton. *Friends in Feathers.* Pictorial cloth. Garden City, 1917. First edition. $75.

PORTER, Gene Stratton. *The Song of the Cardinal.* Illustrated by the author's camera studies. Buckram. Indianapolis, (1903). First edition. $50-$60. Author's first book.

PORTER, Jane. *The Scottish Chiefs: A Romance.* 5 vols., boards. London, 1810. First edition, with errata leaf at end of Vol. 1. $400-$500.

PORTER, Katherine Anne. See F., M. T.

PORTER, Katherine Anne. *A Christmas Story.* Illustrated by Ben Shahn. Oblong cloth. New York, (1967). One of 500, signed by both author and artist. $85-$100.

PORTER, Katherine Anne. *Flowering Judas.* Boards and cloth. New York, (1930). First edition. One of 600. In glassine dust jacket. $125-$150. New York, (1935). Cloth. First augmented edition, first printing. In dust jacket. $40-$60 .

PORTER, Katherine Anne. *French Song Book.* Blue boards and cloth. (Paris, 1933.) First edition. One of 595, signed. In dust jacket. $200-$300. Another issue: One of 15 on Spanish paper, signed. $350-$450.

PORTER, Katherine Anne. *Hacienda.* Cloth. (New York, 1934.) First edition. One of 895, signed. With errata slip. Boxed. $150-$175.

PORTER, Katherine Anne. *The Leaning Tower and Other Stories.* Cloth. New York, (1944). First edition. In dust jacket. $25-$35.

PORTER, Katherine Anne. *Noon Wine.* Decorated boards, paper label. Detroit, 1937. First edition. One of 250, signed. Boxed. $125-$175.

PORTER, Katherine Anne. *Outline of Mexican Popular Arts and Crafts.* Cloth. (Los Angeles), 1922. First edition. $300-$400.

PORTER, Katherine Anne. *Pale Horse, Pale Rider.* Light-blue cloth. New York, (1939). First edition, first printing (so indicated). In dust jacket. $50-$75.

PORTER, Katherine Anne. *Selected Short Stories.* Wrappers. (New York, 1945.) Armed Services Edition. $25-$35.

PORTER, Katherine Anne (translator). *The Itching Parrot.* By José Joaquín Fernández de Lizardi. Cloth. New York, 1942. First edition. In dust jacket. $50.

PORTER, Lavinia Honeyman. *By Ox Team to California.* Portrait. Cloth. Oakland, 1910. First edition. One of 50. $450-$600.

PORTER, William Sidney (or, later, Sydney). See Henry, O. Also see *The O. Henry Calendar.*

*PORTRAIT and Biographical Album of Henry County, Iowa.* Three-quarters leather. Chicago, 1888. $125-$150.

*PORTRAIT and Biographical Album of Jo Daviess County, Illinois.* Three-quarters leather. Chicago, 1889. $125-$150.

*PORTRAIT and Biographical Album of Otoe and Cass Counties, Nebraska.* Three-quarters leather. Chicago, 1889. $150-$175.

*PORTRAIT and Biographical Album of Will County, Illinois.* Three-quarters leather. Chicago, 1890. $100-$125.

*PORTRAIT and Biographical Record of Dickinson, Saline, McPherson and Marion Counties, Kansas.* Three-quarters leather. Chicago, 1893. $150-$175.

*PORTRAIT and Biographical Record of Sheboygan County, Wisconsin.* Three-quarters leather. Chicago, 1894. $100-$125.

POSEY, Alex. *The Poems of Alex Posey, Creek Indian Poet.* Arranged by Mrs. Minnie L. Posey. Cloth. Topeka, 1910. First edition. $35-$50.

POSNER, David. *Love as Image.* Wrappers. London, 1952. First edition. One of 150. $75-$100.

POSNER, David. *A Rake's Progress.* 17 plates. Half cloth. London, (1967). First edition, with errata leaf. $150-$200.

POSNER, David. *S'un Casto Amor.* Wrappers. Oxford, 1953. First edition. One of 30. $150.

POST, Melville Davisson. *The Corrector of Destinies.* Cloth. New York, (1908). First edition. In dust jacket. $150-$175. Lacking jacket, $100-$125.

POST, Melville Davisson. *Uncle Abner.* Cloth. New York, 1918. First edition. In dust jacket. $150-$175. Lacking jacket, $100-$125.

POSTON, Charles D. *Apache Land.* Portrait and views. Cloth. San Francisco, 1878. First edition. $125-$175.

POSTON, Charles D. *Speech of the Hon. Charles D. Poston, of Arizona, on Indian Affairs.* 20 pp., printed wrappers. New York, 1865. $750-$850.

*POSTSCRIPT to the Statement Respecting the Earl of Selkirk's Settlement Upon the Red River, in North America.* (Caption title.) 28 pp. (195-222), plain wrappers. (Montreal, 1818.) (By John Halkett.) $500-$750. Also, $450 (A, 1969).

POTT, J. S. *A Plain Statement of Fact, etc.* (Claims of Florida inhabitants against British forces.) 16 pp., half morocco. London, 1838. $200-$250.

POTTER, Beatrix. *Ginger and Pickles.* Illustrated by the author. Pictorial boards. London, 1909. First edition. $75-$100. New York, 1909. Boards. First American edition. $35-$50.

POTTER, Beatrix. *The Pie and the Patty-Pan.* Illustrated in color by the author. Pictorial boards. London, 1905. First edition. $100-$125. New York, 1905. Illustrated. Boards. $20-$40.

POTTER, Beatrix. *The Roly-Poly Pudding.* Illustrated in color by the author. Cloth. London. (1908). First edition. $100-$150.

POTTER, Beatrix. *The Story of the Fierce Bad Rabbit.* Illustrated by the author. Panoramic wallet-style cloth binding. London, 1906. First edition. $150-$250.

POTTER, Beatrix. *The Story of Miss Moppet.* Illustrated by the author. Panoramic wallet-style cloth. London, 1906. First edition. $200-$300.

POTTER, Beatrix. *The Tailor of Gloucester.* Frontispiece, 15 color illustrations by the author. Pink boards, rounded spine. (London, 1902.) First trade edition, with misprints on pages 26 and 34. $500 and up. Also, $420 (A, 1977). Another edition, privately printed: (London, 1902). Limited to 500. $900 and up.

POTTER, Beatrix. *The Tale of Benjamin Bunny.* Illustrated in color by the author. Boards. London, 1904. First edition. $150-$250.

POTTER, Beatrix. *The Tale of the Flopsy Bunnies.* Illustrated in color by the author. Boards. London, 1909. First edition. $100-$150.

POTTER, Beatrix. *The Tale of Mrs. Tiggy-Winkle.* Frontispiece and 26 colored illustrations by the author. Boards. London, 1905. First edition. $150-$200.

POTTER, Beatrix. *The Tale of Peter Rabbit.* Colored frontispiece, 41 illustrations in black and white by the author. Boards, flat spine. London, (1901). First edition; with copyright undated (privately printed). One of 250. $2,000 and up. Also, $1,840 (A, 1977). (London), 1902. Boards, rounded spine. First edition, second issue (also privately printed). One of 200. $1,250 and up. London, 1902. First published edition (trade edition). $300-$400. Also, $200 (A, 1977).

POTTER, Beatrix. *The Tale of Pigling Bland.* Illustrated in color by the author. Boards. London, 1913. First edition. $100-$150.

POTTER, Beatrix. *Wag-by-Wall.* Illustrated. Cloth. London, 1944. One of 100. In dust jacket. $350-$500.

POTTER, Jack. *Lead Steer and Other Tales.* Illustrated. Pictorial wrappers. Clayton, N. M., 1939. First edition. $40-$50.

POTTER, Theodore Edgar. *Autobiography.* 3 portraits. Cloth. (Concord, N.H., 1913.) First edition. $50-$60.

POTTLE, Frederick A. *Boswell and the Girl from Botany Bay.* Boards and cloth. New York, 1937. One of 500. In dust jacket. $35-$50.

POTTLE, Frederick A. *The Literary Career of James Boswell.* Cloth. Oxford, 1929. First edition. In dust jacket. $50-$60.

POUND, Ezra. See P.,E.; Bosschere, Jean de; Cavalcanti, Guido; Fenollosa, Ernest; Thornton, Richard. Also, see *The Book of the Poets' Club; The Catholic Anthology; Des Imagistes.*

POUND, Ezra. *A Lume Spento.* Green wrappers. (Venice), 1908. First edition. $6,500-$7,500. Also, an inscribed and corrected presentation copy, $18,000 (A, 1977). Author's first book. Milan, (1958). Stiff gray wrappers. One of 2,000. In dust jacket. $50. (New York, 1965.) First American edition. $35.

POUND, Ezra. *ABC of Reading.* Red cloth. London, 1934. First edition. In dust jacket. $100-$150. New Haven, 1934. Green cloth. First American edition. In dust jacket. $75-$100. Norfolk, Conn., 1951. New Directions. Cloth. In dust jacket. $15-$20.

POUND, Ezra. *Antheil and the Treatise on Harmony.* Red wrappers. Paris, 1924. Three Mountains Press. First edition. One of 40 on Arches paper. $400-$500. Also, $375 (A, 1977). Ordinary issue: One of 560. $250-$300. Chicago, 1927. Brown cloth. First American edition. In dust jacket. $50-$75.

POUND, Ezra. *Antologia.* Wrappers. Rome, 1956. One of 100. $150-$200.

POUND, Ezra. *Canto CX.* Frontispiece drawing of Pound. Wrappers. (Cambridge, 1965.) First edition. One of 80. $100-$150.

POUND, Ezra. *Cantos LII-LXXI.* Black cloth. London, (1940). First edition. In dust jacket. $100-$150. Norfolk, (1940). Black cloth. First American edition. One of 500 with envelope and pamphlet, *Notes on Ezra Pound's Cantos, Structure and Rhetoric.* $75-$100. Another issue: One of 500 without the envelope. $50-$60.

POUND, Ezra. *Canzoni.* Gray cloth. London, 1911. First edition, first binding. $200-$300.

POUND Ezra. *Canzoni & Ripostes.* Brown boards, London, 1913. (First edition sheets of *Canzoni* and *Ripostes* bound with new title page and half title.) $100-$150.

POUND, Ezra. *Carta da Visita.* Decorated wrappers. (Rome), 1942. First edition. $100-$150.

POUND, Ezra. *Diptych Rome–London.* Folio, boards. (Norfolk, 1957—actually 1958.) New Directions. One of 125, signed. Boxed. $400-$500. (London, 1957, i.e. 1958). Faber & Faber. One of 50, signed. $400-$500. Milan, (1957, i.e. 1958). One of 25, signed. $400-$500. (These books were issued simultaneously as part of a total edition of 200 produced at the Officina Bodoni in Verona, Italy.)

POUND, Ezra. *A Draft of the Cantos 17-27.* Initials by Gladys Hynes. Folio, red vellum boards. London, 1928. First edition. One of 70 on Roma paper. $1,000-$1,500. Also, $950 (A, 1977). (There were also 4 copies on vellum, signed by the author and the artist, 5 on Japan paper, signed by Pound, 15 on Whatman paper. The 15 on Whatman paper were bound in green vellum, the others being variously bound or unbound, according to the Pound bibliographer Donald M . Gallup.)

POUND, Ezra. *A Draft of the Cantos XXXI-XLI.* Black cloth. London, (1935). First English edition (of *Eleven New Cantos*). In dust jacket. $50-$60.

POUND, Ezra. *A Draft of XVI. Cantos.* Three-quarters white vellum and boards (later in red vellum). Paris, 1925. First edition. One of 70 on Roma paper (of an edition of 90). $2,750-$3,000. Another issue: One of 15 on Whatman paper. $3,000 and up. (A few copies were in folded, gathered, unbound sheets. There were also 5 copies on Japan paper, signed by Pound. Value: obviously higher, but I have no record.)

POUND, Ezra. *A Draft of XXX Cantos.* Beige linen. Paris, 1930. Hours Press. One of 200. $750-$1,000. Also, $800 (A, 1977). Another issue: Red-orange leather. One of 10 on Texas Mountain paper, signed. $2,750 (A, 1977). (Note: There were also 2 on vellum for Pound.) New York, (1933). Black cloth. First American edition. In dust jacket. $200-$300. London, (1933). Black cloth. First English edition. In dust jacket. $150-$200.

POUND, Ezra. *Drafts and Fragments of Cantos CX-CXVII.* Folio, red cloth, paper labels; New York, (1968). New Directions and Stone Wall Press. First edition. With errata slip. One of 310, signed. Boxed. $300-$400. Also, $300 (A, 1977). New York, 1968. Cloth. Trade edition. In dust jacket. $10-$12.50.

POUND, Ezra. *Eleven New Cantos XXXI-XLI.* Black cloth. New York, (1934). First edition. In dust jacket. $75-$100. Norfolk, (1940). Black cloth. In dust jacket. $35-$50.

POUND, Ezra. *Exultations.* Maroon boards. London, 1909. First edition. $200-$250. Also, $200 (A, 1977).

POUND, Ezra. *The Fifth Decad of Cantos.* Black cloth. London, (1937). First edition. In dust jacket. $100-$125. New York, (1937). Black cloth. First American edition. In dust jacket. $50-75.

POUND, Ezra. *Gaudier-Brzeska: A Memoir.* Illustrated. Gray-green cloth. London, 1916.

First edition. $150-200. American issue: Olive green cloth. $100-$150. London, (1939). Green cloth. $100-$125. Milan, (1957). Wrappers. First state, with "Episten" uncorrected. $50-$75.

POUND, Ezra. *Homage to Sextus Propertius*. Blue boards. London, (1934). First separate edition. In dust jacket. $75-$100.

POUND, Ezra. *How to Read*. Red cloth. London, (1931). First edition. In dust jacket. $75-$100. Le Beausset, France, (1932). Wrappers. $150.

POUND, Ezra. *Imaginary Letters*. Stiff printed white wrappers. Paris, 1930. Black Sun Press. First edition. One of 300. In glassine dust jacket. Boxed. $125-$175. Another issue: One of 50 on vellum, signed. Boxed. $500-$750. (There were also 25 copies not for sale.)

POUND, Ezra. *Indiscretions; or, Une Revue de Deux Mondes*. Gray boards and yellow cloth. Paris, 1923. Three Mountains Press. First edition. (300 printed.) $300-$400. Also, $275 (A, 1977); proof copy, unbound, $308 (A, 1966).

POUND, Ezra. *Instigations*. Blue cloth. New York, (1920). First edition. In dust jacket. $150-$200.

POUND, Ezra. *Lustra*. Frontispiece portrait. Tan cloth. (London, 1916.) First edition. One of 200. $250-$350. London, 1916. Tan cloth. Second impression, with altered text. $100-$125. New York, 1917. Blue cloth. First American edition. One of 60. In dust jacket. $250-$300. Second impression: Yellow boards. In dust jacket. $100-$175.

POUND, Ezra. *Make it New: Essays*. Green cloth. London, (1934). First edition. In dust jacket. $150. New Haven, 1935. Tan cloth. First American edition. In dust jacket. $80-$100.

POUND, Ezra. *Patria Mia*. Brown cloth. Chicago, (1950). First edition. In dust jacket. $35-$50.

POUND, Ezra. *Pavannes and Divagations*. Brown cloth. (Norfolk, 1958.) New Directions. First edition. In dust jacket. $25-$35.

POUND, Ezra. *Pavannes and Divisions*. Frontispiece. Dark-blue cloth. New York, 1918. First edition, first binding. In dust jacket. $125-$150. Later binding, gray cloth, same date. In dust jacket. $80-$100.

POUND, Ezra. *Personae*. Drab boards. London, 1909. First edition, first issue (with binding as described). $175-$225. New York, 1926. Dark blue cloth. First American edition. In dust jacket. $150.

POUND, Ezra. *Personae and Exultations*. Boards, London, 1913. First (combined) edition. In glassine dust jacket. $100-$150.

POUND, Ezra. *The Pisan Cantos*. Black cloth. (New York, 1948.) First edition. In dust jacket. $50-$75. London, (1949). Black cloth. First English edition. In dust jacket. $50

POUND, Ezra. *Poems 1918-1921, Including Three Portraits and Four Cantos*. Boards and vellum. New York, (1921). First edition. In dust jacket. $150-$250.

POUND, Ezra. *Polite Essays*. Red cloth. London, (1937). First edition. In dust jacket. $75-$100.

POUND, Ezra. *Provenca: Poems Selected from "Personae," "Exultations and "Canzoniere."* Tan boards. Boston, (1910). First edition, first issue, with boards stamped in dark brown instead of green. In dust jacket. $300-$350.

POUND, Ezra. *Quia Pauper Amavi*. Boards and cloth, paper label. London, (1919). Egoist, Ltd. First edition. One of 110 on handmade paper, signed. (Issued without dust jacket.) $750-$1,000. Also, $200 (A, 1977). First trade edition: One of 500. $125-$150.

POUND, Ezra. *A Quinzaine for This Yule*. Wrappers. (London, 1908.) First edition, first issue, with "Weston St. Llewmy" for "Weston St. Llewmys" in line 6 on page 21. $750-$1,000. Second issue, corrected. $500-$750. Also, $308 (A, 1966).

POUND, Ezra. *Redondillas, or Something of That Sort.* Blue boards, linen spine, label. (New York 1967.) New Directions. Grabhorn-Hoyem printing. One of 110, signed. In dust jacket. $400-$500.

POUND, Ezra. *Ripostes.* Streaky gray cloth. London, 1912. First edition. $150-$200. London, 1915. Wrappers. Fourth issue. (400 copies). $100-$125.

POUND, Ezra. *Section: Rock-Drill.* Gray boards. Milan, 1955. First edition. One of 500. (New York, 1956.) Black cloth. First American edition. In dust jacket. $35. London, (1957). Black cloth. First English edition. In dust jacket. $35.

POUND, Ezra. *Selected Poems.* Introduction by T.S. Eliot. Gray boards. London, (1928). First edition. One of 100, signed. $600-$750. Also, $500 (A, 1977). Trade edition: Green cloth. In dust jacket. $85-$100.

POUND, Ezra. *Seventy Cantos.* Black cloth. London, (1950). First English collected edition. In dust jacket. $50-$60.

POUND, Ezra. *The Spirit of Romance.* Olive-brown cloth. London, (1910). First edition, first binding. In dust jacket. $125-$175. Norfolk, (1953). New Directions. Cloth. In dust jacket. $30-$50.

POUND, Ezra. *Thrones.* Tan boards. Milan, 1959. First edition. One of 300. In glassine dust jacket. $75-$125. London, (1960). Red cloth. First English edition. In dust jacket. $30-$40. (Norfolk, 1959). New Directions. Black cloth. First American edition. In dust jacket. $25.

POUND Ezra. *Umbra.* Gray boards and cloth. London, 1920. First edition. In dust jacket. $100-$150. Another issue: Boards, parchment. One of 100, signed. $750-$1,000. Also, $800 (A, 1976).

POUND, Ezra (editor). *Active Anthology.* Red-brown cloth. London, (1933). First edition. In dust jacket. $175-$200.

POUND, Ezra (translator). *Cathay.* Printed wrappers. London, 1915. First edition. $300-$400. Also, $325 (A, 1977).

POUND, Ezra (translator). *Confucius: The Unwobbling Pivot and The Great Digest.* Wrappers. (Norfolk), 1947. New Directions. First edition, without Chinese text. $75-$100. (Norfolk, 1951.) Black cloth. New edition, with Chinese text and with title altered to read *Confucius: The Great Digest and The Unwobbling Pivot.* In dust jacket. $30-$40.

POUND, Ezra (translator). *The Sonnets and Ballate of Guido Cavalcanti.* Boards, vellum paper spine. Boston, (1912). First edition. In dust jacket. $150-$200. Lacking jacket, $125. London, 1912. Gray cloth. First English edition. $75-$100.

POUND, Ezra (translator). *Ta Hio: The Great Learning.* Translated from Confucius' works. Wrappers. Seattle, 1928. First edition. $65-$75. Norfolk, (1936, i.e. 1938). Wrappers. $50.

POWELL, Anthony. *Afternoon Men.* Cloth. London, 1931. First edition. In dust jacket. $75-$100. Author's first novel.

POWELL, Anthony. *Caledonia: A Fragment.* Boards and cloth. London, (1934). First edition. In dust jacket. $100-$150.

POWELL, Anthony. *From a View to a Death.* Cloth. London, 1933. First edition. In dust jacket. $75-$100.

POWELL, Anthony. *Venusberg.* Cloth. London, 1932. First edition. In dust jacket. $50-$75.

POWELL, C. Frank. *Life of Gen. Zachary Taylor.* 96 pp., wrappers. New York, 1846. First edition. $100-$125.

POWELL, H. M. T. *The Santa Fe Trail to California, 1849-1852.* Edited by Douglas S. Watson. Maps and other illustrations. Half morocco. San Francisco, (1931). Grabhorn Press. One of 300. $850-$1,050. Also, $700 and $575 (A, 1977).

POWELL, J. W. *Canyons of the Colorado.* Illustrated, including 10 folding plates. Cloth. Meadville, Pa., 1895. First edition. $250-$350. (About 100 copies printed.)

POWELL, Lawrence Clark. *The Alchemy of Books.* Decorated boards. Los Angeles, (1954). Ward Ritchie Press. First edition. $35-$50.

POWELL, Lawrence Clark. *Robinson Jeffers, the Man and His Work.* Foreword by Robinson Jeffers. Decorations by Rockwell Kent. Cloth, paper label. Los Angeles, 1934. First edition. One of 750. In dust jacket. $50-$75.

POWELL, Willis J. *Tachyhippodamia, or, Art of Quieting Wild Horses in a Few Hours.* Half leather and marbled boards. New Orleans, 1838. First edition. $100-$125.

POWER, Tyrone. *Impressions of America.* 2 plates. 2 vols., boards and linen. London, 1836. First edition. $250-$350. Philadelphia, 1836. 2 vols., cloth. First American edition. $150-$200.

POWERS, J. F. *Prince of Darkness and Other Stories.* Cloth. New York, 1947. First edition. In dust jacket. $40-$60. Author's first book.

POWERS, Stephen. *Afoot and Alone: A Walk from Sea to Sea by the Southern Route.* 12 plates. Cloth. Hartford, 1872. First edition. $150-$250.

*POWESHEIK County, Iowa: A Descriptive Account of Its Climate, Soil, etc.* Woodcut township map. 36 pp., printed wrappers. Montezuma, Iowa, 1865. $300-$350.

POWYS, John Cowper. *Autobiography.* Portrait frontispiece. Brown cloth. London, (1934). First edition. In dust jacket. $40-$50.

POWYS, John Cowper. *Ballads and Other Poems.* Boards. London, 1893. First edition. $80-$100. Author's first book.

POWYS, John Cowper. *Confessions of Two Brothers.* Cloth. Rochester, 1916. First edition. In dust jacket. $40-$60.

POWYS, John Cowper. *Ducdame.* Cloth. London, 1925. First English edition. In dust jacket. $40-$50.

POWYS, John Cowper. *In Defense of Sensuality.* Cloth. London, 1930. First edition. In dust jacket. $50-$60.

POWYS, John Cowper. *Odes and Other Poems.* Cloth. London, 1896. First edition. $200-$300.

POWYS, John Cowper. *The Owl, the Duck and—Miss Rowe! Miss Rowe!* Boards. Chicago, 1930. Black Archer Press. First edition. One of 250, signed. Boxed. $80-$100.

POWYS, John Cowper. *Poems.* Boards. London, 1899. First edition. $175-$250.

POWYS, John Cowper. *Psychoanalysis and Morality..* Half vellum. San Francisco, 1923. Grabhorn printing. One of 500, signed. $60-$75.

POWYS, John Cowper. *Wolf Solent.* 2 vols., cloth. New York, 1929. First edition. In dust jacket. $40-$60.

POWYS, Llewellyn. *The Book of Days.* 12 etchings. Half green morocco. London, 1927. Golden Cockerel Press. One of 55, signed, with an extra set of plates. $250-$400. Ordinary copies (245 of 300): $150-$200.

POWYS, Llewellyn. *Glory of Life.* Woodcuts by Robert Gibbings. Vellum and cloth. (London, 1934.) Golden Cockerel Press. One of 275. $200-$250. Another issue: One of 2 on vellum. $1,000-$1,500.

POWYS, T. F. *Fables.* 4 drawings by Gilbert Spencer. Buckram. London, 1929. One of 750, signed. $50. New York, (1929). Cloth. In dust jacket. $25.

POWYS, T. F. *Goat Green, or The Better Gift.* Half morocco. London, 1937. Golden Cockerel Press. One of 150, signed. $80-$110.

POWYS, T. F. *The House with the Echo.* Cloth. London, 1928. First edition. In dust jacket. $30-$35.

POWYS, T. F. *An Interpretation of Genesis.* Boards. London, 1929. First edition. One of 490, signed. In dust jacket. Boxed. $50-$75. New York, 1929. White boards. First American edition. One of 260, signed. In glassine dust jacket. Boxed. $50-$75.

POWYS, T. F. *The Key of the Field.* Woodcut frontispiece. Buckram. London, 1930. First edition. One of 550, signed. In dust jacket. $60-$75.

POWYS, T. F. *Mr. Weston's Good Wine.* Illustrated. Cloth. London, 1927. One of 660, signed. In dust jacket. $75-$100.

POWYS, T. F. *Soliloquies of a Hermit.* Boards and cloth. London, 1918. First English edition (of *The Soliloquy of a Hermit*). In dust jacket. $50.

POWYS, T. F. *The Soliloquy of a Hermit.* Cloth. New York, 1916. First edition. In dust jacket. $100-$125. Author's first book.

POWYS, T. F. *Two Stories.* Illustrated with wood engravings. Half leather. Hastings, England, 1967. First edition. One of 25 signed by the illustrator Reynolds Stone. In slipcase. $100-$150.

POWYS, T. F. *The Two Thieves.* Half cloth. London, 1932. First edition. One of 85 signed. In dust jacket. Boxed. $75-$100.

POWYS, T. F. *Unclay.* Half buckram. London, 1931. One of 160, signed. In dust jacket. $75-$100.

POWYS, T. F. *Uncle Dottery.* Illustrated by Eric Gill. Half vellum and green linen. Bristol, England, 1930. First edition. One of 300, signed. In dust jacket. $100-$125. Same issue: One of 50, with an extra set of engravings. $150-$200.

POWYS, T. F. *Uriah on the Hill.* Buckram. Cambridge, 1930. First edition. One of 85, signed. In dust jacket. $125-$150. Ordinary copies: $35.

POWYS, T. F. *When Thou Wast Naked.* London, 1931. Golden Cockerel Press. One of 500, signed. $125-$150.

*PRACTICAL Guide for Emigrants to North America (A).* Folding map in color. 57 pp., printed wrappers. London, 1850. (By George Nettle.) First edition. $150-$175.

*PRAIRIE (The): A Tale,* By the Author of *The Spy.* 3 vols., boards and cloth, paper labels. London, 1827. (By James Fenimore Cooper.) First edition. $550. Philadelphia, 1827. 2 vols., boards, paper labels. First American edition, with copyright notices corrected by slip pasted in. $400-$500. Paris, 1827. 2 vols., half leather. Worn, $250 (A, 1974). New York, 1940. Limited Editions Club. $40-$45.

*PRAIRIEDOM: Rambles and Scrambles in Texas.* By A. Suthron. Map. Cloth. New York, 1845. (By Frederick Benjamin Page.) First edition. $500-$1,000. New York, 1846. Second edition. $250-$350.

PRATT, Anne. *The British Grasses and Sedges.* 35 hand-colored plates. Green cloth. London. (1859). First edition. $85-$100.

PRATT, Parley P. *Late Persecution of the Church of Jesus Christ, of Latter Day Saints.* Cloth. New York, 1840. $175-$225.

*PRECAUTION: A Novel.* 2 vols., boards, or leather. New York, 1820. (By James Fenimore Cooper.) First edition, with errata leaf. $3,000-$5,000, possibly more. Cooper's first book.

*PRÉCIS Touchant la Colonie du Lord Selkirk, sur La Rivière Rouge, sa Destruction en 1815 et 1816, et le Massacre du Gouverneur Semple et de Son Parti.* Boards, Montreal, 1818. (By John Halkett.) First edition. $300-$350.

PRESCOTT, George Bartlett. *The Speaking Telephone.* Illustrated. Cloth, New York, 1878. First edition. $75.

PRESCOTT, William H. *The History of the Conquest of Mexico.* Maps, other illustrations. 3 vols., cloth. New York, 1843. First edition. $200-$300.

PRESCOTT, William H. *The History of the Conquest of Peru.* Illustrated. 2 vols., cloth. New York, 1847. First American edition, first issue, with no period after "integrity," line 20, page 467, Vol. II. $200-$250. Later, $150-$200. Mexico, 1957. Limited Editions Club. Leather. Boxed. $125.

*PRESIDENT Lincoln Campaign Songster (The).* 72 pp., printed wrappers. New York, (1864). First edition. $100-$150.

PRESTON, Lieut.-Col. William. *Journal in Mexico, 1 Nov. 1847 to 25 May 1848.* 48 pp., morocco. No place, no date (modern printing). $150-$300, possibly more.

PREWETT, Frank. *Poems.* Wrappers. (Richmond, England, 1928.) Hogarth Press. First edition. $25.

PRICE, George F. *Across the Continent with the 5th Cavalry.* 4 portraits. Pictorial cloth. New York, 1883. First edition. $125-$150.

PRICE, R. K. *Astbury, Whieldon, and Ralph Wood Figures, and Toby Jugs.* 68 plates, including 18 in color. Half buckram. London, 1922. One of 500. In dust jacket. $200-$300.

PRICE, Reynolds. *Late Warning.* Wrappers, paper label. New York, 1968. First edition. One of 176, signed. $25-$35.

PRICE, Reynolds. *A Long and Happy Life.* Cloth. New York, 1962. First edition. In dust jacket. $30-$40. Author's first novel.

PRICHARD, G. W. *Bureau of Immigration of the Territory of New Mexico. Report of San Miguel County.* Folding view. 30 pp., wrappers. Las Vegas, 1882. $150-$200.

PRICHARD, James C. *An Analysis of the Egyptian Mythology.* Boards. London, 1819. $75-$100.

PRICHARD, James C. *A Treatise on Diseases of the Nervous System.* Part 1 (all published). Half leather. London, 1822. First edition. $150-$200.

PRICHARD, James C. *A Treatise on .Insanity.* Leather. London, 1835. First edition. $150-$250. Philadelphia, 1837. $100-$150.

*PRIDE and Prejudice.* By the Author of *Sense and Sensibility.* 3 vols., blue boards, paper labels. London, 1813. (By Jane Austen.) First edition, with November ads and with ruled lines in half title of Vol. 3 1-2/5 inches (1 inch in second edition). $4,000-$5,000. Also, $4,000 (A, 1974). London, 1813. Second edition. $1,000 and up. New York, 1940. Limited Editions Club. $80-$100.

PRIEST, Josiah. *Stories of the Revolution.* Folding plate. 32 pp., half calf. Albany, 1836. $100-$125.

PRIEST, Josiah. *A True Narrative of the Capture of David Ogden.* (Cover title.) Woodcut. Self-wrappers. Lansingburgh, 1840. First edition. $125-$150.

PRIESTLEY, J. B. *Brief Diversions.* Boards and cloth. Cambridge, 1922. First collected edition. In dust jacket. $75.

PRIESTLEY, J. B. *The Chapman of Rhymes.* Wrappers. London, 1918. First edition. $400 and up. Also, $350 (A, 1977). Author's first book.

PRIESTLEY, J. B. *Faraway.* Morocco. London, (1932). First edition. $100-$125.

PRIESTLEY, J. B. *The Town Major of Miraucourt.* Vellum. London, 1930. First edition. One of 525, signed. $100-$125.

*PRIMAVERA: Poems by Four Authors.* Wrappers. Oxford, 1890. First edition. $40-$50. (Note: Contains poems by Stephen Phillips, Laurence Binyon, and others.)

*PRINCE Dorus; or, Flattery Put Out of Countenance.* Colored plate. Stiff blue or yellow wrappers. London, 1811. (By Charles Lamb.) First edition. $1,000 and up. London, 1818. Yellow-brown wrappers. $400 and up. London, 1889. 9 hand-colored illustrations. Half vellum. $100 and up.

PRINDLE, Cyrus. *Memoir of the Rev. Daniel Meeker Chandler.* Cloth. Middlebury, 1842. $75-$100.

PRITCHETT, R. T. *Historical and Ethnographical Smokiana.* Illustrated in color. London, 1890. First edition. $200-$250.

PRITTS, Joseph. *Mirror of Olden Time Border Life.* 13 plates (17 in a few copies). Cloth. Abingdon, Va., 1849. $75-$100, possibly more.

*PROCEEDINGS of Congress, in 1796, on the Admission of Tennessee as a State, into the Union.* 15 pp., sewed. Detroit, 1835. $150-$200.

*PROCEEDINGS of a Convention to Consider the Opening of the Indian Territory, Held at Kansas City, Mo., Feb. 8, 1888.* 80 pp., wrappers. Kansas City, 1888. $200-$300.

*PROCEEDINGS of the First Annual Session of the Territorial Grange of Montana.* Diamond City, 1875. $300-$400.

*PROCEEDINGS of a General Meeting Held at Chester Courthouse, Nov. 18, 1831.* 16 pp., sewed. Columbia, S.C., 1832. $100-$150.

*PROCEEDINGS of the Harbor and River Convention, Held in Chicago, July 5th, 1847.* 79 pp., wrappers. Chicago, 1847. First edition. $350.

*PROCEEDINGS of a Meeting, and Report of a Committee of Citizens in Relation to Steamboat Disasters in the Western Lakes.* 22 pp., sewed. Cleveland, 1850. $100-$125.

*PROCEEDINGS of the National Ship Canal Convention.* Wrappers. Chicago, 1863. First edition. $100-$125.

*PROCEEDINGS of the Republican National Convention, Held at Chicago. May 16, 17 and 18, 1860.* 153 pp., wrappers. Albany, 1860. $300-$350. Another edition: Chicago, 1860. 44 pp., sewed. $150-$200.

*PROCEEDINGS of the St. Louis Chamber of Commerce, in Relation to the Improvement of the Navigation of the Mississippi River.* 44 pp., sewed. St. Louis, 1842. $100-$125.

*PROCEEDINGS of Sundry Citizens of Baltimore, Convened for the Purpose of Devising the Most Efficient Means of Improving the Intercourse Between That City and the Western States.* 38 pp., sewed. Baltimore, 1827. $200-$300.

PROCTOR, Thomas H. *The Banker's Dream.* Pictorial wrappers. Vineland, N.J., 1895. First edition. $50.

*PROGRESSIVE Men of Southern Idaho.* Frontispiece by Charles M. Russell, other illustrations. Leather. Chicago, 1904. First edition. $300-$350.

PROKOSCH, Frederic. *Age of Thunder.* Cloth. New York, (1945). First edition. One of 30, signed, sheet of original ms. bound in. $100-$125.

PROKOSCH, Frederic. *Death at Sea: Poems.* Cloth. New York, 1940. First edition. One of 55, signed, sheet of original ms. bound in. Boxed. $100-$150.

PROKOSCH, Frederic. *Night of the Poor.* Cloth. New York, 1939. First edition. In dust jacket. $25.

PROKOSCH, Frederic. *Nine Days to Mukalla.* Cloth. New York, 1953. First edition. In dust jacket. $25.

PROKOSCH, Frederic. *Three Songs—Three Images.* 2 vols., wrappers. New Haven, 1932. One of 10 large paper copies. $200-$300.

*PROMETHEUS Bound.* Translated from the Greek of Aeschylus. And *Miscellaneous Poems by the Translator.* Dark-blue cloth, paper label on spine. London, 1833. (By Elizabeth Barrett Browning.) First edition. $100-$150.

PROPERT, W. A. *The Russian Ballet in Western Europe, 1909-1920.* Illustrated, including color plates. Boards and cloth. London, 1921. First edition. One of 500. $225-$250. (Note: There were 150 copies issued for America.)

PROSCH, J. W. *McCarver and Tacoma.* 2 plates. Cloth. Seattle, (1906). First edition. $50-$75.

*PROSE and Poetry of the Live Stock Industry of the United States. Vol. 1.* (All published.) Leather. Denver and Kansas City, (1905). (Edited by James W. Freeman.) First edition. $3,000-$4,000, possibly more. New York, 1959. Half leather. Boxed. $100.

*PROSPECTUS of Hope Gold Company.* (Gold dirt lode in Gilpin County, Colorado.) 25 pp., wrappers, New York, 1864. $125-$150.

*PROSPECTUS of the Deadwood Gulch Hydraulic Mining Co. of Deadwood Gulch, Lawrence County, Black Hills, of the Territory of Dakota.* Folding map. 12 pp., wrappers. Deadwood, 1882. $150-$200.

*PROSPECTUS of the Leadville & Ten Mile Narrow Gauge Railway Company of Leadville, Col.* (Cover title.) 20 pp., printed wrappers. Leadville, 1880. $250-$300.

PROSPERO and Caliban. *The Weird of the Wanderer.* Dark blue cloth. London, 1912. (By Baron Corvo [Frederick William Rolfe] and Charles Harry Pirie-Gordon.) First edition. In dust jacket. $250-$350.

PROTEUS. *Sonnets and Songs.* Cloth. London, 1875. (By Wilfrid Scawen Blunt.) First edition. $150-$250. Author's first book.

PROUST, Marcel. *47 Unpublished Letters from Marcel Proust to Walter Berry.* White wrappers. Paris, 1930. Black Sun Press. One of 200 on Arches paper. Boxed. $150-$200. (Note: There was also another issue of 15, including an original autograph letter, but in most cases the original letter has been removed by autograph collectors.)

*PROVOST (The).* Boards, marbled spine, paper label. Edinburgh, 1822. (By John Galt.) First edition. $100-$125.

*PSALMAU Dafydd. Yn ol William Morgan.* Decorated paper covers, morocco spine. (Newtown, Wales, 1929.) Gregynog Press. One of 200. $250-$300. (Note: *The Psalms of David* in Welsh.)

*PUGET SOUND Business Directory and Guide to Washington Territory, 1872.* 3 colored plates of ads. Boards and leather. Olympia, (1872). First edition. $400.

PULITZER, Ralph. See Burke, John.

PURDY, James. *Don't Call Me by My Right Name and Other Stories.* Blue-gray printed wrappers. New York, 1956. First edition. $75-$100. Author's first book.

PURDY, James. *63: Dream Palace.* Printed wrappers. New York, 1956. First edition. $50-$75.

PURVIANCE, Levi. *The Biography of David Purviance.* Cloth. Dayton, 1848. First edition. $50-$60.

*PUSS in Boots.* Illustrated in color. 10 pp., pictorial boards. New York, (1880's). McLoughlin book with overlays on center spread. $75-$100.

PUTNAM, Arthur Lee. *Ned Newton; or The Fortunes of a New York Bootblack.* Wrappers. New York, 1890. (By Horatio Alger, Jr.) Leather-clad paperback. First edition. $50-$65. Another edition: Cloth (later). American Publishers Corp. $30-$35.

PUTNAM, Arthur Lee. *A New York Boy.* Wrappers. New York, 1890. (By Horatio Alger, Jr.) Leather-clad paperback. First edition. $50-$75. Another edition: Cloth (later). American Publishers Corp. $35-$40.

PUTNAM, Arthur Lee. *Tom Tracy.* Wrappers. New York, 1888. (By Horatio Alger, Jr.) First edition, with Munsey imprint on title page. $50-$60. Another edition (later): Wrappers. Leather-clad. $35. Another (later): Cloth. Lovell, publisher. $40-$50.

*PUT'S Golden Songster.* 64 pp., wrappers. San Francisco, (1858). $50-$75.

PUZO, Mario. *The Dark Arena.* Cloth. New York, (1955). First edition. In dust jacket. $25-$35. Author's first book.

PUZO, Mario. *The Godfather.* Cloth. New York, (1969). First edition. In dust jacket. $35-$40.

PYLE, Howard. *The Garden Behind the Moon.* Illustrated by the author. Cloth. New York, 1895. First edition. $50-$60.

PYLE, Howard. *Howard Pyle's Book of the American Spirit.* Edited by Merle Johnson and Francis J. O'Dowd. Illustrated, including color plates, by Pyle. Boards and cloth. New York, 1923. First edition, with "B-X" on copyright page. In dust jacket. $150-$200. Another issue: One of 50 signed by the editors. In dust jacket. $250-$300. Also, one of 6 signed copies, with an original Pyle drawing for the book. $650 in a 1978 cataogue.

PYLE, Howard. *Howard Pyle's Book of Pirates.* Edited by Merle Johnson. Illustrated, including color plates, by Pyle. Boards and cloth. New York, 1921. First edition, with "D-V" at foot of copyright page. In dust jacket. $150-$175. Another issue: One of 50 on vellum, signed by Johnson. In dust jacket. Boxed. $250-$350.

PYLE, Howard. *Men of Iron.* New York, 1892. Illustrated by Pyle. Cloth. First edition, first issue (1-1/16 inches across top of covers). $100-$150. Second issue. $50-$75.

PYLE, Howard. *The Merry Adventures of Robin Hood.* Illustrated, including color plates, by Pyle. Full leather. New York, 1883. First edition. $200-$250. London, 1883. Cloth. First English edition. $50-$75. Author's first book. New York, 1933. Illustrated by N.C. Wyeth and with 2 drawings by Andrew Wyeth. Cloth. Brandywine Edition. In dust jacket. $150-$250. (Later New York editions in 1935 and 1942 are worth almost as much if in dust jackets and fine.)

PYLE, Howard. *A Modern Aladdin.* Illustrated by Pyle. Cloth. New York, 1892. First edition. $100-$125.

PYLE, Howard. *Otto of the Silver Hand.* Illustrated by the author. Half calf and cloth. New York, 1888. First edition. $250-$350. Also, $190 (A, 1976). London, 1888. Pictorial cloth. First English edition. $100-$150.

PYLE, Howard. *Pepper and Salt.* Illustrated by the author. Pictorial buckram. New York, 1886. First edition. $150-$175. Also, $80 (A, 1976); $70 (A, 1974).

PYLE, Howard. *The Price of Blood.* Colored illustrations by Pyle. Pictorial boards and cloth. Boston, 1899. First edition, first binding, with unlettered spine. $100-$150. Second binding, spine lettered. $75-$100.

PYLE, Howard. *Rejected of Men.* Illustrated by Pyle. Cloth. New York, 1903. First edition, with "Published June, 1903" on copyright page. In dust jacket. $75-$100.

PYLE, Howard. *The Ruby of Kishmoor.* Illustrated. Cloth. New York, 1908. First edition. In dust jacket. $50-$75.

PYLE, Howard. *Sabbath Thoughts.* 2 Pyle illustrations. Wrappers. (New York, 1928.). First edition. One of 20. $100-$125. Another issue: One of 6 large paper copies. $200-$250.

PYLE, Howard. *Stolen Treasure.* Illustrated. Cloth. New York, 1907. First edition, first issue, with "Published May, 1907" on copyright page. In dust jacket. $100-$125.

PYLE, Howard. *The Story of the Champions of the Round Table.* Cloth. New York, 1905. First edition. In dust jacket. $135-$150.

PYLE, Howard. *The Story of the Grail and the Passing of Arthur.* Illustrated by the author. Cloth. New York, 1910. First edition. In dust jacket. $100-$150.

PYLE, Howard. *The Story of Jack Ballister's Fortunes.* Illustrated by Pyle. Cloth. New York, 1895. First edition. $50-$75.

PYLE, Howard. *The Story of King Arthur and His Knights.* Illustrated by Pyle. Cloth. New York, 1903. First edition. In dust jacket. $135-$150.

PYLE, Howard. *The Story of Sir Launcelot and His Companions.* Illustrated by Pyle. Cloth. New York, 1907. First edition. In dust jacket. $150-$165.

PYLE, Howard. *Within the Capes.* Illustrated by Pyle. Cloth. New York, 1885. First edition, first issue (cloth). $80-$100. Later issue: Wrappers: $50-$60.

PYLE, Howard. *The Wonder Clock.* Illustrated by Pyle. Half leather. New York, 1888. First edition. $150-$250.

PYLE, Howard. *Yankee Doodle.* Illustrated by Pyle. Pictorial boards. New York, 1881. First edition. $200-$250. Also, $160 (A, 1976). First book illustrated by Pyle.

PYNCHON, Thomas. *The Crying of Lot 49.* Cloth. Philadelphia, (1966). First edition. In dust jacket. $60-$80.

PYNCHON, Thomas. *Gravity's Rainbow.* Cloth. New York, (1973). First edition. In dust jacket. $35-$45. Same: Wrappers. $25-$30.

PYNCHON, Thomas. *V.* Cloth. Philadelphia, (1963). First edition. In dust jacket. $150-$200. Author's first book. Copies in wrappers—publisher's advance issue. $350.

PYNE, W. H. *The History of the Royal Residences of Windsor Castle, St. James's Palace, Carlton House, Kensington Palace, Hampton Court, Buckingham House, and Frogmore.* 100 colored engravings. 3 vols., morocco, gilt. London, 1819. First edition, first issue, with pre-publication watermarks. $2,000-$3,000. Another issue: Large paper. $3,000 and up. (Note: Bound copies are made up of the original 25 parts, which appeared in wrappers.)

PYRNELLE, Louise-Clarke. *Diddie, Dumps, and Tot, or Plantation Child-Life.* Pictorial cloth. New York, 1882. First edition. $200-$300.

# Q

*QUAKER Partisans (The)*. Cloth. Philadelphia, 1869, (By William Gilmore Simms?) First edition. $100-$125.

*QUARTETTE*. By Four Anglo-Indian Writers. Wrappers. Lahore, India, 1885. (By Rudyard Kipling and his sister, mother, and father.) First edition. $1,500-$2,000. Also, some defects, $1,100 (A, 1974).

QUEEN, Ellery. *The Chinese Orange Mystery*. Cloth. New York, 1934. (By Frederic Dannay and Manfred B. Lee.) First edition. In dust jacket. $50-$60.

QUEEN, Ellery. *The Devil to Pay*. Cloth. New York, 1938. (By Frederick Dannay and Manfred B. Lee.) First edition. In dust jacket. $50-$60.

QUEEN, Ellery. *The Dutch Shoe Mystery*. Cloth. New York, 1931. First edition. In dust jacket. $50-$75.

QUEEN, Ellery. *The Egyptian Cross Mystery*. Cloth. New York, 1932. (By Frederick Dannay and Manfred B. Lee.) First edition. In dust jacket. $50-$75.

QUEEN, Ellery. *The Spanish Cape Mystery*. Cloth. New York, 1935. (By Frederick Dannay and Manfred B. Lee.) First edition. In dust jacket. $50-$60.

QUEEN, Ellery (editor). *The Misadventures of Sherlock Holmes*. Frontispiece by F.D. Steele. Cloth. Boston, 1944. (Edited by Frederic Dannay and Manfred B. Lee.) First edition. In dust jacket. $100-$150.

QUEENY, Edgar M. *Prairie Wings: Pen and Camera Flight Studies*. Illustrated. Cloth. New York, 1946. In dust jacket. $200-$225. Another issue: Morocco. One of 225, signed. $500-$600.

*QUENTIN Durward*. 3 vols., boards and cloth, paper labels. Edinburgh, 1823. (By Walter Scott.) First edition. $100-$150.

QUICKFALL. *Western Life, and How I Became a Bronco Buster*. Portrait. 96 pp., pictorial wrappers. London, (1890). (By Bob Grantham?) First edition. $400-$500. Also, $300 (A, 1968).

QUILLER-COUCH, Sir Arthur. See Rackham, Arthur, *Book of Pictures*.

QUILLER-COUCH, Sir Arthur. *The Golden Pomp*. Half morocco. London, 1895. $35.

QUILLER-COUCH, Sir Arthur. *In Powder and Crinoline*. Illustrated by Kay Nielsen, including 24 color plates. Boards, buckram spine. London, (about 1913). $300-$400. Another issue: Vellum. One of 500, signed. $600-$1,000.

QUILLER-COUCH, Sir Arthur. *The Sleeping Beauty and Other Fairy Tales*. 30 colored plates by Edmund Dulac. Cloth. London, (about 1910). $200-$300. Another issue: Morocco. One of 1,000, signed. $250-$350.

QUIN, Edward. *An Historical Atlas*. 21 maps. Folio, boards. London, 1830. $500.

QUINN, Seabury. *Roads*. Black cloth. Illustrated. Sauk City, Wis., 1948. Arkham House. In dust jacket. $50.

QUIZ. *The Grand Master, or Adventures of Qui Hi? in Hindostan: A Hudibrastic Poem in Eight Cantos*. Folding frontispiece, 26 plates by Thomas Rowlandson. Boards. London, 1816. (By William Combe.) First edition, with errata slip and leaf containing pages 31-32. $500-$600.

# R

R., J. *Poems*. Cloth. (London), 1850. (By John Ruskin.) First edition. $500-$600.

RACKHAM, Arthur. *The Arthur Rackham Fairy Book*. Illustrated, including color. London, (1933). One of 460, signed. Boxed. $500-$650.

RACKHAM, Arthur. *Arthur Rackham's Book of Pictures*. Edited by Sir Arthur Quiller-Couch. Illustrated, including color. Cloth. London, 1913. First edition. In dust jacket. $200-$250. Another issue: One of 1,030 signed by Rackham. In dust jacket. $400-$500. Another: One of 30, inscribed and with an original drawing. $750-$1,000. New York, (1914). Cloth. American edition. In dust jacket. $400-$500. London, (1927). Cloth. In dust jacket. $200-$300.

RACKHAM, Arthur (illustrator). *The Fairy Tales of the Brothers Grimm*. 40 colored plates. Cloth. London, 1900. First Rackham edition. $200-$250. London, 1909. Cloth. $200-$300. Another issue: Vellum. One of 750, signed. $550-$750. New York, 1909. Cloth. $200-$300.

RACKHAM, Bernard. *The Ancient Glass of Canterbury Cathedral*. 21 plates in color and 80 in monochrome. Buckram. London, 1949. $100-$175.

RACKHAM, Bernard, and Read, Herbert. *English Pottery*. Cloth. London, 1924. First edition. In dust jacket. $75-$100. Another issue: Pigskin. One of 75, signed. $150-$225.

RADER, J.L. *South of Forty*. Cloth. Norman, Okla., 1947. First edition (so stated). $50-$75.

RAFINESQUE, C.S. *Circular Address on Botany and Zoology*. 36 pp., sewed. Philadelphia, 1816. $175-$225.

RAFINESQUE, C.S. *A Life of Travels and Researches in North America and South Europe*. 148 pp., wrappers. Philadelphia, 1836. First edition. $400-$500.

RAFINESQUE, C.S. *Medical Flora*. 100 plates, printed in green. 2 vols., boards. Philadelphia, 1828-30. First edition. $1,250-$1,500.

RAHT, Carlysle Graham. *The Romance of Davis Mountains and Big Bend Country*. Map, 13 plates. Cloth. El Paso, (1919). First edition. In dust jacket. $75-$85.

*RAILROAD to San Francisco*. (Caption title.) No place, no date (1849). (By P.P.F.De-Grand.) $125-$150.

RAINE, Kathleen. *Six Dreams and Other Poems*. Illustrated. Boards. London, 1968. First edition. One of 100, signed. $50.

RAINE, Kathleen. *Stone and Flower*. Illustrated. Cloth. London, (1943). First edition. In dust jacket. $35-$50. Author's first book.

RAINE, William MacLeod. *Cattle Brands: A Sketch of Bygone Days in the Cow-Country*. 8 pp., wrappers. Boston, (1920). First edition. $60-$75.

RAINE, William MacLeod. *A Daughter of Raasay*. Illustrated. Cloth. New York, (1902). First edition. In dust jacket. $150-$200. Lacking jacket. $75-$100. Author's first book.

RAINES, C. W. *A Bibliography of Texas*. Cloth. Austin, Tex., 1896. First edition. $100-$200. Facsimile reprint: Houston, 1955. Cloth. One of 500. Boxed. $25.

RALFE, J. *The Naval Chronology of Great Britain*. 60 colored plates. 3 vols., London, 1820. First edition. $2,500-$3,000, possibly more.

RALPH, Julian. *On Canada's Frontier*. Illustrated. Cloth. New York, 1892. First edition. $100-$125.

RAMAL, Walter. *Songs of Childhood*. Frontispiece. Decorated blue cloth and vellum. London, 1902. (By Walter De La Mare.) First edition. In dust jacket. $600-$750. De La Mare's first book.

RAMIREZ, D. José F. *Memorías, Negociaciones y Documentos, etc.* Boards, or wrappers. Mexico City, 1853. $150-$200.

RAMSAY, David. *The History of South Carolina*. 2 folding maps. 2 vols., half leather. Charleston, 1809. First edition. $300-$400.

RAMSDELL, Charles W. *Reconstruction in Texas*. 324 pp., wrappers. New York, 1910. First edition. Wrappers: $100-$150. Cloth. $60-$75.

RAMSEY, Alexander. *Message of Governor Ramsey*. (On the Sioux uprising.) Wrappers. St. Paul, 1862. First edition. $150-$250.

RAMSEY, J.G.M. *The Annals of Tennessee*. Folding map and plan. Leather, or cloth. Charleston, 1853. First edition. $100-$150. Philadelphia, 1853. Cloth. Second edition. $75. Philadelphia, 1860. Cloth. $50. Chattanooga, 1926. Cloth. $50.

RANCK, George W. *History of Lexington, Kentucky*. Illustrated. Cloth. Cincinnati, 1872. First edition. $75-$100.

RAND, Ayn. *Atlas Shrugged*. Cloth. New York, 1957. First edition. In dust jacket. $40-$60.

RAND, Ayn. *The Fountainhead*. Cloth. Indianapolis, (1943). First edition. In dust jacket. $60-$75.

RANDALL, Thomas E. *History of the Chippewa Valley*. Cloth. Eau Claire, Wis., 1875. First edition. $75-$100.

RANKIN, M. Wilson. *Reminiscences of Frontier Days*. Frontispiece. Boards. Denver, (1938). First edition. $100-$125.

RANSOM, John Crowe. See *Armageddon, etc.*

RANSOM, John Crowe. *Chills and Fever*. Batik boards, cloth spine, paper label. New York, 1924. First edition. In dust jacket. $150-$250.

RANSOM, John Crowe. *Grace After Meat*. Boards, paper label. London, 1924. First edition. One of 400. $250-$400.

RANSOM, John Crowe. *Poems About God*. Brown boards, paper label. New York, 1919. First edition. $250-$350. Author's first book.

RANSOM, John Crowe. *Selected Poems*. Cloth. New York, 1945. First edition. In dust jacket. $75-$100.

RANSOM, John Crowe. *Two Gentlemen in Bonds*. Decorated boards, cloth spine, paper label. New York, 1927. First edition. In dust jacket. $125-$175.

RANSOM, John Crowe. *The World's Body*. Cloth. New York, 1938. First edition. In dust jacket. $50-$75.

RANSOM, Will. *Private Presses and Their Books*. Illustrated. Cloth. New York, 1929. First edition. One of 1,200. In dust jacket. $125-$150. New York, 1963. Limited edition. $125-$150.

RANSOME, Arthur. *The Elixir of Life*. Cloth. London, 1915. First edition. $50-$75.

RANSOME, Arthur. *Oscar Wilde: A Critical Study.* Cloth. London, 1912. First edition. $50-$75.

RAREY, J. S. *The Modern Art of Taming Wild Horses.* Wrappers. Columbus, Ohio, 1856. First edition. $400-$600. Austin, 1856. 62 pp., wrappers. Third edition, revised and corrected. $100 and up.

RATHBONE, Frederick. *Old Wedgwood.* Illustrated, including color plates. Half morocco. London, 1898. First edition. One of 200. $750-$1,000.

*RAVENSNEST: or, The Redskins.* 3 vols., boards, green or blue cloth spine. London, 1846. (By James Fenimore Cooper.) First English edition of *The Redskins.* $200-$300.

RAWLINGS, Marjorie Kinnan. *The Yearling.* Decorations by Edward Shenton. Cloth. New York, 1938. First edition, with Scribner's "A" on copyright page. In dust jacket. $75-$125. New York, 1939. Illustrated. Cloth. One of 770. In dust jacket. Boxed. $150-$225.

RAWSTORNE, Lawrence. *Gamonia: or the Art of Preserving Game.* 15 colored aquatints. Green morocco. London, 1837. First edition, with errata slip at end. $500-$600. London, 1929. 15 colored plates. Morocco. One of 125 on large paper. $150.

RAYMOND, Dora Neill. *Captain Lee Hall of Texas.* Map, illustrations. Cloth. Norman, Okla., 1940. First edition. In dust jacket. $35-$50.

*R. B. Adam Library Relating to Dr. Samuel Johnson and His Era (The).* 4 vols., half cloth. Buffalo, 1929-30. First edition. One of 500 (for first 3 vols.) and 225 (for Vol. 4). In dust jackets. $300-$350.

READ, C. Rudston. *What I Heard, Saw and Did at the Australian Gold Fields.* Large folding map, tinted lithograph plates. Cloth. London. 1853. First edition. $175-$250.

READ, Herbert. See Rackham, Bernard.

READ, Herbert. *Eclogues.* Illustrated. Boards and cloth. London, 1919. Beaumont Press. One of 50. $50-$75.

READ, Herbert. *English Stained Glass.* Colored frontispiece, 70 full-page plates. Cloth. London, 1926. First edition. $50-$75.

READ, Herbert. *Mutations of the Phoenix.* Half cloth. London, 1923. First edition. $75-$100.

READ, Herbert. *Staffordshire Pottery Figures.* Plates (6 colored). Cloth. London, 1929. First edition. In dust jacket. $80-$110.

READ, Herbert, and others. *Surrealism.* Plates. Cloth. London, 1936. First edition. $75-$100.

READ, Opie. *An American in New York.* Pictorial red cloth. Chicago, 1905. Autographed edition. $25-$35.

READ, Opie. *An Arkansas Planter.* Illustrated by W. W. Denslow and Ike Morgan. Pictorial green cloth. Chicago, (1896). First edition. $35-$50.

READ, Opie. *Bolanyo.* Illustrated. Cloth. Chicago, 1897. First edition. $25-$35.

READ, Thomas Buchanan. *A Summer Story: Sheridan's Ride and Other Poems.* Cloth. Philadelphia, 1865. First edition. $35.

READE, Charles. *The Cloister and the Hearth.* 4 vols., cloth. London, 1861, First edition, first issue, without ads and with words transposed on page 372 of Vol. 2. $600-$750. New York, 1861. Cloth. First American edition. $100-$125. New York, 1932. Limited Editions Club. Cloth. In dust jacket. Boxed. $35-$40.

READE, Charles. *The Course of True Love Never Did Run Smooth.* Pictorial boards, or cloth. London, 1857. First book edition. $50-$75.

READE, Charles. *"It Is Never Too Late to Mend."* 3 vols., cloth. London, 1856. First edition. $50-$75.

READINGS in Crabbe's *"Tales of the Hall."* Red or green cloth. Guildford, England, 1879. (By Edward Fitz Gerald.) First edition. $75-$100.

REAGAN, John H. *Memoirs, with Special Reference to Secession and the Civil War.* 4 plates. Cloth. New York, 1906. $50-$75.

REAL *Life in Ireland.* 19 hand-colored aquatints. Boards. London, 1821. (By Pierce Egan.) First edition. $400-$500. London, 1829. Calf. Fourth edition. $200-$300.

REAL *Life in London.* By an Amateur. 32 colored plates by Alken, Rowlandson, etc. 21 parts in wrappers. London, 1821-22. (Imitation of Pierce Egan, but not by Egan.) First edition. $600-$800. London, 1821-22. 32 colored plates. 2 vols., boards. First book edition. (Often with 2 extra plates.) $500-$600. Another issue: Morocco. Printed on large paper. $600-$750. (Note: There were numerous later editions.)

RECIO, Jesus T. *Tomochie! Episodios de la Companía de Chihuahua, 1893.* Boards and leather. Rio Grande City, Tex., 1894. $300-$500.

RÉCIT des Évenéments qui ont eu Lieu sur le Territoire des Sauvages. Boards. Montreal, 1818. (By Simon McGillivray.) $250-$300.

RECREATIONS. Boards, parchment spine. (London, 1923.) (By Siegfried Sassoon.) First edition. One of 75. $150. Another issue: One of 6 on large paper. $300-$400.

RED Rover (The): A Tale. By the Author of *The Pilot.* 3 vols., wrappers (?). Paris, 1827. (By James Fenimore Cooper.) First edition. (No copy in wrappers noted.) Half calf, $200-$300. London, 1827. 3 vols., boards (?). First English edition. (No copy in boards noted.) Half calf. $200-$300. Philadelphia, 1828. 2 vols., blue-gray boards, paper labels. First American edition. (Vol. 2 dated 1827.) $300-$500.

REDMOND, Pat. H. *History of Quincy (Ill.) and Its Men of Mark.* Cloth. Quincy, 1869. $100-$150.

REDPATH, James, and Hinton, Richard J. *Hand-book to Kansas Territory and the Rocky Mountains' Gold Region.* 3 maps in color on 2 large folding sheets. Cloth. New York, 1859. First edition. $450-$500.

REDSKINS (The). By the Author of *The Pathfinder.* 2 vols., printed brown wrappers. New York, 1846. (By James Fenimore Cooper.) First edition. $350-$500. (For first English edition, see *Ravensnest.*)

REED, Andrew, and Matheson, James. *A Narrative of the Visit to the American Churches by the Deputation from the Congregational Union of England and Wales.* 4 plates, folding map. 2 vols., leather. London, 1835. First edition. $250-$300.

REED, J.W. *Map of and Guide to the Kansas Gold Region.* Map. 24 pp., printed wrappers. New York, 1859. First edition. $3,000-$3,500.

REED, John. *The Day in Bohemia.* Printed wrappers. New York, 1913. First edition. One of 500. Boxed. $200-$225.

REED, John. *Insurgent Mexico.* Cloth. New York, 1914. First edition. In dust jacket. $75-$100.

REED, John. *Sangar: To Lincoln Steffens.* Boards. Riverside, Conn., 1913. First separate edition. Limited. Boxed. $100-$150. Author's first book.

REED, John. *Tamburlaine and Other Verses.* Boards. Riverside, Conn., 1917. First edition. One of 450 (of an edition of 500). $125-$150. Another issue: One of 50 on handmade paper. In tissue dust jacket. $250-$350. Trade edition: In dust jacket. $60.

REED, John. *Ten Days That Shook the World.* Illustrated. Cloth. New York, 1919. First edition. In dust jacket. $150-$175. Lacking jacket, $75-$100.

REED, S.G. *A History of the Texas Railroads.* Blue cloth. Houston, (1941). Limited, signed edition. $150-$300.

REED, Silås. *Report of . . . Surveyor General of Wyoming Territory, for the Year 1871.* Tables. 46 pp., wrappers. Washington, 1871. First edition. $250-$300.

REED, Talbot Baines. *History of the Old English Letter Foundries.* Illustrated. Half leather. London, 1887. First edition. $65-$85. London, (1952). Cloth. In dust jacket. $75-$100.

REED, Wallace P. *History of Atlanta, Georgia.* 46 portraits. 2 parts in one, cloth. Syracuse, 1889. First edition. $75-$100.

REED, William. *Life on the Border, Sixty Years Ago.* 120 pp., wrappers. Fall River, Mass., 1882. First edition. $50-$75.

REES, William. *Description of the City of Keokuk.* 24 pp., printed self-wrappers. Keokuk, Iowa, 1854. First edition. $225-$250. Keokuk, 1855. 22 pp., with wrapper title. Second edition. $100-$135.

REES, William. *The Mississippi Bridge Cities: Davenport, Rock Island and Moline.* Woodcut frontispiece. 32 pp., sewed. (Rock Island, Ill.). 1854. First edition. $150-$200.

REESE. Lizette Woodworth. *A Branch of May: Poems.* Cloth. Baltimore. 1887. First edition. $150-$200. Author's first book. Portland, Me., 1920. Mosher Press. Boards. One of 450. Boxed. $25-$35.

REESE, Lizette Woodworth. *A Handful of Lavender.* Decorated cloth and parchment. Boston, 1891. First edition. $50-$75.

REESE, Lizette Woodworth. *White April and Other Poems.* Cloth. New York, (about 1930). First edition. In dust jacket. $35-$40.

*REFORMED Practice of Medicine (The).* 2 vols. in one, boards. Boston, 1831. First edition. $200-$225. Rebound in cloth, $60 (A, 1972).

*REGULATIONS and List of Premiums of the Jerauld County Agricultural and Industrial Society for the First Fair to Be Held at Wessington Springs, D.T.* 16 pp., wrappers. Wessington Springs, Dakota Territory, 1884. $125-$150.

*REGULATIONS for the Uniform and Dress of the Army of the United States.* 25 chromolithographs. 13 pp., cloth. Philadelphia, 1851. $500 and up.

REICHEL, Anton. *The Chiaroscurists of the XVI-XVII-XVIII Centuries.* 111 full-color reproductions. Folio, boards. Cambridge, no date. $400-$500.

REID, A.J. *The Resources and Manufacturing Capacity of the Lower Fox River Valley.* Folding map and panorama, plates. 56 pp., wrappers. Appleton, Wis., 1874. First edition. $75-$100.

REID, Forrest. *Apostate.* Cloth. London, (1926). First edition. One of 50, signed. $75-$100.

REID, Forrest. *Illustrators of the Sixties.* Illustrated. Buckram. London, 1928. First edition. In dust jacket. $150-$200.

REID, J. M. *Sketches and Anecdotes of the Old Settlers and New Comers.* 187 pp., wrappers. Keokuk, Iowa, 1876. First edition. $300-$350.

REID, John C. *Reid's Tramp, or A Journal of the Incidents of Ten Months Travel Through Texas, New Mexico, Arizona, Sonora, and California.* Cloth. Selma, Ala., 1858. First edition. $4,000-$5,000, possibly more.

REID, Mayne. *The Headless Horseman.* 20 plates. 2 vols., cloth. London, (1886). (By Thomas M. Reid.) First book edition. $400-$500.

REID, Mayne. *No Quarter!* 3 vols., cloth. London, 1888. First edition. (By Thomas M. Reid.) $150-$250.

REID, Mayne. *Osceola the Seminole*. Cloth. New York, (1858). (By Thomas M. Reid.) First American edition. $100-$150.

REID, Mayne. *The Quadroon; or, A Lover's Adventures in Louisiana*. 3 vols., orange cloth. London, 1856. (By Thomas M. Reid.) First edition. $250-$350.

REID, Mayne. *The White Chief*. 3 vols, cloth. London, 1855. (By Thomas M. Reid.) First edition. $150-$175.

REID, Mayne. *The Wild Huntress*. 3 vols., cloth. London, 1861. (By Thomas M. Reid.) First edition. $150-$200.

REID, Mayne. *The Wood-Rangers*. 3 vols., cloth. London, 1860. (By Thomas M. Reid.) First edition. $175-$200.

REID, Samuel C., Jr. *The Scouting Expeditions of McCulloch's Texas Rangers*. 12 plates and plan. Cloth. Philadelphia, 1847. First edition. $300-$350. Philadelphia, 1848. Cloth. $500-$750. Philadelphia, 1859. Cloth. $100-$125. Philadelphia, 1860. Cloth. $75-$100.

REID, Thomas M. See Reid, Mayne.

*REIGN of Terror in Kanzas (The)*. 34 pp., wrappers. Boston, 1856. (By Charles W. Briggs.) First edition. $600-$750.

*RELIEF Business Directory. Names and New Locations in San Francisco, Oakland, Berkeley and Alameda of 4,000 San Francisco Firms and Business Men*. 64 pp., wrappers. Berkeley, May, 1906. $200-$300. (Issued after the great earthquake and fire of 1906.)

*REMARKS Addressed to the Citizens of Illinois, on the Proposed Introduction of Slavery*. 14 pp., disbound. (Vandalia?, 1824?) (By Morris Birkbeck.) $3,000-$3,500.

REMARQUE, Erich Maria. *All Quiet on the Western Front*. Buckram. London, (1929). First edition in English. In dust jacket. $50-$75. Boston, 1929. Gray cloth. First American edition. In dust jacket. $15-$20. (Note: The first edition in German, *Im Westen Nichts Neues*, Berlin, 1929., wrappers, is worth roughly $100-$150 if in fine condition.) New York, 1969. Limited Editions Club. Cloth. Boxed. $60-$75.

REMARQUE, Erich Maria. *The Road Back*. Illustrated. Cloth. London, (1931). First edition in English. In dust jacket. $65-$100.

REMBRANDT VAN RIJN, H. *The Complete Work of Rembrandt*. Text by W.A. von Bode, assisted by C. Hofstede de Groot, from the German translation by Florence Simmonds. 595 large, 21 small reproductions, 4 facsimiles of letters. 8 vols., folio, half brown morocco. Paris, 1897-1906. One of 75 on Holland paper. $1,000-$1,250.

REMINGTON, Frederic. *Crooked Trails*. 49 plates. Pictorial tan cloth. New York, 1898. First edition, In dust jacket. $150-$250.

REMINGTON, Frederic. *Done in the Open*. Introduction by Owen Wister. Illustrations by Remington. 90 pp., folio, cream-colored pictorial boards. New York, 1902. First edition, first issue, with Russell imprint and with "Frederick" instead of "Frederic" on front cover. $200-$250. Another issue: Suede leather. One of 250, signed. $750-$1,000. Later issue: New York, 1902. Collier imprint. Half cloth. $75-$100. New York, 1903. Half cloth. $50-$75.

REMINGTON, Frederic. *Drawings*. 61 plates. Oblong folio, pictorial boards and cloth. New York, 1897. First edition. Boxed. $150-$250. Another issue: Suede leather. One of 250, signed. $1,000-$1,200. Also, $750 (A, 1977). New York, 1898. Cloth. $400-$500.

REMINGTON, Frederic. *Frederic Remington's Own West*. Edited by Harold McCracken. Colored frontispiece, other illustrations. Cowhide. New York, (1960). First edition. One of 167 signed by McCracken. Boxed. $200-$300. Trade edition: Cloth. In dust jacket. $30-$50.

REMINGTON, Frederic. *Frontier Sketches*. Illustrated by the author. Oblong, pictorial boards. Chicago, (1898). First edition. $250-$300.

REMINGTON, Frederic. *John Ermine of the Yellowstone*. Brown cloth. New York, 1902. First edition. $75-$100. (Note: First edition copies, as well as reprints, misspell the author's name "Reminigton" on the spine.)

REMINGTON, Frederic. *Men with the Bark On*. Illustrated by the author. Pictorial orange-tan cloth. New York, 1900. First edition, first issue, ⅞ inch thick (later 1-⅛ inches). $85-$125.

REMINGTON, Frederic. *Pony Tracks*. Illustrated by the author. Brown decorated cloth, or leather. New York, 1895. First edition. Cloth. Also, a presentation copy, $500 (A, 1977). Leather: $300-$375. Author's first book.

REMINGTON, Frederic. *A Rogers Ranger in the French and Indian War*. Printed wrappers. (New York), 1897. First edition. $75-$100.

REMINGTON, Frederic. *Sundown Leflare*. Illustrated by the author. Brown pictorial cloth. New York, 1899. First edition. $75-$85.

REMINGTON, Frederic. *The Way of an Indian*. Illustrated by the author. Cloth. New York, 1906. First edition, first issue, February, crimson cloth, yellow lettering with "Fox, Duffield & Company" on spine and page 9 so numbered. $175-$250. Second issue copies: $125-$150.

*REMINISCENCES of a Campaign in Mexico*. Map, frontispiece. Cloth. Nashville, 1849. (By John R. Robertson.) First edition. $125-$150.

REMSBURG, John E. and Remsburg, George J. *Charley Reynolds, Soldier, Hunter, Scout and Guide*. Portrait. Cloth. Kansas City, 1931. First book edition. One of 175. $50-$60.

REMY, Jules and Benchley, Julius. *A Journey to Great Salt Lake City*. Map, 10 plates. 2 vols., cloth. London, 1861, First edition in English. $175-$200. (The first edition, *Voyage au pays des Mormons*, Paris, 1860, was issued in both cloth and wrappers and is valued in the $250-$350 range.)

RENFROW, W.C. *Oklahoma and the Cherokee Strip*. Folding map. 16 pp., wrappers. Chicago, 1893. $75-$100.

RENNER, Frederic G. *Charles M. Russell: Paintings, Drawings, and Sculpture in the Amon G. Carter Collection. A Descriptive Catalogue*. Illustrated, including color. Decorated cloth. Austin, (1966). First edition. One of 200, signed, and with an extra color plate and a portfolio of color plates laid in. Boxed. $300-$400.

*REPLY to the Essay on Population, by the Rev. T.R. Malthus (A)*. Leather-backed gray boards. London, 1807. (By William Hazlitt.) First edition. $300-$350.

*RÉPONSE a une Addresse de la Chambre des Communes, en date du 23 Avril 1869, Demandant un Rapport Indiquant le Progrès qui ont été faits dans L'Ouverture d'une Communication entre Fort William et l'Etablissement de la Rivière Rouge . . . Par Ordre Hector L. Langevin, Secrétaire d'État*. 88 pp., half morocco. Ottawa, 1869. $250-$300.

*REPORT from a Select Committee of the House of Representatives, on the Overland Emigration Route from Minnesota to British Oregon*. Printed wrappers, marbled spine. St. Paul, Minn., 1858. $600-$750.

*REPORT from the Select Committee on the Hudson's Bay Company*. 3 elephant folio colored folding maps by Arrowsmith. Half morocco. London, 1857. First edition. $400-$500. (Note: There was also an advance issue in wrappers, 2 parts, same date, catalogued in the 1950's by a New York dealer at $250. Estimated current value: $500 and up.)

*REPORT of a Committee Appointed by the Trustees of the Town of Milwaukee, Relative to the Commerce of That Town and the Navigation of Lake Michigan*. 12 pp., sewed. Milwaukee, 1842. (By I.A. Lapham and F. Randall.) $350-$400.

*REPORT of the Board of Canal Commissioneres, to the General Assembly of Ohio*. Sewed. Columbus, Ohio, 1824. $150-$200.

*REPORT of the Board of Directors of Internal Improvements of the State of Massachusetts, on the Practicability and Expediency of a Rail-Road from Boston to the Hudson River, and from Boston to Providence.* 6 folding plans. Boston, 1829. $100-$150.

*REPORT of the Board of Internal Improvements for the State of Kentucky, and Reports of the Engineers.* 47 pp., sewed. (Frankfort, Ky., 1836.) $100-$125.

*REPORT of the Canal Commissioners, to the General Assembly of Ohio.* 54 pp., stitched. Columbus, 1825. $45. Another issue, 66 pp., sewed. $75-$100.

*REPORT of the Commissioner of Public Buildings, with the Documents Accompanying the Same.* 36 pp., stitched. (Madison, Wis., 1842.) (By John Smith.) $60-$100.

*REPORT of the Committee to Whom Was Referred, on the 26th Ultimo, the Consideration of the Expediency of Accepting from the State of Connecticut, a Cession of Jurisdiction of the Territory West of Pennsylvania, Commonly Called the Western Reserve of Connecticut.* 31 pp., calf. (Philadelphia), 1800. $125-$150.

*REPORT of the General Assembly upon the Subject of the Proceedings of the Bank of the U.S., Against the Officers of State.* 37 pp., sewed. Columbus, Ohio, 1820. $100-$125.

*REPORT of the Proceedings Connected with the Disuptes Between the Earl of Selkirk and the North-West Company.* Half leather. London, 1819. (Samuel Hull Wilcocke, editor.) $650-$750. Montreal, 1819. Calf. $650-$750.

*REPORT of the Secretary of the Interior, Communicating . . . the Report of J. Ross Browne, on the Late Indian War in Oregon and Washington Territories.* 66 pp., stitched. Washington, 1858. First edition. $100-$150.

*REPORT of the Trial of Frederick P. Hill, etc.* 60 pp., wrappers. Chicago, 1864. (Allan Pinkerton, editor.) First edition. $125-$150.

*REPORT on the Committee of the Society of Arts.* Engraved folding plate and 5 engraved full-page reproductions. Boards. London, 1819. $50-$60.

*REPORT on the Governor's Message, Relating to the "Political Situation," "Polygamy," and "Governmental Action."* 13 pp., wrappers. Salt Lake, 1882. $125-$150.

*REPORT on the Subject of a Communication between Canandaigua Lake and the Erie Canal, Made at a Meeting of the Citizens.* 23 pp., sewed. Canandaigua, N.Y., 1821. $75-$100.

*REPORT Relative to the Excitements, on the Part of British Subjects, of the Indians to Commit Hostility Against the U.S., and the Late Campaign on the Wabash.* 43 pp., sewed. Washington City, 1812. $75-$100.

*REPORTS and Resolutions of the General Assembly of the State of South Carolina.* Gathered, not sewed, but punched for stitching. Columbia, 1863. $75-$100.

*REPORTS of the Committee of Investigation Sent in 1873, by the Mexican Government, to the Frontier of Texas.* 3 folding maps. Boards and leather. New York, 1875. $200-$300.

*REPORTS of Territorial Officers of the Territory of Colorado.* Wrappers. Central City, 1871. $100-$125.

REPPLIER, Agnes. *Books and Men.* Boards and cloth. Boston, 1882. First edition. $40-$50. Author's first book.

REPTON, Humphry. *Observations on the Theory and Practice of Landscape Gardening.* Portrait frontispiece and 27 plates, 10 in full color. Contemporary leather. London, 1803. First edition. $1,000-$1,500. London, 1805. $1,000-$1,500.

*RESIGNATION: An American Novel by a Lady.* 2 vols., marbled boards and calf. Boston, 1825. (By Sarah Ann Evans.) First edition, with errata leaf in Vol. 1. $200-$250.

*RESOURCES and Development of the Territory of Washington.* Folding map. 72 pp., sewed. Seattle, 1886. $100-$150.

*RESOURCES of Arizona (The)*. 71 pp., wrappers. (Florence, Ariz., 1881). (By Patrick Hamilton.) First edition. $100-$200. Prescott, Ariz., 1881. 120 pp., printed wrappers. (Author named.) Second edition. $75-$100. (Note: There were later editions, including a San Francisco edition of 1883, which Howes calls a "second" edition.)

REVERE, Joseph W. *A Tour of Duty in California*. 6 plates, folding map. Cloth. New York, 1849. First edition. $200-$250.

*REVIEW of the Opinion of the Supreme Court in the Case of Cohen vs. Virginia, etc*. 78 pp., stitched. Steubenville, Ohio, 1821. (By Charles Hammond.) $150-$175.

REXROTH, Kenneth. *The Art of Worldly Wisdom*. Green boards and cloth. Prairie City, Ill., 1949. First edition. Signed by the author. Errata slip laid in. $175. Sausalito, Calif., 1953. Boards. Second edition. $40.

REXROTH, Kenneth. *In What Hour*. Blue cloth. New York, 1940. First edition. In dust jacket. $65. Author's first book.

REXROTH, Kenneth. *The Signature of All Things*. Boards. (New York, 1950.) First edition. In dust jacket. $35-$45.

REYNARDSON, C.T.S. Birch. *'Down the Road' or Reminiscences of a Gentleman Coachman*. Colored lithographs. Cloth. London, 1875. First edition. $100-$150. Second edition, same date. $100-$150.

REYNOLDS, H.D. (editor). *Wells Cathedral*. Frontispiece, 4 plans (one folding), a folding table, 8 plates and text illustrations. Folio, morocco. London, (1881). $75-$100.

REYNOLDS, J.N. *Voyage of the United States Frigate Potomac*. Illustrated. Half leather. New York, 1835. First edition. $75-$100.

REYNOLDS, John. *My Own Times*. Portrait. Cloth. Illinois (Belleville), 1855. First edition. $350-$450.

REYNOLDS, John. *The Pioneer History of Illinois*. Cloth. Belleville, 1852. First edition. $275-$350.

REYNOLDS, John. *Sketches of the Country on the Northern Route from Belleville, Ill., to the City of New York, and back by the Ohio Valley*. Black cloth. Belleville, 1854. First edition. $600-$750.

REZANOV, Nicolai P. *The Rezanov Voyage to Nueva California in 1806*. Edited by Thomas C. Russell. 5 plates. Half cloth. San Francisco, 1926. One of 200. $65-$75.

REZNIKOFF, Charles. *Five Groups of Verse*. Cloth. New York, (1927). First edition. One of 375. In dust jacket. $40-$50.

REZNIKOFF, Charles. *Going To and Fro and Walking Up and Down*. Cloth. New York, (1941). First edition. In dust jacket. $40-$50.

REZNIKOFF, Charles. *Jerusalem the Golden*. Cloth. New York, (1934). First edition. In dust jacket. $50-$60.

REZNIKOFF, Charles. *Nine Plays*. Cloth. New York, (1927). First edition. One of 400. In dust jacket. $40.

REZNIKOFF, Charles. *Rhythms*. Wrappers. Brooklyn, (1918). First edition. $300-$500. Author's first book.

RHODES, Eugene Manlove. *The Best Novels and Stories of Eugene Manlove Rhodes*. Cloth. Boston, 1949. First edition. In dust jacket. $30-$40.

RHODES, Eugene Manlove. *Beyond the Desert*. Cloth. Boston, 1934. First edition, with dated title page. In dust jacket. $50-$60.

RHODES, Eugene Manlove. *Bransford in Arcadia*. Cloth. New York, 1914. First edition. In dust jacket. $35-$50.

RHODES, Eugene Manlove. *The Desire of the Moth.* Cloth. New York, 1916. First edition. In dust jacket. $150-$175.

RHODES, Eugene Manlove. *Good Men and True.* Cloth. New York, 1910. First edition. In dust jacket. $100-$125. Author's first book.

RHODES, Eugene Manlove. *The Little World Waddies.* Cloth. Chico, Calif., (1946). First edition. In dust jacket. $85-$125.

RHODES, Eugene Manlove. *Once in the Saddle and Paso Por Aqui.* Cloth. Boston, 1927. First edition. In dust jacket. $40-$50.

RHODES, Eugene Manlove. *The Proud Sheriff.* Cloth. Boston, 1935. First edition. In dust jacket. $35-$45.

RHODES, Eugene Manlove. *Say Now Shibboleth.* Boards and cloth. Chicago, 1921. Book Fellows. First edition. One of 400. In tissue dust jacket. $100-$135.

RHODES, Eugene Manlove. *Stepsons of Light.* Cloth. Boston, (1921). First edition. In dust jacket. $40-$560.

RHODES, Eugene Manlove. *The Trusty Knaves.* Cloth. Boston, 1933. First edition. In dust jacket. $40-$50.

RHODES, Eugene Manlove. *West Is West.* Frontispiece. Cloth. New York, 1917. First edition. In dust jacket. $50-$60.

RHODODAPHNE: *or The Thessalian Spell: A Poem.* Blue boards. London, 1818. (By Thomas Love Peacock.) First edition. $300-$350.

RICARDO, David. *On the Principles of Political Economy, and Taxation.* Contemporary calf. London, 1817. First edition. $5,000 and up. Also, $4,750 (A, 1977). Georgetown, D.C., 1819. Half leather. First American edition. $200-$300.

RICE County: *Its Resources.* 20 pp., wrappers. Faribault, Minn., 1869. $150-$200.

RICH, Adrienne Cecile. *Ariadne: A Play in Three Acts and Poems.* 59 pp., blue wrappers. (Baltimore), 1939. First edition. In tissue dust jacket. Inscribed, $2,250 in a 1976 catalogue; $1,750 in a 1978 catalogue. (Note: The poet's first published work, despite her disavowals.)

RICH, Adrienne Cecile. *A Change of World.* Foreword by W. H. Auden. Boards. New Haven, 1951. First edition. In dust jacket. $50-$60. Author's first book as an adult.

RICH, Adrienne Cecile. *The Diamond Cutters and Other Poems.* Cloth. New York, (1955). First edition. In dust jacket. $75-$100.

RICH, Adrienne Cecile. *Snap-Shots of a Daughter-in-Law.* Boards and cloth. New York, (1963). First edition. In dust jacket. $30-$35.

RICHARD Hurdis; *or, the Avenger of Blood.* 2 vols., cloth, paper labels. Philadelphia, 1838. (By William Gilmore Simms.) First edition. $150-$175.

RICHARDS, Laura E. *Captain January.* Gray boards, white cloth spine. Boston, 1891. First edition, first state, with typography and presswork note at foot of copyright page. $50-$75.

RICHARDS, Laura E. *Five Mice in a Mouse-Trap.* Cloth. Boston, 1880. First edition. $150-$175.

RICHARDS, Thomas Addison. *American Scenery Illustrated.* Morocco. New York, (1854). First edition. $150-$200.

RICHARDS, Thomas Addison. *Georgia Illustrated.* Plates. 44 pp., leather. Penfield, Ga., 1842. First edition. $150-$175.

RICHARDS, Thomas Addison. *The Romance of American Landscape.* 16 engravings. Morocco. New York, (1854). First edition. $150-$200.

RICHARDSON, Dorothy. *Pointed Roofs*. Cloth. London, 1915. First edition. $40-$60. Author's first book.

RICHARDSON, Maj. John. *Eight Years in Canada*. Cloth. Montreal, 1847. $150-$250.

RICHARDSON, Rupert N. *The Comanche Barrier to South Plains Settlement*. Illustrated. Cloth. Glendale, Calif., 1933. $100-$150.

RICHARDSON, Rupert N., and Rister, C.C. *The Greater Southwest*. Cloth. Glendale, 1934. First edition. $75-$100.

RICHARDSON, William H. *The Journal of William H. Richardson: A Private Soldier in Col. Doniphan's Command*. 84 pp., wrappers. Baltimore, 1847. First edition. $4,000-$5,000, possibly more. New York, 1848. Third edition. $500-$750.

RICHEY, James H. *A Trip Across the Plains in 1854*. 8 pp., wrappers. (Richey, Calif., 1908.) First edition. $75-$100.

RICHMOND, C.W., and Vallette, H. F. *A History of Du Page County, Illinois*. Cloth. Chicago, 1857. First edition. $150-$200.

*RICHMOND During the War; Four Years of Personal Observation*. Cloth. New York, 1867. (By Sally A. Brock.) First edition. $100-$125.

RICHTER, Conrad. *Brothers of No Kin and Other Stories*. Red cloth. New York, (about 1924). First edition. In white (first) dust jacket. $250-$350. In later (orange) jacket. $200. Author's first book.

RICHTOFEN, Walter, Baron Von. *Cattle-Raising on the Plains of North America*. Cloth. New York, 1885. First edition. $200-$300.

RIDGE, John R. See Yellow Bird. Also see *The Life of Joaquin Murieta*.

RIDGE, John R. *Joaquin Murieta, the Brigand Chief of California*. Color plates, folding reward poster facsimile. Boards. San Francisco, 1932. Grabhorn printing. One of 400. $75-$85.

RIDGE, John R. *The Life and Adventures of Joaquin Murieta the Celebrated California Bandit*. Printed wrappers. San Francisco, (1874). Third (?) edition. $375 (A, 1968). (Note: This edition included a separate title page—*Career of Tiburcio Vasquez*—and is listed by Howes as a reprint of the third edition, which he records as published in 1871.) For first edition, see Yellow Bird (pseudonym).

RIDGE, Lola. *Firehead*. Half morocco. New York, 1929. First edition. One of 30, signed. $50-$75. Trade edition: In dust jacket. $10-$15.

RIDING, Laura. *Americans*. Boards and cloth. No place, 1934. Primavera Press. One of 200. $50-$60.

RIDING, Laura. *The Close Chaplet*. Boards, paper label. New York, (1926). First edition. $125-$150. Author's first book.

RIDING, Laura. *Collected Poems*. Cloth. New York, 1938. First American edition. In dust jacket. $35-$50.

RIDING, Laura. *Four Unposted Letters to Catherine*. Boards and leather. Paris, (1930). Hours Press. First edition. One of 200, signed. In glassine dust jacket. $50-$60.

RIDING, Laura. *Laura and Francesca*. Decorated blue boards and cloth. Deya, Majorca, 1931. Seizin Press. First edition. One of 200, signed. In glassine dust jacket. $60-$80.

RIDING, Laura. *The Life of the Dead*. Illustrated by John Aldridge. Stiff wrappers. London, (1933). First edition. One of 200, signed. $250-$300.

RIDING, Laura. *Lives of Wives*. Green cloth. London, (1939). First edition. In dust jacket. $75-$85.

RIDING, Laura. *Love as Love, Death as Death.* Tan or gray cloth. London, 1928. Seizin Press (its first book). First edition. One of 175, signed. $125-$150.

RIDING, Laura. *Progress of Stories.* Cloth. London, (1935), First edition. In dust jacket. $135-$150.

RIDING, Laura. *The Second Leaf.* Wrappers (actually a broadside folded to make 4 leaves). Deya, 1935. Seizin Press. First edition. Limited (fewer than 100). $60-$80.

RIDING, Laura. *Though Gently.* Decorated boards and cloth. Deya, 1930. Seizin Press. First edition. One of 200, signed. In glassine dust jacket. $100-$150.

RIDING, Laura. *Twenty Poems Less.* Half leather and boards. Paris, 1930. Hours Press. First edition. One of 200, signed. In glassine dust jacket. $100-$150.

RIDING, Laura. *Voltaire.* Wrappers. London, 1927. First edition. $300-$350.

RIDING, Laura, and Graves, Robert. *A Pamphlet Against Anthologies.* Cloth. New York, 1928. First edition. In dust jacket. $75-$85.

RIDING, Laura, and Graves, Robert. *A Survey of Modernist Poetry.* Boards and cloth. London, 1927. First edition. In dust jacket. $75-$85.

RIDINGS, Sam P. *The Chisholm Trail.* Folding map. Cloth. Guthrie, Okla., (1936). First edition. In dust jacket. $75-$100.

RIDLER, Anne (editor). *The Little Book of Modern Verse.* Preface by T. S. Eliot. Cloth. London, 1941. First edition. In dust jacket. $35-$45.

*RIENZI, The Last of the Tribunes.* 3 vols., boards. London, 1835. (By Edward Bulwer-Lytton.) First edition, with errata slips for Vols. 2 and 3 tipped into Vol 2. $300-$400.

RILEY, James Whitcomb. See Johnson, Benj. F. (of Boone).

RILEY, James Whitcomb. *Character Sketches, The Boss Girl, A Christmas Story, and Other Sketches.* Cloth, or printed wrappers. Indianapolis, 1886. First edition, first printing, with copyright notice in the name of Riley and an exclamation point after "sir" in line 5 of page 9. Cloth: $75-$100. Wrappers: $75-$100.

RILEY, James Whitcomb. *The Flying Islands of the Night.* Illustrated. Cloth. Indianapolis, 1892. First edition. In vellum dust jacket. $100.

RILEY, James Whitcomb. *Green Fields and Running Brooks.* Cloth. Indianapolis, 1893. First edition, first state, with "Miles on mile," line 1 of page 16. $25-$35.

RILEY, James Whitcomb. *Poems Here at Home.* Cloth, or vellum. New York, 1893. First edition, first state, with "girls" spelled correctly in line 5 on page 50. In dust jacket. $50-$65.

RILEY, James Whitcomb. *Rhymes of Childhood.* Cloth. Indianapolis, 1891. First edition, first state, with child's head illustrated on front cover. $50-$85.

RILEY, James Whitcomb, and Nye, Edgar W. (Bill). *Nye and Riley's Railway Guide.* Cloth. Chicago, 1888. First edition. $50-$75.

RIMBAUD, Arthur. See Schwartz, Delmore.

RINEHART, Mary Roberts. *The Man in Lower Ten.* Illustrated by Howard Chandler Christy. Cloth. Indianapolis, (1909). First edition. In dust jacket. $50-$75.

RINEHART, Mary Roberts, and Hopwood, Avery. *The Bat: A Novel from the Play by Mary Roberts Rinehart and Avery Hopwood.* Cloth. New York, (1926). First edition. In dust jacket. $50-$60. (Note: Believed to have been written by Stephen Vincent Benét.)

*RINGAN Gilhaize.* 3 vols., boards. Edinburgh, 1823. (By John Galt.) First edition. $200-$250.

RINGWALT, John Luther (editor). *American Encyclopedia of Printing.* Cloth. Philadelphia, 1871. First edition. $100-$150.

RISTER, Carl Coke. *The Southwestern Frontier, 1865-1881.* Cloth. Cleveland, 1928. First edition. $75-$100.

*RIVER Dove (The); with Some Quiet Thoughts on the Happy Practice of Angling.* 14 engravings. Half leather. (London?, about 1845.) (By John L. Anderdon.) One of 25 privately printed. $250-$300.

RIVERS, Elizabeth. *Stranger in Aran.* Illustrations (4 in color) by author. Boards, linen spine. Dublin, 1946. Cuala Press. One of 280. In dust jacket. $60-$80.

*ROB of the Bowl.* 2 vols., cloth, paper labels on spines. Philadelphia, 1838. (By John Pendleton Kennedy.) First edition. $150-$200.

*ROB ROY.* 3 vols., boards, paper labels. Edinburgh, 1818. (By Sir Walter Scott.) First edition. $200-$300.

ROBB, John S. See *Streaks of Squatter Life, etc.*

ROBB, John S. *Kaam, or Daylight.* Pictorial wrappers. Boston, 1847. First edition. $300-$400. Also, $200 (A, 1968).

ROBBINS, Aurelia. *A True and Authentic Account of the Indian War, etc.* 28 pp., wrappers. New York, 1836. $150-$200.

ROBERTS, Mrs. D.W. *A Woman's Reminiscences of Six Years In Camp with the Texas Rangers.* Illustrated. 64 pp., wrappers. Austin, (1928). First edition. $50-$75.

ROBERTS, Elizabeth Madox. *Black Is My Truelove's Hair.* Boards, green buckram spine. New York, 1938. First edition. One of 175, signed. Boxed. $35-$45.

ROBERTS, Elizabeth Madox. *A Buried Treasure.* Green buckram. New York, 1931. First edition. One of 200, signed. Boxed. $35-$40.

ROBERTS, Elizabeth Madox. *The Great Meadow.* Green buckram. New York, 1930. First edition. One of 295 large paper copies, signed. Boxed. $35-$40.

ROBERTS, Elizabeth Madox. *In the Great Steep's Garden.* Wrappers, (Colorado Springs, 1915.) First edition. $35-$50. Author's first book.

ROBERTS, Elizabeth Madox. *Under the Tree.* Boards. New York, 1922. First edition. In dust jacket. $50-$60.

ROBERTS, Kenneth. *Arundel.* Dark-blue cloth. Garden City, 1930. First edition (so indicated on copyright page). In dust jacket. $50-$75.

ROBERTS, Kenneth. *Europe's Morning After.* Decorated cloth. New York, (about 1921). First edition, first issue, with "B-V" on copyright page. In dust jacket. $65-$85. Author's first book.

ROBERTS, Kenneth. *Lydia Bailey.* Cloth. Garden City, 1947. First edition. Gray buckram. One of 1,050, signed, with a page of the ms., with corrections in Roberts' hand, laid in. In dust jacket. Boxed. $60-$85. Trade edition: Cloth. In dust jacket. $15.

ROBERTS, Kenneth. *Northwest Passage.* Dark-green cloth. Garden City, 1937. First edition (so indicated on copyright page). In dust jacket. $25-$35. Another issue: 2 vols., cloth. One of 1,050, signed. In dust jackets. Boxed. $200-$300.

ROBERTS, Kenneth. *Oliver Wiswell.* Cloth. New York, 1940. First edition (so indicated). 2 vols., cloth. One of 1,050, signed. $100-$150. Trade edition: Cloth. $15.

ROBERTS, Kenneth. *Rabble in Arms.* Cloth. Garden City, 1933. First edition (so indicated on copyright page). In dust jacket. $100-$125.

ROBERTS, Kenneth. *Sun Hunting*. Illustrated. Blue-green cloth. Indianapolis, (1922). First edition. In dust jacket. $75-$100.

ROBERTS, Kenneth. *Trending into Maine*. Illustrated by N.C. Wyeth. Tan buckram. New York, 1938. First edition, with "Published June 1938" on copyright page. In dust jacket. $25. Another issue: Cloth. One of 1,075 signed. Boxed. $200-$300. With an extra set of the Wyeth plates, $300-$400.

ROBERTS, Kenneth. *Why Europe Leaves Home*. Cloth. (Indianapolis, 1922.) First edition. $60-$75.

ROBERTS, Oran M. *A Description of Texas*. 8 colored plates, 5 double-page maps. Cloth. St. Louis, 1881. First edition.$100-$150. ·

ROBERTS, W. H. *Northwestern Washington*. Folding map. 52 pp., wrappers. Port Townsend, Wash., 1880. First edition. $150-$200.

ROBERTSON, John W. *Francis Drake and Other Early Explorers Along the Pacific Coast*. 28 maps. Illustrations by Valenti Angelo. Vellum and boards. San Francisco, 1927. Grabhorn Press. One of 1,000. $75-$100.

ROBERTSON, Wyndham, Jr. *Oregon, Our Right and Title*. Folding map. Boards and cloth, or printed wrappers. Washington, 1846. First edition. Either binding: $1,000-$1,500.

ROBIDOUX, Mrs. Orral M. *Memorial to the Robidoux Brothers*. Map. 16 plates. Cloth. Kansas City, 1924. First edition. $80-$100.

ROBINSON, Charles Edson. *A Concise History of the United Society of Believers Called Shakers*. Illustrated. Boards and calf. East Canterbury, N.H., (1893). $150-$175.

ROBINSON, Charles N. *Old Naval Prints, Their Artists and Engravers*. 106 full-page plates, 24 in color. Cloth. London, 1924. In dust jacket. $200-$225.

ROBINSON, Edwin Arlington. *Amaranth*. Cloth. New York, 1934. First edition. Large paper issue, one of 226, signed. $35-$50. Trade edition: Green cloth. In dust jacket. $25.

ROBINSON, Edwin Arlington. *Avon's Harvest*. Light maroon boards and cloth. New York, 1921. First edition. In dust jacket. $25-$35.

ROBINSON, Edwin Arlington. *Captain Craig: A Book of Poems*. Cloth, paper label. Boston, 1902. First edition, first issue, with copyright line and "Published October, 1902" on copyright page. One of 125 untrimmed. $100-$150.

ROBINSON, Edwin Arlington. *Cavender's House*. Cloth. New York, 1929. First edition. One of 500, signed. In slipcase. $50. Trade edition: Cloth. In dust jacket. $10.

ROBINSON, Edwin Arlington. *The Children of the Night*. Muslin. Boston, 1897. First edition. One of 50 on Japan vellum. $1,000-$1,500. Also, $1,100 (A, 1974). Another issue: Cloth. One of 500 on Batchworth laid paper. In dust jacket. $250-$350.

ROBINSON, Edwin Arlington. *Dionysus in Doubt*. Cloth-backed boards. New York, 1925. First edition. One of 350 large paper copies, signed. $50-$60. Trade edition: Cloth. First issue, with gray (instead of white) labels. In dust jacket. $15-$25.

ROBINSON, Edwin Arlington. *Fortunatus*. Boards, paper label. Reno, 1928. Grabhorn printing. First edition. One of 171 signed. $150-$250. One of 12 on brown paper, signed, for presentation. $500-$750.

ROBINSON, Edwin Arlington. *The Glory of the Nightingales*. Cloth. New York, 1930. First edition. One of 500, signed. Boxed. $35-$75. Trade edition: Green cloth. In dust jacket. $10.

ROBINSON, Edwin Arlington. *King Jasper*. Introduction by Robert Frost. Cloth. New York, 1935. First edition. One of 250 large paper copies. $65-$85. Trade edition: Cloth. In dust jacket. $15-$20.

ROBINSON, Edwin Arlington. *Lancelot*. Gray-green cloth. New York, 1920. First edition. In dust jacket. $25. (Later binding in red.) Second-issue title page: One of 450 for the Lyric Society. $40-$60.

ROBINSON, Edwin Arlington. *The Man Against the Sky*. Dark-red cloth. New York, 1916. First edition, first state, with top edges gilt. In dust jacket. $50-$60.

ROBINSON, Edwin Arlington. *The Man Who Died Twice*. Boards and cloth. New York, 1924. First edition. One of 500, signed. Boxed. $35-$50. Trade edition: Red cloth. In dust jacket. $15.

ROBINSON, Edwin Arlington. *Matthias at the Door*. Green cloth. New York, 1931. First edition, first state, with no punctuation at end of fifth line from bottom of page 97. One of 500, signed. Boxed. $40-$60. Trade edition: Cloth. In dust jacket. $10-$15.

ROBINSON, Edwin Arlington. *Merlin*. Red cloth. New York, 1917. First edition, first state, with "only philosophy" (instead of "one philosophy") in line 8 of page 79. In dust jacket. $30-$35.

ROBINSON, Edwin Arlington. *Modred: A Fragment*. Boards and cloth. New York, 1929. First edition. One of 250, signed. In slipcase. $75-$100.

ROBINSON, Edwin Arlington. *Nicodemus*. Cloth. New York, 1932. First edition. One of 235 large paper copies, signed. $50-$60.

ROBINSON, Edwin Arlington. *The Porcupine*. Cloth. New York, 1915. First edition, first state, with top edges gilt and with rules and lettering on front cover in gold. Erratum slip. In dust jacket. $40-$50.

ROBINSON, Edwin Arlington. *The Prodigal Son*. Wrappers. New York, 1929. First edition. One of 475. $50.

ROBINSON, Edwin Arlington. *Roman Bartholow*. Boards and cloth. New York, 1923. First edition. One of 750, signed. In dust jacket. $40-$60. Trade edition: Cloth. In dust jacket. $10.

ROBINSON, Edwin Arlington. *Sonnets 1889-1927*. Boards and cloth. New York, 1928. First edition. One of 561. $40-$50. Another issue: One of 9 on green paper. $175-$250.

ROBINSON, Edwin Arlington. *Talifer*. Cloth. New York, 1933. First edition. One of 273 large paper copies, signed. $50. Trade edition: Cloth. In dust jacket. $15-$20.

ROBINSON, Edwin Arlington. *Three Poems*. Cloth. Cambridge, Mass., 1928. First (pirated) edition. One of 15 copies. $50-$100.

ROBINSON, Edwin Arlington. *The Three Taverns*. Maroon cloth. New York, 1920. First edition. In dust jacket. $25-$35.

ROBINSON, Edwin Arlington. *The Torrent and the Night Before*. Blue wrappers. (Cambridge, Mass.), 1896. First edition. $750-$1,000, possibly more. Also, inscribed by Robinson, $1,400 (A, 1977); $1,900 (A, 1974). Author's first book. New York, 1928. One of 110, signed. $100-$200.

ROBINSON, Edwin Arlington. *The Town Down the River*. Dark-green silk. New York, 1910. First edition. In dust jacket. $50.

ROBINSON, Edwin Arlington. *Tristram*. Half cloth. New York, 1927. First edition, first state, with "rocks" for "rooks," line 2 on page 86. One of 350 large paper copies, signed. Boxed. $100-$150. Trade and Literary Guild editions: Cloth. In dust jacket. $15-$20. (Note: The Guild issue, preceding the trade, has "rooks," not "rocks.")

ROBINSON, Edwin Arlington. *Van Zorn*. Dark-maroon cloth. New York, 1914. First edition, first state, with top edges gilt and with cover lettering in gold. In dust jacket. $35-$50.

ROBINSON, J.A. *The White Rover*. 100 pp., wrappers. New York, no date. $75-$100.

ROBINSON, Dr. J. H. *Rosalthe: Or, The Pioneers of Kentucky*. Wrappers. Boston, 1853. First edition. $100-$125.

ROBINSON, Jacob. *Sketches of the Great West.* 71 pp., wrappers. Portsmouth, N.H., 1848. First edition. $4,500-$5,000.

ROBINSON, John, and Dow, George F. *The Sailing Ships of New England, 1607-1907.* 3 vols., cloth. Series I, II, and III. Salem, 1922-24-28. $200-$250.

ROBINSON, Lennox (editor). *A Little Anthology of Modern Irish Verse.* Blue boards, linen back, paper label. Dublin, 1928. Cuala Press. First edition. One of 300. In plain dust jacket. $60-$75.

ROBINSON, Rowland Evans. See *Forest and Stream Fables.*

ROBINSON, Rowland Evans. *Uncle 'Lisha's Shop.* Cloth. New York, 1887. First edition. $35-$50. Author's first book.

ROBINSON, William Davis. *Memoirs of the Mexican Revolution.* Boards. Philadelphia, 1820. First edition. $150-$300. London, 1821. 2 vols., half linen. $150-$175.

ROBSON, John S. *How a One Legged Rebel Lives, or a History of the 52nd Virginia Regiment.* Wrappers. Richmond, 1876. $100.

ROCHESTER, John Wilmot, Earl of. *Collected Works.* Edited by John Hayward. Boards and buckram. London, 1926. Nonesuch Press. $100-$125. Another issue: Boards and vellum. One of 75. $200.

ROCK, Marion T. *Illustrated History of Oklahoma.* 90 plates. Cloth. Topeka, 1890. First edition. $200-$300.

RODD, Rennell. *Rose Leaf and Apple Leaf.* Introduction by Oscar Wilde. Vellum. Philadelphia, 1882. First edition. De luxe issue. $200-$300. London, 1904. Wrappers. One of 200. $100-$135.

RODENBOUGH, Theodore F. *Uncle Sam's Medal of Honor.* Cloth. New York, (1886). First edition. $50-$75.

RODITI, Edouard. *Prison Within Prison.* Wrappers. Prairie City, Ill., (1941). First edition. $150-$250.

RODRÍGUEZ DE SAN MIQUEL, Juan. *Documentos Relativos al Piadoso Fondo de Misiones para Conversión y Civilización de las Numerosas Tribus Barbaras de la Antigua y Nueva California.* 60 pp., calf. Mexico, 1845. First edition. $350-$450. Another edition, same date, 28 pp. added. Wrappers. $300-$400.

RODRÍGUEZ DE SAN MIQUEL, Juan. *Segundo Cuaderno de Interesantes Documentos Relativos a los Bienes del Fondo Piadoso de Misiones, para Conversión y Civilización de las Tribus Barbaras de las Californias.* 32 pp., wrappers. Mexico, 1845. $400-$600.

ROE, Azel Stevens. *James Montjoy: or I've Been Thinking.* 2 parts, wrappers. New York, 1850. First edition. $50-$75.

ROE, Edward Payson. *Barriers Burned Away.* Cloth. New York, 1872. First edition. $35-$50.

ROETHKE, Theodore. See *Ten Poets.*

ROETHKE, Theodore. *Collected Poems.* Cloth. New York, 1966. First edition. In dust jacket. $30-$40.

ROETHKE, Theodore. *Open House.* Cloth. New York, 1941. First edition. One of 1,000. In dust jacket. $200-$225. Author's first book.

ROETHKE, Theodore. *Sequence Sometimes Metaphysical.* Illustrated. Boards. Iowa City, (1963). First edition. One of 330. Boxed. $200-$250. Another issue: One of 60, signed. $300-$550.

ROETHKE, Theodore. *The Waking: Poems 1933-1953.* Cloth. Garden City, 1953. In dust jacket. $75-$100.

ROETHKE, Theodore. *Words for the Wind*. Cloth. London, 1957. First edition. In dust jacket. $50-$75. Garden City, 1958. Cloth. First American edition. In dust jacket. $30-$45.

ROGERS, A.N. *Communication Relative to the Location of the U.P.R.R. Across the Rocky Mountains Through Colorado Territory*. Wrappers. Central City, Colo., 1867. $450-$500.

ROGERS, Robert. *Journals of Maj. Robert Rogers*. Edited by Franklin B. Hough. Map. Cloth. Albany, 1883. $75-$100.

ROGERS, Samuel. *Human Life: A Poem*. Boards. London, 1819. First edition, first issue, with Bensley misprint on pages 4 and 100. $50-$75.

ROGET, Peter Mark. *Thesaurus of English Words*. Cloth. Boston, 1854. First American edition. $100-$150.

ROLFE, Fr. *Don Tarquinio*. Violet cloth. London, 1905. First edition, first binding. $200-$350.

ROLFE, Fr. *Hadrian the Seventh*. Cloth. London, 1904. First edition, first issue, purple cloth; title and drawing stamped in white. $300-$450. Second issue, title and drawing blind-stamped. $250-$300.

ROLFE, Frederick William. See Corvo, Baron; Corvo, Frederick Baron; Prospero and Caliban.

ROLLINS, Philip Ashton. *Jinglebob*. Illustrated in color by N.C. Wyeth. Cloth. New York, 1930. First edition. In dust jacket. $35.

ROLLINS, Philip Ashton (editor). *The Discovery of the Oregon Trail*. New York, 1935. In dust jacket. $30-$40.

ROLLINSON, John K. *History of the Migration of Oregon-Raised Herds to Mid-Western Markets: Wyoming Cattle Trails*. Plates, maps, colored frontispiece by Frederic Remington. Cloth. Caldwell, Idaho, 1948. First edition. One of 1,000, signed. $50-$75.

ROLLINSON, John K. *Hoofprints of a Cowboy and a U.S. Ranger*. Cloth. Caldwell, 1941. First edition. In dust jacket. $35-$50.

*ROLLO Learning to Talk*. Woodcut illustrations. Decorated cloth. Philadelphia, 1841. (By Jacob Abbott.) New edition (of *The Little Scholar Learning to Talk*, 1835). $50.

ROLPH, J. Alexander. *Dylan Thomas: A Bibliography*. 16 pp., of plates. Cloth. London, (1956). First edition. In dust jacket. $35-$50.

*ROMANCE of Indian History: or, Thrilling Incidents in the Early Settlement of America*. 24 pp., wrappers. New York, (185-?). (By Adam Poe.) $35-$50.

RONSARD, Pierre de. *Florilège des Amours*. 126 lithographs by Henri Matisse. Lithograph on paper cover, folio, in slipcase designed by Matisse. Paris, 1948. Albert Skira. One of 250 signed by the artist. $4,000 and up.

ROOD, Hosea W. *Story of the Service of Co. E*. Cloth. Milwaukee, 1893. $75-$100.

ROOSEVELT, Eleanor. *This I Remember*. Frontispiece and plates. Buckram. New York, (1949). First edition. One of 1,000 on large paper, signed. Boxed. $50-$75. Trade edition: Cloth. In dust jacket. $10-$15.

ROOSEVELT, Eleanor. *This Is My Story*. Buckram. New York, 1937. First edition. One of 258, signed. $75-$125.

ROOSEVELT, Franklin D. *The Democratic Book, 1936*. Illustrated. Folio, wrappers. (Philadelphia), 1936. Limited edition, signed by F.D.R. $150-$250.

ROOSEVELT, Franklin D. *The Happy Warrior: Alfred E. Smith*. 40 pp., black cloth, orange label. Boston, 1928. First edition. In dust jacket. $60-$75.

ROOSEVELT, Franklin D. *Looking Forward.* Wrappers. New York, (1933). First edition. One of 100. $100-$150. Trade edition: Cloth. In dust jacket. $20-$25.

ROOSEVELT, Franklin D. *Whither Bound?* 34 pp., cloth. Boston, 1926. First edition. In dust jacket. $75-$100. Author's first book.

ROOSEVELT, Franklin D. (editor). *Records of the Town of Hyde Park.* Cloth. No place, 1928. One of 100, with limitation notice written out and signed by F.D.R. $150-$200.

ROOSEVELT, Theodore. *American Ideals and Other Essays.* Cloth. New York, 1897. First edition. $25.

ROOSEVELT, Theodore. *American Problems.* Portrait in silhouette. Wrappers. New York, 1910. First edition. $50.

ROOSEVELT, Theodore. *Big Game Hunting in the Rockies and on the Great Plains.* 55 etchings. Signed frontispiece. Full tan buckram. New York, 1899. First edition. One of 1,000, signed. $300-$400.

ROOSEVELT, Theodore, *Hunting Trips of a Ranchman.* 20 plates. Buckram. New York, 1885. First edition. Limited Medora Edition of 500. $200-$350. New York, 1886. Cloth. First trade edition. $35-$45.

ROOSEVELT, Theodore. *Letter . . . Accepting the Republican Nomination for President of the United States.* 32 pp., self-wrappers. (New York), 1902. First edition. $75-$100.

ROOSEVELT, Theodore. *List of Birds Seen in the White House Grounds.* 4 pp., leaflet. (Washington), 1908. First edition. $150-$200.

ROOSEVELT, Theodore. *Naval War of 1812.* Cloth. New York, 1882. First edition. $35-$50. (Note: Second edition so indicated on title page.)

ROOSEVELT, Theodore. *Outdoor Pastimes of an American Hunter.* 49 plates. Half calf and boards. New York, 1905. First edition. One of 260 signed. In dust jacket. $275-$350.

ROOSEVELT, Theodore. *Ranch Life and the Hunting-Trail.* Illustrated by Frederic Remington. All edges gilt, light-colored, coarse weave, tan buckram, cover design in green and gold. New York, (1888). First edition. $100-$150.

ROOSEVELT, Theodore. *The Rough Riders.* Cloth. New York, 1899. First edition. $50-$75.

ROOSEVELT, Theodore. *Some American Game.* Wrappers. New York, 1897. First edition. $150-$200.

ROOSEVELT, Theodore. *Theodore Roosevelt: An Autobiography.* Illustrated. Cloth. New York, 1913. First edition. In dust jacket. $40-$60.

ROOSEVELT, Theodore. *The Wilderness Hunter.* Tan or brown cloth. New York, (1893). First edition, with chapter headings in brown. $30-$40. Another issue: Cloth. One of 200, signed. $200-$250.

ROOSEVELT, Theodore. *The Winning of the West.* 4 vols., cloth. New York, 1889-96. First edition. (Vol. 1: 1889; Vol. 2: 1889; Vol. 3: 1894; Vol. 4: 1896.) First edition, first issue, with "diame-" as last word on page 160 and "ter" as first word on page 161. $150-$200. New York, 1900. Illustrated. 4 vols. $75-$100. Another issue: Half morocco. One of 200 with a page of ms. $300-$400, possibly more.

ROOSEVELT, Theodore, and Minot, H.D. *The Summer Birds of the Adirondacks.* 4 pp., leaflet. (New York, 1877.) First edition. $200-$250. Roosevelt's first published separate work.

ROOT, Frank A., and Connelley, William E. *The Overland Stage to California.* Illustrated. Map. Pictorial cloth. Topeka, 1901. First edition. $125-$150.

ROOT, Riley. *Journal of Travels from St. Josephs* (sic) *to Oregon, etc.* 143 pp., printed wrappers and cloth spine. Galesburg, Ill., 1850. First edition. $2,500-$3,000, possibly more.

ROOT, Riley. *Musical Philosophy*. 20 pp., wrappers. Galesburg, Ill., 1866. First edition. $75-$125.

ROSE, Victor M. *Ross' Texas Brigade*. Illustrated. Louisville, 1881. First edition. $850-$1,000.

*ROSE Garden of Omar Khayyam (The)*. Miniature book, magnifying glass, proof sheet and text "A Thimbleful of Books," contained in a case. Worcester, Mass., 1932. $100-$150.

ROSEN, Peter. *Pa-Ha-Sa-Pah, or The Black Hills of South Dakota*. 27 plates. Pictorial cloth. St. Louis, 1895. First edition. $125-$175.

ROSENBACH, A.S.W. *Early American Children's Books*. Edited by A. Edward Newton. Hand-colored plates. Full blue morocco. Portland, Me., 1933. One of 88, signed. Boxed. $500-$650. Another issue: Half morocco. One of 585 signed. Boxed. $300-$450.

ROSENBERG, Isaac. *Poems*. Portrait. Cloth. London, 1922. First edition. In dust jacket. $75-$125.

ROSENTHAL, Leonard. *The Kingdom of the Pearl*. Illustrated in color by Edmund Dulac. Boards and vellum. New York, (1920). One of 100 signed by Dulac. In dust jacket. $250-$350. Another issue. Boards and cloth. In dust jacket. One of 675. In dust jacket. $200-$250.

ROSS, Alexander. *Adventures of the First Settlers on the Oregon or Columbia River*. Frontispiece (in some copies), folding map. Cloth. London, 1849. First edition. Without frontispiece. $250-$350. With frontispiece, $400-$600.

ROSS, Alexander. *Fur Hunters of the Far West*. Map, 2 plates. 2 vols., cloth. London, 1855. First edition. $500-$750.

ROSS, Alexander. *The Red River Settlement*. Frontispiece. Cloth. London, 1856. First edition. $150-$200.

ROSS, Calvin. *Sky Determines*. Cloth. New York, 1934. First edition. In dust jacket. $35-$50.

ROSS, Harvey L. *The Early Pioneers and Pioneer Events of the State of Illinois*. Portrait. Cloth. Chicago, 1898. First edition. $75-$100.

ROSS, John. *Narrative of a Second Voyage in Search of a Northwest Passage*. 25 plates (9 in color), folding map, charts. Cloth. London, 1825. First edition. $400-$500.

ROSSETTI, Christina. *Poems*. Chosen by Walter de la Mare. Wood-engraving portrait by R.A. Maynard. Printed on Japanese vellum. Red morocco, by the Gregynog bindery. Newtown, Wales, 1930. Gregynog Press. One of 25 specially bound. Boxed. $600-$750. Ordinary issue: Boards and calf. One of 300. $200-$250.

ROSSETTI, Christina. *The Prince's Progress and Other Poems*. Cloth. London, 1866. First edition. $150-$175.

ROSSETTI, Christina. *Speaking Likenesses*. Illustrated. Blue cloth. London, 1874, First edition, first binding. $75-$150.

ROSSETTI, Christina. *Verses*. Boards. Hammersmith (London), 1906. Eragny Press. One of 175 on paper. In dust jacket. $400.

ROSSETTI, Dante Gabriel. *Ballads and Narrative Poems*. Woodcut title and initials. Limp vellum with ties. London, 1893. Kelmscott Press. One of 310. $200-$300.

ROSSETTI, Dante Gabriel. *Ballads and Sonnets*. Boards. London, 1881. First edition. One of 25 on large paper. $300-$350. Ordinary issue: Blue cloth. $75-$100.

ROSSETTI, Dante Gabriel. *The Blessed Damozel*. Illustrated by Kenyon Cox. Folio, cloth.

New York, 1886. Large paper, printed in sepia. $75-$125. Portland, 1895. Morocco. One of 725. $50-$75. London, 1898. Vale Press. Oblong, boards. One of 310. $200-$250. Another issue: Cloth. One of 65 on vellum. $200-$300. Portland, 1901. Boards. One of 450. $80-$100. London, 1903. Illustrated by James Guthrie. Vellum. One of 5 on vellum. $1,500-$2,000.

ROSSETTI, Dante Gabriel. *Hand and Soul.* Wrappers. London, 1869. First separate edition. $300-$400. London, 1895. Kelmscott Press. Woodcut title and borders. Vellum. One of 525. $200-$250. Another issue: One of 10 on vellum, printed for England. $2,000-$2,500. London, 1899. Vale Press. Morocco. One of 210. In dust jacket. $400-$600. Portland, Me., 1906. Mosher Press. Wrappers. $50.

ROSSETTI, Dante Gabriel. *Poems.* Printed wrappers. (London, 1869.) First edition, privately printed. $1,000 and up. London, 1870. Cloth. First published edition. $75-$100. Another issue: Half vellum. One of 25 on Whatman paper. $400-$500. London, 1904. Plates. 2 vols., half morocco. $100-$150. Another issue: 2 vols., vellum. One of 30. $300-$400. Portland, 1892. Mosher Press. One of 450. $35-$75. New York, 1903. Edited by Elizabeth L. Cary. Illustrated. 2 vols., blue cloth. $40-$60.

ROSSETTI, Dante Gabriel. *Sonnets and Lyrical Poems.* Woodcut title and borders by William Morris. Printed in black and red. Vellum with ties. London, 1894. Kelmscott Press. One of 310. $350-$450.

ROSSI, Filippo. *Italian Jewelled Arts.* Illustrated. Cloth. New York, 1954. $50-$75. London, 1957 (actually 1958). Illustrated. Cloth. $50-$75.

ROSSI, Mario M. *Pilgrimage in the West.* Boards and linen. Dublin, 1933. Cuala Press. One of 300. $60-$75.

ROTH, Henry. *Call It Sleep.* Cloth. New York, 1934. First edition. In dust jacket. $200-$500. (A copy in jacket sold for $850 at Goodwin sale in New York, April, 1978.)

ROTH, Philip. *Goodbye, Columbus.* Black cloth. Boston, 1959. First edition. In dust jacket. $75-$100. Author's first book.

ROTHERT, Otto A. *The Outlaws of Cave-in-Rock.* 10 maps and plans. Cloth. Cleveland, 1927. First edition. In dust jacket. $65-$85.

ROYALL, Anne. See *Sketches of History, Life, and Manners, in the United States.*

ROYALL, Anne. *The Tennessean.* Boards. New Haven, 1827. First edition. $285.

ROYIDIS, Emmanuel. *Pope Joan.* Translated by Lawrence Durrell. Cloth. London, (1954). First edition. In dust jacket. $35-$50.

*RUBAIYAT of Omar Khayyam. The Astronomer-Poet of Persia.* Translated into English verse. Brown wrappers. London, 1859. (Translated by Edward Fitz Gerald.) First edition. (250 copies printed.) $7,500-$12,500. Also, $10,500 (A, 1976). Madras, India, 1862. Limp green cloth. One of 50 reprinted from the London first edition with a note by M. Garcin de Tassy. $1,000 and up. London, 1868. Wrappers. Second English edition. $600-$1,000. London, 1872. Half dark-red cloth and leather. Third edition. $300-$400. London, 1879. Frontispiece. Half cloth. Fourth edition. $200-$300. London, 1896. Ashendene Press. Wrappers. One of 50. $1,000-$1,500. Portland, Me., 1899. Illustrated by Austin O. Spare. Wrappers. $300-$400. (Cambridge, Mass.) 1900. Boards and buckram. One of 300 printed by Bruce Rogers. $200-$400. London, 1901. Vale Press. Illustrated by Charles Ricketts. Half cloth. One of 310. $200-$250. Another issue: One of 10 on vellum. $800-$1,000. Portland, 1902. Mosher Press facsimile. One of 200. $100. London, 1909. Illustrated by Edmund Dulac. Vellum. One of 750 signed by the artist. Boxed. $200-$300. London, (1910). Edited by A. C. Benson. Pictorial vellum. $75-$100. Another issue: Illuminated. One of 25 signed by the artists. $750-$1,000. Also, $475 (A, 1973). New York, (1912). 21 color photograph reproductions. Full morocco. $150. London, 1913. Riccardi Press. Vellum. One of 10 on vellum. $1,000 and up. London, 1920. Illustrated by Blanche McManus. Vellum. One of 21 on vellum. $350-$450. Also, $225 (A, 1977). London, 1936. Illustrated by Stephen Gooden. Half morocco. One of 125 signed by Gooden. Boxed. $225-$250. (Also, a 1940 edition by Gooden, same value range.) London, 1938. Golden Cockerel Press. Illustrated. Buckram. One of 300. $150-$200. Another issue: Morocco. One of 30, with extra engravings. $600-$800, possibly more. New York, 1940. Heritage Press. Color plates by Arthur Szyk. Pictorial padded calf and marbled boards. $150. London, 1958. Golden Cockerel Press. Illustrated by J. Yunge Bateman. Pictorial morocco. One of 75 specially bound, with an extra set of plates. Boxed. $400-$500. (Note: There have been numerous other editions of this classic work since its first appearance in 1859. Consult the British and American auction records for a more exhaustive survey.)

RUBEK, Sennoia. *The Burden of the South, in Verse*. Frontispiece. Printed wrappers. New York, (about 1864). (By John Burke.) $50-$60.

RUDD, Dan A., and Bond, Theo. *From Slavery to Wealth: The Life of Scott Bond*. Illustrated. Cloth. Madison, Ark., 1917. First edition. $75-$100.

*RUINED Deacon (The): A True Story*. By a Lady. Printed wrappers. Boston, 1834. (By Mary L. Fox.) First edition. $100-$125.

RUKEYSER, Muriel. *Elegies*. Boards. No place, (1949). First edition. One of 300 signed. In slipcase. $40-$60.

RUKEYSER, Muriel. *The Green Wave*. Cloth. New York, 1948. First edition. In dust jacket. $40-$50.

RUKEYSER, Muriel. *Theory of Flight*. Cloth. New Haven, 1935. First edition. In dust jacket. $100-$125.

*RULES and Orders of the House of Representatives of the Territory of Washington, 1864-5*. 32 pp., wrappers. Olympia. Washington Territory, 1864. $100-$200, possibly more.

*RULES and Regulations of the Utah and Northern Railway, for the Government of Employees*. Calf. Salt Lake City, 1879. $100-$200.

*RULES for the Government of the Council of Wisconsin Territory*. 10 pp., plain wrappers. Madison, Wis., 1843. $50-$60. Madison, 1845, 11 pp., plain wrappers. $100-$125.

*RULES for the Government of the House of Representatives of Wisconsin Territory*. 10 pp., plain wrappers. Madison, 1845. $100-$125.

*RULES, Regulations, and By-Laws of the Board of Commissioners to Manage the Yosemite Valley and Mariposa Big Tree Grove*. 23 pp., wrappers. Sacramento, 1885. $150-$200.

RUNYON, Damon. *The Tents of Trouble*. Flexible cloth. New York, (about 1911). First edition. $50-$75. Author's first book.

RUPP, I. Daniel. *History of the Counties of Berks and Lebanon*. 3 plates Sheep. Lancaster, Pa., 1844. First edition. $75-$100.

RUPP, I. Daniel. *History of Lancaster County, Pennsylvania*. Illustrated. Sheep. Lancaster, 1844. First edition. $100-$125.

RUPPANEER, Antoine. *Hypodermic Injections in the Treatment of Neuralgia, Gout, and Other Diseases*. Cloth. Boston, 1865. First edition. $500-$750.

RUPPIUS, Otto. *Das Vermächtnis des Pedlars. Roman aus dem Amerikanischen Leben*. Half leather. St. Louis, 1859. $50-$100.

RUPPIUS, Otto. *Der Prairie-Teufel. Roman aus dem Amerikanischen Leben*. Half leather. St. Louis, 1861. $75-$125.

RUPPIUS, Otto. *Geld und Geist. Roman aus dem Amerikanischen Leben*. Leather. St. Louis, 1860. $50-$60.

RUSK, Fern H. *George Caleb Bingham*. Illustrated. Cloth. Jefferson City, Mo., 1917. One of 500. $50-$75.

RUSKIN, John. Special Note: Many of the works once attributed to Ruskin have turned out to be Thomas J. Wise forgeries. The following brief list is representative of Ruskin's major endeavors.

RUSKIN, John. See R., J. Also, see Greenaway, Kate (illustrator), *Dame Wiggins of Lee.*

RUSKIN, John. *The Elements of Drawing.* Cloth. London, 1857. First edition. $75-$100.

RUSKIN, John. *The King of the Golden River.* Illustrated by Richard Doyle. Boards. London, 1851. First edition. $300-$400. New York, 1930. Illustrated. Black calf. One of 50, each with a holograph letter, signed by Ruskin, tipped in. Boxed. $250-$300. London, (1932). Illustrated by Arthur Rackham. Vellum. Boxed. $250-$350. Trade edition: $100-$150.

RUSKIN, John. *The Nature of Gothic: A Chapter of the Stones of Venice.* Preface by William Morris. Illustrated. Vellum with ties. London, 1892. Kelmscott Press. One of 500. $300-$400.

RUSKIN, John. *The Political Economy of Art.* Cloth. London, 1857. First edition. $150-$200.

RUSKIN, John. *The Seven Lamps of Architecture.* 14 plates. Cloth. London, 1849. First edition. $150-$200.

RUSKIN, John. *The Stones of Venice.* Illustrated. 3 vols., cloth. London, 1851-53. First edition. $300-$400.

RUSKIN, John. *Unto This Last: Four Essays on the First Principles of Political Economy.* Vellum. London, 1907. Doves Press. One of 300. $500-$600. Another issue: One of 25 on vellum. Boxed. $2,500-$3,000.

RUSSELL, Alex J. *The Red River Country, Hudson's Bay and North-west Territories, etc.* Folding map. Wrappers. Ottawa, 1869. First edition. $150-$200. Montreal, 1870. Folding map, 8 folding plates. Wrappers. Third edition. $150-$200.

RUSSELL, Charles M. (illustrator). See *How the Buffalo Lost His Crown.*

RUSSELL, Charles M. *Back-trailing on the Old Frontiers.* 16 full-page drawings. 56 pp., pictorial wrappers. Great Falls, Mont., 1922. First edition. $150-$200.

RUSSELL, Charles M. *Good Medicine.* Introduction by Will Rogers. Illustrated by the author. Cloth. New York, 1930. First edition. In dust jacket. $100-$150. Another issue: Half buckram. One of 134 on large paper. $500-$600. Another issue: Blue buckram. One of 59 copies for presentation. $1,000-$1,500.

RUSSELL, Charles M. *More Rawhides.* Illustrated by the author. 60 pp., pictorial wrappers. Great Falls, 1925. First edition. $125-$175.

RUSSELL, Charles M. *Pen and Ink Drawings.* 2 vols., oblong boards and cloth. Pasadena, (1946). First edition. $85-$135.

RUSSELL, Charles M. *Pen Sketches.* 12 plates. Oblong, leatherette. Great Falls, (1898). First edition. $1,000-$1,500.

RUSSELL, Charles M. *Rawhide Rawlins Stories.* Illustrated by the author. Pictorial wrappers. Great Falls, 1921. First edition. $125-$175. Another issue: Full limp leather. Presentation copy. $600.

RUSSELL, Charles M. *Trails Plowed Under.* Cloth. New York, 1927. First edition. In dust jacket. $75-$100.

RUSSELL, George W. See E., A.

RUSSELL, Morris C. *Western Sketches. Trail Echoes. Straws of Humor.* (Cover title.) Portrait. Wrappers, cord ties. Lake City, Minn., 1904. First edition, signed by the author. $250-$300.

RUSSELL, Osborne. *Journal of a Trapper.* 105 pp. (Boise, 1914.) First edition. $350-$400.

Boise, (1921). Second edition. 149 pp., cloth. $100-$125. (Portland, Ore.), 1955. Champoeg Press. One of 750. $35-$45.

RUSSELL, Peter (editor). *A Collection of Essays . . . to Be Presented to Ezra Pound on His 65th Birthday.* Portrait frontispiece. Tan cloth. London, (1950). First edition. In dust jacket. $50-$60.

RUSSELL, W. Clark. *The Tale of the Ten.* 3 vols., cloth. London, 1896. First edition. $160.

RUSSELL, W. Clark. *The Wreck of the "Grosvenor."* 3 vols., cloth. London, 1877. First edition. $400.

RUST, Margaret. *The Queen of the Fishes.* 16 woodcuts, 4 colored, by Lucien Pissarro. Vellum. Epping, England, 1894. Eragny Press. One of 150 on vellum. $800-$1,000. Also, $600 (A, 1977). (Note: The first book produced by this press.)

*RUTH Whalley; or, The Fair Puritan.* (Cover title.) 72 pp., pink wrappers. Boston, 1845. (By Henry William Herbert.) $150-$200. (Note: In some copies the author is listed as "William Henry Herbert." There is also said to be an 1844 edition.)

RUTHERFORD, Ernest. *Radio-Activity.* Illustration. Cloth. Cambridge, 1904, First edition. $250-$300.

RUTTENBER, E. M. *History of the County of Orange: With a History of the Town and City of Newburgh.* Plates, maps. Newburgh, N.Y., 1875. First edition. $80-$100.

RUXTON, George F. *Life in the Far West.* Cloth. Edinburgh, 1849. First edition. $75-$100. New York, 1849. Cloth. $50-$75.

RYAN, Abram Joseph. *Father Ryan's Poems.* Portrait and one illustration. Cloth. Mobile, 1879. First edition. $100-$150. Author's first book.

# S

S., E. W., and M., S.W. *The Children's Hour.* Illustrated. Cloth. Philadelphia, 1864. (By Elizabeth W. Sherman and S. Weir Mitchell.) First edition. $125-$175.

S., P.B. *Zastrozzi: A Romance.* Dark blue-gray boards, drab cloth spine, paper label. London, 1810. (By Percy Bysshe Shelley.) First edition. $2,000-$3,000, possibly more. (No copies in original binding for public sale in many years.) London, 1955. Golden Cockerel Press. Plates. Morocco. One of 60 on vellum with duplicate set of 8 plates. Boxed. $200-$350. Another issue: Boards. One of 200. Boxed. $75-$100.

S., S. *Vigils.* Frontispiece by Stephen Gooden. Full morocco. (Bristol), 1934. (By Siegfried Sassoon.) First edition. One of 23 signed by the author and the artist. $300-$350. Another issue: One of 272 signed by Sassoon. $100-$125.

S., S. H. *Nine Experiments.* Green wrappers. Hampstead, England, 1928. (By Stephen Spender.) First edition. One of about 18 copies issued. Bad presswork required filling in some letters by hand in ink. In cloth case, with leather label. $2,100. (This copy, catalogued by a New York dealer in 1968, belonged to Spender's sister-in-law. An inscribed copy was offered by a New York dealer in 1973 at $5,000.)

SABIN, Edwin L. *Building the Pacific Railway.* Cloth. Philadelphia, 1919. First edition. In dust jacket. $50-$60.

SABIN, Edwin L. *Kit Carson Days (1809-1868).* Maps, plates. Brown cloth. Chicago, 1914. First edition. $75-$125. Chicago, 1919. Second edition. $50. New York, 1935. 2 vols., cloth. Revised edition. One of 1,000. $50. One of 200, signed. $100-$125.

*SABINE and Rio Grande Railroad Co. Memorial of Duff Green, President.* 50 pp. Washington, 1860. $75-$150, possibly more.

*SACRED Writings of the Apostles and Evangelists of Jesus Christ, etc. (The).* New Testament translation by George Campbell, James McKnight, and Philip Doddridge. Preface by Alexander Campbell. Contemporary calf. Buffaloe, Brooke County, Va., 1826. First edition. $150-$200.

*SACK and Destruction of the City of Columbia, S.C.* Wrappers. Columbia, 1865. (By William Gilmore Simms.) First edition. Up to $500.

SACKVILLE-WEST, Victoria. *The Edwardians.* Half vellum. (London), 1930. First edition. One of 125, signed. (Issued without dust jacket.) $100-$125.

SACKVILLE-WEST, Victoria. *The Garden.* Cloth. London, 1946. First edition. One of 750, signed. In plain white dust jacket. $100-$125.

SACKVILLE-WEST, Victoria. *Nursery Rhymes.* Vellum and cloth. London, 1947. First edition. One of 25, signed. $75-$100.

SACKVILLE-WEST, Victoria. *Sissinghurst.* Boards. London, 1931. First edition. One of 500, signed. $35-$50.

SACKVILLE-WEST, Victoria. *Twelve Days.* Illustrated. Marbled cloth. London, 1928. First edition. In dust jacket. $50-$60.

SADLEIR, Michael. *Forlorn Sunset.* Frontispiece. Purple morocco. London, 1947. First edition. One of 25, signed. $100-$120.

SADLEIR, Michael. *Hyssop*. Cloth. London, (1915). First edition. In dust jacket. $50-$60. Author's first novel.

SADLEIR, Michael. *XIX Century Fiction: A Bibliographical Record*. Illustrated. 2 vols., cloth. London, (1951). First edition. One of 1,025. $350-$400.

SAGE, Rufus B. *Scenes in the Rocky Mountains*. Half calf. Philadelphia, 1847. Second edition. $150-$300. (For first edition, see title entry.)

SAGE, Rufus B. *Wild Scenes in Kansas and Nebraska, the Rocky Mountains, etc.* Half leather. Philadelphia, 1855. Third ("revised") edition (of *Scenes in the Rocky Mountains*, which see under title entry). $75-$100.

SAGRA, Ramón de la. *Historia Económica-Política y Estadistica de la Isla de Cuba*. Wrappers. Havana, 1831. First edition. $175-$200.

ST. CLAIR, Maj. Gen. (Arthur). *A Narrative of the Manner in Which the Campaign Against the Indians, in the Year 1791, Was Conducted*. Boards. Philadelphia, 1812. First edition. $250-$275. Half morocco. $175-$250.

*ST. IRVYNE; or, The Rosicrucian: A Romance*. By a Gentleman of the University of Oxford. Drab boards, green cloth spine. London, 1811. (By Percy Bysshe Shelley.) First edition. $1,000 and up.

ST. JOHN, James Augustus, and D'Avennes, Emile Prisse. *Oriental Album*. 30 full-page color plates. Elephant folio, half morocco. London, 1848. $500-$800.

ST. JOHN, John R. *A True Description of the Lake Superior Country*. 2 folding maps. Printed cloth. New York, 1846. First edition. $300-$350.

*ST. RONAN'S Well*. 3 vols., boards. Edinburgh, 1824. (By Sir Walter Scott.) First edition. $100-$150.

SAINT-EXUPÉRY, Antoine de. *The Little Prince*. Translated from the French by Katherine Woods. Illustrated in color by the author. Cloth. New York, (1943). First American edition. One of 525, signed. In dust jacket. $375-$450. Trade edition, in English: In dust jacket. $100-$125. Trade edition, in French, as *Le Petit Prince*: In dust jacket, $100-$125.

SAINT-EXUPÉRY, Antoine de. *Night-Flight*. Translated by Stuart Gilbert. Wrappers. Paris, 1932. In cellophane dust jacket. $50-$75. New York, 1932. Cloth. First American edition. In dust jacket. $50-$60.

SAINTSBURY, George. *Notes on a Cellar-Book*. Parchment paper boards and cloth. London, 1921. First edition. One of 500, signed. $50.

SAISSY, Jean-Antoine. *An Essay on the Diseases of the Internal Ear*. Frontispiece. Sheep. Baltimore, 1829. First American edition. $50-$75.

SAKI. *Reginald*. Red cloth. London, (1904). (By H.H. Munro.) First edition. $40-$60.

SAKI. *The Westminster Alice*. Green wrappers. London, (about 1902). (By H.H. Munro.) First edition. $25-$35.

*SALAMAN and Absal: An Allegory*. Translated from the Persian of Jami by Edward Fitz Gerald. Frontispiece. Blue cloth. London, 1856. First edition. $150-$200.

*SALATHIEL: A Story of the Past, the Present, and the Future*. 3 vols., half calf. London, 1828. (By the Rev. George Croly.) First edition. $100-$150.

SALAZAR Ylarregui, José. *Datos de los Trabajos Astronómicos y Topográficos, Dispuestos en Forma de Diario*. 2 folding maps. Blue wrappers. Mexico, 1850. First edition. $600-$850.

SALE, Edith Tunis. *Manors of Virginia in Colonial Times*. 49 plates. Cloth. Philadelphia, 1909. First edition. $75-$100.

SALINGER, J.D. See Barrows, R.M., *The Kit Book for Soldiers, Sailors, and Marines*.

SALINGER, J.D. *The Catcher in the Rye.* Black cloth. Boston, 1951. First edition (so stated). In presumed first-issue dust jacket without book-club slug. $150-$250. Author's first book.

SALINGER, J.D. *Nine Stories.* Cloth. Boston, (1953). First edition. In dust jacket. $150-$200.

SALINGER, J.D. *Raise High the Roof Beam, Carpenters, and Seymour: An Introduction.* Cloth. Boston, (1959). First edition, first issue, without dedication page. In dust jacket. $90-$100. Second issue, with dedication page tipped in in front of half title. $25-$35. Third issue, with dedication correctly placed. $15.

SALISBURY, Samuel. *A Descriptive, Historical, Chemical and Therapeutical Analysis of the Avon Sulphur Springs, Livingston County.* 95 pp., sewed. Rochester, 1845. $75-$100.

SALLEY, Alexander S., Jr. *The History of Orangeburg County.* Folding map, portrait. Cloth. Orangeburg, S.C., 1898. First edition. $75-$100.

SALMONY, Alfred. *Sculpture in Siam.* Collotype plates. Full morocco. London, 1925. One of 25. $150-$175. Trade edition: Cloth. $60. Paris, 1925. Printed wrappers. $50-$75.

SALPOINTE, John B. *A Brief Sketch of the Mission of San Xavier del Bac with a Description of Its Church.* 20 pp., wrappers. San Francisco, 1880. First edition. $150-$175.

SALPOINTE, John B. *Soldiers of the Cross.* Portrait, 45 plates. Cloth. Banning, Calif., 1898. First edition. $125-$150.

*SALT Lake City Directory and Business Guide (The).* Folding map, folding view. 53-219 pp., as issued, boards. Salt Lake City, 1869. (By Edward L. Sloan.) First edition. $150-$250.

SALTEN, Felix. *Bambi, A Life in the Woods.* Illustrated by Kurt Wiese. Pictorial boards. New York, 1928. First edition. In dust jacket. $50-$60.

SALTER, James. *The Hunters.* Cloth. New York, (1956). First edition. In dust jacket. $35-$45. Author's first novel.

SALTER, William. *Memoirs of Joseph W. Pickett.* Brown cloth. Burlington, Iowa, 1880. First edition. $50-$75.

SALTUS, Edgar. *Balzac.* Cloth, paper label. Boston, 1884. First edition. $40-$50. Author's first book.

SALZMANN, C.G. *Gymnastics for Youth.* 9 plates. Boards. London, 1800. First English edition. $200-$250. Philadelphia, 1802. First American edition. Leather. $100-$150. Philadelphia, 1803. 10 plates. Calf. $75-$100.

*SAN BERNARDINO County, California, Illustrated Description of.* 34 pp., printed wrappers. San Bernardino, 1881. $175-$200.

*SAN BERNARDINO County, California. Ingersoll's Century Annals of San Bernardino County, 1769-1904.* Full leather. Los Angeles, 1904. $100-$150.

*SAN FRANCISCO Bay and California in 1776.* Maps and facsimiles. 7 pp., boards. Providence, 1911. (By Pedro Font.) One of 125. $200-$300.

*SAN FRANCISCO Board of Engineers: Report upon the City Grades.* 27 pp., wrappers. San Francisco, 1854. $150-$175.

*SAN FRANCISCO Directory for the Year 1852-53.* Frontispiece, double-page map. Half leather. San Francisco, 1852. First edition. $750-$1,000.

*SAN FRANCISCO Vigilance Committee of 1856—Three Views: William T. Coleman, William T. Sherman and James O'Meara.* Illustrated. Fabrikoid. (Los Angeles, 1971.) First edition. $35.

SANBORN, Ralph, and Clark, Barrett H. *A Bibliography of the Works of Eugene O'Neill.*

Illustrated. Cloth. New York, 1931. First edition. One of 500. $50-$75. (Note: Contains previously unpublished work by O'Neill.)

SANDBURG, Carl. See Sandburg, Charles A.; Wright, Philip Green.

SANDBURG, Carl. *Abraham Lincoln: The Prairie Years*. Illustrated. 2 vols., blue cloth. New York, (1926). First edition, so stated on copyright page. In dust jackets. Boxed. $50. Large paper issue. 2 vols., boards and cloth. First state, with line 9 on page 175 of Vol. 1 reading "ears" instead of "eyes." One of 260, signed. In dust jackets. Boxed. $300-$400. Later, "ears" corrected, $200-$300.

SANDBURG, Carl. *Abraham Lincoln: The War Years*. Illustrated. 4 vols., blue cloth. New York, (1939-41). First edition, so stated. In dust jackets. Boxed. $75-$100. Large paper issue: Brown buckram. One of 525 sets on all rag paper, numbered and signed. In dust jackets. Boxed. In dust jackets. $200-$250.

SANDBURG, Carl. *Always the Young Strangers*. Cloth. New York. (1953). First edition. $20-$25. Another issue. Cloth. One of 600 on large paper, signed. Boxed. $75-$100.

SANDBURG, Carl. *The American Songbag*. Red Cloth. New York, (1927). First edition. In dust jacket. $30-$40.

SANDBURG, Carl. *Bronze Wood*. Frontispiece. 8 pp., orange boards. (San Francisco, 1941.) Grabhorn Press. First edition. One of 195. In dust jacket. $75-$125.

SANDBURG, Carl. *Chicago Poems*. Cloth. New York, 1916. First edition, with ads at back dated "3'16." In dust jacket. $100-$135. The poet's first book, aside from the pamphlet *In Reckless Ecstasy*.

SANDBURG, Carl. *The Chicago Race Riots*. Printed wrappers. New York, 1919. First edition. $100-$150.

SANDBURG, Carl. *Cornhuskers*. Boards. New York, 1918. First edition, first state, with page 3 so numbered at foot of page. In dust jacket. $50-$75.

SANDBURG, Carl. *Early Moon*. Cloth. New York, (1930). First edition, first printing, so indicated on copyright page. In dust jacket. $35-$50.

SANDBURG, Carl. *Good Morning, America*. Cloth. New York, 1928. First edition. In dust jacket. $15-$25. Limited issue: Cloth. One of 811, signed. $60-$75. (Note: A few were printed on blue paper.)

SANDBURG, Carl. *Lincoln Collector*. Illustrated. Cloth. New York, (1949). First edition. $15-$20. Large paper issue: Cloth. Signed. $50-$75.

SANDBURG, Carl. *A Lincoln and Whitman Miscellany*. Cloth. Chicago, 1938. First edition. One of 250. $50-$75.

SANDBURG, Carl. *Mary Lincoln, Wife and Widow*. Cloth. New York, (1932). First edition, first printing (so indicated on copyright page). $15. Large paper issue: One of 260, signed. $50-$65.

SANDBURG, Carl. *M'Liss and Louie*. Wrappers. Los Angeles, 1929. First edition. One of 125. $150-$200.

SANDBURG, Carl. *The People, Yes*. Cloth. New York, (1936). First edition, first printing (so indicated on copyright page). In dust jacket. $30-$40. Large paper issue: One of 270, signed. In slipcase. $75-$100.

SANDBURG, Carl. *Potato Face*. Boards and cloth. New York, (1930). First edition (so stated). In dust jacket. $40-$60.

SANDBURG, Carl. *Remembrance Rock*. Cloth. New York, (1948). First edition. In dust jacket. $20-$25. Another issue: 2 vols., buckram. One of 1,000, signed. In tissue dust jackets. Boxed. $100-$135.

SANDBURG, Carl. *Rootabaga Pigeons*. Illustrated. Pictorial cloth. New York, (1923). First edition. In dust jacket. $50-$75.

SANDBURG, Carl. *Rootabaga Stories.* Illustrated by Maud and Miska Petersham. Pictorial cloth. New York, (1922). First edition. In dust jacket. $75-$100.

SANDBURG, Carl. *Slabs of the Sunburnt West.* Cloth. New York, (1922). First edition, first issue, with text ending at the foot of page 75. In dust jacket. $50-$60.

SANDBURG, Carl. *Smoke and Steel.* Green boards. New York, 1920. First edition. In dust jacket. $100-$150.

SANDBURG, Carl. *Steichen, the Photographer.* Illustrated. Cloth. New York, (1929). First edition. One of 925, signed by author and artist. $400-$600.

SANDBURG, Charles A. *In Reckless Ecstasy.* Wrappers. Galesburg, Ill., 1904. (By Carl Sandburg.) First edition. $1,500 and up. Author's first book.

SANDERS, Daniel C. *A History of the Indian Wars with the First Settlers of the United States.* Sheep. Montpelier, Vt., 1812. First edition. $150-$200.

SANDERS, Capt. John. *Memoir on the Military Resources of the Valley of the Ohio.* 19 pp., unbound. Pittsburgh, 1845. First edition. $125-$150. Washington, 1845. 24 pp., unbound, $100-$150.

SANDOZ, Mari. *The Battle of the Little Bighorn.* Half morocco. New York, 1966. First edition. One of 249, signed. $100-$125.

SANDOZ, Mari. *The Beaver Men.* Illustrated. Half leather. New York, (1964). First edition. In dust jacket. $15. Another issue: Cloth. One of 185, signed. $100-$125.

SANDOZ, Mari. *The Cattlemen.* Illustrated. Cloth. New York, (1958). First edition. In dust jacket. $15-$20. Advance presentation copy, signed. $50-$75. Another issue: Half cloth. One of 199, signed. Boxed. $100-$125.

SANDOZ, Mari. *Crazy Horse.* Illustrated. Cloth, New York, 1942. First edition. In dust jacket. $60-$75.

SANDOZ, Mari. *Old Jules.* Illustrated. Cloth. Boston, 1935. First edition. In dust jacket. $25-$35. Author's first book

SANDOZ, Mari. *Old Jules Country.* Folding map. Illustrated by Bryan Forsyth. Half leather. New York, 1965. One of 250 signed and specially bound. $100-$125.

SANDOZ, Maurice. *The Maze.* Illustrated by Salvador Dali. Cloth. Garden City, 1945. First edition. In dust jacket. $75-$125.

SANDOZ, Maurice. *On the Verge.* Illustrated in color by Salvador Dali. Cloth. Garden City, (1959). First edition. In dust jacket. $75-$100.

SANDS, Frank. *A Pastoral Prince: The History and Reminiscences of Joseph Wright Cooper.* Illustrated. Pictorial cloth. Santa Barbara, 1893. First edition. $100-$150.

SANFORD, Nettle. *History of Marshall County, Iowa.* 5 plates. Cloth. Clinton, 1867. $125-$150.

SANSOM, Joseph. *Sketches of Lower Canada, Historical and Descriptive.* Frontispiece view of Quebec. Boards. New York, 1817. First edition. $175-$225.

SANSOM, William. *A Bed of Roses.* Cloth. London, 1954. Hogarth Press. First edition. In dust jacket. With wrap-around band. $25-$35.

SANTAYANA, George. See *Lines on Leaving the Bedford St. Schoolhouse.*

SANTAYANA, George. *Lucifer.* Cloth. Chicago, 1899. First edition. $75-$85. Cambridge, Mass., 1924. Black cloth. One of 450. $80-$100.

SANTAYANA, George. *Poems.* Cloth. London, (1922). First edition. One of 100, signed. $175-$250.

SANTAYANA, George. *Sonnets and Other Verses.* Buckram. Cambridge, Mass., 1894.

First edition. One of 450. $75-$100. Another issue: Limp vellum. One of 50 on vellum. $250-$335. Author's first book.

SANTEE, Ross. *Men and Horses*. Illustrated. Cloth. New York, (1926). First edition. In dust jacket. $80-$100. Author's first book.

SANTLEBEN, August. *A Texas Pioneer*. Cloth. New York, 1910. First edition. In dust jacket. $150-$250.

SAPPINGTON, John. *The Theory and Treatment of Fevers*. Calf. Arrow Rock, Mo., 1844. $200-$225.

SARA, Col. Delle. *Silver Sam; or, the Mystery of Deadwood City*. 166 pp., wrappers. New York, (1877). $100-$125.

SARGENT, Charles Sprague. *The Silva of North America*. Illustrated. 14 vols., printed boards. Boston, 1890-1902. First edition. In dust jackets. $1,500-$2,000.

SARGENT, Charles Sprague (editor). *Plantae Wilsonianae: an Enumeration of the Woody Plants Collected in Western China by E.H. Wilson*, 3 vols., half morocco. Cambridge, Mass., 1913-17. $200-$250.

SARGENT, George B. *Notes on Iowa*. Map. 74 pp., cloth. New York, 1848. First edition. $750-$1,000.

SAROYAN, William. See Edward VIII; Miller, Henry.

SAROYAN, William. *A Christmas Psalm*. Rose boards, white cloth spine. San Francisco, (1935). Grabhorn Press. First edition, with greeting card and envelope, as issued, laid in. One of 200, signed. $80-$100.

SAROYAN, William. *Contes*. 8 colored woodcuts. Pictorial wrappers. (Paris, 1953.) One of 100, signed. $150-$200.

SAROYAN, William. *The Daring Young Man on the Flying Trapeze*. Gray cloth, paper label. New York, 1934. First edition. In dust jacket. $75-$100. Author's first book.

SAROYAN, William. *The Fiscal Hoboes*. Boards. New York, 1949. First edition. One of 250, signed. $100-$150. (Also issued in wrappers.)

SAROYAN, William. *Fragment*. Folio, wrappers. (San Francisco, 1938.) First edition. One of 150, signed. $150-$200.

SAROYAN, William. *Harlem as Seen by Hirschfeld*. Illustrated. Folio, cloth. New York, (1941). First edition. One of 1,000. In slipcase. $300-$400.

SAROYAN, William. *Hilltop Russians in San Francisco*. 30 colored plates by Pauline Vinson. Boards and cloth. San Francisco, 1941. Grabhorn Press. (Issued without dust jacket.) $150.

SAROYAN, William. *My Name is Aram*. Illustrated. Cloth. New York, (1940). First edition. In dust jacket. $50-$75.

SAROYAN, William. *A Native American*. Illustrated. Cloth. San Francisco, 1938. First edition. One of 450, signed. (Issued without dust jacket.) $75-$100.

SAROYAN, William. *Saroyan's Fables*. Illustrated by Warren Chappell. (New York), 1941. First edition. One of 1,000, signed. Boxed. $50-$65.

SAROYAN, William. *A Special Announcement*. Cloth. New York, 1940. First edition. One of 250, signed. In tissue dust wrapper. $250-$300.

SAROYAN, William. *Those Who Write Them and Those Who Collect Them*. Printed wrappers. Chicago, 1936. Black Archer Press. One of 50. $50-$75. (Note: There are variant colored wrappers; no priority.)

SAROYAN, William. *Three Times Three*. Cloth. Los Angeles, (1936). First edition. One of 250, signed. In dust jacket. $75-$100.

*SARTOR Resartus.* (Reprinted from *Fraser's Magaine.*) Various bindings: calf, morocco, etc. (London), 1834. First edition. (By Thomas Carlyle.) One of about 48, 50, or 58 (bibliographers differ) privately printed for the author's friends. In full morocco, $750-$1,000, possibly more. Also, old calf, inscribed to the author's brother, $750 (A, 1969). London, 1838. Boards and calf. First published English edition. $100-$150. London, 1907. Doves Press. Vellum. One of 300. $400-$600.

SASSOON, Siegfried. See Kain, Saul; Lyre, Pinchbeck; S., S. Also see *Lingual Exercises for Advanced Vocabularians; Memoirs of a Fox-Hunting Man; Memoirs of an Infantry Officer; Orpheus in Diloeryum; Poems; Recreations.*

SASSOON, Siegfried. *An Adjustment.* Frontispiece. Wrappers. Royston, England, 1955. First edition. One of 150 initialed by the author. Boxed. $100-$125.

SASSOON, Siegfried. *Counter-Attack and Other Poems.* Wrappers. London, 1918. First edition. $75-$100. New York, (1918). First American edition. In dust jacket. $25-$35.

SASSOON, Siegfried. *Emblems of Experience.* Wrappers. Cambridge, 1951. First edition. One of 75 signed. $175.

SASSOON, Siegfried. *The Heart's Journey.* Boards and parchment. New York, 1927. First edition. One of 500. In dust jacket. $50-$100. Another issue: One of 9 on green paper. In dust jacket. $100-$150. London, 1938. Blue cloth. First English trade edition. In dust jacket. $15-$20.

SASSOON, Siegfried. *Nativity.* Wrappers. New York, 1927. First American edition. One of 27 to obtain copyright. $325 (A, 1977).

SASSOON, Siegfried. *The Old Huntsman and Other Poems.* Boards. London, 1917. First edition, with errata slip. In dust jacket. $100-$150.

SASSOON, Siegfried. *The Path to Peace.* Boards and vellum. Worcester, 1960. One of 500. $150-$200. Another issue: One of 20 gilded by Margaret Adams. $300-$400.

SASSOON, Siegfried. *Picture Show.* Boards. (Cambridge), 1919. First edition. One of 200. In plain dust jacket. $150-$200. Presentation copy inscribed to Edith Sitwell, $600 (in a 1977 English catalogue).

SASSOON, Siegfried. *The Redeemer.* Unnumbered leaves, unbound. Cambridge, 1916. One of about 250. $150-$200.

SASSOON, Siegfried. *Satirical Poems.* Cloth. London, 1926. First edition. In dust jacket. $80-$100.

SASSOON, Siegfried. *Sherston's Progress.* Buckram. London, 1936. First edition. One of 300, signed. $150-$200.

SASSOON, Siegfried. *Something About Myself.* Wrappers. Worcester, 1966. First edition. One of 250. $150-$200.

SASSOON, Siegfried. *The Tasking.* Boards and cloth. London, 1964. First edition. One of 100, signed. $300-$400.

SASSOON, Siegfried. *To the Red Rose.* Green boards. London, 1931. First edition. One of 400, signed. $75-$100.

SASSOON, Siegfried. *War Poems.* Red cloth. London, 1919. First edition. In dust jacket. $100-$150.

*SATANSTOE; or, The Littlepage Manuscripts.* By the Author of *Miles Wallingford.* 2 vols., printed yellow wrappers. New York, 1845. (By James Fenimore Cooper.) First American edition. $500-$750. London, 1845. 3 vols., boards, paper label. First edition. $200-$250. (Note: Cooper's name appeared on the title page of this edition.)

SATTERLEE, M.P. *A Detailed Account of the Massacre by the Dakota Indians of Minnesota in 1862.* Wrappers. Minneapolis, 1923. $100-$150.

SAUER, Martin. *An Account of a Geographical and Astronomical Expedition to the North-*

*ern Parts of Russia.* Folding map, 14 plates. Boards and calf. London, 1802. First edition. $600-$750.

SAUNDERS, James E. *Early Settlers of Alabama.* Part I. (All published). Cloth. New Orleans, 1899. First edition. $150-$250.

SAUNDERS, Louise. *The Knave of Hearts.* Illustrated in color by Maxfield Parrish. Pictorial cloth. New York, 1925. First edition. In plain buff dust jacket. $400-$550. Lacking jacket, $300-$400. (Note: We have seen one mint copy in a special box, as distributed by A.L. Burt of Chicago. Scribner was the publisher.)

SAUNDERS, Marshall. *Beautiful Joe: An Autobiography.* Mottled olive cloth. Philadelphia, 1894. First edition, first issue, with American Baptist Publication Society imprint. $75-$100.

SAUVAN, Jean-Baptiste-Balthazar. *Picturesque Tour of the Seine, from Paris to the Sea.* Map, colored vignette title and tailpiece, 24 colored aquatint plates. Half morocco. London, 1821. First edition. $2,000-$3,000. Another issue: One of 50 on large paper. $3,000-$3,500.

SAVAGE, Timothy. *The Amazonian Republic, Recently Discovered in the Interior of Peru.* Boards, paper label. New York, 1842. First edition. $100-$125.

SAVAGE, William. *Practical Hints on Decorative Printing.* Illustrated with colored woodcuts. Boards, paper label. London, 1822, First edition. One of 227. $2,500.

SAVONAROLA, Hieronymus. *Epistola de Contemptu Mundi.* Illustrated. Red morocco. London, 1894. Kelmscott Press. One of 150. $300-$400. Another issue: One of 6 on vellum. $1,500.

*SAVOY (The): An Illustrated Quarterly.* Illustrations by Aubrey Beardsley. 8 parts. (All published.) Decorated boards and wrappers. London, 1896. $500-$600.

SAWYER, C. J., and Darton, F. J. Harvey. *English Books, 1475-1900: A Signpost for Collectors.* Illustrated. 2 vols., buckram. London, 1927. $125-$175.

SAWYER, Eugene T. *The Life and Career of Tiburcio Vasquez.* Printed wrappers. San Jose, 1875. First edition. $300-$400. Oakland, 1944. Grabhorn Press. Boards and cloth. One of 500. $40-$60.

SAWYER, Lorenzo. *Way Sketches.* Illustrated. Cloth. New York, 1926. One of 385. $40-$60. Large paper issue: Boards, parchment spine. One of 35. $75-$100.

SAWYER, Ruth. *Roller Skates.* Illustrated by Valenti Angelo. Pictorial cloth. New York, 1936. First edition. $30-$40.

SAXE, John Godfrey. *Progress: A Satirical Poem.* Printed boards. New York, (1846). First edition. $50-$85. Author's first book.

SAXON, Lyle, *Lafitte the Pirate.* Colored frontispiece. Cloth. New York, (1930). First edition. In dust jacket. $40-$50.

SAYERS, Dorothy. *Gaudy Night.* Cloth. London, 1935. First edition. In dust jacket. $50-$60.

SAYERS, Dorothy. *Lord, I Thank Thee.* Wrappers. Stamford, Conn., 1942. Overbrook Press. First edition. One of 100. $75-$100.

SAYERS, Dorothy. *The Other Six Deadly Sins.* Wrappers. London, (1943). First edition. $25-$30.

SCAMMON, Charles M. *The Marine Mammals of the North-Western Coast of North America, etc.* 27 plates. Cloth. San Francisco, 1874. First edition. $600-$750.

*SCENES in the Rocky Mountains, Oregon, California, New Mexico, Texas and Grand Prairies.* By a New Englander. Folding map. Printed wrappers, or cloth. Philadelphia, 1846. (By Rufus B. Sage.) First edition. Either binding: $750-$1,000. (Note: For later editions, see Sage, Rufus B.)

SCHARF, John Thomas. *History of the Confederate States Navy.* 42 plates. Boards. New York, 1887. First edition. $150-$175. Albany, 1894. Cloth. Second edition. $75-$125.

SCHARF, John Thomas. *History of Delaware.* Illustrated. 2 vols., half morocco. Philadelphia, 1888. First edition. $150-$200.

SCHARF, John Thomas. *History of Maryland.* Folding charts and maps. Illustrated. 3 vols., half leather. Baltimore, 1879. First edition. $200.

SCHARF, John Thomas. *History of Westchester County, New York.* Illustrated. 2 vols., cloth. Philadelphia, 1886. First edition. $150-$200.

SCHARF, John Thomas. *History of Western Maryland.* Map, 109 plates, table. 2 vols., cloth. Philadelphia, 1882. First edition. $150-$200.

SCHARMANN, H.B. *Overland Journey to California.* Portrait. Cloth. (New York, 1918.) First edition in English. $150-$200.

SCHATZ, A.H. *Opening a Cow Country.* Plates, maps. Wrappers. Ann Arbor, 1939. First edition. $100-$150.

SCHLEY, Frank. *American Partridge and Pheasant Shooting.* Illustrated. Cloth. Frederick, Md., 1877. First edition. $50-$75.

SCHMIDT, Gustavus. *The Civil Law of Spain and Mexico.* Cloth. New Orleans, 1851. First edition. $350-$450.

SCHMITZ, Joseph M. *Texan Statecraft, 1836-1845.* Cloth. San Antonio, 1941. One of 200. $35-$50.

SCHOBERL, Frederic. *Picturesque Tour from Geneva to Milan, by Way of the Simplon.* Map, 36 color plates. Cloth, or boards. London, 1820. First edition. $800-$1,000, possibly more. (Note: This book illustrates rather typically the astonishingly sharp and large rise in the value of fine color plate books over the last half dozen years. In the last edition of this *Handbook* it was recorded as in the $200-$250 range at retail. As recently as 1971 a copy sold at auction for $65. In 1972 there were two sales at auction—for $117 and $170. In 1975 there were two auction prices recorded—one at $590 and another at $675.)

SCHOEPF, Johann David. *Travels in the Confederation.* Translated and edited by Alfred J. Morrison. Portrait, 2 facsimiles. 2 vols., cloth. Philadelphia, 1911. First American edition (and first in English). $75-$100.

SCHOOLCRAFT, Henry R. *An Address Delivered Before the Was-ah Ho-de-no-son-ne, or New Confederacy of the Iroquois.* 48 pp., sewed. Rochester, 1846. First edition. $150-$175.

SCHOOLCRAFT, Henry R. *Algic Researches.* 2 vols., cloth. New York, 1839. First edition. $250-$300.

SCHOOLCRAFT, Henry R. *A Discourse Delivered on the Anniversary of the Historical Society of Michigan.* 44 pp., wrappers. Detroit, 1830. First edition. $150-$250.

SCHOOLCRAFT, Henry R. *Historical and Statistical Information Respecting the . . . Indian Tribes, etc.* Numerous maps, plates, and tables. 6 vols., cloth. Philadelphia, 1851-57. First edition. $1,500-$2,500. (For reprint, see Schoolcraft, *Information Respecting the History, etc.*)

SCHOOLCRAFT, Henry R. *The Indian Tribes of the United States.* Edited by Francis S. Drake. 100 plates. 2 vols., buckram. Philadelphia, 1884. First edition. $150-$175. London, 1885. 2 vols., cloth. $75-$125. (A condensation from Schoolcraft.)

SCHOOLCRAFT, Henry R. *Information Respecting the History, Condition, and Prospects of the Indian Tribes of the United States.* Illustrated. 6 vols., cloth. Philadelphia, 1853-57. Reprint of *Historical and Statistical Information.* $1,500-$2,000.

SCHOOLCRAFT, Henry R. *Inquiries Respecting the History . . . of the Indian Tribes of the United States.* (Caption title.) Printed wrappers. (Washington, about 1847-50.) $500-$600.

SCHOOLCRAFT, Henry R. *Journal of a Tour into the Interior of Missouri and Arkansaw*. Folding map. Leather. London, 1821. First edition. $150-$200.

SCHOOLCRAFT, Henry R. *The Myth of Hiawatha, and Other Oral Legends*. Cloth. Philadelphia, 1856. First edition. $75-$100.

SCHOOLCRAFT, Henry R. *Narrative of an Expedition Through the Upper Mississippi to Itasca Lake*. 5 maps. Cloth, paper label. New York, 1834. First edition. $150-$200.

SCHOOLCRAFT, Henry R. *Narrative Journal of Travels Through the Northwestern Regions of the U.S., etc*. Engraved title page, folding map, 7 plates. Boards. Albany, 1821. First edition, with errata slip. $200-$250.

SCHOOLCRAFT, Henry R. *Personal Memoirs of a Residence of 30 Years with the Indian Tribes*. Portrait (not in all copies). Cloth. Philadelphia, 1851. First edition. $100-$135.

SCHOOLCRAFT, Henry R. *Travels in the Central Portions of the Mississippi Valley*. 5 maps and plates. Boards. New York, 1825. First edition. $125-$150.

SCHOOLCRAFT, Henry R. *A View of the Lead Mines of Missouri*. 3 plates. Boards. New York, 1819. First edition. $150-$175.

SCHOOLCRAFT, Henry R., and Allen, James. *Expedition to North-West Indians*. (Caption title.) Map. 68 pp., modern wrappers. (Washington, 1834.) $200-$250.

SCHRANTZ, Ward L. *Jasper County, Missouri, in the Civil War*. Frontispiece, 9 plates. Cloth. Carthage, Mo., 1923. $60-$75.

SCHREIBER, Georges (editor). *Portraits and Self-Portraits*. Illustrated, by the editor. Cloth. Boston, 1936. First edition. In dust jacket. $40-$50. (Includes first publication of autobiographical pieces by Hemingway, Frost, Wolfe, and others.)

SCHREINER, Olive. See Iron, Ralph.

SCHULTZ, Christian. *Travels on an Inland Voyage, etc*. Portrait, 2 (sometimes 3) plates, 4 (sometimes 5) maps. 2 vols., leather. New York, 1810. First edition. $300-$350.

SCHUYLER, James. *Salute*. Original silk screen prints by Grace Hartigan. Folio, boards. New York, (1960). First edition. One of 200, signed. $150. The poet's first book.

SCHWARTZ, Delmore. See *The Poet's Pack*.

SCHWARTZ, Delmore, *Genesis: Book One*. Cloth. (New York), 1943. New Directions. First edition. In dust jacket. $50-$75.

SCHWARTZ, Delmore. *In Dreams Begin Responsibilities*. Cloth. Norfolk, Conn. (1938). First edition. In dust jacket. $100-$150. Author's first book.

SCHWARTZ, Delmore. *Shenandoah*. Wrappers, or boards. Norfolk, (1941). First edition. Boards: $50-$75. Wrappers: $30-$40.

SCHWARTZ, Delmore (translator). *A Season in Hell*. (By Arthur Rimbaud.) Beige cloth. Norfolk, Conn., (1939). First trade edition (750 copies.) In dust jacket. $40-$50. Another issue: Special edition. Patterned boards and cloth. One of 30. Boxed. In spider-web glassine jacket. $125-$150.

SCHWATKA, Frederick. *Four Summers in Alaska*. Illustrated. Cloth. St. Louis, 1892. First edition. $50-$75.

SCHWAB, John Christopher. *The Confederate States of America, 1861-1865*. Cloth. New York, 1901. First edition. $75-$100.

SCHWERDT, C. F. G. R. *Hunting, Hawking, Shooting*. 382 plates, including many in color. 4 vols., folio, full or half morocco. London, 1928-37. One of 300, signed. $1,850-$2,000.

SCHWETTMAN, Martin W. *Santa Rita, the University of Texas Oil Discovery*. 43 pp., wrappers. (Austin?), 1943. First edition. $50-$100.

SCLATER, P. L., and Hudson, W. H. *Argentine Ornithology*. 20 color plates. 2 vols., blue-gray boards. London, 1888-89. First edition. One of 200, signed. $1,500-$2,000.

SCORESBY, William, Jr. *Journal of a Voyage to the Northern Whale-Fishery*. 8 maps and plates. Boards, paper label. Edinburgh, 1823. First edition. $250-$350.

SCOT, Reginald. *The Discoverie of Witchcraft*. Edited by Montague Summers. Cloth, or morocco and buckram. (London), 1930. One of 1,275. $100-$125. In dust jacket. $75-$125.

SCOTT, James L. *A Journal of a Missionary Tour Through Pennsylvania*. Decorated cloth. Providence, 1843. First edition. $250-$350.

SCOTT, John. *The Indiana Gazetteer*. 143 pp., leather. Centreville, Ind., 1826. First edition. $500-$600.

SCOTT, John. *Partisan Life with Col. John S. Mosby*. Illustrated. Cloth. New York, 1867. First edition. $65-$75. London, 1867. First English edition. $50-$60.

SCOTT, Michael. See *Tom Cringle's Log*.

SCOTT, Peter. *Morning Flight*. 16 color plates. Cloth. London, 1935. First edition. One of 750, signed. In dust jacket. $250-$300. $200-$250.

SCOTT, Peter. *Wild Chorus*. Illustrated by the author, including mounted color plates. Blue cloth. London, (1938). First edition. One of 1,250, signed. In dust jacket. Boxed. $300-$400.

SCOTT, R.F. *Last Expedition*. Illustrated, including folding maps and color plates. 2 vols., cloth. London, 1913. First edition. $75-$125.

SCOTT, Sir Walter. See Clutterbuck, Captain. Also see *The Abbot; Anne of Geierstein; The Antiquary; The Fortunes of Nigel; Guy Mannering; Harold the Dauntless; Ivanhoe; Kenilworth; The Monastery; Quentin Durward; Rob Roy; Saint Ronan's Well; Waverley; Woodstock*.

SCOTT, Sir Walter. *The Field of Waterloo*. Brown wrappers. Edinburgh, 1815. First edition. $50-$100.

SCOTT, Sir Walter. *Halidon Hill: A Dramatic Sketch, from Scottish History*. 109 pp., drab wrappers. Edinburgh, 1822. First edition. $100-$150.

SCOTT, Sir Walter. *The Lady of the Lake*. Portrait. Boards. London, 1810. First edition. $400-$500. Large paper issue: $500-$750.

SCOTT, Sir Walter. *The Lay of the Last Minstrel*. Boards, paper label. Edinburgh, 1805. First edition. $400-$600.

SCOTT, Sir Walter. *Marmion*. Boards. London, 1808. First edition. $200-$250.

SCOTT-MONCRIEF, Charles Kenneth: See Lear, P. G. and L. O.

SCRIPPS, J.L. *The Undeveloped Northern Portion of the American Continent*. 20 pp., printed wrappers. Chicago, 1856. First edition. $300-$350. Another, plain wrappers. $200-$250.

SCROPE, William. *The Art of Deer-Stalking*. 12 plates. Wrappers. London, 1838. First edition. $400-$500. Rebound in half leather. $300.

SCROPE, William. *Days and Nights of Salmon Fishing in the Tweed*. 13 plates. Wrappers. London, 1843. First edition. $500-$600. Rebound, $300-$400.

SEALSFIELD, Charles. *The Cabin Book; or, Sketches of Life in Texas*. Wrappers. New York, 1844. (By Karl Postl.) First American edition. $750-$1,000. London, 1852. Cloth. First English edition. $250-$300. (Note: This book appeared first in the German language in 1841. Howes lists the first edition as published in Zurich; Thomas W. Streeter located an 1841 Leipzig edition. Value: $2,000?)

SEAVER, Edwin. *The Company*. Cloth. New York, 1930. First edition. In dust jacket. $40-$50.

SEAVER, James E. *A Narrative of the Life of Mrs. Mary Jemison, Who Was Taken by the Indians in the Year 1755, etc.* Boards. Canandaigua, N.Y., 1824. First edition. $600-$1,000. Howden, 1826. Boards. First English edition. $400-$500.

SECONDTHOUGHTS, Solomon. *Quodlibet*. Cloth. Philadelphia, 1840. (By John Pendleton Kennedy.) First edition. $100-$150.

SEDGWICK, Catharine M. *The Linwoods; or "Sixty Years Since" in America*. 2 vols., cloth, paper labels. New York, 1835. First edition. $75-$100.

SEDGWICK, John. *Correspondence of John Sedgwick*. 2 vols., cloth. (New York), 1902-03. First edition. One of 300. $50-$75.

SEEGER, Alan. *Poems*. Dark-brown cloth. New York, 1916. First edition. In dust jacket. $50-$60. Author's first book.

SEELIGSON, Mrs. Leila. *A History of Indianola*. 16 pp., wrappers. Cuero, Tex., (1930-31.) $35-$75.

SELBY, Julian A. *Memorabilia and Anecdotal Reminiscences of Columbia, S.C.* Portrait. Cloth. Columbia, 1905. First edition. $50-$75.

SELDEN, George. *The Cricket in Times Square*. Illustrated by Garth Williams. Cloth. New York, (1960). First edition. In dust jacket. $25-$35.

*SELECT Views in Sicily*. 36 full-page colored aquatint plates. Folio, half leather. London, 1825. (By Achille Etienne de la Salle Gigault.) $1,000-$1,500.

SELKIRK, (Thomas Douglas), Earl of. *A Sketch of the British Fur Trade in North America*. Boards. London, 1816. First edition. $1,000-$1,500. London, 1816. Second edition. $750-$1,000.

SELTZER, Charles Alden. *The Council of Three*. Cloth. New York, 1900. First edition. $50-$60. Author's first book.

*SENIOR Tabula*. Printed wrappers. Oak Park, Ill., June, 1917. (Includes "Class Prophecy," by Ernest Hemingway.) $500-$750. Also, $500 (A, 1977).

*SENSE and Sensibility*. By a Lady. 3 vols., blue or pink boards, paper labels. London, 1811. (By Jane Austen.) First edition, with ruled lines of half title in Vol. 1 measuring 4/5 inch (1-1/7 inches in second edition). $15,000 and up. Also, bindings defective, $5,500 (A, 1974). Rebound copies, $1,000-$3,000. London, 1813. 3 vols, boards. Second edition. $1,000 and up.

SEREDY, Kate. *The White Stag*. Lithographs by the author. Cloth. New York, 1937. First edition. In dust jacket. $30-$40.

SERVICE, Robert W. *Rhymes of a Red Cross Man*. Cloth. Toronto, 1916. First edition. $35-$50.

SERVISS, Garrett P. *A Columbus of Space*. Illustrated. Cloth. New York, 1911. First edition. $50-$75.

SETON, Ernest Thompson. *Animal Heroes*. Illustrated. Cloth. New York, 1905. First edition. $65-$75.

SETON, Ernest Thompson. *Life Histories of Northern Animals*. Illustrated. 2 vols., cloth. New York, 1909. First edition. Boxed. $125-$175. London, 1910. 2 vols. cloth. $75-$150.

SETON, Ernest Thompson. *Studies in the Art Anatomy of Animals*. Illustrated. Cloth. London, 1896. First edition. $150-$200.

SETON, Ernest Thompson. *Wild Animals I have Known*. 200 drawings by the author. Pictorial cloth. New York, 1898. First edition, first issue, without the words "The Angel whispered don't go" in the last paragraph on page 265. $100-$150. London, (1898). Cloth. First English edition. $75-$100. New York, 1900. Illustrated. One of 1,000, signed. $75-$125.

SETON-THOMPSON, Ernest. *The Birch-Bark Roll of the Woodcraft Indians.* Illustrated. 71 pp., birchbark wrappers. New York, 1906. First separate edition. $50-$65.

SETON-THOMPSON, Ernest. *Boy Scouts of America: A Handbook of Woodcraft, Scouting, and Life-craft.* Pictorial wrappers. New York, 1910. First edition, "probably earlier state," with printer's slug on copyright page. $125-$150.

SEUSS, Dr. *And to Think That I Saw it on Mulberry Street.* Illustrated in color by the author. Pictorial boards. New York, 1937. (By Theodore Geisel.) First edition. In dust jacket. $150-$175. Author's first nonsense book for children.

SEUSS, Dr. *The Seven Lady Godivas.* Color illustrations. Pictorial cloth. New York, (1939). (By Theodore Geisel.) First edition. In dust jacket. $50-$75.

*SEVEN and Nine Years Among the Camanches and Apaches.* Plates. Cloth. Jersey City, 1873. (By Edwin Eastman.) First edition. $75-$100.

*SEVEN Little Sisters Who Live on the Round Ball That Floats in the Air (The).* Illustrated. Decorated cloth. Boston, 1861. (By Jane Andrews.) First edition. $100-$125.

*SEVEN Pillars of Wisdom (The).* Specimen sheets. Half red buckram, vellum spine. New York, 1926. (By T.E. Lawrence.) First American (copyright) edition, with author's name accidentally omitted from title page. One of 24 (stated 22), of which 10 were offered for sale at $10,000 each. $2,500-$3,500. Another issue: Out of series. One of 2 specially bound in three-quarters blue buckram for George H. Doran, the publisher, as presentation copies. $5,000 or more. (For first edition, see entry under Lawrence.)

*SEVENTY-SIX . . . (A Novel).* 2 vols., contemporary boards. Baltimore, 1823. (By John Neal.) First edition. $200-$250.

SEWALL, Rufus King. *Sketches of St. Augustine.* 6 plates. 69 pp., cloth. New York, 1848. First edition. $100-$200. Pages 39 and 40 removed, as with most copies. $60-$80.

SEWARD, W.H. *Communication upon the Subject of an Intercontinental Telegraph, etc.* Folding map. 52 pp., wrappers. Washington, 1864. First edition. $500-$600.

SEWELL, Anna. *Black Beauty.* Blue, red, or brown cloth. London, (1877). First edition. $600-$750. Boston, (1890). Orange printed wrappers, or buff boards. First American edition. Wrappers. $100-$150. Boards: $85-$125. London, 1915. Illustrated in color by Lucy Kemp-Welch. Cloth. One of 600, signed. $150-$250.

SEXTON, Anne. *All My Pretty Ones.* Cloth. Boards and cloth. Boston, 1962. First edition. In dust jacket. $35-$45.

SEXTON, Anne. *The Book of Folly.* Boards and cloth. Boston, 1972. First edition. One of 500, signed. $40-$50.

SEXTON, Anne. *To Bedlam and Part Way Back.* Boards and cloth. Boston, 1960. First edition. In dust jacket. $50-$75. Author's first book.

SEXTON, Lucy Ann (Foster), and Foster, Mrs. Roxana C. *The Foster Family: California Pioneers.* Cloth. (Santa Barbara, 1925.) Enlarged (first?) edition. $125-$150.

SEYD, Ernest. *California and Its Resources.* 2 plates (some tinted), 2 folding maps. Cloth. London, 1858. First edition. $200-$250.

SEYMOUR, E. S. *Emigrant's Guide to the Gold Mines of Upper California.* Folding map. 104 pp., wrappers. Chicago, 1849. First edition. $2,000-$2,500.

SEYMOUR, E. S. *Sketches of Minnesota.* Printed wrappers, or cloth. New York, 1850. First edition. Wrappers: $100-$125. Cloth: $75-$100.

SEYMOUR, Silas. *A Reminiscence of the Union Pacific Railroad*. Plates. Printed wrappers. Quebec, 1873. First edition. $175-$225.

SEYMOUR, W.D. *The Isthmian Routes*. 27 pp., sewed. New York, 1863. First edition. $150-$200.

SEYMOUR, William N. *Madison Directory and Business Advertiser*. Map. Leather. Madison, Wis., 1855. First edition. $175-$225.

SCHACKLETON, E. H. *The Heart of the Antarctic*. Illustrated, including color plates and folding maps. 2 vols., cloth. London, 1909. First edition. $75-$100. Limited issue: 3 vols., signed by all in the Shore party. One of 300. $1,000-$1,250.

SHAFFER, Ellen. *The Garden of Health*. Illustrated. Folio, boards and linen. (San Francisco, 1957.) Book Club of California. One of 300, with a leaf from the 1499 *Hortus Sanitatis*. In dust jacket. $150-$200.

SHAFFER, Ellen. *The Nuremberg Chronicle . . . A Monograph*. Illustrated. 61 pp., pictorial cloth. Los Angeles, 1950. Plantin Press. One of 300, with an original leaf from the *Chronicle* (1497). $300-$400.

SHAHN, Ben (illustrator). *Haggadah for Passover*. Text in Hebrew and English. Unbound sheets in white wrappers, in a white parchment box. Illustrated, including 14 color plates. Paris, (1966). Trianon Press. One of 292 signed by Shahn. $1,000-$1,250.

*SHAKESPEARE Rare Print Collection*. Edited by Seymour Eaton. 146 plates, 12 parts, portfolio (New York), 1900. Connoisseur Edition. $50-$85.

SHAKESPEARE, William. *Antony and Cleopatra*. Printed in red and black. Vellum. London, 1912. Doves Press. One of 200. $250-$350. Another issue: specially bound in morocco by the Doves Bindery. $1,500-$2,000. San Francisco, 1960. Grabhorn Press. Illustrated in color by Mary Grabhorn. Folio, parchment. One of 185. $200-$250.

SHAKESPEARE, William. *As You Like It*. Illustrated in color by Hugh Thomson. Morocco. London, (1909). $50-$75. Another issue: Vellum with ties. One of 500 signed by Thomson. $150-$200.

SHAKESPEARE, William. *Comedies, Histories and Tragedies*. Introduction and census of copies by Sidney Lee. Facsimile from the 1st Folio edition. Folio, cloth. Oxford, 1901. One of 1,000, signed. Boxed. $150-$250.

SHAKESPEARE, William. *Coriolanus*. Vellum. London, 1914. Doves Press. One of 200. $300-$350. Another issue: One of 15 on vellum, specially bound in morocco by the Doves Bindery. $3,000-$4,000.

SHAKESPEARE, William. *Cymbeline*. Illustrated. Cloth. London, 1923. Shakespeare Head Press. One of 450. $60-$80. Another issue: Morocco. One of 100. $150-$250.

SHAKESPEARE, William. *Hamlet, Price of Denmark*. In Spanish and English. Illustrated in color by Anthony Salo. Printed on cork, bound in goatskin. Barcelona, (1930). One of 100. $400-$600. Editions in English: London, no date. 30 color plates by W.G. Simmonds. Vellum. One of 250 signed by the artist. $150-$250. London, 1909. Doves Press. Printed in red and black. Vellum or white pigskin. One of 250. $500-$750. Another issue: One of 15 on vellum: $4,000-$5,000. Weimar, Germany, 1930. Cranach Press.Illustrated by Edward Gordon Craig. Boards. One of 300. $1,500-$2,000. New York, (1933). Limited Editions Club. $100-$125.

SHAKESPEARE, William. *Julius Caesar*. Vellum. London, 1913. Doves Press. One of 200. $250-$350. Another issue: One of 15 on vellum. $2,500-$3,000. San Francisco, 1954. Grabhorn Press. Illustrated by Mary Grabhorn. Folio, half leather. One of 180. $175-$200.

SHAKESPEARE, William. *King Lear*. Edited by G. K. Chesterton. 10 plates. Cloth. San Francisco, (1930). $50-$75. San Francisco, 1959. Grabhorn Press. Illustrated in color by Mary Grabhorn. Cloth. One of 180. $150-$175. London, 1963. 16 plates by Oskar Kokoschka. Folio, unsewn sheets, in box. One of 275, signed. $800-$1,000. Another issue: Pigskin. With an added signed lithograph. $1,250-$1,500.

SHAKESPEARE, William. *Lucrece*. Limp vellum. London, 1915. Dove Press. One of 175 on paper. $225.

SHAKESPEARE, William. *Macbeth*. Illustrations in color by Mary Grabhorn. Boards, leather spine. (San Francisco, 1952.) One of 180. Boxed. $175-$200.

SHAKESPEARE, William. *The Merry Wives of Windsor*. Illustrated by Hugh Thomson. Pictorial vellum, silk ties. London, 1910. One of 350, signed. $150-$200.

SHAKESPEARE, William. *A Midsummer-Night's Dream*. Illustrated by Arthur Rackham. Full white vellum with ties. London, 1908. One of 1,000 signed by Rackham. $350-$500. Trade edition: Gold-stamped cloth. $200-$250. New York, 1908. Gray boards, green cloth. First American edition. $250-$300. San Francisco, 1955. Illustrated in color by Mary Grabhorn. Parchment. One of 180. Boxed. $150-$200.

SHAKESPEARE, William. *Othello*. Portraits in color by Mary Grabhorn. Boards, leather spine. San Francisco, 1956. One of 185. $150-$200.

SHAKESPEARE, William. *The Poems of William Shakespeare*. Edited by F. S. Ellis. Limp vellum with ties. London, 1893. Kelmscott Press. One of 500. $600-$750. London, 1899. Essex House. Limp vellum with ties. One of 450. $150-$200. Stamford, Conn., 1939. Folio, half leather. One of 150. Boxed. $200-$250. New York, 1941. Limited Editions Club. 2 vols., pictorial boards. $75-$100.

SHAKESPEARE, William. *Poems and Sonnets*. Morocco. London, 1960. Golden Cockerel Press. One of 100. $250-$300. Another issue: Buckram. One of 470. $150.

SHAKESPEARE, William. *The Rape of Lucrece*. Printed in red and black. Text from the first edition. Vellum. London, 1915. Doves Presss. One of 175. $300-$350. Another issue: Specially bound in morocco by the Doves Bindery. $1,000 and up.

SHAKESPEARE, William. *Richard the Third*. Colored woodcuts by Mary Grabhorn. Vellum. San Francisco, 1953. Grabhorn Press. One of 180. Boxed. $150-$250.

SHAKESPEARE, William. *Songs from Shakespeare's Plays*. Half morocco. Verona, Italy, (1974). One of 300. Boxed. $150.

SHAKESPEARE, William. *Sonnets*. Vellum. London, 1909. Doves Press. One of 250. $450-$700. London, 1913. Morocco. One of 15 on vellum. $750-$1,000. London, 1929. Full morocco. One of 1,000. $75-$150. (Los Angeles, 1974.) Plantin Press. Boards. One of 120. $250.

SHAKESPEARE, William. *The Taming of the Shrew*. 7 drawings in color by Valenti Angelo. Folio, cloth. San Francisco, 1967. Grabhorn printing. $100.

SHAKESPEARE, William. *The Tempest*. 40 color plates by Edmund Dulac. Vellum with ties. London, 1908. One of 500 signed by Dulac. $250-$450. Another issue: Pictorial cloth. $100-$150. London (1926). Vellum. 21 color plates by Rackham. One of 520 signed by Rackham. In dust jacket. $600-$750, possibly more. Trade issue: Cloth. In dust jacket. $90-$150. San Francisco, 1951. Grabhorn Press. Illustrated by Mary Grabhorn. Half cloth. One of 160. $150.

SHAKESPEARE, William. *Twelfth Night*. 29 engravings. Folio, morocco and boards. Waltham Saint Lawrence, 1932. Golden Cockerel Press. One of 275. $250-$300.

SHAKESPEARE, William. *Venus and Adonis*. Vellum. London, 1912. Doves Press. One of 200. $400-$500. Another issue: One of 15 on vellum, specially bound by the Doves Bindery. $2,500-$3,000. Rochester, 1931. Illustrated by Rockwell Kent. One of 75 (of an edition of 1,250) signed, together with 21 mounted illustrations. Boxed as a set. $300-$500. Without the extra plates, $125-$150.

SHAPIRO, Karl. *Poems*. Cloth. Baltimore, 1935. First edition. One of 200 signed. $700-$800. Author's first book.

SHAPIRO, Karl. *Trial of a Poet*. Cloth. New York, (1947). One of 250, signed. In tissue dust jacket. Boxed. $50-$65. Trade edition: In dust jacket. $15-$20.

SHAPIRO, Karl. *V-Letter and Other Poems.* Tan cloth. New York, (1944). First edition. In dust jacket. $30-$40.

SHARAN, James. *The Adventures of James Sharan.* Leather. Baltimore, 1808. First edition. $175.

*SHARON Against Terry. In the Circuit Court of the United States, 9th Circuit, District of California.* Half morocco. San Francisco, no date. $125-$150.

SHARP, Margery. *The Rescuers.* Illustrated by Garth Williams. Cloth. Boston, (1959). First edition. In dust jacket. $25-$35.

SHATTUCK, Lemuel. *A History of the Town of Concord.* Folding map. Half leather. Boston, 1835. First edition. $75-$100.

SHAW, Edward. *Civil Architecture.* 95 engravings. Calf. Boston, 1831. First edition. $100-$150. Boston, 1832. 97 plates. Second edition. $50-$75. Boston, 1836. 100 plates. Sheep. Fourth edition. $50-$100.

SHAW, Edward. *The Modern Architect.* 65 plates. Cloth. Boston, 1855. First edition. $75-$100.

SHAW, Edward. *Rural Architecture.* 52 plates. Calf. Boston, 1843. First edition. $50-$75.

SHAW, George Bernard. See Harris, Frank. Also see *This Is the Preachment on Going to Church.*

SHAW, George Bernard. *Androcles and the Lion.* Printed wrappers. London, 1913. First edition, with title page reading: "Rough Proof—Unpublished." One of 50 privately printed. $400-$500. Also, $350 (A, 1977). London, 1916. Cloth. (With *Overruled* and *Pygmalion* added to title.) In dust jacket. $50-$75.

SHAW, George Bernard. *Augustus Does His Bit.* Wrappers. (London, 1916.) "Rough Proof—Unpublished " $100-$150.

SHAW, George Bernard. *Back to Methuselah: A Metabiological Pentateuch.* Light gray-green cloth. London, 1921. First edition. In dust jacket. $75-$100. New York, 1939. Limited Editions Club. Cloth. $35-$40.

SHAW, George Bernard. *Cashel Byron's Profession.* Printed blue wrappers. (London), 1886. First edition. $300-$350. Author's first book.

SHAW, George Bernard. *A Discarded Defence of Roger Casement.* Wrappers. London, 1922. First edition. One of 25. $200-$300.

SHAW, George Bernard, *The Doctor's Dilemma, Getting Married, and The Shewing Up of Blanco Posnet.* Cloth. London, 1911. First edition. In dust jacket. $75-$100.

SHAW, George Bernard. *Geneva.* Illustrated by Topolski. Cloth. London, (1939). First edition. In dust jacket. $25.

SHAW, George Bernard. *Great Catherine.* Wrappers. London, 1914. First edition, imprinted on front cover: "Rough Proof—Unpublished." $200 (A, 1977).

SHAW, George Bernard. *Heartbreak House, Great Catherine, and Playlets of the War.* Cloth. London, 1919. First edition. In dust jacket. $40-$50.

SHAW, George Bernard. *How to Settle the Irish Question.* Blue printed wrappers. Dublin, (1917). First edition. $50-$60. Second issue: Green wrappers. $40-$50.

SHAW, George Bernard. *The Intelligent Woman's Guide to Socialism.* Green cloth. London, 1928. First edition. $50-$75.

SHAW, George Bernard. *The Irrational Knot.* Blue cloth. London, 1905. First edition. $35-$50. New York, 1905. First American edition. $25-$30.

SHAW, George Bernard. *John Bull's Other Island and Major Barbara.* Green cloth. London, 1907. First edition, first issue, with Archibald Constable & Co. imprint on title page. $25-$35.

SHAW, George Bernard. *Love Among the Artists*. Cloth. Chicago, 1900. First edition. $65-$75.

SHAW, George Bernard. *Man and Superman*. Green cloth. Westminster (London), 1903. First edition. $50-$60. New York, 1962. Limited Editions Club. Illustrated. Pictorial cloth. Boxed. $75-$85.

SHAW, George Bernard. *Mrs. Warren's Profession: A Play in Four Acts*. Cloth. London, 1902 First edition. $40-$60.

SHAW, George Bernard. *On the Rocks*. Printed wrappers. (London), 1933. "First Rough Proof—Unpublished." $150-$250. Another issue: "First Revise After Rehearsal—Unpublished." Printed wrappers. $150-$200.

SHAW, George Bernard. *Passion, Poison and Petrifaction*. Printed wrappers. New York, (1907). First edition. $100-$150. (Note: This first appeared in *Harry Furniss' Christmas Annual*, London, 1905, which in the current market is valued at around $100.)

SHAW, George Bernard. *The Perfect Wagnerite*. Blue and tan cloth. London, 1898. First edition. $75-$100.

SHAW, George Bernard. *Plays: Pleasant and Unpleasant*. Portrait. 2 vols., green cloth. London, 1898. First edition. $75-$100. Chicago, 1898. 2 vols., cloth. First American edition. $35-$50.

SHAW, George Bernard. *The Political Madhouse in America and Nearer Home: A Lecture*. Wrappers. (London), 1933. Proof copy of the first English edition. $100-$150. London, 1933. Boards. First published English edition. $30-$50.

SHAW, George Bernard. *Press Cuttings*. Pink wrappers. London, 1909. First edition, first issue, with "Price One Shilling" at bottom of front cover. $50-$60. New York, 1909. Wrappers. First American copyright edition. One of 25. $200-$250. Another issue: One of 50. $100-$125.

SHAW, George Bernard. *Pygmalion: A Romance in Five Acts*. Printed wrappers. London, 1913. First edition, first issue, with title page reading: "Rough Proof, Unpublished." $600-$800. (London), 1914. Wrappers. Second edition. $300-$350.

SHAW, George Bernard. *The Quintessence of Ibsenism*. Dark-blue cloth. London, 1891. First edition, first binding. $75-$100. Later binding: Gray-green cloth. $50-$75.

SHAW, George Bernard. *Saint Joan: A Chronicle Play*. Blue-gray wrappers. London, 1923. First edition, first issue, with title page reading "Rough Proof, Unpublished." $400-$600. London, 1924. Cloth. First published edition. In dust jacket. $75-$100. London, (1924). Illustrated by Charles Ricketts. Folio, boards and cloth. First illustrated edition. One of 750. In dust jacket. $100-$125.

SHAW, George Bernard. *The Sanity of Art*. Printed brown wrappers. London, 1908. First edition. $50-$75. Another issue: Boards and cloth. $25.

SHAW, George Bernard. *Shaw Gives Himself Away: An Autobiographical Miscellany*. Frontispiece woodcut portrait. Dark-green morocco, inlaid with red leather. Newtown, Wales, 1939. Gregynog Press. One of 300. $300-$350. Another issue: One of 12 bound by George Fisher. $750-$1,000.

SHAW, George Bernard. *The Shewing Up of Blanco Posnet*. 36 pp., printed wrappers. New York, 1909. First (copyright) edition. One of 25. $250-$350.

SHAW, George Bernard. *Three Plays for Puritans*. Plates. Green cloth. London, 1901. First edition. $30-$40. Chicago, 1901. Cloth. First American edition. $30-$40.

SHAW, George Bernard. *An Unsocial Socialist*. Scarlet cloth. London, 1887. First edition, first state, with title of Shaw's first novel incorrectly given on title page and with publisher's name spelled wrong on spine. $200-$250. Second state, with novel's title corrected and with publisher's name on spine stamped over. $150-$200.

SHAW, George Bernard. *War Issues for Irishmen: An Open Letter to Col. Arthur Lynch from Bernard Shaw.* Gray wrappers. Dublin, 1918. First edition. $400-$600. (Suppressed.)

SHAW, George Bernard. *Widowers' Houses: A Comedy.* Blue-green cloth. London, 1893. First edition. $100-$135.

SHAW, Henry. *The Decorative Arts, Ecclesiastical and Civil, of the Middle Ages.* 41 engravings, 18 in color. Half leather. London, 1851. First edition. $200-$225.

SHAW, Henry. *Dresses and Decorations of the Middle Ages.* Hand-colored plates and other illustrations. 2 vols., folio, boards. London, 1843. First edition. $400-$600. Another issue: Three-quarters morocco. One of 12 on large paper. $850-$1,000.

SHAW, Henry. *Examples of Ornamental Metal Work.* 50 plates. Boards. London, 1836. First edition. $150-$250.

SHAW, Henry, and Madden, Sir Frederic. *Illuminated Ornaments Selected from Manuscripts and Early Printed Books.* Illustrated. Boards. London, 1833. First edition. $400-$600. Large paper issue: Boards and leather. $600-$800.

SHAW, Irwin. *Sailor Off the Bremen.* Cloth. New York, 1939. First edition. In dust jacket. $35-$50.

SHAW, Joshua. *United States Directory for the Use of Travellers and Merchants, etc.* Leather. Philadelphia, (1822). First edition. $350-$500.

SHAW, R. C. *Across the Plains in Forty-nine.* Portrait. Cloth. Farmland, Ind., 1896. First edition. $125-$150.

SHAW, T. E. (adopted name). See Homer; Lawrence, T.E.

SHAY, Frank (editor). *Contemporary One-Act Plays of 1921.* Green cloth. Cincinnati, (1922). First edition. In dust jacket. $50-$75. (Note: Includes Eugene O'Neill's *The Dreamy Kid*—first book appearance of the play.)

SHEA, John Gilmary. *Early Voyages Up and Down the Mississippi.* Boards. Albany, N.Y., 1861. First edition. $60-$75. Large paper issue: $100-$125. Albany, (1902). Boards. Facsimile reprint. $75.

SHEA, John Gilmary. *A History of the Catholic Church Within . . . the United States.* Illustrated. 4 vols., cloth. New York, 1886-92. First edition. $100-$150.

SHELDON, Charles M. *In His Steps: "What Would Jesus Do?"* Brown and white printed wrappers, Chicago, 1897. First edition. $250-$500. (One of the best-selling novels of American publishing history; rare in original wrappers.)

SHELLEY, Mary W. See *Falkner; The Fortunes of Perkin Warbeck; Frankenstein; Lodore; Valperga; The Last Man.*

SHELLEY, Percy Bysshe. See *S., P. B.* Also see *History of a Six Weeks' Tour, etc.; St. Irvyne; Epipsychidion.*

SHELLEY, Percy Bysshe. *Adonais: An Elegy on the Death of John Keats.* 25 pp., blue ornamental wrappers. Pisa, Italy, 1821. First edition. $10,000 and up. Also, rebound $5,250 (1974); $6,000 (A, 1971); $3,300 (A, 1970). Cambridge (London), 1829. Green wrappers. Second (first English) edition. $2,000 and up. Also, $525 (A, 1965). Rebound, $550 (A, 1974).

SHELLEY, Percy Bysshe. *Alastor; or, The Spirit of Solitude: and Other Poems.* Boards, paper label on spine. London, 1816. First edition. $2,000 and up. Also, rebound in calf, $780 (A, 1971).

SHELLEY, Percy Bysshe. *The Cenci.* Wrappers, or boards. (Leghorn), Italy, 1819. First edition. (250 copies.) $3,000-$4,000. Also, one of "a few" copies on thin paper, in original wrappers, $1,900 (A, 1977). (Most copies are on heavier paper.) London, 1821. Wrappers. First English edition. $400-$600.

SHELLEY, Percy Bysshe. *The Complete Works of Percy Bysshe Shelley.* 10 vols., cloth, vellum spines. London, 1926-27. One of 780. Boxed. $350.

SHELLEY, Percy Bysshe. *Hellas: A Lyrical Drama.* Stiff drab wrappers. London, 1822. First edition. $1,000 and up.

SHELLEY, Percy Bysshe. *Laon and Cythna.* Boards. London, 1818. First edition, first issue, with four-line quotation from Pindar on half title. $3,000 and up. Second issue, same date, without Pindar lines. Boards. $2,000 and up. Also, $950 (A, 1974); $1,000 (A, 1971).

SHELLEY, Percy Bysshe. *Letters from Percy Bysshe Shelley to J. H. Leigh Hunt.* Edited by Thomas J. Wise. 2 vols., cloth. London, 1894. First edition. (30 copies.) $200-$250. Another issue: Morocco. One of 6 on vellum. $600-$1,000.

SHELLEY, Percy Bysshe. *Letters of Percy Bysshe Shelley.* With an Introductory Essay by Robert Browning. Dark-red cloth. London, 1852. First edition. $200-$250. (Suppressed as forgeries.)

SHELLEY, Percy Bysshe. *The Masque of Anarchy: A Poem.* Preface by Leigh Hunt. Gray-blue boards. London, 1832. First edition, with white spine label lettered vertically "Shelley's Masque." $400-$600.

SHELLEY, Percy Bysshe. *Miscellaneous Poems.* Boards. London, 1826. First edition. $400-$600.

SHELLEY, Percy Bysshe. *On the Vegetable System of Diet.* Cloth. London, 1929. First edition. One of 12. $250-$350, possibly more.

SHELLEY, Percy Bysshe. *Poems. (Poetical Works.)* 3 vols., vellum. (Hammersmith, 1894-95.) Kelmscott Press. (250 copies.) $1,000-$1,250. (London, 1901-02.) Vale Press. Decorations by Charles Ricketts. 3 vols., white buckram. $200-$250. London, 1914. Doves Press. Limp vellum. One of 200.ʻ$400-$600.

SHELLEY, Percy Bysshe. *Poems and Sonnets.* Edited by Charles Alfred Seymour. 74 pp., parchment wrappers. Philadelphia, 1887. (Thomas J. Wise piracy.) One of 30. $400-$500.

SHELLEY, Percy Bysshe. *Posthumous Poems.* Boards, paper label on spine. London, 1824. First edition, first issue, without errata leaf. $400-$600.

SHELLEY, Percy Bysshe. *Prometheus Unbound.* Blue-gray boards, paper label. London, 1820. First edition, first issue, with "Miscellaneous" misprinted "Misellaneous" in table of contents. $2,000-$2,500. Also, $1,000 (A, 1977). Second issue, with misprint corrected. $1,500-$2,000. London, 1904. Essex House Press. Morocco. One of 20 on vellum. Boxed. $1,000 and up. Another issue: Limp vellum. One of 200 on paper. $150-$200.

SHELLEY, Percy Bysshe. *Queen Mab: A Philosophical Poem.* Boards. London, 1813. First (privately printed) edition. $10,000 and up. Shelley removed the title, dedication, and imprint from many copies. An unmutilated copy, with hinges split, was sold at auction for $6,000 in June, 1976. London, 1821. Boards. Second (first published) edition. $200-$300. New York, 1821. Boards. First American edition. $100-$150.

SHELLEY, Percy Bysshe. *The Revolt of Islam.* Blue boards, white paper label on spine. London, 1817 (actually 1818). First edition, first issue, incorrectly dated on title page. $2,500-$3,500. Also, $1,850 (A, 1977). London, 1818. Second issue, correctly dated. $1,000 -$2,000. London, 1829. Second edition. $750-$1,000.

SHELLEY, Percy Bysshe. *Rosalind and Helen.* Drab wrappers. London, 1819. First edition, with 2 ad leaves at end. $500-$750.

SHELLEY-ROLLS, Sir John C. E. *Yachts of the Royal Yacht Squadron, 1815-1932.* Buckram. London, 1933. First edition. $100-$150.

SHELTON, Frederick William. See Admirari, Nil

SHEPARD, A.K. *The Land of the Aztecs.* Cloth. Albany, 1859. First edition. $100-$150.

SHEPARD, Ernest H. *Fun and Fantasy.* Introduction by A.A. Milne. 7 color plates. Cloth. London, (1927). First edition. One of 150, signed. $135-$175. Trade edition: Boards. $50-$60.

SHEPARD, Odell. *A Lonely Flute.* Boards. Boston, 1917. First edition. In dust jacket. $30-$50. Author's first book.

*SHEPPARD Lee.* Written by Himself. 2 vols., floral cloth. New York, 1836. (By Robert Montgomery Bird.) First edition. $150-$250.

SHEPPERD, Tad. *Pack & Paddock.* Illustrated. Boards. New York, (1938). Derrydale Press. First edition. One of 950. $80-$100.

SHERIDAN, Philip H. *Outline Descriptions of the Posts in the Military Division of the Missouri, etc.* Maps, including a folding map. Cloth. Chicago, 1872. First edition. $150-$200.

SHERMAN, Elizabeth Ware. See S., E.W., and M., S. W.

SHERWELL, Samuel. *Old Recollections of an Old Boy.* Portrait. Cloth. New York, 1923. First edition. $75-$100.

SHERWOOD, J. Ely. *California: Her Wealth and Resources.* 40 pp., wrappers. New York, 1848. First edition. $1,200.

SHIEL, M. P. *Prince Zaleski.* Decorated purple cloth. London, 1895. First edition, with two ad catalogues at back. $150-$200.

SHIEL, M. P. *The Purple Cloud.* Cloth. London, 1929. First edition. One of 105 signed. $150.

SHIEL, M. P. *Shapes in the Fire.* Cloth. London, 1896. First edition. $100-$150.

SHIELDS, G.O. *The Battle of the Big Hole.* 8 plates. Cloth. New York, 1889. First edition. $75-$100.

SHILLIBEER, Lieut. J. *A Narrative of the Briton's Voyage to Pitcairn's Island.* 16 etchings (not 18 as title erroneously states.) Contemporary boards. Taunton, 1817. First edition, with errata leaf and instructions to the binder. $150-$200. London, 1817. 11 plates. Boards. Second edition. $100. London, 1818. 12 plates. Half calf. Third edition. $100.

SHINN, Charles Howard. *Mining Camps.* Cloth. New York, 1885. First edition. $125-$150.

SHINN, Charles Howard. *Pacific Rural Handbook.* Cloth. San Francisco, 1879. First edition. $100-$125.

SHIPMAN, Mrs. O. L. *Taming the Big Bend.* Folding map, 4 plates. Cloth. (Marfa, Tex., 1926.) First edition. $250-$350.

SHOBER, G. A. *A Choice Drop of Honey from the Rock Christ, or a Short Word of Advice to All Saints and Sinners.* 30 pp., wrappers. New Market, Va., 1811. $100-$150.

SHOEMAKER, James. *Directory of the City of Mankato, and Blue Earth County.* Printed boards. Mankato, Minn., 1888. $125-$150.

*SHORT History of Gen. R. E. Lee (A).* 15 pp., pictorial wrappers, miniature. New York, 1888. $50-$75.

*SHORT History of T. J. Jackson (A).* 15 pp., pictorial wrappers, miniature. New York, 1888. $50-$75.

*SHOWMAN'S Series III (The): Theatre Picture Book.* Pop-up book with colored folding scenes. Pictorial boards. New York, (about 1885). $100-$150.

SHUTE, Henry A. *The Real Diary of a Real Boy.* Cloth. Boston, 1902. First edition. $100-$150.

SIDNEY, Margaret. *Five Little Peppers and How They Grew.* Green, blue, or brown pictorial cloth. Boston, (1880). (By Harriet M. S. Lothrop.) First edition, first state, with 1880 copyright and with caption on page 231 reading "said Polly." $200-$300.

SIDNEY, Sir Philip. *The Defence of Poesie and Certain Sonnets.* Engraved portrait. Limp vellum, with ties. Bedford Park, Chiswick, 1906. Caradoc Press. One of 14 (of an edition of 364) printed in red and black on vellum. $400-$600. Ordinary issue: Boards. One of 350. $100-$150.

SIEBERT, Wilbur Henry. *Loyalists in East Florida.* 6 maps and plates. 2 vols., buckram. DeLand, Fla., 1929. First edition. One of 355. $175-$200.

*SIEGE of Corinth (The).* Drab wrappers. London, 1816. (By George Gordon Noel, Lord Byron.) First edition. $400-$500.

SILL, Edward Rowland. *The Venus of Milo and Other Poems.* Printed cream wrappers. Berkeley, 1883. First edition, with copyright stamp on title page. $50-$75.

SILLIMAN, Benjamin. *A Description of the Recently Discovered Petroleum Region in California.* (Cover title.) Printed wrappers. New York, 1864. First edition. $750-$1,000.

SILLIMAN, Benjamin. *Report upon the Oil Property of the Philadelphia and California Petroleum Co.* 2 maps. 36 pp., wrappers. Philadelphia, 1865. First edition. $300-$400, possibly more.

SILLITOE, Alan. *The Loneliness of the Long Distance Runner.* Cloth. London, 1959. First edition. In dust jacket. $40-$50.

SILURIENSIS, Leolinus. *The Anatomy of Tobacco.* White parchment boards. London (1884). (By Arthur Machen.) First edition. $50-$75. Author's first book (aside from the anonymous privately printed pamphlet *Eleusinia,* Hereford, Wales, 1881, of which only one copy is known).

*SILVER Mines of Virginia and Austin, Nevada.* 19 pp., wrappers. Boston, 1865. $300-$350.

SIMMS, Jeptha R. *The American Spy, or Freedom's Early Sacrifice.* 63 pp., wrappers. Albany, 1846. First edition. $50-$75.

SIMMS, Jeptha R. *History of Schoharie County.* Plates. Cloth. Albany, 1845. First edition. $100-$150.

SIMMS, Jeptha R. *Trappers of New York.* 4 plates. Cloth. Albany, 1850. First edition. $50-$75. Albany, 1860. Red buckram. $40-$50.

SIMMS, William Gilmore. See *Atalantis; Beauchampe; Border Beagles; Carl Werner; The Damsel of Darien; Grouped Thoughts and Scattered Fancies; Guy Rivers; The Lily and the Totem; Martin Faber; Mellichampe; The Partisan; Pelayo; Richard Hurdis; Sack and Destruction of Columbia, S.C.; The Wigwam and the Cabin; The Yemassee.*

SIMMS, William Gilmore. *Areytos; or, Songs of the South.* Wrappers. Charleston, 1846. First edition. $100-$125.

SIMMS, William Gilmore. *The Cassique of Accabee.* Wrappers. Charleston, 1849. First edition. $150-$200.

SIMMS, William Gilmore. *Egeria; or, Voices of Thought and Counsel for the Woods and Wayside.* Cloth. Philadelphia, 1853. First edition. $50-$75.

SIMMS, William Gilmore. *Father Abbott; or, The Home Tourist.* Wrappers. Charleston, 1849. First edition. $100-$125.

SIMMS, William Gilmore. *The Forayers; or, The Raid of the Dog-Days.* Cloth. New York, 1855. First edition. $100-$125.

SIMMS, William Gilmore. *Helen Halsey; or, the Swamp State of Conelachita.* Wrappers. New York, 1845. First edition. $200-$300.

SIMMS, William Gilmore. *The History of South Carolina*. Cloth. Charleston, 1840. First edition. $150-$200.

SIMMS, William Gilmore. *The Life of Chevalier Bayard*. Frontispiece, other illustrations. Cloth. New York, 1847. First edition. $100-$125.

SIMMS, William Gilmore. *The Life of Francis Marion*. Cloth. New York, 1844. First edition. $75-$100.

SIMMS, William Gilmore. *Lyrical and Other Poems*. Cloth. Charleston, 1827. First edition. $300-$500. Author's first book.

SIMMS, William Gilmore. *Marie De Berniere*. Cloth. Philadelphia, 1853. First edition. $75-$100.

SIMMS, William Gilmore. *Norman Maurice; or, The Man of the People*. Wrappers. Richmond, Va., 1851. First edition. $300-$350.

SIMMS, William Gilmore. *Poems: Descriptive, Dramatic, Legendary and Contemplative*. 2 vols., cloth. Charleston, 1853. First edition. $250-$300. New York, 1853. 2 vols., cloth. $175-$200.

SIMMS, William Gilmore. *Southward Ho! A Spell of Sunshine*. Cloth. New York, 1854. First edition. $100-$150.

SIMMS, William Gilmore. *The Spartanburg Female College Oration*. Wrappers. Spartanburg, S.C., 1855. First edition. $150-$200.

SIMMS, William Gilmore (editor). *War Poetry of the South*. Cloth. New York, 1866. First edition. $75-$100.

*SIMONIDEA*. Blue boards. Bath, England, (1806). (By Walter Savage Landor.) First edition. $150-$200.

*SIMPLE Truths in Verse, for the Amusement and Instruction of Children, at an Early Age*. Illustrated. Boards. Baltimore, (about 1820). (By Mary Belson Elliot.) First American edition. $50-$60.

SIMPSON, Elizabeth M. *Bluegrass Houses and Their Traditions*. Illustrated. Cloth. Lexington, 1932. First edition. In dust jacket. $50-$75.

SIMPSON, George. *Journal of Occurrences in the Athabasca Department, etc*. Edited by E. E. Rich. Cloth. Toronto, 1938. One of 550. $100-$175.

SIMPSON, George. *Narrative of a Journey Round the World, During the Years 1841 and 1842*. Portrait, folding map. 2 vols., cloth. London, 1847. First edition. $250-$300.

SIMPSON, Harold B. *Gaines Mill to Appomattox*. Illustrated. Full leather. Waco, Tex., 1963. First edition. One of 50, signed. $100-$125.

SIMPSON, Henry I. *The Emigrant's Guide to the Gold Mines*. Folding map. 30 pp., wrappers. New York, 1848. First edition. $3,000-$3,500.

SIMPSON, Gen. James H. *Coronado's March in Search of the Seven Cities of Cibola*. Map. 34 pp., wrappers. Washington, 1884. $100-$125.

SIMPSON, Capt. James H. *Report of Explorations Across the Great Basin of the Territory of Utah. etc*. Folding map, plates, errata leaf. Cloth. Washington, 1876. First edition. $100-$135.

SIMPSON, James H. *Journal of a Military Reconnaissance, from Santa Fe, N.M., to the Navajo Country*. Folding map, 75 plates (23 colored). Cloth. Philadelphia, 1852. First separate printing. $175-$200.

SIMPSON, James H. *Report from the Secretary of War . . . and Map of the Route from Fort Smith, Ark., to Santa Fe, N.M.* (Caption title.) 4 folding maps. Stitched. (Washington, 1850.) First edition. Senate issue. $100-$150. House issue: One folding map. 2 plates. $100-$150.

SIMPSON, James H. *Report of the Secretary of War . . . and Map of Wagon Roads in Utah.* (Caption title.) Large folding map. (Washington, 1859.) First edition. $150-$200.

SIMPSON, Louis. *The Arrivistes: Poems, 1940-1949.* Wrappers. New York, (1949). First edition. $100-$110. Author's first book.

SIMPSON, Thomas. *Narrative of the Discoveries on the Northwest Coast of America.* 2 folding maps. Cloth. London, 1843. First edition. $400-$500.

SINCLAIR, Upton. *A Home Colony. A Prospectus.* 23 pp., wrappers. New York (1906). First edition. $40-$50.

SINCLAIR, Upton. *The Jungle.* Green cloth. New York, 1906. First edition, first issue, with Doubleday imprint and with the "1" in date on copyright page in perfect type. $85-$100. Later issue: New York, 1906. Jungle Publishing Co. First state, with unbroken type on copyright page and with "Sustainers' Edition" note tipped in. $50-$60. Later state, type broken on copyright page, $10-$15.

SINCLAIR, Upton. *Oil!* Printed wrappers. Long Beach, (1927). First edition $35-$50.

SINGLETON, Arthur. *Letters from the South and West.* Stiff wrappers, or boards. Boston, 1824. (By Henry Cogswell Knight.) First edition. $200-$250.

SINJOHN, John. *From the Four Winds.* Olive-green cloth. London, 1897. (By John Galsworthy.) First edition. One of 500. $500-$600. Also, $450 (A, 1977). Author's first book.

SINJOHN, John. *Jocelyn.* Cloth. London, 1898. (By John Galsworthy.) First edition, first issue, with "you" for "my" on page 257, third line from bottom. $300-$400.

SINJOHN, John. *A Man of Devon.* Blue cloth. Edinburgh and London, 1901. (By John Galsworthy.) First edition, with ads dated "4/01." $300-$400.

SINJOHN, John. *Villa Rubein.* Cherry-red cloth. London, 1900. (By John Galsworthy.) First edition. $300-$400.

SIRINGO, Charles A. *A Cowboy Detective.* Illustrated. Pictorial cloth. Chicago, 1912. First edition, first issue, published by Conkey. $75-$100. Another binding: Special first issue presentation copies, in pebble-grained leather (unrecorded in bibliographies), inscribed by Siringo. $400-$500. Second issue, same date. 2 vols., wrappers. $150.

SIRINGO, Charles A. *History of "Billy the Kid."* 142 pp., stiff pictorial wrappers. (Santa Fe, 1920.) First edition. $125-$175.

SIRINGO, Charles A. *A Lone Star Cowboy.* Illustrated. Pictorial cloth. Santa Fe, 1919. First edition. $75-$100.

SIRINGO, Charles A. *Riata and Spurs.* 16 plates. Pictorial cloth. Boston, 1927. First edition, first issue, with "1927" on title page. In dust jacket. $125-$150. Lacking jacket, $50-$75. Boston (1927). Pictorial cloth. Second issue, with many changes. $50-$75.

SIRINGO, Charles A. *A Texas Cowboy, or, Fifteen Years on the Hurricane Deck of a Spanish Pony.* Illustrated, including chromolithographic frontispiece in color. Wrappers, or black pictorial cloth. Chicago, 1885. First edition. Wrappers: $2,500 (sale price of the only copy known in wrappers). Cloth: $750-$1,500. Chicago, 1886. Siringo & Dobson. 8 plates, 347 pp. Second edition. $150-$200. Another edition, same place and date: Rand McNally, same collation. Third edition. $100-$150. New York, (1886). Wrappers. $100-$150.

*SIR Ralph Esher: or, Adventures of a Gentleman of the Court of Charles II.* 3 vols., boards. London, 1832. (By Leigh Hunt.) First edition. $150-$200.

*SISTER Years (The); Being the Carrier's Address, to the Patrons of the Salem Gazette, for the First of January, 1839.* (Cover title.) 8 pp., printed self-wrappers. Salem, Mass., 1839. (By Nathaniel Hawthorne.) First edition. $350-$500, possibly more.

SITGREAVES, Lorenzo. *Report of an Expedition down the Zuni and Colorado Rivers.* 79 plates, folding map. Cloth. Washington, 1853. First edition. $150-$250. Washington, 1874. Second edition. $70 (A, 1973).

SITWELL, Edith. *Alexander Pope.* Illustrated. Yellow buckram. London, 1930. First edition. One of 220, signed. In dust jacket. Boxed. $75-$100.

SITWELL, Edith. *Collected Poems.* Cloth. London, 1930. One of 320, signed. In dust jacket. $150-$200. Trade edition: Cloth. In dust jacket. $75-$100.

SITWELL, Edith. *Facade.* Colored frontispiece. Boards. London, 1920. First edition. One of 150, signed. $150-$250. London, 1922. Boards. Second edition. $150-$200.

SITWELL, Edith. *Five Poems.* Cloth. London, 1928. First edition. One of 275, signed. $75-$100.

SITWELL, Edith. *In Spring.* 3 wood engravings by Edward Carrick. Green boards, yellow label. London, 1931. First (special) edition. (15 copies signed by author and artist and one stanza in author's handwriting.) In tissue dust jacket. $100-$125. Another issue: One of 350, signed. $35-$50.

SITWELL, Edith. *Jane Barston, 1719-1746.* Yellow boards. London, 1931. One of 250, signed. $80-$100.

SITWELL, Edith. *The Mother and Other Poems.* Wrappers. Oxford, 1915. First edition. $250-$375. Author's first book. (500 copies issued.)

SITWELL, Edith. *The Pleasures of Poetry.* First, Second, and Third Series. 3 vols., cloth. London, 1930-31-32. First editions. In dust jackets. $200-$250.

SITWELL, Edith. *Popular Songs.* Boards. London, 1928. First edition. One of 500, signed. $100-$125.

SITWELL, Edith. *Street Songs.* Cloth. London, 1942. First edition. In dust jacket. $30-$40.

SITWELL, Edith. *The Wooden Pegasus.* Boards and cloth. Oxford, 1920. First edition. In dust jacket. $35-$50.

SITWELL, Edith, and Sitwell, Osbert. *Twentieth Century Harlequinade.* Cloth. Oxford, 1916. First edition. One of 500. $50-$75.

SITWELL, Osbert. *At the House of Mrs. Kinfoot.* Wrappers. London, 1921. First edition. One of 101, signed. $100-$125.

SITWELL, Osbert. *Before the Bombardment.* Cloth. London, 1926. First edition. In dust jacket. $50-$75.

SITWELL, Osbert. *The Collected Satires and Poems of Osbert Sitwell.* Portrait frontispiece. Cloth. (London), 1931. First edition. Limited and signed. $40-$50.

SITWELL, Osbert. *England Reclaimed.* Buckram. London, 1927. First edition. One of 165, signed. In dust jacket. $50-$60.

SITWELL, Osbert. *Miss Mew.* Half linen and boards. (London), 1929. First edition. One of 101, signed. $100-$125.

SITWELL, Osbert. *Who Killed Cock-Robin?* Boards. London, 1921. First edition. In dust jacket. $50-$60.

SITWELL, Osbert. *The Winstonburg Line: 3 Satires.* Pictorial wrappers. London, 1919. First edition. $75-$100. Author's first book.

SITWELL, Sacheverell. *The Cyder Feast and Other Poems.* Yellow buckram. (London), 1927. One of 165, signed. $75-$100.

SITWELL, Sacheverell. *Doctor Donne and Gargantua.* Wrappers. Kensington. 1921. First edition. One of 101, signed. $100-$135. London, 1930. Boards. One of 200, signed. $75-$100.

SITWELL, Sacheverell. *The People's Palace.* Frontispiece. Wrappers. Oxford 1918. First edition. (400 copies.) $50-$60.

SITWELL, Sacheverell. *Two Poems, Ten Songs.* Decorated boards. London, 1929. First edition. One of 275, signed. $50-$60.

SITWELL, Sacheverell, and Lambert, Constant. *The Rio Grande.* Boards. London, 1929. First edition. One of 75, signed. $75-$10. Unsigned (but numbered), $50-$60.

SITWELL, Sacheverell; Blunt, Wilfred; and Synge, Patrick M. *Great Flower Books, 1700-1900.* 36 plates, 20 in color. Folio, half morocco. London, 1956. First edition. One of 295 signed by the authors. Boxed. $750-$1,000. Another issue: Half cloth. One of 1,750. $400-$500.

SITWELL, Sacheverell; Buchanan, Handasyde; and Fisher, James. *Fine Bird Books, 1700-1900.* 38 plates in color, 36 in black and white. Folio, half morocco. London, 1953. One of 295 signed by the three authors. $750-$1,000. Another issue: Buckram and boards. One of 2,000. $450-$650.

*SIX to One; A Nantucket Idyl.* Tan or gray cloth. New York, 1878. (By Edward Bellamy.) First edition, first state, cloth. $150-$200. Later state, printed wrappers. $75-$100.

*SIXTY Years of the Life of Jeremy Levis.* 2 vols., boards, cloth spines, paper labels. New York, 1831. (By Laughton Osborn.) First edition. $75-$100.

SKEFFINGTON, F. J. C., and Joyce, James A. *Two Essays.* 4 leaves, pink printed wrappers. Dublin, (1901). First edition. Joyce's first published book, containing his essay "The Day of the Rabblement." $2,500-$3,000. Also, $1,700 and $2,200 (A, 1977).

SKELTON, John. *The Tunning of Elynour Rummynge.* Illustrated by Leonard Baskin. Boards. Worcester, Mass., 1953. Gehenna Press. One of 118. $400-$500.

*SKETCH of the Geographical Rout [sic] of a Great Railway . . . Between the Atlantic States and the Great Valley of the Mississippi.* Folding map. 16 pp., wrappers. New York, 1829. (By William C. Redfield.) First edition. $250-$300.

*SKETCH of the History of South Carolina, etc. (A).* Cloth. Charleston, 1856. (By William James Rivers.) First edition. $75-$125.

*SKETCH of Old England (A).* By a New England Man. 2 vols., printed boards. New York, 1822. (By James Kirke Paulding.) First edition. $200-$300.

*SKETCH of St. Anthony and Minneapolis.* Frontispiece, 4 plates, map. 32 pp., wrappers. St. Anthony, 1857. First edition. With errata slip. $400-$500.

*SKETCH of the Seminole War, and Sketches During the Campaign.* Leather. Charleston, 1836. First edition. $200-$300.

*SKETCHES by "Boz."* Illustrated by George Cruikshank. 3 vols. (First Series, 1836, 2 vols., dark-green cloth; Second Series, 1837, pink cloth.) London, 1836-37. (By Charles Dickens.) First edition. $1,500-$2,500. Author's first book. London, 1837-39. 20 parts, pictorial pink wrappers. $5,000-$10,000. Also, some plates stained, $5,000 (A, 1976). (Complete sets with all ads and wrappers in the first state are rare. Imperfect sets are available at much lower prices than are quoted here.)

*SKETCHES by a Traveller.* Calf. Boston, 1830. (By Silas P. Holbrook.) First edition. $125-$150.

*SKETCHES, Historical and Descriptive of Louisiana.* Boards and calf. Philadelphia, 1812. (By Amos Stoddard.) First edition. $200-$250.

*SKETCHES of History, Life and Manners in the United States.* By a Traveller. Woodcut frontispiece view. Boards. New Haven, 1826. (By Anne Royall.) First edition. $350-$400.

*SKETCHES of the History of Ogle County, Ill.* 88 pp., wrappers. Polo, Ill., 1859. (By Henry R. Boss). First edition. $100-$150.

*SKETCHES of Mission Life Among the Indians of Oregon.* Frontispiece and 4 plates. Cloth. New York, 1854. (By H. K. W. Perkins ? or Z. A. Mudge ?) First edition. $250.

*SKETCHES of Springfield.* By a Citizen. 49 pp., plus 21 pp. of ads, wrappers. Springfield, Ohio, (1852). $100-$150.

*SKETCHES of the West, or the Home of the Badgers.* Folding map. 48 pp., wrappers. Milwaukee, 1847. (By Josiah B. Grinnell.) Second edition (of *The Home of the Badgers,* which see under Grinnell's pseudonym, Oculus). $350-$400.

SKINNER, B. F. *Walden Two.* Cloth. New York, 1948. First edition. In dust jacket. $35-$50.

SLAUGHTER, Mrs. Linda W. *The New Northwest.* 24 pp., wrappers. Bismarck, 1874. First edition. $1,500-$2,000, possibly more.

SLOAN, Edward L. (editor). *Salt Lake City: Gazetteer and Directory.* Cloth. Salt Lake City, 1874. $150-$200.

SLOAN, Roberts. *Utah Gazetteer and Directory of Logan, Ogden, Provo and Salt Lake Cities.* Cloth. Salt Lake City, 1884. $150-$200.

SLOCUM, Joshua. *Sailing Alone Around the World.* Cloth. New York, 1900. First edition. $125-$150.

SLOCUM, Joshua. *Voyage of the Destroyer from New York to Brazil.* 47 pp., wrappers. Boston, 1894. First edition. $75-$100.

SMART, Stephen F. *Leadville, Ten Mile . . . And All Other Noted Colorado Mining Camps.* 2 folding maps. 56 pp., printed wrappers. Kansas City, 1879. First edition. $400-$600. (For a similar work, see Willis Sweet entry.)

SMEDLEY, Frank E. See *Frank Fairleigh.*

SMEDLEY, William. *Across the Plains in '62.* Map and portrait. 56 pp., boards. (Denver, 1916.) First edition. $100-$125.

SMITH, Alexander. *Poems.* Cloth. London, 1853. First edition, with inserted ads dated November, 1852. $50-$60. Author's first book.

SMITH, Alice R. H., and Smith, D. E. H. *The Dwelling Houses of Charleston.* Illustrated. Cloth. Philadelphia, 1917. First edition. $75-$125.

SMITH, Arthur D. Howden. *Porto Bello Gold.* Cloth. New York, (1924). First edition. In dust jacket. $50-$60.

SMITH, Ashbel. *Reminiscences of the Texas Republic.* Cloth. Galveston, 1876. First edition. One of 100. $750-$1,000.

SMITH, Buckingham (translator). *Narratives of the Career of Hernando de Soto in the Conquest of Florida.* Folding map. Boards. New York, 1866. One of 75. $400-$500. (See also De Soto, Hernando.)

SMITH, Buckingham (translator). *Rudo Ensayo, tentativa de una Provencional Descripción Geographica de la Provincia de Sonora.* 208 pp., printed gray wrappers. San Agustin (St. Augustine, Fla.), 1863. (By Juan Nentuig?) First edition. One of 10 large paper copies. $750-$1,000. Regular issue: One of 160. $500-$600. (Note: Actually printed in Albany, N.Y.)

SMITH, Charles H. *The History of Fuller's Ohio Brigade, 1861-1865.* Illustrated. Cloth. Cleveland, 1909. $50-$75.

SMITH, Charles Hamilton. *Orders of Knighthood.* Title and 74 watercolor drawings of knights, some with manuscript captions beneath. Folio, half red morocco. London, (about 1830). $800-$1,200.

SMITH, Charles Hamilton. *Selections of the Ancient Costume of Great Britain & Ireland.* 60 full-page color plates. Boards. London, 1814. $700-$1,000. London, 1815. Half morocco. $600-$750.

SMITH, Clark Ashton. *The Abominations of Yondo.* Cloth. Sauk City, 1960. First edition. In dust jacket. $50-$75.

SMITH, Clark Ashton. *The Dark Chateau.* Cloth. Sauk City, 1951. First edition. In dust jacket. $200-$250.

SMITH, Clark Ashton. *The Double Shadow and Other Fantasies.* (Cover title.) 30 pp., wrappers. (Auburn, Calif., 1933.) First edition. $50-$75. Presentation copy, signed with author's corrections. $100.

SMITH, Clark Ashton. *Genius Loci and Other Tales.* Cloth. Sauk City, 1948. First edition. In dust jacket. $50-$75.

SMITH, Clark Ashton. *Lost Worlds.* Cloth. Sauk City, 1944. First edition. In dust jacket. $125-$175.

SMITH, Clark Ashton. *Odes and Sonnets.* Preface by George Sterling. Decorations by Florence Lundborg. Blue boards, tan cloth spine, paper label. San Francisco, 1918. First edition. One of 300. $100-$125.

SMITH, Clark Ashton. *Out of Space and Time.* Cloth. Sauk City, 1942. First edition. In dust jacket. $100-$125.

SMITH, Clark Ashton. *Poems in Prose.* Illustrated. Cloth, Sauk City, 1964. First edition. In dust jacket. $50-$60.

SMITH, Clark Ashton. *Spells and Philtres.* Cloth. Sauk City, 1958. First edition. In dust jacket. $250-$300.

SMITH, Clark Ashton. *The Star-Treader and Other Poems.* Buff pictorial boards. San Francisco, 1912. First edition. In dust jacket. $100-$150. Author's first book.

SMITH, Emma (editor). *A Collection of Sacred Hymns for the Church of the Latter Day Saints.* Marbled boards and cloth. Kirtland, Ohio, 1835. First edition. $4,000-$5,000. Also, $2,000 (A, 1968).

SMITH, F. Hopkinson. *American Illustrators.* Folio, 5 parts, printed wrappers in printed board folder. New York, 1892. First edition. One of 1,000. $100-$125.

SMITH, F. Hopkinson. *Colonel Carter of Cartersville.* Cloth. Boston, 1891. First edition, first issue, with no mention of the book in ads. $100-$125.

SMITH, F. Hopkinson, *Venice of Today.* 21 colored plates, 12 plain plates. Half morocco. New York, 1896. First book edition. $75-$100. Another issue: One of 118 on handmade paper. $300-$400. New York, 1902. Half morocco. $150-$200. (Note: This title first appeared in 20 paperbound parts in 1895. I have noted no copies for sale in modern times.)

SMITH, Frank Meriweather (editor). *San Francisco Vigilance Committee of '56.* 83 pp., wrappers. San Francisco, 1883. First edition. $150-$250. Rebound in cloth, $100-$150.

SMITH, Harry B. *First Nights and First Editions.* Cloth. Boston, 1931. First edition. One of 260, signed. In dust jacket. $60-$75.

SMITH, Harry B. *A Sentimental Library.* Half vellum. (New York), 1914. First edition. In dust jacket. $100-$150.

SMITH, J. Calvin. *A New Guide for Travelers Through the United States.* Folding map in color. Cloth, or leather. New York, 1846. $125-$150. New York, 1848. $75-$100.

SMITH, J. Calvin. *The Western Tourist and Emigrant's Guide.* Colored folding map. Cloth, or leather. New York, 1839. First edition. $100-$150. New York, 1845. $75-$100.

SMITH, James E. *A Famous Battery and Its Campaigns, 1861-64.* Cloth. Washington, 1892. First edition. $75-$100.

SMITH, James F. *The Cherokee Land Lottery, etc.* Contemporary calf. New York, 1838. First edition. $250-$300.

SMITH, Jodie (editor). *History of the Chisum War.* Illustrated. Stiff pictorial wrappers. (Electra, Tex., 1927.) (By Ike Fridge.) First edition. $100-$150.

SMITH, John Thomas. *Antiquities of Westminster.* Illustrated, including color plates. 2 vols., half leather. London, 1807-(09). First edition. $600-$750. Also, $400 (A, 1977).

SMITH, John Thomas. *Cries of London, Exhibiting Several of the Itinerant Traders of Antient and Modern Times.* Portrait and 30 hand-colored etchings. Half leather and cloth. London, 1839. First edition. $200-$250. Another issue: Large paper. $300-$400.

SMITH, Johnston. *Maggie: A Girl of the Streets.* Yellow printed wrappers. (New York, 1893.) (By Stephen Crane.) First edition. $5,000-$6,000. Also, $3,500 and $3,000 (A, 1973). (For the second edition, see the entry under Crane, Stephen.)

SMITH, Joseph, Jr. See *A Book of Commandments.*

SMITH, Joseph, Jr. *The Book of Mormon.* Leather. Palmyra, N.Y., 1830. First edition, first issue, with two-page preface and testimonial leaf at end and without index. $2,500-$3,000. Author's first book. Second issue, without testimonials, etc. $2,000-$2,500. Kirtland, Ohio, 1837. Second edition. $750-$1,000. Nauvoo, Ill., 1840. Third edition. $500-$600. Liverpool, 1841. Leather. First English edition. $750 and up. Nauvoo, 1842. Fourth American edition. $150-$200. New York, 1869. In Deseret (Mormon) alphabet. $100-$125. Plano, Ill. 1874. $75-$100.

SMITH, Joseph, Jr. *Te Buka A Mormona.* Translated by Frank Cutler and others. Cloth. Salt Lake City, 1904. First edition of *The Book of Mormon* in Tahitian. $100-$150.

SMITH, Joseph, Jr., and others (editors). *Doctrine and Covenants of the Church of the Latter Day Saints.* Leather. Kirtland, 1835. First edition. $2,500-$3,000. New York, 1869. In Deseret alphabet. Printed boards, leather spine. $100-$150.

SMITH, Kate Douglas. *The Story of Patsy. A Reminiscence.* 27 pp., wrappers. San Francisco, 1883. (By Kate Douglas Wiggin.) First edition. $100-$150. Author's first separate publication.

SMITH, Lillian. *Killers of the Dream.* Cloth. New York, 1949. First edition. In dust jacket. $25-$35.

SMITH, Logan Pearsall. *Unforgotten Years.* Cloth. London, 1938. First edition. In dust jacket. $25.

SMITH, Logan Pearsall. *The Youth of Parnassus and Other Stories.* Blue Cloth. London, 1895. First edition, first issue. Author's first book. $55.

SMITH, Michael. *A Geographical View, of the Province of Upper Canada, and Promiscuous Remarks upon the Government, etc.* 107 pp., wrappers. Hartford, 1813. First edition. $175-$225.

SMITH, Moses. *History of the Adventures and Sufferings of Moses Smith.* 2 plates. Boards. Brooklyn, N.Y., 1812. First edition. $100-$125. Albany, 1814. 2 plates. Calf. $75-$100.

SMITH, Nathan. *A Practical Essay on Typhous Fever.* Half calf. New York, 1824. First edition. $300-$350.

SMITH, Patti. *Kodak.* Wrappers (Philadelphia, 1972). First edition. One of 100 signed. $75-$100.

SMITH, Platt. *The Dubuque Claim Case; in the Supreme Court of the United States.* 20 pp., wrappers. Dubuque, 1852. $150-$175.

SMITH, Mrs. Sarah. *A Journal Kept by Mrs. Sarah Foote Smith While Journeying with Her People from Wellington, Ohio, to Footeville, Town of Nepeuskun, Winnebago County, Wis., April 15 to May 10, 1846.* Boards, paper label. (Kilbourn, Ohio, 1905.) $100-$150.

SMITH, Sydney Goodsir. *Orpheus and Eurydice.* Hand-colored plates. Pictorial wrappers. Edinburgh, 1955. First edition. One of 50, signed. $50-$65.

SMITH, Thorne. *Biltmore Oswald: The Diary of a Hapless Recruit.* Pictorial boards. New York, (1918). First edition. In dust jacket. $50-$75. Author's first book.

SMITH, Thorne. *Topper: An Improbable Adventure.* Red cloth. New York, 1926. First edition. In dust jacket. $40-$60.

SMITH, W. L. G. *Life at the South; or, Uncle Tom's Cabin As It Is.* Cloth. Buffalo, 1852. First edition. $100-$150.

SMITH, Wallace. *Garden of the Sun: A History of the San Joaquin Valley, 1772-1939.* Cloth. Los Angeles, (1939). First edition. $50-$65.

SMITH, William H. *History of Canada.* Folding table. 2 vols., boards, paper labels, Quebec, 1815 (actually 1826). First edition. $400-$500. Later edition: (Quebec, 1827.) 2 vols., half morocco. $400-$500.

SMITH, William H. *Smith's Canadian Gazeteer.* Map and plates. Cloth. Toronto, 1846. First edition, first issue, with numbers instead of place names on the map. $175-$200. Later issue, same year, map with place-names. $125-$150.

SMITH, William Henry. *A Political History of Slavery.* Portrait. 2 vols., cloth. New York, 1903. First edition. $75-$100.

SMITH, William Jay. *Poems.* Cloth. New York, 1947. First edition. In dust jacket. $50. Author's first book.

SMITH, William Russell. *Reminiscences of a Long Life.* Vol 1. (All published.) 8 portraits (not 9, as called for). Cloth. Washington, (1889). First edition. $75-$100.

SMITHWICK, Noah. *The Evolution of a State.* 5 plates. Cloth. Austin, (1900). First edition. $75-$125, possibly more. Another issue: One of 10, signed. $1,000 and up.

SMYTH, Henry de Wolf. *A General Account of . . . Methods of Using Atomic Energy for Military Purposes.* Wrappers. Washington, 1945. First (official) edition. $800-$1,200. London, 1945. (*Atomic Energy: A General Account.*) Wrappers. First English edition. $150-$250.

SMYTHE, Henry. *Historical Sketch of Parker County and Weatherford, Texas.* Cloth. St. Louis, 1877. First edition. $650.

*SNARLEYYOW, or The Dog Fiend.* 3 vols., boards. London, 1837. (By Frederick Marryat.) First edition. $150-$200. Philadelphia, 1837. 2 vols., cloth. First American edition. (Published with by-line "F. Marryat.") $50-$75.

SNELLING, William J. See *Tales of the Northwest.*

SNELLING, William J. *The Polar Regions of the Western Continent Explored.* Contemporary calf. Boston, 1831. First edition. $175-$200.

SNODGRASS, W. D. *Heart's Needle.* Cloth. New York, 1959. First edition. In dust jacket. $75-$100. Author's first book.

SNOW, C. P. *Death Under Sail.* Cloth. London, (1932). First edition. In dust jacket. $50-$60.

SNOW, C.P. *The New Men.* Cloth over boards. London, 1954. First edition. In dust jacket. $25-$35.

SNYDER, Gary. *The Back Country.* Cloth. London, (1967). First edition. One of 100, signed. In dust jacket. $50-$75. Trade edition: $20.

SNYDER, Gary. *The Blue Sky.* Oblong, wrappers. New York, 1969. First edition. One of 126, signed. $40-$60.

SNYDER, Gary. *The Fudo Trilogy.* Illustrated. Boards and cloth. Berkeley, 1973. First edition. One of 108, signed. In glassine dust jacket. $50-$75.

SNYDER, Gary. *Myths and Texts.* Illustrated. Decorated wrappers. New York, (1960). First edition. $30-$40. Author's second book.

SNYDER, ‚Gary. *A Range of Poems.* Cloth or wrappers. London, (1966). First edition, either format. $30-$40. Another issue: 100 numbered copies, 50 signed. $75 unsigned; $100-$110 signed.

SNYDER, Gary. *Regarding Wave.* Cloth. Iowa City, (1969). First edition. One of 280, signed. (Issued without dust jacket.) $35-$50.

SNYDER, Gary. *Riprap.* Japanese-style blue and white wrappers. (Ashland, Mass.), 1959. Origin Press. First edition. $150-$200. Author's first book.

SNYDER, Gary. *Six Sections from Mountains and Rivers Without End.* Green cloth. London, (1967). Fulcrum Press. One of 100 on sage Glastonbury paper, signed. In dust jacket. $50-$75.

SNYDER, Gary. *Three Worlds, Three Realms, Six Roads.* Illustrated. Wrappers. Marlboro, Vt., (1966). First edition. One of 200. $50-$60.

SNYDER, Gary (translator). *The Wooden Fish: Basic Sutras & Gathas of Rinzai Zen.* Prepared by Kanetsuki Gutetsu and Gary Snyder. Wrappers. (Kyoto, Japan), 1961. First edition, with errata slip laid in. $400-$450.

*SOLDIER'S Story of the War (A).* 9 plates (some copies without plates). Cloth. New Orleans, 1874. (By Napier Bartlett.) First edition, with plates. $100-$150.

SOMBRERO *(The).* Quarter-Centennial Number. Yearbook of the Class of 1895, University of Nebraska. White and red cloth. Lincoln, Neb., (1894). First edition. $400-$600. Also, $400 (A, 1977). First edition. $400-$500. (Note: Contains Willa Cather's and Dorothy Canfield's prize story "The Fear That Walks by Noonday.")

*SOME Antiquarian Notes.* 56 pp., red wrappers. Naples, 1907. (By Norman Douglas.) First edition. One of 250. $200-$250.

*SOMEBODY Had to Do Something.* Wrappers. Los Angeles, 1939. First edition. $150. (Contains tributes to James P. Lardner, killed in the Spanish Civil War, including material by Ernest Hemingway and Ring Lardner, Jr.)

*SOME Imagist Poets.* Printed wrappers. Boston, 1915. (Edited by Amy Lowell.) First edition. $75-$100. London, 1915. Pink printed wrappers. First English edition. $75-$100. Other annual numbers: Boston, 1916. Boards. First edition. $50-$75. Boston, 1917. Boards. First edition. In dust jacket. $50.

*SONG of Roland (The).* Translated by Isabel Butler. 7 hand-colored illustrations by Bruce Rogers. Boards, vellum spine. (Cambridge, Mass., 1906.) One of 220. First edition. $250-$350.

*SONGS of the Class of MDCCCXXIX.* Cream-yellow wrappers. Boston, 1854. First edition. (Contains 3 poems by Oliver Wendell Holmes.) About 6 copies are known to exist; none has appeared for sale in many years. Boston, 1859. Second edition, with 8 Holmes poems. $50-$75.

SONN, Albert H. *Early American Wrought Iron.* Illustrated. 3 vols., Cloth. New York, 1928. First edition. In dust jackets. $400. Also, $300 (A, 1977).

SOULE, Frank; Gihon, Frank; and Nisbet, James. *The Annals of San Francisco.* 6 plates, 2 maps. Leather. New York, 1855. First edition. $300-$400. Palo Alto, 1966. Facsimile reprint. Cloth. $75. Another issue: Morocco. One of 60. $100-$125.

*SOUTH Carolina Jockey Club (The).* Cloth. Charleston, 1857. (By John B. Irving.) First edition. $150-$200.

*SOUTHERN Business Directory and General Commercial Advertiser (The).* Vol. 1. (All published.) Illustrated. Charleston, 1854. $125-$150.

*SOUTHERN Business Guide, 1881-82.* Illustrated. Cloth. New York. 1882. $100-$125.

*SOUTHERN History of the War.* Illustrated. Cloth. New York, 1863. First edition. $200-$275.

*SOUTHERN Primer (The).* Illustrated. Wrappers. Richmond, 1860. $150-$175.

SOUTHEY, Robert. *All for Love; and The Pilgrim to Compostella.* Cloth, paper label. London, 1829. First edition. $75-$100.

SOUTHEY, Robert. *Omniana, or Horae Otiosiores.* 2 vols., boards. London, 1812. First edition. $200.

*SOUTH-WEST (The).* By a Yankee. 2 vols., cloth, paper labels. New York, 1835. (By Joseph Holt Ingraham.) First edition. $250-$350. Author's first book.

SOWELL, A. J. *Early Settlers and Indian Fighters of Southwest Texas.* 12 plates. Cloth. Austin, 1900. First edition. $300-$400, possibly more.

SOWELL, A. J. *Rangers and Pioneers of Texas.* Illustrated. Pictorial cloth. San Antonio. 1884. First edition. $500-$750.

SPALDING, C. C. *Annals of the City of Kansas.* 7 plates. Cloth. Kansas City, 1858. First edition. $1,000-$1,250.

SPARGO, John. *Anthony Haswell: Printer, Patriot, Ballader.* 35 facsimiles. Half morocco. Rutland, Vt., 1925. First edition. One of 300. $100-$125.

SPARGO, John. *The Potters and Potteries of Bennington.* Boards. Boston, 1926. First edition. One of 800. $40-$50.

SPARK, Muriel. *Not to Disturb.* Illustrated. Boards and cloth. London, 1971. One of 500, signed, with an original etching by Michael Ayrton. In glassine dust jacket. $50-$60.

SPARK, Muriel. *The Prime of Miss Jean Brodie.* Cloth. London, 1961. First edition. In dust jacket. $35-$50.

SPARROW, Walter Shaw. *A Book of Sporting Painters.* 138 illustrations, some in color. Buckram. London, (1931). First edition. $100-$150. Another issue: One of 125 with 2 extra plates. $200-$300.

SPARROW, Walter Shaw. *British Sporting Artists, from Barlow to Herring.* 27 color plates, other illustrations. Cloth. London (1922). First edition. $100-125. Limited issue: Buckram. One of 95, signed. $250-$350.

SPAVERY (compiler). *The Harp of a Thousand Strings: or, Laughter for a Lifetime.* Illustrated. Cloth. New York, (1858). (By George Washington Harris.) First edition, first printing, with frontispiece in black and gray and with imprints of Craighead and Jenkins on copyright page. $400-$600. (The pen name Spavery in this case was used for Harris' pseudonym "Samuel Putnam Avery." The engravings are attributed on the title page to "S.P. Avery." The book contains a reprint, unsigned, of an early English magazine prose piece by Lewis Carroll. The reprinting—the first of any of Carroll's work anywhere—was unauthorized.)

SPEARS, John R. *Illustrated Sketches of Death Valley and Other Borax Deserts of the Pacific Coast.* Printed wrappers or cloth. Chicago, 1892. First edition. $50-$75.

*SPECIMENS.* 54 pp., pink wrappers, stitched. (Canyon City, Ore. 1868.) (By Joaquin Miller—preface signed "C.H. Miller.") First edition. $3,000-$3,500. Also, an inscribed copy, $1,900 (A, 1976). Author's first book—rigorously suppressed by him.

*SPECIMENS: A Stevens-Nelson Paper Catalogue.* (Specimen sheets of fine papers, with text.) Half goatskin and boards. (New York, about 1950-53). Boxed. $300-$350.

SPEED, Thomas. *The Wilderness Road.* Map. Cloth. Louisville, 1886. First edition. $75-$100.

SPEER, Emory. *The Banks County Ku-Klux.* 60 pp., wrappers. Atlanta, 1883. First edition. $150-$175.

SPENCER, Elizabeth. *Fire in the Morning.* Red cloth. New York, 1948. First edition. In dust jacket. $125. Author's first novel.

SPENCER, Mrs. George E. *Calamity Jane: A Story of the Black Hills.* Frontispiece. Wrappers. New York, (about 1887). (By William L. Spencer.) First edition. $250.

SPENCER, Herbert. *Education: Intellectual, Moral, and Physical.* Cloth. New York, 1861. First edition. In slipcase. $40-$50.

SPENCER, Herbert. *The Principles of Biology.* 2 vols., cloth. London, 1864-67. First edition. $300-$400.

SPENCER, Herbert. *Social Statics.* Cloth. London, 1851. First edition. $50-$75. Author's first book.

SPENCER, J. W. *Reminiscences of Pioneer Life in the Mississippi Valley.* Portrait. Cloth. Davenport, Iowa, 1872. First edition. $100-$150.

SPENCER, O.M. *Indian Captivity: A True Narrative of the Capture of, etc.* Gray wrappers. Washington, Pa., 1835. First edition (?). $500-$600. New York, 1835. $500-$600. New York, 1836. Third edition. $75-$100.

SPENDER, Stephen. See S., S. H.

SPENDER, Stephen. *The Burning Cactus.* Cloth. London, 1936. First edition, first issue, with first and final leaves blank. In dust jacket. $40-$50.

SPENDER, Stephen. *The Generous Days.* Boards and calf. Boston, 1969. First edition. One of 50, signed. $80-$100. London, 1971. First English edition. In dust jacket. $15-$20.

SPENDER, Stephen. *Poems.* Black cloth. London, (1933). First edition. In dust jacket. $75-$100.

SPENDER, Stephen. *Returning to Vienna 1947.* Wrappers. (London, 1947.) Banyan Press. One of 500, signed. $60-$75.

SPENDER, Stephen. *Ruins and Visions: Poems.* Blue-green cloth. London, (1942). First edition. In dust jacket. $75-$100. New York, (1942). Red cloth. First American edition. In dust jacket. $30-$40.

SPENDER, Stephen. *Twenty Poems.* Wrappers. Oxford, (1930). First edition. One of 135. $150-$200. Signed copies (75 of the 135), $250-$300.

SPENDER, Stephen. *Vienna.* Cloth. London, 1934. First edition. In dust jacket. $35-$50.

SPENSER, Edmund. *The Faerie Queene.* Folio, half leather and vellum. Chelsea (London), 1923. Ashendene Press. One of 180. $850-$1,250.

SPENSER, Edmund. *Minor Poems.* London, 1925. Ashendene Press. One of 200 on paper. $600-$800. Another issue: One of 15 on vellum. $2,500-$3,000.

SPENSER, Edmund. *The Shepheardes Calender.* 12 woodcuts. Boards and linen. London, 1896. Kelmscott Press. One of 225. $450-$750. Another issue: One of 6 on vellum. (In a special morocco binding.) $6,500 in a 1977 catalogue. London, 1930. Cresset Press. Boards, vellum spine. One of 350. In dust jacket. $150.

SPEYER, Leonora. *Holy Night: A Yuletide Masque.* Designs by Eric Gill. Stiff blue decorated wrappers. New York, 1919. One of 500. $35-$50. Author's first book.

SPICER, Jack. *After Lorca.* Wrappers (San Francisco, 1957.) First edition. One of 500. $110. Author's first book.

SPICER, Jack. *Lament for the Makers.* Wrappers. (Oakland, 1962.) First edition. One of 100. $175-$200.

SPIELMANN, M. H. and Laynard, G. S. *Kate Greenaway.* 53 colored plates, other illustrations. White cloth. London, 1905. One of 500 with an original pencil sketch by Kate Greenaway inserted. $400-$500. Trade edition: Purple cloth. $75-$100.

SPILLANE, Mickey. *I, the Jury*. Cloth. New York, 1947. First edition. In dust jacket. $40-$50. Author's first book.

SPILMAN, The Rev. T. E. *Semi-Centenarians of Butler Grove Township, Montgomery County (Illinois)*. Boards and cloth. (Butler), 1878. First edition. $100-$125.

*SPIRIT of the Age (The)*. Boards, paper label. London, 1825. (By William Hazlitt.) First edition. $75-$100.

*SPORTS of Childhood (The)*. 18 pp., wrappers. Northampton, Mass. (about 1830-40). First edition (?). $50-$75. (Henderson, in *Early American Sports*, also lists a New Haven edition of about 1839.)

*SPORTSMAN'S Portfolio of American Field Sports (The)*. 20 full-page wood engravings, title page vignette, illustration at end. Oblong wrappers. Boston, 1855. First edition. $200-$250.

SPOTTS, David L. *Campaigning with Custer*. Map, 13 plates. Cloth. Los Angeles, 1928. First edition. One of 800 (Howes says all but about 300 burned). $150-$200.

SPRAGUE, John T. *The Origin, Progress, and Conclusion of the Florida War*. Folding map, 8 plates. Cloth. New York, 1848. First edition. $150-$175.

SPRAGUE, John T. *The Treachery in Texas*. 35 pp., wrappers. New York, 1862. First edition. $75-$100.

*SPRING: Infancy,—The Spring of Life*. 8 woodcuts. 16 pp., pictorial wrappers. New York, (about 1815-20). (Children's toybook published by Samuel S. Wood.) $100-$150.

SPRING, Agnes Wright. *The Cheyenne and Black Hills Stage and Express Routes*. Map, 17 plates. Cloth. Glendale, Calif., 1949. First edition. $75-$100.

SPRING, Agnes Wright. *Seventy Years: A Panoramic History of the Wyoming Stock Growers Association*. Illustrated. Stiff pictorial wrappers. (Cheyenne), 1942. First edition. $75-$100.

SPRUNT, James. *Chronicles of the Cape Fear River*. Half leather. Raleigh, 1914. First edition. $60-$75.

*SPY (The): A Tale of the Neutral Ground..* By the Author of *Precaution*. 2 vols., boards, paper labels. New York, 1821. (By James Fenimore Cooper.) First edition. $10,000-$12,500. (Note: There are said to be only three known sets in original boards. John H. Jenkins, bookseller, of Austin, tells me one of these sets was stolen from his stock in 1976.) New York, 1963. Limited Editions Club. Cloth. $40-$50.

SPYRI, Johannes. *Heidi*. Translated by Louise Brooks. Cloth. Boston, 1885. First American edition. $150-$175. Also, $70 (A,1976).

SQUIER, E. G., and Davis, E.H. *Ancient Monuments of the Mississippi Valley*. Map, 48 plates. Folio, cloth. Washington, 1848. First edition. $75-$100. New York, 1848. Second issue. $75-$100.

SQUIRE, Watson C. *Resources and Development of Washington Territory*. Folding map. 72 pp., wrappers. Seattle, 1886. First edition. $75-$100.

STAFFORD, William E. *Down in My Heart*. Green cloth. Elgin, Ill., (1947). First edition. In dust jacket. $75-$100. Author's first book.

STAFFORD, William E. *Traveling Through the Dark*. Cloth. New York, (1962). First edition, with National Book Award sticker on cover. In dust jacket. $35-$45.

STANARD, Mary Newton. *Colonial Virginia*. 93 plates. Cloth. Philadelphia, 1917. First edition. Limited. $85.

STANLEY, David S. *Diary of a March from Fort Smith, Ark., to San Diego, Calif., Made in 1853.* 37 pp., multigraphed. No place, no date. In cloth case. $150-$175.

STANLEY, F. *The Grant That Maxwell Bought.* Map, 15 plates. Cloth. (Denver, 1952.) (By Father Stanley Crocchiola.) First edition. One of 250, signed. $175-$200.

STANLEY, F. *The Las Vegas Story.* Illustrated. Cloth. (Denver, 1951.) (By Father Stanley Crocchiola.) First edition. $50-$75.

STANLEY, F. *One Half Miles from Heaven, or, The Cimmaron Story..* 155 pp., wrappers. Denver, 1949. (By Father Stanley Crocchiola.) First edition. $60-$75.

STANSBURY, P. *A Pedestrian Tour of 2,300 Miles, in North America, etc.* 9 plates. Boards. New York, 1822. First edition. $150-$175.

STANTON, Schuyler. *Daughters of Destiny.* Red cloth. Chicago, (1906). (By L. Frank Baum.) First edition. $75-$100.

STAPLEDON, Olaf. *Latter-Day Psalms.* Cloth. Liverpool, 1914. First edition. In dust jacket. $200-$250.

STAPP, William P. *The Prisoners of Perote.* Wrappers, or cloth. Philadelphia, 1845. First edition. Wrappers: $450-$500. Cloth: $350-$450.

*STAR City of the West (The): Pueblo and Its Advantages.* 24 pp., folded. Pueblo, Colo., 1889. $125-$150.

STARBUCK, Alexander. *History of the American Whale Fishery, etc.* 6 plates. Cloth. Waltham, Mass., 1878. First edition. $200-$250. (Its first appearance was as Part IV, *Report of the U.S. Commissioner of Fish and Fishing,* Washington, 1878, catalogued in 1967 by a Boston dealer at $87.50.) New York, 1964. 2 vols., half leather. Boxed. One of 50. $200-$300. Trade edition: 2 vols., cloth. Boxed. $35-$50.

STARKEY, James. *Reminiscences of Indian Depredations.* 25 pp., wrappers. St. Paul, 1891. First edition. $150-$175.

STARR, Julian. *The Disagreeable Woman.* Green cloth. New York, 1895. (By Horatio Alger, Jr.) First edition. $600-$800. Also, $475 (A, 1975).

STARRETT, Vincent. *Ambrose Bierce.* Boards and cloth. Chicago, 1920. First edition. One of 250. $35-$50.

STARRETT, Vincent. *Arthur Machen: A Novelist of Ecstasy and Sin.* Boards and cloth. Chicago, 1918. First edition. One of 250. $100-$150. Author's first book.

STARRETT, Vincent. *Et Cetera: A Collector's Scrap-Book.* Half cloth. Chicago, 1924. First edition. One of 625. $75-$85.

STARRETT, Vincent. *Flame and Dust.* Half cloth. Chicago, 1924. First edition. One of 450. In dust jacket. $35-$50.

STARRETT, Vincent. *Persons from Porlock and Other Interruptions.* Boards. Chicago, 1938. One of 399, signed. In dust jacket. $40-$50.

STARRETT, Vincent. *The Private Life of Sherlock Holmes.* Illustrated. Cloth. New York, 1933. First edition. In dust jacket. $50-$60.

STARRETT, Vincent. *Stephen Crane: A Bibliography.* Half cloth. Philadelphia, 1923. First edition. One of 300. In dust jacket. $75-$100.

STARRETT, Vincent. *The Unique Hamlet.* Boards. Chicago, 1920. First edition. One of 250. $250-$350.

STARRETT, Vincent (editor). *In Praise of Stevenson.* Boards and cloth. Chicago, 1919. First edition. One of 300. $50-$60.

*STATE of Indiana Delineated (The).* Boards, leather spine, printed label on cover. New

York, 1838. First edition. (Published by J. H. Colton to accompany his separately published map, which is inserted in some copies.) $350-$450. With the map, $500 and up.

*STATEMENT Respecting the Earl of Selkirk's Settlement of Kildonan, upon the Red River, in North America.* Folding map. 125 pp., boards. London, (about 1817). (By John Halkett.) First edition. $400-$500. London, 1817. Second (enlarged) edition. 194 pp., boards. With title altered to *Statement Respecting the Earl of Selkirk's Settlement upon the Red River, in North America.* $350-$400.

STAUFFER, David McN., and Fielding, Mantle. *American Engravers Upon Copper and Steel.* Illustrated. 3 vols., boards and cloth. New York and Philadelphia, 1907-17. Vols. 1 and 2, limited to 350 copies (1907); Vol. 3, limited to 220, signed by Fielding (1917). The 3 vols., complete. $300-$400. Incomplete set, Vols. 1 and 2 only, $250-$300. Vol. 3 only, $75-$100. (Note: T. H. Gage published an *Artist's Index to Stauffer*, Worcester, 1921, which is sometimes offered with the three-volume set. The value of the *Index* is roughly $80 in the current market.)

STEAD, William T. *If Christ Came to Chicago.* Pictorial wrappers. Chicago, 1894. First edition. $100-$150.

*STEAM-BOAT (The).* Boards, marbled cloth spine. Edinburgh, 1822. (By John Galt.) First edition. $200-$250.

STEARNS, Samuel. *The American Herbal or Materia Medica.* Calf. Walpole, N.H., 1801. First edition. $500-$600.

STEDMAN, Edmund C. *Poems, Lyrical and Idyllic.* Cloth. New York, 1860. First edition. $25-$35. Author's first book.

STEDMAN, Edmund C. *Songs and Ballads.* Morocco. New York, 1884. First edition. One of 100 on Japan paper. Boxed. $45-$50.

STEDMAN, John G. *Narrative of a Five Years' Expedition Against the Revolted Negroes of Surinam in Guiana on the Wild Coast of America.* 80 full-page colored engravings, map. 2 vols., marbled boards and calf. London, 1813. Third edition. $400-$500.

STEEDMAN, Charles J. *Bucking the Sagebrush.* 3 portraits, folding map, 9 Charles M. Russell plates. Pictorial cloth. New York, 1904. First edition. In dust jacket. $150-$175.

STEEL, Flora A. *English Fairy Tales Retold.* Illustrated in color by Arthur Rackham. Vellum. London, 1918. One of 500 signed by Rackham. $400-$600. Trade edition: Cloth. $125-$150. New York, 1918. Half cloth. $150-$300.

STEELE, James W. *The Klondike.* Illustrated, 2 maps. 80 pp., pictorial gray wrappers. Chicago, 1897. First edition. $150-$200.

STEELE, James W. *The Sons of the Border.* Cloth. Topeka, 1873. First edition. $80-$100.

STEELE, John. *Across the Plains in 1850.* 7 plates. Cloth. Chicago, 1930. Caxton Club. First edition. $75-$100.

STEELE, John. *In Camp and Cabin: Mining Life and Adventure, in California, etc.* 81 pp., printed wrappers. Lodi, Wis., 1901. First edition. $250-$300.

STEELE, Oliver G. *New and Corrected Map of Michigan.* Colored folding map, leatherbound. Buffalo, (1834). $100-$135.

STEELE, R. J., and others (compilers). *Directory of the County of Placer.* Boards and calf. San Francisco, 1861. $600-$750.

STEELE, Zadock. *The Indian Captive.* Calf. Montpelier, Vt., 1818. First edition. $350-$500.

STEFFENS, Lincoln. *John Reed Under the Kremlin.* Introduction by Clarence Darrow. Wrappers. Chicago, 1922. First edition. One of 235. $100-$200.

STEFFENS, Lincoln. *The Shame of the Cities.* Cloth. New York, 1904. First edition. $75-$100. Author's first book.

STEGNER, Wallace. *The Big Rock Candy Mountain*. Cloth. New York, 1943. First edition. In dust jacket. $35.

STEIN, Gertrude. See Cerwin, Herbert; Toklas, Alice B.

STEIN, Gertrude. *Absolutely Bob Brown, or, Bobbed Brown*. Wrappers. Pawlet, Vt., 1955. Banyan Press. First edition. One of 52. In plain white envelope. $200-$250.

STEIN, Gertrude. *An Acquaintance with Description*. Oyster-white linen. London, 1929. Seizin Press. First edition. One of 225, signed. In glassine dust jacket. $300-$500.

STEIN, Gertrude. *Before the Flowers of Friendship Faded Friendship Faded*. Wrappers. Paris, (1931). First edition. One of 118, signed (of an edition of 120). In glassine dust jacket. $600-$800. Also, $500 (A, 1977).

STEIN, Gertrude. *Blood on the Dining Room Floor*. Half buckram and boards. (Pawlet, Vt., 1948.) Banyan Press. One of 626. In glassine dust jacket. Boxed. $100-$175.

STEIN, Gertrude. *A Book Concluding with As a Wife Has a Cow: A Love Story*. 4 lithographs (one in color) by Juan Gris. Wrappers. Paris, (1926). One of 102, signed. In glassine dust jacket. $1,750-$2,500. Another issue: One of 10 on Japon vellum, signed. $5,500 (A, 1977).

STEIN, Gertrude. *Chicago Inscriptions*. Stiff wrappers, stapled. (Chicago), 1934. First edition. $300-$400.

STEIN, Gertrude. *Composition As Explanation*. Green boards. London, 1926. Hogarth Press. First edition. $85-$150.

STEIN, Gertrude. *Dix Portraits*. Translated by G. Hugnet and Virgil Thomson. Illustrated by Picasso and others. Decorated wrappers. Paris, (1930). First edition. One of 10 on Japon vellum, signed, and with an autograph page of text by Miss Stein. In glassine jacket. $1,500 (A, 1977). Other issues: One of 25 on Holland paper, signed by author and translators. In glassine dust jacket. $400-$600. One of 65 on Velin d'Arches paper, signed. In dust jacket. $350-$400. Trade copies: One of 402 on Alfa paper without illustrations. In printed dust jacket plus glassine jacket. $50-$100.

STEIN, Gertrude. *An Elucidation*. (Cover title.) Wrappers. (Paris), 1927. First edition. $75-$100. (Issued as a supplement to *Transition* magazine after having been printed there with errors.)

STEIN, Gertrude. *The Geographical History of America or The Relation of Human Nature to the Human Mind*. Black and white cloth. (New York, 1936.) First edition. In dust jacket. $300-$400.

STEIN, Gertrude. *Geography and Plays*. Foreword by Sherwood Anderson. Cloth and boards. Boston, (1922). First edition, first binding, with lettering on front cover. In dust jacket. $350-$500. Second binding, cover unlettered. $100-$150.

STEIN, Gertrude. *Have They Attacked Mary. He Giggled*. (A Political Caricature.) Woodcut. Printed red wrappers. (West Chester, Pa., 1917.) First edition. One of 200. $600-$700. Also, $500 (A, 1977).

STEIN, Gertrude. *How to Write*. Boards, paper label on spine. Paris, (1931). First edition. One of 1,000. (Issued without dust jacket.) $100-$125.

STEIN, Gertrude. *Lectures in America*. Frontispiece. Beige cloth. New York, (1935). First edition. In dust jacket. $150-$300. Also, $225 (A, 1975).

STEIN, Gertrude. *Lucy Church Amiably*. Boards. Paris, 1930. First edition. In plain brown paper dust jacket. $200-$225.

STEIN, Gertrude. *The Making of Americans*. Wrappers. (Dijon, 1925.) First edition. One of 500. $600-$750. Another issue: One of 5 on vellum, with a letter by Miss Stein inserted. $5,600 (A, 1975). New York, 1926. Cloth. First American edition. In dust jacket. $750-$1,000. Also, $450 (A, 1977); $500 (A, 1975).

STEIN, Gertrude. *Matisse, Picasso, and Gertrude Stein, with Two Shorter Stories.* Wrappers. Paris, (1932). First edition. In glassine dust jacket. Boxed. $175-$200.

STEIN, Gertrude. *Morceaux Choisis de la Fabrication des Américains.* Portrait frontispiece by Christian Bérard. Wrappers. Paris, (1929). First edition. One of 95 signed by author and illustrator. In glassine jacket. $400-$500. Also, $300 (A, 1977). Another issue: One of 400 (not signed). $200-$250. Also, presentation copy, inscribed, $550 (A, 1977). Another issue: One of 5 on Japon vellum, with a manuscript page by Miss Stein. Signed by artist and author. $3,000-$4,000.

STEIN, Gertrude. *Narration: Four Lectures.* Introduction by Thornton Wilder. Blue, black, and gilt cloth. Chicago, (1935). First edition. One of 120 signed by Stein and Wilder. Boxed. $400-$500. Ordinary edition (unsigned): Orange cloth. In orange dust jacket. $75-$125.

STEIN, Gertrude. *On Our Way.* Introduction by Robert A. Wilson. Wrappers. New York, 1959. First edition. One of 100. $75-$100.

STEIN, Gertrude. *Operas and Plays.* Wrappers. Paris, (1932). First edition. Boxed. $200-$300. Signed by Stein, $450 (in a 1977 catalogue).

STEIN, Gertrude. *Paris France.* Rose cloth. London, (1940). First edition. In dust jacket. $50. New York, 1940. Rose cloth. First American edition, first binding. In dust jacket. $35. Second binding, red pebbled cloth. In dust jacket. $15-$25. New York, 1940. Blue cloth. Second American edition. In dust jacket. $20.

STEIN, Gertrude. *Picasso.* Illustrated. Pictorial wrappers. Paris, 1938. First edition. $100-$125. London, (1938). Rose-colored cloth. First English edition. In dust jacket. $30-$40.

STEIN, Gertrude. *Portrait of Mabel Dodge at the Villa Curonia.* Stitched wrappers. (Florence, 1912.) First edition, with imprint at foot of last page. $400-$600.

STEIN, Gertrude. *Portraits and Prayers.* Pictorial cloth. New York, (1934). First edition. In cellophane dust jacket. $150-$200.

STEIN, Gertrude. *A Primer For the Gradual Understanding of Gertrude Stein.* Edited by Robert B. Haas. Boards. Los Angeles, 1971. First edition. One of 60 specially bound copies with Stein's autograph. In glassine jacket. Boxed. $110-$155.

STEIN, Gertrude. *Tender Buttons. Objects. Food. Rooms.* Boards, paper label. New York, 1914. First edition. (Issued without dust jacket.) $300-$350.

STEIN, Gertrude. *Things as They Are: A Novel in 3 Parts.* Cloth. Pawlet, Vt., 1950. First edition. One of 516. (Issued without dust jacket.) $100-$150.

STEIN, Gertrude. *Three Lives.* Blue cloth. New York, 1909. First edition. (1,000 printed; issued without dust jacket.) $1,000-$1,250. Also, $500 (A, 1975); $550 (A, 1974). Author's first book. New York and London, 1915. First English edition. $750-$1,000. Also $500 (A, 1977). (300 issued from American sheets, with new title page.)

STEIN, Gertrude. *Useful Knowledge.* Cloth. New York, (1928). First edition. In dust jacket. $200-$250. London, (1928). First English edition. In dust jacket. $150-$200.

STEIN, Gertrude. *A Village Are You Ready Yet Not Yet.* Illustrated by Élie Lascaux. Wrappers. Paris, (1928). First edition. One of 102, signed. In glassine dust jacket. $400-$500. Another issue: One of 10 on Japon vellum signed. $950 (A, 1977).

STEIN, Gertrude. *What Are Masterpieces?* Portrait frontispiece. Blue cloth. (Los Angeles, 1940.) First edition. In dust jacket. $100-$150. Another issue: One of more than 50, signed. In dust jacket. $400-$500.

STEIN, Gertrude. *The World is Round.* Illustrated by Clement Hurd. Boards. New York, (1939). First edition. One of 350, signed. Boxed. $300-$400. Trade edition: Blue boards. In dust jacket. $50-$75. London, (1939). First English edition. Red cloth. In dust jacket. $50.

STEINBECK, John. See Cerwin, Herbert. Also, see *El Gabilan.*

STEINBECK, John. *Bombs Away.* Blue cloth. New York, 1942. First edition. In dust jacket. $40-$50.

STEINBECK, John. *Cannery Row.* Yellow cloth. New York, 1945. First edition. In dust jacket. $75. Advance copy: Wrappers. $500, possibly more. Also, $275 (A, 1977).

STEINBECK, John. *Cup of Gold: A Life of Henry Morgan, Buccaneer, with Occasional Reference to History.* Orange cloth. New York, 1929. First edition, first issue, with "First Published, August, 1929" on copyright page, and with top edges stained. In dust jacket. $1,000-$1,250. (A copy in worn dust jacket, offered along with a second issue copy and a second edition, both with worn jackets, brought $1,100 at the second Jonathan Goodwin sale in New York in October, 1977.) Author's first book. New York, (1936). Blue cloth. Second edition. In dust jacket. $25-$35.

STEINBECK, John. *East of Eden.* Green buckram. New York, 1952. First edition. One of 1,500, signed. Boxed. $200-$250. Trade edition: Cloth. In dust jacket. $35-$45.

STEINBECK, John. *The First Watch.* Wrappers. (Los Angeles), 1947. First edition. One of 60 in mailing envelope. $1,500-$2,000. Also, $1,100 (A, 1977).

STEINBECK, John. *The Forgotten Village.* Tan cloth. New York, 1941. First edition, first issue, with "First published in May 1941" on copyright page. In dust jacket. $50-$60.

STEINBECK, John. *The Grapes of Wrath.* Pictorial beige cloth. New York, (1939). First edition, with yellow top edges, with "First published in April, 1939" on copyright page, and with first edition notice on front flap of dust jacket. In dust jacket. $150-$175. Also, a set of uncorrected galley proofs, $1,700 (A, 1977); also, a clothbound salesman's dummy copy, $1,100 (A, 1977). London, (1939). First English edition. In dust jacket. $50. New York, 1940. Limited Editions Club. 2 vols., grass cloth and leather. Boxed. $200-$250.

STEINBECK, John. *How Edith McGillcuddy Met RLS.* Boards and cloth, paper labels. Cleveland, 1943. Rowfant Club (Grabhorn printing). First edition. One of 152. $1,000-$1,500. Also, $1,100 (A, 1977).

STEINBECK, John. *In Dubious Battle.* Orange cloth. New York, (1936). First edition. In dust jacket. $150-$175. Another issue: Beige cloth. One of 99, signed. Boxed. $1,000-$1,250. Also, $950 (A, 1977).

STEINBECK, John. *John Steinbeck Replies.* 4-page leaflet, unbound. (First page is letter to Steinbeck by L. M. Birkhead. Pages 2 and 3 are Steinbeck's reply.) (New York, 1940.) $75. (See following entry for a reprint.)

STEINBECK, John. *A Letter by John Steinbeck to the Friends of Democracy.* Boards, paper label. Stamford, Conn., 1940. First edition with this title. One of 350 by the Overbrook Press. $75-$100. (A reprint of *John Steinbeck Replies.)*

STEINBECK, John. *A Letter from John Steinbeck.* Printed wrappers. (San Francisco), 1964. First edition. One of 150. $100-$125.

STEINBECK, John. *The Log from the Sea of Cortez.* Red cloth. New York, 1951. Revised edition of *Sea of Cortez,* with a new 67-page chapter, "About Ed Ricketts." In dust jacket. $35-$50. (See Steinbeck, and Ricketts, *Sea of Cortez.)*

STEINBECK, John. *The Long Valley.* Rust-colored cloth, natural cloth spine. New York, 1938. First edition. In dust jacket. $85-$125.

STEINBECK, John. *The Moon is Down.* Blue cloth, top edges stained blue. New York, 1942. First edition, first issue, without printer's name on copyright page and with large period between "talk" and "this" in line 11 on page 112. In dust jacket. $75-$100.

STEINBECK, John. *Nothing So Monstrous: A Story.* Donald McKay drawings, decorated boards, cloth spine. (New York), 1936. First edition. One of 370. In tissue dust jacket. $400-$500. Also, $325 (A, 1977).

STEINBECK, John. *Of Mice and Men.* Tan cloth. New York, (1937). First edition, first state, with "'and only moved because the heavy hands were / pendula" at page 9, second and third lines from bottom of page. In dust jacket. $75-$100. Second state, lines 2 and 3 from bottom of page 9 corrected. $30-$40. London, (1937). Cloth. First edition. In dust jacket. $60-$80. Also, "proof copy" in printed wrappers, $60 (A, 1963).

STEINBECK, John. *The Pastures of Heaven*. Green cloth. New York, 1932. First edition, first issue, with Brewer, Warren & Putnam imprint. In dust jacket. $500-$750. Second issue, with Robert O. Ballou imprint. In dust jacket, with a 4-page Ballou brochure, *The Neatest Trick of the Year*. $150-$200. Another, no brochure, in dust jacket, $75. (Note: Johnson notes a later issue with Covici-Friede imprint.) New York, (1945). Wrappers. Armed Services Edition. $20-$25.

STEINBECK, John. *The Red Pony*. Decorated flexible beige cloth. New York, 1937. First edition. One of 699, signed. Boxed. $300-$400. Another issue: One of 26 lettered copies. $850. New York, 1945. Beige cloth. First illustrated edition. In slipcase. $35.

STEINBECK, John. *A Russian Journal*. Boards and cloth. New York, 1948. First edition. In dust jacket. $50-$75.

STEINBECK, John. *Saint Katy the Virgin*. Printed boards, cloth spine. (New York, 1936.) First edition. One of 199, signed. (Issued as a Christmas greeting by Covici-Friede with greeting slip inserted.) In glassine dust jacket. $1,000 and up. Also, bottom edges rubbed, $950 (A, 1977).

STEINBECK, John. *"Their Blood Is Strong."* Pictorial wrappers. San Francisco, 1938. First edition. $300-$350.

STEINBECK, John. *To a God Unknown*. Green cloth. New York, (1933). First edition, first issue, with Robert O. Ballou imprint. In dust jacket. $250-$300. Second issue, with Covici-Friede imprint. In dust jacket. $100-$150.

STEINBECK, John. *Tortilla Flat*. Tan cloth. New York, (1935). First edition. In dust jacket. $135-$150. Advance issue of 500, in wrappers: $500 and up. Also, $375 (A, 1977).

STEINBECK, John. *Vanderbilt Clinic*. Illustrated. Wrappers. (New York, 1947.) First edition. $40-$60.

STEINBECK, John. *The Wayward Bus*. Brown cloth. New York, 1947. First edition. In dust jacket. $40-$50. London, (1947). Red cloth. First English edition. In dust jacket. $20-$30.

STEINBECK, John. *The Winter of Our Discontent*. Cloth. New York, (1961). First edition. In dust jacket. $35. Another issue: One of 500, signed. In dust jacket. $100-$150.

STEINBECK, John, and Ricketts, Edward F. *Sea of Cortez*. Illustrated, including maps. Cloth. New York, 1941. First edition. In dust jacket. $150-$175. Also, a clothbound salesman's dummy copy, $650 (A, 1977). (See Steinbeck, *The Log from the Sea of Cortez*.)

STEPHENS, Alexander H. *A Constitutional View of the Late War Between the States*. Map, plates. 2 vols., cloth. Philadelphia, 1868-70. First edition. $50-$75.

STEPHENS, Alexander H. *Speech in January, 1861, Before the Georgia State Convention*. 12 pp., wrappers. Baltimore, 1864. $50-$75.

STEPHENS, Mrs. Ann S. *Malaeska: The Indian Wife of the White Hunter*. Printed orange wrappers. New York, (1860). First edition, first issue, with covers 6-5/8 × 4-1/2 inches, and without woodcut on cover. $300-$500.

STEPHENS, Ann Sophia. *High Life in New York*. Wrappers. (New York, 1843.) First edition. $100-$150. Author's first separate book.

STEPHENS, Ann Sophia (editor). *The Portland Sketch Book*. Cloth. Portland, Me., 1836. First edition. $35-$50. Author's first book appearance.

STEPHENS, James. See Esse, James.

STEPHENS, James. *The Charwoman's Daughter.* Cloth. London, 1912. First edition. In dust jacket. $40-$50.

STEPHENS, James. *Collected Poems.* Boards and vellum. London, 1926. One of 500 large paper copies, signed. $75-$85.

STEPHENS, James. *The Crock of Gold.* Green cloth. London, 1912. First edition. In dust jacket. $150-$250. London, 1926. Illustrated. Half vellum. One of 525, signed. $150-$200. New York, 1942. Limited Editions Club. Cloth. $50-$60.

STEPHENS, James. *Etched in Moonlight.* Light-blue cloth. London, 1928. First edition. In dust jacket. $50-$75. New York, 1928. Half cloth. First American edition. One of 750, signed. In dust jacket. $50-$75.

STEPHENS, James. *Green Branches.* Wrappers. Dublin, 1916. First edition. One of 500, signed. $75-$85. New York, 1916. Half vellum. First American edition. One of 500. $30-$40.

STEPHENS, James. *The Insurrection in Dublin.* Cloth. London, 1916. First edition. $40-$60.

STEPHENS, James. *Insurrections.* Brown boards. Dublin, 1909. First edition. In dust jacket. $75-$100.

STEPHENS, James. *Irish Fairy Tales.* Illustrated by Arthur Rackham. Vellum and boards. London, 1920. First edition. One of 520, signed by Rackham. $400-$600. Trade issue: Cloth. $150-$200.

STEPHENS, James. *Julia Elizabeth.* Decorated boards. New York, 1929. First edition. One of 861, signed. $30-$40.

STEPHENS, James. *Little Things.* Boards and cloth. Freelands, (1924). First edition. One of 25, signed. $75-$100. Another issue: Printed wrappers. One of 200, signed. $65-$85.

STEPHENS, James. *Optimist.* Illustrated. Boards and cloth. Gaylordsville, N.Y., 1929. First edition. One of 89, signed. $100-$175.

STEPHENS, James. *A Poetry Recital.* Boards. London, 1925. First edition. In dust jacket. $40-$50.

STEPHENS, John L. *Incidents of Travel in Central America, Chiapas and Yucatan.* Folding map, other maps and plans, 68 plates, other illustrations. Half-leather. London, 1841. First edition. $150-$200.

STEPHENS, Lorenzo Dow. *Life Sketches of a Jayhawker of '49.* 6 plates. 68 pp., printed wrappers. (San Jose), 1916. First edition. $125-$150.

STERLING, George. *The Caged Eagle and Other Poems.* Cloth. San Francisco, 1916. First edition. $75-$80.

STERLING, George. *Ode on the Opening of the Panama-Pacific International Exposition.* Boards and cloth. San Francisco, 1915. First edition. One of 525. $50-$60.

STERLING, George. *The Testimony of the Suns and Other Poems.* Black cloth. San Francisco, 1903. First edition. $75-$100. Author's first book. San Francisco, 1927. John Henry Nash printing. Folio, boards. One of 300. (Facsimile of title poem with comments by Ambrose Bierce.) $75-$100.

STERLING, George. *To a Girl Dancing.* Printed boards or wrappers. (San Francisco, 1921.) Grabhorn Press. First edition. $150-$200.

STERLING, George. *Truth.* Blue paper boards, cloth spine, two paper labels. Chicago, 1923. First edition. One of 285, signed. $50-$60.

STERLING, George; Taggard, Genevieve; and Rorty, James. *Continent's End: An Anthology of Contemporary California Poets.* Boards, pigskin spine. San Francisco, 1925. Book Club of California. First edition. One of 600. In half morocco slipcase. $60-$75.

STEVENS, C. A. *Berdan's United States Sharpshooters in the Army of the Potomac.* Illustrated. Cloth. St. Paul, 1892. $150-$175.

STEVENS, George W. *Adventures, American Anecdotes, Biographical, Historical and Descriptive.* Cloth, printed label. Dansville, 1845. First edition. $75-$100.

STEVENS, Isaac I. *Campaigns of the Rio Grande and of Mexico.* 108 pp., wrappers. New York, 1851. First edition. $200-$350, possibly more.

STEVENS, Isaac I. *A Circular Letter to Emigrants Desirous of Locating in Washington Territory.* 21 pp., sewed. Washington, 1858. First edition. $250-$350.

STEVENS, Wallace. See *Harvard Lyrics; An Ordinary Evening in New Haven; Verses from the Harvard Advocate.*

STEVENS, Wallace. *The Auroras of Autumn.* Blue cloth. New York, 1950. First edition. In dust jacket. $75-$85.

STEVENS, Wallace. *The Collected Poems of Wallace Stevens.* Brown cloth. New York, 1954. First collected edition. One of 2,500. In dust jacket. $100-$125.

STEVENS, Wallace. *Harmonium.* Checkered boards; later, striped boards. New York, 1923. First edition, first binding. In dust jacket. Either binding: $400-$600. Also, inscribed but lacking jacket, $350 (A, 1977). Third binding: Blue cloth. In dust jacket. $200-$300, possibly more. Author's first book. New York, 1931. Cloth. In dust jacket. $150.

STEVENS, Wallace. *Ideas of Order.* Cloth, New York, 1935. First edition. One of 165 signed. In dust jacket. $850 (A, 1976). New York, 1936. First edition (so called) first binding, striped cloth. In dust jacket. $150-$200. (Later bindings in boards.)

STEVENS, Wallace. *The Man with the Blue Guitar & Other Poems.* Cloth. New York, 1937. First edition. In dust jacket. $150-$175. New York, 1952. Cloth. In dust jacket. $75.

STEVENS, Wallace. *The Necessary Angel.* Green cloth. New York, 1951. First edition. In dust jacket. $75-$100.

STEVENS, Wallace. *Notes Toward a Supreme Fiction.* Cloth. Cummington, Mass., 1942. First edition. One of 193. In acetate dust jacket. $350-$400. Another issue: One of 80, signed. $1,000-$1,500. Also, $1,100 (A, 1977).

STEVENS, Wallace. *Opus Posthumous.* Cloth. New York, 1957. First edition. In dust jacket. $35-$50.

STEVENS, Wallace. *Owl's Clover.* Wrappers. New York, (1936). First edition. One of 105 signed. $2,500-$3,000. Also, $3,250 (A, 1976); advance copy signed by the publisher, $1,700 (A, 1977).

STEVENS, Wallace. *Parts of a World.* Boards. New York, 1942. First edition. In dust jacket. $150-$200.

STEVENS, Wallace. *A Primitive Like an Orb.* Illustrated by Kurt Seligmann. Olive-green wrappers. New York, 1948. First edition. One of 500. $150-$175.

STEVENS, Wallace. *Raoul Dufy: A Note.* 4 pp., wrappers. (New York, 1953.) First edition. One of 200. $150-$200.

STEVENS, Wallace. *Selected Poems.* Black boards. London, (1952). First edition. $200-$250. (Suppressed because it was unauthorized.)

STEVENS, Wallace. *Three Academic Pieces.* Boards. (Cummington), 1947. First edition. One of 102 signed (of an edition of 246). $800-$900. Also, spine faded. $550 (A, 1977).

STEVENS, Wallace. *Transport to Summer.* Green boards and cloth. New York, 1947. First edition. In dust jacket. $100-$125.

STEVENS, Walter B. *Through Texas: A Series of Interesting Letters.* Illustrated. Wrappers. (St. Louis), 1892. First edition. $75-$100.

STEVENS, William. See *The Unjust Judge.*

STEVENS & Conover. *Branch County Directory and Historical Record.* Cloth. Ann Arbor, 1871. $100-$125.

STEVENSON, B. F. *Letters from the Army.* Cloth. Cincinnati, 1864. $50-$60.

STEVENSON, R. Randolph, M.D. *The Southern Side: or, Andersonville Prison.* Cloth. Baltimore, 1876. $100-$125.

STEVENSON, Robert Louis. See *The Pentland Rising.*

STEVENSON, Robert Louis. *Across the Plains.* Cream-colored cloth. London, 1892. First edition. One of 100 on large paper. $100-$150.

STEVENSON, Robert Louis. *Ballads.* Portraits. Blue cloth. London, 1890. First edition. $50-$60. Another issue: White cloth. One of 100 on large paper. $100-$125.

STEVENSON, Robert Louis. *The Black Arrow.* Red cloth. London, 1888. First English edition. $50-$75.

STEVENSON, Robert Louis. *Catriona, A Sequel to "Kidnapped."* Blue cloth. London, 1893. First edition. $75-$85.

STEVENSON, Robert Louis. *A Child's Garden of Verses.* Blue cloth. London, 1885. First edition. $400-$500. Also, covers discolored, $220 (A, 1977).

STEVENSON, Robert Louis. *Diogenes at the Saville Club.* Boards. Chicago, 1921. First edition. One of 150. $50-$60. Another issue: Vellum. One of 5 on vellum. $200-$225.

STEVENSON, Robert Louis. *Edinburgh, Picturesque Notes.* Etchings and vignettes. Folio, cloth. London, 1879. First edition. $40-$60.

STEVENSON, Robert Louis. *Familiar Studies of Men and Books.* Pictorial green cloth. London, 1882. First edition. $100-$125. (Note: De Ricci notes a large paper reprint of 100 copies in 1888.)

STEVENSON, Robert Louis. *Father Damien.* Wrappers, stapled. Sydney, Australia, 1890. First edition. One of 25. $1,150 (in a 1974 American catalogue). Also, $600 (A, 1977). Edinburgh, 1890. Unbound sheets in board portfolio. One of 30 on vellum. $150-$200. Also, $65 (A, 1976). London, 1890. Wrappers. First published edition. $150-$200. Oxford, 1901. Printed wrappers. One of 299 on vellum. $200-$250. Portland, Me., 1905. Vellum. One of 4 on vellum. $250-$350. San Francisco, 1930. John Henry Nash printing. 2 vols., half vellum. $50-$100.

STEVENSON, Robert Louis. *A Footnote to History: Eight Years of Trouble in Samoa.* Frontispiece. Blue or green cloth. London, 1892. First edition. $100-$150.

STEVENSON, Robert Louis. *The Graver & the Pen, or Scenes from Nature with Appropriate Verses.* Woodcuts. Gray wrappers. Edinburgh, (1882). First edition. $500 and up. Also, $360 (A, 1977).

STEVENSON, Robert Louis. *An Inland Voyage.* Frontispiece by Walter Crane. Blue cloth. London, 1878. First edition. $150-$200. Author's first novel. Stamford, Conn., 1938. Overbrook Press. 25 plates by Jean Hugo. Half calf. One of 150. $75-$100.

STEVENSON, Robert Louis. *Island Nights' Entertainments.* 28 illustrations. Cloth. London, 1893. First English edition, first issue, with changes in ink in price list of Stevenson's works. $125-$150.

STEVENSON, Robert Louis. *Kidnapped.* Folding frontispiece map. Cloth. (London), 1886. First edition. (Issued in various colors of cloth—blue, red, brown, and green—with blue as first.) Blue cloth, first issue, with the reading "business" in line 11 of page 40, etc. $200-$400. Second issue, in bright red cloth, with the reading "pleasure" on line 11 of page 40, etc. $100-$200. (Later binding in green cloth.) New York, 1938. Limited Editions Club. Cloth. $30-$40. (Note: De Ricci records a "very scarce" London trade issue, undated, in advance of the first edition.)

STEVENSON, Robert Louis. *The Master of Ballantrae*. Red cloth. London, 1889. First edition. $75-$100. (There was also a "trial" edition of only 10 copies published in London in wrappers in 1888, according to De Ricci. A copy was sold at auction for $615 at Sotheby's in 1915.) New York, 1965. Limited Editions Club. Boxed. $40-$50.

STEVENSON, Robert Louis. *Memoirs of Himself*. Boards. Philadelphia, 1912. First edition. One of 45 on Whatman paper. $100-$150.

STEVENSON, Robert Louis. *The Merry Men and Other Tales and Fables*. Decorated blue cloth. London, 1887. First edition, with 32 pages of ads at end dated September, 1886. $75-$100.

STEVENSON, Robert Louis. *A Mountain Town in France*. Gray wrappers. New York, 1896. First edition. One of 350. $100-$125.

STEVENSON, Robert Louis. *New Arabian Nights*. 2 vols., green cloth. London, 1882. First edition, first issue, with yellow end papers in Vol. 1. $150-$200.

STEVENSON, Robert Louis (Thomas J. Wise forgery). *On the Thermal Influence of Forests*. Blue wrappers. Edinburgh: Neill and Co., 1873 (1895?). First edition. $250.

STEVENSON, Robert Louis. *Pan's Pipes*. Glazed red boards. (Boston), 1910. First separate edition. One of 500. Boxed. $80-$100.

STEVENSON, Robert Louis. *Prince Otto, a Romance*. Decorated cloth. London, 1885. First edition, with ads dated January. $150-$175.

STEVENSON, Robert Louis. *St. Ives*. Cloth. New York, 1897. First edition. $50-$75. London, 1898. Slate-colored cloth. First English edition. $100-$125.

STEVENSON, Robert Louis. *The Silverado Squatters*. Decorated green cloth. London, 1883. First edition, first issue, with 32-page catalogue dated 1883 at back. $150-$250. There was also a 10-copy trial issue of Chapter 1, 14 pages, green wrappers, London, (1883), published for copyright: $725 (A, 1952); inscribed copy, $2,400 (A, 1946). San Francisco, 1952. Grabhorn Press. Boards and cloth. One of 900. In original plain wrapper. $100-$150.

STEVENSON, Robert Louis. *The South Seas: A Record of Three Cruises*. Cloth. London, 1890. First edition. One of about 20 or 22 copies privately printed for copyright purposes. $1,000-$2,000. (Note: De Ricci noted this book in wrappers and in red cloth.)

STEVENSON, Robert Louis. *A Stevenson Medley*. Cloth. London, 1899. First edition. One of 300. $75-$100.

STEVENSON, Robert Louis (Thomas J. Wise forgery). *The Story of a Lie*. Folded sheets. London, 1882. First edition. (Withdrawn before publication.) $300 and up.

STEVENSON, Robert Louis. *The Strange Case of Dr. Jekyll and Mr. Hyde*. Printed wrappers, or pink cloth. London, 1886. First English edition, first issue, in wrappers, with the date on front cover altered in ink from 1885 to 1886. $400-$500. Cloth: $200-$300. New York, 1886. Wrappers, or cloth. First edition. Wrappers: $200-$250. Cloth: $150-$200. New York, 1952. Limited Editions Club. Marbled boards. Boxed. $40-$50.

STEVENSON, Robert Louis. *The Suicide Club*. Illustrated. Wrappers over boards. New York, (1941). First edition. One of 86 (of 100), signed by the artist Karl Schrag and issued with an extra set of the 18 etchings. Boxed. $150.

STEVENSON, Robert Louis. *Thomas Stevenson: Civil Engineer*. Wrappers. (London), 1887. First edition. $200. (A Thomas J. Wise forgery.)

STEVENSON, Robert Louis. *Ticonderoga*. Vellum boards. Edinburgh, 1887. First edition. One of 50. $400-$500. (A Wise forgery.)

STEVENSON, Robert Louis. *Travels with a Donkey in the Cevennes.* Frontispiece by Walter Crane. Green cloth. London, 1879. First edition. $400-$500. New York, 1957. Limited Editions Club. $40-$50.

STEVENSON, Robert Louis. *Treasure Island.* Green, gray, blue, or rust-colored cloth. London, 1883. First edition, first state, with ads dated July, 1883. $600-$750. Also, $440 (A, 1977). Boston, 1884. Frontispiece map, illustrated. Pictorial cloth. First American (and first illustrated) edition. $500-$600. London, 1885. Illustrated. Red cloth. First English illustrated edition. $150-$250. (Note: The McCutcheon sale catalogue, New York, 1926, No. 563, erroneously calls this the first illustrated edition.) London, 1927. Illustrated by Edmund Dulac. Vellum. One of 50, signed. $400-$500. Trade edition: Cloth. $200-$300. New York, (1927). Dulac illustrations. Cloth. First American trade edition. In dust jacket. $100-$125. Philadelphia, 1930. Illustrated by Lyle Justis. Tan cloth. First printing. In dust jacket and slipcase. $40-$60. New York, 1941. Limited Editions Club. Cloth. $75-$100. Extra lithograph bound in, $125. London, 1949. Illustrated by Mervyn Peake. In dust jacket. $100-$125.

STEVENSON, Robert Louis. *Underwoods.* Green cloth. London, 1887. First edition, with July ads at back. $50-$75. Large paper issue: White buckram. One of 50. $75-$100.

STEVENSON, Robert Louis. *Vailima Letters.* 2 vols., green buckram. Chicago, 1895. First edition. $50-$75. Large paper issue: One of 100. $100-$150.London, 1895. Terra-cotta cloth. First English edition. $40-$60. Large paper issue: Cloth. One of 125. $100-$125.

STEVENSON, Robert Louis. *Virginibus Puerisque and Other Papers.* Orange cloth, beveled edges. London, 1881. First edition, with ads dated "8.80." $75-$125. New York, 1893. Etched portrait by G. Mercier. Blue-green boards, paper label. One of 212. $75-$100. London, 1910. Florence Press. Illustrated by Norman Wilkinson. Vellum. One of 12 on vellum. $750-$1,000. Another issue: One of 250. $50-$75.

STEVENSON, Robert Louis. *The Weir of Hermiston.* Blue buckram. London, 1896. First edition, with March ads. $75-$100.

STEVENSON, Robert Louis, and Henley, William Ernest. *Macaire: A Melodramatic Farce in Three Acts.* Printed wrapers. Edinburgh, 1885. First edition. $200-$250. Chicago. 1895. American copyright edition. $100-$150.

STEVENSON, Robert Louis, and Osbourne, Lloyd. *The Ebb Tide.* Cloth. Chicago, 1894. First edition. $40-$50. London, 1894. Pictorial cloth. First English edition, first issue, with 20 pages of ads at back. $40-$50.

STEVENSON, Robert Louis, and Osbourne, Lloyd. *The Wrecker.* Illustrated. Blue cloth. London, 1892. First edition. $40-$50.

STEVENSON, Robert Louis, and Van De Grift, Fanny. *More New Arabian Nights. The Dynamiter.* Cloth, or green pictorial wrappers. London, 1885. First edition. Either binding: $150-$200.

STEWART, Sir William Drummond. See *Altowan.*

STEWART, William F. *Last of the Filibusters.* 85 pp., pictorial wrappers. Sacramento, 1857. First edition. $650-$750.

STIFF, Col. Edward. *The Texan Emigrant.* Folding map. Cloth, Cincinnati, 1840. First edition. $350-$500.

STILL, James. *Hounds on the Mountain.* Cloth. New York, 1937. First edition. One of 700. In dust jacket. $50-$60.

STILL, James. *River of Earth.* Cloth. New York, 1940. First edition. In dust jacket. $35-$50.

STILLMAN, Jacob D. B. B. *The Horse in Motion, as Shown by Instantaneous Photography.* 107 plates, 9 in color, by Eadweard Muybridge. Cloth. Boston, 1882. First edition. $600-$750. Also, $350 (A, 1975). London, 1882. Cloth. $350-$400.

STILLMAN, Samuel. *Select Sermons on Doctrinal and Practical Subjects.* Illustrated. Calf. Boston, 1808. $50-$75.

STILLWELL, Margaret Bingham. *Gutenberg and the Catholicon of 1460.* Folio, cloth. New York, 1936. With an original leaf of the Catholicon printed by Gutenberg in 1460. In slipcase. $1,000-$1,500. Also, $1,100 (A, 1974).

STIPP, G. W. (compiler). *The Western Miscellany.* Calf. Xenia, Ohio, 1827. First edition. $3,500-$4,000. Also, $1,700 (A, 1967).

STOBO, Maj. Robert. *Memoirs of Maj. Robert Stobo.* 78 pp., boards. London, 1800. First edition. $250-$350. Pittsburgh, 1854. Folding frontispiece, map. Cloth. First American edition. $200-$250.

STOCKTON, Frank R. *The Casting Away of Mrs. Lecks and Mrs. Aleshine.* Cloth, or wrappers. New York, (1886). First edition, first issue, with signatures (divisions of paper) at pages 9, 25, 49, 57, 73, 81, 97, 105, 121, and 125. Wrappers, first state, with ads for *Century* and *St. Nicholas* magazines: $100-$150. Cloth, first state, half inch across top of covers: $50-$60.

STOCKTON, Frank R. *The Floating Prince and Other Fairy Tales.* Cloth. New York, 1881. First edition. $135-$175.

STOCKTON, Frank R. *The Great War Syndicate.* Printed wrappers. New York, 1889. First edition, published by Collier. $50-$75.

STOCKTON, Frank R. *The Lady, or the Tiger? and Other Stories.* Pictorial gray and brown cloth. New York, 1884. First edition. $75-$100.

STOCKTON, Frank R. *Rudder Grange.* Pictorial red or green cloth. New York, 1879. First edition, first issue, with 18 chapters and no ads or reviews of this title. $50-$65.

STOCKTON, Frank R. *A Storyteller's Pack.* Illustrated. Green cloth. New York, 1897. First edition. $40-$50.

STOCKTON, Frank R. *Tales Out of School.* Illustrated. Cloth. New York, 1876. First edition. $40-$50.

STOCKTON, Frank R. *Ting-a-Ling.* Illustrated. Pictorial purple cloth. New York, 1870. First edition. $125-$200. Author's first book.

STOCKTON, Frank R. *What Might Have Been Expected.* Pictorial cloth. New York, 1874. First edition. $50-$75.

STODDARD, Maj. Amos. *Sketches, Historical and Descriptive of Louisiana.* Boards. Philadelphia, 1812. First edition. $200-$250.

STODDARD, Herbert L. *The Bob-White Quail.* Illustrated. Cloth. New York, 1931. First edition. One of 260, signed, and with an original signed by Frank W. Benson. $300-$400.

STODDARD, Richard Henry. *Abraham Lincoln: An Horatian Ode.* Wrappers. New York, (1865). First edition. $50-$60.

STODDARD, William O. *Little Smoke: A Tale of the Sioux.* Illustrated by Frederick S. Dellenbaugh. Pictorial cloth. New York, 1891. First edition. $75-$100.

STOKER, Bram. *Dracula.* Yellow cloth. Westminister (London), 1897. First edition, first issue, without ads. $300-$400, possibly more. Second issue, with ads at back. $100-$150. New York, 1965. Limited Editions Club. Boxed. $60-$80.

STOKER, Bram. *The Lady of the Shroud.* Cloth. London, 1909. First edition. $75-$100.

STOKES, I. N. Phelps. *The Iconography of Manhattan Island.* Many plates, some in color. 6 vols., half vellum. New York, 1915-28. First edition. One of 360. In dust jackets. Boxed. $2,000-$3,000. Another issue: One of 42 on Japan vellum. $3,000-$4,000.

STOKES, I. N. Phelps, and Haskell, Daniel C. *American Historical Prints: Early Views of American Cities.* Illustrated. Cloth. New York, 1932. $150-$250. New York, 1933. Cloth. $100-$150.

STONE, Charles P. *Notes on the State of Sonora.* 28 pp., printed wrappers. Washington, 1861. First edition. $300-$350.

STONE, George C. *A Glossary of the Constitution, Decoration and Use of Arms and Armour.* Cloth. Portland, Me., 1934. First edition. $75-$100. De luxe issue: Leather. One of 35. $100-$150. New York, 1961. Facsimile edition. Buckram. One of 500. $40-$60.

STONE, Herbert Stuart. *First Editions of American Authors.* Cloth. Cambridge, Mass., 1893. First edition. One of 450, signed. $35-$50. Another issue: One of 50 on large paper, signed. $75-$100.

STONG, Phil. *Horses and Americans.* Cloth. New York, 1939. First edition. In dust jacket. $25. Author's autograph edition: Buckram. $50-$75.

STOREY, David. *This Sporting Life.* Cloth. (London, 1960.) First edition. In dust jacket. $75-$100. Author's first book.

*STORIES from the Harvard Advocate.* Half morocco. Cambridge, Mass., 1896. First edition. $40-$50.

*STORY of Cripple Creek (A), the Greatest Gold Mining Camp on Earth.* Folding map. 28 pp., wrappers. (Denver, 1896.) First edition. $100-$125.

*STORY of Louis Riel, Rebel Chief (The).* Illustrated. Cloth. Toronto, 1885. (By J. E. Collins.) First edition. $100-$125.

*STORY of the Three Bears (The).* Illustrated by Harrison Weir and John Absolon. 12 leaves, yellow hand-covered wrappers. New York, (about 1870). $40-$60.

STOTZ, Charles Morse. *The Early Architecture of Western Pennsylvania.* Cloth. Pittsburgh, 1936. First edition. $50-$75.

STOUT, Rex. *How Like a God.* Purple cloth. New York, 1929. First edition. In dust jacket. $50-$75. Author's first book.

STOWE, Harriet Beecher. See Beecher, Harriet Elizabeth.

STOWE, Harriet Beecher. *A Key to Uncle Tom's Cabin.* Cloth, or wrappers. Boston, 1853. First edition. Wrappers: $50-$75. Cloth: $25-$50.

STOWE, Harriet Beecher. *Uncle Sam's Emancipation.* Cloth. Philadelphia, 1853. First edition. $50-$75.

STOWE, Harriet Beecher. *Uncle Tom's Cabin.* Title vignette, 6 plates. 2 vols., pictorial wrappers, or 2 vols., cloth. Boston, 1852. First edition, first printing, first issue, wrappers, with slug of Hobart and Robbins on copyright page. $5,000 and up. (The Paul Hyde Bonner copy, with the spines gauzed, brought $1,025 at auction in 1934. No comparably fine copy in wrappers seems to have been offered since.) First printing, second issue (cloth) binding, $1,250 and up. Also, "Gift" binding of gilt-decorated brown cloth, $4,500 in a 1975 catalogue. (For price ranges on numerous other copies—defective, rebound, and in various "gift" bindings—see the current auction records in *American Book-Prices Current.)* London, 1852. Cassell imprint. Illustrated by George Cruikshank. 13 parts, pictorial wrappers. First English edition. $200-$300. London, 1852. Cloth. First English book edition, with Cassell imprint. $150-$250. London, 1852. 40 plates. Cloth. C. H. Clarke, publisher. $75-$100. New York, 1938. Limited Editions Club. Marbled boards and leather. $60-$85.

STRACHEY, Lytton. *Books and Characters.* Portrait. Green cloth. London, 1922. First edition. In dust jacket. $35-$50.

STRACHEY, Lytton. *Elizabeth and Essex.* Half cloth. New York, 1928. One of 1,060, signed. $75-$85.

STRACHEY, Lytton. *Portraits in Miniature.* Half cloth. London, 1931. First edition. Limited and signed issue. $100-$110. Trade issue: Buckram. In dust jacket. $20-$25.

STRAHORN, Mrs. Carrie A. *15,000 Miles by Stage.* Numerous illustrations, including 4 in color by Charles M. Russell. Cloth. New York, 1911. First edition. $150-$200. New York, 1915. Second edition. $100-$150.

STRAHORN, Robert E. *The Hand-book of Wyoming, and Guide to the Black Hills and Big Horn Regions.* 14 plates. 272 pp., printed wrappers. Cheyenne, 1877. First edition. $400-$600. Also, in cloth: $250-$300.

STRAHORN, Robert E. *Montana and Yellowstone National Park.* 101 pp., flexible cloth wrappers, plus 14 pp. ads. Kansas City, 1881. First edition. $200-$225.

STRAHORN, Robert E. *To the Rockies and Beyond.* Folding map. Wrappers. Omaha, 1878. First edition. $300-$350. Also in cloth: $225. Omaha, 1879. Second edition. $150-$200. Chicago, 1881. Third edition. $100-$150.

STRAND, Mark. *Sleeping With One Eye Open.* Cloth. Iowa City, 1963. Stone Wall Press. First edition. One of 225. In acetate dust jacket. $50-$60. Author's first book.

STRANG, James J. *The Book of the Law of the Lord.* 80 pp., cloth. (Kansas City, 1927.) $150-$200. (For earlier editions, see title entry.)

STRANGE, Edward F. *The Colour-Prints of Hiroshige.* 16 colored, 36 plain plates. Buckram. London, 1925. In dust jacket. $150-$200. Another issue: Vellum. One of 250. $200-$250.

*STRANGER in Lowell (The).* Wrappers. Boston, 1845. (By John Greenleaf Whittier.) First edition. $100-$200.

*STRANGER'S Guide to St. Louis, or What to See and How to See It.* Folding map. Cloth. St. Louis, 1867. First edition. $150-$200.

STRATTON, R. B. *Captivity of the Oatman Girls, etc.* 231 pp., printed wrappers. San Francisco, 1857. Second edition of *Life Among the Indians* (entry following). $500-$750. Chicago, 1857. (Reprint.) $250-$350. New York, 1858. 3 plates. Cloth. Third edition, enlarged. $250-$300.

STRATTON, R. B. *Life Among the Indians.* Illustrated. 183 pp., wrappers. San Francisco. 1857. First edition. $2,500-$3,000. San Francisco, 1935. Grabhorn Press. Plates. Half cloth. One of 550. $75-$100. (See preceding entry.)

STRAUSS, David Friedrich. *The Life of Jesus.* 3 vols., blue-green cloth. London, 1846. (Translated by George Eliot [Mary Ann Evans].) First edition. $200-$300. Author's first book.

*STREAKS of Squatter Life, and Far-West Scenes.* Illustrated by F. O. C. Darley. Half calf. Philadelphia, 1847. (By John S. Robb). First edition. $150-$250.

STREETER, Edward. *Dere Mable: Love Letters of a Rookie.* Pictorial boards. New York, (1918). First edition. In dust jacket. $25-$35. Author's first book.

STREETER, Floyd Benjamin. *Prairie Trails and Cow Towns.* 12 plates. Cloth. Boston, (1936). First edition. $100-$150.

STREETER, Thomas W. See *Americana—Beginnings.*

STREETER, Thomas W. *Bibliography of Texas.* 5 vols. (Part I, 2 vols; Part II, one vol.; Part III, 2 vols.), cloth. Cambridge, Mass., 1955-56-60. First edition. One of 600. In dust jackets. $600-$750. Parts I and II, 3 vols. $300-$350. Part III, 2 vols. $200-$250.

STREETER, Thomas W. (sale). *The Celebrated Collection of Americana Formed by the Late Thomas Winthrop Streeter.* 8 vols., blue boards (including index), or blue cloth. New York, 1966-69. $400-$500. (An indispensable reference. The copies in boards, while first, are less desirable than cloth because the cheap bindings deteriorate rapidly.)

STREETT, William B. *Gentlemen Up.* Illustrated, including color. Green cloth. New York, 1930. Derrydale Press. First edition. One of 850. In dust jacket. $100-$125. Another issue: Half morocco. One of 75 signed, with a signed etching. $750-$1,000. Also, $700 (A, 1977).

STRIBLING, T. S. *The Cruise of the Dry Dock*. 4 color illustrations. Green cloth. Chicago, (1917). First edition. In dust jacket. $75-$100. Author's first book.

STRICKLAND, William. *Reports on Canals, Railways, Roads, and Other Subjects*. Plates. Oblong, boards and leather. Philadelphia, 1826. First edition. $500-$600. Also, $400 (A, 1977).

*STRICTURES on a Voyage to South America, as Indicated by the "Secretary of the (Late) Mission" to La Plata, etc*. By a Friend of Truth and Sound Policy. 108 pp., printed wrappers. Baltimore, 1820. (By H. M. Brackenridge.) $125-$150.

STRONG, L. A. G. *The Jealous Ghost*. Cloth. London, 1930. First edition. One of 75, signed. In dust jacket. $75-$100.

STRONG, Gen. W. E. *A Trip to the Yellowstone National Park in July, August, and September, 1875*. 2 folding maps, 7 signed photos, 7 plates. Half morocco. Washington, 1876. First edition. $600-$750. (Note: In some copies there are fewer than 7 signatures of the participants in this hunting trip.)

STRUTT, Joseph. *A Complete View of the Dress and Habits of the People of England*. 151 colored engravings. 2 vols., half morocco. London, 1842. $350-$450.

STRUTT, Joseph. *Glig-Gamena Angel-Deod, or The Sports and Pastimes of the English People*. 40 colored plates. Contemporary calf. London, 1801. $450-$600, possibly more. London, 1810. Second edition. $200-$250.

STUART, Granville. *Forty Years on the Frontier*. 15 plates. 2 vols., cloth. Cleveland, 1925. First edition. $125-$150.

STUART, Jesse. *Beyond Dark Hills*. Cloth. New York, 1938. First edition. In dust jacket. $100-$175.

STUART, Jesse. *Foretaste of Glory*. Cloth. New York, 1946. First edition. In dust jacket. $75-$100.

STUART, Jesse. *Harvest of Youth*. 80 pp. Howe, Okla., (1930). First edition. $1,000 and up. Author's first book.

STUART, Jesse. *Man with a Bull-Tongue Plow*. Cloth. New York, 1934. First edition. In dust jacket. $250-$350.

STUART, Jesse. *Taps for Private Tussie*. Cloth. New York, 1943. First edition. In dust jacket. $75-$125. New York, (1943). Illustrated by Thomas Hart Benton. In dust jacket. $35-$50.

STUART, Jesse. *Trees of Heaven*. Cloth. New York, 1940. First edition. In dust jacket. $100-$150.

STUART, Joseph A. *My Roving Life*. Illustrated. 2 vols., boards and cloth. Auburn, Calif., 1895. First edition. $1,000-$1,250.

STUDER, Jacob H. *The Birds of North America*. 119 colored lithographs after Jasper. Cloth, or leather. Columbus, Ohio, 1878. First edition. $100-$125. New York, 1881. $35-$50. New York, 1895. Morocco. $35-$50. New York, 1903. Cloth. $40-$50.

STURGIS, Thomas. *Common Sense View of the Sioux War*. 52 pp., wrappers. Cheyenne, 1877. First edition. $150-$200.

STYRON, William. *The Confessions of Nat Turner*. Cloth. New York, (1967). First edition. One of 500, signed. Boxed. $35-$50. Trade edition: In dust jacket. $15.

STYRON, William. *Lie Down in Darkness*. Brown cloth. Indianapolis, (1951). First edition. In dust jacket. $75-$85. Author's first book.

STYRON, William. *This Quiet Dust*. Printed blue wrappers. (New York, 1968.) First edition. $40-$50.

SUÁREZ Y Navarra, Juan. *Defensa que el Licenciado José G. P. Garay Hizo ante el Juez Primero de lo Civil, Don Gayetano Ibarra, etc.* 64 pp., sewed. Mexico, 1849. $300-$350.

SUGDEN, Alan V. *A History of English Wallpaper, 1509-1914.* 70 color plates and 190 halftone illustrations. Folio, blue buckram. New York, (1925). First edition. In dust jacket. Boxed. $250-$350.

SULLIVAN, Frank. *The Life and Times of Martha Heppelthwaite.* Yellow cloth. New York, 1926. First edition. In dust jacket. $30-$40. Author's first book.

SULLIVAN, Louis H. *A System of Architectural Ornament.* Illustrated. Folio, half cloth. New York, 1924. First edition. One of 1,000. $300-$400.

SULLIVAN, Maurice S. *The Travels of Jedediah Smith.* Map, 12 plates. Pictorial cloth. Santa Ana, Calif., 1934. First edition. $150-$200.

SULLIVAN, W. John L. *Twelve Years in the Saddle for Law and Order on the Frontiers of Texas.* 13 plates. Cloth. Austin, 1909. First edition. $100-$200.

SULZBERGER, Cyrus. *The Resistentialists.* Cloth. New York, (1962). First edition. In dust jacket. $200-$250. (Suppressed.)

SUMMERFIELD, Charles. *The Rangers and Regulators of the Tanaha.* Frontispiece, plates. Cloth. New York, (1956). (By Alfred W. Arrington.) First edition. $65-$85.

SUNDERLAND, LaRoy. *Mormonism Exposed and Refuted.* 54 pp., printed wrappers. New York, 1838. First edition. $1,500-$2,000.

*SUNDRY Documents Referring to the Niagara and Detroit River Railroad.* 8 pp., wrappers. (Albany?, 1845.) (By W. H. Merritt.) $75-$100.

*SUPERIOR Court of the City and County of San Francisco (In the ) . . . Sarah Althea Sharon, Plaintiff, vs. William Sharon, Defendant.* Half morocco. San Francisco, (about 1884). $100-$150.

*SUPERNATURALISM of New England (The).* Printed wrappers. New York, 1847. (By John Greenleaf Whittier—his name on cover but not on title page.) First edition. $200-$250.

SURTEES, Robert Smith. See *"Ask Mamma"; The Analysis of the Hunting Field; Handley Cross; Hawbuck Grange; Mr. Facey Romford's Hounds; Mr. Sponge's Sporting Tour; Jorrocks' Jaunts and Jollities; "Plain or Ringlets?"*

SUTHERLAND, Thomas A. *Howard's Campaign Against the Nez Perce Indians.* 48 pp., wrappers. Portland, Ore., 1878. First edition. $750-$1,000.

SUTRO, Adolph. *The Mineral Resources of the United States.* Folding map, plates. Cloth. Baltimore, 1868. First edition. $100-$125.

SUTRO, Adolph. *The Sutro Tunnel and Railway to the Comstock Lode in Nevada.* 2 folding maps. 37 pp., printed wrappers. London, 1873. $100-$125.

SUTTER, Johann August. *Diary of Johann August Sutter.* Edited by Douglas S. Watson. 3 colored plates, 3 facsimiles. Boards. San Francisco, 1932. First edition. One of 500. $75-$100.

SUTTER, Johann August. *New Helvetia Diary.* 2 color plates, facsimile, map. Half cloth. San Francisco, 1939. Grabhorn Press. One of 950. $75-$100.

SUTTON, J. J. *History of the 2nd Regiment, West Virginia Cavalry Volunteers.* Cloth. Portsmouth, Ohio, 1892. $100-$125.

SWADOS, Harvey. *Out Went the Candle.* Cloth. New York, 1955. First edition. In dust jacket. $50-$60. Author's first book.

*SWALLOW BARN, or A Sojourn in the Old Dominion,* 2 vols., half cloth and boards, paper labels. Philadelphia, 1832. (By John Pendleton Kennedy.) First edition. $200-$300. Author's first book.

SWAMP Outlaws (The), or the Lowery Bandits of North Carolina. 84 pp., wrappers. New York, (1872). $125-$150.

SWAN, Alonzo M. Canton: Its Pioneers and History. Cloth. Canton, Ill., 1871. First edition. $100-$125.

SWAN, Alonzo M. Life, Trial, Conviction, Confession and Execution of John Osborn, the Murderer of Mrs. Adelia Mathews, etc. 85 pp., wrappers. Peoria, 1872. First edition. $100. Peoria, 1873. 95 pp., wrappers. Second edition. (Name of the murderer changed to John Marion Osborne.) $50 and up.

SWAN, James G. The Northwest Coast. Folding map, plates. Cloth. New York, 1857. First edition. $100-$125.

SWASEY, William F. The Early Days and Men of California. Portrait, 2 plates. Cloth. Oakland, (1891). First edition. $125-$150.

SWEET, Willis. The Carbonate Camps, Leadville and Ten-Mile, of Colorado. Maps and plates. 83 pp., pictorial wrappers. Kansas City, 1879. First edition. $250-$350. (For a similar work, see Stephen F. Smart entry.)

SWIFT, Jonathan. Gulliver's Travels. 12 color plates by Arthur Rackham. Cloth. London, 1909. One of 750 signed by Rackham. $400-$600. New York, 1929. Limited Editions Club. $60-$80. London, 1925. Golden Cockerel Press. Illustrated by David Jones. 2 vols., buckram. One of 30 signed by the artist. $1,000-$1,250. Ordinary copies: One of 450. $200-$350. London, 1930. Cresset Press. 12 colored engravings by Rex Whistler. 2 vols., morocco and boards. One of 195. In slipcase. $2,000-$3,000.

SWINBURNE, Algernon Charles. Note: So many of the books and pamphlets once attributed to Swinburne have turned out to be forgeries by Thomas J. Wise that the listing of them here would constitute a bibliographical nightmare for both compiler and reader. For this reason, I have listed here only a few of the better known items of Swinburniana.

SWINBURNE, Algernon Charles. See The Children of the Chapel.

SWINBURNE, Algernon Charles. Astrophel and Other Poems. Cloth. London, 1894. First edition, first issue, with February ads. $50-$75.

SWINBURNE, Algernon C. Atalanta in Calydon: A Tragedy. White cloth. London, 1865. First edition, with only 111 pages. $600-$800, possibly more. London, 1894. Kelmscott Press. Woodcut title, initials, etc. Vellum, silk ties. One of 250. $500-$600. London, 1923. Medical Society. Boards. $25.

SWINBURNE, Algernon Charles. Border Ballads. Edited by Thomas J. Wise. Facsimiles of manuscripts. Half vellum. Boston, 1912. Bibliophile Society. One of 477. $25-$30.

SWINBURNE, Algernon Charles. Chastelard: A Tragedy. Cloth. London, 1865. First edition, first issue, Moxon imprint and November ads. $100-$135. London, 1878. Second edition. $20-$25.

SWINBURNE, Algernon Charles. Erechtheus: A Tragedy. Cloth. London, 1876. First edition. $75-$85.

SWINBURNE, Algernon Charles. The Jubilee. Wrappers. London, 1887. First edition. One of 25 printed on paper. $150-$250.

SWINBURNE, Algernon Charles. Laus Veneris. Illustrated. Cloth. London, 1948. Golden Cockerel Press. One of 650. $75-$125. Another issue: One of 100 specially bound. $200-$300.

SWINBURNE, Algernon Charles. Lucretia Borgia. Illustrated. Full leather. (London), 1942. Golden Cockerel Press. One of 30 specially bound with manuscript facsimile. $300. Another issue: One of 320. $150.

SWINBURNE, Algernon Charles. *Marino Faliero, A Tragedy.* Green cloth. London, 1885. First edition, with 32 pages of ads. $50-$60.

SWINBURNE, Algernon Charles. *Pasiphae: A Poem.* Illustrated. Buckram. (London, 1950.) Golden Cockerel Press. One of 500. $35-$50. Another issue: Vellum. One of 100 specially bound. $200-$250.

SWINBURNE, Algernon Charles. *Poems and Ballads.* Cloth. London, 1866. First edition, first issue, with E. Moxon imprint. $300-$350. Second issue with J. C. Hotten imprint. $150-$250. London, 1889. Cloth. $15.

SWINBURNE, Algernon Charles. *Poetical Fragments.* Wrappers. London, 1916. One of 25, signed by Clement Shorter. $75-$125.

SWINBURNE, Algernon Charles. *The Queen-Mother. Rosamond. Two Plays.* Slate-gray cloth, white spine label. London, 1860. First edition, first issue, with "A. G. Swinburne" on spine. $200-$300. Author's first book.

SWINBURNE, Algernon Charles. *Rosamond, Queen of the Lombards.* Boards. London, 1899. First edition. $50-$60.

SWINBURNE, Algernon Charles. *A Song of Italy.* Boards, green cloth, purple end papers. London, 1867. First edition, with 24 pages of ads at beginning and end. $100-$150. Portland, Me., 1904. Mosher Press. One of 10 on vellum. $150-$200.

SWINBURNE, Algernon Charles. *Songs Before Sunrise.* Blue-green cloth. London, 1871. First edition. $75-$100. Large paper issue: Morocco. One of 25. $500-$600. Portland, 1901. Mosher Press. One of 4 on vellum. $300. London, 1909. Florence Press. Levant morocco extra. One of 12 on vellum. $750-$1,000. Another issue: vellum. One of 600. $200-$225.

SWINBURNE, Algernon Charles. *The Springtide of Life: Poems of Childhood.* 9 color plates, numerous text illustrations by Arthur Rackham. Half vellum. London, 1918. One of 765 signed by Rackham. $500-$600. Trade edition: Cloth. $100-$125.

SWINBURNE, Algernon Charles. *Under the Microscope.* Wrappers. London, 1872. First edition, with suppressed leaf laid in. $250-$550.

SWINBURNE, Algernon Charles. *William Blake: A Critical Essay.* Illustrated. Cloth. London, 1868. First edition, first issue, with the word "Zamiel" below woodcut on title page. $100-$150.

SWISHER, James. *How I Know.* Plates. Cloth. Cincinnati, 1880. First edition. $100-$125. Cincinnati, 1881. Second edition. $75-$100.

*SWISS Family Robinson (The).* 2 vols., boards. New York, 1832. (By Johann David Wyss.) First American edition. $300-$500. New York, 1963. Limited Editions Club. $40-$50.

SYDENHAM, Thomas. *The Works of Thomas Sydenham, M.D.* Calf. Philadelphia, 1809. First American edition. $200-$300.

SYMONDS, John Addington. *Animi Figura.* Cloth. London, 1882. First edition. $35-$50.

SYMONDS, John Addington. *The Escorial: A Prize Poem.* Wrappers. Oxford, 1860. First edition. $150-$250. Author's first book.

SYMONDS, John Addington. *Essays Speculative and Suggestive.* 2 vols., cloth. London, 1890. First edition. $75-$85.

SYMONDS, John Addington. *In the Key of Blue and Other Prose Essays.* Light-blue or cream cloth. London, 1893. First edition, with 15 pages of ads at end. $75-$125. (The blue cloth binding is scarce.) Another issue: Vellum. One of 50 on large paper. $250-$350.

SYMONDS, John Addington. *The Life of Michael Angelo Buonarotti.* 2 vols., cloth. London, 1893. First edition. $50-$75.

SYMONDS, John Addington. *The Renaissance.* Wrappers. Oxford, 1863. First edition. $100-$125.

SYMONDS, John Addington. *Renaissance in Italy.* 7 vols., cloth. London, 1880-86. (First issue copies of *The Age of Despots, The Revival of Learning,* and *The Fine Arts* without stars on spines.) $250-$350.

SYMONDS, John Addington. *The Sonnets of Michael Angelo Buonarroti and Tommaso Campanella.* Translated into rhymed English. Dark blue cloth. London, 1878. First edition. $50-$75.

SYMONDS, John Addington. *Wine, Women and Song: Mediaeval Latin Students' Songs.* Cloth. London, 1884. First edition. $40-$50. Another issue: Vellum. One of 50 on large paper. $100-$125.

SYMONDS, John Addington. *Walt Whitman: A Study.* 5 plates. Cloth. London, 1893. First edition. $75-$100.

SYMONDS, Mary, and Preece, Louisa. *Needlework Through the Ages.* 8 color plates, 96 other plates. Half vellum. London, 1928. $350-$400.

SYMONS, A. J. A. *Aubrey Beardsley.* Cloth. London, 1898. First edition. $75. Another issue: One of 150 on large paper. $100-$135.

SYMONS, A. J. A. *The Quest for Corvo.* Black cloth. London, (1934). First edition. In dust jacket. $100.

SYMONS, Arthur. *An Introduction to the Study of Browning.* Green cloth. London, 1886. First edition. $75. Author's first book.

SYMONS, Arthur. *Silhouettes.* London, 1892. Gray boards. First edition. One of 250. $50-$60. Another issue: One of 25 on large paper, signed. $100-$150.

SYNGE, John M. *The Aran Islands.* Drawings. Cloth. Dublin, 1906. First edition. In dust jacket. $200-$300. Dublin, 1907. Illustrated by Jack B. Yeats. $100-$125. Another issue: One of 150 on large paper, signed by Synge and Yeats. $400-$600.

SYNGE, John M. *Deirdre of the Sorrows: A Play.* Preface by W. B. Yeats. Boards, linen spine. Dundrum, Ireland, 1910. Cuala Press. First edition. One of 250. $150-$200. New York, 1910. Boards and cloth. One of 50. $600-$750. (All except five on vellum and five on handmade paper were reported destroyed by the publisher, John Quinn).

SYNGE, John M. *A Few Personal Recollections, with Biographical Notes by John Masefield.* Cloth. Dundrum, 1913. Cuala Press. First edition. One of 350. $85-$125.

SYNGE, John M. *In the Shadow of the Glen.* Pale-gray printed wrappers. New York, 1904. First edition. One of 50 published for copyright purposes. $1,000-$2,000. Also, $900 (A, 1977). Author's first book. (For first English edition, see *The Shadow of the Glen.)*

SYNGE, John M. *The Playboy of the Western World.* Portrait. Cloth. Dublin, 1907. First edition. $150-$200. Another issue: White linen. One of 25 on handmade paper. $500-$600.

SYNGE, John M. *Poems and Translations.* Blue boards, tan linen spine, paper label. Dundrum, 1909. Cuala Press. One of 250. $100-$125. New York, 1909. Boards and cloth. One of 50. $100-$125.

SYNGE, John M. *The Shadow of the Glen. Riders to the Sea.* Printed green wrappers. London, 1905. First English edition. $75-$125. (For first edition, see *In the Shadow of the Glen.)* Synge's first commercially published book.

SYNGE, John M. *The Tinker's Wedding.* Rust-colored cloth, beige spine. Dublin, 1907. First edition. In dust jacket. $150-$200.

SYNGE, John M. *The Well of the Saints.* Wrappers. London, 1905. First edition, first issue. $150-$200. London, 1905. Boards and cloth. Second issue, with introduction by William Butler Yeats. $50-$100. New York, 1905. One of 50. First American edition. $100-$125.

SYNGE, John M. *The Works of John Millington Synge.* Portraits. 4 vols., cloth. Dublin, 1910. First edition. $200-$225. Boston, 1912. 4 vols., cloth. $100-$125.

SYNTAX, Doctor. *Doctor Syntax in Paris.* 18 colored plates by Williams. Boards. London, 1820. (By William Combe?) First edition. $400-$500.

SYNTAX, Doctor. *The Life of Napoleon: A Hudibrastic Poem in 15 Cantos.* 30 color plates by George Cruikshank. Boards. London, 1815. (By William Combe.) First edition. $500-$750.

SYNTAX, Doctor. *The Tour of Doctor Syntax Through London.* 19 colored plates. 8 parts, wrappers. London, 1820. (Sometimes attributed to William Combe, but not by him, says De Ricci.) First edition. $1,000 and up. London, 1820. Boards. First book edition. $250-$350.

SYNTAX, Doctor. *The Tours* . . . (1st, 2d, and 3d.) (By William Combe.) *The Tour of Doctor Syntax in Search of the Picturesque.* Frontispiece, title page, and 29 colored plates by Thomas Rowlandson. Boards. London, 1812. First edition. *The Tour of Doctor Syntax in Search of Consolation.* 24 colored plates by Rowlandson. Boards. London, 1820. First edition. *The Tour of Doctor Syntax in Search of a Wife.* 24 colored plates by Rowlandson. Boards. London, (1821-22). First edition. Copies in original boards are rare, few having been at public sale since the 1940's. Estimated value today: $5,000 and up. Copies in bindings: $1,000-$2,000 and up. Many later editions and mixed sets at lower prices show the continuing popularity of the series. They include the 3-vol. *Tours of Doctor Syntax.* 80 color plates by Rowlandson. Pink boards, paper labels, uncut. London, 1823. First miniature edition, with printed title issued in Vol. 2 only. $100-$300.

*SYRACUSE Poems, 1963-1969.* Edited by George P. Elliott. Cloth. Syracuse, (1970). First edition. In dust jacket. $25 and up. (Contains poems by W. D. Snodgrass and others. Some copies signed by contributors: $40-$50.)

SZYK, Arthur (artist). *Ink and Blood: A Book of Drawings.* Text by Struthers Burt. 74 plates. Morocco. New York, 1946. First edition. One of 1,000 signed by Szyk. Boxed. $175-$200

# T

TABB, John Banister. *Lyrics.* Boards. Boston, 1897. First edition. One of 5 on china paper. $100 and up. Other issues: One of 50 on handmade paper. $35-$50. One of 500. $10-$15.

TABB, John Banister. *Poems.* Cloth. (Baltimore, 1882.) First edition. $35-$50. Author's first book.

TABULA. Vol. XXII, No. 3. Pictorial wrappers. Oak Park, Ill., April, 1916. (Includes Ernest Hemingway's story "A Matter of Colour.") $750-$1,000. Also, covers stained, $750 (A, 1977). Vol. XXIII, No. 3. Decorated wrappers. Oak Park, March, 1917. (Includes three Hemingway poems.) $750-$1,000. Also, spine chipped, $650 (A, 1977).

TACITUS, C. Cornelius. *De Vita et Moribus Julii Agricolae Liber.* Vellum. London, 1900. Doves Press. One of 225. $200-$300. In special morocco binding by the Doves Bindery. $1,000-$1,500. First book printed at the Doves Press.

TAFT, Robert. *Artists and Illustrators of the Old West.* Illustrated. Cloth. New York, 1953. First edition. In dust jacket. $50-$60. Later, in dust jacket. $10.

TAFT, Robert. *Photography and the American Scene: A Social History, 1839-89.* Cloth. New York, 1938. First edition. In dust jacket. $100-$150. New York, 1942. Cloth. In dust jacket. $50-$75.

TAGGARD, Genevieve. *For Eager Lovers.* Boards, paper labels, New York, 1922. First edition. In dust jacket. $75-$100. Author's first book.

TAGGARD, Genevieve. *The Life and Mind of Emily Dickinson.* Boards. New York, 1930. First edition. One of 200 uncut copies. $75-$100. Ordinary copies: $30-$40.

TAGGARD, Genevieve (editor). *May Days: An Anthology of Masses-Liberator Verse, 1912-1924.* Cloth. New York, 1925. First edition. In dust jacket. $40-$50.

TAGORE, Rabindranath. *The Post Office: A Play.* Preface by William Butler Yeats. Boards and cloth. Dundrum, Ireland, 1914. Cuala Press. One of 400. $60-$85. New York, 1914. Blue cloth. First American edition. $30-$40.

TALBOT, Theodore. *The Journals of Theodore Talbot.* Edited by Charles H. Carey. Cloth. Portland, Me., 1931. First edition. $45-$60.

TALES of the Northwest; or, Sketches of Indian Life and Character. By a Resident from Beyond the Frontier. Boards. Boston, 1830. (By William J. Snelling.) First edition. $350-$400. Author's first book.

TALES of Terror; with an Introductory Dialogue. Engraved half title. Wrappers. London, 1801. (By Matthew G. Lewis.) First edition. $150-$200. London, 1808. Half leather. Second edition. $75-$100.

TALES of Travels West of the Mississippi. Map. Illustrated. Boards and cloth. Boston, 1830. (By William J. Snelling.) First edition. $350-$400.

TALLAHASSEE Girl (A). Cloth. Boston, 1882. (By Maurice Thompson.) First edition. $75-$100.

TALLAPOOSA Land, Mining and Manufacturing Co., Haralson County. Map. 32 pp., wrappers. Tallapoosa, Ga., 1887. $100-$125.

TALLENT, Annie D. *The Black Hills; or The Last Hunting Grounds of the Dakotahs.* 50 plates. Cloth, or half leather. St. Louis, 1899. First edition. Either binding: $100-$150.

*TAMERLANE and Other Poems.* By a Bostonian. Printed wrappers. Boston, 1827. (By Edgar Allan Poe.) First edition. $100,000 and up. Also, a copy described as "the finest known" brought $123,000 at auction in New York in 1974. (Note: Exact facsimiles exist which require careful examination to distinguish from the original.) London, 1884. Vellum. One of 100. $100-$150. San Francisco, 1923. 2 vols., boards (folio plus a smaller facsimile volume). One of 150. $200-$300.

TANNER, Henry S. *A Brief Description of the Canals and Railroads of the United States.* Maps. 31 pp., cloth. Philadelphia, 1834. First edition. $150-$200. Second edition, same place and date. 63 pp., 2 plates, map. $75-$100. New York, 1840. Enlarged edition. (*A Description, etc.*) 3 maps, 2 diagrams, 272 pp. $250-$300.

TANNER, Henry S. *A New American Atlas.* 16 double-page and 2 large folding maps. Folio, half leather. Philadelphia, 1823. First edition. $1,500-$2,000.

TARASCON, Louis A. *An Address to the Citizens of Philadelphia, on the Great Advantages Which Arise from the Trade of the Western Country, etc.* 13 pp., wrappers. Philadelphia, 1806. First edition. $750-$1,000.

TARASCON, Louis A., and others. *Petition . . . Praying the Opening of a Wagon Road from the River Missouri, North of the River Kansas, to the River Columbia.* 12 pp., sewed. Washington, 1824. $150-$200.

TARBELL, Ida M. *The History of the Standard Oil Company.* Illustrated. 2 vols., cloth. New York, 1904. First edition. $100-$125.

*TARCISSUS: The Boy Martyr of Rome, in the Diocletian Persecution, A.D. CCCIII.* (By Baron Corvo [Frederick William Rolfe]). 4 leaves, printed gray wrappers. (Saffron Walden, Essex, England, 1880—actually 1881.) First edition. $2,000-$2,500, possibly more. Also, stained, $1,700 (A, 1977); $2,375 (A, 1971)—a record price. Author's first book.

TARG, William (editor). *Carrousel for Bibliophiles.* Red cloth. New York, 1947. First edition. In dust jacket. $35-$50.

TARG, William (editor). *Bibliophile in the Nursery.* Illustrated. Cloth. Cleveland, (1957). First edition. In dust jacket. $40-$60.

TARKINGTON, Booth. *Christmas This Year.* Manuscript facsimile and full-page plate. Wrappers. (Los Angeles, 1945.) First edition. One of 52. $40-$50.

TARKINGTON, Booth. *The Fascinating Stranger and Other Stories.* Boards. Garden City, 1923. First edition. One of 377, signed. In dust jacket. $25-$35. Trade edition: $10.

TARKINGTON, Booth. *The Gentleman from Indiana.* Pictorial green cloth, top stained green. New York, 1899. First edition, first issue, with "eye" as last word in line 12, page 245; with line 16 reading "so pretty". $150-$200. Author's first published book.

TARKINGTON, Booth. *Lady Hamilton and Her Nelson.* Cloth. New York, 1945. First edition. One of 300, signed. In dust jacket. $85-$100.

TARKINGTON, Booth. *Monsieur Beaucaire.* Illustrated. Red cloth, gilt top. New York, 1900. First edition, first issue, with Gilliss Press seal on page after end of text exactly 1/2 inch in diameter. $100-$125.

TARKINGTON, Booth. *Penrod.* Illustrated by Gordon Grant. Cloth: first, blue mesh; second, blue ribbed cloth. Garden City, 1914. First edition, first state, with page viii so numbered and with "sence" for "sense" in third line from bottom of page 19. In dust jacket. $500-$1,000. Also, $950 (A, 1977).

TARKINGTON, Booth. *Penrod and Sam.* Illustrated by Worth Brehm. Pictorial light-green cloth. Garden City, 1916. First edition, first issue, with perfect type on pages 86, 141, 144, 149, and 210. In dust jacket. $100-$150. Lacking jacket, $50-$60.

TARKINGTON, Booth. *Seventeen.* Cloth or leather. New York, (1916). First edition, first issue, with letters "B-Q" beneath copyright notice. In dust jacket. $100-$125. Lacking jacket, $50-$60.

TARKINGTON, Booth. *The Two Vanrevels*. Cloth. New York, 1902. First edition. In dust jacket. $60-$80. Lacking jacket, $20. Another issue (later): White boards. One of 500, signed. 40-$60. Another issue: Brown boards (also with first edition notice). One of 500, signed. $40-$60. Some from this issue lacking first edition notice, $20-$25.

TARRANT, Sgt. E. *The Wild Riders of the 1st Kentucky Cavalry*. Cloth. Louisville, (1894). $175-$200.

TATE, Allen. *Jefferson Davis, His Rise and Fall*. Cloth, paper label. New York, 1929. First edition. In dust jacket. $50-$65.

TATE, Allen. *The Mediterranean and Other Poems*. Wrappers. New York, 1936. First edition. One of 165 on Strathmore all-rag paper, signed. Boxed. $300-$500. Another issue: Cloth. Signed but not numbered. $200-$300.

TATE, Allen. *Mr. Pope and Other Poems*. Cloth, paper labels. New York, 1928. First edition. In dust jacket. $200-$300.

TATE, Allen. *On the Limits of Poetry*. Cloth. New York, 1948. First edition. In dust jacket. $40-$60.

TATE, Allen. *Poems, 1928-1931*. Cloth. New York, 1932. First edition, with "A" on copyright page. In cellophane dust jacket with printed flaps. $60-$80.

TATE, Allen. *Reason in Madness*. Green cloth. New York, 1941. First edition. In dust jacket. $50-$60.

TATE, Allen. *Stonewall Jackson, the Good Soldier: A Narrative*. Cloth, paper labels. New York, 1928. First edition. In dust jacket. $50-$75. Author's first separate book.

TATE, Allen. *Two Conceits for the Eye to Sing, If Possible*. Wrappers, paper label. Cummington, Mass., 1950. First edition. One of 300. $50-$60.

TATE, Allen. *The Winter Sea: A Book of Poems*. Decorated cloth. Cummington, 1944. First edition. One of 300. In dust jacket. $75-$100.

TATE, James. *Cages*. Wrappers. Iowa City, 1966. First edition. One of 45, $50-$60. Author's first book.

TATE, James. *Hottentot Ossuary*. Cloth. Cambridge, Mass., 1974. First edition. One of 50, signed. In dust jacket. $30-$40.

TATTERSALL, C. E. C. *A History of British Carpets*. 116 plates (55 in color). Buckram. London, (1934). First edition. $150-$250.

TATTERSALL, George. *The Pictorial Gallery of English Race Horses*. 90 plates. Cloth. London, 1850. First edition. $750-$1,000.

TAUNTON, Thomas Henry. *Portraits of Celebrated Racehorses*. 463 plates. 4 vols., half morocco. London, 1887-88. First edition. $750-$1,000.

TAYLOR, Bayard. *Eldorado, or, Adventures in the Path of Empire, etc*. 8 lithograph views. 2 vols., cloth. New York, 1850. First edition, with list of illustrations in Vol. 2 giving Mazatlan at page 8 instead of page 80. $400-$500. New York, 1850. 2 vols., cloth. Second edition, with Mazatlan reference corrected. $200-$300. New York, 1850. 2 vols. in one, cloth, no plates. $75-$100. London, 1850. 2 vols., cloth. First English edition. $150-$200.

TAYLOR, Bayard. *Ximena and Other Poems*. Boards. Philadelphia, 1844. First edition. $75-$100. Author's first book.

TAYLOR, F. *A Sketch of the Military Bounty Tract of Illinois*. 12 pp., boards and calf. Philadelphia, 1839. First edition. $175-$200.

TAYLOR, F. W. *The Principles of Scientific Management*. 118 pp., green cloth. New York, 1911. First edition. $750-$1,000. Later, enlarged issue, red cloth. $200-$250.

TAYLOR, James W. *Northwest British America and Its Relations to the State of Minnesota.* Map. Cloth. St. Paul, 1860. First edition. $1,250-$1,500.

TAYLOR, James W. *The Sioux War.* Wrappers. St. Paul, 1862. First edition. $850. St. Paul, 1863. Second edition. $400-$500.

TAYLOR, Jane and Ann. *Little Ann and Other Poems.* Illustrated in color by Kate Greenaway. Pictorial boards and cloth. (London, about 1883-84.) Published by Warne. $225-$300.

TAYLOR, John W. *Iowa, the "Great Hunting Ground" of the Indian; and the "Beautiful Land" of the White Man.* 16 pp., printed wrappers. Dubuque, 1860. First edition. $250-$300.

TAYLOR, Joseph Henry. *Beavers—Their Ways and Other Sketches.* 20 plates. Cloth. Washburn, N. D., 1904. First edition. $85-$100.

TAYLOR, Joseph Henry. *Sketches of Frontier and Indian Life.* 12 plates. Half leather and boards. Pottstown, Pa., 1889. First edition. $300-$400.

TAYLOR, Joseph Henry. *Twenty Years on the Trap Line.* 8 plates. 154 pp., boards and calf. Bismarck, N. D., 1891. First edition. $200-$225. Second edition, same place and date. 173 pp., maroon cloth. $100-$150.

TAYLOR, Lee M. *The Texan; A Tale of Texas.* Cloth. (Texas), 1908. With pages 171-174 removed (as in all copies noted). $50-$75.

TAYLOR, Oliver I. *Directory of Wheeling and Ohio County.* 2 plates, including tinted frontispiece. Half leather. Wheeling, W. Va., 1851. First edition. $100-$150.

TAYLOR, Peter. *A Long Fourth and Other Stories.* Cloth. New York, (1948). First edition. In dust jacket. $40-$50. Author's first book.

TAYLOR, Philip Meadows. *Confessions of a Thug.* 3 vols., boards. London, 1839. First edition. $400-$500. Author's first book.

TAYLOR, Thomas U. *Fifty Years on Forty Acres.* Illustrated. Cloth. Austin (?), 1938. First edition. $50-$100.

TAYLOR, Thomas U. *Jesse Chisholm.* Illustrated. Cloth. Bandera, Tex., (1939). First edition. $75-$150.

TAYLOR and Tallmadge. *The Bill to Authorize the People of Missouri to Form a Constitution and State Government.* 16 pp., sewed. No place, (1819). $150-$200.

TAYLOR, Zachary. *Letters of Zachary Taylor from the Battle-Fields of the Mexican War.* Half cloth. Rochester, 1908. One of 300. $75-$100.

TEASDALE, Sara. *Love Songs.* Cloth. New York, 1917. First edition. In dust jacket. $50-$60.

TEASDALE, Sara. *Sonnets to Duse and Other Poems.* Boards, paper labels. Boston, 1907. First edition. $150-$175. Author's first book.

TEASDALE, Sara. *Stars To-Night.* Illustrated by Dorothy P. Lathrop. Cloth. New York, 1930. First edition. One of 150, signed. In dust jacket. $75-$100.

*TEHAUNTEPEC Railway: Its Location Features and Advantages Under the LaSere Grant of 1869.* Folding map. Cloth. New York, 1869. $100-$125.

*TEMPLAR (The). To Which Is Added "Tales of the Passaic."* By a Gentleman of New York. Half calf. Hackensack, N.J., 1822. First edition. $150-$250.

*TEN Poets.* Oblong, decorated wrappers. (Seattle, 1962.) First edition. One of 37 (of an edition of 537) specially bound and signed by the ten poets, including Theodore Roethke. $50-$75.

*TEN Thousand a-Year.* 6 vols., boards, paper labels. Philadelphia, 1840-41. (By Samuel

Warren.) First edition, first issue, without volume number on title page of Vol. 1. $300-$400. Second issue, with volume number on title page of first volume. $150-$200. Edinburgh, 1841. 3 vols., dark brown or plum-colored cloth. First English edition. $150-$200.

TENNYSON, Alfred, Lord. See *Helen's Tower; In Memoriam; Poems by Two Brothers.*

TENNYSON, Alfred, Lord. *Carmen Saeculare; An Ode in Honour of the Jubilee of Queen Victoria.* Wrappers. London, 1887 (actually about 1895). $150-$250. (A suspected Thomas J. Wise forgery.)

TENNYSON, Alfred, Lord. *Enoch Arden.* Green cloth. London, 1864. First edition, first issue, with ads dated August, 1864. $150-$200. Boston, 1864. Brown cloth. First American edition. $50-$75.

TENNYSON, Alfred, Lord. *Idylls of the King.* Green cloth. London, 1859. First edition, first issue, with verso of title page a blank. $100-$150. London, 1868. Illustrations after Gustave Doré. Folio, cloth. $100-$150. New York, 1952. Limited Editions Club. Illustrated by Lynd Ward. Boxed. $50-$60.

TENNYSON, Alfred, Lord. *Maud, and Other Poems.* Green cloth. London, 1855. First edition, with yellow end papers and 8 pages of ads dated July, 1855, and a last leaf advertising Tennyson's books. $75-$150. (Note: Contains first printing of "The Charge of the Light Brigade.") London, 1893. Kelmscott Press. One of 500. $300-$400. London, 1905. Essex House. One of 125 on vellum. $300-$400.

TENNYSON, Alfred, Lord. *Poems.* Boards, white spine label. London, 1833 (actually 1832). First edition. $400-$500. London, 1842. 2 vols., boards. $500-$750. London, 1857. Cloth. First illustrated edition. $300-$400. London, 1889. Illustrated by Lear. Folio, half morocco. One of 100 proof copies on Japan paper, signed by Tennyson. $500-$750.

TENNYSON, Alfred, Lord. *Poems, Chiefly Lyrical.* Drab or pink boards, white spine label. London, 1830. First edition, first issue, with page 91 misnumbered 19. $400-$500. Author's first separate book of poems.

TENNYSON, Alfred, Lord. *Poems MDCCCXXX. MDCCCXXXIII.* Printed blue wrappers. (London), 1862. Pirated edition. $400-$500. Also, $180 (A, 1972).

TENNYSON, Alfred, Lord. *The Sailor Boy.* Cream-colored printed wrappers. London, 1861. First edition. $200-$250. (A Wise forgery.)

TENNYSON, Alfred, Lord. *Seven Poems and Two Translations.* Vellum. London, 1902. Doves Press. One of 325. $400-$600. Another issue: One of 25 on vellum. Boxed. $1,500-$2,000, possibly more.

TENNYSON, Alfred, Lord. *Tiresias and Other Poems.* Cloth. London, 1885. First edition. $75-$150. Northampton, Mass., no date. Engraved title page, 5 etchings, one in color, by Leonard Baskin. One of 150, signed. Boxed. $250-$350.

TENNYSON, Charles. *Sonnets and Fugitive Pieces.* Boards, or cloth. Cambridge, 1830. First edition. $100-$125.

TENNYSON, Frederick. *Days and Hours.* Cloth. London, 1854. First edition. $50-$60. Author's first book.

TENNYSON, Frederick. *Poems of the Day and Year.* Frontispiece portrait, woodcut title page. Red cloth. London, 1895. First edition. $40-$50.

TERHUNE, Albert Payson. *Caleb Conover, Railroader.* Cloth. New York, 1907. First edition. In dust jacket. $50-$60. Author's first book.

TERHUNE, Albert Payson. *Lad of Sunnybank.* Cloth. New York, 1929. First edition. In dust jacket. $35-$50.

*TERRITORY of Wyoming (The); Its History, Soil, Climate, Resources, etc.* 84 pp., printed wrappers. Laramie City, Wyoming Territory, 1874. (By J. K. Jeffrey.) First edition. $500-$750.

*TEXAS Almanac (The)*. Wrappers. Galveston, 1857. (First of this series.) $1,000. Other issues: 1859, $750; 1860, $750; 1861, $750; 1867, $350; 1868, $300; 1870, $250.

*TEXAS, the Home for the Emigrant from Everywhere*. Folding map. 43 pp., printed wrappers. Houston, 1875. (By J. B. Robertson.) First edition. $150-$200. St. Louis, 1876. $75-$100.

THACHER, J. B. *Christopher Columbus*. Plates. 3 vols., half vellum. New York, 1903-04. $200-$225. Another issue; 3 vols in 6, plus portfolio of facsimiles of published accounts of the voyages of Columbus. $300-$500.

THACHER, James. *Observations on Hydrophobia*. Hand-colored plate. Full leather. Plymouth, Mass., 1812. First edition. $200-$250.

THACKERAY, William Makepeace. See Marvy, Louis; Pendennis, Arthur; Titmarsh, M. A.; Wagstaff, Theophile. Also see *King Glumpus; The Yellowplush Correspondence; The Loving Ballad of Lord Bateman; The History of Henry Esmond*.

THACKERAY, William Makepeace. *The Adventures of Philip on His Way Through the World*. 3 vols., brown cloth. London, 1862. First edition. $150-$250.

THACKERAY, William Makepeace. *The Book of Snobs*. Illustrated by the author. Green pictorial wrappers. London, 1848. First edition, first issue, with page 126 misnumbered 124. $150-$200. New York, 1852. Cloth. First American edition. $75-$100.

THACKERAY, William Makepeace. *The English Humourists of the Eighteenth Century*. Blue marbled cloth. London, 1853. First edition, first or second issues. $100-$150. New York, 1853. First American edition. $50-$75.

THACKERAY, William Makepeace. *The Four Georges*. Illustrated. Cloth. New York, 1860. First edition. $125-$175. London, 1861. First English edition, first issue, with November ads and with title page reading "Sketches of Manners, Morals, Court, and Town Life." $125-$175.

THACKERAY. William Makepeace. *The Great Hoggarty Diamond*. Vignette on title page. Cloth. New York, (1848). First edition, first issue, with "82 Cliff Street" on title page (later "306 Pearl Street"). $100-$150.

THACKERAY, William Makepeace. *The History of Pendennis*. 46 full-page plates and other illustrations by the author. 24 parts in 23, printed yellow wrappers. London, 1848-50. First edition. $300-$500. London, 1849-50. 2 vols., cloth. First book edition. $200-$250. New York, 1855. Illustrated. 2 vols., black cloth. First American edition, $100-$150.

THACKERAY, William Makepeace. *The Orphan of Pimlico, and Other Sketches*. Illustrated by Thackeray. Boards. London, 1876. First edition. $200-$500. (Note: There is much hairsplitting over the various states of the plates, and this picayunishness affects prices on this item.)

THACKERAY, William Makepeace. *Vanity Fair: A Novel Without a Hero*. Illustrated by the author. 20 parts in 19, yellow pictorial wrappers. London, 1847-48. First edition, first issue, with the heading in rustic type on page 1, woodcut of the Marquis of Steyne on page 336 (later omitted), and the reading "Mr. Pitt" on page 453 (later "Sir Pitt"). $3,000 and up. (As with most nineteenth century books issued in parts, there are complicated bibliographical "points" in identifying issues and states of the edition. Perfect sets, with all "correct" points and required advertisements, are extremely rare, and most sets offered for sale are in one way or other defective or in mixed states. Thus the price range is wide and scarcely predictable.) London, 1848. Cloth. First book edition, first issue, with engraved title page date of 1849. $500-$750. New York, 1931. Limited Editions Club. 2 vols., boards. Boxed. $80-$100.

THACKERAY, William Makepeace. *The Virginians: A Tale of the Last Century*. 24 parts, printed yellow wrappers. London, 1857-59. First edition. $750-$1,000 and up. (See the note concerning "points" in the *Vanity Fair* entry above.) London, 1858-59. 2 vols., cloth. First book edition. $200-$250.

*THADEUS Amat and Others Against Mexico: Argument for the Defense Before the Honor-*

*able Umpire.* 50 pp., unbound. (Washington, 1876.) Original signatures, unbound, unopened. $75-$100.

THAXTER, Celia. *An Island Garden.* Illustrated by Childe Hassam. Cloth. Boston, 1894. First edition. $100-$150. London, 1894. Cloth. $100.

THAXTER, Celia. *Poems.* Brown cloth. New York, 1872. First edition. $50. Author's first book.

THAYER, William N. *The Pioneer Boy, and How He Became President.* Illustrated. Cloth. Boston, 1863. First edition. $35-$50.

THEOCRITUS. *The Idylls.* Translated by Andrew Lang. 20 color plates after drawings by W. Russell Flint. 2 vols., vellum. London, 1922. One of 500. $300-$350. Another issue: Boards and cloth. One of 500. In dust jackets. $150-$200.

THERION, The Master. *The Book of Thoth.* 8 color plates, 78 other illustrations. Half morocco. (London), 1944. (By Aleister Crowley.) First edition. One of 200, signed. $125-$150.

*THIS Is the Preachment on Going to Church.* Vellum. East Aurora, N.Y., 1896. (By George Bernard Shaw.) First edition. One of 26 on Japan paper. $100-$125. Another issue: Half cloth. $40-$50. (Note: These are pirated items issued by Elbert Hubbard.)

THISSELL, G. W. *Crossing the Plains in '49.* 11 plates. Cloth. Oakland, 1903. First edition. $150-$175.

THOM, Adam. *A Charge Delivered to the Grand Jury of Assiniboia, 20th February, 1845.* 44 pp., printed wrappers. London, 1848. $150-$300.

THOM, Adam. *The Claims to the Oregon Territory Considered.* 44 pp., sewed. London, 1844. First edition. $175-$200.

THOMAS, David. *Travels Through the Western Country in the Summer of 1816.* Folding map. Errata slip. Boards or cloth. Auburn, N.Y., 1819. First edition. $300-$350.

THOMAS, Dylan. *Adventures in the Skin Trade.* Black cloth. London, (1955). First separate edition, first issue, with "First published in Great Britain 1955" on verso of title page. In dust jacket. $100-$125.

THOMAS, Dylan. *Adventures in the Skin Trade and Other Stories.* Gray cloth. (New York or Norfolk, Conn., 1955.) New Directions. First edition. In dust jacket. $60-$75.

THOMAS, Dylan. *Caseg Broadsheet No. 5. From in Memory of Ann Jones.* (Caption title.) One sheet, quarto, printed one side only. Llanllechid (Llandyssul, South Wales), (1942). First edition. One of 500. $150-$200.

THOMAS, Dylan. *A Child's Christmas in Wales.* Pale-gray printed boards. Norfolk, (1954). First (separate) edition. (A Christmas token of New Directions, Thomas' American publisher, 1955.) In dust jacket. $75-$125.

THOMAS, Dylan. *Collected Poems 1934-1952.* Portrait. Dark-blue cloth. London, (1952). First English edition, "ordinary" issue, with "First published 1952" on verso of title page. In dust jacket. $100-$125. Proof copy, same place and date, pale-green wrappers printed in black, lacking dedication and without the poem "Paper and Sticks." 65 copies printed. $200-$300. Limited issue, same place and date: Full dark-blue morocco. One of 65, signed. $1,000-$1,250. Also, $850 (A, 1977). London, 1954. Light-brown canvas. Reader's Union edition. In dust jacket. $50. (Later issues are in finer brown cloth.)

THOMAS, Dylan. *The Collected Poems of Dylan Thomas.* Blue cloth. (New York, 1953.) New Directions. First American edition (of *Collected Poems 1934-1952*), first issue, with "daughters" misprinted "daughers" in last line on page 199. In dust jacket. $80-$100. (Note: Some first edition copies, identifiable as indicated, have dust jackets imprinted "second printing," because, as the publishers have stated in a letter to me, "we simply ran out of dust jackets.")

THOMAS, Dylan. *Conversation About Christmas.* Wrappers (6 leaves stapled, including printed covers). (New York), 1954. First separate edition. $50-$75.

THOMAS, Dylan. *Deaths and Entrances.* Orange cloth. London, (1946). First edition, with "First published 1946" on verso of title page. In dust jacket. $75-$150. (Note: Not as scarce as it once was believed to be.)

THOMAS, Dylan. *The Doctor and the Devils.* Red cloth. London, (1953). First published edition, with "First published 1953" on verso of title page. $50-$60. New Directions imprint: (New York, or Norfolk, 1953.) Red cloth, First American edition, first issue, identical with English edition except for substitution of New Directions imprint for Dent, etc. In dust jacket. $50-$60. Second issue, gray cloth, with "Second printing" on dust jacket. $20-$30. Proof copies (unpublished): London, (1947). First edition, first issue, in cork-colored wrappers, with date on verso of title page (35 printed). $350-$450. Also, with revisions in Thomas' hand, $960 (A, 1969). London, (1953). Green wrappers (97 printed). Second issue of the proofs. $200-$300.

THOMAS, Dylan. *18 Poems.* Black cloth. London, (1934). First edition, first issue, with flat spine and lacking leaf between half title and title page. In dust jacket. $350-$500. Same imprint, second issue, with rounded back and with leaf between half title and title (published 1936). In dust jacket. $150-$200. Author's first book. London, (about 1940). Second (?) edition (unrecorded by J. Alexander Rolph, *Dylan Thomas: A Bibliography*, but appearing in two binding variants in the Feinberg sale in 1968). Blue or green boards and cloth. In dust jacket. $40-$50. London, (about 1942). Fortune Press imprint. Red buckram. Rolph's second edition, with a John Banting pencil sketch laid in, $62 (A, 1971). Later issue, green boards and cloth: In dust jacket. $35-$50.

THOMAS, Dylan. *The Hand.* Colored drawing by Frederic Prokosch as frontispiece. Wrappers. Venice, Italy, 1939. One of 3 (of an edition of 10) on Arches paper. $1,500-$2,000.

THOMAS, Dylan. *In Country Sleep and Other Poems.* Green boards. (New York or Norfolk, 1952.) New Directions. First edition. With picture of Thomas attached to title page. In dust jacket. $75-$100. Limited edition, same imprint: Buff-gray cloth. One of 100, signed. In dust jacket? Boxed. $500-$750. Also, box worn, $450 (A, 1977).

THOMAS, Dylan. *The Map of Love: Verse and Prose.* Portrait frontispiece by Augustus John. Fine-grained mauve cloth, gilt, top edges purple. London, (1939). First edition, first issue (mauve cloth). In dust jacket. $150-$200. Second issue, plum-colored cloth (published 1947). Third issue, purple cloth (published 1948). Fourth issue, purple cloth, unstained top edges. (The second and third issues were 250 copies each as against 1,000 for the first issue and 500 for the fourth, according to Rolph.)

THOMAS, Dylan. *New Poems.* 32 pp., unnumbered, mauve boards, or mauve wrappers. Norfolk, (1943). First edition. Boards: $35. Wrappers: $75. (Note: This actually is a second printing, the entire first printing having been destroyed, according to Rolph.)

THOMAS, Dylan. *Portrait of the Artist as a Young Dog.* Cloth. London, (1940). First edition, first issue, with "First published 1940" on verso of title page. In dust jacket. $150-$200. Proof copy, printed wrappers. $300-$400. Also, $225 (A, 1968). Norfolk, (1940). Brick-red cloth. First American edition. In dust jacket. $50-$60. Norfolk, (1950). Yellow cloth. Second printing (so stated). $35. London, 1948. Guild Books. Wrappers. First printing. $25-$35.

THOMAS, Dylan. *A Prospect of the Sea.* Blue cloth. London, (1955). First edition, with "First published July, 1955" on verso of title page. In dust jacket. $75-$100. Proof copy (so imprinted) in wrappers, $100-$150. Second edition, same date. In dust jacket. $25-$35.

THOMAS, Dylan. *Quite Early One Morning: Broadcasts.* Portrait frontispiece. Blue cloth. London, (1954). First edition, first issue, with full stop after "sailors" at end of verse 5 on pages 3 and 11. In dust jacket. $65-$85. New Directions imprint: (New York, 1954.) Gray cloth. First American edition, first issue, without note of later impression on dust jacket. $35-$50.

THOMAS, Dylan. *Selected Writings of Dylan Thomas.* Pinkish mauve cloth. (Norfolk, 1946.) First edition, without printing number on front flap of dust jacket. In dust jacket. $50.

THOMAS, Dylan. *Twenty-five Poems.* Gray boards. London, (1936). First edition. One of 730. In dust jacket. $250-$275. Also, proof copy containing only 23 poems, $500 (A, 1976).

THOMAS, Dylan. *Twenty-six Poems*. Decorated boards, canvas spine, paper label. (New York or Norfolk, 1950.) First edition. New Directions. One of 87, signed. Boxed. $500-$750. There were also 10 copies printed on Japan vellum (2 for Thomas, the rest for New Directions, his American publisher); no copies noted for sale. London, (1949). First English edition,· identical (save for Dent imprint) with the American edition, which preceded it by three months. One of 50, signed, for the English market. Boxed. $575 (A, 1971).

THOMAS, Dylan. *Under Milk Wood*. Light-brown cloth. London, (1954). First edition, with "First published 1954" on verso of title page. In dust jacket. $85-$100. "Advance proof copy," wrappers. $500-$600. Also, $400 (A, 1977). New Directions imprint: (New York, 1954.) Mulberry-brown cloth. First American edition. In dust jacket. $50-$75.

THOMAS, Dylan. *The World I Breathe*. Light-brown buckram. Norfolk, (1939). First edition, first issue, with single star on either side of Thomas' name on title page and on spine (later copies having five stars on either side). $250-$350.

THOMAS, Edward. See Eastaway, Edward.

THOMAS, Edward. *Chosen Essays*. Wood engravings. Blue morocco. Newtown, Wales, 1926. Gregynog Press. One of 33 thus bound, (from a limited edition of 350.) $600-$750. Another issue: Buckram. One of 317. $150-$200.

THOMAS, Edward. *Selected Poems*. Buckram. Newtown, Wales, 1927. Gregynog Press. One of 275 on vellum. $200-$250.

THOMAS, Henry W. *History of the Doles-Cook Brigade, Army of Northern Virginia*. Cloth. Atlanta, 1903. First edition. $75-$100.

THOMAS, Hugh. *The World's Game*. Cloth. London, 1957. First edition. $35-$50. Author's first book.

THOMAS, Isaiah. *The History of Printing in America*. 2 plates, 3 facsimiles. 2 vols., calf. Worcester, Mass., 1810. First edition. $750 and up. Albany, 1874. Cloth. Second edition. $200-$250. Barre, Mass., 1972. Imprint Society. Edited by Marcus A. McCorison. One of 1,950, signed by the editor, with a leaf from the first edition of 1810. $200-$225.

THOMAS, Isaiah. *Isaiah Thomas's Catalogue of English, Scotch, Irish, and American Books*. Half leather. Worcester, 1801. First edition. $400-$500. Also, worn and chipped, some writing on title page, $160 (A, 1971).

THOMAS, Jerry. *The Bar-Tender's Guide*. Cloth. New York, 1862. First edition. $100-$150.

THOMAS, Joseph B. *Hounds and Hunting Through the Ages*. Cloth. New York, 1928. First edition. Derrydale Press. One of 750. $150-$200. New York, 1929. Second edition. One of 250. $100-$150.

THOMAS, Lowell. *The First World Flight*. Illustrated. Half vellum. Boston, 1925. First edition. One of 575 signed by Thomas and the aviators. $75-$100.

THOMAS, P.J. *Founding of the Missions*. Map, plates. Cloth. San Francisco, 1877. First edition. $100-$150.

*THOMAS Wolfe Memorial (The)*. Illustrated. Decorated wrappers. Asheville, (1949). First edition. $40-$50. (Issued to raise funds for a Thomas Wolfe Memorial Arts Center.)

THOMPSON, A.C. *Preludes*. Green cloth. London, 1875. (By Alice Meynell.) First edition, first issue, with brown end papers. $75. Author's first book (republished later under the name Alice Meynell as *Poems*, which see under her name).

THOMPSON, Capt. B.F. *History of the 112th Regiment of Illinois Volunteer Infantry, 1862-1865*. Cloth. Toulon, Ill., 1885. First edition. $100-$125.

THOMPSON, Daniel Pierce. See *The Adventures of Timothy Peacock, Esquire; The Green Mountain Boys*.

THOMPSON, Daniel Pierce. *May Martin*. Cloth. Montpelier, Vt., 1835. First edition. $200-$250.

THOMPSON, Daniel Pierce (editor). *The Laws of Vermont, 1824-34, Inclusive.* Calf. Montpelier, 1835. First edition. $100-$125. Author's first book.

THOMPSON, David. *David Thompson's Narrative of His Explorations in Western America: 1784-1812.* Edited by J.B. Tyrell. 23 maps and plates. Cloth. Toronto, 1916. Champlain Society. First edition. One of 550. $600-$750.

THOMPSON, David. *History of the Late War, Between Great Britain and the U.S.A.* Boards or leather. Niagara, U.C. (Upper Canada), 1832. First edition. $150-$250.

THOMPSON, Edwin P. *History of the First Kentucky Brigade.* 6 plates. Cloth. Cincinnati, 1868. First edition. $175-$200.

THOMPSON, Francis. *Poems.* Decorated boards. London, 1893. First edition. With ads at back dated October. One of 500. $100. Another issue: Vellum. One of 12, signed. $250. Author's first book.

THOMPSON, Francis. *Sister-Songs: An Offering to Two Sisters.* Green cloth. London, 1895. First edition, with ads at back dated 1895. (First published edition of *Songs Wing-to-Wing.*) $75-$100.

THOMPSON, Francis. *Songs Wing-to-Wing: An Offering to Two Sisters.* (Cover title.) Wrappers. London, (1895). First edition, first issue (of *Sister-Songs*), with no title page and no dedication leaf. $250-$300.

THOMPSON, Kay. *Eloise.* Drawings by Hilary Knight. Boards. New York, 1955. First edition. In dust jacket. $60-$75.

THOMPSON, Maurice. See *A Tallahassee Girl.*

THOMPSON, Maurice. *Alice of Old Vincennes.* Green cloth, pictorial label on front cover. Indianapolis, (1900). First edition, first issue, with running headline in bold-face capital letters and no page of "Acknowledgment" at end of text. In dust jacket. $100-$125. Lacking jacket, $35-$45. Advance publisher's presentation copy, with printed label so stating, blue-gray cloth, pictorial label. In dust jacket. $150-$200. Lacking jacket, $100-$125.

THOMPSON, Maurice. *Hoosier Mosaics.* Cloth. New York, 1875. First edition. $75-$85. Author's first book.

THOMPSON, Maurice. *The Story of Louisiana.* Cloth. Boston, (1888). First edition. $50-$60.

THOMPSON, Maurice. *The Witchery of Archery.* Cloth. New York, 1878. First edition. $75-$100.

THOMPSON, R.A. *Central Sonoma: A Brief Description of the Township and Town of Santa Rosa, Sonoma County, California.* Printed wrappers. Santa Rosa, Calif., 1884. First edition. $175-$200.

THOMPSON, R.A. *Conquest of California.* Portrait, 3 plates. 33 pp., wrappers. Santa Rosa, 1896. First edition. $75-$100.

THOMPSON, R.A. *Historical and Descriptive Sketch of Sonoma County, California.* Map. Printed wrappers. Philadelphia, 1877. First edition. $150-$250.

THOMPSON, R.A. *The Russian Settlement in California Known as Fort Ross.* 2 plates, other illustrations. 34 pp., wrappers. Santa Rosa, 1896. First edition. $200-$250.

THOMPSON, Ruth Plumly. *The Gnome King of Oz.* Illustrated. Cloth. Chicago, (1927). First edition. $100-$150.

THOMPSON, Lieut. S.D. *Recollections with the 3rd Iowa Regiment.* Cloth. Cincinnati, 1864. $125-$150.

THOMPSON, William. *To the Committee on Election. Ought the Kanesville Vote in August, 1848, to Have Been Allowed?* 19 pp., boards and calf. (Iowa City?), 1850. $350-$400.

THOMSON, James [1700-48]. *The Seasons*. Engravings by F. Bartolozzi and P.W. Tomkins. Contemporary calf. London, 1807. $100-$125.

THOMSON, James [1834-82]. *The City of Dreadful Night*. Cloth. London, 1880. First edition. One of 40 on large paper. $200-$250. Ordinary issue: $50-$60.

THOMSON, James [1834-82]. *Vane's Story, Weddah, etc.* Cloth. London, 1881. First edition. $40-$60.

THOREAU, Henry David. *Autumn: From the Journal of Henry D. Thoreau*. Cloth. Boston, 1892. First edition. $100-$125.

THOREAU, Henry David. *Cape Cod*. Purple cloth. Boston, 1865 (actually 1864). First edition, with no pagination on title page and leaf following. $350-$500. Also, with spine faded and frayed, $250 (A, 1974). Boston, 1896. Colored illustrations by Amelia M. Watson. 2 vols., decorated cloth. $150-$200.

THOREAU, Henry David. *Early Spring in Massachusetts: From the Journal of Henry D. Thoreau*. Boston, 1881. First edition. $50-$60.

THOREAU, Henry David. *Excursions*. Engraved portrait. Green cloth. Boston, 1863. First edition. $200-$250.

THOREAU, Henry David. *Familiar Letters*. Edited by Franklin B. Sanborn. Green cloth. Boston, 1894. First edition. $30-$40. Another issue: One of 150 on large paper. $75-$100.

THOREAU, Henry David. *The First and Last Journeys of Thoreau*. Edited by Franklin B. Sanborn. Engraved limitation plate in Vol. 1., engraved portrait of Thoreau in Vol. 2, manuscript facsimiles. 2 vols., brown boards and parchment. Boston, 1905. First edition. One of 10 on vellum. In slipcase. $300-$350. Ordinary copies: One of 479. $35-$50.

THOREAU, Henry David. *Letters to Various Persons*. Cloth. Boston, 1865. First edition. $75-$85.

THOREAU, Henry David. *The Maine Woods*. Green cloth, chocolate end papers. Boston, 1864. First edition, first issue, with one-leaf ad of *Atlantic Monthly* at end reading "The Thirteenth Volume." $200-$400. Also, faded, spine worn, $175 (A, 1974).

THOREAU, Henry David. *Poems of Nature*. Cloth. Boston, 1895. First edition. $75-$100.

THOREAU, Henry David. *Sir Walter Raleigh*. Three-quarters calf. Boston, 1905. First edition. One of 489. Boxed. $50-$75.

THOREAU, Henry David. *Summer: From the Journal of Henry D. Thoreau*. Double-page frontispiece map. Green cloth. Boston, 1884. First edition. $100-$125.

THOREAU, Henry David. *Walden or, Life in the Woods*. Cloth. Boston, 1854. First edition, with "post" for "port" on page 24, "single spruce" for "double spruce" on page 137, and "white spruce" for "black spruce" on page 217. (Tipped-in ads range from April to December; April ads presumably are earliest.) With April ads: $1,250-$2,000. With May ads: $800-$1,200. Later ads, 1854: $500 and up. London, 1884. Cloth, paper label. First English edition. $100-$200. Edinburgh, 1884. Cloth, paper label. $100-$150. Boston, 1909. 2 vols., half vellum. One of 488. $150-$200. Chicago, 1930. Lakeside Press. Illustrated. Half buckram. One of 1,000. $75-$100. New York, 1936. Limited Editions Club. Boards. Boxed. $150-$250.

THOREAU, Henry David. *A Week on the Concord and Merrimack Rivers*. Brown cloth, yellow end papers. Boston, 1849. First edition, with 3 lines dropped at bottom of page 396—usually written in with pencil by Thoreau. $2,000 and up. Also, binding badly frayed, $1,400 (A, 1977). (Note: The 3 lines are missing in all copies issued.) Author's first book. Boston, 1862. Cloth. Second edition. (Remaindered sheets of first edition with a new title page.) $200-$300.

THOREAU, Henry David. *Winter Animals*. Boards. Westport, Conn., 1928. First edition. One of 60. $75-$85.

THOREAU, Henry David. *Winter: From the Journal of Henry D. Thoreau*. Cloth. Boston, 1888 (actually 1887). First edition. $75-$100.

THOREAU, Henry David. *A Yankee in Canada, with Anti-Slavery and Reform Papers.* Cloth. Boston, 1866. First edition. $400-$500. (Contains "Civil Disobedience.")

THORNTON, Alfred. See *The Adventures of a Post Captain.*

THORNTON, J. Quinn. *Oregon and California in 1848.* Folding map. 2 vols., cloth. New York, 1849. First edition. $250-$300. New York, 1855. 2 vols., cloth. $100-$150.

THORNTON, Richard (editor). *Recognition of Robert Frost: Twenty-Fifth Anniversary.* Cloth. New York, (1937). First edition. In dust jacket. $75. (Includes tributes by Pound and other poets.)

THORNTON, Robert John. *Botanical Extracts, or Philosophy of Botany.* 2 vols. of text, 2 vols. of copperplates, together, 4 vols., atlas folio, contemporary calf. London, 1810. $1,000-$1,500.

THORNTON, Robert John. *The Temple of Flora.* Engraved title with vignette, colored frontispiece, 28 colored and 2 uncolored plates. Contemporary morocco. London, 1812. $2,000-$3,000.

*THOUGHTS on the Destiny of Man.* 96 pp., wrappers. (Harmony, Ind.), 1824. (By Father George Rapp.) First edition. $600-$750.

*THOUGHTS on the Proposed Annexation of Texas to the United States.* 55 pp., wrappers. New York, 1844. (By Theodore Sedgwick.) First edition. $100-$150.

*THOUSAND Miles in a Canoe from Denver to Leavenworth (A).* Wrappers. Bushnell, Neb., 1880. (By W.A. Spencer.) First edition. $300-$350.

THRALL, The Rev. Homer S. *A Pictorial History of Texas.* Folding map. Leather, or cloth. St. Louis, 1878. First edition. $100-$150. St. Louis, 1879. Cloth. Fourth edition. $75-$150.

THRALL, The Rev. S.C. *The President's Death: A Sermon Delivered at Christ Church.* 12 pp., wrappers. New Orleans, 1865. First edition. $125-$150.

*THREE Monographs.* 56 pp., light-brown printed wrappers. Naples, Italy, 1906. (By Norman Douglas.) First edition. One of 250. $100-$150.

THUCYDIDES. *The History of the Peloponnesian War.* Translated by Benjamin Jowett Folio, white pigskin. London, 1930. Ashendene Press. One of 260 printed on paper. $1,250-$1,500. Another issue: One of 20 on vellum. $4,000-$6,000.

THURBER, James. *The Owl in the Attic and Other Perplexities.* Illustrated. Introduction by E.B. White. Yellow cloth. New York, 1931. First edition. In dust jacket. $40-$50.

THURBER, James. *The Thirteen Clocks.* Illustrated in color by Mark Simont. Boards and cloth. New York, (1950). First edition, first printing, Simont credit line on title page in black (later red). $40-$50. (Note: The illustrator's first name, Marc, is misspelled "Mark.")

THURBER, James, and White, E.B. *Is Sex Necessary? Or Why You Feel the Way You Do.* Illustrated. Green boards, black cloth spine. New York, 1929. First edition. In dust jacket. $40-$50. Thurber's first book.

THURMAN, Wallace. *The Blacker the Berry: A Novel of Negro Life.* Brown cloth. New York, 1929. First edition. Lacking dust jacket but inscribed, $125 (in a 1976 catalogue).

THWAITES, Reuben Gold. *Historic Waterways: Six Hundred Miles of Canoeing Down the Rock, Fox, and Wisconsin Rivers.* Cloth. Chicago, 1888. First edition. $75-$100. Author's first book.

TILLSON, Christina Holmes. *Reminiscences of Early Life in Illinois by Our Mother.* 4 plates. Cloth. (Amherst, Mass., about 1872). First edition. $750-$1,000.

TIMLIN, William M. *The Ship That Sailed to Mars.* Cloth. London, 1923. First edition. In dust jacket. $600-$750. Also, in torn dust jacket, $420 (A, 1977).

TIMMONS, Wilbert H. *Morelos of Mexico: Priest, Soldier, Statesman.* Illustrated by José Cisneros. Cloth. El Paso, 1963. "Pesos" edition. One of 500, signed. In dust jacket. Boxed. $75-$100.

*TIMOLEON.* 70 pp., printed buff wrappers. New York, 1891. (By Herman Melville.) Caxton Press. First edition. One of 25. Copies with Melville's signature pasted in, $510 (A, 1944), $375 (A, 1945). (No recent sales noted.)

*TIMOTHY Crump's Ward; or, The New Years Loan and What Came of It.* Purple cloth, or wrappers. Boston, 1866. (By Horatio Alger, Jr.) First edition. Published by Loring. Wrappers: $2,500 or more. Cloth: $2,000 or more.

TIPTON, R.B. *Directory of Marshalltown.* Printed boards. Marshalltown, Iowa, 1884. $100-$125.

TITMARSH, M.A. [Michael Angelo] (editor). *Comic Tales and Sketches.* 12 tinted plates. 2 vols., black or brown cloth. London, 1841. (By William Makepeace Thackeray.) First edition. $300-$400.

TITMARSH, M.A. *Doctor Birch and His Young Friends.* 16 color plates by the author. Wrappers. London, 1849. (By William Makepeace Thackeray.) First edition. $200-$300.

TITMARSH, M.A. *The Irish Sketch-Book.* Wood engravings. 2 vols., green cloth. London, 1843. (By William Makepeace Thackeray.) First edition. $200-$300. First book of which Thackeray acknowledged authorship.

TITMARSH, M.A. *Jeames's Diary; or, Sudden Riches.* Woodcuts. Wrappers. New York, 1846. (By William Makepeace Thackeray.) First edition. $1,000 and up. Very rare, with only 3 copies known to bibliographers.

TITMARSH, M.A. *The Kickleburys on the Rhine.* 15 illustrations in color by the author. Wrappers. London, 1851. (By William Makepeace Thackeray.) First edition. $200-$300.

TITMARSH, M.A. *"Our Street."* 16 color plates. Wrappers. London, 1848. (By William Makepeace Thackeray.) First edition. $200-$300.

TITMARSH, M.A. *The Second Funeral of Napoleon: In Three Letters to Miss Smith, of London, and the Chronicle of the Drum.* Frontispiece, 3 plates, picture of Napoleon on front cover. Wrappers. London, 1841. (By William Makepeace Thackeray.) First edition, first issue, with six lines of shading on the cheek of Napoleon on front cover. $500 and up. (Note: A copy of this rarity was sold in 1914 for $825. The so-called "second issue" apparently is a reprint, done about 1880, according to De Ricci, and with the illustrations lithographed. Its value is nominal.)

TITTSWORTH, W.G. *Outskirt Episodes.* Portrait (tipped to title page). Red cloth. (Avoca, Iowa, 1927.) First edition. In dust jacket. $150-$200.

TODD, The Rev. John. *The Lost Sister of Wyoming.* Frontispiece. Cloth. Northampton, Mass., 1842. First edition. $50-$75.

TODD, Ruthven. *Over the Mountain.* Cloth. London, 1939. First edition. In dust jacket. $50-$75.

TODHUNTER, John. *A Sicilian Idyll.* Illustrated by Walter Crane. Vellum and boards. London, 1890. One of 50, signed. $100-$150.

TOKLAS, Alice B. *The Autobiography of Alice B. Toklas.* Blue cloth. New York, (1933). (By Gertrude Stein.) First edition, published by Harcourt, Brace. In dust jacket. $100-$125. (Note: Gertrude Stein was not identified on title pages as the author until the paperback editions of the 1950's and 1960's. Also, it should be noted that the Literary Guild edition of 1933, although proclaiming itself a "first edition," is not such.)

TOLKIEN, J.R.R. *Farmer Giles of Ham.* Illustrated, including 2 color plates. Boards. London, 1949. First edition. In dust jacket. $100-$125.

TOLKIEN, J.R.R. *The Hobbit.* Illustrated by the author. Green cloth. London, (1937). First edition. In dust jacket. $750-$1,000, possibly more.

TOLKIEN, J.R.R. *The Lord of the Rings.* Illustrated by the author. 3 vols., red cloth. London, 1954-54-55. First edition. In dust jackets. $650-$750. (Note: This famous trilogy consists of the uniformly bound first editions, dated as shown, of *The Fellowship of the Rings, The Two Towers,* and *The Return of the King.* Later issues have sometimes been offered, incorrectly, as first editions.)

TOLKIEN, J.R.R. *A Middle Earth Vocabulary.* Wrappers. Oxford, 1922. First edition. $200-$250. Author's first book.

TOLSTOY, Leo. *Anna Karenina.* Cloth. New York, 1886. First edition in English. $250. New York, 1933. Limited Editions Club. 2 vols. Boxed. $60-$70. Another issue, 1951: 2 vols. Boxed. $50.

TOLSTOY, Leo. *War and Peace.* Translated from the French by Clara Bell. 6 vols., decorated brown cloth. New York, 1886. First edition in English. $750-$1,000. New York, 1938. Limited Editions Club. 6 vols. $80-$100.

TOLSTOY, Leo. *Where God Is Love Is.* Wrappers. London, 1924. Ashendene Press. One of about 200 issued as a Christmas token from St. John and Cicely Hornby. $500 and up.

*TOM Brown at Oxford.* 3 vols., blue cloth. Cambridge, 1861. (By Thomas Hughes.) First edition. $400-$500. Second edition, same date: $150-$200.

*TOM Brown's School Days.* By an Old Boy. Blue cloth. Cambridge, 1857. (By Thomas Hughes.) First edition. $400-$500.

*TOM Cringle's Log.* 2 vols., cloth. London, 1833. (By Michael Scott.) First edition. $150-$200.

TOMKINSON, G.S. *A Select Bibliography of the Principal Modern Presses . . . in Great Britain and Ireland.* Illustrated. Boards and cloth. London, 1928. First edition. $125-$165.

TOMLINSON, Charles. *Relations and Contraries.* Wrappers. (Aldington, Kent, England, 1951.) First edition. $30-$35. Author's first book.

TOMLINSON, H.M. *All Our Yesterdays.* Boards and cloth. New York, 1930. First edition. One of 350. $75. Trade edition: Black cloth. In dust jacket. $15-$20. London, (1930). Cloth. First English edition. One of 1,025, signed. $50-$60. Trade edition: Cloth. First issue, with error in running head on page 67. In dust jacket. $15-$20.

TOMLINSON, H.M. *Ports of Call.* Cloth. London, 1942. Corvinus Press. One of 30, signed. Boxed. $75-$100.

TOMLINSON, H.M. *The Sea and the Jungle.* Frontispiece. Green cloth. London, (1912). First edition, first issue, with 10 ad leaves at back. In dust jacket. $150-$200. Author's first book. London, or New York, 1930. Illustrated by Clare Leighton. Cloth. One of 515, signed. In dust jacket. $60-$75. Trade edition: Boards and cloth. In dust jacket. $15.

TOMLINSON, H.M. *Under the Red Ensign.* Cloth. London, 1926. First edition. In dust jacket. $30-$50.

TOOMER, Jean. *Essentials.* Black cloth, paper labels. Chicago, 1931. First edition. One of 1,000. In dust jacket. $125-$150.

TOOMER, Jean. *The Flavor of Man.* Wrappers. Philadelphia, (1949). First edition. $100.

*TOPOGRAPHICAL Description of the State of Ohio, Indian Territory, and Louisiana (A).* 5 plates, errata slip. Calf, or sheep. Boston, 1812. (By Jervis Cutler.) First edition. $500-$600.

TOPONCE, Alexander. *Reminiscences of Alexander Toponce, Pioneer, 1839-1923.* 14 plates. Fabrikoid. (Ogden, Utah, 1923.) First edition. $85-$100.

TOPPING, E.S. *The Chronicles of the Yellowstone.* Folding map. Cloth. St. Paul, 1883. First edition. $100-$125.

*TOPSYS & Turveys.* 31 leaves with colored illustrations. Oblong folio, pictorial boards. New York, 1893. (By Peter Newell.) First edition. $150-$200. Author's first book.

TORNEL, José Maria (translator). *Diario Histórico del Ultimo Viaje que Hizo M. de La Sale para Descubrir el Desembocadero y Curso del Missicipi.* Boards. New York, 1831. $200-$350.

TORRENCE, Ridgely. *The House of a Hundred Lights.* Gold-decorated boards. Boston, 1900. First edition. $80-$100. Author's first book.

TORY, Geoffroy. *Champ Fleury.* Translated by George B. Ives. Vellum and boards. New York, 1927. Grolier Club. Printed by Bruce Rogers. One of 7 on larger paper (of an edition of 397). $750-$1,000. Regular issue: One of 390. In dust jacket. Boxed. $300-$400.

*TOUR of Doctor Prosody (The).* 20 colored plates by C. Williams and W. Read. Boards. London, 1821. $400-$500. (Note: Sometimes attributed to William Combe, but not by him, according to De Ricci.)

*TOUR of the Prairies (A).* By the Author of *The Sketch-Book.* Boards, or cloth. London, 1835. (By Washington Irving.) First edition. $200-$300. Philadelphia, 1835. Blue or green cloth, paper label. First American edition, first state, without "No. 1" on the label. $250-$400. Second state. $100-$125.

*TOUR Through Part of Virginia in the Summer of 1808 (A).* 31 pp. New York, 1809. (By John E. Caldwell.) First edition. $175-$200.

TOWER, Col. Reuben. *An Appeal to the People of New York in Favor of the Construction of the Chenango Canal, etc.* 32 pp., sewed. Utica, 1830. First edition. $100-$125.

TOWLER, J(ohn). *The Silver Sunbeam: A Practical and Theoretical Text-Book on Sun-Drawing and Photographic Printing.* Cloth. New York, 1864. First edition. $300-$400. "Second thousand" (second printing), same date, $200-$250. New York, 1870. Seventh edition. $100. New York, 1879. Ninth edition. With mounted original Artotype by Bierstadt. $200.

TOWNSEND, George Alfred. *The Real Life of Abraham Lincoln.* Frontispiece. 15 pp., printed wrappers. New York, 1867. First edition. $75-$100.

TOWNSEND, John K. *Narrative of a Journey Across the Rocky Mountains.* Cloth. Philadelphia, 1839. First edition. $400-$500.

TOWNSHEND, John K. *Sporting Excursions in the Rocky Mountains.* Engraved frontispieces. 2 vols., full leather. London, 1840. First English edition of the preceding item, with the author's name spelled "Townshend" instead of "Townsend"). $250-$350.

TOWNSHEND, R.B. *The Tenderfoot in New Mexico.* Illustrated. Cloth. London, (1923). First edition. $50.

*TOWNSHIP Maps of the Cherokee Nation.* 130 maps. Folio, cloth. Muskogee, Okla., no date. $150-$200.

TRACY, J.L. *Guide to the Great West.* 2 maps. Cloth. St. Louis, 1870. First edition. $150-$175.

*TRAGEDY of Count Alarcos (The).* Wrappers, or cloth. London, 1839. (By Benjamin Disraeli.) First edition. Wrappers. $150-$250. Cloth: $150-$200.

TRAIN, M. *Ray Burton: A Chicago Tale.* Wrappers. Chicago, 1895. First edition. $50-$75.

*TRAITS of American Indian Life and Character.* By a Fur Trader. 6 plates. Half cloth. San Francisco, 1933. (By Peter Skene Ogden or Duncan Finlayson.) Grabhorn printing. One of 500. $75-$100.

*TRANSACTIONS of the Chicago Academy of Sciences. Vol. 1, Part 1, and Vol. 1, Part 2.* Plates, lithographs, folding map, separate title page for Part 2. Half leather. Chicago. 1867 and 1869. First edition. (All published.) $500 and up.

*TRANSCRIPT of Record of Proceedings Before the Mexican and American Mixed Claims Commission with Relation to the "Pious Fund of the Californias."* Washington, 1902. $60-$75.

*TRANSITION Stories.* Edited by E. Jolas and R. Sage. Pictorial boards and cloth. New York. 1929. First edition. One of 100. In dust jacket. $250-$300.

TRAUBEL, Horace L. (editor). *At the Graveside of Walt Whitman: Harleigh, Camden, New Jersey, March 30th, and Sprigs of Lilac.* 37 pp., printed gray wrappers. (Philadelphia), 1892. First edition. $100-$125.

TRAUBEL, Horace L. (editor). *Camden's Compliment to Walt Whitman.* Frontispiece. Red cloth. Philadelphia, 1889. First edition. $100-$125.

*TRAVELS of Capts. Lewis and Clarke (The).* Folding map and 5 portraits of Indians. Calf. Philadelphia, 1809. First edition. $350-$450. (Note: A spurious work. For authentic first edition see entry under Lewis' name.)

*TRAVELS in Louisiana and the Floridas, in the Year, 1802.* Translated from the French by John Davis. Boards, paper label. New York, 1806. (By Berquin-Duvallon.) First edition in English. $750-$1,000.

TRAVEN, B. *The Bridge in the Jungle.* Green cloth. New York, 1938. First American edition. In dust jacket. $35-$50.

TRAVEN, B. *The Death Ship: The Story of an American Sailor.* Cloth. London, 1934. First edition in English. In dust jacket. $100-$110. New York, 1934. Black cloth. First American edition, first printing. In dust jacket. $85-$135. Author's first book.

TRAVEN, B. *Der Schatz der Sierra Madre.* Orange-colored pictorial cloth. Berlin, 1927. First edition (of *The Treasure of the Sierra Madre*). $150-$200.

TRAVEN, B. *The General from the Jungle.* Cloth. London, (1954). First edition in English. In dust jacket. $75-$100.

TRAVEN, B. *The Rebellion of the Hanged.* Black cloth. New York, 1952. First American edition. In dust jacket. $40-$50.

TRAVEN, B. *The Treasure of the Sierra Madre.* Cloth. London, 1934. First edition in English. In dust jacket. $150. New York, 1935. Cloth. First American edition. In dust jacket. $50-$60.

TRAVERS, P.L. *Mary Poppins.* Illustrated by Mary Shepard. Pictorial cloth. (London, 1934.) First edition. In dust jacket. $150. New York, (1934). Pictorial blue cloth. In dust jacket. $75. Author's first book.

TREADWELL, Edward F. *The Cattle King.* 4 plates. Cloth. New York, 1931. First edition. In dust jacket. $50-$75. Boston, 1950. Cloth. $20-$35.

*TREATISE on Tennis (A).* By a Member of the Tennis Club. Folding engraved diagram of court. Boards. London, 1822. (By Robert Lukin.) First edition. $250-$350.

*TREATY Between the United States and the Chasta and Other Tribes of Indians.* Wrappers. (Washington, 1855.) (By Joel Palmer.) $100-$150.

*TREATY Between the United States and the Comanche and Kiowa Tribes of Indians . . . Proclaimed May 26, 1866.* 8 pp., folio. (Washington, 1866.) $100-$150.

*TREATY Between the United States and the Creek and Seminole Tribes of Indians . . . Ratified March 6, 1845.* 6 pp., folio. (Washington, 1845.) $100-$150.

*TREATY Between the United States and the Klamath and Moadoc Tribes and Yahooskin Band of Snake Indians . . . Proclaimed Feb. 17, 1870.* 8 pp., folio. (Washington, 1870.) $150-$175.

*TREATY Between the United States and the Nez Perce Tribe of Indians . . . Proclaimed April 20, 1867.* 10 pp., folio. (Washington, 1867.) $150-$175.

TRELAWNY, Edward John. See *The Adventures of a Younger Son*.

TRENT, William. *Journal of Captain William Trent from Logstown to Pickawillany, A.D. 1752*. Cloth. Cincinnati, 1871. First edition. $50-$75.

TRIAL *of Impeachment of Levi Hubbell*. Contemporary calf. Madison, Wis., 1853. First edition. $100-$125.

TRIALS *of A. Arbuthnot and R.C. Ambrister (The), Charged with Exciting the Seminole Indians to War Against the United States of America*. 80 pp., morocco. London, 1819. First edition. $300-$350.

TRIBES *and Temples: A Record of the Expedition to Middle America Conducted by the Tulane University of Louisiana in 1925*. 2 vols., cloth. New Orleans, 1926. $50.

TRIBUNE *Book of Open Air Sports (The)*. Edited by Henry Hall. Illustrated. Pictorial cloth. New York, 1887. First edition. $150-$200. (Note: This is the first book composed by linotype.)

TRIBUNE *Tracts No. 6, Life of Abraham Lincoln*. 32 pp., sewed. New York, 1860. (By John Locke Scripps.) $50. (Note: This book first appeared in an undated Chicago edition of 1860, 32 pp., under the caption title *Life of Abraham Lincoln*. That edition is rare, worth $1,000 and up.)

TRIGGS, J.H. *History and Directory of Laramie City, Wyoming Territory*. 91 pp., printed wrappers. Laramie City, 1875. First edition. $650-$1,000.

TRIGGS, J.H. *History of Cheyenne and Northern Wyoming, etc*. Folding map. 144 pp., printed wrappers. Omaha, 1876. First edition. $650-$1,000.

TRIPLER, Eunice. *Some Notes of Her Personal Recollections*. Illustrated. Cloth. New York, 1910. First edition. $100-$125.

TRIPLETT, Frank. *The Life, Times and Treacherous Death of Jesse James*. Plates. Pictorial cloth. Chicago, 1882. First edition. $200-$250.

TRIPP, C.E. *Ace High: The Frisco Detective*. Introduction by David Magee. Illustrated. Boards and cloth. San Francisco, 1948. Grabhorn Press. One of 500. $50-$60.

TRISTRAM, W. Outram. *Coaching Days and Coaching Ways*. Pictorial cloth. London, 1888. First edition. Large paper issue. $100-$150. Regular issue: $60-$80. London, 1893. One of 250. $100-$125. London, 1924. Illustrated. Leather. $100-$150.

TROLLOPE, Anthony. See *Nina Balatka; On English Prose Fiction as a Rational Amusement*.

TROLLOPE, Anthony. *The American Senator*. 3 vols., pinkish ochre cloth. London, 1877. First edition, first binding. $150-$250.

TROLLOPE, Anthony. *Australia and New Zealand*. 8 colored maps. 2 vols., cloth. London, 1873. First edition, first issue, with dark green end papers. $200-$250.

TROLLOPE, Anthony. *An Autobiography*. Portrait. 2 vols., cloth. Edinburgh, 1883. First edition, first issue, with smooth (not ribbed) red cloth covers. $100-$150.

TROLLOPE, Anthony. *Ayala's Angel*. 3 vols., orange cloth. London, 1881. First edition. $500-$600.

TROLLOPE, Anthony. *Barchester Towers*. 3 vols., cloth. London, 1857. First edition, first binding, brown cloth. $1,000-$1,250. Second binding, tan cloth, with 24 pp. of ads dated October, 1860. $900 (A, 1974). New York, (1859?). 2 vols. in one, purple-brown cloth. First American edition, without printer's imprint on back of title page. $200-$300. New York, 1958. Limited Editions Club. Boxed. $40.

TROLLOPE, Anthony. *The Belton Estate*. 3 vols., scarlet cloth. London, 1866. First edition. $1,000-$1,500. Also, $950 (A, 1974); $650 (A, 1970).

TROLLOPE, Anthony. *The Bertrams*. 3 vols., dark gray-purple cloth. London, 1859. First edition. $1,000-$1,500. Also, $1,300 (A, 1974); $550 (A, 1970).

TROLLOPE, Anthony. *Can You Forgive Her?* Illustrated. 20 parts, buff wrappers. London, 1864-65. First edition. $500-$600. London, 1864-(65). 2 vols., crimson cloth. First book edition. $300-$400.

TROLLOPE, Anthony. *Castle Richmond*. 3 vols., dark purple-gray cloth. London, 1860. First edition, first binding, without line under the author's name on spine, first issue text (as defined in the Michael Sadleir bibliography). $750-$1,000. Also, second issue, with line under author's name on spine and ads in Vol. 3 dated May. $400-$600. New York, 1860. Green cloth. First American edition. $200-$250.

TROLLOPE, Anthony. *The Claverings*. Illustrated. Wrappers (26 chapters only). New York, 1866. First edition. $400-$500. Another edition: New York, 1866 (actually 1867). Gray lilac cloth. First complete edition. $250-$300. London, 1867. Illustrated. 2 vols., bright green cloth. First English edition. $400-$500.

TROLLOPE, Anthony. *Doctor Thorne*. 3 vols., gray-purple cloth. London, 1858. First edition. $400-$600. Second edition, same date. $250-$300.

TROLLOPE, Anthony. *The Duke's Children*. 3 vols., blue-green cloth. London, 1880. First edition. $300-$400. New York, 1880. Stitched, as issued. $400-$500.

TROLLOPE, Anthony. *An Editor's Tales*. Pinkish-brown cloth. London, 1870. First edition. $100-$150.

TROLLOPE, Anthony. *The Eustace Diamonds*. Printed wrappers, or cloth. New York, 1872. First edition. Either binding: $500-$750. London, 1873. 3 vols., brown cloth, spine title in gold. First English edition, correct binding. $750-$1,000.

TROLLOPE, Anthony. *The Fixed Period*. 2 vols., red cloth. Edinburgh, 1882. First edition. $250-$300.

TROLLOPE, Anthony. *Framley Parsonage*. Millais illustrations. 3 vols., gray-purple cloth. London, 1861. First edition. $500-$750. (Note: Copies with April ads at end of Vol. 3 preferred.)

TROLLOPE, Anthony. *The Golden Lion of Granpere*. Reddish-brown cloth. London, 1872. First edition. $200-$250. New York, 1872. Illustrated. Wrappers. $400-$500.

TROLLOPE, Anthony. *He Knew He Was Right*. Illustrated by Marcus Stone. 32 parts, gray-green wrappers. London, 1868-69. First edition. $750-$1,000. New York, 1869. Illustrated. 2 vols., wrappers. First American edition. $300-$400. London, 1869. Illustrated. 2 vols., green cloth. First English book edition. $400-$500.

TROLLOPE, Anthony. *How the "Mastiffs" Went to Iceland*. Illustrated. Blue cloth. London, 1878. First edition. $300-$350.

TROLLOPE, Anthony. *Hunting Sketches*. Red cloth. London, 1865. First edition, with May ads. $150-$200.

TROLLOPE, Anthony. *John Caldigate*. 3 vols., cloth. London, 1879. First edition, first binding, lilac-gray cloth. $300-$500.

TROLLOPE, Anthony. *The Kellys and the O'Kellys*. 3 vols., boards. London, 1848. First edition. $1,000 and up. Also, rebound in half morocco, $950 (A, 1970). New York, 1860. Cloth. First American edition. $300-$400.

TROLLOPE, Anthony. *Kept in the Dark*. Frontispiece by Millais. 3 vols., olive-brown cloth. London, 1882. First edition. $300-$400.

TROLLOPE, Anthony. *La Vendee: An Historical Romance*. 3 vols., boards, or cloth. London, 1850. First edition, first issue, with verso of title pages blank. Either binding: $1,000-$1,500. Also, boards, $750 (A, 1970).

TROLLOPE, Anthony. *Lady Anna*. 2 vols., red-brown cloth. London, 1874. First edition. $300-$400.

TROLLOPE, Anthony. *The Landleaguers*. 3 vols., green cloth. London, 1883. First edition. $150-$250.

TROLLOPE, Anthony. *The Last Chronicle of Barset*. Illustrated. 32 parts, pictorial wrappers. London, 1866-67. First edition. $800-$1,000. London, 1867. 32 plates. 2 vols., blue cloth. First book edition. $400-$600. Rebound in leather, $200. New York, 1867. Illustrated. Cloth. First American edition. $75-$100. (Note: Both the parts issue and the book issue of the English first edition are complicated books with confusing issue points; see the Michael Sadleir bibliography.)

TROLLOPE, Anthony. *The Life of Cicero*. 2 vols., dark-red cloth. London, 1880. First edition, first issue, with black end papers. $100-$150.

TROLLOPE, Anthony. *London Tradesmen*. Boards and cloth. London, 1927. First edition. One of 530. In glassine dust jacket. $35-$50.

TROLLOPE, Anthony. *Lotta Schmidt and Other Stories*. Maroon cloth. London, 1867. First edition. $200-$300.

TROLLOPE, Anthony. *The Macdermots of Ballycloran*. 3 vols., dark brown cloth. London, 1847. First edition, first issue (with 1847 on title page). $5,000-$10,000. Also, contemporary morocco, $2,300 (1974). Author's first book. London, 1848. Cloth. Second issue (with 1848 title page). $1.000 and up.

TROLLOPE, Anthony. *Marion Fay*. 3 vols., yello-ochre cloth. London, 1882. First edition. $500-$600. New York, 1882. Illustrated. Wrappers. First American edition. $300-$400.

TROLLOPE, Anthony. *Miss Mackenzie*. 2 vols., dark-green cloth. London, 1865. First edition. $200-$250.

TROLLOPE, Anthony. *North America*. 2 vols., pinkish maroon cloth. London, 1862. First edition, with October ads. $250-$350. New York, 1862. Gray cloth. First American (pirated) edition. $100-$125.

TROLLOPE, Anthony. *Orley Farm*. Illustrated by J.E. Millais. 20 parts, buff wrappers. London, 1861-62. First edition. $750 and up. London, 1862. 2 vols., purple-brown cloth. First book edition. $250-$500. (Note: As with *The Last Chronicle of Barset*, this is an extremely complex book to sort out bibliographically; see Sadleir's bibliography.)

TROLLOPE, Anthony. *The Prime Minister*. 8 parts, gray wrappers, or brown cloth. London, 1876. First edition. $750 and up. London, 1876. 4 vols., red-brown cloth. First book edition. $250-$350.

TROLLOPE, Anthony. *Rachel Ray*. 2 vols., pinkish red cloth. London, 1863. First edition, first issue, with volume numbers on spines in roman (not block) type. $500-$750.

TROLLOPE, Anthony. *Ralph the Heir*. Illustrated. 19 parts, buff wrappers. London, 1870-71. First edition. $3,000 (A, 1970). London, 1871. 3 vols., brown cloth. $200-$250.

TROLLOPE, Anthony. *Sir Harry Hotspur of Humblethwaite*. Scarlet-orange cloth. London, 1871. First edition. $200-$250. (For issue points, see Sadleir.) New York, 1871. Cherry-red or green cloth. First American edition. $200-$250.

TROLLOPE, Anthony. *The Small House at Allington*. Illustrated by Millais. 2 vols., green cloth. London, 1864. First edition, first issue, with "hobbledehoya" in first line of page 33. $750-$1,000.

TROLLOPE, Anthony. *South Africa*. Folding map in color. 2 vols., scarlet cloth. London, 1878. First edition. $200-$300.

TROLLOPE, Anthony. *The Struggles of Brown, Jones, and Robinson*. Wrappers. New York, 1862. First edition. $1,000 and up. Also, worn and repaired, $550 (A, 1970). London, 1870. Illustrated. Brown cloth. First English and first illustrated edition. $200-$250.

TROLLOPE, Anthony. *Tales of All Countries*. (First and Second series.) 2 vols., blue cloth. London, 1861 and 1863. First editions. $400-$600.

TROLLOPE, Anthony. *Thompson Hall*. Illustrated. Pictorial boards. London, 1885. First separate edition. $100-$150.

TROLLOPE, Anthony. *The Three Clerks*. 3 vols., boards, blue cloth spine, labels. London, 1858. First edition. $1,000 and up. Also, variant issue; Cloth. $800 (A, 1970). New York, 1860. Plum-colored cloth. First American edition. $200-$300.

TROLLOPE, Anthony. *Travelling Sketches*. Scarlet cloth. London, 1866. First edition. $100-$125.

TROLLOPE, Anthony. *The Vicar of Bulhampton*. Illustrated. 11 parts, decorated gray-blue wrappers. London, 1869-70. First edition. $400-$600. London, 1870. Brown cloth. First book edition. $200-$300.

TROLLOPE, Anthony. *The Warden*. Brown cloth. London, 1855. First edition, first binding, with 24 pages of ads dated September, 1854. $1,000 and up. Also, $700 (A, 1974). New York, 1862. Wrappers. First American edition. $400-$500. Also, spine repaired, $250 (A, 1970).

TROLLOPE, Anthony. *The Way We Live Now*. Illustrated. 20 parts, pictorial wrappers. London, 1874-75. First edition. $400-$600. London, 1875. 2 vols., green cloth. First book edition. $300-$400.

TROLLOPE, Anthony. *Why Frau Frohmann Raised Her Prices, and Other Stories*. 2 vols., green cloth. London, 1882. First edition. $400-$500. Also, $275 (A, 1970).

TROLLOPE, Frances. See *Domestic Manners of the Americans*.

TROLLOPE, Frances. *Uncle Walter*. 3 vols., boards and cloth, paper labels. London, 1852. First edition. $200-$250.

TROLLOPE, Frances. *The Vicar of Wrexhill*. 3 vols., boards, paper labels. London, 1837. First edition. $200-$300.

TROLLOPE, T. Adolphus. *A Summer in Brittany*. Edited by Frances Trollope. 14 plates, 2 in color. 2 vols., purple cloth. London, 1840. First edition. $200-$225.

TROWBRIDGE, John Townsend. See Creyton, Paul.

TROWBRIDGE, John Townsend. *Cudjo's Cave*. Pictorial half title. Cloth. Boston, 1864. First edition, first printing, listing the "L'Envoy" as beginning on page 503 (later, page 501). $125-$150.

TROWBRIDGE, John Townsend. *Jack Hazard and His Fortunes*. Cloth. Boston, 1871. First edition. $75-$100.

TROWBRIDGE, John Townsend. *The South: A Tour of Its Battlefields and Ruined Cities*. Cloth. Hartford, 1866. First edition. $50-$75.

TRUETT, Velma Stevens. *On the Hoof in Nevada*. Portraits, other illustrations. Oblong pictorial buckram. Los Angeles, 1950. First edition. $75-$100.

TRUMAN, Maj. Ben. C. *Life, Adventures and Capture of Tiburcio Vasquez, the Great California Bandit and Murderer*. Frontispiece map. 44 pp., pictorial wrappers. Los Angeles, 1874. First edition. $500-$600. Los Angeles, 1941. Cloth and leather. One of 100. $50-$75.

TRUMAN Benjamin C. *Occidental Sketches*. Cloth. San Francisco, 1881. First edition. $50-$75.

TRUMAN, Harry S. *Mr. Citizen*. Cloth. (New York, 1960.) First edition. One of 1,000, signed. Boxed. $100-$125. Trade edition: In dust jacket. $75.

TRUMBO, Dalton. *Eclipse*. Cloth. London, (1935). First edition. In dust jacket. $150-$200. Author's first book.

TRUMBO, Dalton. *Johnny Got His Gun.* Yellow cloth. Philadelphia, (1939). First edition. In dust jacket. With wraparound band. $60-$80.

TSA TOKE, Monroe. *The Peyote Ritual.* 15 color plates. Boards and cloth. San Francisco, 1957. Grabhorn Press. One of 325. $295.

TUCKER, Beverley. *The Partisan Leader.* Printed wrappers. Richmond, 1862. Reprint of the anonymous 1836 novel forecasting the Civil War. $200.

TUCKER, E. *History of Randolph County, Indiana.* Half leather and cloth. Chicago, 1882. First edition. $75-$100.

TUCKER, H.S.G. *Introductory Lecture Delivered by the Professor of Law in the University of Virginia, at the Opening of the Law School.* 24 pp., half leather. Charlottesville, 1841. First edition. $75-$100.

TUCKER, Dr. Joseph C. *To the Golden Goal, and Other Sketches.* Cloth. San Francisco, 1895. First edition. One of 50. $100-$150.

TUER, Andrew W. *History of the Horn-Book.* With 7 facsimile hornbooks in pockets. 2 vols., vellum. London, 1896. First edition. $600-$750. London, 1897. 2 vols., brown buckram. With 3 facsimile hornbooks. $300-$400.

TUER, Andrew W. *Pages and Pictures from Forgotten Children's Books.* Illustrated. Cloth. London, 1898-99. First edition. $100-$150.

TUFTS, James. *A Tract Descriptive of Montana Territory.* Map. 15 pp., folded sheets. New York, 1865. First edition. One of 24 on fine paper. $200-$300. Another issue: Sewed. $300-$400.

TULLIDGE, Edward W. *The History of Salt Lake City and Its Founders.* 33 plates. Half morocco. Salt Lake City, (about 1886). $100-$125. (Note: The first edition, with 3 plates, was published 1883-84, according to Howes.)

TURNER, Frederick Jackson. *The Significance of the Frontier in American History.* 34 pp., wrappers. Madison, Wis., 1894. First separate edition. $1,000.

TURNER, Mary Honeyman Ten Eyck. *These High Plains.* Portrait and plates. Cloth, pictorial label. Amarillo, 1941. First edition. One of 150. $100-$150.

TURNER, Orsamus. *History of the Pioneer Settlement of Phelps and Gorham's Purchase.* Boards and leather. Rochester, 1851. First edition. $100-$135.

TURNER, T.G. *Gazetteer of the St. Joseph Valley.* Frontispiece and plate. Cloth. Chicago, 1867. First edition. $100-$150.

TURNER, T.G. *Turner's Guide from the Lakes to the Rocky Mountains.* Cloth. Chicago, 1868. First edition. $100-$150.

TURNLEY, Parmenas T. *Reminiscences of Parmenas T. Turnley, from the Cradle to Three-Score and Ten.* 6 plates. Cloth. Chicago, (1892). First edition. $125-$175.

TURRILL, H.B. *Historical Reminiscences of the City of Des Moines.* Double-page frontispiece plate and 7 other plates. 144 pp., printed dark blue wrappers. Des Moines, 1857. First edition. $150-$200.

TUTTLE, C.R. *History of Grand Rapids.* Cloth. Grand Rapids, 1874. First edition. $100-$150.

TUTTLE, J.H. *Wam-dus-ky: A Descriptive Record of a Hunting Trip to North Dakota.* Illustrated. Cloth. Minneapolis, 1893. First edition. $400-$500.

TWAIN, Mark. See Harte, Bret, and Twain, Mark. Also see *Date 1601; What is Man?*

TWAIN, Mark. *Adventures of Huckleberry Finn.* Illustrated. Pictorial red cloth. London, 1884. (By Samuel Langhorne Clemens.) First edition (preceding the American first). $500-$600. New York, 1885. Green or blue cloth (or various leathers), green cloth being most common. First American edition, first issue, with "was" for "saw" in line 23, page

57; with "Him and another man" given in list of illustrations as being on page 88, and with page 283 on a stub. Blue cloth: $1,500-$2,500. Also, blue cloth, $1,050 (A, 1975); $1,500 (A, 1960). Green cloth: $1,000-$1,500. Also, $850 (A, 1974). First issue copies, in publisher's sheepskin, with first state (suppressed) of the Silas Phelps illustration with the suggestive distortion of the fly on Phelps' trousers: $1,500-$2,500. Average copies in the green or blue binding sell in the $400-$600 range at retail, with defective copies bringing less. (The prospectus for this work, with samples of text and binding, sells in the $500-$750 range.) New York. 1933. Limited Editions Club. Boxed. $60-$75. New York, 1942. Limited Editions Club. Boxed. $75-$85.

TWAIN, Mark. *The Adventures of Tom Sawyer.* Illustrated. Red cloth. London, 1876. (By Samuel Langhorne Clemens.) First edition (preceding the American first). $400-$500. Toronto, 1876. Illustrated. Decorated plum-colored cloth. First Canadian edition (also preceding the American). $400-$500. Hartford, 1876. Illustrated. Blue cloth (or various leathers). First American edition, first issue, printed on calendered paper, with versos of half title and preface blank. Copies in cloth: $1,500-$2,500, possibly more. Also, $1,400 (A, 1962); $1,500 (A, 1960). Copies in half leather: $2,000 and up. Also, $1,300 (A, 1976); $1,400 (A, 1974). Copies in full sheepskin: $1,500-$2,500. Rebacked copy, $2,000 in a late fall 1977 bookshop catalogue. Second issue, lacking the two blank pages: Cloth. $200-$300. New York, 1939. Limited Editions Club. Boxed. $60-$80.

TWAIN, Mark. *The American Claimant.* Illustrated. Gray-green cloth. New York, 1892. (By Samuel Langhorne Clemens.) First edition. $75-$100.

TWAIN, Mark. *Be Good, Be Good: A Poem.* (Cover title.) 4 pp., French-folded, printed in green. New York, 1931. (By Samuel Langhorne Clemens.) First edition. $125-$150. Another issue: One of 10 or 12 printed in blue on vellum. $300.

TWAIN, Mark. *The Celebrated Jumping Frog of Calaveras County, and Other Sketches.* Edited by John Paul. Cloth, various colors. New York, 1867. (By Samuel Langhorne Clemens.) First edition, first issue, with perfect "i" in "this" in last line on page 198 and with page of yellow tinted ads preceding title page. $1,000-$1,500. (Note: The latter price, the highest I have noted, was for a copy with the gold-stamped frog in a vertical position, head pointing up, in the center of the front cover. There is some controversy as to the priority of the bindings in respect to the placement of the frog on the cover. A copy with the frog at the lower left corner brought $1,200 at auction in 1974.) Second issue, with type in "this" on page 198 broken or worn, no ad leaf present. $300-$400. Also, $140 (A, 1975). London, 1867. Yellow wrappers. First English edition. $350-$450. Author's first book.

TWAIN, Mark. *Christian Science.* Illustrated. Red cloth. New York, 1907. (By Samuel Langhorne Clemens.) First edition, first issue, with perfect "W" in "Why," line 14 on page 5. $50-$60.

TWAIN, Mark. *Concerning Cats: Two Tales.* Boards and cloth. San Francisco, 1959. (By Samuel Langhorne Clemens.) Grabhorn printing for the Colt Press. One of 450. $75.

TWAIN, Mark. *A Connecticut Yankee in King Arthur's Court.* Illustrated. Green cloth (or various leathers). New York, 1889. (By Samuel Langhorne Clemens.) First edition, first issue, with "S" before "King" in the caption on page 59. $200-$350. New York, 1949. Limited Editions Club. Boxed. $50-$60.

TWAIN, Mark. *A Curious Dream.* Pictorial yellow boards. London, (1872). (By Samuel Langhorne Clemens.) First edition, first printing, with end papers blank. $150-$200.

TWAIN, Mark. *The Curious Republic of Gondour.* Yellow boards. New York, 1919. (By Samuel Langhorne Clemens.) First edition. In dust jacket. $75-$100.

TWAIN, Mark. *A Double-Barrelled Detective Story.* Illustrated by Lucius Hitchcock. Red cloth. New York, 1902. (By Samuel Langhorne Clemens.) First edition. In dust jacket. $200-$250. Also, $130 (A, 1974).

TWAIN, Mark. *Editorial Wild Oats.* Illustrated. Red cloth. New York, 1905. (By Samuel Langhorne Clemens.) First edition. $50-$75.

TWAIN, Mark. *Eve's Diary.* Illustrated. Red cloth. New York, 1906. (By Samuel Langhorne Clemens.) First edition. $40-$50.

TWAIN, Mark. *Extracts from Adam's Diary.* Illustrated. Red cloth. New York, 1904. (By Samuel Langhorne Clemens.) First separate edition. $40-$50.

TWAIN, Mark. *Eye Openers.* Light yellow pictorial wrappers, or cloth. London, (1871). (By Samuel Langhorne Clemens.) J.C. Hotten, publisher. First edition, unauthorized, with ads at end dated 1871. Wrappers: $200-$250. (Cloth copies less scarce.) London, ("after 1875"). Ward, Lock & Co., publishers. Cloth. $50-$75.

TWAIN, Mark. *Following the Equator.* Illustrated. Blue cloth (or various leathers). Hartford, 1897. (By Samuel Langhorne Clemens.) First edition, first issue, with Hartford imprint only (New York added later). In leather or half leather: $100-$200. Cloth: $100-$125. Salesman's prospectus, with binding samples: $300-$400. Hartford, 1898. Cloth. One of 250, signed (of which only about 60 are said to have been bound). $400-$500. Also, $450 (A, 1974).

TWAIN, Mark. *A Horse's Tale.* Illustrated by Lucius Hitchcock. Red cloth. New York, 1907. (By Samuel Langhorne Clemens.) First edition. $35-$50. Also, $40 (A, 1974). London, 1907. Red cloth. First English edition. $20-$30.

TWAIN, Mark. *How to Tell a Story and Other Essays.* Red cloth. New York, 1897. (By Samuel Langhorne Clemens.) First edition. $75-$100.

TWAIN, Mark. *The Innocents Abroad or, The New Pilgrim's Progress.* Illustrated. Black cloth (or various leathers). Hartford, 1869. (By Samuel Langhorne Clemens.) First edition, first issue, without page references on page xvii and xviii and lacking illustration on page 129. Cloth, $150-$250. Prospectus for salesmen: $500 and up. (Note: A first issue copy with the rare three-page prospectus *Excursion to the Holy Land,* used in the first chapter, brought $225 at auction in 1974.) London, (1870). Wrappers. First English edition. $150-$200. Hartford, 1876. Illustrated. Decorated cloth. $150-$200.

TWAIN, Mark. *Letters from the Sandwich Islands.* Edited by G. Ezra Dane. Colored illustrations. Half cloth. San Francisco, 1937. (By Samuel Langhorne Clemens.) Grabhorn Press. First edition. One of 550. $75-$100.

TWAIN, Mark. *Life on the Mississippi.* Illustrated. Pictorial red cloth. London, 1883. (By Samuel Langhorne Clemens.) First edition. $100-$150. Boston, 1883. Brown cloth (or various leathers.) First American edition, first issue, with drawing of author in flames on page 441 and with caption on page 443 reading "The St. Louis Hotel." $250-$350. Later, with the reading "St. Charles Hotel," $150-$200. Prospectus for the American edition: $400-$500.

TWAIN, Mark. *The Love Letters of Mark Twain.* Edited by Dixon Wecter. Buckram. New York, 1949. First edition. One of 155. In dust jacket. Boxed. $300-$350.

TWAIN, Mark. *The Man That Corrupted Hadleyburg and Other Stories and Essays.* Illustrated. Red cloth. New York, 1900. (By Samuel Langhorne Clemens.) First edition, first state, with line reading "Page 2" on plate opposite page 2. $100-$150. Later, without "Page 2," $15-$20. London, 1900. Yellow cloth. First English edition. $100-$125.

TWAIN, Mark. *Mark Twain's (Burlesque) Autobiography and First Romance.* Cloth, or printed self-wrappers (with cover title). New York, (1871). (By Samuel Langhorne Clemens.) First edition, first issue, without Ball, Black & Co. ad on verso of title page. Wrappers: $200-$250. Cloth: $100-$150.

TWAIN, Mark. *Mark Twain's Library of Humor.* Illustrated by E.W. Kemble. Brown cloth. New York, 1888. (By Samuel Langhorne Clemens.) First edition, first state, with index of titles arranged in order of appearance. $100-$200.

TWAIN, Mark. *Mark Twain's Sketches, New and Old.* Illustrated. Blue cloth (or various leathers). Hartford, 1875. (By Samuel Langhorne Clemens.) First collected edition, first state, with paragraph "From *Hospital Days*" at page 299 and (in some copies) erratum slip at that page. $200-$250. Second issue, "From *Hospital Days*" not present. $100-$150. (Also, see Twain, *Number One: Mark Twain's Sketches, etc.*)

TWAIN, Mark. *A Murder, A Mystery, and A Marriage.* Printed gray wrappers. (New York), 1945. (By Samuel Langhorne Clemens.) First edition. One of 16. $500 and up. Also, $450 (A, 1974).

TWAIN, Mark. *The Mysterious Stranger: A Romance.* Illustrated by N.C. Wyeth. Black cloth, with color illustration pasted on front cover. New York, (1916). (By Samuel Langhorne Clemens.) First edition, with copyright page code letters "K-Q." In dust jacket. $100-$135. Lacking dust jacket, $50-$75.

TWAIN, Mark. *The Notorious Jumping Frog of Calaveras County.* Boards and cloth. New York, 1932. (By Samuel Langhorne Clemens.) One of 200. In tissue dust jacket. $50. New York, 1970. Limited Editions Club. Boxed. $40.

TWAIN, Mark. *Number One: Mark Twain's Sketches. Authorised Edition.* Illustrated. 32 pp., pictorial pale-blue or green wrappers. New York, (1874). (By Samuel Langhorne Clemens.) First edition, first state, with back cover blank. $400-$500. Also, $225 (A, 1974). Second state, ad on back cover. $100-$150.

TWAIN, Mark. *Old Times on the Mississippi.* Gray wrappers. Toronto, 1876. (By Samuel Langhorne Clemens.) First edition, first issue, in wrappers (later, cloth). $200-$300. Cloth: $150-$200.

TWAIN, Mark. *The £1,000,000 Bank-Note and Other New Stories.* Frontispiece. Pictorial tan cloth. New York, 1893. (By Samuel Langhorne Clemens.) First edition. $40-$60. London, 1893. Cloth. First English edition, with March ads. $100-$150.

TWAIN, Mark. *The Pains of Lowly Life.* (Cover title.) 8 pp., printed red or green wrappers (title in blue). (London), 1900. (By Samuel Langhorne Clemens.) First edition. $250-$300.

TWAIN, Mark (so designated on binding, but not on title page). *Personal Recollections of Joan of Arc.* Red buckram. New York, 1896. (By Samuel Langhorne Clemens.) First edition, first state, with ads listing third and fourth volumes of *Memoirs of Barras* as "just ready." $100-$150. London, 1896. Red cloth. First English edition, with Twain's name on title page. Issued simultaneously with American edition. $50-$75.

TWAIN, Mark. *The Prince and the Pauper.* Illustrated. Pictorial red cloth. London, 1881. (By Samuel Langhorne Clemens.) First edition, first issue, with ads dated November. $150-$200. Montreal, 1881. Blue cloth. First (?) edition. (Blanck says, "Probably simultaneous with the London edition.") $250-$300. Boston, 1882. Green cloth (or various leathers). First American edition, first issue, with Franklin Press imprint on copyright page. $250-$300. (Note: This complicated book also exists in its American first edition in an issue of "6 or 8" copies—Twain was uncertain when he signed a copy for the New York Public Library—on China paper, with white linen binding. Value: $2,000 and up? There was also supposed to be, Twain indicated, a Montreal issue in wrappers, but Blanck had not seen one. Value: $1,000 and up?) New York, 1964. Limited Editions Club. Boxed. $80-$100.

TWAIN, Mark. *Pudd'nhead Wilson: A Tale.* Illustrated. Red cloth. London, 1894. (By Samuel Langhorne Clemens.) First English edition (of *The Tragedy of Pudd'nhead Wilson,* which see). $50-$75.

TWAIN, Mark. *Pudd'nhead Wilson's Calendar for 1894.* (Cover title.) 16 pp. (3 × 2½ inches), printed yellow wrappers. (Dawson's Landing, Mo., *i.e.,* New York, 1893,) (By Samuel Langhorne Clemens.) First edition. $750-$1,000. Also, $600 (A, 1974).

TWAIN, Mark. *Punch, Brothers, Punch!* Pictorial wrappers, or cloth. New York, (1878). By Samuel Langhorne Clemens.) First edition, first issue, with Twain's name in Roman capitals on title page. Wrappers: $200-$300. Cloth: $150-$250.

TWAIN, Mark. *Queen Victoria's Jubilee.* Illustrated. Printed white boards. (New York (?), 1910.) (By Samuel Langhorne Clemens.) First edition. One of 195. $150-$200.

TWAIN, Mark. *Roughing It.* Illustrated. Black cloth (or various leathers). Hartford, 1872. (By Samuel Langhorne Clemens.) First American edition, first issue, with no words missing in lines 20 and 21 of page 242. $100-$150. Later issue, words missing on page 242. $40. Kentfield, Calif., 1953. Boards. One of 200. $100-$125.

TWAIN, Mark. *The Stolen White Elephant.* Decorated red cloth. London, 1882. First edition. $100-$125. Boston, 1882. Tan cloth. First American edition. $50-$60.

TWAIN, Mark. *To the Person Sitting in Darkness.* (Cover title.) 16 pp., self-wrappers. (New York, 1901.) (By Samuel Langhorne Clemens.) First edition. $250-$300.

TWAIN, Mark. *Tom Sawyer Abroad, Tom Sawyer, Detective, and Other Stories.* Illustrated by Dan Beard. Red cloth. New York, 1896. (By Samuel Langhorne Clemens.) First edition. $500-$600. Also, spine faded, $375 (A, 1974).

TWAIN, Mark. *The Tragedy of Pudd'nhead Wilson.* Illustrated. Brown cloth (or leather). Hartford, 1894. (By Samuel Langhorne Clemens.) First American edition. $250-$300. (For English first edition, see Twain, *Pudd'nhead Wilson.*)

TWAIN, Mark. *A Tramp Abroad.* Illustrated. Black cloth (or various leathers.) Hartford, 1880. (By Samuel Langhorne Clemens.) First edition, first state, with frontispiece entitled "Moses," not "Titian's Moses." $300-$400. Also, $225 (A, 1974). London, 1880. Red cloth. First English edition. $100-$150.

TWAIN, Mark. *A True Story.* Illustrated. Green or terra-cotta cloth. Boston, 1877. (By Samuel Langhorne Clemens.) First edition, first binding, with J R O monogram on front cover. $500-$600. Also, $425 (A, 1974). (Later issues have monogram H O.)

TWAIN, Mark. *What Is Man?* Blue cloth. London, 1910. (By Samuel Langhorne Clemens.) First English edition. $75-$100. (For first edition, see title entry.)

TWAIN, Mark (editor). *Tom Sawyer Abroad.* By Huck Finn. Edited by Mark Twain. Illustrated by Dan Beard. Tan cloth. New York, 1894. (By Samuel Langhorne Clemens.) First American edition. $150-$200. (Note: The English first edition of the same year, red cloth, preceded the American first and is currently valued in the $75-$100 range.)

TWAIN, Mark, and Warner, Charles Dudley. *The Gilded Age.* Illustrated. Black cloth (or various leathers). Hartford, 1873. (By Samuel Langhorne Clemens and Warner.) First edition, first issue, without an illustration on page 403. $300-$350. Later state. Illustration on page 403, $100-$150. Prospectus for the book: $650 and up.

TWEEDIE, William. *The Arabian Horse: His Country and People.* 10 plates, 25 text illustrations, maps and tables. Green decorated cloth. London, 1894. $200-$300. Large paper issue: Half morocco. One of 100. $400-$500.

*TWELVE Mormon Homes Visited in Succession on a Journey Through Utah to Arizona.* Cloth. Philadelphia, 1874. (By Elizabeth D. Kane.) First edition. $150.

*TWENTY Letters to Joseph Conrad.* 12 pamphlets, wrappers. London, 1926. First edition. One of 220 sets. Boxed. $200.

*TWENTY Poems.* White buckram. London, 1909. First edition. One of 25. $150-$200. (Note: Supposedly contains four poems by George Meredith.)

*TWIN Cities Directory and Business Mirror for the Year 1860, Including the Cities of Davenport, Iowa; Rock Island, Ill., and Moline, Ill.* Vol. 1. Cloth. Davenport, 1859. (E. Coy & Co., publisher.) $200-$250.

TWINING, Elizabeth. *Illustrations of the Natural Order of Plants, Arranged in Groups.* 160 colored lithograph plates. 2 vols., tall folio, half morocco. London, 1849. $5,000 and up.

TWITCHELL, Ralph Emerson. *The Leading Facts of New Mexican History.* Folding maps, color frontispiece, other illustrations. 2 vols., cloth. Cedar Rapids, Iowa, 1911-12. First edition. One of 1,500. $150-$200.

TWITCHELL, Ralph Emerson. *Old Santa Fe.* Illustrated. Cloth. (Santa Fe., 1925.) First edition. $50-$75.

*TWO Admirals (The): A Tale.* By the Author of *The Pilot.* 2 vols., purple muslin, paper labels. Philadelphia, 1842. (By James Fenimore Cooper.) First American edition. $300-$400. London, 1842. 3 vols., boards and cloth, paper labels. First edition. (Issued under Cooper's name.) $200-$250.

*TWO Generals (The).* 8 pp., printed on a single sheet, unbound. No place, no date (1868?). (By Edward Fitz Gerald.) First edition. $200 and up.

*TWO Rivulets.* See Whitman, Walt.

*TWO Years Before the Mast. A Personal Narrative of Life at Sea.* (Harpers' Family Library No. CVI.) Tan, black, or gray cloth. New York, 1840. (By Richard Henry Dana, Jr.) First edition, first issue, with perfect "i" in the word "in," first line of copyright notice. $2,000-$3,000, possibly more. Also, $2,250 (A, 1974). Second issue: $500 and up. Boston, 1869. Cloth. Revised edition. $150 and up. Boston, 1911. Illustrated. 2 vols., boards. $150 and up. Chicago, 1930. Lakeside Press. Illustrated by Edward A. Wilson. Pictorial linen. One of 1,000. Boxed. $85-$125. New York, 1936. Grabhorn printing. Illustrated. Boards. One of 1,000. In dust jacket. $60-$85. New York, 1947. Limited Editions Club. Cloth. Boxed. $45-$60.

TYLER, Daniel. *A Concise History of the Mormon Battalion in the Mexican War.* Full leather. (Salt Lake City), 1881 (actually 1882). First edition. $250-$350.

TYLER, Parker (editor). *Modern Things.* Purple and white cloth. New York, (1934). First edition. In dust jacket. $100-$135.

TYNAN, Katherine. *Twenty One Poems.* Selected by W. B. Yeats. Blue boards and linen. Dundrum, Ireland, 1907. Dun Emer Press. One of 200. $75-$85.

TYNDALE, William (translator). *The Boke off the Revelacion off Sanct Jhon the Devine, Done into Englysshe.* Vellum. London, 1901. Ashendene Press. One of 54. $1,000-$1,250.

TYNDALL, John. *Essays on the Floating-Matter of the Air in Relation to Putrefaction and Infection.* Cloth. London, 1881. First edition. $200-$300.

*TYPES of Successful Men in Texas.* Red leather. Austin, Tex., 1890. $100-$150.

TYSON, James L., M.D. *Diary of a Physician in California.* 92 pp., printed wrappers. New York, 1850. First edition. $400-$500. Oakland, Calif., 1955. One of 500. $40-$50.

TYSON, Philip T. *Geology and Industrial Resources of California.* Folding maps, charts, tables. Cloth. Baltimore, 1851. $75-$100.

TYSON, Robert A. *History of East St. Louis.* Folding map and folding view of stockyards. 152 pp., wrappers. East St. Louis, 1875. First edition. $300-$350.

# U

UDELL, John. *Incidents of Travel to California, Across the Great Plains.* Portrait, errata leaf. Cloth. Jefferson, Ohio, 1856. First edition. $250-$300.

UDELL, John. *Journal of John Udell, Kept During a Trip Across the Plains.* Vignette portrait. 47 pp., printed wrappers. Jefferson, 1868. Second edition. $1,250-$1,500. Los Angeles, 1946. Edited by Lyle H. Wright. Half morocco. One of 35 signed by Wright. $35-$50. Another issue: Cloth. One of 750. $20-$25. (Note: The first edition of Udell's *Journal*, 45 pp., printed wrappers, including cover title, appeared in Suisun City, Calif., in 1859 and is known in only one surviving copy. The following facsimile was published by Yale University in 1952.) (New Haven, 1952.) Printed wrappers. One of 200. $35-$50.

ÚLTIMAS *Communicaciones entre el Gobierno Mexicano y el Enviado Estraordinario y Ministro Plenipotenciario nombrado por el de los Estados Unidos, sobre la Cuestión de Tejas, etc.* 22 pp., printed wrappers. Mexico, 1846. $750-$1,000.

UNCLE *Abe's Republican Songster.* Wrappers. San Francisco, 1860. $100-$150.

UNDER *the Greenwood Tree.* 2 vols., green cloth. London, 1872. (By Thomas Hardy.) First edition. $400-$500.

UNIFORM *and Dress of the Army of the Confederate States.* 15 plates by Ernest Crehen. 5 pp., boards, paper label. Richmond, 1861. First edition, first issue, with black-and-white plates. $400-$600. Second issue, same date, with 9 of the 15 plates in color, plus errata slip and tipped-in colored strip illustrating field caps. $1,000-$1,500.

UNITED *States Enrollment Laws (The), for Calling Out the National Forces.* Wrappers. New York, 1864. $75-$100.

UNITED *States "History" as the Yankee Makes and Takes It.* By a Confederate Soldier. 99 pp., yellow wrappers. Glen Allen, 1900. (By John Cussons.) $100-$125.

UNJUST *Judge (The).* By a Member of the Ohio Bar. Cloth. Mansfield, Ohio, 1854. (By William Stevens.) First edition. $75-$100.

UPDIKE, D. B. *Notes on the Merrymount Press and Its Work.* Cloth. Cambridge, Mass., 1934. First edition. One of 500. $100-$135.

UPDIKE, John. *Bath After Sailing.* Wrappers, paper label. (Stevenson, Conn.). First edition (after broadside publication). One of 125, signed. $50-$75.

UPDIKE, John. *Bech: A Book.* Cloth. New York, 1970. First edition. One of 500, signed. In dust jacket. Boxed. $35-$50. Trade edition: In dust jacket. $15.

UPDIKE, John. *The Carpentered Hen and Other Tame Creatures.* Boards and cloth. New York, (1958). First edition. In dust jacket. $150-$200. Author's first book (poems).

UPDIKE, John. *Dog's Death.* Broadside poem. (Cambridge, Mass.), 1965. First edition. One of 100, signed. $75-$125.

UPDIKE, John. *The Indian.* Wrappers. (Marvin, S.D., 1971.) First edition. $25.

UPDIKE, John. *The Music School.* Boards. New York, 1966. First edition, first issue, with transposed lines in the poem on page 46. In dust jacket. $50-$75.

UPDIKE, John. *The Poorhouse Fair.* Boards and cloth. New York, 1959. First edition. In dust jacket. $75-$85. Author's first novel.

UPDIKE, John. *Rabbit, Run.* Boards and cloth. New York, 1960. First edition. In dust jacket. $50-$60.

UPDIKE, John. *The Same Door.* Boards and cloth. New York, 1959. First edition. In dust jacket. $75-$125.

UPDIKE, John. *Three Texts from Early Ipswich.* Wrappers. Ipswich, Mass., 1968. First edition. One of 50, signed. $85-$125. Trade edition: Not signed. $25.

UPDIKE, John. *Warm Wine.* Wrappers. New York, 1973. First edition. One of 276, signed. $35-$40.

UPHAM, Samuel C. *Notes from Sunland, on the Manatee River, Gulf Coast of South Florida.* Frontispiece. 83 pp., printed wrappers. Braidentown, Fla., 1881. First edition. $150-$200. Second edition (so stated), same date. $100-$125.

*UPS and Downs: A Book of Transformation Pictures.* Illustrated in color. 16 pp., with pull slides to change pictures (a movable book). Boards. London, (about 1890). $100-$150.

URREA, José. *Diario de las Operaciones Militares de la División que al Mando del Gen. José Urrea Hizo la Campana de Tejas.* Half leather. Victoria, Mexico, 1838. First edition. $1,500-$2,500. Also, $800 (A, 1966)—the Streeter copy.

# V

*VAGABOND (The): A New Story for Children.* 16 pp., wrappers. Hartford, 1819. (By Samuel Griswold Goodrich.) First edition. $100-$150.

VAIL, Alfred. *Description of the American Electro-Magnetic Telegraph.* 14 wood engravings, 24 pp., unbound. Washington, 1845. First edition. $75-$100.

VAIL, Issac Newton. *Alaska: Land of the Nugget. Why?* 68 pp., wrappers. Pasadena, 1897. $100-$125.

VAIL, Isaac Newton. *Ophir's Golden Wedge.* 36 pp., wrappers. Pasadena, 1893. $75-$125.

VALENTIA, George, Viscount. *Voyages and Travels to India, Ceylon, the Red Sea, Abyssinia, and Egypt, 1802-6.* 69 engraved views and folding maps. 3 vols., boards. London, 1809. First edition. Large paper issue: $350-$500, possibly more. Ordinary issue: $300-$400. Rebound in leather, $200-$400.

VALENTINER, Wilhem R. *Rembrandt Paintings in America.* 175 plates. Half morocco. New York, 1931. First edition. In dust jacket. $50-$60. Limited issue: Full morocco. One of 200, signed. $100-$135.

VALÉRY, Paul. *Album de Vers Anciens 1890-1900.* Wrappers. Paris, 1920. First edition. One of 150. In glassine dust jacket. $80.

VALÉRY, Paul. *Eupalinos, or The Architect.* Translated by William M. Stewart. Buckram. London, 1932. One of 250, signed. $100-$135.

VALÉRY, Paul. *Introduction to the Method of Leonardo Da Vinci.* Translated by Thomas McGreevey. Boards. London, 1929. One of 50. $100-$125.

*VALPERGA: Or, the Life and Adventures of Castruccio, Prince of Lucca.* 3 vols., blue-gray boards. London, 1823. (By Mary Wollstonecraft Shelley.) First edition, without half titles. $2,000-$2,500. Also, $1,300 (A, 1977).

VAN CLEVE, Mrs. Charlotte O. C. *"Three Score Years and Ten"; Life-Long Memories of Fort Snelling, Minn., and Other Parts of the West.* Portrait. Cloth. (Minneapolis), 1888. First edition. $50-$75.

VANDERBILT, William K. *Taking One's Own Ship Around the World.* 19 color plates. 112 photographs. Half (or full) morocco. New York, 1929. One of 200. Boxed. $65-$75.

VANDERBILT, William K. *To Galapagos on the Ara.* (New York, 1926.) Boards and leather. One of 900. $50-$75. Another issue: New York, 1927: Boards and calf. One of 500. $200.

VANDERBILT, William K. *West Made East with the Loss of a Day.* 7 color plates, 13 charts. Cloth. New York, 1933. One of 800. $50-$75. Another issue: Half morocco. One of 200 on Rives paper. $75-$100.

VAN DE WATER, Frederic F. *Glory Hunter: A Life of Gen. Custer.* 2 maps, 13 plates. Cloth. Indianapolis, (1934). First edition. In dust jacket. $40-$50.

VAN DOREN, Mark. *Spring Thunder and Other Poems.* Boards. New York, 1924. First edition. $30-$40. Author's first book.

VAN DYKE, T. S. *The Advantages of the Colony of El Cajon, San Diego County, and the*

*Superiority of Its Fruit Lands.* Large folding map. 32 pp., wrappers. San Diego, 1883. $150-$175.

VAN LOON, Hendrik Willem. *The Story of Mankind.* Illustrated by the author. Cloth, pictorial label. (New York), 1921. First edition. In dust jacket. $100-$125. Lacking jacket, worn, $50.

VAN TRAMP, John C. *Prairie and Rocky Mountain Adventures.* 61 plates. Leather. Columbus, Ohio, 1858. First edition. $125-$150. Columbus, 1867. Leather. $50-$60. Columbus, 1870. Leather. $50-$60.

VAN VECHTEN, Carl. *Firecrackers: A Realistic Novel.* Boards and cloth. New York, 1925. First edition. One of 205, signed. Boxed. $65-$75.

VAN VECHTEN, Carl. *Music After the Great War.* Cloth, paper label. New York, 1915. First edition. In dust jacket. $50-$75. Author's first book.

VAN VECHTEN, Carl. *Nigger Heaven.* Decorated cloth, printed spine label. New York, 1926. First edition. One of 205, signed. Boxed. $75.

VAN VECHTEN, Carl. *Parties.* Lemon-yellow vellum, silver decorations. New York, 1930. One of 250, signed. In dust jacket. $55. Trade edition: Yellow cloth. In dust jacket. $15-$20.

VAN VECHTEN, Carl. *Spider Boy: A Scenario for a Moving Picture.* Half cloth. New York, 1928. First edition. One of 220. Boxed. $100. Another issue: Red vellum. One of 75 on vellum. Boxed. $100-$150.

VAN VECHTEN, Carl. *The Tattooed Countess.* Boards and cloth. New York, 1924. First edition. One of 150, signed. Boxed. $50. Trade edition: Cloth. In dust jacket. $15.

VAN VECHTEN, Carl. *The Tiger in the House.* Half cloth. New York, 1920. First edition. In dust jacket. $30-$40.

VAN VLIET, Gen. S. *Table of Distances in the Department of the Missouri.* 3 folding maps, folding table. 20 pp., wrappers. Washington, 1874. $125-$150.

VAN VOGT, A. E. *Slan: A Story of the Future.* Cloth. Sauk City, Wis., 1946. Arkham House. First edition. In dust jacket. $75-$100.

VAN WYCK, Frederick. *Keskachauge, or the First White Settlement on Long Island.* 6 maps, 55 plates. Cloth. New York, 1924. First edition. $50-$60.

VAN ZANDT, Nicholas Biddle. *A Full Description of the Soil, Water, Timber, and Prairies of Each Lot, or Quarter Section of the Military Lands Between the Mississippi and Illinois River.* 127 pp., plus separately issued folding map. boards and calf. Washington City, 1818. First edition. $3,500-$4,000.

VARTHEMA, Ludovico de. *The Itinerary of . . . in Southern Asia.* Maps, illustrations. Half vellum. London, 1928. Limited edition. $50-$75.

VAUGHAN, Henry. *Poems.* Illustrated. Boards. (Newtown, Wales), 1924. Gregynog Press. One of 500. $150-$250.

VAUGHAN, Dr. John. *A Concise History of the Autumnal Fever, Which Prevailed in the Borough of Wilmington, in the Year 1802.* 32 pp., wrappers. Wilmington, Del., 1803. First edition. $175-$200.

VAUGHAN, Robert. *Then and Now, or 36 Years in the Rockies.* Illustrated. Pictorial cloth. Minneapolis, 1900. First edition. $65-$75.

VEBLEN, Thorstein. *The Theory of the Leisure Class.* Green cloth. New York, 1899. First edition. $250-$300.

VEDDER, Elihu. *Doubt and Other Things.* Illustrated by Vedder. Parchment. Boston, 1922. First edition. One of 500. Boxed. $75-$100.

VEGA CARPIO, Lope Félix de (attributed to). *The Star of Seville.* Translated by Henry Thomas. Half morocco. Newtown, Wales, 1935. Gregynog Press. One of 175. $250-$300.

VELASCO, José Francisco. *Sonora: Its Extent, Population, Natural Productions, Indian Tribes, Mines, Mineral Lands, etc.* Translated by William F. Nye. Cloth. San Francisco, 1861. First American edition. $150-$175.

VENABLE, W. H. *Beginnings of Literary Culture in the Ohio Valley.* Cloth. Cincinnati, 1891. First edition. $75-$100.

*VENTURE (The):* An Annual of Art and Literature. 23 plates. Pictorial cloth. London, 1905 (actually 1904). First edition. ("Two Songs," included here, is James Joyce's first appearance in a clothbound book.) $250-$300.

VERGA, Giovanni. *Little Novels of Sicily.* Translated by D. H. Lawrence. Red cloth, spine label. New York, 1925. First edition, first binding. In dust jacket. $35-$50.

VERGA, Giovanni. *Mastro—Don Gesualdo.* Translated by D. H. Lawrence. Cloth. New York, 1923. First edition. In dust jacket. $35-$50. London, 1925. Cloth. First English edition. In dust jacket. $20-$25.

VERINO, Ugolino. *Vita di Santa Chiara Vergine.* Printed in black and red. 4 facsimile pages. White vellum. London, 1921. Ashendene Press. One of 236. $400-$600. Another issue: Full red vellum. One of 10 on vellum. $1,500-$2,000.

VERNE, Jules. *Five Weeks in a Balloon.* Red cloth. New York, 1869. First American edition. $75-$100. Verne's first book.

VERNE, Jules. *From the Earth to the Moon.* Illustrated. Cloth. London, 1873. First English edition. $100-$125. New York, 1874. Illustrated. Cloth. First American edition. $75-$100.

VERNE, Jules. *The Fur Country; or, Seventy Degrees North Latitude.* 100 full-page illustrations. Pictorial cloth. Boston, 1874. First American edition. $75-$100.

VERNE, Jules. *Mistress Branican.* Illustrated, including 2 maps and 12 colored engravings. Pictorial red cloth. Paris, no date. First edition. $75-$125.

*VERSES by Two Undergraduates.* Wrappers. (Cambridge, Mass.), 1905. (By Van Wyck Brooks and John Hall Wheelock.) First edition. $50-$75. First book for both authors.

*VERSES from the Harvard Advocate.* Cloth. Cambridge, 1906. First edition. $75-$100. (Note: Contains five poems by Wallace Stevens.)

*VERSES on Various Occasions.* Cloth. London, 1868. (By John Henry, Cardinal Newman.) First edition. $75-$150.

VESPUCCI, Amerigo. *Letter of Amerigo Vespucci Describing His Four Voyages to the New World.* Map in color, illustrations by Valenti Angelo. Vellum. San Francisco, 1926. One of 250. Boxed. $125-$200.

VESTAL, Stanley. *Big Foot Wallace.* Illustrated. Cloth. Boston, 1942. (By Walter S. Campbell.) First edition. In dust jacket. $50-$60.

VICENTIO, Ludovico. *The Calligraphic Models of Ludovico degli Arrighi, Surnamed Vicentio.* Edited by Stanley Morrison. 64 pp., facsimile. Montagnola (Paris), 1926. One of 300. $400-$500.

VIDAL, Gore. *In a Yellow Wood.* Cloth. New York, 1947. First edition. In dust jacket. $75.

VIDAL, Gore. *The Judgment of Paris.* Cloth. New York, 1962. First edition. In dust jacket. $25-$35.

VIDAL, Gore. *The Season of Comfort.* Cloth. New York, 1949. First edition. In dust jacket. $25-$35.

VIDAL, Gore. *Williwaw.* Cloth. New York, 1946. First edition. In dust jacket. $75-$100. Author's first book.

VILLA, José Garcia. *Footnote to Youth*. Cloth. New York, 1933. First edition. In dust jacket. $45. Author's first book.

*VINDICATION of the Recent and Prevailing Policy of Georgia in Its Internal Affairs, etc. (A)*. 90 pp., wrappers (?). Athens, Ga., 1827. (By Augustin S. Clayton.) First edition. $250-$300.

VIRGIL. *Les Georgiques*. In Latin and French. 122 woodcuts by Aristide Maillol. 2 vols., loose sheets, printed wrappers, in 2 slipcases, plus matching case with 2 extra sets of the woodcuts. Paris, 1937-43-(50). One of the special sets from the edition of 750 with the extra plates. $1,000-$1,500. Ordinary issue: One of 750. $500-$750.

*VIRGINIA Illustrated*. Cloth. New York, 1857. (By David Hunter Strother.) First edition. $100-$150.

*VIRGINIA Speller and Reader (The)*. Boards. Richmond, 1865. $250-$300.

VISCHER, Edward. *Missions of Upper California*. 15 plates. Wrappers. San Francisco, 1872. First edition. $300-$350.

VISCHER, Edward. *Sketches of the Washoe Mining Region*. Cloth portfolio with 29 mounted plates (25 numbered) and 24 pp. of text, wrappers. San Francisco, 1862. First edition. $1,500-$2,000. Also, $1,100 (A, 1968)—the Streeter copy (catalogued "24 pp., 24 plates"). (Note: Another copy was offered in a Boston dealer's catalogue in 1957 as with 25 numbered plates and four other mounted plates at $850. Howes' *U.S.-iana* calls for 26 plates.)

*VISIT to Texas (A)*. Folding map in color, 4 plates. Cloth. New York, 1834. (Attributed to Col. W. W. Morris and Dr. M. [or E.] Fisk[e]?) First edition. $325-$500. New York, 1836. Cloth. Second edition, with plates omitted. $275-$400.

VISSCHER, William Lightfoot. *"Black Mammy": A Song of the Sunny South*. Illustrated. Cloth. Cheyenne, 1885. First edition. $75-$100. Author's first book.

VISSER, H. F. E. *Asiatic Art*. Illustrated, including color frontispiece. Black cloth. New York, (1948). First edition. In dust jacket. $75-$100.

VIVIAN, George. *Scenery of Portugal and Spain*. 35 hand-colored plates. Half morocco. London, 1839. First edition. $1,000-$1,500.

VIVIAN, George. *Spanish Scenery*. Engraved title, 27 other plates. Half morocco. London, 1838. First edition. $400-$600.

*VIVIAN Grey*. 5 vols., boards, paper labels. London, 1826. (By Benjamin Disraeli.) First edition. $400-$500. Author's first novel.

VIZETELLY, Henry. *A History of Champagne*. Illustrated. Cloth. London, 1882. First edition. $200.

*VOIAGE and Travaile of Sir John Maundeville (The)*. Illuminated by Valenti Angelo. Red morocco. New York, 1928. Grabhorn Press (Random House). One of 150. $600-$800.

*VOICE of Scotland (The)*. See MacDiarmid, Hugh.

VOLNEY, C. F. *A View of the Soil and Climate of the United States*. 2 folding plates, 2 folding maps. Leather. Philadelphia, 1804. First American edition. $200-$250.

VOLTAIRE, Jean François Marie Arouet de. *Candide*. Translated by Richard Aldington. Illustrated by Rockwell Kent and colored by hand. Cloth, leather spine. New York, 1928. Limited edition. One of 95, signed. Boxed. $400-$600. Ordinary issue (not hand-colored): Buckram. One of 1,470 signed by Kent. $125-$200. Another copy, with the "exceedingly rare" suppressed plate (copulation) and a letter from Bennett Cerf explaining its exclusion from the first Random House book. $600 (in a 1978 catalogue).

VON HAGEN, Victor W. *The Aztec and Maya Papermakers*. Illustrated, including paper samples. Cloth. New York, 1943. First edition. One of 220, signed. $300-$400.

VON OETTINGEN, B. *Horse Breeding in Theory and Practice.* Cloth. London, 1909. $75-$100.

VONNEGUT, Kurt, Jr. *Cat's Cradle.* Two-toned cloth. New York, (1963). First edition. In dust jacket. $40-$50.

VONNEGUT, Kurt. Jr. *Mother Night.* Wrappers. Greenwich, Conn., (1962). Fawcett Publications. First edition. $30-$40.

VONNEGUT, Kurt, Jr. *Player Piano.* Cloth. New York, 1952. First edition, with the Scribner seal and "A" on copyright page. In dust jacket. $65-$95.

VONNEGUT, Kurt, Jr. *The Sirens of Satan.* Pictorial wrappers. (New York, 1959.) First edition. $50-$75. Boston, 1961. Cloth. first hardbound edition. In dust jacket. $40-$50.

VONNEGUT, Kurt, Jr. *Slaughterhouse-Five.* Cloth. (New York, 1969). First edition, first printing. In dust jacket. $40-$50.

VOORHEES, Luke. *Personal Recollections of Pioneer Life on the Mountains and Plains of the Great West.* Portrait. 75 pp., cloth. Cheyenne, (1920). First edition. $125-$150.

*VOYAGE to Mexico and Havanna (A); Including Some General Observations on the United States.* By an Italian. Half calf. New York, 1841. (By Charles Barinetti.) First edition. $225-$250.

VOYNICH, E. L. *The Gadfly.* Red or brown cloth. New York, 1897. First American edition. $50-$60.

# W

W., E. B. *The Lady is Cold: Poems by E. B. W.* Boards. New York, 1929. (By E. B. White.) First edition. In dust jacket. $75-$100. Author's first book.

WADSWORTH, Edward. *The Black Country.* Introduction by Arnold Bennett. 20 drawings and signed woodcut frontispiece. Cloth. London, 1920. One of 50 on Japan vellum, with special additional woodcut. $500-$600. Ordinary copies: In dust jacket. $100-$125.

WAGNER, Lieut. Col. A. L., and Kelley, Comm. J. D. *The United States Army and Navy: Their Histories, etc.* 43 colored plates. Oblong folio, leatherette. Akron, Ohio, 1899. First edition. $200-$250.

WAGNER, Henry R. *Bullion to Books.* Illustrated. Cloth. Los Angeles, 1942. First edition. In dust jacket. $100-$150.

WAGNER, Henry R. *The Cartography of the Northwest Coast of America to the Year 1800.* 2 vols., folio, cloth. Berkeley, 1937. First edition. In dust jackets. Boxed. $250-$350.

WAGNER, Henry R. *The Plains and the Rockies.* Boards and cloth. San Francisco, 1920. First edition (suppressed). With 6-page pamphlet of corrections. $200-$250. San Francisco, 1921. Boards. First published edition. $50-$75. Another issue: Half vellum. 40 photostat reproductions. One of 50. $100-$150. San Francisco, 1937. Revised by C. L. Camp. Grabhorn Press. Cloth. Second edition. One of 600. $200-$225. Columbus, Ohio, 1953. Cloth. Third edition. $100-$150. Another issue: Boards. De luxe edition. One of 75. Boxed. $200-$225.

WAGNER, Henry R. *Sir Francis Drake's Voyage Around the World.* Maps, plates. Cloth. San Francisco, 1926. First edition. $75-$100. Another issue: Three-quarters morocco. One of 100 signed and extra-illustrated. $200-$250.

WAGNER, Henry R. *Sixty Years of Book Collecting.* Portrait frontispiece. Boards. (Los Angeles), 1952. First edition. One of 200. $100-$150.

WAGNER, Henry R. *Spanish Explorations in the Strait of Juan de Fuca.* Maps, illustrations. Cloth. Santa Ana, Calif., 1933. First edition. One of 425. $200-$250. Another issue: Vellum. One of 25, signed and extra-illustrated. $300-$325.

WAGNER, Henry R. *The Spanish Southwest, 1542-1794.* Half morocco. Berkeley, 1924. First edition. One of 100. $350-$450. Another issue: Vellum. One of 20, signed and extra-illustrated. $500-$600. Albuquerque, 1937. 2 vols., half vellum. $200-$250.

WAGNER, Henry R. *The Spanish Voyages to the Northwest Coast of America.* Maps, plates. Cloth. San Francisco, 1929. First edition. $200-$250. Another issue: Vellum. One of 25, signed and extra-illustrated. $350-$450.

WAGNER, Henry R. (editor). *California Voyages, 1539-1541.* Cloth. San Francisco, 1925. First edition. $75-$125.

WAGNER, Richard. *The Flying Dutchman.* Vellum. London, 1938. Corvinus Press. One of 130. Boxed. $100-$150.

WAGNER, Richard. *The Rhinegold & The Valkyrie.* Translated by Margaret Armour. 34 color plates by Arthur Rackham. Vellum. London, 1910. One of 1,150 signed by the artist. $350-$500. London, 1910. Cloth. Trade edition. $125-$200. New York, 1910. Cloth. American trade edition. $125-$200. London, (1920). Cloth. $150-$200. London, (1939). Cloth. $65-$100.

WAGNER, Richard. *Siegfried and the Twilight of the Gods*. Translated by Margaret Armour. Illustrated by Arthur Rackham. Pictorial vellum. London, 1911. One of 1,150, signed. In half morocco slipcase. $400-$550. London, 1911. Cloth. Trade edition. $150-$200. London, 1924. Cloth. $100-$150.

WAGSTAFF. A. E. (editor). *Life of David S. Terry*. 5 plates. Cloth. San Francisco, 1892. First edition. $75-$100.

WAGSTAFF, Theophile. *Flore et Zephyr: Ballet Mythologique*. 9 tinted plates (including cover title) by the author. Wrappers. London, 1836. (By William Makepeace Thackeray.) First edition. $500-$750, possibly more. Author's first separate publication.

WAIN, John. *Mixed Feelings! Nineteen Poems*. Wrappers. Reading, England, 1951. First edition. One of 120. $100-$135. $500-$750, possibly more. Author's first book.

WAKEFIELD, John A. *History of the War Between the United States and the Sac and Fox Nations of Indians, etc.* Cloth. Jacksonville, Ill., 1834. First edition. $400-$500.

WAKEFIELD, H. Russell. *The Clock Strikes Twelve*. Cloth. Sauk City, Wis., 1946. First edition. In dust jacket. $25-$40.

WAKEFIELD, Maj. Paul L. (compiler). *Campaigning Texas*. 156 pp., wrappers. Austin, 1932. One of 50. $100-$125.

WAKEFIELD, Priscilla. *A Family Tour Through the British Empire*. Contemporary calf, leather label. Philadelphia 1804. First American edition. $100-$125.

WAKOSKI, Diane. *Coins and Coffins*. Printed wrappers. (New York, 1962). First edition. $75-$100. Author's first printed book.

WAKOSKI, Diane. *The Diamond Merchant*. Gray cloth, paper label. Cambridge, Mass., (1968). First edition. One of 99, signed. In dust jacket. $75-$85.

WAKOSKI, Diane. *Discrepancies and Apparitions*. Cloth. Garden City, 1966. First edition. In dust jacket. $25-$35.

WAKOSKI, Diane. *The Lament of the Lady Bank Dick*. Boards. Cambridge, (1969). First edition. One of 109, signed. In glassine dust jacket. $75-$85.

WAKOSKI, Diane. *The Magellanic Clouds*. Boards. Los Angeles, 1970. Black Sparrow Press. One of 250, signed. In acetate dust jacket. $35-$45. Another issue: Wrappers. $10.

WAKOSKI, Diane. *On Barbara's Shore*. Boards. Los Angeles, 1971. First edition. One of 100, signed. In acetate dust jacket. $50-$75. Another issue: Wrappers. $10.

WAKOSKI, Diane. *Thanking My Mother for Piano Lessons*. Wrappers. Mt. Horeb, Wis., 1969. One of 250. $30-$40.

WALCOTT, Mary Vaux. *North American Wildflowers*. 400 color plates. 5 vols., cloth portfolios. Washington, 1925-29. One of 500, signed. Boxed. $300-$500. Also, $150 (A, 1977).

WALDROP, Keith. *Songs from the Decline of the West*. Calf. Mt. Horeb, (1970). First edition. One of 120. $60.

WALGAMOTT, Charles S. *Reminiscences of Early Days*. Plates. 2 vols., cloth. (Twin Falls, Idaho, 1926-27.) First edition. $100-$150.

WALGAMOTT, Charles S. *"Six Decades Back."* Cloth. Caldwell, Idaho, 1936. Second edition (of *Reminiscences of Early Days*.) $50-$75.

WALKER, Charles D. *Biographical Sketches of the Graduates and Élèves of the Virginia Military Institute Who Fell During the War between the States*. Cloth. Philadelphia, 1875. $75-$100.

WALKER, George. *The Costume of Yorkshire*. Text in English and French. Colored frontispiece and 40 colored aquatint plates. Folio, contemporary morocco. London, 1814.

First edition in book form. $1,000-$2,000. Leeds, 1885. Half morocco. Facsimile of 1814 edition. One of 600. $500-$750.

WALKER, Tacetta. *Stories of Early Days in Wyoming: Big Horn Basin.* Illustrated. Cloth. Casper, Wyo., (1936). First edition. $35-$50.

WALL, Bernhardt. *Ten Etched Poems: First Series.* Boards, paper label. New York, 1924. First edition. One of 50, signed. $50-$75.

WALL, W. G. *Wall's Hudson River Portfolio.* 21 color plates. Oblong atlas folio, boards and calf. New York, (about 1826). First edition. $4,000-$5,000, possibly more. (Note: The last two sales noted at auction were in 1948: copies without title page, $1,700 each.) New York, 1828. Second edition (or state), without title page. $4,000-$5,000, possibly more.

WALLACE, Dexter. *The Blood of the Prophets.* Boards. Chicago, 1905. (By Edgar Lee Masters.) First edition. $75-$100.

WALLACE, Ed. R. *Parson Hanks.* Wrappers. Arlington, Tex., (1906?). First edition. $75-$100.

WALLACE, Edgar. *The Four Just Men.* Frontispiece. Yellow cloth. London, 1905. First edition, first issue, with folding frontispiece plate and "Solution" leaf at end. $80-$100.

WALLACE, Edgar. *The Mission That Failed! A Tale of the Raid and Other Poems.* Wrappers. (Cape Town, 1898.) First edition. $300-$400. Author's first book.

WALLACE, Edgar. *Writ in Barracks.* Cloth. London, 1900. First edition. $50-$75.

WALLACE, Lew. *Ben-Hur: A Tale of the Christ.* Light-blue floral cloth. New York, 1880. First edition, first issue, with dated title page, six-word dedication. $150-$200. (Copies in brown cloth and other colors are considered later issues.) New York, 1960. Limited Editions Club. Boxed. $40-$50.

WALLACE, Lew. *The Fair God.* Cloth. Boston, 1873. First edition, first state on thin paper, bound in beveled boards. $60-$80. Author's first book.

WALPOLE, Horace. *Memoires of the Last Ten Years of the Reign of George the Second.* 11 plates. 2 vols., boards. London, 1822. First edition. $150.

*WALTER Kennedy: An American Tale.* Boards, leather spine label. London, 1805. (By John Davis.) First edition. $500-$600.

WALTER, William W. *The Sharp Sickle: Text Book of Eschatology.* Cloth. Aurora, Ill., (1938). First edition. Boxed. $50.

WALTERS, Henry. *Incunabula Typographica.* Illustrated, including facsimiles. Calf. Baltimore, 1906. $100-$150.

WALTERS, L. D. O. (compiler). *The Year's at the Spring: An Anthology of Recent Poetry.* Illustrated by Harry Clarke. Vellum. London, 1920. One of 250 signed by Clarke. $500-$650.

WALTERS, Lorenzo D. *Tombstone's Yesterdays.* Illustrated. Cloth. Tucson, 1928. First edition. $60-$100.

WALTHER, C. F., and Taylor, I. N. *The Resources and Advantages of the State of Nebraska.* (Cover title.) Folding map. 27 pp., wrappers. (Omaha, 1871.) First edition. $175-$200.

WALTON, Izaak (or Isaac), and Cotton, Charles. *The Compleat* [or *Complete*] *Angler.* (Note: As with many classic works, there have been innumerable editions of this since its first publication in 1653. A representative group of nineteenth- and twentieth-century editions is listed here.) New York, 1847. Edited by George W. Bethune. 2 portraits, 2 plates, other illustrations. 2 parts bound in one vol., light-tan cloth, horizontal red stripes. First American edition. Large paper issue, with proof impressions of plates. $400-$600. Ordinary issue: $150-$250. London, 1824-25. Proof impressions of plates on

India paper. 2 vols., green morocco. $150-$300. London, (1880). Vellum. Facsimile edition by Elliott Stock. One of 6 printed on vellum. $400-$500. New York, 1880. Half morocco. One of 100 large paper copies. Sixth Bethune edition. $150-$200. London, 1888. Edited by R. B. Marston. Printed on India paper. 2 vols., green morocco. "Lea & Dove Edition." One of 250. $600-$800. (Also, $1,500 at auction in 1975—"sold as photographica"!) London, 1902. Edited by G. A. B. Dewar. India paper. 2 vols., green vellum or morocco. "Winchester Edition." One of 150. $400-$500. London, 1905. Caradoc Press. One of 350. $150-$200. Cambridge, Mass., 1909. Boards. Designed by Bruce Rogers. One of 440. $75-$100. London, 1929. Nonesuch Press. Full morocco. One of 1,600. $175-$200. London, (1931). Illustrated by Arthur Rackham. Vellum. One of 775 signed by Rackham. $400-$600. Trade edition: Cloth. $150-$200. Philadelphia, (1931). American trade edition. In dust jacket. $150-$200.

WALTON, W. M. *Life and Adventures of Ben Thompson, the Famous Texan.* 15 plates, 229 pp., pictorial wrappers. Austin, 1884. First edition. $750-$1,000.

WANDREI, Donald. *Dark Odyssey.* Illustrated. Cloth. St. Paul, (1931). First edition. One of 400, signed. In dust jacket. $100-$125.

WANDREI, Donald. *The Eye and the Finger.* Cloth. (Sauk City, Wis.), 1944. First edition. In dust jacket. $100-$125.

WANDREI, Donald. *Poems for Midnight.* Illustrated. Cloth. Sauk City, 1964. First edition. In dust jacket. $50-$75.

WANDREI, Donald. *The Web of Easter Island.* Cloth. Sauk City, 1948. First edition. In dust jacket. $40-$50.

*WAR in Florida (The).* By a Late Staff Officer. Folding map. 2 plates. Green cloth. Baltimore, 1836. (By Woodburn Potter.) First edition. $175-$225.

*WAR in Texas (The).* By a Citizen of the United States. 57 pp., printed wrappers. Philadelphia, 1836. (By Benjamin Lundy.) First edition under this title (but second, enlarged, edition of an earlier pamphlet of the same date. *The Origin and True Causes of the Texas Rebellion*). $125-$250. Philadelphia, 1837. 64 pp., wrappers (or sewed). $100-$200.

WARD, D. B. *Across the Plains in 1853.* (Cover title.) Portrait. 55 pp., printed wrappers. (Seattle, 1911.) First edition. $125-$150.

WARD, Lynd. *God's Man: A Novel in Woodcuts.* 143 plates, no text. Pictorial boards and cloth. New York, (1929). First edition. In dust jacket. $75-$100. Another issue: One of 409, signed. Boxed. $150-$200.

WARD, Lynd. *Vertigo: A Novel in Woodcuts.* Pictorial cloth. New York, 1937. First edition. In dust jacket. $75-$85.

WARDER, T. B., and Catlett, J. M. *Battle of Young's Branch, or, Manassas Plain.* 2 folding maps. Wrappers, or half leather. Richmond, 1862. First edition. Wrappers: $175-$225. Half leather: $150-$175.

WARE, Eugene. *The Indian War of 1864.* Frontispiece. Cloth. Topeka, 1911, First edition. $100-$125.

WARE, Eugene. *The Lyon Campaign in Missouri.* Cloth. Topeka, 1907. First edition. $50-$75.

WARE, Joseph E. *The Emigrants' Guide to California.* Folding map. 56 pp., cloth. St. Louis, (1849). First edition. $2,500-$3,000 The last two copies to sell at auction lacked the map: $1,000 (1948); $500 (1968)—the Streeter copy, offered later at retail for $1,000.

WARING, Robert Lewis. *As We See It.* Cloth. Washington, 1910. First edition. $50-$75.

WARNER, Charles Dudley. *Backlog Studies.* Illustrated. Boards. Cambridge, Mass., 1899. One of 250, signed. $40-$50.

WARNER, Charles Dudley. *My Summer in a Garden.* Cloth. Boston, 1871. First edition. $50-$60. Author's first book.

WARNER, Col. J. J.; Hayes, Benjamin; and Widney, Dr. J. P. *An Historical Sketch of Los Angeles County.* 88 pp., printed wrappers. Los Angeles, 1876. First edition. $150-$200. Los Angeles, 1936. Boards and cloth. $50-$75.

WARNER, M. M. *Warner's History of Dakota County, Nebraska.* Plates. Cloth. Lyons, Neb., 1893. First edition. $100-$125.

WARNER, Matt, and King, Murray E. *The Last of the Bandit Riders.* Illustrated. Pictorial cloth. Caldwell, Idaho, 1940. First edition. In slipcase. $50.

WARNER, Susan B. See Wetherell, Elizabeth.

WARNER and Foote. *Directory of Carroll County (Iowa).* 48 pp., wrappers. Minneapolis, 1884. $100-$125.

WARRE, Henry J. *Sketches in North America and the Oregon Territory.* Map, 20 colored views (on 16 sheets). Large folio, boards. (London, 1848.) First edition. $9,500-$10,000. Also, $4,600 (A, 1971), for copy lacking spine; $4,000 and $3,500 (A, 1969).

WARREN, Edward. *A Doctor's Experiences in Three Continents.* Cloth. Baltimore, 1855. $75-$100.

WARREN, Edward. *An Epitome of Practical Surgery for Field and Hospital.* Boards and cloth. Richmond, 1863. First edition. $175-$225.

WARREN, John. *The Conchologist.* 34 plates, 17 colored. Morocco. Boston, 1834. First edition. $100-$125.

WARREN, John C. *Etherization: With Surgical Remarks.* Cloth. Boston, 1848. First edition. $200-$250.

WARREN, Robert Penn. *Blackberry Winter.* Illustrated. Boards, paper label. (Cummington, Mass.), 1946. First edition. One of 280 on Arches paper, signed. $150-$200.

WARREN, Robert Penn. *Eleven Poems on the Same Theme.* Printed wrappers. Norfolk, Conn., (1942). First edition. $50-$75. Another issue: Boards. $75-$100.

WARREN, Robert Penn. *John Brown: The Making of a Martyr.* Cloth. New York, 1929. First edition. In dust jacket. $200-$350. Author's first book.

WARREN, Robert Penn. *Night Rider.* Cloth. Boston, 1939. First edition. In dust jacket. $65-$75.

WARREN, Robert Penn. *Selected Poems: New and Old, 1923-1966.* Cloth. New York, (1966). First edition. One of 250, signed. In dust jacket. Boxed. $50-$75. Trade edition: In dust jacket. $10.

WARREN, Robert Penn. *Selected Poems: 1923-1943.* Cloth. New York, (1944). First edition. In dust jacket. $50-$75.

WARREN, Robert Penn. *Thirty-six Poems.* Wrappers. New York, 1935. First edition. One of 165, signed. $75-$100.

WARREN, Samuel. See *Ten Thousand a-Year.*

WASHBURNE, The Rev. Cephas. *Reminiscences of the Indians.* Cloth. Richmond, (1869). First edition. $200-$300.

WASHINGTON, Booker T. *The Future of the American Negro.* Cloth. Boston, 1899. First edition. $50-$75. Author's first book.

WASHINGTON, Booker T. *Up from Slavery: An Autobiography.* Cloth. New York, 1901. First edition. $50-$75. New York, 1970. Limited Editions Club. Boxed. $30-$40.

WASSON, George S. *Sailing Days on the Penobscot.* Boards and cloth. Salem, Mass., 1932. One of 97 on rag paper. $150-$200. Trade edition: Cloth. In dust jacket. $75-$85.

WASSON, R. Gordon. *The Hall Carbine Affair.* Illustrated. Half morocco. Danbury, Conn., 1971. One of 250. Boxed. $200.

WASSON, R. Gordon. *Soma: Divine Mushroom of Immortality.* Illustrated, including color plates. Half morocco. New York, 1968. First edition. One of 680. Boxed. $450-$500.

WASSON, Valentina Pavlona, and Wasson, R. Gordon. *Mushrooms, Russia and History.* Color plates, folding maps and plates. 2 vols., folio, buckram. New York, (1957). First edition. One of 521. Boxed. $1,250-$1,500.

*WATER Witch (The), or The Skimmer of the Seas.* By the Author of *The Pilot.* 3 vols., boards, paper labels. Dresden, 1830. (By James Fenimore Cooper.) First edition. $2,000 and up. London, 1830. 3 vols., brown boards, paper labels. First English edition. $300-$400. Philadelphia, 1831. Blue or tan boards. First American edition. $150-$250.

WATERS, Frank. *Leon Gaspard.* Illustrated, including color, by Gaspard. Cloth. Flagstaff, Ariz., 1964. First edition. One of 500, signed. Boxed. $85-$100. Trade edition: In dust jacket. $15.

WATERS, Frank. *Masked Gods: Navaho and Pueblo Ceremonialism.* Illustrated. Cloth. Albuquerque, 1950. First edition. In dust jacket. $25-$35.

WATERLOO, Stanley. *The Seekers.* Red cloth. Chicago, 1900. First edition. $50-$75.

WATERLOO, Stanley. *The Story of Ab.* Illustrated. Cloth. Chicago, 1897. First edition. $100-$125.

WATERLOO, Stanley. *The Wolf's Long Howl.* Pictorial cloth. Chicago, 1899. First edition. $50-$75.

WATKINS, C. L. *Photographic Views of the Falls and Valley of Yo-Semite.* Map and 52 (or 62?) mounted photographs. Folio, morocco. San Francisco, 1863. First edition. $10,000-$15,000. Also, $4,500 (A, 1971).

WATKINS, Lucy. *The History and Adventures of Little James and Mary.* 15 pp., wrappers. Philadelphia, (1810). $100-$125.

WATKINS, Lura W. *Early New England Potters and Their Wares.* Illustrated. Cloth. Cambridge, Mass., 1950. $40-$50.

WATSON, Douglas S. *West Wind: The Life Story of Joseph Reddeford Walker.* Plates, folding map. Boards. Los Angeles, 1934. First edition. One of 100. $300-$400. Trade edition: $150-$200.

WATSON, Douglas S. (editor). *California in the Fifties.* 50 views. Oblong folio, cloth. San Francisco, 1936. One of 850. In dust jacket. $125-$150.

WATSON, Douglas S. (editor). *The Spanish Occupation of California.* Illustrated. Boards and cloth. San Francisco, 1934. Grabhorn Press. One of 550. $100-$150.

WATSON, Frederick. *Hunting Pie.* Illustrated. Boards. New York, (1938). Derrydale Press. First edition. One of 750. $75-$100.

WATSON, William. *The Eloping Angels.* Cloth. London, 1893. First edition. One of 250. $25-$35. Trade edition: Cloth. $15.

WATSON, William. *Epigrams of Art, Life and Nature.* Cloth. Liverpool, 1884. First edition. One of 50. $50-$60.

WATSON, William. *Excursions in Criticism.* Boards. London, 1893. First edition. One of 50. $35-$50. Trade edition: Cloth. $15-$20.

WATSON, William. *The Father of the Forest and Other Poems.* Frontispiece portrait. Cloth. London, 1895. First edition. One of 75. $35-$50.

WATSON, William. *Odes and Other Poems.* Cloth. London, 1894. First edition. One of 75. $35-$50.

WATSON, William. *The Purple East: A Series of Sonnets on England's Desertion of Armenia.* Frontispiece. Cloth. London, 1896. First edition. One of 75. $35-$50.

WATSON, William. *Wordsworth's Grave and Other Poems.* Frontispiece. Boards. London, 1890. First edition. $25-$30.

WATTS, W. J. *Cherokee Citizenship and a Brief History of Internal Affairs in the Cherokee Nation.* (Cover title.) Portrait. Wrappers. Muldrow, Indian Territory (Okla.), 1895. $150-$200.

WATTS, W. W. *Old English Silver.* 307 plates. Cloth. New York, 1924. First American edition. $80-$125. London, 1924. Cloth. First English edition. $125-$150. One of 40 in leather binding. $200-$300.

WAUGH, Alec. *Hot Countries.* Illustrated by Lynd Ward. Pictorial cloth. New York, (1930). First edition. In dust jacket. $50-$75.

WAUGH, Evelyn. *Basil Seal Rides Again.* Cloth. Boston, (1963). First American edition. One of 1,000, signed. $75-$85. London, 1963. Cloth. One of 750, signed. $100-$125.

WAUGH, Evelyn. *Black Mischief.* Cloth. London, 1932. First trade edition. In dust jacket, with Book Society wraparound band. $100-$135. Large paper issue: Purple cloth. One of 250, signed. (Issued without dust jacket.) $200-$275.

WAUGH, Evelyn. *Decline and Fall.* Illustrated. Cloth. London, 1928. First edition. In dust jacket. $250-$300. Lacking jacket. $150-$175.

WAUGH, Evelyn. *A Handful of Dust.* Frontispiece. Cloth. London, 1934. First edition. In dust jacket. $65-$85. Another issue: Wrappers. One of 12 signed. $850-$1,250.

WAUGH, Evelyn. *The Holy Places.* Woodcuts by Reynolds Stone. Morocco. London, 1952. First edition. One of 50, signed. In dust jacket. $300-$400.

WAUGH, Evelyn. *Labels: A Mediterranean Journal.* Illustrated. Light-blue cloth. (London), 1930. First edition. One of 110, signed, specially bound with a leaf of the original manuscript. $400-$500. Trade edition: Cloth. In dust jacket. $100-$125.

WAUGH, Evelyn. *Love Among the Ruins.* Illustrated. Decorated cloth. London, 1953. First edition. One of 350, signed. In glassine dust jacket. $250-$350.

WAUGH, Evelyn. *The Loved One.* Illustrated by Stuart Boyle. Buckram. London, (1948). First edition. One of 250, signed. (Issued without dust jacket.) $150-$200. Trade issue. In dust jacket. $30-$50. Boston, 1948. Gray cloth. First American edition. In dust jacket. $40-$50.

WAUGH, Evelyn. *P. R. B.: An Essay on the Pre-Raphaelite Brotherhood.* Boards and linen. London, 1926. First edition, with errata slip. $750-$1,000. Also, inscribed, $1,010 (A, 1974).

WAUGH, Evelyn. *Scoop.* Cloth. London, (1938). First edition. In dust jacket, with Book Society band. $60-$100.

WAUGH, Evelyn. *Vile Bodies.* Cloth. London, 1930. First edition. In dust jacket. $150-$200. Lacking jacket, $75-$100.

WAUGH, Evelyn. *Waugh in Abyssinia.* Cloth. London, (1936). First edition. In dust jacket. $75-$125.

WAUGH, Evelyn. *Wine in Peace and War.* Illustrations. by Rex Whistler. Decorated boards. London, (1949). First edition. In plain dust jacket. $100-$125. Another issue: Leather. One of 100 signed. $200-$250.

WAUGH, Lorenzo. *Autobiography of Lorenzo Waugh.* illustrated. Cloth. Oakland, 1883. First edition. $50-$65.

*WAVERLEY; or, 'Tis Sixty Years Since.* 3 vols., boards, paper labels, Edinburgh, 1814. (By Sir Walter Scott.) First edition, first issue, with "our" instead of "your" in first line on page 136 in Vol. II. $3,500-$4,000. Also, $2,250 (A, 1974). Only a few copies known in original boards. One was catalogued by an English dealer early in 1970 at $3,600. Acceptable rebound copies in contemporary leather range in price up to $500 or more at retail.

WAYLAND, John W. *History of Rockingham County.* Plates. Buckram. Dayton, Va., 1912. $75-$125.

WAYLAND, John W. *Historic Homes of Northern Virginia and the Eastern Panhandle of Western Virginia.* Cloth. Staunton, Va., 1937. First edition. $45-$60.

WEARY, Ogdred. *The Beastly Baby.* Illustrated. Wrappers. (New York, 1962.) (By Edward Gorey.) First edition. $200-$300.

WEATHERLY, Frederick Edward. *Magic Pictures: A Book of Changing Scenes.* 16 pp., with pull slides to change pictures (a movable book). Pictorial cloth. London, (about 1890). $100-$150.

WEATHERLY, Frederick Edward. *Pretty Polly: A Novel Book for Children.* 4 double-page 3-dimensional color plates. Half cloth. London, (about 1895). First edition. $150.

WEAVER, John V. A. *In American—Poems.* Boards. New York, 1921. First edition. In dust jacket. $35-$50. Author's first book.

WEBB, Mary. *The Chinese Lion.* Decorated boards, red cloth spine, red label on front cover. London, 1937. First edition. One of 350. Boxed. $85-$100.

WEBB, Mary. *The Golden Arrow.* Cloth. London, 1916. First edition. In dust jacket. $300-$350. Also, $225 (A, 1977). Author's first book.

WEBB, Mary. *Gone to Earth.* Dark-red cloth. London, (1917). First edition. In dust jacket. $175-$200.

WEBB, Mary. *The House in Dormer Forest.* Green cloth. London, (1920). First edition. In dust jacket. $100-$135.

WEBB, Mary. *Precious Bane.* Green cloth. London, (1924). First edition. In dust jacket. $200-$350. Second edition, same date. Cloth. In dust jacket. $150-$200.

WEBB, Mary. *Seven for a Secret: A Love Story.* Green cloth. London, (1922). First edition. In dust jacket. $150-$200.

WEBB, Mary. *The Spring of Joy: A Little Book of Healing.* Cloth. London, 1917. First edition. In dust jacket. $100-$125.

WEBB, Sidney. *Soviet Communism: A New Civilisation?* Boards. (London, 1935.) First edition. $50-$75.

WEBB, Walter Prescott. *The Great Plains.* Illustrated. Cloth. Boston, (1931). First edition, first issue, with error in heading of Chapter 2. In dust jacket. $75-$100.

WEBB, Walter Prescott. *The Texas Rangers.* Illustrated. Cloth. Boston, 1935. First edition. In dust jacket. $100-$125. Another issue: Half leather. One of 205, signed. Boxed. $300-$500.

WEBBER, C. W. *The Hunter-Naturalist; Romance of Sporting, or Wild Scenes and Wild Hunters.* Engraved title page and 9 colored lithographs, other illustrations. Cloth, leather spine and corners. Philadelphia (1851). First edition. $250-$300.

WEBBER, C. W. *Wild Scenes and Song Birds.* 20 colored plates. Morocco. New York, 1854. First edition. $175-$200. New York, 1855. Cloth. $75-$100.

WEBER, Max. *Cubist Poems.* Wrappers. London, 1914. First edition. $150-$250.

"WEBFOOT." *Fore and Aft; Or, Leaves from the Life of an Old Sailor.* Illustrated. Cloth. Boston, 1871. (By William D. Phelps.) First edition. $125-$150.

WEBSTER, Daniel. *A Discourse in Commemoration of the Lives and Services of John*

*Adams and Thomas Jefferson.* 62 pp., printed brown wrappers. Boston, 1826. First edition. $50-$60.

WEBSTER, George G. See Hall, J. L.

WEBSTER, Jean. *Daddy-Long-Legs.* Illustrated by the author. decorated cloth. New York, 1912. First edition. In dust jacket. $100-$125. Lacking jacket, $40-$50.

WEBSTER, Noah. *An American Dictionary of the English Language.* Portrait. 2 vols., light-brown boards, linen spines, paper labels. New York, 1828. First edition. With two-page ad leaf laid in. $1,500-$2,000. Rebound copies, $750 and up.

WEBSTER, Noah. *A Compendious Dictionary of the English Language.* Full leather, leather spine label. Hartford, 1806. First edition. $400-$500, possibly more.

WEBSTER, Noah. *A Dictionary of the English Language Compiled for the Use of Common Schools in the United States.* Calf, red morocco label. New Haven, 1807. First edition. $200 and up.

WEIDMAN, Jerome. *I Can Get It for You Wholesale.* Cloth. New York, 1937. First edition. In dust jacket. $25-$30. Author's first book.

WEIZMANN, Chaim. *Trial and Error.* 2 vols., cloth. New York, (1949). First edition. One of 500, signed. $150-$250. Trade edition: In dust jacket. $15.

WELBY, Adlard. *A Visit to North America.* 14 plates. Leather. London, 1821. First edition. $500-$750.

WELCH, Denton. *Maiden Voyage.* Frontispiece portrait. Cloth. London, 1943.·First edition. In dust jacket. $50-$75. Author's first book.

WELCH, Lew. *Courses.* Leather. San Francisco, 1968. First edition. $60.

WELLS, H. G. *Ann Veronica.* Cloth. London, 1909. First edition. $40-$65.

WELLS, H. G. *Brynhild.* Cloth. London, 1937. First edition. In dust jacket. $35-$45.

WELLS, H. G. *Certain Personal Matters.* Cloth. London, 1898. First edition. $75-$100.

WELLS, H. G. *The Country of the Blind.* Wood engravings. Orange vellum. London, 1939. Golden Cockerel Press. One of 30, signed. $250-$350. Ordinary copies: One of 280. $100-$125.

WELLS, H. G. *The First Men in the Moon.* Illustrated by Claude Shepperson. Dark-blue cloth. London, 1901. First edition, first issue, gilt lettering on cover. $200-$250. Second issue, lettering in black. $125-$150.

WELLS, H. G. *Floor Games.* Illustrated. Pictorial cloth. London, 1911. First edition, first state, pages 8½ inches tall. In dust jacket. $100-$150.

WELLS, H. G. *The Food of the Gods.* Cloth. London, 1904. First edition, first issue, with ads dated "20/7/04." In dust jacket. $200-$250. Lacking dust jacket, $125. New York, 1904. Olive cloth. First American edition. $35-$50.

WELLS, H. G. *Guide to the New World.* Cloth. London, 1941. First edition. In dust jacket. $25-$35.

WELLS, H. G. *The History of Mr. Polly.* Illustrated. Cloth. London, (1910). First edition, first issue, with "Trepanned" on page 8 of ads at back. In dust jacket. $85-$100.

WELLS, H. G. *The Invisible Man.* Red cloth. London, 1897. First edition, first issue, page (1) numbered page 2 in error. $150-$200. New York, 1897. Cloth. First American edition. $50-$65. New York, 1967. Limited Editions Club. Cloth. Boxed. $40.

WELLS, H. G. *The Island of Doctor Moreau.* Brown cloth. London, 1896. First edition, with 32 pp. of ads in back. $200-$300.

WELLS, H. G. *The Mind at the End of Its Tether.* Cloth. London, (1945). First edition. In dust jacket. $35-$45.

WELLS, H. G. *The Sea Lady.* Cloth. London, 1902. First edition. $30-$40.

WELLS, H. G. *Select Conversations with an Uncle (Now Extinct) and Two Other Reminiscences.* Cloth. London, 1895. First edition. $200-$300. Wells' first literary work.

WELLS, H. G. *Tales of Space and Time.* Olive cloth. London, 1900 (actually 1899). $250-$350. Also, $180 (A, 1976).

WELLS, H. G. *Text-Book of Biology.* 2 vols., dark green cloth. London, (1893). First edition, first binding. $300-$400. Also, $190 (A, 1976). (Note: Brown cloth is a later binding.) Author's first book.

WELLS, H. G. *The Time Machine.* Gray cloth. London, 1895. First edition, first issue, with ads at back and purple stamping on cloth. $250-$350. Second issue: No ads; cloth lettered in brown. $100-$150. (A simultaneous issue in wrappers, without ads, also is recorded.)

WELLS, H. G. *Tono-Bungay.* Green cloth. London, 1909. First edition. $35-$50.

WELLS, H. G. *The War in the Air.* 16 plates. Pictorial blue cloth. London, 1908. First edition. In dust jacket. $350-$500. Also, $275 (A, 1976).

WELLS, H. G. *The War of the Worlds.* Cloth. London, 1898. First edition. $200-$300.

WELLS, H. G. *When the Sleeper Wakes.* 3 plates. Cloth. London, 1899. First edition. $150-$250. New York, 1899. Green cloth. First American edition. $75-$100.

WELLS, H. G. *The Wonderful Visit.* Red cloth. London, 1895. First edition. $250-$350. New York, 1895. Green cloth. First American edition. $75-$100.

WELLS, H. G. *The World of William Clissold.* 3 vols., cloth. London, 1926. First edition. One of 198, signed. $150-$200.

WELLS, H. G. *The World Set Free.* Cloth. London, 1914. First edition. In dust jacket. $100-$150.

WELLS, William, and Onken, Otto. *Western Scenery; or, Land and River, Hill and Dale, in the Mississippi Valley.* Pictorial title page, 19 full-page lithographic views, 52 pp. of text. Boards and calf. Cincinnati, 1851. First edition. $2,500-$5,000.

WELLS, Winifred. *The Hesitant Heart.* Lavender boards. New York, 1919. First edition. $30-$40. Author's first book.

WELTY, Eudora. *A Curtain of Green.* Brown cloth. Garden City, 1941. First edition. In dust jacket. $60-$85. Author's first book.

WELTY, Eudora. *Delta Wedding.* Brown cloth. New York, (1946). First edition. In dust jacket. $35-$50.

WELTY, Eudora. *The Golden Apples.* Cloth. New York, (1949). First edition. In dust jacket. $40-$50.

WELTY, Eudora. *Losing Battles.* cloth. New York, (1970). First edition. In dust jacket. $20-$25. Another issue: One of 300, signed. $75-$100.

WELTY, Eudora. *Music from Spain.* Decorated boards, paper spine label. Greenville, Miss., 1948. First edition. One of 775, signed. Issued without dust jacket. $125-$175.

WELTY, Eudora. *The Optimist's Daughter.* Cloth. New York, (1972). First edition. In dust jacket. $15-$20. Limited edition: One of 300, signed. Boxed. $75-$110.

WELTY, Eudora. *A Pageant of Birds.* Wrappers. (New York, 1974.) First edition. One of 326, signed. $30-$40.

WELTY, Eudora. *Place in Fiction.* Cloth. New York, 1957. First edition. One of 300, signed. $35-$50.

WELTY, Eudora. *The Robber Bridegroom.* Blue cloth. Garden City, 1942. First edition. In dust jacket. $40-$50.

WELTY, Eudora. *Short Stories.* Boards. New York. (1949). First edition. One of 1,500. In glassine dust jacket. $40-$50.

WELTY, Eudora. *A Sweet Devouring.* Wrappers. New York, 1969. First edition. One of 176, signed. $30-$40.

WELTY, Eudora. *Three Papers on Fiction.* Wrappers. Northampton, Mass., 1962. First edition. $35-$45.

WENTWORTH, Lady Judith Anne. *The Authentic Arabian Horse and His Descendants.* 26 color plates, numerous other illustrations. Blue cloth. London, (1945). First edition. In dust jacket. $150-$200. London, 1962. Second edition. In dust jacket. $75-$100. New York, 1962. Cloth. In dust jacket. $75-$100.

WENTWORTH, Lady Judith Anne. *Thoroughbred Racing Stock and Its Ancestors.* 21 color plates. Red buckram. London, 1938. First edition. In dust jacket. $150-$200. London, (1960). Second edition. In dust jacket. Boxed. $75-$100.

*WEPT of Wish Ton-Wish (The): A Tale.* By the Author of *The Pioneers.* 2 vols., boards, paper labels. Philadelphia, 1829. (By James Fenimore Cooper.) First American edition. $150-$250. (For first edition, see *The Borderers.*)

WERTH, John J. *A Dissertation on the Resources and Policy of California.* 87 pp., cloth. Benicia, 1851. First edition. $600.

WESCOTT, Glenway. *The Babe's Bed.* Cloth. Paris, 1920. First edition. One of 375 signed. $125-$175. Another issue: One of 18 on parchment. $300-$400.

WESCOTT, Glenway. *The Bitterns: A Book of Twelve Poems.* Black wrappers with printed silver design. Evanston, Ill., (1920). First edition, signed. In cloth folding case. $300-$400. Author's first book.

WESCOTT, Glenway. *A Calendar of Saints for Unbelievers.* Illustrated by Pavel Tchelitchew. Half morocco. Paris, 1932. First edition. One of 40, signed. Boxed. $400-$500. Another issue: Cloth. One of 695. In glassine dust jacket. Boxed. $150-$250.

WESCOTT, Glenway. *Good-bye, Wisconsin.* Boards and cloth. New York, 1928. First edition. One of 250, signed. $75-$100. Trade edition: Cloth. In dust jacket. $30-$40.

WESCOTT, Glenway. *The Grandmothers.* Cloth-backed boards. New York, 1927. First edition. One of 250, signed. Boxed. $60-$75. Trade edition: Cloth. In dust jacket. $30-$40.

WESCOTT, Glenway. *Natives of Rock, XX Poems: 1921-1922.* Boards. New York, 1925. First edition. One of 25 on vellum. Boxed. $150-$200. Another issue: One of 550 plain copies. In glassine dust jacket. Boxed. $30-$40.

WEST, Anthony. *On a Dark Night.* Cloth. London, 1951. First edition. In dust jacket, with Book Society wraparound band. $25-$35.

WEST, Goldsmith B. *The Golden Northwest.* Illustrated. Cloth. Chicago, 1878. First edition. $50-$75.

WEST, John C. *A Texan in Search of a Fight.* 189 pp., wrappers. Waco, 1901. First edition. $150-$200.

WEST, Nathanael. *A Cool Million.* Light tan cloth. New York, (1934). First edition, first binding. In dust jacket. $250-$350. Also, "probably an advance issue or trial binding in russet cloth without publisher's name at bottom of spine," $85 (A, 1970). (Note: Green cloth is a later binding.)

WEST, Nathanael. *The Day of the Locust.* Cloth, paper label. New York, (1939). First edition. In dust jacket. $200-$250.

WEST, Nathanael. *The Dream Life of Balso Snell.* Printed stiff wrappers. Paris, (1931). Contact Editions. First edition. One of 485 numbered copies. In tissue dust jacket.

$750-$1,000. Also, $600 (A, 1977). (Note: Fifteen copies were bound in blue and white or dark blue cloth. Value: $1,000 and up). Author's first book.

WEST, Nathanael. *Miss Lonelyhearts*. Cloth. New York, (1933). Liveright, publisher. First edition. In dust jacket. $300-$500. New York, (1933). Harcourt, Brace. "New edition." In dust jacket. $75.

WEST, Rebecca. *The Return of the Soldier*. Cloth. New York, 1918. First edition. In dust jacket. $35-$50.

WESTCOTT, Edward Noyes. *David Harum*. Yellow cloth. New York, 1898. First edition, first state, with perfect "J" in "Julius" in next to last line of page 40. $65-$100. Author's first book. New York, (1900). First illustrated edition. White boards. One of 750. In dust jacket. $50-$75.

WESTERN *Agriculturist (The) and Practical Farmer's Guide*. Frontispiece, plates. Leather. Cincinnati, 1830. $150-$200.

WESTERN *Reserve Register for 1852, (The)*. Cloth. Hudson, Ohio. 1852. First issue. $100-$150.

WESTON, Edward (photographer). *California and the West*. (By Charis Wilson Weston and Edward Weston.) Illustrated. Cloth. New York (1940). First edition. In dust jacket. $100-$150.

WESTON, Edward (photographer). *Edward Weston*. 40 plates. Half vellum. New York, 1932. First edition. One of 550 signed by Weston. $400-$500.

WESTON, Edward (photographer). *Fifty Photographs*. (By Weston and others.) Half cloth. New York, (1947). First edition. One of 1,500, initialed by Weston. In dust jacket. $400-$500.

WESTON, Edward (photographer). *My Camera on Point Lobos*. Illustrated. Folio, spiral binding. Yosemite National Park and Boston, 1950. First edition. In dust jacket. $150-$250.

WESTON, Silas. *Four Months in the Mines of California; or, Life in the Mountains*. 24 pp., printed wrappers. Providence, 1854. Second edition (of *Life in the Mountains*). $350-$400. (See below.)

WESTON, Silas. *Life in the Mountains: or Four Months in the Mines of California*. 36 pp., printed wrappers. Providence, 1854. First edition. $500-$750.

WESTROPP, M. S. Dudley. *Irish Glass*. 40 plates. Buckram. London, (about 1920-21?). $100-$135.

*WESTWARD Ho!* 2 vols., cloth. New York, 1832. (By James Kirke Paulding.) First edition. $150-$250.

WETHERBEE, J., Jr. *A Brief Sketch of Colorado Territory and the Gold Mines of That Region*. 24 pp., printed wrappers. Boston, 1863. First edition. $1,750-$2,500.

WETHERELL, Elizabeth. *Queechy*. 2 vols., cloth. New York, 1852. (By Susan B. Warner.) First edition. $100-$150. London, 1852. 2 vols., cloth. First English edition. $75-$100.

WETHERELL, Elizabeth. *The Wide, Wide World*. 2 vols., cloth. New York, 1851. (By Susan B. Warner.) First edition, first issue, brown cloth. $150-$200. Later, blue cloth. $100-$150. London, 1853. 2 vols., red cloth. First English edition. $50-$60.

WETMORE, Alphonso (compiler). *Gazetteer of the State of Missouri*. Frontispiece and folding map. Cloth. St. Louis, 1837. First edition. $300-$400.

WEYMAN, Stanley J. *A Gentleman of France*. 3 vols., green cloth. London, 1893. First edition. $150-$200.

WEYMAN, Stanley J. *The House of the Wolf*. Decorated gray cloth. London, 1890. First edition. $75-$100. Author's first book.

WHALING *Directory of the United States in 1869.* Colored flags. Cloth. New Bedford, Mass., 1869. $200-$300.

WHARTON, Clarence. *Remember Goliad.* 61 pp., boards. Houston, 1931. One of 100. $75-$125.

WHARTON, Edith. See Jones, Edith Newbold.

WHARTON, Edith. *Ethan Frome.* New York, 1911. First edition, first issue, with top edges gilt and perfect type in last line of page 135. In dust jacket. $150-$200. New York, 1922. Boards. One of 2,000. $75-$85. (New York), 1939. Limited Editions Club. Cloth. Boxed. $40-$50.

WHARTON, Edith. *Quartet: Four Stories.* Boards. Kentfield, Calif., 1975. Allen Press. One of 140. $175-$225.

WHARTON, Edith. *Twelve Poems.* Buckram and boards. London, 1926. Medici Society. First edition. One of 130, signed. In dust jacket. $125-$200.

*WHAT Is Man?* Gray-blue boards, green-black leather label on spine. New York, 1906. (By Samuel Langhorne Clemens.) First edition, first issue, with "thinks about" as last line of page 131. One of 250. In tissue dust jacket. Boxed. $400-$500. Second issue with "thinks about it," $150-$200. (Note: The First English edition, London, 1910, cloth, identifies Twain as author. See Twain, *What Is Man?*)

WHEAT, Carl I. *Books of the Gold Rush.* Illustrated. Pictorial boards and cloth. San Francisco, 1949. Grabhorn Press. First edition. One of 500. $100-$200.

WHEAT, Carl I. *Mapping the Trans-Mississippi West.* Illustrated. 5 vols. in 6 vols., folio, buckram, leatherette spine. San Francisco, 1957-63. Grabhorn Press. First edition. One of 1,000. $850-$1,000.

WHEAT, Carl. I. *The Maps of the California Gold Region, 1848-1857.* 26 maps. Folio, cloth. San Francisco, 1942. Grabhorn Press. First edition. One of 300. $500-$750. Another issue: Three-quarters calf. One of 22, with map by Gibbs added. $800-$1,000.

WHEAT, Carl I. *The Pioneer Press of California.* Boards and cloth. Oakland, 1948. First edition. One of 450. $50-$75.

WHEAT, Marvin T. See Cincinnatus.

WHEATLEY, Phillis. *Memoir and Poems of Phillis Wheatley, a Native African and a Slave.* Cloth, red paper label on front cover. Boston, 1834. Reprint of the London edition of 1773. $75-$100.

WHEELER, Edward L. *Deadwood Dick's Doom; or, Calamity Jane's Last Adventure.* 16 pp., self-wrappers. New York, 1881. Beadle's Half-Dime Library. First edition. $50-$75. New York, 1887. Beadle's Pocket Library. Reprint. $25.

WHEELER, Ella. *Drops of Water: Poems.* Purple cloth. New York, 1872. (By Ella Wheeler Wilcox.) First edition. $50. Author's first book.

WHEELER, William. *In Memoriam: Letters of William Wheeler.* Illustrated. Cloth. (Cambridge, Mass.), 1875. First edition. $65-$100.

WHEELER, William Ogden (compiler). *The Ogden Family in America.* 2 vols., cloth. Philadelphia, 1907. $75-$100.

*WHERE Men Only Dare to Go, or, The Story of a Boy Company.* By an Ex-Boy. Frontispiece. Cloth. Richmond, 1885. (By Royall W. Figg.) $100-$125.

WHILLDIN, M. *A Description of Western Texas.* 28 plates, folding map. 120 pp., pictorial wrappers. Galveston, 1876. First edition. $225-$400, possibly more.

WHITAKER, Arthur Preston (editor). *Documents Relating to the Commercial Policy of Spain in the Floridas.* 7 maps and plates. Cloth. DeLand, Fla., 1931. First edition. One of 360. $60-$75.

WHITAKER, Fess. *History of Corporal Fess Whitaker.* Illustrated. Cloth. Louisville, Ky., 1918. First edition. $50-$75.

WHITE, Diana. *The Descent of Ishtar.* Frontispiece. Boards, paper label. London, 1903. Eragny Press. One of 226. In dust jacket. $380-$425.

WHITE, E. B. See W., E. B. Also, see Thurber, James.

WHITE, E. B. *Charlotte's Web.* Illustrated by Garth Williams. Pictorial cloth. New York, (1952). First edition. In dust jacket. $100-$125.

WHITE, E. B. *Stuart Little.* Illustrated by Garth Williams. Pictorial cloth. New York, (1945). First edition. In dust jacket. $100-$125.

WHITE, The Rev. George. *Statistics of the State of Georgia.* Map. Cloth. Savannah, 1849. First edition, with errata leaf. $100-$150.

WHITE, Gilbert. *The Writings of Gilbert White of Selborne.* Wood engravings by Eric Ravilious. 2 vols., gray buckram. London, 1938. Nonesuch Press. One of 850. Boxed. $300-$400.

WHITE, Joseph M. *A New Collection of the Laws . . . of Great Britain, France and Spain.* 2 vols., cloth. Philadelphia, 1839. $150-$200.

WHITE, Owen P. *Out of the Desert.* Illustrated. Cloth. El Paso, 1923. First edition. $75-$85.

WHITE, Owen P. *Trigger Fingers.* Cloth. New York, 1926. First edition. In dust jacket. $50-$75.

WHITE, Philo. *Agricultural Statistics of Racine County.* 16 pp., wrappers. Racine, Wis., 1852. Presentation copy from author. $150-$200.

WHITE, Stewart Edward. *Arizona Nights.* 7 color illustrations by N.C. Wyeth. Cloth. New York, 1907. First edition. In dust jacket. $150. Lacking jacket, $60-$75.

WHITE, Stewart Edward. *The Claim Jumpers.* Cloth, printed wrappers, or marbled boards with leather spine. New York, 1901. First edition. Wrappers: $50-$75. Cloth or boards: $30-$50. Author's first book.

WHITE, T. H. See Aston, James.

WHITE, T H. *The Elephant and the Kangaroo.* Cloth. London, 1948. First edition. In dust jacket. $30-$40.

WHITE, T. H. *Loved Helen and Other Poems.* Black cloth. London (1939). First edition. In dust jacket. $150. Author's first book under his own name.

WHITE, T. H. *Mistress Masham's Repose.* Illustrated. Cloth. New York, (1946). First edition, first issue, brown end papers. In dust jacket. $50-$75.

WHITE, T. H. *The Sword in the Stone.* Cloth. London, 1938. First edition. In dust jacket. $50-$60.

WHITE, William Allen. *The Court of Boyville.* Illustrated by Orson Lowell and Gustav Verbeek. Pictorial buckram. New York, 1899. First edition. $75-$100.

WHITE, William Allen. *The Real Issue.* Buckram. Chicago, 1896. First edition. $35-$50. Author's first book.

WHITE, William Allen, and Paine, Albert Bigelow. *Rhymes by Two Friends.* Illustrated. Blue cloth. Fort Scott, Kan., (1893). First edition. $100-$150. White's first book appearance.

WHITEHEAD, Charles E. *Wild Sports in the South.* Illustrated. Cloth. New York, 1860. First edition. $75-$100.

WHITEHEAD, Henry S. *Jumbee and Other Uncanny Tales.* Cloth. (Sauk City, Wis.), 1944. First edition. In dust jacket. $100-$125.

WHITELY, Ike. *Rural Life in Texas.* 82 pp., wrappers. Atlanta, 1891. First edition. $600-$1,000.

WHITMAN, Walt. See *Leaves of Grass; Leaves of Grass Imprints.*

WHITMAN, Walt. *After All, Not to Create Only.* 11 folio numbered sheets, printed on one side only, stitched. (Washington, 1871.) First edition, first (proof) issue. Very rare in proof state. Estimated value: $500 and up. The last copy at auction, along with a 4-line Whitman poem in author's hand, brought $200 (1951). Boston, 1871. Green, maroon, or brown cloth. First book edition. $100-$150. Another issue: Limp cloth wrappers. $200.

WHITMAN, Walt. *An American Primer.* Illustrated. Edited by Horace Traubel. Boards, vellum spine. Boston, 1904. First edition, first binding. One of 500. $50-$75. Second issue and binding, blue cloth. $35-$50.

WHITMAN, Walt. *As a Strong Bird on Pinions Free. And Other Poems.* Green cloth. Washington, 1872. First edition. $200-$250. (Note: Although "Leaves of Grass" appears in small letters above this title, this is not one of the later editions of the book of the same title.)

WHITMAN, Walt. *Autobiographia, or The Story of a Life.* Gray cloth. New York, 1892. First edition, with Charles L. Webster imprint. $40-$50.

WHITMAN, Walt. *The Book of Heavenly Death.* Compiled from *Leaves of Grass* by Horace Traubel. Portrait. Boards, paper label. Portland, 1905. Mosher Press. One of 50 on Japan vellum. In dust jacket. Boxed. $100-$110. Another issue: One of 500. $25-$30.

WHITMAN, Walt. *Calamus: A Series of Letters, Written During the Years 1868-1880 . . . to a Young Friend (Peter Doyle).* Cloth. Boston, 1897. First edition. $125-$150. Another issue: Boards, cloth back, paper label. One of 35 on large paper. $150-$200.

WHITMAN, Walt. *Complete Poems and Prose, 1855-1888.* Portrait title page, one plate. Half cloth and boards, paper label. (Philadelphia, 1888-89.) First edition. One of 600, signed. $500-$600.

WHITMAN, Walt. *Criticism: An Essay.* Gray boards, paper label. Newark, 1913. First edition. One of 100. $75-$100.

WHITMAN, Walt. *Franklin Evans; or The Inebriate.* (By Walter Whitman.) 31 pp., pamphlet without covers. New York, 1842. First edition. Issued as a supplement to the *New World.* $2,800 (A, 1972). Whitman's first separately published work. (Note: According to Wayne Somers, consignor of this copy, one of two known in this state, the pamphlet exists in two states, of which this copy, with 6½ cents as the price on front, is the second. The first state copies, of which there are also only two known, bore a price of 12½ cents. The last copy in this state was sold at auction in 1945.)

WHITMAN, Walt. *The Gathering of the Forces.* Edited by Cleveland Rogers and John Black. 2 vols., boards. New York, 1920. First edition. Limited. In dust jackets. $100-$150.

WHITMAN, Walt. *Good-Bye, My Fancy. 2d Annex to Leaves of Grass.* Phototype portrait. Green or maroon cloth. Philadelphia, 1891. First edition. $100-$125. Large paper issue: $300-$500. Also, $200 (A, 1977).

WHITMAN, Walt. *The Half-Breed and Other Stories.* Edited by T.O. Mabbott. Illustrated. Half cloth. New York, 1927. First edition. One of 155. $60-$80. Another issue: One of 30 with illustrations signed in proof by the artist, Allen Lewis. $100-$135.

WHITMAN, Walt. *Lafayette in Brooklyn.* Boards. New York, 1905. First edition. One of 235 numbered copies. $40-$60. Another issue: One of 15 on Japan vellum. $100-$125.

WHITMAN, Walt. *Letters Written by Walt Whitman to His Mother.* Greenish-gray wrappers. New York, 1902. First edition. Only 5 copies printed. $500-$750.

WHITMAN, Walt. *Memoranda: Democratic Vistas.* Light-green wrappers. Washington, 1871. First edition, later printing (the first did not have Whitman's name on title page but only in copyright notice). $200-$300. (For first printing, see the title entry.)

WHITMAN, Walt. *Memoranda During the War.* 2 portraits. Red-brown cloth, green end papers. Camden, N.J., 1875-76. First edition, first printed page beginning "Remembrance Copy" and with space below for autograph (all copies signed). $500-$750. Another issue, without the portraits and the leaf headed "Remembrance Copy": $250-$350.

WHITMAN, Walt. *New York Dissected: A Sheaf of Recently Discovered Newspaper Articles.* Cloth. New York, 1936. First edition. One of 750. $35-$50.

WHITMAN, Walt. *Notes & Fragments.* Edited by Richard Maurice Bucke. Blue pebbled cloth. (London, Ont., Canada), 1899. First edition. One of 225 signed by Bucke. $50-$75.

WHITMAN, Walt. *November Boughs.* Frontispiece portrait. Maroon or green cloth. Philadelphia, 1888. First edition. $100-$150. Large paper issue: Dark green cloth, or limp red or blue cloth. $150-$200.

WHITMAN, Walt. *Pictures: An Unpublished Poem.* Boards, paper label. New York, 1927. First edition. One of 700. $75-$85.

WHITMAN, Walt. *Poems by Walt Whitman.* Edited by William Michael Rossetti. Frontispiece portrait. Ad leaf pasted in. Cloth, gilt panel on cover. London, 1868. First edition, first issue, without price on spine. $60-$85.

WHITMAN, Walt. *Poems from Leaves of Grass.* 24 colored illustrations by Margaret Cook. Green cloth. London, 1913. First edition, first issue, without gold decorations on cover and spine. In dust jacket. $75-$85.

WHITMAN, Walt. *Rivulets of Prose.* Edited by Carolyn Wells and Alfred F. Goldsmith. Cloth. New York, 1928. First edition. One of 499. $50-$75.

WHITMAN, Walt. *Specimen Days & Collect.* Light-blue wrappers or yellow cloth. Philadelphia, 1882-83. First edition, first issue, with Rees Welsh & Co. imprint. $75-$100. Philadelphia, 1883. Cloth. David McKay imprint. First edition, second issue. $50-$75.

WHITMAN, Walt. *Two Rivulets.* Portrait frontispiece, signed "Walt Whitman." Half calf. Camden, 1876. First edition. $250-$300. Also, $150 (A, 1974). Another issue: "Centennial Edition." One of 100. $500-$600.

WHITMAN, Walt. *The Uncollected Poetry and Prose of Walt Whitman.* Illustrated. 2 vols., green cloth. Garden City, 1921. First edition. In dust jackets.$60-$75.

WHITMAN, Walt. *Walt Whitman's Diary in Canada.* Edited by W. S. Kennedy. Gray boards and vellum. Boston, 1904. First edition. One of 500. $50-$75. Second issue, blue cloth: $15-$25.

WHITMAN, Walt. *Walt Whitman's Drum-Taps.* Brown cloth. New York, 1865. First edition, first issue, with only 72 pages. $400-$500. Also, $375 (A, 1976). New York, 1865-66. Second issue, with 24 more pages and separate title page, "Sequel, etc." $200-$300.

WHITMAN, Walt. *Walt Whitman's Workshop.* Gray boards and cloth. Cambridge, Mass., 1928. First edition. One of 750. $75-$100.

WHITMAN, Walt. *The Wound Dresser.* Edited by Richard Maurice Bucke. Red buckram. Boston, 1898. First edition, first printing, with 1897 copyright notice. $100-$125. Large paper issue: One of 60 signed by Bucke. $150-$200.

WHITMER, David. *An Address to All Believers in Christ.* 77 pp., wrappers. Richmond, Mo., 1887. First edition. $125-$150.

WHITNEY, Henry C. *Life on the Circuit with Lincoln.* 67 plates. Cloth. Boston, (1892). First edition. $50-$75.

WHITNEY, J. D. *The Auriferous Gravels of the Sierra Nevada of California.* Folding maps and plates. Cloth. Cambridge, Mass., 1880. First edition. $125-$150.

WHITNEY, J. D. *The Yosemite Book.* 28 photographic plates, 2 maps. Half leather. New York, 1868. First edition. (250 printed.) $3,000-$4,000.

WHITNEY, J. H. E. *The Hawkins Zouaves.* Cloth. New York, 1866. First edition. $75-$100.

WHITTIER, John Greenleaf. See Dinsmoor, Robert, *Incidental Poems.* Also see *Justice and Expediency; Leaves from Margaret Smith's Journal; Moll Pitcher; The Stranger in Lowell; The Supernaturalism of New England.* (Note: Whittier's numerous publications, with all the complicated [and sometimes confusing] bibliographical points, are exhaustively covered in Thomas F. Currier's *A Bibliography of John Greenleaf Whittier,* Cambridge, Mass., 1937. The list here includes representative scarce and important items.)

WHITTIER, John Greenleaf. *At Sundown.* Pea-green cloth. Cambridge, 1890. First edition. One of 250, with facsimile autograph presentation slip. $50-$60.

WHITTIER, John Greenleaf. *The Captain's Well.* Illustrated by Howard Pyle. 4 pp., leaflet, imitation alligator leather binding. Supplement to New York *Ledger,* January 11, 1890. First edition. $100-$150.

WHITTIER, John Greenleaf. *The Demon Lady.* 8 pp., wrappers. No place, 1894. One of 25. $75.

WHITTIER, John Greenleaf. *The King's Missive, and Other Poems.* Portrait. Reddish-brown cloth. Boston, 1881. First edition. $30-$50.

WHITTIER, John Greenleaf. *Legends of New England.* Boards and cloth, paper label. Hartford, 1831. First edition, first state, with next to last line on page 98 reading "the go" for "they go." $100-$150. Author's first book.

WHITTIER, John Greenleaf. *Miriam and Other Poems.* Frontispiece. Cloth. Boston, 1871. First edition, first issue, with publisher's monogram on spine. $50-$75.

WHITTIER, John Greenleaf. *Mogg Megone: A Poem.* Slate-colored cloth. Boston, 1836. First edition. $150-$200. Also, $125 (A, 1974).

WHITTIER, John Greenleaf. *The Panorama, and Other Poems.* Cloth. Boston, 1856. First edition, without ads. $40-$50.

WHITTIER, John Greenleaf. *Poems.* Leather, or cloth. Philadelphia, 1838. First edition. $65-$85. New York, 1945. Limited Editions Club. Boxed. $30-$35.

WHITTIER, John Greenleaf. *Poems Written During the Progress of the Abolition Question in the United States.* Frontispiece. Cloth. Boston, 1837. First edition, first issue, 96 pp. $100-$150. Second issue, 103 pp. $50-$75.

WHITTIER, John Greenleaf. *A Sabbath Sane.* Printed wrappers. Boston, 1854. First edition. $30-$40.

WHITTIER, John Greenleaf. *Snow-Bound.* Green, blue, or terra-cotta cloth. Boston, 1866. First edition, first issue, with last page of text numbered "52" below printer's slug. $400-$500. Also, $180 (A, 1976). New York, 1930. Limited Editions Club. Boards and cloth. Boxed. $30-$40.

WHITTOCK, Nathaniel. *The Decorative Painters' and Glaziers' Guide.* Plates, many colored. Leather. London, 1827. First edition. $200-$300. London, 1828. Second edition. $150-$200. London, 1832. Third edition. $100-$150. London, 1841. Half leather. $250.

*WHO'S Who In America.* Cloth. Chicago, 1899. First edition. $50-$75.

WHYTE-MELVILLE, George John. See *Market Harborough.*

WHYTE-MELVILLE, George John. *"Bones and I."* Brown cloth. London, 1868. First edition. $50-$75.

WHYTE-MELVILLE, George John. *Digby Grand: An Autobiography.* 2 vols., cloth. London, 1853. First edition. $75-$100. Author's first novel.

WHYTE-MELVILLE, George John. *The Queen's Maries: A Romance of Holyrood.* 2 vols., lilac cloth. London, 1862. First edition. $60-$80.

WHYTE-MELVILLE, George John. *Rosine.* Frontispiece, 7 plates. Cloth. London, 1877. First edition. $50-$75.

WHYTE-MELVILLE, George John. *Sister Louise, or The Story of a Woman's Repentance.* Frontispiece, 7 plates. Cloth. London, 1876. First edition. $75-$100.

WIAT (or Wyatt), Sir Thomas. *Poems.* Edited by A. K. Foxwell. Portrait, 10 facsimiles. 2 vols., cloth. London, 1913. $75-$100.

WICKERSHAM, James. *Is It Mt. Tacoma or Rainier—What Do History and Tradition Say?*

WIENER, Norbert. *Cybernetics.* Cloth. New York, (1948). First edition. In dust jacket. $150.

WIENERS, John. *Ace of Pentacles.* Boards. New York, 1964. First edition. One of 75, signed, with manuscript portion tipped in. In glassine dust jacket. $30-$50. Another issue: Leather. One of 12 signed, with a poem tipped in. $100. Trade edition: Wrappers. $7.50-$10.

WIENERS, John. *Youth.* Stiff wrappers. New York, 1970. First edition. One of 126, signed, plus an unknown number of copies not for sale. $35-$50.

WIERZBICKI, F. P. *California as It Is and as It May Be.* 60 pp., glazed lavender wrappers. San Francisco, 1849. First edition, with errata leaf. (The first book written and published in California.) $6,000-$10,000. Also, rebound in half cloth, $3,600 (A, 1973). (Note: The most recent sale of a copy in original wrappers was in 1945, when the C. G. Littell copy brought $475 at auction; it is now in the Everett D. Graff collection at the Newberry Library, Chicago. A Newberry duplicate, rebound in half morocco, with title page bearing part of the author's presentation inscription, brought $3,500 at auction in 1968.) San Francisco, 1849. 76 pp., errata, saffron wrappers. Second edition. $3,000 and up. Also, defective, $1,000 (A, 1971); $2,600 (A, 1968)—the Streeter copy. San Francisco, 1933. Grabhorn Press. Boards and cloth. One of 500. In dust jacket. $75-$100.

WIGGIN, Kate Douglas. See Smith, Kate Douglas.

WIGGIN, Kate Douglas. *Children's Rights: A Book of Nursery Logic.* Cloth. Boston, 1892. First edition. $35.

WIGGIN, Kate Douglas. *Rebecca of Sunnybrook Farm.* Green pictorial cloth. Boston, 1903. First edition, first issue, with publisher's imprint on spine in type only 1/16 inch high. $50-$75.

*WIGWAM and the Cabin (The).* First Series. Wrappers. New York, 1845. (By William Gilmore Simms.) First edition. $500-$750. Later: With the Second Series. 2 vols. in one, cloth. New York, 1845. $100-$200. (Note: The Second Series in wrappers has not appeared for sale in many years.)

WILBARGER, J. W. *Indian Depredations in Texas.* 38 plates (37 listed). Pictorial cloth. Austin, 1899. First edition. $250-$400. Austin, 1890. Second edition. $100-$200. Austin, 1933. Facsimile. Pictorial cloth. $60-$80.

WILBUR, Homer (editor). *Meliboeus-Hipponax. The Biglow Papers.* Cloth, or glazed boards. Cambridge, Mass., 1848. (By James Russell Lowell.) First edition, first issue, with George Nichols only as publisher. $150-$200.

WILBUR, Richard. *The Beautiful Changes and Other Poems.* Cloth. New York, (1947). First edition. In dust jacket. $100-$135. Author's first book.

WILBUR, Richard. *Seed Leaves: Homage to R. F.* Illustrated by Charles E. Wadsworth. Wrappers, paper label. Boston, 1974. First edition. One of 160 signed by poet and artist. In portfolio wrappers. $75-$100.

WILBUR, Richard. *Things of This World.* Cloth. New York, 1956. First edition. In dust jacket. $25-$35.

WILBUR, Richard (compiler). *A Bestiary*. Illustrated by Alexander Calder. Pictorial buckram. New York, (1955). First edition. One of 750, signed. Boxed. $200-$300. Another issue: Folio, half morocco. One of 50 signed by author and artist and with a signed pen-and-ink drawing by Calder. $800-$1,250.

WILCOX, Ella Wheeler. See Wheeler, Ella.

WILDE, Oscar. See C. 3.3.; Young, Dal. Also see *Children in Prison; An Ideal Husband; The Importance of Being Earnest*.

WILDE, Oscar. *The Birthday of the Infanta*. Illustrated by Alastair. Wrappers. Paris, 1928. Black Sun Press. First edition. One of 9 on vellum, with an original drawing. $600 (A, 1977).

WILDE, Oscar. *De Profundis*. Blue buckram. London, (1905). First English edition, first issue, with ads dated February. $85-$110. Later, ads dated March. $50-$75. Large paper issues: White cloth. One of 200 on handmade paper. $200-$250. One of 50 on Japan vellum. Boxed. $300-$400. London, (1949). Introduction by Vyvyan Holland. Morocco. One of 200 signed by Holland. $75-$100.

WILDE, Oscar. *The Duchess of Padua*. Wrappers. New York, (actually Paris), (1905). First published edition in English. (Pirated.) $75. London, (1908). Buckram. First published English edition. One of 1,000. $50-$75. (Note: About 20 copies of this play were privately printed in London in 1883 for theater use. One of the surviving copies was sold at auction for $2,300 in London in 1973.)

WILDE, Oscar. *The Fisherman and His Soul*. Illustrations and initials in color, illuminated in gold. Boards and silk. (San Francisco, 1939.) Grabhorn Press. One of 200. $150-$200.

WILDE, Oscar. *The Happy Prince and Other Tales*. Illustrated by Walter Crane and Jacomb Hood. Vellum boards. London, 1888. First edition. $150-$200. Another issue: One of 75, signed. $1,000-$1,250. Also, boxed, back hinge cracked. $550 (A, 1977).

WILDE, Oscar. *A House of Pomegranetes*. 4 plates. White cloth, green cloth spine. London, 1891. First edition. $400-$500. Also, "virtually pristine," $350 (A, 1975). London, 1915. Color plates by Jessie M. King. Decorated cloth. $300-$400.

WILDE, Oscar. *Impressions of America*. Stiff wrappers. Sunderland, 1906. First edition. One of 500. $100-$125. Another issue: One of 50 on handmade paper. $200-$225.

WILDE, Oscar. *Intentions*. Moss-green cloth. London, 1891. First edition. $100-$150.

WILDE, Oscar. *Lady Windermere's Fan: A Play About a Good Woman*. Reddish-brown linen. London, 1893. First edition. $150-$200. Large paper issue: One of 50. $400-$500. Also, spine and fly leaves darkened, $300 (A, 1977). Paris, 1903. Cloth. Pirated edition published by Leonard Smithers. One of 250. $50-$75. New York, 1973. Limited Editions Club. Boxed. $40-$50.

WILDE, Oscar. *Lord Arthur Savile's Crime & Other Stories*. Salmon-colored boards. London, 1891. First edition. $75-$100.

WILDE, Oscar. *Newdigate Prize Poem. Ravenna. Recited in the Theatre, Oxford, June 26, 1878*. 16 pp., printed wrappers. Oxford, 1878. First edition, with Oxford University seal on title page and cover. $300-$400. Also, inscribed to Robert Browning, $2,000 (A, 1977). Author's first book.

WILDE, Oscar. *Oscariana. Epigrams*. Printed wrappers. (London), 1895. First edition. $100-$150.

WILDE, Oscar. *The Picture of Dorian Gray*. Rough gray beveled boards, vellum spine. London, (1891). First edition, with letter "a" missing from "and" on page 208 in eighth line from the bottom. In dust jacket. $1,000-$1,500. Also, with crudely repaired jacket, $950 (A, 1977). Another issue: One of 250, signed. (Error corrected.) $500 and up.

WILDE, Oscar. *Poems*. White parchment boards. London, 1881. First edition, first issue, with the word "maid" in line 3, stanza 2, page 136. One of 250. $300-$400. Boston, 1881. Cloth. First American edition. $100-$125. London, 1892. Violet cloth. One of 220, signed. $400-$500. Paris, 1903. Buckram. One of 250. $75-$100.

WILDE, Oscar. *Salome: Drame en Un Acte.* Purple wrappers. Paris, 1893. First edition. $100-$150. Another issue: One of 50 on Van Gelder paper. $750-$1,000. Also, inscribed, $1,500 (A, 1977). London, 1894. Illustrated by Aubrey Beardsley. Decorated cloth. First English edition. One of 500. $250-$350. Large paper issue: One of 100 on vellum. $200 and up. London, 1904. Beardsley illustrations. Boards. One of 250. Pirated edition, suppressed. $200-$250. Paris, 1922. Illustrated by Alastair. Pictorial wrappers. In glassine dust jacket. $200-$250. San Francisco, 1927. Grabhorn Press. Illustrated. Boards. One of 195. Boxed. $100-$150. New York, 1938. Limited Editions Club. 2 vols., cloth. Boxed. $100-$150.

WILDE, Oscar. *The Soul of Man.* Light-brown printed wrappers. London, 1895. First edition. One of 50. $400-$500.

WILDE, Oscar. *The Soul of Man Under Socialism.* Boards, green linen spine. Boston, 1910. First "authorized" American edition. $75-$125.

WILDE, Oscar. *The Sphinx.* Decorations by Charles Ricketts. Vellum. London, 1894. First edition. One of 250. $750-$1,000. Another issue: One of 25 on large paper (issued later, with Boston firm of Copeland and Day added to London imprint). $1,000 and up. London, 1920. Illustrated by Alastair. Cloth. One of 1,000. $200-$350.

WILDE, Oscar. *Vera; or, The Nihilists.* Gray wrappers. London, 1880. First edition (issued privately). $4,000-$6,000. Very rare, with a $570 auction record, 1920. A presentation copy sold for $375 in the early 1950's and when reoffered in the 1959 auction season brought $650. (New York), 1882. Wrappers. Second edition (first American edition), privately issued. $300-$400. London, 1902. Wrappers. One of 200. $150-$200.

WILDE, Oscar. *A Woman of No Importance.* Cloth. London, 1894. First edition. $100-$150. De luxe edition: Cloth. One of 50 on fine paper. $500-$600.

WILDER, Laura Ingalls. *Farmer Boy.* Illustrated by Helen Sewell. Pictorial cloth. New York, 1933. First edition. In dust jacket. $125-$150.

WILDER, Laura Ingalls. *Little House on the Prairie.* Illustrated by Helen Sewell. Pictorial cloth. New York, 1935. First edition. In dust jacket. $125-$150.

WILDER, Laura Ingalls. *On the Banks of Plum Creek.* Illustrated by Helen Sewell and Mildred Boyle. Pictorial cloth. New York, 1937. First edition. In dust jacket. $125-$150.

WILDER, Thornton. *The Angel That Troubled the Waters.* Blue boards and cloth. New York, 1928. First edition. One of 775, signed. In dust jacket. $60-$75. London, 1928. Blue cloth. First English edition. One of 260, signed. In dust jacket. $100-$135.

WILDER, Thornton. *The Bridge of San Luis Rey.* Tan cloth. London, 1927. First edition (preceding American edition by a few days). In dust jacket. $100-$125. Also, signed copy, $50 (A, 1970). New York, 1927. Cloth. First American edition, "preliminary issue," with title page printed only in black. In dust jacket. $300-$400. Also, in dust jacket, $250 (A, 1960); lacking jacket, $120 (A, 1960). Regular trade issue, title page printed in green and black: In dust jacket. $50-$75. New York, 1929. Illustrated by Rockwell Kent. Pictorial cloth, leather label. One of 1,100 signed by Wilder and Kent. Boxed. $50-$75.

WILDER, Thornton. *The Cabala.* Blue figured cloth or tan figured cloth. New York, 1926. First edition, first printing, with "conversation" for "conversion" in line 13, page 196. Blue (only a few copies issued): In dust jacket. $150-$200. Tan: In dust jacket. $75-$125. Author's first book.

WILDER, Thornton. *The Ides of March.* Cloth. New York, 1948. First edition. One of 750, signed. In dust jacket. $75-$85. Trade edition: Cloth. In dust jacket. $25.

WILDER, Thornton. *James Joyce, 1882-1941.* Wrappers. Aurora, N. Y., no date. First edition. One of 150. $40-$50.

WILDER, Thornton. *The Long Christmas Dinner and Other Plays in One Act.* Boards, imitation vellum spine. New Haven, 1931. First edition. One of 525, signed. In dust jacket. Boxed. $60-$80. Trade edition: Brick cloth. In dust jacket. $25-$35.

WILDER, Thornton. *The Merchant of Yonkers.* Cloth, paper labels. New York, 1939. First edition, first printing (so indicated on copyright page). In dust jacket. $60-$80.

WILDER, Thornton. *The Woman of Andros*. Cloth. New York, 1930. First edition. In dust jacket. $60-$80. London, 1930. Cloth. First English edition. One of 260, signed. In dust jacket. $100-$150. Trade edition: In dust jacket. $25-$35.

WILKES, Charles. *Synopsis of the Cruise of the United States Exploring Expedition During the Years 1838-42*. Folding map. 56 pp., wrappers. Washington, 1842. First edition. $350-$500.

WILKES, Charles. *Western America, Including California and Oregon*. 3 folding maps. Printed tan wrappers. Philadelphia, 1849. First edition. $400-$500.

WILKES, George. *The History of Oregon, Geographical and Political*. Folding map. 127 pp., printed wrappers. New York, 1845. First edition. $1,000-$1,250.

WILKESON, Samuel. *Wilkeson's Notes on Puget Sound*. 47 pp., wrappers. (New York, 1870?) First edition. $50-$75.

WILKINSON, Gen. James. *Memoirs of My Own Times*. 9 folding tables, 3 folding facsimiles. 4 vols., boards and calf. Philadelphia, 1816. First edition, including atlas of 19 maps and plans. $750-$1,000, possibly more. Also, worn, $250 (A, 1972); $1,000 (A, 1967)—the Thomas W. Streeter copy.

WILL, George F. *Notes on the Arikara Indians and Their Ceremonies*. 48 pp., wrappers. Denver, 1934. Old West Series. One of 75. $75-$100.

WILLARD, John Ware. *A History of Simon Willard, Inventor and Clockmaker*. Cloth. (Boston), 1911. One of 500. $300-$325. Also, $200 (A, 1977).

WILLCOX, R. N. *Reminiscences of California Life*. Cloth. (Avery, Ohio), 1897. First edition. $75-$125.

WILLETT, William M. (editor). *A Narrative of the Military Actions of Col. Marmus Willett*. Portrait, plan, facsimile letter. Half leather. New York, 1831. First edition. $275.

WILLEY, S. H. *An Historical Paper Relating to Santa Cruz, California*. 37 pp., printed wrappers. San Francisco, 1876. First edition. $150-$175.

WILLIAMS, Alpheus F. *The Genesis of the Diamond*. 221 plates, 30 colored. 2 vols., buckram. London, 1932. First edition. $150-$300.

WILLIAMS, Charles. *Poems of Conformity*. Cloth. London, 1917. First edition. In dust jacket. $50-$60. Author's first book?

WILLIAMS, Charles. *War in Heaven*. Cloth. London, 1930. First edition. In dust jacket. $40-$50. Author's first novel.

WILLIAMS, Mrs. Ellen. *Three Years and a Half in the Army*. Cloth. New York, (1885). First edition. $100-$150.

WILLIAMS, G. T. *Receipts and Shipments of Livestock at Union Stock Yards for 1890*. 40 pp., wrappers. Chicago, 1891. $300-$400.

WILLIAMS, Jesse. *A Description of the United States Lands of Iowa*. Folding map in color. Green cloth. New York, 1840. First edition. $600-$800.

WILLIAMS, John G. *The Adventures of a Seventeen-Year-Old Lad*. Cloth. Boston, 1894. First edition. $100-$150.

WILLIAMS, John Lee. *The Territory of Florida*. Folding map, portrait, 2 plates. Cloth. New York, 1837. First edition. $200-$250. New York, 1839. Cloth. $75-$100.

WILLIAMS, John Lee. *A View of West Florida*. Folding map. Boards and leather. Philadelphia, 1827. First edition. $150-$200.

WILLIAMS, John R. *Biographical Sketch of the Life of William G. Greene, of Menard County, Ill.* 18 pp., cloth. No place, 1874. $60-$75.

WILLIAMS, Joseph. *Narrative of a Tour from the State of Indiana to the Oregon Territory.*

48 pp., plain blue wrappers. Cincinnati, 1843. First edition. $5,000-$7,500. Also, $3,000 (A, 1968)—the Streeter copy, with front wrapper only. New York, 1921. Cloth. One of 250. $50-$60.

WILLIAMS, Margery. *The Velveteen Rabbit or How Toys Become Real.* Illustrated by William Nicholson. Pictorial boards. London, 1922. First edition. $500-$600. Spine ends chipped, name in crayon on half title, $300.

WILLIAMS, O. W. *In Old New Mexico, 1879-1880: Reminiscences of Judge O. W. Williams.* 48 pp., wrappers. No place, no date. $100-$150.

WILLIAMS, R. H. *With the Border Ruffians.* Illustrated. Cloth. New York, 1907. First American edition. $75-$100. London, 1907. First English edition. $50-$60.

WILLIAMS, Tennessee. *American Blues.* Printed wrappers. (New York, 1948.) First edition, first issue, with "85¢" as price and with author's name misspelled on cover. $85-$125. Second issue, name corrected. $35.

WILLIAMS, Tennessee. *Baby Doll.* Cloth. (New York, 1956.) First edition. In dust jacket. $50-$60. London, 1957. Boards. First English edition. In dust jacket. $25.

WILLIAMS, Tennessee. *Battle of Angels.* Printed wrappers (comprising double number, Nos. 1 and 2, of *Pharos,* Spring, 1945). (Murray, Utah, 1945.) First edition. $200-$250. Author's first book.

WILLIAMS, Tennessee. *Cat on a Hot Tin Roof.* Tan cloth. (Norfolk, Conn., 1955.) First edition. In dust jacket. $35-$50.

WILLIAMS, Tennessee. *The Glass Menagerie.* Rust or blue cloth. New York, 1945. First edition, first printing (so stated). In dust jacket. $75-$100.

WILLIAMS, Tennessee. *Grand: A Short Story.* Cloth. New York, 1964. First edition. One of 300, signed. In glassine dust jacket. $125-$150.

WILLIAMS, Tennessee. *Hard Candy: A Book of Stories.* Patterned boards, cloth spine. (Norfolk, 1954.) First edition. Limited. Boxed. $50-$60. (Norfolk, 1959.) First trade edition. In dust jacket. $20.

WILLIAMS, Tennessee. *I Rise in Flames, Cried the Phoenix.* Boards and cloth. Norfolk, (1952). First edition. One of 300, signed (of an edition of 310). Boxed. $200-$300. Another issue: One of 10 on Umbria paper, signed. Boxed. $750-$1,000.

WILLIAMS, Tennessee. *In the Winter of Cities: Poems.* White parchment boards, gilt. (Norfolk, 1956.) First edition. One of 100 signed. In slipcase. $200-$350. Trade edition: Patterned boards and cloth. In dust jacket. $30-$50.

WILLIAMS, Tennessee. *One Arm and Other Stories.* Boards, vellum spine. (Norfolk, 1949.) First edition. One of 50, signed. Boxed. $400-$500. Trade edition: Boards and cloth. Boxed. $100. (Note: Most of the first edition copies bear a tipped-in title leaf with the copyright in Williams' name, but about 20 are said to exist with an integral title leaf with an incorrect copyright credit by New Directions. In 1977 a New York dealer listed one of these at $285.)

WILLIAMS, Tennessee. *The Roman Spring of Mrs. Stone.* Marbled boards, vellum spine. (Norfolk, 1950.) First edition. One of 500, signed. Boxed. $150-$175. Trade edition: Black cloth. In dust jacket. $20-$25.

WILLIAMS, Tennessee. *The Rose Tattoo.* Rose cloth. (New York or Norfolk, 1951.) First edition, first binding. In dust jacket. $50-$60.

WILLIAMS, Tennessee. *A Streetcar Named Desire.* Pink decorated boards. (Norfolk, 1947.) First edition. In dust jacket. $100-$150. Same place and date: Fifth printing, with text revised. In dust jacket. $30-$50.

WILLIAMS, Tennessee. *Summer and Smoke.* Blue cloth. (Norfolk, 1948.) First edition. In dust jacket. $40-$60.

WILLIAMS, Tennessee. *27 Wagons Full of Cotton and Other One-Act Plays.* Light-gray cloth. (Norfolk, 1946.) First edition. In dust jacket. $40-$60. (Norfolk), 1953. Third edition. Buckram. (First appearance of two plays, *Something Unspoken* and *Talk to Me Like the Rain.*) In dust jacket. $25.

WILLIAMS, Tennessee. *The Two-Character Play.* Cloth. (New York, 1969.) First edition. One of 350, signed. Boxed. $80-$100. (There was no trade edition.)

WILLIAMS, Tennessee, and Windham, Donald. *You Touched Me! A Romantic Comedy.* Green boards. New York, (1947). First edition. In dust jacket. $100-$125. Same: In gray printed wrappers. $100-$125.

WILLIAMS, Thomas J. C. *A History of Washington County* (Maryland). 2 vols., cloth. (Hagerstown), 1906. First edition. $80-$100.

WILLIAMS, William Carlos. See Ginsberg, Allen; Loy, Mina.

WILLIAMS, William Carlos. *Al Que Quiere! A Book of Poems.* Yellow boards. Boston, 1917. First edition. In glassine dust jacket. $350-$450. (Some copies in tan boards, slightly larger, with author's name "Willams" on spine. No priority. A copy in a frayed dust jacket was sold at auction in 1977 for $300.)

WILLIAMS, William Carlos. *The Broken Span.* Stiff paper wrappers. Norfolk, Conn., (1941). First edition. No. 1 of the Poet of the Month series. In dust jacket. $75.

WILLIAMS, William Carlos. *The Build-Up.* Boards and cloth. New York, (1952). First edition. In dust jacket. $80-$100.

WILLIAMS, William Carlos. *The Clouds, Aigeltinger, Russia, &.* Cloth, paper label on spine. (Aurora, N.Y., and Cummington, Mass.), 1948. First edition. One of 310. $200. One of 60 (of the same issue), signed. Boxed. $300-$400.

WILLIAMS, William Carlos. *The Cod Head.* Wrappers, with label. San Francisco, 1932. First edition. One of 125 signed. $250-$350.

WILLIAMS, William Carlos. *The Collected Later Poems.* Buckram. (Norfolk, 1950.) New Directions. First edition. One of 100, signed. Boxed. $250-$300. Trade edition: Cloth. In dust jacket. $40-$60.

WILLIAMS, William Carlos. *Collected Poems, 1921-1931.* Preface by Wallace Stevens. Cloth. New York, 1934. First edition. In dust jacket. $100-$125.

WILLIAMS, William Carlos. *The Complete Collected Poems 1906-1938.* Buckram. Norfolk, (1938). First edition. One of 50, signed. Boxed. $400-$450. Trade edition: Buckram. In dust jacket. $50-$60.

WILLIAMS, William Carlos. *The Desert Music and Other Poems.* Boards and cloth. New York, (1954). First edition. One of 100, signed. In glassine dust jacket. Boxed. $200-$300.

WILLIAMS, William Carlos. *An Early Martyr and Other Poems.* Wrappers. New York, 1935. First edition. One of 145, signed (of an edition of 165). In glassine dust jacket and green slipcase. $450-$550. (20 copies on special paper were issued in a yellow slipcase for presentation.)

WILLIAMS, William Carlos. *Go Go. (Manikin No. 2).* Stiff printed wrappers. New York, (1923). First edition. In publisher's envelope. (150 copies printed.) $750-$1,000. Also, $1,000 (A, 1977).

WILLIAMS, William Carlos. *The Great American Novel.* Boards and cloth, paper label. Paris, 1923. Three Mountains Press. First edition. One of 300. $200-$300.

WILLIAMS, William Carlos. *In the American Grain.* Buckram. New York, 1925. First edition. In dust jacket. $75-$100.

WILLIAMS, William Carlos. *In the Money.* Cloth. Norfolk, (1940). First edition. In dust jacket. $50-$60.

WILLIAMS, William Carlos. *The Knife of the Times and Other Stories*. Cloth, paper labels. Ithaca, (1932). First edition. One of 500. In dust jacket. $300-$400. Also, $300 (A, 1977).

WILLIAMS, William Carlos. *Kora in Hell: Improvisations*. Frontispiece. Gray boards. Boston, 1920. First edition. In dust jacket. $150-$225.

WILLIAMS, William Carlos. *Life Along the Passaic River*. White cloth. Norfolk, 1938. First edition. In dust jacket. $75-$100.

WILLIAMS, William Carlos. *A Novelette and Other Prose*. Printed green wrappers. (Toulon, 1932.) First edition. $200-$300. Also, covers faded, $175 (A, 1977).

WILLIAMS, William Carlos. *Paterson*. (Books 1, 2, 3, 4, and 5.) 5 vols., cloth. (New York, 1946-48-49-51-58). First editions. In dust jackets. $500-$750. Also, $600 (A, 1977). (Books 1-4 were limited to 1,000 copies; Book 5 bears no limitation notice.)

WILLIAMS, William Carlos. *The Pink Church*. Printed wrappers. Columbus, Ohio, 1949. First edition. One of 400. $150-$200. Another state: One of 25 (from the same issue), signed. $400-$450.

WILLIAMS, William Carlos. *Poems*. 22 pp., printed brown wrappers. (Rutherford, N.J.), 1909. First edition, first state, with "of youth himself, all rose-y-clad," in line 5 of first poem. (100 copies printed, of which two are known.) Second state, with "of youth himself all rose-yclad." (100 copies printed, about 12 known.) Either state: $10,000-$15,000, possibly more. (An inscribed presentation copy in the second state was sold for $16,000 at the first Jonathan Goodwin auction in New York in March, 1977. Another copy was offered in a 1978 catalogue at $16,500.)

WILLIAMS, William Carlos. *The Selected Letters*. Boards and cloth. New York, no date (1957). First edition. One of 75, signed. Boxed. $300-$325.

WILLIAMS, William Carlos. *Sour Grapes*. Boards, paper label. Boston, 1921. First edition. In dust jacket. $300-$350. (Note: Author's name on spine label only.)

WILLIAMS, William Carlos. *Spring and All*. Printed wrappers. (Paris, 1923.) First edition. One of 300. In glassine dust jacket. $350-$450. Also, $300 (A, 1977).

WILLIAMS, William Carlos. *The Tempers*. Boards. London, 1913. First edition. In glassine dust jacket. $500-$750. Author's first hardbound book.

WILLIAMS, William Carlos. *A Voyage to Pagany*. Cloth. New York, 1928. First edition. In dust jacket. $200-$250.

WILLIAMS, William Carlos. *The Wedge*. Boards. (Cummington), 1944. First edition. One of 380. In glassine dust jacket. $175-$200.

WILLIAMS, William Carlos. *White Mule*. Buckram. Norfolk, 1937. First edition. In dust jacket. $150-$200.

WILLIAMSON, George C. *The History of Portrait Miniatures*. 107 plates. 2 vols., folio, white cloth. London, 1904. One of 500. $350-$400. One of 50 with hand-colored plates. $600-$800.

WILLIAMSON, Henry. *The Patriot's Progress*. Wood engravings by William Kermode. Half vellum. London, (1930). First edition. One of 350, signed. Boxed. $35-$50.

WILLIAMSON, Hugh. *The History of North Carolina*. Folding map. 2 vols., calf. Philadelphia, 1812. First edition. $200.

WILLIAMSON, James J. *Mosby's Rangers*. Cloth. New York, 1896. First edition. $75-$100. New York, 1909. Cloth. Second edition. $50-$75.

WILLIS, Nathaniel Parker. *American Scenery*. 117 views by W.H. Bartlett. 2 vols., cloth or leather. London, 1840. First edition. $500-$600.

WILLIS, Nathaniel Parker. *Sketches*. Glazed boards and cloth, paper label. Boston, 1827. First edition. $75-$100. Author's first book.

WILLIS, William L. *History of Sacramento County.* Illustrated. Three-quarters leather. Los Angeles, 1913. $150-$175.

WILLMOTT, Ellen Ann. *The Genus Rosa.* Colored and plain plates. 25 parts, gray wrappers. London, (1910)-14. First edition. $1,500 and up. London, 1914. 2 vols. $800-$1,000, possibly more.

WILLOUGHBY, Edwin Elliott. *The Making of the King James Bible.* 31 pp., folio, boards and cloth. Los Angeles, 1956. Plantin Press. One of 290, with a leaf from a 1611 Bible. $150-$225.

WILLYAMS, Cooper. *A Voyage up the Mediterranean in HMS "Swiftsure."* 42 plates, folding map. Calf. London, 1802. First edition. $1,000 and up. With plates colored, $1,500 and up.

WILSON, Angus. *The Wrong Set and Other Stories.* Cloth. London, 1949. First edition. In dust jacket. $50-$75. Author's first book.

WILSON, Edmund. *Axel's Castle.* Cloth, paper label. New York, 1931. First edition. In dust jacket. $50-$75.

WILSON, Edmund. *The Boys in the Back Room.* Cloth, paper label. San Francisco, 1941. Colt Press. First edition. One of 100, signed. In acetate dust jacket. $150-$200. Trade edition: Boards and cloth, paper label. In dust jacket. $50-$75.

WILSON, Edmund. *Memoirs of Hecate County.* Green cloth. Garden City, 1946. First edition. In dust jacket. $40-$60.

WILSON, Edmund. *Note Books of Night.* Cloth. San Francisco, 1942. Colt Press. First edition. In dust jacket. $50-$75.

WILSON, Edmund. *Poets, Farewell!* Cloth. New York, 1929. First edition. In dust jacket. $75.

WILSON, Edmund. *This Room & This Gin & These Sandwiches.* Wrappers. New York, 1937. First edition. $75-$100.

WILSON, Edmund. *To the Finland Station.* Cloth. New York, 1940. First edition. In dust jacket. $50-$85.

WILSON, Edmund, and Bishop, John Peale. *The Undertaker's Garland.* Cloth. New York, 1922. First edition. In dust jacket. $100-$125. Another issue: Boards. One of 50 for "bookseller friends." $150. Wilson's first book.

WILSON, Elijah N. *Among the Shoshones.* 8 plates. Red cloth. Salt Lake City, (about 1910). First (suppressed) edition, with 222 pages. $150-$200. Second edition, same place and date, 247 pages. $50-$75.

WILSON, Harry Leon. *Ruggles of Red Gap.* Illustrated. Cloth. Garden City, 1915. First edition. In dust jacket. $50-$60.

WILSON, Harry Leon. *Zigzag Tales from the East to the West.* Illustrated by C. Jay Taylor. Cloth. New York, 1894. Decorated wrappers, or cloth. Wrappers: $75-$100. Cloth: $50. Author's first book.

WILSON, John Albert. *History of Los Angeles County, California.* Illustrated. Leather and cloth. Oakland, 1880. First edition. $300-$400.

WILSON, Sir John. *The Royal Philatelic Collection.* Edited by Clarence Winchester. 12 color facsimiles, 48 monochrome plates, other illustrations. Full red morocco. London, 1952. First edition. $150-$300.

WILSON, Obed G. *My Adventures in the Sierras.* Portrait. Cloth. Franklin, Ohio, 1902. First edition. $75-$100.

WILSON, Richard L. *Short Ravelings from a Long Yarn, or Camp and March Sketches of the Santa Fe Trail.* Edited by Benjamin F. Taylor. Illustrated. Printed boards. Chicago, 1847. First edition. $3,600-$4,200. Santa Ana, Calif., 1936. Cloth. $50-$75.

WILSON, Robert. *The Travels of Robert Wilson: Being a Relation of Facts*. Portrait, plates. Mottled calf. London, 1807. $200-$300.

WILSON, Woodrow. *Congressional Government*. Cloth. Boston, 1885. First edition, first issue, with publisher's monogram on spine. $75-$100. Author's first book.

WILSON, Woodrow. *George Washington*. Illustrated. Cloth. New York, 1897. First edition. $50-$75.

WILTSEE, Ernest A. *Gold Rush Steamers (of the Pacific)*. Illustrated. Cloth. San Francisco, 1938. Grabhorn Press. One of 500. $100-$150.

WINDELER, B. C. *Elimus*. 12 designs by Dorothy Shakespear. Gray boards. Paris, 1923. Three Mountains Press. First edition. One of 300. $75-$100.

WINDELER, Bernard. *Sailing Ships and Barges of the Western Mediterranean and the Adriatic Seas*. Map. 17 hand-colored copperplate engravings by Edward Wadsworth. Cloth. London, 1926. One of 450. Boxed. $200-$250.

*WING-and-Wing (The)*. By the Author of *The Pilot*. 2 vols., printed terra-cotta wrappers. Philadelphia, 1842. (By James Fenimore Cooper.) First American edition (of the novel issued first in London under the title *The Jack O'Lantern* and under Cooper's name; see author entry). $100-$250. Later issue, wrappers dated 1843. $100-$150.

WINKLER, A. V. *The Confederate Capital and Hood's Texas Brigade*. Illustrated. Cloth. Austin, 1894. First edition. $75-$125.

WINSHIP, George Parker. *The First American Bible*. Cloth. Boston, 1929. Merrymount Press. One of 157 with a leaf from John Eliot's Indian Bible of 1663. $250-$275.

WINSHIP, George Parker. *William Caxton*. Boards, vellum spine. London, 1909. Doves Press. One of 54 for the Club of Odd Volumes (from an edition of 300). $250-$300. Others, not of this series, $200-$250. Another issue: Specially bound in dark orange morocco. Boxed. $500 and up.

WINSHIP, George Parker (editor). *The Journey of Francisco Vazquez de Coronado, 1540-1542*. Cloth. San Francisco, 1933. One of 550. $100-$150.

*WINTER Ship (A)*. Leaflet. Edinburgh, 1960. (By Sylvia Plath.) First edition. $150-$250. Author's first published work.

*WINTER in the West (A)*. By a New Yorker. 2 vols., cloth. New York; 1835. (By Charles Fenno Hoffman.) First edition. $150-$175. Author's first book.

WINTERS, Yvor. *Before Disaster*. Printed green wrappers. Tryon, N.C., 1934. First edition. $75-$100.

WINTERS, Yvor. *The Immobile Wind*. Wrappers. Evanston, (1921). First edition. $200-$250. Author's first book.

WINTERS, Yvor. *The Magpie's Shadow*. Printed blue wrappers. Chicago, 1922. First edition. $200-$300.

WINTERS, Yvor. *Maule's Curse: Seven Studies in the History of American Obscurantism*. Blue cloth. Norfolk, (1938). First edition. In dust jacket. $50-$75.

WINTERS, Yvor. *The Proof*. Decorated boards. New York, 1930. First edition. In dust jacket. $50-$60.

WIRT, Mrs. E. W. *Flora's Dictionary*. 58 hand-colored plates. Morocco. Baltimore, 1837. $500-$600. Baltimore, 1855. Cloth. $400-$500.

*WISDOM of Jesus (The), the Son of Sirach. Commonly called Ecclesiasticus*. Orange vellum, silk ties. London, 1932. One of 328. Ashendene Press. $800-$1,250. Another issue: One of 25 printed on vellum. Morocco. $5,000 and up.

WISE, George. *Campaigns and Battles of the Army of Northern Virginia*. 2 portraits. Cloth. New York, 1916. First edition. $100-$150.

WISLIZENUS, Frederick A. *A Journey to the Rocky Mountains in the Year 1839.* Folding map. Boards and cloth. St. Louis, 1912. First edition. One of 500. $100-$150.

WISLIZENUS, Frederick A. *Memoir of a Tour to Northern Mexico.* 3 folding maps. Boards. Washington, 1848. First edition. $150-$250.

WISTAR, Casper. *A System of Anatomy for the Use of Students of Medicine.* 2 vols., boards. Philadelphia, 1811-14. First edition. $200-$250.

WISTAR, Isaac Jones. *Autobiography of Isaac Jones Wistar, 1827-1905.* Folding map, portrait, plates. 2 vols., boards and cloth, leather spine labels. Philadelphia, 1914. First edition. One of 250. $250-$300. Philadelphia, 1937. Illustrated. Buckram. $50.

WISTER, Owen. *The Virginian.* Illustrated. Yellow pictorial cloth. New York, 1902. First edition. In dust jacket. $100-$125. New York, 1911. Illustrated by Frederic Remington and Charles M. Russell. Boards. One of 100. Boxed. $800-$1,000. New York, 1930. Limited Editions Club. Cowhide. $30-$40.

WITHERS, Alexander S. *Chronicles of Border Warfare.* Leather. Clarksburg, Va., 1831. First edition. $250-$300. Cincinnati, 1895. Cloth. $75-$100.

WODEHOUSE, P. G. *The Pothunters.* Cloth. London, 1902. First edition. In dust jacket. $200-$250. Author's first book.

WOIWODE, Larry. *What I'm Going to Do, I Think.* Cloth. New York, (1969). First edition. In dust jacket. $40-$60. Also, advance copy in dust jacket for the book. $100. Author's first book.

WOLF, Edwin, II, and Fleming, John. *Rosenbach: A Biography.* Illustrated. Cloth. Cleveland, (1960). First edition. One of 250, signed. Boxed. $100-$125. Trade edition: In dust jacket. $35-$45.

WOLFE, Humbert. *Cursory Rhymes.* Illustrated by Albert Rutherston. Cloth. London, 1927. One of 500, signed. $25-$35.

WOLFE, Humbert, *The Silver Cat and Other Poems.* Boards. New York, 1928. One of 780. In dust jacket. $25-$35.

WOLFE, Humbert. *The Uncelestial City.* Cloth. London, 1930. First edition. One of 400, signed. In dust jacket. $35.

WOLFE, Thomas. See Dashiell, Alfred; Koch, Frederick H.; Schreiber, Georges. Also see *Thomas Wolfe Memorial, (The).*

WOLFE, Thomas. *America.* Wrappers. (San Mateo, Calif., 1942.) Published by the Greenwood Press. First separate edition. One of 150. $100.

WOLFE, Thomas. *The Crisis in Industry.* 14 pp., printed wrappers. Chapel Hill, N.C., 1919. First edition. $400-$500. Author's first separate work.

WOLFE, Thomas. *The Face of a Nation.* Cloth. New York, 1939. First edition. In dust jacket. $40-$60. (Scribner and Literary Guild issues were simultaneous.)

WOLFE, Thomas. *From Death to Morning.* Brown cloth. New York, 1935. First edition, first binding, with code letter "A" on copyright page. In dust jacket. $75-$100.

WOLFE, Thomas. *From Of Time and the River America.* Chicago. 1942. $40-$50. (Privately reprinted section from *Of Time and the River,* done by a class in typography. See *America* entry.)

WOLFE, Thomas. *Gentlemen of the Press.* Cloth, paper label. Chicago, (1942). First edition. One of 350. $80-$125.

WOLFE, Thomas. *The Hills Beyond.* Cloth. New York, (1941). First edition. In dust jacket. $40-$60.

WOLFE, Thomas. *Look Homeward, Angel.* Blue cloth, gilt. New York, 1929. First edition, first issue, with seal of Scribner Press on copyright page. In first state dust jacket with Wolfe's picture on back. $400-$600. Also, $250 (A, 1974). Author's first novel. In later dust jacket, $100 and up at retail. London, 1930. Cloth. In dust jacket. $125-$150. New York, 1947. Illustrated by D. Gorsline. Cloth. First illustrated edition. In dust jacket. $35-$50. New York, (1963). Reprint of Gorsline edition. In dust jacket. $20-$25.

WOLFE, Thomas. *Mannerhouse: A Play in a Prologue and Three Acts.* Black cloth. New York, 1948. First edition. One of 500. In dust jacket. Boxed. $60-$100. Trade edition: Cloth. In dust jacket. $15-$20.

WOLFE, Thomas. *A Note on Experts: Dexter Vespasian Joyner.* Cloth. New York, 1939. First edition. One of 300. In glassine dust jacket. $200-$300. Also, $225 (A, 1977).

WOLFE, Thomas. *Of Time and the River.* Black cloth. New York, 1935. First edition, with "A" on copyright page. In dust jacket. $80-$100.

WOLFE, Thomas. *The Story of a Novel.* Cloth. New York, 1936. First edition, with "A" on copyright page. In dust jacket. $40-$60.

WOLFE, Thomas. *To Rupert Brooke.* 4 leaves, printed wrappers. (Paris), 1948. One of 100 used as a Christmas greeting. $100-$150.

WOLFE, Thomas. *The Web and The Rock.* Blue cloth. New York, 1939. First edition, first printing. In dust jacket. $50-$75.

WOLFE, Thomas. *You Can't Go Home Again.* Cloth. New York, (1940). First edition, first printing. In dust jacket. $50-$75. London, (1947). First English edition. In dust jacket. $50-$75.

*WOMAN'S Daring; As Shown by the Testimony of the Rock. Recorded by an Exultant Woman and a Hugh-millerated Man.* 24 pp., unbound (self-wrappers with cover title?). (Annisquam, Mass.?, 1872). First edition. Last leaf crudely mended, $250. (Note: Contains a contribution by Thomas A. Janvier, his first book appearance.)

*WONDERFUL Providence (A), in Many Incidents at Sea.* 24 pp., wrappers. Buffalo, 1848. (By Capt. Elijah Holcomb.) First edition. $35-$50.

*WONDERFUL Stories of Fuz-Buz the Fly and Mother Grabem the Spider (The).* 9 engraved plates. Half morocco. Philadelphia, 1867. (By S. Weir Mitchell.) First edition. One of 170 on large paper. $500-$600. Also, $350 (A, 1976). First trade edition: Cloth. $150-$200.

WOOD, Arnold. *A Bibliography of "The Complete Angler."* Vellum, cloth ties. New York, 1900. First edition. One of 120. $100-$150. Another issue: One of 18 on vellum. $400-$450.

WOOD, Charles Erskine. *A Masque of Love.* 87 pp., boards. Chicago, 1904. First edition. $50. Author's first book.

WOOD, Mrs. Henry. *East Lynne.* 3 vols., violet cloth. London, 1861. First edition. $500-$750.

WOOD, James H. *The War, Stonewall Jackson, His Campaigns and Battles, The Regiment, as I Saw Them.* Cloth. Cumberland, Md., (about 1910). $100-$150.

WOOD, John. *Journal of John Wood.* 76 pp., printed wrappers. Chillicothe, Ohio, 1852. First edition. $3,500-$5,000. Columbus, Ohio, 1871. 112 pp., printed wrappers. Second edition. $400-$600.

WOOD, R.E. *Life and Confessions of James Gilbert Jenkins: the Murderer of 18 Men.* Illustrated. 56 pp., wrappers. Napa City, 1864. First edition. $100-$200.

WOOD, Silas. *A Sketch of the First Settlement of the Several Towns on Long Island.* Half leather. Brooklyn, 1824. First edition. $250.

WOOD, W. D. *Reminiscences of Reconstruction in Texas.* 58 pp., wrappers. (San Marcos, Tex.) 1902. First edition. $100-$200.

WOOD, William. *Zoography, or the Beauties of Nature Displayed.* Aquatint plates by William Daniell. 3 vols., calf. London, 1807. First edition. $300-$400.

WOODMAN, David, Jr. *Guide to Texas Emigrants.* Map, plate. Light-blue cloth. Boston, 1835. First edition. $2,000-$2,500, possibly more.

WOODRUFF, W. E. *With the Light Guns in '61-'65.* Cloth. Little Rock, 1903. First edition. $150-$250.

WOODS, Daniel B. *Sixteen Months at the Gold Diggings.* Cloth. New York, 1851. First edition. $250-$350.

WOODS, John. *Two Years' Residence . . . on the English Prairie, in the Illinois Country.* 2 maps and plan. Boards. London, 1822. First edition. $750-$1,000. (Howes says there are possibly earlier, less desirable, issues with only one or only two maps.)

WOODSON, W. H. *History of Clay County, Missouri.* Cloth. Topeka, 1920. $60-$80.

*WOODSTOCK.* 3 vols., boards. Edinburgh, 1826. (By Sir Walter Scott.) First edition. $150-$300.

WOODWARD, John, and Burnett, George. *A Treatise on Heraldry.* 56 plates, many colored, other illustrations. 2 vols., cloth or half morocco. Edinburgh, 1892. $100-$200. Edinburgh, 1896. 66 plates, many colored, etc. 2 vols., half leather. One of 325. $150-$250.

WOODWARD, W.E. *Bunk.* Cloth. New York, 1923. First edition. In dust jacket. $40-$50. Author's first book.

WOODWARD, William. *The Gallant Fox: A Memoir.* Color plates, charts, pedigrees. Red morocco. New York, 1931. Derrydale Press. One of 25 in leather (No. 1). $9,500 in a 1977 catalogue. (25 copies are said to have been bound in wrappers.)

WOODWORTH, Samuel. *The Champions of Freedom, or the Mysterious Chief.* 2 vols., boards. New York, 1816-18. $100-$150.

WOOLF, Leonard. *Stories of the East.* Buff Wrappers. Richmond, England, 1921. Hogarth Press. First edition. $60-$80.

WOOLF, Leonard. *The Village in the Jungle.* Cloth. London, 1913. First edition. In dust jacket. $75-$100. London, 1931. Cloth. First Hogarth Press edition. In dust jacket. $40-$50.

WOOLF, Virginia. See Cameron, Julia M.

WOOLF, Virginia. *Beau Brummell.* Boards and cloth. New York, 1930. First edition. One of 550, signed. Boxed. $200-$275.

WOOLF, Virginia. *Between the Acts.* Cloth. London, 1941. Hogarth Press. First edition. In dust jacket. $75-$100. New York, (1941). Cloth. First American edition. In dust jacket. $40-$50.

WOOLF, Virginia. *The Captain's Death Bed.* Brown cloth. London, 1950. First edition. In dust jacket. $40-$60. New York, 1950. Blue cloth. First American edition. In dust jacket. $40-$50.

WOOLF, Virginia. *The Common Reader.* White boards and cloth. London, 1925. Hogarth Press. First edition. In dust jacket. $150-$250. London, 1932. Cloth. Second Series (same title). In dust jacket. $150. New York, 1948. Blue cloth. First and Second Series in one volume. First American edition thus. In dust jacket. $25.

WOOLF, Virginia. *Flush: A Biography.* Illustrated by Vanessa Bell. Buff cloth. London, 1933. Hogarth Press. First edition. In dust jacket (imprinted "Large Paper Edition"). $100-$125. Ordinary issue: $50-$60.

WOOLF, Virginia. *Hours in a Library.* Frontispiece. Boards and cloth. New York, (1957). First edition. In glassine dust jacket. $40-$60.

WOOLF, Virginia. *Jacob's Room*. Yellow cloth. Richmond, 1922. Hogarth Press. First edition. In dust jacket. $175-$275. Also, one of about 40, signed, with subscriber's list, $400-$500.

WOOLF, Virginia. *Kew Gardens*. Woodcut by Vanessa Bell. Wrappers. Richmond, 1919. Hogarth Press. First edition, first issue, with correction slip pasted to imprint at end. $750-$1,000. Also, $1,400 (A, 1977.) Second issue, "Richard Madley for the Hogarth Press." $400-$500. London, (1927). Hogarth Press. Boards. One of 500. In dust jacket. $150-$250.

WOOLF, Virginia. *The Mark on the Wall*. (Cover title—no title page.) White wrappers. Richmond, 1919. "Second edition" (actually first separate edition, having previously appeared in *Two Stories*, published jointly with her husband Leonard Woolf). $250-$350.

WOOLF, Virginia. *Mr. Bennett and Mrs. Brown*. White wrappers. London, 1924. Hogarth Press. First edition. In dust jacket. $100-$150.

WOOLF, Virginia. *Mrs. Dalloway*. Cloth. London, 1925. First edition. In dust jacket. $200-$300. New York, 1925. Orange cloth. First American edition. In dust jacket. $75-$100.

WOOLF, Virginia. *The Moment and Other Essays*. Cloth. London, 1947. Hogarth Press. First edition. In dust jacket. $50-$75.

WOOLF, Virginia. *Monday or Tuesday*. Woodcuts by Vanessa Bell. Decorated boards and cloth. Richmond, 1921. Hogarth Press. First edition. $200-$300.

WOOLF, Virginia. *Night and Day*. Cloth. London, 1919. First edition. In dust jacket. $300-$350.

WOOLF, Virginia. *On Being Ill*. Vellum and cloth. (London), 1930. Hogarth Press. First edition. One of 250, signed. In dust jacket. $400-$600.

WOOLF, Virginia. *Orlando: A Biography*. Brown, or orange, cloth. London, 1928. Hogarth Press. First English edition, first issue, brown cloth. In dust jacket. $125-$150. Second issue: $75-$125. New York, 1928. Plates. Black cloth. First American edition. One of 861, signed. $175-$250.

WOOLF, Virginia. *A Room of One's Own*. Cloth. New York and London, 1929. First edition. One of 492, signed. (Of this edition, 100 were reserved for Great Britain. All copies bore both New York, Fountain Press, and London, Hogarth Press, imprints. I have found no record of a New York dust jacket, although the London copies were provided with pink jackets.) $250-$350.

WOOLF, Virginia. *Street Haunting*. Boards and blue or green morocco. San Francisco, 1930. Grabhorn Press. One of 500, signed. Boxed. $300-$350.

WOOLF, Virginia. *Three Guineas*. 5 plates. Yellow cloth. London, 1938. Hogarth Press. First edition. In dust jacket. $65-$100.

WOOLF, Virginia. *To the Lighthouse*. Blue cloth. London, 1927. Hogarth Press. First edition. In dust jacket. $200-$300. New York, (1927). Cloth. First American edition. In dust jacket. $75-$125.

WOOLF, Virginia. *The Voyage Out*. Cloth. London, 1915. First edition. In dust jacket. $400-$500. New York, 1920. Cloth. First American edition. In dust jacket. $200-$250. London, 1927. Cloth. First Hogarth Press edition. In dust jacket. $50-$100.

WOOLF, Virginia. *The Waves*. Purple cloth. London, 1931. Hogarth Press. First edition. In dust jacket. $150-$200. New York, (1931). Cloth. First American edition. In dust jacket. $60-$80.

WOOLF, Virginia. *A Writer's Diary*. Orange cloth. London, 1953. First edition. In dust jacket. $75-$100. New York, 1954. Pink cloth. First American edition. In dust jacket. $30-$40.

WOOLF, Virginia. *The Years*. Green cloth. London, 1937. Hogarth Press. First edition. In dust jacket. $100-$150.

WOOLF, Virginia, and Woolf, L. S. *Two Stories*. Wrappers or paper-backed cloth. Richmond, 1917. Hogarth Press. First edition. $1,000-$1,500. First book of the Hogarth Press.

WOOLWORTH, James M. *Nebraska in 1857*. Colored folding map. Printed cloth. Omaha, 1857. First edition. $400-$600, possibly more.

WOOTEN, Dudley G. (editor). *A Comprehensive History of Texas, 1865 to 1897*. 23 plates. 2 vols., leather. Dallas, 1898. First edition. $300-$400.

WORDSWORTH, William. *See Grace Darling; Kendel and Windermere Railway, etc.; Lyrical Ballads; Ode Performed in the Senate-House*.

WORDSWORTH, William. *A Decade of Years: Poems, 1798-1807*. Printed in red and black. Limp vellum. London, 1911. Doves Press. One of 200. $350-$500. Another issue: One of 12 on vellum. $1,500-$2,000.

WORDSWORTH, William. *The Excursion, Being a Portion of the Recluse, a Poem*. Drab boards. London, 1814. First edition. $300-$400.

WORDSWORTH, William. *A Letter to a Friend of Robert Burns*. Wrappers. London, 1816. First edition. $200-$300.

WORDSWORTH, William. *Memorials of a Tour on the Continent, 1820*. Boards. London, 1822. First edition. $350-$500. Also, worn, $200 (A, 1977).

WORDSWORTH, William. *Ode on the Intimations of Immortality*. Colored frontispiece by Walter Crane. Vellum. London, 1903. Essex House Press. One of 150 on vellum. $200-$300.

WORDSWORTH, William. *Peter Bell, a Tale in Verse*. Frontispiece. 88 pp., drab wrappers, paper label on back. London, 1819. First edition. $800-$1,000. Also, rebacked, worn, $450 (A, 1977).

WORDSWORTH, William. *Poems*. 2 vols., boards, paper labels. London, 1807. First edition, first issue, with period after "Sonnets" on page (103) of Vol. 1 and "fnuction" on page 98 of Vol. 2. $1,250-$1,500. London, 1815. 2 vols., boards, with frontispiece added to each volume. $300-$400. London, (1902). Vale Press. 6 woodcuts. White buckram. One of 310. $150-$250.

WORDSWORTH, William. *The Prelude, or Growth of a Poet's Mind: An Autobiographical Poem*. Dark-red cloth. London, 1850. First edition. $100-$150. London, 1915. Doves Press. Vellum. One of 155. $400-$500. Another issue: One of 10 on vellum. $1,500-$2,000.

WORDSWORTH, William. *The River Duddon: A Series of Sonnets*. Boards and cloth. London, 1820. First edition. $150-$200.

WORDSWORTH, William. *Thanksgiving Ode, January 18, 1816*. Dark-green wrappers. London, 1816. First edition. $200-$250.

WORDSWORTH, William. *The Waggoner: A Poem, to Which Are Added, Sonnets*. Drab wrappers, label. London, 1819. First edition. $200-$300.

WORDSWORTH, William. *The White Doe of Rylstone*. Frontispiece. Drab boards, paper label. London, 1815. First edition. $750-$1,000. Also, worn, $375 (A, 1977).

WORDSWORTH, William. *Yarrow Revisited, and Other Poems*. Drab boards, paper label on spine, or cloth. London, 1835. First edition, with inserted errata slip. Either binding: $400-$500, possibly more.

WORK, John. See Lewis, W.S., and Phillips, P.C.

WRIGHT, Austin Tappan. *Islandia*. Beige buckram. New York, (1942). First edition. First issue, with Farrar & Rinehart insignia on copyright page. In dust jacket. With Basil Davenport prospectus pamphlet *An Introduction to Islandia*, $150-$250. Lacking jacket but with prospectus, $75-$100. Lacking both jacket and pamphlet, $50-$75.

WRIGHT, Crafts J. *Official Journal of the Conference Convention Held at Washington City, February, 1861.* Wrappers. Washington, 1861. $100-$150.

WRIGHT, E.W. (editor). *Lewis and Dryden's Marine History of the Pacific Northwest.* Plates. Morocco. Portland, 1895. First edition. $200-$250.

WRIGHT, Frank Lloyd. See Gannet(t), William C., *The House Beautiful.*

WRIGHT, Frank Lloyd. *An Autobiography.* Illustrated. Cloth. New York, 1932. First edition. $150-$200.

WRIGHT, Frank Lloyd. *Buildings, Plans and Designs.* 100 plates, loose in half cloth portfolio. New York, (1963). Limited edition. $250-$300.

WRIGHT, Frank Lloyd. *Drawings for a Living Architecture.* 200 drawings by the author (75 colored). Oblong folio, cloth. New York, 1959. Signed by the author. In dust jacket. $500-$750.

WRIGHT, Frank Lloyd. *The Future of Architecture.* Illustrated. Cloth. New York, 1953. First edition. In dust jacket. $75-$100.

WRIGHT, Frank Lloyd. *Genius and the Mobocracy.* Illustrated by Louis H. Sullivan. Cloth. New York, (1949). First edition. In dust jacket. $100.

WRIGHT, Frank Lloyd. *The Japanese Print.* Illustrated. Orange wrappers. Chicago, 1912. First edition (suppressed). $750-$1,000. (Note: All except about 50 burned by the publisher when Wright protested the binding.) First published edition: Printed boards. One of 35 on vellum. $400-$500. Ordinary issue: $100-$150.

WRIGHT, Frank Lloyd. *On Architecture.* Edited by Frederick Gutheim. Cloth. New York, 1941. First edition. In dust jacket. $65-$85.

WRIGHT, Harold Bell. *The Shepherd of the Hills.* Illustrated. Cloth. Chicago, 1907. First edition, with "Published, September, 1907" on copyright page. $150-$250. (Burt printings are later.)

WRIGHT, Harold Bell. *That Printer of Udell's: A Story of the Middle West.* Illustrated by John Clithero Gilbert. Pictorial cloth. Chicago, 1903. First edition. $40-$60. Author's first book.

WRIGHT, Harry. *Harry Wright's Pocket Base Ball Score Book, No. 1.* Cloth, paper label. Boston, 1876. $100-$150.

WRIGHT, Isaac. *Wright's Family Medicine.* Sheepskin. Madisonville, Tenn., 1833. $125.

WRIGHT, James. *The Branch Will Not Break.* Cloth. Middletown, Conn., (1963). First edition. In dust jacket. $25-$30.

WRIGHT, James. *The Green Wall.* Foreword by W.H. Auden. Boards. New Haven, 1957. First edition. In dust jacket. $40-$50. Author's first book.

WRIGHT, John Lloyd. *My Father Who Is on Earth.* Gray cloth. New York, (1946). First edition. In dust jacket. $35-$50.

WRIGHT, Joseph (editor). *The English Dialect Dictionary.* 6 vols., half morocco. London, 1898-1905. First edition. $200-$300. New York, 1962. 6 vols., cloth. Reprint. $150-$200.

WRIGHT, Philip Green. *The Dreamer.* Foreword by Charles A. Sandburg. White boards. Galesburg, Ill., (1906). First edition. $300-$400. (Carl Sandburg's first prose writing—set, printed and bound, but not published, two years before his first book, *In Reckless Ecstasy.)*

WRIGHT, Richard. *How "Bigger" Was Born.* Printed wrappers. (New York, 1940.) First edition. $40-$50.

WRIGHT, Richard. *Native Son.* Dark-blue cloth, stamped in red. New York, 1940. First edition, first binding. In yellow and green (first) dust jacket. $75-$100. Second binding, gray cloth: In grayish (second) dust jacket. $25-$30.

WRIGHT, Richard. *The Outsider*. Cloth. New York, (1953). First edition. In dust jacket. $30-$40.

WRIGHT, Richard. *Uncle Tom's Children. Four Novellas*. Red cloth. New York, 1938. First edition. In dust jacket. $100-$125. Author's first book. (Note: *Uncle Tom's Children: Five Long Stories*, same place and year, is a revised edition. Value: In jacket. $25-$35.)

WRIGHT, Robert M. *Dodge City, the Cowboy Capital*. Colored frontispiece, 40 plates. Cloth. (Wichita, 1913.) First edition, with 344 pp. $175-$200. Second edition, same place and date, 342 pp., black-and-white portrait. $50-$60.

WRIGHT, Capt. T.J. *History of the 8th Regiment, Kentucky Volunteer Infantry*. Cloth. St. Joseph, 1880. $150-$250.

WRIGHT, William. See De Quille, Dan.

WROTH, Lawrence C. *The Early Cartography of the Pacific*. Folding facsimile maps. Cloth. New York, 1934. First edition. One of 100. $100-$150.

*WYANDOTTE; or, The Hutted Knoll*. 3 vols., boards. London, 1843. (By James Fenimore Cooper.) First edition. $200-$300. Philadelphia, 1843. 2 vols., wrappers. First American edition. $250-$350.

WYATT, M.D. *The Art of Illuminating*. Illustrated. Decorated brown cloth, or morocco. London, 1860. First edition. $200-$300.

WYATT, Sir Thomas. See Wiat, Sir Thomas.

WYETH, John A. *Life of Gen. Nathan Bedford Forrest*. 55 plates, maps. Cloth. New York, 1899. First edition. $75-$100.

WYETH, John B. *Oregon; or A Short History of a Long Journey*. 87 pp., printed wrappers. Cambridge, Mass., 1833. First edition, first issue, with half title. (Very rare with wrappers intact.) $1,500-$2,000. Also, $1,200 (A, 1974). Cleveland, 1906. Cloth. Reprint (with John K. Townsend's *Journey Across the Rockies to the Columbia*). $35-50.

WYLIE, Elinor. See *Incidental Numbers*.

WYLIE, Elinor. *Angels and Earthly Creatures: A Sequence of Sonnets*. Decorated wrappers. Henley-on-Thames, 1928. First edition. One of 51 numbered copies. About half of this edition were signed, the rest left unsigned at the author's death. In dust jacket, signed. $750 and up. Unsigned, $500 and up. Also, $425 (A, 1977). New York, 1929. Portrait. Black cloth. First American edition (and first commercially published). One of 200. Boxed. $75-$100.

WYLIE, Elinor. *Collected Poems*. Cloth. New York, 1932. First edition. In dust jacket. $30-$50.

WYLIE, Elinor. *Mr. Hodge & Mr. Hazard*. Blue buckram. New York, 1928. First edition. One of 145 (actually 150), signed. Boxed. $80-$100.

WYLIE, Elinor. *Nets to Catch the Wind*. Cloth. New York, 1921. First edition, first issue, on unwatermarked paper. In dust jacket. $100-$150. Also, $120 (A, 1974). (First book under her name.)

WYLIE, Elinor. *The Orphan Angel*. Boards and cloth. New York, 1926. One of 160 on rag paper, signed. Boxed. $100-$125. Another issue: One of 30 on vellum, signed. $200-$250.

WYLIE, Elinor. *Trivial Breath*. Boards. New York, 1928. First edition, with "In" for "An" in line 9 of page 13. One of 100, signed. 75-$125.

WYLIE, Elinor. *The Venetian Glass Nephew*. Boards. New York, 1925. First edition, first issue, without publisher's monogram on copyright page. One of 250, signed. $50-$75.

# X

XENOPHON. *Cyropaedia: The Institution and Life of Cyrus, the First of That Name, King of Persians.* Translated by Philemon Holland. (Reprint of 1632 edition.) Folio, goatskin, Newtown, Wales, 1936. Gregynog Press. One of 150. $1,000-$1,250. Special issue: One of 15 bound by George Fisher. Morocco. $2,500 and up.

# Y

*YALE Book of Student Verse, 1910-1919 (The).* Boards. New Haven, 1919. First edition. $50-$60. (Note: Includes poems by Stephen Vincent Benét, Wilder, MacLeish, and others.)

YATES, Edmund Hodgson. *My Haunts and Their Frequenters* Illustrated. Wrappers. London, 1854. First edition. $50. Author's first book.

*YE Minutes of Ye CLXXVIIth Meeting of Ye Sette of Odd Volumes.* Transcribed by John Todhunter. Printed wrappers. (London, 1896.) One of 154. $300-$400.

*YEAR of Scandal: How The Washington Post Covered Watergate and the Agnew Crisis.* Compiled by Laura Longley Babb. Illustrated. Quarto, blue cloth. Washington, 1973. First edition. One of 100 for presentation. $850 and up.

YEARY, Mamie. *Reminiscences of the Boys in Gray, 1861-1865.* Cloth. Dallas, 1912. First edition. $125-$250.

YEATS, John Butler. *Early Memories.* Preface by W.B. Yeats. Boards and linen. Dundrum, Ireland, 1923. Cuala Press. One of 500. $60-$100.

YEATS, John Butler. *Further Letters.* Selected by Lennox Robinson. Boards and linen. Dundrum, 1920. Cuala Press. One of 400. $60-$100.

YEATS, John Butler. *La la Noo.* Boards and linen. Dublin, 1943. Cuala Press. One of 250. In dust jacket. $100-$125.

YEATS, John Butler. *Passages from the Letters of John Butler Yeats.* Selected by Ezra Pound. Boards and linen. Dundrum, 1917. Cuala Press. One of 400. $100-$150.

YEATS, William Butler. See Allingham, William; Bax, Clifford; Dunsany, Lord; Ganconagh; Gogarty, Oliver St. John; Gregory, Lady. Also see *Agnes Tobin.*

YEATS, William Butler. *The Bounty of Sweden*. Boards and linen. Dublin, 1925. Cuala Press. One of 400. In glassine dust jacket. $100-$150.

YEATS, William Butler. *The Cat and the Moon and Certain Poems*. Boards and linen. Dublin, 1924. Cuala Press. First edition. One of 500. $100-$150.

YEATS, William Butler. *Cathleen ni Houlihan*. Vellum, silk ties. London, 1902. Caradoc Press. First edition. One of 8 on Japan vellum. $1,000-$1,500. First regular edition: Cream-colored boards, leather spine. (300 copies.) $500-$600.

YEATS, William Butler. *The Celtic Twilight*. Olive-green cloth. London, 1893. First edition, first binding, with publisher's name on back in capital letters. $150-$200. Later binding, capitals and lower case lettering, $100-$150.

YEATS, William Butler. *Collected Works*. Portraits. 8 vols., buckram. Stratford-on-Avon, 1908. $600-$800, possibly more.

YEATS, William Butler. *The Countess Kathleen*. Frontispiece. Japan vellum boards. London, 1892. First edition. One of 30 signed by the publisher. $450-$650. Another issue: Dark-green boards, parchment spine. One of 500. $200-$250. London, 1919. Wrappers. Revised edition. $75-$100.

YEATS, William Butler. *The Cutting of an Agate*. Green boards. New York, 1912. First edition. In dust jacket. $75. Lacking jacket, $35-$50. London, 1919. Dark-blue cloth. First English edition. In dust jacket. $50-$60.

YEATS, William Butler. *The Death of Synge, and Other Passages from an Old Diary*. Boards and linen. Dublin, 1928. Cuala Press. First edition. One of 400. In dust jacket. $65-$100.

YEATS, William Butler. *Deirdre*. Gray boards, green cloth spine, paper label. London, 1907. First edition, with printer's imprint on page 48. $75-$100.

YEATS, William Butler. *Discoveries: A Volume of Essays*. Blue boards and linen. Dundrum, 1907. Dun Emer Press. First edition. One of 200. $125-$175.

YEATS, William Butler. *Dramatis Personae.* Boards and linen. Dublin, 1935. Cuala Press. One of 400. In dust jacket. $100-$150. New York, 1936. In dust jacket. $75-$125.

YEATS, William Butler. *Eight Poems*. Wrappers. London, 1916. Morland Press. $75-$100.

YEATS, William Butler. *Essays*. Cloth. London, 1924. First edition. In dust jacket. $100-$175. New York, 1924. Boards and cloth. One of 250, signed. $200-$300.

YEATS, William Butler. *Essays: 1931 to 1936*. Boards and linen. Dublin, 1937. Cuala Press. One of 300. In dust jacket. $125-$200.

YEATS, William Butler. *Estrangement: Being Some Fifty Thoughts from a Diary Kept by William Butler Yeats*. Boards and linen. Dublin, 1926. Cuala Press. First edition. One of 300. In dust jacket. $65-$125.

YEATS, William Butler. *Four Years*. Boards and linen. Dundrum, 1921. Cuala Press. First edition. One of 400. $100-$150.

YEATS, William Butler. *A Full Moon in March*. Dark-green cloth. London, 1935. First edition. In dust jacket. $100-$125.

YEATS, William Butler. *The Golden Helmet*. Gray boards. New York, 1908. First edition. One of 50. $200-$300.

YEATS, William Butler. *The Green Helmet and Other Poems*. Gray boards and linen. Dundrum, 1910. Cuala Press. One of 400. With erratum slip. $150-$200. New York, 1912. Boards. First American edition. $25.

YEATS, William Butler. *The Hour Glass*. Unbound. London, 1903. First edition. (12 copies issued; without covers.) $2,000 and up. (The scarcest of all Yeats items. An inscribed copy brought $170 at auction in 1941; no other sales noted.) New York, 1904. Blue cloth.

$150-$200. Another issue: Parchment. One of 100 on Japan vellum. $300-$350. (Dublin, 1914.) Cuala Press. Gray wrappers. (50 copies.) $1,000-$1,250.

YEATS, William Butler. *The Hour Glass, Cathleen ni Houlihan, The Pot of Broth: Being Volume Two of Plays for an Irish Theatre.* Gray boards and green cloth. London, 1904. First English edition. $75-$100.

YEATS, William Butler. *Ideas of Good and Evil.* Green boards and cloth. London, 1903. First edition. $75-$100. Dublin, 1905. Boards and linen. Second edition. $35-$50.

YEATS, William Butler. *If I Were Four-and-Twenty.* Boards and linen. Dublin, 1940. Cuala Press. One of 450. In dust jacket. $100-$150.

YEATS, William Butler. *In the Seven Woods.* Printed in red and black. Linen. Dundrum, 1903. Dun Emer Press. First edition. One of 325. In tissue dust jacket. $100-$150. Signed by Yeats, $175. (First book from the Dun Emer Press.)

YEATS, William Butler. *John Sherman and Dhoya.* See Ganconagh.

YEATS, William Butler. *The King of the Great Clock Tower, Commentaries and Poems.* Boards and linen, paper label. Dublin, 1934. Cuala Press. One of 400. $150.

YEATS, William Butler. *The King's Threshold.* Gray boards. New York, 1904. First edition. One of 100, signed. Boxed. $527.50 (A, 1975).

YEATS, William Butler. *The Land of Heart's Desire.* Purple-pink wrappers. London, 1894. First edition. $150-$200. Chicago, 1814 (actually 1894). Gray boards. First American edition. One of 450. $75-$100. Portland, Me., 1903. Boards. One of 100 on vellum, signed by the publisher, Thomas B. Mosher, $50-$60.

YEATS, William Butler. *Last Poems and Plays.* Green cloth. London, 1940. First trade edition (after 500-copy Cuala Press edition of *Last Poems and Two Plays).* In dust jacket. $75-$100. New York, 1940. Cloth. First American edition. In dust jacket. $75-$100.

YEATS, William Butler. *Last Poems and Two Plays.* Boards and linen. Dublin, 1939. Cuala Press. One of 500. In dust jacket. $100-$150.

YEATS, William Butler. *Later Poems.* Light-green cloth. London, 1922. First edition. $85-$100. New York, 1927. Boards. First American edition. One of 250, signed. In glassine jacket. Boxed. $100-$150. Trade issue: Cloth. $15-$20.

YEATS, William Butler. *Michael Robartes and the Dancer.* Printed in red and black. Boards and linen. Dundrum, 1920. Cuala Press. First edition. One of 400. $125-$175.

YEATS, William Butler. *Modern Poetry.* Bright-green wrappers. London, 1936. First edition. One of 1,000. $100-$150. (Scarce despite the limitation; the Yeats bibliographer Allan Wade says hundreds of copies were destroyed by incendiary bombs.)

YEATS, William Butler. *Mosada. A Dramatic Poem.* Brown wrappers. Dublin, 1886. First edition. $5,000 and up. Also, $3,500 (A, 1971); $2,296 (A, 1962); inscribed by Yeats, $3,750 (A, 1963). Author's first book. Dublin, 1943. Cuala Press. Cream-colored parchment wrappers. One of 50. In dust jacket. $800-$1,000 (Note: This poem was first published in the *Dublin University Review,* June, 1886, Vol. 2, No. 6, original decorated wrappers.)

YEATS, William Butler. *New Poems.* Boards and linen. Dublin, 1938. Cuala Press. One of 450. In glassine dust jacket. $100-$150.

YEATS, William Butler. *Nine Poems.* Wrappers. London, 1918. First edition. One of 25. $300-$500.

YEATS, William Butler. *October Blast: Poems.* Boards and linen. Dublin, 1927. Cuala Press. One of 350. In dust jacket. $150-$200.

YEATS, William Butler. *On the Boiler.* Pictorial blue-green wrappers. Dublin, (1939). Cuala Press. Second edition. (Only about 4 copies of the first edition were printed, according to Mrs. Yeats.) $30-$65.

YEATS, William Butler. *A Packet for Ezra Pound.* Boards and linen. Dublin, 1929. Cuala Press. One of 425. In plain dust jacket. $250-$350.

YEATS, William Butler. *Pages from a Diary Written in Nineteen Hundred and Thirty.* Yellow boards and linen. Dublin, 1944. Cuala Press. One of 280. In dust jacket. $100-$150.

YEATS, William Butler. *Per Amica Silentia Lunae.* Dark-blue cloth. London, 1918. First edition. In dust jacket. $75-$125.

YEATS, William Butler. *The Player Queen.* Wrappers. London, 1922. First separate edition. $100-$125.

YEATS, William Butler. *Plays and Controversies.* Boards and cloth. New York, 1924. One of 250, signed. Boxed. $100-$150.

YEATS, William Butler. *Plays for an Irish Theatre.* Illustrated. Boards. London, 1911. First edition, first issue, with white end papers. $75-$125.

YEATS, William Butler. *Plays in Prose and Verse.* Boards and cloth. New York, 1924. One of 250, signed. In dust jacket. $50-$100.

YEATS, William Butler. *Poems.* Light-brown cloth. London, 1895. First edition. One of 25 printed on vellum, signed by Yeats. $650-$1,000. Trade edition: 750 copies. $150-$200. Second issue: Boston imprint of Copeland & Day added to title page. $150-$200. London, 1899. Dark-blue cloth. Second English edition. $100-$150. London, 1901. Dark-blue cloth. Third English edition. $65. London, 1904. Fourth English edition. $50-$60. Inscribed by Yeats, $325 in a dealer's catalogue and listed as "first edition." London, 1908. Cloth. Fifth English edition. $50-$100. London, 1912. Pictorial blue cloth. Sixth English edition. $75-$100. Dublin, 1935. Blue wrappers. Cuala Press. One of 30. $400-$500. London, 1949. 2 vols., olive-green cloth. Definitive Edition. One of 375, signed. Boxed. $500-$600. Also, $450 (A, 1970).

YEATS, William Butler. *Poems Written in Discouragement, 1912-1913.* Dark-gray wrappers, stitched with red cord. Dundrum, 1913. Cuala Press. One of 50. $1,000 and up. Also, $550 (A, 1971).

YEATS, William Butler. *The Poetical Works of William Butler Yeats.* 2 vols., dark-blue cloth. New York, 1906-07. First edition. $75-$100.

YEATS, William Butler. *Responsibilities and Other Poems.* Dark-blue cloth. London, 1916. First edition. $85-$150. New York, 1916. Gray boards and cloth. First American edition. In dust jacket. $60-$80.

YEATS, William Butler. *Responsibilities: Poems and a Play.* Gray boards and linen. Dundrum, 1914. Cuala Press. First edition. One of 400. $125-$175.

YEATS, William Butler. *Reveries over Childhood and Youth.* With a blue board portfolio containing a colored plate and 2 portraits. Gray boards and linen. Dundrum, 1915. Cuala Press. One of 425. $150-$200. New York, 1916. Cloth. First American edition. $35-$50. London, 1916. Dark-blue cloth. First English edition. $50-$75.

YEATS, William Butler. *The Secret Rose.* Illustrated by John Butler Yeats. Dark-blue cloth. London, 1897. First edition, first binding, with "Lawrence & Bullen" on spine. $75-$100.

YEATS, William Butler. *A Selection from the Love Poetry of William Butler Yeats.* Gray boards and linen. Dundrum, 1913. Cuala Press. One of 300. $100-$150.

YEATS, William Butler. *Seven Poems and a Fragment.* Gray boards and linen. Dundrum, 1922. Cuala Press. First edition. One of 500. $100-$150.

YEATS, William Butler. *The Shadowy Waters.* Dark-blue cloth. London, 1900. First edition. $75-$100. New York, 1901. Gray boards. First American edition. $50-$100.

YEATS, William Butler. *Stories of Michael Robartes and His Friends.* 2 woodcut illustrations. Boards and linen. Dublin, 1931. First edition. Cuala Press. One of 450. In dust jacket. $100-$200.

YEATS, William Butler. *Stories of Red Hanrahan*. Blue boards and linen. Dundrum, 1904. Dun Emer Press. First edition. One of 500. In dust jacket. $100-$150. Signed by Yeats, $175. Also, signed by Yeats and dated, $425 (A,1970).

YEATS, William Butler. *Synge and the Ireland of His Time*. Gray boards and linen. Dundrum, 1911. Cuala Press. First edition. One of 350. $100. Signed by Yeats, $175.

YEATS, William Butler. *The Tables of the Law. The Adoration of the Magi*. Portrait frontispiece. Buckram. (London), 1897. First edition. One of 110. $400-$500. London, 1904. Blue wrappers. First unlimited edition. $50-$75. Stratford-on-Avon, 1914. Shakespeare Head Press. Cloth. Second unlimited edition. One of 510. $75-$85.

YEATS, William Butler. *Three Things*. Blue boards. London, 1929. First edition. One of 500 large paper copies, signed. $75. Trade issue (Ariel Poems): Blue wrappers. (Cover title only.) $10-$15.

YEATS, William Butler. *The Tower*. Pictorial cloth. London, 1928. First edition. In dust jacket. $75-$125. New York, 1928. Green cloth. First American edition. In dust jacket. $75-$100.

YEATS, William Butler. *Two Plays for Dancers*. Green boards and linen. (Dundrum), 1919. parchment. London, 1922. First edition. One of 1,000 signed. In dust jacket. $150-$200.

YEATS, William Butler. *Two Plays for Dancers* Green boards and linen. (Dundrum), 1919. Cuala Press. First edition. One of 400. $85-$150.

YEATS, William Butler. *The Variorum Edition of the Poems of William Butler Yeats*. Buckram. New York, 1957. First edition. One of 825, signed. Boxed. $350-$400.

YEATS William Butler. *A Vision*. Blue boards. London, 1925. First edition. One of 600, signed. $275.

YEATS, William Butler. *The Wanderings of Oisin and Other Poems*. Dark-blue cloth. London, 1889. First edition, first binding. One of 500. $500-$750. Author's first regularly published hardbound book.

YEATS, William Butler. *The Wild Swans at Coole, Other Verses, and a Play in Verse*. Dark-blue boards and linen. Dundrum, 1917. Cuala Press. First edition. One of 400. $150-$200. London, 1919. Dark-blue cloth. In dust jacket. $50-$75. New York, 1919. Blue boards. First American edition. In dust jacket. $50-$60.

YEATS, William Butler. *The Wind Among the Reeds*. Dark-blue cloth. London, 1899. First edition, first issue, without correction slip. $150-$200. Second issue, same date, with correction slip. $40-$60.

YEATS, William Butler. *The Winding Stair*. Dark-blue cloth. New York, 1929. Fountain Press. First American edition. One of 642, signed. In dust jacket. $150-$200. (Another New York edition of 1929, unpublished, bears the imprint of Crosby Gaige. Sheets of this edition, signed by Yeats, brought $275 at auction in 1971. A Chicago bookseller listed a set at $2,000 late in 1977.) London, 1933. Olive-green cloth. First English edition (with *And Other Poems* added to title). In dust jacket. $75-$100. New York, 1933. Cloth. First American edition. In dust jacket. $25-$35.

YEATS, William Butler. *Words for Music Perhaps and Other Poems*. Blue boards and linen. Dublin, 1932. Cuala Press. One of 450. In dust jacket. $100-$200.

YEATS, William Butler. *The Words upon the Window Pane: A Play in One Act*. Blue boards and linen. Dublin, 1934. Cuala Press. First edition. One of 350. In dust jacket. $100-$150.

YEATS, William Butler (editor). *Fairy and Folk Tales of the Irish Peasantry*. Cloth. London, 1888. First edition, with errata slip. $100-$150.

YEATS, William Butler, and Johnson, Lionel. *Poetry and Ireland: Essays*. Boards and linen. Dundrum, 1908. Cuala Press. First edition. One of 250. $85-$125.

YELLOW BIRD. *The Life and Adventures of Joaquin Murieta*. 2 plates. 90 pp., wrappers. San Francisco, 1854. (By John R. Ridge.) First edition. $20,000 and up (?). Howes: "One copy known." $10,000 at auction (1967)—the Streeter copy. (For later editions, see *The Life of Joaquin Murieta*; also see Ridge, John R.)

*YELLOWPLUSH Correspondence (The).* Boards and cloth, paper label. Philadelphia, 1838. (By William Makepeace Thackeray.) First edition, with text starting at page 13, as issued. $300-$350. First publication in book form of any of Thackeray's works.

*YEMASSEE (The): A Romance of Carolina.* 2 vols., cloth, paper labels. New York, 1835. (By William Gilmore Simms.) First edition, first issue, with copyright notice pasted in Vol. 1. $400-$600.

YOAKUM, Henderson K. *History of Texas.* Folding document, 4 maps, 5 plates. 2 vols., half calf. New York, 1855. First edition. $600-$1,000. New York, 1856. 2 vols., cloth. Second edition. $300-$400.

YOST, Karl. *Charles M. Russell, the Cowboy Artist: A Bibliography.* Illustrated. Cloth. Pasadena, (1948). First edition. One of 500. In slipcase. $50.

YOST, Karl, and Renner, Frederic G. *A Bibliography of the Published Works of Charles M. Russell.* Illustrated, including color. Leather. Lincoln, Neb., (1971). First edition. One of 600 (actually more), with an extra color plate, signed by Renner. In dust jacket. $50-$60. Another issue: Cloth. In dust jacket. $25.

YOSY, A. *Switzerland.* 50 colored engravings. 2 vols., boards. London, 1815. First edition. $1,250-$1,500. London, 1816. 2 vols. $800-$1,500.

YOUNG, Andrew W. *History of Chautauqua County, New York.* Half morocco. Buffalo, 1875. First edition. $100-$125.

YOUNG, Ansel. *The Western Reserve Almanac for the Year 1844.* 32 pp., wrappers. Cleveland, (1843). $100-$200.

YOUNG, Dal. *Apologia pro Oscar Wilde.* Printed wrappers. London, (1895). First edition. $75-$100.

*YOUNG Duke (The).* By the author of *Vivian Grey.* 3 vols., boards, paper spines with labels. London, 1831. (By Benjamin Disraeli.) First edition, first issue, with half titles to Vols. 2 and 3 and advertisement leaf at end of Vol. 3. $300-$400.

YOUNG, Harry (Sam). *Hard Knocks: A Life Story of the Vanishing West.* 25 plates. Boards. Portland, 1915. First edition. $75-$100. Chicago, (1915). Only 18 plates. Cloth. Reprint edition. $35-$50.

YOUNG, John. *An Address to the Senior Class, Delivered at the Commencement in Centre College, September 22, 1831.* 15 pp., sewed. Danville, Ky., 1831. $75-$100.

YOUNG, John R. *Memoirs.* 4 portraits. Cloth. Salt Lake City, 1920. First edition. $100-$125.

YOUNG, Philip. *History of Mexico.* Sheep. Cincinnati, 1847. First edition. $125-$150. Cincinnati, 1848. Cloth. Second edition. $60-$75.

YOUNG, R.M. *Argument of Attorney for the Occupants of Portage City Against the State of Wisconsin.* 62 pp., wrappers. (Washington, 1857.) $75-$100.

YOUNGBLOOD, Charles. L. *Adventures of Chas. L. Youngblood During Ten Years on the Plains.* Portrait. Cloth. Boonville, Ind., 1882. First edition. $200-$250.

# Z

ZACCARELLI, John. *Zaccarelli's Pictorial Souvenir Book of the Golden Northland.* Oblong, Wrappers. Dawson, (1908). $35-$50.

ZAMACOIS, Niceto de. *El Buscador de Oro en California.* 81 pp., wrappers. Mexico, 1855. $40.

*ZAMORANO 80 (The): A Selection of Distinguished California Books.* Cloth. Los Angeles, 1945. First edition. One of 500. $75-$125.

ZAVALA, Lorenzo de. *Ensayo Historico de las Revoluciones de Mexico, etc.* 2 vols. (Vol. 1, Paris, 1831.) Vol. 2, New York, 1832. First edition. $500-$800.

*ZONES of the Earth (The).* 12 color plates. Oblong folio, cloth portfolio with pictorial cover. London, 1845. $25.

ZUCKER, A. E. *The Chinese Theater.* Plates, 4 original paintings in color on silk, other illustrations. Pictorial cloth. Boston, 1925. First edition. One of 750. $100-$150.

ZUKOFSKY, Louis. See *Columbia Verse: 1897-1924.*

ZUKOFSKY, Louis. *"A" 1—12.* Cloth. (Ashland, Mass.), 1959. First edition. With note by W. C. Williams. One of 200. Errata slip laid in. In glassine dust jacket. $100-$150.

ZUKOFSKY, Louis. *"A"—14.* Cloth. (London, 1967.) One of 250, signed. In dust jacket. $35-$50.

ZUKOFSKY, Louis. *Barely and Widely.* Oblong, wrappers. New York, 1958. First edition. One of 300, signed. $45-$60.

ZUKOFSKY, Louis. *First Half of "A"—9.* Manila envelope. New York, privately printed, no date. "First Edition, Limited to 55 Autographed Copies." $200-$250. Author's first book.

ZUKOFSKY, Louis. *5 Statements For Poetry.* 58 pp., mimeographed, pale blue wrappers, stapled. No place, 1958. First edition. (About 110 produced.) $100-$150.

ZUKOFSKY, Louis. *I Sent Thee Late.* (Cambridge, Mass., 1965.) First edition. One of 20, signed. In original envelope. $75-$100.

ZUKOFSKY, Louis. *It Was.* Cloth. (Kyoto, Japan, 1961.) First edition. One of 50, signed. $45.

ZUKOFSKY, Louis. *Iyyob.* Oblong, wrappers. London, (1965). Turret Books. One of 100 signed. $75.

ZUKOFSKY, Louis. *Prepositions.* Cloth. London, (1967). First edition. One of 150, signed. In dust jacket. $35-$50.

ZUKOFSKY, Louis. *A Test of Poetry.* Cloth. Brooklyn, 1948. First edition. In dust jacket. $35-$50.

ZUKOFSKY, Louis. *An Unearthing.* Wrappers. (Cambridge, 1965.) First edition. One of 77, signed. $50-$90.

ZUKOFSKY, Louis (editor). *An "Objectivist's" Anthology.* Wrappers. (Dijon, France), 1932. First edition. $75-$100. (Contributors include T. S. Eliot, William Carlos Williams.)